Javier Lopez Xinyi Huang
Ravi Sandhu (Eds.)

Network and System Security

7th International Conference, NSS 2013
Madrid, Spain, June 3-4, 2013
Proceedings

Volume Editors

Javier Lopez
University of Malaga, Computer Science Department
ETSI Informatica, Campus de Teatinos, 29071 Malaga, Spain
E-mail: jlm@lcc.uma.es

Xinyi Huang
Fujian Normal University
School of Mathematics and Computer Science
No. 32 Shangsan Road, 350007 Fuzhou, China
E-mail: xyhuang81@gmail.com

Ravi Sandhu
University of Texas at San Antonio
Institute for Cyber Security
One UTSA Circle, San Antonio, TX 78249, USA
E-mail: ravi.sandhu@utsa.edu

ISSN 0302-9743
e-ISSN 1611-3349
ISBN 978-3-642-38630-5
e-ISBN 978-3-642-38631-2
DOI 10.1007/978-3-642-38631-2
Springer Heidelberg Dordrecht London New York

Library of Congress Control Number: 2013938835

CR Subject Classification (1998): K.6.5, C.2.0-4, E.3, H.2.7, D.4.6, K.4.4, C.3, C.4

LNCS Sublibrary: SL 4 – Security and Cryptology

Typesetting: Camera-ready by author, data conversion by Scientific Publishing Services, Chennai, India

Printed on acid-free paper

Springer is part of Springer Science+Business Media (www.springer.com)

Lecture Notes in Computer Science 7873

Commenced Publication in 1973
Founding and Former Series Editors:
Gerhard Goos, Juris Hartmanis, and Jan van Leeuwen

Preface

NSS 2013, the 7th International Conference on Network and System Security, was held in Madrid, Spain, during June 3–4, 2013. The conference was organized and supported by the Universidad Autonoma de Madrid, Spain.

NSS constitutes a series of events covering research on all theoretical and practical aspects related to network and system security. The aim of NSS is to provide a leading edge forum to foster interaction between researchers and developers within the network and system security communities, and to give attendees an opportunity to interact with experts in academia, industry, and governments.

In response to the call for papers, 176 papers were submitted to NSS 2013. These papers were evaluated on the basis of their significance, novelty, technical quality, and practical impact. The review and discussion were held electronically using EasyChair. From the papers submitted, 41 full papers (less than 24%) were selected for inclusion in this Springer volume. Additionally, 17 short papers and 13 industrial track papers were invited to the conference program and also for inclusion in the volume.

The conference also featured two keynote speeches, one by Arun Ross entitled "Biometrics: The Future Beckons" and one by Wanlei Zhou entitled "Authentication, Privacy, and Ownership Transfer in Mobile RFID Systems".

We are very grateful to the people whose work ensured a smooth organization process: Javier Ortega-Garcia (Full Professor), Julian Fierrez (Associate Professor), and Javier Eslava (Electrical Engineer) for taking care of the local organization, and Yu Wang for managing the conference website.

Last but certainly not least our thanks go to all authors who submitted papers and all attendees. We hope you enjoy the conference proceedings!

June 2013

Javier Lopez
Xinyi Huang
Ravi Sandhu

Organization

General Chairs

Javier Ortega-Garcia	Universidad Autonoma de Madrid, Spain
Jiankun Hu	University of New South Wales Canberra, Australia
Elisa Bertino	Purdue University, USA

Program Chairs

Javier Lopez	University of Malaga, Spain
Xinyi Huang	Fujian Normal University, China
Ravi Sandhu	University of Texas at San Antonio, USA

Industry Track Program Chairs

Xinyi Huang	Fujian Normal University, China
Roberto Di Pietro	Roma Tre University of Rome, Italy
Al-Sakib Khan Pathan	International Islamic University, Malaysia

Steering Chair

Yang Xiang	Deakin University, Australia

Publicity Chairs

Kejie Lu	University of Puerto Rico at Mayaguez, Puerto Rico
Roberto Di Pietro	Roma Tre University of Rome, Italy
Al-Sakib Khan Pathan	International Islamic University, Malaysia

Publication Chair

Xu Huang	University of Canberra, Australia

Workshop Chairs

Shui Yu	Deakin University, Australia
Yulei Wu	Chinese Academy of Sciences, China

International Advisory Committees

Robert Deng	Singapore Management University, Singapore
C.-C. Jay Kuo	University of Southern California, USA
Peter Mueller	IBM Zurich Research, Switzerland
Makoto Takizawa	Seikei University, Japan
Yi Mu	University of Wollongong, Australia
Vijay Varadharajan	Macquarie University, Australia

Program Committees

Rafael Accorsi	University of Freiburg, Germany
Gail-Joon Ahn	Arizona State University, USA
Eric Alata	LAAS-CNRS, France
Man Ho Au	University of Wollongong, Australia
Joonsang Baek	KUSTAR, UAE
Marina Blanton	University of Notre Dame, USA
Carlo Blundo	Universtà degli Studi di Salerno, Italy
Zhenfu Cao	Shanghai Jiao Tong University, China
Barbara Carminati	University of Insubria, Italy
Marco Casassa Mont	Hewlett-Packard Labs, UK
Jordi Castella-Roca	Universitat Rovira i Virgili, Spain
David Chadwick	University of Kent, UK
Xiaofeng Chen	Xi'dian University, China
Mauro Conti	University of Padua, Italy
Frederic Cuppens	Télécom Bretagne, France
Jesus Diaz Verdejo	University of Granada, Spain
Xuhua Ding	Singapore Management University, Singapore
Xiaolei Dong	Shanghai Jiao Tong University, China
Wenliang Du	Syracuse University, USA
Jose M. Fernandez	Ecole Polytechnique de Montreal, Canada
Jordi Forne	Universitat Politecnica de Catalunya, Spain
Keith Frikken	Miami University, USA
Steven Furnell	Plymouth University, UK
Alban Gabillon	University of French Polynesia, France
Joaquin Garcia-Alfaro	Télécom SudParis, France
Pedro Garcia-Teodoro	University of Granada, Spain
Gabriel Ghinita	University of Massachusetts at Boston, USA
Dieter Gollmann	Hamburg University of Technology, Germany
Juan Gonzalez Nieto	Queensland University of Technology, Australia
Dawu Gu	Shanghai Jiao Tong University, China
Xu Huang	University of Canberra, Australia
Limin Jia	Carnegie Mellon University, USA
James Joshi	University of Pittsburgh, USA
Sokratis Katsikas	University of Piraeus, Greece
Stefan Katzenbeisser	TU Darmstadt, Germany

Muhammad Khurram Khan	King Saud University, Kingdom of Saudi Arabia
Shinsaku Kiyomoto	KDDI R&D Laboratories Inc., Japan
Costas Lambrinoudakis	University of Piraeus, Greece
Adam J. Lee	University of Pittsburgh, USA
Jin Li	Guangzhou University, China
Shengli Liu	Shanghai Jiao Tong University, China
Giovanni Livraga	Università degli Studi di Milano, Italy
Der-Chyuan Lou	Chang Gung University, Taiwan
Fabio Martinelli	IIT-CNR, Italy
Carlos Maziero	Federal Technological University, Brazil
Wojciech Mazurczyk	Warsaw University of Technology, Poland
Qun Ni	Google Inc, USA
Jaehong Park	University of Texas at San Antonio, USA
Gerardo Pelosi	Politecnico di Milano, Italy
Gregorio Martinez Perez	University of Murcia, Spain
Guenther Pernul	University of Regensburg, Germany
Alexander Pretschner	Technische Universität München, Germany
Indrakshi Ray	Colorado State University, USA
Arturo Ribagorda	University Carlos III Madrid, Spain
Ning Shang	Qualcomm Research, USA
Charalabos Skianis	University of the Aegean, Greece
Miguel Soriano	Universitat Politecnica de Catalunya, Spain
Anna Squicciarini	The Pennsylvania State University, USA
Hung-Min Sun	National Tsing Hua University, Taiwan
Willy Susilo	University of Wollongong, Australia
Qiang Tang	SnT, University of Luxembourg, Luxembourg
Juan E. Tapiador	Universidad Carlos III de Madrid, Spain
Dan Thomsen	Smart Information Flow Technologies, USA
Mahesh Tripunitara	University of Waterloo, Canada
Traian Marius Truta	Northern Kentucky University, USA
Alexander Uskov	Bradley University, USA
Alexandre Viejo	Universitat Rovira i Virgili, Spain
Jaideep S. Vaidya	Rutgers University, USA
Guilin Wang	University of Wollongong, Australia
Haining Wang	College of William and Mary, USA
Huaxiong Wang	Nanyang Technological University, Singapore
Lingyu Wang	Concordia University, Canada
Jian Weng	Jinan University, China
Duncan S. Wong	City University of Hong Kong, Hong Kong, China
Qianhong Wu	Universitat Rovira i Vergili, Spain
Li Xu	Fujian Normal University, China
Shouhuai Xu	University of Texas at San Antonio, USA
Xun Yi	Victoria University, Australia

Additional Reviewers

Bagus Santoso
Andrea Saracino
Angelo Spognardi
Xiao Tan
Raylin Tso
Nikos Vrakas
Lusha Wang
Yifei Wang
Yujue Wang
Samer Wazan
Michael Weber
Sheng Wen
Tobias Wüchner
JiaXu
Saman Taghavi Zargar
Zhenxin Zhan
Jiang Zhang
Jun Zhang
Mengyuan Zhang
Yihua Zhang
Yubao Zhang
Nan Zheng

Table of Contents

NSS 2013 Regular Papers

Network Security: Modeling and Evaluation

Network Security: Security Protocols and Practice

Network Security: Network Attacks and Defense

System Security: Malware and Intrusions

System Security: Applications Security

System Security: Security Algorithms and Systems

Cryptographic Algorithms I

Cryptographic Algorithms II

Privacy

Key Agreement and Distribution

NSS 2013 Short Papers

NSS 2013 Industrial Track Papers

Stochastic Traffic Identification for Security Management: eDonkey Protocol as a Case Study

Rafael A. Rodríguez-Gómez, Gabriel Maciá-Fernández, and Pedro García-Teodoro

Department of Signal Theory, Telematics and Communication,
CITIC - ETSIIT, University of Granada
C/ Periodista Daniel Saucedo Aranda s/n E-18071
{rodgom,gmacia,pgteodor}@ugr.es

Abstract. Traffic identification is a relevant issue for network operators nowadays. As P2P services are often used as an attack vector, Internet Service Providers (ISPs) and network administrators are interested in modeling the traffic transported on their networks with behavior identification and classification purposes. In this paper, we present a stochastic detection approach, based on the use of Markov models, for classifying network traffic to trigger subsequent security related actions. The detection system works at flow level considering the packets as incoming observations, and is capable of analyze both plain and encrypted communications. After suggesting a general structure for modeling any network service, we apply it to eDonkey traffic classification as a case study.

After successfully evaluating our approach with real network traces, the experimental results evidence the way our methodology can be used to model normal behaviors in communications for a given target service.

1 Introduction

Traffic characterization and modeling is fundamental for management purposes, as this allows a number of supervision activities: services performing and planning, fault diagnosis, security control, among others. Specifically, as P2P services are often used as an attack vector to communications and users, it would be interesting to estimate a behavioral model for this kind of transmissions. This way, we would be able to determine the occurrence of deviations in the observed behavior and, from them, to conclude the appearance of non-legitimate events from the security perspective of the system.

Three main issues should be highlighted regarding a typical traffic classification process:

- *Traffic parameterization*: Several features have been studied in the literature to represent network traffic in order to model and subsequently classify the observed events as belonging to different classes [1] [2].
- *Analysis level*: Once the traffic is parameterized, two main different levels are considered in the literature to carry out the identification or classification

J. Lopez, X. Huang, and R. Sandhu (Eds.): NSS 2013, LNCS 7873, pp. 1–13, 2013.

process [3]: flow-based analysis, and packet-based analysis. In the flow-based case the goal is to classify each flow as belonging or not to a given service. On the other hand, in packet-based analysis the objective is to classify each individual packet.

- *Identification process*: Finally, the schemes involved in performing the identification itself cover a broad range of techniques. From simple heuristics or indicators to complex data mining or pattern learning algorithms.

Regarding the aforementioned aspects, this paper presents an efficient approach for traffic classification, with the following characteristics which constitute the main contributions of this work:

1. First of all, a flow-based approach is considered at the analysis level. For that, the source and destination ports of each packet are used to define a flow or communication.
2. To carry out the flow level representation, each packet in the flow is considered as an incoming observation to the system. For that, every packet is parameterized as a three-dimensional vector: <*psize, itime, chdir*>, where *psize* is the packet size, *itime* is the inter-arrival time, and *chdir* represents the change of direction in the flow.
3. Finally, the modeling and classification of a given flow is based on the disposal of a Markov model representing the communications belonging to the associated service.
4. Taking this classification methodology as a base, two main benefits are obtained. First, the monitored traffic could be classified as belonging to different types, *e.g.*, P2P, HTTP, SMTP, VoIP, etc. Second, as the modeling approach relies on the estimation of the normal behavior of the target service, the detection of behavioral deviations allows us to conclude the occurrence of non-legitimate events from the security perspective.

The rest of the paper is organized as follows. Section 2 deals with the related work in the field of traffic classification, specially regarding the particular modeling considered here: hidden Markov models. In Section 3 the fundamentals of Markov modeling for classification purposes are described. After that, our specific parameterization and Markov model structure for traffic classification is discussed in Section 4. The evaluation of this traffic detection approach is carried out by analyzing some traffic datasets in Section 5 Finally, some main conclusions regarding this work are drawn in Section 6.

2 Related Work

Most of the existent research in the field of traffic classification can be divided into three groups: *(i)* based on well-known port, *(ii)* based on packet content, and *(iii)* based on flow features. Several studies highlight the low effectiveness of port-based identification for present network traffic [4]. To address the problems related to this type of classification, several techniques based on packet content have been proposed. Given the limitations of previous traffic classification techniques, the research community focused on the third type of traffic classification: based on flow features.

In this paper, we propose a technique for traffic modeling and identification based on flow features and on the use of Markov models. There is no much contributions in the field of traffic classification based on Markov modeling, but in the following, we present the most relevant ones and compare them with respect to our proposal.

The authors in [5], use Markov modeling to collect the behaviour of a specific flow. The observations for the model are control packets, *e.g.* SYN, ACK, PSH, etc. They need a high number of control packets in a flow to be able to classify it with high accuracy. For example, to differentiate HTTP flows from HTTPS at least 50 control packets are necessary to achieve 90% of true detection rate with more than 10% of false positive rate. Our approach is independent of the number of packets in a flow and moreover, is able to achieve higher detection results.

Wright et al. [6] follow a similar design to that used for protein sequence alignment. The authors use a left-right HMM with a number of states equal to the mean number of non-zero payload packets in a flow of the target protocol. The obtained true detection rates vary from 58.20% to 92.90%, and the false positive rates from 7.90% to 0.62%. As we will show in the experimental section our approach achieves much higher detection results.

Dainotti et al. model in [7] present a different model per service to be classified. An important weak point of this contribution is the reduced dataset used both in training and detection stages. For example, AoM is trained with only 4 flows and evaluated with 2, and eDonkey is trained with 109 and evaluated with 82. Instead, our training and evaluation use more than 240 thousands of eDonkey flows, reaching a higher true detection rate and a similar false positive one.

In probability theory, Markov modeling refers to a stochastic model that assumes the Markov property for a given process. That is, the probability of future states depends only upon the present state, not on the sequence of events that preceded it.

The strength of Markov modeling relies on its capacity to represent the dynamic behavior of a system. This way, it has been successfully applied in a number of fields since its introduction in 1954 [8], which range from speech recognition to medicine, from seismology to engineering [9]. In this variety of fields, two main types of models appear: Markov chains and hidden Markov models (HMM). In the first case, each state of the system is modeled through a random variable that changes over time, that is there exists a state associated to each variable/observation. Instead, a HMM is a Markov chain for which the state is only partially observable, that is observations are related to the state of the system, but they are typically insufficient to precisely determine the state.

HMMs are the dominant technique in the context of classification and pattern recognition [10], so that we focus our attention on this type of modeling in the rest of the section, as it constitutes the basis of our proposal for traffic classification in this paper.

3 Fundamentals of Markov Modeling for Classification

3.1 General Concepts in HMM

Given a discrete time Markov chain with a finite set of states $S = \{s_1, s_2, ..., s_N\}$, a HMM is defined as the tuple $\lambda = (\Pi, A, B)$, where

1. $\Pi = \{\pi_1, \pi_2, ..., \pi_N\}$ is the initial probability vector, that is the probability that the *ith* state is the first one in the sequence: $\pi_i = P(q_1 = s_i), i \in [1, ..., N]$
2. $A = [a_{ij}]$ is the transition probably matrix, each term representing the probability of the transition from the *ith* state at time t to the *jth* state at time $t+1$: $a_{ij} = P(q_{t+1} = s_j | q_t = s_i), i, j \in [1, ..., N]$
3. $B = [b_{jk}]$ is the probability observation matrix, that is the probability that the *kth* observation occurs in the state i at t: $b_{ik} = P(o_t = v_k | q_t = s_i), i \in [1, ..., N], k \in [1, ..., M]$

3.2 HMM-Based Classification

Classification with HMM implies solving two main problems: *decoding* and *training*. Decoding refers to the determination of the sequence of states Q of λ associated to the sequence O observed. For that, the Viterbi algorithm [11] is used to calculate the a-posteriori probability:

$$Q = \underset{Q'}{argmax} P(Q'|O, \lambda) = \underset{Q'}{argmax} P(O|Q', \lambda)$$

where

$$P(O|Q', \lambda) = \pi_{q_1} b_{q_1 o_1} \prod_{t=2}^{T} a_{q_{t-1} q_t} b_{q_t o_t} \tag{1}$$

On the other hand, training is about how to estimate the parameters Π, A and B which define the model associated to the target system. Although several training procedures can be found in the literature with this aim, the Baum-Welch algorithm [12] is the most used one.

To reduce the size of the observation space, and thus the complexity of the parameterization of the observations of the system a *vector quantization* process (VQ) is involved. Two main issues should be highlighted regarding the VQ process: *(i)* the quantization algorithm to be used (K-means is widely accepted), and *(ii)* the distance measure to determinate the proximity between two observations (Euclidean distance is the most common).

Summarizing, a HMM-based classification process follows the general scheme shown in Fig. 1. Every event in the system is first parameterized by using a multi-dimensional vector. Then, a training stage from a given (pre-recorded) dataset of observations is initially performed. The main purpose in the training stage is

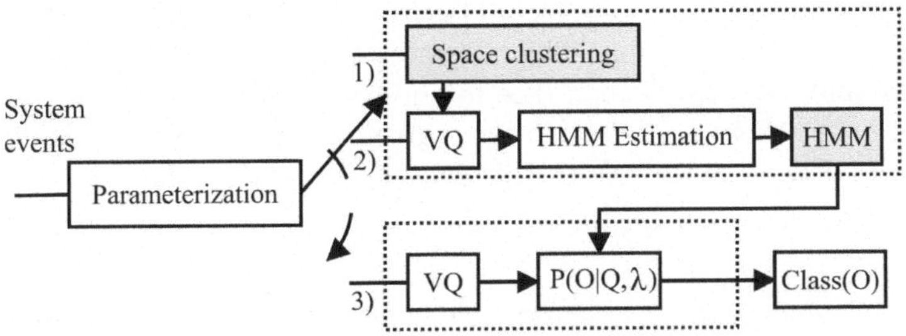

Fig. 1. General scheme for a HMM-based classification

the estimation of the parameters which define the HMM. Once the training of the system is complete, the classification of each sequence of VQ observations occurred is dealt with as follows:

1. The associated generation probability is first obtained according to (1), that is the sequence is decoded.
2. This probability is compared with a given detection threshold, P_{th}, so that the observation is considered as generated by the model if the probability threshold is surpassed, and not otherwise.

4 Detection System Overview

In an identification system based on Markov models it is necessary to specify: *(i)* the network traffic features that should be used as observations for the Markov model, and *(ii)* the Markov model itself (*i.e.*, states, transitions, etc).

4.1 Model Observations: Preprocessing

Our traffic classification approach relies on a flow identification basis. Here, we consider that a flow [13] is the bidirectional traffic identified by the tuple <source-IP-address, source-port, destination- IP-address, destination-port, IP-protocol>, where source and destination are interchangeable to allow bidirectional traffic. Since we are interested in the detection of application traffic, we specifically focus on packets containing high level information.

Each flow is specified in terms of a sequence of packets and every packet constitutes an incoming observation. A task before introducing observations to our system is a preprocessing stage which is composed of three modules: *(i)* parameterization, *(ii)* normalization, and *(iii)* vector quantization.

Parameterization. The election of the vector features is a key issue and it directly influences on the discerning capability of the system.

First, it is desirable that the selected features are independent of the transmission mode for the information. This allows the detection of both plain and encrypted communications. Second, the features should be representative enough, in the sense that their combination for a given service should be as different as possible from other services. With this criteria in mind we suggest the following three features:

1. *Inter-arrival time (itime):* it is defined for a packet as the difference, in seconds, between the arrival time of that packet and the arrival time of the previous one in the same flow.
2. *Payload size (psize):* it is the size, in bytes, of the information carried out by a packet.
3. *Change of direction (chdir):* this feature takes a value '1' for a given packet if it travels in the opposite direction than the previous packet in the same flow. Otherwise, it takes a value '-1'.

Both *inter-arrival time* and *payload size* are two common characteristics. However, up to our knowledge, *change of direction* has never been used to characterize network packets in the field of traffic classification. This feature allows to characterize UDP and TCP based protocols. This is due to the fact that it does not assume the existence of a server or a client.

Normalization. The normalization module is aimed at giving the same dynamic range for the three extracted features of a packet. The selected range is [-1,1], so that the *change of direction* should not be modified. With regard to the *inter-arrival time* feature, we first apply a logarithmic transformation to reduce the dynamic range of time [14]. Then, we normalize the obtained value by mean shifting and auto-scaling. The normalization is expressed as $v_s = (v_o - \mu)/\sigma$, where v_s is the scaled value, v_o the original value, and μ and σ the mean and standard deviation of the values to be scaled. For the *payload size* feature, only the mean shifting and auto-scaling transformation is applied.

To apply this normalization the mean and standard deviation of the expected payload size and the logarithm of the inter-arrival time should be calculated. The estimation of these values is done from the training dataset.

Vector Quantization. We finally carry out a quantization process on the obtained vectors of features for every observation (packet) in a flow. The vector quantization process used in our system is based on the K-means algorithm [15], in such a way that all the possible combinations of values for the three features are reduced to K possible vectors. These vectors are the most representative centroids for clustering the data contained in the training dataset. Regarding the metric used for the distance, we select the Euclidean metric.

From the K-clustered space, each incoming feature vector will be replaced by the centroid of the nearest cluster. Summarizing, an incoming packet, after this preprocessing stage, will be a sequence of indexes which are the observations of the HMM.

4.2 HMM Structure

The key feature of the proposed detection methodology is the use of a Markov model to describe traffic corresponding to a given protocol/service. Although the specific definition of the parameters of the Markov model depends on the protocol to be detected in the following a generic model to represent most of the communication services is proposed:

1. *Initial dialog:* This represents the start of the communication. Frequently in this step, the members of the communication interchange an identifier that will be used afterwards. For example, in the case of SSH, it is necessary to carry out an user authentication request which is responded by the corresponding answer.
2. *Information exchange:* Here, the participants transmit the information that constitutes the main purpose of the communication, e.g., file transfer, web page retrieval, email sending, etc. Thus, it is expected that the bulk of the packets in the flow are transferred in this step.
3. *Termination:* After the information exchange step, it is usual that many protocols exchange some messages with the aim of finalizing the communication. SSH protocol is an example of this.

An important issue in the design of our Markov model is the variability in the number of packets (observations) of different flows, even for a same protocol/service. To consider in our model this variability we define the *information exchange* step as re-executable. Finally, note that the *initial dialog* and the *termination* are two steps executed only once in the model.

4.3 HMM for the Detection of eDonkey Flows

With the aim of exploring the proposed generic model in a case study, we have carried out an adaptation to build a detection system for the eDonkey protocol.

The eDonkey protocol presents some features that makes it suitable to highlight the potential of our proposal. First of all, it is a P2P protocol and thus, a node can act both as a client and as a server. Secondly, eDonkey is a protocol used to shared files and, thus, it uses flows plenty of data and also flows with a reduced number of short size packets. Finally, eDonkey allows two communication modes: encrypted and plain communications. For these reasons, eDonkey flows present a high variability which make them hard to be modeled.

The eDonkey protocol communicates through TCP and UDP. However, TCP flows represent more than 95% of the total eDonkey flows and more than 99% of the transmitted bytes[1]. Thus, we focus our detection in eDonkey TCP flows.

The proposed Markov model is shown in Fig. 2. The first and the last steps are composed of two states each one and there exists only a possible transition between them. This is due to the own behavior of the protocol. The messages interchanged during the *initial dialog* step are the `Hello` (represented by state

[1] These percentages have been extracted studying the traces described in Section 5.

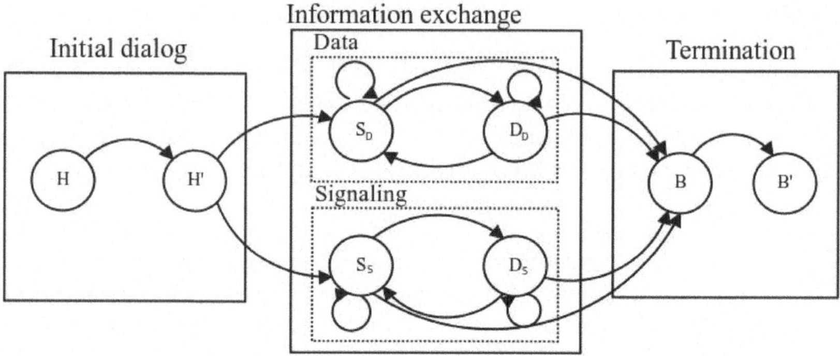

Fig. 2. HMM for modeling eDonkey protocol

H) and `Hello answer` (state H'). The messages transmitted in the *termination* step are `Start upload request` (state B) and `Queue rank` (state B').

Regarding to the *information exchange* step we cannot define a state for every packet in the flow, as there is a variable number of packets in different flows. Now, we define two possible ways: *(i)* one for data flows (high number of packets with a high size per packet), and *(ii)* the other one for signaling flows (reduced number of packets with a low size per packet). Each one of these flows are composed of two states, one representing signaling packets (S), and the other (D) data packets. The transitions defined here allow a variable number of packets in every transfer, and all the possible combinations between these two types of packets. Finally, the transition to the *termination* step can occur also from both signaling or data states.

5 Experimental Evaluation

Here we describe the experimental evaluation done for assessing the validity of the proposed approach.

5.1 Datasets

Two groups of network traces have been used to carry out the evaluation of the proposed detection system. The principal features of these traces are exposed now.

- *eDonkey traffic traces, eD-DB:* This trace is composed of the eDonkey traffic generated by a node during 45 days (during of 2011). In order to simulate a normal user behavior, this client connected to the eDonkey network during 5 hours each day. aMule 2.2.6 version [16] was used as eDonkey application. The client was connected to the eDonkey server called *se-Master Server 1*. To cover a wide range of different eDonkey peers to communicate with, we selected files to download and share with a high, medium and low number of peers sharing them.

These network traces contain 240,851 TCP flows and 7,003 UDP flows, all of them belonging to the eDonkey protocol. Among the total amount of TCP flows, 22,409 are obfuscated. All these communications were carried out between more than 12 thousands of different IPs and they transferred more than 20GB in the download direction and uploaded more than 25GB.

– *Middle East University trunk traces, ME-DB:* This trace is taken in a network trunk of a Middle East University. It contains all the traffic generated during 48 hours (November of 2010). In summary, there are around 73,000 IPs and 300 million packets transmitted.

  We analyze the entire trace using deep packet inspection (`OpenDPI` [17]), the most common protocols that appear being: Bittorrent, HTTP, DNS, SSL, and RTP. The eDonkey protocol is not present in these traces, due to the fact that the P2P file sharing applications used in this Middle East University are based on Bittorrent protocol, and also maybe because the obfuscation techniques used by the protocol does not allow the deep packet inspector to identify it.

To train the model we need to provide eDonkey flows to the model and, thus, we use a specific subset of the eD-DB trace. For the tuning of the system, we use a dataset which contains the rest of eD-DB plus a subset of ME-DB. Moreover, it should be remarked that a cross-validation process is carried out with 9 parts used to train and 1 to test.

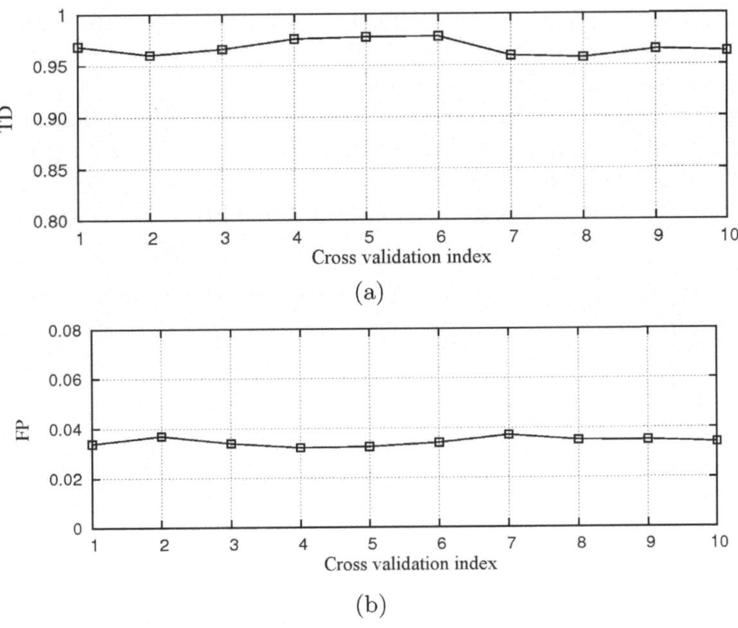

Fig. 3. TD (a) and FP (b) obtained in the cross validation process

5.2 Analysis of Real eDonkey Flows

A first step in our validation process is to carry out a preliminary evaluation to check if real eDonkey flows behave as expected. To carry out this evaluation, we have monitored the evolution of the 240,851 TCP flows in eD-DB, in order to check which are the two first and the two last packets in the communication. As we are monitoring the contents of the flows, and many of them are obfuscated by means of cyphering, we have modified the aMule eDonkey client.

As a result of this inspection, we have confirmed that, in 99.89% of the flows, the two first packets correspond to the `HELLO` and `HELLO answer` messages. Moreover, 96.24% of the flows contain, as the two last packets, the `Start upload request` and the `Queue rank` messages. We have checked that these percentages does not reach 100% due to the existence of incomplete flows in the trace.

These results confirm us the correctness in the selection of two states for both the initial dialog and the termination steps of the generic model when particularized for eDonkey.

5.3 Detection Results

Next we are interested in checking if the proposed detection system achieves the expected detection rates. For the preprocessing of the observations, we have used K-means with a value $K = 32$ and the distance metric was the Euclidean one.

In Fig. 3, we show the results extracted from the cross validation process. Fig. 3(a) shows the results obtained for the true detection rate, while the false positives rates are shown in Fig. 3(b). We can see that our system is able to achieve more than 95% of true detection with around 4% of false positives.

Now we carry out the validation of our system with the validation dataset. Here we study the dependency of the quality of the detection with respect to the selection of the detection threshold, P_{th}. To do this, we carry out the detection with several different values of P_{th} in the probability margin [0.0293,0.3488].

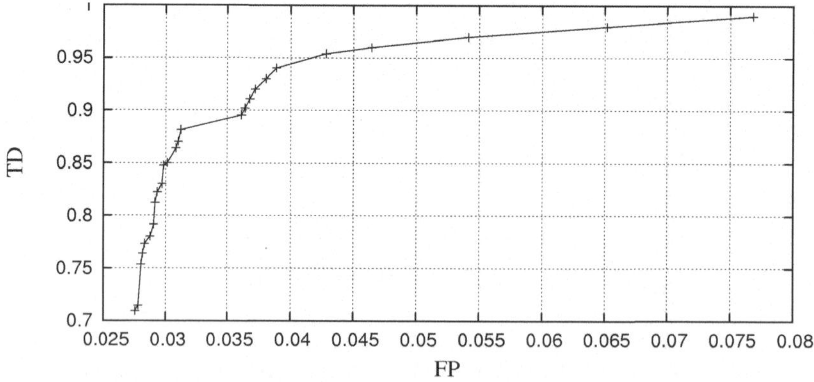

Fig. 4. ROC curve of the eDonkey detection

Table 1. False positive rates for the detection of eDonkey when other protocols are analyzed

	Total flows	**FP rate**
HTTP	710,037	0.036
Multimedia streaming (RTP)	58,509	0.001
P2P file sharing	215,203	0.017

The results of this study are presented as a ROC curve in Fig. 4. As it can be seen, there exists a wide range of TD rate (between 0.9 and 0.95) in which the system gives a small range of false positive values (from 0.036 to 0.038). Note that the results obtained from the validation dataset does not differ substantially from those obtained from the cross validation in the training phase, what leads us to the conclusion that our model generalizes well.

As we mentioned, eD-DB contains both obfuscated and plain flows. Specifically, the TD with eDonkey obfuscated flows is 96.6% and 94.2% for not obfuscated ones. These results demonstrate the independence of the system and the encryption of the target protocol.

Once we have demonstrated that our stochastic model for eDonkey represents conveniently the corresponding flows, an additional detection experiment is carried out to study how behavioral deviations in subsequent observed flows can be used to classify them as generated by other different protocols/services than eDonkey. In particular, we have chosen three groups of services in the ME-DB trace: *(i)* HTTP, *(ii)* multimedia streaming protocols (RTP), and *(iii)* P2P file sharing protocols. The last type of traffic is collected here to show not only the classification capability of our proposal but also its ability to discriminate between *normal* P2P traffic (eDonkey) and *abnormal* P2P traffic (non-eDonkey).

The results obtained from this evaluation are shown in Table 1. Here, we can see the total amount of flows and the rate of false positives yielded by our detection system. Note that, our system is able to distinguish flows from other files sharing applications and from multimedia streaming giving a very low false positive rate. Finally, HTTP is also well discarded by the detection system, yielding an acceptable false positive rate.

Summarizing, all the detection results obtained show the higher performance of our approach in comparison with similar schemes in the literature, as discussed along Section 2. This way, our stochastic traffic identification system can be used both as a multi-protocol classifier and as an anomaly-based detection scheme with security purposes.

6 Conclusions and Future Work

In this paper, we introduce a stochastic methodology based on the use of Markov models to classify network traffic. First, a generic HMM is contributed, which relies on a flow-based detection and the consideration of every packet in the flow as an incoming observation for the system. After that, the model is particularized to represent eDonkey communications as a particular case study. For that, different key issues are discussed: vector parameterization and normalization, system structure, etc.

To validate our classification proposal several experiments with eDonkey and non-eDonkey network traces are carried out. The results obtained show that our approach is able to detect normal eDonkey flows with high accuracy, both in terms of true detection rate and false positive rate. Even when the processed flows are obfuscated or belong to a different P2P file sharing protocol, like bitTorrent or Gnutella, the proposed detection system achieves really good detection results.

This work could be seen as a proof of concept of the capabilities of stochastic traffic identification techniques in the field of security management. Due to the extremely hard task of having a complete and current P2P attack database we choose to detect a specific P2P protocol. We assume that if we are able of distinguishing a particular P2P protocol (eDonkey) from other P2P protocols with the same purpose (file sharing), we will be able of distinguishing, for example, a P2P protocol used by P2P bots to communicate between them from normal P2P traffic. However, there is much work still to be done, in the following we present some future research:

- To use our classification proposal to differentiate traffic generated by a P2P botnet from the normal P2P traffic.
- To extend the modeling to other different services, in order to check the versatility of the proposed detection system.
- To develop and evaluate a continuous variant of the HMMs (CHMM). In this case, each feature vector is not associated with a discrete centroid in the VQ, but with a probability density function.

Acknowledgements. This work has been partially supported by Spanish MICINN through project TEC2011-22579.

References

1. Jin, Y., Duffield, N., Erman, J., Haffner, P., Sen, S., Zhang, Z.L.: A Modular Machine Learning System for Flow-Level Traffic Classification in Large Networks. ACM Trans. Knowl. Discov. Data 6(1), 4:1–4:34 (2012)
2. Chen, H., Zhou, X., You, F., Wang, C.: Study of Double-Characteristics-Based SVM Method for P2P Traffic Identification. In: 2010 Second International Conference on Networks Security Wireless Communications and Trusted Computing (NSWCTC), vol. 1, pp. 202–205 (April 2010)
3. Callado, A., Kamienski, C., Szabo, G., Gero, B., Kelner, J., Fernandes, S., Sadok, D.: A Survey on Internet Traffic Identification. IEEE Communications Surveys & Tutorials 11(3), 37–52 (2009)
4. Dainotti, A., Pescape, A., Claffy, K.: Issues and future directions in traffic classification. IEEE Network 26(1), 35–40 (2012)

5. Dahmouni, H., Vaton, S., Rossé, D.: A markovian signature-based approach to IP traffic classification. In: Proceedings of the 3rd Annual ACM Workshop on Mining Network Data, MineNet 2007, pp. 29–34. ACM, New York (2007)
6. Wright, C.V., Monrose, F., Masson, G.M.: On Inferring Application Protocol Behaviors in Encrypted Network Traffic. J. Mach. Learn. Res. 7, 2745–2769 (2006)
7. Dainotti, A., de Donato, W., Pescape, A., Salvo Rossi, P.: Classification of Network Traffic via Packet-Level Hidden Markov Models. In: Global Telecommunications Conference, IEEE GLOBECOM 2008, pp. 1–5. IEEE (November 2008)
8. Markov, A., Nagorny, N.: The theory of algorithms. Mathematics and its applications: Soviet series. Kluwer Academic Publishers (1988)
9. Dymarski, P.: Hidden Markov Models, Theory and Applications. InTech (2011)
10. Fink, G.: Markov models for pattern recognition: from theory to applications. Springer (2008)
11. Forney, G.J.: The Viterbi algorithm. Proceedings of the IEEE 61(3), 268–278 (1973)
12. Baum, L.E., Petrie, T., Soules, G., Weiss, N.: A Maximization Technique Occurring in the Statistical Analysis of Probabilistic Functions of Markov Chains. The Annals of Mathematical Statistics 41(1), 164–171 (1970)
13. Thompson, K., Miller, G., Wilder, R.: Wide-area Internet traffic patterns and characteristics. IEEE Network 11(6), 10–23 (1997)
14. Feldmann, A.: Characteristics of TCP Connection Arrivals. Technical memorandum, AT&T Labs Research (1998)
15. Johnson, R.A., Wichern, D.W. (eds.): Applied multivariate statistical analysis. Prentice-Hall, Inc., Upper Saddle River (1988)
16. AMULE: aMule, `http://www.amule.org` (last accessed: January 2013)
17. OpenDPI: OpenDPI, `http://www.opendpi.org` (last accessed: January 2013)

A Technology Independent Security Gateway for Real-Time Multimedia Communication

Fudong Li[1], Nathan Clarke[1,2], and Steven Furnell[1,2]

[1] Centre for Security, Communications and Network Research (CSCAN), School of Computing & Mathematics, Plymouth University, Plymouth, PL4 8AA, United Kingdom
info@cscan.org

[2] School of Computer and Information Science, Edith Cowan University, Perth, Western Australia

Abstract. With currently more than 178 million users worldwide, the demand on real-time multimedia communication services (e.g. VoIP, video conference) grows steadily. However, whilst the protocols utilised in such communications are standardised, internal aspects are not. For example, if calling parties utilise incompatible media codecs or security mechanisms, a real-time multimedia communication cannot be established. The latter would result in either a failure to establish a connection or a plaintext connection that leaves the communication open to attacks. This paper proposes a novel technology independent security gateway for real-time multimedia communications which offers ciphering assistance for these terminals when they have incompatible security mechanisms and/or media codecs, allowing them to communicate in a seamless and secure manner despite their incompatibilities. The proposed security gateway operates across standard IP protocols and provides a flexible, scalable and robust system that is capable of managing the ciphering requirements of a modern communications system.

Keywords: IMS, security gateway, SIP, cross-ciphering.

1 Introduction

With the foundation laid by the IP Multimedia Subsystem (IMS), Internet users can establish real-time multimedia calls not only within the Internet Protocol (IP) world but also interconnect with terminals from other types of communication networks, such as the traditional telephony network and Terrestrial Trunked Radio (TETRA) networks. For instance, users can utilise their IMS terminals to participate a business video conference, make a Voice over IP (VoIP) call to a normal telephone and even communicate to a police officer's TETRA terminal in a life threaten situation [1]. In comparison with other communication networks, the IMS architecture provides a cheap, flexible and convenient communication channel to many Internet users. Indeed, with currently more than 178 million subscribers worldwide, the demand on real-time multimedia communication services grows steadily on a yearly basis [2].

J. Lopez, X. Huang, and R. Sandhu (Eds.): NSS 2013, LNCS 7873, pp. 14–25, 2013.

In order to facilitate the high demand for real-time multimedia communication services, various types of terminals have been developed by different providers around the world [3]. Within the IMS architecture, it is universal that these terminals rely upon the Session Initiation Protocol (SIP) for call setup and control in the signalling plane and the Real-time Transport Protocol (RTP) or Secure RTP (SRTP) for media transmission in the media plane [4-6]. However, they can utilise various types of codecs to encode and decode the media and different security mechanisms to secure the media transmission. As a result, in addition to the existing mismatch issues among terminals from different communication networks (e.g. between IMS and TETRA), this may also create incompatibility issues (e.g. early call termination during the setup phase in the signalling plane) between various IMS terminals.

Regarding the challenge posed by incompatible codecs, many media gateways have been devised in the media plane for the purpose of transcoding (i.e. converts media data from the format of one codec into another's), enabling two terminals to establish a communication despite utilising different codecs and/or from different network domains [7]. For instance, Asterisk which is one of the most popular open source media gateways supports more than 10 popular codecs enabling various transcoding options, such as facilitating an IMS terminal which utilises G.711 codec to communicate a normal mobile phone terminal which employs Adaptive Multi-Rate Narrowband (AMR-NB) codec [8]. Another example, by utilising its own media gateway, Skype, one of the most well-known proprietary VoIP applications, can establish communication with landline telephones despite utilising different codecs.

When users utilise different media security mechanisms within terminals to communicate with one another, a call cannot be established in normal circumstances unless in plain text (i.e. RTP format). However, it is well documented that unprotected real-time media traffic is open to eavesdropping and man-in-the-middle attacks [9]. By utilising these tricks, attackers can collect user's sensitive information (e.g. bank account details) and then abused them. As a result, a security gateway, which can provide ciphering support (i.e. transforms encrypted data from one format to another), is required to ensure the communication can be established and protected between security mechanisms and/or media codecs incompatible terminals. In comparison with the maturity of the media gateway, little work has been carried out on investigating the need of a security gateway. Therefore, this paper proposes a novel technology independent security gateway for real-time multimedia services that can provide ciphering support for terminals with incompatible security controls allowing them to communicate in a safe and secure fashion.

This paper begins by presenting the popularity and importance of the real-time multimedia services. The paper then proceeds to describe existing gateways that support real-time multimedia services. In section 3, a novel technology independent security gateway for real-time multimedia communication is proposed and details of its components, capabilities, working modes and challenges are thoroughly described and discussed. The paper finishes by highlighting the future development of the security gateway.

2 Existing Gateways for Real-Time Multimedia Services

In order to allow real-time multimedia services to run smoothly between incompatible terminals and/or different types of communication networks, a gateway which provides media and/or security support is required (as illustrated in Figure 1). During a call setup phase, control elements (e.g. Serving Call Session Control Function (S-CSCF)) of a communication network (e.g. IMS) examine the capability of the caller and callee's terminals and decide whether the assistance of the gateway is required; if it is required, the element of the signalling plane will notify the Resource Function Controller of the gateway and exchange configuration parameters with it for setting up both the incoming and outgoing legs. Once the call setup phase is completed, the Resource Function Processor of the gateway will provide the media and/or ciphering support in a transparently manner allowing two terminals to communicate despite their incompatibility.

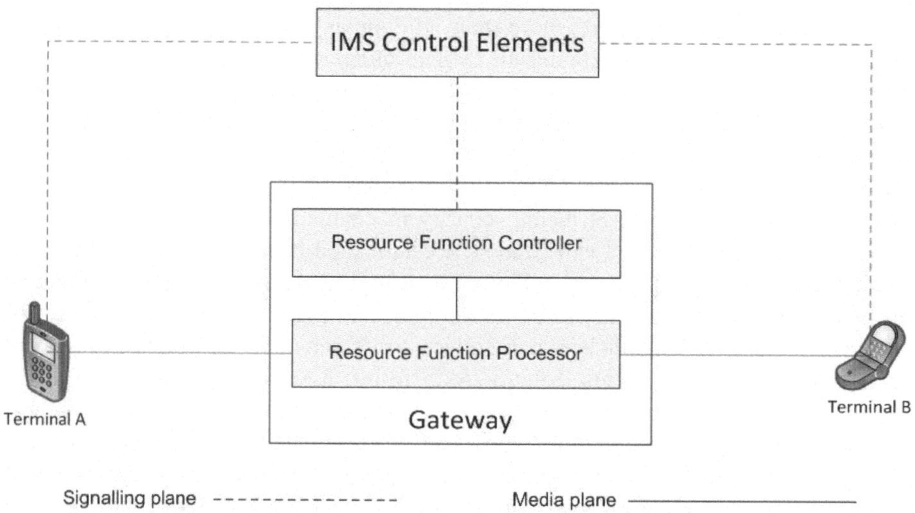

Fig. 1. A generic gateway for real-time multimedia services

Based upon the functionality, a gateway can be either categorised as a media gateway or a security gateway.

A media gateway is dedicated to provide media support when terminals have incompatible codecs. It is further divided into a Media Resource Function Controller (MRFC) and a Media Resource Function Processor (MRFP) [10]. The MRFC is a signalling node that is in charge of interpreting information coming from the signalling plane and also controlling the MRFP; the MRFP is a media plane node that is utilised to transparently perform media transcoding process if required. Ideally, the media gateway should be equipped with as many codecs as possible, to support a wide range of transcoding tasks.

The idea of the media gateway was first proposed in 1999 by [11], describing a VoIP call being established between terminals from Asynchronous Transfer Mode (ATM), IP and Integrated Services Digital Network (ISDN) networks despite the incompatibility of the terminals. Since then much research in the field of media gateways have been carried out to provide interoperability between incompatible terminals from the same or different networks, including: [12-16]. In addition to the work performed by the research community, telecommunication bodies and manufacturers have also contributed significantly towards the maturity of the media gateway. For instance, 3rd Generation Partnership Project (3GPP) has published a series of technical reports (e.g. 3GPP TS 29.232 (from release 4 to 12) on regulating the functionalities of the media gateway [17]. Also, Cisco, one of the world leading networking equipment manufacturers, has a wide range of gateways, which can support multimedia communication [18]. Nevertheless, it is not authors' intention to discussion the capability and performance of these existing media gateways, but to highlight the amount of work have been given in the area of media gateway.

A security gateway is designed for providing ciphering support when terminals have different security mechanisms and/or incompatible codecs. Similar to the media gateway, it should also have two components: Security Resource Function Controller (SRFC) and Security Resource Function Processor (SRFP). The SRFC is a signalling node that communicates with other controlling functions in the signalling plane and also controls the SRFP. In order to provide ciphering assistance, the security gateway should also support as many security mechanisms as possible.

With the purpose of providing security for the real-time multimedia traffic, several media gateways are equipped with security mechanisms to support SRTP traffics. [19] describes a security gateway that provides secured communications for terminals that do not support any security controls within its local network. As a result, the call is transported in plain text between the security gateway and the security incompatible terminal, allowing anyone on the same local network to listen to the conversation via a network monitoring tool (e.g. Wireshark). Asterisk, one of the most popular open source media gateways, offers terminals with same security compatibilities to establish secured communication [20]; nonetheless, it cannot provide any cross-ciphering support for terminals with incompatible security mechanisms. Skype, one of the most popular proprietary VoIP applications, utilises AES encryption to secure end-to-end Skype-to-Skype calls [21]; however, it does not support interoperability with any other proprietary or open source VoIP applications. In addition, as these existing gateways are designed predominately for the purpose of transcoding, it would be difficult for them to provide sufficient security support to these high demands real-time multimedia services. Therefore, a dedicated security gateway that can provide ciphering support allowing interoperability between incompatible terminals is required for real-time multimedia services.

In the next section, a novel security gateway that can provide interoperability support for incompatible terminals will be proposed and fully described, along with its internal components and functionalities.

3 A Technology Independent Security Gateway for Real-Time multimedia communication

With the purpose of enabling a wide range of incompatible terminals to securely communicate with each other at a high level of performance, a novel technology independent security gateway (TI-SGW) for real-time multimedia service is proposed. In order to provide the ciphering support in a secure and timely fashion, a number of internal modules of the TI-SGW architecture have been devised and are illustrated in Figure 2.

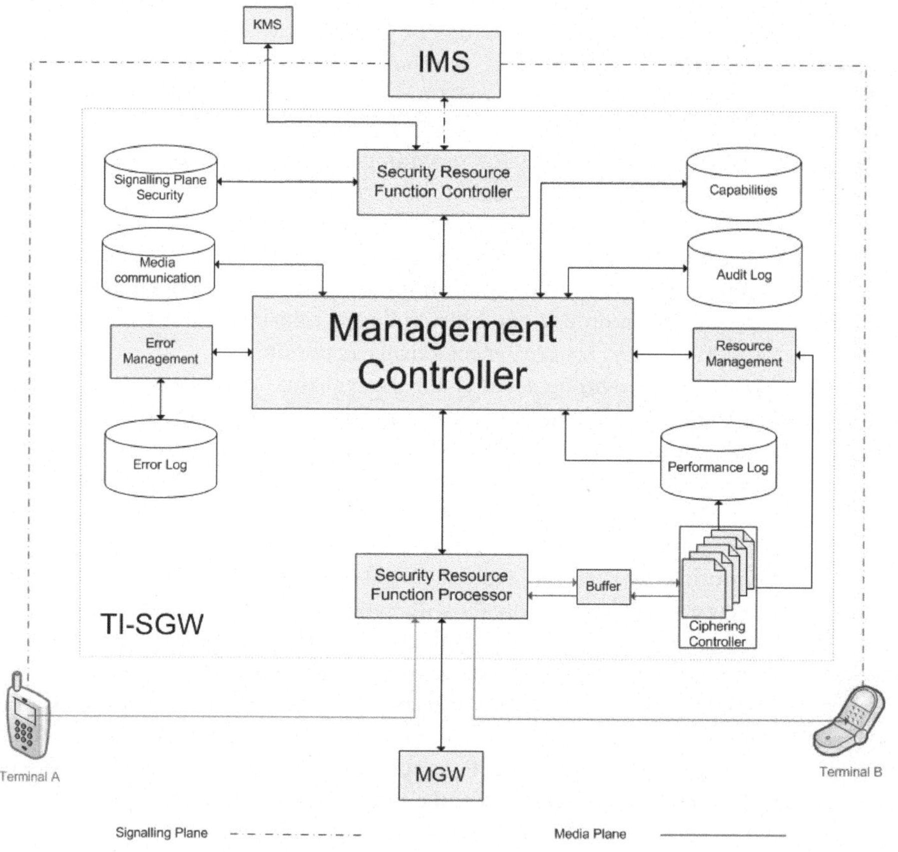

Fig. 2. TI-SGW Architecture

The architecture is largely divided into three areas: the signalling, media and management segments. For the signalling plane, its principal responsibility is to securely establish signalling communication with the IMS controlling system. From the IMS controlling system, the TI-SGW can obtain all the parameters required to set up a seamless media plane ciphering process for both calling parties upon request.

The media plane is responsible for identifying incoming media flows, applying appropriate ciphering on the media and forwarding it to the appointed receivers in a secure and timely manner. The Management segment of the TI-SGW controls both the media and signal plane interfaces and also provides resource management, error control, performance monitoring and accountability functionalities.

3.1 Components of the TI-SGW Architecture

The following sections describe each of the architectural components in more detail, providing an overview of its role and the relationship between components.

Security Resource Function Controller (SRFC) is mainly responsible for establishing mutual authentication with the IMS signalling plane and determining the parameters for setting up media plane security when any ciphering assistance is required. Two functions have been designed to achieve these responsibilities:

- Authentication function (TI-SGW-AF)
- Media plane security setup function (TI-SGW-MPS)

The TI-SGW-AF is employed to facilitate all signalling plane security setup procedures between the TI-SGW and the IMS signalling plane, including mutual authentication, key establishment and security association setup [22]. In addition, the TI-SGW-AF is utilised to perform the mutual authentication process between the TI-SGW and a Key Management Server (KMS). This permits the TI-SGW to securely request and retrieve keys and tickets from the KMS when a KMS is utilised as the key management solution. All details to assist the setup of authentication processes are stored in the Signalling Plane Security database.

The TI-SGW-MPS is responsible for configuring the security associations for the setup of media transmissions between the TI-SGW and a real-time multimedia terminal. When ciphering assistance is requested, the TI-SGW-MPS selects an appropriate set of crypto suite and key management solutions from a capability list to set up both the incoming and outgoing calling legs. Also, all the information which is related to the configuration, such as caller and callee's contact details (e.g. IP addresses), their crypto suites and key management solutions, will be securely stored in the Media Communication database as a reference for the later ciphering process in the media plane.

Security Resource Function Processor (SRFP) is the interface of the TI-SGW to any media transmissions. Upon receiving the media traffic, the SRFP inspects it based upon the information stored in the Media Communication database for obtaining details (e.g. cipher keys) which will be utilised for requesting computing resources (e.g. storage and processing power) to establish the ciphering process. Once the ciphering process is completed, the SRFP will send the processed media to the appointed receiver. Details of the whole process will then be stored in the Audit Log for the purpose of accounting.

Resource Management is employed to manage the allocation of computer processing resource for the ciphering process. It constantly monitors the resource, and reserves and distributes it based upon each ciphering request. At the same time, it also gathers all necessary security parameters (e.g. crypto suites) from each request and passes it onto the ciphering process. This will enable the ciphering process to be taken smoothly and also enable the TI-SGW to scale up accordingly with large volumes of media connections.

Ciphering Controller serves the TI-SGW by providing the actual ciphering and deciphering process. Upon receiving the media data, it decrypts the media on the incoming leg by utilising crypto suites and cipher keys that are used by the caller; and then encrypts the plain text media by employing crypto suites and ciphering key which are utilised by the callee. As the TI-SGW is designed to serve multiple incoming communications, the ciphering function operates in a multitasking manner. All details of ciphering process (e.g. cipher suites and time of ciphering process) will be stored in the Performance Log storage for the purpose of valuation of the ciphering process. For media connections that also require a change in codec, the deciphered text is sent to a media gateway (MGW) for transcoding prior to the re-ciphering process.

Error Management provides oversight and control of internal errors that can arise from any unexpected events that may be experienced. Controls will ensure errors within any of the architectural components are identified and reported. All details of the error event will be stored in the Error Log for the purpose of accountability.

Management Controller is the primary controller of the TI-SGW that regulates the system and liaises between components. Apart from overseeing the entire ciphering process, it is also responsible for managing the ciphering capability of the TI-SGW and the feedback of the ciphering process; both tasks are carried out by the Capability List function and the Performance Enquiries function respectively.

- **Capability List function:** By default, the TI-SGW is equipped with various crypto suites and key exchange solutions that are utilised to assist the ciphering process. During the setup process of these security mechanisms, details of them are extracted by the Capability list function and then stored in the Capabilities storage. This is utilised to assist the negotiation of the media plane security during the call setup process.
- **Performance Enquiries function:** is utilised to present answers to any enquires regarding the performance of the ciphering process which is stored in the Performance Log storage, such as which crypto suite was utilised, how long a typical ciphering process takes, what the memory and processing consumptions are for a particular ciphering task. The primary propose of this function is to ensure the ciphering process is undertaken in a timely manner and in accordance with Quality of Experience (QoE) expectations. The resulting audit is useful in identifying particular issues with crypto suites and performance. For instance, security policies could be amended based upon particular performance characteristics of certain crypto suites.

3.2 Ciphering Capability of the TI-SGW

As mentioned in the previous section, the main task of the TI-SGW is to provide ciphering assistance. In order to offer the assistance whenever it is requested, the TI-SGW needs to support as many real-time multimedia security mechanisms as possible. It is well established that these security mechanisms utilise the SRTP as the fundamental protocol for securing the real-time multimedia traffic and the SRTP employs a number of crypto suites and key exchange solutions to achieve that. Therefore, all the crypto suites and key exchange solutions which the TI-SGW should support are described in the following section.

Crypto Suites of the TI-SGW. A crypto suite is a combination of encryption and message authentication code (MAC) algorithms that provide confidentiality, integrity and authentication for data. The default encryption method for the SRTP is Advanced Encryption Standard (AES) which can operate in two modes: Segmented Integer Counter Mode AES (AES_CM) and AES in f8-mode [6]; while the default message authentication and integrity method for the SRTP is HMAC-SHA1 [6]. By utilising the combination of encryption methods, message authentication and integrity solutions, in addition to various key lengths, a number of crypto suites (as demonstrated in Table 1) can be obtained [23-24]. Furthermore, it is envisaged that the TI-SGW should also provide support for future releases of crypto suites for the SRTP, enabling future compatibility and longevity of the system.

Table 1. A list of crypto suites of the SRTP

Crypto suites
AES_CM_128_HMAC_SHA1_80
AES_CM_128_HMAC_SHA1_32
AES_F8_128_HMAC_SHA1_80
AES_192_CM_HMAC_SHA1_80
AES_192_CM_HMAC_SHA1_32
AES_256_CM_HMAC_SHA1_80
AES_256_CM_HMAC_SHA1_32

Key Exchange Solutions of the TI-SGW. A number of key exchange protocols have been proposed to manage the key exchange between terminals to enable the establishment of the SRTP communication [25]. The decision as to whether the assistance of the TI-SGW should be required is decided by the IMS signalling plane. Any potential key exchange protocols of the TI-SGW must be indicated and initialized in the IMS signalling plane, otherwise the call which is meant to be supported by the TI-SGW cannot be established. Therefore, key management solutions that utilize the media plane for advertising their usage will not be supported by the TI-SGW. Based upon these premises, the IT-SGW will support the following key exchange protocols: Session Description Protocol (SDP) Security Descriptions for Media Streams (SDES) [23], MIKEY pre-shared key (MIKEY-TICKET) [26], MIKEY-public key encryption (MIKEY-IBAKE) [27], IMS Authentication and Key Agreement (AKA) [25], Otway-Rees based key management solution [25] and ZRTP [28]. In addition, the

TI-SGW should be easily adaptable with any future key exchange solutions that also utilize the IMS signalling plane for initialization of the key management.

3.3 Operational Modes of the TI-SGW

When two terminals share common codecs and security mechanisms, the media flow can be directly established between them. While two terminals do not have common security mechanisms and/or codecs, the TI-SGW and/or MGW will be required in the media flow to provide ciphering and/or transcoding support respectively allowing interoperability between the two incompatible terminals. The usage of the MGW is required only when two calling parties do not share common codecs. In comparison, the need of the TI-SGW will be compulsory in the following three scenarios:

1. Two terminals do not share same security mechanisms but same codec.
2. Two terminals do not share same security mechanisms or same codec.
3. Two terminals do share same security mechanisms but not same codec.

Each of these scenarios defines one working mode of the TI-SGW. As a result, the TI-SGW has three working modes accordingly to the above scenarios:

- Cross-ciphering mode **without** the presence of the MGW.
- Cross-ciphering mode **with** the presence of the MGW.
- Mono-ciphering mode **with** the presence of the MGW.

3.4 Challenges of the TI-SGW

The proposed the TI-SGW can provide ciphering support for the real-time multimedia services whenever it is required. Hence, this solution can ensure that the real-time multimedia services are protected during a session despite terminals may have incompatible security mechanisms and/or codecs. Nonetheless, there are a number of challenges that the TI-SGW has both internally and externally.

For the internal challenges, they are related to the TI-SGW itself, including the security mechanism, multitasking and performance:

- Security mechanisms: the TI-SGW needs to be regularly updated with any newly released security mechanisms to ensure that the gateway can provide maximum ciphering support for the real-time multimedia services.
- Multitasking: the TI-SGW is required to simultaneously handle multiple ciphering jobs if required. These jobs can be concurrently carried out in various working modes of the TI-SGW. In addition, should operational requirements exceed a singular TI-SGW, a load-balancing approach with multiple TI-SGWs can be implemented.
- Performance: as the real-time multimedia services require a high level of demand on performance. The TI-SGW has to be able to complete the ciphering job in a timely manner to minimise the impact that is introduced by the encryption and decryption process.

For the external challenges, they are the surrounding environments and factors which affect the TI-SGW, including:

- Upgrading of the IMS control element: the IMS control element (e.g. SCSCF) is required to be equipped with an intelligent function which can intercept and analyse the SDP message, detect the need of the TI-SGW and configure it for the ciphering support.
- Regulations: efforts of standardisation bodies and industrial forums are also required for setting up new standards and regulations to govern the development of the TI-SGW and avoid any incompatibilities between any future security gateways.

All of the aforementioned challenges are critical for the development of the TI-SGW as any of them can affect the role that the TI-SGW is designed to complete, enabling a secured communication channel between media security mechanisms and codecs incompatible terminals to be established.

4 Conclusions and Future Work

The paper has identified the need for a technology independent security gateway that is capable of meeting the needs of incompatible security requirements in an efficient and effective manner. The proposed TI-SGW has been devised to incorporate a series of management control functions that permit various performance and accountability functions in addition to providing wide-spread security compatibility.

In the next phase of the research, a prototype of the designed security gateway that can provide ciphering assistance for incompatible terminals of real-time multimedia services will be developed. This will be incorporated within a complete inter-domain IMS/TETRA-based system that will permit an operational evaluation of the system. With respect to performance, a series of experiments will be devised to study the ciphering, multitasking and performance capabilities of the security gateway.

Acknowledgements. The research leading to these results has received funding from the European Union Seventh Framework Programme (FP7/2007-2013) under grant agreement 284863 (FP7 SEC GERYON).

References

1. Aiache, H., Knopp, R., Koufos, K., Salovuori, H., Simon, P.: Increasing Public Safety Communications Interoperability: The CHORIST Broadband and Wideband Rapidly Deployable Systems. In: IEEE International Conference on Communications Workshops, ICC Workshops 2009, June 14-18, pp. 1–6 (2009), doi:10.1109/ICCW.2009.5208003
2. Infonetics Research: VoIP services market growing strong as businesses seek flexibility, easier management (2012), http://www.infonetics.com/pr/2012/VoIP-UC-Services-Market-Forecast-and-SIP-Trunking-Survey-Highlights.asp

3. Myvoiprovider: Top 100 VoIP Provider World Ranking (2012), http://www.myvoipprovider.com/en/Top_100_VoIP_Providers
4. Rosenberg, J., Schulzrinne, H., Camarillo, G., Johnston, A., Peterson, J., Sparks, R., Handley, M., Schooler, E.: SIP: Session Initiation Protocol. RFC3261, IETF (2002), http://www.ietf.org/rfc/rfc3261.txt
5. Schulzrinne, H., Casner, S., Frederick, R., Jacobson, V.: RTP: A Transport Protocol for Real-Time Applications. RFC3550, IETF (2003), http://www.ietf.org/rfc/rfc3550.txt
6. Baugher, M., McGrew, D., Naslund, M., Carrara, E., Norrman, K.: The Secure Real-time Transport Protocol (SRTP). RFC 3711, IETF (2004), http://www.ietf.org/rfc/rfc3711.txt
7. Voip-Info: VoIP Gateways (2012), http://www.voip-info.org/wiki/view/VoIP+Gateways
8. Asterisk: Codec Modules (2012), https://wiki.asterisk.org/wiki/display/AST/Codec+Modules
9. Keromytis, A.D.: A Comprehensive Survey of Voice over IP Security Research. IEEE Communications Surveys & Tutorials 14(2), 514–537 (2012), doi:10.1109/SURV.2011.031611.00112
10. 3GPP TS 24.147: Conferencing using the IP Multimedia (IM) Core Network (CN) subsystem; Stage 3, release 11 (2012), http://www.3gpp.org/ftp/Specs/html-info/24147.htm
11. Grilo, A.M., Carvalho, P.M., Medeiros, L.M., Nunes, M.S.: VTOA/VoIP/ISDN telephony gateway. In: 1999 2nd International Conference on ATM, ICATM 1999, pp. 230–235 (1999), doi:10.1109/ICATM.1999.786807
12. Conte, A., Anquetil, L.P., Levy, T.: Experiencing Megaco protocol for controlling non-decomposable VoIP gateways. In: Proceedings of the IEEE International Conference on Networks (ICON 2000), pp. 105–111 (2000), doi:10.1109/ICON.2000.875776
13. Castello, F.C., Balbinot, R., Silveira, J.G., Santos, P.M.: A robust architecture for IP telephony systems interconnection. In: 2003 IEEE Pacific Rim Conference on Communications, Computers and Signal Processing, PACRIM, August 28-30, vol. 2, pp. 593–596 (2003), doi:10.1109/PACRIM.2003.1235851
14. Yoo, H.K., Kang, B.R.: A media stream processing of VoIP media gateway. In: The 9th Asia-Pacific Conference on Communications, APCC 2003, September 21-24, vol. 1, pp. 91–94 (2003), doi:10.1109/APCC.2003.1274318
15. Guo, Y., Liang, M., Guo, Y., Zhang, L.: A design scheme of PSTN media gateway. In: Proceedings of the 2004 7th International Conference on Signal Processing, ICSP 2004, August 31-September 4, vol. 3, pp. 2651–2654 (2004), doi:10.1109/ICOSP.2004.1442327
16. Kang, T., Bae, H., Kim, D., Kim, D.: SIP/SDP signaling of media gateway with transcoding function in converged network. In: The 6th International Conference on Advanced Communication Technology, vol. 2, pp. 842–845 (2004), doi:10.1109/ICACT.2004.1292988
17. 3GPP TS 29.232: Media Gateway Controller (MGC) - Media Gateway (MGW) interface; Stage 3 (2012), http://www.3gpp.org/ftp/Specs/html-info/29232.htm
18. Cisco: Voice and Unified Communications (2012), http://www.cisco.com/en/US/products/sw/voicesw/products.html
19. Li, J.S., Tzeng, J.J., Kuo, C.M.: Building Security Gateway. In: International Conference on Information Networking, ICOIN 2009, January 21-24, pp. 1–3 (2009)
20. Asterisk: Secured calling tutorial (2011), https://wiki.asterisk.org/wiki/display/AST/Secure+Calling+Tutorial

21. Skype: Privacy and Security (2012), https://support.skype.com/en/faq/FA31/does-skype-use-encryption
22. 3GPP TS 33.203: 3G security; Access security for IP-based services (2012), http://www.3gpp.org/ftp/Specs/html-info/33203.htm
23. Andreasen, F., Baugher, M., Wing, D.: Session Description Protocol (SDP) Security Descriptions for Media Streams, RFC 4568, IETF (2006), http://www.ietf.org/rfc/rfc4568.txt
24. McGrew, D.: The Use of AES-192 and AES-256 in Secure RTP, RFC 6188, IETF (2011), http://www.ietf.org/rfc/rfc6188.txt
25. 3GPP TR 33.828: IP Multimedia Subsystem (IMS) media plane security (2012), http://www.3gpp.org/ftp/Specs/html-info/33828.htm
26. Mattsson, J., Tian, T.: MIKEY-TICKET: Ticket-Based Modes of Key Distribution in Multimedia Internet KEYing (MIKEY), RFC6043, IETF (2011), http://www.ietf.org/rfc/rfc6043.txt
27. Cakulev, V., Sundaram, G.: MIKEY-IBAKE: Identity-Based Authenticated Key Exchange (IBAKE) Mode of Key Distribution in Multimedia Internet KEYing (MIKEY), RFC 6267, IETF (2011), http://www.ietf.org/rfc/rfc6267.txt
28. Zimmermann, P., Johnston, A. (ed.), Callas, J.: ZRTP: Media Path Key Agreement for Unicast Secure RTP, RFC 6189, IETF (2011), http://www.ietf.org/rfc/rfc6189.txt

Efficient Attribute Based Access Control Mechanism for Vehicular Ad Hoc Network

Y. Sreenivasa Rao and Ratna Dutta

Department of Mathematics
Indian Institute of Technology Kharagpur
Kharagpur-721302, India
{ysrao,ratna}@maths.iitkgp.ernet.in

Abstract. In this work, we provide a solution to help mitigate the problem of the large ciphertext size in designing access control mechanism using Attribute Based Encryption (ABE) for vehicular communications. Our approach is to use access policy in Disjunctive Normal Form (DNF) enabling the *length of ciphertext* linear in the number of conjunctions instead of number of attributes in the access policy. This reduces communication overhead in contrast to the existing works in the area. The proposed scheme is computationally efficient as it requires only a *constant number of pairings* during encryption and decryption. Vehicles can validate their secret attribute-keys obtained from the Central Authority (CA) as well as from an Road Side Unit (RSU) individually. Remarkably, our approach allows vehicles to send multiple messages in a single ciphertext. Our scheme is collusion-resistant, secure under compromised RSUs and is proven to be secure in generic group model.

Keywords: vehicular ad hoc network, access control, attribute based encryption, disjunctive normal form, generic group model.

1 Introduction

The development of Vehicular Ad Hoc Network (VANET) allows vehicles to communicate on roads to increase awareness of their environment and thereby optimize road safety, comfortable road traffic and efficient utilization of infotainment services. However, concerns over loss of privacy and message authentication is an overwhelming barrier to the adoption of VANET by consumers. For example, a selfish user can send a bogus traffic message to reduce traffic on the road he is taking, thereby more traffic on another road in the network. The main security issues addressed in VANET include message authentication, entity authentication, location privacy, trust management and revocation [12], [19]. Message authentication is an active area of research in the literature [16], [17], [18]. Location privacy is another crucial security issue in VANET. An excellent way to assuage location privacy is to assign to each vehicle a set of unrelated pseudonyms. Along with each pseudonym, a public and secret key pair is also assigned by a Central Authority (CA) to respective vehicle. Access control in

J. Lopez, X. Huang, and R. Sandhu (Eds.): NSS 2013, LNCS 7873, pp. 26–39, 2013.

VANET has received very little attention so far [10, 11, 13–15] and is an interesting avenue of research. Adoption of Attribute Based Encryption (ABE) can satisfactorily address the access control concerns for VANET. ABE is a generalization of Identity Based Encryption (IBE) proposed by Shamir [1]. The first ABE scheme was proposed in [2] by Sahai and Waters. Subsequently, there have been various ABE schemes in the literature [3]-[9]. In ABE, each user is ascribed a set of descriptive attributes, while secret key and ciphertext are associated with an access policy or a set of attributes. Decryption is then successful only when the attributes of ciphertext or secret key satisfy the access policy.

In this work we focus on designing a computationally efficient access control scheme with low communication overhead for vehicular ad hoc network adapting Müller et al. [8] concept of distributed attribute based encryption. Our access control policies are expressed in Disjunctive Normal Form (DNF) wherein each conjunction consists of static and dynamic attributes of selected vehicles which are all monitored essentially by one RSU. An attribute which remains the same during a long period of time is called *static* (e.g. vehicle type, manufacturing year) whereas if it changes frequently, it is called *dynamic* (e.g. road name, lane number). A vehicle can disseminate data in terms of DNF formula over attributes issued from CA and any chosen set of RSUs. Our approach enables a vehicle to communicate with any number of vehicles which are monitored by different RSUs. The length of ciphertext is proportional to the number of conjunctions occur in the DNF access policy instead of the number of attributes in it. This reduces communication cost significantly when compared to the existing access control schemes [10] and [11] for VANET. On a more positive note, the number of required pairing operations in our scheme is constant. If the communication amongst vehicles is limited to one RSU's range, the computation and communication costs of our construction are constant. In this case, our approach utilizes only three exponentiations and two pairing operations during encryption and decryption, respectively, in addition with one pre-computed pairing during system setup. Moreover, it uses constant length ciphertexts to transmit data.

Another interesting feature of the proposed scheme is that it can send different messages simultaneously to different vehicles through a single ciphertext, thus reduces network traffic significantly. In our system, vehicles can validate their secret attribute keys obtained from the CA as well as from an RSU individually. To achieve location privacy, each vehicle is assigned a set of unrelated pseudonyms by the CA. Our scheme has a collusion resistance capability and is secure in the presence of compromised RSUs. We analyze security of our scheme in the generic bilinear group model. In the proposed scheme, no RSU can alone decrypt any ciphertext and any RSU may join the network by simply publishing the public keys of its dynamic attributes. The security against collusion attacks is not addressed by [10] and this scheme does not withstand attacks mounted by compromised RSU. The scheme in [11] is collusion resistant and provides security against compromised RSUs. However, no formal security proofs are given in [10], [11] in existing security models. Our scheme is proven to be collusion resistant, secure against compromised RSUs and is supported by formal security proof in the generic group model.

2 Preliminary

Definition 1 (Bilinear Groups). *Let $\mathbb{G}$ and $\mathbb{G}_T$ be multiplicative cyclic groups of prime order p. Let g be a generator of $\mathbb{G}$. A mapping $e : \mathbb{G} \times \mathbb{G} \to \mathbb{G}_T$ is said to be bilinear if $e(u^a, v^b) = e(u, v)^{ab}$, for all $u, v \in \mathbb{G}$ and $a, b \in \mathbb{Z}_p$ and non-degenerate if $e(g, g) \neq 1_T$ (where, 1_T is the unit element in $\mathbb{G}_T$). We say that $\mathbb{G}$ is a bilinear group if the group operation in $\mathbb{G}$ can be computed efficiently and there exists $\mathbb{G}_T$ for which the bilinear map $e : \mathbb{G} \times \mathbb{G} \to \mathbb{G}_T$ is efficiently computable. Notice that the map e is symmetric since $e(g^a, g^b) = e(g, g)^{ab} = e(g^b, g^a)$.*

2.1 Communication Model

Following [10] and [11], a VANET consists of a Central Authority (CA), a number of Road Side Units (RSUs) and several Vehicles which are equipped with a wireless communication device, called an On-Board Unit (OBU). Each vehicle can be considered as a node. Each node in the network is assigned a set of pseudonyms to preserve location privacy, by the CA. Two or more pseudonyms cannot be linked together. Each node is capable of changing pseudonyms from time to time. The CA provides each node a set of public keys and secret *node-keys* corresponding to the set of pseudonyms of the node. The CA also distributes static attributes along with the corresponding secret *attribute-keys* to all nodes. All the attributes and keys issued by the CA are preloaded into OBU. The attribute and key distribution is carried out over a secure communication channel between nodes and the CA.

The network has several RSUs each of which is responsible for a specified region, called *communication range* of that RSU. Each RSU has a set of dynamic attributes. When a node enters within the communication range of an RSU, the RSU gives it certain dynamic attributes along with corresponding secret *attribute-keys* through a secure communication channel between them after receiving the public key associated with current pseudonym of the node. RSUs can also send messages to a set of selected nodes in the network for authorized access.

2.2 DNF Access Policy

Let $\mathcal{S}$ be the universe of static attributes, $\mathcal{R}$ be the set of all RSUs and $\mathcal{D}^j$ be the set of dynamic attributes of RSU R_j. Assume that $\mathcal{S} \cap \mathcal{D}^j = \emptyset$, for all j and $\mathcal{D}^{j_1} \cap \mathcal{D}^{j_2} = \emptyset$, for $R_{j_1}, R_{j_2} \in \mathcal{R}$ with $j_1 \neq j_2$, which means that every static attribute is different from every dynamic attribute and the attributes chosen by two different RSUs are all different from each other.

Suppose a vehicle $\mathsf{v_s}$ wants to send a message to a set V_1 of vehicles which are in region of RSU R_1 and a set V_2 of vehicles which are in region of RSU R_2. Then $\mathsf{v_s}$ creates one conjunction, say $(\bigwedge_{w \in W_1} w)$, on a set W_1 of some static and dynamic attributes of the vehicles in V_1 and another conjunction, say $(\bigwedge_{w \in W_2} w)$, on a set W_2 of some static and dynamic attributes of the vehicles in V_2, and then $\mathsf{v_s}$ formulates the DNF access policy as $W = (\bigwedge_{w \in W_1} w) \bigvee (\bigwedge_{w \in W_2} w)$. We note here that the first conjunction is committed to RSU R_1 and second conjunction is committed to RSU R_2. A receiver vehicle $\mathsf{v_r}$ which is in region of RSU R_1 first finds the respective conjunction in the access policy W, which is $(\bigwedge_{w \in W_1} w)$ in this case, and then checks whether the conjunction is satisfied by the attribute set that it possesses. This means all attributes occurring in W_1 should match with the attributes that $\mathsf{v_r}$ possesses. If this is not the case, the vehicle will be unable to decrypt the message, otherwise it decrypts the message.

If a vehicle wants to communicate with a set of selected nodes belonging to one RSU's region, the access policy contains only one conjunction while the set of selected nodes belong to k different RSU regions, the access policy contains k conjunctions wherein each conjunction is meant for one RSU region. Note that two conjunctions may serve one RSU region. In this case, any vehicle in the region of that RSU satisfies two conjunctions and can randomly select one of them in order to recover a message. To specify the access policy for a ciphertext, we use the following notation: $W = \bigvee_{l=1}^{k} (\bigwedge_{w \in W_l} w)$ which is an **OR**-gate on k conjunctions and each conjunction is an **AND**-gate on some attributes; where W_l is a set of attributes occurring in the l-th conjunction of the DNF representation of the access policy W. All dynamic attributes occurring in one conjunction are essentially belong to one RSU, i.e., each conjunction in W is dedicated to exactly one RSU in the network.

For example, when a vehicle wants to send a message to other vehicles in the network regarding the road situation (e.g. a car accident is ahead), it decides firstly the intended vehicles (e.g. ambulance, police car, breakdown truck) and then formulates an associated access policy W over some attributes, e.g. $W = (\mathsf{ambulance} \wedge \mathsf{road1}) \vee (\mathsf{policecar} \wedge \mathsf{road1} \wedge \mathsf{lane2}) \vee (\mathsf{breakdowntruck} \wedge \mathsf{road2})$. The vehicle uses the public keys of the attributes occurring in the access policy to encrypt the message and transmits the ciphertext.

Definition 2 (Satisfiability). *Given a set of attributes A and an access policy W, A satisfies W, denoted as $A \models W$ if and only if $W_l \subset A$, for some l, $1 \leq l \leq k$, and otherwise A does not satisfy W. In the case where the access policy W possesses one conjunction say $W = \bigwedge_{w \in W'} w$, the satisfiability condition is defined as : A* satisfies *W if and only if $W' \subset A$. In this context, W is a monotone access policy.*

2.3 Security Model

Following [8], we define our security model in terms of a game which is carried out between a challenger and an adversary, where the challenger plays the role of the CA and all RSUs.

Setup. The challenger runs the Setup algorithm and gives all public parameters to the adversary.

Query Phase 1. The adversary is allowed to make queries for public and secret node-keys of an arbitrary number of nodes with several different pseudonyms. For each node the adversary can request an arbitrary number of public and secret attribute-keys of static and dynamic attributes that the node has. Since every node has a set of different pseudonyms, the adversary can query for secret attribute-keys of the same node with different pseudonyms.

Challenge. The adversary submits two messages M_0 and M_1 and an access policy W such that none of the nodes whose keys have been queried before in Query Phase 1 satisfy the access policy W. If attributes of any such node from Query Phase 1 satisfies the access policy W, the challenger aborts, otherwise the challenger flips a random coin $\mu \in \{0,1\}$, and encrypts M_μ under W. The ciphertext is then given to the adversary.

Query Phase 2. Query Phase 1 is repeated. In addition, the adversary can also request for more secret attribute-keys of the nodes that he has already queried in Query Phase 1 and 2. If any secret attribute-key that would give the respective node a set of attributes satisfying W, then the challenger aborts.

Guess. The adversary outputs a guess bit $\mu' \in \{0,1\}$ for the challenger's secret coin μ and wins if $\mu' = \mu$.

The advantage of an adversary $\mathcal{A}$ in this game is defined as $\mathsf{Adv}_{\mathcal{A}} = |\Pr[\mu' = \mu] - \frac{1}{2}|$, where the probability is taken over all random coin tosses of both adversary and challenger.

Definition 3. *A scheme is secure in the above game if all polynomial time adversaries have at most a negligible advantage in the security parameter κ.*

3 Proposed Access Control Scheme

Our scheme consists of (1) System Initialization,(2) Key Generation, (3) Encryption and (4) Decryption. Let $\mathcal{N}$ be the set of all nodes and $\mathcal{R}$ be the set of all RSUs.

(1) System Initialization. This algorithm in turn consists of three algorithms: (a) *GlobalSetup*, (b) *CASetup* and (c) *RSUSetup*.

(a) *GlobalSetup.* This algorithm takes as input the implicit security parameter κ. The CA chooses a prime number p, a bilinear group $\mathbb{G}$, a generator $g \in \mathbb{G}$ and a bilinear map $e : \mathbb{G} \times \mathbb{G} \to \mathbb{G}_T$, where $\mathbb{G}$ and $\mathbb{G}_T$ are multiplicative groups of same prime order p. The CA selects a random point $Q \in \mathbb{G}$, a random exponent $y \in \mathbb{Z}_p$ and computes $g^y, Y = e(g,g)^y$. The global public parameters of the system are *params* $=\langle p, \mathbb{G}, \mathbb{G}_T, e, g, Q, Y\rangle$ and the global secret key of the system is $\mathsf{gk} = g^y$.

(b) *CASetup.* The CA defines the universe of static attributes $\mathcal{S}$. For each static attribute $s \in \mathcal{S}$, the CA chooses a random exponent $t_s \in \mathbb{Z}_p$ and computes $P_s = g^{t_s}$. The public key of CA is $\mathsf{PubCA} = \{P_s : s \in \mathcal{S}\}$ and the master secret key of CA is $\mathsf{MkCA} = \{t_s : s \in \mathcal{S}\}$.

(c) *RSUSetup.* Each RSU $R_j \in \mathcal{R}$ has a set of dynamic attributes $\mathcal{D}^j$, R_j chooses a random exponent $t_d \in \mathbb{Z}_p$, for each dynamic attribute $d \in \mathcal{D}^j$ and computes $P_d = g^{t_d}$. The public key of R_j is $\mathsf{PubRSU}_j = \{P_d : d \in \mathcal{D}^j\}$ and the master secret key of R_j is $\mathsf{MkRSU}_j = \{t_d : d \in \mathcal{D}^j\}$.

(2) Key Generation. This algorithm consists of two algorithms (a) *CAKeyGen* and (b) *RSUKeyGen* which are described below.

(a) *CAKeyGen*
  - For each node $n_i \in \mathcal{N}$, the CA chooses a keyed hash function $\mathcal{H}_{\mathsf{key}_i} : \{0,1\} \to \mathbb{Z}_p$ from a hash family, which we model as random oracle. For each pseudonym p_{it} of the node n_i, the CA computes a public and secret node-key pair as $\mathsf{PK}_{p_{it}} = g^{\mathcal{H}_{\mathsf{key}_i}(p_{it})}$ and $\mathsf{NodeSK}_{p_{it}} = \mathsf{gk} \cdot Q^{\mathcal{H}_{\mathsf{key}_i}(p_{it})}$, respectively; these public keys $\mathsf{PK}_{p_{it}}$ are made available to every participant in the network including RSUs and secret node-keys $\mathsf{NodeSK}_{p_{it}}$ are secretly issued to respective nodes in the network. All key_i are kept secret for the CA itself.
  - The CA issues each node $n_i \in \mathcal{N}$ a set of static attributes $\mathcal{S}_i$ through a secure communication channel between them.
  - For each pseudonym p_{it}, the CA also issues secretly a set of secret attribute-keys $\{\mathsf{AttrSK}_{s,p_{it}} = g^{t_s \cdot \mathcal{H}_{\mathsf{key}_i}(p_{it})} : s \in \mathcal{S}_i\}$, where each $t_s \in \mathsf{MkCA}$ to the node n_i.

(b) *RSUKeyGen*
  - When a node with a pseudonym p_{it} enters the communication range of an RSU R_j, R_j gives secretly the node a set of dynamic attributes $\mathcal{D}_i^j$.
  - Next, the RSU R_j issues secretly a set of secret attribute-keys $\{\mathsf{AttrSK}_{d,p_{it}} = (\mathsf{PK}_{p_{it}})^{t_d} : d \in \mathcal{D}_i^j\}$, where each $t_d \in \mathsf{MkRSU}_j$, to the node n_i. Note that $\mathsf{AttrSK}_{d,p_{it}} = (\mathsf{PK}_{p_{it}})^{t_d} = g^{t_d \cdot \mathcal{H}_{\mathsf{key}_i}(p_{it})}$.

(3) Encryption

- Suppose n_i wants to communicate with k different categories of vehicles belonging to k' different communication regions, where $k' \leq k$. Then the access policy in DNF is

$$W = \bigvee_{l=1}^{k} \left(\bigwedge_{w \in W_l} w \right) \tag{1}$$

  where W_l denotes the set of attributes in the l-th conjunction of W, $1 \leq l \leq k$. Note that $W_1, W_2, \ldots, W_k$ are not necessarily pairwise disjoint sets although all W_l are distinct and contain both static and dynamic attributes.
- Choose a random exponent $r \in \mathbb{Z}_p$ and compute

$$C = M \cdot Y^r, \widetilde{C} = g^r, \text{ for each } 1 \leq l \leq k, C_l = (Q \cdot \prod_{w \in W_l} P_w)^r. \tag{2}$$

- The ciphertext is $\mathsf{CT} = \langle W, C, \widetilde{C}, \{C_l\}_{l=1}^k \rangle$.

(4) Decryption

- Suppose the attribute set $A_{p_{it}}$ of the node n_i with pseudonym p_{it} satisfies the l-th conjunction of W, i.e., $W_l \subset A_{p_{it}}$. Then n_i aggregates the secret attribute-keys corresponding to the attributes in W_l and computes $K_l = \mathsf{NodeSK}_{p_{it}} \cdot \prod_{a \in W_l} (\mathsf{AttrSK}_{a,p_{it}})$.
- Now, n_i computes $C \cdot e(\mathsf{PK}_{p_{it}}, C_l)/e(K_l, \widetilde{C})$, which returns the message M.

A couple of remarks are in order.

Remark 1. (*Constant length ciphertext*)
Suppose a node n_i decides on a group of nodes which are all monitored by single RSU to send a message M. This restricts the encryption algorithm to communication region of one RSU, thereby the access policy consists only of a single conjunction which is of the form $W = \bigwedge_{w \in W'} w$. Then the ciphertext $\mathsf{CT} = \langle W, C, \widetilde{C}, C' \rangle$, which is constant in length, where $C = M \cdot Y^r, \widetilde{C} = g^r, C' = (Q \cdot \prod_{w \in W'} P_w)^r$.

The node n_i with pseudonym p_{it} recovers the message M only when $W' \subset A_{p_{it}}$. The node n_i computes $K = \mathsf{NodeSK}_{p_{it}} \cdot \prod_{a \in W'} (\mathsf{AttrSK}_{a,p_{it}})$ and recovers the message M by computing $C \cdot e(\mathsf{PK}_{p_{it}}, C')/e(K, \widetilde{C})$.

Remark 2. (*Packing many messages in a single ciphertext*)
Suppose node n_i would like to send different messages to each category of vehicles. Let $M_1, M_2, \ldots, M_k$ be k messages which may or may not be distinct. In order to send simultaneously all these messages to different categories of nodes by broadcasting a single ciphertext, n_i first defines an access policy W given in Eq. (1) over a set of attributes associated with the selected nodes in the network. All dynamic attributes occurring in one conjunction are essentially belong to one RSU. For each l-th conjunction, n_i chooses a random exponent $r_l \in \mathbb{Z}_p$ and computes the ciphertext $\mathsf{CT} = \langle W, \{C_{l,1}, C_{l,2}, C_{l,3}\}_{l=1}^{k} \rangle$, where $C_{l,1} = M_l \cdot Y^{r_l}, C_{l,2} = g^{r_l}, C_{l,3} = (Q \cdot \prod_{w \in W_l} P_w)^{r_l}$.

If the attribute set $A_{p_{it}}$ of the node n_i with pseudonym p_{it} satisfies the l-th conjunction of W, i.e., $W_l \subset A_{p_{it}}$, then n_i aggregates the secret attribute-keys corresponding to the attributes in W_l and computes $K_l = \mathsf{NodeSK}_{p_{it}} \cdot \prod_{a \in W_l} (\mathsf{AttrSK}_{a,p_{it}})$. Then n_i recovers the respective message M_l by computing $C_{l,1} \cdot e(\mathsf{PK}_{p_{it}}, C_{l,3})/e(K_l, C_{l,2})$.

4 Security

Theorem 1. *Our scheme resists collusion attacks made between any number of nodes.*

Proof. Our scheme is said to be collusion-resistant if no two or more nodes can combine their secret attribute-keys in order to decrypt a message that they are not entitled to decrypt alone. Let us assume that nodes can collude and have secret attribute-keys such that the associated attributes satisfy the l-th conjunction of the access policy $W = \bigvee_{l=1}^{k} (\bigwedge_{w \in W_l} w)$, for some l, $1 \leq l \leq k$. The encryption algorithm blinds the message M with $e(g, g)^{yr}$, where g is a generator of the group $\mathbb{G}$, y and r are two random elements chosen from $\mathbb{Z}_p$. In order to recover the message M, the decryptor, say n_i, needs to compute the blinding term $e(g, g)^{yr}$ by pairing the secret node-key $\mathsf{NodeSK}_{p_{it}}$ of pseudonym p_{it}, secret attribute-keys, $\mathsf{AttrSK}_{w,p_{it}}$ for the pseudonym p_{it} with the respective ciphertext components $C, \widetilde{C}$ and C_l, for some l. To this end, n_i introduces terms of the form $e(g^{t_w \mathcal{H}_{\mathsf{key}_i}(p_{it})}, \widetilde{C}) = e(g^{t_w \mathcal{H}_{\mathsf{key}_i}(p_{it})}, g^r)$. If $W_l \subset A_{p_{it}}$, for some $l, 1 \leq l \leq k$, then the node n_i can recover the blinding term from the following computation

$$\frac{e\left(K_l, \widetilde{C}\right)}{e(\mathsf{PK}_{p_{it}}, C_l)} = \frac{e(g^y Q^{\mathcal{H}_{\mathsf{key}_i}(p_{it})}, g^r) \cdot \prod_{w \in W_l} e(g^{t_w \mathcal{H}_{\mathsf{key}_i}(p_{it})}, g^r)}{e(g^{\mathcal{H}_{\mathsf{key}_i}(p_{it})}, Q^r) \cdot \prod_{w \in W_l} e(g^{\mathcal{H}_{\mathsf{key}_i}(p_{it})}, g^{r t_w})} = e(g,g)^{yr}.$$

If two nodes n_1 and n_2 with different pseudonyms p_{1t} and p_{2t} respectively, at time t, try to collude and combine their secret attribute-keys, then there will be some terms of the form $e(g^{t_w \mathcal{H}_{\mathsf{key}_1}(p_{1t})}, g^r)$ and some terms of the form $e(g^{t_w \mathcal{H}_{\mathsf{key}_2}(p_{2t})}, g^r)$ and these terms will not cancel with each other, thereby preventing the recovery of the blinding term $e(g,g)^{yr}$, so is the message M. This demonstrates that our scheme is collusion-resistant. □

Theorem 2. *Our construction is secure against corrupted RSUs unless the static attributes of a node in communication range of the corrupted RSU match with static attributes occur in the respective conjunction of the corrupted RSU in the access policy W given in Eq.(1).*

Proof. Note that the access policy is $W = \bigvee_{l=1}^{k} \left(\bigwedge_{w \in W_l} w\right)$, where the l-th conjunction $(\bigwedge_{w \in W_l} w)$, for $1 \leq l \leq k$, is meant for an RSU $R_j \in \mathcal{R}$ and contains both static and dynamic attributes. As a more systematic approach, the set of attributes in each conjunction and the attribute set of each node could be partitioned into static and dynamic attributes as follows. For each l, $1 \leq l \leq k$, let $W_l = W_l^S \cup W_l^D$; where W_l^S and W_l^D, respectively, are the set of static and dynamic attributes occurring in the l-th conjunction of W with $W_l^S \cap W_l^D = \emptyset$. Each node n_i with pseudonym p_{it} has an attribute set $A_{p_{it}}$ which can be written as $A_{p_{it}} = A_{p_{it}}^S \cup A_{p_{it}}^D$, where $A_{p_{it}}^S = \mathcal{S}_i$ and $A_{p_{it}}^D = \mathcal{D}_i^j$, for some RSU $R_j \in \mathcal{R}$ with $A_{p_{it}}^S \cap A_{p_{it}}^D = \emptyset$. Then node n_i is authorized node if and only if the attribute set $A_{p_{it}}$ of n_i satisfies the access policy W, i.e., if and only if $W_l \subset A_{p_{it}}$ for some $l, 1 \leq l \leq k$, i.e., if and only if $W_l^S \subset A_{p_{it}}^S$ and $W_l^D \subset A_{p_{it}}^D$, for some l, $1 \leq l \leq k$.

Suppose an RSU $R_{j'}$ is compromised. This means that it reveals the master secret key t_d of each attribute $d \in \mathcal{D}^{j'}$. Consequently, the secret attribute-key $\mathsf{AttrSK}_{d,p_{it}}$, for each $d \in \mathcal{D}^{j'}$ is known to every node that is monitored by $R_{j'}$. In turn, the following key information is available to every node n_i with pseudonym p_{it} in the communication range of $R_{j'}$.

- $\mathsf{PK}_{p_{it}}, \mathsf{NodeSK}_{p_{it}}$
- $\mathcal{S}_i, \{\mathsf{AttrSK}_{s,p_{it}} : s \in \mathcal{S}_i\}$, where $A_{p_{it}}^S = \mathcal{S}_i$
- $\mathcal{D}^{j'}, \{\mathsf{AttrSK}_{d,p_{it}} : d \in \mathcal{D}^{j'}\}$, where $A_{p_{it}}^D = \mathcal{D}_i^{j'} \subset \mathcal{D}^{j'}$

Suppose the l-th conjunction of the access policy W is meant for the RSU $R_{j'}$. Consequently, all nodes in communication range of $R_{j'}$ can be divided into the following four categories according to the satisfiability condition of the access policy W: (i) $W_l^S \subset A_{p_{it}}^S$ and $W_l^D \subset A_{p_{it}}^D$ (ii) $W_l^S \not\subset A_{p_{it}}^S$ and $W_l^D \subset A_{p_{it}}^D$ (iii) $W_l^S \not\subset A_{p_{it}}^S$ and $W_l^D \not\subset A_{p_{it}}^D$ (iv) $W_l^S \subset A_{p_{it}}^S$ and $W_l^D \not\subset A_{p_{it}}^D$.

In the compromised RSU scenario, security totally depends on static attributes because of the fact that all the secret dynamic attribute-keys of respective RSU are revealed, thereby the second satisfiability condition on dynamic attributes is immaterial. In the first category all nodes are authorized, thereby can decrypt a message. All the nodes in second and third category are unauthorized so that they cannot recover a message since their attribute sets do not satisfy the first satisfiability condition on static attributes. Although the nodes in the fourth category are not satisfying the access policy W corresponding to the ciphertext $\mathsf{CT} = \langle W, C, \widetilde{C}, \{C_l\}_{l=1}^k \rangle$, they can still recover a message M as follows.

(i) In order to recover a message, n_i first needs to compute K_l. Note that $K_l = \mathsf{NodeSK}_{p_{it}} \cdot \prod_{s \in W_l^S} (\mathsf{AttrSK}_{s,p_{it}}) \cdot \prod_{d \in W_l^D} (\mathsf{AttrSK}_{d,p_{it}})$. Since $W_l^S \subset A_{p_{it}}^S$ and n_i has $\{\mathsf{AttrSK}_{s,p_{it}} : s \in \mathcal{S}_i = A_{p_{it}}^S\}$, it can compute $\prod_{s \in W_l^S} (\mathsf{AttrSK}_{s,p_{it}})$. As all the secret dynamic attribute-keys $\mathsf{AttrSK}_{d,p_{it}}, d \in \mathcal{D}^{j'}$ are disclosed by the compromised RSU $R_{j'}$, the node n_i can also compute $\prod_{d \in W_l^D} (\mathsf{AttrSK}_{d,p_{it}})$, thereby can compute K_l.

(ii) Now, similar to the decryption algorithm, n_i can recover the message M from the following computation $C \cdot e(\mathsf{PK}_{p_{it}}, C_l)/e\left(K_l, \widetilde{C}\right) = M$.

Thus, not every node belongs to $R_{j'}$'s communication range can recover a message, only the nodes whose static attributes satisfy the condition $W_l^S \subset A_{p_{it}}^S$ irrespective of the second satisfiability condition on dynamic attributes namely $W_l^D \subset A_{p_{it}}^D$. Hence the theorem. □

Remark 3. We point out here that the construction proposed in [11] guarantees the same security as ours against compromised RSUs as stated in Theorem 2, i.e., the unauthorized nodes of fourth category as classified in the proof of this theorem will be able to decrypt the ciphertext which they are not entitled to in [11] also and hence does not provide full security against compromised RSUs.

Theorem 3. *Our scheme is secure in the generic group model.*

Proof. Without loss of generality, we can assume that all RSUs are non-corrupt in our security proof. We follow the structure of the security proof in [8]. In our security game, say Game_1, the adversary $\mathcal{A}$ has to distinguish between $X_0 = M_0 \cdot e(g,g)^{yr}$ and $X_1 = M_1 \cdot e(g,g)^{yr}$. We can alternatively consider a modified game, say Game_2 as follows: **Setup, Query Phase 1** and **Query Phase 2** are similar to Game_1, but changes will be made in **Challenge** phase. After receiving an access policy W subject to the condition mentioned in the Challenge phase, the challenger flips a random coin $b \in \{0,1\}$ and generates a ciphertext based on the access policy W, wherein the ciphertext component C is computed as $C = e(g,g)^{yr}$ if $b = 1$ and $C = e(g,g)^{\delta}$ if $b = 0$, where δ is uniformly and independently chosen from $\mathbb{Z}_p$, and other ciphertext components are computed according to Eq. (2). Then we have the following claim.

Claim 1: If there is an adversary $\mathcal{A}_1$ that has advantage $\mathsf{Adv}_{\mathcal{A}_1}$ to win Game_1, then there is an adversary $\mathcal{A}_2$ who wins Game_2 with advantage $\mathsf{Adv}_{\mathcal{A}_2}$ such that $\mathsf{Adv}_{\mathcal{A}_1} \leq 2 \times \mathsf{Adv}_{\mathcal{A}_2}$.

Proof of Claim 1: Suppose there is an adversary $\mathcal{A}_1$ who has an advantage $\mathsf{Adv}_{\mathcal{A}_1}$ to win Game_1. According to $\mathcal{A}_1$, we can construct an adversary $\mathcal{A}_2$ as follows: In **Setup**, **Query Phase 1** and **Query Phase 2**, $\mathcal{A}_2$ forwards all messages he receives from $\mathcal{A}_1$ to the challenger and all messages from the challenger to $\mathcal{A}_1$. In the **Challenge** phase, $\mathcal{A}_2$ receives two messages M_0 and M_1 from $\mathcal{A}_1$ and the challenge ciphertext CT (which contains C that is either $e(g,g)^{yr}$ or $e(g,g)^{\delta}$) from the challenger. Now, $\mathcal{A}_2$ flips a random coin $\mu \in \{0,1\}$ and computes $C' = M_\mu \cdot C$ and finally sends the resulting ciphertext CT' to the adversary $\mathcal{A}_1$. **Guess:** $\mathcal{A}_1$ outputs his guess $\mu' \in \{0,1\}$ on μ. If $\mu' = \mu$, $\mathcal{A}_2$ outputs as its guess $b' = 1$; otherwise he outputs $b' = 0$.

- In the case where $b = 1$, CT' is a correct ciphertext of M_μ. Consequently, $\mathcal{A}_1$ can output $\mu' = \mu$ with the advantage $\mathsf{Adv}_{\mathcal{A}_1}$, i.e., $\Pr[\mu' = \mu | b = 1] = \frac{1}{2} + \mathsf{Adv}_{\mathcal{A}_1}$. Since $\mathcal{A}_2$ guesses $b' = 1$ when $\mu' = \mu$, we get $\Pr[b' = b | b = 1] = \frac{1}{2} + \mathsf{Adv}_{\mathcal{A}_1}$.
- In the next case where $b = 0$, the challenge ciphertext CT is independent of the messages M_0 and M_1, so $\mathcal{A}_1$ cannot obtain any information about μ. Therefore, $\mathcal{A}_1$ can output $\mu' \neq \mu$ with no advantage, i.e., $\Pr[\mu' \neq \mu | b = 0] = \frac{1}{2}$. Since $\mathcal{A}_2$ guesses $b' = 0$ when $\mu' \neq \mu$, we get $\Pr[b' = b | b = 0] = \frac{1}{2}$.

Thus, we have $\mathsf{Adv}_{\mathcal{A}_2} = \left|\Pr[b' = b] - \frac{1}{2}\right| \geq \frac{1}{2} \cdot (\frac{1}{2} + \mathsf{Adv}_{\mathcal{A}_1}) + \frac{1}{2} \cdot \frac{1}{2} - \frac{1}{2} = \frac{\mathsf{Adv}_{\mathcal{A}_1}}{2}$. This proves the claim 1.

This claim demonstrates that any adversary that has a non-negligible advantage in Game_1 can have a non-negligible advantage in Game_2. We shall prove that no adversary can have non-negligible advantage in Game_2. From now on, we will discuss the advantage of the adversary in Game_2, wherein the adversary must distinguish between $Y_0 = e(g,g)^{yr}$ and $Y_1 = e(g,g)^{\delta}$.

To simulate the modified security game Game_2, we use the generic bilinear group model described in [4]. Consider two injective random maps $\psi, \psi_T : \mathbb{Z}_p \rightarrow \{0,1\}^{\lceil 3\log(p) \rceil}$. In this model every element of $\mathbb{G}$ and $\mathbb{G}_T$ is encoded as an arbitrary random string from the adversary's point of view, i.e., $\mathbb{G} = \{\psi(x) : x \in \mathbb{Z}_p\}$ and $\mathbb{G}_T = \{\psi_T(x) : x \in \mathbb{Z}_p\}$. The adversary is given three oracles to compute group operations of $\mathbb{G}$, $\mathbb{G}_T$ and to compute the bilinear pairing e. The input of all oracles are string representations of group elements. The adversary is allowed to perform group operations and pairing computations by interacting with the corresponding oracles only. It is assumed that the adversary can make queries to the group oracles on input strings that were previously been obtained from the simulator or were given from the oracles in response to the previous queries.

We use the notations $g^x := \psi(x)$ and $e(g,g)^x := \psi_T(x)$ throughout our proof. During *GlobalSetup* time, the simulator chooses two random exponents $y, q \in \mathbb{Z}_p$ and gives $g = \psi(1), Q = \psi(q)$ and $e(g,g)^y = \psi_T(y)$ to the adversary. When the adversary requests public and secret node-key of a node n_i with pseudonym p_{it} for the first time, the simulator chooses a unique random value $u_{it} \in \mathbb{Z}_p$, which simulates the term $\mathcal{H}_{\mathsf{key}_i}(p_{it})$, queries the group oracle for $g^{\mathcal{H}_{\mathsf{key}_i}(p_{it})}$ and $g^y \cdot Q^{\mathcal{H}_{\mathsf{key}_i}(p_{it})}$, and returns $\mathsf{PK}_{p_{it}} = \psi(u_{it})$ and $\mathsf{NodeSK}_{p_{it}} = \psi(y + q \cdot u_{it})$ to the adversary. The association between values u_{it} and nodes n_i is stored in UList for subsequent queries in the future. When the adversary requests for public key of an attribute a of the node n_i, the simulator chooses a new, unique random value $t_a \in \mathbb{Z}_p$, computes g^{t_a} using respective group oracle and gives $P_a = \psi(t_a)$ to the adversary. We note here that the attribute a might be either static or dynamic attribute. If the adversary requests for a secret attribute-key of an attribute a of the node n_i with pseudonym p_{it}, the simulator supplies $\mathsf{AttrSK}_{a,p_{it}} = \psi(u_{it}t_a)$ to the adversary. If u_{it} has not been stored in UList before, it is determined as above.

When the adversary specifies an access policy W for a challenge ciphertext CT, the simulator first chooses a random $r \in \mathbb{Z}_p$. The simulator then flips a random coin b and if $b = 1$, he sets $\delta = yr$, otherwise δ is set to be a random value from $\mathbb{Z}_p$. The simulator finally computes the components of challenge ciphertext CT by using group oracles as follows: $C = \psi_T(\delta), \widetilde{C} = \psi(r), C_l = \psi(b_l r + qr)$, for all $1 \leq l \leq k$. Recall that $b_l = \sum_{w \in W_l} t_w$. The ciphertext $\mathsf{CT} = \langle W, C, \widetilde{C}, \{C_l\}_{l=1}^k \rangle$ is sent to the adversary.

We note that if the adversary requests for a secret attribute-keys for a set of attributes that satisfies the access policy W, the simulator aborts.

The adversary now can have in his hand, all values that consists of encodings of random values $\delta, 1, y, q, u_{it}$ and t_a, and combination of these values given by the simulator or results of queries on combination of these values to the oracles. In turn, we can see that each query of the adversary is a multivariate polynomial in the variables δ, y, q, u_{it} and t_a. We keep track of the polynomials PList used to query the oracles. We assume that any pair of the adversary's queries on two different polynomials result in two different answers. This assumption is false only when our choice of the random encodings of the variables ensures that the difference of two query polynomials evaluates to zero. Similar to the security proof in [9], this assumption occurs with overwhelming probability. In the following we will condition that no such random collisions occur.

Under this condition, we consider how the adversary's views differ between two cases: $\delta = yr$ if $b = 1$ and δ is random, if $b = 0$. If we prove that the views are identically distributed for both cases, then any adversary cannot distinguish them in the generic bilinear group model. We prove this by contradiction. Let us assume that the views are *not* identically distributed. The adversary's views can only differ when there exist two queries which are equal in the view where $\delta = yr$, and unequal in the view where δ is random. Since δ only appears as $C = \psi_T(\delta)$ and elements of ψ_T cannot be used as input of pairing, the adversary can make queries involving δ which are only of the form: $q_1 = c_1\delta + q_1'$ and $q_2 = c_2\delta + q_2'$, for some q_1' and q_2' that do not contain δ, and for some constants c_1 and c_2. This implies that $c_1 yr + q_1' = c_2 yr + q_2'$ and it gives $q_2' - q_1' = (c_1 - c_2)yr$. We may then conclude that the adversary can construct the query cyr, for some constant $c \neq 0$.

Claim 2: The adversary cannot construct a query of the form $\psi_T(cyr)$.

Table 1. Possible adversary's query terms in $\mathbb{G}_T$

u_{it}	$u_{it}u_{it^*}$	$(y+qu_{it})(y+qu_{it^*})$	$b_l r$
$y+qu_{it}$	$u_{it}y+qu_{it}u_{it^*}$	$yb_l+qu_{it}b_l$	$b_l b_{l'} r+qrb_l$
b_l	$u_{it}b_l$	$yr+u_{it}qr$	r^2
r	$u_{it}r$	$(y+qu_{it})(b_l r+qr)$	$b_l r^2+qr^2$
$b_l r+qr$	$u_{it}qr+u_{it}b_l r$	$b_l b_{l'}$	$(b_l r+qr)(b_{l'}r+qr)$

Proof of Claim 2: To prove this claim, we examine the information given to the adversary during the simulation. Since all r and y are random, the only way that the adversary can construct $\psi_T(cyr)$ is by pairing two elements of $\mathbb{G}$ using the pairing oracle. We observe that b_l can be constructed by querying the multiplication oracle for encodings of the terms containing t_a for all $a \in W_l$.

In Table 1, first column represents the adversary's information received from the simulator during simulation and the next three columns represent all combinations, as results of pairing oracle, of the terms listed in the first column. So, the queries listed in Table 1 are all possible queries of the adversary. The only appearance of yr in the above table is $yr+u_{it}qr$. In order to make a query for yr, the adversary has to eliminate the additional term $u_{it}qr$. The adversary can cancel this term by using $u_{it}qr+u_{it}b_l r$, which leaves behind the term $u_{it}b_l r$. The only way $u_{it}b_l r$ can be constructed is by querying the pairing oracle for encodings of the terms containing $u_{it}b_l$ and r. Since $b_l = \sum_{w \in W_l} t_w$ and $\mathsf{AttrSK}_{w,p_{it}}$ are the only appearances of $u_{it}t_w$, in order to construct $u_{it}b_l$ the adversary multiplies representations of $\mathsf{AttrSK}_{w,p_{it}}$ which results in a query of the form

$$\sum_i \left(c_i u_{it} \sum_a c_{a,i} t_a \right), \tag{3}$$

for some constants $c_i, c_{a,i}$. Note that i stands for node n_i in Eq. (3). Recall from our security game Game_1 that the adversary cannot have all secret attribute-keys corresponding to any one node n_i that satisfies any conjunction of the challenge access policy W. As a consequence, Eq. (3) yields no information about $u_{it}b_l$. Therefore, the adversary cannot construct a term of the form $\psi_T(yr)$ and thus cannot break the system.

Thus, we have shown that the adversary cannot make a query of the form cyr, for any c, without having a sufficient set of attributes that satisfy the access policy W. This contradicts our assumption that the adversary's views in the modified game Game_2 are not identically distributed and therefore, the adversary has no non-negligible advantage in Game_2, so is in the original game Game_1. □

5 Performance

We compare our scheme with the existing schemes in Table 2 and Table 3. Here $E_{\mathbb{G}}$ stands for the number of exponentiations in a group $\mathbb{G}$, $E_{\mathbb{G}_T}$ denotes the number of exponentiations in a group $\mathbb{G}_T$, P_e is the number of pairing computations, α is the number of attributes in the access policy W, β denotes the

Table 2. Comparison of Computation Costs

	Key Generation	Encryption			Decryption		
Scheme	$E_{\mathbb{G}}$	$E_{\mathbb{G}}$	$E_{\mathbb{G}_T}$	P_e	$E_{\mathbb{G}}$	$E_{\mathbb{G}_T}$	P_e
[10]	$2\Gamma + 2$	$2\alpha + 2$	2	-	-	$\mathcal{O}(\beta)$	$\mathcal{O}(\beta)$
[11]	2Γ	3α	$2\alpha + 1$	1	-	$\mathcal{O}(\beta)$	$\mathcal{O}(\beta)$
Proposed	$\Gamma + 2$	$k + 1$	1	-	-	-	2

Table 3. Comparison of Communication Overheads

Scheme	Secret Key Size	Ciphertext Size	Expressiveness of Access Policy
[10]	$(2\Gamma + 1)B_{\mathbb{G}}$	$(2\alpha + 3)B_{\mathbb{G}} + B_{\mathbb{G}_T} + \tau$	AND
[11]	$(\Gamma)B_{\mathbb{G}}$	$(2\alpha)B_{\mathbb{G}} + (\alpha + 1)B_{\mathbb{G}_T} + \tau$	Boolean formula
Proposed	$(\Gamma + 2)B_{\mathbb{G}}$	$(k + 1)B_{\mathbb{G}} + B_{\mathbb{G}_T} + \tau$	DNF

number of attributes satisfying the access policy W, k stands for the number of conjunctive terms in the access policy W, $B_{\mathbb{G}}$ stands for bit size of an element in $\mathbb{G}$, $B_{\mathbb{G}_T}$ stands for bit size of an element in $\mathbb{G}_T$, Γ denotes the number of attributes associated with secret key of a node and τ is size of an access policy.

The number of pairing computations in [10] and [11] is linear in the minimum number of attributes required for decryption whereas our scheme uses only two pairing computations. If we restrict our scheme to one communication region of RSU like [10], our access policy consists of one conjunction, i.e., $k = 1$, then the access policy is a monotone access policy, the ciphertext is of constant length, has constant computation cost and constant communication cost. We note here that all receivers essentially belong to one RSU, however the sender may or may not belong to the same RSU unlike [10].

The length of ciphertexts in [10] and [11] is linear in the number of attributes, α, occurring in the access policy. On the other hand, our access policy consists of k conjunctions so the length of ciphertext grows linearly with k, thereby making our scheme more efficient than [10] and [11] as k is significantly smaller than α. For example, if an access policy in DNF contains ρ conjunctive terms and each conjunction contains η different attributes, then $k = \rho$, but $\alpha = \rho \times \eta$.

6 Conclusion

In this work, we have proposed an access control paradigm for vehicular communications that enables only the authorized users to decrypt a message. Our proposed construction is efficient as it requires only a constant number of pairings during encryption and decryption, while having a significant improvement in the communication overhead as compared to the existing schemes. We have shown that our scheme resists collusion attacks and is secure against compromised RSUs. The security of our scheme is proven under generic group model. Our approach provides secret key verification. Moreover, it develops a mechanism for packing multiple messages in a single ciphertext.

References

1. Shamir, A.: Identity-Based Cryptosystems and Signature Schemes. In: Blakely, G.R., Chaum, D. (eds.) CRYPTO 1984. LNCS, vol. 196, pp. 47–53. Springer, Heidelberg (1985)
2. Sahai, A., Waters, B.: Fuzzy Identity-Based Encryption. In: Cramer, R. (ed.) EUROCRYPT 2005. LNCS, vol. 3494, pp. 457–473. Springer, Heidelberg (2005)
3. Goyal, V., Pandey, O., Sahai, A., Waters, B.: Attribute Based Encryption for Fine-Grained Access Control of Encrypted Data. In: ACM Conference on Computer and Communications Security, pp. 89–98 (2006)
4. Bethencourt, J., Sahai, A., Waters, B.: Ciphertext-Policy Attribute-Based Encryption. In: IEEE Symposium on Security and Privacy, pp. 321–334 (2007)
5. Emura, K., Miyaji, A., Nomura, A., Omote, K., Soshi, M.: A Ciphertext-Policy Attribute-Based Encryption Scheme with Constant Ciphertext Length. IJACT 2(1), 46–59 (2010)
6. Chase, M.: Multi-authority Attribute Based Encryption. In: Vadhan, S.P. (ed.) TCC 2007. LNCS, vol. 4392, pp. 515–534. Springer, Heidelberg (2007)
7. Chase, M., Chow, S.S.M.: Improving Privacy and Security in Multi-Authority Attribute-Based Encryption. In: Proceedings of the 16th ACM Conference on Computer and Communications Security (CCS 2009), pp. 121–130 (2009)
8. Müller, S., Katzenbeisser, S., Eckert, C.: Distributed Attribute-Based Encryption. In: Lee, P.J., Cheon, J.H. (eds.) ICISC 2008. LNCS, vol. 5461, pp. 20–36. Springer, Heidelberg (2009)
9. Lewko, A., Waters, B.: Decentralizing Attribute-Based Encryption. In: Paterson, K.G. (ed.) EUROCRYPT 2011. LNCS, vol. 6632, pp. 568–588. Springer, Heidelberg (2011)
10. Huang, D., Verma, M.: ASPE: Attribute-Based Secure Policy Enforcement in Vehicular Ad Hoc Networks. Ad Hoc Networks 7(8), 1526–1535 (2009)
11. Ruj, S., Nayak, A., Stojmenovic, I.: Improved Access Control Mechanism in Vehicular Ad Hoc Networks. In: Frey, H., Li, X., Ruehrup, S. (eds.) ADHOC-NOW 2011. LNCS, vol. 6811, pp. 191–205. Springer, Heidelberg (2011)
12. Mishra, B., Nayak, P., Behera, S., Jena, D.: Security in Vehicular Adhoc Networks: A Survey. In: ICCCS 2011, pp. 590–595. ACM, New York (2011)
13. Huang, D., Hong, X., Gerla, M.: Situation-Aware Trust Architecture for Vehicular Networks. IEEE Communications Magazine 48(11), 128–135 (2010)
14. Chen, N., Gerla, M., Hong, D.H.X.: Secure, Selective Group Broadcast in Vehicular Networks using Dynamic Attribute Based Encryption. In: Ad Hoc Networking Workshop, Med-Hoc-Net, pp. 1–8 (2010)
15. Lo-Yao, Y., Yen-Cheng, C., Jiun-Long, H.: ABACS: An Attribute-Based Access Control System for Emergency Services over VANETs. IEEE Journal on Selected Areas in Communications 29(3), 630–643 (2011)
16. Studer, A., Shi, E., Bai, F., Perrig, A.: TACKing Together Efficient Authentication, Revocation, and Privacy in VANETs. In: 6th Annual IEEE Conference on Sensor, Mesh and Ad Hoc Communications and Networks, pp. 484–492 (2009)
17. Hao, Y., Chengcheng, Y., Zhou, C., Song, W.: A Distributed Key Management Framework with Cooperative Message Authentication in VANETs. IEEE Journal on Selected Areas in Communications 29(3), 616–629 (2011)
18. Ming-Chin, C., Jeng-Farn, L.: PPAS: A Privacy Preservation Authentication Scheme for Vehicle-to-Infrastructure Communication Networks. In: CECNet, pp. 1509–1512 (2011)
19. Subir, B., Md. Mahbubul, H., Jelena, M.: Privacy and Anonymity in VANETs: A Contemporary Study. Ad Hoc and Sensor Wireless Networks 10(2-3), 177–192 (2010)

Evaluation of Detecting Malicious Nodes Using Bayesian Model in Wireless Intrusion Detection

Yuxin Meng[1], Wenjuan Li[2], and Lam-for Kwok[1]

[1] Department of Computer Science, College of Science and Engineering, City University of Hong Kong, Hong Kong, China
ymeng8@student.cityu.edu.hk

[2] Computer Science Division, Zhaoqing Foreign Language College, Guangdong, China
wenjuan.anastatia@gmail.com

Abstract. Wireless sensor network (WSN) is vulnerable to a wide range of attacks due to its natural environment and inherent unreliable transmission. To protect its security, intrusion detection systems (IDSs) have been widely deployed in such a wireless environment. In addition, trust-based mechanism is a promising method in detecting insider attacks (e.g., malicious nodes) in a WSN. In this paper, we thus attempt to develop a trust-based intrusion detection mechanism by means of Bayesian model and evaluate it in the aspect of detecting malicious nodes in a WSN. This Bayesian model enables a hierarchical wireless sensor network to establish a map of trust values among different sensor nodes. The hierarchical structure can reduce network traffic caused by node-to-node communications. To evaluate the performance of the trust-based mechanism, we analyze the impact of a fixed and a dynamic trust threshold on identifying malicious nodes respectively and further conduct an evaluation in a wireless sensor environment. The experimental results indicate that the Bayesian model is encouraging in detecting malicious sensor nodes, and that the trust threshold in a wireless sensor network is more dynamic than that in a wired network.

Keywords: Intrusion Detection, Network Security, Wireless Sensor Network, Trust Computation, Bayesian Model.

1 Introduction

A wireless sensor network (WSN) is usually composed of a number of small, resource-limited, autonomous sensor nodes (SNs) to transmit data to a main location and provide access points for human interface. Such networks nowadays are being widely used in many fields such as agriculture [4], transportation [7] and homeland security [13]. Due to its natural environments (i.e., deployed in a hostile environment) and inherent unreliability of transmission, a WSN is vulnerable to a wide range of attacks (e.g., DoS) [5]. Attackers can exploit rogue access points within an organization or poorly configured hotspots to launch attacks [16]. For example, an attacker can gain access to wireless user's data by placing an unauthorized access point.

To mitigate the above problems, intrusion detection systems (IDSs) [16] have been widely implemented aiming to protect a WSN. Generally, an IDS can be classified as:

J. Lopez, X. Huang, and R. Sandhu (Eds.): NSS 2013, LNCS 7873, pp. 40–53, 2013.

misuse-based IDS and anomaly-based IDS. The misuse-based detection [20] (or called *signature-based detection*) looks for network attack sequences or events through matching them with its stored signatures[1]. The detection capability is as good as the available signatures. The anomaly-based detection [12], on the other hand, detects anomalies by comparing current network events with pre-defined normal traffic behavior on the network. In this case, sensor nodes can monitor their deployed network for deviations and produce alerts when anomalies are discovered.

However, an IDS suffers from some inherent issues (i.e., generating a lot of false alarms [1,24]). In a wireless environment, due to limitations of resource restrains such as computational power, memory of a SN, traditional complex security mechanism is difficult to be implemented in a WSN [19]. Specifically, attacks in a WSN can be categorized into *outsider attacks* and *insider attacks*. Authentication is used as a defense mechanism against the outsider attacks (e.g., spoofing), while the insider attacks (e.g., malicious nodes) are more difficult to identify [2]. In this paper, we develop a trust-based intrusion detection mechanism by using Bayesian model to compute trust values for each node in a hierarchical WSN, and this mechanism can then detect malicious nodes by selecting an appropriate trust threshold. The hierarchical structure can be used to reduce network traffic caused by node-to-node communications. The contributions of our work can be summarized as below:

- We develop a trust-based intrusion detection mechanism by means of Bayesian model to compute trust values and detect malicious nodes in a WSN, which relies on a scalable hierarchical structure including sensor nodes (SNs) and cluster heads (CHs). The SNs can initially record trust information during the node-to-node communication, and a CH collects trust reports from all SNs and calculates comprehensive trust values for all nodes in its effective range (e.g., clusters). Malicious nodes can be identified by selecting an appropriate trust threshold.
- We further conduct a simulation in a WSN to identify an appropriate trust threshold for detecting a malicious node. By computing and analyzing the trust values of 10 clusters, we point out that the trust threshold in a wireless network is more dynamic than that in a wired network.
- In the experiment, we evaluate the performance of the Bayesian model in a WSN with a fixed trust threshold and a dynamic threshold respectively. The results illustrate that this model is encouraging in detecting malicious nodes by selecting an appropriate trust threshold, with an acceptable false positive rate and false negative rate. Additionally, we compare and analyze the current findings with our previous results obtained in a wired network [18], and present possible overhead with respect to our developed trust-based intrusion detection mechanism.

The remaining parts of this paper are organized as follows. In Section 2, we review some related work about trust calculation and trust management in a WSN. We describe the details of calculating trust values using Bayesian model in Section 3. In Section 4, we conduct a simulation to choose an appropriate (initial) trust threshold. We perform an evaluation and present the experimental results in Section 5. Finally, we conclude our work with future directions in Section 6.

[1] A *signature* is a kind of descriptions to describe a known attack or exploit.

2 Related Work

In computer science, the notion of *trust* has been extensively studied, which is borrowed from the social science literature attempting to evaluate and predict the behavior of target objects [11]. In a WSN, a lot of trust-based mechanisms regarding trust computation and trust management have been developed [8].

Probst and Kasera [21] presented a distributed approach that established reputation-based trust among sensor nodes to identify malfunctioning, malicious sensor nodes and minimize their impact on applications. Their proposed method could compute statistical trust values and a confidence interval around the trust, based on sensor node behavior. Wang *et al.* [22] presented a novel intrusion detection mechanism based on the Trust Model (called *IDMTM*) for mobile Ad hoc networks. To judge whether it is a malicious node, they evaluated the trust values using two concepts: Evidence Chain (EC) and Trust Fluctuation (TF). They further indicated that the *IDMTM* could greatly decrease the false alarm rate by efficiently utilizing the information collected from the local node and the neighboring nodes. Later, Chen *et al.* [6] proposed an event-based trust framework model for WSNs, which used watchdog scheme to observe the behavior in different events of these nodes and broadcast their trust ratings. In their work, different events of a sensor node have different trust-rating values, that is, a sensor node could have several trust-rating values stored in its neighbor nodes. Zahariadis *et al.* [28] proposed a secure routing protocol (ATSR) by adopting the geographical routing principle to cope with the network dimensions, and the ATSR could detect malicious neighbors based on a distributed trust model incorporating both direct and indirect trust information.

For trust management, Shaikh *et al.* [23] proposed a new lightweight Group-based Trust Management Scheme (GTMS) employing clusters for wireless sensor networks. The GTMS evaluated the trust of a group of SNs and worked on two topologies: *intra-group topology* where distributed trust management approach was used and *intergroup topology* where centralized trust management approach was adopted. Then, Zhang *et al.* [29] proposed a dynamic trust establishment and management framework for hierarchical wireless sensor networks. Their framework takes into account direct and indirect (group) trust in trust evaluation as well as the energy associated with sensor nodes in service selection. Their approach also considers the dynamic aspect of trust by developing a trust varying function which can be used to give greater weight to the most recently obtained trust values during the trust calculation. In addition, their approach has the capability of considering movement of nodes from one cluster to another. The hierarchical structure (e.g., base station, clusters, sensor nodes) used in our work is very similar to their work.

Later, Guo *et al.* [14] presented a trust management framework to generate trust values by using Grey theory and Fuzzy sets. The total trust value in their work was calculated by using relation factors and weights of neighbor nodes, not just by simply taking an average value. Bao *et al.* [2] proposed a trust-based IDS scheme by utilizing a hierarchical trust management protocol for clustered wireless sensor networks. They considered a trust metric including both quality of service (QoS) trust and social trust for detecting malicious nodes. They further developed an analytical model based on stochastic Petri nets for performance evaluation and a statistical method for calculating the false alarm probability. Their experimental results showed that an optimal trust threshold for minimizing false positives and false negatives was existed, and that this optimal trust threshold could differ based on the anticipated WSN lifetime. Their extended work [3] showed that their trust-based IDS algorithm outperformed traditional anomaly-based IDS techniques (e.g., weighted summation-based IDS and fixed width data clustering-based IDS) in the detection probability while maintaining sufficiently low false positives (i.e., less than 5%). Several other work about trust management protocols can be referred to [9], [10], [17] and [25].

Different from the above articles, in this work, we mainly attempt to compute trust values of sensor nodes by means of Bayesian model and further develop a trust-based intrusion detection mechanism in a hierarchical WSN. This mechanism can compute trust values for each node and detect malicious nodes by means of a trust threshold. To the best of our knowledge, the Bayesian model used in our work has not been explored in a WSN. Based on the results in our previous work [18], we additionally compare the effect of this Bayesian model with its applications in a wired network.

3 Our Proposed Method

In this section, we introduce the architecture of hierarchical (clustered) wireless sensor networks, describe the calculation of trust values using Bayesian model for sensor nodes and present our developed trust-based intrusion detection mechanism.

3.1 Hierarchical Wireless Sensor Network

A hierarchical (clustered) WSN is usually composed of multiple clusters, in which each cluster contains a cluster head (CH) and a number of sensor nodes (SNs). In this network, a cluster head is assumed to have more computational power and energy resources than a sensor node. We present the typical architecture of a hierarchical WSN in Fig. 1. In this model, a WSN consists of a base station, several cluster heads and a number of clusters (e.g., Cluster 1, Cluster 2,..., Cluster N) grouped by multiple sensor nodes.

The cluster head in each cluster can be selected by using election protocols [27]. The clusters can be grouped based on various criteria [29] such as location and communication range or using several cluster algorithms [15]. Generally, a sensor node forwards its data (or information) to its corresponding cluster head and the cluster head then forwards the data to the base station. The basic assumptions for a clustered WSN are described as below:

- All sensor nodes and cluster heads are stationary, and the physical location and communication range of all nodes in the hierarchical WSN are known.
- All the sensor nodes and cluster heads have unique identities and all SNs are organized into clusters.
- The base station is a central control authority and virtually has no resource constraints. In addition, the base station is fully trusted by all nodes.
- Cluster heads have more computational power and more memory compared to other sensor nodes in the WSN.
- The base station communicates with the cluster head and each cluster head manages all the sensor nodes in its own group.

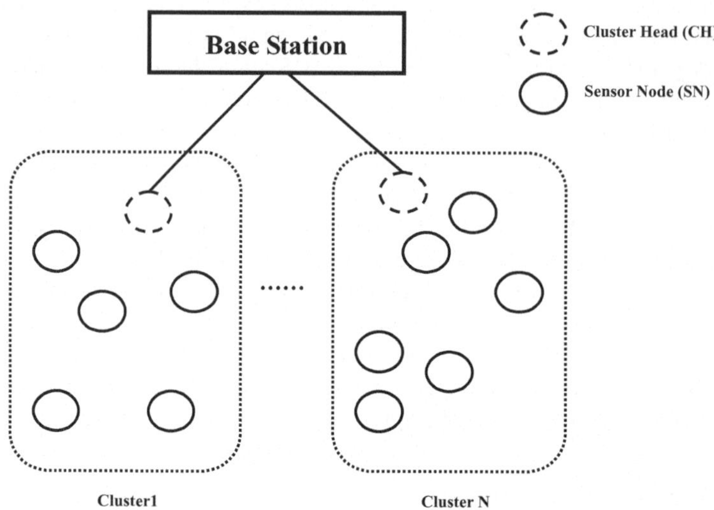

Fig. 1. The typical architecture of hierarchical wireless sensor network

In this work, our mechanism implements a misuse-based IDS in each node and calculates their trust values by means of Bayesian model. With the rapid development of computer networks, we further assume that: all sensor nodes can be deployed with a misuse-based IDS (i.e., constructing a *wireless misuse-based detection sensor*) and have the basic capability of launching the process of signature matching.

3.2 Bayesian Model

In statistics, Bayesian Model (or called *Bayesian inference*) is a method of inference in which Bayes' rule is utilized to update the probability estimate for a hypothesis as additional evidence [26]. The objective of using the *Bayesian Model* in our work is to calculate the trust values for sensor nodes (and cluster heads) in a clustered WSN. This model is based on a major assumption described as follows:

- *Assumption.* We assume that all packets sent from a node are independent from each other. That is, if one packet is found to be a malicious packet, the probability of the following packet being a malicious packet is still $1/2$.

This probability assumption indicates that the attacks can appear in various forms, either in one packet or in a number of packets. To derive the calculation of trust values. We assume that N packets are sent from a node, of which k packets are proven to be *normal*. Next, we provide some terms as those described in our previous work [18].

$$P(n_i : normal) = p \quad (means\ the\ probability\ of\ the\ i^{th}\ packet\ is\ normal.)$$

$$V_i \quad (means\ that\ the\ i^{th}\ packet\ is\ normal.)$$

$$n(N) \quad (means\ the\ number\ of\ normal\ packets.)$$

In terms of the analysis in work [11,26] and the above assumption, we can assume that the distribution of observing $n(N) = k$ is governed by a Binomial distribution[2], which can be described as below.

$$P(n(N) = k|p) = \binom{N}{k} p^k (1-p)^{N-k} \tag{1}$$

In this case, our final objective is to estimate the probability: $P(V_{N+1} = 1|n(N) = k)$ (determining whether the $N + 1$ packet is normal or not). We can use the approach of *Bayesian Inference* to calculate this probability. Based on the Bayesian theorem, we can have the following probability distribution.

$$P(V_{N+1} = 1|n(N) = k) = \frac{P(V_{N+1} = 1, n(N) = k)}{P(n(N) = k)} \tag{2}$$

For the above equation, we apply marginal probability distribution[3] and we then can have two equations:

$$P(n(N) = k) = \int_0^1 P(n(N) = k|p) f(p) \cdot dp \tag{3}$$

$$P(V_{N+1} = 1, n(N) = k) = \int_0^1 P(n(N) = k|p) f(p) p \cdot dp \tag{4}$$

There is no prior information about p, so that we assume that p is determined by a uniform prior distribution $f(p) = 1$ where $p \in [0, 1]$. Therefore, using equation (1), (2), (3) and (4), we can have the following equation:

$$P(V_{N+1} = 1|n(N) = k) = \frac{\int_0^1 P(n(N) = k|p) f(p) p \cdot dp}{\int_0^1 P(n(N) = k|p) f(p) \cdot dp} = \frac{k+1}{N+2} \tag{5}$$

Therefore, trust values (denoted t_{value}) can be calculated based on equation (5) for all nodes in a WSN (i.e., obtaining the number of normal packets k and the total number of packets N). In terms of the trust values calculated for each node (i.e., constructing a map of trust values), a potential malicious node can be identified by giving an appropriate trust threshold. Note that a node can be regarded as a malicious node by only sending one malicious packet, but our approach has the capability of evaluating the trust of a node based on its long-term performance.

3.3 Trust-Based Intrusion Detection Mechanism

As described above, trust values can be calculated based on equation (5). To obtain the trust value for a certain node, we therefore should record the total number of its sent

[2] Binomial distribution is the discrete probability distribution that represents the number of successes in a sequence of n independent, which the possibility of each n is the same p.

[3] Marginal distribution of a subset of random variables is the probability distribution of the variables contained in the subset.

packets and the number of normal packets. In current mechanism, we use a misuse-based IDS (e.g., Snort) to identify malicious packets (i.e., the number of malicious packets is m) so that the number of normal packets can be computed as: $k = N - m$. As the nature of the misuse-based detection, malicious packets can be detected by means of signature matching between incoming payloads and stored IDS signatures.

Maliciousness. Based on equation (5), we can determine a malicious node by using a *trust threshold*. If we set the *trust threshold* to $T \in [a, b]$ (the selection of the *threshold* will be discussed later), then we can judge a malicious node as follows:

- If $t_{value} \in T$, then the corresponding node is regarded to be a normal node.
- If t_{value} is not in T, then the corresponding node is regarded to be a malicious (or untrusted) node.

Trust Value of a Node. In a hierarchical WSN, each sensor could have two main functions: sensing and relaying. Sensors collect and gather data and then transmit the collected information to the cluster head directly in one hop or by relaying via a multi hop path. Sensors transmit or relay data only via short-haul radio communication. It is also assumed that each cluster head (CH) has the capability of reaching and controlling all the sensor nodes in its cluster. Each cluster head can receive the data from different sensor nodes, and it then processes, extracts and sends the data to the base station.[4]

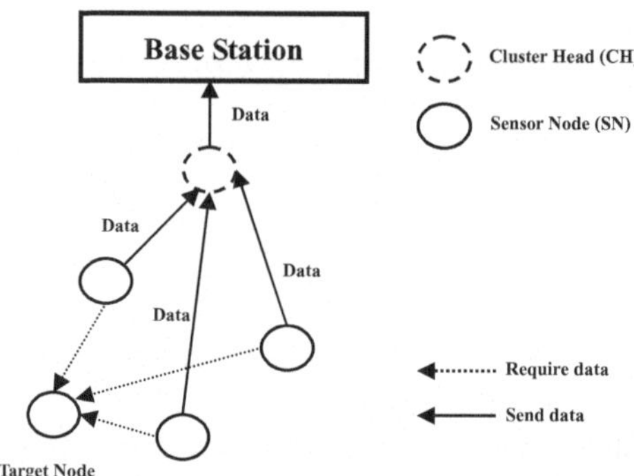

Fig. 2. Trust calculation in a hierarchical wireless sensor network

In Fig. 2, we give an example of calculating trust values for a target node in a hierarchical WSN. Each sensor node will deploy a misuse-based IDS to examine incoming packets. The calculation of node's trust values is based on a time window t. The time window usually consists of several time units. The sensor nodes in a cluster record the information (e.g., the number of sent packets, the number of malicious packets) about other nodes in each time unit and then send the information to its cluster head. After several time units elapse, the time window slides to the right (e.g., one time unit), and

[4] In this structure, the trust of a cluster head (CH) can be evaluated by the base station.

the sensor nodes can drop the data collected during the earliest unit aiming to reduce the storage consumption. The cluster head receives the data and then calculates the trust values for the target node during a selected time period, as shown in Fig. 2, based on equation (5). Later, the cluster head sends data to the base station.

Specifically, the cluster head will periodically request the trust state for a target node and thus can establish a map of trust values. In response, all sensor nodes in the cluster forward the recorded information to the cluster head. Suppose there are n sensor nodes, the cluster head can then establish a map of trust values as follows:

$$T_{map} = [t_{value,i}] \quad (i = 1, 2, ..., n)$$

Where T_{map} represents the matrix (or *map*) of trust values in the cluster, and $t_{value,i}$ represents the trust values for sensor node i. If a trust threshold is given, then the cluster head can quickly identify malicious nodes based on the matrix. In the mechanism, bad behavior of a node (i.e., sending malicious packets) can reduce its trust value greatly. For a sensor node, its trust value can be computed by its cluster head, while for a cluster head, its trust value can be computed by the base station.

4 Trust Threshold

To efficiently detect a malicious node using the Bayesian model, a trust threshold should be identified in advance. According to equation (5), we can find that if k becomes bigger, then the t_{value} will become larger. Because k (the number of normal packets) is always smaller than N (the total number of incoming packets), the range of t_{value} is belonging to the interval of [0,1]. In this case, the best scenario for t_{value} is that its value infinitely close to 1, which means that a node is more credible by sending most normal packets. On the other hand, if t_{value} declines, it means that malicious packets are detected for that node during the node-to-node communications.

We define a as the lower limit of the threshold, thus, the trust threshold can be initially presented as [a,1]. In order to determine the lower limit a, we simulate a clustered WSN with the purpose of identifying an appropriate trust threshold. The simulated WSN consists of 100 sensor nodes (SNs) and 10 cluster heads (CHs) uniformly distributed in a 110m$\times$110m area. The duration of a time unit for calculating the trust values is initially set to 10 minutes. To evaluate the trust threshold, we performed the experiment for a day by randomly selecting 5 clusters. The average trust values for each cluster are presented in Fig. 3.

The average trust values are calculated by using the trust values of all sensor nodes in a cluster within an hour[5]. In the figure, it is visible that each cluster has a different range of trust values. Take *Cluster 1* for an example, its trust values are ranged from 0.856 to 0.937, whereas for *Cluster 2*, its trust values are ranged from 0.742 to 0.912. For the *Cluster 3*, *Cluster 4* and *Cluster 5*, the corresponding trust values are in the range from 0.785 to 0.904, from 0.765 to 0.931, and from 0.731 to 0.893 respectively.

[5] In this simulation, we consider an *hour* is an appropriate time unit for our mechanism to collect trust information, whereas the time duration can be configured based on real settings.

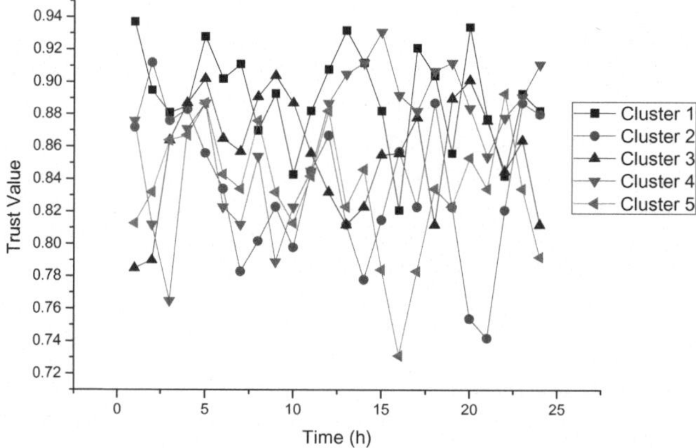

Fig. 3. The average trust values for 5 clusters in the simulated WSN

As shown in Fig. 3, it is visible that the trust values are very dynamic in different clusters. For the other 5 remaining clusters, we conduct the same simulation and find that their trust values are mainly ranged from 0.724 to 0.916. In [18], we evaluated the trust values calculated by means of the Bayesian model in a wired network and found that the corresponding trust values are ranged from 0.75 to 0.92. In this scenario, the results show that the trust values in a wireless sensor network are more dynamic than in a wired network. Based on the simulation results, we set the lower limit a to 0.72 so that the (initial) trust threshold for the simulated WSN is [0.72,1]. If the trust value of a node is below this threshold, then this node can be regarded as a malicious node.

Note that the lower limit a may be varied in different network deployment (i.e., the characteristics of traffic may be distinct). In this work, we can only say that $a = 0.72$ is an appropriate value regarding our simulated WSN. Whether it is suitable for other WSNs needs to be verified in our future experiments.

5 Evaluation

In this section, we evaluate the performance of our proposed trust-based intrusion detection mechanism on the simulated WSN. In particular, we mainly conducted two experiments by using a fixed and a dynamic trust threshold respectively:

- *Experiment1*. This experiment evaluated the performance of our proposed method by using a fixed trust threshold of [0.72,1]. During the experiment, we launched some wireless attacks and malicious packets by means of testing tools[6] (i.e., flooding the WSN with deauthentication packets-WVE-2005-0045).
- *Experiment2*. This experiment evaluated the performance of our proposed method by implementing a dynamic trust threshold, which would be updated in every time

[6] `http://code.google.com/p/wireless-intrusion-detection-system-testing-tool/`

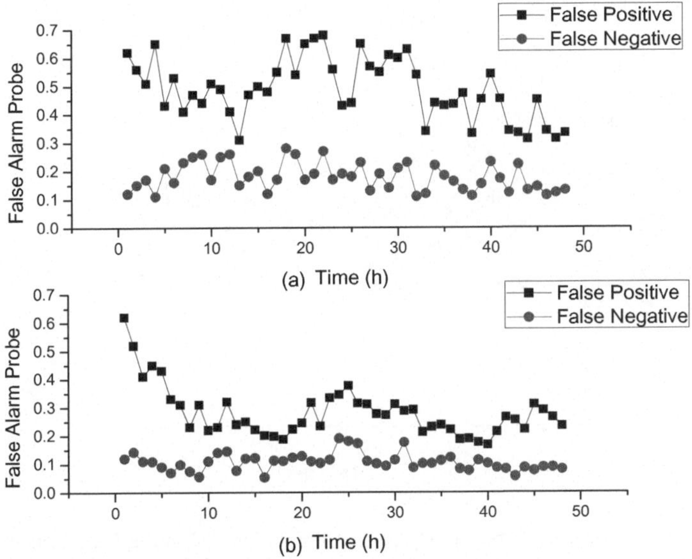

Fig. 4. The false positive rates and the false negative rates for (a) the *Experiment1* and (b) the *Experiement2*

unit. The dynamic trust threshold for each cluster is an average trust value computed by all nodes in that cluster during the latest time unit. As being deployed in the same WSN, we attempt to compare the performance of the fixed trust threshold and the dynamic trust threshold.

5.1 Experiment1

In this experiment, a fixed trust threshold of [0.72,1] is used. The sensor nodes may randomly send malicious packets by using the wireless IDS testing tools. Therefore, a sensor node in a cluster may become a malicious node by sending a number of malicious packets. The experiment was conducted for 2 days. The false positive rates and the false negative rates are described in Fig. 4 (a).

In the figure, the false positive rates are ranged from 0.31 to 0.68 while the false negative rates are ranged from 0.11 to 0.28. The results show that the false alarm rate is very fluctuant and a bit high regarding the fixed trust threshold. The main reason is that the traffic in a WSN is very dynamic whereas the fixed trust threshold cannot reflect the traffic changes in the WSN.

5.2 Experiment2

In this experiment, we used a dynamic trust threshold for each cluster. The dynamic trust threshold is an average trust value computed by all nodes in its cluster during the latest time unit. Through analyzing the same WSN data, the false positive rates and the false negative rates are described in Fig. 4 (b).

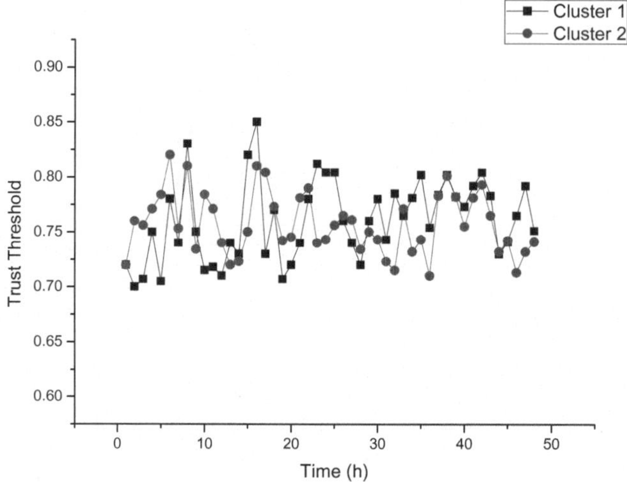

Fig. 5. The trust threshold for cluster 1 and cluster 2 in the *Experiement2*

In the figure, it is visible that the false positive rates and the false negative rates are greatly reduced. For the false positive rates, the rate-range is maintained from 0.2 to 0.3 excluding the first several hours. The range for the false negative rate is from 0.05 to 0.15. These experimental results indicate that the use of dynamic trust thresholds can significantly reduce the false alarm rate and keep the rate at a relatively stable level. The reason is that the dynamic trust threshold can vary with the latest traffic changes in a cluster and can more accurately reflect the current network traffic.

In Fig. 5, we illustrate an example of computing dynamic trust thresholds for cluster 1 and cluster 2 during the experiment. It is easily visible that the trust thresholds for these two clusters are varied. For the cluster 1, the trust threshold is ranged from 0.705 to 0.812, while for the cluster 2, the trust threshold is ranged from 0.713 to 0.82. This situation is similar to other clusters.

5.3 Discussion

The above experimental results indicate that, by employing the mechanism of computing the trust threshold in an adaptive way, the false positive rates and false negative rates for detecting malicious nodes can be greatly reduced and maintained at a stable level. However, as compared to our previous results obtained in a wired network environment [18] (where the false positive rate is about 0.084 and the false negative rate is about 0.068), the false alarm rate achieved in this work is still a bit higher. This comparison reflects that the traffic in a wireless network is more dynamic than that in a wired network. In other words, it is more difficult to model the traffic by means of the Bayesian model in a wireless sensor network than in a wired network environment.

To enhance the detection performance of our proposed trust-based intrusion detection mechanism, several additional measures (e.g., energy consumption, cooperativeness) could be used to compute a weighted trust value. During the experiments, we also find that the implementation of a misuse-based IDS brings less burden on a sensor node since all nodes can perform the process of signature matching well. Next, we briefly analyze possible overhead with respect to our developed mechanism.

Communication Overhead. We assume the worst case scenario: every sensor node wants to communicate with every other node in the cluster and every cluster wants to communicate with the other clusters in the WSN. If there are N_{ct} clusters and the average size of a cluster is S, then the maximum communication overhead within a cluster is $2S(S-1)(S-2)$ (since a node sends $S-2$ and receives $S-2$ packets by communicating with other $S-1$ nodes), while the maximum communication overhead between clusters is $2N_{ct}(N_{ct}-1)$ (i.e., a cluster should send a request to the base station when communicates with another cluster). Thus, the maximum communication overhead in the WSN is: $N_{ct}[2S(S-1)(S-2)] + 2N_{ct}(N_{ct}-1)$.

Storage Overhead. For sensor nodes, each of them needs to store a $2 * (S-1)$ matrix to record the information (i.e., the number of malicious packets and the total number of packets) of other nodes. For the cluster head, it needs to store a $(S-1) * (S-1)$ matrix (i.e., recording information sent from other nodes) and a $1 * (s-1)$ matrix.

Computation Overhead. In current mechanism, the trust calculation is conducted in the cluster head. To compute the trust values, the cluster head begins by establishing a $(S-1) * (S-1)$ matrix to record collected information sent from sensor nodes, and then computes one $1 * (S-1)$ matrix of trust values.

Note that in this work, our goal is to compute and evaluate the trust values of WSN nodes by using the Bayesian model. A detailed comparison of our proposed mechanism with other existing solutions in the aspect of CPU cycle, memory consumption and communication overhead will be investigated in our future work.

6 Conclusion and Future Work

In this paper, we proposed a trust-based intrusion detection mechanism by means of Bayesian model to detect malicious nodes in a hierarchical wireless sensor network. The Bayesian model enables a hierarchical wireless sensor network to establish a map of trust values among different sensor nodes. In particular, the sensor nodes collect and sent data about other nodes to its corresponding cluster head. The cluster head can calculate the trust values for all nodes in its cluster, and the base station can calculate the trust values for all cluster heads. We then evaluated the trust mechanism in a simulated WSN and identified an initial trust threshold that can be used at the beginning of detecting malicious nodes. In the evaluation, we conducted two experiments to explore the effect of a fixed trust threshold and a dynamic trust threshold. The experimental results show that the way of dynamically computing trust thresholds can greatly reduce both the false positive rates and the false negative rates, and maintain the false alarm rate at a lower and more stable level. We also find that the traffic in a wireless sensor network is more dynamic than that in a wired network by comparing our current results with our previous work in a wired network environment.

Our work is developed at an early stage and there are many possible topics for our future work. One is to implement our approach into a more larger wireless sensor network and validate the results obtained in this work. Future work could also include exploring how to effectively identify a trust threshold, and applying other measures (e.g., energy consumption) in calculating a weighted trust threshold. In addition, future work could include investigating the impact of the number of clusters and the time unit on the calculation of trust values, and conducting a comparative performance analysis of existing trust-based IDS mechanisms.

References

1. Axelsson, S.: The Base-rate Fallacy and the Difficulty of Intrusion Detection. ACM Transactions on Information and System Security 3(3), 186–205 (2000)
2. Bao, F., Chen, I.-R., Chang, M., Cho, J.-H.: Trust-Based Intrusion Detection in Wireless Sensor Networks. In: Proceedings of the 2011 IEEE International Conference on Communications (ICC), pp. 1–6 (2011)
3. Bao, F., Chen, I.-R., Chang, M., Cho, J.-H.: Hierarchical Trust Management for Wireless Sensor Networks and its Applications to Trust-Based Routing and Intrusion Detection. IEEE Transactions on Network and Service Management 9(2), 169–183 (2012)
4. Beckwith, R., Teibel, D., Bowen, P.: Report from the Field: Results from an Agricultural Wireless Sensor Network. In: Proceedings of the 29th Annual IEEE International Conference on Local Computer Networks, pp. 471–478 (2004)
5. Chen, X., Makki, K., Yen, K., Pissinou, N.: Sensor Network Security: A Survey. IEEE Communication Surveys & Tutorials 11(2), 52–73 (2009)
6. Chen, H., Wu, H., Hu, J., Gao, C.: Event-based Trust Framework Model in Wireless Sensor Networks. In: Proceedings of the 2008 International Conference on Networking, Architecture, and Storage (NAS), pp. 359–364 (2008)
7. Cheung, S.-Y., Varaiya, P.: Traffic Surveillance by Wireless Sensor Networks: Final Report. California PATH Research Report, UCB-ITS-PRR-2007-4. Institue of Transportation Studies, University of California, Berkeley (2007), http://www.its.berkeley.edu/publications/UCB/2007/PRR/UCB-ITS-PRR-2007-4.pdf
8. Cho, J.-H., Swami, A., Chen, I.-R.: A Survey on Trust Management for Mobile Ad Hoc Networks. IEEE Communications Surveys & Tutorials 13(4), 562–583 (2011)
9. Daabaj, K., Dixon, M., Koziniec, T., Lee, K.: Trusted Routing for Resource-Constrained Wireless Sensor Networks. In: Proceedings of the 2010 IEEE/IFIP International Conference on Embedded and Ubiquitous Computing (EUC), pp. 666–671 (2010)
10. Ganeriwal, S., Balzano, L.K., Srivastava, M.B.: Reputation-based Framework for High Integrity Sensor Networks. ACM Transitions on Sensor Network 4(3), 1–37 (2008)
11. Gonzalez, J.M., Anwar, M., Joshi, J.B.D.: A Trust-based Approach against IP-Spoofing Attacks. In: Proceedings of the 9th International Conference on Privacy, Security and Trust (PST 2011), pp. 63–70 (2011)
12. Ghosh, A.K., Wanken, J., Charron, F.: Detecting Anomalous and Unknown Intrusions Against Programs. In: Proceedings of the 1998 Annual Computer Security Applications Conference (ACSAC), pp. 259–267 (1998)
13. Grilo, A., Piotrowski, K., Langendoerfer, P., Casaca, A.: A Wireless Sensor Network Architecture for Homeland Security Application. In: Ruiz, P.M., Garcia-Luna-Aceves, J.J. (eds.) ADHOC-NOW 2009. LNCS, vol. 5793, pp. 397–402. Springer, Heidelberg (2009)

14. Guo, J., Marshall, A., Zhou, B.: A New Trust Management Framework for Detecting Malicious and Selfish Behaviour for Mobile Ad Hoc Networks. In: Proceedings of the 10th IEEE International Conference on Trust, Security and Privacy in Computing and Communications (TrustCom), pp. 142–149 (2011)
15. Gupta, G., Younis, M.: Performance Evaluation of Load-Balanced Clustering of Wireless Sensor Networks. In: Proceedings of the 10th International Conference on Telecommunications (ICT), pp. 1577–1583 (2003)
16. Hutchison, K.: Wireless Intrusion Detection Systems. SANS GSEC Whitepaper, 1–18 (2005), `http://www.sans.org/reading_room/whitepapers/wireless/wireless-intrusion-detection-systems_1543`
17. Liu, K., Abu-Ghazaleh, N., Kang, K.-D.: Location Verification and Trust Management for Resilient Geographic Routing. Journal of Parallel and Distributed Computing 67(2), 215–228 (2007)
18. Meng, Y., Kwok, L.-F., Li, W.: Towards Designing Packet Filter with a Trust-Based Approach Using Bayesian Inference in Network Intrusion Detection. In: Keromytis, A.D., Di Pietro, R. (eds.) SecureComm 2012. LNICST, vol. 106, pp. 203–221. Springer, Heidelberg (2013)
19. Mishra, A., Nadkarni, K., Patcha, A.: Intrusion Detection in Wireless Ad-Hoc Networks. IEEE Wireless Communications 11(1), 48–60 (2004)
20. Porras, P.A., Kemmerer, R.A.: Penetration State Transition Analysis: A Rule-based Intrusion Detection Approach. In: Proceedings of the 8th Annual Computer Security Applications Conference (ACSAC), pp. 220–229 (1992)
21. Probst, M.J., Kasera, S.K.: Statistical Trust Establishment in Wireless Sensor Networks. In: Proceedings of the 2007 International Conference on Parallel and Distributed Systems (ICPADS), pp. 1–8 (2007)
22. Wang, F., Huang, C., Zhang, J., Rong, C.: IDMTM: A Novel Intrusion Detection Mechanism based on Trust Model for Ad-Hoc Networks. In: Proceedings of the 22nd IEEE International Conference on Advanced Information Networking and Applications (AINA), pp. 978–984 (2008)
23. Shaikh, R.A., Jameel, H., d'Auriol, B.J., Lee, H., Lee, S., Song, Y.J.: Group-based Trust Management Scheme for Clustered Wireless Sensor Networks. IEEE Transactions on Parallel and Distributed Systems 20(11), 1698–1712 (2009)
24. Sommer, R., Paxson, V.: Outside the Closed World: On Using Machine Learning for Network Intrusion Detection. In: Proceedings of the 2010 IEEE Symposium on Security and Privacy, pp. 305–316 (2010)
25. Sun, Y., Luo, H., Das, S.K.: A Trust-Based Framework for Fault-Tolerant Data Aggregation in Wireless Multimedia Sensor Networks. IEEE Transactions on Dependable and Secure Computing 9(6), 785–797 (2012)
26. Sun, Y., Yu, W., Han, Z., Liu, K.: Information Theoretic Framework of Trust Modeling and Evaluation for Ad Hoc Networks. IEEE Journal on Selected Areas in Communications 24(2), 305–317 (2006)
27. Younis, O., Fahmy, S.: HEED: A Hybrid Energy Efficient, Distributed Clustering Approach for Ad Hoc Sensor Network. IEEE Transaction on Mobile Computing 3(3), 366–379 (2004)
28. Zahariadis, T., Trakadas, P., Leligou, H.C., Maniatis, S., Karkazis, P.: A Novel Trust-Aware Geographical Routing Scheme for Wireless Sensor Networks. Wireless Personal Communications, 1–22 (2012)
29. Zhang, J., Shankaran, R., Orgun, M.A., Varadharajan, V., Sattar, A.: A Dynamic Trust Establishment and Management Framework for Wireless Sensor Networks. In: Proceedings of the 2010 IEEE/IFIP International Conference on Embedded and Ubiquitous Computing (EUC), pp. 484–491 (2010)

Model the Influence of Sybil Nodes in P2P Botnets

Tianzuo Wang*, Huaimin Wang, Bo Liu, and Peichang Shi

School of Computer Science, National University of Defense Technology, ChangSha, China
{tianzuow,pcshi.nudt}@gmail.com, whm_w@163.com,
boliu615@yahoo.com.cn

Abstract. Sybil attacks are suitable to mitigate P2P botnets, and the effects depend on the influences of Sybil nodes. However, the problem of how to evaluate the influences of Sybil nodes is rarely studied. Considering Kademlia based botnets, we formulate a model to evaluate the influence of Sybil nodes during the publishing of commands. Simulation results show the correctness of this model, and it is found that the percentage of Sybil nodes in the botnet, the value of K, and the size of the botnet are three important factors which significantly affect the influence of Sybil nodes. For defenders who want to determine how many sybil nodes should be inserted to achieve the goal of mitigation, this model can provide valuable guidance.

Keywords: P2P botnets, Sybil, mitigation, influence, model, Kademlia.

1 Introduction

Botnets are complex, flexible and efficient platforms for network attacks, and are threatening the Internet severely. Recent years, for the absence of single point of failure, more and more botnets are built on P2P, e.g., Storm [1], Waledac [2] and Conficker [3].

Attacking the publishing of commands can efficiently mitigate P2P botnets. For the botmaster of a P2P botnet, in order to control the whole botnet, he has to deliver commands to all the bots through two stages. First, the botmaster publishes the commands on certain root nodes. Second, commands are spreaded to all the bots. The efficient way to mitigate P2P botnets is to disrupt the first stage, because it is in the upstream of the control over the botnet. The earlier the delivery of commands is blocked, the better the effect of mitigation will be.

In P2P botnets, the delivery of commands is resilient to eliminating bots, but is vulnerable to Sybil attacks. A Sybil node originally means an entity that has multiple identities, and now in general, the fake identities are also called Sybil nodes [4]. Douceur [5] et al. pointed out that in a purely decentralized network without a centric authority, it is almost impossible to completely solve the problem of Sybil attacks. Even though some approaches [4, 6, 7] have been proposed to relieve the problem of Sybil attacks, usually, they are not suitable to P2P botnets.

In P2P botnets, the mitigation effect of Sybil nodes is usually exerted through responding to inquiring bots with misleading messages. From existing methods [8-10]

* Corresponding author.

J. Lopez, X. Huang, and R. Sandhu (Eds.): NSS 2013, LNCS 7873, pp. 54–67, 2013.

which use Sybil nodes to mitigate P2P botnets, we concluded that the effect of mitigation depends on the probability that bots inquire Sybil nodes during their activities. We call this probability the influence of Sybil nodes in P2P botnets.

If there is a model that can predict the influence of Sybil nodes, proper suggestions will be provided to the practical mitigation. However, there are no such models as far as we know.

This paper studies the influence of Sybil nodes on the publishing of commands. Taking Kademlia [11] based botnets (e.g. Storm, Overbot [12] and TLD-4[1]) as the most important case, through the analysis of some critical factors that affect the influence of Sybil nodes, a prediction model is proposed to calculate the probability for bots to inquire Sybil nodes during the publishing of commands. This model has been validated by our experiments. In accord with our model, simulations show that the percentage of Sybil nodes in the Kademlia-botnet, the value of K, and the size of the botnet are three important factors which significantly affect the influence of Sybil nodes. Big values of these factors will lead to large influence of Sybil nodes.

The reason that we focus on Kademlia based botnets is that Kademlia is often adopted by botmasters to construct their P2P botnets, for example, Storm botnet, Waledac botnet and Conficker botnet all utilized Kademlia protocol to construct their P2P overlays. Further, structured P2P protocols have much in common, so the study on Kademlia based botnets can also shed lights on mitigating other kinds of structured P2P botnets.

The rest of this paper is organized as follows. In Section 2, the background on the Kademlia protocol is presented. In Section 3, the prediction model of the influence of Sybil nodes are deduced. In Section 4, the results of experiments are analyzed, and our model is validated. Related work is reviewed in Section 5, and the paper is concluded in Section 6.

2 Background

2.1 Route List of Kademlia

Kademlia is a kind of structured P2P protocol. Between a structured P2P network and an unstructured one, the efficiency of searching is one of the most important differences. Unstructured P2P protocols often adopt flooding algorithm to search, and make use of TTL (Time To Live) to limit the massive requesting messages generated. This kind of searching not only is inefficient for the directionless inquiries, but also may miss the targets because of the limit of TTL. Structured P2P protocols provide the nodes with the information about the structure of the network, so that the publisher can store objects in specific locations and the nodes can issue directed searching for those objects. It is necessary for structured P2P nodes to determine the distances to the target objects, so each node or object need to be assigned an ID.

---

[1] http://www.securelist.com/en/analysis/204792180/TDL4_Top_Bot

Kademlia is based on the DHT (Distributed Hash Table) mechanism. In Kademlia, each node is assigned a distinct nodeID, and each object is assigned an objectID (also called key). These IDs are usually generated by a 160 bit SHA-1 function. Objects are stored on K nodes whose nodeIDs are nearest to the ObjectIDs, and the distances are calculated by the XOR operation. Because this kind of distance is symmetric, from the messages received, nodes can get useful information about the structure of network. So compared with other protocols like Chord [13], Kademlia is more fault-tolerant and flexible.

Each Kademlia node maintains a route list called "k-buckets". Take the 160-bit ID as an example. For each $i \in [0, 160)$, a node stores a peer list (called a "k-bucket") no longer than K, which is used to store information of peers whose distances to it are located in $[2^i, 2^{i+1})$. Fig. 1 shows the structure of the route list of node A. The line, with $nodeID_A$ as the starting point and $nodeID_A \oplus (2^{160}-1)$ as the ending point, represents the reordered nodeID space which is a result of the XOR operations between $nodeID_A$ and all the nodeIDs in the nodeID space. Kademlia nodes update their route list through the method of "piggy backing", which means that once a message from another node B arrives, the information of node B will be used to update the "k-buckets".

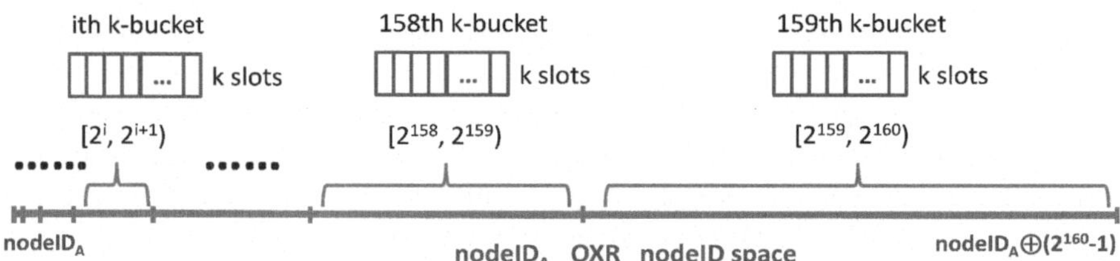

Fig. 1. K-buckets of node A

2.2 RPCs of Kademlia

Kademlia is formed mainly by four RPCs (Remote Procedure Call), including PING, STORE, FIND_NODE and FIND_VALUE.

Kademlia based botnets construct their C&C (Command and Control) mechanisms with these four RPCs. Botmasters use FIND_NODE and STORE to publish the C&C information (i.e. commands), and bots use FIND_VALUE to get the target objects. We are to analyze the influence of Sybil nodes on the publishing of C&C information, so the mechanism of publishing is detailed here.

Table 1. Four fundamental RPCs

Name of RPC	Description
PING	Detects if one node is alive.
STORE	Asks one node to store a <key, value> pair. The key is the objectID, and the value is the content or its index.
FIND_NODE	Asks one node for its K neighbor nodes nearest to a certain ID.
FIND_VALUE	Finds the value indexed by a certain key.

2.3 Publishing of the C&C Information

To publish a <key, value> pair, one node W has to find the K nearest nodes to key first, and this process is called "node lookup". After that, the STORE RPC will be used to store this pair on each of the K nodes. The K nearest nodes is also called root nodes for key. During node lookup, the initiator W will firstly select α nearest nodes to key in its own k-buckets, and then issue FIND_NODE RPCs to them concurrently and asynchronously. If no response is received from one node, the information of this node will be deleted from the k-buckets. This process will be repeated to find the root nodes.

```
Input: Ckey, C&C information
Output: K-list
Construct a K-list which consists of K nearest bots to Ckey in k-buckets;
While( there are bots not requested in K-list)
{
Request the nearest unrequested bot(bot_u) for its K nearest neighbors(K-neighbors);
Wait for K-neighbors from bot_u;
If ( no response from bot_u)
{
      Delete bot_u from K-list;
}
      Else
{
            K-list = K nearest bots from K-list and K-neighbors;
      }
}
Store(K-list, C&C information)
```

Fig. 2. Algorithm of Publishing in Kademlia

If no nearer nodes are received in a round of α FIND_NODE RPCs, the node W will take the K nearest nodes to its knowledge as the possible root nodes. At the moment, W has to send FIND_NODE to all the nodes not inquired among the nearest K ones. After receiving the responses of the K nodes, the process of node lookup ends. Fig. 2 shows the algorithm of publishing in Kademlia, and the K-list contains the K nearest nodes to the current knowledge of node W. For the sake of simplicity, α is set 1 here.

Whatever complex C&C mechanisms are adopted by Kademlia based botnets, the delivery of C&C information have to make use of this publishing process of Kademlia. When publishing <CKey, C&C information> into the botnet, the publishing node W has to find the K nearest nodes to CKey first, and then store the <CKey, C&C information> pair on these nodes respectively. In a Kademlia-based botnet, the CKey is often a rendezvous value between bots and the botmaster.

3 Prediction Model of Influence

3.1 Concepts and Assumptions

For the convenience of description, some concepts are presented here.

Publishing path: the set of all the nodes that are visited during a publishing activity.

Meet a Sybil during publishing: there is at least one Sybil in the publishing path.

A Sybil-meet pub: a publishing activity that meet a Sybil.

Confronting space: the smallest nodeID subspace which contains the nodes in the K-list.

Target space: the smallest nodeID subspace that contains the K root nodes.

Inquiry round: a round of inquiries begins with the sending of α requests, and ends with the receiving of α responses or timeouts.

For simplicity but without loss of generality, we assume the Kademlia-botnet as the assumption 1, which constitute the basic scenario for the deduction of our model.

Assumption 1. The size of the Kademlia based botnet is M, and the percentage that Sybil nodes take in the botnet is x. The bots and Sybil nodes are both distributed in the nodeID space randomly, and Sybil nodes are as active as bots. <CKey, C&C information> is to be published into the botnet by the botmaster through node W.

According to the feature of structured P2P protocols, the confronting space will shrink after each round of α FIND_NODE inquiries. The node lookup process can be considered as a process that the confronting space shrinks gradually onto the target space. So, we propose assumption 2.

Assumption 2. Before the confronting space has already shrunk onto the target space, the inquiries of FIND_NODE RPCs are issued round after round. In each round, α FIND_NODE RPCs are issued asymmetrically, and this round does not end until all the α inquiries are responded or timeout. Until the previous round ends, the new round would not start. Once the confronting space shrinks onto the target space, the K root nodes will be inquired one by one.

Normally, the target space should always be located in the confronting space. According to the assumption 1, the distribution of nodes can be roughly considered uniform, thus the size of the subspace represented by each node is also roughly equal. During each round, the node W selects α nodes from the K-list, and sends them FIND_NODE messages. The space represented by the α nodes is α/K of the current confront space. Each of the inquired nodes will return the K nearest nodes to CKey in their route list, so node W will get the information of α*K nodes. Then from the α*K nodes, W will select K nearest nodes to CKey to update the K-list, so the space would shrink to K/(α*K). Thus, we can get the ideal shrinking rate U of confronting space in each round.

$$U = 1/(\frac{\alpha}{K} \cdot \frac{K}{\alpha \cdot K}) = K \tag{1}$$

Thus, assumption 3 is made as below.

Assumption 3. After each round of inquiries, the size of confronting space shrinks to its 1/U. In this paper, U is called the shrinking rate, and its value is considered to be constantly K.

3.2 Deduction of the Model

According to the assumptions above, if the number of nodes located in the initial confronting space is M0, the number of inquiry rounds needed for the confronting space to shrink onto the target space will be $R=\log_k M0-\log_K K$, which means that there will be $\alpha*R$ inquiries. When the confronting space is the same as the target space, other K inquiries are still needed for each node in the K-list. Thus, $\alpha*R+K$ inquiries are needed during the whole process of publishing.

According to the assumption 1, the probability to visit a Sybil in each inquiry is x, so the probability for the node W to meet at least one Sybil during publishing is $1-(1-x)^{\alpha*R+K}$.

Now, it is clear that if we can calculate the probability distribution of M0, we will be able to get the total probability for W to meet a Sybil during the publishing of <CKey, C&C information>. This total probability is the influence of Sybil nodes.

In this paper, we name the k-bucket of $[2^i, 2^{i+1})$ the NO_(i) k-bucket, and name $[2^i, 2^{i+1})$ the NO_(i) k-bucket scope. It can be proved that the length of the path from one node to any node in its NO_(i) k-bucket scope is the same in the sense of statistics, which means that probability is the same to meet with Sybil nodes when searching for any node in the NO_(i) k-bucket scope. In this sense, we can take the k-bucket scope which contains the target space as the initial confronting space.

Assume the nodeID contains L bits. M is the size of the botnet according to assumption 1. If the target space is located in the NO_(i) k-bucket scope, the size of the initial confronting space would be 2^i, so M0 would be $M*2^i/2^L=M*2^{i-L}$.

Thus, the probability distribution of M0 is determined by the distribution of the target space. If for each k-bucket scope of the node W, we can calculate the probability that the target space is located in it, we will get the probability distribution of M0.

According to the protocol of Kademlia, when the node W publishes <CKey, C&C information>, the target space is determined by CKey. If CKey is located in its NO_(L-i) k-bucket scope, and if the target space is no larger than the NO_(L-i) k-bucket scope, the target space is in the NO_(L-i) k-bucket scope. The size of the smallest k-bucket scope that contains the target space should be no smaller than K.

The probability that the target space is located in the NO_(L-h) k-bucket is $P_h=2^{L-h}/2^L=2^{-h}$, because the probability that CKey is located in the NO_(L-h) k-bucket is $P_h=2^{L-h}/2^L=2^{-h}$. In this situation, M0 equals $M/2^h$. If we can identify the smallest k-bucket scope that can accommodate the target space, we will get the probability distribution of the target space.

The proportion taken by the NO_(i) k-bucket scope in the total space is $2^{-(L-i)}$. The proportion taken by the target space in the total space is $K/M=2^{-\log_2(M/K)}$, so the index of the smallest k-bucket scope containing the target space should be $L-\lfloor\log_2(M/K)\rfloor$, which means the smallest k-bucket containing the target space is $NO\_(L-\lfloor\log_2(M/K)\rfloor)$.

Thus, we get the distribution of M0 as well as the probability to meet a Sybil for the node W when publishing, as is shown in Table II.

The probability that the node W itself is located in the target space is $1/2^{\lfloor\log_2(M/K)\rfloor}\approx K/M$, and in this situation, the publishing path would not include a Sybil node unless there is a Sybil node in the other K-1 root nodes. In this situation, the probability to meet a Sybil during publishing is $1-(1-x)^{K-1}$. According to the analysis above, for each node which is publishing commands, the average probability to meet a Sybil during publishing is P.

$$P=\sum_{i=1}^{\left\lfloor \log_2 \frac{M}{K} \right\rfloor} \frac{1}{2^i}\cdot(1-(1-x)^{\alpha\cdot\log_K \frac{M}{2^i\cdot K}+K})+\frac{K}{M}\cdot(1-(1-X)^{K-1}) \tag{2}$$

It can be find out that with the increase of the size of network, the Sybil percentage or the K value, the probability to meet a Sybil during publishing increases.

Table 2. Distribution of the probability to meet a Sybil during publishing

i	Probability that target space is in the NO_(L-i) k-bucket scope.	Number of nodes in initial confronting space	Number of inquiry rounds	Probability to meet a Sybil during publishing
1	1/2	$M_1=M/2$	$R_1 = \log_K M_1 - \log_K K$	$P_1 = 1-(1-x)^{\alpha\cdot R_1+K}$
2	$1/2^2$	$M_2=M/2^2$	$R_2 = \log_K M_2 - \log_K K$	$P_2 = 1-(1-x)^{\alpha\cdot R_2+K}$
3	$1/2^3$	$M_3=M/2^3$	$R_3 = \log_K M_3 - \log_K K$	$P_3 = 1-(1-x)^{\alpha\cdot R_3+K}$
...	...	...	...	...
h	$1/2^h$	$M_h=M/2^h$	$R_h = \log_K M_h - \log_K K$	$P_h = 1-(1-x)^{\alpha\cdot R_h+K}$
...	...	...	...	...
$\lfloor \log \frac{M}{K} \rfloor$	$1/2^{\lfloor \log_2 \frac{M}{K} \rfloor}$	$M_{\lfloor \log_2 \frac{M}{K} \rfloor} = M/2^{\lfloor \log_2 \frac{M}{K} \rfloor}$	$R_{\lfloor \log_2 \frac{M}{K} \rfloor} = \log_K M_{\lfloor \log_2 \frac{M}{K} \rfloor} - \log_K K$	$P_{\lfloor \log_2 \frac{M}{K} \rfloor} = 1-(1-x)^{\alpha\cdot R_{\lfloor \log_2 \frac{M}{K} \rfloor}+K}$

4 Experiments and Validation

In order to validate this model, a number of simulation experiments are conducted. There are some important variables to consider in experiments: the size of the Kademlia-botnet (n_size), the number of Sybil nodes (n_sybil), the number of bots (n_bot), the proportion taken by Sybil nodes (Sybil percentage), the number of Sybil-meet pub (np_sybil), the total number of publishing (np_total), the proportion of Sybil-meet pub (Sybil-meet-pub rate) and so on. In fact, P in equation (2) is the Sybil-meet-pub rate estimated through the model. The following conditions are satisfied.

n_size = n_sybil + n_bot
Sybil percentage = n_sybil / n_size
Sybil-meet-pub rate = np_sybil / np_total

4.1 Simulation Platform

Our experiments are carried out on our simulation tool based on PeerSim [14]. PeerSim is a well-known open sourced simulation tool written in JAVA for P2P networks, and Furlan and Bonani implemented Kademlia protocol for PeerSim. Based on these works, we devised the Kademlia protocol implementation and added certain functions into PeerSim. Thus we got a simulation platform for Kademlia-botnets, which can simulate the publishing of C&C information and calculate the results we concern. PeerSim supports two kinds of simulation modes, one is cycle-based which is efficient but ignores the transport layer in the communication protocol stack, the other is event-based which is less efficient than the former but supports transport layer simulation. Our simulation platform works upon the event-based mode.

Parameters such as Sybil percentage, n_bot and K (which determines the number of bots to return when receiving FIND_NODE message in Kademlia) are the most important to be set. Under each set of parameters, the simulator runs for 20 times and the average of results are adopted.

During each time of the simulations, at least two publishing activities are issued by every node in the botnet, and the objectIDs for the publishing activities are generated by the simulator randomly. For example, if there are 2000 nodes in the network, 4000 searching actions will be issued. The value of np_sybil and np_total are recorded accumulatively, and the mitigation rate is calculated at the end of each time of simulation. The requests for C&C information are issued concurrently and asynchronously. The concurrent number is set 3, which means that at most three requests from a bot can exist simultaneously in the network.

4.2 Results and Analysis

1) Impact of Sybil percentage

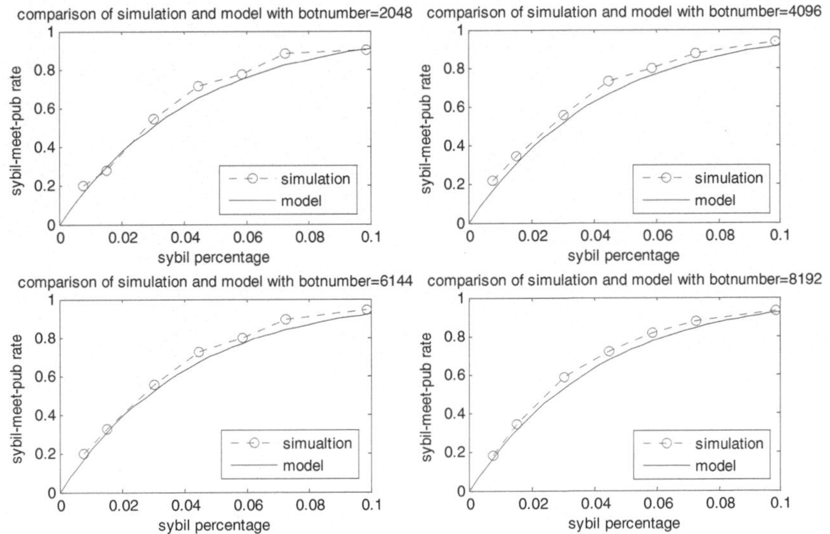

Fig. 3. Impact of Sybil percentage

To check whether this model can correctly reflect the impact of Sybil percentage on the Sybil-meet-pub rate, simulations are carried out with the value of n_bot being respectively 2048, 4096, 6144 and 8192. The value of K is set 20, and the comparison between the results of experiments and the prediction of the model is shown in Fig. 3. The dotted line represents the results of simulation, and the active line represents the prediction of the model, and the two curves fit well. This means that this model can reflect the impact of Sybil percentage well.

According to the model, the Sybil-meet-pub rate should increase obviously with the increase of Sybil percentage, which is verified in the experiments. The reason is that with the increase of the density of Sybil nodes, the probability for a bot to meet a Sybil in the iterative inquiries during publishing will also increase.

2) Impact of the Botnet Size

In order to check whether this model can correctly reflect the impact of botnet size on the Sybil-meet-pub rate, simulations are carried out under different Sybil percentages. In experiments, the value of K is set 20, and the results are shown in Fig. 4. In Fig. 4(a), the results with bot number being respectively 2048, 8192 and 16384 are compared, and in Fig. 4(b), the comparison predicted by our model is made. Both results demonstrate that the Sybil-meet-pub rate increases with the enlargement of the botnet. The reason for this phenomenon is that with the enlargement of the botnet, the average length of paths would increase, which makes the number of inquiry rounds increase and results in the increase of Sybil-meet-pub rate.

The impact of the botnet size is more obviously shown in Fig. 4(c) and Fig. 4(d). The experimental results are represented by the dotted line, and the prediction results are represented by the active line. The errors between two kinds of results are always below 10%, which means the model can effectively reflect the impact of botnet size on the Sybil-meet-pub rate.

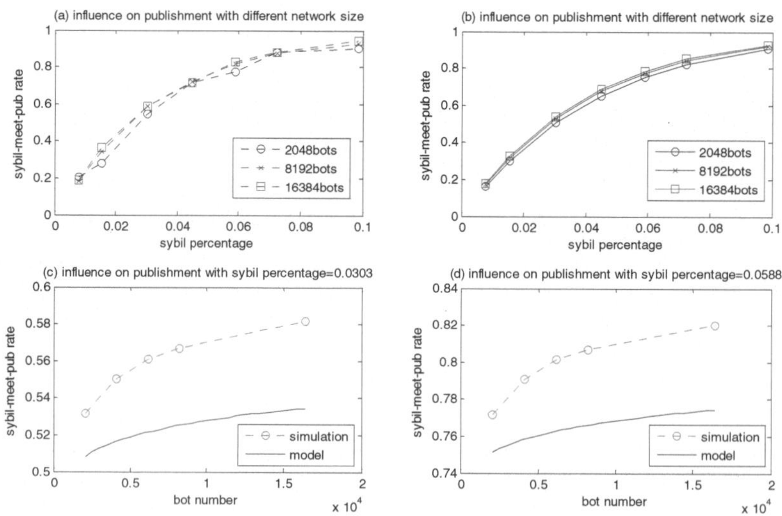

Fig. 4. Impact of the botnet size

The fact that Sybil-meet-pub rate increases with the enlargement of the botnet implies that for large scale Kademlia-botnets, Sybil nodes can do better in counter attacking.

3) Impact of the K Value

In order to check whether this model can correctly reflect the impact of the value of K on the Sybil-meet-pub rate, simulations are carried out under different K values. In experiments, the n_bot is set 4096, and the results are shown in Fig. 5. Fig. 5(a) demonstrates the relationship between Sybil-meet-pub rate and Sybil percentage during simulations, with the value of K being set 8, 10, 16, 20 and 32 respectively. Fig. 5(b) shows the results calculated by the model. The relationships between different curves in Fig. 5(a) are nearly the same with that in Fig. 5(b).

Fig. 5(c) and Fig. 5(d) demonstrate the relationships between Sybil-meet-pub rate and the K value, and it is more obviously displayed that Sybil-meet-pub rate increases with the growth of the K value. According to calculation, the errors between the results of experiments and that of model are always below 10%, which indicates that our model can correctly reflect the impact of the K value on the Sybil-meet-pub rate.

The impact of the K value implies that for botmasters, the smaller K should be adopted; while for the defenders, a bigger K is preferred.

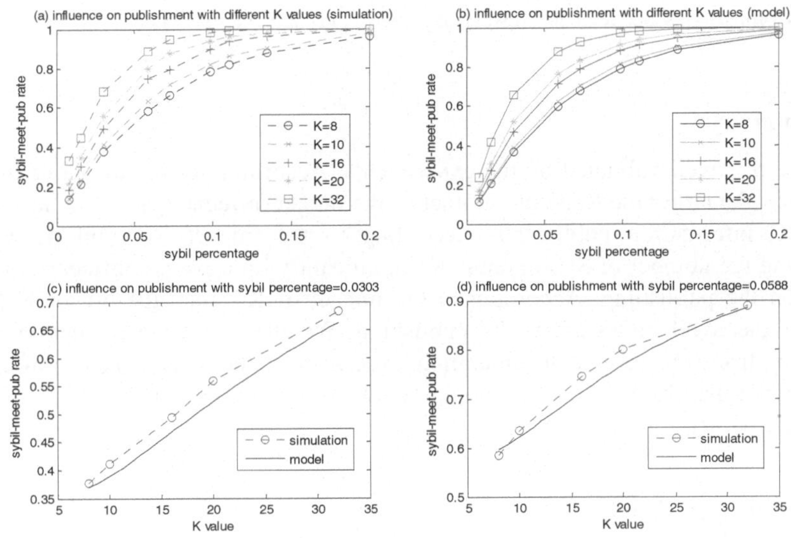

Fig. 5. Relationships between the K value and the Sybil-meet-pub rate

The relationship between the Sybil-meet-pub rate and the value of K is showed in Fig. 6, with Sybil percentage being 1/K. According to the prediction of our model, when the Sybil percentage equals 1/K, the Sybil-meet-pub rate would be high, as is shown by the active line in Fig. 6. This is because there would be one Sybil node in every K nodes in average. The dotted line in Fig. 6 shows the results of experiments. The errors between the results of experiments and that of the model are always below 10%, which means that the prediction of our model is acceptable.

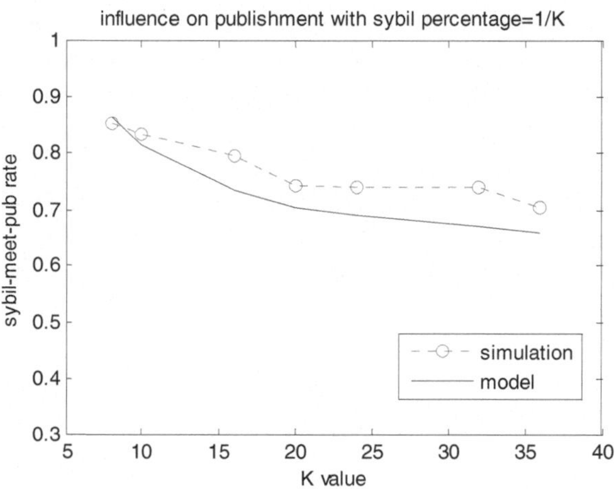

Fig. 6. Comparisons between the results of experiments and model when Sybil percentage = 1/K

4) Summary

Our model is well validated by the experiments. According to the impact of the network size, the larger the Kademlia-botnet is, the bigger influence the Sybil nodes have on C&C information publishing. According to the impact of Sybil percentage, increasing the number of Sybil nodes can significantly improve the influence of Sybil nodes on the publishing. According to the impact of K value, the bigger K is, the stronger the Sybil nodes affect the publishing. Whether from the prediction of our model or from the results of simulation experiments, the same conclusion can be summarized that the Sybil attack should be taken as an important method to mitigate Kademlia-botnets.

5 Related Work

Although many methods have already been proposed to defend against Sybil nodes [4, 6, 7], Douceur [5] pointed out an important fact that it is hard for a large scale network without a centralized authority to solve the problem of Sybil attacks.

Davis [9, 10] et al. did quantitative researches about the effect of Sybil attacks on the C&C mechanism of Storm botnet. In their simulation experiments, a lot of Sybil nodes were added into the botnet, and the Sybil nodes always responded to the inquirer with error messages which would cheat bots to stop searching. The results of the experiments demonstrated that the Sybil nodes could mitigate the delivery of C&C information obviously, with no need to predict the keys used by the botmaster. However, the impacts of some important parameters (such as the size of the botnet and the value of K) were not studied, and no prediction model was proposed to calculate the effect of Sybil attacks, which is important for mitigation in practice.

Holz et al. [8] proposed a method to separate a part of the P2P botnet from the rest. To eclipse a particular keyword CKey, they position a certain number of fake nodes closely around CKey, i.e., the DHT IDs of the nodes are closer to the hash value of CKey than that of any other regular peers. They then announce these nodes to regular peers in order to "poison" their routing lists and to attract all the route requests for CKey. However, this method can only be effective to the particular key at a moment.

In fact, the method of Holz is a kind of eclipse attack[15]. Eclipse attack is an important pattern of the Sybil attack. Singh et al.[16] pointed out that the effect of the eclipse attack depends on the in-degrees of Sybil nodes, so they proposed a method to defend against Sybil nodes by limiting the degrees of nodes in the network. In their method, the in-degrees of all nodes are nearly the same, including the Sybil nodes.

Ping Wang et al. [17] proposed a good mathematical model to estimate the probability that bots inquire at least one Sybil nodes during their network activities. However, there are at least four import differences between the model in [17] and that in this paper. First, the number of inquiry rounds, which is a critical value for the model, was directly estimated in [17], rather than calculated as in this paper. Second, the model in [17] is only for one node, but our model of equation (2) is for the whole botnet, which may give more valuable guidance. Third, the impacts of some critical parameter, such as Sybil percentage, the size of botnet and the value of K, were not clarified in [17]. Further, the model in [17] was not verified by experiments.

In this paper, we studied the influence of Sybil nodes under the most restrict limitation: the degrees of Sybil nodes are no higher than bots. In fact, the prediction of our model is a lower limit for the influence of Sybil nodes; once the Sybil nodes have high in-degrees than bots, the influence will be enhanced obviously.

6 Conclusion

The mitigation of P2P botnets is a relatively challenging problem in the field of security research, and Sybil attacks should be regarded as a powerful method to counter attack P2P botnets. However, it is rarely studied how to evaluate the influence of Sybil nodes in P2P botnets, especially during the publishing of C&C information.

Since Kademlia is very suitable to build large P2P networks and there have already been some typical P2P botnets based on it, we take the Kademlia based botnet as the object of our study. In this paper, the features of C&C information publishing in Kademlia botnets are analyzed, and then some important concepts and assumptions are presented. Based on the study of the impacts of some important factors, a predition model is proposed to evaluate the influence of Sybil nodes on the C&C information publishing. This model is validated by extensive simulations.

As a future work, the influence of Sybil nodes under different preconditions, for example, Sybil nodes are more active than bots, or Sybil nodes are distributed in the botnet in different manners, will be studied. These researches are to provide better suggestions for the mitigation of P2P botnets.

Acknowledgements. This research was supported by National Grand Fundamental Research 973 Program of China under Grant No.2011CB302600: "Basic Research on Effective and Trustworthy Internet-Based Virtual Computing Environment (iVCE)".

References

1. Grizzard, J.B., Sharma, V., Nunnery, C., Kang, B.B.H.: Peer-to-peer botnets: overview and case study. In: 1st Conference on First Workshop on Hot Topics in Understanding Botnets, p. 1. USENIX Association (2007)
2. W32.waledac threat analysis, `http://www.symantec.com/content/en/us/enterprise/media/security_response/whitepapers/W32_Waledac.pdf`
3. Shin, S., Gu, G., Reddy, N., Lee, C.P.: A large-scale empirical study of conficker. IEEE Transactions on Information Forensics and Security 7, 676–690 (2012)
4. Yu, H., Kaminsky, M., Gibbons, P.B.: SybilGuard: defending against sybil attacks via social networks. SIGCOMM Comput. Commun. Rev. 36(4), 267–278 (2006)
5. Douceur, J.R.: The sybil attack. In: Druschel, P., Kaashoek, M.F., Rowstron, A. (eds.) IPTPS 2002. LNCS, vol. 2429, pp. 251–260. Springer, Heidelberg (2002)
6. Yang, Z., Wilson, C., Wang, X., Gao, T., Zhao, B.Y.: Uncovering social network sybils in the wild. In: The 2011 ACM SIGCOMM Conference on Internet Measurement Conference, pp. 259–268. ACM Press, New York (2011)
7. Yu, H., Gibbons, P.B.: SybilLimit: A near-optimal social network defense against sybil attacks. IEEE/ACM Transactions on Networking 18(3), 885–898 (2010)
8. Holz, T., Steiner, M., Dahl, F., Biersack, E., Freiling, F.: Measurements and mitigation of peer-to-peer-based botnets: a case study on storm worm. In: 1st USENIX Workshop on Large-Scale Exploits and Emergent Threats, pp. 1–9. USENIX Association (2008)
9. Davis, C.R., Fernandez, J.M., Neville, S.: Optimising sybil attacks against P2P-based botnets. In: 4th International Conference on Malicious and Unwanted Software, pp. 78–87. IEEE Press, New York (2009)
10. Davis, C.R., Fernandez, J.M., Neville, S., McHugh, J.: Sybil attacks as a mitigation strategy against the storm botnet. In: 3rd International Conference on Malicious and Unwanted Software, pp. 32–40. IEEE Press, New York (2008)
11. Maymounkov, P., Mazières, D.: Kademlia: A peer-to-peer information system based on the XOR metric. In: Druschel, P., Kaashoek, M.F., Rowstron, A. (eds.) IPTPS 2002. LNCS, vol. 2429, pp. 53–65. Springer, Heidelberg (2002)
12. Starnberger, G., Kruegel, C., Kirda, E.: Overbot-a botnet protocol based on kademlia. In: 4th International Conference on Security and Privacy in Communication Networks. ACM Press, New York (2008)
13. Stoica, I., et al.: Chord: A scalable peer-to-peer lookup service for internet applications. ACM SIGCOMM Computer Communication Review 31(4), 149–160 (2001)
14. Montresor, A., Jelasity, M.: PeerSim: A Scalable P2P Simulator. In: 9th International Conference on Peer-to-Peer Computing, pp. 99–100. IEEE Press, New York (2009)

15. Singh, A., Ngan, T.-W.J., Druschel, P., Wallach, D.S.: Eclipse attacks on overlay networks: Threats and defenses. In: 25th IEEE International Conference on Computer Communications. IEEE Press, New York (2006)
16. Singh, A., Castro, M., Druschel, P.: Defending against eclipse attacks on overlay networks. In: 11th Workshop on ACM SIGOPS European Workshop, p. 21. ACM Press, New York (2004)
17. Wang, P., Wu, L., Aslam, B., Zou, C.C.: A Systematic Study on Peer-to-Peer Botnets. In: International Conference on Computer Communications and Networks, San Francisco. IEEE Press, New York (2009)

A Novel Security Protocol for Resolving Addresses in the Location/ID Split Architecture

Mahdi Aiash

School of Science and Technology, Middlesex University,
London, UK
M.Aiash@mdx.ac.uk

Abstract. The Locator/ID Separation Protocol (LISP) is a routing architecture that provides new semantics for IP addressing. In order to simplify routing operations and improve scalability in future Internet, the LISP uses two different numbering spaces to separate the device identifier from its location. In other words, the LISP separates the 'where' and the 'who' in networking and uses a mapping system to couple the location and identifier. This paper analyses the security and functionality of the LISP mapping procedure using a formal methods approach based on Casper/FDR tool. The analysis points out several security issues in the protocol such as the lack of data confidentiality and mutual authentication. The paper addresses these issues and proposes changes that are compatible with the implementation of the LISP.

Keywords: Location/ID Split Protocol, Casper/FDR, Future Internet, Address Resolving.

1 Introduction

Since the public Internet first became part of the global infrastructure, its dramatic growth has created a number of scaling challenges. Among the most fundamental of these is helping to ensure that the routing and addressing systems continue to function efficiently as the number of connected devices increases. To deal with these issues, a number of proposals have been described in the literature such as the LINA, ILNP [1] [2] and the addressing scheme proposed by Aiash et al in [3] [4]. Unlike IP addresses, which combines hosts' locations and identifiers in a single numbering space, the proposals adopted the concept of ID/Location split with uses two separate numbering spaces; one specifies the host's identifier while the other defines its location.

An IETF working group along with the research group at Cisco, are working on the Locator/ID Separation Protocol (LISP) [10]. This protocol shows a great potential; firstly, in addition to dealing with addressing and routing issues, it considers issues like security, QoS, multi-casting and mobility in different environments such as cloud computing and Next Generation Networks (NGNs) [5]. Secondly, large amount of research papers and Internet drafts have been produced by Cisco and the LISP working group which describe the progress in the

J. Lopez, X. Huang, and R. Sandhu (Eds.): NSS 2013, LNCS 7873, pp. 68–79, 2013.

design of the LISP [6]. Thirdly, some of the routing and addressing concepts of the LISP have already been implemented in the new Cisco Nexus 7000 Series Switches. Due to these reasons, this paper considers the LISP protocol as an example of the new routing/addressing schemes for future Internet and investigates the security of this protocol.

A key concept of the LISP is that end-systems (hosts) operate the same way they do today. The IP addresses that hosts use for sending and receiving packets do not change. In LISP terminology, these addresses are called Endpoint Identifiers (EIDs). Routers continue to forward packets based on IP destination addresses, the IP addresses of gateway routers or LISP-capable routers at the edge of end-sites are referred to as Routing Locators (RLOCs). To map hosts' EIDs to the authoritative RLOC, the LISP assumes the existence of a mapping or address resolving system that consists of a Map Server (MS) and a distributed database to store and propagate those mappings globally. The functionality of the mapping system goes through two stages:

1. Registration Stage: in this stage, the Map Server learns the EIDs-to-RLOC mappings from an authoritative LISP-Capable Router and publishes them in the database.
2. Addresses resolving Stage: the Map Server (Ms) accepts Map-Requests from routers, looks up the database and returns the requested mapping.

These two stages will be explained in more details in section 2.2.

Currently, the research concentrates mainly on defining the LISP architecture as well as the structure of the packets such as the Map-Request and Map-Reply messages. However, the security-related research is still at an early stage, the research in [7] [8] have highlighted potential threats as an introduction to come up with the required security mechanisms. These research efforts have not defined specific attacks against the deployment of the LISP. Therefore, this paper uses formal methods approach based on the well developed CASPER/FDR [15] tool to investigate the security of implementing the LISP architecture. Our main concern here is the security of the address resolving stage (stage 2), where a LISP-capable router approaches the Map Server with a Map-Request message and expects the required EID-to-RLOC mapping in a Map-Replay message.

This study adds the following contributions: firstly, using formal methods approach, it discovers and describes possible attacks against the implementation of the LISP architecture. Secondly, to fix these problems, the paper proposes feasible solution that is in line with the goals of the LISP's security requirements as defined in [8]. The proposed solution has been formally verified using Casper/FDR. We believe that, this paper will help researchers and developers to realize some of the actual security threats and use the proposed solution as a guideline to come up with the most complete security solutions.

The rest of the paper is organised as follows: Section 2 describes related work in the literature. Section 3 formally analyses the security of the basic address procedure of the LISP, then using a progressive approach, it explains and formally verifies the refinement stages, which led to the final version of the secure protocol. The paper is concludes in Section 4.

2 Related Work

2.1 An Overview of The LISP

To improve routing scalability while facilitating flexible address assignment in multi-homing and mobility scenarios, the LISP describes changes to the Internet architecture in which IP addresses are replaced by routing locators (RLOCs) for routing through the global Internet and by endpoint identifiers (EIDs) for identifying network sessions between devices [9]. As shown in Fig 1, three essential components exist in the LISP environment: the LISP sites (EID space), the non-LISP sites (RLOC space), and the LISP Mapping System which comprises Map Servers and databases.

– **The LISP sites (EID space):** they represent customer end-sites in exactly the same way that end-sites are defined today. However, the IP address in the EID space are not advertised to the non-LISP sites, but are published into the LISP Mapping Systems which performs the EID-to-RLOC mapping. The LISP functionalities is deployed on the site's gateway or edge routers. Therefore, based on their roles, two types of routers are defined: firstly, the Ingress Tunnel Routers (ITRs) which receive packets from hosts and send LISP packets toward the Map Server. Secondly, the Egress Tunnel Routers (ETRs) which receive LISP packets from the Map Server and pass them to hosts [10] [9].
– **Non-LISP sites (RLOC space):** it represents current sites where the IP addresses are advertised and used for routing purpose.
– **LISP Mapping Systems:** These are represented by Map Servers (MS) and a globally distributed database that contains all known EID prefixes to RLOC mappings. Similar to the current Domain Name System (DNS), the Mapping systems are queried by LISP-capable devices for EID-to-RLOC mapping.

2.2 Interactions with Other LISP Components

The functionality of the LISP goes through two stages:

1. **The EID Prefix Configuration and ETR Registration Satge**
As explained in [11], an ETR publishes its EID-prefixes on a Map Server (MS) by sending LISP Map-Register messages which includes the ETR's RLOC and a list of its EID-prefixes. Initially, it has been presumed that prior to sending a Map-Register message, the ETR and Map Server must be configured with a shared secret or other relevant authentication information. Upon the receipt of a Map-Register from an ETR, the Map Server checks the validity of the Map-Register message and acknowledges it by sending a Map-Notify message. When registering with a Map-Server, an ETR might request a no-proxy reply service which implies that the Map Server will forward all the EID-to-RLOC mapping requests to the relevant ETR rather than dealing with them.

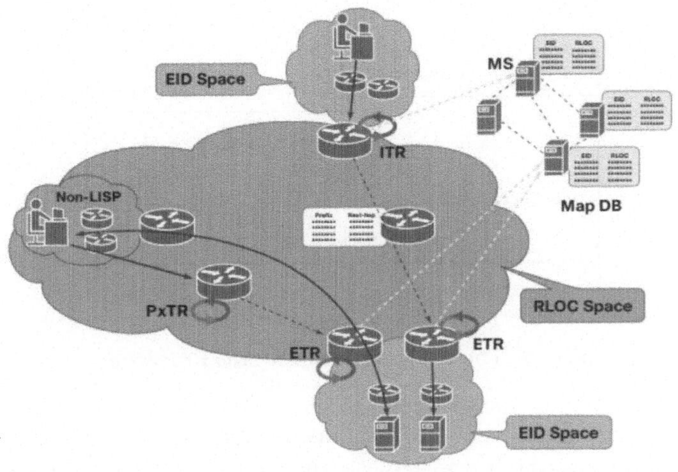

Fig. 1. The LISP Network Architecture Design [9]

The registration stage, shown in Fig 2, is vulnerable to serious security threats such as replay and routing table poisoning attacks. A detailed security analysis of this stage has been presented in another work of our group in [12].

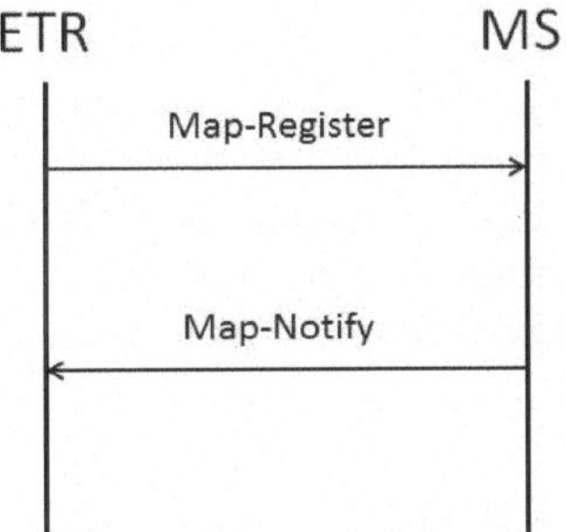

Fig. 2. The ETR Registration Process

2. **The Address Resolving Stage:** Once a Map Server has EID-prefixes registered by its client ETRs, it will accept and process Map-Requests. In response to a Map-Request (sent from an ITR), the Map Server first checks to see if the required EID matches a configured EID-prefix. If there is no match, the Map Server returns a negative Map-Reply message to the ITR. In case of a match, the Map Server re-encapsulates and forwards the resulting Encapsulated Map-Request to one of the registered ETRs which will return Map-Replay directly to the requesting ITR as shown in Fig 3.

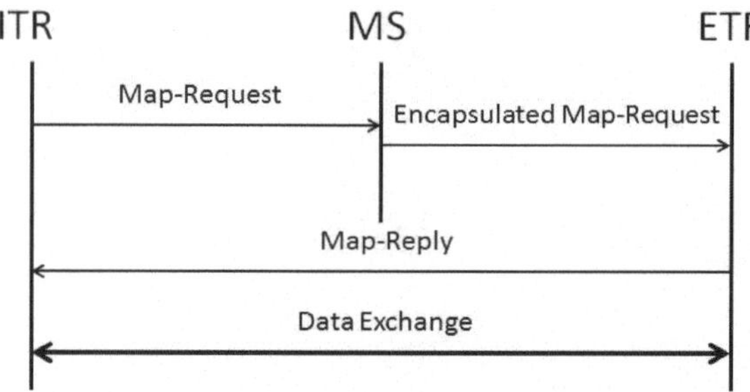

Fig. 3. The No Proxy Map Server Processing

The LISP working group in [10] has defined the structure of all the LISP Packets including the Map-Request, the Map-Notify, the Map-Register and the MAP-Reply. However, for the security analysis in section 3, only security-related parameters of the LISP messages are explicitly mentioned.

2.3 Verifying Security Protocols Using Casper/FDR

Previously, analysing security protocols used to be done using two stages. Firstly, modelling the protocol using a theoretical notation or language such as the CSP [13]. Secondly, verifying the protocol using a model checker such as Failures-Divergence Refinement (FDR) [14]. However, describing a system or a protocol using CSP is a quite difficult and error-prone task; therefore, Gavin Lowe [15] has developed the CASPER/FDR tool to model security protocols, it accepts a simple and human-friendly input file that describes the system and compiles it into CSP code which is then checked using the FDR model checker. Casper/FDR has been used to model communication and security protocols as in [16], [17]. The CASPER's input file that describes the systems consists of eight headers as explained in Table 1.

Table 1. The Headers of Casper's Input File

The Header	Description
# Free Variables	Defines the agents, variables and functions in the protocol
# Processes	Represents each agent as a process
# Protocol Description	Shows all the messages exchanged between the agents
# Specification	Specifies the security properties to be checked
# Actual Variables	Defines the real variables, in the actual system to be checked
# Functions	Defines all the functions used in the protocol
# System	Lists the agents participating in the actual system with their parameters instantiated
# Intruder Information	Specifies the intruder's knowledge and capabilities

3 Analysing the Security of the Address Resolving Procedure

3.1 System Definition

As shown in Fig 3, and based on the notations in Table 2, the procedure of the mapping procedure goes as follows:

Msg1. ITR→ MS : ITR, N1, MapRequest, h(ITR, N1, MapRequest)

The ITR sends a Map-Request message which includes a 4-byte random nonce (N1) and the addresses of the ITR. The ITR expects to receive the same nonce in the Map-Reply message.

Msg2. MS→ ETR : ITR, N1, MapRequest, h(ITR, N1, MapRequest)

The Map Server (MS) encapsulates Msg1 and passes it to the relevant ETR as Msg2.

Msg3. ETR→ ITR : ETR, N1, MapReply, h(ETR, N1, MapReply)

The ETR composes Msg3 which includes a Map-Reply and the received nonce (N1). Upon receiving this message, the ITR checks the included nonce and only when the check succeeds, the ITR authenticates the ETR.

Table 2. Notation

The Notation	Definition
ITR	The Ingress Tunnel Router in the source EID Space
ETR	The Egress Tunnel Router in the destination EID Space
MS	The Map Server
N1	The Nonce
h(m)	Hash value of the message (m)
{m}{K}	The message (m) being encrypted with the key (K)

3.2 Formal Analysis of the Basic Mapping Procedure

To formally analyse the basic mapping procedure, we simulate the system using Casper/FDR tool. A Casper input file describing the system in Figure 3 was prepared. for conciseness, only the #Specification and the #Intruder Information headings are described here, while the rest are of a less significance in terms of understanding the verification process.

The security requirements of the system are defined under the # Specification heading. The lines starting with the keyword **Secret** define the secrecy properties of the protocol. The `Secret(ITR, N1, [Ms, ETR])` specifies the N1 nonce as a secret between ITR, Ms and ETR. The lines starting with **Agreement** define the protocol's authenticity properties; for instance `Agreement(ETR, ITR, [N1])` specifies that, the ETR is correctly authenticated to ITR using the random number N1. The `WeakAgreement(ITR, Ms)` assertion could be interpreted as follows: if ITR has completed a run of the protocol with Ms, then Ms has previously been running the protocol, apparently with ITR.

```
#Specification
Secret(ITR, N1, [Ms, ETR])
WeakAgreement(ITR, Ms)
WeakAgreement(ITR, ETR)
WeakAgreement(ETR, ITR)
Agreement(ETR, ITR, [N1])
```

The # Intruder Information heading specifies the intruder identity, knowledge and capability. The first line identifies the intruder as Mallory, the intruder knowledge defines the Intruder's initial knowledge, i.e., we assume the intruder knows the identity of the participants and can fabricate Map Request and Map Reply messages.

```
#Intruder Information
Intruder = Mallory
IntruderKnowledge = {ITR, ETR, Ms, Mallory, mapRequest, mapReply}
```

After generating the CSP description of the systems using Casper and asking FDR to check the security assertions. The following attacks were found:

1. The First attack is against the `WeakAgreement(ITR, Ms)` assertion, and it goes as follows:
   ```
   1. ITR -> I_Ms : ITR, N1, mapRequest, h(ITR, N1, mapRequest)
   1. I_ETR -> Ms : ETR, N1, mapReply, h(ETR, N1, mapReply)
   2. Ms -> I_ETR : ETR, N1, mapReply, h(ETR, N1, mapReply)
   ```
   Where the notations I_ Ms, I_ETR and I_ITR represent the case where the Intruder impersonates the Ms, ETR and ITR, respectively. This is an active Man-in-the-Middle attack; the Intruder blocks the first message and composes message two, acting as the ETR. Upon receiving this message, the Map Sever mistakenly believes that the message came from ETR and hence replies with a Map-Replay message, which will be intercepted by the Intruder.
2. The second attack compromises three assertions `Secret(ITR, N1, [Ms, ETR])`, `Agreement(ETR, ITR, [N1])`, `WeakAgreement(ETR, ITR)`, and it goes as follows:
   ```
   1. ITR -> I_Ms : ITR, N1, MapRequest, h(ITR, N1, MapRequest)
   3. I_ETR -> ITR : ETR, N1, MapReply, h(ETR, N1, MapReply)
   The intruder knows N1
   ```

In this attack, the intruder intercepts the first message and replays to the ITR acting as ETR. Since there is no encryption, the Intruder acquires the nonce N1 and uses it to impersonate ETR; consequently, the ITR runs this process believing it is with ETR while in reality it is with the Intruder. Furthermore, the basic protocol uses the nonce N1 to authenticate the ETR to the ITR. However, it does not provide any approach to authenticate the ITR to the ETR.

The discovered attacks are due to the lack of security in the transaction between the participating parties. Therefore, the following subsections will propose security measures to address the discovered attacks.

3.3 The First Proposed Enhancement

The first discovered attack in section 3.2 was due to the exposure of the nonce (N1). Therefore, to stop this attack, there is a need to secure the (ITR-MS) and the (MS-ETR) connections. As explained in section 2, for the Registration process, it is presumed that LISP-Capable routers (ITR, ETR) and MS have already agreed on secret keys. Similarly, we will presume that these keys will be used to secure the transactions in the resolving procedure. Hence, two pre-configured secret keys: (K1) is shared between ITR and MS, and (K2) is shared between the MS and ETR. The enhanced version of the protocol looks as follows:

Msg1. ITR→ MS : {ITR, N1, MapRequest, h(ITR, N1, MapRequest)}{K1}
Msg2. MS→ ETR : {ITR, N1, MapRequest, h(ITR, N1, MapRequest)}{K2}
Msg3. ETR→ ITR : ETR, N1, MapReply, h(ETR, N1, MapReply)

We modelled the new version of the protocol with Casper and checked it with FDR, the following attack against the secrecy assertion was discovered.

```
1a. ITR -> I_Ms : {ITR, N1, mapRequest, h(ITR, N1, mapRequest)}{K1}
1b. I_ITR -> Ms : {ITR, N1, mapRequest, h(ITR, N1, mapRequest)}{K1}
2a. Ms -> I_ETR : {ITR, N1, mapRequest, h(ITR, N1, mapRequest)}{K2}
2b. I_Ms -> ETR : {ITR, N1, mapRequest, h(ITR, N1, mapRequest)}{K2}
3a. ETR -> I_ITR : ETR, N1, mapReply, h(ETR, N1, mapReply)
3b. I_ETR -> ITR : ETR, N1, mapReply, h(ETR, N1, mapReply)
The intruder knows N1
```

Here, the Intruder passively replays the messages between the participants. This attack could be interpreted as follows: the ITR will complete running the protocol believing that it was with the ETR, while it was with the Intruder instead. Similarly, the ETR will believe it has been running the protocol with the ITR, while in reality it was with the Intruder. Again, this attack is ascribed to the exposure of the nonce (N1), which highlight the need for securing the direct transaction between the ITR and ETR. Also, there is a need to propose an authentication mechanism, through which the ETR can authenticate the ITR.

3.4 The Final Enhancement: The Proposed AKA Protocol

In order to secure the direct connection between the ITR and ETR, and to achieve a mutual authentication between them. We propose an Authentication and Key Agreement (AKA) protocol that does not require major modifications to the basic LISP protocol. The proposed AKA protocol is based on the Challenge-Response paradigm and it goes as follows:

Msg1. ITR→ MS:{ITR,N1,MapRequest,K3,h(ITR, N1,MapRequest,K3)}{K1}
Msg2. MS→ ETR:{ITR,N1,MapRequest,K3, h(ITR,N1,MapRequest,K3)}{K2}

The ITR composes Msg1 and includes a freshly generated secret key (K3) to be used by the ETR to encrypt the Map-Reply packet. This message is forwarded by the MS towards the ETR.

Msg3. ETR→ ITR:{ETR, N1, N2 MapReply, h(ETR, N1,N2 MapReply)}{K3}

Upon receiving the Map-Request in Msg2, the ETR replies with a Map-Reply message with a challenge nonce (N2). The message is encrypted using the suggested key (K3).

Msg4. ITR → ETR : {N2}{K3}

The ITR returns the challenge (N2) encrypted using the key (K3). The ETR will check the returned challenge to authenticate ITR.

To verify the proposed AKA protocol, we prepared a Casper file that describes the protocol (the full Casper input file is shown in the Appendix). To check the mutual authentication, the `Agreement(ITR, ETR, [N2])` assertion has been added to the # Specification heading as shown below:

```
#Specification
Secret(ITR, N1, [Ms, ETR])
WeakAgreement(ITR, Ms)
WeakAgreement(ITR, ETR)
WeakAgreement(ETR, ITR)
Agreement(ETR, ITR, [N1])
Agreement(ITR, ETR, [N2])
```

We simulated this security considerations with Casper and asked FDR to check for attacks. Casper/FDR failed to find attacks against any of the checked assertions as shown in Fig 4.

Protocol Analysis: The main goals of the proposed protocol are to achieve mutual authentication between ETR and ITR and to secure the direct connection between them. Furthermore, it is crucial to achieve these goals with a minimum modification to the basic LISP. The security-related goals could be

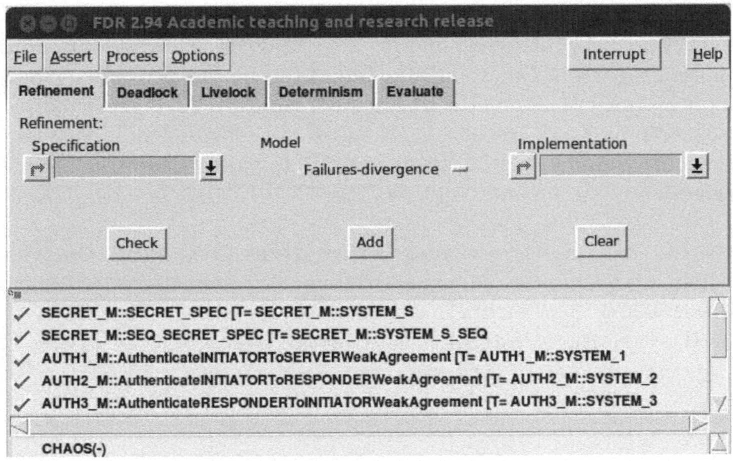

Fig. 4. The FDR Verification

achieved using different protocols, examples of there are the Internet Key Exchange (IEK) [18], and Virtual Private Network (VPN) protocols such as the Internet Protocol Security (IPsec) [19]. However, these protocols will increase the number of exchanged messages significantly, At least five extra messages in the case of IKE and more than this in the case of IPSec (based on the IPSec mode). Furthermore, packets-encapsulation due to the tunnelling process in VPN protocols will lead to adding extra headers to the LISP packets which make them incompatible with the current implementation of the LISP-capable devices.

The fact that the formal verification of the proposed protocol, using Casper/ FDR, found no attacks against any of the checked assertions, implies that the protocol successfully achieves a number of crucial security requirements such as mutual authenticating the participating parties and maintaining the secrecy of the session key between the ITR and ETR. Furthermore, the protocol does not require major modification to the basic LISP transactions and no extra headers are needed for packets encapsulation.

4 Conclusion

This paper analysed the security of the address resolving process in LISP protocol. Analysing and verifying the basic LISP using Casper/FDR shows that the protocol is vulnerable to authentication and secrecy attacks. Therefore, a new security protocol was introduced in this article, the article described the refinement stages of the protocol along with the discovered attacks. The final version of the proposed protocol was proven to be secure and to comply with the design of the LISP protocol.

References

1. Ishiyama, I., Uehara, K., Esaki, H., Teraoka, F.: LINA: A New Approach to Mobility in Wide Area Networks. IEICE Trans. Commun. E84-B(8) (August 2001)

2. Atkinson, R.J.: ILNP Concept of Operations, internet Draft (July 27, 2011)
3. Mapp, G., Aiash, M., Crestana Guardia, H., Crowcroft, J.: Exploring Multi-homing Issues in Heterogeneous Environments. In: 1st International Workshop on Protocols and Applications with Multi-Homing Support (PAMS 2011), Singapore (2010)
4. Aiash, M., Mapp, G., Lasebae, A., Phan, R., Augusto, M., Vanni, R., Moreira, E.: Enhancing Naming and Location Services to support Multi-homed Devices in Heterogeneous Environments. In: Proc. The CCSIE 2011, London, UK, July 25-27 (2011)
5. Cisco Nexus 7000 Series Switches, Cisco Nexus 7000 LISP Overview Video, http://www.cisco.com/en/US/prod/collateral/iosswrel/ps6537/ps6554/ps6599/ps10800/LISP_VDS.html (last accessed on January 13, 2013)
6. Locator/ID Separation Protocol (lisp) Working Group, http://datatracker.ietf.org/wg/lisp/charter/ (last accessed on January 13, 2013)
7. Cisco Locator/ID Separation Protocol Security At-A-Glance, http://www.cisco.com/en/US/prod/collateral/iosswrel/ps6537/ps6554/ps6599/ps10800/at_a_glance_c45-645204.pdf (last accessed on January 13, 2013)
8. Maino, F., Ermagan, V., Cabellos, A., Saucez, A., Bonaventure, O.: LISP-Security (LISP-SEC). Internet-Draft (September 12, 2012)
9. Cisco Locator/ID Separation Protocol Revolutionary Network Architecture to Power the Network, http://www.cisco.com/en/US/prod/collateral/iosswrel/ps6537/ps6554/ps6599/ps10800/aag_c45-635298.pdf (last accessed on January 13, 2013)
10. Farinacci, D., Fuller, V., Meyer, D., Lewis, D.: Locator/ID Separation Protocol (LISP). Internet-Draft (November 13, 2012)
11. Farinacci, D., Fuller, V.: LISP Map Server Interface. Internet-Draft (March 4, 2012)
12. Aiash, M., Al-Nemrat, A., Preston, D.: Securing Address Registration in Location/ID Split Protocol Using ID-Based Cryptography. In: Tsaoussidis, V., Kassler, A., Koucheryavy, Y., Mellouk, A. (eds.) WWIC 2013. LNCS, vol. 7889, pp. 129–139. Springer, Heidelberg (2013)
13. Goldsmith, M., Lowe, G., Roscoe, A.W., Ryan, P., Schneider, S.: The modelling and analysis of security protocols. Pearson Ltd. (2010)
14. Formal Systems, Failures-divergence refinement. FDR2 user manual and tutorial, Version 1.3 (June 1993)
15. Lowe, G., Broadfoot, P., Dilloway, C., Hui, M.L.: Casper: A compiler for the analysis of security protocols, 1.12 edn. (September 2009)
16. Aiash, M., Mapp, G., Lasebae, A., Phan, P., Loo, J.: Casper: A formally verified AKA protocol for vertical handover in heterogeneous environments using Casper/FDR. EURASIP Journal on Wireless Communications and Networking 2012, 57 (2012)
17. Aiash, M., Mapp, G., Lasebae, A., Phan, P., Loo, J.: A Formally Verified Device Authentication Protocol Using Casper/FDR. In: 11th IEEE International Conference on Trust, Security and Privacy in Computing and Communications (TrustCom), June 25-27 (2012)
18. Harkins, D., Carrel, D.: The Internet Key Exchange (IKE). Request for Comments: 2409 (November 1998)
19. Kent, S., Atkinson, R.: IP Encapsulating Security Payload (ESP). Request for Comments: 2406 (November 1998)

Appendix: The Final Version of the Protocol

```
#Free variables
Itr, Etr : Agent
na, nb, seq2, n1, n2 : Nonce
K1, K2: PreSharedKey
Ms: Server
K3: SessionKey
MappRequest,MappReply: Messages
InverseKeys = (K3,K3),(K2, K2), (K1, K1)
h : HashFunction
#Processes
INITIATOR(Itr,Ms,Etr,n1, MappRequest, K1, K3)
SERVER(Ms, Etr, K1, K2)
RESPONDER(Etr, MappReply, K2, n2)
#Protocol description
0. -> Ms : Itr
1. Itr -> Ms : {Itr, n1,MappRequest, K3, h(Itr, n1, MappRequest)}{K1}
2. Ms -> Etr : {Itr, n1,MappRequest, K3, h(Itr, n1, MappRequest)}{K2}
3. Etr -> Itr : {Etr, n1,MappReply,n2, h(Etr, n1, MappReply)}{K3}
4. Itr -> Etr : {n2}{K3}
#Specification
Secret(Itr, n1, [Ms, Etr])
WeakAgreement(Itr, Ms)
WeakAgreement(Itr, Etr)
WeakAgreement(Etr, Itr)
Agreement(Etr, Itr, [n1])
Agreement(Itr, Etr, [n2])
#Actual variables
itr, etr, Mallory : Agent
Na, Nb, Seq2, N1, N2 : Nonce
k1, k2: PreSharedKey
ms: Server
mappRequest,mappReply: Messages
InverseKeys = (k2, k2), (k1, k1), (k3,k3)
k3: SessionKey
#System
INITIATOR(itr,ms, etr, N1, mappRequest, k1, k3)
SERVER(ms, etr, k1, k2)
RESPONDER(etr, mappReply, k2, N2)
#Intruder Information
Intruder = Mallory
IntruderKnowledge = {itr, etr, ms, Mallory, mappRequest, mappReply}
```

The OffPAD: Requirements and Usage

Kent Are Varmedal[1], Henning Klevjer[1], Joakim Hovlandsvåg[1], Audun Jøsang[1], Johann Vincent[2], and Laurent Miralabé[3]

[1] Department of Informatics, University of Oslo
[2] ENSICAEN, GREYC, F-14032 Caen, France
[3] TazTag, 2 Allée Gustave Eiffel, Campus de Ker Lann, 35170 Bruz, France
{kentav,hennikl,joakimsh,josang}@ifi.uio.no,
johann.vincent@ensicaen.fr, lm@taztag.com

Abstract. Strong authentication for online service access typically requires some kind of hardware device for generating dynamic access credentials that are often used in combination with static passwords. This practice have the side effect that users fill up their pockets with more and more devices and their heads with more and more passwords. This situation becomes increasinlgy difficult to manage which in turn degrades the usability of online services. In order to cope with this situation users often adopt insecure *ad hoc* practices that enable them to practically manage their different identities and credentials. This paper explores how one single device can be used for authentication of user to service providers and server to users, as well as provide a range of other security services.

1 Introduction

Over the last decade there has been a radical evolution in procedures for authentication. Before the Internet revolution and the invention of the World Wide Web, system passwords were typically simple, physical keys were still the most widely used method to access offices, and bills were still being paid by signing pieces of paper. Today, computer systems are globally interconnected and exposed to millions of host, physical access control to offices is typically based on electronic access cards, and sensitive documents e.g. for financial transactions are now digital, which require digital signatures instead of hand-written signatures. In order for this evolution to remain secure and sustainable there are strong requirements for authentication of entities. By taking into account the distinction between system entity (client or server) and legal/cognitive entity (person or organisation) there are in fact two entities on each side of a communication session, as illustrated in Fig.1.

The distinction between the human user and the client system on the user side, as well as between the SP organisation and the server system on the server side, leads to the conclusion that each of the 4 entities can be authenticated in 2 different ways leading to 8 different classes of peer entity authentication between the two sides, as illustrated in Fig.1 and described in Table 1 and Table 2 below.

For online services applications the entity authentication classes [S → U] and [U → S] are the most relevant because of the need for end-to-end security. In the

J. Lopez, X. Huang, and R. Sandhu (Eds.): NSS 2013, LNCS 7873, pp. 80–93, 2013.

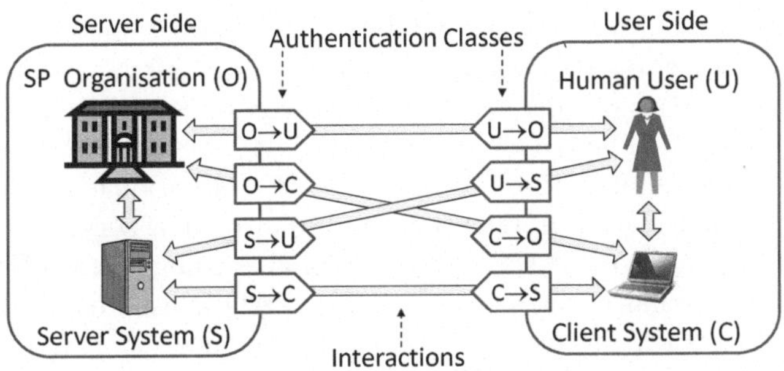

Fig. 1. General entity authentication classes

Table 1. Classes of authentication of user side entities by server side entities

Class	Authentication by server side: Origin and Target
[O → U]	The SP organisation (O) authenticates the human user (U)
[O → C]	The SP organisation (O) authenticates the user client (C)
[S → U]	The server system (S) authenticates the human user (U) (commonly called *user authentication*)
[S → C]	The server system (S) authenticates the user client (C)

Table 2. Classes of authentication of server side entities by user side entities

Class	Authentication by user side: Origin and Target
[U → O]	The human user (U) authenticates the SP organisation (O)
[U → S]	The human user (U) authenticates the server system (S) (which can be called *Cognitive Server Authentication*)
[C → O]	The user client (C) authenticates the SP organisation (O)
[C → S]	The user client (C) authenticates the server system (S)

typical case where a human user accesses an online service, semantic end-to-end communication takes place between the human user (U) and the server system (S). It is therefore pragmatic to require mutual authentication between those two entities. Traffic encryption and authentication between the server system (S) and user client (C) typically provides communication confidentiality, but can not provide cognitive server authentication in a meaningful way.

In case of one-factor user authentication based on static passwords, corporate computer networks and online service providers typically require long, complex and unique passwords. Two-factor authentication is often required for access to sensitive online services and for physical access to buildings, where one of the factors is a dynamic credential generated by a device, such as an OTP (One-Time Password). Two-factor authentication typically combines "something you know" (the password) with "something you have" (the authentication device).

Personal authentication devices combined with static passwords have been used by online banks, e-governments and other online service providers for several years. The device is usually an OTP-generator, or a smart card (with reader) of varying complexity. The reason for service providers to use two-factor authentication is to have a higher level of authentication assurance. Some banks offer smart phone authentication applications to log into their services.

In [14], Jøsang and Pope describe the Personal Authentication Device (PAD), a secure device external to the computer. The PAD is used as an identity management system to which the user authenticates once (with a PIN, password or similar), and for one *session*[1]. The user can authenticate to every supported service automatically using the PAD as his identity manager. This is done by transient (replay protected) challenge-response communication between the PAD and the remote server, through the user's computer.

Service providers have identities that also need adequate management. Interestingly, technologies for service provider authentication are very different from those of user authentication, because e.g. user authentication (class [S → U]) mainly takes place on the application layer, whereas traditional server authentication (class [C → S]) mainly takes place on the transport layer.

In [16], Klevjer *et al.* describe a more secure PAD, the physically decoupled OffPAD, which supports mutual authentication between user and server, as well as user-centric identity management, i.e. secure and usable management of digital identities and credentials on the OffPAD rather than in the user's brain. The OffPAD supports management and authentication of both user and service provider identities. It should be (mostly) offline and contain a secure element, to protect its contents and the privacy of the user.

The idea of having a secure device to do different kinds of authenticated operations is also proposed in a position paper by Laurie and Singer [17]. The so-called "Nebuchadnezzar" is a device that can run multiple security applications such as authentication and transaction signing. Another device similar to the OffPAD is the Pico by Frank Stajano, which is designed to replace passwords everywhere[21]. Stajano describes a number of different solutions where the Pico can be used instead of a password or PIN, such as client authentication to websites, logging into one's home computer or unlocking a screen saver.

In this paper we will first present some requirements for an OffPAD, followed by descriptions of different applications that can be implemented with contemporary technology. Finally, the limitations of the device are addressed.

2 Requirements

The OffPAD is an Offline Personal Authentication Device. The security requirements specified for the Nebuchadnezzar device [17] are aimed at the operating system on the device and can easily be transferred to the concept of an OffPAD. The system requirements they propose to the device is to have a securely built operating system, with a bullet-proof kernel that can run multiple applications

[1] Limited to either time or connection.

which can interact with untrusted systems. The user interface of such a device must be non-spoofable and it should be able to attest to the software is running. The device is not for general purpose (e.g. it does not run a web browser). The device has to support cryptographic functions and being updateable.

Klevjer *et al.* [16] describe that the OffPAD should also have limited connectivity, a secure element and access control. The requirement of limited connectivity can be met by using NFC or other physically activated (contactless) communication. Other (live) means of communications may be appropriate, depending on the required assurance level. The infrastructure for secure messaging and storage in a secure element is described in ISO 7816-4.[10] For access to the OffPAD, the user must unlock the device by using a PIN, pass phrase, biometrics or other adequate authentication credentials, which prevents unauthorized users from activating the device.

The OffPAD must also be tamper resistant, so that an attacker with physical access to the device cannot easily access information stored on the OffPAD or alter any of the OffPADs characteristics. A possible design of the OffPAD is illustrated in Fig.2 below.

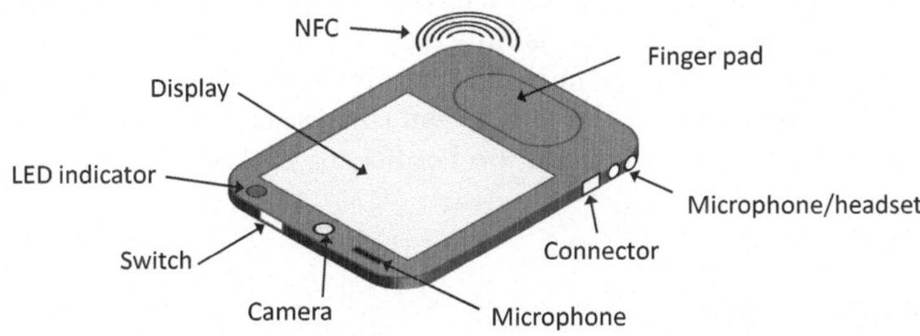

Fig. 2. OffPAD design

The OffPAD may have several interfaces for communication. Microphone and camera may be used for voice and face recognition, and a fingerprint reader may be used for both authenticating to the device and elsewhere.

Communication

Some form of electronic communication is essential for practical integration of the OffPAD into online authentication. Options for electronic communication technologies are listed in table 3. The OffPAD must be restricted with regard to connectivity, and should remain *offline* as much as possible, meaning that it should only be able to communicate securely, in controlled formats and in short, restricted time periods. This decoupling from networks improves security on the device, as it is less vulnerable to outside attacks. Any specific electronic communication technology described in the list above should normally be disconnected, and should only be connected whenever it is needed for authentication or for

Table 3. OffPAD communication technologies

NFC	Short point-to-point connections over limited range.
Bluetooth	Medium range point-to-point communication.
ZigBee	Longer point-to-point connections with low power consumption and transmission range up to 100 m[4].
WiFi	Communication that over the Internet.
USB	Wired connection, can also be used to charge the device's battery (but this will make the OffPAD online).

management of the device. However, the connection should be fast and easy to set up, which might exclude WiFi and Bluetooth.

NFC with a backup USB connection is probably the most suitable communication technology for the OffPAD. Both technologies are fast, USB guarantees (physically) that the correct device is connected, and NFC gives high visual assurance that the correct device is connected. This limits the threat of a man-in-the-middle attack when connecting an OffPAD to a computer.

The first connection to the OffPAD builds upon the concept of Trust-On-First-Use (TOFU), also known as leap-of-faith. On first use there is no cryptographic way to verify that the connection is only between the device and the software, this must be based on trust (or faith) in the physically observed set-up. On the first connection some kind of pairing between the device and computer occurs, so that the subsequent connections can be verified to be between the same device and computer.

3 Services

One OffPAD may be used for a number of different security services simultaneously. With a simple menu system the user can select which service she wants to use. Each service can also be used in different environments (e.g. locations), where either the OffPAD can detect the environment or the user can select it depending on the type of application and communication protocol.

3.1 Digitally Signed Bank Transactions

Normally, when doing online banking, the user can review information on a transaction in the web browser window before confirming and submitting the transaction. The data shown on the screen in such a scenario is vulnerable to change by a man-in-the-browser (MITB). The integrity of the transaction data may be broken (e.g. the amount and receiver account may be changed) before being submitted to the bank's server. With an OffPAD, the transaction data may be signed with the bank's private key and be presented on the device's screen. This data may be verified on the trusted device by validating the signature using the bank's public key. Alternatively, a photo of the browser window may be taken with the OffPAD camera, and the text from the photo analysed with OCR

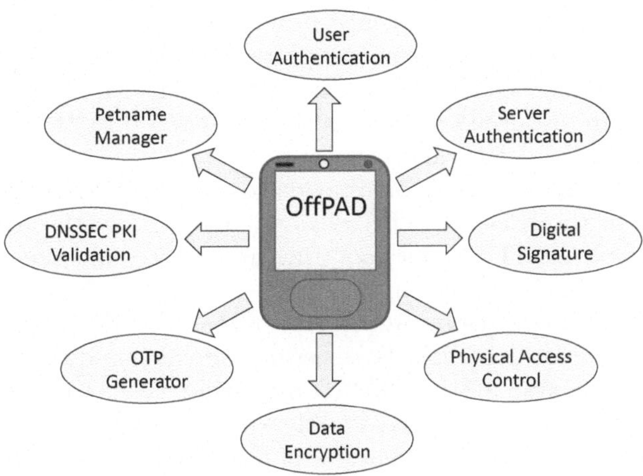

Fig. 3. Multi usage device

(Optical Character Recognition) software. The resulting text may be compared with the expected transaction details. This ensures that the specified transaction data received by the server is exactly as specified by the user, and that it is consistent with what is presented in the client's browser window [1].

Another way to keep the user from signing malformed transaction data, is by having the OffPAD display all the information that is to be signed, e.g. the amount and destination of a bank transfer. Studies have shown that users do not check all the details before confirming such transactions, especially when long rows of numbers are involved, and only a few of them are wrong[18]. The OffPAD would then require a simple keyboard, and the protocol would need to support the OffPAD to be able to not only sign data, but also to generate and modify transactions.

3.2 User Authentication

People who frequently use online services will typically accumulate a large number of online identities and related passwords, and managing these quickly becomes impossible. The OffPAD may be used to manage and authenticate a user to a system in a secure way. This would improve usability by providing a tool for identity management, and would also improve security in several respects. In a traditional scenario where the user types his password, or the password is decrypted by a password manager (e.g. LastPass[2]), the password is exposed in the computer's memory and is vulnerable to attacks such as key logging or memory inspection. A solution for password authentication using an OffPAD is proposed by Klevjer *et al.* in [16], consisting of an extension to the original *HTTP Digest Access Authentication* scheme specified as a part of the HTTP standard

[2] http://lastpass.com

in [8]. User credentials are stored in a hashed format on both the server and the OffPAD. When the client requests a protected resource, the server responds with an authentication challenge, which on the client side is hashed with the user credentials and returned to the server. The server does the same challenge-response calculations locally, and compares the result and the response. If the two values match and the user corresponds to an authorized entity, the user is granted access to the resource. This can be done securely through an insecure channel, such as over HTTP, not requiring an extra connection to the server, just a browser plugin or extension.

The OffPAD may be used as an authenticator to servers that supports challenge-response authentication protocols. For existing systems that do not want to change their authentication system, the OffPAD may still be able to provide the server with the credentials. This, however, would require the use of HTTPS or another protection mechanism, as the username and password would be sent in plaintext from the OffPAD to the user's computer.

3.3 Validation of DNSSEC

DNSSEC is a mechanism for confirming the validity of a domain name system (DNS) record using asymmetric cryptography. DNSSEC rests on a hierarchic PKI where the public key of the DNSSEC root is globally known and acknowledged. The OffPAD can store a copy of the DNSSEC root public key, and get all the other required DNS-records from the computer. Then the OffPAD can validate each record and alert the user if validation fails.

The validation process of DNSSEC is quite simple and described in [3, 2]. Each resource record (RR) in DNS has a Resource Record Signature (RRSIG) containing the signature for the current record. This signature can be authenticated with the public key stored in the DNSKEY RR. A digest of the DNSKEY is stored in a Delegation Signer (DS) RR in the parent DNS zone[3], which in turn has a RRSIG. The validation process propagates all the way to the root.

For services that take the advantage of DNSSEC and stores their server certificate in the new TLSA resource record[9], would also make the OffPAD able to validate the server certificate through DNSSEC instead of or in addition to X.509. The TLSA RR is a resource record that gives you enough information to be able to validate the targeted server certificate, and it also tells you if you should validate it through X.509 or not. Public keys for other usage could also be stored in DNSSEC, in other RR types.

To be able to validate a server through DNSSEC, the OffPAD must be fed the chain of RRs, keys and their respective signatures. This must come from the untrusted computer when the authentication should take place. Man-in-the-middle attacks are still not a threat, since the whole chain of data is indirectly signed by the root node's key, which must be pre installed on the OffPAD.

[3] A DNS zone is a collection of RR that is administrated by the same entity, thus signed with the same DNSKEY.

3.4 Server Authentication

There are multiple ways for an attacker to lure a victim to access a fake website with phishing attacks. Users are normally not well aware of the possible threats, and will in many cases not notice that the fake website is not the intended website, even if the user tries to inspect the server certificate [13]. To make it easy for the user to verify that she is connected to the correct service, the user can use a *petname system* [22, 7]. The petname system allows the user to associate server identities with personally recognisable identifiers such as a logo, name or tune, which are called petnames. Having a personally recognisable petname enables the user to easily validate the identity of the service. If the user navigates to a web site and there is a mismatch between its identifier and the one stored, the system should alert the user, or ask the user to add a new petname for the new service. Petname systems protects users from falling victim to phishing attacks[7].

As proposed by Ferdous *et al.*[6], the Petname system can be implemented on an OffPAD, validating the service being accessed. This will make the Petname system more user-friendly, since the user only needs to manage one central collection of petnames. DNSSEC combined with a petname system can give a quite strong service authentication, which gives a good base for the Server Authentication Assurance as proposed by Jøsang *et al.* [12].

3.5 Generation of One-Time Passwords

Several service providers that offer two factor authentication use one-time passwords (OTP) generated by a device. An OTP is considered to be a dynamic password, and is typically combined with a static password for authentication to an online service. The OTP is generated as a function of a secret string of bytes and either a timestamp or a counter value. Standards exist for how these functions can be implemented, e.g. Time-Based One-Time Password Algorithm (TOTP) [20] and HMAC-Based One-Time Password Algorithm (HOTP) [19].

Both TOTP and HOTP works by taking pseudorandom bytes from a HMAC[4] using a shared secret key and the time or counter value as input. The resulting string of pseudorandom bytes is the OTP. The key and the expected time or counter value are known to the service provider so that it can perform the same calculations and compare the received OTP with the locally computed OTP. The simplicity of the OTP mechanism makes it possible to install any practical number of different OTP services on the same OffPAD, to manage OTP-based authentication for access to different service providers.

3.6 Encryption and Decryption of Messages

E-mail is still widely used for exchanging private and confidential information between people. While the user's connection to the mail server might be encrypted,

[4] Hash-based Message Authentication Code.

the connection between different mail servers is not. This is problematic when it comes to "forgotten passwords" request, where some service providers send a temporary password in plain text, or a time limited link to reset the password. Sometimes the forgotten current password is even resent in clear. A solution is to let the service provider encrypt a message containing a password reset code with the public key for the OffPAD, so that it can only be decrypted by the OffPAD. This ensures that only the correct user can reset his password.

This can also be used to encrypt and decrypt other messages for the user, e.g. notifications from a bank. It is particularly useful were the user's computer is considered compromised.

3.7 Physical Access Control

Physical access control based on NFC technology is increasing in popularity. An OffPAD with passive NFC capability can support physical access control in the same way that standard NFC-enabled identity cards do, but can also support more advanced functionality, e.g. using personal stored fingerprints or other biometric information. A fingerprint can be scanned and validated on the OffPAD instead of on a central system, which enhances convenience, hygiene and privacy for the user. After matching the fingerprint the OffPAD can send an assertion to the access control system. If the user is authenticated on the OffPAD, she might not need to enter her PIN-code on the keypad by the door, limiting the possibility for an attacker to observe the PIN-code.

4 Limitations

The OffPAD is primarily intended to be a security device. Since complexity is the enemy of security it implies that the OffPAD should be simple and be limited in functionality. In contrast to smart phones or tablets that are designed to be open and have maximum connectivity and flexibility, the OffPAD should be a closed platform and have strictly controlled connectivity. This design principle is aimed at reducing the attack surface. The challenge is to offer adequate usability despite these limitations.

4.1 Deployment and Updating Applications on the OffPAD

A challenge for the OffPAD is to upgrade the software on the device itself, as known bugs can make the OffPAD vulnerable, and even the process of updating the software might create vulnerabilities. There is a number of ways to update software, including the use of physical service stations, but this is quite impractical and it is hard for a user to build trust relations with such stations even if they are completely trustworthy.

The easiest, and still secure method for updates, is through the user's computer. Where the user (or OffPAD driver) downloads update files and transfer them to the OffPAD. If these files are signed, the OffPAD can validate the files and their source before running them. This is somewhat similar to how application distribution systems for smart phones work.

4.2 Controlled Connectivity

One of the requirements for the OffPAD is to enforce strictly controlled connectivity, e.g. by not having a direct connection to the Internet, and by enforcing time limits for connections to client computers or to other systems. The user should explicitly activate a connection, the OffPAD should clearly indicate when a connection is active, and should indicate when the connection ends. Typically, every connection should not last longer than one second at a time, just enough to exchange authentication information. If the communication takes much longer the user is likely to leave the OffPAD connected to the client computer which would introduce new attack vectors.

The short connection time requires either high transmission rate, or small amounts of data, or a combination of both. The standard for NFC [11] describes two communication modes: passive and active. Passive means that the target entity does not have a power source itself. It gets its power from a radio frequency (RF) field generated by the other part in the communication (the initiator). In active communication, both entities have a power source and the initiator and target alternate between making the RF field. The top speed is defined to be up to 424 kbit/s for passive mode and up to 6780 kbit/s for active mode. This limits the amount of data to transferred, but will probably not introduce any practical constraints for the security services mentioned here. Services that need to send or receive relatively large amounts of data might need to use active mode.

4.3 Driver Software and Browser Plug-ins

The OffPAD is intended to communicate with a variety of computer systems using one or several of the communication technologies listed in Table3. For each communication modality, specific software driver is needed, which *a priori* will be installed by the OffPAD hardware manufacturer. In case software update of any of the drivers is needed it is important that the driver can be securely obtained, and that it is easy to install.

Communication between the client computer and the OffPAD requires drivers and software installed on the client computer. It is important for the software to not introduce new security vulnerabilities to the host computer. A client computer must be used to transfer data to the OffPAD, and in case the client computer has been infected with malware the data to be transferred to the OffPAD could give attackers some information about the OffPAD, and potentially an opportunity to compromise the OffPAD itself. This can be prevented with pairing, where the user physically operates the client computer to initialise the pairing process. The pairing process can be done using Diffie-Hellman key exchange[5], where both the client computer and the OffPAD select unique keys for each other. As the user starts the pairing process and observes that there is only the host and the OffPAD, this gives a small chance for a *man-in-the-middle-attack* (unless the *man* is already in the host system).

If there is malicious code on the host computer (in the drivers, browser plug-in or other places), applications that base themselves on information from the host may take wrong actions. Applications where the information is validated with a public key, with DNSSEC for instance, can be secure even if the host computer is compromised.

4.4 Protecting the OffPAD in Case of Theft

Even if there is strong access control on the device it is challenging to protect against all forms of attacks when the device is in the hands of the attacker, but some security measures can provide relatively robust protection against compromise. It should not be possible to rapidly do an exhaustive search through the entire PIN code space, or rapidly try many different fingerprints. A limit of e.g. 3 attempts can e.g. trigger a delay of e.g. 10 minutes before the OffPAD can be accessed again.

5 Commercial Adoption

The OffPAD might be relatively expensive to produce compared to a simple OTP-calculator, but as mentioned already some banks and institutions are already deploying relatively advanced devices to the public, such as card readers with a display and keypad. With an OffPAD as a general purpose security device many more security services can be supported and the resulting security for online transactions will be higher than that which can be achieved with most of the calculators used today.

The challenge is to get the average Internet users to discover the advantages of adopting this device for all their security solutions, and therefore to be willing to pay for it. Since the OffPAD is not a web-browser, an MP3-player or gaming console, people would probably not carry it with them everywhere, as they typically do for mobile phones. Adoption would certainly be increased in case different service providers and system developers (e.g. Facebook, Google, Microsoft and Apple) decided to promote an OffPAD, or a protocol supported by the OffPAD. But initially, it will most likely be companies with high security requirements that will see the need for having people use a device like the OffPAD.

5.1 Using a Mobile Phone as the OffPAD

Modern mobile phones, or smart phones, are packed with advanced features and must be considered a "general purpose computing platform". This certainly provides great flexibility and support for many new business models, but it also opens up many new attack vectors. From 2010 to 2011 Juniper MTC reported a 155% increase in malware on mobile phones [15]. It should be noted that all the different mobile phone operating system manufacturers are trying to make their system more secure. At the same time the market pressure enforces them to provide more connectivity and more flexibility into their devices, which necessarily also introduces new vulnerabilities. This makes a normal mobile phone unreliable for high security applications.

It is important that the user can be assured that she is interacting with the operating system and not an application pretending to be the operating system. Windows Phone, iOS and Android[5] have a “trusted path” button that ensures that the user is directed to the home screen and not to an application.

The French company TazTag has introduced a mobile phone (TPH-ONE) [23] based on Android, and also integrates a secure element which can be accessed in a secure state. The secure element can potentially offer some of an OffPAD's functionality, by providing identity management and security services.

6 Conclusion

In this paper we describe the OffPAD as a general purpose security device for all types of users, which can replace or complement the different multi-factor authentication devices that already exist. This paper also describes specific security services that can be implemented on the OffPAD. It can be integrated with many of the existing systems and can offer a general security solution for the client and user side, both in enterprise and private settings.

7 Future Work

Prototypes for the different security services mentioned in this paper are currently being developed. User experiments are planned to test if security services offered by the OffPAD are superior to solutions that already exist. Still to be developed are solutions for updating software and the operating system. The security enhanced smart phone produced by TazTag will be tested to see if the security of the operating systems and hardware can meet the requirements for an OffPAD. For instance, it must be possible to switch between the OffPAD functionality and the normal smart phone context using a physical switch on the device.

Acknowledgements. The work reported in this paper has been partially funded by Franco-Norwegian Foundation Project 1/11-FNS, and by the EUREKA Project 7161 Lucidman.

References

[1] Alzomai, M., Alfayyadh, B., Jøsang, A.: Display Security for Online Transactions. In: The 5th International Conference for Internet Technology and Secured Transactions, ICITST 2010 (2010)

[2] Arends, R., et al.: Protocol Modifications for the DNS Security Extensions. RFC 4035 (Proposed Standard). Updated by RFCs 4470, 6014. Internet Engineering Task Force (March 2005), http://www.ietf.org/rfc/rfc4035.txt

[5] It is possible to change the workings of the “Home” button in the settings for Android, so it might be possible for an application to change the function of this button.

[3] Arends, R., et al.: Resource Records for the DNS Security Extensions. RFC 4034 (Proposed Standard). Updated by RFCs 4470, 6014. Internet Engineering Task Force (March 2005), http://www.ietf.org/rfc/rfc4034.txt
[4] Baker, N.: ZigBee and Bluetooth strengths and weaknesses for industrial applications. Computing Control Engineering Journal 16(2), 20–25 (2005)
[5] Diffie, W., Hellman, M.: New directions in cryptography. IEEE Transactions on Information Theory 22(6), 644–654 (1976)
[6] Ferdous, M.S., Jøsang, A., Singh, K., Borgaonkar, R.: Security Usability of Petname Systems. In: Jøsang, A., Maseng, T., Knapskog, S.J. (eds.) NordSec 2009. LNCS, vol. 5838, pp. 44–59. Springer, Heidelberg (2009)
[7] Ferdous, M.S., Jøsang, A.: Entity Authentication & Trust Validation in PKI using Petname Systems. In: Elçi, A., et al. (eds.) Theory and Practice of Cryptography Solutions for Secure Information Systems (CRYPSIS). IGI Global (2013) ISBN: 9781466640306
[8] Franks, J., et al.: HTTP Authentication: Basic and Digest Access Authentication. RFC 2617 (Draft Standard). Internet Engineering Task Force (June 1999), http://www.ietf.org/rfc/rfc2617.txt
[9] Hoffman, P., Schlyter, J.: The DNS-Based Authentication of Named Entities (DANE) Transport Layer Security (TLS) Protocol: TLSA. RFC 6698 Proposed Standard. Internet Engineering Task Force (August 2012), http://www.ietf.org/rfc/rfc6698.txt
[10] Identification cards - Integrated circuit cards - Part 4: Organization, security and commands for interchange. Norm (2005), http://www.iso.org/iso/iso_catalogue_catalogue_tc/catalogue_detail.htm?csnumber=36134 (visited on April 01, 2013)
[11] ISO. Information technology – Telecommunications and information exchange between systems – Near Field Communication – Interface and Protocol (NFCIP-1). ISO 18092. International Organization for Standardization, Geneva, Switzerland (2004)
[12] Jøsang, A., et al.: Service provider authentication assurance. In: 2012 Tenth Annual International Conference on Privacy, Security and Trust (PST), pp. 203–210 (2012)
[13] Jøsang, A.: Trust Extortion on the Internet. In: Meadows, C., Fernandez-Gago, C. (eds.) STM 2011. LNCS, vol. 7170, pp. 6–21. Springer, Heidelberg (2012)
[14] Jøsang, A., Pope, S.: User Centric Identity Management. In: AusCERT Conference 2005 (2005)
[15] Inc. Juniper Networks. Juniper Mobile Threat Report 2011. Tech. rep. Juniper Networks, Inc. (2011)
[16] Klevjer, H., Varmedal, K.A., Jøsang, A.: Extended HTTP Digest Access Authentication. In: Fischer-Hübner, S., de Leeuw, E., Mitchell, C. (eds.) IDMAN 2013. IFIP AICT, vol. 396, pp. 83–96. Springer, Heidelberg (2013)
[17] Laurie, B., Singer, A.: Choose the red pill and the blue pill: a position paper. In: Proceedings of the 2008 Workshop on New Security Paradigms, pp. 127–133. ACM (2009)
[18] Jøsang, A., AlZomai, M., AlFayyadh, B., McCullagh, A.: An Experimental Investigation of the Usability of Transaction Authorization in Online Bank Security Systems. In: Proceedings of the Australasian Information Security Conference (AISC 2008), vol. 81, Wollongong, Australia (2008)
[19] M'Raihi, D., et al.: HOTP: An HMAC-Based One-Time Password Algorithm. RFC 4226 (Informational). Internet Engineering Task Force (December 2005), http://www.ietf.org/rfc/rfc4226.txt

[20] M'Raihi, D., et al.: TOTP: Time-Based One-Time Password Algorithm. RFC 6238 (Informational). Internet Engineering Task Force (May 2011), http://www.ietf.org/rfc/rfc6238.txt

[21] Stajano, F.: Pico: No More Passwords! In: Christianson, B., Crispo, B., Malcolm, J., Stajano, F. (eds.) Security Protocols 2011. LNCS, vol. 7114, pp. 49–81. Springer, Heidelberg (2011)

[22] Stiegler, M.: An Introduction to Petname Systems (2005), http://www.skyhunter.com/marcs/petnames/IntroPetNames.html (visited on December 04, 2012)

[23] TazTag. Mobility Products, http://taztag.com/index.php?option=com_content&view=article&id=104 (visited on November 20, 2012)

Information-Oriented Trustworthiness Evaluation in Vehicular Ad-hoc Networks

Sashi Gurung[1], Dan Lin[1], Anna Squicciarini[2], and Elisa Bertino[3]

[1] Department of Computer Science, Missouri University of Science and Technology
{sgy99,lindan}@mst.edu

[2] College of Information Sciences & Technology, Pennsylvania State University
asquicciarini@ist.psu.edu

[3] Department of Computer Science, Purdue University
bertino@cs.purdue.edu

Abstract. In Vehicular Ad-Hoc Networks (VANETs), applications are typically realized by forwarding and exchanging messages among vehicles. The integrity and trustworthiness of messages directly impacts the quality of the applications. Though there have been extensive works on authentication protocols in VANETs, authentication can only certify message origin but cannot guarantee that the identity holders will send truthful and accurate messages. Therefore, in this paper, we propose a novel trust model to directly evaluate the trustworthiness of the content of a message received from other vehicles. The model is built based on various factors such as content similarity, content conflict and route similarity. Trustworthiness of message content will be evaluated at the individual vehicle level and will not introduce any additional architectural assumptions. We have conducted extensive experiments and the results indicate both efficiency and effectiveness of the proposed approach.

1 Introduction

The integration of on-board computers (e.g., engine control units) and positioning devices (e.g., GPS receivers), along with communication capabilities based on the use of Dedicated Short Range Communications (DSRC) radios, have made vehicular ad hoc networks (VANETs) one of the most promising commercial applications of mobile ad hoc networking. In VANETs, vehicles are able to communicate with one another, thereby creating a large network with vehicles acting as the network nodes.

VANETs, originally created to enhance safety on the road using cooperative collision warning via vehicle-to-vehicle (V2V) communication [8], are now a predominant and widely powerful technology. The scope of VANET now range from driving assistance to mobile entertainment [10, 18]. For example, a vehicle may send inquiries to vehicles around certain landmarks to obtain the up-to-date parking information, the condition of a road, or convenient lodging; vehicles can exchange files via pure V2V communication. Messages can be propagated through multiple hops and the typical one-hop communication range is 300 meters.

For these VANET applications to be effective and beneficial to drivers, a possibly large number of messages among vehicles is exchanged and forwarded. The integrity

J. Lopez, X. Huang, and R. Sandhu (Eds.): NSS 2013, LNCS 7873, pp. 94–108, 2013.

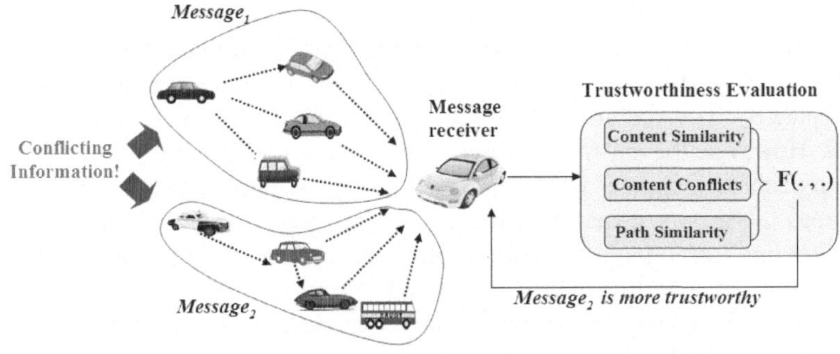

Fig. 1. Real-time Message Content Validation in VANETs

and trustworthiness of these messages critically impacts the quality of the applications. Henceforth, messages' content should be vouched and verified prior to being distributed. Otherwise, VANET nodes may purposely or accidentally send fake messages that disrupt the traffic, with potentially dramatic consequences, including loss of human lives. In particular, without proper controls, an adversary may easily exploit the VANET mobility and short-term connections to cheat on his temporary and short-lived neighbors and gain personal benefit. A victim may find out that the received message was malicious or misleading too late to avoid the loss caused by the wrong information, be it in terms of time, information or other resources. For example, a driver may already be stuck in a traffic jam and not able to reroute when he realized that the message he received via VANETs was incorrect.

Due to the unique contextual and network settings of VANETs, solutions for information validation in alternative domains such as P2P and social network environments [1, 2, 6, 7, 12, 13, 23], are not suitable. For example, in social network sites, users typically gain reputation if they contribute correct information. Based on one's reputation (and possibly content analysis [2]), other users can determine whether his information is trustworthy. However, reputation is established using a stable network over a relatively long period of time (a day, a week or even longer), and neither one of them exists in VANETs. In VANETs, even if an individual keeps a historical database of vehicles that he traveled along with, the database may not be useful since he may not come across the same vehicles again in the future. Moreover, compared to social networks, the mobility of vehicles imposes strict time constraints on making informed decisions. Notice that authentication protocols are also not sufficient, as they can only certify message origin but cannot guarantee that the identity holder will send truthful and accurate messages in VANETs.

In this paper, we propose a Real-time Message Content Validation (RMCV) scheme. It empowers each individual vehicle with the capability of evaluating the trustworthiness of the possibly large amount of messages received in VANETs, without relying on any infrastructure support such as road-side units or central servers. The core of the RMCV scheme is an *information-oriented* trust model which assigns each message a trust score indicating the estimated probability of the message being true. The proposed trust model considers a variety of factors that have impact on the trustworthiness of messages, including message content similarity, content conflict and message routing path similarity. Figure 1 shows an overview of the system. Suppose that one vehicle (the one in the center of the image) wants to know the traffic condition at one road that it will soon pass by. The vehicle sent its query via the VANET and received six response messages. However, the six messages contain conflicting information of one another. The group of three messages (denoted by $Message_1$) claimed that there was a traffic jam whereas the group of the other three messages (denoted by $Message_2$) claimed that there was no traffic jam. It becomes difficult for the querying vehicle to tell which message is more trustworthy. In this situation, the proposed RMCV system will help analyze the received six messages and compute the trust scores for the messages based on the trust model. If the trust score of $Message_2$ is much higher than that of $Message_1$, the RMCV system would inform the user that $Message_2$ is probably telling the truth.

We have implemented the RMCV scheme and conducted extensive experiments by simulating various scenarios. We also compare our model with the state-of-the art [16]. The experimental results demonstrate the efficiency and effectiveness of our work.

The rest of the paper is organized as follows. Section 2 gives a brief review on related works. Section 3 presents the proposed trust model. Section 4 reports experimental studies. Finally, Section 5 concludes the paper.

2 Related Work

Existing works on information trustworthiness in VANETs can be classified into three main categories [22]: (i) entity-oriented trust model; (ii) data-centric trust model; and (iii) combined trust model.

In entity-oriented trust model, trustworthiness of information is estimated based on trustworthiness of the message sender. For example, in [15], Raya et al. utilized static infrastructure such as a Certification Authority (CA) to evict malicious vehicles in VANETs. A critical assumption they have made is the existence of an honest majority in the attacker's neighborhood. This will allow vehicles to trust their honest neighbors in order to evict attackers. They proposed two methods for misbehaving node revocation by the CA. The first one is called RTC (Revocation of the Trust Component) which deprives the misbehaving node from its cryptographic keys; thus confirming that all its messages are disregarded by all other legal nodes. However, RTC is not robust against a sophisticated adversary that controls the communication link between the CA and the TC. The other method that they propose is a localized MDS (Misbehavior Detection System) and the LEAVE (Local Eviction of Attackers by Voting Evaluators) protocol. The main principle of LEAVE is that the neighbors of the misbehaving vehicle temporarily evict it. In [9,11], a vehicle needs to build up a profile of each vehicle it comes in contact with. The vehicle evaluates the trustworthiness of its peers based on its past interactions and then determines whether the information received is trustworthy or not based on the sender's profile. However, entity-oriented trust models have the following common limitations. First, VANET is a very dynamic environment and relationships among entities do not last for long, which causes difficulties to collect enough evidences to trust an interacting entity. Second, even if an entity is trustworthy and honestly forwarded a message it received, we still do not know whether the message itself is correct.

To address limitations in entity-oriented trust models, recent work proposed to evaluate message content directly rather than just validating the identities of message senders. The most related work is by Raya et al. [16] who use Bayesian inference and Dempster-Shafer theory to evaluate the evidences received regarding an event occurrence. Their approach relies on the availability of trust scores of individual evidence (i.e., message) related to an event. However, the calculation of trust scores of individual messages is presented as a black box which is considered system dependent. Our work should be distinguished from it in the following aspects. First, we design specific functions to compute the trust score for each message rather than just a framework. Second, we explore a more thorough set of factors including similarity among message routing paths, rather than information received from directly interacting nodes [16].

Last, the combined trust model [3, 5, 14] aims to determine trustworthiness of the messages based on opinions provided by other peer vehicles. The basic idea is to suggest a vehicle to trust a message that has been evaluated to be trustworthy by many other trusted peer vehicles. When a vehicle provided many trusted opinions, the vehicle's honesty value will be increased (i.e., the vehicle becomes more trusted). This is an iterative process and similar to the true fact discovery problem in Internet [4, 21] an approach to evaluate Data Trustworthiness based on Data Provenance. However, such model has similar limitations of the entity-oriented model. Also, this model assumes the existence of certain methods for the peer vehicles to evaluate the trustworthiness of message content, while we actually develop the specific approach for evaluating the message content.

3 Information-Oriented Trustworthiness Evaluation

In this section, we first give an overview of the proposed Real-time Message Content Validation (RMCV) scheme, and then elaborate on each step of the scheme and the associated trust model.

The core of the RMCV is an information-oriented trust model which estimates the trustworthiness of message content by taking into account a variety of VANET-specific dimensions, such as who handled the message at what location and what time. The RMCV scheme consists of two main components: (i) Message Classification; and (ii) Information-oriented Trust Model. The outcome of the scheme is a "trustworthiness" value associated to each received message.

The model applies to information inquiry or information sharing applications, for which we adopt the following format of messages:

Definition 1. *Let $Msg(loc_q, loc_{int}$, etype, info, t_e, mpath) be a message transmitted in VANETs for information inquiry or sharing:*

- loc_q: *The location of the query issuer or the entity to receive the shared information.*
- loc_{int}: *The querying location that the query issuer would like to know about the information, or the location of the shared information.*
- *etype: The event type which could be "traffic condition", "road condition", "coupon", etc.*
- *info: The information about the location loc_{int}, which could be the query results or shared information.*

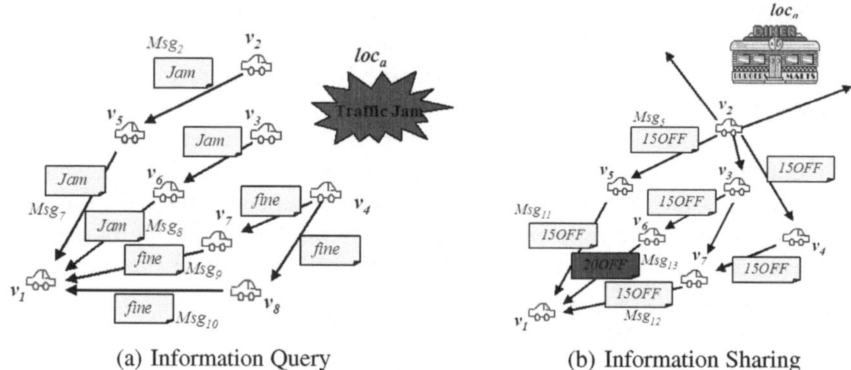

(a) Information Query

(b) Information Sharing

Fig. 2. Example Scenarios

- t_e*: The time the query results or the shared information is available.*
- *mpath: This records the message propagation path. It is in the form of [(*loc_{s_1}*,* t_{s_1}*),(*loc_{s_2}*,* t_{s_2}*), ...), which means a vehicle at* loc_{s_1} *generated the message* Msg *at* t_{s_1} *and then the message was forwarded by the vehicle at* loc_{s_2} *at* t_{s_2}*, and so on. We assume the locations of senders and message sending time are stamped by a tamper-proof device installed in the vehicle.*

Figure 2(a) illustrates an example scenario of information inquiry. Vehicle V_1 at location loc_1 initiates a query on traffic condition at location loc_a. The query message is in the form of $Msg_1(loc_1, loc_a,$ "traffic", NULL, NULL, [(loc_1, t_1)]), where two fields *info* and t_e are waiting to be answered. The query was propagated to vehicles (V_2, V_3, V_4) close to the querying location loc_a. V_2 and V_3 honestly reported that there was a traffic jam by sending back the messages Msg_2 and Msg_3 respectively:

Msg_2(loc_1, loc_a, "traffic", "traffic jam", t_2, [(loc_2, t_2)])

Msg_3(loc_1, loc_a, "traffic", "traffic jam", t_3, [(loc_3, t_3)])

However, a malicious node V_4 who lied that the traffic was fine and sent the following message: Msg_4(loc_1, loc_a, "traffic", "traffic fine", t_4, [(loc_4, t_4)]). Further, in order to make the message appear trustworthy, V_4 forwarded the message to multiple vehicles (V_7 and V_8) instead of the one close to V_1. A malicious vehicle may not know how many other malicious vehicles out there. Thus vehicle V_4 has to spread his messages to more vehicles otherwise his false messages can be easily ruled out based on a simple majority vote by V_1.

Upon receiving the messages initially sent by V_2, V_3 and V_4, the querying vehicle V_1 needs to analyze the conflicting information carried by the messages and figure out which one to trust. Our proposed RMCV scheme can be executed by V_1 to conduct the trust evaluation, and we expect that the true messages provided by V_2 and V_3 will receive higher trust scores.

The RMCV scheme also works for scenarios wherein one would like to share information with others. As shown in Figure 2(b), the owner of vehicle V_2 would like to share a coupon from a restaurant that he/she just visited. Thus, V_2 broadcasts the coupon code to other vehicles using message Msg_5, where loc_q is set to NULL as this is a broadcasting message: Msg_5(NULL, loc_a, "coupon", "15% off code of TJ Restaurant 15OFF", t_5, [(loc_2, t_5)]).

During the message propagation, some malicious nodes may purposely modify the coupon code to be invalid such as given by Msg_{13}. However, the malicious node would not be able to fake location and time information (i.e., $mpath$) which is directly generated by vehicle's tamper proof device by using techniques such as [17]. For a vehicle which receives multiple coupon messages, it will again utilize the RMCV scheme to help identify the more trustworthy version: Msg_{11}(NULL, loc_a, "coupon", "15% off code of TJ Restaurant 15OFF", t_6, [(loc_2, t_5),(loc_5, t_6]).

3.1 Message Classification

In VANETs, one vehicle may receive multiple messages with different and possibly contrasting information from different vehicles during a short period of time. These messages may be related to different events (or different queries) occurring at same or different places. Therefore, the first step is to identify the messages describing the same event from the potentially large amount of received messages so that the analysis can be conducted separately for each event.

One may think of using clustering algorithms to cluster these messages. Messages corresponding to the same event may be similar or conflicting, if spurious or inaccurate messages are included. Direct adoption of conventional clustering algorithms is likely to put these related but conflicting messages in different groups, and hence affect the construction of the trust model. For example, applying a conventional K-means clustering algorithm to messages received by the vehicle V_1 illustrated in Figure 2, three clusters may be obtained: cluster C_1 (containing messages of "traffic jam"), cluster C_2 of messages about "traffic fine", and cluster C_3 for the coupon code. Such clustering did not provide any hint that information in C_1 and C_2 is in fact responding to the same query and they are conflicting. Moreover, the cluster of C_3 did not identify the false coupon code either since the messages are very much similar in terms of content and other values of other components (e.g., location, event type) in the messages.

Thus, in order to better classify messages disseminated in VANETs, we propose a two-level clustering algorithm. The first level clustering groups messages describing the same event regardless the message content. To achieve this, we cluster messages based on their similarity on the three components: loc_{int}, t_e, and $etype$. Specifically, two messages (Msg_i and Msg_j) would be placed in the same cluster if they satisfy all the following conditions:

- $D_l(loc_{int_i}, loc_{int_j}) \leq \rho_d$: D_l is the Euclidean distance of two locations. This condition requires that the two messages are reporting events not further than distance ρ_d so that we may infer that the two messages are likely to be about the same event. In this work, we select ρ_d to be the width of a road which is about 20 meters for a three-lane road.
- $|t_{e_i} - t_{e_j}| \leq \rho_t$: Messages sent from the same locations may not refer to the same event. For example, messages responding to different queries may be sent from the same location at different timestamps. Therefore, we use the time threshold ρ_t to constraint the consideration within messages sent during nearby timestamps. In the

experiments, we set ρ_t to be 30s within which most query results would not have big changes. For example, traffic condition would not change a lot within 30s.

- $etype_i = etype_j$: Two messages about the same event obviously need to have the same event type.

For each cluster obtained from the first level clustering, we further conduct the second level clustering that aims to identify conflicting information regarding the same event. The second-level clustering is conducted mainly by examining the message content, i.e., the similarity between the value of component (*info*) in the message. To compute the similarity of message content, we first extract the keywords from *info* of a message by excluding articles ("a", "an", "the") and connection words that do not carry important information. For example, given a message "there is no traffic jam", we convert it to a set of keywords {"no", "traffic", "jam"}. Then, we sort the keywords in the set in the alphabetical order. After that, we apply the edit distance [19] and WordNet [20] to compute the distance between keywords belonging to two messages. The distance calculation of two keyword sets KW_1 and KW_2 consists of three steps:

1. We first identify the pairs of keywords that fully match each other and remove them from further consideration.
2. Next, we consider if the remaining keywords in the two sets are pairs of synonyms based on WordNet. We remove all such pairs.
3. For remaining keywords, we pair the keywords in KW_1 and KW_2 which have small edit distance, and sum up the obtained edit distance (denoted as D_{ed}).
4. If there is any keyword left unpaired, such as when the two keyword sets have different number of keywords, we sum up the total characters of the unpaired keywords and add to D_{ed}.

If the distance (D_{ed}) between two message content is smaller than ρ_{info}, the two messages will be put in the same cluster. To ensure that conflicting information would have a high probability to be placed in different clusters, we adopt a strict threshold ρ_{info} which is set to 2 (the length of an important keyword "no"). For example, suppose that KW_1={"no", "traffic", "jam"} and KW_2={"traffic", "congestion"}. After sorting the keywords in each set, step 1 removes the matching keyword "traffic". Step 2 removes the synonyms "jam" and "congestion". Step 3 is skipped since there is no more pair left. Step 4 returns the final distance $D_{ed} = 2$ which is the length of the remaining keyword "no". It is worth noting that due to variety of the ways to express the same information, the distance here is just an estimation and may not be always accurate in some cases when messages have same meaning but are expressed in very different ways. The discussion on advanced natural language processing is out of the scope of this paper.

To obtain a better understanding of the whole process of the message classification, let us step through the example scenarios given in Figure 2. Vehicle V_1 received 7 messages which are Msg_7, Msg_8, ..., Msg_{13}. Suppose that t_e in all the messages are fairly close to one another, i.e., the difference less than ρ_t. Applying the three conditions on loc_{int}, t_e and $etype$, we obtain the following two clusters after the first-level clustering:

$C_1 = \{Msg_7, Msg_8, Msg_9, Msg_{10}\}$, $C_2 = \{Msg_{11}, Msg_{12}, Msg_{13}\}$.

This is because messages in C_1 report the same type of event "traffic" at the same location loc_a almost at same time, while messages in C_2 are about coupon information at loc_a.

Next, we conduct second-level clustering for C_1 and C_2 respectively. The cluster C_1 is further divided into two clusters based on the message content:
$C_{11} = \{Msg_7, Msg_8\}, C_{12} = \{Msg_9, Msg_{10}\}$.
Similarly, the cluster C_2 is also divided into two clusters based on the content:
$C_{21} = \{Msg_{11}, Msg_{12}\}, C_{22} = \{Msg_{13}\}$.

3.2 Information-Oriented Trust Model

After the message classification, the next task is to determine which group of messages are truth-telling. To achieve this, we design an information-oriented trust model. The overall process is to identify the factors that may be indicative of message trustworthiness, and then quantify their impact and integrate their effects to generate an overall trustworthiness score that can be easily understood by end users for making decisions. To this end, we identify three important factors that affect message trustworthiness, which are *content similarity*, *content conflict* and *routing path similarity*. In what follows, we explain why they are important, how they affect the trust score. Finally, we derive the trust model based on these factors.

Effect of Content Similarity. Given a group of messages associated to a same event, similar messages are generally considered to be supportive to one another. Moreover, similar to daily life conversations, the more people supporting the same fact, the more likely the fact would have some true ground. Though this observation may not always hold as we will discuss later in Section 3.2, it is certainly an important factor to be considered when judging the trustworthiness of a message. To model these two effects, we use two parameters. The first parameter is the maximum distance ($maxD_c$) of content between two messages in the same cluster. It quantifies the similarity of information in the same cluster. The smaller the distance, the higher support level of the information given by each other. The second parameter is the number of messages (N_c) in the cluster which models the second effect: the more messages in the cluster, the higher support the message received. The two parameters are then integrated to compute the support value by using Equation 1.

$$Support(c) = \frac{e^{\frac{N_c}{N_e}}\left(\frac{3}{2} - \frac{maxD_c}{\rho_{ed}}\right)}{\frac{2}{3}e} \tag{1}$$

We now explain the rationale behind Equation 1.

- In the first part of the formula, N_e is the total number of messages regarding the event. Dividing N_c by N_e is for the purpose of obtaining a normalized value ranging in 0 and 1, since $0 \leq N_c \leq N_e$. Such normalization helps make values obtained from different clusters of messages comparable. The effect of N_c is then modeled by an exponential function $e^{\frac{N_c}{N_e}}$. The reason to choose the exponential function is that the resulting value grows faster when the effect becomes more dominant. This maps the following scenario. For groups of few number of messages (e.g., two or three messages), it is hard to say one group is more trustworthy than the other just because of it has one more supportive message. Therefore, such groups will have very close trust scores. When the number of messages in a group is much bigger, the trust score will grow much faster using the exponential function, and this represents that the probability of the message being true is higher.

- In $\frac{maxD_c}{\rho_{ed}}$, $maxD_c$ is normalized to the range of 0 to 1 by using the possible maximum distance ρ_{ed}. Recall that ρ_{ed} is the threshold used to determine whether two messages can be placed in the same cluster. The value $\frac{3}{2}$ is used for two purposes. First, it reverses the effect of $\frac{maxD_c}{\rho_{ed}}$ so that when the difference of messages is greater, the trust score would be lower. Second, it ensures that the second part will have certain effect on the overall trust score even if it reaches the maximum distance. In particular, when messages in the cluster are the same, i.e., $maxD_c = 0$, the second part returns a value 1.5. In contrast, when $maxD_c = 1$, the second part returns value 0.5.
- The value obtained from the product of the previous two components ranges from $\frac{1}{2}$ to $\frac{3}{2}e$. By dividing the product by $\frac{3}{2}e$, the final similarity score is normalized to be less than 1. It is always greater than 0 since messages in the same cluster are expected to have at least some similarity.

Effect of Routing Path Similarity. It is likely for one to trust a message which has a large number of other similar messages as the support. However, considering content similarity may not be sufficient to determine the trustworthiness of the message since in some cases a large number of messages may also cause illusion. An extreme case is that if all messages have the same origin and the origin is a malicious vehicle, these messages should not be trusted. From the example shown in Figure 2, the vehicle V_1 received two groups of conflicting messages about the traffic condition. These two groups of messages have equal content similarity scores according to Equation 1 in Section 5, making it difficult to tell which is more trustworthy. However, if observed closely, one may notice that the group of false messages (Msg_9 and Msg_{10} are actually provided by the same source vehicle, while the group of true messages (Msg_7 and Msg_8) have different source providers. Following a general assumption that majority of people are honest, it is less likely that the majority of people purposely provide wrong information. Therefore, the probability of multiple source providers reporting the same wrong information is expected to be lower than that of a single source provider in most cases. More generally speaking, if similar messages share more common nodes during their routing paths, the risk of messages being tampered increases.

Based on the above discussion, we model the effect of routing path similarity by using three parameters: the number of messages (N_c) in the cluster, the number of the origins of the messages (N_{src}), and the number of distinct vehicles (N_{dif}) in the routing paths of messages in the same cluster. Then, we design the path similarity function based on the following guidelines:

- If there are a large number of source providers (N_{src}), the message routing paths are less likely to be similar.
- If there are common vehicles in multiple paths and the common vehicle is malicious, all messages forwarded by the malicious vehicle may be tampered. To model this, the more distinct vehicles (N_{dif}) involved in the same cluster of messages, the lower path similarity should be.

The following equation sums up the above effects:

$$Path_c = 1 - (0.5\frac{N_{src}}{N_c} + 0.5\frac{N_{dif}}{N_{all}}) \tag{2}$$

In Equation 2, N_{all} denotes the total number of vehicle nodes involved in forwarding the messages in the cluster C. If the same vehicle occurs in different paths, each of its occurrence would be counted to N_{all}. Then, $\frac{N_{dif}}{N_{all}}$ yields the percentage of the distinct vehicles in the routing paths. Though this percentage also reflects the difference of source providers to certain degree, we still put an equal weight (0.5) to the number of source providers due to its importance.

We now use the example in Figure 2 to illustrate the steps of computing the path similarity. In cluster $C_{11} = \{Msg_7, Msg_8\}$, the routing paths are the following:

$Msg_7 : V_2 - V_5$; $Msg_8 : V_3 - V_6$.

Observe that in the above two ($N_c = 2$) messages, there are two different sources ($N_{src} = 2$), four different nodes ($N_{dif} = 4$), and total four nodes ($N_{all} = 4$). Therefore, the $Path_c = 1 - (0.5 \cdot \frac{2}{2} + 0.5 \cdot \frac{4}{4})$=0, which means the paths are totally different.

In cluster $C_{12} = \{Msg_9, Msg_{10}\}$, the routing paths are the following:

Msg_9:$V_4 - V_7$; $Msg_{10} : V_4 - V_8$.

Accordingly, we have $N_c = 2$, $N_{src} = 1$, $N_{dif} = 3$, and $N_{all} = 4$. Then, plug in the numbers to Equation 2, we obtain $Path_c = 1 - (0.5 \cdot \frac{1}{2} + 0.5 \cdot \frac{3}{4})$ = 0.375, which has a higher path similarity score compared to cluster C_{11}.

The path similarity serves as a penalty value to the support value of a cluster of messages. The more similar the routing paths of messages in the same cluster, the less support to each other will be considered. In other words, the more independent of routing paths, the less probability of messages being tampered. We revise the Equation 1 as follows:

$$Support'(c) = (1 - Path_c) \cdot Support(c) \tag{3}$$

Effect of Content Conflict. The analysis of messages referring to a same event, may result in more than one cluster of messages. Messages in different clusters indicate the inconsistency of the information of the event. As shown in the example of Figure 2, one cluster of messages claim there is traffic jam while the other claim the traffic is fine. It is obvious that content conflict has a negative impact on the trustworthiness of messages, and the more conflicting messages the heavier impact. Specifically, let C_1, ..., C_k be the clusters of messages regarding the same event. For each cluster of messages, we compute a conflicting value Con_{ci} given by Equation 4.

$$Con_{c_i} = \frac{e^{\frac{\sum_{j=1}^{k} Support'_{cj} - Support'_{ci}}{\sum_{j=1}^{k} Support'_{cj}}}}{e} \tag{4}$$

A higher conflicting value will be obtained if there are more messages against current cluster C_i. The conflicting value is 0 if there is not any conflicting clusters. Here, the exponential function is adopted for the same purpose of amplifying the effect.

Final Trust Score. To obtain the final trust score $trust(c)$, we integrate the conflicting value to the support score Support'(c). In particular, the conflicting value is used to further penalize the support value as given by the following equation.

$$trust(c) = \frac{(e^{\xi} - e^{\xi \cdot Con_c})Support'(c)}{e^{\xi} - 1} \tag{5}$$

We model it based on the following rationale. When the conflicting value is small, its effect should not be very dominant. In this way, if there exist few false messages, these false messages would not affect the overall trustworthiness of the true messages. When the conflicting value is big, its effect grows faster as it is more likely that the information in the cluster being affected is not true regarding the existence of a large number of opponents. Therefore, as can be seen from Equation 5, $e^{\xi \cdot Con_c}$ models the impact of the conflicting value whereby the exponential function along with a parameter ξ make the resulting value grow faster with the increase of Con_c. Here, ξ is a positive value that helps adjust the importance of the conflicting value, and it is set to e in the experiments. Finally, the score is normalized to range 0 to 1 by multiplying $\frac{1}{e^{\xi}-1}$. The higher the trust score, the more trustworthy the message may be.

Finally, we summarize the overall process of estimating the trustworthiness of a message. Given a bunch of messages received by vehicle V within a short time interval ρ_t, the RMCV scheme first clusters messages according to the events, and then further clusters messages based on their content. After that, trust scores are computed for all the clusters of messages. For clusters of the same event, the one which received the highest trust score is selected. If its trust score is above an experience threshold (e.g., 0.5), the system would report that the content of this cluster may be trustworthy. Otherwise, the system would report that none of the received messages are trustworthy.

In addition, we introduce one more interesting scenario that can also be handled by our approach. Suppose that a vehicle V_x sends the following two messages:

- Msg_{x1}: At time t_1, there is a traffic jam between exits 25 and 30 in HWY 65.
- Msg_{x2}: At time t_2, there is no traffic jam between exits 25 and 30 in HWY 65.

It may be the case that between t_1 and t_2 things have changed, or it could be the case that a vehicle can only observe some partial view and later on may see a complete view and send a different message for correction.

For the given scenario, our RCMV will deal with it as follows:

- Case 1: Suppose that t_2 is far from t_1 (e.g., 30 minutes later). All messages (including the one from vehicle V_x and others) about traffic jam sent around time t_1 would be considered as message for one event. We compare these messages to see if there was a real traffic jam at t_1. Messages sent around t_2 will be considered as another event (no jam) which could be true if the traffic was clear at t_2.
- Case 2: Suppose that t_2 is close to t_1 (e.g., only a couple of minutes different), and there is in fact no traffic jam but vehicle V_x made a wrong observation at t_1. In this case, the message of "traffic jam" will be considered as a conflicting message. Assuming that majority is honest, we expect to have more messages of "no traffic jam" around timestamp t_1, so that the receiver would not be confused.

4 Experimental Study

In this section, we first present the experimental settings and then reports a comparative study of our approach against the existing work.

The implementation is written in JAVA and conducted in a desktop of 64-bit Intel(R) Xeon(R) E5630 2.53GHz machine. We simulate the message disseminated in VANETs as follows. We adopt a parameter that controls the number of hops N_{hop} between the source provider and the query issuer (or the last message receiver) being considered. In the experiments, we vary N_{hop} from 1 to 5. At each hop, we generate 100 vehicles. For each event, we randomly select one hop and then select δ percent of malicious vehicles. For the vehicles at the first hop, we generate true messages about several events for honest vehicles, and conflicting messages for malicious vehicles. Honest vehicles will honestly forward whatever messages they receive to one vehicle at the next hop, while malicious vehicles will modify the received messages and forward them to multiple vehicles (ranging from 1 to N_f) at the next hop.

We compare our approach with the work by Raya et al. [16] which is the latest representative work on data-centric trust establishment in VANETs. As their work is based on Bayesian Inference, we denote it as BI in the experiment figures. Since the BI work only considers a single event, we limit the messages to one event when comparing to them. Also, the BI work assumes the existence of trust scores (probability of trustworthiness) of each message for computing the final trust score of the event. In the simulation in their work, they assume the probability of trustworthiness of individual messages follows a Beta distribution with the mean equals to 0.6 and 0.8. We adopt the same parameters for their work in our experiments.

4.1 Experimental Results

In the first two rounds of experiments, we examine the properties of our RMCV, and in the last round of experiments, we compare our approach with the BI work in terms of the ability of preventing attack.

Efficiency. In the first round of experiments, we aim to evaluate the efficiency of our RMCV scheme. Unlike the BI work which assumes the existence of scores of individual messages and just computes one equation for the final trust score, our RMCV scheme offers detailed steps to obtain the trust scores of individual messages. These steps include message classification and routing path similarity analysis. In Figure 3(a), we report the total time taken by the RMCV scheme from messages being received till the trust score being computed. We vary the total number of messages from 100 to 1000 that a vehicle received during ρ_t. There are five hops along each routing path. It is not surprising to see that the processing time increases with the number of messages to be handled. This is because the more messages, the more time needed for message classification and path analysis. We also observe that the time for processing 1000 messages is really short (less than 50ms), which indicates that our scheme is feasible and efficient to meet the strict time constraint in real-time applications.

Effect of Conflicting Value and Path Similarity on Trustworthiness Score. In this experiment, we show how conflicting values and path similarity values affect the over-

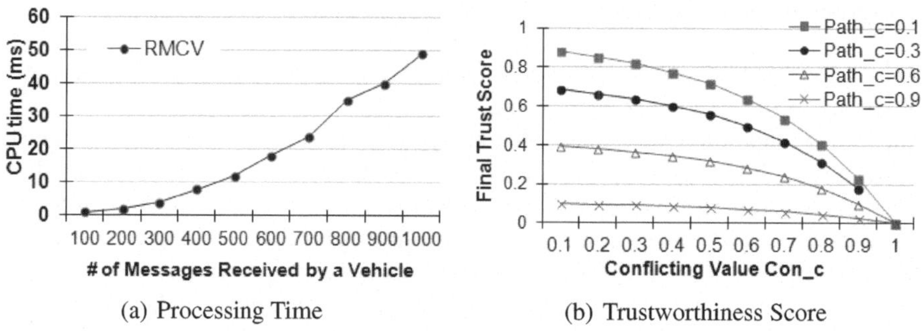

(a) Processing Time

(b) Trustworthiness Score

Fig. 3. The RMCV Approach

all trustworthiness score. From Figure 3(b), we can see that the trustworthiness score decreases with the increase of conflicting values or path similarity values. More importantly, the trust score drops faster when the conflicting value and path similarity value become larger. Thus, the model is tolerant to cases when there are few false reports (i.e., conflicting information), and becomes more sensitive when the number of false reports increases.

Impact of False Messages on Vehicles Accepting True Messages. We now proceed to compare our approach with the BI work. We examine the effect of increase in the percentage of false messages per vehicle to the percentage of good vehicles accepting true messages. We ran a simulation of 1000 rounds for a group of 100 vehicles. The results are reported in Figure 4. From the figure, we can see that when the amount of false messages is less than 50%, both the BI work and our RCMV approach can very well identify false reports, yielding close to 100% acceptance rate of true messages. However, once there are more than 50% false messages, the BI work results in very low (close to 0%) acceptance rate of true messages. In fact, the BI work almost downgrades to a majority vote. In contrast, our RCMV approach yields much better performance even if there are many false messages. This is attributed to the way we model the conflicting information and path similarity. Specifically, since false messages tend to have higher path similarity scores, the penalty score from path similarity decreases the impact of the large amount of false messages on making the final decision.

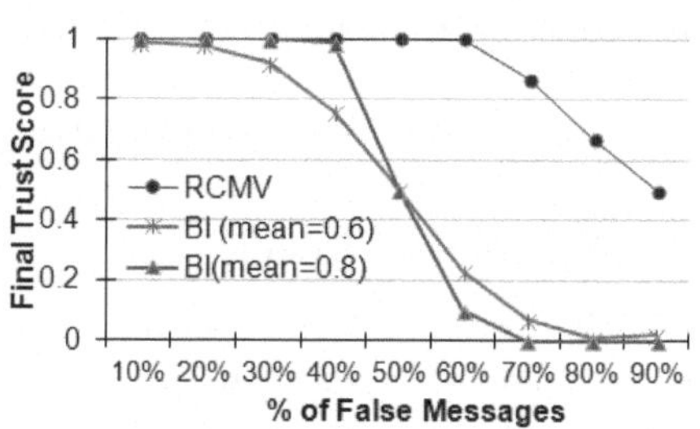

Fig. 4. RCMV vs. BI

5 Conclusion

This paper presents a novel information-oriented scheme for evaluating trustworthiness of messages disseminated in VANETs, which incorporates content similarity, content conflict and route similarity into the trust model to best suit the dynamics of VANET environment. In the future, we aim to integrate in-depth message content analysis techniques to further improve the accuracy.

References

1. Buchegger, S., Boudec, J.-Y.L.: A robust reputation system for peer-to-peer and mobile ad-hoc networks. In: Workshop on the Economics of Peer-to-Peer Systems (2004)
2. Castillo, C., Mendoza, M., Poblete, B.: Information credibility on twitter. In: ACM World Wide Web Conference, pp. 675–684 (2011)
3. Chen, C., Zhang, J., Cohen, R., Ho, P.: A trust-based message propagation and evaluation framework in vanets. In: Proceedings of the Int. Conf. on Information Technology Convergence and Services (2010)
4. Dai, C., Lin, D., Bertino, E., Kantarcioglu, M.: An approach to evaluate data trustworthiness based on data provenance. In: Jonker, W., Petković, M. (eds.) SDM 2008. LNCS, vol. 5159, pp. 82–98. Springer, Heidelberg (2008)
5. Dotzer, F., Fischer, L., Magiera, P.: Vars: A vehicle ad-hoc network reputation system. In: Sixth IEEE International Symposium on a World of Wireless Mobile and Multimedia Networks, WoWMoM 2005, pp. 454–456. IEEE (2005)
6. Eschenauer, L., Gligor, V.D., Baras, J.: On Trust Establishment in Mobile *Ad-Hoc* Networks. In: Christianson, B., Crispo, B., Malcolm, J.A., Roe, M. (eds.) Security Protocols 2002. LNCS, vol. 2845, pp. 47–66. Springer, Heidelberg (2004)
7. Ganeriwal, S., Srivastava, M.: Reputation-based framework for high integrity sensor networks. In: ACM Workshop on Security of Ad Hoc and Sensor Networks, pp. 66–77 (2004)
8. Gerla, M., Gruteser, M.: Vehicular networks: Applications, protocols, and testbeds. In: Emerging Wireless Technologies and the Future Mobile Internet, pp. 201–241 (2011)
9. Gerlach, M.: Trust for vehicular applications. In: Proceedings of the Eighth International Symposium on Autonomous Decentralized Systems, pp. 295–304. IEEE Computer Society, Washington, DC (2007)
10. Mathur, S., Jin, T., Kasturirangan, N., Chandrasekaran, J., Xue, W., Gruteser, M., Trappe, W.: Parknet: drive-by sensing of road-side parking statistics. In: Proceedings of the 8th International Conference on Mobile Systems, Applications, and Services (MobiSys 2010), pp. 123–136 (2010)
11. Minhas, U., Zhang, J., Tran, T., Cohen, R.: Towards expanded trust management for agents in vehicular ad-hoc networks. International Journal of Computational Intelligence Theory and Practice (IJCITP) 5(1) (2010)
12. Mundinger, J., Boudec, J.-Y.L.: Reputation in self-organized communication systems and beyond. In: Workshop on Interdisciplinary Systems Approach in Performance Evaluation and Design of Computer & Communications Systems, p. 3 (2006)
13. Nakajima, Y., Watanabe, K., Hayashibara, N., Enokido, T., Takizawa, M., Deen, S.M.: Trustworthiness in peer-to-peer overlay networks. In: IEEE International Conference on Sensor Networks, Ubiquitous, and Trustworthy Computing, p. 8 (2006)
14. Patwardhan, A., Joshi, A., Finin, T., Yesha, Y.: A data intensive reputation management scheme for vehicular ad hoc networks. In: 2006 Third Annual International Conference on Mobile and Ubiquitous Systems: Networking & Services, pp. 1–8. IEEE (2006)
15. Raya, M., Papadimitratos, P., Aad, I., Jungels, D., Hubaux, J.-P.: Eviction of misbehaving and faulty nodes in vehicular networks. IEEE Journal on Selected Areas in Communications 25(8), 1557–1568 (2007)

16. Raya, M., Papadimitratos, P., Gligor, V.D., Hubaux, J.-P.: On datacentric trust establishment in ephemeral ad hoc networks. In: IEEE International Conference on Computer Communications, INFOCOM (2008)
17. Richter, J., Kuntze, N., Rudolph, C.: Security digital evidence. In: IEEE International Workshop on Systematic Approaches to Digital Forensic Engineering, pp. 119–130 (2010)
18. Tonguz, O.K., Boban, M.: Multiplayer games over vehicular ad hoc networks: A new application. Ad Hoc Networks 8(5), 531–543 (2010)
19. Wagner, R.A., Fischer, M.J.: The string-to-string correction problem. J. ACM 21(1), 168–173 (1974)
20. WordNet, `http://wordnet.princeton.edu/`
21. Yin, X., Han, J., Yu, P.S.: Truth Discovery with Multiple Conflicting Information Providers on the Web. In: Proc. of ACM SIGKDD, pp. 1048–1052 (2007)
22. Zhang, J.: A survey on trust management for vanets. In: 2011 IEEE International Conference on Advanced Information Networking and Applications (AINA), pp. 105–112 (March 2011)
23. Zouridaki, C., Mark, B.L., Hejmo, M., Thomas, R.K.: Robust Cooperative Trust Establishment for MANETs. In: ACM Workshop on Security of Ad Hoc and Sensor Networks, pp. 23–34 (2006)

Using Trusted Platform Modules for Location Assurance in Cloud Networking

Christoph Krauß[1] and Volker Fusenig[2]

[1] Fraunhofer Research Institution for Applied and Integrated Security (AISEC)
Parkring 4, 85748 Garching, Germany
christoph.krauss@aisec.fraunhofer.de
[2] Siemens AG
Otto-Hahn-Ring 6, 81739 Munich, Germany
volker.fusenig@siemens.com

Abstract. In cloud networking users may want to control where their virtual resources are stored or processed, e.g., only in western Europe and not in the US. Cloud networking is the combined management of cloud computing and network infrastructures of different providers and enables dynamic and flexible placement of virtual resources in this distributed environment. In this paper, we propose a mechanism for verifying the geographic location of a virtual resource. Our approach uses Trusted Platform Modules (TPM) to identify physical machines and a trusted authority which verifies the actual location. In addition, our approach enables the verification of the trustworthiness of the machine of the cloud operator.

Keywords: Security, Cloud Networking, TPM, Location.

1 Introduction

Nowadays, cloud computing is used for various applications and offers the possibility to flexibly allocate and use scalable and cheap computing, storage, or networking resources. The resources are offered at different abstraction layers, known as Infrastructure-as-a-Service (IaaS), where the pure hardware functionalities are offered (e.g., Amazon's EC2 [2]), Platform-as-a-Service (PaaS), where a platform is offered on which applications can be run on (e.g., Google's AppEngine [4]), and Software-as-a-Service (SaaS), where ready-to-use applications are offered (e.g., Google Docs [5]). A company which wants to use cloud services can either roll-out its own cloud infrastructure for its own usage (private cloud), it can use cloud infrastructure of other cloud operators (public cloud), or it can use a combination of these two use models (hybrid cloud).

A new approach called cloud networking combines the classical cloud computing with advanced networking functionality and intelligent management of both. A cloud networking provider is responsible for the management of virtual resources, i.e., to move the virtual resources to a cloud operator and to instantiate network connections at network operators. The cloud networking provider

J. Lopez, X. Huang, and R. Sandhu (Eds.): NSS 2013, LNCS 7873, pp. 109–121, 2013.

has contracts with both, the cloud networking users and the cloud and network operators, takes care of the billing in both directions, and is able to globally optimize the placement of virtual resources, e.g., reduce latency for accessing virtual resources, choose the cheapest cloud and network operator, or minimize the network load.

For both, static cloud computing and cloud networking, virtual resources can be placed on cloud infrastructures that are not under control of the user. Therefore, the user might want to define a security policy which gives rules on how the data contained in the virtual resource must be handled. The cloud network provider has to choose a cloud operator that has the capability to fulfill the security policy of the user and the cloud operator has to implement these security policies on its cloud infrastructure. However, the user has no means to verify whether a cloud operator really follows these security policies or just claims to follow the policies.

One important policy is the guarantee that data is stored and processed only at a defined geographic location [18], e.g., only in western Europe and not in the US or other countries. This is of particular interest for some companies because of some regulations such as the US patriot or similar acts. However, for a cloud operator it may be beneficial to move the user's data to another location where storage space and computation are cheaper. Thus, a mechanism is required which enables the verification whether the actual location complies to the defined security policy of the user. Some approaches have been proposed to address this issue [11,10,17]. However, they are all based on the measurement of round trip times which results in high error rates [19].

In this paper, we introduce a mechanism for detecting the geographic location of a virtual resource to prevent a cloud operator to move the virtual resources of a user to an undesired location. Our approach uses Trusted Platform Modules (TPM) which are placed on the physical machines in the cloud infrastructure as unique identifier. The geographic position of these TPMs is verified by a trusted authority. Users can use the TPM to reliably locate their virtual resources and to verify that the actually used system of the cloud infrastructure is trustworthy, i.e., is not maliciously manipulated by the cloud operator or someone else.

The rest of the paper is organized as follows. First, we provide relevant background of the TPM and the used functionalities in our approach in Section 2. Then, we introduce our approach on geolocating virtual resources based on TPMs in Section 3 and discuss the security of our approach in Section 4. In Section 5, we show related work on geolocating techniques and other techniques to place resources at untrusted cloud operators. Finally, in Section 6 we conclude our work and discuss ongoing work.

2 Background on TPM-Mechanisms

The TPM is the core of the TCG specifications [23] and provides functionalities of a smartcard, i.e., protected storage for cryptographic keys and hardware enhanced calculation engines for random number generation, key generation, hash computation, and RSA operations. Although the TPM chip was not specified as necessarily being tamper-resistant, many hardware vendors offer security mechanisms for preventing tampering and the unauthorized extraction of protected keys, such as active security sensors.

When an owner first activates a platform, the TPM is initialized using the `TPM_TakeOwnership` command which requires physical presence at the system. An owner password is set which is required to access the TPM. This process cannot be executed remotely and a new initialization requires physical presence and a special reset sequence.

The manufacturer pre-configures an individual so-called Endorsement Key (EK) pair on the TPM and a corresponding certificate at the trusted platform. The EK and the certificate can be used to clearly identify a specific TPM. The private part of the key pair EK_{priv} is non-migratable, i.e., the private key is always protected by the TPM and must not leave its protected storage. Due to security and privacy reasons, EK_{priv} cannot be used to perform signatures. EK_{priv} can only be used to decrypt sensitive data which has been encrypted with the public part EK_{pub}, e.g., to perform attestations. The certificate of the EK is called *EK Credential*. It contains EK_{pub} and is signed with the private key of the TPM manufacturer attesting the validity of the TPM and the EK.

In addition to the EK Credential, a trusted platform is delivered with *Conformance Credentials* and the *Platform Credential* to provide assurance that its components have been constructed to meet the requirements of the TCG Specifications. The Conformance Credentials are issued by an evaluation service (e.g., platform manufacturer, vendor, or independent lab) to confirm that design and implementation of the Trusted Building Blocks (TBB) comply with the TPM specification. The Platform Credential is issued by the platform manufacturer, vendor or an independent entity to provide evidence, that the platform contains a TPM as described by the EK Credential.

To perform signatures, an owner can generate an Attestation Identity Key (AIK) pair which is an alias for the EK. It is usually used to prove the authenticity of the TPM to a third party without revealing the actual identity (i.e., the EK) of the TPM. The private part of the AIK AIK_{priv} is also non-migratable, just like EK_{priv}. The AIK is solely a signature key, and is never used for encryption. It is used to sign information generated internally by the TPM. The TPM can create a virtually unlimited number of AIKs. An AIK key pair can be created using the `TPM_MakeIdentity` command. To prove that an AIK is tied to valid Endorsement, Platform and Conformance credentials, a certificate called *AIK Credential* is used. The AIK Credential creation process uses an external certification authority (CA) for this purpose. The TPM sends a request, signed with the AIK_{priv}, containing EK Credential, Conformance Credentials, Platform Credential, and public part of the generated AIK AIK_{pub}. If the credentials are valid, the CA generates the AIK Credential and sends it encrypted with EK_{pub} (from the EK Credential) back to the trusted platform.

Since there could be a very large number of keys, possibly more than can be stored within the TPM, many keys such as AIKs can be stored externally, e.g., on a hard disk. Every externally stored key is encrypted by the TPM's Storage Root Key (SRK) which is also a non-migratable RSA key pair and builds the Root of Trust for Storage. An SRK can be changed when a new user takes ownership of the TPM.

The TPM also offers so-called Platform Configuration Registers (PCRs), which are used to store platform-dependent configuration values. These registers are initialized on power up and are used to store software integrity values. Software components (BIOS, bootloader, operating system, applications) are measured by the TPM before execution and the corresponding hash-value is then written to a specific PCR by extending the previous value:

$$Extend(PCR_N, value) = SHA1(PCR_N || value) \tag{1}$$

SHA1 refers to the cryptographic hash function used by the TPM and || denotes a concatenation. The trust anchor for a so-called trust-chain is the *Core Root of Trust Measurement* (CRTM), which resides in the BIOS and is first executed when a platform is powered up. The CRTM then measures itself and the BIOS, and hands over control to the next software component in the trust-chain. For every measured component, an event is created and stored in the Stored Measurement Log (SML). The PCR values can then be used together with the SML to attest the platform's state to a remote entity using for example the *Integrity Measurement Architecture (IMA)* proposed in [20]. To initiate an attestation, a verifier creates a Nonce and sends it to the attesting system. The TPM of this system creates a signature of the Nonce and the PCR values using an AIK and sends signature and Nonce together with the SML back to the challenger. The verifier can verify the signature and compare these values with reference values to see if the system integrity is trustworthy.

3 TPM-Based Location Assurance

The general idea of our approach is to use the TPM of the physical machine as a trust-anchor for validating the geo-position of virtual machines. The identity of a TPM is registered together with its actual geographic location at a Certification Authority (CA). A user starts a software client running in the virtual machine to initiate an attestation protocol to clearly identify the identity of the TPM and verify the location with the help of the CA. In addition, the attestation protocol ensures that nobody has tampered with the software components running on the machine, i.e., BIOS, bootloader, hypervisor etc.

In the following, we first describe the setting we assume for our protocol for TPM-based Location Assurance before we describe our protocol in detail.

3.1 Setting

Figure 1 shows the setup we assume for the TPM-based location assurance. The virtual machine VM_1 of a user runs on a machine of a cloud operator CO at some specific geographic location. The cloud operator provides a machine with

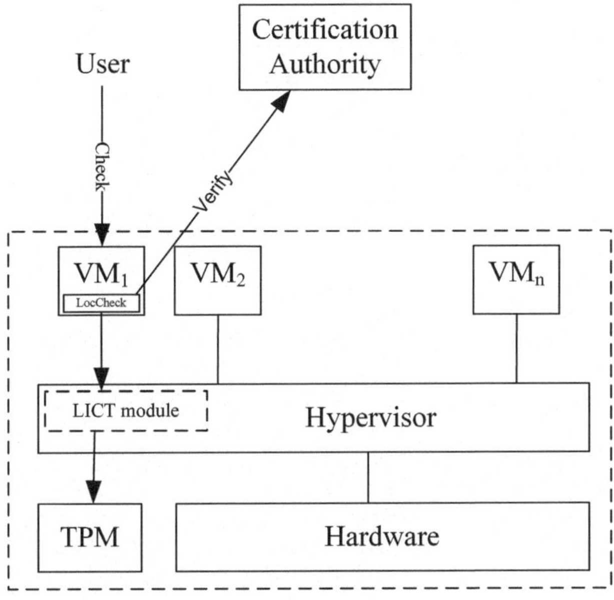

Fig. 1. Setup

a TPM. On top of the hardware runs the hypervisor which executes the VMs of the different users. The TPM of the machine can be accessed by all VMs running on this machine via a `LICT` module which provides functionalities for Location verification and Integrity Check as well as a TPM driver. The module is part of the hypervisor and manages the access of the different users to the TPM for location assurance and implements the necessary parts of an IMA (cf. Section 2) to ensure that the hypervisor and the `LICT` module is not manipulated. A `LocCheck` client running within the VM of a user uses the `LICT` module to get the unique identity of the TPM. The identity of the TPM is registered with the location of the physical machine at a trusted CA. By contacting the CA, the location of the TPM and the machine can be verified. We assume that the location of the machine is verified during some anyway performed regular system inspection by some trusted service provider (or the CA itself). For example, this could be part of an anyway performed security audit according to ISO/IEC 27001 which is repeated in regular intervals. For the sake of simplicity, we assume that the CA also maintains a database with fingerprints of trustworthy software components which is required by the IMA. This could also be realized by another third party. Furthermore, we assume that the communication between user, cloud operator, and CA is secured using mechanisms such as IPsec or TLS.

3.2 Protocol

The protocol is divided into two phases: *Initialization* and *Verification Phase.* The Initialization Phase is usually performed only once when a cloud operator sets up

Table 1. Protocol Steps: Initialization Phase

1a.	`LICT` → TPM:	`TPM_TakeOwnership`
1b.	`LICT` → TPM:	`TPM_MakeIdentity`
1c.	TPM	Generate (AIK_{priv}, AIK_{pub})
1d.	TPM	$AR = AIK_{pub}, EC, PC, CC$
1d.	TPM	$RSA\_Sign(AR \mid EK_{priv}) = Sig$
2.	`LICT` → CA:	AR, Sig
3a.	CA	Verify Credentials
3b.	CA	Verify $RSA\_Verify(Sig \mid EK_{pub}) = AR$
3c.	CA	Generate AC
3d.	CA	Generate K
3e.	CA	$RSA\_Enc(K \mid EK_{pub})$
3f.	CA	$Sym\_Enc(AC \mid K)$
4.	CA → `LICT`:	$RSA(K \mid EK_{pub}), Enc(AC \mid K)$
5a.	`LICT` → TPM:	`TPM_ActivateIdentity`
5b.	TPM	Decrypt K
5c.	TPM	Decrypt AC
6a.	`LICT` → TPM:	`TPM_Quote`$(h_{AIK}, pass_{AIK}, loc_M, S_{PCR})$
6b.	TPM	$RSA\_Sign(loc_M, S_{PCR} \mid AIK_{priv}) = SigL$
6c.	`LICT` → CA:	loc_M, PCR[S_{PCR}], SML, $SigL$
7a.	CA	Verify $SigL$
7b.	CA	Verify platform integrity
7c.	CA	Verify loc_M
7d.	CA	Mark loc_M of M as verified

a new machine to register the machine (with the integrated TPM) and location at the CA. We adapted the AIK Credential Generation process for this purpose. During the Initialization Phase, the CA also verifies the trustworthiness of the machine by means of an attestation protocol. After the CA has verified that the alleged location of the machine is correct and that the system is trustworthy, users of the machine can also verify the location by executing the Verification Phase of the protocol.

Initialization Phase. When a new machine M is set up by a cloud operator CO, the `LICT` module initiates the following protocol steps (cf. Table 1).

First, the `TPM_TakeOwnership` command is executed to initialize the TPM and the owner password *pass* to access the TPM is set and stored in the `LICT` module. Next, the `TPM_MakeIdentity` command is invoked to cause the TPM to generate an AIK key pair (AIK_{priv}, AIK_{pub}). A key handle h_{AIK} is associated with this RSA key pair, since multiple AIK pairs can be generated on a TPM. When generating the keys another password $pass_{AIK}$ is set, which is required to use AIK_{priv}.

An AIK-Request AR containing the AIK public key AIK_{pub}, Endorsement Credential EC, Platform Credential PC, and Conformance Credential CC is generated and signed by the TPM using EK_{priv}. The TPM sends this signature Sig and AR to the `LICT` module which forwards them to the CA. Since the endorsement credential contains the public endorsement key EK_{pub}, the AIK key pair is exclusively bound to the TPM. The LICT module stores *pass*, h_{AIK}, $pass_{AIK}$, AIK_{pub}, and all credentials for future use.

After receiving this message, the CA verifies the validity of the credentials (cf. Section 2) and of the signature Sig. If both verifications pass, the CA generates an AIK Credential AC, i.e., AIK_{pub} is signed with the private key of the CA. AC is encrypted with a symmetric encryption scheme Sym_Enc using a generated session key K. Note that TPMs use symmetric encryption and decryption only internally for purposes such as session key encryption or encryption of externally stored data. The session key K itself is RSA-encrypted with EK_{pub} and sent together with AC to the LICT module.

The LICT module calls the TPM_ActivateIdentity command to decrypt the session key K using EK_{priv}. Thus, this operation ensures that only the TPM is able to decrypt AC in the next step.

Now the LICT module starts the registration of the claimed location loc_M of the machine M at the CA. As stated in the setting, we combine this location registration process with a check of the platform integrity and an attestation to enable the CA to verify that nobody has tampered with the machine M, i.e., BIOS, Bootloader, Hypervisor, and LICT module are trustworthy (cf. Section 2). The TPM is requested to sign the location loc_M and the set of PCR values S_{PCR} used for measurements by the IMA during the boot process using the just generated AIK_{priv} by invoking the TPM_Quote command. The key handle h_{AIK} is used as parameter to point to the correct AIK and the password $pass_{AIK}$ to get permission to use the key. The message to the CA contains the location loc_M, the set of PCR values PCR[S_{PCR}], the Stored Measurement Log *SML*, and the signature $SigL$.

When the CA receives this message, it first verifies the validity of the signature using AIK_{pub}. Next, the SML is validated against the PCR values and the individual measurements are validated using the fingerprint database to verify that the platform is trustworthy. After the location is verified by some external party, e.g., during an anyway performed audit, the CA marks this machine (with its TPM) and its location as verified.

After the initialization phase, the AIK key pair of the TPM installed in CO's machine is successfully registered at the CA with its current location and can be used in the subsequent verification phase.

Verification Phase. The protocol steps of the Verification Phase are shown in Table 2.

When a user U wants to verify that his virtual machine VM_1 (cf. Fig. 1) is indeed running on a machine of the cloud operator CO at the alleged location and is still trustworthy, he chooses randomly several memory areas $MA_1, \dots, MA_n$ of its virtual resource VM_1 (cf. Fig. 2) and sends a pointer MA to their locations as input to initialize the LocCheck client. During every verification, different memory areas $MA_1, ..., MA_n$ are chosen. Including these memory locations in the verification process, renders relay attacks pointless (cf. Section 4).

Table 2. Protocol Steps: Verification Phase

0. User → `LocCheck`:	Memory areas MA
1a. `LocCheck` → `LICT`:	Request AIK
1b. `LICT` → `LocCheck`:	AIK_{pub}
1c. `LocCheck`	Generate $hash(MA)$
1d. `LocCheck` → CA:	$hash(MA)$, AIK_{pub}
2a. CA	Select S_{PCR}
2b. CA → `LocCheck`	S_{PCR}
2c. `LocCheck` → `LICT`	MA, S_{PCR}
3a. `LICT`	Generate $hash(MA)$
3a. `LICT` → TPM:	`TPM_Quote`$(h_{AIK}, pass_{AIK}, hash(MA), S_{PCR})$
3b. TPM	$RSA\_Sign(hash(MA), S_{PCR} \mid AIK_{priv}) = SigMA$
3c. TPM → `LICT`	PCR[S_{PCR}], $SigMA$
4a. `LICT` → `LocCheck`	PCR[S_{PCR}], SML, $SigMA$
4b. `LocCheck` → CA:	PCR[S_{PCR}], SML, $SigMA$
5a. CA	Verify $SigMA$
5b. CA	Verify platform integrity
5c. CA	Verify loc_M marked as verified
5d. CA	Verify $hash(MA)$
6a. CA → `LocCheck`	Location loc_M confirmed
6b. `LocCheck` → User	Location loc_M confirmed

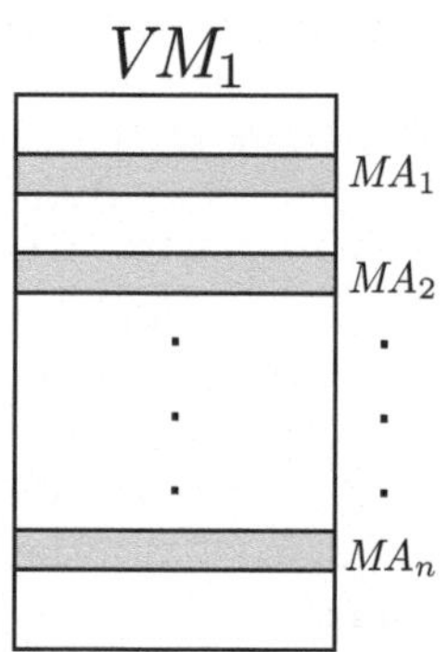

Fig. 2. Memory Areas included in the verification

Next, the `LocCheck` client requests the public AIK AIK_{pub} of the TPM from the `LICT` module and sends the public AIK and the hash over the memory areas $hash(MA_1, \ldots, MA_n)$ to the CA with the request to confirm the location. The public AIK is used as the identifier of the TPM.

When the CA receives AIK_{pub}, it looks in its database which PCR values are required to attest the platform integrity of the machine M and sends the set of identifiers of the PCRs S_{PCR} back to the `LocCheck` client. The `LocCheck` client sends S_{PCR} and the pointer to the memory areas MA to the `LICT` module.

The LICT module builds the hash value $hash(MA) = hash(MA_1, \ldots, MA_n)$ over the memory areas denoted by MA and uses the TPM_Quote command to request the TPM to sign $hash(MA)$ and the PCR values listed in S_{PCR} with AIK_{priv}. Again, the key handle h_{AIK} is used as parameter to point to the correct AIK and the password $pass_{AIK}$ to get permission to use the key. The TPM sends the signature $SigMA$ over $hash(MA)$ and the PCR values as well as the PCR values themselves PCR[S_{PCR}] to the LICT module.

Next, the LICT module sends this data together with the *SML* to the LocCheck client which directly forwards this message to the CA.

The CA verifies the validity of the signature, the platform integrity, that the location loc_M is marked as verified, and that hash of the memory areas calculated by LocCheck and the signed one of LICT are the same. If all verifications pass, the CA uses its own private key to sign a confirmation message for the stated location loc_M and sends it to the LocCheck client which forwards this message to the User. Finally, the User uses the public key of the CA to verify the signature of the confirmation message and verifies that the location loc_M is indeed the location he requested.

4 Security Discussion

In this section, we discuss the security of our protocol. We assume a cloud operator behaves adversarial and tries to move virtual resources to another location which might be cheaper and helps him saving costs.

For our protocol, we assume that the locations of the TPMs are verified and that they are indeed at their alleged location stored at the CA. Furthermore, we assume that the adversary can neither circumvent the tamper-protection mechanisms of the TPM to read out cryptographic keys nor break any cryptographic mechanisms, e.g., forge signatures without knowing the key or inverting hash functions.

Basically, there exist two ways how the adversary could attack our protocol: he can either try to forge the location of a machine or perform a relay attack.

In the first case, the adversary tries to forge the location of a machine to be compliant with the user's policy. Since the result of the initialization phase is verified during an audit, he can only attack during the verification phase. To pass the verifications of the CA in steps 5a to 5d (cf. Table 2) and to generate $SigMA$, direct access to AIK_{priv}, which is securely stored in the TPM, is required. The adversary would need to circumvent the tamper-protection mechanisms of the TPM, to get access to AIK_{priv} which is a contradiction to our above stated assumption. Alternatively, the adversary could remove the (motherboard with the) TPM from the machine and install it in another machine at another location. However, this would be detected at the latest during the next audit. Thus, the audit should be performed in regular intervals to make this attack uneconomical for the adversary since he needs to regularly uninstall, ship, and reinstall (motherboards with) TPMs.

In the latter case, the adversary could use two machines to perform a relay attack. Machine M_A is located at a correct location according to the user's policy and is not modified and operates correctly. The adversarial cloud operator has its own virtual resource VM_x running on this machine. In addition, he sets up another machine M_B at a location not compliant to the user's policy. On M_B, the hypervisor and the $\mathtt{LICT_B}$ module are modified to forward the protocol requests to a modified $\mathtt{LocCheck_x}$ client running in VM_x on M_A. Using this construction, the adversary could move the user's VM_1 from M_A to M_B and relay all protocol messages and the verification would still pass. To address this issue, we adapted the idea of software-based attestation [9] in our protocol by extending the verification over the virtual resource VM_1. The TPM of a machine generates in steps 3a to 3c (cf. Table 2) the signature SigMA over the hash of the memory regions $MA_1, \ldots, MA_n$ of the respective virtual machine. To pass this verification on machine M_A, the virtual machine VM_x of the adversary must be identical to the user's virtual machine VM_1 running on M_B. Thus, a relay attack is pointless for an adversary, since he always needs to maintain a copy of VM_1 at M_A and in addition requires additional resources at machine M_B.

On general problem of attestation, which is not specific to our solution, is Time-of-check Time-of-use (TOCTOU). This means that between the verification and the use of a machine, the state of the machine could be changed by the adversary. Thus, we propose that the verification process is regularly repeated.

5 Related Work

There exist several regulations on the placement and the access to digital data. The European data protection law [1] restricts the placement of data to juristic borders. Both, a Gartner report on assessing the security of cloud infrastructures [15] and an ENISA report on general risks in cloud computing [12], highlight the importance of data location and its jurisdiction in cloud computing. On the other hand the US Patriot Act [13] gives US governmental institutions the right to access digital data if it is located in the US or it is located at a data center that belongs to a US company.

Policy enforcement in cloud computing is addressed by the cloud audit group [3]. The cloud audit community works on automation of audit, assertion, assessment, and assurance in cloud computing. Iskander et al. [16] introduces mechanisms on the enforcement of authentication policies. The same does Vimercati et al. [24] by selective resource sharing enforced by encryption. Basescu et al. [8] defines a security management framework for specifying and enforcing security policies. However, none of the work give means for checking if the security policies are fulfilled. The work in this paper concentrates on the assurance of the location of a virtual resource, which can be part of a security policy.

Another approach to restrict access to data in the cloud is homomorphic encryption [14]. Homomorphic encryption allows to process encrypted data. By applying this technique to cloud computing the confidentiality of processed data can be guaranteed. At the time of writing homomorphic encryption only works for a restricted set of operations and is not applicable to cloud computing.

A similar approach is secure multiparty computation (SMC) [21,25]. In SMC the data to be processed is distributed over different cloud operators and processed cooperatively so that none of the operators have all information to reveal the original data. Because of efficiency reasons and because it does not support all operations, SMC is not applicable to cloud computing.

Another geolocation technique used in the internet is the use of network coordinate systems [11,10,17]. By measuring the round trip times of ping messages sent from different known locations in the internet to one destination, network coordinate systems estimate the geoposition of a device. For using this technique no trust in the hypervisor is needed because a VM can directly be accessed. However, Ries et al. [19] show that this approach works in general but gives a high error rate which makes it useless for reliably checking the geoposition of virtual resources in cloud computing.

Work on how to use TPMs in cloud computing environments already exist [22] but concentrates only on using the TPM for encryption.

6 Conclusion

Cloud computing and cloud networking is widely used and users might want to define security policies how their data is handled. One important aspect is the location where data is stored and processed, e.g., only in western Europe and not in the US or other countries. This is of particular interest for some companies because of regulations such as the US patriot act. In this paper, we propose a mechanism based on Trusted Platform Modules and a trusted third party to enable users to verify the actual location of their virtual resources and the trustworthiness of the machine of the cloud operator. An attestation protocol is used to verify the platform configuration of the machine of the cloud operator and to uniquely identify the TPM of the machine. The actual location of the TPM and data to attest the platform integrity of machines of cloud operators are stored at a trusted third party which is contacted during the attestation. Our security discussion shows that our approach provides an adequate level of security. In contrast to previously proposed approaches, our approach enables a reliable location verification, however, with the additional costs for a TPM and the overhead for the location audits.

We are currently working on the implementation of our location assurance mechanism for cloud networking. A standard PC, equipped with a TPM according to the TPM specification 1.2 [23], is used for the machine of the cloud operator running Xen [7] as hypervisor. The `LICT` module is implemented as a Back-End in the *dom0* domain with a native device driver to access the TPM. The corresponding Front-End Device Driver implements the `LocCheck` client in the unprivileged virtual machines (*domU*) of the users. To verify the platform integrity of the machine, we use Trusted GRUB [6] as bootloader and implement the IMA [20] mentioned in Chapter 2. The CA will be implemented on another machine using self signed certificates and the communication will be secured using OpenSSL to set up a TLS tunnel between the machines.

References

1. Directive 2002/58/EC of the European Parliament and of the Council of 12 July 2002 concerning the processing of personal data and the protection of privacy in the electronic communications sector (directive on privacy and electronic communications). Official Journal of the European Union (L201), 0037–0047 (2002)
2. Amazon Virtual Private Cloud (July 2012), http://aws.amazon.com/ec2/
3. CloudAudit: A6 - The Automated Audit, Assertion, Assessment, and Assurance API (July 2012), http://cloudaudit.org
4. Google App Engine (July 2012), https://developers.google.com/appengine/
5. Google Docs (July 2012), http://docs.google.com
6. Trusted GRUB website (July 2012), http://projects.sirrix.com/trac/trustedgrub
7. Xen website (July 2012), http://xen.org/
8. Basescu, C., Carpen-Amarie, A., Leordeanu, C., Costan, A., Antoniu, G.: Managing data access on clouds: A generic framework for enforcing security policies. In: AINA, pp. 459–466. IEEE Computer Society (2011)
9. Castelluccia, C., Francillon, A., Perito, D., Soriente, C.: On the difficulty of software-based attestation of embedded devices. In: Proceedings of the 16th ACM Conference on Computer and Communications Security, CCS 2009, pp. 400–409. ACM (2009)
10. Chen, Y., Xiong, Y., Shi, X., Deng, B., Li, X.: Pharos: A decentralized and hierarchical network coordinate system for internet distance prediction. In: GLOBECOM, pp. 421–426 (2007)
11. Dabek, F., Cox, R., Kaashoek, F., Morris, R.: Vivaldi: A decentralized network coordinate system. In: SIGCOMM, pp. 15–26 (2004)
12. ENISA. Cloud computing security risk assessment. Technical report, European Network and Information Security Agency, ENISA (2009)
13. Fraser, D.: The canadian response to the USA Patriot Act. IEEE Security Privacy 5(5), 66–68 (2007)
14. Gentry, C.: Fully homomorphic encryption using ideal lattices. In: STOC 2009: Proceedings of the 41st Annual ACM Symposium on Theory of Computing, pp. 169–178. ACM, New York (2009)
15. Heiser, J., Nicolett, M.: Assessing the security risks of cloud computing. Technical report, Gartner (2008)
16. Iskander, M.K., Wilkinson, D.W., Lee, A.J., Chrysanthis, P.K.: Enforcing policy and data consistency of cloud transactions. In: Proceedings of the Second International Workshop on Security and Privacy in Cloud Computing, ICDCS-SPCC 2011. IEEE Computer Society, Washington, DC (2011)
17. Ng, T.S.E., Zhang, H.: Towards global network positioning. In: Proceedings of the First ACM SIGCOMM Workshop on Internet Measurement, pp. 25–29 (2001)
18. Peterson, Z.N.J., Gondree, M., Beverly, R.: A position paper on data sovereignty: the importance of geolocating data in the cloud. In: Proceedings of the 3rd USENIX Conference on Hot Topics in Cloud Computing, HotCloud 2011 (2011)
19. Ries, T., Fusenig, V., Vilbois, C., Engel, T.: Verification of data location in cloud networking. In: Proceedings of the First International Workshop on Cloud Service Quality Measurement and Comparison, CSQMC 2011. IEEE Computer Society (2011)
20. Sailer, R., Zhang, X., Jaeger, T., van Doorn, L.: Design and implementation of a tcg-based integrity measurement architecture. In: Proceedings of the 13th Usenix Security Symposium (2004)

21. Shamir, A.: How to share a secret. Commun. ACM 22, 612–613 (1979)
22. Trusted Computing Group. Cloud computing and security - a natural match. Technical report, Trusted Computing Group (2010)
23. Trusted Computing Group. TPM Main Specification (2011)
24. De Capitani di Vimercati, S., Foresti, S., Jajodia, S., Paraboschi, S., Pelosi, G., Samarati, P.: Encryption-based policy enforcement for cloud storage. In: Proceedings of the 2010 IEEE 30th International Conference on Distributed Computing Systems Workshops, ICDCSW 2010, pp. 42–51 (2010)
25. Yao, A.C.: Protocols for secure computations. In: Proceedings of the 23rd Annual Symposium on Foundations of Computer Science, SFCS 1982, pp. 160–164. IEEE Computer Society, Washington, DC (1982)

Tracing Sources of Anonymous Slow Suspicious Activities

Harsha K. Kalutarage, Siraj A. Shaikh, Qin Zhou, and Anne E. James

Digital Security and Forensics (SaFe) Research Group
Department of Computing, Faculty of Engineering and Computing
Coventry University
Coventry, CV1 5FB, UK
{kalutarh,aa8135,cex371,csx118}@coventry.ac.uk

Abstract. Tracing down anonymous slow attackers creates number of challenges in network security. Simply analysing all traffic is not feasible. By aggregating information of large volume of events, it is possible to build a clear set of benchmarks of what should be considered as normal over extended period of time and hence to identify anomalies. This paper provides an anomaly based method for tracing down sources of slow suspicious activities in Cyber space. We present the theoretical account of our approach and experimental results.

1 Introduction

As computer networks scale up in terms of number of nodes and volume of traffic, analysing slow attack activity, deliberately designed to stay beneath the threshold, becomes ever more difficult. Traditional attackers relied more on brute force attacks. However, increasingly nowadays attackers are trying to remain undetected and to steal information over and over again, adopting a much more patient type of structure to compromise a network. An attacker may take days, weeks or months to complete the attack life cycle against the target host. Attacks may blend into the network noise in order to never exceed detection thresholds and to exhaust detection system state. Such persistent attacks are known as slow attacks. For example [3,2] present tools and technique to perform such attacks. Our previous work [17] presents a detection algorithm for such attacks, based on the underlying assumption that attack activity can be attributed to a meaningful specific source. This assumption is not valid for anonymous slow attackers. Identifying the source of such an attack requires tracing the packets back to the source hop by hop. Current approaches for tracing these attacks require the tedious continued attention and cooperation of each intermediate Internet Service Provider (ISP). This is not always easy given the world-wide scope of present day Networks [8].

This paper presents a methodological way to trace anonymous slow activities to their approximate sources by prioritizing evidence acquisition. First, we map paths from victim to all possible networks as a tree. And then each path is profiled in a Bayesian framework [23,15] and highest scored path is selected to

J. Lopez, X. Huang, and R. Sandhu (Eds.): NSS 2013, LNCS 7873, pp. 122–134, 2013.

move towards. Experimental results are promising proposed approach eliminates all but a handful of nodes that could be the source of the suspicious activity.

The paper is organised as follows. Section 2 presents a brief overview of related work. Theoretical account of the underlying methodology is presented in Section 3. A novel tracing algorithm is presented in Section 4. Experimental set-up (including two scenarios), and their outcomes are presented in Sections 5 and 6 respectively. Section 7 concludes the paper.

2 Related Work

Tracing back is one of the most difficult problems in network security. There is a lot of research being conducted in this area (refer to survey papers [4,19]). Deterministic packet marking and Out-of-band approaches are not relevant to this work. Burch and Cheswick control flooding tests network links between routers to approximate the source [8]. Sager and Stone suggest to log packets at key routers and then use data mining techniques to determine the path that the packets traversed [16,25]. The upside of the property is that it can trace an attack long after the attack has completed. As it is obvious, downside is this approach is not scalable. Snoeren et al. propose marking within the router, to reduce the size of packet log and provide confidentiality, hash-based logging is proposed [5]. Savage et al. suggest probabilistically marking packets as they traverse through routers [24]. They propose that the router mark the packet with either the routers IP address or the edges of the path that the packet traversed to reach the router. With router based approaches, the router is charged with maintaining information regarding packets that pass through it. Most of above approaches are focus on DDoS attacks. Since our interest is not on events related to quick attacks, our work differs from all above works.

As Davidoff and Ham claim flow record analysis techniques are statistical in nature, but exceptionally powerful and very useful [13]. Especially, in slow attack environments where full content captures are limited by the amount of disk space and processing power. The purpose of flow record collection is to store a summary of information about the traffic flows across the network, which lets devices to save records for much longer than full packet captures. There are number of open source and commercialised flow record collection and analysed tools [6,12,9,21] at present while some switches (Cisco catalyst), routers and firewalls (current revisions of Cisco) support flow record generation and exportation [13]. A typical flow record of existing tools may include IP addresses, ports & flags, protocols, date, time, and the amount of data transmitted in each flow. It is possible to use suspicious events related to these parameters as inputs to our profiling method, but has not limited to flow records elements only. Any suspicious event in the scene is an important input to our profiling method. For example alerts of multiple login failures or an execution of cmd.exe are also interested and important events to our method. Essentially the profiling technique used in our approach combines all suspicious events in the scene into a single score using a Bayesian technique. This evidence fusion is especially important for scalable solutions. It scales well our approach to very large networks with high throughput. Most of existing flow analysis tools collect, analyse, interpret and present data of above parameters separately without combining them. Hence our approach is certainly different to existing flow record analysis techniques, though our's too is statistical in nature.

Chivers et al. use Bayes formula for combining evidence from multiple sources, to provide a scalable solution to identify suspicious slow insider activities [11,10]. Authors profile all nodes in the target network against the time line, and distinguish between anomaly and normal behaviours by setting a control (base line). Most deviant node from the control is identified as the attacker. Kalutarage et al. similarly motivated, but show that such a decision criteria is not valid for situations where there are more than one attacker in a same subnet with higher variations of node behaviours [17]. Since it can be affected by even dimensions of the drawing canvas, Kalutarage et al. claim standardisation of profile scores should be performed before any comparison. Authors use Z-Scores, instead of row profile scores, together with concept of statistical normality for this task [17,18]. In [17], they use evidence fusion and aggregation (in a Bayesian framework) as the profiling method and have discussed the necessity and possibility to integrate contextual information with the detection. However Chivers et al. themselves identify a need for a different decision criteria other than the maximum score function method they used.

Phillip et al.'s work [7] is a much more similar study to Chivers et al.s work. In [7], users are profiled according to their behaviour and that information is used to identify users who require further investigations. Streilein et al. use multiple neural network classifiers to detect stealthy probes [26]. Evidence accumulation as a means of detecting slow activities has been proposed in [27]. That work differs from us as it uses a counting algorithm and also in its decision criteria. In next section we explain why simple counting approach is not suitable herein.

3 Profiling Method

Profiling plays a key role in our approach. We use a probabilistic approach for this task. Because, such approaches performs well in noisy environments than deterministic approaches. The environment we are working is noisy due to two types of uncertainties (*motivation* and *source*) of each event of interest.

The motivation behind an event is not always easy to judge. Some suspicious events can be appeared as a part of attack signatures as well as could be originated from normal network activities. For example, a major router failure could generate many ICMP unreachable messages; an alert of multiple login failures could result from a forgotten password. An execution of cmd.exe could be a part of malicious attempt or a legitimate as it is frequently used by malicious programs to execute commands while it is also frequently used by legitimate users during their normal day-to-day operations. By just looking at such an event you cannot simply judge its motivation that it is a part of malicious attempt or not. As Davidoff and Ham claim other information (contextual/multivariate) can be used to narrow down the meaning of such an event [13]. For example suspicious port scanning activity may have the following characteristics: a single source address, one or more destination addresses, and target port numbers increasing incrementally. When fingerprinting such traffic, we examine multiple elements and develop a hypothesis for the cause of behaviour on that basis. We use a multivariate approach handling the above uncertainty.

There is no guarantee on publicly visible source of an event is to be the true source. As mentioned in [14], to remain anonymous, the attacker attempts to either disguise the elements that characterize the attack or hide the source of its acts. The localization process becomes evermore difficult when the attacker employs various proxy methods (e.g. Generic port routing, HTTP, Socks, IRC etc) and zombie (e.g. bots) nodes. Manipulation of TCP/IP elements (e.g. IP Spoofing), using relay or random routing (e.g. Tor networks, Crowds, Freenet systems etc) approaches can help an attacker protecting her location. Proliferation of weakly encrypted wireless networks could also help an attacker getting anonymous locations. In nature, some security monitoring parameters (e.g. bandwidth) do not have the source information.

The critical challenge is how to keep information about activities of each node over an extended period of time while acknowledging above uncertainties? As a solution we propose to use an incremental approach in a Bayesian framework which updates normal node profiles dynamically based on changes in behaviour.

3.1 The Bayesian Paradigm

The posterior probability of the hypothesis H_k given that E is given by the well-known formula:

$$p(H_k/E) = \frac{p\,(E/H_k)\,.p(H_k)}{p(E)} \tag{1}$$

In order to fit this formula into our case, let H_k : hypothesis that kth node is an attacker, $E = \{E_1{=}e_1, E_2{=}e_2, E_3{=}e_3, ..., E_m{=}e_m\}$ is the set of all suspicious evidence observed against node k during time t from m different independent observation spaces. Here P(E) is the probability of producing suspicious events by node k, but on its own is difficult to calculate. This can be avoided by using the law of total probability and reformatted (1) as:

$$p(H_k/E) = \frac{p\,(E/H_k)\,.p(H_k)}{\sum\limits_i p(E/H_i).p(H_i)} \tag{2}$$

For independent observations, the joint posterior probability distribution:

$$p(H_k/E) = \frac{\prod\limits_j p(e_j/H_i).p(H_k)}{\sum\limits_i \prod\limits_j p(e_j/H_i).p(H_i)} \tag{3}$$

Once we observed E from node k, to calculate the posterior probability of node k being an attacker $p(H_k/E)$, it is necessary to estimate:

1. the likelihood of the event E given the hypothesis H_i, *i.e.*$p(E/H_i)$ and,
2. the prior probability $p(H_i)$, where $n \geq i > 0$.

Assuming that we know the prior and likelihoods, it is obvious that (3) facilitates to combine evidence from multiple sources to a single value (posterior probability) which describes our belief, during a short observation period, that node k is an attacker given E. Aggregating short period estimations over time helps to accumulate relatively weak evidence for long periods. This accumulated probability term $\sum_t p(H_k/E)$ (t is time) is then divided by number of nodes behind the target node (i.e. n_k - size of the subnet behind node k, if there is one) and, known as profile value hereafter, can be used as a measurement of the level of suspicion for node k at any given time. Schultz et al. claim that profiling suspected insiders provides one of the best ways of reverse engineering an attacker [22]. Although there are some significant differences between the characteristics of insiders and outsiders, profiling can still be used effectively in tracing down anonymous slow attackers at any location in the Network, if the topological information is available. Let:

$$c_{kt} = \frac{\sum_t p(H_k/E)}{n_k} \tag{4}$$

is the cumulative node score of kth node at time t. Then

$$z_{kt} = \frac{c_{kt} - \bar{c_t}}{\sigma_t} \tag{5}$$

is the Z-score of node k at time t. where $\bar{c_t} = \frac{\sum_i c_{it}}{n}$, $\sigma_t = \sqrt{\frac{\sum_i (c_{it} - \bar{c_t})^2}{n-1}}$, and $i = 1, 2, 3, ..., n$.

Calculating standardised node profiles (Z-scores) as shown in (4) and (5) above, instead of node profiles themselves, will resolve the comparison issues discussed in Section 2.

4 Tracing Algorithm

Here we present our algorithm for tracing slow suspicious nodes by prioritising the likely source of evidence. The tracing algorithm has two segments: *tree formation* and *tree traversal.*

4.1 Tree Formation

Tree formation is the process of building an equivalent tree structure for a given attack scenario. Victim node is the starting point. Gateway node to the victim is considered as the root of the tree and all immediate visible nodes (either internal or external) to the root are considered as children of the root. If a given child is a host node in the network then it becomes a leaf of the tree. Else, if it is a gateway, it becomes a parent node of the tree and all immediate visible nodes to that node is attached as its children. This process is continued until the entire topology is covered (see Figure 2).

```
ϑ: Tree;
ω: A node;
τ: Set of all nodes in the given topology;
input  : Topological information together with victim's location
output: Tree structure for the given attack scenario
Initialize the tree ϑ to have the root as the gateway of the victim;
List all nodes into the list τ;
/* attached each node to the tree*/;
tree-construction(ϑ,τ);
foreach node ω in τ do
    if num-of-hops-between(ϑ,ω)==1 then
        insert ω into ϑ;
    end
end
foreach ϑ.child do
    tree-construction(ϑ.child,τ)
end
```

Algorithm 1. Tree formation for a given attack scenario

4.2 Tree Traversal

Once the equivalent tree structure is built, proposed tree traversal algorithm is applied. To traverse a non-empty tree, perform the following operations recursively at each node, starting from the root of the tree, until suspected node is found.

1. Visit the parent node
2. Compute profile scores for all children of the parent (as in section 3.1)
3. Traverse the highest profile scored sub tree (if an attacker node is found, backtrack to the parent)
4. Traverse next highest profile scored sub trees (only sub trees significantly deviate from rest of nodes of same parent)

The algorithm continues working towards a built tree node by node, narrow downing the attack source to one network and then to a node. At this point we can run more standard trace back methods by contacting the entity which controls that network, if it is beyond our control.

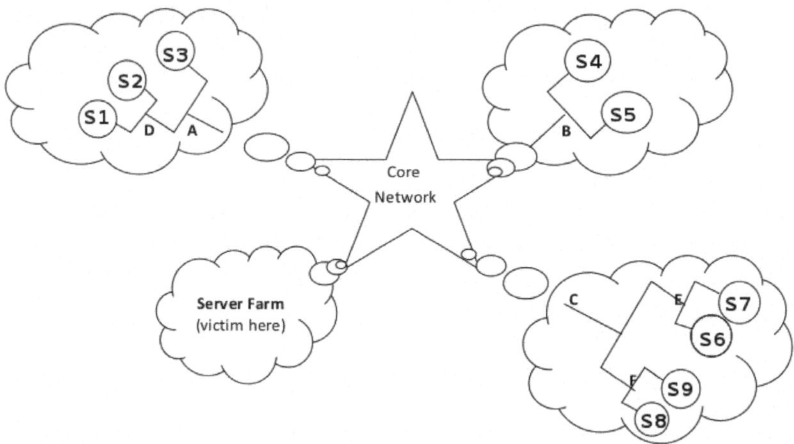

Fig. 1. Network topology used for the experiment. For the particular scenario presented in this paper, subnet sizes are: S1(25), S2(25), S3(50), S4(25), S5(15), S6(25), S7(25), S8(5), S9(5), Server farm(10).

```
input  : A Tree constructed for anonymous slow attack scenario
output: A node where attacker is located
proposed-traverse(ϑ);
while not found do
    visit node ω;
    if node ω is a leaf then
        return;
    else
        profile all children of node;
        proposed-traverse(node.top_scored_child);
        proposed-traverse(node.next_scored_child);
    end
end
```

Algorithm 2. Tree traversal (pointer representation)

5 Experiment

To test the proposed approach, we have formulated number of scenarios and have conducted series of experiments. Figure 1 presents the network topology used for our experiments. Its equivalent tree structure is presented in figure 2.

5.1 Scenario

Suppose that security staff have noticed someone's suspicious activity on a node in the server farm (see Figure 1) for sometime. Though they have a packet

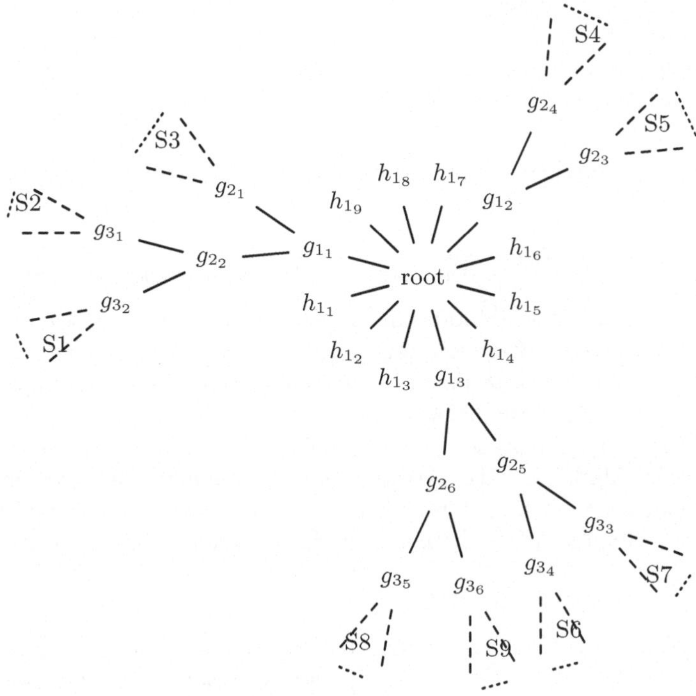

Fig. 2. Tree structure. *root* is the victim's gateway, g_{i_j} - a gateway node, h_{i_j} - a host node, i-level of the tree, j- a node number. Dashed rectangles represent a collection of leaves relevant to hosts in each subnet.

capture of the activity, they can't figure out what's going on, whether those events are a result of simple user mistakes or a malicious attempt. Origin of packets seems to be fake and the time gap between two consecutive events of that particular activity seems to be significantly high.

5.2 Implementation

We implemented the above scenario in a simulated environment and run the proposed approach until the attacker is found. ns3 [20] was used to build above topology and to generate the traffic patterns of interest. Poison arrival model was assumed. Inter arrival time gap between two consecutive events was modelled as an exponential. Each simulation was run for a reasonable time period to ensure that enough traffic was generated (over one million events). Two cases were considered: single and multiple attackers. In single attacker case, an attacker was located at a node in subnet S6. And in multiple attackers case, three attackers were located one in each in three different subnets S6, S5 and S3.

Attacker Modelling. If λ_s, λ_n are mean rates of generating suspicious events by suspicion and normal nodes respectively, we ensured maintaining $\lambda_s = (\lambda_n \pm$

$3\sqrt{\lambda_n}$) and $\lambda_n(\leq 0.1)$ sufficiently smaller for all our experiments to characterise slow suspicious activities which aim at staying beneath the threshold and hiding behind the background noise. $\sqrt{\lambda_n}$ is the standard deviation of rates of suspicious events generated by normal nodes.

Parameter Estimation. Prior probabilities and Likelihoods are assigned as follows.

$$p(H_m) = p(H_n) = \frac{1}{Number\, of\, nodes\, in\, the\, target\, network} \tag{6}$$

Equation (6) assumes that all nodes in the scene have a same prior belief (equally likely) to be subverted. However, this is not the case in many situations. One node may have a higher prior belief of suspicion than another. A node attached to a Public Zone (PZ) in the network may have a higher chance to be subverted than a node in a Special Access Zone (SAZ) (refer to Network Security Zones Implementation Model in [1]). We followed the equally likely assumption for the single attacker case. But, for multiple attacker case, we assumed there is a slightly higher chance (55%) sitting back the attacker at a node outside to the server-farm.

$$p(e_j/H_m) = p(e_j/H_n) = k \tag{7}$$

for all j, m, n and m $\neq$ n. (7) explains the likelihood of producing event e_j by any node, if it was subverted. For the purpose of demonstration, we assigned arbitrary values ($\leq$1) for k for the certain types of events we produced in the simulation. However it can be estimated as follows. If e_j is an event such as UDP scan or land attack which cannot be expected from a non-subverted node, then k can be assigned to one. However, k cannot always be one, as described in section 2 there are some suspicious events (e.g. an alert of multiple login failures) can be a part of attack signatures as well as could be originated from normal network activities. The question is how to estimate $p(e_j/H_m)$, i.e. the true positives ratio, if e_j becomes such an observation? One possible answer would be using IDS evaluation datasets such as ISCX 2012 or DARPA as corpus and using similar techniques used in the natural language processing domain [17]. Chivers et al. claim that, in some cases, the historical rate of occurrences of certain attacks is known and can be used to estimate the likelihood that certain events derive from such attacks or it may be sufficient to quantify these frequencies, in a similar way to estimating risk likelihoods, to an accuracy of an order of magnitude. As Davidoff and Ham claim the biggest challenge for anyone who analyses network traffic is the absence of large publicly available data sets for research and comparison. However according to them, within an organization, it is entirely possible to empirically analyse day-to-day traffic and build statistical models of normal behaviour.

6 Results

Figures 3 and 4 present Z-score graphs created at each step in the process of tracing suspicious node(s). Step 1 graph in Figure 3 is created at the root of the

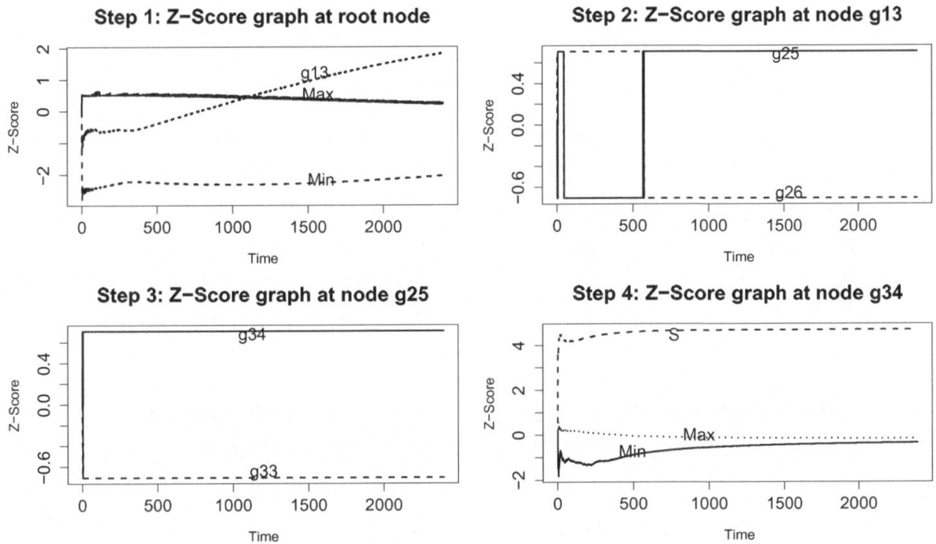

Fig. 3. Z-Score graphs at each node until the attacker is found for one attacker case

derived tree. Min and Max represent the minimum and maximum Z-scores of all visible nodes (11 in total, except g_{1_3}) to the root at each time point. As step 1 suggested moving towards g_{1_3}, step 2 graph was created at node g_{1_3}, and so on. Finally search is narrow downing to the subnet S6. Step 4 graph is created at S6's gateway node g_{3_4}. In that graph, S represents the Z-scores corresponded to the true attacker we located in that subnet. Min and Max represent the minimum and maximum Z-scores of all other nodes in subnet S6. A similar manner should be followed in interpreting graphs in Figure 4.

One of interesting features of above graphs: if the subnet size is sufficiently large (≥ 30), they follows the characteristics of statistical normality clearly (see step 4 in Figure 3 and steps 3,6,8 in Figure 4). A node lies outside to the ± 3 in the Z-score graph can be considered as an outlier from the majority (normality). For very small size subnets, it is possible to see a significant deviation of attacker node from the normal nodes though its value does not go beyond ± 3, and hence identifying the attacker or finding directions to her location is possible.

Proposed approach is independent from the subnet size. Increasing (or decreasing) the subnet sizes, but keeping the same topological structure, does not change the number of steps required in tracing the suspicious node. Table 1 presents travel sequences for tracing single and multiple attackers. In multiple attackers case, once an attacker is found, tracing algorithm should be back tracked to its immediate parent node and should proceed with next highest Z-scored sub tree (if it deviates significantly from the majority), to find other suspicious nodes. Step 1 of Figure 4 depicts such a situation. After step 3 and 6, algorithm back tracks to step 1.

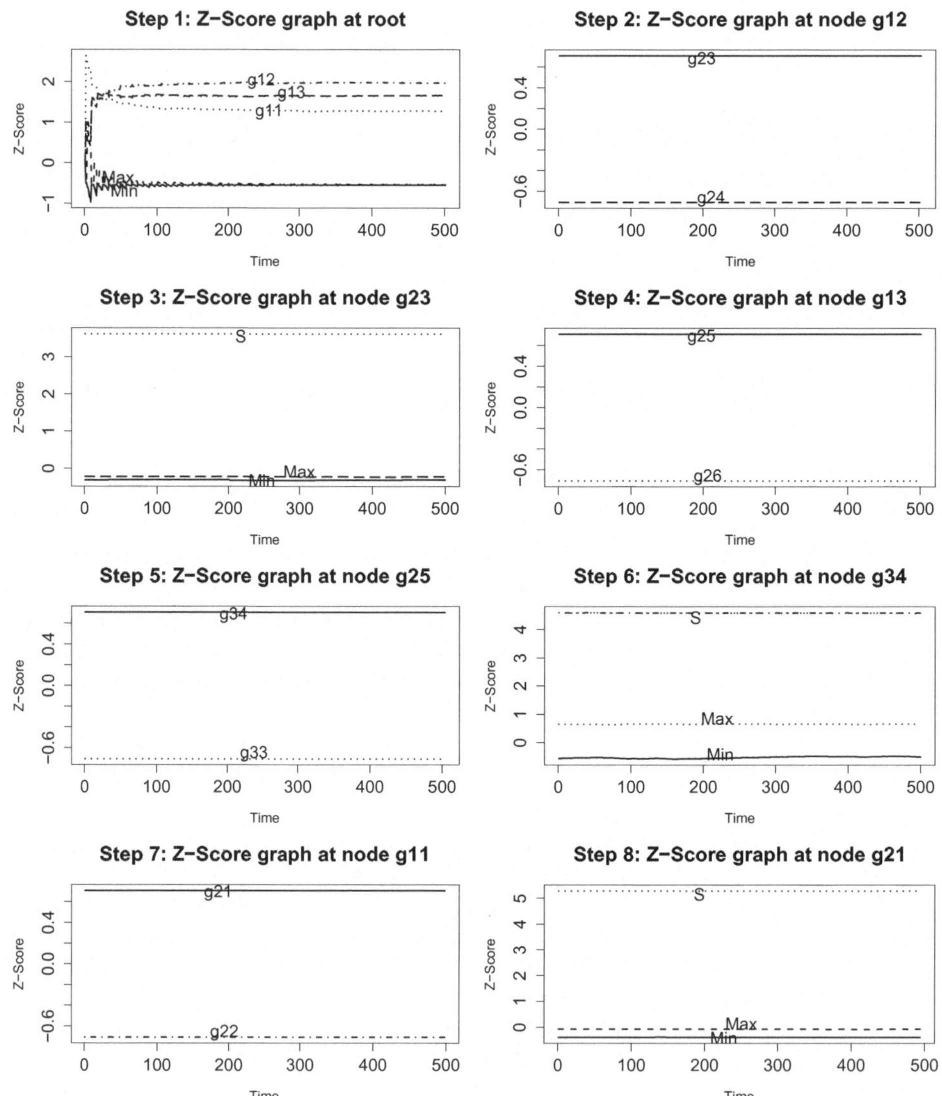

Fig. 4. Z-Score graphs at each node until the attacker is found for multiple attackers case

Table 1. Traversal sequences in tracing attackers

Scenario	Travel sequence (until all attackers are found)
Single attacker: Attacker is at a node in subnet S6	root, g_{1_3}, g_{2_5}, g_{3_4}
Multiple attackers: Attackers are at a node in subnets S3, S5 and S6	root, g_{1_2}, g_{2_3}, root, g_{1_3}, g_{2_5}, g_{3_4},root, g_{1_1}, g_{2_1}

7 Conclusion

Proposed approach changes its traversal sequence according to the suspicious traffic. As a result, suspicious node comes forward in the sequence and probability of trapping it early becomes high. Proposed approach assumes that attacker is not moving to other networks as a part of launching the attack. However attributing collusion activities still remain unsolved. We acknowledge that use of sophisticated attack activities such as use of bot-nets, throwaway systems and distributed sources makes it very difficult to attribute slow attacks. Of further interest is to determine the target of such activity. In future we will investigate methods to profile such nodes, where we adapt our profiling algorithm to profile target nodes for possible slow and suspicious activities, as a defensive mechanism. The underlying principle remains the same: we trade in state for computation.

References

1. Baseline Security Requirements for Network Security Zones in the Government of Canada (June 2007), http://www.cse-cst.gc.ca/its-sti/publications/itsg-csti/itsg22-eng.html#a42
2. Defend your network from slow scanning (March 2013), http://www.techrepublic.com/blog/security/defend-your-network-from-slow-scanning/361
3. Slowloris http dos (March 2013), http://ha.ckers.org/slowloris/
4. John, A., Sivakumar, T.: DDoS: Survey of Traceback Methods. International Journal of Recent Trends in Engineering 1(2) (May 2009)
5. Snoeren, A.C., Partridge, C., Sanchez, L.A., Jones, C.E., Tchakountio, F., Schwartz, B., Kent, S.T., Strayer, W.T.: Single-packet ip traceback. IEEE/ACM Trans. Netw. (2002)
6. Argus: Argus, the network audit record generation and utilization system (December 2012), http://www.qosient.com/argus/
7. Bradford, P.G., Brown, M., Self, B., Perdue, J.: Towards proactive computer system forensics. In: International Conference on Information Technology: Coding and Computing. IEEE Computer Society (2004)
8. Burch, H., Cheswick, B.: Tracing Anonymous Packets to Their Approximate Source. In: Proc. 2000 of USENIX LISA Conference (2000)
9. CERT Network Situational Awareness Team, Silk, the system for internet-level knowledge (December 2012), http://tools.netsa.cert.org/silk

10. Chivers, H., Clark, J.A., Nobles, P., Shaikh, S.A., Chen, H.: Knowing who to watch: Identifying attackers whose actions are hidden within false alarms and background noise. Information Systems Frontiers 15(1), 17–34 (2013)
11. Chivers, H., Nobles, P., Shaikh, S.A., Clark, J., Chen, H.: Accumulating evidence of insider attacks. In: MIST 2009 (In conjunction with IFIPTM 2009) CEUR Workshop Proceedings (2009)
12. Miller, D.: Softflowd, flow-based network traffic analyser (December 2012), http://www.mindrot.org/projects/softflowd/
13. Davidoff, S., Ham, J.: Network Forensics: Tracking Hackers through Cyberspace. Prentice Hall (2012)
14. de Tangil Rotaeche, G.S., Palomar, E., Garnacho, A.R., Álvarez, B.R.: Anonymity in the service of attackers. In: UPGRADE 2010, pp. 27–30 (2010)
15. Fienberg, S.E., Kadane, J.B.: The presentation of bayesian statistical analysis in legal proceedings. The Statistician 32, 88–98 (1983)
16. Sager, G.: Security fun with ocxmon and cflowd. In: Internet 2 Working Group (1998)
17. Kalutarage, H.K., Shaikh, S.A., Zhou, Q., James, A.E.: Sensing for suspicion at scale: A bayesian approach for cyber conflict attribution and reasoning. In: 4th International Conference on Cyber Conflict (CYCON 2012), pp. 1–19 (2012)
18. Kalutarage, H.K., Shaikh, S.A., Zhou, Q., James, A.E.: How do we effectively monitor for slow suspicious activities? In: Proceedings of the International Symposium on Engineering Secure Software and Systems (ESSoS-DS 2013) CEUR Workshop Proceedings (2013), http://ceur-ws.org/Vol-965/paper06-essos2013.pdf
19. Mitropoulos, S.: Network forensics: towards a classification of traceback mechanisms. In: Workshop of the 1st International Conference on Security and Privacy for Emerging Areas in Communication Networks (2005)
20. NS3 Development Team, Ns3 discrete-event network simulator for internet systems (2011), http://www.nsnam.org/
21. ProQueSys, Flowtraq, for effective monitoring, security, and forensics in a network environment (December 2012), http://www.flowtraq.com/corporate/product/flowtraq
22. Schultz, E.E., Shumway, R.: Incident response: A strategic guide for system and network security breaches Indianapolis. New Riders (2001)
23. Smith, A.F.M.: Present position and potential developments: Some personal views bayesian statistics. Journal of the Royal Statistical Society 147(2), 245–259 (1984)
24. Stefan, S., David, W., Anna, K., Tom, A.: Network support for ip traceback. IEEE/ACM Transactions on Networking 9(3), 226–237 (2001)
25. Stone, R.: CenterTrack: An IP overlay network for tracking DoS floods. In: USENIX Security Symposium (2000)
26. Streilein, W.W., Cunningham, R.K., Webster, S.E.: Improved detection of low profile probe and novel denial of service attacks. In: Workshop on Statistical and Machine Learning Techniques in Computer Intrusion Detection (2002)
27. Heberlein, T.: Tactical operations and strategic intelligence: Sensor purpose and placement. Net Squared Inc., Tech. Rep. TR-2002-04.02 (2002)

Static Analysis for Regular Expression Denial-of-Service Attacks

James Kirrage, Asiri Rathnayake, and Hayo Thielecke

University of Birmingham, UK

Abstract. Regular expressions are a concise yet expressive language for expressing patterns. For instance, in networked software, they are used for input validation and intrusion detection. Yet some widely deployed regular expression matchers based on backtracking are themselves vulnerable to denial-of-service attacks, since their runtime can be exponential for certain input strings. This paper presents a static analysis for detecting such vulnerable regular expressions. The running time of the analysis compares favourably with tools based on fuzzing, that is, randomly generating inputs and measuring how long matching them takes. Unlike fuzzers, the analysis pinpoints the source of the vulnerability and generates possible malicious inputs for programmers to use in security testing. Moreover, the analysis has a firm theoretical foundation in abstract machines. Testing the analysis on two large repositories of regular expressions shows that the analysis is able to find significant numbers of vulnerable regular expressions in a matter of seconds.

1 Introduction

Regular expression matching is a ubiquitous technique for reading and validating input, particularly in web software. While pattern matchers are among the standard techniques for defending against malicious input, they are themselves vulnerable. The root cause of the vulnerability is that widely deployed regular expression matchers, like the one in the Java libraries, are based on *backtracking* algorithms, rather than the construction of a Deterministic Finite Automaton (DFA), as used for lexers in compiler construction [13,2]. One reason for relying on backtracking rather than a DFA construction is to support a more expressive pattern specification language commonly referred to as "regexes". Constructs such as back-references supported by such regex languages go beyond regular and even context-free languages and are known to be computationally expensive [1]. However, even if restricted to purely regular constructs, backtracking matchers may have a running time that is exponential in the size of the input [6], potentially causing a regular expression denial-of-service (ReDoS) attack [19]. It is this potentially exponential runtime on pure regular expressions (without backreferences) that we are concerned about in this paper. Part of our motivation is that, for purely regular expressions, the attack could be defended against by avoiding backtracking matchers and using more efficient techniques [7,26] instead.

J. Lopez, X. Huang, and R. Sandhu (Eds.): NSS 2013, LNCS 7873, pp. 135–148, 2013.

For a minimalistic example [6], consider matching the regular expression `a**` against the input string `a`... `a b`, with n repetitions of `a`. A backtracking matcher takes an exponential time [6] in n when trying to find a match; all matching attempts fail in the end due to the trailing `b`. For such vulnerable regular expressions, an attacker can craft an input of moderate size which causes the matcher to take so long that for all practical purposes the matcher fails to terminate, leading to a denial-of-service attack. Here we assume that the regular expression itself cannot be manipulated by the attacker but that it is matched against a string that is user-malleable.

While the regular expression `a**` as above is contrived, one of the questions we set out to answer is how prevalent such vulnerable expressions are in the real world. As finding vulnerabilities manually in code is time consuming and error-prone, there is growing interest in automated tools for static analysis for security [14,5], motivating us to design an analysis for ReDoS.

Educating and warning programmers is crucial to defending against attacks on software. The standard coverage of regular expressions in the computer science curriculum, covering DFAs in courses on computability [13] or compiler construction [2], is not necessarily sufficient to raise awareness about the possibility of ReDoS. Our analysis constructs a series of attack strings, so that developers can confirm the exponential runtime for themselves.

This paper makes the following contributions:

1. We present an efficient static analysis for DoS on pure regular expressions.
2. The design of the tool has a firm theoretical foundation based on abstract machines [20] and derivatives [4] for regular expressions.
3. We report finding vulnerable regular expressions in the wild.

In Section 2, we describe backtracking regular expression matchers as abstract machines, so that we have a precise model of what it means for a matching attempt to take an exponential number of steps. We build on the abstract machine in designing our static analysis in Section 3, which we have implemented in OCaml as described in Section 4. Experimental results in testing the analysis on two large corpora of regular expressions are reported in Section 5. Finally, Section 6 concludes with a discussion of related work and directions of further research. The code of the tool and data sets are available at this URL:
`http://www.cs.bham.ac.uk/~hxt/research/rxxr.shtml`

2 Regular Expression Matching by Backtracking

This and the next section present the theoretical basis for our analysis. Readers primarily interested in the results may wish to skim them.

We start with the following minimal syntax for regular expressions:

$e ::= \varepsilon$	Empty expression
$\mathtt{a}$	Constant, where a is an input symbol
$e_1 \cdot e_2$	Concatenation
$e_1 \mid e_2$	Alternation
e^*	Kleene star

The $\cdot$ in concatenation $e_1 \cdot e_2$ is usually omitted, except when it is useful for emphasis, as in a syntax tree. Following the usual parser construction methods [2], we can define a parser which is capable of transforming (parsing) a given regular expression into an AST (abstract syntax tree) which complies with the above grammar. As an example, the AST constructed by such a parser for the regular expression $(a \mid b)^*c$ can be visualized in the following manner:

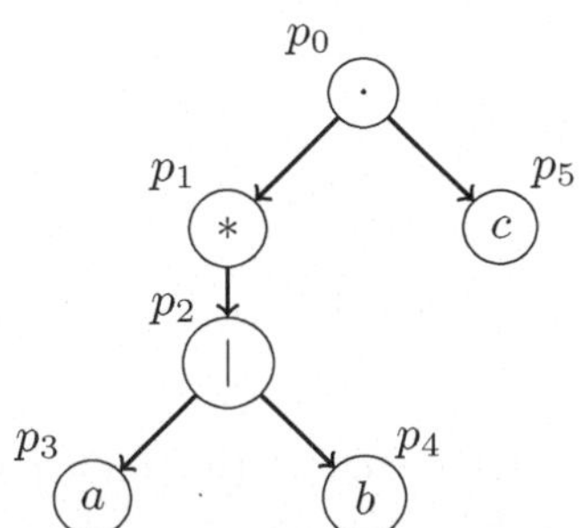

p	$\pi(p)$
p_0	$p_1 \cdot p_5$
p_1	${p_2}^*$
p_2	$p_3 \mid p_4$
p_3	a
p_4	b
p_5	c

Notice that we have employed a pointer notation to illustrate the AST structure; this is quite natural given that in most programming languages, such an AST would be defined using a similar pointer-based structure definition. Each node of this AST corresponds to a unique sub-expression of the original regular expression, the relationships among these nodes are given on the table to the right. We have used the notation $\pi(p)$ to signify the dereferencing of the pointer p with respect to the heap π in which the above AST is constructed. A formal definition of π was avoided in order to keep the notational clutter to a minimum, interested readers may refer [20] for a more precise definition of π.

Having parsed the regular expression into an AST, the next step is to construct an NFA structure that allows us to define a backtracking pattern matcher. While there are several standard NFA construction techniques [2], we opt for a slightly different construction which greatly simplifies the rest of the discussion. The idea is to associate a continuation pointer `cont` with each of the nodes in the AST such that `cont` points to the *following* (continuation) expression for each of the sub-expressions in the AST. In other words, `cont` identifies the "next sub-expression" which must be matched after matching the given sub-expression. More formally, `cont` is defined as follows:

Definition 1. *Let* `cont` *be a function*

$$\mathtt{cont} : \mathrm{dom}(\pi) \rightarrow (\mathrm{dom}(\pi) \cup \{\mathtt{null}\})$$

Such that,

- *If* $\pi(p) = (p_1 \mid p_2)$, *then* $\mathtt{cont}\, p_1 = \mathtt{cont}\, p$ *and* $\mathtt{cont}\, p_2 = \mathtt{cont}\, p$
- *If* $\pi(p) = (p_1 \cdot p_2)$, *then* $\mathtt{cont}\, p_1 = p_2$ *and* $\mathtt{cont}\, p_2 = \mathtt{cont}\, p$
- *If* $\pi(p) = (p_1)^*$, *then* $\mathtt{cont}\, p_1 = p$
- $\mathtt{cont}\, p_0 = \mathtt{null}$, *where* p_0 *is the pointer to the root of the AST.*

The following example illustrates the NFA constructed this way for the regular expression $(a \mid b)^*c$:

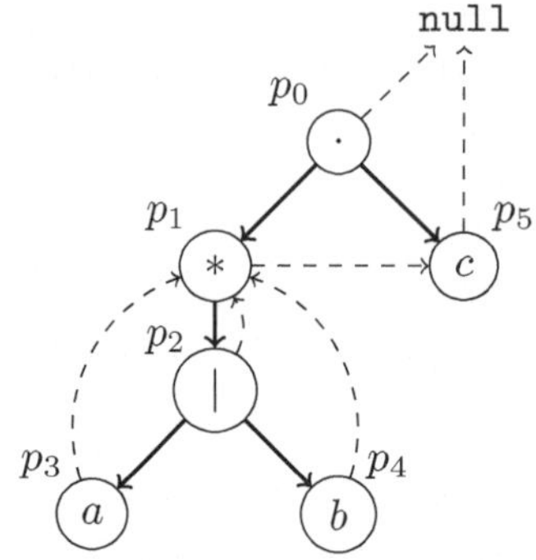

p	$\pi(p)$	cont p
p_0	$p_1 \cdot p_5$	null
p_1	$p_2{}^*$	p_5
p_2	$p_3 \mid p_4$	p_1
p_3	a	p_1
p_4	b	p_1
p_5	c	null

Here the dashed arrows identify the cont pointer for each of the AST nodes. Readers familiar with Thompson's construction [26,2] will realize that the resulting NFA is a slightly pessimized version of that resulting from Thompson's algorithm. The reason for this pessimization is purely of presentational nature; it helps to visualize the NFA as an AST with an overlay of a cont pointer mesh so that the structure of the original regular expression is still available in the AST portion. Furthermore, this presentation allows the definitions and proofs to be presented in an inductive fashion with respect to the structure of the expressions.

With the NFA defined, we present a simple non-deterministic regular expression matcher in the form of an abstract-machine called the PWπ machine:

Definition 2. *A configuration of the PWπ machine consists of two components:*

$$\langle p \,;\, w \rangle$$

The p component represents the current sub-expression (similar to a code pointer) while w corresponds to the rest of the input string that remains to be matched. The transitions of this machine are as follows:

$$\begin{aligned}
\langle p \,;\, w \rangle &\rightarrow \langle p_1 \,;\, w \rangle \textit{ if } \pi(p) = (p_1 \mid p_2) \\
\langle p \,;\, w \rangle &\rightarrow \langle p_2 \,;\, w \rangle \textit{ if } \pi(p) = (p_1 \mid p_2) \\
\langle p \,;\, w \rangle &\rightarrow \langle q \,;\, w \rangle \textit{ if } \pi(p) = p_1{}^* \wedge \texttt{cont}\, p = q \\
\langle p \,;\, w \rangle &\rightarrow \langle p_1 \,;\, w \rangle \textit{ if } \pi(p) = p_1{}^* \\
\langle p \,;\, w \rangle &\rightarrow \langle p_1 \,;\, w \rangle \textit{ if } \pi(p) = (p_1 \cdot p_2) \\
\langle p \,;\, aw \rangle &\rightarrow \langle q \,;\, w \rangle \textit{ if } \pi(p) = a \wedge \texttt{cont}\, p = q \\
\langle p \,;\, w \rangle &\rightarrow \langle q \,;\, w \rangle \textit{ if } \pi(p) = \varepsilon \wedge \texttt{cont}\, p = q
\end{aligned}$$

The initial state of the PWπ machine is $\langle p_0 \,;\, w \rangle$, where p_0 is the root of the AST corresponding to the input expression and w is the input string. The machine may terminate in the state $\langle \texttt{null} \,;\, w'' \rangle$ where it has matched the original regular *expression against some prefix* w' *of the original input string* w *such that* $w = w'w''$*. Apart from the successful termination, the machine may also terminate if it enters into a configuration where none of the above transitions apply.*

The PWπ machine searches for a matching prefix by non-deterministically making a choice whenever it has to branch at alternation or Kleene nodes. While this machine is not very useful in practice, it allows us to arrive at a precise model for backtracking regular expression matchers. Backtracking matchers operate by attempting all the possible search paths in order; this allows us to model them with a stack of PWπ machines. We call the resulting machine the PWFπ machine:

Definition 3. *The PWFπ machine consists of a stack of PWπ machines. The transitions of the PWFπ machine are given below:*

$$\frac{\langle p\,;\,w\rangle \to \langle q\,;\,w'\rangle}{\langle p\,;\,w\rangle :: f \to \langle q\,;\,w'\rangle :: f} \qquad \frac{\langle p\,;\,w\rangle \not\to}{\langle p\,;\,w\rangle :: f \to f}$$

$$\frac{\langle p\,;\,w\rangle \to \langle q_1\,;\,w\rangle \qquad \langle p\,;\,w\rangle \to \langle q_2\,;\,w\rangle}{\langle p\,;\,w\rangle :: f \to \langle q_1\,;\,w\rangle :: \langle q_2\,;\,w\rangle :: f}$$

The initial state of the PWFπ machine is $[\langle p_0\,;\,w\rangle]$*. The machine may terminate if one of the PWπ machines locates a match or if none of them succeeds in finding a match. In the latter case the PWFπ machine has exhausted the entire search space and determined that the input string cannot be matched by the regular expression in question.*

The PWFπ machine allows us to analyze backtracking regular expression matchers at an abstract level without concerning ourselves about any implementation specific details. More importantly, it gives an accurate cost model of backtracking matchers; the number of steps executed by the PWFπ machine corresponds to the amount of work a backtracking matcher has to perform when searching for a match. In the following sections we employ these ideas to develop and implement our static analysis.

3 Static Analysis for Exponential Blowup

The problem we are aiming to solve is this: given a regular expression e, represented as in Section 2, are there input strings x, y, and z, such that:

1. Reading x takes the machine to a pointer p_0 that is the root of a Kleene star expression.
2. Reading the input w takes the machine from p_0 back to p_0, and in at least two different ways, that is, along two different paths in the NFA.
3. Reading the input z when starting from p_0 causes the match to fail.

We call x the *prefix*, w the *pumpable* string by analogy with pumping lemmas in automata theory [13], and z the *failure suffix*.

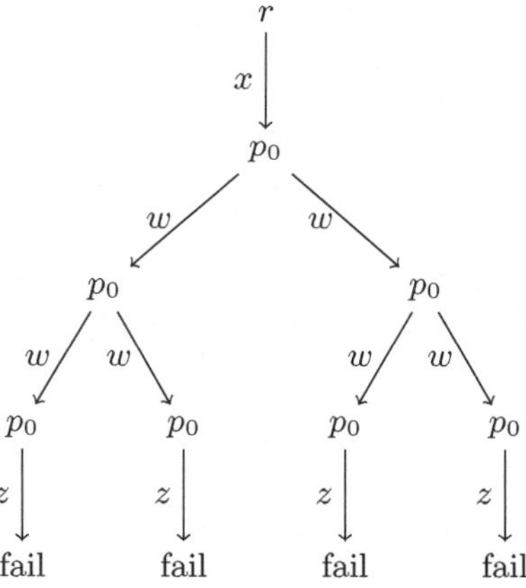

Fig. 1. The search tree for $x\,w\,w\,y$

From these three strings, malicious inputs can be constructed: the n-th malicious input is $x\,w^n\,z$. Figure 1 illustrates the search tree that a backtracking matcher has to explore when w is pumped twice. Because w can be matched in two different ways, the tree branches every time a w is read from the input. All branches fail in the end due to the trailing z, so that the matcher must explore the whole tree.

To state the analysis more formally, we will need to define paths in the matcher.

Definition 4. *A path of pointers,* $t : p \xrightarrow{w} q$ *is defined according to the following inductive rules:*

- *For each pointer* p, $[p] : p \xrightarrow{\varepsilon} p$ *is a path (identity).*
- *If* $t : p \xrightarrow{w} q$ *is a path and there exists a PWπ transition such that:*

$$\langle q \,;\, w' w_1 \rangle \to \langle q' \,;\, w_1 \rangle$$

Then $t \cdot [q'] : p \xrightarrow{ww'} q'$ *is also a path.*

Lemma 1. *The path* $t : p \xrightarrow{w} q$ $(q \neq p)$ *exists if and only if a PWπ run exists such that:*

$$\langle p \,;\, ww' \rangle \to \cdots \to \langle q \,;\, w' \rangle$$

Lemma 1 associates a unique string w with each path of pointers (the sub-string matched by the corresponding PWπ run). However, note that the inverse of this implication does not hold; there can be input strings for which we may find more than one PWπ run. In fact, it is this property of paths that leads us to the main theorem of this paper:

Theorem 1. *For a given Kleene expression* p_0 *where* $\pi(p_0) = p_1{}^*$, *if at least two paths exist such that* $t_1 : p_1 \xrightarrow{w} p_0$, $t_2 : p_1 \xrightarrow{w} p_0$ *and* $t_1 \neq t_2$, *then a regular expression involving* p_0 *exhibits* $o(2^n)$ *runtime on a backtracking regular expression matcher for input strings of the form* $xw^n z$ *where* x *is a sub-string matching the prefix of* p_0 *and* z *is such that* $xw^n z$ *fails to match the overall expression.*

While a formal proof of Theorem 1 is outside of the scope of this paper, we sketch its proof with reference to Figure 1. The prefix x causes the PWFπ machine to advance into a state where it has to match p_0 against the remainder of the input string, which leads to the branching of the search tree. Finally, the suffix z at the end of the input causes each search path to fail, which in turns forces the PWFπ machine to backtrack and explore the entire search tree before concluding that a match cannot be found. For the complexity, note that each additional pumping increases the size of the input by a constant (the length of w) whereas it doubles the size of the binary subtree given by the w branches, as well as the number of failed attempts to match z at the end. If there are more than 2 ways to match the pumpable string, say b, then b rather than 2 becomes the base of the exponent, but 2 is still a lower bound. The matching of the prefix x at the beginning contributes a constant to the runtime, which can be disregarded relative to the exponential growth. Thus the lower bound for the number of steps is exponential.

3.1 Generating the Pumpable String

The most important step in generating an attack string for a vulnerable regular expression is to generate the pumpable string w in $xw^n z$ (for some Kleene sub-expression). In order to arrive at the machine for building the pumpable string, we must first introduce several utility definitions. Note that in the remainder of this discussion, p_0 refers to a Kleene expression such that $\pi(p_0) = p_1{}^*$.

Definition 5. *For a given pointer* p, *the operation* $\Box p$ *(called evolve) is defined as:*

$$\Box p = [q \mid \exists t.t : p \xrightarrow{\varepsilon} q \wedge \exists a.\pi(q) = a]$$

Notice that the result of $\Box p$ *is a list of pointers.*

Definition 6. *The function* $\mathcal{D}_a(P)$, *(called derive) is defined on a list of pointers* P *and an input symbol* a *according to the following rules:*

$$\mathcal{D}_a([\,]) = [\,]$$

$$\mathcal{D}_a(h :: t) = \begin{cases} \mathcal{D}_a(t) & \text{if } \pi(h) = b, b \neq a \\ q :: \mathcal{D}_a(t) & \text{if } \pi(h) = a \wedge \texttt{cont}\, h = q \\ \mathcal{D}_a(\Box h \cdot t) & \text{otherwise.} \end{cases}$$

The definition $\mathcal{D}_a(P)$ is analogous to Brzozowski's derivatives of regular expressions [4]. In essence, the analysis computes derivatives of a Kleene expression in order to find two different matcher states for the same input string.

Definition 7. *A wP frame is defined as a pair (w, P) where w is a string and P is a list of pointers. A non-deterministic transition relation is defined on wP frames as follows:*

$$\frac{\mathcal{D}_a(P) \neq []}{(w, P) \to (w\,a, \mathcal{D}_a(P))}$$

Definition 8. *The HFπ machine has configurations of the following form:*

$$\langle H\ ;\ f \rangle$$

Here H (history) represents a set of (sorted) pointer lists and f is a list of wP frames. A deterministic transition relation defines the behavior of this machine as follows:

$$\frac{(w, P) \to (wx_0, P_0) \quad \ldots \quad (w, P) \to (wx_n, P_n) \quad \forall i.x_i \in \Sigma \quad P_i \notin H}{\langle H\ ;\ (w, P) :: f \rangle \to \langle H \cup \{P_0, \ldots, P_n\}\ ;\ f \cdot [(wx_0, P_0), \ldots, (wx_n, P_n)] \rangle}$$

The initial configuration of the HFπ machine is $\langle \emptyset\ ;\ [(\varepsilon, [p_1])] \rangle$ and the machine can terminate in either of the following two configurations:

$$\langle H\ ;\ [] \rangle$$

$$\langle H\ ;\ (w, P) :: f \rangle \text{ where } \exists p', p'' \in P.\ \exists t', t''.\ t' : p' \xrightarrow{\varepsilon} p_0 \wedge t'' : p'' \xrightarrow{\varepsilon} p_0$$

In the former configuration the machine has determined the Kleene expression in question to be non-vulnerable while in the latter it has derived the pumpable string w.

3.2 Generating the Prefix and the Suffix

For a regular expression of the form $e_1\,({e_2}^*)\,e_3$, apart from a pumpable string w, we must also generate a prefix x and a suffix z. The intention is that x would lead the matcher to the point where it has to match ${e_2}^*$, after which we can pump many copies of w to increase the search space of the matcher. However, a successful exploit also needs a suffix z that forces the matcher to fail and so to traverse the entire search tree.

Generating the prefix and the suffix might at first appear to be straightforward, since x and z can be generated from e_1 and e_3 such that x is in the language of e_1 and z is not in the language of e_3. However, upon closer inspection we realize that the choice of x and z can have un-intended effects on the final outcome of the match, as it is possible that e_1 could match part of the pumped string w^n in addition to the intended sub-string x. A similar situation could occur with e_2 and z. In other words, x, w and z are dependent on each other in complicated ways. Writing $e \downarrow y$ for e matches y, we have the following conditions:

$$e_1 \downarrow x \qquad e_2 \downarrow w \text{ (with multiple traces)} \qquad e_1\,{e_2}^*\,e_3 \not\downarrow x\,w^n\,z$$

At present, we have chosen not to solve this problem in full generality, but resolve to employ heuristics that find prefixes and suffixes for many practical expressions, as illustrated in the results section.

4 Implementation of the Static Analysis

We have implemented the HFπ machine described in Section 3 using the OCaml programming language. OCaml is well suited to programming abstract syntax, and hence a popular choice for writing static analyses. One of the major obstacles faced with the implementation is that in order to be able to analyze real-world regular expressions, it was necessary to build a sophisticated parser. In this regard, we decided to support the most common elements of the Perl / PCRE standards, as these seem to be the most commonly used (and adapted) syntaxes. It should be noted that the current implementation does not support back-references or look-around expressions due to their inherent complexity; it remains to be seen if the static analysis proposed in this work can be adapted to handle such "regexes". However, as it was explained earlier, exponential vulnerabilities in pattern specifications are not necessarily dependent on the use of back-references or other advanced constructs (although one would expect such constructs to further increase the search space of a backtracking matcher). A detailed description of the pattern specification syntax currently supported by the implementation has been included in the resources accompanying this paper.

The implementation closely follows the description of the HFπ machine presented in Section 3. The history component H is implemented as a set of sorted integer lists, where a single sorted integer list corresponds to a list of nodes pointed by the pointer list P of a wP frame (w, P). This representation allows for quick elimination of looping wP frames. While the size of H is potentially exponential in the number of nodes of a given Kleene expression, for practical regular expressions we found this size to be well within manageable levels (as evidenced in the results section).

A technical complication not addressed in the current work is that the PWFπ machine (and naive backtracking matching algorithms in general) can enter into infinite loops for Kleene expressions where the enclosed sub-expression can match the empty string, i.e., where the sub-expression is nullable [9,12]. A similar problem occurs in the HFπ machine during the $\Box p$ operation. We have incorporated a variation of the technique proposed by Danvy and Nielsen [9] for detecting and terminating such infinite loops into the OCaml code for the $\Box p$ function, so that it terminates in all cases.

5 Experimental Results

The analysis was tested on two corpora of regexes (Figure 1). The first of these was extracted from an online regex library called *RegExLib* [21], which is a community-maintained regex archive; programmers from various disciplines submit their solutions to various pattern matching tasks, so that other developers can reuse these expressions for their own pattern matching needs. The second corpus was extracted from the popular intrusion detection and prevention system *Snort* [25], which contains regex-based pattern matching rules for inspecting

Table 1. Experimental results with RegExLib and Snort

	RegExLib	Snort
Total patterns	2994	12499
Analyzable (only regular constructs)	2213	9408
Uses Kleene star	1103	2741
Pumpable Kleene and suffix found	127	15
Pumpable Kleene only	20	4
No pumpable Kleene	2066	9389
Max HFπ steps	509	256
Total classification time (Intel Core 2 Duo 1.8 MHz, 4 GB RAM)	40 s	10 s

IP packets across network boundaries. The contrasting purposes of these two corpora allow us to get a better view of the seriousness of exponential vulnerabilities in practical regular expressions.

The regex archive for RegExLib was only available through the corresponding website [21]. Therefore, as the first step the expressions had to be scraped from their web source and adapted so that they can be fed into our tool. These adaptations include removing unnecessary white-space, comments and spurious line breaks. A detailed description of these adjustments as well as copies of both adjusted and un-adjusted data sets have been included with the resources accompanying this paper (also including the Python script used for scraping). The regexes for Snort, on the other hand, are embedded within plain text files that define the Snort rule set. A Python script (also included in the accompanying resources) allowed the extraction of these regexes, and no further processing was necessary.

The results of the HFπ static analysis on these two corpora of regexes are presented in Table 1. The figures show that we can process around 75% of each of the corpora with the current level of syntax support. Out of these analyzable amounts, it is notable that regular expressions from the RegExLib archive use the Kleene operator more frequently (about 50% of the analyzable expressions) than those from the Snort rule set (close to 30%). About 11.5% of the Kleene-based RegExLib expressions were found to have a pumpable Kleene expression as well as a suitable suffix, whereas for Snort this figure stands around 0.55%.

The vulnerabilities reported range from trivial programming errors to more complicated cases. For an example, the following regular expression is meant to validate time values in 24-hour format (from RegExLib):

```
^(([01][0-9]|[012][0-3]):([0-5][0-9]))*$
```

Here the author has mistakenly used the Kleene operator instead of the `?` operator to suggest the presence or non-presence of the value. This pattern works perfectly for all intended inputs. However, our analysis reports that this expression is vulnerable with the pumpable string "13:59" and the suffix "/". This result gives the programmer a warning that the regular expression presents a DoS security risk if exposed to user-malleable input strings to match.

For a moderately complicated example, consider the following regular expression (again from RegExLib):

```
^([a-zA-z]:((\\([-*\.*\w+\s+\d+]+)|(\w+)\\)+)(\w+.zip)|(\w+.ZIP))$
```

This expression is meant to validate file paths to zip archives. Our tool identifies this expression as vulnerable and generates the prefix "z:\ ", the pumpable string "\zzz\" and the empty string as the suffix. This is probably an unexpected input in the author's eye, and this is another way in which our tool can be useful in that it can point out potential mis-interpretations which may have materialized as vulnerabilities.

It is worth noting that the HFπ machine manages to classify both the corpora (the analyzable portions) in a matter of seconds on modest hardware. This shows that our static analysis is usable for most practical purposes, with the average classification time for an expression in the range of micro-seconds. The two extreme cases for which the machine took several seconds for the classification are given below (only the respective Kleene expressions):

```
([\d\w][-\d\w]{0,253}[\d\w]\.)+

([^\x00]{0,255}\x00)*
```

Here counting expressions `[-\d\w]{0,253}` and `[^\x00]{0,255}` were expanded out during the parsing phase. The expansion produces a large Kleene expression, which naturally requires more analysis during the HFπ simulation. However, it should be noted that such expressions are the exception rather than the norm.

Finally, it should be mentioned that all the vulnerabilities reported above were individually verified using a modified version of the PWFπ machine (which counts the number of steps taken for a particular matching operation). A sample of those vulnerabilities was also tested on the Java regular expression matcher.

6 Conclusions

We have presented a static analysis to help programmers defend against regular expression DoS attacks. Large numbers of regular expressions can be analysed quickly, and developers are given feedback on where in their regular expressions the problem has been identified as well as examples of malicious input.

As illustrated in Section 5, the prefix, pumpable string and failure suffix can be quite short. If their length is, say, 3, 5 and 0 characters, then an attacker only needs to spend a very small amount of effort in providing a malicious input of length 3+5*100 characters to cause a matching time in excess of 2^{100} steps. Even if a matching step takes only a nanosecond, such a running time takes, for all intents and purposes, forever. The attacker can still scale up the attack by pumping a few times more and thereby correspondingly multiplying the matching time.

The fact that the complexity of checking a regular expression for exponential runtime may be computationally expensive in the worst case does not necessarily imply that such an analysis is futile. Type checking in functional languages like ML and Haskell also has high complexity [16,23], yet works efficiently in practice because the worst cases rarely occur in real-world code. There are even program analyses for undecidable problems like termination [3], so that the worst-case running time is infinite; what matters is that the analysis produces results in enough cases to be useful in practice. It is a common situation in program analysis that tools are not infallible (having false positives and negatives), but they are nonetheless useful for identifying points in code that need attention by a human expert [10].

6.1 Related Work

A general class of DoS attacks based on algorithmic complexities has been explored in [8]. In particular, the exponential runtime behavior of backtracking regular expression matchers has been discussed in [6] and [22]. The seriousness of this issue is further expounded in [24] and [18] where the authors demonstrate the mounting of DoS attacks on an IDS/IPS system (Snort) by exploiting the said vulnerability. The solutions proposed in these two works involve modifying the regular expressions and/or the matching algorithm in order to circumvent the problem in the context of IDS/IPS systems. We consider our work to be quite orthogonal and more general since it is based on a compile-time static analysis of regular expressions. However, it should be noted that both of those works concern of regexes with back-references, which is a feature we are yet to explore (known to be NP-hard [1]).

While the problem of ReDoS has been known for at least a decade, we are not aware of any previous static analysis for defending against it. A handful of tools exist that can assist programmers in finding such vulnerable regexes. Among these tools we found Microsoft's SDL Regex Fuzzer [17] and the RegexBuddy [15] to be the most usable implementations, as other tools were too unstable to be tested with complex expressions.

While RegexBuddy itself is not a security oriented software, it offers a debug mode, which can be used to detect what the authors of the tool refer to as *Catastrophic Backtracking* [11]. Even though such visual debugging methods can assist in detecting potential vulnerabilities, it would only be effective if the attack string is known in advance—this is where a static analysis method like the one presented on this paper has a clear advantage.

SDL Fuzzer, on the other hand, is aimed specifically at analyzing regular expression vulnerabilities. While details of the tool's internal workings are not publicly available, analyzing the associated documentation reveals that it operates fuzzing, i.e., by brute-forcing a sequence of generated strings through the regular expression in question to detect long running times. The main disadvantage of this tool is that it can take a very long time for the tool to classify a given expression. Tests using some of the regular expressions used in the results section above revealed that it can take up to four minutes for the Fuzzer to classify certain expressions. It is an inherent limitation of fuzzers for exponential runtime DoS attacks that the finding out if something takes a long time by running it takes a long time. By contrast, our analysis statically analyzes an expression without ever running it. It is capable of classifying thousands of regular expressions in a matter of seconds. Furthermore, the output produced by the SDL Fuzzer only reports the fact that the expression in question failed to execute within a given time limit for some input string. Using this generated input string to pin-point the exact problem in the expression would be quite a daunting task. In contrast, our static analysis pin-points the exact Kleene expression that causes the vulnerability and allows programmers to test their matchers with a sequence of malicious inputs.

6.2 Directions for Further Research

In further work, we aim to broaden the coverage of our tool to include more regexes. Given its basis in our earlier work on abstract machines [20] and derivatives [4], we aim for a formal proof of the correctness of our analysis. We intend to release the source code of the tool as an open source project. More broadly, we hope that raising awareness of the dangers of backtracking matchers will help in the adoption of superior techniques for regular expression matching [7,26,20].

References

1. Aho, A.V.: Algorithms for Finding Patterns in Strings. In: van Leeuwen, J. (ed.) Handbook of Theoretical Computer Science, vol. A, pp. 255–300. MIT Press, Cambridge (1990)
2. Aho, A.V., Lam, M., Sethi, R., Ullman, J.D.: Compilers - Principles, Techniques and Tools, 2nd edn. Addison Wesley (2007)
3. Berdine, J., Cook, B., Distefano, D., O'Hearn, P.W.: Automatic termination proofs for programs with shape-shifting heaps. In: Ball, T., Jones, R.B. (eds.) CAV 2006. LNCS, vol. 4144, pp. 386–400. Springer, Heidelberg (2006)
4. Brzozowski, J.A.: Derivatives of Regular Expressions. J. ACM 11(4), 481–494 (1964)
5. Chess, B., McGraw, G.: Static analysis for security. IEEE Security & Privacy 2(6), 76–79 (2004)
6. Cox, R.: Regular Expression Matching Can Be Simple and Fast (but is slow in Java, Perl, Php, Python, Ruby, ...) (January 2007), `http://swtch.com/~rsc/regexp/regexp1.html`
7. Cox, R.: Regular expression matching: the virtual machine approach (December 2009), `http://swtch.com/~rsc/regexp/regexp2.html`
8. Crosby, S.A., Wallach, D.S.: Denial of Service via Algorithmic Complexity Attacks. In: Proceedings of the 12th USENIX Security Symposium, Washington, DC (August 2003)
9. Danvy, O., Nielsen, L.R.: Defunctionalization at Work. In: Proceedings of the 3rd ACM SIGPLAN International Conference on Principles and Practice of Declarative Programming, PPDP 2001, pp. 162–174. ACM, New York (2001)

10. Dowd, M., McDonald, J., Schuh, J.: The Art of Software Security Assessment: Identifying and Preventing Software Vulnerabilities. Addison Wesley (2006)
11. Goyvaerts, J.: Runaway Regular Expressions: Catastrophic Backtracking (2009), http://www.regular-expressions.info/catastrophic.html
12. Harper, R.: Proof-Directed Debugging. J. Funct. Program. 9(4), 463–469 (1999)
13. Hopcroft, J.E., Ullman, J.D.: Introduction to Automata Theory, Languages and Computation. Addison-Wesley (1979)
14. Livshits, V.B., Lam, M.S.: Finding security vulnerabilities in java applications with static analysis. In: Proceedings of the 14th Conference on USENIX Security Symposium, vol. 14, p. 18 (2005)
15. Just Great Software Co. Ltd. RegexBuddy (2012), http://www.regexbuddy.com/
16. Mairson, H.G.: Deciding ML typability is complete for deterministic exponential time. In: Proceedings of the 17th ACM SIGPLAN-SIGACT Symposium on Principles of Programming Languages, pp. 382–401. ACM (1989)
17. Microsoft. SDL Regex Fuzzer (2011), http://www.microsoft.com/en-gb/download/details.aspx?id=20095
18. Namjoshi, K., Narlikar, G.: Robust and Fast Pattern Matching for Intrusion Detection. In: Proceedings of the 29th Conference on Information Communications, INFOCOM 2010, pp. 740–748. IEEE Press, Piscataway (2010)
19. The Open Web Application Security Project (OWASP). Regular Expression Denial of Service - ReDoS (2012), https://www.owasp.org/index.php/Regular_expression_Denial_of_Service_-_ReDoS
20. Rathnayake, A., Thielecke, H.: Regular Expression Matching and Operational Semantics. In: Structural Operational Semantics (SOS 2011). Electronic Proceedings in Theoretical Computer Science (2011)
21. RegExLib.com. Regular Expression Library (2012), http://regexlib.com/
22. Roichman, A., Weidman, A.: Regular Expression Denial of Service (2012), http://www.checkmarx.com/white_papers/redos-regular-expression-denial-of-service/
23. Seidl, H., et al.: Haskell overloading is DEXPTIME-complete. Information Processing Letters 52(2), 57–60 (1994)
24. Smith, R., Estan, C., Jha, S.: Backtracking Algorithmic Complexity Attacks Against a NIDS. In: Proceedings of the 22nd Annual Computer Security Applications Conference, ACSAC 2006, pp. 89–98. IEEE Computer Society, Washington, DC (2006)
25. Sourcefire. Snort, IDS/IPS (2012), http://www.snort.org/
26. Thompson, K.: Programming Techniques: Regular Expression Search Algorithm. Communications of the ACM 11(6), 419–422 (1968)

Next-Generation DoS at the Higher Layers: A Study of SMTP Flooding

Gabriel Cartier, Jean-François Cartier, and José M. Fernandez

École Polytechnique de Montréal
Montréal, Québec, Canada
{gabriel.cartier,jean-francois.cartier,jose.fernandez}@polymtl.ca

Abstract. In this paper, we study distributed denial of service (DDoS) attacks that establish connections at the higher layers of the protocol stack, in order to maximize resource depletion on the targeted servers. In particular, we concentrate on attacks directed at SMTP applications on incoming mail servers. We first describe our experiments on the feasibility of such attacks on two widely used SMTP server applications: Microsoft Exchange 2010 and Postfix 2.8. The results show that both applications can survive relatively strong attacks, if configured properly. Although it was shown that Microsoft Exchange 2010 handles the attacks better than Postfix, both applications can benefit from hardened configurations.

In particular, we show the efficacy of their connection timeout mechanisms as a protection against this kind of DoS attack. We first show that default timeout parameters give weak protection for Postfix, but that Exchange's default throttling policy makes attacks ineffective. We then statically modify the timeout value and other parameters in Postfix in order to measure their impact on the performance under an SMTP flood attack. The results obtained allow us to make recommendations about optimal configurations in terms of quality of service for legitimate clients.

1 Introduction

Denial of service (DoS) attacks were once considered one of the most dangerous threats on the Internet. Significant amounts of research was conducted to improve their detection and prevention. However, just as DoS research seemed to have fallen out of fashion, DoS attacks against Estonia, CNN, Georgia, Iran and more recently the attacks by the hacktivist group called *Anonymous*, have showed that not only DoS attacks are still a real threat, but also that they have evolved and they have become more effective against existing countermeasures. Even if it seems that most DoS attacks are still largely based on SYN floods, others try to exhaust bandwidth of their victim by sending multiple ping packets or UDP packets. Another type is those that try to exhaust server resources by sending properly formed application traffic that will be handled and force extensive resource allocation by the targeted application, for example, by sending multiple HTTP GET requests to a Web server. These latter type of attack is

J. Lopez, X. Huang, and R. Sandhu (Eds.): NSS 2013, LNCS 7873, pp. 149–163, 2013.

potentially more insidious because this kind of traffic is harder to discriminate from legitimate traffic and filtering it can have a stronger impact on legitimate users. Given the increased financial and political significance of DoS attacks, it becomes necessary to study the current and potential future impact of such newer types of attacks. We also need to consider the ones that have not yet been reported to prevent them from causing damage in the future.

While these application-targeting attacks have been traditionnaly less common, they are not new. There have been attacks of this kind targetting websites as early as October 2003, such as reported in [16]. Most of the research on application-layer DoS has focused on HTTP flood [17,21,14], with much less attention having been paid to the potential consequences of such attacks on SMTP servers. Also, while many different ways of attacking the application layer have been studied, our research especially focuses on idling the connection to max out the resources given for a TCP connection. However, while there has been little work on DoS protection of SMTP servers *per se*, much research has been conducted on their protection against unwanted SPAM traffic [9,10,8,13,12]. Numerous hardware and software solutions are available that can help mitigate spam on SMTP servers. However, these are not necessarily well suited to defend against STMP floods where the attacker's objective is not to send spam mail traffic, but to prevent anybody from sending legitimate mail. In particular, an SMTP flood does not need to send messages with a particular pattern or message, and in some cases (as we shall see) might not need to send any properly formatted mail at all! In addition, the deployment of spam protection counter-measures could in fact worsen the situation by increasing resource consumption and decrease the level of DoS protection.

Some noteworthy previous work on SMTP DoS attacks is that of Bencsath *et al.* [3,4], whose work includes a comparative study of DoS resilience on SMTP servers. The main difference, however, is that the attack model described is one where the attackers send multiple e-mails to the MTA. Although this research is similar to ours, our paper is broader in that it focuses on different aspects of the server to evaluate the performance under an attack, not just the number of simultaneous connections. Also, we demonstrate that with an attack that is easier to mount than sending multiple mails, we can still exhaust the server relatively easily. More recently, Still and McCreath [19] published a comparison of different solutions for DDoS protection against SMTP server. The work of Bencsath *et al.* is referred to and the conclusion is that the implementation of its push back router technique would help in mitigating DDoS attacks.

More precisely, the attack scenario that we consider in this paper is composed of an attacker owning multiple machines (e.g. zombies in a botnet) and opening multiple SMTP connections to the targeted server. Once a connection is established, the bad clients will idle until a certain timeout is reached after which the server closes the connection. Our claim is that every non-completed SMTP connection uses resources on the server. Whether it is the memory, the number of threads created or the number of process started, resources are bounded in a system and one of them will be the ultimate limiting factor or bottleneck.

When the server exhausts all its resources, it will stop accepting new SMTP connections, thus creating a denial of service. Our research is thus essentially an improvement on the work of Bencsath, in that we demonstrate that with a simpler to mount DoS, we can easily exhaust the server resources. Furthermore, our results are potentially more general, in that this kind of idling attack could more easily applied to other applications such as HTTP servers.

The main objective of this research is to evaluate the performance of various SMTP applications with an adaptive behaviour against SMTP flood attacks and to propose solutions that would improve their resilience against such attacks. By analyzing as examples Microsoft Exchange 2010 on Windows Server 2008 and Postfix 2.8 on Linux 2.6, we aim to answer the following questions:

- How good is the performance of these applications, with their default settings, while under an SMTP flood attack?
- Is it possible to optimize their configuration parameters, especially the timeout, to achieve better results in this case?
- Is the mechanism described and implemented in our previous work on SYN flood [7,6,5] suitable to protect these applications against SMTP flood?

Our work and results attempting to answer these questions are presented in the rest of the paper as follows. Section 2 presents the SMTP applications that we studied. We discuss its viability when aimed at SMTP applications, based on preliminary experiments that we performed. We cover those in Section 3, where we describe our testing methodology first and then present our experimental setup. We then present our experimental results and a discussion follows about their interpretation and relevance. We also briefly discuss the use of SPAM filters as DoS counter-measures in the light of these results. Finally, we summarize our results, provide recommendations on protection against these attacks, and discuss directions for future work in Section 4.

2 SMTP Flood Attacks

As discussed in our previous work [5], the attack described in this paper can be viewed as an extension of the SYN flood attack at the higher layers of the protocol stack. While in general IP address spoofing is not possible, this type of flooding has the advantage of forcing the target to commit more resources.

For our research, we studied two SMTP server applications: Microsoft Exchange 2010 and Postfix 2.8. Microsoft Exchange 2010 is the latest version of the Exchange serie. We chose the latter because it is quite commonly used and although it is a complex application providing much more than e-mail services, we decided that, if properly configured, we would get better results than the much simpler (and deprecated) Microsoft SMTP Service. More importantly, both these applications implement a defence mechanism when under stress. We ran Exchange on a Windows Server 2008 machine. On the Linux side, Postfix is one of the most widely used SMTP servers. We chose it for its simplicity, its popularity and because it offers most of the functionalities of every other SMTP server application running on Linux. Postfix also seemed a good choice, given the fact that its creator, Wietse Venema, is a well established security researcher and hence the application was built with a big emphasis on security. As such, it's often recognized as the best alternative to sendmail.

There have been several surveys comparing the various SMTP server applications [18,15,20]. Our choices are mostly confirmed with those surveys except for Sendmail and Exim, that are stated to be the most popular. One survey shows that sendmail is still the most widely used application for SMTP servers, but the article is dated of 2007. Nonetheless, we decided not to choose since it is not being updated anymore and its popularity seems to lower drastically. We also noted that qmail is renowned for being one of the most secure SMTP server applications. We did not experiments on this particular application because it is not widely used due to its complexity. Our Postfix server was run on a machine with Ubuntu 9.04 Server Edition, Kernel version 2.6.27.7.

As a preliminary step, we decided to conduct proof-of-concept experiments to verify whether SMTP flood was viable in practice with the two applications chosen and, in the case where it would be, to determine what the limiting factor was. Our results show that, indeed, a successful SMTP flood is possible on both applications, but the limiting factor differs from one to the other.

2.1 Preliminary Analysis of Microsoft Exchange 2010

Our initial analysis covered a study of the relevant configuration settings, and determining which can be modified and which cannot. The most interesting parameter is without doubt the connection timeout whose default value is 5 minutes and is customizable down to as low as 10 seconds. The only other interesting parameter is the maximum number of users since, which can be modified, but is set to 5000 by default; a value we chose to keep for our initial tests. For these tests, the application was run on a server with 4 Gb of memory and two quad-core processors with 2.00 GHz clock speed. Using 7 similar machines running Ubuntu, we flooded the server with completed TCP connections.

The Windows Reliability and Performance Monitor [11] that comes with Windows Server 2008 showed that the server can indeed handle a maximum of 5000 opened TCP connections. When this limit is reached, the server denies any new connection by first sending a timeout message and then by immediately closing the connection with a FIN packet. At its maximum capacity, the application still runs in only one process and a small number of threads have been created. However, a lot of memory is used by the process. Our hypothesis was that the application allocates significant amount of memory when a TCP connection completes. We then modified the default number of maximum number of users to unlimited to determine the limiting factor in this case. When the number of simultaneous users is set to unlimited, the server can handle to as many as about 61000 connections. With the server accepting an unlimited number of connections and even putting it through an attack of as many as 1000 connections per second, it manages to serve the legitimate connection with a success rate of almost 100%. We can thus conclude that the attack is possible but not effective. It is still interesting to see that the limiting factor is, as we thought, the memory that is almost completely used when the server reaches the maximum connections. We can also note that the attackers failure rate starts going up and then stops at an average of 12000 connections refused. After that, the server keeps on handling the attackers without refusing them. Exchange 2010 implements a throttling policy that changes its settings for specific users that seems to abuse the system. Since the attackers create connections and idle them, when the server is saturated, Exchange starts throttling the maximum number of concurrent connections which is by default set to 20. Although the server handles the attack efficiently, further experiments shows that lowering the default timeout value is improving the efficiency rate to almost 100%.

2.2 Preliminary Analysis of Postfix

In the case of Postfix, the timeout can also be modified: its default value is 5 minutes and in this case it can be adjusted in seconds. It is also interesting to note that Postfix have numerous timeout settings providing the server maximum flexibility such as a timeout before receiving the HELO command or the MAIL FROM command. Like in Exchange, the maximum number of connections is configurable and its default is set to 50. Another interesting configuration parameter of Postfix is the maximum number of processes it can start. Indeed, Postfix starts daemon processes to handle connections to the server. We decided to keep its default value of 100 for our tests. We flooded Postfix using the same method as for Exchange. We then set the maximum number of connections to unlimited and our experiments show that it can handle a maximum of 202 connections with its default process settings. We then set the maximum number of processes to 1000 in the Postfix configuration and ran the test again. This time, the server could handle 6108 connections. By giving different values to this setting, our tests showed that the limiting factor in Postfix is indeed the maximum number of processes it can create. Table 1 summarizes the results from our preliminary analysis of Microsoft SMTP Service and Postfix. It is important to note that the maximum number of connections that the application can handle is inferred by the limiting factor and is thus dependent on the specifications of the machine it is running on.

In summary, our preliminary experiments demonstrated that Exchange and Postfix have different limiting factors (memory vs. number of processes)and that both restrict the number of simultaneous TCP connections. Although Exchange is highly resilient to such an attack, we showed that this inferred capacity is

Table 1. Default timeout value, maximum number of connections with default parameters and the limiting factor for Microsoft SMTP Service and Postfix

SMTP server app.	Default timeout	Maximum conn.	Limiting factor
Microsoft Exchange	5 minutes	61000	Memory
Postfix	5 minutes	202	Number of processes

relatively small and that, together with high timeout values, Postfix can be easily flooded by an attacker using a low quantity of its resources.

3 Performance Analysis Experiments

To evaluate the performance of SMTP applications against SMTP flood and in order to make recommendations on timeout optimization techniques, we conducted three different experiments. The first experiment was aimed at evaluating the performance of SMTP server applications with their default settings while under an SMTP flood attack. The second experiment shows the impact of the timeout value on their performance and aims at finding the best timeout value. We also discuss the adaptive techniques of both applications when under stress and their effectiveness against such an attack. The first part of this section presents the testing methodology we used. The next part explains our experimental setup. We then describe in detail each of the experiments and present and discuss the results obtained.

3.1 Testing Methodology

For each of our experiments, we generated two kinds of traffic: malicious traffic and legitimate traffic. The malicious clients open a TCP connection with the server and then idle until they are disconnected after the timeout is reached. Legitimate clients open a connection with the server and then send an email of a size between 1 Kb and 2 Mb. This choice was motivated by the analysis of mail server logs from the École Polytechnique de Montréal for a six weeks period in 2009, that showed that 90% of emails were between 20 bytes and 500 Kb. Every test was done on both the Microsoft Exchange server and the Postfix server. For each of them, the only interesting performance metric is the connection success rate of the legitimate clients which can be defined as

$$\phi = \frac{\varphi_c}{\varphi_c + \varphi_f + \varphi_t}$$

where ϕ is the connection success rate, φ_c is the number of SMTP sessions completed for all legitimate clients, φ_f is the number of failed SMTP sessions, and φ_t is the number of timed-out SMTP sessions. A client completes its session when it gets on the server, sends its message, and then disconnects with the QUIT command. A session fails when the client cannot get on the server because it is unavailable, that is, because it is full. Finally, a session times out when the server disconnects the client when it has been idle for the timeout value.

3.2 Experimental Setup

SMTP Servers. We tested both Microsoft Exchange and Postfix 2.8 in our experiments. Microsoft Exchange 2010 was installed on a machine running the 32 bits version of Windows Server 2008 and Postfix 2.8 was installed on a machine running the 32 bit version of Ubuntu 9.04 Desktop Edition with Linux 2.6 kernel. Both machines have the same specifications: 4 GB of RAM and two Intel Xeon E5405 quad-core processors with a clock speed of 2.00 GHz.

Malicious and Legitimate Traffic Generator. Both malicious and legitimate traffic were generated using a home-made application that connects to the server. For malicious traffic, it idles the connections infinitely and for legitimate connections it sends an email of varying size. The malicious machines consisted of 10 physical machine from a cluster, each connected with a 1 Gbps ethernet connection to the switch. Since the legitimate clients produce considerably less traffic, we used 5 machines from the cluster to generate the traffic.

Both the malicious and the legitimate clients connected to a command and control server that sent them specific details on the attack traffic to generate. The legitimate clients typically connected following a Poisson distribution with 10 conn/s. For the attackers, the connections followed either a Poisson or a burst distribution with an attack rate betwee 10 and 1000 conn/s. Both attackers and legitimate clients keep tally the number of connections attempts, whether successful, refused or timed out. Moreover, network traffic traces (PCAP files) were kept for each run for further analysis, as required.

Network Setup. To connect all these machines together and create a network, we used a Linksys SRW2016 16-port gigabit switch. Figure 1 illustrates the network connections.

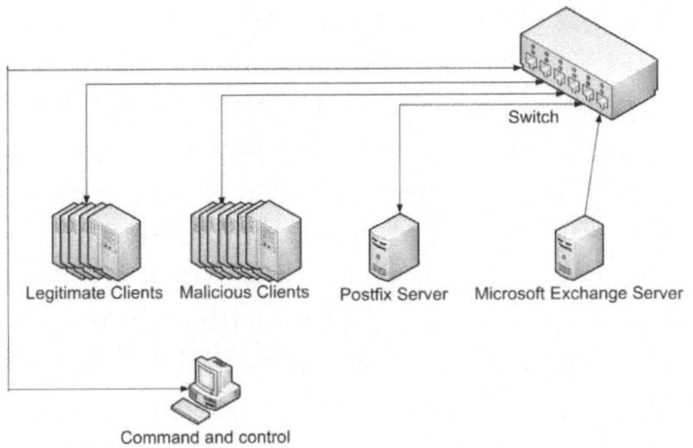

Fig. 1. Network connections of the experimental setup

The command and control was used to send the commands to the legitimate and malicious clients and controlled the testing. Both SMTP servers were always up and running during every experiment, even when the other server was tested. The SMTP servers were handling the emails themselves, storing them inside the proper mailboxes. We chose this scenario for its simplicity and the fact that the bottleneck would not be caused by the relaying to another server.

3.3 Experiments Conducted and Results

Performance Analysis of SMTP Applications with Default Settings. The first experiment is measures the performance of SMTP applications with their default timeout settings during an STMP flood attack. For this experiment, we kept the default settings for Postfix but modified the number of connections to unlimited for Exchange. Although we did the experiment with all the default settings on Exchange, the results are predictable and uninteresting. The server stops receiving connections when the default maximum of 5000 is reached and the failure rates start increasing afterward. For the default timeout values with unlimited connections, the connection rate of legitimate clients was set to 10 conn/s and set to follow a Poisson distribution. The malicious connection rate was also Poisson, since it represents an attack with little or no coordination where the attacker just gives orders to all machines to constantly attack his victim. Our main performance metric, the connection success rate of the legitimate clients, was computed for the connection arrival rate of malicious clients, also called attack strengths, of 10, 100 and 1000 conn/s.

For both applications, each test was set to last five times the timeout delay, with a minimum of 10 minutes. For each malicious connection arrival rate, a minimum of five runs were completed. In the cases where the standard deviation of the results was not within 5% of the mean, additional runs were performed.

To compute the legitimate connection success rate, we used the statistics generated by our application. Additionally, during all the tests a network trace was taken with the switch allowing us to analyze the attacks *a posteriori* for cross-verification of results. The data from our application was recorded a specified time intervals (1 second, by default). The metrics we decided to use for the statistics are the number of failed and succeeded malicious sessions and the number of disconnected, failed and succeeded legitimate connections. In the case of legitimate connections, it may happen that the client gets disconnected during his session due to the volume of requests. We decided not to evaluate the delays created while the server is under attack because of how we built our setup. The fact that the clients are connected almost directly to the server through the switch, the delays are thus negligible. We also believe that the number of failed legitimate connections is more interesting as it shows that the server simply cannot handle any more clients. It is important to note that the number of failed connections on the attacker is calculated based on the completed connections, there is thus a delay before the failed connections starts growing. Figure 2 shows these statistics for the first 10 minutes of an attack with a malicious connection arrival rate of 10 conn/s.

We can see in Fig. 2 that sessions start failing almost immediately. Indeed, the Postfix server, as mentioned in Section 2.2, does not allow more than 202 simultaneous connections with the default settings. Although the failure rate of the attacker is almost constantly growing, the server does not allow any legitimate connection, it is quite evidently unable to serve the clients. It also interesting to note that at about 5 minutes, the legitimate clients connections seems to peak and stops growing for almost the end of the test. This behaviour could be

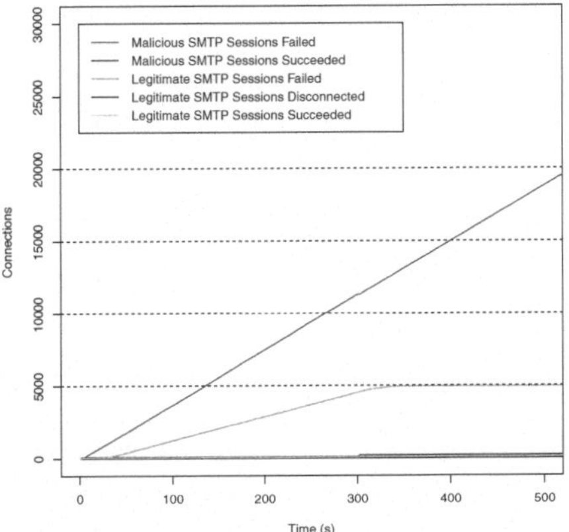

Fig. 2. Statistics on STMP sessions with Postfix, attacked by malicious clients at 10 conn/s

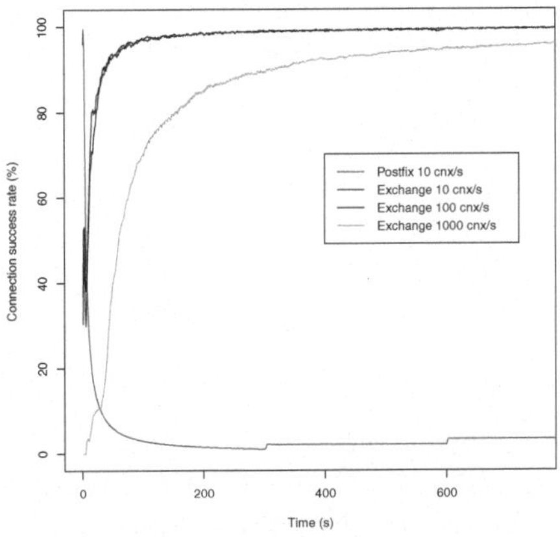

Fig. 3. Variation of legitimate connection success rate for different attack strengths for Exchange

explained by the fact that Postfix is completely flooded and cannot even complete the TCP handshake. The legitimate clients application is not behaving the same way the attacker does because it uses POSIX sockets while the attackers use RAW sockets. That behaviour is noticeable throughout the test but does not affect the results because it is clear that the server is not allowing any other kind of connections at this point.

For the Exchange server, we ran the initial tests by modifying the default value of the maximum concurrent connections which we set to unlimited. Figure 3 shows the variation of the success rate of the legitimate connections for the Postfix server and the Exchange Server. The successful rate of Exchange seems counter intuitive in the graph, but it is mainly because a connection cannot be counted as successful until it completes. There is thus a delay in the sum of the successful rate, but it is still clear from Fig. 3 that Exchange is highly resilient to such an attack, and this, even with its default timeout settings. In the case of Postfix, since the server capacity is low (202 conn.), the legitimate connection success rate is already below 5% at an attack strength of 10 conn/s. For this reason, we did not experiment higher malicious clients connection arrival rates for Postfix. As Table 2 summarizes the legitimate connection success rates by presenting their final values, that is at the end of the experiment, for each case.

Fine Tuning the SMTP Applications. As it was demonstrated earlier, Postfix is unable to subsist an attack as low as 10 connections per seconds with its default settings. The application allows us to fine tune many settings to be able to get the best performances possible. Since we were able to determine that the number of created process by Postfix was the bottleneck, it is fair to assume that increasing this number will give us a better performance for the same attack rate. As there is no maximum value for this setting, we ran multiple tests by increasing it 10 times for each test. Given that the default is 100 processes,

Table 2. Final legitimate connection success rate for different malicious connection arrival rates on Microsoft Exchange and Postfix

	SMTP server application	
	MS Exchange	Postfix
Attack strength (conn/s)	ϕ (%)	ϕ (%)
10	98.40	3.83
100	98.35	–
1000	90.11	–

we ran an attack of 10 conn/s with maximum numbers of processes created of 100, 1000, 10000 and 100000. Figure 4 displays that an efficiency of almost 55% can be achieved by fine tuning this parameters. It becomes obvious that there is a point where increasing the number of processes is not helping performance, i.e. beyond 10,000 processes, but rahter slightly decreasing it. Consequently, we thus kept this value at 10,000 for subsequent tests.

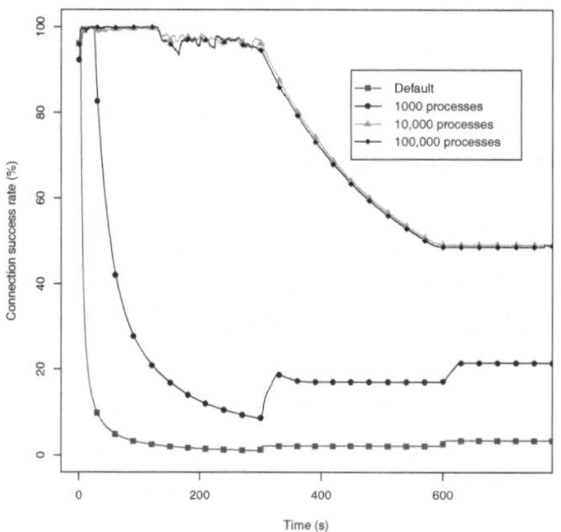

Fig. 4. Legitimate success rate, as a variation of the number of processes Postfix can create

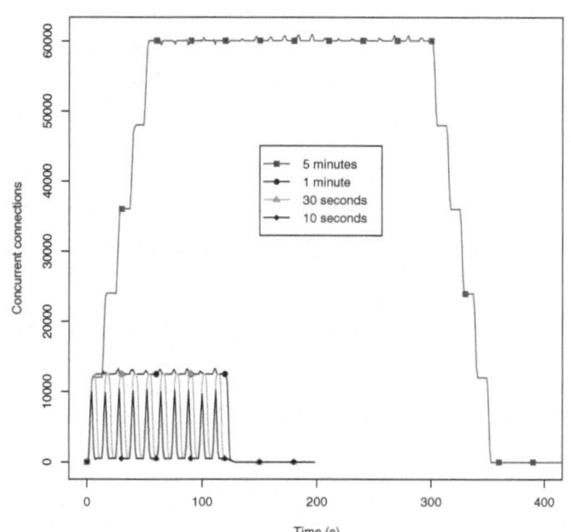

Fig. 5. Number of concurrent connections based on the timeout value for Exchange

As mentioned earlier, both applications implement adaptive behaviour that adjusts some parameters when the server is under great loads. For Exchange, this worked out of the box, as the preliminary tests demonstrated that an attack with rates as high as 1000 conn/s were highly ineffective against the server with its default timeout values. The throttling policy of Exchange is simply limiting the number of concurrent connections to a specific IP when under load. The policies are applied to a specific service and new policies can be added for extra safety. Nonetheless, it is still interesting to see what would be the effects of modifying the timeout value. It is obvious that the rate of successful connection could only benefit from lowering the timeout, but since the rate is already high with the default value, we could neglect its change. Figure 5 shows a significant improvement in the number of concurrent connections when tuning the timeout. Not only is it helping to keep the server load lower, but it also provides a better quality of service to the legitimate clients. This small tuning coupled with the throttling policy of Exchange makes it highly resilient to DDoS attacks.

Postfix also has a stress adaptive behaviour which, in our case, did not work directly. While the Postfix documentation states that versions 2.5 and later of Postfix implement the stress adaptive behaviour should automatically starts without closing current sessions when under load [2], we ran our test by forcing the stress adaptive behaviour. This does not have significant effect on our results as the switch between the normal mode of operation to the stress adaptive behaviour is negligible. For our first experiment, we decided to keep the stress adaptive settings to their default which in this case results in lowering the timeout delay to 10 seconds [1]. We attacked the server with 3 different strengths: 10 conn/s, 100 conn/s and finally 1000 conn/s.

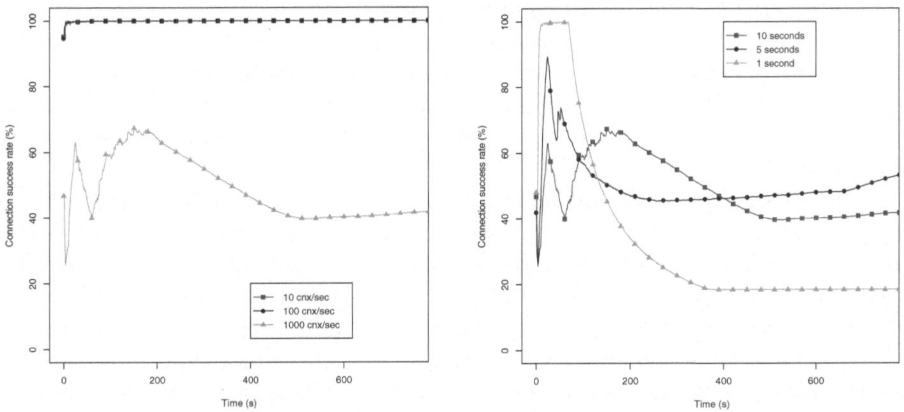

Fig. 6. Success rate with different attack strengths on Postfix under stress

Fig. 7. Success rate with different timeout values on Postfix under stress

Figure 6 shows clearly that the stress adaptive behaviour implemented by Postfix offers improved protection for a DDoS attack. Even with the default timeout values under stress, the server is able to serve about 50% of the legitimate connections. Postfix allows the customization of the timeout value to as low as 1s. Since it was clear that an uncoordinated attack of strength lower than 1000 conn/s was not efficient, we lowered the timeout to 5 and 1 second and tested how the success rate of our legitimate clients was to change. Figure 7 shows the results of this experiment.

Table 3. Final legitimate connection success rate for different malicious connection arrival rates on different timeout values under stress for Postfix

	Postfix timeout values under stress		
Attack strength (conn/s)	10 secs	5 secs	1 sec
10	99.99	–	–
100	99.98	–	–
1000	46.43	71.21	18.43

3.4 Discussion

The results from our first experiment showed that Postfix with its default value is weak against SMTP flood attacks. Although in the first experiment Postfix did not go into stress adaptive behaviour, we can guess that any Postfix setup with a version before 2.5 (before the automatic stress adaptive behaviour was implemented) would get extremely weak performances. With the stress adaptive behaviour and some fine tuning, we were able to get a 46% success rate for an attack of 1000 conn/s, a great improvement compared to the weak 3.83% that the default settings offers at 10 conn/s. Postfix profits largely from the increase of processes but also from the stress adaptive feature. Even if we did not test the server with a general timeout value lower than the default 300 seconds, we can easily guess that the results would show significant improvement based on the results of the Exchange experiment and the results of the under stress Postfix experiment.

One interesting point is that in Fig. 7, and its associated numerical results in Table 3, the curve for timeout of 1 second seems promising at first but starts going downhill after about 2 minutes and then stays at about 20%. This can be explained by the fact that at a 1 second delay, the server keeps handling numerous new connections and closing other ones, at some point the server seems frozen and does not accept any other connections for quite some time. It is hard to explain exactly how the server behaves but we can assume that the server is too busy handling the connections and thus keeping a 5 second timeout is a better solution. It is also more appropriate for real life settings as large emails could take more than 5 seconds to send. Giving these results, the question that needs to be asked is *Should the default timeout value of SMTP applications be lowered?* We believe so. First, our experiments show that lower timeout values give a better protection against SMTP flood. Second, lowering the timeout value will not affect the QoS of the server.

Indeed, for all of our experiments, we only experienced a couple of timeout for the legitimate clients. xThat is because the timer that checks for the timeout gets reset each time a packet is received by the client. Generally speaking, to send an email, the client needs five commands: EHLO, MAIL FROM, RCPT TO, DATA and QUIT. After the DATA command, the client sends its actual mail content. Each command is some bytes long, so the time between receptions of each command is negligible. The only data with a significant size that could be sent is the actual mail. However, packets are fragmented on a network, and their fragments size is equal to the MTU (Maximum Transmission Unit). The MTU on Ethernet is 1500 bytes, and is said to be at least 576 bytes on the Internet. Therefore the waiting time upon reception of a packet from a client is the time it takes to send a maximum of roughly 1 Kb. Even with a very low bandwidth, this is very unlikely to take more than a (very) few seconds, unless the other party is down, in which case the connection better be closed soon. Some SMTP server applications, such as Postfix, offer the possibility of setting a timeout value for each SMTP command. However, this does not give better protection to SMTP flood attacks, since the timeout is also reset upon the reception of each packet. To the best of our knowledge, Microsoft Exchange 2007 and higher and qMail are the only applications which implement a per session timeout. In this case, this timeout value could have an important impact on the protection against SMTP flood and it is part of our future work to investigate this application. Nonetheless, default timeout settings should be lowered in SMTP applications since it increases the security against SMTP flood without reducing the QoS.

4 Conclusion and Future Work

In this paper, we have conducted a study of a newer kind of DoS attacks, TCP application flooding attacks. For this type of attack, the aggressor tries to exhaust the resources on a server by opening a large number of TCP connections and let them idle until they get disconnected when a certain timeout value is reached. We argued that TCP connection flooding cannot be successful when it is aimed at the transport layer alone. In order to be efficient, such attacks need to be aimed at the application layer. We focused our work on incoming SMTP servers, in which case the attack is named SMTP flood.

In order to evaluate the performance of SMTP applications against SMTP flood, we then conducted three different kind of experiments on two famous SMTP server applications: Microsoft Exchange 2010 and Postfix 2.8. The first experiment was aimed at evaluating the performance of SMTP server applications with their default settings. The second experiment showed the impact of fine tuning various parameters to get the best performance for Postfix. The last experiment aimed at demonstrating the benefits of modifying the timeout values for both Postfix and Exchange and also validate that the throttling and stress adaptive behaviour was an asset to both applications. The results we obtained allowed us to answer the three research questions of our study.

In the case of Microsoft Exchange, even with the default settings, the server is highly resilient to an SMTP flood attack. Postfix showed devastating results as the server could not resist an attack of as many as 10 conn/s. However, by just adjusting a few parameters, we were able to get a better resistance to attacks as high as 1000 conn/s. Afterward, we have showed that for both Exchange and Postfix, modifying the timeout greatly increases the performance of the server. In the case of Exchange, although the server resist an attack with its default settings, it is clear that much better performance can be achieved with lowering the timeout values. In the case of Postfix, modifying the stress adapted timeout value will benefit the server although with the default settings, it still offers a much better defence than the normal timeout. We believe that in light of these results, advanced techniques such as dynamic timeout management presented in [7,6,5] improve the performance of the servers. The implementations are similar to the one we proposed and we have shown their performance against an SMTP flood attack.

This study was not only intended to evaluate the threat of SMTP flood attacks, but also to help prevent against them. It showed that SMTP flood attacks can be avoided by modifying the timeout value of the SMTP server. We demonstrated that the latest version of both Postfix and Exchange offer a good counter-measure when under stress. We would recommend for system administrator to change the default timeout value to as low as 30 seconds although lower settings can be used. It will increase the server's performance against SMTP flood attack without degrading the service to legitimate users since timeouts are likely to never occur as it has been demonstrated above. As a matter of fact, timeout value higher than a few tens of seconds should never be used except testing purpose since it really has no desirable positive effects.

As part of future work, we intend to construct a mathematical model of attack and performance against SMTP flood attacks. It could then be used to extend our results to other parts of the parameter space not yet explored by our experiments on current applications and (e.g. shorter timeout values, higher legitimate traffic rates). This would help us discover what parameter changes or policies would be more effective, and drive the development of a new generation of more DoS-resistant SMTP applications. Indeed, many other SMTP servers applications are available, and testing some others such as qmail or Exim which are widely used. Qmail is known as the most secure server, and Exim implements a dynamic rate limiting worth testing in a future work. Finally, as mentioned above, TCP connection flooding attacks can be aimed at any high level TCP application. It would thus be important to apply our methodology to other applications such as HTTP and compare our results with that of previous work on Web server DoS-resilience.

References

1. Postfix Documentation (2008), `http://www.postfix.org/documentation.html`
2. Postfix Stress Adaptive Documentation (2012), `http://www.postfix.org/STRESS_README.html`
3. Bencsath, B., Vajda, I.: Protection against DDoS attacks based on traffic level measurements. In: 2004 International Symposium on Collaborative Technologies and Systems, pp. 22–28 (2004)
4. Bencsath, B., Ronai, M.A.: Empirical analysis of denial of service attack against SMTP servers. In: 2007 International Symposium on Collaborative Technologies and Systems (2007)
5. Boteanu, D., Fernandez, J.M.: An exhaustive study of queue management as a DoS counter-measure. Tech. rep., École Polytechnique de Montréal (2008)

6. Boteanu, D., Fernandez, J.M., McHugh, J.: Implementing and testing dynamic timeout adjustment as a DoS counter-measure. In: Quality of Protection Workshop, QoP (2007)
7. Boteanu, D., Fernandez, J.M., McHugh, J., Mullins, J.: Queue management as a DoS counter-measure? In: Garay, J.A., Lenstra, A.K., Mambo, M., Peralta, R. (eds.) ISC 2007. LNCS, vol. 4779, pp. 263–280. Springer, Heidelberg (2007)
8. Brodsky, A., Brodsky, D.: A distributed content independent method for spam detection. In: HotBots 2007: Proceedings of the First Conference on First Workshop on Hot Topics in Understanding Botnets, p. 3. USENIX Association, Berkeley (2007)
9. Jung, J., Sit, E.: An empirical study of spam traffic and the use of DNS black lists. In: Proceedings of the 4th ACM SIGCOMM Conference on Internet Measurement, pp. 370–375. ACM, New York (2004)
10. Luo, H., Fang, B., Yun, X.: Anomaly detection in SMTP traffic. In: ITNG 2006: Proceedings of the Third International Conference on Information Technology: New Generations, pp. 408–413. IEEE Computer Society, Washington, DC (2006)
11. Microsoft TechNet: Windows Reliability and Performance Monitor (2008), `http://technet.microsoft.com/en-us/library/cc755081(WS.10).aspx`
12. Nagamalai, D., Dhinakaran, C., Lee, J.: Multi layer approach to defend DDoS attacks caused by spam. In: International Conference on Multimedia and Ubiquitous Engineering, MUE 2007, pp. 97–102. IEEE (2007)
13. Nagamalai, D., Dhinakaran, C., Lee, J.: Novel mechanism to defend DDoS attacks caused by spam. Arxiv preprint arXiv:1012.0610 (2010)
14. Ranjan, S., Swaminathan, R., Uysal, M., Knightly, E.: DDoS-resilient scheduling to counter application layer attacks under imperfect detection. In: Proceedings of 25th IEEE International Conference on Computer Communications, INFOCOM 2006, pp. 1–13 (2006)
15. Simpson, K., Bekman, S.: Fingerprinting the World's Mail Servers (2007), `http://www.oreillynet.com/pub/a/sysadmin/2007/01/05/fingerprinting-mail-servers.html`
16. Srivatsa, M., Iyengar, A., Yin, J., Liu, L.: A middleware system for protecting against application level denial of service attacks. In: van Steen, M., Henning, M. (eds.) Middleware 2006. LNCS, vol. 4290, pp. 260–280. Springer, Heidelberg (2006)
17. Srivatsa, M., Iyengar, A., Yin, J., Liu, L.: Mitigating application-level denial of service attacks on web servers: A client-transparent approach. ACM Trans. Web 2(3), 1–49 (2008)
18. Still, M., McCreath, E.: Inferring relative popularity of SMTP servers. In: Proc. of the USENIX LISA (2007)
19. Still, M., McCreath, E.: DDoS protections for SMTP servers. International Journal of Computer Science and Security (IJCSS) 4(6), 537 (2011)
20. stillhq.com: SMTP survey results 2010 (2010), `http://www.stillhq.com/research/smtpsurveys_feb2010.html`
21. Xie, Y., Yu, S.Z.: Monitoring the application-layer DDoS attacks for popular websites. IEEE/ACM Trans. Netw. 17(1), 15–25 (2009)

Towards Hybrid Honeynets via Virtual Machine Introspection and Cloning

Tamas K. Lengyel, Justin Neumann, Steve Maresca, and Aggelos Kiayias

University of Connecticut, Computer Science & Engineering Department,
Storrs, CT 06269, USA
{tamas.lengyel,justin.neumann,steven.maresca,aggelos.kiayias}@uconn.edu
http://www.cse.uconn.edu/

Abstract. We present a scalable honeynet system built on Xen using virtual machine introspection and cloning techniques to efficiently and effectively detect intrusions and extract associated malware binaries. By melding forensics tools with live memory introspection, the system is resistant to prior in-guest detection techniques of the monitoring environment and to subversion attacks that may try to hide aspects of an intrusion. By utilizing both copy-on-write disks and memory to create multiple identical high-interaction honeypot clones, the system relaxes the linear scaling of hardware requirements typically associated with scaling such setups. By employing a novel routing approach our system eliminates the need for post-cloning network reconfiguration, allowing the clone honeypots to share IP and MAC addresses while providing concurrent and quarantined access to the network. We deployed our system and tested it with live network traffic, demonstrating its effectiveness and scalability.

Keywords: Honeypot, Honeynet, Introspection, Virtual Machine, Network Security, Memory Forensics, Malware Analysis.

1 Introduction and Background

In the last decade there have been significant efforts to push high-interaction honeypots (HIHs) to virtualized environments. Virtualized environments provide many benefits for HIHs as they simplify containment and isolation of infections while providing easy and convenient methods for reverting a compromised HIH to a clean state. Furthermore, virtual environments enable real-time monitoring of the execution, disk and memory of the virtual HIHs, providing a direct way to observe infections as they occur and their effects on the compromised systems.

In order for these observations to provide meaningful, high-level state information, one must tackle a semantic-gap problem: given a virtual machine identify the features that are relevant to malware analysis, cf. [3][5]. While primarily system-call interception based approaches have been employed [7][4][8], recent advances in virtual machine introspection (VMI) techniques based purely upon memory observation have been shown to be an effective and practical solution

J. Lopez, X. Huang, and R. Sandhu (Eds.): NSS 2013, LNCS 7873, pp. 164–177, 2013.

[15]. Memory based VMI can enable a transparent and tamper resistant view into the state of a HIH, without revealing the presence of the monitoring environment [12].

While memory introspection based honeypot operations have been shown to be effective, the deployment of the technique on a large-scale honeynet setup presents numerous obstacles. Virtual HIHs provide complete systems and application code for an attacker, thus, a scaling issue arises as the hardware requirements increase linearly with the number of HIHs. Furthermore, networking challenges are present when creating quarantined network connectivity to identical HIH clones without internal "in-guest" network reconfiguration. In-guest network reconfiguration would inadvertently lead to changing the initial memory state of the HIH, making comparative analyses of the HIHs more difficult from a pure memory perspective. This issue leads to the "clone-routing" problem, which asks for a way to concurrently route packets to multiple clones that have identical network configurations.

In this paper we present a practical honeynet deployment utilizing a pure virtual machine memory introspection approach. The system takes advantage of recent developments in the open-source Xen hypervisor to effectively tackle the scalability problem with multiple operating systems as honeypots. We also present a novel approach to the "clone-routing" problem using the open-source Honeybrid engine that enables us to deploy clone HIHs simultaneously without requiring in-guest network reconfiguration.

2 Related Work

While many research papers have been published about implementing IDS and Honeypot solutions based on VMI techniques [7][9], the majority of these techniques approach the semantic-gap problem by intercepting system calls through the virtual machine monitor (VMM). These approaches, while effective, are vulnerable to in-guest detection of the monitoring environment by observation of the time-skew introduced by the system call interception [1][14]. In the following we highlight prior work that focuses on the memory scaling and introspection aspects of VMI based IDS and Honeypot solutions.

In 2005, Vrable et. al. implemented a highly scalable honeynet system named Potemkin using the Xen VMM [16]. Potemkin solved the scaling issue associated with running a large number of nearly identical VMs by introducing memory sharing that de-duplicates identical memory pages present across the VMs.While Potemkin was limited to paravirtualized (PV) Linux systems, later works, such as SnowFlock [11], support fully virtualized (HVM) systems as well. As of the latest version of Xen, Potemkin-style VM cloning of fully virtualized systems is now natively supported, enabling the creation of dense honeynet systems using a wide range of operating systems [10].

In 2008, Srivastava et. al. implemented a VMI-based firewall called VMwall using the Xen VMM [15]. VMwall captured network flows in the most privileged domain (Dom0) and correlated them with processes running within a VM by using the XenAccess library. VMwall accomplishes the correlation by extracting information from data-structures of the guest Linux kernel. In 2011, Dolan-Gavitt et. al. noted that the same functionality can be achieved by utilizing forensics tools, such as Volatility, which in conjunction with XenAccess allows the inspection of guest kernel data-structures [13].

In 2012, Biedermann et. al. presented a dynamic honeypot cloning system using CoW techniques for cloud platforms which enabled incoming attack traffic to be redirected to a stripped-down clone of the Linux VM under attack [2]. The clone honeypot system's memory was monitored to detect new processes spawning in the honeypot. This monitoring worked in concert with parsing of log files inside the clone's filesystem to detect relevant information about ongoing events. While the cloning techniques' performance was comparable to SnowFlock, the VMI techniques employed were susceptible to in-guest subversion attacks because an exploit could unhook its process structure from the kernel. Furthermore, the use of a production VM as the base for a clone honeypot raises security and manageability concerns, as all sensitive information in the original VM has to be found and stripped out during the cloning procedure. While Biedermann et al. explain stripping the contents of the filesystem as part of the cloning procedure, one must also take into account the non-trivial problem of stripping the CoW RAM of sensitive information as well, otherwise the clone honeypot could leak sensitive information.

In 2012, building upon the XenAccess successor library LibVMI , Volatility and LibGuestFS Lengyel et. al. implemented a pure memory observation based Honeypot monitor, VMI-Honeymon, which was capable of automatically detecting and extracting infections from a Windows XP HIH VM [12]. By taking advantage of Volatility's memory scanning approach for state reconstruction, VMI-Honeymon was shown to be increasingly resistant against kernel manipulation techniques used to evade detection in the monitored VM. VMI-Honeymon was deployed in a hybrid honeypot architecture using Honeybrid, which provided improved resiliency against DoS attacks, such as SYN-floods, while at the same time expanded the range of malware captures by utilizing the low-interaction honeypot (LIH) Dionaea as a fall-back system.

3 System Architecture and Design

Our system is a direct extension VMI-Honeymon, focusing on improving the stealth and tamper resistance of the original VMI-Honeymon system and fusing it with Potemkin-style dense VM deployment. The following is an in-depth description of our system.

3.1 Hybrid Setup

Drawing from the operational experiences with the original VMI-Honeymon system, we opted to use a similar hybrid setup with Honeybrid and Dionaea as our LIH. The hybrid honeypot setup fuses the benefits of low- and high-interaction honeypots to enable efficient use of available resources. In the hybrid setup all incoming connections are handled by the LIH first, utilizing HIHs only when needed to bypass the problem of wasting HIH resources on scans or handling a SYN-flood. The hybrid setup also provides a highly configurable firewall to monitor and contain potential intrusions. Figure 1 shows an overview of our setup.

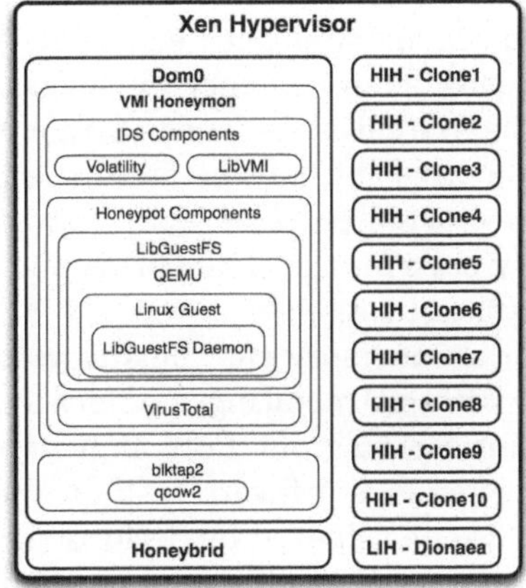

Fig. 1. VMI-Honeymon System Version 2

While the LIH provides DoS resiliency and emulated services in case the HIH resources are exhausted, the HIHs provide native systems and application code for intrusions. The HIHs are controlled by VMI-Honeymon and are periodically scanned with Volatility or when a network event is detected by Honeybrid. The use of Volatility in conjunction with LibVMI simplifies the state-reconstruction of various HIHs, including Windows XP, Vista and 7 as Volatility provides optimized routines for memory scanning and kernel data-structure fingerprinting for these operating systems.

The Volatility plugins can be characterized by their approach to state reconstruction: scanning or non-scanning plugins. The scanning plugins operate by performing a search for pool tag headers in the VM's memory, while non-scanning plugins operate by following standard kernel data-structures and paths. The trade-off between these two types of plugins is between performance and evasion resistance: scanning the entire memory of a VM takes longer, especially with large memory spaces, but is less likely to miss structures that are unhooked or hidden from the kernel. The Volatility scans in our experiments were limited to running only scanning plugins, which include: open files (filescan), open sockets (sockscan), network connections (connscan), processes (psscan), kernel modules (modscan), drivers (driverscan), mutexes (mutantscan), threads (thrdscan) and registry hives (hivescan).

To avoid introducing heavy memory latency that may lead to side-channel attacks potentially revealing the presence of the monitoring environment by measuring fluctuations in memory bandwidth, VMI-Honeymon was extended to include a limitation on running parallel memory scans to a pre-defined maximum concurrency level.

3.2 Memory Sharing

To achieve dense HIH deployment while avoiding the linear memory requirements associated with running multiple HIHs we take advantage of Xen's native memory sharing subsystem. Memory sharing enable the creation of nearly identical clones that transparently share the memory pages that have not changed during HIH execution. The system is designed so that the origin (parent) VM is paused, and all clones created initially point to the parent's static memory. When a clone writes to memory, Xen performs a copy-on-write (CoW) routine and duplicates the memory page for the clone, providing an optimized use of the overall memory of the physical host.

Recent developments of the memory sharing subsystem enables the creation of nearly identical clones without requiring modifications to Xen itself. While the subsystem is capable of carrying out Potemkin-style flash-cloning of VMs, implementing such cloning remains a future task on the official Xen roadmap. Nevertheless, cloning can also be achieved by performing the standard snapshot-and-restore routine with the XenLight library and de-duplicating the memory pages of the clone afterwards. While the approach is suboptimal, it is sufficient for evaluating the nature of several HIHs in a memory sharing setup.

A key aspect in performing the XenLight (XL) snapshot-restore routine is that the snapshot operation is performed only once when a VM is being designated as a honeypot origin. This snapshot operation also encompasses the scanning of the VM's memory with Volatility and performing a full filesystem fingerprinting with LibGuestFS, so that later infections can be correlated to a known clean-state of the honeypot. By taking advantage of features in the XL utility, the restore routine is further customized, so that the memory snapshot is restored with a dynamically created configuration to place the clone system on a QEMU copy-on-write (qcow2) filesystem.

3.3 Clone-Routing

While the combination of CoW RAM and filesystem enables the creation of identical clones, from a networking perspective, the identical clones pose a new challenge: the network interface in each clone will also remain identical, sharing both the MAC and IP address of the original VM. Placing these clones on the same network bridge leads to MAC and IP collisions that prevents proper routing. Both Potemkin and SnowFlock solve the problem of clone-routing by performing post-cloning IP reconfiguration of the VMs. However, this approach is untenable for a memory introspection based system: such reconfiguration will inadvertently change the initial state of the memory in the clone, leading to noisy analysis results when comparing memory states between the clone and its origin. This 'noise' is caused by the process of unpausing the VM to alter settings, which inadvertently allows suspended processes to resume execution, subsequently causing potentially substantial deviation from the original memory state. It could be argued that unpausing the VM for reconfiguration would alter the state so minimally that it does not appreciably impact the analysis goal. Nevertheless, eliminating any opportunity for the introduction of otherwise avoidable noise appears to be a sensible approach to reach our objectives.

To ensure the creation of truly identical clones and enable pure comparison between a clone and the origin, we retain the MAC and IP of the original VM for each clone. To do so, each clone is placed upon a separate network bridge to provide isolation for the MAC of the clone and avoid a collision. As seen in Figure 2, the clone's bridge is also attached to the VM that runs Honeybrid. This solution enables us to avoid collisions on the bridge, but requires custom routing to be setup on the Honeybrid VM that can identify clones based on the network interface they are attached to instead of their (identical) IP and MAC addresses.

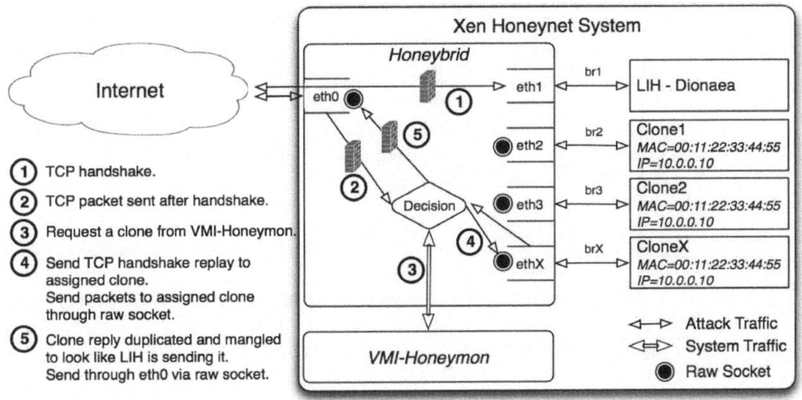

Fig. 2. Clone routing layout - externally initiated

In order to provide transparent connection switching between the LIH and an HIH, Honeybrid acts as a man-in-the-middle. Using iptables, each incoming connection in the Honeybrid VM is DNATed to the LIH and then queued to be processed by Honeybrid. Each TCP connection performs the TCP handshake with the LIH, and if the connection sends any additional packets, Honeybrid evaluates if the connection should be switched to an HIH. The evaluation is performed in conjunction with VMI-Honeymon where Honeybrid asks for a random available clone from VMI-Honeymon through an SSH tunnel. When there is one available, VMI-Honeymon responds with the clone's name and Honeybrid looks up the clone's interface from the pre-defined configuration file. If VMI-Honeymon reports that all HIHs are taken, the attacker's IP is pinned to use Dionaea. When the connection is switched to an HIH, Honeybrid replays the TCP handshake with the HIH. The incoming packets bound to the LIH thereafter are duplicated and modified to be directed to the clone and transmitted through a raw socket bound to the clone's network interface. The use of raw sockets forces the incoming packets to egress on the proper bridge. Packets from the HIH in return are also duplicated and modified to look like the packet was sent by the LIH.

For connections that are initiated from a clone, which happens for example when an exploit performs a reverse TCP connection, Honeybrid must be aware to route incoming packets for that connection back to the clone that initiated the connection. We use additional routing tables to specify which interface each clone is bound to and by using iptables marks and ip rules we can direct incoming reply packets to specific routing tables which in effect lead to specific clones, shown in Figure 3. We utilize Honeybrid to set the iptables mark on the reply packets by looking up Honeybrid's internal NAT table to identify the original source of the connection. An alternate approach would be to use iptables' CONNMARK save and restore feature to restore connection marks on the packets. We opted to use Honeybrid for this task as it allows for a potential configuration where internally initiated connections are dynamically switched between honeypots as well.

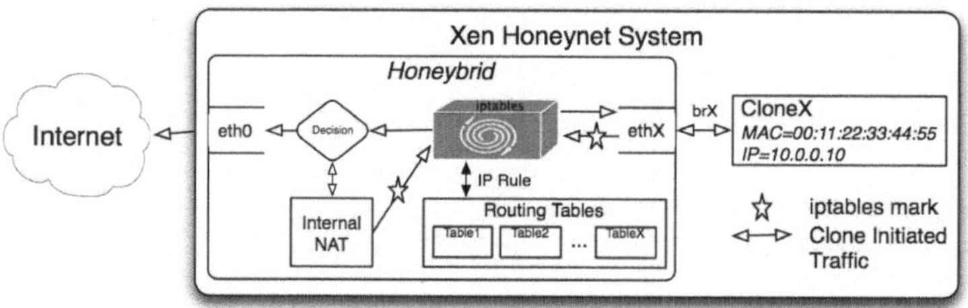

Fig. 3. Clone routing layout - internally initiated

Since currently the network setup requires manual configuration of the routing tables, network interfaces, iptables marks and ip rules, we used a pre-defined pool of clones for testing. This choice was made for our initial testing purposes and it should be noted that by using Xen's network hotplug features it would be possible to add new clones to the honeynet on-the-fly.

4 Operational Experiences

We have conducted several tests and experiments which are discussed in the following section. The tests were focused on the scalability of the memory sharing subsystem when used with Windows XP SP2 x86, Windows XP SP3 x86, and Windows 7 SP1 x86 clones. The experiments were conducted on a single server with the following hardware specs: second generation Intel i7-2600 quad-core CPU, Intel DQ67SW motherboard and 16GB DDR3 1333Mhz RAM. In our tests the Windows systems were running with the minimum recommended memory, which is 128MB RAM for Windows XP x86, and 1GB RAM for Windows 7 SP1 x86.

4.1 Idle Clones

An important aspect of our intrusion detection approach and of effective memory sharing is to limit the memory changes that are not related to an incoming attack. While in Windows XP the number of background processes that generate unrelated memory changes are limited to a handful of services (automatic updates, NTP, background disk defragmentation and background auto-layout), in Windows 7 the number of such services have increased significantly. The effect of these background services on Windows 7 is significant as even within two minutes the amount of shared memory decreases below 25%, effectively requiring over 750MB RAM to be allocated to the clone. At the same time, the clone itself reported only using 26% of its available memory, therefore the allocated CoW memory pages had only short-lived purposes.

By disabling background services which required the allocation of unnecessary resources and polluted our Volatility scans, we were able the minimize the resources allocated to idle clones. The disabled Windows 7 services include prefetch, superfetch, BITS, RAC, indexing, offline files and font cache. Figure 4 shows the resulting memory sharing state of the clones when idle, in terms of shared memory and Figure 5 in terms of additional RAM allocated to the Windows 7 SP1 clones. It is important to note that disabling too many services in the HIH will inevitably impact the attack surface of the HIH, as these services may contain vulnerabilities that could be looked for and/or exploited by the attacker. Since the services we disabled were not listening for incoming connections on the network we deemed their absence to be a reasonable trade-off from a network intrusion perspective. Further examining this performance / detection trade-off is an interesting question that can be tackled in future work.

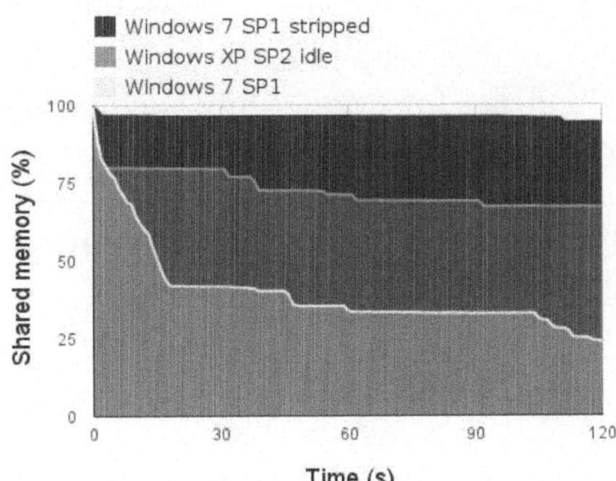

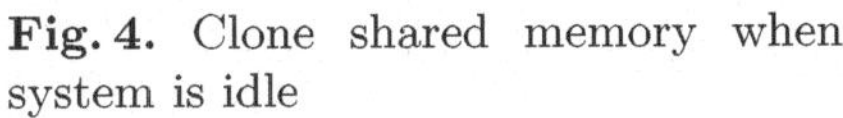
Fig. 4. Clone shared memory when system is idle

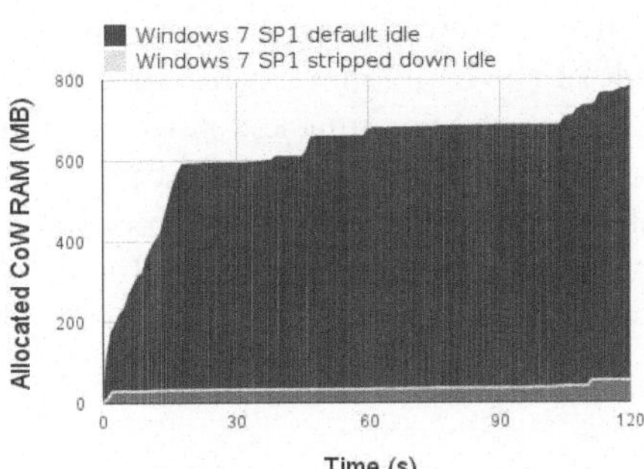

Fig. 5. CoW RAM allocated when system is idle

4.2 SMB and RDP

The second set of tests we ran on our system were targeting open services in our clones, namely the standard SMB and Remote Desktop services as both of these services have known vulnerabilities. The RDP sessions had significant impact on the RAM allocated to both the Windows XP and Windows 7 clones, reducing the amount of shared memory to 25% in case of the Windows XP clone and 50% for the Windows 7 clone, as seen in Figure 6. In terms of actual RAM allocation, the Windows 7 clone's 50% memory allocation translates to allocating 500MB RAM for the clone, while the Windows XP clone at 75% required 96MB RAM.

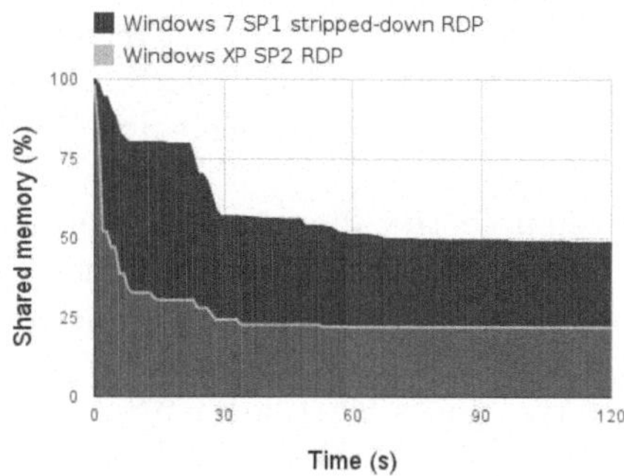

Fig. 6. Clone shared memory after RDP connection

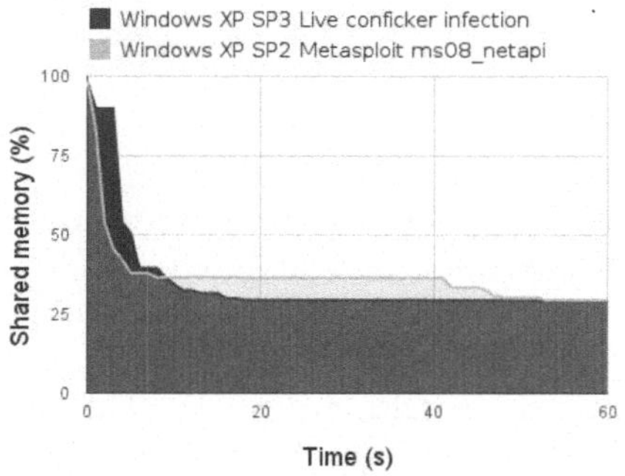

Fig. 7. Clone shared memory after SMB exploitation

The SMB tests were only conducted on Windows XP clones as Windows 7 SP1's SMB stack has no publicly available exploit. We used a manual Metasploit exploit session (ms08_067_netapi) to benchmark the effect on the Windows XP clone when used with a meterpreter payload that performs a reverse TCP call-back. This exploit was chosen because Conficker uses the same vulnerabilities, which has been observed many times during our live tests. Figure 7 shows the result of the benchmark compared to a live Conficker infection. Only the first 60 seconds were benchmarked since the Conficker infection performed a connection attempt to a third party at that point, triggering our pause-scan-revert operation with VMI-Honeymon. The Windows XP clones retained 25% of their memory in a shared state, which translates to saving 32MB of RAM.

4.3 Live Sessions

Our experiments were conducted using multiple HIH back-ends drawn from a pool of clones consisting of five Windows XP SP3 x86 and five Windows 7 SP1 x86 VMs. Each Windows VM was configured with the firewall, automatic updates, time synchronization and memory paging turned off and remote desktop enabled. Windows 7 had additional adjustments as described previously in Section 4.1.

For the live captures we utilized a single IP on a university network with all firewall ports open. Over two weeks of activity, we recorded a total of 52761 connections out of which 6207 were forwarded to an HIH. Currently we forward any incoming connection that passes the TCP handshake to an HIH (if one is available), regardless of whether the HIH is actually listening on the port the attack is targeting. In this way, 1466 forwarded connections never actually established real communication with the HIHs, because these connections targeted ports that were closed (MsSQL, MySQL, SSH, HTTP, VNC).

For the live sessions, one aspect we were interested in was the concurrency of active clones and the amount of memory savings achieved due to CoW RAM. Figure 8 and Figure 9 shows the breakdown of the concurrency that occurred in our system. Figure 10 and 11 show the distribution of the memory remaining shared at the end of the clones' life cycle.

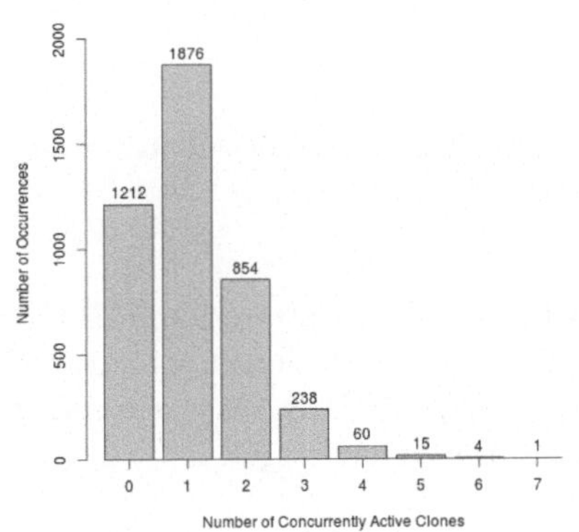

Fig. 8. Clone activity by number of occurrences

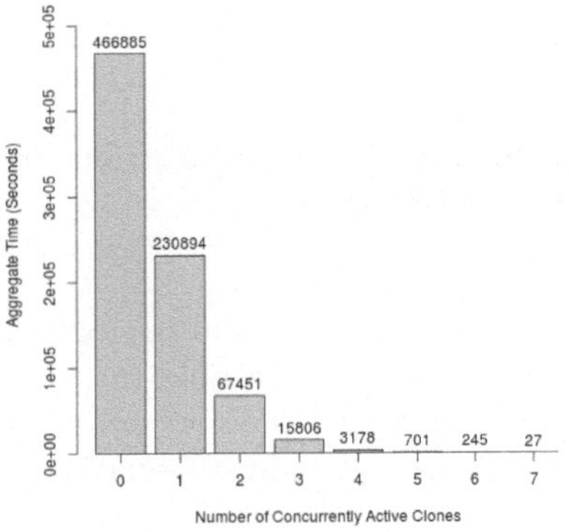

Fig. 9. Clone activity by time spent in each state

While VMI-Honeymon is configurable to scan the clones periodically during their life-span, we decided to limit such scans to a single instance which happens when the clone reaches its maximum allowed life-span or when a network event is detected. The maximum life-span was set at two minutes, which is cut short if the clone initiates a connection to an IP other than the attacker's. The highest concurrency of active clones was observed as seven, therefore our pool of ten clones was never depleted. The HIHs were actively handling incoming attack traffic 41% of the time during our experiment.

By using the information gathered during these sessions we calculate the projected memory savings when running multiple clones concurrently, shown in Figure 12 and Figure 13. From these projections it is clear that the savings are more significant when the base memory of the HIH is large, as in the case of Windows 7 SP1, allowing for a larger percentage of the overall memory to remain shared. We estimate that we would be able to run 40 Windows 7 SP1 clones concurrently and not run out of memory even if all forty clones were three standard deviations above the observed average memory allocation with our 16GB RAM

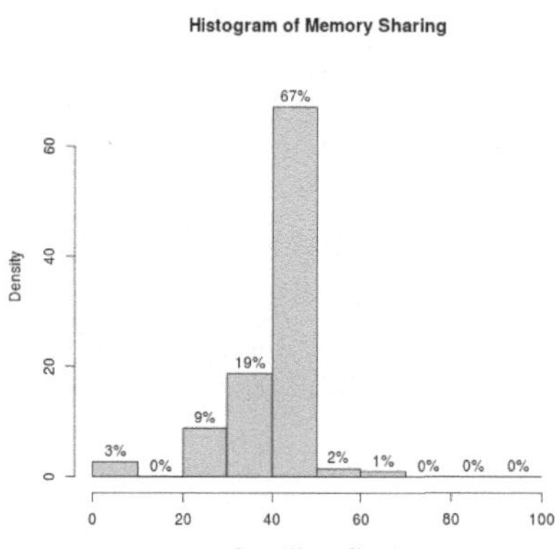

Fig. 10. Shared memory distribution of Windows XP SP3

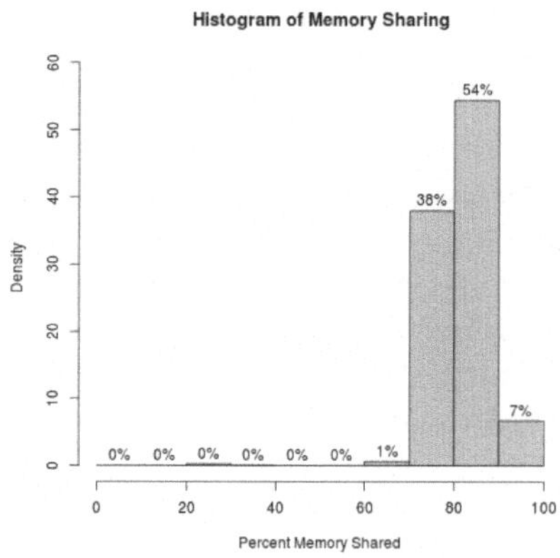

Fig. 11. Shared memory distribution of Windows 7 SP1

limitation (this would still use only 13.34GB RAM out of the available 16GB). Similarly, we would be able to run 140 Windows XP SP3 clones concurrently and not run out of memory which would allocate 14.6GB RAM assuming all clones are three standard deviations above the observed average.

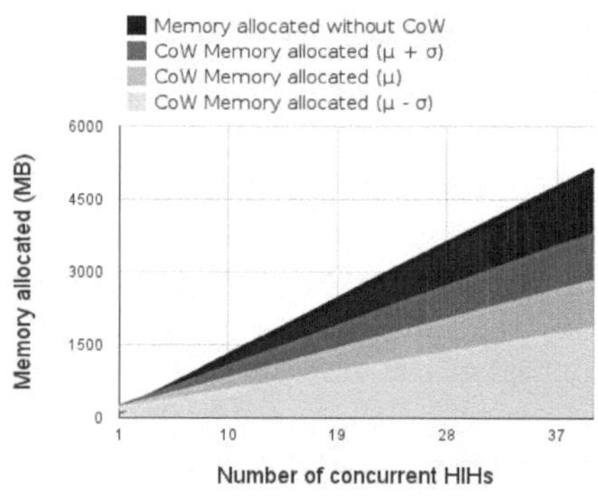

Fig. 12. Projected memory savings of Windows XP SP3. μ=75.52MB σ=10.1MB

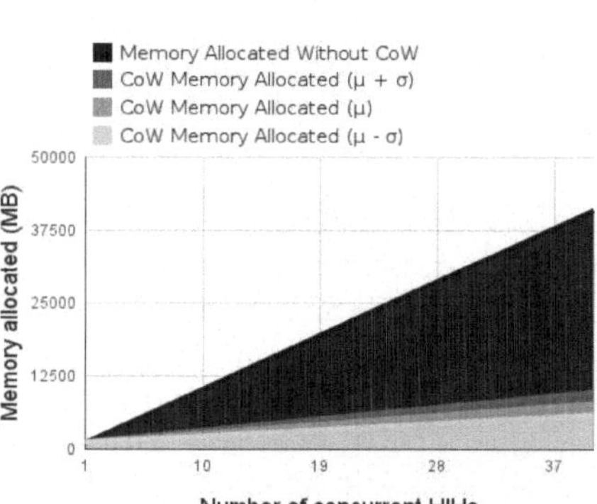

Fig. 13. Projected memory savings of Windows 7 SP1. μ=170.94MB σ=48.3MB

The malware samples we obtained were all Conficker variants verified by VirusTotal and all of the samples were extracted from the Windows XP HIHs. Nevertheless, we have observed several intrusions in our Windows 7 HIHs as well, which resulted in the clones trying to perform DNS queries. The service exploited during these attack sessions were against the SMB server running on port 445. To allow these intrusions to further interact with the HIH to potentially drop a payload we will be refining our firewall policy to allow some DNS queries and to allow connections to the IP's mapped in the DNS response (with certain rate-limiting applied as to avoid potential malware propagation from within the honeynet).

5 Future Work

Attackers wishing to DoS our system could produce slightly-interactive SYN-flood like traffic which would step just past the initial handshake, causing an HIH to be deployed for every connection, depleting our pre-defined pool of available HIHs. Another DoS approach could use the compromised HIHs to make small changes throughout the memory of the VM in order to produce changes in as many memory pages as possible, making Xen CoW RAM less effective and diminishing the benefits of the memory deduplication. Both of these issues require the system to be modified so that safety checks are included that mitigate these problems. The slightly interactive connection problem could be avoided by dynamically shortening the life-span of the clone when network inactivity is detected instead of running it for a pre-defined period of time. The memory dedup attack could be potentially mitigated by dynamically checking the concurrency of the clones running in the system and their memory sharing stage to automatically pause and halt clones whose memory sharing is approaching a critical state.

While our cloning routine is effective and required no changes to Xen, it can clearly be improved. Further work is necessary to be able to perform flash-cloning rather than restoring the entire memory image to the clone just to be discarded by the memory sharing. Similarly, instead of running a pre-defined pool of clones, it would be beneficial to allow the pool to dynamically balloon up and down to match the incoming attack rate. This inevitably requires Honeybrid to be able to automatically add and remove clones from its routing engine, which could be achieved by careful cordination with VMI-Honeymon and by utilizing Xen's network hotplug features.

Although Volatility's memory scanning and fingerprinting routines are already optimized, there is more room for improvement. Currently each Volatility scan has to evaluate the target memory from start to end independently of one-another. Combining the scans in such a way that Volatility detects all structures by traversing the memory only once would improve performance considerably. However, it should be noted that the pool tag headers that these scans rely on can still be manipulated by rootkits and therefore a more robust scanning approach should be taken into consideration that uses, for example, data-structure invariants for fingerprinting [6].

Building upon the nature of Xen's CoW RAM it would be possible to direct Volatility to examine only the specific memory regions which have changed during the execution of the HIH, drastically reducing the memory space the scans have to evaluate. Furthermore, through Xen's memory events subsystem, these directed and combined Volatility scans can potentially allow for real-time monitoring of the HIHs, instead of the current one-time evaluation at the end of the clone's life cycle.

Our current experiments were performed using a single IP on a university network but, as we have shown, the system is capable of effective scaling and it is possible to utilize a darknet to increase the rate of the incoming connections. Furthermore, our experiments focused on x86 versions of Windows XP and Windows 7, but as Volatility supports both 64-bit versions of these operations systems, as well as Linux, it is possible to use these OSs as HIHs as well in future experiments.

6 Conclusion

We have shown a practical solution to deploying a scalable honeynet system on Xen using virtual machine introspection techniques to detect intrusions and extract associated malware binaries. By melding forensics tools with live memory introspection the system remains effectively transparent to in-guest detection of the monitoring environment and is increasingly resilient against in-guest subversion attacks. By utilizing both copy-on-write disks and memory, the system mitigates the linear increase in hardware requirements typically associated with running multiple virtual HIH. Additionally, our novel routing approach eliminates the need for post-cloning network reconfiguration of the HIHs. While our implementation is an effective and practical solution to achieve scalable and automated malware capture, both opportunities and challenges remain for future enhancements.

References

1. Bahram, S., Jiang, X., Wang, Z., Grace, M., Li, J., Srinivasan, D., Rhee, J., Xu, D.: Dksm: Subverting virtual machine introspection for fun and profit. In: Proceedings of the 2010 29th IEEE Symposium on Reliable Distributed Systems, SRDS 2010, pp. 82–91. IEEE Computer Society, Washington, DC (2010), http://dx.doi.org/10.1109/SRDS.2010.39
2. Biedermann, S., Mink, M., Katzenbeisser, S.: Fast dynamic extracted honeypots in cloud computing. In: Proceedings of the 2012 ACM Workshop on Cloud Computing Security Workshop, CCSW 2012, pp. 13–18. ACM, New York (2012), http://doi.acm.org/10.1145/2381913.2381916
3. Chen, P.M., Noble, B.D.: When virtual is better than real. In: Proceedings of the Eighth Workshop on Hot Topics in Operating Systems, HOTOS 2001, pp. 133–138. IEEE Computer Society, Washington, DC (2001), http://dl.acm.org/citation.cfm?id=874075.876409
4. Dinaburg, A., Royal, P., Sharif, M.I., Lee, W.: Ether: malware analysis via hardware virtualization extensions. In: Ning, P., Syverson, P.F., Jha, S. (eds.) ACM Conference on Computer and Communications Security, pp. 51–62. ACM (2008), http://doi.acm.org/10.1145/1455770.1455779

5. Dolan-Gavitt, B., Leek, T., Zhivich, M., Giffin, J.T., Lee, W.: Virtuoso: Narrowing the semantic gap in virtual machine introspection. In: IEEE Symposium on Security and Privacy, pp. 297–312. IEEE Computer Society (2011), http://doi.ieeecomputersociety.org/10.1109/SP.2011.11
6. Dolan-Gavitt, B., Srivastava, A., Traynor, P., Giffin, J.: Robust signatures for kernel data structures. In: Proceedings of the 16th ACM Conference on Computer and Communications Security, CCS 2009, pp. 566–577. ACM, New York (2009), http://doi.acm.org/10.1145/1653662.1653730
7. Garfinkel, T., Rosenblum, M.: A virtual machine introspection based architecture for intrusion detection. In: NDSS. The Internet Society (2003), http://www.isoc.org/isoc/conferences/ndss/03/proceedings/papers/13.pdf
8. Hofmeyr, S.A., Somayaji, A., Forrest, S.: Intrusion detection using sequences of system calls. Journal of Computer Security 6, 151–180 (1998), http://dl.acm.org/citation.cfm?id=1298084
9. Jiang, X., Wang, X., Xu, D.: Stealthy malware detection and monitoring through VMM-based "out-of-the-box" semantic view reconstruction. ACM Trans. Inf. Syst. Secur. 13(2) (2010), http://doi.acm.org/10.1145/1698750.1698752
10. Lagar-Cavilla, H.A.: Xen-devel: Cloning a vm and copy-on-write deduplicating memory using cow page sharing in xen 4+ (February 2, 2012), http://lists.xen.org/archives/html/xen-devel/2012-02/msg00259.html
11. Lagar-Cavilla, H.A., Whitney, J.A., Scannell, A.M., Patchin, P., Rumble, S.M., de Lara, E., Brudno, M., Satyanarayanan, M.: Snowflock: rapid virtual machine cloning for cloud computing. In: Proceedings of the 4th ACM European Conference on Computer Systems, EuroSys 2009, pp. 1–12. ACM, New York (2009), http://doi.acm.org/10.1145/1519065.1519067
12. Lengyel, T.K., Neumann, J., Maresca, S., Payne, B.D., Kiayias, A.: Virtual machine introspection in a hybrid honeypot architecture. In: Proceedings of the 5th USENIX Conference on Cyber Security Experimentation and Test, CSET 2012, p. 5. USENIX Association, Berkeley (2012), http://dl.acm.org/citation.cfm?id=2372336.2372343
13. Payne, B.D., Lee, W.: Secure and flexible monitoring of virtual machines. In: ACSAC, pp. 385–397. IEEE Computer Society (2007), http://ieeexplore.ieee.org/xpls/abs_all.jsp?arnumber=4413005
14. Pék, G., Bencsáth, B., Buttyán, L.: nether: in-guest detection of out-of-the-guest malware analyzers. In: Proceedings of the Fourth European Workshop on System Security, EUROSEC 2011, pp. 3:1–3:6. ACM, New York (2011), http://doi.acm.org/10.1145/1972551.1972554
15. Srivastava, A., Giffin, J.T.: Tamper-resistant, application-aware blocking of malicious network connections. In: Lippmann, R., Kirda, E., Trachtenberg, A. (eds.) RAID 2008. LNCS, vol. 5230, pp. 39–58. Springer, Heidelberg (2008), http://dx.doi.org/10.1007/978-3-540-87403-4_3
16. Vrable, M., Ma, J., Chen, J., Moore, D., Vandekieft, E., Snoeren, A.C., Voelker, G.M., Savage, S.: Scalability, fidelity, and containment in the potemkin virtual honeyfarm. In: Proceedings of the Twentieth ACM Symposium on Operating Systems Principles, SOSP 2005, pp. 148–162. ACM, New York (2005), http://doi.acm.org/10.1145/1095810.1095825

MADS: Malicious Android Applications Detection through String Analysis

Borja Sanz, Igor Santos, Javier Nieves, Carlos Laorden, Iñigo Alonso-Gonzalez, and Pablo G. Bringas

S^{3}Lab, DeustoTech Computing, University of Deusto, Bilbao, Spain
{borja.sanz,isantos,jnieves,claorden,pablo.garcia.bringas}@deusto.es, ialonso@opendeusto.es

Abstract. The use of mobile phones has increased in our lives because they offer nearly the same functionality as a personal computer. Besides, the number of applications available for Android-based mobile devices has also experienced a importat grow. Google offers to programmers the opportunity to upload and sell applications in the Android Market, but malware writers upload their malicious code there. In light of this background, we present here Malicious Android applications Detection through String analysis (MADS), a new method that extracts the contained strings from the Android applications to build machine-learning classifiers and detect malware.

Keywords: malware, android, machine learning, security.

1 Introduction

Smartphones have become very popular. They allow us to check the email, to browse the Internet, or to play games with our friends, wherever we are. But, in order to take advantage of every possibility these devices may offer, applications have to be previously installed in the devices.

In the past, the installation of applications was a source of problems for the users because there was not a centralised site for users to download their applications and they used to search them in the Internet. Several operating systems like Symbian, in an attempt to avoid piracy and protect the device, used an authentication protocol that certified the application and, usually, caused several inconveniences to the users (e.g., they could not install applications although they had bought them).

Nowadays, new methods for the distribution and installation have appeared thanks to the widely used Internet connection in mobile devices. Therefore, users can install any application they want, avoiding the connection of the device to a personal computer. The App Store of Apple was the first online store to bring this new paradigm to novel users. The model was praised and it became very successful, leading to other vendors such as RIM, Microsoft or Google to adopt the same business model and developing application stores for their devices. These factors have led a large number of developers to focus on these platforms.

J. Lopez, X. Huang, and R. Sandhu (Eds.): NSS 2013, LNCS 7873, pp. 178–191, 2013.

However, malware has also arrived to the application markets. To this end, both Android and iOS have different approaches to deal with malicious software. According to their response to the US Federal Communication Commission's July 2009[1], Apple applies a very strict review process by at least two reviewers. Android, on the other hand, relies on its security permission system and on the user's sound judgement. Unfortunately, users have usually no security consciousness and they do not read required permissions before installing an application.

Both the AppStore and Android Market include in their terms of service, clauses that do not allow developers to upload malware to their markets but both markets have hosted malware. Therefore, we can conclude that both models by themselves are insufficient to ensure safety and other methods must be developed in order to enhance the security of the devices.

Machine learning classification has been widely used in malware detection [1–5]. Several approaches [6, 7] have been presented that focus on classifying executables specifying the malware category (e.g., Trojan horses, worms or viruses) or even the malware family.

Regarding Android, the number of new malware samples is also increasing exponentially and several approaches have already been proposed to detect malware. Shabtai et al. [8] built several machine learning models using as features: the count of elements, attributes and namespaces of the parsed Android Package File (.apk). To validate their models, they selected features using three selection methods: Information Gain, Fisher Score and Chi-Square. Their approach achieved 89% of accuracy classifying applications into only 2 categories: tools or games.

There are other proposals that use dynamic analysis for the detection of malicious applications. Crowdroid [9] is an approach that analyses the behaviour of the applications. Blasing et al. [10] created AASandbox, which is a hybrid dynamic-static approximation. The dynamic part is based on the analysis of the logs for the low-level interactions obtained during execution. Shabtai and Elovici [11] also proposed a Host-Based Intrusion Detection System (HIDS) which uses machine learning methods that determines whether the application is malware or not. Google has also deployed a framework for the supervision of applications called Bouncer. Oberheide and Miller [12] revealed how the system works: it is based in QEMU and it performs both static and dynamic analysis.

In light of this background, we present MADS (Malicious Android applications Detection through String analysis), a novel approach for detection of malware in Android. This method employs the strings contained in the disassembled Android applications, constructing a bag of words model in order to train machine-learning algorithms to provide detection of malicious applications.

In summary, our main contributions are: (i) we present a new technique for the representation of Android applications, based on the bag of words model formed by the strings contained in the disassembled application; (ii) we adapt well-known machine learning classifiers to provide detection of malicious applications

[1] `http://online.wsj.com/public/resources/documents/wsj-2009-0731-FCCApple.pdf`

in Android; and (iii)we found out that machine-learning algorithms can provide detection of malicious applications in Android using the strings contained in the disassembled application as features.

The reminder of this paper is organised as follows. Section 2 presents and details MADS, our new approach to represent applications in order to detect malware in Android. Section 3 describes the machine-learning algorithms we have used. Section 4 describes the empirical evaluation of our method. Finally, section 5 discusses the obtained results and outlines the avenues of further work in this area.

2 Representation of Applications Using String Analysis

One of the most widely-used techniques for classic malware detection is the usage of strings contained in the files [13, 2]. This technique extracts every character strings within an executable file. The information that may be found in these strings can be, for example, options in the menus of the application or malicious URLs to connect to. In this way, by means of an analysis of these data, it is possible to extract valuable information in order to determine whether an application is malicious or not.

The process that we followed in MADS is the following. We start by disassembling the application using the open-source Android disassembler `smali`[2]. Hereafter, we search for the `const-string` operation code within the disassembled code.

Using this disassembler, the representation of Android binaries are semantically richer than common desktop binaries. For example, the strings extraction in desktop binaries are complex and it is usual that malware writers obfuscate them to hide relevant information. Instead, the obfuscation of strings in the binaries of Android is more difficult, given the internal structure of the binaries in this platform.

In order to conform the strings, we tokenise the found symbols using the classic separators (e.g., dot, comma, colon, semi-colon, blank space, tab, etc.). In this way, we construct a text representation of an executable $\mathcal{E}$, that is formed by strings s_i, such as $\mathcal{E} = (s_1, s_2, ..., s_{n-1}, s_n)$ where n is the number of strings within a file.

$\mathcal{C}$ is the set of Android executables $\mathcal{E}$, $\{\mathcal{E} : \{s_1, s_2, ...s_n\}\}$, each comprising n strings $s_1, s_2, \ldots, s_n$, we define the weight $w_{i,j}$ as the number of times the string s_i appears in the executable $\mathcal{E}_j$ if s_i is not present in $\mathcal{E}$, $w_{i,j} = 0$. Therefore, an application $\mathcal{E}_j$ can be represented as the vector of weights $\boldsymbol{\mathcal{E}_j} = (w_{1,j}, w_{2,j}, ...w_{n,j})$.

In order to represent a string collection, a common approach in text mining area is to use the Vector Space Model (VSM) [14], which represents documents algebraically, as vectors in a multidimensional space.

This space consists only of positive axis intercepts. Executables are represented by a string-by-executable matrix, where the $(i, j)^{th}$ element illustrates the association between the ith string and the jth executable. This association

[2] `http://code.google.com/p/smali/`

reflects the occurrence of the ith string in executable j. Strings can represent can be individually weighted, allowing the strings to become more or less important within a given executable or the executable collection $\mathcal{C}$ as a whole.

We used the *Term Frequency – Inverse Document Frequency* (TF–IDF) [15] weighting schema, where the weight of the ith string in the jth executable, denoted by $weight(i, j)$, is defined by:

$$weight(i, j) = tf_{i,j} \cdot idf_i \tag{1}$$

where *term frequency* $tf_{i,j}$ is defined as:

$$tf_{i,j} = \frac{n_{i,j}}{\sum_k n_{k,j}} \tag{2}$$

where $n_{i,j}$ is the number of times the string s_i appears in a executable $\mathcal{E}_j$, and $\sum_k n_{k,j}$ is the total number of strings in the executable $\mathcal{E}_j$. The inverse term frequency idf_i is defined as:

$$idf_i = \log\left(\frac{|\mathcal{C}|}{|\mathcal{C} : t_i \in \mathcal{E}|}\right) \tag{3}$$

where $|\mathcal{C}|$ is the total number of executables and $|\mathcal{C} : s_i \in \mathcal{E}|$ is the number of executables containing the string s_i.

Once we have characterised the application, we must classify it. In order to achieve it, we use machine learning algorithms. These algorithms allow us to, given a training dataset, assign a category (i.e., malware or goodware) to a sample under evaluation.

3 Machine-Learning Algorithms

Machine-learning is an active research area within *Artificial Intelligence* (AI) that focuses on the design and development of new algorithms that allow computers to reason and decide based on data [16].

Machine-learning algorithms can commonly be divided into three different types depending on the training data: supervised learning, unsupervised learning and semi-supervised learning. For supervised algorithms, the training dataset must be labelled (e.g., the class of an executable) [17]. Unsupervised learning algorithms try to determine how data are organised into different groups named clusters. Therefore, data do not need to be labelled [18]. Finally, semi-supervised machine-learning algorithms use a mixture of both labelled and unlabelled data in order to build models, improving the accuracy of solely unsupervised methods [19].

Because executables can be properly labelled, we use supervised machine-learning; however, in the future, we would also like to test unsupervised and semi-supervised methods for detection of malware in Android.

3.1 Bayesian Networks

Bayesian Networks [20], which are based on the *Bayes Theorem*, are defined as graphical probabilistic models for multivariate analysis. Specifically, they are directed acyclic graphs that have an associated probability distribution function [21]. Nodes within the directed graph represent problem variables (they can be either a premise or a conclusion) and the edges represent conditional dependencies between such variables. Moreover, the probability function illustrates the strength of these relationships in the graph [21].

The most important capability of Bayesian Networks is their ability to determine the probability that a certain hypothesis is true (e.g., the probability of an executable to be malware) given a historical dataset.

3.2 Decision Trees

Decision Tree classifiers are a type of machine-learning classifiers that are graphically represented as trees. Internal nodes represent conditions regarding the variables of a problem, whereas final nodes or leaves represent the ultimate decision of the algorithm [22].

Different training methods are typically used for learning the graph structure of these models from a labelled dataset. We use *Random Forest*, an ensemble (i.e., combination of weak classifiers) of different randomly-built decision trees [23], and *J48*, the WEKA [24] implementation of the *C4.5* algorithm [25].

3.3 K-Nearest Neighbour

The *K-Nearest Neighbour* (KNN) [26] classifier is one of the simplest supervised machine-learning models. This method classifies an unknown specimen based on the class of the instances closest to it in the training space by measuring the distance between the training instances and the unknown instance.

Even though several methods to choose the class of the unknown sample exist, the most common technique is to simply classify the unknown instance as the most common class amongst the K-nearest neighbours.

3.4 Support Vector Machines (SVM)

SVM algorithms divide the n-dimensional space representation of the data into two regions using a *hyperplane*. This hyperplane always maximises the *margin* between those two regions or classes. The margin is defined by the farthest distance between the examples of the two classes and computed based on the distance between the closest instances of both classes, which are called *supporting vectors* [27].

Instead of using linear hyperplanes, it is common to use the so-called *kernel functions*. These kernel functions lead to non-linear classification surfaces, such as polynomial, radial or sigmoid surfaces [28]

4 Experimental Results

In this section we describe the empirical validation of our method for Android malware applications detection.

4.1 Dataset Description

In this subsection, we detail how the dataset has been composed. The requirements that the final dataset has to meet are the following: (i) it must be heterogeneous, showing the diversity in the types of applications that are available in the Android market; and (ii) it must be proportional to the number of samples that already exist of each type of application, to this end, two different datasets were created: one composed of the benign applications and other composed of malicious software.

Malicious Software. To compile the malware dataset, the samples were obtained from the company VirusTotal[3]. VirusTotal offers a series of services called VirusTotal Malware Intelligence Services, which allow researchers to obtain samples from their databases.

To generate the dataset, we first selected the samples. Initially, we collected 2,808 samples. Next, we normalised the values given by the different antivirus vendors. The goal of this step was to determine their reliability detecting malware in Android.

To this end, we assumed that every sample that was detected as an specific piece of malware (i.e., already cataloged, not generic) by at least one antivirus was malware. Then, we evaluated the detection rate of each antivirus engine with respect to the complete malware dataset:

$$a_w = \frac{n}{n_t} \tag{4}$$

where n is the number of samples detected by the antivirus and n_t is the total number of each antivirus detecting malware on the Android platform. Then, we evaluated each malware sample taking into account the weights of each antivirus.

For this evaluation, we applied the next metric:

$$m_w = \sum a_w |\forall a \in \mathcal{A} \tag{5}$$

being $\mathcal{A} = (a_1, a_2, , a_\ell)$ the set of the weights of the antivirus computed before, for the antiviruses that detect the sample. Therefore, m_w rates the detection taking into account the antiviruses that detect the sample.

We determined a threshold below which a sample cannot enter the dataset, in order to ensure that the samples belonging to it are relevant enough. The threshold was set empirically to 0.1, which provided us a total number of 1,202 malware samples. Besides, we focused on the results given by the different antiviruses to determine whether the samples were actually Android-based applications. This

[3] http://www.virustotal.com

was performed using the naming convention of the different antivirus engines. Finally, we also removed any duplicated samples.

We finally acquired a malware dataset composed of 333 unique samples. According to the report elaborated by LookOut[4], this dataset represents the 75% of the malware that existed in July, 2011.

Benign Software. To generate this dataset, we gathered 1,811 Android samples of diverse types. To classify them adequately, we categorised them using the same scheme that Android market follows. To this extent, we categorised the applications by means of an unofficial library called android-market-api[5]. Once the samples were classified, we selected a subgroup of samples to be part of the final benign software dataset. The employed methodology was the following:

Table 1. Number of samples for each category.

Category	Samples	Category	Samples
Arcade and Action	32	Multimedia & Video	23
Books	10	Music & Audio	12
Business	1	News & magazines	7
Card Games	2	Personalisation	6
Casuals	10	Photography	6
Comics	1	Productivity	27
Communication	20	Puzzles	16
Education	0	Races	2
Enterprise	4	Sales	3
Entertainment	16	Society	25
Finance	3	Sports	5
Health	3	Tools	80
Libraries & Demos	2	Transportation	2
Lifestyle	4	Travels	8
Medicine	1	Weather	2

Total number of benign applications: 333

1. *Determine the number of total samples.* To facilitate the training of the machine-learning models, it is usually desirable for both categories to be balanced. Therefore, given that the number of malware samples is inferior to the benign category, we opted to reduce the number of benign applications to 333.
2. *Determine the number of samples for each benign category.* Second, we decided to follow the proportion present in the Android market and, therefore, selected the number of applications accordingly.
3. *Types of application.* There are different types of applications: native ones (developed by means of the Android SDK), web (developed through HTML,

[4] `https://www.mylookout.com/_downloads/lookout-mobile-threat-report-2011.pdf`

[5] `http://code.google.com/p/android-market-api/`

JavaScript and CSS) and widgets (simple applications displayed in the Android desktop). All these applications have different features. To generate the dataset, we made no distinction in the type of application and included samples of the different types in the final dataset.

4. S*election of the samples for each category.* Once the number of applications for each category was determined, we selected the applications randomly using a Monte Carlo sampling method, avoiding different versions of the same application.

Following this methodology, we constructed the benign dataset. The number of samples for each category is shown in Table 1.

4.2 Configuration

For the evaluation of the different machine learning algorithms we used the tool WEKA (Waikato Environment for Knowledge Analysis) [24]. Specifically, the algorithms used in this tool can be seen in Table 2. In those cases in which no configuration parameters are specified, the configuration used was the default.

Table 2. Configuration of the algorithms

Used Algorithms	Configuration
NaïveBayes	N/A
Bayessian Network	K2 and TAN
SVM	Polynomial and Normalised Polynomial Kernel
KNN	K: 1, 3 and 5
J48	N/A
RandomForest	N = 10, 50 and 100

The dataset was divided using the k-cross-validation technique [29, 30]. It divides k times the input dataset in k complementary subsets using one shaping sample data set, called test set, while the rest of subsets forming the joint training. To obtain the error ratio for the final sample, the arithmetic mean of the error rates obtained for each of the k iterations is calculated.

4.3 Evaluation

The evaluation was performed by measuring the following metrics:

– **True Positive Ratio (TPR)**

$$TPR = \frac{TP}{TP + FN} \tag{6}$$

where TP is the number of malware cases correctly classified (true positives) and FN is the number of malware cases misclassified as legitimate software (false negatives).

– **False Positive Ratio (FPR)**

$$FPR = \frac{FP}{FP + TN} \tag{7}$$

where FP is the number of benign software cases incorrectly detected as malware and TN is the number of legitimate executables correctly classified.

– **Accuracy.** It is the total number of the classifier's hits divided by the number of instances in the whole dataset:

$$Accuracy = \frac{TP + TN}{TP + FN + FP + TN} \tag{8}$$

– **Area under the ROC Curve (AUC).** AUC establishes the relation between false negatives and false positives [31]. The ROC curve is obtained by plotting the TPR against the FPR.

4.4 Results

Table 3 shows the obtained results for the tested algorithms.

Table 3. Obtained results

Algorithm	*TPR*	*FPR*	*AUC*	*Accuracy (%)*
Naïve Bayes	0.93	0.17	0.90	88.07%
Bayesian Network: K2	0.71	0.13	0.89	78.68%
Bayesian Network: TAN	0.83	0.11	0.94	86,09%
SVM: Poly	0.93	0.03	0.95	94.70%
SVM: NPoly	0.77	0.04	0.86	86.45%
KNN K=1	0.35	0.02	0.84	66.24%
KNN K=3	0.22	0.03	0.82	59.85%
KNN K=5	0.17	0.03	0.79	56.75%
KNN K=10	0.08	0.04	0.77	51.77%
J48	0.83	0.12	0.86	85.54%
Random Forest N=10	0.92	0.13	0.96	89.74%
Random Forest N=50	0.93	0.09	0.97	91.81%
Random Forest N=100	0.94	0.09	0.97	92.04%

The best results were obtained the Random Forest configured with 100 trees, obtaining an AUC of 0.97 and an accuracy of 92.04%. Regarding TPR, this classifier can detect the 94% of the malware, whilst a 9% of the legitimate applications are misclassified. TPR and FPR establish the cost of misclassification. It is important to set the cost of false negatives ($1 - TPR$) and false positives, in other words, establish whether is better to classify a malware as legitimate or to classify a benign software as malware. In particular, if our framework is devoted to detect new and unknown malware, one may think that it is more important to detect more malware than to minimise false positives. However, for commercial reasons, one may think just the opposite: a user can be bothered if their legitimate applications are flagged as malware. Therefore, we consider that the importance of the cost is established by the way our framework will be used. If it is used as a complement to standard anti-malware systems then we should focus on minimising false positives. Otherwise, if the framework is used within antivirus laboratories to decide which executables should be further analysed then we should minimise false negatives (or maximise true positives). To tune the proposed method, we can apply two techniques: (i) whitelisting and blacklisting or (ii) cost-sensitive learning. White and black lists store a signature of an executable in order to be flagged either as malware (blacklisting) or benign software (whitelisting). On the other hand, cost-sensitive learning is a machine-learning technique where one can specify the cost of each error and the classifiers are trained taking into account that consideration [32].

4.5 Comparison with Related Work

To combat the problem of malware that has risen in recent years in Android, researchers have begun to explore this area, using the experience acquired in other platforms.

"Andromaly" [33], a framework for detecting malware on Android mobile devices, is one of these examples. This framework collected 88 features and events and, then, applied machine-learning algorithms to detect abnormal behaviours. Their dataset was composed of 4 self-written malware, as well as goodware samples, both separated into two different categories (games and tools). Their approach achieved a 0.99 area under ROC curve and 99% of accuracy. Despite these results, their framework had to collect a huge number of features and events, overloading the device and, consequently, draining the battery. Our approach only needs information extracted from .apk files, making the extraction process almost trivial. Although our results are not as sound as theirs, our approach requires less computational effort and our dataset is larger and sparser in malware samples than theirs.

On the other hand, Peng et al. [34] ranks the risks in Android using probabilistic generative models. They selected the permissions of the applications as key feature. Specifically, they chose the top 20 most frequently requested permissions in their dataset, composed by 2 benign software collections, obtained from the Google Play (157,856 and 324,658 samples, respectively) and 378 unique samples of malware. They obtained a 0.94 area under ROC curve as best result. We complemented the information provided by the permissions with the uses-features, enhancing the results and approaching them to those obtained by previous methods.

5 Discussion and Conclusions

Smartphones are a first class citizen nowadays. Unfortunately, malware writers are focused in this devices too. Malware detection techniques have moved from desktop to mobile devices. The main difference between both environment are the available resources. Despite the evolution of the last years, current smartphones have several limitations (i.e., computational performance or battery life). Due to these limitations, the application of various techniques used in the desktop environment to smartphones is doubtful.

In this paper we propose a new method for detecting Android malware using string features to train machine-learning techniques. In order to validate our method, we collected several malware samples of Android applications. Then, we extracted the aforementioned features for each application and trained the models, evaluating each configuration. Random Forest was the best classifier obtaining very high accuracy levels. Nevertheless, there are several considerations regarding the viability of our approach.

The use of supervised machine-learning algorithms for the model training, can be a problem in itself. In our experiments, we used a training dataset that is very small when compared with commercial antivirus databases. As the dataset size grows, so does the issue of scalability. This problem produces excessive storage requirements, increases time complexity and impairs the general accuracy of the models [35]. To reduce disproportionate storage and time costs, it is necessary to reduce the original training set [36]. In order to solve this issue, *data reduction* is normally considered an appropriate preprocessing optimisation technique [37, 38]. Such techniques have many potential advantages such as reducing measurement, storage and transmission; decreasing training and testing times; confronting the *curse of dimensionality* to improve prediction performance in terms of speed, accuracy and simplicity and facilitating data visualisation and understanding [39, 40]. Data reduction can be implemented in two ways. On the one hand, *Instance Selection* (IS) seeks to reduce the evidences (i.e., number of rows) in the training set by selecting the most relevant instances or re-sampling new ones [41]. On the other hand, *Feature Selection* (FS) decreases the number of attributes or features (i.e., columns) in the training set [42]. Both IS and FS are very effective at reducing the size of the training set and helping to filtrate and clean noisy data, thereby improving the accuracy of machine-learning classifiers [43, 44].

Besides, our method has several limitations due to the representation of executables. In this way, because the bag of words model is based on the frequencies with which strings appear within executables, malware writers may start modifying their techniques to evade filters. For example, in the field of spam filtering, *Good Word Attack* is a method that modifies the term statistics by appending a set of words that are characteristic of legitimate e-mails, thereby bypassing spam filters. In case that happens in our domain, we can adopt some of the methods that have been proposed, such as *Multiple Instance Learning* (MIL) [45]. MIL divides an instance or a vector in the traditional supervised learning methods into several sub-instances and classifies the original vector based on the sub-instances [46].

Morever, because of the static nature of the proposed method, it cannot counter *packed* malware. Packed malware is the result of cyphering the payload of the executable and deciphering it when the executable is finally loaded into memory. Indeed, static detection methods can deal with packed malware only by using the signatures of the packers. Accordingly, dynamic analysis seems a more promising solution to this problem [47]. Forensic experts are developing reverse engineering tools over Android applications, from which researchers could retrieve new features to enhance the data used to train the models.

Future work of this Android malware detection tool is oriented in three main directions. First, we will enhance the representation of data using data reduction techniques. Second, we will explore several attacks to this statistical model and propose solutions. Finally, we will use dynamically extracted features in order to improve our method.

Acknowledgements. This research was partially supported by the Basque Government under the research project 'BRANKA4U: Evolución de los servicios bancarios hacia el futuro' granted by the ETORGAI 2011 program.

References

1. Schultz, M., Eskin, E., Zadok, F., Stolfo, S.: Data mining methods for detection of new malicious executables. In: Proceedings of the 2001 IEEE Symposium on Security and Privacy, S&P, pp. 38–49. IEEE (2001)
2. Santos, I., Devesa, J., Brezo, F., Nieves, J., Bringas, P.G.: OPEM: A static-dynamic approach for machine-learning-based malware detection. In: Herrero, Á., Snášel, V., Abraham, A., Zelinka, I., Baruque, B., Quintián, H., Calvo, J.L., Sedano, J., Corchado, E. (eds.) Int. Joint Conf. CISIS'12-ICEUTE'12-SOCO'12. AISC, vol. 189, pp. 271–280. Springer, Heidelberg (2013)
3. Santos, I., Nieves, J., Bringas, P.G.: Semi-supervised learning for unknown malware detection. In: Abraham, A., Corchado, J.M., González, S.R., De Paz Santana, J.F. (eds.) International Symposium on DCAI. AISC, vol. 91, pp. 415–422. Springer, Heidelberg (2011)
4. Santos, I., Laorden, C., Bringas, P.G.: Collective classification for unknown malware detection. In: Proceedings of the 6th International Conference on Security and Cryptography (SECRYPT), pp. 251–256 (2011)
5. Santos, I., Brezo, F., Ugarte-Pedrero, X., Bringas, P.G.: Opcode Sequences as Representation of Executables for Data-mining-based Unknown Malware Detection. Information Sciences 231, 64–82 (2013) ISSN: 0020-0255, doi:10.1016/j.ins.2011.08.020
6. Rieck, K., Holz, T., Willems, C., Düssel, P., Laskov, P.: Learning and classification of malware behavior. In: Zamboni, D. (ed.) DIMVA 2008. LNCS, vol. 5137, pp. 108–125. Springer, Heidelberg (2008)
7. Tian, R., Batten, L., Islam, R., Versteeg, S.: An automated classification system based on the strings of trojan and virus families. In: Proceedings of the 4th International Conference on Malicious and Unwanted Software (MALWARE), pp. 23–30 (2009)
8. Shabtai, A., Fledel, Y., Elovici, Y.: Automated static code analysis for classifying android applications using machine learning. In: Proceedings of the International Conference on Computational Intelligence and Security (CIS), pp. 329–333 (2010)
9. Burguera, I., Zurutuza, U., Nadjm-Tehrani, S.: Crowdroid: behavior-based malware detection system for android. In: Proceedings of the 1st ACM Workshop on Security and Privacy in Smartphones and Mobile Devices, pp. 15–26. ACM (2011)

10. Blasing, T., Batyuk, L., Schmidt, A., Camtepe, S., Albayrak, S.: An android application sandbox system for suspicious software detection. In: Proceedings of the 5th International Conference on Malicious and Unwanted Software (MALWARE), pp. 55–62 (2010)
11. Shabtai, A., Elovici, Y.: Applying behavioral detection on android-based devices. In: Cai, Y., Magedanz, T., Li, M., Xia, J., Giannelli, C. (eds.) Mobilware 2010. LNICST, vol. 48, pp. 235–249. Springer, Heidelberg (2010)
12. Oberheide, J., Miller, J.: Dissecting the android bouncer. In: SUMERCON 2012 (2012), http://jon.oberheide.org/files/summercon12-bouncer.pdf
13. Santos, I., Penya, Y., Devesa, J., Bringas, P.G.: N-Grams-based file signatures for malware detection. In: Proceedings of the 11th International Conference on Enterprise Information Systems (ICEIS), vol. AIDSS, pp. 317–320 (2009)
14. Baeza-Yates, R.A., Ribeiro-Neto, B.: Modern Information Retrieval. Addison-Wesley Longman Publishing Co., Inc, Boston (1999)
15. Salton, G., McGill, M.: Introduction to modern information retrieval. McGraw-Hill, New York (1983)
16. Bishop, C.: Pattern recognition and machine learning. Springer, New York (2006)
17. Kotsiantis, S., Zaharakis, I., Pintelas, P.: Supervised machine learning: A review of classification techniques. Frontiers in Artificial Intelligence and Applications 160, 3 (2007)
18. Kotsiantis, S., Pintelas, P.: Recent advances in clustering: A brief survey. WSEAS Transactions on Information Science and Applications 1(1), 73–81 (2004)
19. Chapelle, O., Schölkopf, B., Zien, A.: Semi-supervised learning. MIT Press (2006)
20. Pearl, J.: Reverend bayes on inference engines: a distributed hierarchical approach. In: Proceedings of the National Conference on Artificial Intelligence, pp. 133–136 (1982)
21. Castillo, E., Gutiérrez, J.M., Hadi, A.S.: Expert Systems and Probabilistic Network Models, Erste edn., New York, NY, USA (1996)
22. Quinlan, J.: Induction of decision trees. Machine Learning 1(1), 81–106 (1986)
23. Breiman, L.: Random forests. Machine Learning 45(1), 5–32 (2001)
24. Garner, S.: Weka: The Waikato environment for knowledge analysis. In: Proceedings of the 1995 New Zealand Computer Science Research Students Conference, pp. 57–64 (1995)
25. Quinlan, J.: C4.5 programs for machine learning. Morgan Kaufmann Publishers (1993)
26. Fix, E., Hodges, J.L.: Discriminatory analysis: Nonparametric discrimination: Small sample performance. Technical Report Project 21-49-004, Report Number 11 (1952)
27. Vapnik, V.: The nature of statistical learning theory. Springer (2000)
28. Amari, S., Wu, S.: Improving support vector machine classifiers by modifying kernel functions. Neural Networks 12(6), 783–789 (1999)
29. Kohavi, R.: A study of cross-validation and bootstrap for accuracy estimation and model selection. In: International Joint Conference on Artificial Intelligence, vol. 14, pp. 1137–1145. Lawrence Erlbaum Associates Ltd. (1995)
30. Devijver, P., Kittler, J.: Pattern recognition: A statistical approach. Prentice/Hall International (1982)
31. Singh, Y., Kaur, A., Malhotra, R.: Comparative analysis of regression and machine learning methods for predicting fault proneness models. International Journal of Computer Applications in Technology 35(2), 183–193 (2009)
32. Elkan, C.: The foundations of cost-sensitive learning. In: Proceedings of the 2001 International Joint Conference on Artificial Intelligence, pp. 973–978 (2001)

33. Shabtai, A., Kanonov, U., Elovici, Y., Glezer, C., Weiss, Y.: Andromaly: a behavioral malware detection framework for android devices. Journal of Intelligent Information Systems, 1–30 (2012)
34. Peng, H., Gates, C., Sarma, B., Li, N., Qi, Y., Potharaju, R., Nita-Rotaru, C., Molloy, I.: Using probabilistic generative models for ranking risks of android apps. In: Proceedings of the 2012 ACM Conference on Computer and Communications Security, pp. 241–252. ACM (2012)
35. Cano, J., Herrera, F., Lozano, M.: On the combination of evolutionary algorithms and stratified strategies for training set selection in data mining. Applied Soft Computing Journal 6(3), 323–332 (2006)
36. Czarnowski, I., Jedrzejowicz, P.: Instance reduction approach to machine learning and multi-database mining. In: Proceedings of the 2006 Scientific Session Organized during XXI Fall Meeting of the Polish Information Processing Society, Informatica, ANNALES Universitatis Mariae Curie-Skłodowska, Lublin, pp. 60–71 (2006)
37. Pyle, D.: Data preparation for data mining. Morgan Kaufmann (1999)
38. Tsang, E., Yeung, D., Wang, X.: OFFSS: optimal fuzzy-valued feature subset selection. IEEE Transactions on Fuzzy Systems 11(2), 202–213 (2003)
39. Torkkola, K.: Feature extraction by non parametric mutual information maximization. The Journal of Machine Learning Research 3, 1415–1438 (2003)
40. Dash, M., Liu, H.: Consistency-based search in feature selection. Artificial Intelligence 151(1-2), 155–176 (2003)
41. Liu, H., Motoda, H.: Instance selection and construction for data mining. Kluwer Academic Pub. (2001)
42. Liu, H., Motoda, H.: Computational methods of feature selection. Chapman & Hall/CRC (2008)
43. Blum, A., Langley, P.: Selection of relevant features and examples in machine learning. Artificial Intelligence 97(1-2), 245–271 (1997)
44. Derrac, J., García, S., Herrera, F.: A First Study on the Use of Coevolutionary Algorithms for Instance and Feature Selection. In: Corchado, E., Wu, X., Oja, E., Herrero, Á., Baruque, B. (eds.) HAIS 2009. LNCS (LNAI), vol. 5572, pp. 557–564. Springer, Heidelberg (2009)
45. Dietterich, T., Lathrop, R., Lozano-Pérez, T.: Solving the multiple instance problem with axis-parallel rectangles. Artificial Intelligence 89(1-2), 31–71 (1997)
46. Maron, O., Lozano-Pérez, T.: A framework for multiple-instance learning. In: Advances in Neural Information Processing Systems, pp. 570–576 (1998)
47. Kang, M., Poosankam, P., Yin, H.: Renovo: A hidden code extractor for packed executables. In: Proceedings of the 2007 ACM Workshop on Recurring Malcode, pp. 46–53 (2007)

X-TIER: Kernel Module Injection

Sebastian Vogl, Fatih Kilic, Christian Schneider, and Claudia Eckert

Technische Universität München, München, Germany
{vogls,kilic,chrschn,eckert}@sec.in.tum.de

Abstract. In spite of the fact that security applications can greatly benefit from virtualization, hypervisor-based security solutions remain sparse. The main cause for this is the semantic gap, which makes the development of hypervisor-based security applications cumbersome, error-prone, and time-consuming. In this paper, we present X-TIER, a framework that enables hypervisor-based security applications to bridge the semantic gap by injecting kernel modules from the outside into a running virtual machine (VM). While previous approaches bridge the semantic gap by reading kernel objects from memory, X-TIER goes beyond such work and allows the injected code to manipulate the guest operating system (OS) state and even call kernel functions without sacrificing the overall security. We have implemented a prototype of X-TIER on the x86 architecture that supports module injection for Windows and Linux guests. The evaluation of our system shows that kernel module injection only incurs a very small performance overhead, leaves no traces within the guest system, and provides access to all exported guest OS data structures and functions. Consequently, the mechanism is well-suited for creating hypervisor-based security applications.

Keywords: Security, Virtual Machine Introspection, Semantic Gap.

1 Introduction

Virtualization provides essential security properties such as isolation and introspection that are predestined for the development of novel and robust security applications [8]. Nevertheless, hypervisor-based security applications remain sparse. The main reason for this is the semantic gap. While hypervisor-based security applications have access to the complete virtual hardware state, the semantic knowledge of the guest OS that is necessary to interpret the binary view of this state is essentially lost. Without this knowledge, hypervisor-based security mechanisms can neither access the data structures of the guest OS nor invoke guest functions that operate on these data structures. As a result, the development of hypervisor-based security applications becomes cumbersome, error-prone, and time-consuming. Although researchers have proposed various methods to narrow this semantic gap [2,5,6,7,11,15], reconstructing the complete semantic view of the guest OS remains an open problem. This is especially true when it comes to a practical approach that not only bridges the semantic gap, but

J. Lopez, X. Huang, and R. Sandhu (Eds.): NSS 2013, LNCS 7873, pp. 192–205, 2013.

does so efficiently, securely, and supports the development of hypervisor-based security mechanisms in a straight forward manner.

In this paper, we present X-TIER, a framework that allows security applications residing within the hypervisor to inject kernel modules, also referred to as kernel drivers, into a running VM. An injected module will thereby, similar to a module that was loaded by the OS, be able to access all exported guest OS data structures and functions. In contrast to a normally loaded module, however, an injected module will be inaccessible to any other code residing within the VM. Even in the case that the injected module invokes a guest OS function, the function will neither be aware of the existence of the module nor be able to access any data of the module besides its function arguments. In fact, if a module constrains itself to only reading state information, its execution leaves no detectable traces within the VM (with the exception of timing attacks). A module may, however, apply selective changes to the state, for example, to remove a rootkit from a compromised system. Consequently, our system provides a secure and elegant way for hypervisor-based security applications to bridge the semantic gap.

X-TIER is not targeted at a particular OS or kernel module file format. Instead, it aims to provide a general and secure mechanism for module injection on the x86 architecture. Our framework achieves this goal by making use of a converter that transforms an existing module into a universal binary format that we call the X-Format. This step can either happen on-the-fly as the module is injected or ahead of time and requires no changes or re-compilation of existing kernel modules. Once a module has been converted to the X-Format (in the following referred to as X-Module), it can be injected into any VM as long as the guest OS provides the same API as the OS that the original module has been compiled for. This design enables X-TIER to support any OS for a particular hardware platform as long as it is known to the converter.

To support a wide range of security applications, X-TIER is capable of periodically injecting X-Modules into a VM as well as injecting X-Modules in reaction to a specific event. In addition, our system offers a hypercall-based communication channel that enables injected modules to communicate with X-TIER or a security application that resides on the hypervisor level. This communication channel makes it particularly easy to transfer information obtained by an injected module to the hypervisor.

We implemented a prototype of X-TIER for the x86 architecture that relies on full hardware virtualization and is based on the KVM hypervisor. To demonstrate the possibilities of our approach, we created an on-access virus scanner for Linux as well as multiple Linux and Windows modules that retrieve security relevant information from within a guest system. The experiments that we conducted show that the proposed mechanism is not only able to securely bridge the semantic gap for Linux and Windows guests, but also incurs only a very small performance overhead (4.30% for Linux and 2.76% for Windows guests in the worst case in our experiments) which makes it well-suited for the creation of security applications.

In summary, this paper makes the following contributions:

- We specify a uniform binary format, the X-Format, for injectable kernel modules on the x86 architecture (Section 2.1).
- We show how a kernel module can be injected and executed within the context of a guest OS in a secure way (Section 2.2).
- We present an intuitive communication mechanism that allows X-Modules to transfer arbitrary information to the hypervisor (Section 2.3).
- We demonstrate the effectiveness and efficiency of our approach with our prototype implementation, X-TIER, and its evaluation (Section 3).

2 System Design

The overall design of X-TIER is shown in Figure 1. Before a kernel module can be injected by the *injector* it must be transformed into an X-Module by the *converter*. The key difference between a kernel module and an X-Module is that the latter provides its own loader code, which enables an X-Module to execute from an arbitrary memory address without having to rely on an external loader. By converting a kernel module into an X-Module, we can thus separate the loading of a module from the injection of a module, which allows our framework to obtain two essential properties: First, we can provide a general mechanism for hypervisor-based code injection on the x86 architecture. This is due to the fact that the *injector* does not require any knowledge about the guest OS or an X-Module to be able to inject and execute it. Second, our system will be able to support a wide-range of OSs, since the *converter* is the only component of X-TIER that must actually be able to handle different module file formats. Consequently, all that needs to be done to support an additional OS is to add a handler to the *converter* that can transform kernel modules for the OS into X-Modules. In the following the *converter*, the *injector*, and the *communication* component of our system will be covered in a subsection of their own.

2.1 Converter

The task of the *converter* is to transform an existing kernel module into an X-Module. The binary format of an X-Module is the *X-Format*. The motivation behind the X-Format is to provide a single common structure for module injection in which existing kernel module formats such as the Linux Executable and Linkable Format (ELF) and the Windows Portable Executable (PE) format can be embedded. This is achieved by defining a wrapper format, the X-Format, that is capable of encapsulating all of the different existing module formats. By wrapping the existing formats into a common structure, it can be guaranteed that all modules provide the same interface and fulfill the necessary requirements for use with our system independent of their original format.

The common structure of the X-Format is shown in the underpart of Figure 1. As one can see, it consists of four main parts. At the beginning of the X-Format

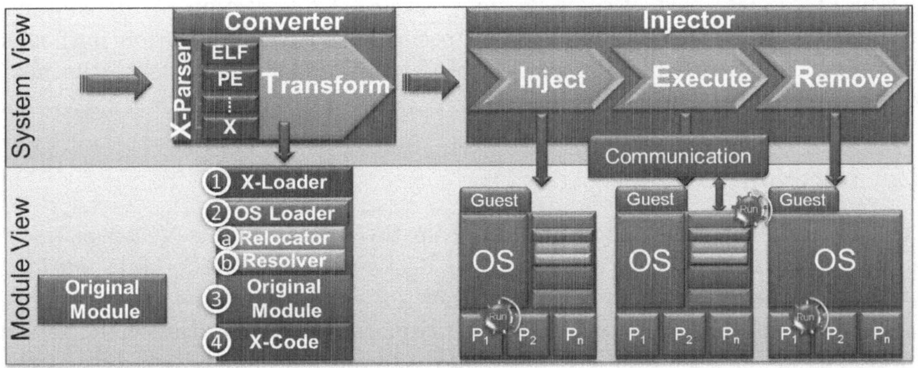

Fig. 1. The architectural view of our system is shown in the upper-half of the picture, while the underpart shows the effects of the architectural components on a kernel module that is injected into a VM

resides the X-Loader (1). The X-Loader functions as the common entry point for all modules in X-Format and also controls the execution of the preprocessing phase of a module. Similar to normal executables, kernel modules must usually be preprocessed before they can be executed. This preprocessing is normally conducted by the OS when a kernel module is loaded. Since we inject kernel modules from the outside into a VM without the support of the guest OS, the necessary preprocessing steps have to be executed by our system.

Although preprocessing code varies from OS to OS, it encompasses in general at least two steps that are reflected in the design of the X-Format: Relocation (2a) and symbol resolution (2b). Relocation is required since kernel modules are usually position independent and can be loaded to an arbitrary memory address. To support this functionality, a position independent module provides a list of addresses that have to be updated when the module is loaded. During relocation this list is processed and the given addresses are adjusted according to the base address of the module.

Besides relocation, symbol resolution is the second common step that is usually executed by the module loader. As the name suggests, the purpose of this step is to resolve the addresses of any external kernel symbols that the module uses. How this resolution is performed heavily depends on the OS and will for the sake of brevity be omitted in this paper.

After the loader code follows the kernel module (3) itself. The loader code will patch this module at runtime. When the X-Loader finally transfers the control to the entry point of the module, which is a user-specified function, it will be ready to execute from its current memory location. Since the X-Loader invokes the entry point of the module, control will be returned to the X-Loader once the entry point function has been executed. Thus, the X-Loader is not only the entry point of an X-Module, but also the exit point. This enables the X-Loader to notify our system when a module has finished its execution and can be removed.

Finally, the last part of the X-Format is the X-Code section (4). It contains wrapper functions that are required for security and communication purposes. We defer a more detailed description of these wrapper functions to the next section and to Section 2.3 respectively.

2.2 Injection

The process of injecting an X-Module from the outside into a VM consists of three individual steps that are shown in Figure 1. First, the module must be loaded into the memory of the guest. Then the actual execution phase begins, where the control flow of the VM is altered and execution is transferred to the injected module. This phase is particularly important for the security of the proposed mechanism, since it must be ensured that the X-Module is protected from foreign accesses during its execution within a potentially malicious guest. Finally, the injected module must be removed from the guest after it has finished its execution. In the following, each of these steps will be discussed in more detail.

Module Injection. X-TIER supports three injection modes: *count-based* injection, which injects a module exactly *n*-times, *interval-based* injection, where a module is repeatedly injected after a certain period of time, and *event-based* injection, where a module is injected based on an event. However, in the interest of space we will not cover all the details of the individual injection modes. Instead we will only focus on the common injection process.

To inject an X-Module from the hypervisor into a VM, the module must be loaded into the guest's memory. This is basically a twofold process. In the first step, we have to select the guest physical memory regions that will be used to hold the data, code, stack, and external function area of the injected module. In the case of X-TIER, this is accomplished by adding additional guest physical memory for each of these memory areas to the VM at runtime as has been proposed by Gu et al. [9]. The external function area is thereby an additional memory area that is required during external function calls and will be covered in more detail in the following section of the paper.

In the second step, a virtual memory mapping has to be established for the newly added guest physical memory areas such that they can be accessed by the hardware. This is realized by directly updating the guest's page tables, which are accessible through the CR3 register.

Module Execution. Once a module has been loaded into the memory of a VM, it must be securely executed within the context of the guest. While the execution of a module can be triggered by simply setting the instruction pointer (EIP) of the guest to the injected module, isolating the module from other code within the VM is a hard problem. Our system uses two separate techniques to achieve this goal: *runtime isolation* and *function call unmapping*. Both of these techniques will be described in more detail below. For the sake of simplicity, we will assume a `cdecl` calling convention and a single core VM. We discuss how these techniques can be applied to multi-core systems in Section 3.4.

The main idea behind runtime isolation is to execute an injected module *atomically* within the guest. This requires that our system disables timer interrupts within the VM by unsetting the interrupt enable flag (IF) within the RFLAGS register. Consequently, the injected module will no longer be interrupted during its execution. However, other guest OS code could still be executed in the case of an exception or an external interrupt. To avoid this problem, X-TIER further intercepts all exceptions and interrupts that occur within the VM on the hypervisor level by enabling every bit in the exception bitmap [10] and setting the Interrupt Descriptor Table Register (IDTR) base to 32 as suggested by Pfoh et al. [14], respectively. This will constrict the execution of the VM to the injected module. All other code within the VM will effectively be frozen during the runtime of the module. Even in the event of an exception or an interrupt, no guest OS code will be executed.

The only problem that remains is the handling of external function calls. If the injected module invokes an external function, this function will have access to the module's code and data regions in spite of runtime isolation. X-TIER solves this problem by temporarily unmapping an injected module from the guest's memory whenever an external function is invoked. For this purpose, the converter adds an individual wrapper for each external function that is used by a module to the X-Code section of an X-Module and additionally modifies each external function call such that it will invoke the wrapper. As a result, all external function calls within an X-Module will actually invoke wrapper functions.

Once invoked, it is the task of the wrapper to prepare the external function call. In particular, this means that the wrapper must copy all data structures that will be required by the external function and reside within the module's data area to a memory region that will be accessible to the function. During this process, the wrapper must also update any pointers that are used within the data structures such that they no longer point to the original data structures but to their copies. Our system uses the external function area for this purpose, which has been reserved by X-TIER during the module injection and is used as stack region during external function calls.

After the necessary data was copied, the wrapper will modify the function arguments that were provided by the module such that every reference points to the copied data structures. Finally, it will modify the stack pointer (ESP) to point to the external function region, place the modified function arguments into the correct register and stack locations as it would do if it would invoke the external function, and use the communication channel of our framework (see next section) to notify X-TIER of the function call. Thereby the wrapper will also provide X-TIER with the address of the external function, which the wrapper in turn obtains during the symbol resolution phase of the X-Module.

Upon receiving the notification that an external function is about to be executed, X-TIER will first unmap the injected module from the VM's memory by marking all memory regions of the module as not present within the

Extended Page Tables (EPT). Next, it will reenable interrupts and invoke the external function from the hypervisor by pushing the current EIP on the stack and setting the EIP to the specified address. This will trigger the execution of the external function within the VM. As soon as the external function returns, an EPT violation will occur, since X-TIER placed a return address on the stack that is no longer accessible. If the current EIP coincides with the value that our system pushed on the stack, this event will be interpreted as the return of the external function call. In this case our system will reenable the interception of interrupts and will return the control to the wrapper. The wrapper will then restore the stack and copy the possibly modified function arguments back from the external function area to their original location. Finally, the wrapper returns control to the X-Module which concludes the external function call.

Module Removal. When the injected module has finished its execution, the hypervisor component needs to be notified that the module can be removed and control can be returned to the VM. In our system, this is realized through the X-Loader component. Since the X-Loader invokes the entry point of the injected module, control will be returned to it as soon as the function returns. Once the X-Loader regains control of the execution, it will notify X-TIER that the injected module has finished its execution and can be removed.

During the module removal phase, all changes that were applied during module injection must be reverted. First, all modifications that were made to the guest pages tables will be undone. In the next step, the now unmapped physical memory regions of the injected module are removed from the VM. Finally, the original values of all general purpose registers are restored. This last step completes the module removal and enables the VM to resume its execution from the last EIP before the injection.

2.3 Communication

The system we described so far provides the possibility to inject kernel modules into a VM at runtime. However, without a mechanism to communicate with the hypervisor, the information that is obtained by an injected module is confined within the VM. In this section, we will first describe the basic communication channel that our system provides, before we explain how it can be used in conjunction with output functions to transfer information to the hypervisor.

Communication Channel. X-TIER provides a hypercall mechanism that enables an injected module to notify the hypervisor about specific events such as external function calls. To execute a hypercall, an injected module places the numerical representation of the event which it wants to communicate to the hypervisor into a predefined command register, e.g. EAX, and invokes an interrupt. Due to runtime isolation, the invocation of the interrupt will lead to a VM exit. Based on the interrupt number and the value of the command register, X-TIER can identify the communication attempt from the module and handle the event.

Function Call Translation. Although the above described hypercall mechanism is well-suited to inform our system about certain events, it cannot easily be used to send information obtained by an injected module such as the list of currently running processes to the hypervisor. A more intuitive approach would be to make use of an output function for this purpose. As an example, consider the `printk` function, which is an output function of the Linux kernel that basically provides the same functionality as the well-known C function `printf`. If a developer of a kernel module could simply use `printk` statements to transfer information from an injected module to the hypervisor, modules that retrieve information from the guest could be easily implemented. X-TIER provides this functionality by making use of a technique we refer to as *function call translation*.

The main idea of function call translation is to redirect a function call occurring within a VM to an equivalent function call that is executed on the host system or a different VM. To illustrate this technique, let us once more consider a call to a `printk` function occurring within a VM. Let us further assume that we want to translate this function call to an equivalent `printk` function call that occurs on the host system instead of the guest system. X-TIER achieves this by executing the following steps:

1. Intercept the in-guest call to `printk` from the hypervisor before it occurs. X-TIER already provides this functionality, since `printk` is an external function that will lead to the invocation of a wrapper function and a VM exit.
2. Obtain the arguments of the in-guest `printk` call, which either reside on the guest's stack and/or within the guest's general purpose registers depending on the architecture and the guest OS.
3. Translate the guest virtual address referenced by each pointer argument to the corresponding host virtual address.
4. Finally, move the now translated arguments to the appropriate stack and/or general purpose registers on the host system and invoke `printk`.

X-TIER currently uses function call translation to translate all calls to output functions occurring within an injected module to calls to output functions that are executed on the host system instead. In particular calls to `printk` (Linux) and `DbgPrint` (Windows) functions that are executed by an X-Module are translated to calls to `printf` on the host system. Notice, however, that the proposed mechanism of function call translation is general and could be applied to arbitrary function calls. Moreover function call translation is completely transparent to the developer of a kernel module.

3 Evaluation

We implemented a prototype of our X-TIER framework for the x86 architecture that is based on the Linux KVM hypervisor. In this section, we describe the experiments that we conducted with this prototype to evaluate the performance of our approach and state the results that we obtained. In addition, we present an example application that demonstrates the possibilities of module injection

Table 1. The X-Modules that were used to conduct the performance evaluation

Name	*Description*
`tasklist`	Shows the running processes.
`lsmod`	Prints a list of the loaded modules.
`netstat`	Displays the open TCP and UDP connections for each process.
`files`	Prints a list of all open files for each process.

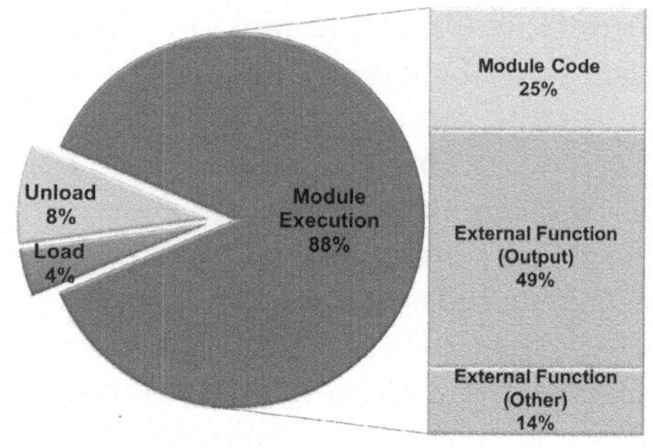

Fig. 2. The average execution time distribution of all modules shown in Table 1

and will discuss the security properties of X-TIER as well as the limitations of the current prototype.

3.1 Performance

We used four different kernel modules that extract typical security relevant information from within a guest system to empirically evaluate X-TIER. The name of these modules as well as a description of their functionality is shown in Table 1. Each of the modules was implemented for Linux and Windows. To test function call translation, each module was designed to print the information that it obtains using `printk` (Linux) and `DbgPrint` (Windows), respectively.

For the purpose of implementation, compilation, and injection of the kernel modules, we used two VMs. The virtual hardware configuration of both VMs consisted of a single virtual CPU, 512 MB of guest physical memory, and a 20 GB virtual hard disc. As OSs we chose the 64-bit version of Ubuntu 11.04 Server and the 32-bit version of Windows 7 Professional SP1. We purposely selected a 64-bit OS and a 32-bit OS for the VMs to verify that our framework is generic enough to handle both system types. The host OS was Ubuntu 12.04 64-bit running on a machine with an Intel Core i7-2600 3.4 GHz CPU and 8 GB RAM.

The modules were compiled with gcc 4.6.3 (Linux) and Build Utility 6.1 (Windows), respectively. While we used the default flags to compile the Windows modules, we compiled the Linux modules with the option `mcmodel=large`. This flag instructs the compiler to reserve 8 bytes for each address within the module code instead of 4 bytes. Although this option is not required, it allows us to inject a Linux module anywhere within the 64-bit virtual address space.

After compilation, we used X-TIER's converter to transform each module into an X-Module. The mean time required for the conversion was 55ms for a Windows module and 7ms for a Linux module. On average the resulting X-Modules had an increased size of 14% (Windows) and 17% (Linux).

To measure the performance of X-TIER, we compiled (Linux) or respectively extracted (Windows) the Linux 3.6 Kernel Image, a 467 MB tar file, within the guest. In the process, we repeatedly injected one of the modules into the VM

Table 2. Results of the experiments. The columns show for each module its average run-times of the injection (LOAD), execution (EXEC), and removal (UNLOAD) phase in ms, the total number of injections (IN), of external function calls (FUNC) and calls to output functions (OUT), and the total overhead that the modules' injection incurred.

Experiment		*Run-time* [ms]			*Result*			
OS	*Module*	LOAD	EXEC	UNLOAD	IN	FUNC	OUT	*Overhead*
Win	`tasklist`	0.11	1.21	0.16	1047	0	31531	**0.15%**
Win	`lsmod`	0.11	7.21	0.16	1051	140975	144128	**0.80%**
Win	`netstat`	0.10	2.93	0.23	1182	0	30322	**0.28%**
Win	`files`	0.13	25.38	0.16	1030	469939	528131	**2.76%**
Linux	`tasklist`	0.30	2.43	0.59	2925	0	209581	**0.18%**
Linux	`lsmod`	0.30	0.49	0.61	2957	0	38990	**0.05%**
Linux	`netstat`	0.30	0.45	0.64	2967	0	21603	**0.05%**
Linux	`files`	0.32	12.37	0.79	2954	523098	451233	**1.08%**
Linux	`LxS`	0.24	5.18	0.52	28330	3944284	89058	**4.30%**

at intervals of one second. The information that was obtained by an injected module was printed on the host system using function call translation. Thereby, each call to an output function within a module lead to an individual VM exit. No output data was buffered within the module to increase the performance. This experiment was repeated for each of the modules and the resulting run-time overhead was measured from the hypervisor.

The results of the experiments are shown in Table 2. On average, each module was injected 2950 times on Linux and 1078 times on Windows. The highest performance overhead was introduced by the `files` modules, which led to a overhead of 1.08% and 2.76% respectively. The reason for this is that these modules had the longest run-time within the VMs. The more time a module requires to execute, the longer all other code within the guest will be frozen and consequently the higher will be the resulting performance impact. As Figure 2 shows, the run-time itself is heavily influenced by the number of external functions that a module invokes. This is a result of the fact that the invocation of an external function leads to at least one VM exit, which is a costly operation. Since output functions account for almost 50% of the run-time in the current implementation, we expect that the performance of our prototype could be considerably increased by buffering output data within the guest system instead of processing each call to an output function individually.

In summary, the experiments show that our system is capable of effectively bridging the semantic gap by injecting normally created kernel modules from the hypervisor. The overhead of the approach is very small even if a module is frequently injected into a VM. The performance impact of the injection mainly depends on the execution time of the injected module, which in-turn is influenced by the number of external functions that the module invokes.

3.2 Example Application

We implemented an on-access virus scanner for Linux using X-TIER that we call LxS. This virus scanner consists of two parts: a hypervisor component and a kernel module. The kernel module is injected by X-TIER every time a file is executed within the VM using the `execve` system call. In this particular case, we trap this event by setting a debug breakpoint on the address of the `execve` system call using the debug registers of the x86 architecture. Notice, however, that this mechanism is independent of X-TIER. Intercepting in-guest events in a secure manner is beyond the scope of our framework.

Once the kernel module has been injected, it reads the file that should be executed, calculates its SHA-1 hash, and transfers the file name as well as the SHA-1 hash to the hypervisor component using function call translation. The hypervisor component will then compare the calculated hash to a virus database and signal to the injected module whether the file is malicious or benign. In the first case, the module will deny access to the file by returning an error code, while the module will invoke the original `sys_execve` function in the latter case, which will trigger the execution of the file. This mechanism is completely transparent to the guest OS and cannot be evaded.

We tested the above described virus scanner once more by monitoring the compilation of the Linux kernel. Thereby we used a clam-av database that contained 45039 SHA-1 hashes to check the executed binaries. The results of this experiment are shown in Table 2. As one can see, the virus scanner application tested 28330 executables during compilation and only incurred an overhead of 4.30%. In addition, we verified the detection mechanism of the approach by executing serveral malicious files including the adore-ng rootkit, the suckit rootkit, the mood-nt rootkit, and the enyelkm rootkit. In all cases, the access to the malicious files was denied. No false positives were observed.

3.3 Security

From a security standpoint, one of the most important properties of virtualization is isolation. Isolation ensures that a security application that runs on the hypervisor level cannot be accessed by code running in a VM. By injecting a module into a VM and executing it within the context of the guest, we break this isolation. Ideally, however, a module that was injected into a VM should have the exact same security properties that it would have if it was running outside of the guest. X-TIER achieves this by making use of *runtime isolation* and *function call unmapping*.

Runtime isolation restricts the execution of the guest system to the injected module and the guest code that it invokes. Any code that is not explicitly required by the X-Module will be frozen during its execution. This effectively isolates the module within the VM. Even in the case that the X-Module is faulty, exceptions will not be handled by the guest system, but on the hypervisor level as they would if the module would run outside of the guest. The only way to disable the proposed lightweight isolation mechanism is to reenable the timer-interrupts within the guest system by setting the IF flag, which is the *only* mechanism that is used by our system that cannot be protected from the hypervisor. However, due to the fact the injected module controls the virtual CPU, this can only be done by the module itself. Therefore we do not consider this to be an issue.

While runtime isolation is sufficient to protect the execution of an injected module, it cannot ensure a module's isolation if the module itself invokes an external function. This is why X-TIER temporarily unmaps an X-Module from the guest system when it calls an external function. Since this unmapping is realized with the help of the EPT and the EPT can only be modified by the hypervisor, the proposed mechanism of function call unmapping can reliably isolate a module during external function calls. To be useful in practice, however, our system does not extend this isolation to the function arguments. That is an external function will be able to access and modify its function arguments arbitrarily even if they reside within the module's data region. Although the access of an external function will be restricted to the function arguments alone, this provides a small attack surface. This attack surface, however, is not limited to our system, but rather inherent to the problem of invoking untrusted code. In fact, if the module would reside on the hypervisor level and would invoke a function within a guest system, the same problem would exist. Nevertheless, our system reduces the attack surface by using individual wrapper functions for each external function. Rather than updating all arguments after an external function call, each wrapper only updates the function arguments within a module's data region that a specific function is supposed to modify.

Finally, it is worth to emphasize that the execution of an injected module leaves no traces within a guest system unless the module purposely modifies the state of the guest. This is due to the fact that our system only operates on memory regions that will be removed once a module finished its execution. As a result, an injected module that constrains itself to only reading data structures within a guest system can only be detected based on timing attacks, since it is atomically executed and leaves no traces.

3.4 Limitations

There currently exist two limitations within our prototype. First of all, our prototype is not yet able to operate on multi-core systems. To support multi-core systems, the concept of runtime isolation must be expanded such that an X-Module cannot be accessed during its execution from one of the other cores. A possible solution to this problem would be to disable the interrupts on all CPUs and to put the additional cores into busy waiting loops while the X-Module executes on a single core. As a result, all other CPUs would be idle during the execution of an X-Module, which would affect the performance of the approach.

Second, there is a single functional limitation that our system places on the creation of kernel modules. Since X-TIER injects a kernel module from the hypervisor without involving the guest OS, specific OS data structures that are related to the module itself will not be created within the guest OS. For instance, an X-Module will not be able to use the `__this_module` (Linux) or respectively the `DriverObject` (Windows) variable, because the internal OS data structures that usually exist for each loaded module will not be available for an X-Module. In fact, if these data structures would exist, the guest OS would be aware of the existence of the injected module, which is why they are not created by X-TIER.

4 Related Work

The semantic gap [3] is a fundamental problem that every hypervisor-based security application faces. Existing approaches that try to bridge this gap can roughly be divided into in-band delivery approaches, out-of-band delivery approaches, and derivative approaches [13]. In-band delivery approaches, as the one presented within this paper, rely on an in-guest component to bridge the semantic gap. Lares [12] and SIM [16] use this in-guest component to actively monitor an untrusted VM. In contrast to X-TIER, however, both approaches do not dynamically inject the in-guest component and are unable to invoke guest OS functions without compromising the security of the system. SADE [4] is also capable of injecting a kernel agent into a VM at runtime, but it relies on guest OS functions to reserve the necessary virtual memory space for the in-guest agent and does not protect the agent during its execution. Process Implanting [9] provides the possibility to inject statically linked binaries into the address space of a victim process running within a VM, where they will be executed in the context of the victim process. Unlike injected modules, implanted processes are unable to access kernel data structures or functions directly and additionally require a trusted guest OS. Finally, SYRINGE [1] aims to provide hypervisor-based security applications with the possibility to inject secure function calls into a VM. For this purpose, SYRINGE monitors the complete execution of all injected function calls within the guest system and verifies that only trusted code is executed. In contrast to SYRINGE, X-TIER provides access to both guest OS functions and data structures. In addition, our system does not place any restrictions on the code that can be executed by an injected module. Instead it guarantees the isolation of a module even if it invokes hostile functions.

5 Conclusion

We proposed X-TIER, a framework that allows a security application residing on the hypervisor level to inject kernel modules into a VM at runtime. Our system makes use of runtime isolation and function call unmapping to execute an injected module isolated within the context of an untrusted guest system. Nevertheless, injected modules are able to access all exported guest OS data structures and can even invoke guest OS functions without sacrificing isolation or compromising their security. Consequently, our system enables hypervisor-based security applications to securely bridge the semantic gap.

Prior to injection, X-TIER converts modules into our uniform X-Format. This step requires no changes or recompilation of existing kernel modules and allows our system to support multiple OSs while remaining extensible. In addition,

X-TIER provides an intuitive communication channel that allows injected modules to send and receive information from a security application residing on the hypervisor level.

Our prototype implementation of X-TIER is capable of injecting kernel modules into Windows and Linux guests. The evaluation of our system shows that the performance impact of module injection is small even for frequently injected modules. Due to its functionality, security, and performance, X-TIER is very well-suited for creating hypervisor-based security applications as has been demonstrated with the implementation of an on-access virus scanner for Linux.

References

1. Carbone, M., Conover, M., Montague, B., Lee, W.: Secure and robust monitoring of virtual machines through guest-assisted introspection. In: Balzarotti, D., Stolfo, S.J., Cova, M. (eds.) RAID 2012. LNCS, vol. 7462, pp. 22–41. Springer, Heidelberg (2012)
2. Carbone, M., Cui, W., Lu, L., Lee, W., Peinado, M., Jiang, X.: Mapping kernel objects to enable systematic integrity checking. In: Proc. of 16th ACM Conf. on Computer and Communications Security, pp. 555–565. ACM (2009)
3. Chen, P.M., Noble, B.D.: When virtual is better than real. In: Proc. of the 8th Workshop on Hot Topics in Operating Systems. IEEE (2001)
4. Chiueh, T., Conover, M., Lu, M., Montague, B.: Stealthy deployment and execution of in-guest kernel agents. In: BlackHat USA (2009)
5. Dolan-Gavitt, B., Leek, T., Zhivich, M., Giffin, J., Lee, W.: Virtuoso: Narrowing the semantic gap in virtual machine introspection. In: Proc. of Symp. on Sec. & Priv. IEEE (2011)
6. Dolan-Gavitt, B., Srivastava, A., Traynor, P., Giffin, J.: Robust signatures for kernel data structures. In: Proc. of Conf. on Comp. and Comm. Sec. ACM (2009)
7. Fu, Y., Lin, Z.: Space traveling across VM: Automatically bridging the semantic gap in virtual machine introspection via online kernel data redirection. In: Proc. of Symp. on Sec. & Priv. IEEE (2012)
8. Garfinkel, T., Rosenblum, M.: A virtual machine introspection based architecture for intrusion detection. In: Proc. of NDSS Symposium (2003)
9. Gu, Z., Deng, Z., Xu, D., Jiang, X.: Process implanting: A new active introspection framework for virtualization. In: Proc. of 30th SRDS. IEEE (2011)
10. Intel, Inc., Intel 64 and IA-32 Architectures Software Developer's Manual (2011)
11. Jiang, X., Wang, X., Xu, D.: Stealthy malware detection and monitoring through VMM-based "out-of-the-box" semantic view reconstruction. ACM Trans. Inf. Syst. Secur. 13(2), 12:1–12:28 (2010)
12. Payne, B.D., Carbone, M., Sharif, M., Lee, W.: Lares: An architecture for secure active monitoring using virtualization. In: Proc. of Sec. & Priv. IEEE (2008)
13. Pfoh, J., Schneider, C., Eckert, C.: A formal model for virtual machine introspection. In: Proc. of 2nd Workshop on Virtual Machine Security. ACM (2009)
14. Pfoh, J., Schneider, C., Eckert, C.: Nitro: Hardware-based system call tracing for virtual machines. In: Iwata, T., Nishigaki, M. (eds.) IWSEC 2011. LNCS, vol. 7038, pp. 96–112. Springer, Heidelberg (2011)
15. Schneider, C., Pfoh, J., Eckert, C.: Bridging the semantic gap through static code analysis. In: Proceedings of EuroSec 2012 Workshop. ACM (2012)
16. Sharif, M.I., Lee, W., Cui, W., Lanzi, A.: Secure in-VM monitoring using hardware virtualization. In: Proc. of Conf. on Comp. and Comm. Sec. ACM (2009)

Leveraging String Kernels for Malware Detection

Jonas Pfoh, Christian Schneider, and Claudia Eckert

Technische Universität München
Computer Science Department
Munich, Germany
{pfoh,schneidc,eckertc}@in.tum.de

Abstract. Signature-based malware detection will always be a step behind as novel malware cannot be detected. On the other hand, machine learning-based methods are capable of detecting novel malware but classification is frequently done in an offline or batched manner and is often associated with time overheads that make it impractical. We propose an approach that bridges this gap. This approach makes use of a support vector machine (SVM) to classify system call traces. In contrast to other methods that use system call traces for malware detection, our approach makes use of a string kernel to make better use of the sequential information inherent in a system call trace. By classifying system call traces in small sections and keeping a moving average over the probability estimates produced by the SVM, our approach is capable of detecting malicious behavior online and achieves great accuracy.

Keywords: Security, Machine Learning, Malware Detection, System Calls.

1 Introduction

Detecting malware is an ever present challenge in the field of security. Traditionally, malware detection makes use of signature-based methods. That is, known malware samples are analyzed to create a repository of signatures which are then matched against a static object to determine whether the particular object is infected with malware. While this approach is straightforward, it has two fundamental issues. The first stems from the static nature of the analysis. A static analysis indicates that it is performed on an inert object, that is, an object that is not being executed or in any other way active. Malware authors take advantage of this fact by obfuscating the inert object in such a way that it no longer matches any of the the signatures in the repository. However, when executed, the actions of the active process prove malicious. This may be achieved by simple packing and unpacking of the malicious portions of the object or by more advanced polymorphism techniques.

The second issue with such an approach is a result of its reliance on signatures. These signatures must be generated prior to a successful match, which makes

J. Lopez, X. Huang, and R. Sandhu (Eds.): NSS 2013, LNCS 7873, pp. 206–219, 2013.

such an approach disadvantageous in situations where no prior sample existed for signature generation. For example, novel malware that makes use of so-called "0-day" exploits (exploits which have not yet been seen in the wild) are difficult to detect with a signature-based method. To address these issues, dynamic machine learning-based analysis has often been considered in various forms [1–5].

In a dynamic analysis, the behavior of the malware is analyzed rather than the inert object. This circumvents traditional code obfuscation as the behavior remains malicious and it is this behavior that is analyzed. Obfuscating behavior becomes much more difficult as the malicious act must be carried out in some form. That is, one can attempt to conceal their intentions, but once the malicious act is carried out, this behavior is ideally observable and can be acted upon. Furthermore, machine learning techniques lend themselves well to malware detection as such techniques make an attempt to generalize and learn the features of malware that differentiate them from benign software. This can then also be applied to novel malware, thus countering the threat of 0-day exploits.

While dynamic approaches show much promise they are not immune to shortcomings of their own. While obfuscating behavior is more difficult than obfuscating code, it is not impossible. Depending on how the behavior of a process is modeled, dynamic analysis is generally vulnerable to a class of attacks called mimicry attacks [6, 7]. This class of attack attempts to "act benign" while secretly carrying out some malicious action. Additionally, the large time complexity combined with the massive amount of data that needs to be classified often makes a practical solution difficult.

In this paper we model process behavior though system call traces and present a practical machine learning-based method for malware detection. Specifically, we make use of a support vector machine (SVM) in combination with a string kernel function called a string subsequence kernel (SSK) [8]. This kernel function has properties that lend themselves well to malware detection in spite of mimicry attacks. Additionally, we present a novel method for classifying the behavior of processes in an online manner. Finally, we present an evaluation of our approach which includes several comparisons with other machine learning methods for malware detection.

2 Background

For the classification of system call traces, we make use of support vector machines (SVMs) [9]. SVMs are a maximal margin hyperplane classifiers. That is, given a training set $X = \{(\mathbf{x_m}, y_m)\}_{m=1}^{M}$, where $\mathbf{x_m}$ is a training vector and y_m is the associated class +1 or −1, the SVM identifies the hyperplane for which the separation between the most relevant training vectors (i. e., the support vectors) and the hyperplane is maximized, then classifies new vectors based on their relation to this hyperplane. The hyperplane is represented by a weight vector $\mathbf{w} \in \mathbb{R}^D$ and a variable $b \in \mathbb{R}$ and is formally defined for some $C > 0$ in the following optimization problem:

$$\begin{aligned} \underset{\mathbf{w},\xi,b}{\text{minimize}} \quad & \frac{\|\mathbf{w}\|^2}{2} + \frac{C}{M}\sum_{m=1}^{M} \xi_m \\ \text{subject to} \quad & y_m(\langle \mathbf{w}, \mathbf{x}_m \rangle + b) \geq 1 - \xi_m, m = 1, \cdots, M \end{aligned} \tag{1}$$

where ξ_i represents slack variables that are responsible for preventing an overfitting of the model.

By introducing a Lagrangian with multipliers $\alpha_m \geq 0$, the training phase determines which training vectors will become support vectors. Then, the classification occurs by comparing the test vector to each support vector and measuring the similarity. The decision function f is formally defined as:

$$f(\mathbf{x}) = \text{sgn}(g(\mathbf{x})) \tag{2}$$

where

$$g(\mathbf{x}) = \sum_{m=1}^{M} y_m \alpha_m \langle \mathbf{x}, \mathbf{x}_m \rangle + b \tag{3}$$

Here the dot product ($\langle \mathbf{a}, \mathbf{b} \rangle$) plays the role of the kernel function, which measures the similarity between the two vectors. For simple geometric classification, a dot product may suffice as a measure of similarity. However, for detecting malware through system call traces, a more complex kernel function is necessary. This kernel function must be carefully chosen for a given domain and is discussed in further detail in Section 2.1.

While SVMs produce a binary result as seen in (2), it is often beneficial to work with a posterior probability $P(y = 1|g(x))$ based on $g(x)$ defined in (3). Such a posterior probability is especially helpful when the output is to be combined with other factors to reach a final decision.

Several methods for probability estimation have been proposed. We make use of a method proposed by Platt [10]. Platt's method estimates the posterior probability by using the following sigmoid function:

$$P(y = 1|g(x)) = \frac{1}{1 + e^{Ag(x)+B}} \tag{4}$$

where A and B are found by minimizing the negative logarithmic likelihood of the training data.

2.1 Kernel Function

In looking for a kernel function, we begin by examining the nature of the input itself. The input consists of a string (i. e., sequence) of system call numbers. For the language processing domain, string kernels were introduced to classify texts or strings [8]. In essence, our input is very similar, though instead of classifying strings over the roman alphabet, for example, we are interested in classifying strings over the alphabet of all system calls. That is, we define our alphabet, Σ, as all possible system calls and a string is a sequence $s \in \Sigma^*$ of letters (i. e., system calls). Based on this similarity, we choose a string kernel for our method.

Specifically, we choose to use the string subsequence kernel (SSK) [8]. This kernel measures the similarity between inputs by considering the number of common *subsequences*. A subsequence allows for non-matching, interior letters between its elements, though the kernel penalizes the similarity as this number of interior letters increases. For example, the string ABC would clearly match on the string ABC, but it would also match on the string $AaaaBbbbCccc$, though with a lower similarity measure due to the interior aaa and bbb. This property of the kernel is especially attractive as a sequence of system calls may contain interior system calls that might be irrelevant to the malicious nature of the sequence.

The SSK is formally defined as:

$$k(s,t) = \sum_{u \in \Sigma^n} \sum_{\mathbf{i}:u=s[\mathbf{i}]} \sum_{\mathbf{j}:u=t[\mathbf{j}]} \lambda^{l(\mathbf{i})+l(\mathbf{j})} \tag{5}$$

where n is the size of the subsequence and $\lambda \in (0,1)$ is the decay factor used to weight the contribution of the match based on the number of interior letters. The notation $u = s[\mathbf{i}]$ denotes that u is a subsequence of s for which there exist indices $\mathbf{i} = (i_1, \ldots, i_{|u|})$, with $1 \leq i_1 < \cdots < i_{|u|} \leq |s|$, such that $u_j = s_{i_j}$, for $j = 1, \ldots, |u|$. Finally, $l(\mathbf{i})$ represents the length of the subsequence including interior letters.

3 Method

We begin this section by arguing for system call traces as a model for process behavior. We present the observation that a process in complete isolation cannot perform any malicious action on the rest of the system. Hence, in order for a process to act maliciously it must interact in some manner with the rest of the system and if the isolation mechanism in place is sound, this interaction must take place through the interface provided by the operating system (OS) (i. e., system calls). System calls are necessary to perform actions such as file operation, network communication, inter-process communication, etc. As a result of the above observation, system call traces are often used to model process behavior [1, 3, 4].

However, previous approaches often make use of polynomial kernels or other methods that do not fully consider the sequence of the system calls [1, 3, 5]. That is, in the most trivial case, the number of times that a system call occurs in the trace is taken into account without considering the order of the system calls. This is most likely due to the fact that string kernels incur a massive time overhead when used with large amounts of data. However, if one can mitigate the increased time overhead, an approach that considers sequential data has the potential to produce very high accuracy rates. Intuitively, considering sequential data is logical. If one were to manually analyze a system call trace, one would consider the order of the system calls in addition to which system call is being executed. In an effort to baseline the time overhead, we began training the SSK with our raw data and broke the test off after two months of running with no result in sight. So with practical analysis as a goal, clearly this time overhead must be addressed.

We address the time overhead of the SSK with the observation that if we are able to classify a process by updating an interim classification value and making a decision before the process has finished, we inherently address online classification while reducing the time overhead by not having to analyze the entire system call trace.

Training. To prepare the training data, we iterate over each individual system call trace and extract contiguous sub-traces of size S starting at random points within the traces. We iterate over all the training traces several times in order to get several sub-traces from each original trace. These size S sub-traces become our training set. We do this for two reasons. First, training the SSK with circa 2000 full-length traces, some of which may contain hundreds of thousands of system calls, takes months even on modern hardware. Second, classifying against a support vector with hundreds of thousands of system calls is equally time consuming. The clear concern is that some of these sub-traces may not be indicative of the class they belong to because they represent a relatively small fraction of the entire trace. However, with enough sub-traces we will eventually collect some that are indicative of the class they belong to. The beauty of a SVM is that it will decide which of the sub-traces to use as support vectors (hopefully those indicative of the training class) and which to disregard.

Classification. The classification works by sliding a window of size S over the system call trace that is to be classified. This sliding window moves forward by $S/2$ elements in the trace for each iteration. Then, for each iteration, probability estimates are taken using Platt's method [10] as described in Section 2 and factored into a cumulative moving average for each class. If we let $p_i = P(y = 1|x_i)$ represent the probability estimate as approximated by (4) for an iteration i, we represent the cumulative moving average after iteration i as:

$$U_i = \frac{p_1 + \cdots + p_i}{i} \tag{6}$$

In addition to calculating the cumulative moving average, we also experimented with a simple moving average of the probability estimates. This is a similar method, though instead of considering all previous window iterations, a simple moving average only considers the last y window iterations in the average (where y may be arbitrarily set). Formally,

$$S_i = \frac{p_{i-y} + \cdots + p_i}{y} \tag{7}$$

where $i \geq y$.

We continue our classification by defining two thresholds $T_1 \in [0.5, 1]$ and $T_{-1} \in [0.5, 1]$. These thresholds are compared to U_i and $1 - U_i$, respectively and if either threshold is exceeded, the classification ends by predicting the class represented by the exceeded threshold. Formally, the decision function is represented as follows:

$$D_i = \begin{cases} 1 & \text{if } U_i > T_1, \\ -1 & \text{if } 1 - U_i > T_{-1}, \\ D_{i+1} & \text{else} \end{cases} \tag{8}$$

Clearly, $U_i > 0.5 \wedge (1 - U_i) > 0.5$ can never be true if $U_i \in [0, 1]$, therefore if $T_1 \in [0.5, 1]$ and $T_{-1} \in [0.5, 1]$, only one single case of the decision function will ever be true for a given iteration. For practicality, if the cumulative moving average never exceeds either threshold and there are no more system calls in the trace, the decision function simply predicts 1 if $U_i > 0.5$ or it predicts -1 otherwise.

4 Evaluation

In this section we present the results of our experiments when testing our SVM-based method for malware detection on real-world data

4.1 Data Collection

We ran this experiment on two sets of sample traces collected from Windows XP SP3. We chose Windows XP as it is a popular commercial OS and numerous malware samples are available for this platform.

The first set of system call traces was collected using Nitro [11], a VMI-based system for system call tracing and trapping. This dataset includes 1943 system call traces of malicious samples taken from VX Heavens[1] and 285 system call traces of benign samples taken from a default Windows XP installation and selected installations of well-known, trusted applications.

The second set of traces is taken from a level slightly above system calls. Windows XP wraps its system calls in APIs that it provides to programmers through system libraries. While these traces are technically at a level slightly above the system calls themselves, they serve the same purpose and demonstrate that our method works at both levels. This dataset was collected by hooking these API functions and was first used by Xiao and Stibor [4]. It consists of 2176 API call traces of malicious samples and 161 API call traces of benign samples.

We chose to introduce the second independent data set for two reasons. First, the second data set makes use of API call traces rather than system call traces directly. This gives us a chance to observe the accuracy of our approach for system calls as well as API calls. The second and perhaps more important reason for including a second data set is to confirm that our method also works on an independent data set that was not collected by us. This strengthens the credibility of our approach as it allows us to present results based on data that

[1] `http://www.vxheavens.com`

others have previously used in similar experiments. In fact, we directly compare the results of our method with that of Xiao and Stibor in Section 5.

One might notice that the amount of benign and malicious samples are somewhat imbalanced. We address this by making use of cross-validation as described in Section 4.2 and by reporting the false positive rate in addition to the recall as seen in Section 4.3.

4.2 Setup

We begin by preparing the training set as described in Section 3. That is, we iterate over the full system call traces and extract random contiguous subsequence of size S (in our experiments $S = 100$). We iterate a number of times as to have 2000 random contiguous subsequences in each training set. We take care that the training samples can be traced back to their original trace as to make sure we properly perform a two-fold cross-validation. That is we are careful that, when testing, we train the SVM with samples that do not come from traces in the testing set. Making use of cross-validation allows us to "simulate" the detection of 0-day malware as the classification is performed on data that was not seen during the training phase.

With the data collected and prepared, we make use of LIBSVM [12] along with a provided string kernel extension to perform both training and classification as described in Section 3. Since the SSK is not implemented in LIBSVM or the string kernel extension, we incorporated the SSK implementation proposed by Herbrich [13]. This implementation had to be further modified such that it accepts an input over an integer alphabet as opposed to a roman letter alphabet used in text classification. It is also important to note that LIBSVM calculates probability estimates by making use of an improved algorithm for minimizing the negative logarithmic likelihood proposed by Lin et al. [14].

With these tools and the data prepared, we set up the experiment as described in Section 3. We also found that it was necessary to factor several values into the moving average before checking either threshold. This allows the moving average to factor in the first several iterations before a decision is made. For this reason we always factor the probability estimates for the first 10 iterations in our moving average before we begin considering the thresholds.

4.3 Results

For each experiment, P represents the number of positive (malicious) samples and N represents the number of negative (benign) samples. The variables associated with tuning our detection mechanism (n, λ, T_{-1}, T_1) are experimentally optimized. A discussion of each of these variables can be found below. Then, as each experiment runs, we collect the number of correctly and incorrectly classified results as true positives (TP), true negatives (TN), false positives (FP), and false negatives (FN). With this information we calculate the classification measures presented in Table 1 and Table 2 and discussed below. Finally, we also present the number of average iterations (the average number of times the SVM

Table 1. Experimental results for *system call trace dataset* ($P = 1943$, $N = 285$)

Test Num.	n	λ	T_{-1}	T_1	Avg.	TP	FP	TN	FN	Average Iterations
1	**3**	**0.50**	**0.50**	**0.75**	**CMA**	**1929**	**11**	**274**	**14**	**13.2608**
2	4	0.50	0.50	0.75	CMA	1910	15	270	33	29.4753
3	5	0.50	0.50	0.75	CMA	1903	20	265	40	19.7244
4	3	0.25	0.50	0.75	CMA	1702	17	268	241	209.4165
5	3	0.75	0.50	0.75	CMA	1902	14	271	41	120.6194
6	3	0.40	0.50	0.75	CMA	1919	12	273	24	14.1831
7	3	0.60	0.50	0.75	CMA	1929	14	271	14	22.4475
8	3	0.50	0.50	0.50	CMA	1941	35	250	2	10.8406
9	3	0.50	0.50	0.75	SMA	1869	7	278	74	11.3321
10	3	0.50	1.00	0.90	SMA	1906	48	237	37	722.3012

Test Num.	FP Rate $\frac{FP}{N}$	Recall $\frac{TP}{P}$	Precision $\frac{TP}{TP+FP}$	Accuracy $\frac{TP+TN}{P+N}$	F-Measure $\frac{2}{\frac{1}{\text{Precision}}+\frac{1}{\text{Recall}}}$
1	**0.0386**	**0.9928**	**0.9943**	**0.9888**	**0.9936**
2	0.0526	0.9830	0.9922	0.9785	0.9876
3	0.0702	0.9794	0.9896	0.9731	0.9845
4	0.0596	0.8760	0.9901	0.8842	0.9295
5	0.0491	0.9789	0.9927	0.9753	0.9857
6	0.0421	0.9876	0.9938	0.9838	0.9907
7	0.0491	0.9928	0.9928	0.9874	0.9928
8	0.1228	0.9990	0.9823	0.9834	0.9906
9	0.0246	0.9619	0.9963	0.9636	0.9788
10	0.1684	0.9810	0.9754	0.9618	0.9782

classifier had to be called until either threshold was met) and the type of moving average (CMA = cumulative moving average, SMA = simple moving average) used in each experiment.

We began by considering the threshold values. These values are quite important as they most directly affect the average number of iterations it takes to make a decision. As the thresholds rise, so does the average number of iterations in general. However, if a threshold is too low, the number of false positives and/or negatives rises. In addition, we noticed that our SVM was much more sensitive to malicious samples than it was to benign samples. That is, the average of the malicious probability estimates rose much more quickly to 1 for malicious samples than the average of the benign probability estimates for benign samples. We speculate that this is due to the fact that the traces from the malicious samples are more similar to one another than the traces from the benign samples. That is, the diversity among the benign samples is higher due to the fact that while malicious behavior is generally easier to define, benign behavior is simply "everything else".

We next considered the size n of the subsequence that the kernel function looks for in the traces being compared. What we observed is that as we increased n from the initial value of 3, the classification measures for both datasets became worse. This may seem somewhat counterintuitive. However, n is very dependent

Table 2. Experiment results for *API call trace dataset* ($P = 2176$, $N = 161$)

Test Num.	n	λ	T_{-1}	T_1	Avg.	TP	FP	TN	FN	Average Iterations
1	**3**	**0.6**	**0.5**	**0.75**	**CMA**	**2029**	**19**	**142**	**147**	**37.2174**
2	3	0.5	0.5	0.75	CMA	1971	19	142	205	31.3479
3	3	0.4	0.5	0.75	CMA	1699	15	146	477	32.8015
4	4	0.5	0.5	0.75	CMA	1660	20	141	516	29.1656
5	5	0.5	0.5	0.75	CMA	1697	18	143	479	32.2657
6	3	0.5	0.5	0.75	SMA	1456	16	145	720	14.1694
7	3	0.5	0.7	0.9	SMA	1961	21	140	215	51.3697

Test Num.	FP Rate $\frac{FP}{N}$	Recall $\frac{TP}{P}$	Precision $\frac{TP}{TP+FP}$	Accuracy $\frac{TP+TN}{P+N}$	F-Measure $\frac{2}{\frac{1}{\text{Precision}}+\frac{1}{\text{Recall}}}$
1	**0.1180**	**0.9324**	**0.9907**	**0.9290**	**0.9607**
2	0.1180	0.9057	0.9905	0.9042	0.9462
3	0.0932	0.7808	0.9912	0.7895	0.8735
4	0.1242	0.7629	0.9881	0.7706	0.8610
5	0.1118	0.7799	0.9895	0.7873	0.8723
6	0.0993	0.6691	0.9891	0.6851	0.7982
7	0.1304	0.9012	0.9894	0.8990	0.9432

on S (the size of the window). Since the SSK function does not compute distance between matched subsequences, it must look for exact subsequence matches and as n approaches S, the probability that two subsequences of size n exist in two separate traces of relatively small size decreases.

We then began to experiment with various values for $\lambda \in (0, 1)$. λ is the decay factor used to weight the contribution of the match based on the number of interior letters. That is, as λ approaches 1, interior letters are increasingly penalized. We were surprised by the drastic increase in the average number of iterations it took for a decision to be reached as λ moved away from 0.5. This can most dramatically be seen for values $\lambda = 0.25$ and $\lambda = 0.75$ in Table 1. We found that these values caused the probability estimates to remain closer to 0.5, this caused the decision function to take longer when the probability estimates where favoring the malicious (i. e., "+1") class, as this threshold is set to 0.75.

Finally, we considered using simple moving averages as opposed to cumulative moving averages to make a classification. We found that using a cumulative moving average performed slightly better than a simple moving average. We reasoned that because the average number of iterations is so low when using the cumulative moving average, the success of two methods would not differ greatly if all other factors remained the same. One would expect to see a greater difference in the performance of the two methods if the average number of iterations is much higher. This is supported by the API call dataset in which the average number of iterations is higher and the success of the two methods differ more greatly. In both cases, however, the experiments that made use of a cumulative moving average performed better.

Table 3. A comparison of results from various machine learning approaches to malware detection using system call traces. The □ symbol indicates that the information is not available.

	Author	Approach	FP Rate	Recall	Accuracy
1	Pfoh et al.	SVM+SSK (syscalls)	0.0386	0.9928	0.9888
2	Pfoh et al.	SVM+SSK (API)	0.1180	0.9324	0.9290
3	Rieck et al. [3]	SVM+Poly	□	□	0.88
4	Rieck et al. [3]	SVM+Poly (extended)	□	□	0.76
5	Liao and Vemuri [15]	kNN (total)	0.0	0.917	□
6	Liao and Vemuri [15]	kNN (novel)	0.0	0.75	□
7	Xiao and Stibor [4]	STT	0.4286	0.9955	0.9721
8	Xiao and Stibor [4]	STT+SVM	0.3748	0.9997	0.9790

After having experimentally optimized the various variables, we see that $n = 3$, $\lambda = 0.5$, $T_{-1} = 0.5$, $T_1 = 0.75$, and using a cumulative moving average produces the best results for the system call datasets. We show that these values contribute to a 99.28% recall, a 99.43% precision, a 98.88% accuracy, and a 99.36% F-measure, with only a 3.86% false positive rate. We performed more thorough testing on the system call data set as it is the data we collected and it is the system call traces that our system focuses on rather than API call traces. We tested our method on the second dataset (i. e., the API call dataset) to strengthen our claim that our approach performs well. For this dataset, we produced the best results with $n = 3$, $\lambda = 0.6$, $T_{-1} = 0.5$, $T_1 = 0.75$. With these inputs, our approach produced a 93.24% recall, a 99.07% precision, a 92.90% accuracy, and a 96.07% F-measure, with a 11.80% false positive rate.

5 Related Work

In this section, we compare the results of our approach with those of other approaches. To our knowledge, there are no other approaches that make use of string kernels with SVMs, however we compare our approach with another SVM-based approach, a k-nearest neighbor approach, and an approach that makes use of probabilistic topic models.

5.1 SVM/Polynomial Kernel Function

The first approach we will compare our results with is the work of Rieck et al. [3]. This approach models the system trace by counting the frequency of each system call. The frequency of a system call becomes the weight of that particular system call and this information is stored in a separate vector for each trace. These vectors can then be introduced as arguments to a kernel function. In this case, Rieck et al. make use of a polynomial kernel.

For their testing, they made use of a corpus of 10,072 malware samples divided into 14 malware families. The results of this approach can be seen in Table 3, lines

3 and 4. Line 3 represents a round of testing the authors did using normal cross-validation as is the case in our testing, while line 4 represents testing that took place with an extended dataset that included malware that belonged to none of the malware families along with benign processes. We see that, comparatively, our approach is more accurate. This is not surprising as the approach used by Rieck et al. does not consider any sequential information at all.

5.2 *k*-Nearest Neighbor Classifier

Liao and Vermuri [15] present an approach that makes use of a k-nearest neighbor (kNN) classifier. A kNN classifier makes use of frequencies by storing the frequency of a single system call on a per-trace basis. That is, to train such a classifier each trace is processed and the frequency with which each system call is used is stored per trace. In order to classify an unknown trace, the classifier computes the k most similar traces from the training set and classifies the unknown trace based on the labels associated with the k most similar traces. In this instance, the authors make use of the cosine similarity.

For their experimentation, the authors made use of 5,285 benign traces and 24 malicious traces. When training, they used 16 of the 24 malicious traces. This leads to a situation in which the results in line 5 of Table 3 include the same 16 of 24 traces when testing as when training. Clearly, the classifier classified these 16 traces 100% correctly. Therefore, the results on line 6 of Table 3 represent results that are a better measure of the approach. Despite this, our approach achieves a higher recall than both approaches and the 0% false positive rate for each test can be attributed to the fact that there are far more benign traces than malicious traces.

5.3 Probabilistic Topic Model

Finally, Xiao and Stibor present an interesting approach that makes use of the supervised topic transition (STT) model. This approach assigns system calls to topics. That is, the algorithm groups the system calls based on co-occurrence. The model is then built by modeling the topic transitions rather than the system call transitions that one might expect.

This approach makes use of an algorithm that iteratively alternates between a Gibbs sampling approach and a gradient descent approach to update the topic assignment and the topic transition model in parallel to train the algorithm. The classification then takes place by generating a topic transition model for the unknown trace and probabilistically predicting a label.

In addition to a pure STT approach, the authors also considered a classifier that makes use of a SVM. In this instance, the same training method is used, however the topic transitions are fed into a SVM. This SVM makes use of a Radial Basis Function (RBF) kernel.

In their experimentation, the authors made use of the same API call dataset we used and tested several methods. The two most successful are described here and the results are depicted in Table 3. Line 7 represents the pure STT approach while line 8 represents the approach in which the authors combined their STT model with a SVM classifier. While this approach performs slightly better than our approach when considering the recall, the fact that they report a 37% and 43% false positive rate favors our approach in this regard.

6 Discussion

In this section we discuss the applicability of our approach to online scenarios and discuss the impact of mimicry attacks on our approach.

6.1 Online Classification

As mentioned in Section 3, our method inherently lends itself to online classification due to the fact that it considers additional system calls as they are produced by the process (i. e., while the process is still running). However, we must also consider the time overhead. The issue with classifying an entire system call trace using the SSK is that a single trace may be hundreds of thousands of system calls long and examining two traces of this length for matching subsequences will clearly lead to a large time overhead. We solve this problem by keeping the lengths (S) of the traces that we input into the SVM relatively small (100 system calls).

By setting S to a relatively small value we make the use of the SSK feasible. However, in order for our classification to be accurate, we need to iterate over some number of windows before a final decision can be made. That is, we must still consider the number of iterations that it takes our method to make a decision. As is shown in Table 1, the average number of iterations for the experiment with the highest accuracy is 13.26, while in Table 2 the average number of iterations for the experiment with the highest accuracy is 37.22. That is, our method of classification can make a decision after only considering a relatively small number of system calls, which significantly reduces the time overhead and allows for online classification.

One may criticize the point that our approach does not consider the entire trace, however all such approaches must address this practical problem somehow. The problem is that one may have to wait an indefinite amount of time for a process to finish. For example, a permanently resident process will only end execution once the system is shut down. That is, practically, one will always have to set a maximum trace length to address this and other approaches do this arbitrarily [16] while our approach makes use of the given thresholds to determine when to stop.

6.2 Mitigating Mimicry Attacks

Mimicry attacks [6, 7] are a class of attacks in which either an adversary drowns the individual steps necessary for delivering the malicious payload in "benign steps" or an adversary "acts benign" for a certain amount of time before delivering a malicious payload.

While this class of attacks is certainly a concern for any system that models program behavior through system call traces, the use of the SSK significantly raises the bar against this type of attack. As mentioned in Section 2.1, the SSK matches on subsequences, where the definition of a subsequence allows for interior system calls. In a simple case, if we consider the system call sequence "12,19,39" to be indicative of malicious behavior, a mimicry attack might try to fool the security mechanism by introducing interior "benign" system calls. For example, the attacker might augment the malicious program such that the system call trace was as follows: "**12**,17,13,**19**,32,**39**". This may be enough to fool signature-based or simple "bag of words" approaches to malware detection, but the beauty of the SSK is that it, by design, will still match on these traces.

On the other hand, if an adversary decides to "act benign" for a time before delivering a payload, our approach may miss the payload if either threshold has been met. The solution for this is simply to raise the threshold. In the most extreme case, one could raise the threshold for the benign class to 1.0. This will result in a system that continuously scans a trace and will only exit if a malicious classification is made. Such an approach would also be applicable in detecting injected code (e. g., shellcode). Due to the fact that any process will be scanned until the threshold for malicious activity is reached, any benign process that is injected with malicious code will also be potentially detected. In order for such an approach to be successful one would most likely have to consider the simple moving average of the probability estimates as described in Section 3. We performed such a test on our system call data and were able to produce 96% accuracy as can be seen in Table 1.

7 Conclusion

This paper proposes a novel method for practical malware detection with system calls using the SSK. We address the large time overhead generally associated with such an approach by considering the moving average of probability estimates over a sliding window. This moving average is then compared to a threshold to predict a class.

Our experimentation shows that this method is both accurate and considerably reduces the time overhead associated with using the SSK for this domain. We test our method on two separate datasets and the fact that our method shows promising results for both datasets makes us confident that this method is universally applicable. Additionally, we compare our approach with other machine learning-based approaches and could show that our approach performs very well in comparison. Finally, we argue that our approach raises the bar against mimicry attacks through the use of the SSK and our threshold mechanism.

References

1. Rieck, K., Trinius, P., Willems, C., Holz, T.: Automatic analysis of malware behavior using machine learning. Technical report, Berlin Institute of Technology (2009)

2. Kolter, J.Z., Maloof, M.A.: Learning to detect and classify malicious executables in the wild. Journal of Machine Learning Research 7, 2721–2744 (2006)
3. Rieck, K., Holz, T., Willems, C., Düssel, P., Laskov, P.: Learning and classification of malware behavior. In: Zamboni, D. (ed.) DIMVA 2008. LNCS, vol. 5137, pp. 108–125. Springer, Heidelberg (2008)
4. Xiao, H., Stibor, T.: A supervised topic transition model for detecting malicious system call sequences. In: Proceedings of the Workshop on Knowledge Discovery, Modeling and Simulation. ACM, New York (2011)
5. Schultz, M.G., Eskin, E., Zadok, E., Stolfo, S.J.: Data mining methods for detection of new malicious executables. In: Proceedings of the IEEE Symposium on Security and Privacy, pp. 38–49. IEEE, Washington, DC (2001)
6. Wagner, D., Dean, D.: Intrusion detection via static analysis. In: Proceedings of the IEEE Symposium on Security and Privacy, pp. 156–168. IEEE, Washington, DC (2001)
7. Wagner, D., Soto, P.: Mimicry attacks on host-based intrusion detection systems. In: Proceedings of the ACM Conference on Computer and Communications Security, pp. 255–264. ACM, New York (2002)
8. Lodhi, H., Saunders, C., Shawe-Taylor, J., Cristianini, N., Watkins, C.: Text classification using string kernels. Journal of Machine Learning Research 2, 419–444 (2002)
9. Schölkopf, B., Smola, A.J.: Learning with Kernels: Support Vector Machines, Regularization, Optimization, and Beyond. MIT Press, Cambridge (2001)
10. Platt, J.C.: Probabilistic Outputs for Support Vector Machines and Comparisons to Regularized Likelihood Methods. In: Advances in Large Margin Classifiers, pp. 61–74. MIT Press, Cambridge (2000)
11. Pfoh, J., Schneider, C., Eckert, C.: Nitro: Hardware-based system call tracing for virtual machines. In: Iwata, T., Nishigaki, M. (eds.) IWSEC 2011. LNCS, vol. 7038, pp. 96–112. Springer, Heidelberg (2011)
12. Chang, C.C., Lin, C.J.: LIBSVM: A library for support vector machines. ACM Transactions on Intelligent Systems and Technology 2, 27:1–27:27 (2011), Software available at http://www.csie.ntu.edu.tw/~cjlin/libsvm
13. Herbrich, R.: Learning Kernel Classifiers: Theory and Algorithms. MIT Press, Cambridge (2001)
14. Lin, H.T., Lin, C.J., Weng, R.C.: A note on platt's probabilistic outputs for support vector machines. Machine Learning 68(3), 267–276 (2007)
15. Liao, Y., Vemuri, V.R.: Using text categorization techniques for intrusion detection. In: Proceedings of the USENIX Security Symposium, pp. 51–59. USENIX, Berkeley (2002)
16. Wang, X., Yu, W., Champion, A., Fu, X., Xuan, D.: Detecting worms via mining dynamic program execution. In: Proceedings of the International Conference on Security and Privacy in Communications Networks (2007)

Insiders Trapped in the Mirror Reveal Themselves in Social Media

Miltiadis Kandias, Konstantina Galbogini, Lilian Mitrou, and Dimitris Gritzalis

Information Security & Critical Infrastructure Protection Research Laboratory
Dept. of Informatics, Athens University of Economics & Business
76 Patission Ave., GR-10434, Athens, Greece
{kandiasm,l.mitrou,dgrit}@aueb.gr, gko@entersoft.gr

Abstract. Social media have widened society's opportunities for communication, while they offer ways to perform employees' screening and profiling. Our goal in this paper is to develop an insider threat prediction method by (e)valuating a users' personality trait of narcissism, which is deemed to be closely connected to the manifestation of malevolent insiders. We utilize graph theory tools in order to detect influence of and usage deviation. Then, we categorize the users according to a proposed taxonomy. Thus we detect individuals with narcissistic characteristics and manage to test groups of people under the prism of group homogeneity. Furthermore, we compare and classify users to larger sub-communities consisting of people of the same profession. The analysis is based on an extensive crawling of Greek users of Twitter. As the application of this method may lead to infringement of privacy rights, its use should be reserved for exceptional cases, such as the selection of security officers or of critical infrastructures decision-making staff.

Keywords: Insider Threat, Social Media, Twitter, Narcissism, Personality Profiling, Usage Deviation, Group Homogeneity, Security Officer.

1 Introduction

Information security officers, analysts, and researchers are often asked to tackle hard to deal with problems. That is, they are asked to find appropriate solutions to resource intensive problems, identify the correct analogy between security and functionality, battle a wide range of threats, etc. Research indicates [1] that one of the most demanding problems in cyber and corporate security is the insider threat. In principle, the malevolent insider manifests when a trusted user of the information system behaves in a way that the security policy defines as unacceptable [2]. One should not discriminate between advanced and not advanced users while eligible access to the information system is a prerequisite in order to classify an intruder as an insider threat. For the needs of this work we adopt the following definition [2]: *"Insider threat refers to threats originating from people who have been given access rights to an information system and misuse their privileges, thus violating the information system security policy of the organization"*.

J. Lopez, X. Huang, and R. Sandhu (Eds.): NSS 2013, LNCS 7873, pp. 220–235, 2013.

In this paper we will utilize the multifaceted information that information shared/ revealed in the (context of) social media offer us, in order to propose prediction and deterrence measures against the insider threat. Our goal is to extract conclusions over the users regarding the personality trait of narcissism, which is a common characteristic among insiders. Unfortunately, it is not possible, for us, to evaluate the results of our research on real-life insiders since most of them never face justice [1] and even those cases which have been publicized are related to older incident when social media did not exist.

Furthermore, we propose a method for analyzing existing groups of people. We consider that a homogeneous group consists of users with similar valuations of specific characteristics, in our case the trait of narcissism. A dysfunctional group could lead to conflicts, less appealing working environment, and personal antipathies, which facilitate or even "create" malevolent insiders.

Finally, we introduce a method to compare and classify users to larger groups of users who share the same profession. This way we achieve a more equitable outcome, as we can observe noteworthy usage differentiation between different professions.

We use data crawled by Twitter, so as to analyze the collected users in a graph-theoretic manner. We identify connections between usage patterns and define which users' behavior could be considered as deviating from the average. The use of such method interferes with the personality and privacy rights of the affected persons. Moreover, the ability to rapidly conduct psychometrics for such a large number of people may become a social threat. Thus, we have adopted a privacy-sensitive and pro-employee attitude over the results of this work. The potentially intrusive nature of this method dictates the necessity of its confined application to certain information systems and organizations. This application may be clearly acceptable for selecting security officers, as well as for personnel involved in the decision-making process within security-critical information systems and critical infrastructures.

The paper is organized as follows: in section 2 we refer to existing methods to tackle the insider threat, along with a review of the graph theoretic methodologies utilized in social media analysis. In section 3 we describe the proposed methodology and test environment. In section 4 we describe the adopted graph theoretic approach. In section 5 we describe a method of outlier detection, i.e., we note some common characteristics of the outliers and propose a user's taxonomy. In section 6 we discuss issues that relate to group homogeneity and propose ways to utilize our methodology in smaller or larger groups. Section 7 is dedicated to ethical and law issues. In section 8 we sum up our findings and frame our plans for future work.

2 Relevant Literature and Motivation

For a long time academic and corporate security researchers have been trying to propose solid countermeasures to deal with the insider threat [3]. The battle against the insider threat has three major fronts, i.e., the detection, the prediction, and the prevention of this kind of threats.

Regarding the detection of malevolent insiders, numerous ideas, methods and techniques have been proposed. Intrusion Detection Systems and anomaly detection techniques have been widely utilized [4-5], together with log file analysis [6]. Another detection method uses *honeynets* and *honeytokens* [7]. Host and network sensors have been also proposed to mitigate the problem [8]. The area of insider threat prediction is active, too. In [9-10], various methods and techniques have been proposed to predict insiders. Other approaches include scope-specific attempts in relational databases [11] or highlight the need for both technical and psychological approaches [12]. The psychosocial perspective of the insider is also referred to by Greitzer et al. [13] and Brdiczka et al. [14].

In this work, we gathered data from social media so as to extract results over each user's predispositions. It is important to mention that data is gathered from publicly available information, which results from Twitter communication. The selected data are used for prediction and deterrence purposes, since we analyze each user under the prism of usage deviation with the tool of graph theory. Social media and collaborative environments have been used in the battle against the insider threat [15]. Usage deviation aids in detecting narcissistic behavior through social media popularity and intense usage of the media [16-18]. Interestingly, the psychosocial trait of narcissism is closely related to delinquent behavior, especially regarding the insider threat [19-20]. Shaw et al. [20] were the first to conduct a research on the psychological characteristics of the insider threat. They detected a close connection between malevolent insiders and narcissism, under the prism of the "sense of entitlement" and "lack of empathy". They highlighted that convicted insiders have been found to share this personality trait, which often led to anger and the so called "revenge syndrome". Their results have been supported/strengthened by many psychologists and psychological researches. Butts et al. [19] confirmed the aforementioned by stating that narcissism may motivate malevolent insiders who "*suffer from excess self-importance or preoccupation and have difficulty living up to their own expectations*" due to their inflated self-image. Ego and self-image are considered suspicious personal factors in the manifestation of an insider threat, by the Federal Bureau of Investigation [21].

Twitter is a popular social medium. Data from Twitter are often utilized in order to find out why some users of certain communities distinct from other users of the same communities. A *distinct community* is defined as a set of users who share common characteristics. In [22], Mislove et al. present a large-scale study of multiple online social networks and refer to the small-world phenomenon [23].

An important question for the research with a social medium is *"who is influential in a social network"*. *User influence* can be defined as the ability to convince an audience to engage in a single act. In [24], Cha et al. present ways of measuring someone's influence in Twitter by taking into account his number of mentions, *retweets* and *indegree*. As only a minority of users has the ability to persuade others in a higher level, research shows that influential users have a certain way of expressing themselves via social media, while they decorate their tweets with appropriate sentiment [25].

3 Methodology and Testing Environment

In our work we focus on a Greek community of Twitter, since our research is context sensitive and utilizes ethnological features rooted in locality, thus, we are able to extract results and analyze them appropriately. We provide a graph analysis of this community using specific metrics. We also define the content and measures of user influence. Furthermore, we analyze the different ranks of users, ordered by their influence valuation score, and present the set of users who are outliers both in the whole graph and in smaller communities. The graph theoretic methods are utilized so as to tackle the insider threat under the prism of outlier detection, narcissism detection, and group homogeneity. Our goal is to analyze the collected data, in order to extract useful results about the psychosocial trait of narcissism of the users, as well as the group they belong to inside an organization.

A Twitter user can have more than one label that characterizes her social actions. Thus, there are three types of user categories: (a) follower, i.e., she is followed by someone, (b) following, i.e., she follows someone, and (c) retweeter, i.e., she spreads the speech of someone else via tweets.

Regarding the crawling, as Twitter poses a rate limit for calls towards its API, there are two ways to crawl data from it: (a) by using unauthenticated calls towards its API, and (b) by making calls that must have an embedded OAuth token within their content. In the second case, the OAuth token is used to identify the client who makes the calls and is provided with every user profile. We chose to use the first way, in order to use the REST protocol that simplifies and accelerates the procedure. However, the unauthenticated calls permit 150 requests/hour and are measured against the public IP of the device making the requests. Taking into account the huge amount of information that a single user produces and when the scope is a whole community, one needs to collect a vast amount of data.

As for the algorithmic part of crawling, we used a set of Greek users who had Twitter accounts as initial seeds, and then run a breadth-first search. This set of seeds consisted of 1.500 users. The process of data collection began by crawling the profile data of each user. Then, we distinguished the users who were connected to the initial seeds and collected their data. In order to create a community consisting only of Greeks, we crawled only those users who have published on their profiles that they are Greeks. In case someone had not published such information, we checked the language she used or her *geolocation*. Starting from initial seeds and crawling their followers and followings, a social graph of 1.075.859 distinct users with 7.125.561 connections among them was created. The graph created on the basis that (a) each user is a node, and (b) every connection is a directed edge.

For the test of the data we used the SNAP (snap.stanford.edu) library. We propose three ways to measure user influence and tested these metrics with 41.818 users. As a result, we ranked the users by their scores and we identified ways for distinguishing users who are outliers in a community. The crawling software and the algorithms that detect the influential users are developed in a Java environment. Also, in order to collect the *klout* scores of each user we made calls to their API retrieving messages in *json* type of files.

Regarding the set of 41.818 users, we have managed to collect their full profile. We have both personal and statistical details for each one of them. Furthermore, we kept each user's screen name, id, the description that she wrote about herself, her url, her language, and her *geolocation*. We also kept the state of her profile (protected or not), the number of lists she is participating, the numbers of her following and follower users, all her tweets, the number of her favorites, the number of tweets she has mentioned, and the number of retweets she has made.

4 The Graph-Theoretic Approach

In this section we present the graph analysis of the Twitter dataset, so as to identify the way users tend to behave inside a community, as well as the way an outlier can be identified in the set. Our focus is on developing a method that categorizes newcomers to the community in a given taxonomy.

The structure of the Greek Twitter community is described as follows:

(a). *Strongly connected components*: We performed a depth-first search to find out this type of connection among users. The result was that there is a large such component (153.121 nodes) and several others (significantly smaller). The largest strongly connected component of the graph, where everyone connects to each other, is small.

(b). *Node loneliness*: In order to check if every node is connected to someone else, we ran the Weakly Connected Components algorithm. As a result, 1.075.815 users are connected to someone (99% of the nodes).

(c). *Small world phenomenon*: We calculated the effective diameter of the graph (Fig. 2), i.e., that every user of it is 6 hops away from everyone else [26].

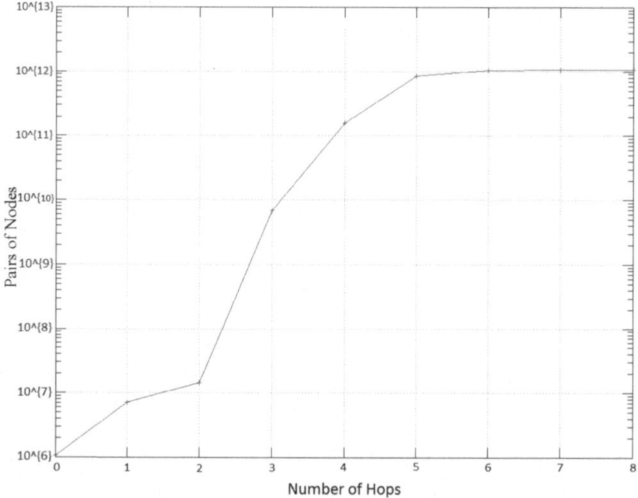

Fig. 1. The *Small World* phenomenon in crawled community

The term user's indegree value indicates the number of users who follow the user, while outdegree value is the number of users to whom she points. Both indegree and outdegree distributions show heavy tails [27-28] for the biggest values of indegree and outdegree values, respectively. Fig. 3 shows the indegree distribution of the graph. The average indegree value is 13.2 followers per user. Only a set of 55.225 (0.05%) nodes have indegree value above average. From this set, 35.807 users (0.033%) have indegree value bigger than the double average degree. In Fig. 4 the outdegree distribution resembles to indegree distribution. The average outdegree value is 11, while only 27.152

(0.02%) users have outdegree value bigger than the average and out of them a small fracture of 19.249 (0.018%) users have outdegree value of twice the average. Intuitive, these leads to the conclusion that there are many users with low indegree and outdegree values, while even fewer users have been found to have high indegree and outdegree values. Based on the above, we argue that the users who spread in usage and create the heavy tails (Fig. 3 and Fig. 4) are outliers.

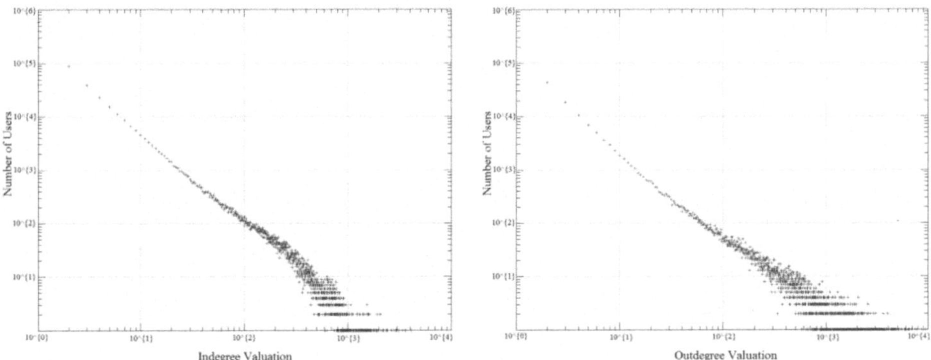

Fig. 2. Indegree distribution

Fig. 3. Outdegree distribution

In order to identify the characteristics of the users in this Twitter community, we used three metrics, i.e. (1) the commonality valuation of the users, (2) their klout score, and (3) the influence valuation of a user. In specific:

(1). we produce a statistical distribution of the *commonality* of the users, i.e., a representation of usage intensity of the specific social media. This utilizes the data collected from the public user profiles. Then, we created a combinatorial function that aggregates the values of seven parameters that emerge from a user's profile, as follows: (a) number of followers, (b) number of followings, (c) number of tweets, (d) number of retweets, (e) number of mentions, (f) number of favorites, and (g) number of lists. We calculated the aggregate value for each user and we sorted their rank. Fig. 5 shows the distribution of usage intensity in Twitter (log-log scale). This demonstrates heavy tail behavior; therefore, there are many users with small usage in Twitter. On the contrary, a much smaller set of users shows intense usage of Twitter.

(2). we reveal the *outliers* in this community by taking into account their "Klout scores" (klout.com). The *klout score* is a metric that represents someone's social media influence. We first crawled the klout scores of each user in the Twitter community, and then we ranked the users according to this score.

(3). we define someone's *influence* by seeking the set of individuals around her - considering her as a central user - rather than her usage intensity in social media. Every user has a specific subset of users which she affects. Thus, we focus on the set of users who are possible candidates to adopt her words by retweeting them. The influential set of each user consists of: (a) followers who directly learn her quotes, (b) her mentioners, (c) retweeters who mention her or repeat her word of mouth, even without following her, and (d) the followers of her last two categories, as there is a possibility to learn about her indirectly. Therefore, we identify the influential sets of each user in the graph and rank them by the size of these sets, taking into consideration only the number of distinct users in each set. We use these ranks of the Greek Twitter Community users in order to observe the minimum, the average, and the maximum values in each case. The average values can reveal the common users of social media, while the maximum values can determine the outliers.

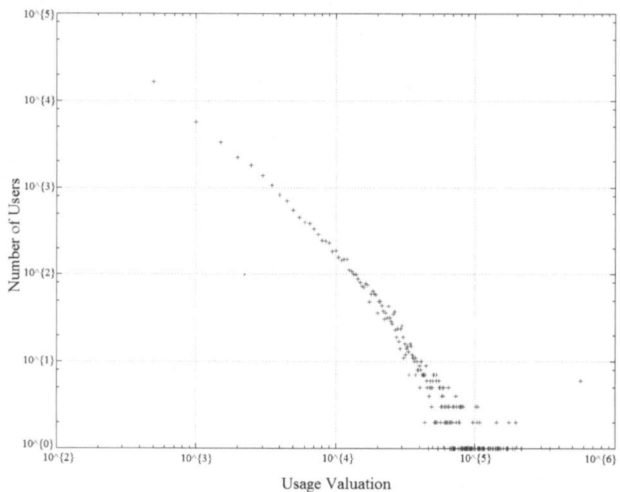

Fig. 4. Usage intensity distribution

We also wish to find out the outlier users in specific Twitter sub-communities. As an example, we defined four sub-communities that were distinguished by each user's job. As Twitter users tend to declare their jobs in the "description field", we crawled their jobs from their profiles. Thus, we created the following sub-communities: (a) Lawyers, (b) IT personnel, (c) Academics and (d) Artists. In Table 1 we have listed the sub-communities that were extracted, the number of users in each community, the minimum and maximum scores for influence and usage valuation, and the klout score.

Table 1. Characteristics and valuations of sub-communities

Category	# of users	Influence valuation	Klout score	Usage valuation
Lawyers	107	34 - 408	10.0 - 61.97	16 - 78930
IT Personnel	832	32 - 351	3.55 - 19.28	21 - 79251
Academic Personnel	144	30 - 503	8.77 - 20.31	45 - 32716
Artists	344	55 - 3604	20.89 - 77.46	11 - 186878

5 Outlier's Common Characteristics and Detection

The proposed approach can be used for the identification of users who perform quite differentiated usage of the specific social media. Our initial hypothesis was that the users' usage distribution would be Gaussian, i.e., few users perform a very limited usage of the media, the vast majority been normally active, and few users been quite popular. The results that refer to the Greek Twitter Community (Fig. 5) indicate that this is not true, i.e., (a) the majority of the Greek users make very poor use of the medium, (b) there are a lot of normally active users, and (c) very few users are popular.

Now we propose a general taxonomy of the Twitter users, the data of whom were crawled and analyzed. According to our findings, the most influential users' influence valuation is between 942 and 3604 and usage valuation is between 21004 and 569000 (Fig. 5). Based on this, users whose sum of the previous values is higher of the threshold of 22000 are classified in a different category of the taxonomy. Furthermore, the majority of the users with usage valuation above 21000 are either real life celebrities or news media. This leads us assume that the "normal" users with high scores should belong to a different category. The proposed categories appear on Table 2.

Table 2. The proposed Twitter user taxonomy

Category	Influence valuation	Klout score	Usage valuation
Loners	0 - 90	3.55 - 11.07	0 - 500
Individuals	90 - 283	11.07 - 26.0	500 - 4500
Known users	283 - 1011	26.0 - 50.0	4500 - 21000
News Media & Personas	1011 - 3604	50.0 - 81.99	21000 - 569000

The question that emerges is "why one should care of the usage differentiation or deviation between the users". Based on the available data, we can spot a threshold above which the users may become quite influential and perform intense medium usage. Therefore, we can define a specific point where a user turns from a normal one to a "media persona". Research has proved that individuals tend to transfer their offline behavior online. Thus, more *extravert* individuals tend to form large groups and communicate easier in the territory of social media, while *introvert* individuals tend to communicate less [29-30]. Furthermore, research work has connected excessive usage of social media to the personality trait of narcissism [16-18].

The connection between narcissism and insider threat has been verified in a number of research works. In specific, research has demonstrated that a narcissistic personality is more vulnerable to become a malevolent insider [19-20]. The first one to make the connection between narcissism and the predisposition towards becoming a malevolent insider was Shaw et al. [20]. In order to determine a user's narcissism and the level of usage differentiation, our method first utilizes a user's fully crawled Twitter profile. Then, this user's influence over a social medium, as well as his overall activity in this medium, is also evaluated. These actions may - in certain cases - be considered intrusive and violate privacy, therefore they should only be performed in the course of a legitimate action.

6 Group Homogeneity

Research clearly indicates that poor relations with co-workers and/or supervisors, as well as dysfunctional working groups not only facilitate the manifestation of insider threats, but also catalyzes an insider's malevolent behavior [15]. Some researchers refer to the need for thorough screening of the employees prior to employment, especially for those who are going to occupy high risk positions [31-32]. As a result, it has been suggested [15] that a background check would be essential, not only regarding a users' criminal background, but also under the prism of work group homogeneity.

Researchers have suggested that management and human resources staff should maintain awareness of users' satisfaction and well-being [33]. An important parameter of employees' satisfaction is the sense of belonging to the group, which depicts the group's homogeneity. Show et al. [31] explains that 90% of insider cases involve serious employment crises and personnel problems prior to the attack. Moreover, destructive group dynamics analysis has identified similar results [14].

Based on the above, a three-step process can be used for user screening and group homogeneity testing. The scope of each step is the following: (a) how well could a new user fit to an existing group, in terms of group homogeneity, (b) how homogeneous is an existing group inside the organization, and (c) how similar is the specific user's social media behavior to other users' of the same profession. Human Resources experts could utilize this screening/testing, in order to assess the employees who may pose the most significant threat on becoming malevolent insiders [13]. This process can be, in principle, utilized for the benefit of both, the employer and the employee. However, as one or more of these steps might be considered privacy-intrusive in certain legal contexts, they must be only performed in the course of a legitimate action.

In order to evaluate how well a newcomer could fit in an existing group, one could check her Twitter account and crawl it. Then, the crawled data could be sent as input to a graph theoretic analysis that calculates her influence on the media and her overall usage valuation. Having a collection of data about the users of the group, one can define a range of acceptable media influence and usage values for the newcomers.

In case we wish to study the homogeneity of a specific group in an organization, we can utilize a fraction of the above process. In specific, we need to crawl each group member's Twitter account and feed the results to the appropriate algorithms. Then, we should analyze the results of each user's influence and usage assessment, so as to decide over the homogeneity of the group.

Another proposal for user screening is to compare each individual with others with the same profession. This technique was feasible to deploy, as it does not need evaluation of real life groups and further authorization by the research subjects. Thus, we collected and analyzed Twitter users who have declared their profession in their profiles. As mentioned before, the profession clusters that we distinguished were referring to Lawyers, IT personnel, Academics, and Artists. The distribution of their Twitter usage is showed in Fig. 6.

Most users follow the general usage pattern and belong to the normal influence/usage groups of the taxonomy. Artists and IT staff have slightly more members classified at the "Media Persona" category of our taxonomy. This is so, as IT staff is more familiar to Information and Communication Technology advances, including social media, while artists are often based on social media to promote their work.

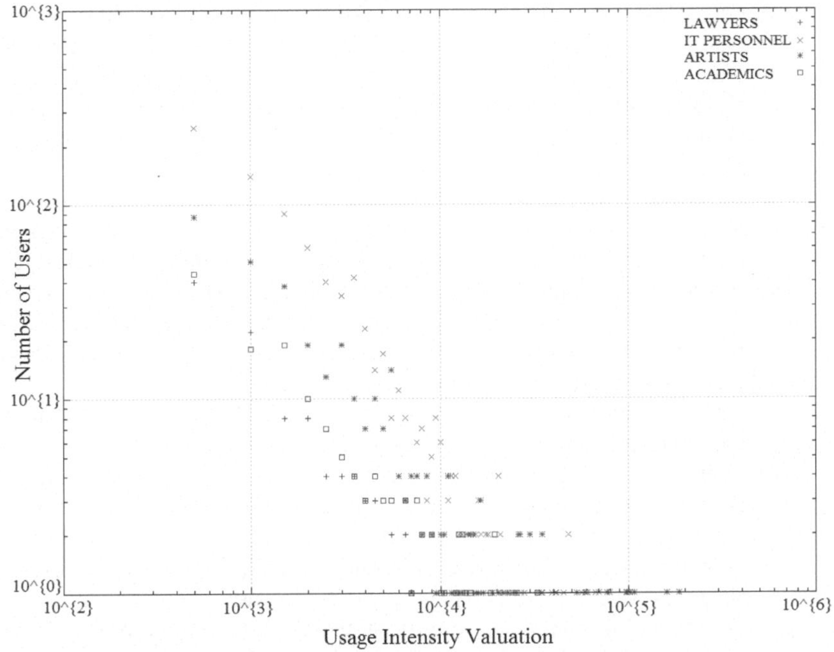

Fig. 5. Usage deviation (Lawyers, IT personnel, Academics, Artists)

7 Ethical and Legal Issues

Online social media profiles, blogs, tweets, and online fora are increasingly monitored by employers searching for information that may provide insight on employees and prospective hires [34-36].A broader and potentially less censored or more honest array of information is easily accessible on the Internet. Taking into consideration the exponentially growing participation in online social networking sites and social media, it is not surprising that employers are searching for unique information about applicants and employees not found with other selection methods. In particular in the US, recent surveys point out lifestyle concerns among the most common reasons for rejecting candidates [37]. Such findings indicate that the once clear lines between the private and the public, as well as the employee's personal and professional life, are gradually blurring as a result of : (a) the "boundary-crossing technologies" [38], (b) the transformation of workplace structure and ethos through ICT, and (c) the radical changes in mass self-communication [39]. In other words, the more private information has become easily accessible and infinitely shareable and transferable, the more monitoring may extent to private spaces, activities, and time [35-36]. Methods (such the proposed in this paper) allows employers to collect and aggregate information, which reflects behavior of the user and her interaction with other users, in order to produce relevant patterns/profiles and anticipate future behaviors and threats.

Employers are, in principle, not prohibited to consider information about a person who is documented in publicly available social media profiles, public posts, or public Twitter accounts. However, both the wide availability of private information, as well as its use beyond the initial context that this information has been produced, may have far reaching effects for the employees' rights and liberties. With regard to the findings referred to in our paper, we should take into consideration that the insider threat prediction and prevention raises ethical and legal issues concerning the protection of employees' privacy, personality, and dignity.

The openness and sharing culture that dominates the online social media reflects a population that does not construct communication on the traditional division between private and public contexts. Many argue that when one publishes something to all comers it is not reasonable to expect (current and future) employers to respect her privacy and freedom of expression and refrain from judging her based on publicly available information [38]. This is true, in particular when employers have legitimate interests to protect their secrets and reputation, and ensure a secure business environment and operation.

On the other hand (informational), privacy responds to the requirement that everyone should be in control of the information concerning her, so as to formulate conceptions of personal identity, values, preferences, goals, and to protect her life choices from public control, social disgrace, or objectification. Individuals tailor their social identities and aim at controlling others' impressions and opinions of them through behavior and performances within particular audiences [38]. Informational privacy offers safeguards to preserve an underlying capacity for autonomous decision - and choice-making [35] and to maintain a variety of social identities and roles. Moreover, privacy is a requirement for maintaining the human condition with dignity and respect. As related to privacy, dignity summarizes, among other principles, the recognition of an individual's personality, non-interference with another's life choices, and the possibility to act and express freely in society. Employer's intrusion into an employee's personal life through "social media background checks" may lead employers to judge opinions and behaviors out of their initial context. De-contextualization is an inherent characteristic of social media that pertains to over-simplification of social relations and the wide dissemination of information [40].

However, as Nissenbaum [41] underlines, the definitive value to be protected by the right to privacy is exactly the "contextual integrity" of a given contextual-self having different behaviors and sharing different information depending on the context. Information gathered through social media analysis is normally not only unintended as application information but often job-irrelevant or, moreover, related to sensitive activities and, consequently, information of the person concerned (religion, political beliefs, etc.) [42]. We should also take into account that this information may be inaccurate or not timely, reflecting a different life-phase of the person. Due to the Internet's excessive and perpetual memory, it is becoming harder and harder for persons to escape their past.

Furthermore we should consider that the social and communication norms which dominate the social media appear not only to lead to projected identities that job applicants may not wish to be seen by potential employers [43] but also to encourage exaggeration, bravado or shameless behavior [44]. Moreover, social media screening may expose employees and candidates to discrimination [37]. Profiling with the aim to gain probabilistic knowledge from data of the past and (to) propose/ predictions and identify risks for the future may infringe privacy as a right to be a multiple personality and carries far-reaching consequences in terms of social selection and unjustified and - often - invisible discrimination. Profiling may indeed entail the risk of formatting and customization of individual behavior that affects her personal autonomy [40]. Extending monitoring to social communication relationships of employees and candidates augments the chances of employers to influence behavior and promote the "well-adjusted employee" [45]. Information gathering about employee performances outside the traditionally conceived work sphere not only increases the dependence on (future) employers but has also a chilling effect on individuals' personality and freedom of speech. This is so, as they may sacrifice "Internet participation to segregate their multiple life performance" [37] and, thus, refrain from expressing themselves.

Employees are routinely asked to sacrifice privacy rights to managerial interests like productivity, prevention and detection of threats and liability risks. Given the workplace belongs to the "public sphere", scholars argue that employees, who are hired to attend company business, cannot have a (subjective) "reasonable expectation of privacy" that society (objectively) accepts and legitimizes. American Courts are reluctant to recognize a workplace privacy right: in any case reasonable expectation of privacy of employees should be judged under all the circumstances and must be reasonable both in inception and scope (Supreme Court, Case O'Connor vs. Ortega). In the employment context privacy, if any, seems to be exchanged for something of commensurate value, like taking or keeping a job [46]. Regarding privacy as a purely bargainable and alienable right ignores the dignity element, inherent in the notion of privacy. The European approach seems diametrically opposite in many respects: Privacy is not conceived as a right to seclusion and intimacy but as a phenomenon, a protectable situation that regards the relationships between a person and its environment/other persons. The European Court of Human Rights (Niemitz v. Germany) rejected the distinction between private life and professional life. According to the Court, European employees have "a right to dignity and a private life that does not stop at the employer's doorstep".

Finally, it has been found that excessive monitoring disturbs the relationship between the employer and the employees. It has been proved that employees whose communications were monitored, suffered from higher levels of depression, anxiety and fatigue than those who were not monitored, within the same organization [36]. The panoptic effect of being constantly monitored even concerning activities that fall out of the workplace frame has negative impacts on the employer-employee relationship that should be based on mutual trust and confidence [47-48].

8 Conclusions and Future Work

In this paper we dealt with the insider threat prediction and prevention. Malevolent insiders and predisposition towards computer crime has been closely linked to the personality trait of narcissism.

Personal data, views, and considerations, often disclosed and referred to in social media, may be used for both, the social good/in the interest of the society (e.g. Forensics, e-commerce, etc.), or in a way that infringes fundamental rights and liberties or private interests (e.g. social engineering, discriminations, etc.) [49-53]. Herein, we proposed a method of outlier detection in social media via influence, usage intensity, and klout score valuation, in order to detect users with narcissistic behavior. We have also proposed a method for group analysis under the prism of group homogeneity, as this homogeneity is a valuable characteristic to deter the manifestation of insider threats. In order to improve the efficiency of our results, we have proposed a way to compare and classify users with communities of users of the same profession. These methods can be used to strengthen legal employee screening and monitoring efficiency within an organization.

To demonstrate the efficiency of the proposed method, we collected a vast amount of data from Twitter. Then, we adopted a specific graph theoretic approach to analyze the crawled data. We focused on a fraction of Twitter users, i.e., a community of 41.818 Greek users. Along with this whole community, we distinguished four smaller sub-communities, which consist of users that share the same profession (lawyers, IT personnel, academic personnel, artists).

Privacy violations may occur, in case someone chooses to apply the proposed method in an illegal or unethical manner. Users' privacy and dignity may be at stake if someone uses the method to promote employee/user discrimination and careless punishment. Therefore, the method should be utilized in the course of a legitimate action. Due to the nature of the employment relationship, in which there is an inherent asymmetry of power, reliance on consent for monitoring and screening is highly questionable. Consent should be confined only to, the very few, cases where the employee has a genuine free choice and is subsequently able to withdraw the consent without detriment [54-55]. Monitoring/screening techniques and psychological tests as indicated in the proposed method have to comply with privacy and data protection principles. According to the core principle of proportionality monitoring/screening must, in all cases, be necessary, appropriate, relevant, and proportionate with regard to the aims that it is pursuing.

The employer's monitoring policy should be tailored to the type and degree of risk the employer faces and the level of tolerated privacy intrusion depends on the nature of the employment as well as on the specific circumstances surrounding and interacting with the employment relationship [48]. To further elaborate on this issue, we propose that the method is applied for security officers and for personnel involved in the decision making process within security-critical information systems and critical infrastructures.

For future work, we plan to focus on locating real life groups inside Twitter and study a number of parameters regarding their behavior, together with each group's dynamics. Furthermore, it is claimed that narcissism is a characteristic that both extravert and introvert individuals share. In this work we located only the extravert ones. Our future plans include the development of methods capable of detecting introvert individuals with minor social media usage who manifest this personality trait.

Acknowledgements. This work has been performed in the framework of the S-Port Project (09SYN-72-650), which is partly funded by the Greek General Secretariat for Research & Technology, under the SYNERGASIA Programme.

References

1. CSO magazine in cooperation with the U.S. Secret Services, Software Engineering Institute CERT Program at Carnegie Mellon University and Deloitte: Cybersecurity watch survey: Cybercrime increasing faster than computes and defenses (2010), http://www.cert.org/blogs/insider_threat/2010/10/interesting_insider_threat_statistics.html
2. Theoharidou, M., Kokolakis, S., Karyda, M., Kiountouzis, E.: The insider threat to information systems and the effectiveness of ISO17799. Computers & Security 24(6), 472–484 (2005)
3. Theoharidou, M., Gritzalis, D.: A Common Body of Knowledge for Information Security. IEEE Security & Privacy 4(2), 64–67 (2007)
4. Liu, A., Martin, C., Hetherington, T., Matzner, S.: A comparison of system call feature representations for insider threat detection. In: Proceedings from the 6th Annual IEEE SMC Information Assurance Workshop, IAW 2005, pp. 340–347. IEEE (June 2005)
5. Kalutarage, H., Shaikh, S., Qin Zhou, A., James, A.: Sensing for suspicion at scale: A Bayesian approach for cyber conflict attribution and reasoning. In: 4th International Conference on Cyber Conflict (CYCON), pp. 1–19. IEEE (June 2012)
6. Magklaras, G., Furnell, S., Papadaki, M.: LUARM: An audit engine for insider misuse detection. International Journal of Digital Crime and Forensics (IJDCF) 3(3), 37–49 (2011)
7. Spitzner, L.: Honeypots: Catching the insider threat. In: Proceedings of 19th Annual Computer Security Applications Conference, pp. 170–179. IEEE (December 2003)
8. Bowen, B.M., Ben Salem, M., Hershkop, S., Keromytis, A., Stolfo, S.J.: Designing host and network sensors to mitigate the insider threat. IEEE Security & Privacy 7(6), 22–29 (2009)
9. Magklaras, G.B., Furnell, S.M.: Insider threat prediction tool: Evaluating the probability of IT misuse. Computers & Security 21(1), 62–73 (2001)
10. Magklaras, G., Furnell, S., Brooke, P.: Towards an insider threat prediction specification language. Information Management & Computer Security 14(4), 361–381 (2006)
11. Yaseen, Q., Panda, B.: Knowledge acquisition and insider threat prediction in relational database systems. In: International Conference on Computational Science and Engineering (CSE), pp. 450–455. IEEE (August 2009)
12. Kandias, M., Mylonas, A., Virvilis, N., Theoharidou, M., Gritzalis, D.: An insider threat prediction model. In: Katsikas, S., Lopez, J., Soriano, M. (eds.) TrustBus 2010. LNCS, vol. 6264, pp. 26–37. Springer, Heidelberg (2010)
13. Greitzer, F., Kangas, L., Noonan, C., Dalton, A., Hohimer, R.: Identifying At-Risk Employees: Modeling Psychosocial Precursors of Potential Insider Threats. In: 45th Hawaii International Conference on System Science (HICSS), pp. 2392–2401. IEEE (January 2012)
14. Brdiczka, O., Liu, J., Price, B., Shen, J., Patil, A., Chow, R., Ducheneaut, N.: Proactive Insider Threat Detection through Graph Learning and Psychological Context. In: IEEE Symposium on Security and Privacy Workshops (SPW), pp. 142–149. IEEE (May 2012)
15. Chen, Y., Nyemba, S., Zhang, W., Malin, B.: Leveraging social networks to detect anomalous insider actions in collaborative environments. In: IEEE International Conference on Intelligence and Security Informatics (ISI), pp. 119–124. IEEE (July 2011)
16. Skues, J., Williams, B., Wise, L.: The effects of personality traits, self-esteem, loneliness, and narcissism on Facebook use among university students. Computers in Human Behavior (2012)

17. Buffardi, L., Campbell, W.: Narcissism and social networking web sites. Personality and Social Psychology Bulletin 34(10), 1303–1314 (2008)
18. Mehdizadeh, S.: Self-presentation 2.0: Narcissism and self-esteem on Facebook. In: Cyberpsychology Behavior Society Network, pp. 357–364 (2010)
19. Butts, J., Mills, R., Peterson, G.: A multidiscipline approach to mitigating the insider threat. In: International Conference on Information Warfare and Security, ICIW (March 2006)
20. Shaw, E., Ruby, K., Post, J.: The insider threat to information systems: The psychology of the dangerous insider. Security Awareness Bulletin 2(98), 1–10 (1998)
21. U.S. Department of Justice, Federal Bureau of Investigation: The insider threat, an introduction to detecting and deterring insider spy (2012), http://www.fbi.gov/about-us/investigate/counterintelligence/the-insider-threat
22. Mislove, A., Marcon, M., Gummadi, K.P., Druschel, P., Bhattacharjee, B.: Measurement and analysis of online social networks. In: Proceedings of the 7th ACM SIGCOMM Conference on Internet Measurement, pp. 29–42. ACM (October 2007)
23. Travers, J., Milgram, S.: An experimental study of the small world problem. In: Sociometry, pp. 425–443 (1969)
24. Cha, M., Haddadi, H., Benevenuto, F., Gummadi, K.: Measuring user influence in Twitter: The million follower fallacy. In: 4th International AAAI Conference on Weblogs and Social Media (ICWSM), vol. 14(1), p. 8 (May 2010)
25. Quercia, D., Ellis, J., Capra, L., Crowcroft, J.: In the mood for being influential on twitter. In: Privacy, Security, Risk and Trust, IEEE 3rd International Conference on Social Computing (SOCIALCOM), pp. 307–314. IEEE (October 2011)
26. Watts, D., Strogatz, S.: The small world problem. In: Collective Dynamics of Small-World Networks, pp. 440–442 (1998)
27. Costa, L., Rodrigues, F., Travieso, G., Boas, P.: Characterization of complex networks: A survey of measurements. Advances in Physics 56(1), 167–242 (2007)
28. Barabasi, A.: The origin of bursts and heavy tails in human dynamics. Nature 435(7039), 207–211 (2005)
29. Ross, C., Orr, E., Sisic, M., Arseneault, J., Simmering, M., Orr, R.: Personality and motivations associated with Facebook use. Computers in Human Behavior 25, 578–586 (2009)
30. Amichai-Hamburger, Y., Vinitzky, G.: Social network use and personality. Computers in Human Behavior 26, 1289–1295 (2010)
31. Shaw, E., Fischer, L.: Ten tales of betrayal: The threat to corporate infrastructure by information technology insiders analysis and observations. Defense Personnel Security Research Center, USA (2005)
32. Shaw, E.: The role of behavioral research and profiling in malicious cyber insider investigations. Digital Investigation 3(1), 20–31 (2006)
33. Frank, L., Hohimer, R.: Modeling human behavior to anticipate insider attacks. Journal of Strategic Security 4(2), 3 (2011)
34. International Working Group on Data Protection in Telecoms: Report and guidance on privacy in social network services. Rome Memorandum. 43rd Meeting, Rome, Italy (March 2008)
35. Mitrou, L., Karyda, M.: Employees' privacy vs. employers' security: Can they be balanced? Telematics and Informatics 23(3), 164–178 (2006)
36. Fazekas, C.: 1984 is Still Fiction: Electronic Monitoring in the Workplace and US Privacy Law. Duke Law & Technology Review, 15 (2004)

37. Broughton, A., Higgins, T., Hicks, B., Cox, A.: Workplaces and Social Networking - The Implications for Employment Relations. Institute for Employment Studies, Brighton (2009)
38. Abril-Sánchez, P., Levin, A., Del Riego, A.: Blurred Boundaries: Social Media Privacy and the 21st Century Employee. American Business Law Journal 49(1), 63–124 (2012)
39. Castells, M.: Communication Power. Oxford University Press (2009)
40. Dumortier, F.: Facebook and Risks of "De-contextualization" of Information. In: Gutwirth, S., et al. (eds.) Data Protection in a Profiled World, pp. 119–137 (2010)
41. Nissenbaum, H.: Privacy as Contextual Integrity. Washington Law Review 79, 119–157 (2004)
42. Davison, K., Maraist, C., Hamilton, R., Bing, M.: To Screen or Not to Screen? Using the Internet for Selection Decisions. Employ Response Rights 24, 1–21 (2012)
43. Smith, W., Kidder, D.: You've been tagged (Then again, maybe not): Employers and Facebook. Business Horizons 53, 491–499 (2010)
44. Slovensky, R., Ross, W.: Should human resource managers use social media to screen job applicants? Managerial and Legal Issues in the USA 14(1), 55–69 (2012)
45. Simitis, S.: Reconsidering the premises of labour law: Prolegomena to an EU regulation on the protection of employees' personal data. European Law Journal 5, 45–62 (1999)
46. Lasprogata, G., King, N., Pillay, S.: Regulation of electronic employee monitoring: Identifying fundamental principles of employee privacy through a comparative study of data privacy legislation in the European Union, US and Canada. Stanford Technology Law Review 4 (2004), http://stlr.stanford.edu/STLR/Article?04_STLR_4
47. UK Information Commissioner: The Employment Practices Data Protection Code (2003)
48. Data Protection Working Party. Opinion 8/2001 on the processing of personal data in the employment context (5062/01/Final) (2001)
49. Gritzalis, D.: A digital seal solution for deploying trust on commercial transactions. Information Management & Computer Security Journal 9(2), 71–79 (2001)
50. Lambrinoudakis, C., Gritzalis, D., Tsoumas, V., Karyda, M., Ikonomopoulos, S.: Secure Electronic Voting: The current landscape. In: Gritzalis, D. (ed.) Secure Electronic Voting, pp. 101–122. Springer (2003)
51. Marias, J., Dritsas, S., Theoharidou, M., Mallios, J., Gritzalis, D.: SIP vulnerabilities and antispit mechanisms assessment. In: Proc. of the 16th IEEE International Conference on Computer Communications and Networks, pp. 597–604. IEEE Press (2007)
52. Mitrou, L., Gritzalis, D., Katsikas, S., Quirchmayr, G.: Electronic voting: Constitutional and legal requirements, and their technical implications. In: Gritzalis, D. (ed.) Secure Electronic Voting, pp. 43–60. Springer (2003)
53. Spinellis, D., Gritzalis, S., Iliadis, J., Gritzalis, D., Katsikas, S.: Trusted Third Party services for deploying secure telemedical applications over the web. Computers & Security 18(7), 627–639 (1999)
54. Mitrou, L., Karyda, M.: Bridging the gap between employee's surveillance and privacy protection. In: Social and Human Elements of Information Security: Emerging Trends and Countermeasures, pp. 283–300. IGI Global, New York (2009)
55. Mitrou, L.: The Commodification of the Individual in the Internet Era: Informational Self-determination or "Self-alienation"? In: Proceedings of 8th International Conference on Computer Ethics Philosophical Enquiry, pp. 466–485. INSEIT, Athens (2009)

On Business Logic Vulnerabilities Hunting: The APP_LogGIC Framework

George Stergiopoulos, Bill Tsoumas, and Dimitris Gritzalis

Information Security and Critical Infrastructure Protection Research Laboratory
Dept. of Informatics, Athens University of Economics and Business (AUEB)
76 Patission Ave., Athens GR-10434, Greece
{geostergiop,bts,dgrit}@aueb.gr

Abstract. While considerable research effort has been put in the identification of technical vulnerabilities, such as buffer overflows or SQL injections, business logic vulnerabilities have drawn limited attention. Logic vulnerabilities are an important class of defects that are the result of faulty application logic. Business logic refers to requirements implemented in algorithms that reflect the intended functionality of an application, e.g. in an online shop application, a logic rule could be that each cart must register only one discount coupon per product. In our paper, we extend a novel heuristic and automated method for the detection of logic vulnerabilitieswhich we presented in a previous publication. This method detects logic vulnerabilities and asserts their criticality in Java GUI applications using dynamic analysis and static together with a fuzzy logic system in order to compare and rank its findings, in an effort to minimize false positives and negatives. An extensive analysis of the code ranking system is given along with empirical results in order to demonstrate its potential.

Keywords: Bug Detection, Vulnerability, Business Logic, Propositional Logic.

1 Introduction

A *software error or fault* is the difference between a computed, observed, or measured value and the true, specified, or theoretically correct value or condition inside the software code [1].A *software vulnerability* is the characteristics and degree of the fatal software-failure occurrence caused by a software fault [2]. An "Application Business Logic Vulnerability" (BLV) is *the flaw present in the faulty implementation of business logic rules within the application code* [3].

In this paper we extend the method presented in [3], formally define its BLV ranking system, and demonstrate empirical results. To do that, we inject logic BLVs in commercial and test bed applications developed in our research lab. In Section 2 we briefly review previous work. In Section 3 we analyze how our framework evaluates potential BLV and ranks them according to a fuzzy analysis process. In Section 4 we formally define the ranking method's rules. Section 5 details our experiments on real-world and lab *Application Under Test* (AUT). Finally, in Section 6 we conclude and describe our plans for future research.

J. Lopez, X. Huang, and R. Sandhu (Eds.): NSS 2013, LNCS 7873, pp. 236–249, 2013.

The task of detecting logic vulnerabilities is inherently difficult, since logic vulnerabilities differ according to the intended functionality of an application. Therefore, it is hard to define a general specification that allows for the discovery of logic vulnerabilities in different applications [5]. Our method to discover BLV extends our previous work [3] and is divided in four steps:

1) Our APP_LogGIC framework uses an Abstract Syntax Tree (AST) from Java compiler to detect points inside the source code that are considered "dangerous" for BLV. According to [5,17], we consider these points to be *input vectors* where data is inserted by the user and *Conditional execution Branches* (CB), i.e. IF-statements, that control the execution flow of an AUT, since these sets of source code points reflect the intent of theprogrammer. According to their position, we rank these points using a "*Severity*" Likert scale in order to rank the risk of having a BLV in each code point of interest.We name this step (1) procedure, "*Information Extraction Method*" (IEM).
2) We use dynamic analysis with the Daikon tool from MIT [14], so as to extract variable rules called *invariants* that describe the intended use of the AUT in source code level. Afterwards, we use scripted execution with static analysis using the JPF tool from NASA [7] to gather all possible execution paths and variable states of an AUT. We combine the results from dynamic analysis and static analysis using a method to find *violations* between the intended use of the AUT and execution states we gathered from static analysis. By *violations*, we mean situations where an invariant rule extracted from dynamic analysis is simultaneously found both TRUE and FALSE in different versions of the same execution path [5] (i.e. static analysis produces variants of the same execution path from different executions. Invariant violations are identified when one version of an execution path violates an invariant AND another version verifies it). These invariant violations are ranked using a "*Vulnerability*" Likert scale that reflects how certain we are that a BLV does exist in this violation of an invariant rule. Step (2) procedure is called "*Invariant-Based Method*" (IBM).
3) APP_LogGIC executes a source code analyzer inside APP_LogGIC called "*Input Vector Analysis Method*" (IVAM), which uses the above mentioned AST tree from (1) to analyze the sanitization checks enforced upon input data held in source code variables. By *sanitization checks* we mean source code control points that check data context in variables (OWASP [17]) states that all input data should be sanitized before use, regardless of the situation. The verification of personal information before providing services and the privacy of such information is of growing concern [4], information usually implemented as input data. IEM ranks AUT's input vectors on the Vulnerability scale according to the type of sanitization used (if any) on variables holding input data; e.g., if a variable that holds input data is never used in a check (say, an IF-statement), this point inside the code is ranked as high as possible in the Vulnerability scale, indicating that a BLV exists on that point.
4) APP_LogGIC implements a Fuzzy Logic system [18] to compute the *Criticality* of variables by using *linguistic rules* of type "If Severity is High and Vulnerability is High then Criticality is High" in order to congregate Severity and Vulnerability values given for each source code point of interest separately. It provides a clear, numerical and graphical measurement on how "certain" APP_LogGIC is that a BLV. The Criticality of a source code variable might be different (e.g. "High" and

"Medium"), according to its point inside the source code in conjunction with the certainty that the variable indeed contains a BLV.

The paper extends previous work by contributing the following:

(a) *A formal presentation of an extendedBLV ranking method presented in* [3], capable of detecting BLV in GUI applications with almost zero false positives on all tests ran, close to how a security analyst would detect potentially dangerous code.

(b) *We limit the Trusted Computing Base (TCB)* needed for our method by proving that all ranking method's rules can be derived by only three axiomatic rules; thus, APP_LogGIC's implementation is small and can be easily proven sound.

(c) *Extensions of APP_LogGIC* to support analysis for nested IFs and complex structures in Java.

(d) *Testing results on real-world Java applications and test beds alike.*We use injection for our proof-of-concept tests, since there is no official application intended as a BLV test bed. We demonstrate APP_LogGIC's capability in detecting all BLV injections on real-world software and lab test beds.We provide descriptions of the BLV injected. We classify these BLV using known vulnerability classification taxonomies [17].

2 Related Work

In *Waler* [5], authors use MIT's Daikon tool to infer a set of behavioral specifications that describe web applications and filter learned specifications. Then, they check whether results from Daikon are enforced or violated by using NASA's Java Pathfinder (JPF) tool [7] for model checking over symbolic input. They identify program paths that, under specific conditions, may indicate the presence of a certain type of web application logic flaws.

A variation of the method is used in APP_LogGIC's step (2), Invariant-Based Method as mentioned earlier. This approach targets only single-execution web applets and does not provide a solution for false negatives/positives. Also, it does not scale well with larger applications.

In [21], a study of logic flaws in web applications is presented, called Execution After Redirect, with a focus on web applets and a specific type of vulnerability, manifesting only in web applications. In [22], authors combine analysis techniques to identify multi-module vulnerabilities in web applications but do not focus on BLV, per se, rather in web application workflow attacks in PHP with state variables and programs that do not contain object-oriented code.

In [3], we presented APP_LogGIC, a tool for detecting and ranking possible BLV close to how a security code advisor would do. The method focuses on GUI applications and heuristically detects BLV in applications using methods from [5] but focuses on GUI applications and also, presents a preliminary deployment of a novel fuzzy ranking method of the source code to detect BLV. Herein we formally define an extended fuzzy ranking system and provide various testing results with it.

3 How APP_LogGIC Works

We provide a brief presentation of each APP_LogGIC method and then give a formal definition of the fuzzy evaluation ranking system. Our framework analyzes GUI applications code with infinite combinations of execution paths (contrary to e.g. Java servlets [5,23]) and identifies variables in source code points that may contain a BLV.

3.1 Invariant-Based Method (IBM)

Dynamic Analysis

IBM monitors the execution of the AUT with input data. By using the Daikon tool [14] we extract a set of traces representing expected application behavior based on the intended use of an AUT, named *invariants* (i.e., logic rules that hold true during execution states intended by the programmer and describe the relationships and restrictions enforced on the application variables). These invariants hold throughout the execution of the method they refer to.

```
---LoginFrame.initComponents():::EXIT
identity == "-1"
```

Fig. 1. Invariant produced by Daikon Dynamic Analysis

In Fig. 1, the line initComponents():::EXIT shows that the invariant <identity> must be equal to “-1”, holding as a rule whenever the LoginFrame.initComponents() method finishes execution. APP_LogGIC builds on [5], by focusing on the invariants for the “IF” branches checks lying inside the AUT code; IBM categorizes the produced invariants by their restriction in branch decisions [3].

Static Analysis

Each application function is a sum of sequential instruction executions (*execution path*). This step uses scripted GUI program executions, so as to produce the execution paths that are necessary to cover the AUT’s functionality [3].

```
VARIABLE: user -> "admin"
        LoginFrame.java:122             : if (user.equals("") && pass.equals(""))
        LoginFrame.java:125             : if (identity.equals("-1")) {
VARIABLE: identity -> "1"
        LoginFrame.java:125             : if (identity.equals("-1")) {
        LoginFrame.java:132             : System.out.println("Login");
VARIABLE: out -> gov.nasa.jpf.ConsoleOutputStream@e5
```

Fig. 2. Execution Path with variable states and variable parsing steps

APP_LogGIC detects points in static analysis execution paths, where a variable described in an invariant rule is used. Then, it records paths that enforce or violate the invariant produced by dynamic analysis. If it finds a path, then checks the rest of the execution paths produced, in search of an alternate version of the same path that violates the same rule, e.g.; back to the Identity invariant case (Fig. 1), the current execution path violates the rule identity == “-1”, as the path finishes with Identity having the value “1”. If another version of the same execution path exists (which finishes with a “-1” state), then the Identity might be a BLV.

3.2 Information Extraction Method (IEM)

The IEM extracts AUT information from a Java C compiler AST, including data entry points (input vectors) so as to refine variables related to possibleBLV. IEM provides structural info about the AUT. The code is represented as a tree, with variables or values as leaves and instructions as nodes [3]. Analysis is fed to IBM and Input Vector Analysis for enhancing the filtering of the invariant rules and JPF execution paths. This way, we only keep invariant rules and execution paths we are interested in, thus lowering APP_LogGIC memory consumption for medium sized AUTs.

3.3 Input Vector Analysis Method

The Input Vector Analysis component monitors the checks enforced on source code variables that hold data from input vectors. It performs structural (REGEX) checks and analyzes: a) the *tainted* variable (i.e. the variable that contains dangerous data) that holds the initial value passed from a vector; b) the structure of the data inside a tainted variable (but not their actual content); and c) occasions where user input is never checked or sanitized in any way [3].

3.4 Fuzzy Logic Ranking System

We use a scalable Fuzzy Logic system [18] to rank possible BLV according to their vulnerability and position in code. A critical point in the source code is *conditional branching*, which has a decision-making ability in its conditional control transfer [5,8] since control flow restrictions and application business logic rules manifest as branch restrictions. All variables *may* be linked with a BLV at the CBs, which are inherently bound to a binary Boolean decision (all branches result to a true/false decision on whether to execute or not).

We define three evaluation scales to classify BLV in source code variables: a) *Severity* (the risk level according to variable position), b) *Vulnerability* (the level of certainty that a vulnerability manifests on the specific variable), and c) *Criticality* (the final result calculated from previous two scales inside the fuzzy logic mechanism). APP_LogGIC uses 1-to-5 Likert scales so as to provide a quantitative way of measuring BLV. A Likert scale captures the intensity of beliefs for a given item by assigning a value from 1-5 and provide a quantitative way of measuring the risk of a specific point in the source code [9]. Each scale maps into 3 groups (Low, Medium, High), with an approximate width of each group of (5/3) = 1,66~1,5 (final ranges: Low in [0…2], Medium in (2…3,5] and High in (3,5…5]).

Severity

Severity aims to assess the importance of source code variables. Each variable is assigned a severity value by taking into account two facts, i.e., the involvement in a CB restriction and the storage of data dependent on the user input. A check on a variable is a control flow operation that constrains this variable on a path; e.g., the IF-statement *if (isAdmin == true) {...}* represents a CB check on "isAdmin" [5]. Source code CBs (and all decision statements) are key points where unintended control-flow deviations occur [5,8]. Thus, the involved variables are classified as important.

By *important variable data* we mean user input data or any data constructed from user input, since improperly validated user input is the underlying root cause for a wide variety of attacks [10]. Table 1 depicts all Likert ranks for the Severity.

Table 1. App_LogGIC's Severity ranks in the Likert scale

Linguistic Value	Condition	Severity Level
Low	Random variable Severity	1
Low	Random variable Severity	2
Medium	Severity for variables used as data sinks (i.e. dataoriginated from user input)	3
Medium	Severity for variables used in a CB **ONCE** on an "IF" branchand/-or a'SWITCH' branch	3
High	Severity for variables used in a CB **TWICE OR MORE** on an "IF" branchand/or a "SWITCH" branch	4
High	Severity for variables used as a data sink **AND** in a CB on an "IF" branchand/or a "SWITCH" branch	5

Random Variable is any variable that is neither used in a CB, nor as a user input data container and gets a value in [1,2], depending on the frequency used inside the source code. The **TWICE OR MORE** condition targets variables used two or more times inside the source code. Intuitively, we consider that variables used in two different CBs have the same risk as those used in, say, ten CBs, since the risk of a CB variable affecting execution paths in two different points is already high enough.

Vulnerability

NIST SP 800-30 defines vulnerability as "*a flaw or weakness in system security procedures, design, implementation, or internal controls that could be exercised acid/violation of the system's security policy*" [11]. APP_LogGIC detects such flaws by assigning a 5-grade Vulnerability level to each variable of interest, i.e. a quantitative confidence level that a BLV exists (Table 2).

Table 2. APP_LogGIC Vulnerability levels in the Likert scale

Linguistic value	Condition	Vulnerability level
Low	No invariant incoherencies or improper check of variables.	0
Medium	Multiple propagation of variable dependent in input data with general checks.	2
Medium	Sound checks in variable but multiple propagation to method variables with relatively improper checks (**Input Vector Method**)	3
High	No check or improper checks in variables depended on input data for branch conditions	4
High	Invariant enforcement AND invariant violation in alternate versions of same execution path (**Invariant-Based Method**)	5

Criticality

Criticality is the final, calculated risk value assigned for each variable, by combining the relevant Severity and Vulnerability ranks. Our tool produces a set of graphs where the combined risk factor of possible BLV is drawn (e.g. Figure 5). It is calculated using Fuzzy Set Theory, using Fuzzy Logic's linguistic variables and IF-THEN rules (Figure 3). For clarity, all scales (Severity, Vulnerability and Criticality) share the same linguistic variables "Low", "Medium" and "High". Criticality is based on Vulnerability and Severity since source code variables might have different values at the same time, according to the Severity and Vulnerability ranks.

IF Severity IS low AND Vulnerability IS low THEN Criticality IS low

Fig. 3. Example of a Fuzzy Logic rule

The Criticality for each variable is calculated separately, as the conjunction between Severity and Vulnerability with one numerical and one fuzzy result:

$$Criticality(x) \quad = Severity(x) \cap Vulnerability(x)$$

This result is calculated by using defuzzification and the Center of Gravity technique. *Defuzzification* is the process of producing a quantifiable result in fuzzy logic, given fuzzy sets (i.e. Severity and Vulnerability values) and corresponding membership degrees (i.e. the involvedness of each fuzzy set presented in Likert values). APP_LogGIC computes a discrete value as output using the *Center of Gravity* technique, across-section calculation of geometrical shapes created by Severity and Vulnerability values. All source code variables of interest are checked separately. Figure 4 shows the way that Fuzzy Logic is used in APP_LogGIC.

First, the results of the Severity and Vulnerability values (1) and (2) calculated using *Table 1* rules, are added together using a fuzzy set membership function (in our case, a conjunction between the sets) (3). Then, defuzzification calculates final values based on percentage (4). These shapes corresponding to Severity and Criticality values are then cut in a straight horizontal line between the top and the bottom, and the top portion is removed. These trapezoids are then superimposed one upon another, forming a single geometric shape. Lastly, the centroid of this shape, called the fuzzy centroid, is calculated. The *x* coordinate of the centroid is the *defuzzified value* [12], which gives a precise measurement of the Criticality in any particular point of interest inside the source code.

2 APP_LogGIC'SFUZZY Ranking Basis

APP_LogGIC calculates *Criticality* as the fuzzy intersection or conjunction (AND) of two fuzzy sets, *Severity* and *Vulnerability*, which are specified by a binary mapping T that aggregates two membership functions as follows: A∩B(x) = T(μA(x), μB(x)), e.g., the binary operator T represents the conjunction of $\mu_A(x)\ and\ \mu_B(x)$ [14]. Next, we define the axiomatic rules used in our method, using premises shown in Table 3 below. The first step is to define the premises needed to express these rules.

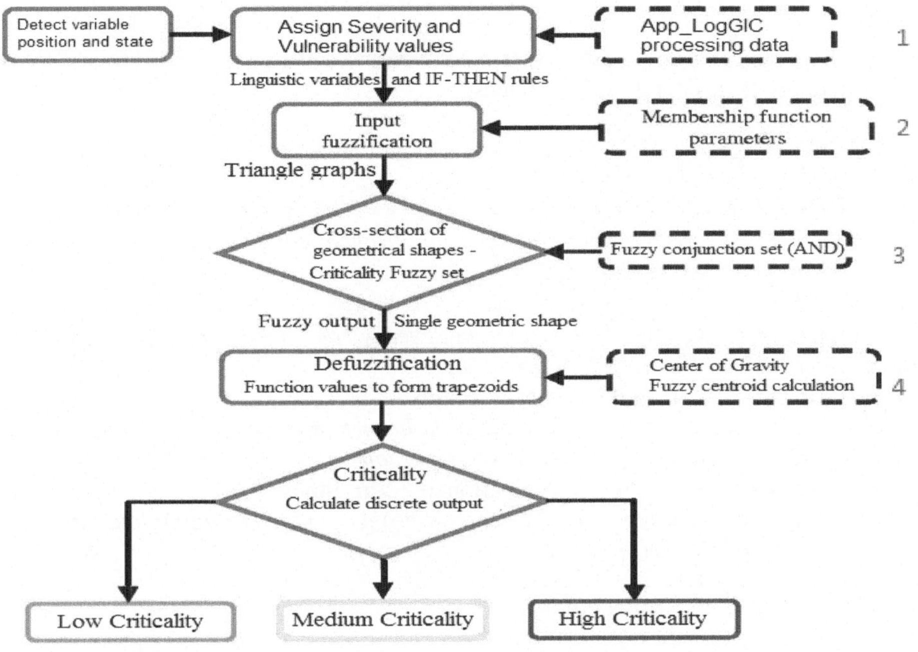

Fig. 4. App_LogGIC's fuzzy computation diagram

Table 3. Mathematical Logic premises used in formal ranking rules

Severity premises		
S_{low}: Severity is "low"	S_{med}: Severity is "medium"	S_{hi}: Severity is "high"
Vulnerability premises		
V_{low}: Vulnerability is "low"	V_{med}: Vulnerability is "medium"	V_{hi}: Vulnerability is "high"

Variable premises	
var_Input: Variable contains input data for potential BLV	violation_inv: Variable violates an implemented invariant
var_Branch: Variable is used in a decision branch (once)	violation_noChecks: Variable has no context or structural checks
var_MultiBranch: Variable is used in different branches >1 times	pass2sink: Variable is being passed along to sinks

Rules for Ranking Severity

Severity ranking takes two aspects into consideration: (1) if a variable exists in a branch statement (control flow check) and (2) if a variable contains input data. Since "High Severity" implies that all characteristics of a set are TRUE, we conclude that a

Medium Severity point (i.e., an element without all set characteristics) cannot be ranked 5/5. Logically, there is a mutual exclusion between the three linguistic variables (Low, Medium, High) in all ranking scales.

Four formal Severity rules expressed in formal mathematical Logic [6] define the base for ranking Severity in variables:

SR1. (**LOCON-1, LOCON-2**) Slow ↔ ¬Var_Input ^ ¬var_Branch

Iff a logical error variable is used neither on a branch, nor on an input data variable, then the Severity of that error is Low.

SR2. Smed ↔ ¬Slow ^ ¬Shi

Iff a logical error variable has a Medium Severity rank, then it can have neither a Low Severity rank, nor a High Severity rank.

SR3. (**LOCON-5**) Var_MultiBranch ↔ Shigh

Iff a variable is used in two or more different branch statements in the source code, then this variable is ranked high on the Severity scale.

SR4. (**LOCON-6**) Shi ↔ var_Branch ^ Var_Input

Iff a logical error variable is used both on a branch and as an input data variable, then the Severity of that error is High.

Rules for Calculating Vulnerability

These four formal Vulnerability rules (VRx) define the base for ranking Vulnerability in source code variables:

VR1. Vlow ↔ ¬violation_inv ^ ¬Violation_noChecks

Iff a branch or input data variable is neither holding any invariant vulnerability flags, nor does it lack sanitization checks, then the Vulnerability level is Low.

VR2. Vmed ↔ ¬Vlow ^ ¬Vhi

Iff a focus variable has a Medium Vulnerability rank, then it can have neither a Low Vulnerability rank, nor a High Vulnerability rank.

VR3. Vhi ↔ violation_inv v (Violation_noChecks)

Iff a focus variable holds any invariant vulnerability rank higher than "0" OR if it is lacking sanitization checks, then the Vulnerability level of that variable is High.

VR4. ¬Vlow ↔ ¬Violation_noChecks ^ pass2sink

Iff a focus variable has robust sanitization checks AND that variable's content is spread to numerous other variables inside the source code, then that variable's Vulnerability level cannot be low.

Calculating Criticality

Table 3 shows all possible results from the IF-THEN linguistic Fuzzy Logic conjunction rule for calculating Criticality. Severity set plays a more important role than the Vulnerability set because we can calculate a variable's Severity value with high precision (points inside the source code of an application are discrete), unlike assigning Vulnerability values, a procedure prone to false positives/negative due to the nature of logical errors themselves; BLV are based on the programmer's coding logic, something relatively difficult to identify patterns, while the source code locations where a variable is used, are discrete. Criticality is a combination (aggregation) of Severity and Vulnerability (**C=SxV**).

Table 4. C = SxV

Vulnerability \ Severity	Low	Medium	High
Low	Low	Low	Medium
Medium	Low	Medium	High
High	Medium	High	High

5 Real-World Application Testing

A comparison between APP_LogGIC and existing tools does not exist at the moment, as there are currently no tools nor frameworks that are able to detect code BLVs or injections for logic vulnerabilities. To demonstrate our approach, we evaluated the effectiveness of APP_LogGIC in detecting BLV on three injected applications, i.e., one real-world application (*CleenSheets*) and two research lab test beds called *LogicBombs* in which we injected BLV. Lab test beds were written as part of this project. All AUTs were coded in Java. Injected BLV used during our experiments were built to match specific categories in a BLV taxonomy developed by *Common Weakness Enumeration*, CWE-840 [17]. APP_LogGIC generates reports for each potential BLV found that contains the variable involved, the method, Class and line number where it manifests.

CleanSheets AUT

Our first test used a real-world application "CleanSheets" [16], an extensible Java GUI spreadsheet. CleanSheets was injected with three (3) types of input vector BLV. The types of BLV injected are common mistakes found at several applications [15], specifically, OWASP has a separate chapter [17] dedicated to this type of vulnerabilities. This AUT uses Java's getText() method to fetch user input data into source code variables. According to APP_LogGIC's ranking system, injections fall into the *Medium* Severity category from Table 1 and *High* Vulnerability category from Table 2 inside the Fuzzy ranking system:

Severity scale

Medium	Severity for variables used as data sinks (i.e. dataoriginated from user input)	**3**

Vulnerability scale

High	No check or improper checks in variables depended on input data for branch conditions	**4**

1) For our first injection, we removed all content-type (sanitization) checks imposed on variables holding input data from the source code (i.e. checks that were imposing restrictions on the variable's data content, in the AUT's case, a series of IF-statements).APP_LogGIC correctly noticed the lack of proper sanitization checks on input data and ranked variables holding data from the "getText()" high (4) on the Vulnerability scale and medium (3) on the Severity scale, since data from variables did not affect a big portion of the total execution path (the possible

diversions were limited, only 1 IF-statement was found capable of diverting the control-flow based on input data from that variable and the execution path would soon return to the same flow no matter what).

2) We injected two more complex variations of an improper sanitization BLV. Specifically, we replaced sanitization statements with ones comparing initialization data to actual variable data, a common logical error since that kind of check proves that a variable has updated memory state compared to the initial, but does not impose any check on whether the updated data are harmful or not. Example:

```
String dataContainer = "";                    // variable initialization
dataContainer = input.getText();              // User input - update variable data
if ( !dataContainer.equals("")) {             // initialization check
```

Our method managed to correctly evaluate and detect the BLV. APP_LogGIC sample output results for one BLV report can be seen in Figure 5.

3) The third injection included keeping the initial sanitization checks. We injected a transfer of input data into other variables in different methods (viral tainting of input data [10]). APP_LogGIC correctly ranked the initial (pre-injection), safe sanitization checks with zero (0) rank on the Vulnerability scale and tracked other methods flow checks using the newly added support for nested-if statements. Due to current limitations concerning state explosion, APP_LogGIC can perform limited deep source code analysis on *taint propagation* (taint propagation is the method in which all input data are considered dangerous (tainted) and are followed inside the source code [10]). For this reason, it ranked this potential BLV with a two (2) rank on the Vulnerability scale, providing a degree of uncertainty.

APP_LogGIC detected javax.swing input fields in the AUT avoiding native method name collisions,detected all control flow checks implemented on input vector variables and ranked the sanitized, safe vectors with a zero vulnerability rank. Thus, APP_LogGIC had no false negative results in this AUT. The above mentioned BLV injected fall in the CWE-754 category, according to the taxonomy: "*The software does not check or improperly checks for unusual or exceptional conditions that are not expected to occur frequently during day to day operation of the softwar* " [17]. APP_LogGIC managed to detect all BLV injections in variables depended on input data. Intuitively, it properly ranked safe, sanitized variables with "Medium-to-High" Severity (as their risk factor due to positioning was High) but with Low (0) Vulnerability rank.

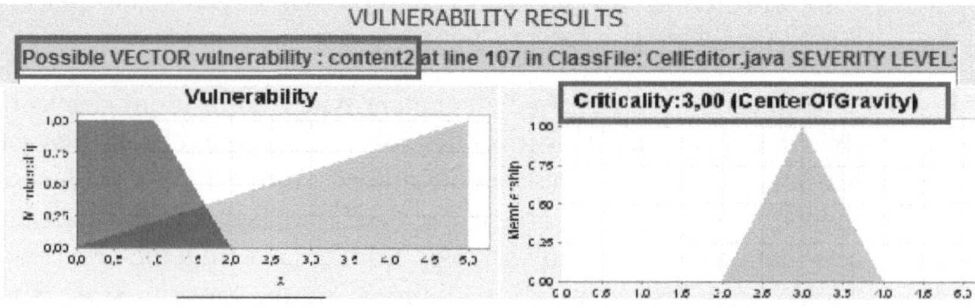

Fig. 5. APP_LogGIC Result graphs (Single BLV)

LogicBombs

We ran APP_LogGIC on two LogicBomb version applications written specifically for this project. *LogicBombs* is a set of functions deploying a sample authentication system that allows users to send and receive money using their own private accounts and supports a "Forgot your Password?" option. This option asks for a valid username and corresponding email and allegedly sends the password to the specific email address.

Our first injection in LogicBombs was to test the Invariant-Based Method (IBM) concerning possible invariant violations. This injection falls into the *Medium* Severity category from Table 1 as the invariant that raised the alert was about a variable used only once in a control-flow check (IF-statement), but ranked *High* on the Vulnerability scale from Table 2 due to a violation detected.

Three versions of the same execution path were found concerning the "*Forgot your Password?*" functionality. Two of them proved that invariant rule "identity", on exiting execution from method *initComponents(),* is *True* and is *enforced* on these two execution paths but one variation of that execution path was violating the invariant (memory state of the variable was *identity == "1"* on that execution path).

--LoginFrame.initComponents():::EXIT *identity == "-1"*

Severity scale

Medium	Severity for variables used in a CB **<u>ONCE</u>** on: o An "IF" branch o A'SWITCH' branch	3

Vulnerability scale

High	Invariant enforcement AND invariant violation in alternate versions of same execution path (**Invariant-Based Method**)	5

The aforementioned BLV injected fall in the CWE-288: *Authentication Bypass Using an Alternate Path or Channel* category, according to the taxonomy: "*A product requires authentication, but the product has an alternate path or channel that does not require authentication*" [17]. APP_LogGIC detected our injection by cross-checking alternate execution paths upon its dynamic analysis invariants and correctly ranked this BLV with "High" Criticality ("High" Vulnerability and "High" Severity).

Similarily, we injected LogicBombs with all BLVused in real-world AUT test CleanSheets in order to test the diversity of our first, preliminary results. Following CleanSheets, the results in LogicBombs were identical to CleanSheets. APP_LogGIC managed to provide the same results with zero false negatives in all injections.

APP_LogGIC framework ran on an Intel Core 2 Duo E6550 PC (2.33 GHz, 4GB RAM). Table 4 shows the execution times for the tools used (including the APP_Log GIC analysis). Dynamic Analysis includes the user time to manually execute the AUT.

Table 5. Execution Times

Type of execution	**Time** (sec) for CleanSheets	**Time** (sec) for LogicBombs
Dynamic Analysis	72.1	26.5
Static Analysis (JPF)	4.8	6.2
APP_LogGIC analysis	68.9	1.2

Limitations

The current version of the framework, though able to detect BLV in real-world and research lab applications, suffers by a number of limitations. The types of vulnerabilities found are limited to those in control flow restrictions found inside an execution path. Also, due to inherent incompatibilities in the Daikon tool, APP_LogGIC does not support analysis of loops ("While" and "For"). AUT dynamic execution must cover all possible paths for the BLV to be discovered.

JPF cannot analyze complex GUIs due to the lack of support from JPF, although progress is being made at the moment from NASA. The use of scripted configuration files limits the amount of execution paths generated and, concurrently, the amount of information for checking the validity of invariants. Moreover, APP_LogGIC support for switch-statement type CBs is lacking. Finally, our approach at the moment cannot detect BLV based on the application variables' context.

6 Conclusions and Further Research

We extended a method for detecting BLV in Java GUI applications using a novel fuzzy ranking system. We formally presented an axiomatic basis on how our fuzzy ranking system works.

In addition, we demonstrated test results that stem from real-world and test bed applications alike. APP_LogGIC managed to correctly analyze AUTs, found possible points that might hold BLV and correctly ranked them, whether these points had a BLV or not.

Ranking results and BLV injected are consistent with the reality of BLV: Real vulnerabilities got high grades in Criticality and well-coded points of interest got zero ranks. Results were classified using a known BLV taxonomy, thus defining a preliminary BLV subset that can be detected by APP_LogGIC.

We extended support for tree-like structure and packaged source code. We injected different types of BLV and demonstrated APP_LogGIC's analysis ability.

We plan to extend our work to "While" and "For" constructs and further define a formal, complete set of possible BLV that can be found with APP_LogGIC.

Also, we are in the process of making a thorough empirical analysis of APP_LogGIC's potential on numerous real-world AUTs and, to address what appears to be a hard part in BLV detection (i.e. the detection of BLV based on the data context), we plan to explore the use semantic constructs such as XBRL [19] or OWL [20] to describe business rules and feedthem to APP_LogGIC.

References

[1] Peng, W., Wallace, D.: Software Error Analysis, National Institute of Standards and Technology, NIST SP 500-209 (December 1993)

[2] Kimura, M.: Software vulnerability: Definition, modeling, and practical evaluation for e-mail transfer software. International Journal of Pressure Vessels and Piping (2006)

[3] Stergiopoulos, G., Tsoumas, B., Gritzalis, D.: Hunting application-level logical errors. In: Barthe, G., Livshits, B., Scandariato, R. (eds.) ESSoS 2012. LNCS, vol. 7159, pp. 135–142. Springer, Heidelberg (2012)

[4] Theoharidou, M., Gritzalis, D.: A Common Body of Knowledge for Information Security. IEEE Security & Privacy 5(2), 64–67 (2007)

[5] Felmetsger, V., Cavedon, L., Kruegel, C., Vigna, J.: Toward automated detection of logic vulnerabilities in web applications. In: Proc. of the 19th USENIX Symposium, USA (2010)

[6] Huth, M., Ryan, M.: Logic in Computer Science: Modeling and Reasoning about Systems. Cambridge University Press (2004)

[7] Mehlitz, P., et al.: Java PathFinder, Ames Research Center, NASA, USA

[8] Freiberger, P., Swaine, M.: Encyclopedia Britannica, Analytical Engine section

[9] Burns, A., Burns, R.: Basic Marketing Research, p. 245. Pearson Education

[10] Haldar, V., Chandra, D., Franz, M.: Dynamic Taint Propagation for Java. In: Proc. of the 21st Annual Computer Security Applications Conference, pp. 303–311 (2005)

[11] NIST SP 800-30, Risk Management Guide for Information Technology Systems

[12] Leekwijck, W., Kerre, E.: Defuzzification: Criteria and classification. Fuzzy Sets and Systems 108, 159–178 (1999)

[13] Foundations of Fuzzy Logic, Fuzzy Operators, Mathworks, `http://www.mathworks.com/help/toolbox/fuzzy/bp7816_-1.html`

[14] Ernst, M., Perkins, J., Guo, P., McCamant, S., Pacheco, C., Tschantz, M., Xiao, C.: The Daikon Invariant Detector User Manual. MIT, USA (2007)

[15] RTCA/DO-178B Software Considerations in Airborne Systems and Equipment Certification (December 1, 1992)

[16] Pehrson, E.: CleanSheets Office Suite (2009), `http://sourceforge.net/projects/csheets/`

[17] OWASP, Common Types of Software Vulnerabilities, `https://www.owasp.org/index.php/Category:Vulnerability`

[18] Cingolani, P.: Open Source Fuzzy Logic library and FCL language implementation, http://jfuzzylogic.sourceforge.net/html/index.html

[19] Fuger, S., et al.: ebXML Registry Information Model, ver. 3.0 (2005)

[20] OWL 2 Web Ontology Language Document Overview, W3C Recommendation (2009)

[21] Doupe, A., Boe, B., Vigna, G.: Fear the EAR: Discovering and Mitigating Execution After Redirect Vulnerabilities. In: Proc. of the 18th ACM Conference on Computer and Communications Security (2011)

[22] Balzarotti, D., Cova, M., Felmetsger, V., Vigna, G.: Multi-module vulnerability analysis of web-based applications. In: Proc. of the 14th ACM Conference on Computer and Communications Security (2007)

Using the Smart Card Web Server in Secure Branchless Banking

Sheila Cobourne, Keith Mayes, and Konstantinos Markantonakis

Smart Card Centre, Information Security Group (SCC-ISG),
Royal Holloway, University of London, Egham, Surrey, TW20 0EX
{Sheila.Cobourne.2008,Keith.Mayes,K.Markantonakis}@rhul.ac.uk

Abstract. In remote areas of developing countries, the mobile phone network may be the only connection with outside organizations such as banks. SMS messages are used in branchless banking schemes such as M-PESA in Kenya, but can be vulnerable to SMS spoofing exploits. This paper proposes a branchless banking system for withdrawal, deposit and transfer transactions, using an application on the phone's tamper-resistant Subscriber Identity Module (SIM) equipped with a Smart Card Web Server (SCWS) and public key cryptography capabilities.

Keywords: Smart Card Web Server, Branchless Banking, Security, Mobile Phone, PKI-SIM.

1 Introduction

In developing countries, banking via mobile phone is popular with low income people, especially where poor infrastructure makes access to conventional bank accounts difficult. SMS messaging is the most common method branchless banking systems use to carry out financial transactions: the most successful service to date is M-PESA, operated by Safaricom in Kenya [1]. This provides cash transactions and fund transfers using SMS messages and a network of authorized agents. However, there have been attacks on M-PESA, where spoofed SMS messages exploited a lack of authentication of bank-originating messages [9]. Also, the underlying GSM network architecture has well documented weaknesses e.g. [28]. An alternative, secure branchless banking scheme is therefore desirable.

One possibility would be to use phone-based online banking: typically the bank's online site is accessed via the phone browser, or a specialized mobile application. However, bank web servers are exposed to all standard online security threats [8], and Distributed Denial of Service attacks (DDoS) [22]. Customer credentials transmitted over the Internet can also be targeted. Additionally, highly sensitive (and valuable) information is stored on the phone, making phone operating systems an attractive target for malware designed to steal credentials [18]. The phone handset is therefore regarded as an untrusted platform.

A mobile phone's Subscriber Identity Module (SIM) could be used to store the banking application and credentials. The SIM is on the Universal Integrated

J. Lopez, X. Huang, and R. Sandhu (Eds.): NSS 2013, LNCS 7873, pp. 250–263, 2013.

Circuit Card (UICC) smart card in mobile phones, and is an application used to access the mobile network [25]. (In this paper, the term SIM will be used generically to represent the smart card used in phone handsets.) The SIM is a tamper-resistant environment, providing secure storage and processing of cryptographic keys. Modern SIMs can have advanced features such as the Smart Card Web Server (SCWS) [11] which introduces web server functionality to the SIM environment and provides a rich interface for the user. Advanced SIMs can also perform public-key processing (PKI-capable SIM), using standardized cryptographic algorithms for encryption/ digital signatures [19,23].

The proposal in this paper uses a PKI-capable SCWS/SIM in a branchless banking scheme, catering for both cash-based transactions and third party transfers using a network of authorized bank agents as intermediaries. The protocols presented here provide security without requiring the customer to obtain expensive equipment: all that is required is an existing phone handset (complete with a standard browser) which can have an advanced SIM installed. No specialized software needs to be installed onto the phone.

The paper is structured as follows: branchless banking security is presented in Section 2 and the security and usability of the SCWS is outlined in Section 3. The entities and assumptions needed for the proposed design are detailed in Section 4. Banking transaction protocols are then described in Section 5 (Withdrawals), Section 6 (Deposits) and Section 7 (Transfers). Section 8 analyzes the security of the proposal, and the paper concludes in Section 9.

2 Branchless Banking Security

Branchless banking services must provide all the security expected of a financial system, but they may have to operate in difficult environments where a number of additional challenges exist. For example, customers could be illiterate, unfamiliar with technology and unable to access conventional text-based user interfaces [26]. Additionally, a different concept of privacy to that found in the developed world means that security credentials will not necessarily be kept secret and equipment may be shared. There may be low levels of trust between participants [27], and mobile network connectivity may be unreliable.

Existing branchless banking schemes use combinations of SMS, Unstructured Supplementary Service Data (USSD) and Interactive Voice Response (IVR) mechanisms to communicate financial and authentication data between parties. For example, M-PESA (Kenya) [1], uses two-factor authentication (i.e. possession of a phone and knowledge of a PIN) with USSD and proprietary security via a SIM Toolkit (STK) application [25], with SMS messages for transaction data: customers are issued with a SIM containing the M-PESA application. Other branchless banking schemes include: EKO Bank (India) [29], ALW/ZMF (India) [12], FSB (not yet deployed) [30], M-ATM (SriLanka) [20], and mChek (India) [2]. Their authentication methods are shown in Table 1.

Security concerns about SMS-based banking schemes exist, however. Many use proprietary security mechanisms (security by obscurity), and there are well

Table 1. Customer Authentication Methods in Branchless Banking Schemes

Scheme	Authentication Mechanism
M-PESA	PIN sent via USSD with proprietary encryption
EKO	6-digit printed nonces combined with user's 4-digit PIN
ALW	Voice/Fingerprint Biometrics
FSB	Voice Biometrics plus scratch-card nonces
M-ATM	PIN/phone no. generate key for encrypted SMS, also SMS Nonces
mChek	6-digit PIN, IVR and SMS One Time Password (OTP)

documented security issues in GSM/3G mobile networks (e.g. [28]). The SMS service operates on a 'best effort' basis: messages can be delayed, dropped or arrive out of order, and they are not usually encrypted. Messages can be spoofed [3]: an attack on M-PESA involved spoofed bank-originating SMS messages (along with knowledge of a secret obtained by social engineering) and caused a security breach which defrauded an agent of 35,000 Kenyan Shillings [9].

Alternatively, a Wireless Application Protocol (WAP) browser on the phone could connect a customer to the bank's web server. Here, authentication credentials are sent over the Internet to the bank for checking; SMS OTP codes are sometimes used as an added security measure. However, transmitted customer credentials can be attacked: and the bank's web server is exposed to all standard Internet security threats, e.g. the Open Web Application Security Project (OWASP) Top Ten [8], or DDoS attacks [22]. Sensitive (i.e. high-value) information is stored on phone handsets, forming attractive targets for malware. Malware can intercept/ suppress SMS messages [13], point to phishing websites and specifically target banking applications, e.g. mobile Zeus trojan [17]. Infection can occur via MMS messages or Bluetooth connections e.g. Commwarrior [4]. The phone cannot be regarded as a trustworthy platform.

SIM-based applications, on the other hand, have many desirable security properties. Access to the SIM is tightly controlled, so it is difficult for malware on a phone to affect a SIM application. The SIM environment is tamper-resistant, which protects against physical attacks. If the SIM is able to perform public key cryptographic operations (PKI-capable) it can use standardized security algorithms [19,23], which is a useful security feature for branchless banking.

Branchless banking systems should meet the following security requirements:

Confidentiality: sensitive information should not be disclosed to unauthorized parties, during processing, in transit, or at rest: this applies to all messages sent to/from the bank, and all information stored on agent/ customer equipment.
Integrity: information must not be tampered with by unauthorized parties during processing, in transit or at rest, and a system must perform its tasks without unauthorized manipulation: this applies to all messages sent to/from the bank, and all information stored and processed on agents' and customers' equipment.
Authentication: all participants in a transaction must be authorized, and all transaction data must be genuine. So, a customer needs assurance that the agent is genuine and authorized to deposit their money in the correct account, an agent

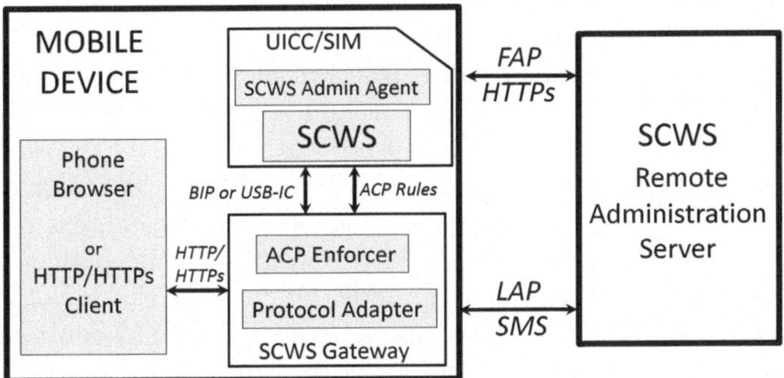

Fig. 1. Smart Card Web Server Architecture (adapted from [10])

must make sure that the individual withdrawing money from an account is not an impostor, and all bank-originating messages must be authenticated.
Availability: a service is not denied to authorized entities: for example, through network connectivity problems, loss of equipment such as phones, or distributed denial of service (DDoS) attacks.
Non-repudiation: none of the participants in a transaction (i.e. agent, customer or bank) can subsequently deny taking part in it.

The next section describes the SCWS environment and its maintenance procedures, which will be used later in a proposed branchless banking solution.

3 The Smart Card Webserver (SCWS)

The Smart Card Web Server (SCWS) is a HTTP 1.1 server implemented on a SIM, standardized by the Open Mobile Alliance (OMA) [11]. The SCWS is owned and operated by the the Mobile Network Operator (MNO), and is only accessible from authorized applications on the phone handset or a trusted Remote Administration Server (RAS) controlled by the MNO or an authorized third party (e.g. a bank). Figure 1 shows the SCWS architecture.

The RAS updates the content of the SCWS using one of two standardized protocols, depending on the amount of data required: small amounts of data are sent by the Lightweight Administration Protocol (LAP) Over-The-Air (OTA); larger amounts of data use the Full Administration Protocol (FAP) via an HTTPs [5] channel between the RAS and SCWS. A FAP session can be initiated by the RAS, or triggered by the SCWS, and is handled by an on-SIM entity, the Administration Agent (AA). If a network connection problem occurs during a FAP session the AA attempts reconnection according to a pre-defined retry policy: if the session is abandoned, an error SMS is sent to the RAS (see [11] for details). The SCWS communicates with the phone browser via HTTP/HTTPs: a JavaCard v.3.0 SIM can do this directly using a TCP/IP stack; for other SIMs, the Bearer Independent Protocol (BIP) is used, via a BIP Gateway. An Access

Control Policy (ACP) Enforcer on the phone restricts local access to the SCWS to authorized applications only.

Applications can be installed and run in the SCWS environment using techniques described in [16]. As the MNO owns and operates the SIM/SCWS, service providers must have a business relationship with the MNO in order to install their applications on the SIM. The use of a Trusted Services Manager (TSM) to manage the business ecosystem has been suggested in the context of supporting Near Field Communication (NFC) applications on mobile phones [14]. Three business models are identified: simple mode, where only the MNO can manage applications on the UICC; delegated mode, where the TSM can manage applications on the UICC but needs a pre-authorization token from the MNO; and authorized mode where the TSM manages a specific area of the UICC without reference to the MNO. (For examples of the key management of these business models, please see [14].) In the SCWS scenario, as the RAS is a trusted entity, the TSM could control it on behalf of a service provider.

The SCWS provides interoperability across phone handsets and operating systems, and can be used to access web content offline using standard phone browsers. This gives a powerful, feature-rich interface, which can incorporate files, images and multimedia as required [7]. This is particularly helpful for illiterate users, where graphical and voice based interactions are more effective than menu-style SIM-toolkit applications [26], or for the visually challenged [31]. Other work uses the SCWS architecture and management to provide DDoS resistant distributed processing (e.g. e-voting [21]).

The tightly controlled SCWS management procedures make a SCWS solution suitable for addressing branchless banking security requirements. This paper therefore proposes a branchless banking system which uses a PKI-capable SIM with SCWS (referred to in future as SCWS-Banking). The next section describe entities and assumptions needed for this.

4 Entities and Assumptions

Entities in the proposed branchless banking system are now described, and their relationship illustrated in Figure 4.

Bank (B): processes all financial transactions, and maintains central databases of customer/agent accounts. It uses the procedures outlined in Section 3 to install its banking application and relevant security credentials on customers' and agents' SCWS/SIMs.(See assumptions below for details of credentials.)
Agent (A): is authorized to process transactions on the bank's behalf.
Customer (C): an individual who performs financial transactions.
Recipient (R): an individual who receives transferred value from a customer.
Smart Card Web Server (SCWS): as described in Section 3. A Java applet running on the SCWS will use relevant credentials and keys present on the SIM, and create dynamic content whenever requested: this applet will be referred to as the SCWS-Banking application throughout this paper.

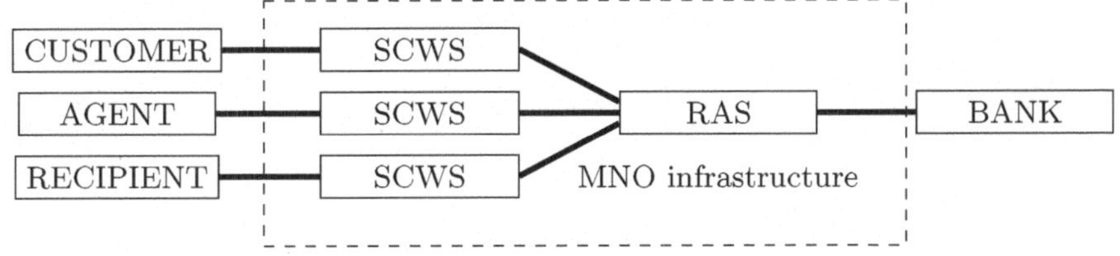

Fig. 2. Entities

Remote Administration Server (RAS): see Section 3. The RAS is a mere conduit between the bank and participants' SCWS/SIMs: it may be part of an MNO, TSM or bank, and passes messages unaltered to/from the bank's transaction processing system, with additional phone/SIM routing information as required. The RAS communicates with each SCWS using FAP/HTTPs sessions: however as HTTPs is not running end-to-end throughout a whole transaction, application level security mechanisms are required to prevent confidential information being visible at the RAS.

Mobile Network Operator (MNO): provides the technical mobile infrastructure and standardized SCWS administration protocols (see Section 3). The MNO provides a managed space on the SCWS/SIM for the bank's exclusive use, as described in [15]: delegated or authorized mode business models could be used to update SIM content. In certain regulatory environments, the MNO can act as the bank by storing value on behalf of the customer: the mobile phone number is the account number, as in M-PESA [1]. The simple mode business model is appropriate here. In this paper, the term 'bank' will be used for both MNO-centric and bank-centric scenarios.

The assumptions underlying the proposed SCWS-Banking system are:

Registration: agents and customers register with the bank, when appropriate identity documents are checked to satisfy banking regulations (e.g. Know Your Customer (KYC), Anti-Money-Laundering (AML) and Countering the Financing of Terrorism (CFT)). In some regulatory environments agents can check and register customers [24]: in others, customers/agents must go to the bank to register. Customers' identity details are stored by the bank for later use. Agents are allocated an Agent ID to display publicly. Customers/agents are issued with SCWS/SIMs, containing the SCWS-Banking application and their account credentials, installed using the procedures outlined in Section 3.

Banking Credentials on SCWS: these are a SCWS PIN (passwords may not be suitable for illiterate customers [26]); two customer public/private key pairs (for key separation purposes, one pair for encryption/decryption and one pair for signing/verifying), with key sizes following recommended guidelines e.g. [6]; and two bank public keys, for encrypting/verifying messages to/from the bank.

Availability of Equipment and Services: it is envisaged that the customer will possess a mobile handset with a browser, but if necessary their SCWS/SIM could be inserted in a shared phone to access SCWS-Banking. An agent must have a phone with SCWS/SIM. It is assumed a mobile phone network is available, although connectivity could be intermittent.

Table 2. Notation

Notation	Description
A	Agent(entity)
AC_X	Account Number for entity X
B	Bank(entity)
BAL_X	Balance in Account AC_X for entity X
BAL'_X	Updated Balance in Account AC_X for entity X
C	Customer(entity)
CH_X	Result of identity check for entity X, value = *true/false*
E_K(Z)	Encryption of data Z with key K
ID_X	Identity of entity X
N_X	Random Nonce generated by entity X
$NAME_X$	Name of entity X, (i.e. a short identifying text)
Ph_X	Phone Number of entity X
$PK_X/\ SK_X$	Public/ Secret Key pair of entity X
R	Recipient(entity)
$S_X/\ V_X$	Signing/ Verification key pair of entity X
Tr	Transaction Type:'W'=Withdrawal, 'D'=Deposit, 'T'=Transfer
TrAmt	Transaction Amount
$TrCount_X$	Transaction Counter for entity X
TrNo	Transaction Number
X→Y:	Message sent from entity X to entity Y
(Z)$Sign_K$	Signature on data Z with signature key K

Access to SCWS-Banking System: customers and agents participating in a SCWS-Banking transaction must first authenticate themselves to the SCWS environment by inputting a PIN to the phone browser.
Account Structure: there is a one-to-one correspondence between a SCWS and a bank account number: this means that a SCWS mobile phone number can be used to uniquely identify a customer or agent.
Trust: the customer does not trust the agent, and vice-versa. The bank and RAS are fully trusted.

The next sections will present SCWS-Banking transaction protocols: withdrawals, deposits and transfers. For simplicity, it is also assumed in the following descriptions that: if any of the protocol validation checks fail an error message is sent to all participants, the transaction is terminated and logged as unsuccessful; all cryptographic keys are checked for validity before use; data is padded according to best practice recommendations before being encrypted using a standardized public key algorithm e.g. RSA [19]; and a standardized digital signature algorithm is used e.g. DSA [23]. The notation used is shown in Table 2.

5 SCWS-Banking Withdrawal Protocol

In a withdrawal, the customer enters transaction details, the bank authorizes them and forwards them on to the agent to authorize in the presence of the customer. Figure 3 shows the messages in a withdrawal transaction.

Step 1: Customer enters data: (*TrAmt*, ID_A). The SCWS-Banking application generates N_C, increments $TrCount_C$ and creates message W1 using PK_B, S_C to encrypt and sign. The SCWS triggers a FAP session, the RAS retrieves message W1 (over HTTPs), adds Ph_C and passes it on to the bank.
W1 C→B: $(E_{PK_B}(Tr, TrAmt, ID_A, N_C, TrCount_C))Sign_{S_C}$

Step 2: Bank authorizes transaction: the bank uses Ph_C to find AC_C, BAL_C, V_C, PK_C, $NAME_C$ and ID_C, and verifies/ decrypts message W1 using relevant keys. The bank checks $TrCount_C$, and uses ID_A to obtain Ph_A, BAL_A, V_A and PK_A. If $TrAmt \leq BAL_C$, the bank generates N_B and *TrNo*, creates message W2 (encrypted/signed with PK_A/S_B) and sends it to the RAS (with Ph_A) to forward on to the agent via FAP/HTTPs.
W2 B→A: $(E_{PK_A}(Tr, TrNo, TrAmt, NAME_C, ID_C, N_B, BAL_A))Sign_{S_B}$

Step 3: Agent authorizes transaction: the agent SCWS-Banking application verifies/decrypts message W2 using $V_B/\ SK_A$, then checks that *TrNo* has not been received before. The agent inputs ID_C, and the SCWS-Banking application checks if ID_C(input) = ID_C(from W2) and sets CH_C: N_B is incremented, N_A is generated, and a transaction log is updated. Message W3 is created, retrieved via RAS/FAP/HTTPs, the RAS adds Ph_A and passes it to the bank.
W3 A→B: $(E_{PK_B}(Tr, TrNo, CH_C, N_B + 1, N_A))Sign_{S_A}$

Step 4: Bank finalizes and confirms transaction: the bank uses Ph_A to obtain agent keys to verify/decrypt message W3. The bank inspects $N_B + 1$ and CH_C: if the CH_C = *true*, *TrAmt* is used to create BAL'_A and BAL'_C. The transaction is logged, then time-stamped confirmation messages are sent to the agent/customer via SMS, and (encrypted and signed) to their SCWS-Banking applications, via RAS/FAP/HTTPs (messages W4A and W4C).
W4A B→A: $(E_{PK_A}(Tr, TrNo, TrAmt, ID_C, N_B + 1, N_A + 1, BAL'_A))Sign_{S_B}$
W4C B→C: $(E_{PK_C}(Tr, TrNo, TrAmt, ID_A, N_C + 1, BAL'_C))Sign_{S_B}$

Step 5: Agent and customer finalize transaction: the SCWS-Banking applications verify/ decrypt message W4A or W4C (as appropriate) from the bank, update the SCWS-Banking files with transaction data, and the transaction is logged. The agent should only give the customer cash once the confirmation mes-

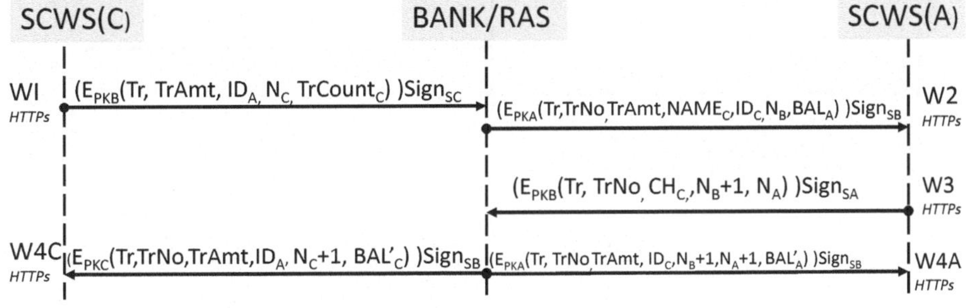

Fig. 3. SCWS-Banking Withdrawal Protocol

sage has arrived from the bank. A paper transaction log is also maintained by the agent, which the customer must sign to acknowledge receipt of the cash.

6 SCWS-Banking Deposit Protocol

A deposit is an agent-initiated transaction similar to a withdrawal, but with the message flow reversed. The deposit protocol messages are shown in Figure 4, and summarized below: again, phone numbers are added to messages between the bank and the RAS for routing purposes.

Step 1: Agent enters data (*TrAmt*, ID_C) (Agent to Bank)
D1 $A \rightarrow B$: $(E_{PK_B}(Tr, TrAmt, ID_C, N_A, TrCount_A))Sign_{S_A}$
Step 2: Bank authorizes transaction (Bank to Customer)
D2 $B \rightarrow C$: $(E_{PK_C}(Tr, TrNo, TrAmt, ID_A, N_B, BAL_C))Sign_{S_B}$
Step 3: Customer authorizes transaction (Customer to Bank)
D3 $C \rightarrow B$: $(E_{PK_B}(Tr, TrNo, CH_A, N_B + 1, N_C))Sign_{S_C}$
Step 4: Bank finalizes and confirms transaction
D4A $B \rightarrow A$: $(E_{PK_A}(Tr, TrNo, TrAmt, ID_C, N_A + 1, BAL'_A))Sign_{S_B}$
D4C $B \rightarrow C$: $(E_{PK_C}(Tr, TrNo, TrAmt, ID_A, N_B{+}1, N_C{+}1, BAL'_C))Sign_{S_B}$

7 SCWS-Banking Transfer Protocol

The bank transfers value *TrAmt* from a customer to a recipient (R), directly if the recipient's account is known, otherwise via an SMS to the recipient for redeeming *TrAmt* from an agent later. Transfer messages are shown in Figure 5.

Step 1: Customer enters data (*TrAmt*, Ph_R) (Customer to Bank)
T1 $C \rightarrow B$: $(E_{PK_B}(Tr, TrAmt, Ph_R, N_C, TrCount_C))Sign_{S_C}$
Step 2: Bank processes transaction (Bank to Customer/ Recipient)
T2R-SMS is sent via SMS to Ph_R if the recipient does not have a SCWS-Banking account: Steps 3 and 4 are also needed in this case.

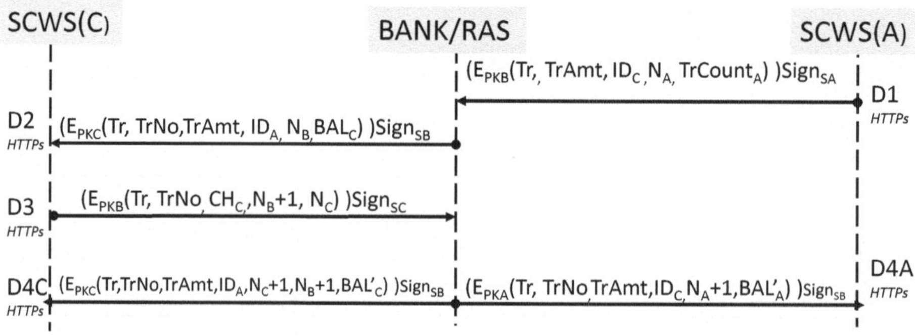

Fig. 4. SCWS-Banking Deposit Protocol

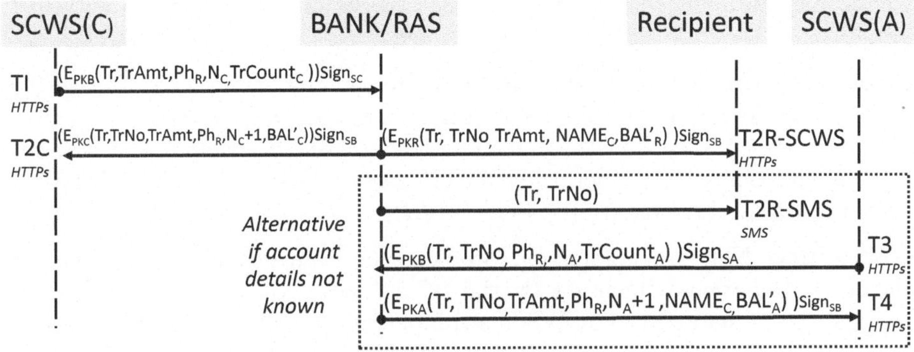

Fig. 5. SCWS-Banking Transfer Protocol

T2C B→C: $(E_{PK_C}(Tr, TrNo, TrAmt, Ph_R, N_C + 1, BAL'_C))Sign_{S_B}$
T2R-SCWS B→R: $(E_{PK_R}(Tr, TrNo, TrAmt, NAME_C, BAL'_R))Sign_{S_B}$
T2R-SMS B→R: (Tr, TrNo)
Step 3: Recipient redeems SMS transfer (Agent to Bank)
The recipient gives the agent Ph_R and *TrNo.*
T3 A→B:$(E_{PK_B}(Tr, TrNo, Ph_R, N_A, TrCount_A))Sign_{S_A}$
Step 4: Bank confirms transaction to agent (Bank to Agent)
The bank obtains full transaction details from its records and instructs the agent to pay the recipient *TrAmt.* $NAME_C$ can be given to the recipient for their records. The agent should also manually record the recipients ID credentials, and maintain a paper transaction log for non-repudiation purposes,
T4 B→A:$(E_{PK_A}(Tr, TrNo, TrAmt, Ph_R, N_A{+}1, NAME_C, BAL'_A))Sign_{S_B}$

8 Security Analysis

The proposal is now discussed with respect to the security requirements set out in Section 2. Potential attacks will be identified and a comparison with the SMS-Banking scheme M-PESA is made.

Addressing Security Requirements

Confidentiality: All information sent between the SCWS, RAS, and phone browser are protected by HTTPs against eavesdropping and man-in-the-middle attacks whilst in transit. As HTTPs is not running end-to-end (there are separate RAS/FAP/HTTPs sessions for each message) application level security is also used to meet security requirements. Public key encryption and the PIN-protected tamper-resistant SCWS environment ensure that sensitive information is kept confidential at all times.

Integrity: Using HTTPs between the RAS/SCWS/phone browser gives reasonable assurance that messages are not tampered with. Digital signatures allow detection of unauthorized changes, and challenge-responses prevent replay attacks. The tamper-resistant SIM makes attacks on data integrity extremely hard.

Authentication: ID credentials are input by the customer/agent and verified by the bank, so imposters will be identified. Digital signatures are used in all messages for assurance that the bank/customer/agent is genuine. The RAS and SCWS authenticate each other using HTTPs. Also, the bank sends confirmations via two separate channels (SMS/ SCWS-FAP).

Availability: Network connection problems encountered during a FAP session are automatically handled by the SCWS on-card Administration Agent (see [11]). Data held on the SCWS is available offline, only accessible via a PIN. Back-office procedures are needed for remote locking/reissue of the SIM/SCWS application and credentials when phones/SIMs are lost/damaged. The SCWS-Banking application and credentials are installed on many SIMs, so DDoS attacks are hard to mount because each phone has to be targeted individually.

Non-Repudiation: Digital signatures provide non-repudiation; also, transaction logs are securely held on both the agent/customer SCWS and centrally by the bank. Paper-based transaction logs are maintained by the agent and signed by the customer to acknowledge each transaction. Bank confirmation messages are sent via two channels, to minimize the likelihood of losing a message.

Potential Attacks: The SCWS is a web server, and as such is vulnerable to most of the attacks identified in the OWASP Top Ten project [8]. Strict filtering of input fields in the phone browser should prevent injection and cross site scripting exploits. Although attacks on the SCWS from the phone browser are theoretically possible, they are not scalable: the attacker needs physical possession of the handset to access the SCWS. Remote attacks on the SCWS are hard, as access to it is only permitted through the trusted RAS. It is difficult for malware on the phone to attack the SCWS, as the ACP enforcer only allows access to authorized applications. Even if the ACP enforcer is compromised, the

Table 3. M-PESA /SCWS-Banking Security Comparison

Security Requirement	M-PESA	SCWS-Banking
Confidentiality	Unencrypted SMS messages, readable from phone's SMS inbox	Encrypted messages, HTTPs, data PIN protected on SCWS
Integrity	Malware could intercept and tamper with SMS messages on phone	Digital Signatures and HTTPs protect integrity
Authentication	Customer is authenticated, bank-originating messages are not	Digital Signatures and physical IDs are used for authentication
Availability	Procedures for lost/stolen phones, but large number of SMS messages could flood mobile network:	Procedures for lost/stolen SIMs: DDoS resistant
Non-repudiation	Messages from bank not authenticated, so no non-repudiation	Digital signatures provide non-repudiation

SCWS has a small attack surface due to its restricted processing capability. Replay attacks, where messages W1/D1/T1 are recorded and subsequently resent to the bank to generate multiple transaction authorization numbers (*TrNo*) are prevented by the use of transaction counters held on the SCWS and checked by the bank. As stated previously, DDoS attacks are hard to mount, although a Denial of Service attack against a single SCWS is feasible but difficult. The RAS is potentially a single point of failure in the SCWS-Banking protocol, as it controls the entire message flow. However, as it is a trusted entity, owned and operated by the MNO, it is subject to tightly controlled management procedures which should make unauthorized usage and attacks difficult.

Comparison with SMS Banking: Table 3 compares the security of SCWS-Banking with M-PESA. It can be seen that M-PESA only partially meets all the identified security requirements, whereas the proposed SCWS-Banking solution satisfies them all.

9 Conclusion

This paper has presented a SCWS-Banking scheme which uses PKI-capable SIMs equipped with a SCWS to process branchless banking withdrawals, deposits and transfers in a secure and user-friendly manner. The main strength of the proposal is that it uses standardized hardware, protocols and communications to protect sensitive information, without the need for specialized equipment and phone applications. All communication to/from the SCWS is done via HTTPs. By storing security information on the tamper-resistant SIM, local authentication of PINs can be done by the SCWS without communicating credentials across a network. All transactions pass through a trusted Remote Administration Server, owned and operated by the MNO or trusted third party. It is hard to mount large scale attacks against the system, as credentials and applications stored on each SIM must be targeted individually. PKI-capable SIMs enable application level public key encryption/ digital signatures to provide authentication and non-repudiation, using keys stored on the tamper-resistant SCWS/SIM. Agents and customers need new advanced SIMs containing the SCWS-Banking application and their account credentials. Even though these are more expensive than conventional SIMs, this is a cheaper overall solution than setting up physical bank branches. All systems present a trade-off between usability and security: a practical implementation would enable performance measurements to be taken for each stage of the protocol, to give an indication how speed of processing will impact the usability of the system, and its suitability for use with various phone handsets. A preliminary security analysis indicates that SCWS-Banking security is higher than that offered by M-PESA. A more detailed security analysis of the protocols would be useful in future to examine their security properties in more depth. However, the initial findings are promising, and the SCWS-Banking proposal meets branchless banking security challenges very well.

References

1. http://www.safaricom.co.ke/
2. http://main.mchek.com/
3. http://www.spoofsms.co.uk/
4. http://www.f-secure.com/v-descs/commwarrior.shtml
5. Hypertext Transfer Protocol over TLS protocol, RFC 2818 (May 2000), http://www.ietf.org/rfc/rfc2818.txt
6. Recommendation for Key Management - Part 1: General (Revised). National Institute of Standards and Technology (NIST) Special Publication 800-57 (March 2007), http://csrc.nist.gov/publications/nistpubs/800-57/
7. Smart Card Web Server: How to bring operators' applications and services to the mass market (February 2009), http://www.simalliance.org/en/resources/white_papers/
8. OWASP Top Ten Project (2010), https://www.owasp.org
9. Security breach at M-PESA: Telco 2.0 crash investigation (2010), http://www.telco2.net/blog/2010/02/security_breach_at_mpesa_telco.html
10. Open Mobile Alliance (2011), http://technical.openmobilealliance.org/comms/pages/oma_2011_ar_scws.html
11. Smartcard-Web-Server, Approved Version 1.1.2, OMA-TS-Smartcard_Web_Server-V1_1_1_2-20120927-A, Open Mobile Alliance (OMA), Version 1.2 (September 2012), http://www.openmobilealliance.org
12. Arora, B., Metz Cummings, A.: A Little World: Facilitating Safe and Efficient M-Banking in Rural India. GIM Case Study No. B051. United Nations Development Programme, New York (2010)
13. Bickford, J., O'Hare, R., Baliga, A., Ganapathy, V., Iftode, L.: Rootkits on smart phones: attacks, implications and opportunities. In: Proceedings of the Eleventh Workshop on Mobile Computing Systems & Applications, HotMobile 2010, pp. 49–54. ACM, New York (2010)
14. GlobalPlatform: GlobalPlatform's Proposition for NFC Mobile: Secure Element Management and Messaging (April 2009), http://www.globalplatform.org/documents/GlobalPlatform_NFC_Mobile_White_Paper.pdf
15. GlobalPlatform: Confidential Card Content Management - GlobalPlatform Card Specification v2.2 - Amendment A v1.0.1 (January 2011)
16. GlobalPlatform: Remote Application Management over HTTP Card Specification v2.2 Amendment B Version 1.1.1 (March 2012)
17. Goodin, D.: ZeuS trojan attacks bank's 2-factor authentication (2012), http://www.theregister.co.uk/2011/02/22/zeus_2_factor_authentication_attack/
18. Juniper Networks Inc.: 2011 Mobile Threats Report (2011)
19. Kaliski, B., Staddon, J.: PKCS# 1: RSA cryptography specifications version 2.0. Tech. rep., RFC 2437 (October 1998)
20. Karunanayake, A., De Zoysa, K., Muftic, S.: Mobile ATM for developing countries. In: Proceedings of the 3rd International Workshop on Mobility in the Evolving Internet Architecture, MobiArch 2008, pp. 25–30. ACM, New York (2008)
21. Kyrillidis, L., Cobourne, S., Mayes, K., Dong, S., Markantonakis, K.: Distributed e-voting using the Smart Card Web Server. In: 2012 7th International Conference on Risk and Security of Internet and Systems (CRiSIS), pp. 1–8 (October 2012)
22. Leyden, J.: HSBC websites fell in DDoS attack last night, bank admits (July 2010), http://www.theregister.co.uk/2012/10/19/hsbc_ddos/

23. Locke, G., Gallagher, P.: FIPS PUB 186-3: Digital signature standard (DSS). Federal Information Processing Standards Publication (2009)
24. Mas, I., Siedek, H.: Banking through networks of retail agents (May 2008), http://www.cgap.org
25. Mayes, K.E., Markantonakis, K. (eds.): Smart Cards, Tokens, Security and Applications. Springer, New York (2008)
26. Medhi, I., Gautama, S., Toyama, K.: A comparison of mobile money-transfer uis for non-literate and semi-literate users. In: Proceedings of the 27th International Conference on Human Factors in Computing Systems, pp. 1741–1750. ACM (2009)
27. Morawczynski, O., Miscione, G.: Examining trust in mobile banking transactions: The case of M-PESA in Kenya. In: Avgerou, C., Smith, M.L., van den Besselaar, P. (eds.) Social Dimensions of Information and Communication Technology Policy. IFIP, vol. 282, pp. 287–298. Springer, Boston (2008)
28. Paik, M.: Stragglers of the herd get eaten: security concerns for GSM mobile banking applications. In: Proceedings of the Eleventh Workshop on Mobile Computing Systems & Applications, pp. 54–59. ACM (2010)
29. Panjwani, S., Cutrell, E.: Usably secure, low-cost authentication for mobile banking. In: Proceedings of the Sixth Symposium on Usable Privacy and Security, p. 4. ACM (2010)
30. Sharma, A., Subramanian, L., Shasha, D.: Secure branchless banking. In: ACM SOSP Workshop on Networked Systems for Developing Regions, NSDR (2009)
31. Thinyane, H., Thinyane, M.: ICANSEE: A SIM based application for digital inclusion of the Visually impaired community. In: Innovations for Digital Inclusions, K-IDI 2009. ITU-T Kaleidoscope, pp. 1–6. IEEE (2009)

Liability for Data Breaches: A Proposal for a Revenue-Based Sanctioning Approach

Maurizio Naldi[1], Marta Flamini[2], and Giuseppe D'Acquisto[1]

[1] Università di Roma Tor Vergata, Roma, Italy
naldi@disp.uniroma2.it, dacquisto@ing.uniroma2.it
[2] Università Telematica Internazionale UNINETTUNO, Roma, Italy
m.flamini@uninettunouniversity.net

Abstract. Data breaches are a rising concern in personal data management. While the damages due to data breaches fall primarily on the end customer, the service provider should be held liable. A sanctioning approach is proposed to promote a greater responsibility by the service provider, where sanctions are proportional to the service providers revenues. The interactions between the customer and the service provider are modelled as a game, where the customer decides the amount of tolerable loss (a proxy for the amount of information released) and the service provider decides the amount of security investment. The solution of the game for a typical scenario shows that sanctions effectively spur the service provider to invest more in security and lead to a reduced data breach probability.

Keywords: Security investments, Data Breaches, Sanctions, Privacy, Security economics.

1 Introduction

Security incidents where customers' personal data are stolen (often to be put to malicious use), a.k.a. data breaches, are rising. After a temporary decrease, the number of compromised records, which went from 361 million in 2008 to 144 million in 2009 [1] marking an all-time low, went back to 174 million in 2011 [2] (which is the second-highest data loss total since Verizon started keeping track in 2004). Large economic interests work behind the scenes: the industry of developing and selling toolkits for exploits alone is worth 100 million dollars a year [3]. And the payoff per victim ranges from $2000 for mass attacks to $80000 for focused attacks, according to Cisco [3].

The ultimate sources of personal data are customers who release them in a variety of contexts. Though we can expect customers to have the most interest to protect their data, they exhibit a peculiar behaviour when valuing their privacy: they are willing to accept money to release their data more than they are willing to pay to protect them [4].

On the other hand, service providers hosting their customer's data can do much to protect them. They can make their systems and transactions more

J. Lopez, X. Huang, and R. Sandhu (Eds.): NSS 2013, LNCS 7873, pp. 264–277, 2013.

secure by investing in security technology. It has however been recognized that security investments must be related to the benefit they provide in reducing the potential loss deriving from a data breach [5]. If the loss deriving from a data breach falls on the customer's shoulders alone, the service provider may have no strong incentive to invest more in security.

Among the possible remedies and countermeasures envisaged in [3], legislation is mentioned as the foremost approach. Though class actions against a sloppy service providers may experience difficulties in proving direct causality relationships in court, regulatory actions are being put forward, e.g., in the European Union.

An approach based on damage sharing, which apportions the damage between the service provider and the customer, has been proposed in [6]. In [7], it has been shown that the policy may be ineffective unless the fraction of damage charged to the service provider is quite large, beyond 60%.

In this paper, we propose an alternative regulatory action, where the sanction is related to the service provider's turnover rather than the damage suffered by the customer. This new approach is finding its way in the European legislation, since a sanctioning approach based on the revenues of the company hosting the data is under examination in the European Parliament [8]. We employ models for the behaviour of both the customer and the service provider and derive a game-theoretic formulation of their interaction. For both stakeholders, we obtain their best response function and show that the game solution can be found numerically. For a typical scenario, we find that the sanctioning approach based on the service provider's turnover is quite effective in leading the service provider to invest more in security and reducing the data breach probability. As a side effect of sanctions, customers have a more relaxed attitude when releasing their personal data.

The paper is organized as follows. In Section 2, we describe the relationship between the behaviour of the two players and the probability of data breaches. The sanctioning approach based on the service provider's turnover is defined in Section 3, leading to the definition and solution of the game in Section 4, while the results of its application to a typical scenario are reported in Section 5. A list of the parameters involved is reported in Table 1.

2 Data Breaches and Security Investments

Customers are led to expose themselves when requiring services, which increases the probability of data breaches At the same time, service providers can mitigate that risk by investing in security. We associate the two phenomena to the stakeholders responsible for them: in the following, we refer to the probability of data breach (and the resulting loss) $P_{\text{db}}^{(\text{c})}$ due to the customer as that originating because of two effects: the release of personal information that is intercepted by an attacker, and the installation of malware of the customer's equipment. The probability $P_{\text{db}}^{(\text{s})}$ will denote instead the probability that a data breach and the associated loss occur due to inadequate investment in security by the service provider. In this section, we provide models for both effects. We largely draw on the models already employed in [6] and [7].

Let's consider first the impact of what the customer itself releases. Rather than considering the amount of information as the driver of the probability of data breaches, we consider the more easily measurable amount L of potential loss as a proxy. That is the loss occurring when a data breach takes place. We assume that it is known, or at least estimated, by both the customer and the service provider. After normalizing the potential loss to the maximum customer's exposure $L_{\max}$, we assume that the following power law holds

$$P_{\mathrm{db}}^{(\mathrm{c})} = P_{\max}^{(\mathrm{c})} \left(\frac{L}{L_{\max}} \right)^{\theta} \qquad \theta \in \mathbb{R}^{+}, \tag{1}$$

where $P_{\max}^{(\mathrm{c})}$ is the probability of breach corresponding to the maximum release of information.

For the probability of data breach due to inadequate investment in security by the service provider, we consider a power law as well. Of course, the curve is now a decreasing one. In the absence of additional investments, the probability of data breaches is $P_{\max}^{(\mathrm{s})}$. When the investment per customer is the maximum envisaged $I_{\max}$, the probability of data breaches decreases by $A \cdot 100\%$, where A is a suitable coefficient, satisfying the inequality $0 < A < 1$, since, no matter the amount of investments in security, the data cannot be granted total security. The resulting power law relationship is

$$P_{\mathrm{db}}^{(\mathrm{s})} = P_{\max}^{(\mathrm{s})} \left[1 - A \left(\frac{I}{I_{\max}} \right)^{k} \right], \tag{2}$$

Since a data breach can occur due to either reason, and independently of each other, the overall probability P_{db} of a data breach and its associated loss can be obtained by the logical OR combination of the two events, leading to

$$\begin{aligned} P_{\mathrm{db}} &= 1 - (1 - P_{\mathrm{db}}^{(\mathrm{c})})(1 - P_{\mathrm{db}}^{(\mathrm{s})}) \\ &= P_{\mathrm{db}}^{(\mathrm{s})} + P_{\mathrm{db}}^{(\mathrm{c})} - P_{\mathrm{db}}^{(\mathrm{s})} \cdot P_{\mathrm{db}}^{(\mathrm{c})}. \end{aligned} \tag{3}$$

3 Sanctioning Procedure

Though investing in security leads to reduced data breaches, service providers do not directly benefit from such a reduction. In the absence of any incentive, investments in security may appear just as a cost item. In this section, we propose a sanctioning procedure that makes service providers liable for data breaches.

In most countries' jurisdictions, sanctions for data breaches are defined through their maximum value, with no reference to the extent of the damage suffered by customers. A survey is reported in [9]. A notable exception is France, where the maximum sanction is stated as a percentage (5%) of the data controller's turnover in the case of a second violation. A sanctioning approach based on the revenues of the company hosting the data is under examination in the European Parliament [8].

Hereafter, we consider a sanctioning regime where the sanction M is proportional both to the expected damage inflicted on the customer and to the revenues of the service provider, through a proportionality factor Ω. Since the revenues are the product of the unit price p and the amount of services q, the resulting sanction is

$$M = \Omega L P_{\mathrm{db}} p q. \tag{4}$$

The sanction is expected to be imposed on the service provider by a regulatory agency. Service providers are therefore led to reduce the probability of data breaches by investing more in security. We consider a strict proportionality rather than a ceiling based on revenues to allow for a fairer treatment of smaller companies. It is to be noted that, through Equation (4), the service provider is held liable and subject to sanctions even when the data breach has occurred due to the customer's fault. In fact, in Equation (4) the overall probability P_{db} of data breach appears, rather than just the service provider-related term $P_{\mathrm{db}}^{(\mathrm{s})}$. Though this treatment may appear as unfair to the service provider, we observe that tracking the root cause of a data breach may prove difficult.

4 A Game-Theoretical Model

In the previous sections, we have seen that opposite forces drive the stakeholders. Customers are led to release more personal information to get more services, but expose themselves to a greater risk of data breaches and subsequent money losses. On the other side, service providers would like to reduce their security investments as much as possible but are forced to invest by a sanctioning procedure that reduces their revenues when data breaches take place. Such contrasts may be formalized by building a game-theoretical model. In this section, we set up such a model, defining the players and their strategical leverages. We show that the game can be solved to provide a rational direction for both stakeholders and the regulatory authority.

We consider a customer who gets services offered through a communications network by a service provider. We do not refer to a specific service, so that what follows can be applied on rather general terms. If services are provided without the service provider asking for personal information, we assume a simple linear relationship between the quantity q of services and their price p:

$$q = \begin{cases} q^* \left(1 - \frac{p}{p^*}\right) & \text{if} \quad p < p^* \\ 0 & \text{if} \quad p \geq p^* \end{cases} \tag{5}$$

where p^* is the maximum price the customer can tolerate (its willingness-to-pay), and q^* is the maximum amount of service the customer is capable to consume, even if the service is free. Examples of demand measurement units are the minutes of conversation for the telephone service, the amount of data transferred, the number of transactions accomplished. In the following, we treat the demand as a continuous quantity, though it is possibly discrete, since this allows us to use continuous calculus tools; the problem is a minor one, since the granularity is so fine that the quantity can be practically considered as continuous.

However, in many cases the service provider is keen on getting come personal information about its customers. This may be due to several reasons: profiling its customers better so as to induce them into buying a wider range of services or even just selling that information to third parties who may in turn use it to target those customers. Whatever the reason, the service provider wishes to get as much personal data as possible and, in order to do so, is willing to reward those customers who release their personal data. Though the rewards may take many forms, we assume here that it basically consists in allowing the customer to get more services at the same price. The impact on the demand function is shown in Fig. 1, so that the demand function takes the following form instead of Equation (5)

$$q = \begin{cases} q^*(1+\alpha)\left(1 - \frac{p}{p^*}\right) & \text{if} \quad p < p^* \\ 0 & \text{if} \quad p \geq p^* \end{cases} \tag{6}$$

The demand in the absence of personal information is multiplied by a factor $1+\alpha$. The coefficient α is a measure of the reward, which is envisaged to be directly related to the amount of personal information released. At the same time, releasing personal data exposes the customer to those data being stolen and put to malicious use. Apart from other consequences, the most apparent result of a data breach is the monetary damage caused to the customer. Here we assume that the relationship between the amount of information released (embodied by α) and the potential monetary loss L is the power law

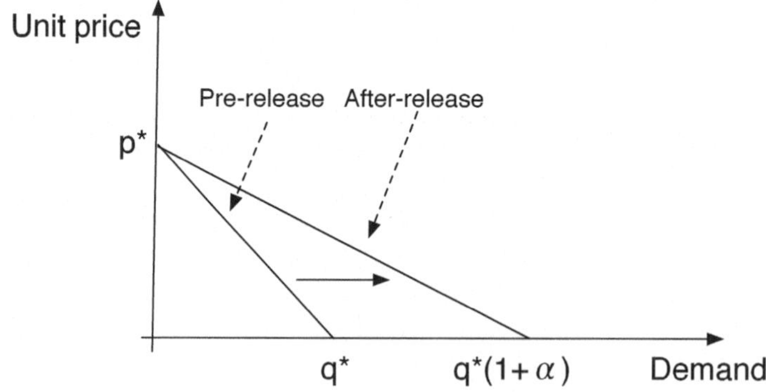

Fig. 1. Demand function

$$\alpha = \alpha_{\max} \left(\frac{L}{L_{\max}} \right)^{\nu} \qquad \nu \in \mathbb{R}^{+}. \tag{7}$$

In Equation (7), the parameter $\nu > 0$ measures the degree of attention to privacy. If $\nu < 1$, the customer releases its information starting with the most potentially damaging, and the additional risk associated to further releases is a decreasing function of the information released. In particular, if $\nu \ll 1$ (i.e., the service provider is privacy-friendly), the customer gains a large benefit (i.e., a large extension of the maximum quantity of services) even for small pieces of the information released (i.e., small potential losses). When $\nu = 1$, we have instead a linear relationship between the information released and the associated economical loss. The case $\nu > 1$ models instead the situation where the customer releases information starting with the least sensitive one. Here we don't support strongly any specific value for the privacy parameter.

Let's consider now the economic quantities that measure the welfare of the two stakeholders: the customer and the service provider. When the customer obtains the services at the unit price p, it gets a surplus given by the excess of its willingness-to-pay with respect to the actual price. If we integrate this surplus over the range of purchased quantity, we obtain the overall customer's surplus, which is lowered by the expected loss due to data breaches. By recalling the demand function (6), we obtain the customer's net surplus

$$S_{\mathrm{c}} = \frac{(p - p^*)^2}{2p^*} q^* \left[1 + \alpha_{\max} \left(\frac{L}{L_{\max}} \right)^{\nu} \right] - LP_{\mathrm{db}}. \tag{8}$$

On the other hand, the service provider gets a profit $p(1 - \gamma)$ for each unit of service it sells, with γ, $0 < \gamma < 1$, being the cost-to-price ratio. But the service provider has to spend a part of its profit to invest in security and pay the sanction (4), so that the net profit of the service provider is

$$\begin{aligned} S_{\mathrm{sp}} &= qp(1 - \gamma) - I - qp\Omega LP_{\mathrm{db}} = qp(1 - \gamma - \Omega LP_{\mathrm{db}}) - I \\ &= q^* p(1 + \alpha) \left(1 - \frac{p}{p^*} \right) (1 - \gamma - \Omega LP_{\mathrm{db}}) - I. \end{aligned} \tag{9}$$

By introducing the normalized variables $X = L/L_{\max}$ and $Y = I/I_{\max}$, we can express the surplus functions (8) and (9) in the following form, which highlights the most relevant variables

$$\begin{aligned} S_{\mathrm{c}} &= \frac{(p - p^*)^2}{2p^*} q^* \left[1 + \alpha_{\max} (X)^{\nu} \right] - LP_{\mathrm{db}}, \\ S_{\mathrm{sp}} &= q^* p(1 + \alpha) \left(1 - \frac{p}{p^*} \right) (1 - \gamma - \Omega L_{\max} X P_{\mathrm{db}}) - I_{\max} Y, \end{aligned} \tag{10}$$

where

$$P_{\mathrm{db}} = 1 - \left(1 - P^{(\mathrm{c})}_{\max} X^{\theta} \right) \left[1 - P^{(\mathrm{s})}_{\max} \left(1 - AY^{k} \right) \right]. \tag{11}$$

Equations (10) show that the two major stakeholders's surpluses are driven in different directions by the two strategic variables on which they can act. The customer is led to reveal as much personal information as it can to get extra services at the same price, but this could expose it to larger losses, which could completely offset that benefit. On the other hand, the service provider can mitigate the sanction by reducing the probability of a data breach through larger investments in security, but this represents an upfront expense, which lowers its profit. The contrasting interests of the service provider and the customer can therefore be modelled as a game, where the strategic variables are respectively the amount of security investments for the service provider and the potential loss (which acts as a proxy for the amount of information revealed) for the customer.

We now wish to solve the game and find the optimal values for the strategic variables. We look first for the best response functions of the two players. We recall that, in a two-player game, the best-response function of player i is the function $Z_i(a_j)$ that, for every given action a_j of player j, assigns an action $a_i = Z_i(a_j)$ that maximizes player i 's payoff. In our case, the actions taken by the two players consist in setting the normalized loss X and the normalized investment Y, and their payoffs are represented by their surpluses, so that their best response functions are

$$
\begin{aligned}
\hat{X} &= \underset{X}{\operatorname{argmax}}\{S_{\mathrm{c}}(X, Y, L_{\max}, I_{\max}, p, p^*, q^*, \alpha_{\max}, P_{\max}^{(\mathrm{c})}, P_{\max}^{(\mathrm{s})}, \theta, A, k, \nu)\}, \\
\hat{Y} &= \underset{Y}{\operatorname{argmax}}\{S_{\mathrm{sp}}(X, Y, L_{\max}, I_{\max}, p, p^*, q^*, \alpha_{\max}, P_{\max}^{(\mathrm{c})}, P_{\max}^{(\mathrm{s})}, \theta, A, k, \gamma, \Omega)\}.
\end{aligned}
\tag{12}
$$

By applying those definitions to the surpluses (10), we obtain the following best response function for the customer

$$
\begin{aligned}
\hat{X} &= X : \left\{ \frac{\partial S_{\mathrm{c}}}{\partial p} = 0 \right\} \\
&= X : Y - \left[\frac{1}{A} - \frac{\Delta X^{\nu-1} - L_{\max} \Lambda X^{\theta}}{\Upsilon(1 - \Lambda X^{\theta})} \right]^{1/k} = 0
\end{aligned}
\tag{13}
$$

where we have used the following positions

$$
\begin{aligned}
\Delta &= \frac{(p^* - \hat{p})^2}{2p^*} q^* \alpha_{\max} \nu, \\
\Lambda &= P_{\max}^{(\mathrm{c})}(1 + \theta), \\
\Upsilon &= P_{\max}^{(\mathrm{s})} A L_{\max},
\end{aligned}
\tag{14}
$$

Here we have preferred to express the best response function in such an implicit form, because writing $\hat{X}$ as a function of Y would result in an awkward expression. The best response for the service provider is instead

$$
\hat{Y} = \left[\Phi X \Omega (1 + \alpha_{\max} X^{\nu}) \left(1 - P_{\max}^{(\mathrm{c})} X^{\theta} \right) \right]^{\frac{1}{1-k}}, \tag{15}
$$

where we use the position

$$\Phi = \frac{q^* p \left(1 - \frac{p}{p^*}\right) L_{\max} A k P_{\max}^{(s)}}{I_{\max}} \tag{16}$$

From the couple of best response functions we can determine the Nash equilibrium: we have to find the pair of actions with the property that player 1's action is a best response to player 2's action, and player 2's action is a best response to player 1's action [10]. A Nash equilibrium is then reached as the solution of the system of two equations (13) and (15). In graphical terms, the Nash equilibrium is the intersection of the curves representing the best response functions. In this case, we must be content with obtaining the Nash equilibrium (if any) through a numerical procedure.

5 Effectiveness of the Sanctioning Approach

In Section 4, we have described the interaction between the customer and the service provider as a strategic game, where the former decides how much information to release and the latter decides how much to invest in security. The solution of the game, represented by the Nash equilibrium, has to be found by a numerical approach. In this section, we analyse the results obtained for a typical scenario and assess the impact of the regulatory intervention.

We consider a typical scenario, represented by the values reported in Table 1, which has been built by gathering gathered data from a variety of sources, including [11], [12], [13], and [14].

In order to assess the effectiveness of the sanctioning approach, we look for some metrics. The ultimate goal of sanctions is to reduce the probability of data

Table 1. Parameters' values for the reference scenario

Parameter	Symbol	Value
Max potential loss	$L_{\max}$	25000 €
Max investment	$I_{\max}$	20 €
Willingness to pay	p^*	350 €
Price	p	200 €
Max service consumption	q^*	7
Max reward coefficient	$\alpha_{\max}$	0.15
Max probability of loss (service provider)	$P_{\max}^{(s)}$	$5 \cdot 10^{-3}$
Max probability of loss (customer)	$P_{\max}^{(c)}$	$5 \cdot 10^{-3}$
Power law exponent (service provider)	k	0.5
Loss probability decrease coefficient	A	0.9
Power law exponent (info release)	ν	0.139
Power law exponent (customer)	θ	0.139

breaches by inducing the service provider to invest more in security. For that purpose, we analyse here the impact of sanctions on the amount of investments in security, the service provider's revenues, and the probability of data breaches.

We analyze first the impact of the sanctioning factor Ω on the game's outcome. In Fig. 2, we see what happens when the sanctioning factor spans two orders of magnitude, from 10^{-4} to $1.9 \cdot 10^{-2}$; that curve represents the locus of equilibria points as the sanctioning factor varies. As desired, raising Ω moves both coordinates of the Nash equilibrium point upwards. If the sanction is more severe, the service provider is induced into investing more in security, since that will reduce the probability of data breaches and will help it avoid sanctions. At the same time, if sanctions are higher, the customer takes a more relaxed attitude and accepts to reveal more personal information (hence, risking more), since it knows that the service provider will be more protective of its data. However, the impact on the two stakeholders is of quite different intensity; more precisely, the impact is much heavier on the service provider than on the end customer. In fact, over the whole range of the sanctioning factor, the strategic leverage exercised by the customer (the amount of tolerable loss) roughly doubles, while the amount of security investment goes from nearly zero to 80% of its maximum envisaged value. After an initial slower ascent, the trend of the curve in Fig. 2 is roughly linear, meaning that the optimal amount of security investment grows as a fixed multiple of the optimal amount of tolerable loss. On the other hand, the impact of the sanctioning factor on either strategic leverage is more than linear. As can be ascertained from Equation (15), the optimal value of security investment grows as the $1/(1-k)$ power of the sanctioning factor; for the values of the typical scenario of Table 1, that means that the security investment has to grow as the square of the sanctioning factor, as shown in Fig. 3.

Since the aim of introducing a sanction is to induce the service provider into investing more in security, the increase of that investment shown in Fig. 2 is a proof of the effectiveness of the sanctioning approach. An additional indication of such effectiveness can be obtained by observing the revenues of the service provider, since the means adopted to act on the service provider is to punish it by curtailing its revenues. In Fig. 4, we report the impact of the sanctioning factor on the service provider's revenues. The effect is quite harsh: by increasing the sanctioning factor up to its maximum value, the revenues are slashed down by a factor of three. This confirms the effectiveness of the approach, though it also signals that it can be overdone.

Since the service provider is heavily affected by sanctions, we have to see if and how much the other stakeholder, i.e., the customer, benefits from the regulatory intervention. We report in Fig. 5 the customer's surplus. The trend is opposite to that experienced by the service provider: when the sanctioning factor rises, the customer's surplus grows. However, the effect is really limited: the whole range of variation of the sanctioning factors results in a mere 0.74% increase of the customer's surplus. We can safely conclude that the sanctioning approach has a heavy negative impact on the service provider without resulting in a significant net benefit for the customer.

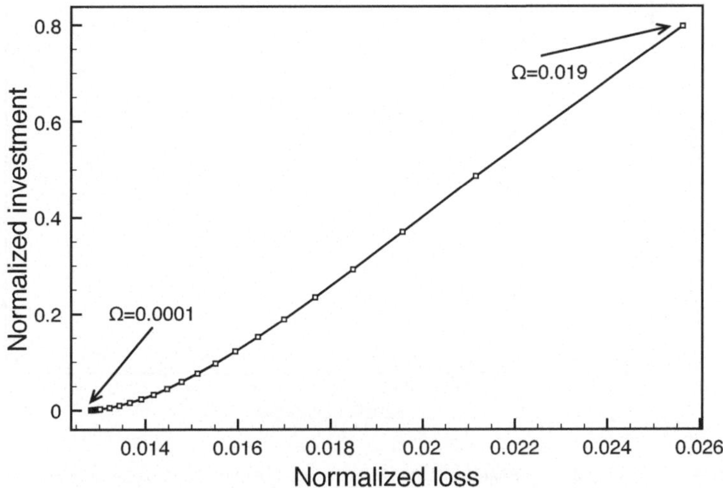

Fig. 2. Impact of the sanctioning factor on equilibrium

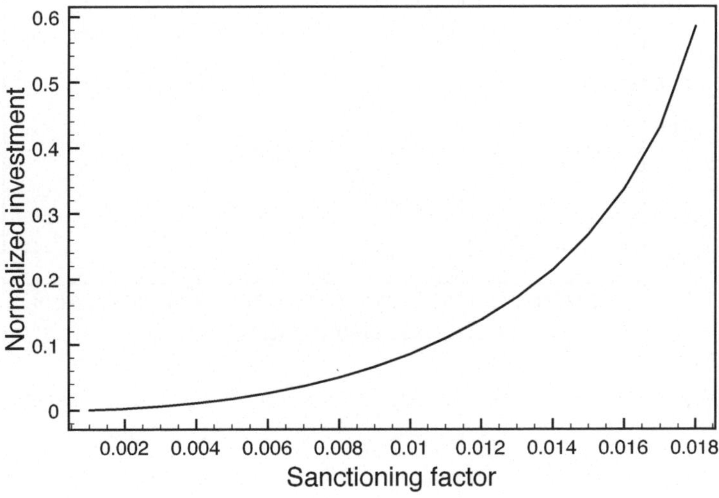

Fig. 3. Impact of the sanctioning factor on investments in security

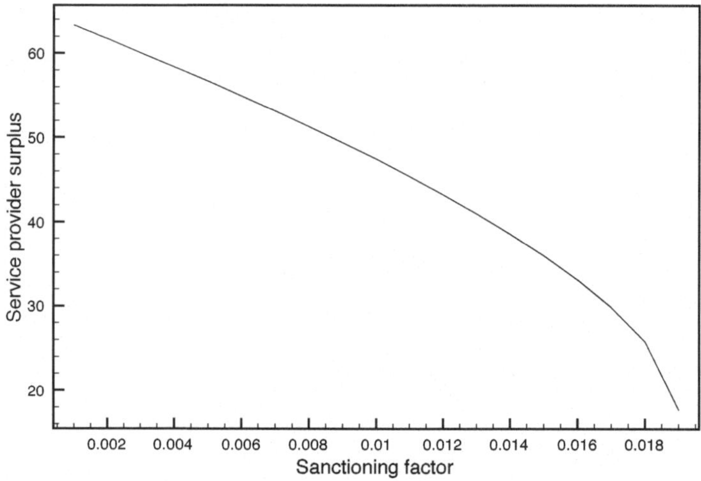

Fig. 4. Impact of the sanctioning factor on the service provider's surplus

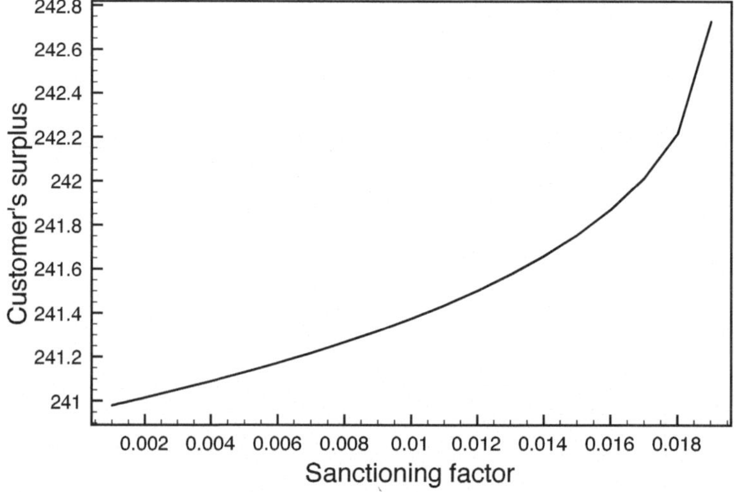

Fig. 5. Impact of the sanctioning factor on the customer's surplus

Finally, we consider the ultimate goal of the sanctioning policy: reducing the probability of data breaches. In our model, that probability is linked to the behaviour of both the service provider and the customer, as embodied by Equations (1), (2), and (3). We expect sanctions to reduce the data breach probability as a by-product of the spur to invest more in security. Actually, in Fig. 6 we see that the contribution to the data breach probability due to the service provider

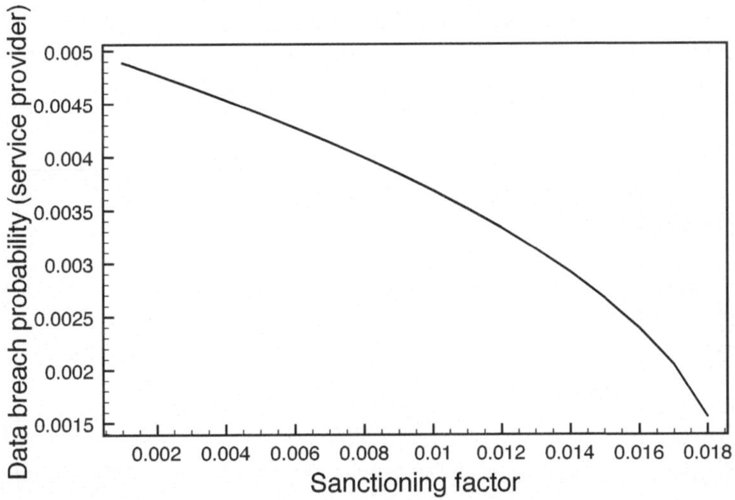

Fig. 6. Impact of sanctions on the the data breach probability ($P_{\text{db}}^{(s)}$)

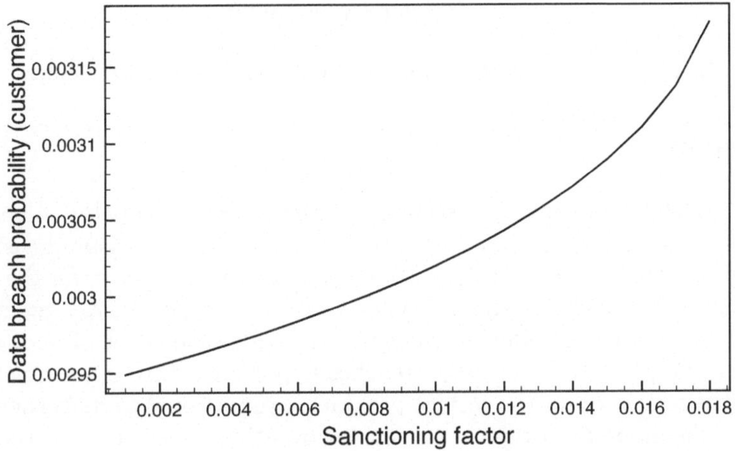

Fig. 7. Impact of sanctions on the data breach probability $P_{\text{db}}^{(c)}$

($P_{\text{db}}^{(s)}$) reduces by a factor of three over the range employed for the sanctioning factor. Hence, the sanctioning policy is effective in spurring a virtuous behaviour on the service provider's side.

On the other hand, the sanctioning policy inspires confidence in the customer, who is led to a more relaxed attitude when releasing its personal data. Its contribution to the overall data breach probability $P_{\text{db}}^{(c)}$ increases as sanctions grow, as shown in Fig. 7, though by a very small amount.

As security is concerned, sanctions have therefore an effect of different sign on the two players. The net effect is shown in Fig. 8; the introduction of sanction leads anyway to a reduction of the data breach probability.

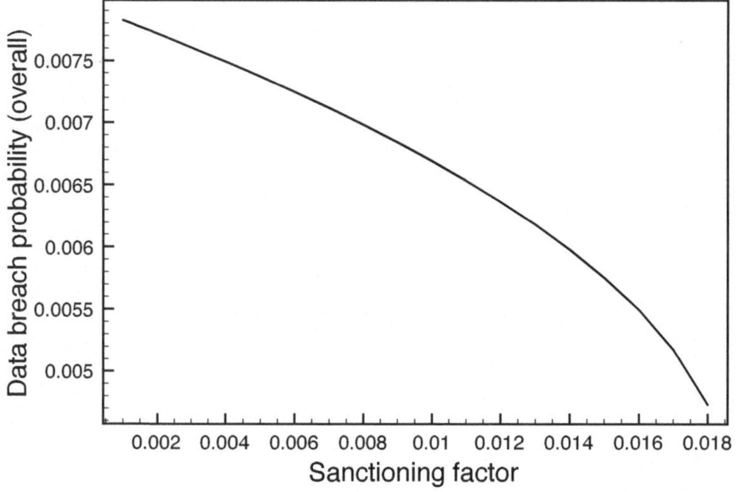

Fig. 8. Impact of sanctions on the overall data breach probability

6 Conclusions

We have modelled the impact of security on the interactions between customers and service providers as a game, where the strategic leverages employed by the two players are the amount of tolerable loss (considered as a proxy for the amount of information released) for the customer and the amount of investments in security for the service provider. In the game, the negative effect of poor security practice on the probability of data breaches is punished through a sanction imposed by the regulator on the service provider, proportional to its turnover. The solution of the game for a typical scenario shows that sanctions lead the service provider to increase its investments in security and reduce the probability of data breaches, while inducing a more relaxed attitude of the customer to release its personal data. While the latter effect may not be positive, the sanctioning approach proves to be effective as a means to promote a greater responsibility of the service provider in dealing with data breaches.

References

1. Verizon Risk Team. 2011 Data Breach Investigations Report. Technical report, Verizon (2011)
2. Verizon Risk Team. 2012 Data Breach Investigations Report. Technical report, Verizon (2011)

3. Hoffmann, L.: Risky business. Commun. ACM 54(11), 20–22 (2011)
4. Acquisti, A., John, L., Loewenstein, G.: What is privacy worth. In: Twenty First Workshop on Information Systems and Economics (WISE), pp. 14–15 (2009)
5. Gordon, L.A., Loeb, M.P.: The economics of information security investment. ACM Trans. Inf. Syst. Secur. 5(4), 438–457 (2002)
6. D'Acquisto, G., Flamini, M., Naldi, M.: A game-theoretic formulation of security investment decisions under ex-ante regulation. In: Gritzalis, D., Furnell, S., Theoharidou, M. (eds.) SEC 2012. IFIP AICT, vol. 376, pp. 412–423. Springer, Heidelberg (2012)
7. D'Acquisto, G., Flamini, M., Naldi, M.: Damage sharing may not be enough: An analysis of an ex-ante regulation policy for data breaches. In: Fischer-Hübner, S., Katsikas, S., Quirchmayr, G. (eds.) TrustBus 2012. LNCS, vol. 7449, pp. 149–160. Springer, Heidelberg (2012)
8. European Commission. Proposal for a Regulation of the European Parliament and of the Council on the protection of individuals with regard to the processing of personal data and on the free movement of such data (General Data Protection Regulation). COM (2012) 11 final (Co-decision procedure) (January 25, 2012)
9. The Practical Law Company. The PLC multi-jurisdictional guide to data protection (June 1, 2012), http://uk.practicallaw.com/5-518-8056#
10. Gibbons, R.: A Primer in Game Theory. Prentice-Hall (1992)
11. Javelin: 2011 identity fraud survey report. Technical report, Javelin Strategy (2011)
12. Osservatorio eCommerce B2c. B2c eCommerce in Italy (in Italian). Technical report, Netcomm-School of Management of Politecnico di Milano (2011)
13. Casaleggio Associati. E-commerce in Italy 2011 (in Italian). Technical report (April 2011), http://www.casaleggio.it/e-commerce/
14. AGCOM (Italian Communications Regulatory Authority). Annual report (2011), http://www.agcom.it

Efficient and Private Three-Party Publish/Subscribe

Giovanni Di Crescenzo[1], Jim Burns[1], Brian Coan[1], John Schultz[3], Jonathan Stanton[3], Simon Tsang[1], and Rebecca N. Wright[2]

[1] Applied Communication Sciences, NJ, USA
{gdicrescenzo,bcoan,stsang,jburns}@appcomsci.com
[2] Rutgers University, NJ, USA
rebecca.wright@rutgers.edu
[3] Spread Concepts, MD, USA
{jschultz,jonathan}@spreadconcepts.com

Abstract. We consider the problem of modeling and designing publish/subscribe protocols that safeguard the privacy of clients' subscriptions and of servers' publications while guaranteeing efficient latency in challenging scenarios (i.e., real-time publication, high data arrival rate, etc.). As general solutions from the theory of secure function evaluation protocols would not achieve satisfactory performance in these scenarios, we enrich the model with a third party (e.g., a cloud server). Our main result is a three-party publish/subscribe protocol suitable for practical applications in such scenarios because the publication phase uses only symmetric cryptography operations (a result believed not possible without the third party). At the cost of only a very small amount of privacy loss to the third party, and with no privacy loss to the publishing server or the clients, our protocol has very small publication latency, which we measured for large parameter ranges to be just a small constant factor worse than a publish/subscribe protocol guaranteeing no privacy.

1 Introduction

Publish/subscribe protocols address the problem of publishing data items to interested participants. In a simple formulation of the problem, a publish/subscribe protocol can be considered a protocol between multiple clients, each with its own interests, and multiple servers with data items and associated topics. The servers would like to distribute a data item to a client if there is a match between the data item's topics and the client's interests. These protocols come in many different formulations and variations, as well surveyed in [1], and find applications in a large number of areas. In many applications, however, privacy is a sensitive issue that may deter from the implementation or use of a publish/subscribe system. For instance, in finance, a publish/subscribe system that allows clients to receive quotes from a stock market server, while revealing the clients' interests, may not only impact clients' privacy but also significantly alter the stock market pricing process and overall integrity.

In this paper, we investigate the modeling and design of publish/subscribe protocols with satisfactory levels of both privacy and efficiency in a challenging scenario of high arrival-rate data and real-time publishing. First, we note that designing a private

J. Lopez, X. Huang, and R. Sandhu (Eds.): NSS 2013, LNCS 7873, pp. 278–292, 2013.

publish/subscribe protocol in the two-party model (i.e., with no third party) using general solutions from the area of secure function evaluation protocols (e.g., [2]) would not meet our efficiency targets, one reason being that such protocols require public-key cryptographic primitives [3], which are significantly more expensive than their private-key cryptography counterparts. Departing from the two-party model and considering a three-party model helps towards efficiency. General solutions in this three-party model (i.e., client, server and third party), such as [4–6], would likely still be not efficient in our scenario because of significant resource requirements (e.g., interaction and/or randomness and/or cryptographic operations) for each gate and each input bit of the circuit associated with the publish/subscribe predicate. Instead, we consider the problem of designing efficient three-party publish/subscribe protocols, possibly at the expense of allowing some minimal privacy leakage to the third party (but not to the server or the clients and not about actual interests, topics or data items).

Our Contribution and Solution Sketch. Under this problem formulation, we design a publish/subscribe protocol that satisfies a highly desirable set of requirements: publication correctness (i.e. clients obtain a data item if their subscription predicate is satisfied by their interests and the data item's topics), privacy against malicious adversaries (i.e., a malicious adversary corrupting any one of client, server or third party cannot extract any information about interests, topics or data items) and efficiency (i.e., the publication, which is the real-time part of the protocol, only requires a small number of private-key cryptography operations).

Our protocol is natural and simple, and uses pseudo-random functions [7] and symmetric encryption as cryptographic primitives (but could be implemented using only information-theoretic tools). Our main technical contribution is that of representing client's interests and data item's topics using two-layer cryptographic pseudonyms, requiring only a few symmetric cryptography operations per (interest,topic) pair, and then directly performing computation over such pseudonyms, by testing equality statements without need for cryptographic operations. The computation of the topic pseudonyms is performed by the server during publication (with a randomizer specific to the data item) and the computation of the interest pseudonyms is split into two phases: the 1st layer is computed by the client during subscription (with a client-specific randomizer) and the 2nd layer is computed by the third party during publication (and given the appropriate randomizer by the server). During publication, the third party can evaluate the client's subscription predicate using interest and topic pseudonyms, *without any further cryptographic operation*. A high-level description can be found in Figure 1.

We prove privacy properties of our protocol using a natural adaptation of the real/ideal security definition approach (frequently used in cryptography), and show that our protocol leaks no information to server and clients, and only minimal information to the third party: the structure of each client's subscription predicate (but not the client's interests) and how many (interest,topic) pairs match. We also describe measurements of the protocol's publication latency, which, for large and practical parameter ranges, is only a small (≤ 6) constant slower than a publish/subscribe system with no privacy.

Related Work. Although there are a number of interesting publish/subscribe protocols with various security or privacy properties (e.g., [8–14]), they do not our combined functionality and privacy requirements for a mixture of reasons, including: a differ-

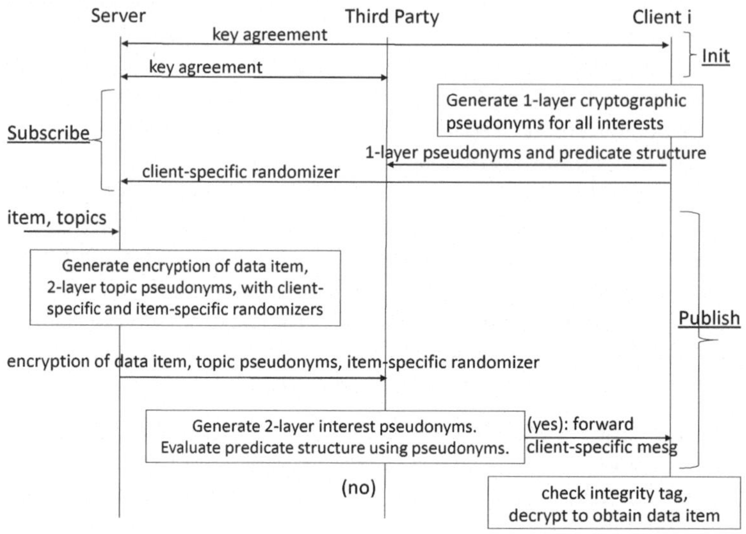

Fig. 1. Informal description of our publish/subscribe protocol

ent participant model (i.e., they typically consider entirely distributed models with no servers or third parties), and a different set of capabilities and functionalities (i.e., they typically target simple rules for content publication). Perhaps the closest solutions to our paper are [8, 12], which use essentially the same participant model as ours. To the best of our knowledge, no previous work presents rigorous modeling of security or privacy requirements for publish/subscribe systems or rigorous proofs that the proposed solutions meet any such requirements.

2 Models and Definitions

In this section we detail definitions of interest during our investigation of private publish/subscribe protocols: data, participant, topology, network and protocol models and publication correctness, privacy and efficiency requirements.

Data Model. We consider the following data objects or structures.

Data items. We represent the published data items as binary strings of length ℓ_d.

Dictionary and topics. To each data item, we associate d keyword tags, also denoted as *topics*, taken from a known set, called the *dictionary*, assumed, for simplicity, to be the set of all ℓ_t-bit strings. To each client, we associate c keyword tags, also denoted as *interests*, taken from the dictionary.

Subscription predicate: for $i = 1, \ldots, n$, a subscription from client C_i is formally represented as a boolean predicate, denoted as p_i, having equality statements of the type "$top_h = int_j$" as inputs, where top_h denotes the h-th topic associated with the current data item and int_j denotes the j-th interest associated with C_i, for $h \in \{1, \ldots, d\}$ and $j \in \{1, \ldots, c\}$. For each subscription predicate p_i, we define the associated *predicate structure* ps_i as the representation of the predicate obtained by replacing each equality statement "$top_h = int_j$" with the pair (h, j). That is, each input to ps_i keeps pointers to the same topic and the same interest as in p_i, but does not explicitly contains the topic and interest strings. (This allows parties to have some workable representation of the predicate, without revealing the actual strings representing interests or topics).

Data items and associated topics are assumed to be streamed (at possibly large speed) to the server. Generalizations to other data arrival scenarios are possible, but not further discussed in this paper. We have, for simplicity, defined length and number variables ℓ_d, ℓ_t, d, c as system parameters with value known to all parties; however, smaller values for specific clients or data items can be accommodated by simple padding techniques.

Participant and Network Model. We consider the following types of participants, all assumed to be *efficient* (i.e., running in probabilistic polynomial-time in a common security parameter, denoted in unary as 1^σ). A *client* is a party that submits subscription updates based on his interests and a specific subscription predicate; we assume there are n parties, denoted as $C_1, \ldots, C_n$; a generic client may also be denoted as C. The *server* is the party, denoted as S, processing submitted data items (and associated topics) and client interests to realize the publish/subscribe functionality. The *third party*, denoted as TP, helps clients and servers to carry out their functions.

Each client is assumed to be capable of communicating with both the server and the third party. All clients are capable to be communicating with each other, but are not required to do so in our proposed protocol. For simplicity, we consider a confidential and authenticated network (this assumption is without loss of generality as parties can use a security protocol like TLS) with no packet loss. Additionally, we also restrict to the scenario where server and third party are assumed to be always connected to the network; clients are allowed to temporarily disconnect from the network (and thus potentially not receive matching data items while disconnected).

Protocol Model. A publish/subscribe protocol includes the following subprotocols:

Init: S and TP may exchange messages with $C_1, \ldots, C_n$, to initialize their data structures and/or cryptographic keys. Formally, on input a security parameter 1^σ, protocol Init returns private outputs for all parties, denoted as $out_S^{in}, out_{TP}^{in}, \{out_C^{in} : \forall C\}$.

Subscribe: C submits his updated subscription (based on C's set of interests and a subscription predicate) to S (and possibly TP) who update their record of C's subscription. Formally, on input a security parameter 1^σ to all parties, and a set of interests $int_1, \ldots, int_c$ and a subscription predicate p_i as private inputs of client C_i, for some $i \in \{1, \ldots, n\}$ protocol $\mathsf{Subscribe}$ returns private outputs for all participants, denoted as $out_S^{su}, out_{TP}^{su}, \{out_C^{su} : \forall C\}$.

Publish: S distributes the data item to each client based on the item's topics and the clients' interests and subscription predicate, possibly in collaboration with TP. In terms of distribution strategy, this protocol follows the so-called 'push mode': as soon as a new data item arrives, it is processed by S and TP and eventually sent to the appropriate subset (or all) of the clients. Formally, on input a security parameter 1^σ to all parties, and a data item m and a set of topics $top_1, \ldots, top_d$ as private inputs of server S, protocol $\mathsf{Publish}$ returns a (possibly empty) data item m as private output for (possibly a subset of the) clients and additional private outputs for all participants, denoted as

$out_S^{pu}, out_{TP}^{pu}, \{out_C^{pu} : \forall C\}$. Generalizations to other distribution strategies, like the so-called 'pull mode', are possible but not further discussed in this paper.

Requirements. Let σ be a security parameter. A function over the set of natural numbers is *negligible* if for all sufficiently large $\sigma \in \mathcal{N}$, it is smaller than $1/p(\sigma)$, for any polynomial p. Two distribution ensembles $\{D_\sigma^0 : \sigma \in \mathcal{N}\}$ and $\{D_\sigma^1 : \sigma \in \mathcal{N}\}$ are *computationally indistinguishable* if for any efficient algorithm A, the quantity $|\text{Prob}[x \leftarrow D_\sigma^0 : A(x) = 1] - \text{Prob}[x \leftarrow D_\sigma^1 : A(x) = 1]|$ is negligible in σ (i.e., no efficient algorithm can distinguish if a random sample came from one distribution or the other). A participant's *view* in a protocol (or a set of protocols) is the distribution of the sequence of messages, inputs and internal random coins seen by the participant while running the protocol (or the set of protocols). We address publish/subscribe protocols that satisfy the following classes of requirements: *correctness* (i.e., correctness of publication of data items to clients with matching predicate and interests), *privacy* (i.e., privacy of data items, interests and topics against all protocol participants, and of the subscription predicate against the third party), and *efficiency* (i.e., minimal time, communication and round complexity). We will use the following requirements.

Publication Correctness: for each data item m and associated topics $top_1, \ldots, top_d$, each client C_i with subscription predicate p_i and interests $int_1, \ldots, int_c$, the probability ϵ that, after an execution of Init on input 1^σ, an execution of Subscribe on input $int_1, \ldots, int_c, p_i$, and an execution of Publish on input $m, top_1, \ldots, top_d$, one of the following two events happens, is negligible in σ: (a) predicate p_i is satisfied by interests $int_1, \ldots, int_c$ and topics $top_1, \ldots, top_d$ but $out_{C_i}^{pu} \neq m$; (b) predicate p_i is not satisfied by interests $int_1, \ldots, int_c$ and topics $top_1, \ldots, top_d$ but $out_{C_i}^{pu} = m$.

Privacy: We use a natural adaptation of the real/ideal and universal composability (see, e.g., [15]) security frameworks, which are commonly used in the cryptography literature. Assume an environment E that delivers private inputs and randomness to all parties, as needed in the publish/subscribe protocol lifetime. For any efficient (i.e., probabilistic polynomial time) adversary Adv corrupting one of the three party types (i.e., client C, server S or third party TP), there exists an efficient algorithm Sim (called the *simulator*), such that for any efficient environment algorithm E, Adv's view in the "real world" and Sim's output in the "ideal world" are is computationally indistinguishable to E, where these two worlds are defined as follows. In the *real world*, runs of the Init, Subscribe and Publish subprotocols are executed, while Adv acts as the corrupted party. In the *ideal world*, each run of the Init, Subscribe and Publish subprotocols is replaced with an 'ideal execution' that is specifically designed to only reveal some 'minimal information', in addition to system parameters, inputs and outputs based on the publish/subscribe funtionality and related condition (see, e.g.,[16]). Here, we choose this minimal information to be the predicate structure ps_i and the evaluation results of the 'interest = topic' equality statements inputs to ps_i for TP (and no additional information for C and S). Thus, we define these ideal executions of Init, Subscribe and Publish as follows:

1. Ideal-Init, on input security parameter 1^σ, returns all system parameters and an *ok* string to all participants.
2. Ideal-Subscribe, on input a predicate p and a sequence of c interests $int_1, \ldots, int_c$ from C, returns a predicate structure ps to TP and an *ok* string to C, S and TP.

3. Ideal-Publish, on input a data item m and a sequence of d topics $top_1, \ldots, top_d$ of known length from S, returns an *ok* string to S and the following for each client C_i: the data item m to C_i if predicate p_i is satisfied by C_i's interests and m's topics $top_1, \ldots, top_d$; and the following to TP: the predicate structure ps_i and bits b_{hj} denoting which pairs (h, j) input to ps_i satisfy "topic(h)=interest(j)" (or not).

Efficiency: The protocol's *latency* is measured as the time taken by a sequential execution of subprotocols Init, Subscribe, Publish (as a function of σ and other system parameters). The protocol's *communication complexity* (resp., *round complexity*) is defined as the length (resp., number) of the messages, as a function of σ and other system parameters, exchanged by C, S and TP during subprotocols Init, Subscribe, Publish. Even if we will mainly focus our analysis on publication latency, our design targets minimization of all the mentioned efficiency metrics.

Although we have focused our formalization on the correctness, privacy and efficiency properties, we note that our design has targeted a number of additional *security* properties, which are however obtained using well-known techniques. Specifically, properties like *confidentiality* of the communication between all participants, message *sender authentication*, message *receiver authentication*, and *communication integrity* protection, can be immediately obtained by using a security protocol like TLS. Other simple and inexpensive steps to add security properties (i.e., to prevent TP to modify the encryption of the data item received by S before transferring it to the appropriate clients) are directly discussed in the presentation of our protocol. In the rest of this document, we describe our protocol, prove that it satisfies the above correctness and privacy requirements, and show some runtime analysis of its efficiency properties.

3 A Simple and Efficient Publish/Subscribe Protocol

In this section we describe our publish/subscribe protocol. We start with a formal statement of the properties of our protocol, then discuss the known and new cryptographic primitives used in the protocol, and give an informal description, a detailed description, and a proof of the properties of our protocol.

Theorem 1. In the model of Section 3.1, there exists (constructively) a publish/subscribe protocol satisfying the following properties:
1. publication correctness with error negligible in security parameter σ;
2. privacy against adversary Adv corrupting S, under no unproven assumption;
3. privacy against adversary Adv corrupting C, under no unproven assumption;
4. privacy against adversary Adv corrupting TP, assuming that F is a family of pseudo-random functions and (KG,E,D) is a secure symmetric encryption scheme.

An important claim of our paper is that our protocol, in addition to satisfying Theorem 1, has desirable performance on all efficiency metrics: round complexity, communication complexity, subscription latency, and, especially, publication latency. Our testing experiments and results on the latter metric can be found in Section 3.2.

3.1 Cryptographic Primitives and Properties Used

Our publish/subscribe protocols use the following cryptographic primitives or tools or approaches: pseudo-random functions [7], symmetric encryption schemes, and 2-layer cryptographic pseudonyms.

Pseudo-random Functions and Secure Symmetric Encryption Schemes. A pseudo-random function F [7] maps a key $k \in \{0,1\}^\kappa$ and an input x to an output $y \in \{0,1\}^\ell$, for some values κ, ℓ suitably related to the security parameter σ, and with the property that to any efficient algorithm making queries to an oracle O, the case $O = F(k,\cdot)$, when k is randomly chosen, is computationally indistinguishable from the case $O = R(\cdot)$, for a random function R with input and output of the same length. For our results, F could be realized using standard cryptographic tools like block ciphers or cryptographic hashing.

A symmetric encryption scheme [17] is a triple (KG,E,D), where KG, the key generation algorithm, returns a key k on input a security parameter 1^κ; E, the encryption algorithm, returns a ciphertext c on input a key k and a message m; D, the decryption algorithm, returns a plaintext m' on input a key k and a ciphertext c. For our results, (KG,E,D) can be realized using textbook schemes based on block ciphers and pseudo-random functions, which satisfy well accepted security notions such as security in the sense of indistinguishability against chosen ciphertext attacks.

Two-Layer Cryptographic Pseudonyms. To protect the privacy of clients' interests and data item's topics, we use cryptographic pseudonyms (possibly involving repeated applications of F) so to later allow TP to perform computation directly on cryptographic pseudonyms, instead of the individual interest and topic bits (as done in other techniques like secure function evaluation). To enable equality checks between client interests and item topics by the third party, the interests and topics' pseudonyms will be defined using the same pseudonym function pF, consisting of repeated application of F, and defined as follows: on input x, function pF returns

$$F(k_{s,tp}, F(k_{s,c(i)}, x|r_i)|s),$$

where $k_{s,c(i)}$ is a key shared between S and C_i, $k_{s,tp}$ is a key shared between S and TP, r_i is a client specific randomizing nonce, and s is a data item specific randomizing nonce. Building on [18], cryptographic pseudonyms use keys shared by different parties and achieve the following: C can generate 1-layer interest pseudonyms, S can generate topic pseudonyms, TP can check whether an interest pseudonym is equal to a topic pseudonym, and leakage of both interests and topics to TP is prevented. Furthermore, the computation of key $k_{s,c(i)}$ is re-randomized at each execution of the Subscribe protocol and for each interest, using a random counter *ctr* and computing $k_{s,c(i),j} = F(k_{s,c(i)}, ctr+j)$, for $j = 1,\ldots,c$. We note that the function pF satisfies the following

Lemma 1. If F is a pseudo-random function the following holds: (1) if interest int_j and topic top_h are equal, then so are the associated interest pseudonym $pF(int_j)$ and topic pseudonym $pF(top_h)$; (2) if the interest int_j and topic top_h are distinct, then the associated interest pseudonym $pF(int_j)$ and topic pseudonym $pF(top_h)$ are computationally indistinguishable from two random and independent strings of the same length. (Hence, they are not different only with negligible probability).

Proof of Lemma. Part (1) of this fact follows from the fact that $pF(int_j)$ is computed from int_j in the same way as $pF(top_h)$ is computed from top_h (i.e., using a triple application of F, based on the same counter ctr, and the same randomizing nonces r_i, s, and the same keys $k_{tp,s}, k_{s,c(i),j}$). Part (2) of this fact follows by observing that when $int_j \neq top_h$, the function pF is pseudo-random (as so is F) and, when evaluated on two distinct inputs, returns two outputs that are computationally indistinguishable from two random strings of the same length. □

In our publish/subscribe protocol, TP can compute 2-layer interest pseudonyms, with help from client and server, and receive 2-layer topic pseudonyms from the server. Later, it can then evaluate the client's subscription predicate using interest and topic pseudonyms as input, without further cryptographic operations. By Lemma 1, this is equivalent, except with negligible probability, to evaluating the client's predicate p_i on input interests and topics, but without any leakage of information about interests or topics to any unintended parties. Depending on the result of the predicate evaluation, TP sends or does not send an encrypted version of the data item to the client, who decrypts it.

The privacy of interests and topics is guaranteed by the computation of cryptographic pseudonyms via pseudo-random functions. The privacy of the data item is guaranteed by use of encryption. We avoid TP to learn correlations among interests in the same subscription (e.g., if the same interest is used more than once) by using an independent key $k_{s,c(i),j}$, computed using a key $k_{s,c(i)}$ and a random counter ctr_i, to compute the pseudonym for each $j = 1, \ldots, c$. We avoid TP to learn correlations among interests in different subscriptions (e.g., if the same interest is used on two different subscriptions) by randomizing the pseudonym computation with random nonce r_i. We avoid TP to learn correlations among topics in different data items (e.g., if the same topic appears on two different data items) by randomizing the pseudonym computation with random nonce s. We achieve high efficiency on publication latency as the Publish subprotocol only requires highly efficient symmetric-key computations.

3.2 Detailed Description

We proceed with a formal description of our publish/subscribe protocol (see Figure 2 for a pictorial description, however omitting some steps for better clarity).

Preliminaries: This protocol assumes a point-to-point secure communication protocol such as TLS to be used for all exchanged communication, and suitable message headers including protocol name, subprotocol name, and unique session, sender and receiver ID's. While for simplicity of presentation, we always refer to a single client C in the description below, we note that in our multiple-client scenario, each client runs C's program described below (using independently chosen random strings), and the other parties repeat their program, described below, for each of the clients (again, using independently chosen random strings).

Init: Server S sets a key length parameter κ (e.g., $\kappa = 128$). Then S and each client C_i, for $i = 1, \ldots, n$, run a secure key-agreement protocol to jointly generate a random and independent key $k_{s,c(i)} \in \{0,1\}^\kappa$ (such a protocol can be built using standard cryptographic protocols [19] or even just requiring S to choose a key and send it to C_i).

Analogously, S and third party TP run a secure key-agreement protocol to jointly generate a random and independent key $k_{s,tp} \in \{0,1\}^{\kappa}$. As a result of these subprotocols, one symmetric key is shared by S and C_i but not by TP, and one key is shared by S and TP but not by any of $C_1, \ldots, C_n$. Moreover, these keys will actually be used as inputs to a pseudo-random function to generate, using standard techniques (e.g., a counter and a block cipher like AES), an arbitrarily large number of pseudo-random keys with the same property (i.e., being shared by only two of the parties).

Subscribe: Let C be a client with interests $int_1, \ldots, int_c$, and a subscription predicate p with predicate structure ps. In this operation, S, TP and client C_i, for some $i \in \{1, \ldots, n\}$, run the following instructions:

1. C_i uniformly and independently chooses a random nonce $r_i \in \{0,1\}^{\ell}$ and a random starting counter $ctr_i \in \{0,1\}^{\ell}$
2. For $j = 1, \ldots, c$, C_i computes pseudo-random key $k_{s,c(i),j} = F(k_{s,c(i)}, ctr_i + j)$ and 1-layer interest pseudonym $ip^i_{j,1} = F(k_{s,c(i),j}, (int_j | r_i))$
3. C_i sends the current subscription predicate structure ps_i and 1-layer pseudonyms $(ip^i_{1,1}, \ldots, ip^i_{c,1})$ to TP
4. C_i sends (r_i, ctr_i) to S
5. TP replaces C_i's 1-layer interest pseudonyms with the just received $(ip^i_{1,1}, \ldots, ip^i_{c,1})$
6. TP replaces C_i's subscription predicate structure with the just received ps_i
7. S replaces C_i's random nonce and counter with the just received (r_i, ctr_i)

Publish: We assume that S receives a new data item m, with topics $top_1, \ldots, top_d$. In this operation, involving S, TP and clients $C_1, \ldots, C_n$, the parties run the following instructions:

1. S uniformly and independently chooses a nonce $s \in \{0,1\}^{\ell}$
2. S computes data item ciphertext $M = E(k, m)$ and $K_i = E(k_{s,c(i)}, k)$, for $i = 1, \ldots, n$
3. For $j = 1, \ldots, c$ and $i = 1, \ldots, n$,
   S computes $k_{s,c(i),j} = F(k_{s,c(i)}, ctr_i + j)$, using last ctr_i received from C_i
4. For each $h = 1, \ldots, d$, $j = 1, \ldots, c$ and $i = 1, \ldots, n$,
   S computes 1-layer topic pseudonym $tp^i_{h,j,1}$ as $= F(k_{s,c(i),j}, top_h | r_i))$
   S computes 2-layer topic pseudonym $tp^i_{h,j,2}$ as $= F(k_{s,tp}, (tp^i_{h,j,1} | s))$
5. S computes tags $tag_i = F(k_{s,c(i)}, M | K_i)$, for $i = 1, \ldots, n$
6. S sends $(M, s, \{tp^i_{h,j,2} : h, j, i\}, \{(K_i, tag_i) : i = 1, \ldots, n\})$ to TP
7. For $i = 1, \ldots, n$,
   for $j = 1, \ldots, c$,
      TP computes 2-layer interest pseudonyms $ip^i_{j,2} = F(k_{s,tp}, (ip^i_{j,1} | s))$
   TP evaluates ps_i on input $\{tp^i_{h,j,2} : h, j, i\}$ and $\{ip^i_{j,2} : j = 1, \ldots, c\}$
   if ps_i evaluates to 1, then TP sends (M, K_i, tag_i) to C_i
   if C_i receives a message (M, K_i, tag_i),
      if $tag_i \neq F(k_{s,c(i)}, M | K_i)$ then C_i returns: "error" and halts.
         else C_i computes $k = D(k_{s,c(i)}, K_i)$, $m = D(k, M)$ and returns: m.

In the rest of this section we discuss why our protocol satisfies publication correctness, privacy and efficiency properties, as defined in Section 2.

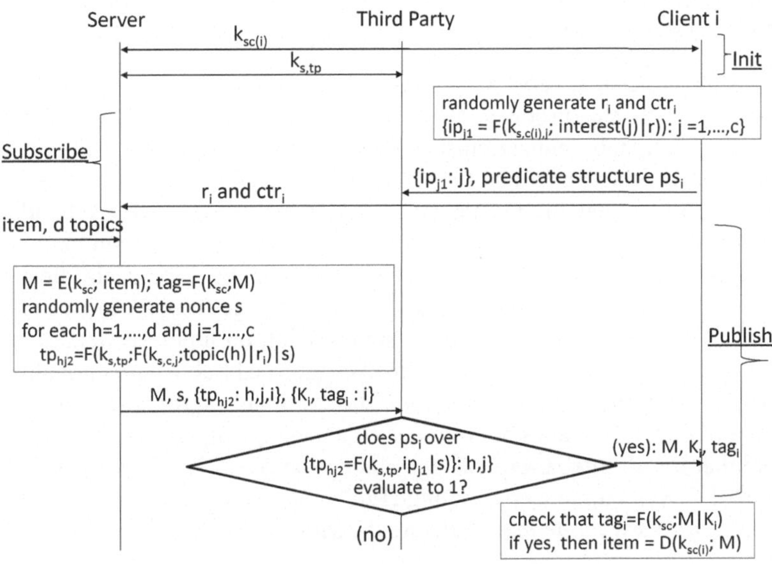

Fig. 2. Our publish/subscribe Protocol

3.3 Properties: Correctness, Privacy and Efficiency

Publication Correctness. We observe that a client C_i receives data item m from TP if the subscription predicate structure ps_i returns 1 when its input equality statements are evaluated over the interest and topic pseudonyms (rather than the interests and topics themselves). However, we note that ps_i returns the same value, except with negligible probability, regardless of whether the equality statements are evaluated over the interest/topic pseudonyms or over the interests/topics. This latter claim, implying the publication correctness property, is implied by observing that there is a polynomial number of interests and topics and by an application of Lemma 1.

Privacy. We achieve privacy against a malicious adversary Adv that corrupts any one of the participants; i.e., either S, or TP, or a client C_i. The protocol only leaks values of global parameter (i.e., length parameters) and the intended protocol functionality outputs (i.e., the data items to the matching clients) to clients or server. To the third party, the protocol only leaks the following: the client's predicate structure, but not the interests, (here, we note that it is not unreasonable for a practical system to have the client's predicate structure as a known protocol parameter), and the bits b_{hj} denoting whether the j-th interest in a client's subscription is equal to the h-th topic associated with a data item (without revealing anything else about interests, topics or data items). Actually, our proof extends to malicious adversaries that corrupts all clients or a subset of them. We divide the formal proof into 3 cases, depending on whether Adv is corrupting S, TP, or a client C_i. In all cases, the simulation of the Init protocol directly follows from the simulation properties of the key agreement protocol used. Thus, we only focus on the Subscribe and Publish subprotocols. Let $m(S, TP)$ denote the message $(M, s, \{tp^i_{h,j,2} : h, j, i\}, \{(K_i, tag_i) : i = 1, \ldots, n\})$ sent from S to TP.

Case Adv=S: Assume an adversary, denoted as Adv, corrupts S. For any such Adv, we show a simulator Sim that produces a view for Adv in the ideal world (while posing as S) that is computationally indistinguishable from Adv's view in the real world (while posing as S), during the execution of the Init, Subscribe and Publish protocols.

To simulate Adv's view in the Subscribe subprotocol, Sim invokes the ideal Subscribe functionality, which only returns an ok string to S, and then randomly chooses a randomizing nonce r_i and a random starting counter ctr_i for each client C_i, for $i = 1, \ldots, n$. Then Sim simulates the subscription message from C_i to S as (r_i, ctr_i).

To simulate Adv's view in the Publish subprotocol, on input the data item m and the associated topics $top_1, \ldots, top_d$, Sim invokes the ideal Publish functionality, which only returns an ok string to S, and then runs Adv on input $m, top_1, \ldots, top_d$ to obtain a message $m(S, TP)$. If S does not return such a message, then Sim simply halts.

We note that for all three protocols, the simulation from Sim is perfect, in that the distribution of Sim's output (representing Adv's view in the ideal world) and the distribution of Adv's view in the real world are the same.

Case Adv=TP: Assume an efficient malicious adversary, denoted as Adv, corrupts TP. For any such Adv, we show a simulator Sim that produces a view for Adv in the ideal world (while posing as TP) that is computationally indistinguishable from Adv's view in the real world (while posing as TP), during the execution of the Init, Subscribe and Publish protocols.

To simulate Adv's view in the Subscribe subprotocol, Sim invokes the ideal Subscribe functionality, which returns client C_i's subscription predicate structure ps_i to TP, and sends ps_i to Adv. Moreover, Sim randomly and independently chooses values $ip^{i,\cdot}_{j,1} \in \{0, 1\}^\ell$, for $j = 1, \ldots, c$, and sends them to Adv.

Finally, to simulate Adv's view in the Publish subprotocol, Sim invokes the ideal Publish functionality, which returns to TP bits b^i_{hj} denoting whether equality "topic(h) = interest(j)" in predicate p_i is satisfied or not. Then, to simulate message $m(S, TP)$, Sim simulates each value in this message's tuple either as a suitable encryption of a random value of the appropriate length (which is known as it is a protocol parameter) or as the output of the appropriate length (also known as a protocol parameter) of a pseudo-random evaluation, as follows. First of all, Sim randomly chooses keys $k', s', k'_{s,c(1)}, \ldots, k'_{s,c(n)}$, a data item m', and hash tags $tag'_1, \ldots, tag'_n$, and computes an encryption $M' = E(k', m')$ and encryptions $K'_i = E(k'_{s,c(i)}, k')$, for $i = 1, \ldots, n$. Furthermore, to simulate the topic pseudonyms, Sim considers each equation "topic(h)=interest(j)" in predicate structure ps_i, for each $i = 1, \ldots, n$. If $b^i_{hj} = 0$ (i.e., the equation does not hold), then Sim uniformly chooses a value $tp^{i,\cdot}_{h,j,2}$. If $b^i_{hj} = 1$ (i.e., the equation holds), then Sim sets value $tp^{i,\cdot}_{h,j,2} = ip^{i,\cdot}_{j,2} = F(k_{s,tp}, (ip^{i,\cdot}_{h,j,1} | s))$. Finally, Sim can simulates $m(S, TP)$ as $(M', s', \{tp^{i,\cdot}_{h,j,2} : h, j, i\}, \{(K'_i, tag'_i) : i = 1, \ldots, n\})$ and the message by TP to clients by simply running Adv's program.

We now show that Sim's output (i.e., Adv's view in the ideal world) and Adv's view in the real world are computationally indistinguishable. With respect to the simulation of subprotocols Subscribe and Publish, we can prove that the simulation is computationally indistinguishable from Adv's view in the real world, as follows. First, we observe that the only differences between the two views are the following:

1. the value M, an encryption of data item m, in Adv's view vs. the value M', an encryption of a random value of the same length, in Sim's output: this difference is proved to be computationally indistinguishable by using the security property of the used symmetric encryption scheme;
2. the values $tag_1, \ldots, tag_n$, where tag_i is a MAC tag of (M, K_i), for $i = 1, \ldots, n$, in Adv's view vs. the randomly chosen values $tag'_1, \ldots, tag'_n$ in Sim's output: this difference is proved to be computationally indistinguishable by using the pseudo-randomness property of the used function F;
3. the 1-layer interest pseudonyms $ip^i_{j,1}$ in Adv's view vs. the randomly chosen values $ip^{i,\cdot}_{j,1}$ in Sim's output: this difference is proved to be computationally indistinguishable by using the pseudo-randomness property of the used function F;
4. conditioned on the interest pseudonyms, the topic pseudonyms $tp^i_{h,j,2}$ in Adv's view vs. the values $tp^{i,\cdot}_{h,j,2}$ in Sim's output: these values are equally distributed when $b^i_{hj} = 1$ (i.e., the equation holds) since they are computed in the same way in both spaces, and are proved to be computationally indistinguishable when $b^i_{hj} = 1$ (i.e., the equation does not hold) by using the pseudo-randomness property of F.

We then observe that by combining the above observations and a standard hybrid argument [17], we can prove that the entire Sim's output and the entire Adv's view in the real world are computationally indistinguishable, assuming the pseudo-randomness property of F and the security of the symmetric encryption scheme used.

Case Adv=C: Assume an adversary, denoted as Adv, corrupts a client C_i. For any such Adv, we show a simulator Sim that produces a view for Adv in the ideal world (while posing as C_i) that is computationally indistinguishable from Adv's view in the real world (while posing as C_i), during the execution of the Init, Subscribe and Publish protocols. To simulate the Subscribe subprotocol, given as input interests $int_1, \ldots, int_c$ and predicate p_i, Sim invokes the ideal Subscribe functionality, which only returns an ok string to C_i, and invokes C to obtain the messages for TP and S. Finally, to simulate the Publish subprotocol, Sim invokes the ideal Publish functionality, possibly obtaining (or not) data item m and topics $top_1, \ldots, top_d$ as output for C_i, depending on whether the predicate p_i is satisfied by topics $top_1, \ldots, top_d$ and interests $int_1, \ldots, int_c$ or not. In the former case, Sim has to simulate the message M, K_i, tag_i from TP and can use data item m to do that perfectly, as follows. Sim computes $M' = E(k_{s,c(i),m})$, randomly chooses key $k' \in \{0,1\}^\kappa$, and computes $K'_i = E(k_{s,c(i)}, k')$ and $tag'_i = F(k_{s,c(i)}, (M'|K'_i))$. By inspection, we see that the simulation of subprotocol Init is perfect, in that the distribution of Sim's output and the distribution of Adv's view in the real world are the same.

Efficiency. While it is easy to verify that our protocol is very efficient on the communication complexity, round complexity and subscription latency metrics, it is of special interest to evaluate the publication latency metric, under varying parameter values. We implemented both our protocol, called P1, and a publish/subscribe protocol, called P0, that performs no additional cryptographic operation, other than using the TLS protocol on all messages between parties. The testing was done on a collection of 6 Dell PowerEdge 1950 processors and one Dell PowerEdge 2950 processor. We divided clients in groups of size 25 each, and each group was run on each of 4 PowerEdge 1950 processors. The server was run on a dedicated 1950 processor, the third party was run on dedicated 1950 processor, and the testing control was run on the 2950 processor. All initialization, subscription, and publication traffic was run over a dedicated gigabit Ethernet LAN. Testing control and collection of timing measurement traffic was isolated on a separate dedicated gigabit Ethernet LAN.

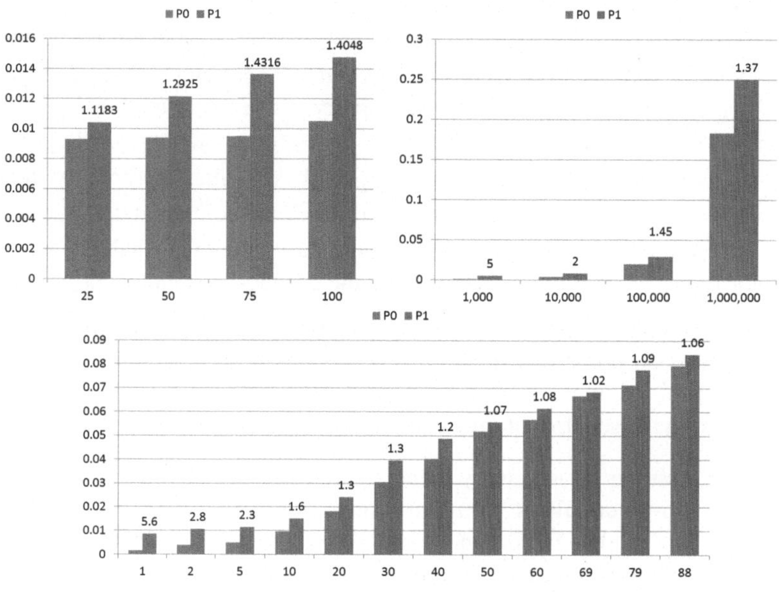

Fig. 3. Publication Latency Measurements for P1 and P0

We compared P1 and P0 under varying values for one of the following parameters: the total number of clients, the length of the data item and the number of matching clients. The initial parameter setting was: 100 clients, 10 matching clients per publication, 10 interests, 10 topics, and 1 publication of a 10K data item per second, where the matching predicate is the OR of all possible equalities between an interest and a topic. (We restricted to this predicate as in our protocol more complex predicates require no additional cryptographic operation other than TLS processing.) Under this setting, in Figure 3, the top left chart reports the max latency vs the number of clients when the latter varies from 25 to 100; the top right chart reports the max latency vs the size of the data item varying from 1K to 1M; the bottom chart reports the max latency vs the number of matching clients varying from 1 to 88. The labels on P1 columns indicate the ratio of the P1 latency to the P0 latency. In all three cases, the P1 latency is at most a small (1.5, 5, and 6, respectively) constant worse than the latency in P0 and scales well as the parameter increases.

Acknowledgements. This work was supported by the Intelligence Advanced Research Projects Activity (IARPA) via Department of Interior National Business Center (DoI/NBC) contract number D12PC00520. The U.S. Government is authorized to reproduce and distribute reprints for Governmental purposes notwithstanding any copyright annotation hereon. Disclaimer: The views and conclusions contained herein are those of the authors and should not be interpreted as necessarily representing the official policies or endorsements, either expressed or implied, of IARPA, DoI/NBC, or the U.S. Government.

References

1. Eugster, P.T., Felber, P., Guerraoui, R., Kermarrec, A.M.: The many faces of publish/subscribe. ACM Comput. Surv. 35(2), 114–131 (2003)
2. Yao, A.C.C.: How to generate and exchange secrets (extended abstract). In: FOCS, pp. 162–167 (1986)
3. Impagliazzo, R., Rudich, S.: Limits on the provable consequences of one-way permutations. In: STOC, pp. 44–61 (1989)
4. Goldreich, O., Micali, S., Wigderson, A.: How to play any mental game or a completeness theorem for protocols with honest majority. In: STOC, pp. 218–229 (1987)
5. Rabin, T., Ben-Or, M.: Verifiable secret sharing and multiparty protocols with honest majority (extended abstract). In: STOC, pp. 73–85 (1989)
6. Feige, U., Kilian, J., Naor, M.: A minimal model for secure computation (extended abstract). In: STOC, pp. 554–563 (1994)
7. Goldreich, O., Goldwasser, S., Micali, S.: How to construct random functions. J. ACM 33(4), 792–807 (1986)
8. Raiciu, C., Rosenblum, D.S.: Enabling confidentiality in content-based publish/subscribe infrastructures. In: SecureComm, pp. 1–11 (2006)
9. Minami, K., Lee, A.J., Winslett, M., Borisov, N.: Secure aggregation in a publish-subscribe system. In: WPES, pp. 95–104 (2008)
10. Shikfa, A., Önen, M., Molva, R.: Privacy-preserving content-based publish/subscribe networks. In: Gritzalis, D., Lopez, J. (eds.) SEC 2009. IFIP AICT, vol. 297, pp. 270–282. Springer, Heidelberg (2009)
11. Tariq, M.A., Koldehofe, B., Altaweel, A., Rothermel, K.: Providing basic security mechanisms in broker-less publish/subscribe systems. In: DEBS, pp. 38–49 (2010)
12. Choi, S., Ghinita, G., Bertino, E.: A privacy-enhancing content-based publish/subscribe system using scalar product preserving transformations. In: Bringas, P.G., Hameurlain, A., Quirchmayr, G. (eds.) DEXA 2010, Part I. LNCS, vol. 6261, pp. 368–384. Springer, Heidelberg (2010)
13. Ion, M., Russello, G., Crispo, B.: Supporting publication and subscription confidentiality in pub/sub networks. In: Jajodia, S., Zhou, J. (eds.) SecureComm 2010. LNICST, vol. 50, pp. 272–289. Springer, Heidelberg (2010)
14. Pal, P., Lauer, G., Khoury, J., Hoff, N., Loyall, J.: P3S: A privacy preserving publish-subscribe middleware. In: Narasimhan, P., Triantafillou, P. (eds.) Middleware 2012. LNCS, vol. 7662, pp. 476–495. Springer, Heidelberg (2012)
15. Canetti, R.: Universally composable security: A new paradigm for cryptographic protocols. In: FOCS, pp. 136–145 (2001)
16. Di Crescenzo, G., Ostrovsky, R., Rajagopalan, S.: Conditional oblivious transfer and timed-release encryption. In: Stern, J. (ed.) EUROCRYPT 1999. LNCS, vol. 1592, pp. 74–89. Springer, Heidelberg (1999)

17. Goldwasser, S., Micali, S.: Probabilistic encryption. J. Comput. Syst. Sci. 28(2), 270–299 (1984)
18. Brickell, E., Di Crescenzo, G., Frankel, Y.: Sharing block ciphers. In: Clark, A., Boyd, C., Dawson, E.P. (eds.) ACISP 2000. LNCS, vol. 1841, pp. 457–470. Springer, Heidelberg (2000)
19. Diffie, W., Hellman, M.E.: New directions in cryptography. IEEE Transactions on Information Theory 22(6), 644–654 (1976)

Marlin: A Fine Grained Randomization Approach to Defend against ROP Attacks

Aditi Gupta[1], Sam Kerr[1], Michael S. Kirkpatrick[2], and Elisa Bertino[1]

[1] Purdue University, West Lafayette IN, USA
{aditi,stkerr,bertino}@purdue.edu
[2] James Madison University, Harrisonburg VA, USA
kirkpams@jmu.edu

Abstract. Code-reuse attacks, such as return-oriented programming (ROP), bypass defenses against code injection by repurposing existing executable code toward a malicious end. A common feature of these attacks is the reliance on the knowledge of the layout of the executable code. We propose a fine grained randomization based approach that modifies the layout of executable code and hinders code-reuse attack. Our solution, *Marlin*, randomizes the internal structure of the executable code, thereby denying the attacker the necessary *a priori* knowledge of instruction addresses for constructing the desired exploit payload. Our approach can be applied to any ELF binary and every execution of this binary uses a different randomization. Our work shows that such an approach is feasible and significantly increases the level of security against code-reuse based attacks.

Keywords: Return-oriented programming, Security, Integrity, Malware.

1 Introduction

The evolution of software exploits, such as buffer overflows and string format vulnerabilities, shows a pattern of an arms race. On one side, stack smashing attacks gave way to heap-based code injection. Defenders countered this with canary words, instruction set randomization, base address randomization, and related techniques [9,10,28,1]. Attackers found ways to bypass these defenses [34,33] and execute their injected malicious code. Defenders then responded with Write-or-Execute ($W \oplus X$), which prevents the execution of injected code. To get around $W \oplus X$, return-into-*libc* and return-oriented programming (ROP) [31,5] attacks were launched that leverage *existing* code rather than injecting their own. In the former case, a corrupted return address is used to jump to a *libc* function, such as `system`. In the latter, the attacker strings together *gadgets* (small sequences of binary instructions) in the existing executable code to perform arbitrary computation.

As these attacks rely on knowing the location of code in the executable and libraries, the intuitive solution is to randomize process memory images. In basic address space layout randomization (ASLR), only the start address of the code

J. Lopez, X. Huang, and R. Sandhu (Eds.): NSS 2013, LNCS 7873, pp. 293–306, 2013.

segment is randomized. However, 32-bit machines provide insufficient entropy, as there are only 2^{16} possible starting addresses, making the system vulnerable to brute-force [32]. While upgrading to 64-bit helps, it is not a universal solution. Specifically, 32-bit (and smaller) architectures will continue to be used as legacy systems and in the area of embedded systems. Furthermore, recent work has demonstrated that an attacker can use information leakage to discover the randomization parameters, thus eliminating the defensive benefits of upgrading [30].

Our approach is to revisit the granularity at which randomization is performed. Rather than randomizing only a single parameter, our technique (*Marlin*) breaks an application binary into function blocks and shuffles them. This significantly increases the entropy of the system; for instance, an application with 500 functions allows for $500! \approx 2^{3767}$ permutations, making brute-force infeasible. Our approach, which can be applied to any ELF binary without requiring source code, is performed transparently at load time to ensure every execution instance is unique. Finally, by paying a (quite reasonable) performance cost up front, Marlin avoids the overhead of on-going monitoring of critical data, such as return addresses, which other systems impose.

We are not the only researchers to have investigated software diversity as ROP attack mitigation. While Section 2.2 offers a detailed comparison, existing approaches suffer from one or more of the following limitations. First, diversification is not done frequently enough. Second, source code or other additional information is required. Third, the granularity of randomization is insufficient, leaving large code chunks unrandomized. Fourth, on-going monitoring imposes significant run-time overhead by introducing additional data structures. Marlin provides strong and efficient defense while addressing these limitations.

After surveying code-reuse attacks and defenses in Section 2, we describe the design of Marlin in Section 3. Section 4 discusses our prototype, which consists of an off-line tool to randomize the binary image of an executable. Section 5 shows the results of various evaluation experiments. Our evaluation of the time to randomize compiled binaries of the SPEC CPU2006 benchmark suite shows the average performance penalty is reasonable. Section 6 highlights both the merits and limitations of Marlin, and we conclude in Section 7.

2 Background and Related Work

The focus of our work is on ROP attacks, which are a special case of code-reuse attacks that leverage existing code in the application binary to execute arbitrary instructions. In this section, we start with a brief summary of these attack techniques and existing defenses. We then summarize critical factors of code-reuse attacks and define our threat model.

2.1 Return-oriented Programming

Return-oriented programming (ROP) is an exploit technique that has evolved from stack-based buffer overflows. In ROP exploits, an attacker crafts a sequence of *gadgets* that are present in existing code to perform arbitrary computation. A gadget is a small sequence of binary code that ends in a `ret` instruction. By carefully crafting a sequence of addresses on the software stack, an attacker can manipulate the `ret` instruction semantics to jump to arbitrary addresses that correspond to the beginning of gadgets. Doing so allows the attacker to perform arbitrary computation. These techniques work in both word-aligned architectures like RISC [4] and unaligned CISC architectures [31]. ROP techniques can be used to create rootkits [19], can inject code into Harvard architectures [16], and have been used to perform privilege escalation in Android [12]. Initiating a ROP attack is made even easier by the availability of architecture-independent algorithms to automate gadget creation [15]. Additionally, the same technique of stringing together gadgets has been used to manipulate other instructions, such as `jmp` and their variants [5,8,3].

2.2 Defenses

Address obfuscation [1], ASLR (*e.g.,* PaX [28]), and Instruction Set Randomization (ISR) aim to defend against code-reuse attacks by introducing randomness into processes' memory images. They randomize with coarse granularity and are subject to brute force attacks [33,32], especially on 32-bit architectures. While upgrading to 64-bit increases the randomization, information leakage can allow an attacker to bypass the defense [30]. Furthermore, for some settings (*e.g.,* embedded devices), upgrading to 64-bit is simply not feasible. While [1] suggests randomizing function blocks as a potential technique (which we employ in Marlin), no further implementation, discussion, or evaluation was attempted.

Researchers have also considered dynamic monitoring defenses. For instance, DROP [6] dynamically compares the execution of `ret` instructions with statistically defined normal program behavior. DynIMA [13] combines TPM memory measurement capabilities with dynamic taint analysis to monitor process integrity. Other approaches store sensitive data (*e.g.,* return addresses) in a protected shadow stack [14,7]. These techniques impose a non-zero performance cost for every checked instruction, yielding non-trivial cumulative overhead. In contrast, Marlin imposes a one-time cost at process start-up and no additional on-going penalty.

Other approaches introduce randomness at compile time. For instance, compilers can be modified to generate code without `ret` instructions [25,22]. These mechanisms, however, fail to handle attacks leveraging `jmp` instructions; furthermore, if a new type of gadget is proposed, the compiler would have to be modified yet again. Alternatively, app store-based diversification [17] and linkage techniques for performance optimization [23,24] can be applied to produce unique executables. However, these techniques do not stop an attacker with a known singular target image, do not help legacy systems, and, in the case of the former, rely on centralized control of software deployment. In contrast, proactive obfuscation [29] applies a semantics-preserving transformation to compiled server applications. Marlin is similar to this work in spirit, but the former aimed at diversifying replicas in distributed systems; as such, their threat model and techniques differed from our own.

Other techniques similar to Marlin have also been proposed to randomize processes. ASLP [21] rewrites the ELF headers and shuffles sections, functions, and variables. As such, ASLP requires relocation information (or recompilation of source code), as well as user input. In contrast, as Marlin randomizes function blocks within the text segment, this additional information is not necessary. Bhatkar *et al.* [2] associates a pointer with every function and adds a layer of indirection to every function call. Unlike Marlin, the function reordering is not done at load time. ILR [18] randomizes the location of every instruction and uses a process-level virtual machine, which imposes a significant on-going performance cost, to find the called code. Pappas *et al.* [26] use in-place randomization that probabilistically breaks 80% of the useful gadgets. However, by shuffling the entire memory image, Marlin provides stronger guarantees, probabilistically breaking all sequences. Furthermore, [18] and [26] do not randomize the binary at *every execution*, which Marlin does. XIFER [11] and STIR [35] defend against ROP by randomizing at the basic block granularity, rather than at the function level. The finer granularity incurs more overhead than Marlin; however, we show that function-level randomization is sufficient to defeat brute force attacks, and the additional granularity is unnecessary.

2.3 Enabling Factors for Code-Reuse Attacks

Based on our survey of ROP attacks and defenses, we have identified a number of distinct characteristics and requirements for a successful exploit. We argue that a defensive technique that undermines these invariants will present a robust protection mechanism against these threats. The fundamental assumption and enabling factor for such attacks is as follows:

The relative offsets of instructions within the application's code are constant. That is, if an attacker knows any symbol's address in the application code, then the location of all gadgets and symbols in application's codebase is deterministic.

2.4 Threat Model

The proposed defense, *Marlin*, is aimed to protect a vulnerable application against code reuse attacks, such as ROP attacks. This application may have a buffer overflow vulnerability that can be leveraged by an attacker to inject the exploit payload. The system is assumed to be protected using $W \oplus X$ policy and the attacker can not inject arbitrary executable code in the stack or the heap. The attacker is assumed to have access to the target binary that has not yet undergone Marlin processing. The attacker is also assumed to be aware of the functionality of Marlin. However, the attacker cannot examine the memory dump of the running process and is unaware of how exactly the code is randomized for the currently executing process image. Our approach protects against both remote and local exploits as long as the attacker is not able to examine the memory of the target process.

1. PARSE SYMBOLS

```
0000 <f1>:
  0000: 55                push %ebp
  0001: e8 00 00 00 08    call 0x0008
  0007: c3                ret
0008 <f2>: ....
0010 <f3>: ....
```

Symbol	Address
f1	0x0
f2	0x8
f3	0x10

2. SHUFFLE FUNCTIONS

```
0000 <f2>: ....
0008 <f1>:
  0008: 55                push %ebp
  0009: e8 00 00 00 08    call 0x0010
  000e: c3                ret
0010 <f3>: ....
```

Symbol	Address
f1	0x8
f2	0x0
f3	0x10

3. JUMP PATCHING

```
0000 <f2>: ....
0008 <f1>:
  0008: 55                push %ebp
  0009: e8 ff ff ff f8    call 0x0000
  000e: c3                ret
0010 <f3>: ....
```

Symbol	Address
f1	0x8
f2	0x0
f3	0x10

Fig. 1. Processing steps in Marlin

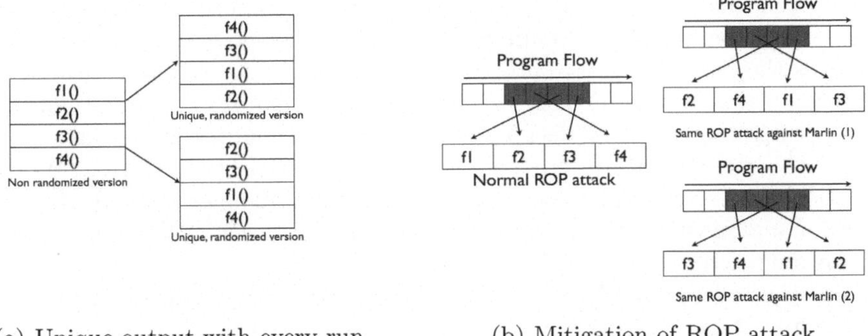

(a) Unique output with every run

(b) Mitigation of ROP attack

Fig. 2. Effect of function block randomization

3 Marlin

Code-reuse attacks make certain assumptions (as discussed in section 2.3) about the address layout of the target application's executable code and shared libraries. Marlin's randomization technique aims at breaking these assumptions by shuffling the function blocks in the binary's `.text` section with *every* execution of this binary. This significantly increases the difficulty of such attacks since the attacker would need to guess the exact permutation being used by the current process image. This shuffling is performed at the granularity of function blocks. Marlin randomizes the target application just before the control is passed over to this application for execution. Thus, every execution of the program results in a different process memory image as illustrated in Figure 2(a). Figure 2(b) illustrates how shuffling the code results in a sequence of gadgets that is not intended by the attacker. We now present Marlin technique in detail.

3.1 Preprocessing Phase

As mentioned above, Marlin randomizes the application binary at the granularity of function blocks. This requires identifying the function blocks in the application binary. Preprocessing phase parses the ELF binary to extract the function symbols and associated information such as start address of the function and length of the function block. However, traditional binaries are typically stripped binaries and do not contain symbol information. In such cases, we first restore the symbol information using an external tool, *Unstrip* [27]. Once the symbol information is restored and identified, we proceed on to the next stage of Marlin processing that randomizes the application binary.

3.2 Randomization Algorithm

Once the function symbols have been identified, Marlin generates a random permutation of this set of symbols. The resulting permutation determines the order in which the `mmap` system calls are issued, which changes the order of the mapped symbols in memory. The function blocks are then shuffled around according to this random permutation. Shuffling the function blocks in an application binary changes the relative offsets between instructions that may affect various jump instructions. These jumps may be either absolute jumps or relative jumps. Relative jumps increment or decrement the program counter by a constant value as opposed to absolute jump that directly jump to a fixed address. When the function blocks are randomized, these jumps will no longer point to the desired location and must be 'fixed' to point to the proper locations. We achieve this by performing *jump patching.*

The randomization algorithm described in Algorithm 1 involves two stages. In the first stage, the function blocks are shuffled according to a certain random permutation. During this shuffling, we keep a record of the original address of the function and also the new address where the function will reside after the binary has been completely randomized. This information is stored in a *jump patching table.* Note that this jump patching table is discarded before the application is given control, thus preventing attacker from utilizing this information to de-randomize the memory layout. In the second stage, the actual jump patching is done where the jump patching table is examined for every jump that needs to be patched. Whenever a relative jump is encountered, the algorithm executes `PatchJump()` method to redirect the jump to the correct address in the binary. `PatchJump()` method takes the current address of the jump and the address of the jump destination to determine the new offset and patch the jump target.

The run-time shuffling of the function blocks prevents multiple instances of the same program from having the same address layout. Thus, to defeat Marlin, an attacker would need to dynamically construct a new exploit *for every instance of every application* which is not possible since the randomized layout is not accessible to attacker. We now discuss the security guarantees offered by Marlin.

Algorithm 1: Code Randomization algorithm

Input : Original program, P
Output: Randomized program, P_R

```
L = All symbols in P
F = A list of forbidden symbols that should not be shuffled
L = L − F
O_L = Ordered sequence of symbols in L
S.Addr_P = Address of symbol S in program P
J.Addr_P = Address of jump instruction J in program P
J.Dest_P = Destination address of jump J in program P
J.Sym = Symbol that J is jumping into
/* Permutation stage */
for Every symbol S ∈ L do
    R = Randomly select another symbol in L
    Swap S and R in O_L
P_R = Permuted program according to symbol order in O_L
/* Jump patching stage */
for Every symbol S ∈ L do
    for Every jump J ∈ S do
        if J is a relative jump to within S then
            /* No action needed */
        else if J is a relative jump to outside S then
            J.Dest_{P_R} =
            J.Dest_P + (J.Sym.Addr_{P_R} − J.Sym.Addr_P) − (S.Addr_{P_R} − S.Addr_P)
            PatchJump(J.Addr_{P_R}, J.Dest_{P_R})
        else if J is an absolute jump then
            PatchJump(J.Addr_{P_R}, J.Dest_{P_R})
```

3.3 Security Evaluation

We now show that our randomization technique significantly increases the brute force effort required to attack the system. In a brute force attack, the attacker will randomly assume a memory layout and craft exploit payload according to that address layout. A failed attempt will usually cause a segmentation fault due to illegal memory access and the crashed process or thread will need to be restarted. We now compute the average number of attempts required by an attacker to succeed. A successful attack is assumed to be equivalent to guessing the correct permutation used for randomization.

In the discussion that follows, let n denote the number of symbols (excluding forbidden symbols) in an application binary. The total number of possible permutations that can be generated for this application is $N = n!$. Let $P(k)$ denote the probability that the attack is successful after the kth attempt. Let X be a random variable denoting the number of brute force attempts after which the attack is successful for the first time (that is, the attacker guesses the correct permutation). We will now estimate the *average* value of X. We consider the following two cases.

Case 1: A failed attempt crashes the process and causes it to be restarted.

In this event, the process will be restarted with a new randomization. The subsequent brute force attempts by an attacker will be independent since he would learn nothing from the past failed attempts. That is, $P(k)$ is constant ($= \frac{1}{N}$) and independent of k. Let $P(k) = p$, $\forall$ k. Then, the average number of attempts before the attack is successful for the first time is

$$\mathrm{E}[X] = (p * 1) + (1 - p) * (1 + \mathrm{E}[X]) = \frac{1}{p}$$
$$\Rightarrow \mathrm{E}[X] = n!$$

Thus, the attacker would have to make an average $n!$ number of attempts to correctly guess the randomized layout and launch a successful ROP attack.

Case 2: A failed attempt crashes a thread of the process and causes only that thread to be restarted.

In this event, since the process is still executing, the memory layout will remain same. Every failed attempt will eliminate one permutation. The probability that first success is achieved at k^{th} attempt is

$$P(k) = \left(\prod_{i=1}^{k-1} \frac{N-i}{N-i+1}\right) * \frac{1}{N-k+1} = \frac{1}{N}$$

The average number of attempts before first success can be computed as

$$\mathrm{E}[X] = \sum_{x=1}^{N} x * P(x) = \sum_{x=1}^{N} x * \frac{1}{N} = \frac{N+1}{2}$$
$$\Rightarrow \mathrm{E}[X] = \frac{n!+1}{2}$$

So, the attacker will need an average $\frac{n!}{2}$ number of brute attempts to correctly guess the randomization and launch successful ROP attack. Given enough time and resources, the attacker can try all possible permutations one after the other and will require at most $n!$ attempts for a successful brute force attack.

As an example, to launch a successful ROP attack against an application with 500 symbols that is protected using Marlin, an average $500! = 2^{3767}$ number of attempts will be required for the first case. This is clearly computationally infeasible. A more extensive evaluation performed using SPEC2006 benchmarks is presented later in Section 5 that demonstrates the effectiveness of our technique.

4 Prototype Implementation

We have implemented a Marlin prototype that can operate on any ELF binary without requiring its source code. As a pre-processing step, we use `objdump`

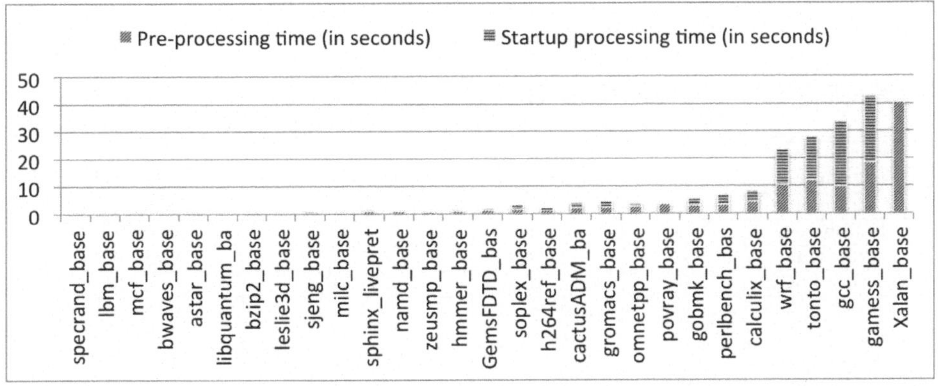

Fig. 3. Overhead measurements of Marlin

utility to obtain a disassembly listing of the application binary that contains the program instructions as well as its internal symbols. These listings are then used to generate a set of parameter files. These parameter files contain a list of symbols (functions) present in the binary, as well as their starting addresses and lengths. Another file is created which lists the addresses where the relative jumps inside functions of interest are located. It is important to note that not every function is considered to be a function of interest, since randomizing certain functions, such as `_start`, will render the binary inoperable. These parameter files are used as input in the next phase of processing that performs the shuffling and jump patching operations. Upon completion, the parameter files are deleted and the the new "marlinized" binary is ready to be run like a normal executable binary.

5 Evaluation

We now describe various experiments to evaluate our *Marlin* prototype. These experiments test three aspects of Marlin. First, we show that Marlin successfully defends against a ROP attack. Second, we study the brute force effort that would be required to circumvent the protection offered by Marlin. Third, we evaluate the processing costs incurred by using Marlin. The experiments were performed on a Linux machine with Intel Core i7 3.40GHz CPU and 8GB RAM. This machine had ASLR and $W \oplus X$ protection enabled while the experiments were being performed. We used SPEC CPU2006 benchmarks to conduct the various experiments. To launch attacks against Marlin-protected binary, we use ROPgadget (v3.3.3) [20], an attack tool that automatically creates exploit payload for ROP attacks by searching for gadgets in an application's executable section.

Effectiveness. We tested the effectiveness of Marlin using a test application that has a buffer overflow vulnerability. This application, `ndh_rop`, was included as a part of the ROPgadget test binaries. We used ROPgadget on this target

Table 1. Brute force effort

Benchmark	Number of Symbols	Time for one attempt (sec)	Avg. # of attempts for successful attack†	Avg. time (sec) for successful attack†
999.specrand	10	0.126	3.63×10^{6}	4.57×10^{5}
470.lbm	26	0.269	4.03×10^{26}	1.08×10^{26}
429.mcf	31	0.269	8.22×10^{33}	2.21×10^{33}
410.bwaves	14	0.385	8.72×10^{10}	3.36×10^{10}
473.astar	97	0.559	9.62×10^{151}	5.38×10^{151}
462.libquantum	106	0.529	1.15×10^{170}	6.06×10^{169}
401.bzip2	79	0.691	8.95×10^{116}	6.18×10^{116}
437.leslie3d	29	1.164	8.84×10^{30}	1.03×10^{31}
458.sjeng	142	1.703	2.69×10^{245}	4.59×10^{245}
433.milc	242	1.408	2.37×10^{473}	3.34×10^{473}
482.sphinx3	335	2.302	1.16×10^{702}	2.66×10^{702}
444.namd	142	2.681	2.69×10^{245}	7.23×10^{245}
434.zeusmp	83	2.399	3.95×10^{124}	9.47×10^{124}
456.hmmer	502	3.269	3.07×10^{1139}	1.00×10^{1140}
459.GemsFDTD	102	4.217	9.61×10^{161}	4.05×10^{162}
450.soplex	918	5.386	1.22×10^{2323}	6.59×10^{2323}
464.h264ref	531	5.532	1.50×10^{1218}	8.31×10^{1218}
436.cactusADM	1299	8.347	2.43×10^{3482}	2.03×10^{3483}
435.gromacs	1098	10.373	4.42×10^{2863}	4.59×10^{2864}
471.omnetpp	2023	7.594	3.19×10^{5811}	2.42×10^{5812}
453.povray	1633	9.039	4.06×10^{4539}	3.68×10^{4540}
445.gobmk	2547	32.019	1.29×10^{7571}	4.12×10^{7572}
400.perlbench	1730	12.625	3.22×10^{4852}	4.07×10^{4853}
454.calculix	1324	18.509	2.16×10^{3560}	3.99×10^{3561}
481.wrf	2883	47.437	6.17×10^{8724}	2.93×10^{8726}
465.tonto	4096	51.328	** $> 1.97\times10^{9997}$	** $> 1.01\times10^{9999}$
403.gcc	4623	50.28	** $> 1.97\times10^{9997}$	** $> 9.92\times10^{9998}$
416.gamess	2893	91.312	2.49×10^{8759}	2.28×10^{8761}
483.xalancbmk	13848	42.903	** $> 1.97\times10^{9997}$	** $> 8.47\times10^{9998}$

† These correspond to the average number of attempts for Case 1 in section 3.3.The values for Case 2 will be approximately half of the value for Case 1.

** We were unable to compute factorial for values larger than 3248. The value used in these columns is 3248!.

application and found 162 unique gadgets. These were sufficient to craft a shell code exploit payload. When this exploit payload was provided as an input to the unprotected binary, it gave us a shell. Next, we randomized this application using Marlin technique and tried to attack it using the same input payload. The attack did not succeed and failed to provide us with a shell.

This highlights the sensitivity of these attacks to slight changes in the address layout. ROP attacks operate under the strong assumption of a static address layout of executable code. Also, notice that in our threat model, the attacker only has access to the unprotected binary and is not aware of the exact permutation that has been used for randomization. So he can only run ROP-gadget on the unprotected test application.

Attacks on Marlin. In section 3.3, we computed the average number of attempts required to successfully attack a "marlinized" binary. We performed an extensive evaluation of this using SPEC CPU 2006 benchmarks. Table 1 shows the number of brute force attempts and the time it takes to craft one exploit. We noticed that around 80% of these benchmarks have more than 80 symbols (indicating an effort of 80! attempts). We observed an average of 1496 symbols and a median of 502 symbols present in these applications. Thus, the number of brute force attempts in a general case can be approximated to $500! \approx 2^{3767}$ attempts which is quite significant. Also, on an average, we observed the time to compute one attack payload is 14.3 seconds.

It is interesting to note that the effectiveness of protection offered by Marlin depends on the modularity of the program. An application that has several function modules will be more secure against brute force attempts when protected with Marlin. If the entire code of an application is organized in few functions, then irrespective of the size of the binary, it will still be quite susceptible to brute force attacks since it would contain large chunks of unrandomized code. Randomizing at finer granularity, for example at the granularity of gadgets or instructions, will solve this issue. However, we believe that randomization breaks the locality principle and the randomized binary may suffer a performance hit. Thus, as a trade off, we chose to randomize at the granularity of function block.

Overhead Analysis. We evaluated the efficiency of Marlin by measuring the overhead incurred while loading an application. We use SPEC CPU2006 benchmarks to conduct this performance evaluation. When an application is loaded, Marlin identifies the function blocks and records information about them (such as start address, length) that is used later in jump patching. This computation is independent of the individual randomizations and referred to as *preprocessing* phase. Next phase involves shuffling the function blocks and patching the jumps. This computation is referred to as *startup processing* phase.

Figure 3 shows the overhead incurred during preprocessing and startup processing phase respectively. The benchmark 483.xalancbmk took significantly longer time to process. This is because it contained 13848 symbols in contrast to a median of 500 symbols by other applications. The average time taken by preprocessing phase was 4.2 seconds, while average time taken by the startup processing phase was 3.3 seconds. It is quite evident from these numbers, that the preprocessing phase is the major contributor to these performance costs.

Since preprocessing phase is independent of individual randomizations, it can be executed just once per application and the results can be stored in database. The randomization phase, that runs with every execution, can read and process information from this database. This simple optimization can greatly improve efficiency of Marlin. Also, the performance hit due to Marlin is incurred only at the load time of the application. Once the application binary has been randomized, it executes like a normal application binary.

6 Discussion

Our proposed solution to defend against code-reuse attacks was to increase the entropy by randomizing the function blocks. One may apply this randomization technique at various levels of granularity - function level, block level or gadget level. The level of granularity to choose is a trade off between security and performance. In our implementation, we implemented the randomization at the function level which is the most coarse granularity amongst the three mentioned above. However, we show that even this coarse level of granularity provides substantial randomization to make brute force attacks infeasible.

Our prototype implementation requires the binary disassembly to contain symbol names, i.e. a non-stripped binary. In practice however, binaries may be stripped and not contain the symbol information. We address this by using external tools such as *Unstrip* [27] that restore symbol information to a stripped binary. Another approach to process stripped binaries is to randomize at the level of basic blocks since they don't require symbol information to be identified. Moving forward, we will explore using basic block level instead of function level as the unit of randomization for Marlin.

7 Conclusion

In this work, we proposed a fine-grained randomization based approach to defend against code reuse attacks. This approach randomizes the application binary with a different randomization for *every run*. We have implemented a prototype of our approach and demonstrated that it is successful in defeating real ROP attacks crafted using automated attack tools. We have also evaluated the effectiveness of our approach and showed that the brute force effort to attack Marlin is significantly high. Based on the results of our analysis and implementation, we argue that fine-grained randomization is both feasible and practical as a defense against these pernicious code-reuse based attack techniques.

Acknowledgments. The work reported in this paper has been partially supported by Sypris Electronics and by NSF under grant CNS-1111512.

References

1. Bhatkar, E., Duvarney, D.C., Sekar, R.: Address obfuscation: an efficient approach to combat a broad range of memory error exploits. In: Proc. of the 12th USENIX Security Symposium, pp. 105–120 (2003)
2. Bhatkar, S., Sekar, R., DuVarney, D.C.: Efficient techniques for comprehensive protection from memory error exploits. In: Proc. of the 14th Conference on USENIX Security Symposium, SSYM 2005, vol. 14, p. 17 (2005)
3. Bletsch, T., Jiang, X., Freeh, V.: Jump-oriented programming: A new class of code-reuse attack. Tech. Rep. TR-2010-8, North Carolina State University (2010)
4. Buchanan, E., Roemer, R., Shacham, H., Savage, S.: When good instructions go bad: generalizing return-oriented programming to risc. In: Proc. of the 15th ACM Conference on Computer and Communications Security, pp. 27–38 (2008)
5. Checkoway, S., Davi, L., Dmitrienko, A., Sadeghi, A.R., Shacham, H., Winandy, M.: Return-oriented programming without returns. In: Proc. of the 17th ACM Conference on Computer and Communications Security, pp. 559–572 (2010)

6. Chen, P., Xiao, H., Shen, X., Yin, X., Mao, B., Xie, L.: DROP: Detecting return-oriented programming malicious code. In: Prakash, A., Sen Gupta, I. (eds.) ICISS 2009. LNCS, vol. 5905, pp. 163–177. Springer, Heidelberg (2009)
7. Chen, P., Xing, X., Han, H., Mao, B., Xie, L.: Efficient detection of the return-oriented programming malicious code. In: Jha, S., Mathuria, A. (eds.) ICISS 2010. LNCS, vol. 6503, pp. 140–155. Springer, Heidelberg (2010)
8. Chen, P., Xing, X., Mao, B., Xie, L.: Return-oriented rootkit without returns (on the x86). In: Soriano, M., Qing, S., López, J. (eds.) ICICS 2010. LNCS, vol. 6476, pp. 340–354. Springer, Heidelberg (2010)
9. Cowan, C., Beattie, S., Johansen, J., Wagle, P.: Pointguard: Protecting pointers from buffer overflow vulnerabilities. In: Proc. of the 12th Usenix Security Symposium (2003)
10. Cowan, C., Pu, C., Maier, D., Hinton, H., Walpole, J., Bakke, P., Beattie, S., Grier, A., Wagle, P., Zhang, Q.: Stackguard: Automatic adaptive detection and prevention of buffer-overflow attacks. In: Proc. of the 7th USENIX Security Symposium, pp. 63–78 (1998)
11. Davi, L., Dmitrienko, A., Nürnberger, S., Sadeghi, A.R.: Xifer: A software diversity tool against code-reuse attacks. In: 4th ACM International Workshop on Wireless of the Students, by the Students, for the Students, S3 2012 (August 2012)
12. Davi, L., Dmitrienko, A., Sadeghi, A.-R., Winandy, M.: Privilege escalation attacks on android. In: Burmester, M., Tsudik, G., Magliveras, S., Ilić, I. (eds.) ISC 2010. LNCS, vol. 6531, pp. 346–360. Springer, Heidelberg (2011)
13. Davi, L., Sadeghi, A.R., Winandy, M.: Dynamic integrity measurement and attestation: towards defense against return-oriented programming attacks. In: Proc. of the 2009 ACM Workshop on Scalable Trusted Computing, pp. 49–54 (2009)
14. Davi, L., Sadeghi, A.R., Winandy, M.: ROPdefender: a detection tool to defend against return-oriented programming attacks. In: Proc. of the 6th ACM Symposium on Information, Computer and Communications Security, pp. 40–51 (2011)
15. Dullien, T., Kornau, T., Weinmann, R.P.: A framework for automated architecture-independent gadget search. In: Proc. of the 4th USENIX Conference on Offensive Technologies, WOOT 2010 (2010)
16. Francillon, A., Castelluccia, C.: Code injection attacks on harvard-architecture devices. In: Proc. of the 15th ACM Conference on Computer and Communications Security, pp. 15–26 (2008)
17. Franz, M.: E unibus pluram: massive-scale software diversity as a defense mechanism. In: Proc. of the 2010 Workshop on New Security Paradigms, NSPW 2010, pp. 7–16 (2010)
18. Hiser, J., Nguyen-Tuong, A., Co, M., Hall, M., Davidson, J.W.: Ilr: Where'd my gadgets go? In: Proc. of the 2012 IEEE Symposium on Security and Privacy, pp. 571–585 (2012)
19. Hund, R., Holz, T., Freiling, F.C.: Return-oriented rootkits: bypassing kernel code integrity protection mechanisms. In: Proc. of the 18th Conference on USENIX Security Symposium, SSYM 2009, pp. 383–398 (2009)
20. Salwan, J.: ROPgadget tool, `http://shell-storm.org/project/ROPgadget/`
21. Kil, C., Jun, J., Bookholt, C., Xu, J., Ning, P.: Address space layout permutation (aslp): Towards fine-grained randomization of commodity software. In: Proc. of the 22nd Annual Computer Security Applications Conference, pp. 339–348 (2006)
22. Li, J., Wang, Z., Jiang, X., Grace, M., Bahram, S.: Defeating return-oriented rootkits with "return-less" kernels. In: Proc. of the 5th European Conference on Computer Systems, pp. 195–208 (2010)

23. MSDN Microsoft: /ORDER (Put Functions in Order), http://msdn.microsoft.com/en-us/library/00kh39zz.aspx
24. MSDN Microsoft: Profile-guided optimizations, http://msdn.microsoft.com/en-us/library/e7k32f4k.aspx
25. Onarlioglu, K., Bilge, L., Lanzi, A., Balzarotti, D., Kirda, E.: G-free: defeating return-oriented programming through gadget-less binaries. In: Proc. of the 26th Annual Computer Security Applications Conference, pp. 49–58 (2010)
26. Pappas, V., Polychronakis, M., Keromytis, A.D.: Smashing the gadgets: Hindering return-oriented programming using in-place code randomization. In: IEEE Symposium on Security and Privacy, pp. 601–615 (2012)
27. Paradyn Project: UNSTRIP (2011), http://paradyn.org/html/tools/unstrip.html
28. PaX Team: PaX, http://pax.grsecurity.net/
29. Roeder, T., Schneider, F.B.: Proactive obfuscation. ACM Trans. Comput. Syst. 28, 1–4 (2010)
30. Roglia, G., Martignoni, L., Paleari, R., Bruschi, D.: Surgically returning to randomized lib(c). In: Annual Computer Security Applications Conference, ACSAC 2009, pp. 60–69 (December 2009)
31. Shacham, H.: The geometry of innocent flesh on the bone: return-into-libc without function calls (on the x86). In: Proc. of the 14th ACM Conference on Computer and Communications Security, pp. 552–561. ACM (2007)
32. Shacham, H., Page, M., Pfaff, B., Goh, E.J., Modadugu, N., Boneh, D.: On the effectiveness of address-space randomization. In: Proc. of the 11th ACM Conference on Computer and Communications Security, pp. 298–307 (2004)
33. Sovarel, A.N., Evans, D., Paul, N.: Where's the feeb? The effectiveness of instruction set randomization. In: Proc. of the 14th Conference on USENIX Security Symposium, vol. 14, p. 10 (2005)
34. Durden, T.: Bypassing PaX ASLR protection. Phrack Magazine 59(9) (June 2002)
35. Wartell, R., Mohan, V., Hamlen, K.W., Lin, Z.: Binary stirring: self-randomizing instruction addresses of legacy x86 binary code. In: Proceedings of the 2012 ACM Conference on Computer and Communications Security, CCS 2012, pp. 157–168. ACM, New York (2012)

Mobile Trusted Agent (MTA): Build User-Based Trust for General-Purpose Computer Platform

Wei Feng[1], Yu Qin[1], Dengguo Feng[1], Ge Wei[2], Lihui Xue[2], and Dexian Chang[1]

[1] Institute of Software Chinese Academy of Sciences
[2] GUANGDONG KAMFU Information & Technology CO., LTD
vonwaist@gmail.com

Abstract. Trusted computing technology can establish trust in the local computer platform by a trusted boot, and can further transfer the trust to a remote verifier through a remote attestation mechanism. However, no standard solution is provided to convey the trust information to users in a friendly manner. Existing methods have no implementation, or need users to buy a specific USB device (an additional purchasing burden for users). To establish user-based trust, we summarize possible solutions and classify the related works according to each solution. After comparing these solutions, we provide a better method "Mobile Trusted Agent (MTA)", which uses a general mobile device as a reliable medium to establish a secure channel between the local user and the remote verifier. Finally, we have implemented MTA using an ARM SoC device and evaluated the performance of the protocol for secure channel. The evaluation results demonstrate that MTA has high quality and flexibility for building user-based trust.

Keywords: Trusted Computing, Remote Attestation, User-Based Trust, Mobile device, ARM.

1 Introduction

Computer has been an indispensable part in our daily life. Using personal computers, users can do many things, like sending or receiving emails, reading or editing confidential documents, shopping online, etc. Sometimes, users have to do these things on their friends' computers or even on public computers. However, computers (especially public computers) are usually not trustworthy, which will compromise user's security and privacy. So before doing any sensitive operations, users need some assurance that the computer is in a "trust" state.

One way to establish trust in a computer is using trusted computing mechanism, which is developed and promoted by the Trusted Computing Group (TCG)[1]. Trusted computing uses a secure chip (like TPM/TCM[1–3]) as a root of trust. The trust state of computer platform can be decided by its software state and configuration, the secure chip will measure all software codes loaded for execution and extend the measurement values to Platform Configuration Registers (PCRs). By remote attestation, TPM/TCM signs PCRs with its

J. Lopez, X. Huang, and R. Sandhu (Eds.): NSS 2013, LNCS 7873, pp. 307–320, 2013.

private key and sends the signature together with the measurement log to a remote verifier. The verifier will verify the signature and the log. If the verification fails, the verifier will send back the symbol 'No'(which means untrusted platform state) to platform, otherwise respond with 'Yes'(which means the platform being used is trustworthy). In this way, trusted computing can establish trust for the whole computer platform.

However, the problem still exists: How do users know the trust state? Currently, many systems based on trusted computing have not considered this problem, or they only suppose that there is a trusted channel to transfer the verification result ('Yes' or 'No') to users. Actually, most of the systems just handle the verification result through a software agent and show the result to users by a display connected to the computer platform. If the agent or the code controlling the display is not secure (e.g. replaced by malware), then the result present to users may not be true. Thus, we need an effective method to show the true state of infected computers to users.

Users usually believe the facts they see with their eyes. We need transfer the true "trust" state to users' eyes, but if the medium (e.g., a software agent) doing this is not trusted, we will fail. If the medium is a hardware agent owned and trusted by users, we can use a more secured method to establish trust for them. So we support to design a trusted agent (acts as the medium) based on a universal commodity hardware for users. In this paper, we give a conclusion about potential solutions and related technologies. After comparing existing solutions, we propose our method Mobile Trusted Agent (MTA), which is based on users' mobile devices. MTA can be used as the trusted medium between the local user and the remote verifier. Furthermore, MTA can also be used as a secure chip for computers without a TPM/TCM. Finally, we have succeeded in implementing such a mobile trusted agent based on an ARM development board Real210[20]. In conclusion, this paper makes the following contributions:

- We summarize and classify existing solutions. After comparing their advantages and disadvantages, we propose our method MTA based on general mobile devices.
- We implement a prototype of MTA using a general ARM development board Real210. We have ported the trusted computing functions and related cryptographic algorithms to our prototype device. Using MTA as the trusted medium, we design, implement and evaluate a protocol for secure channel between the local user and the remote verifier.

Organization: The rest of the paper is organized as follows: First, we present some background knowledge in Section 2. Then, we describe the problem of establishing user-based trust informally in Section 3. Next, we summary and classify possible methods and related work in Section 4, and give our MTA method including the device design, the device usage, the protocol for secure channel and the evaluation of MTA in Section 5. Finally, we conclude the paper in Section 6.

2 Background

Trusted computing uses a secure chip (like TPM/TCM[1–3]) as a *root of trust* for the whole computer platform. When powered[6], the system uses the hardware-based root of trust to initiate the chain of trust by measuring the initial BIOS code.The BIOS then measures and executes the bootloader, and the bootloader, in turn, measures and executes the operating system. Finally the OS might measure and record each application that it executes. Note that system must always measure programs before executing them. All measurements are recorded in a measurement log (or measurement list) and extended into PCRs of secure chip (by TPM_Extend operation). PCRs are protected by the hardware chip and can ensure the credibility of the log, so that PCRs and the log can represent the true state of the whole platform. In this way, trust is transferred from hardware to software and established in the local platform.

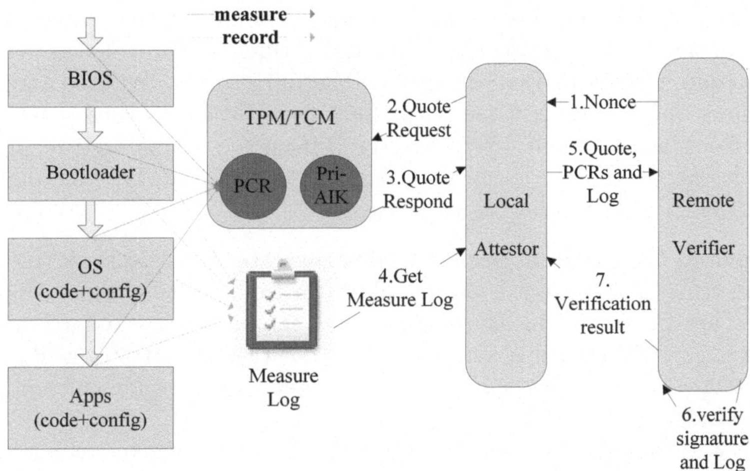

Fig. 1. Trusted Boot and Remote Attestation

Remote attestation can further transfer the local trust to a remote verifier. During the attestation process[6], the verifier supplies the attestor with a nonce to ensure freshness. The attestor then asks the secure chip to generate a Quote (by TPM_Quote operation), which is a digital signature covering the nonce and PCRs. Then the attestor sends the quote with the measure log to the verifier. The verifier then checks the Quote using a public key of Attestation Identity Key (AIK), and then the verifier computes the hash aggregate of the log and compares the result with PCRs. If both succeed, the verifier can ensure the log is truly from the target platform protected by a secure chip. After checking each measurement in the log, the verifier will know whether target platform is trusted. Finally, the verifier sends the verification result back to attestor and the user will know the state of platform he is using.

The exact process of establishing trust in local and transferring trust to remote using trusted computing technology is shown in Fig.1.

3 Problem Description

In this section, we give an informal description of establishing user-based trust. Our goal is to show the truly trust state of platform to its user. But in Fig.1, we don't know how the user gets the verification result. When we implement such an attestation system, we easily find that the objects interacting with the user are displays and keyboards. When the verifier gives the verification result back, it is the attestor (*Local Attestor* in Fig.1) that receives the result and prints it on the display to the user. Note that the attestor is just an agent software. Assuming the whole process in Fig.1 is performed correctly. Actually, the assumption is based on many other hypotheses. For example, the secure chip TPM/TCM is trusted and the private keys of the chip can not be disclosed, PCRs can not be tampered and the chip can defend against physical attack, the remote verifier is trusted and the channel between attestor and verifier is secure. These hypotheses have been adopted by many researches and actual systems. We also assume that users believe the result they see with their eyes. Based on these assumptions, we can infer that the result (step 7 in Fig.1) from the verifier is true, and if the true result can be seen by users, then our goal is achieved. We will analyze the process of Fig.1 in the following two cases:

- **Case 1**. If the platform itself is in a trust state. We can know the attestor is also trusted because it is part of platform configuration. Since all software states are good, the measurements must match with standard values. So the verifier will return a symbol 'Yes'. The trusted attestor will show the result 'Yes' on the display, and user will get the correct result and believe the platform.
- **Case 2**. If the platform itself is not trusted, maybe the attestor is a malware, or maybe some other software codes are controlled by attackers. In this case, the verifier will return the result 'No' and the attestor will get the result. If attestor is replaced by malware, it can print 'Yes' on the display to cheat user. Of course, if some other codes are malwares and attestor is good, it should print 'No'. To print 'Yes' or 'No' is under the control of attacker, so the state transferred to user's eyes may not be true.

If you are the user and your display says 'Yes', will you believe it?I don't think so. From above, we know that the result 'Yes' may come from case 1 and it may cheated by attacker in case 2. User cannot distinguish them.

4 Potential Solutions and Related work

Through the informal analysis above, the key point is to remove the possibility of an untrusted attestor. In this section, we will conclude possible methods to achieve this. We also give some related works about each method.

4.1 Keeping the Computer State Always Trustworthy

From the informal analysis, if only Case 1 can happen, the cheating result from Case 2 can be avoided. An intuitive method is to keep the computer state always trustworthy so that the true trusted state will be transferred to users by remote attestation. However, the computer for daily use can not be always in a trust state. Many researchers propose to create two running environments for each user: secure environment and normal environment. If users want to perform any sensitive operations, the secure environment will be loaded. Because the secure environment can carry a trusted attestor, the users will get the correct result. If users want to do normal tasks, the normal environment can be loaded.

How to create such two environments? The simplest way is to prepare two computers for each user (one for normal user and another for security use). A better method is to create two environments in one physical machine. With the development of virtual technologies, the VMM/hypervisor can separate two virtual machines (VMs), one for secure environment and another for normal use. However, the VMM/hypervisor may become the security bottleneck. To solve this, Keller provides NoHyper[11], which uses existing physical isolation technologies to run two or more operating systems on the same computer. But Keller have not implemented such a NoHype. Here we suggest a good method Lockdown[7], which has implemented such two environments based on Advanced Configuration and Power Interface(ACPI). Users can decide to use any environment by pressing an external button, and an indicator light is used to inform users about the environment they are using. One disadvantage of this method is that the switching time between the two environments is close to reboot time.

4.2 Isolating Attestor

From another point of view, Case 2 leads to possible cheating attacks. The major reason is that the untrusted computer state may influence the code attestor. To address this problem, we need to ensure that the state of attestor will not be influenced by other configurations of the computer platform.

A possible way is to isolate the attestor process from operating system and other applications. Flicker[12] and TrustVisor[13] are two useful systems, which use new features of AMD and Intel's processors to achieve the isolation. AMD's Secure Virtual Machine (SVM)[14] and Intel's Trusted Execution Technology (TXT)[15] can provide Dynamic Root of Trust for Measurement (DRTM) for remote attestation. DRTM can run some security sensitive codes on a relatively isolated environment. Based on DRTM, attestor can run in the isolated environment, and can show the result to user without any cheat. In more detail, even if the state of computer is not trusted, DRTM can ensure that the attestor is not affected. Note that the code running in the isolation environment must be self-contained, and this limits its use for many complex systems. Anyway, it is a good idea to construct an isolation execution environment for safety-sensitive codes, although how to achieve this remains an open problem.

4.3 Using Local Peripherals as Verifier

We know that an untrusted attestor may cheat users by using forged attestation result. The main reason for this is that one function of attestor is showing the returned verification result to users, an untrusted attestor can cheat users by the chance. Thus, we can strip the function out of attestor and integrate it into the trusted verifier. That is, if a trusted party (e.g. verifier) is selected to interact with the users, the true result can be shown.

Now the question is how to integrate the function (of showing the verification result to users) into the verifier. It is impossible for the remote verifier to show the result directly to the local users. Since we cannot force the users to be remote, we can move the remote verifier to local. In Turtles[4], authors have realized the problem and they proposed to implement the verifier as a local USB device, which has a commodity microprocessor and a LED light to show the verification result. They suggest that such a device can act as a local verifier, but they have not implemented such a USB device. Actually, the local USB device is owned and trusted by users and can be used as the secure medium for users. Moreover, in many scenarios like crisis management[23], we cannot assume that a remote verifier is always available and on-line (e.g. intermittent network failures). Therefore, a local verifier is needed. The possible flaw of the method is that it needs users to buy a specialized USB device. Our MTA can be used to implement such a local verifier based on users' mobile devices rather than additional USB devices.

4.4 Establishing Secure Channel between Local Agent and Remote Verifier

From section 4.3, if we choose a trusted entity to notify users and the attacks may be avoided. But a local verifier only suits to some specific scenarios. If we can establish a secure channel between a local trusted agent and the remote verifier, we don't need to move the remote verifier to local. For example, we can add the function of interacting with users to the local TPM itself and use the TPM secure chip as the trusted agent to design a secure channel. But we have no permission to modify an actual hardware TPM which is controlled by its manufacturer, so we plan to design our own trusted device (or agent). One possible way is to integrate the functionalities of TPM into a USB device. In PTM[9, 10], authors have designed and implemented such a USB device. PTM is a cryptographic chip based on USB interface, and it has part functions of trusted computing and can act as a trust root of universal computer platform. In prototype, PTM[9] chooses a Watachdata USB Key with Java Card Runtime Environment and implements TPM commands as a Java Card Applet. But their PTM implementation may not be compatible with TCG specification[1], and the java-based program is not effective for resource-constrained embedded devices. What's more, they need users to buy an additional specialized USB device. Our method MTA is similar with PTM, but we use the C code to implement Trusted Computing abilities and adopt the general mobile device (which has stronger computing power and storage resources than USB device) as the trusted device.

After the design of a local trusted device for users, the question remains how to establish a secure channel between the local trusted agent and the remote verifier. The most effective method is using cryptographic protocols. Now that the trusted device can perform cryptographic operations and trusted computing commands, it is possible to design such a protocol. In PTM[9], they designed a public key protocol and used a little LCD screen to interact with users. But their protocol has not taken full advantage of trusted computing commands and provides no confirmation respond to the remote verifier. As you will see from the next section, MTA is more agile and practical.

5 Our Method: Mobile Trusted Agent

In the above section, we have summarized four kinds of methods. For each method, we have also analyzed some related work. Our method MTA belongs to the fourth method and can also support the third method by using MTA as a local verifier. We focus on the implementation of the fourth method. Thus, in this section we first introduce the design and usage of our trusted device MTA and then give a protocol for secure channel between the local user and the remote verifier. Finally, we describe MTA prototype and overheads evaluation.

5.1 Design of Mobile Trusted Agent

The MTA device should own two major functions: (1)It should provide the necessary cryptographic algorithms and the trusted computing functions. Thus, we can establish a secure channel between the device and the remote verifier; and if necessary, the device can also act as TPM/TCM to provide trusted computing commands for host platform. (2)The device can show the verification result to users friendly. That is to say, the device should be owned and trusted by users, and it can interact with users in an intuitive and physical way.

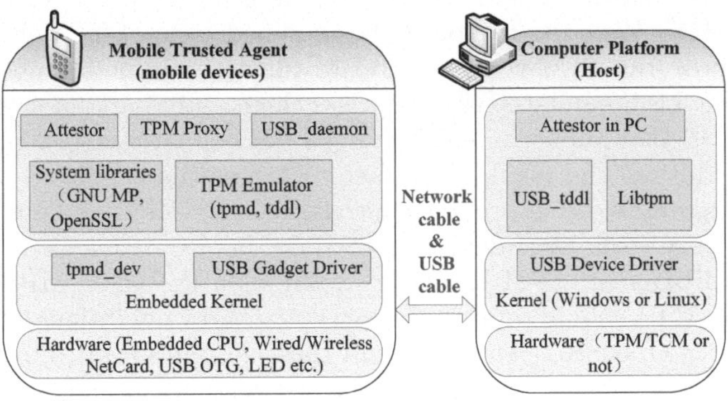

Fig. 2. The design and usage of our Mobile Trusted Agent

Through careful study, we choose the general mobile devices as the basic hardware environment of MTA. Firstly, many mobile devices and embedded systems can provide enough software and hardware resources to design a trusted device. Secondly, we can port the relative cryptography libraries such as OpenSSL to mobile devices, so that they can support the necessary cryptographic operations. We can also transplant the software TPM Emulator [18] to provide the trusted computing commands. Thus, our function (1) can be met. Finally, mobile devices usually support many peripherals like LCD and LED to interact with users, and they also support to ring or vibrate. These are enough to realize our function (2).

The whole design of MTA and its connection with the host platform is shown in Fig.2. The left part of Fig.2 is our trusted device MTA, which is composed of the following modules:

- **Hardware**: It uses the general embedded processor (e.g. ARM processor), which supports the cryptography acceleration and the floating point arithmetic. It also supports many peripherals and we can choose the LED light (or others) to interact with users. The mobile devices are usually equipped with wired/wireless network cards for communication. The USB OTG interface can make MTA look like a removable device for host with USB interface.
- **Kernel**: It needs to compile an embedded kernel for MTA. A USB Gadget Driver is designed in the kernel to enable USB communication between MTA and host.
- **USB gadget driver**: The driver talks over USB to a USB Device Driver running on a host PC. Using the driver, the MTA can act as a TPM-like chip with USB bus for host.
- **USB_dameon**: The module is responsible for listening on the USB gadget driver for incoming TPM commands. Upon the reception of a valid command, it is forwarded to the TPM emulator. After processed by the TPM emulator, USB_dameon returns the corresponding response to the sender of the command.
- **TPM Emulator**: For TPM functions, we use a modified version of TPM Emulator[18]. We cross-compiled the modified code of TPM Emulator and transplanted the TCG-compliant TPM functions into the mobile environment. The TPM emulator[18] comprises three main parts: a user-space daemon (*tpmd*) that implements the actual TPM emulator, a TPM device driver library (tddl) as the regular interface to access the emulator, and a kernel module (*tpmd_dev*) that provides the character device /dev/tpm for low-level compatibility with TPM device drivers.
- **System libraries**: TPM emulator depends on the GNU MP library. Furthermore, MTA should support some cryptography operations, we choose the open source OpenSSL. We need build these system libraries to our device.
- **TPM Proxy**: For TPM access using network, we use IBM's libtpm and proxy[19]. The TPM Proxy is located in the MTA and it keeps listening the requests from libtpm running in the host platform.

- **Attestor**: We implement an attestor module (called $Attestor_{MTA}$) in the embedded environment. When the attestor in PC (called $Attestor_{PC}$) receives the verification result (encrypted), it can't resolve the result and just forwards the ciphertext to $Attestor_{MTA}$. $Attestor_{MTA}$ will decrypt the information and show the result to user with a LED light. Actually, MTA is our trusted device and $Attestor_{MTA}$ (running on MTA) is the function module stripped from the original $Attestor_{PC}$. $Attestor_{MTA}$ is also responsible for establishing a secure channel between MTA and the remote verifier using a well-designed cryptography protocol, which we will introduce in Section 5.3.

The right part of Fig.2 is the general-purpose computer platform that can communicate with MTA by a wired/wireless network cable or a USB cable. Both Windows and Linux hosts can use MTA to build user-based trust, no matter whether there is a TPM/TCM secure chip or not. The specific usage of MTA is described in Section 5.2.

5.2 Usage of Mobile Trusted Agent

According to Fig.2, there are two kinds of communication modes between MTA and the host platform: Network mode and USB mode. For the flexibility of MTA, both of the two modes can be used.

For host equipped with a TPM/TCM, MTA can be used only as the reliable medium to establish a secure channel between the local user and the remote verifier. The protocol is introduced in Section 5.3. For this case, we can use the network mode (wired or wireless) between MTA and host. Attestor module on MTA interacts with the attestor on PC through network mode (TCP/IP). Attestor module on MTA will parse the verification result using the TPM Emulator and show the result to users by a LED light. Fig.3 depicts the usage of MTA as a reliable hardware medium to build user-based trust for general-purpose computer platform.

For host without a TPM or TCM chip, MTA can further acts as the TPM/TCM chip for the host to use trusted computing functions. In this case, both modes can be used. When using network mode, it just depends on the TPM Proxy module

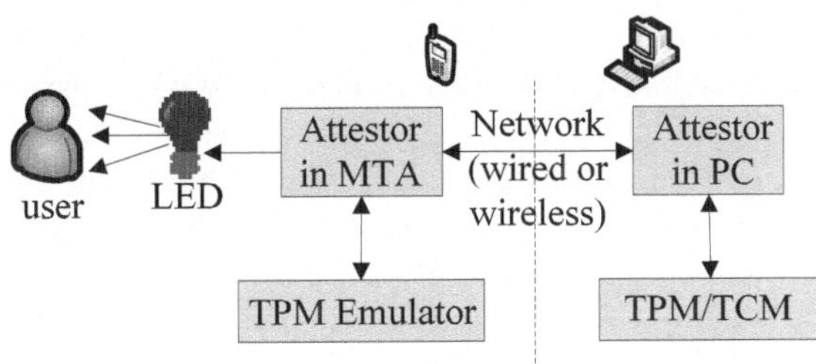

Fig. 3. Use MTA as a trusted agent (or medium)

on the MTA and the Libtpm module on the host. The USB mode depends on the USB_dameon and the USB Gadget Driver on the MTA, and the USB device driver and USB_tddl on the host. The most convenient way to access a TPM is TPM Device Driver Library (TDDL) as specified by the TCG. We have implemented the USB_tddl owning the same interfaces with a TPM TDDL. Thus, through our USB connection, the MTA can act as a TPM/TCM chip, which is affixed to the host with a universal serial bus (USB). Any secure application (e.g. attestor on PC) of host can rely on the two communication modes to use the trusted computing functions of MTA, as described in Fig.4.

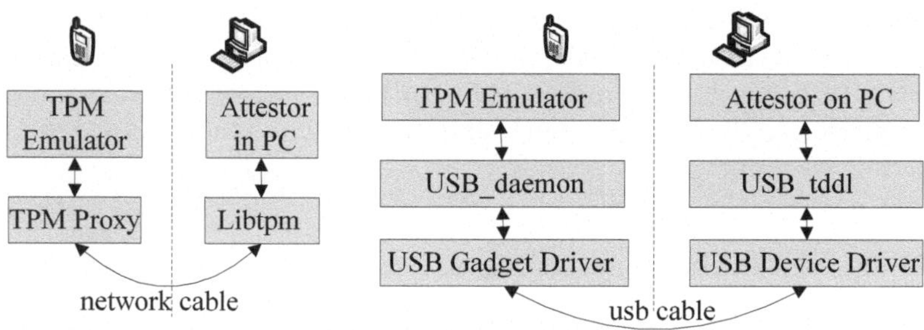

Fig. 4. Two modes for using the trusted computing functions of MTA: the left is network mode and the right is usb mode

5.3 Protocol for Secure Channel

Based on MTA, we design a protocol to establish the secure channel between the device and the remote verifier. We not only use cryptographic operations but also the TPM commands of TPM Emulator. At first, we generate signature key pair $(PubK_{SIG}, PriK_{SIG})$ and binding key pair $(PubK_{BIND}, PriK_{BIND})$ for MTA. The two keys are all non-migratable, 2048 bits RSA keys. The remote verifier knows the public keys $PubK_{SIG}$ and $PubK_{BIND}$ in advance. The public key of the verifier is $PubK_{VER}$, and the private key is $PriK_{VER}$ and they are also 2048 bits RSA keys. VR represents the verification result, Enc is the encryption algorithm, Dec is the decryption algorithm (we use TPM_UnBind command), Sig is the signature algorithm (we use TPM_sign command), Ver is the verification algorithm.

The protocol is shown in Fig.5. The first four steps is based on a standard remote attestation in which a Nonce (for freshness) is sent to host, and the host calls our MTA (instead of TPM/TCM) to produce a quote. Nonce1 is used to request verification result from the remote verifier. ML represents the measurement log. The rest steps consist of the core of secure channel, for which we use a signature scheme combined with an encryption scheme. The signature can prevent forgery of the verification result and the encryption scheme ensures

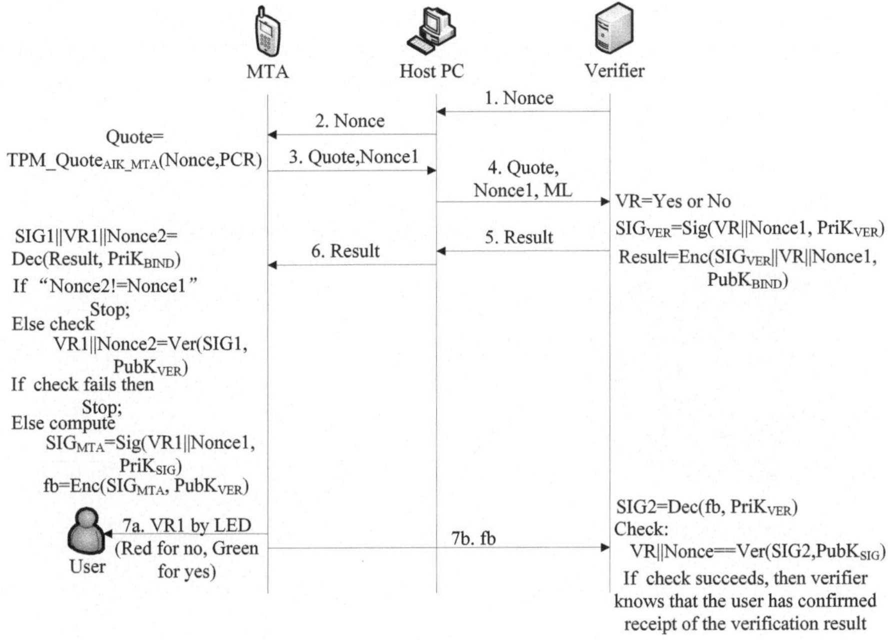

Fig. 5. Protocol for Secure Channel and Confirmation based on MTA

confidentiality. For MTA, it executes one *Dec* operation and one *Ver* operation to obtain the true trust state; after that, it also performs one *Sig* and one *Enc* operation to return a confirmation message. Compared with the protocol in PTM[9], our protocol makes good use of TPM keys and commands. The private parts of binding key and signature key will never leave MTA, so only the MTA with TPM Emulator can perform TPM_UnBind command to obtain the verification result and only the MTA can produce a unforgeable and undeniable signature using TPM_sign command. Furthermore, our protocol adds a confirmation information from users to the verifier and this is very important in many secure applications, especially online transaction. The verifier is usually an online service provider and it may expect to receive the undeniable feedback information (*fb* in Fig.5) from users.

5.4 Prototype and Evaluation of MTA

As ARM processors are adopted by most mobile and embedded devices, we choose ARM development board[20] to implement our MTA prototype. The prototype is called MTA-Real210, which is equipped with a 1GHz ARM Cortex-A8 processor (Samsung's S5PV210), with a 512MB DDR2 memory and 256MB NAND Flash. Our cryptography operations are adapted from the open-source OpenSSL library (openssl-0.9.8g) and TPM commands are from the software-based TPM Emulator[18]. We port the code of TPM Emulator from the x86 architecture to the ARM processor and embedded Linux. Because the processors and kernels are different, we have made some changes to the original TPM Emulator. For TPM access and tests, we adopt IBM's libtpm and proxy[19], a C/C++ interface for trusted computing.

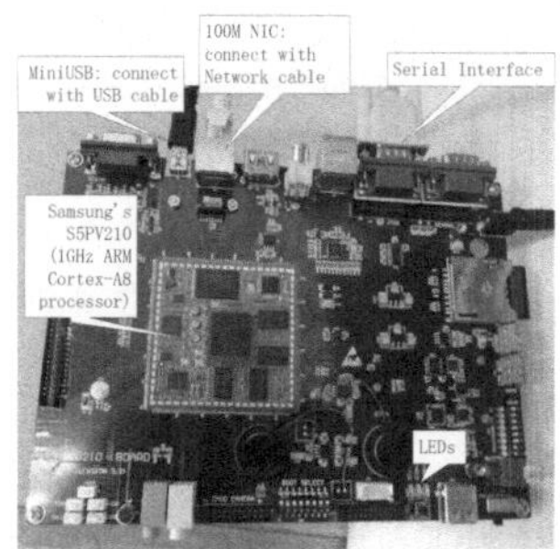

Fig. 6. A picture of the prototype system MTA-Real210

Command or Operation	Time on Real210	Time on Ubuntu
TPM_TakeOwnership	3193ms	424ms
TPM_CreateWrapKey	2637ms	408ms
TPM_LoadKey	314ms	117ms
TPM_Sign	51ms	25ms
RSA_Verify	2.8ms	0.438ms
RSA_BIND	3.3ms	0.66ms
TPM_UnBind	51.9ms	24.9ms

Fig. 7. Evaluation Results

A picture of the prototype system MTA-Real210 is shown in Fig.6. The board has a 100M network card and a MiniUSB (USB OTG) interface, and these are enough for us to implement both the network and the USB modes. For network connection, we started a *TPM Proxy* on the board and the host can use the *libtpm* to access the relative functions (like TPM commands and RSA cryptography operations). For USB connection, we compiled a kernel module *g_serial.ko* (a USB gadget serial driver) for the embedded kernel (Linux-2.6.32) on the board, the gadget serial driver talks over USB to a *CDC ACM driver* (a USB Device Driver) running on a host PC. We wrote the code *USB_daemon* for the board to listen the request from the gadget serial driver, and we also wrote the code *USB_tddl* for the host to use the CDC ACM driver. With the help of these components, MTA-Real210 can act as a TPM/TCM chip used by the host with a USB cable. For interacting with the user, we choose the LEDs on the board. At present, both network and USB connection are running normally.

Using MTA-Real210, we test the execution time of related TPM commands and cryptography operations in the protocol of Fig.5. The cryptography operations executed are: RSA_Verify (this operation verifies the signature using the public key $PubK_{SIG}$) and RSA_BIND (this operation encrypts the verification result using the public key $PubK_{BIND}$). The TPM commands used are: TPM_TakeOwnership, TPM_CreateWrapKey, TPM_LoadKey, TPM_Sign, TPM_UnBind. The first three commands are used to produce related key pairs. The command TPM_Sign is used to produce the signature of the verification result and nonce, and TPM_UnBind is adopted to decrypt the information containing the verification result. All these operations and commands are tested on MTA-Real210. For comparison, we also evaluate the execution time of these operations and commands on our VMware Virtual Machine Ubuntu Linux system with a 2.4GHz Intel(R) Core(TM)2 Duo CPU and 512MB memory. The evaluation results are reported in Figure 7. The *Enc* operation (RSA_BIND) only take 3.3ms and the related *Dec* operation (TPM_UnBind) only needs 51.9ms. The *Sig* operation (TPM_Sign) costs 51ms and Ver operation (RSA_Verify) only needs 2.8ms. The total time of $Attestor_{MTA}$ in the protocol is about 109ms (3.3+51.9+2.8+51). Thus we can conclude that these operations in the mobile and embedded environment are accepted for actual system and our protocol is feasible for mobile and embedded devices.

6 Conclusion and Future Work

This paper presented MTA, a trusted agent that can establish user-based trust for general-purpose computer platform. MTA is designed based on uses' mobile devices, which can use trusted computing commands and cryptographic operations to establish a secure channel for local users and remote verifiers. MTA uses the physical property of mobile devices to interact with users. MTA can also be used to act as the TPM for PCs without any secure chips. Finally, we have implemented MTA using a general ARM development board and evaluated the overheads. Our evaluation results show that MTA is a feasible way for building user-based trust. As the mobile devices may not be secure now, we consider to strengthen our MAT architecture using secure elements (e.g. ARM TrustZone, Smart Card, etc.) for future work.

Acknowledgments. This work has been supported by the National Natural Science Foundation of China (under grants No.91118006 and No.61202414) and the National 973 Program of China (under grants No.2013CB338003). This work has also been supported by Project of "Trusted Terminal System development and Terminal Product Industrialization for Self-help tax service" (under grants No.2011BY100042). We would also like to thank anonymous reviewers for their valuable comments and suggestions to improve the manuscript.

References

1. Trusted Computing Group. Trusted platform module main specification. Version 1.2, Revision 103 (2007)
2. State Cryptography Administration. Functionality and Interface Specification of Cryptographic Support Platform for Trusted Computing (2007)
3. Ryan, M.: Introduction to the TPM 1.2 (March 24, 2009)
4. McCune, J.M., Perrig, A., Seshadri, A., van Doorn, L.: Turtles All The Way Down: Research Challenges in User-Based Attestation. In: Proceedings of the 2nd USENIX Workshop on Hot Topics in Security. USENIX, Boston (2007)
5. Parno, B.: Bootstrapping Trust in a "Trusted" Platform. In: Proceedings of the 3rd USENIX Workshop on Hot Topics in Security, San Jose, CA (July 29, 2008)
6. Parno, B., McCune, J.M., Perrig, A.: Bootstrapping Trust in Commodity Computers. In: Proceedings of the IEEE Symposium on Security and Privacy (May 2010)

7. Vasudevan, A., Parno, B., Qu, N., Gligor, V., Perrig, A.: Lockdown: A Safe and Practical Environment for Security Applications, CMU-CyLab-09-011 (2009)
8. Sparks, E.R.: A security assessment of trusted platform modules. Technical Report TR2007-597, Dartmouth College (2007)
9. Zhang, D., Han, Z., Yan, G.: A Portable TPM Based on USB Key. In: Proceedings of the 17th ACM Conference on Computer and Communications Security, New York, NY, USA (2010)
10. Han, L., Liu, J., Zhang, D.: A Portable TPM Scheme for General-purpose Trusted Computing Based on EFI. In: International Conference on Multimedia Information Networking and Security. IEEE, Wuhan (2009)
11. Keller, E., Szefer, J., Rexford, J., Lee, R.B.: NoHype: Virtualized cloud infrastructure without the virtualization. In: Proc. International Symposium on Computer Architecture (June 2010)
12. McCune, J.M., Parno, B., Perrig, A., Reiter, M.K., Isozaki, H.: Flicker: An Execution Infrastructure for TCB Minimization. In: Proceedings of the ACM European Conference on Computer Systems, Glasgow, Scotland (2008)
13. McCune, J.M., Li, Y., Qu, N., Zhou, Z., Datta, A., Gligor, V., Perrig, A.: TrustVisor: Efficient TCB Reduction and Attestation. In: IEEE Symposium on Security and Privacy (2010)
14. Advanced Micro Devices. AMD64 architecture programmer' manual. System programming, vol. 2. AMD Publication no. 24593 rev.3.14 (September 2007)
15. Intel Corporation. Intel trusted execution technology-software development guide. Document number 315168-005 (June 2008)
16. Aaraj, N., Raghunathan, A., Jha, N.K.: Analysis and design of a hardware/software trusted platform module for embedded systems. ACM Transactions on Embedded Computing Systems 8(1), 1–31 (2008)
17. Aaraj, N., Raghunathan, A., Ravi, S., Jha, A.K.: Energy and Execution Time Analysis of a Software-based Trusted Platform Module. In: Proceedings of the Conference on Design, Automation and Test in Europe. IEEE (2007)
18. Strasser, M.: TPM Emulator, `http://tpm-emulator.berlios.de`
19. Software TPM Introduction (IBM), `http://ibmswtpm.sourceforge.net`
20. Real210, `http://www.realarm.cn/pic/?78_490.html`
21. CodeSourcery ARM EABI toolchain, `https://sourcery.mentor.com/sgpp/lite/arm/portal/subscription?template=lite`
22. Dietrich, K., Winter, J.: Implementation Aspects of Mobile and Embedded Trusted Computing. In: Proceedings of the 2nd International Conference on Trusted Computing, Oxford, UK, April 06-08 (2009)
23. Hein, D.M., Toegl, R., Pirker, M., Gatial, E., Balogh, Z., Brandl, H., Hluchy, L.: Securing mobile agents for crisis management support. In: STC 2012: Proceedings of the Seventh ACM Workshop on Scalable Trusted Computing, pp. 85–90. ACM, New York (2012)

Anomaly Detection for Ephemeral Cloud IaaS Virtual Machines

Suaad Alarifi[2] and Stephen Wolthusen[1,2]

[1] Norwegian Information Security Laboratory,
Department of Computer Science,
Gjøvik University College, Norway
[2] Information Security Group,
Department of Mathematics,
Royal Holloway, University of London, UK
{s.alarifi,stephen.wolthusen}@rhul.ac.uk

Abstract. In public Infrastructure-as-a-Service (IaaS), virtual machines (VMs) are sharing the cloud with other VMs from other organisations. Each VM is under the control of its owner and security management is their responsibility. Considering this, providers should deal with the hosted VMs as potential source of attacks against other VMs and/or against the cloud infrastructure. The cloud model is flexible enough to allow consumers to initiate VMs to perform specific tasks for an hour or two, then terminate; so call VMs short-lived VMs. The provider dilemma here is monitoring these VMs, including short-lived ones, and detecting any change of behaviour on them as a sign of anomaly with a low level of intrusiveness for legal and practical reasons.

In this paper, we therefore propose a hypervisor based anomaly detection system that monitors system calls in between a VM and its host kernel. This host intrusion detection system (HIDS),is able to detect change in behaviour in even short-lived VMs without requiring any prior knowledge of them. To achieve this goal, a Hidden Markov Model (HMM) is used to build the classifier and system calls are analysed and grouped to reflect the properties of a VM-based cloud infrastructure. We also report on the experimental validation of our approach.

Keywords: IDS, HIDS, IaaS security, Cloud Computing Security.

1 Introduction

Cloud computing is a service for providing resources to consumers on demand and allow them to request, increase, and/or shrink the used resources without human intervention from the provider side. Consumers in cloud model access the requested resources through the public Internet (in case of public cloud) or through their private networks (in case of private cloud). The cost model in the cloud is to pay for what is used. The main idea is sharing resources to reduce cost, and virtualization technique is used to allow the sharing. The most popular three cloud services are infrastructure as a service (IaaS), where resources

J. Lopez, X. Huang, and R. Sandhu (Eds.): NSS 2013, LNCS 7873, pp. 321–335, 2013.

such as network, storage and computing power are offered for sharing; platform as a service (PaaS), where platforms are offered for sharing by consumers to develop their applications on them; finally software as a service (SaaS), where applications are offered to consumers. In this research, we focus on the security of public IaaS from the provider side.

The technologies used in IaaS cloud are not new but the combination of technologies and the special cloud features introduce new security requirements and new threats; for instance, one of the main features of cloud network is high data volume, which may require a distributed security system to cope with the high traffic volume. Furthermore, in cloud network there exist some VMs which live for an hour or two to perform specific tasks then terminate. This scenario of using the IaaS cloud to perform specific tasks is popular and it requires security systems that are built and work on the fly. These new threats and special security requirements are discussed in detail in the literature review section.

In IaaS, consumers initiate VMs in the provider network; these VMs are hosted in servers where they are co-located with other VMs owned by other consumers. This introduces the threat of VMs attacking each other (inter-VM attack). In IaaS, each VM is owned and 100% controlled by its owner. Owners might not apply security patches or might use highly vulnerable applications or operating systems. Providers can obligate them to maintain the security of their VMs legally by contract, and technically by monitoring the behaviour of these VMs. Providers can only monitor these VMs from outside because monitoring these VMs from inside requires accessing them or installing agents on them which increase the level of intrusiveness and might introduce legal complications. The providers' dilemma here is hosting these VMs, protecting them, and maintaining the security of the environment without accessing VMs or requiring any prior knowledge of them.

In this paper, we develop a Host Based Intrusion Detection System (HIDS) that monitors the VMs from outside without any prior knowledge of them. The proposed system monitors invoked system calls by the hosted VM. System-calls based HIDS are well established and have been used for long time [1]; however, monitoring system calls in cloud environments is different because of the nature of the cloud and the fact that VMs live in a virtual environment [2]. For instance, in our IaaS cloud environment, Kernel-based Virtual Machine KVM is the main hypervisor; in KVM networks, VMs are communicating with virtual resources using IOCTL system call[1]. Therefore, when dealing with system call based HIDS, it is important to analyse IOCTL system calls, understand its structure, and deal

[1] IOCTL system call stands for input/output control and is used to manipulate a character device via a file descriptor. From Linux man page, IOCTL system call has the following format: Int ioctl(int d, int request, ...). -Int d is the open file descriptor, -Int request is the device-dependent request code. -The third argument is an untyped pointer to memory. It is represented by dots because this pointer could lead to unlimited amount of data, -The return value is zero on success and it could be also used as an output parameter.

with it in a special way. More details about how to analyse IOCTL system call are in [3].

The most important feature of the proposed system is its ability to monitor short-lived VMs, then to detect any anomalies in their behaviour and generate a strong enough anomaly signal.

Many approaches can be used to build a classifier that perform this task. The choice of approach depends on many factors such as the available data for training, the acceptable cost and the nature of collected data. In our environment, only normal non-malicious data are available to train the classifier and this approach is called supervised training.

Training classifiers is a machine learning problem and also is related to the artificial intelligence field. Many methods are used in the literature but the one used here is Hidden Markov Model (HMM).

The rest of the paper is designed as following: section 2 is the literature review. Section 3 is the hypothesis, assumptions and requirements. Section 4 is to describe the used method to build the classifier, the application of the method and the results. Section 5 is the discussion and section 6 is the conclusion and future work.

2 Literature Review

There are three types of HIDS that can be deployed in the cloud, type 1 is the one placed in the host system itself (the place where VMs live and share resources) and it is used to monitor the host. This is a regular HIDS with almost a full knowledge on the structure of the host OS, applications, hardware states, and log files. Type 2 is the one placed in the VMs that are hosted by the host system in the cloud. VMs owners see this HIDS as a regular one but in reality this HIDS monitors virtual machines that work on virtual resources. Type 3 is the one placed in the host machine but is used to monitor the VM lives in that host not the host itself; it is called hypervisor based HIDS and this type works in virtualization based environments such as cloud computing. In this paper we investigate type 3 HIDS (hypervisor based anomaly detection system) that is placed in the host system and used to monitor virtual machines.

The hypervisor based HIDS introduced first in 2003 by Garfinkel and Rosenblum [4]. They design a system called virtual machine introspection, VMI, used to monitor VMs from the host system and detect anomalies. This system came as a solution for the problem of low attack resistance that HIDS usually suffers from. Once the host system is compromised, the attacker can then disable or neutralise the detection system. This problem is common for HIDSs in general [2], [5] and [4]. Researchers in [4] decided to convert the targeted physical machine to virtual ones to be able to separate the HIDS from the targeted machine so if this machine get breached the attacker won't be able to neutralise the HIDS. VMI requires prior knowledge about the VM structure and its OS. It also uses a modified version of VMware to collect some of the required data and monitors hardware states in the VM such as memory pages and registers.

Similar solution, of separating the HIDS from the host using virtualisation, is suggested in [5]. Laureano et al. [5] used a modified version of User-Mode Linux (UML) to collect data from processes inside the VM. UML communicates with the processes inside VM through named pipes and the host operating system synchronises the data flow between them. They analyse system calls using Forrest et al. method from [6] and [7], which is by using a sliding window to register system calls, they have not specify the used length in their paper. It is not also clear which processes they chose to monitor from inside the VM.

Low attack resistance is one of two problems cloud HIDSs suffer from; the second problem is that cloud models usually have high volume of data, [2], [8] and [9], which might cause overloading of the IDS and dropping of data traffic. In [2], researchers believe that these two limitations are critical enough to stop using HIDS in the cloud. They state "a network based IDS would be more suitable for deployment in cloud like infrastructure. NIDS would be placed outside the VM servers on bottle neck of network points such as switch, router or gateway for network traffic monitoring to have a global view of the system" [2]; however we think that this is not a solution because as argued in [10], NIDS cannot deal with attacks from inside the network; for this reason Jiankun and his colleagues state in [10] "an effective IDS should include an HIDS as a complement to the NIDS". Another crucial reason we note for having HIDS is that NIDS cannot detect inter-VM attacks.

For the second problem, which is high volume data in the cloud, many research papers, such as in [8] and [9], suggest distributed IDS (DIDS).

We believe that there is an urgent need for a host intrusion detection system; it allows cloud providers, who have no control at all over what is inside the hosted VMs, to maintain the security of the cloud and to detect any breached or misbehaved VM before being used to attack the infrastructure or neighbouring VMs. Furthermore, it helps providers to draw a security picture for each VM, and this help them to take future decisions for example weather to renew the contract with a specific consumer or not, or whether there is a need to notify a specific consumer to improve his security. The target here is to reduce the level of intrusiveness by monitoring VMs (including short-lived ones) from outside without accessing them or installing any agent for efficiency and legal reasons.

In this research, we monitor VMs from the host system which makes the HIDS safe when the VM is compromised but there is still the threat of compromising the host system and disabling the hypervisor-based IDS. It is important to state here that the suggested system is not an alternative for the NIDS but that it is a complementary system. We also suggest a separate normal behaviour profile for each VM to be able to suit the mobility characteristic of VMs in the cloud. These profiles or small HIDS should be able to migrate with VMs.

In addition to these two problems there is a special requirement for cloud based IDS suggested in [3] which is monitoring VMs with the minimum or no instrumentation within VMs. This requirement is vital as [3] states "this is desirable as VMs may be required to be under exclusive control of the client, and hence not be amenable to internal instrumentation by the IaaS provider".

Furthermore, legal restrictions may bound the acceptable level of instrumentation the provider can perform to the minimum. Reducing the level of instrumentation may also quicken the monitoring process that could allow the detection mechanism to work on the fly as argued by [3].

In previous research [3] we designed, a hypervisor based HIDS more suitable for cloud IaaS environments. The designed HIDS requires no knowledge from inside the hosted VMs; it deals with them as black boxes. It also uses plain KVM to accomplish the task. The representation method for our first HIDS is the low demanding bag of system calls which is a frequency based representation method that requires no probabilities calculation at all. The produced classifier generates very strong anomaly signals with a very high detection rate. However, it needed about 6G of data to train the classifier and 1G for testing. This is a relatively large amount of data and it is acceptable in long term VMs especially gives that high volume of flow data is one of the prominent characteristics of cloud environments [4]. However, for short term VMs there is a need for a classifier that can be build faster even if it consumes more computing resources but not time. The scenario of a machine living for an hour is normal in the cloud especially for VMs that are used for testing purposes or analysing data. For instance, an organisation might have a very large amount of data which require fast analysis once a year to generate annual reports; so instead of buying servers to perform this annual task they initiate hundreds of VMs in the cloud to analyse the data in few hours then terminated.

Requiring more resources to build this classifier rather than time is acceptable in the cloud where resources such as computational power are not scarce because it is the main service the cloud provides. Hence, with these requirements in mind, we modify our first classifier by changing the used machine learning approach and also by changing the part of the data being analysed to reduce noise. Then a new classifier has been produced in the same environment as [3].

Some research papers, such as [11], categorise anomaly detection modelling approaches into two categories: Dynamic approach, which is based on probabilities calculation such as HMM, and static approaches which is based on frequency distributions and the principle of minimum cross entropy such as bag of system calls [12]. Researchers in [11] argue that dynamic modelling approaches are better than static modelling approaches for system call datasets and worse in the shell command datasets. In this research we monitor system calls using Hidden Markov Model (HMM) approach which is a dynamic approach.

HMM is an old but sophisticated representation method. HMM almost always provides a high detection rate and a low minimum false positives but with high computational demand [1] and [13].

There are many research papers about how to improve HMM for anomaly detection by reducing the used power such as in [10], [14] and [15]; however, in this paper, we test a regular HMM and HMM improvements can be tested in future research.

HIDS can be categorised depending on the source of data; it could be log files, hardware status, memory pages, registers, system calls, and/or system files modifications. In this research we are monitoring only system calls for two reasons. First, previous research proves that monitoring system calls gave high efficiency and efficacy to detect anomalies in hosts [6], [12], and [16]. Second, monitoring hardware status or applications log files require installing some agents in the VM or prior knowledge for the VM OS structure which is against the cloud HIDS requirement stated earlier in this section; while system calls invoked by the VM are sent to the host system and they can be intercepted by the HIDS and used to build an identity for each VM and detect abnormality.

Some research papers, such as [17], suggest monitoring only privileged system calls or system calls with high threat, other suggest monitoring only root processes or processes with high privileges [6]. In this paper, one of the methods used to pre-processing data is by categorising them depending on their threat level and another method by only monitoring specific threads in the VM.

3 Hypothesis, Assumptions, and Requirements

The main hypothesis is that a strong anomaly signal can be generated by building a normal behaviour profile for each VM hosted in IaaS cloud model and represented as a single process in the host system using HMM to build a hypervisor based anomaly detection system. The strong anomaly signal is generated when evaluating abnormal sequences of system calls using the generated model and we argue that this model is sufficient to cover even short-lived VMs.

We assume that VMs are not malicious from the beginning, to be able to collect normal data for training the classifier. In the context of our research, this assumption is acceptable because if the monitored VM is malicious from the beginning that means either the owner of this VM is an attacker or the VM get hijacked the moment it starts. These two possibilities are not the security problems we try to investigate here; they are more related to authentication mechanisms and the process of initiating new VM, and it is out of the scope of this paper.

There are two main requirements to be satisfied by the proposed system. First, the required amount of data to train the classifier should be the minimum to be able to build the profile for short-lived VMs in acceptable time. Second, the model should provide acceptable accuracy, detection rate and false positive rate and the acceptable level will be discussed later. There should be also a balance between efficiency and efficacy.

4 Approach

The data used in this research imported from our previous research [3]. Data was collected from IaaS cloud environment based on KVM hypervisor. We collected normal and malicious samples of invoked system calls by hosted virtual machines. Normal samples are used for initializing, training and testing the classifier and malicious samples for testing the classifier. Malicious samples are generated using a DoS attack called 'stress test attack', more details about this attack can be found in [3]. The choice of the attack is not of great importance because what is matter here is the detection of behaviour change whether it is legitimate or by an attack. In cloud environments detecting any change of behaviour suppose to be treated as a strong sign of abnormality because as stated in [3] that "regular best practices for IaaS cloud services would argue against such mixed workloads being deployed in single VM instances". They also observe that "server systems tend to perform similar operations repeatedly, providing a sound training data set".

Another important point to be mentioned here, that the HIDS would not be able to detect attacks that do not change the internal behaviour of the VM's operating system; however, this kind of attacks usually related to network thus they might be detected by the NIDS and that is why we state earlier that both HIDS and NIDS are required.

For analysing system calls, we also use the same method from [3] by considering each IOCTL system call with different first and second arguments as a distinct system call because they request different actions from the kernel. We also apply the idea of adding extra item to the list of system calls called 'other' to cover any rarely used system call; this trick is to save time and space [3] by decreasing the number of states in the model.

The used data set for training and testing was collected from a cloud IaaS environment built in the lab with the minimum acceptable setup for production environments; three VMs were hosted in the cloud and they provide an Enterprise Resource Planning (ERP) service which is popular in the cloud. To obtain sufficient activity, the ERP system "was exercised using a number of different scenarios (more than 30 use cases) for the ERP, which were automated using a scripting mechanism consisting of Python scripts and the Dogtail open source automation framework. The selection of use cases and intervals was performed randomly to mimic realistic usage patterns and to avoid generating spurious similarities among data sets" [3].

In this stage we want to build HMM based classifier that generates matrix representing VMs normal behaviour and detect any occurring change of behaviour.

4.1 Building HMM to Model VM Normal Behaviour

HMM is known to provides a very powerful model to capture the structure of sequential data. It generates two sequences of symbols the first is observable and the second is hidden. The hidden states can be discovered only through the observable states. The probabilities of transition from a hidden state to another and from a hidden state to observable state are represented using two probability density functions. The model is denoted as $\lambda = \{A, B, \pi\}$.

HMM Symbols

- A: is transition matrix of size N*N which stores the probabilities of transition from one state to another and it is row stochastic (the sum of each row is equal to 1).

- B: is the observation matrix of size N*M which stores the probabilities of an observable event occurring given that the system is in a certain hidden state and it is row stochastic too.
- π: is the initial state probabilities of each state being the starting of the sequence. It is of size M and it is row stochastic.
- T: length of the observation sequence (is the number of observations taken)
- S: S_1, S_2... S_N is the set of hidden states with N item
- O: O_1, O_2... O_M is the set of observable states which is the set of used distinct system calls with M item

The collected system call traces of the targeted VM are considered as the observation sequence and each system call as an observation symbol. Before building and training the classifier we need first to specify the size of the HMM. HMM consists of two finite sets of states hidden states set S with N item and observable events set O with M item. It is a common practice in HMM anomaly detection classifiers based on system calls to chose the size of N equal to the size of M equal to the number of distinct system calls, as suggested in [18], and in our case the number of distinct system calls are 25[2]. After specifying the size of the HMM becomes the stage of pre-processing the data to train and test the classifier. We import three samples, two are normal and one is malicious. The first normal sample is used to train the classifier while the second and third are for testing purposes.

Training Steps

- Step 1: Imports a normal samples for training
- Step 2: Processes the sample by removing errors, incomplete system calls and IOCTL system calls with missed first or second arguments. We pre-process data using three methods for comparison purposes.
  - Method one: We consider all system calls invoked by the targeted VM. This method is the main method in this research paper however, we will show the results of method two and three in the result and discussion sections.
  - Methods two: We consider only IOCTL system calls and system calls of threat level one from the list of used system calls. The threat level of each system call was imported from [17] but modified depending on the research environment.
  - Method three: Each VM represented in the system with one process, but this process has many threads or child processes. In this method, only main threads are considered. We define main threads as the thread that

[2] In Linux there are more than 300 system calls but the number 25 come from experiment and it is the same used in [3] where only frequently used system calls are considered which are 24 in our setup and then we add one more item called "other" which represent any rarely used system calls. This technique reduce the number of states in HMM which reduce the computation time significantly. In addition, by experiment we found that other system calls are rarely used.

initiate IOCTL system calls; because in this research environment (KVM based virtual environment), IOCTL system call is the most critical system call in our environment for the reason that VMs communicate with resources in the host kernel using IOCTL.

- Step 3: Take a small part of the normal sample and use it to create the list of used distinct system calls then specify the value of M which is 25 for methods one and three and 8 for method two.
- Step 4: Transfer system calls to vector of numbers; for instance system call 'ioctl(11,0xae80,' represented by number 10 and the system call called 'other' represented by number 24. The list of numbers is representing the items of the observable states O.
- Step 5: Convert all of system calls in the training sample to the corresponding number and divide them into group of k = 6 using sliding window from [13]; k is the number of items in each sequence of system calls and it is a common to choose the value of k = 6 [1]. The following example is to simplify the technique of sliding window; for instance if this is the trace of system calls

  ```
  ['ioctl(5,0xae03' 'ioctl(5,0xae03' 'clone' 'read' 'read']
  ```

  It generates the following sequences if k = 3

  ```
  ['ioctl(5,0xae03' 'ioctl(5,0xae03' 'clone'],
  ['ioctl(5,0xae03' 'clone' 'read'],
  ['clone' 'read' 'read']
  ```

- Step 6: Decide the number of sequences of system calls used to train the classifier. Since this classifier is targeting short-lived VMs, the number of sequences used for training should be kept to the minimum. The number of sequences for training and for testing have been chosen by experiment and is shown later in the section.
- Step 7: After deciding the number of sequences to train the classifier, we train the classifier using Baum-Welch algorithm, which is an expectation maximisation algorithm to find the unknown parameters of HMM; the input of the algorithm is sequences of system calls of size 6 and the output is a trained classifier to be used later for testing
- Step 8: End of training process

The next stage is testing the performance of the classifier.

4.2 Testing the Classifier

To test the classifier we used 1500 traces (1000 are normal and 500 are malicious). We enter them to the classifier and calculate the log-likelihood of each trace and calculate two sets of values; Set1 is the difference between the log-likelihood of 500 normal traces 'TR1' and 500 abnormal traces 'TR2'. Set2 is the difference between the log-likelihood of TR1 (the same normal traces used in Set1) and another 500 normal traces 'TR3'. To label traces as normal or malicious and generate the anomaly signal, two thresholds should be designed. The first threshold 'T1' is to decide if a trace is normal (represented by 0) or mismatch (represented by 1). The value of this threshold is calculated using the following equation:

P1 = the average of difference in log-likelihood of normal samples
P2 = the average of difference in log-likelihood of abnormal samples
The threshold T1 = (P1 - P2)/2

For each entry in TR1 and TR2 we calculate the difference in log-likelihood and compare it to T1; If the difference is less than T1, the value set to '1' and the trace is registered as mismatch otherwise the value set to '0', and the trace is registered as normal.

The second threshold T2 is to decide if a chunk of traces are normal or malicious which make the final decision to send anomaly signal or not. Each chunk of traces contain 10 traces. If a chunk of traces registers over 4 mismatches it is considered as a malicious trace and an alert should be raised; however, by experiment, we found that about 50% of the malicious chunks register 10 out of 10 mismatches, which means all traces in the chunk are malicious. If the chunk has 4 or less mismatches it is considered as normal chunk, however about 60% of normal chunks has 8,9 or 10 out of 10 normal traces on them. Dividing traces into chunks helps to make the classifier work on the fly using small amount of data for detecting anomalies. When the classifier starts processing a chunk and it registers 5 mismatches there is no need to continue processing the rest of the chunk because 5 is enough to label it as malicious and the classifier can ignore the rest of the chunk and move to the next one. The choice of T2 and the number of traces in each chunk are defined by experiment.

The amount of data used to train the classifier are relatively small, we used about 780000 system calls to train the classifier which is about 19 MB of collected data and it contains system calls, their arguments and return values. The traces used for detection are of size about 150 KB which contains 6000 system calls with their arguments and return values. The size of a chunk is equal to 1500 KB and in 50% of the samples the classifier is able to decide if a chunk is malicious or not by checking only the first 750 KB of the chunk.

4.3 Efficacy Analysis

To decide if the system used generates a strong enough anomaly signals or not, we use hypothesis testing.

Hypothesis Testing. Q_1 is number of anomaly signals in malicious samples in comparing with normal sample, and Q_2 is number of anomaly signals in normal sample in comparing with another normal sample.

1. The null hypothesis: $H_0 : Q_1 - Q_2 > 5$
   $H_1 : Q_1 - Q_2 <= 5$ (one sided hypothesis)
2. Assume H_0 is true

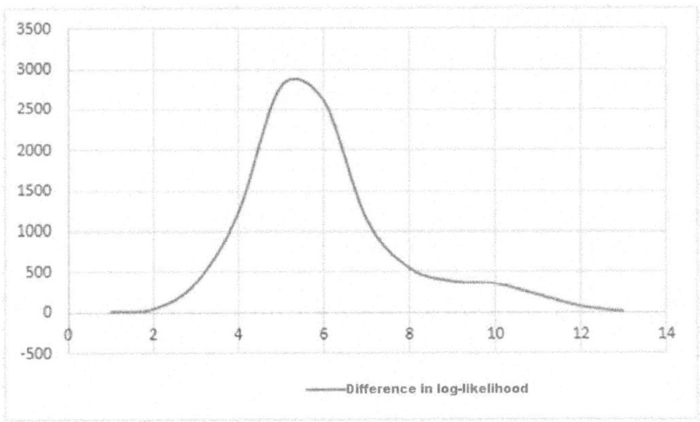

Fig. 1. Difference in log-likelihood between normal and abnormal samples

3. The difference in anomaly signals which is based on the difference in log-likelihood follows approximately normal distribution see Fig. 1
4. Level of significance $\alpha = 0.001$(99.9% confidence level)
5. Find Z scores[3]: $Z_\alpha = Z_{0.001} = -3.09$
6. Find the region of rejection RR which is a set of values less than or equal to α: $(RR <= -3.09)$
7. Collect samples
8. Extract difference in anomalies signals for sequences for each chunk and calculate statistics shown in table 1. N is sample size and μ is the average.

Table 1. Statistics collected from the samples

Normal	Malicious
$N_1 = 8$	$N_2 = 8$
$\mu_1 = 0.625$	$\mu_2 = 9.625$

$SD = \sqrt{\frac{\sigma_1^2}{N_1} + \frac{\sigma_2^2}{N_2}} = 0.320$
$\Delta = 5$ (the value in the null hypothesis)
$\mu = \mu_2 - \mu_1 = 9$ the new centre
$ME = Z_\alpha * SD = Z_{0.001}) * SD = -0.99014$
Range: 8.06 to 9.99
$Z = \frac{\mu - \Delta}{SD} = 12.48303$

9. Draw a conclusion: the test statistics Z = 12.48303 is not in the RR so we retain the null hypothesis

[3] Z Score is a statistical measurement represent the relationship of a score to the mean in a group of scores.

Accuracy, detection rate, and false positive rate criteria are used to measure the efficiency of the detection system. The result of testing 1500 samples with chunk size 10, sequence length 6, each sample contains 1000 sequences and 8 iterations are used to train the classifier is shown in table2

Table 2. Result of testing 1500 samples with chunk size 10, sequence length 6, each sample contains 1000 sequence and 8 iterations

Accuracy	Detection Rate	False Positive Rate
97%	100%	5.66%

4.4 Complexity Analysis

Two main factors are affecting the time and memory complexity of the algorithms. "The time complexity of the Baum-Welch algorithm per iteration scales linearly with the sequence length and quadratically with the number of states. In addition, its memory complexity scales linearly with both sequence length and number of states" [19]. The time complexity is $O(N2k)$ and the memory complexity is $O(Nk)$ [20]. Therefore, to reduce the required computational complexity, we reduce the value of N to an acceptable level. Although Linux has about 326 different system calls, we only consider 25 of them which reduces the time complexity considerably.

4.5 Results

We found that method one provided the best results. Method two, when only IOCTL system calls were monitored, provided a detection rate $\approx$ 83%. For method three, when only main threads were monitored, we found that there are three main threads; the first one provided a very low anomaly signal while the other two fail to distinguish between normal and malicious samples.

The other comparison we made is between different size of training samples of method one. The chunk approach has not been used to provide the results shown in table 3.

Table 3. Different size of training samples

# of System Calls	195000	390000	780000
Detection Rate	$\approx$ 93%	$\approx$ 96%	$\approx$ 97%

After having this primitive results, we decided to use the 780.000 system calls for training then applied the chunk approach which generates the results showed earlier in the section.

5 Discussion

As has been shown earlier, method one detected all of the malicious samples but also labelled some normal chunks as malicious (False Positive rate 5.66%). The FP rate can be lowered by reducing the threshold T1. For instance, instead of dividing the difference in average by 2, as we did, we divide it by 4. This will decrease the FP rate but will increase the False Negative one. Therefore, the choice of this threshold depends on how critical this VM is, in addition to other factors. Providers should design this threshold depending on the nature of their clients, their industry and the geographical area.

We argue that method two fail because IOCTL system calls were not the main system calls to distinguish the 'stress test attack'. Other attacks might be detected by monitoring mainly IOCTL system calls; however, deciding which system call to monitor is a complicated task and going deeper in this track might convert the anomaly detection system to a misuse detection system.

The reason for the failure of task three might be that we monitor the wrong threads. Threads in general are not stable they are created and terminated continually; therefore, the approach of monitoring specific threads under the main process of the VM should be flexible and change with time. More research can be done in this area to find a better definition of 'main threads' rather than (the thread that initiates IOCTL system calls), which is the definition used in this paper. We argue that by monitoring the right threads, the training and detection time will be less and the accuracy will be more.

6 Conclusion

In this research a system call based anomaly detection system was designed using HMM for IaaS public cloud environments to detect anomalies in short-lived VMs traffic. The designed detection system only required about 19 MB of data to train the classifier and less than 150 KB of data for detection. This classifier is based on the fact that VMs in public clouds has a very steady behaviour because of the cost model of the cloud[4] and that their is no need to increase the utilisation of cloud VMs by installing multiple services on them.

Our anomaly detection system successfully detects anomalies without any prior knowledge about the VM from inside, dealing with VMs as black boxes, which is a requirement in public IaaS cloud where VMs are under the full control of their owners.

There are many published papers investigating the area of reducing the cost of HMM; most of the ideas can be applied to our system; however, we have not covered this area in this paper. Also, more research can be done to improve the performance of the classifier by monitoring specific threads, changing the list of

[4] The cost model in the cloud is 'pay for what you use' reduces the importance of increasing servers utilisation by installing multiple services in them. Because instead of doing that consumers can initiate multiple VMs for multiple services and still pay the same.

distinct system calls or improving the representation of IOCTL system calls. Furthermore, system calls arguments can be considered by the classifier to increase the performance. We also think that there is a need for more research to test and find solutions for classifier drafting problem in short-lived VMs. Another interesting problem is how to determine if a newly initiated VM is a short-lived one or not; although this is not a security problem but many security solutions may rely on it. Therefore, we think that there is a need to more research in this area.

References

1. Warrender, C., Forrest, S., Pearlmutter, B.: Detecting intrusions using system calls: Alternative data models. In: IEEE Sympsium on Security and Privacy, pp. 133–145. IEEE Computer Society (1999)
2. Shelke, P.K., Sontakke, S., Gawande, A.D.: Intrusion detection system for cloud computing. International Journal of Scientific and Technology Research 1 (2012)
3. Alarifi, S.S., Wolthusen, S.D.: Detecting anomalies in iaas environments through virtual machine host system call analysis. In: 2012 International Conference for Internet Technology and Secured Transactions, pp. 211–218 (December 2012)
4. Garfinkel, T., Rosenblum, M.: A virtual machine introspection based architecture for intrusion detection. In: Proc. Network and Distributed Systems Security Symposium, pp. 191–206 (2003)
5. Laureano, M., Maziero, C., Jamhour, E.: Intrusion detection in virtual machine environments. In: Proceedings of the 30th EUROMICRO Conference, EUROMICRO 2004, pp. 520–525. IEEE Computer Society, Washington, DC (2004)
6. Forrest, S., Hofmeyr, S.A., Somayaji, A., Longstaff, T.: A sense of self for unix processes. In: Proceedings of the 1996 IEEE Symposium on Security and Privacy, pp. 120–128 (May 1996)
7. Hofmeyr, S.A., Forrest, S., Somayaji, A.: Intrusion detection using sequences of system calls. J. Comput. Secur. 6(3), 151–180 (1998)
8. Vieira, K., Schulter, A., Westphall, C., Westphall, C.: Intrusion detection for grid and cloud computing. IT Professional 12(4), 38–43 (2010)
9. Gul, I., Hussain, M.: Distributed cloud intrusion detection model. International Journal of Advanced Science and Technology 34 (2011)
10. Hu, J., Yu, X., Qiu, D., Chen, H.H.: A simple and efficient hidden markov model scheme for host- based anomaly intrusion detection. Netwrk. Mag. of Global Internetwkg. 23(1), 42–47 (2009)
11. Yan Yeung, D., Ding, Y.: Host-based intrusion detection using dynamic and static behavioral models. Pattern Recognition 36, 229–243 (2003)
12. Kang, D.K., Fuller, D., Honavar, V.: Learning classifiers for misuse and anomaly detection using a bag of system calls representation. In: Proceedings from the Sixth Annual IEEE SMC Information Assurance Workshop, IAW 2005, pp. 118–125 (June 2005)
13. Warrender, C., Forrest, S., Pearlmutter, B.: Detecting intrusions using system calls: Alternative data models. In: IEEE Symposium on Security and Privacy, pp. 133–145. IEEE Computer Society (1999)
14. Sultana, A., Hamou-Lhadj, A., Couture, M.: An improved hidden markov model for anomaly detection using frequent common patterns. In: ICC, pp. 1113–1117. IEEE (2012)

15. Hu, J.: Host-based anomaly intrusion detection. In: Stavroulakis, P.P., Stamp, M. (eds.) Handbook of Information and Communication Security, pp. 235–255. Springer (2010)
16. Mutz, D., Valeur, F., Vigna, G., Kruegel, C.: Anomalous system call detection. ACM Trans. Inf. Syst. Secur. 9(1), 61–93 (2006)
17. Bernaschi, M., Gabrielli, E., Mancini, L.V.: Operating system enhancements to prevent the misuse of system calls. In: Proceedings of the 7th ACM Conference on Computer and Communications Security, CCS 2000, pp. 174–183. ACM, New York (2000)
18. Hoang, X., Hu, J.: An efficient hidden markov model training scheme for anomaly intrusion detection of server applications based on system calls. In: Proceedings of the 12th IEEE International Conference on Networks (ICON 2004), vol. 2, pp. 470–474 (November 2004)
19. Khreich, W., Granger, E., Sabourin, R., Miri, A.: Combining hidden markov models for improved anomaly detection. In: IEEE International Conference on Communications, ICC 2009, pp. 1–6 (June 2009)
20. Khreich, W.: Towards Adaptive Anomaly Detection Systems using Boolean Combination of Hidden Markov Models. PhD thesis, Ecole De Technologie Superieure, Université Du Quebec, Canada (2011)

JShadObf: A JavaScript Obfuscator Based on Multi-Objective Optimization Algorithms

Benoît Bertholon[1], Sébastien Varrette[2], and Pascal Bouvry[2]

[1]Interdisciplinary Centre for Security Reliability and Trust
[2]Computer Science and Communication (CSC) Research Unit
University of Luxembourg
6, rue Richard Coudenhove-Kalergi
L-1359 Luxembourg, Luxembourg
Firstname.Name@uni.lu

Abstract. With the advent of the Cloud Computing (CC) paradigm and the explosion of new Web Services proposed over the Internet (such as Google Office Apps, Dropbox or Doodle just to cite a few of them), the protection of the programs at the heart of these services becomes more and more crucial, especially for the companies making business on top of these services. In parallel, the overwhelming majority of modern websites use the JavaScript programming language as all modern web browsers – either on desktops, game consoles, tablets or smart phones – include JavaScript interpreters making it the most ubiquitous programming language in history. Thus, JavaScript is the core technology of most web services. In this context, this article focuses on novel *obfuscation* techniques to protect JavaScript program contents.

Informally, the goal of obfuscation is to make a program "unintelligible" without altering its functionality, thus preventing reverse-engineering on the program. However, this approach hardly caught attention from the research community after stand-alone obfuscation for arbitrary programs has been proven impossible in 2001. Here we would like to renew this interest with the proposal of JSHADOBF, an obfuscation framework based on evolutionary heuristics designed to optimize *for a given input JavaScript program*, the sequence of transformations that should be applied to the source code to improve its obfuscation capacity. Measuring this capacity is based on the combination of several metrics optimized simultaneously with Multi-Objective Evolutionary Algorithms (MOEAs). Whereas our approach cannot pretend to offer an absolute protection, the objective remains to protect the target program for a sufficiently long period of time. The experiment results initially conducted on a pedagogical example then on JQuery – the most popular and widely used JavaScript library – outperform existing solutions. It demonstrates the validity of the approach and its concrete usage in reference codes used worldwide.

Keywords: Obfuscation, JavaScript Compilation, MOEA.

1 Introduction

The Obfuscation of source code is a mechanism to modify a source code to make it harder to understand by humans even with the help of computing resources. More precisely, the objective is to conceal the purpose of a program or its logic without altering

J. Lopez, X. Huang, and R. Sandhu (Eds.): NSS 2013, LNCS 7873, pp. 336–349, 2013.

its functionality, thus preventing the tampering or the reverse engineering of the program. While this research area used to be popular in the 90's, it has raised far less enthusiasm after stand-alone obfuscation for arbitrary programs has been proven impossible in 2001 [10]. Yet this aversion might change with the recent advent of the Cloud Computing (CC) paradigm and the explosion of new Web Services proposed over the Internet (such as Google Office Apps, Dropbox or Doodle just to cite a few of them). More and more companies are making business on top of such services, with the limitations and drawbacks inherent to this context as part or all the web service are executed in the client browser. That's where obfuscation techniques catch back the interest of the industrial: whereas this approach cannot pretend to offer an absolute protection over time, preventing the reverse-engineering of a program containing the enterprise core business for a certain amount of time definitely makes sense until better techniques (homomorphic encryption etc.) become available.

In this article, we present and detail JSHADOBF, an obfuscation framework based on evolutionary heuristics designed to optimize *for a given input JavaScript program*, the sequence of transformations that should be applied to the source code to improve its obfuscation capacity. Our work focuses here on the JavaScript language as the overwhelming majority of modern websites use the JavaScript programming language. Also, all modern web browsers – either on desktops, game consoles, tablets or smart phones – include JavaScript interpreters making it the most ubiquitous programming language in history. That's probably why a company such as Google heavily uses this language for most of its services (Gmail or Google Docs, just to cite a few). Measuring the obfuscation capacity within JSHADOBF is based on the combination of well known metrics, coming from Software Engineering, which are optimized simultaneously thanks to Multi-Objective Evolutionary Algorithms (MOEAs). We have validated our approach over two concrete examples: one pedagogical (a classical matrix multiplication program) and one more serious on the most popular and widely used JavaScript library, named *JQuery*. We obtained experimental results that outperformed existing solutions. Thus, it demonstrates not only the feasibility of the approach but also its concrete usage in reference codes used worldwide.

This article is organized as follows: section 2 presents the background of this work (from the JavaScript programming language to the notion of Evolutionary Algorithms (EAs) and code obfuscation), and reviews related works. The section 3 describes the JSHADOBF proposal, an EA-based JavaScript Obfuscator. The validation of JSHADOBF on concrete applications is expounded in the section 4 and presents the associated experimental results. Finally, the section 5 concludes the paper and provides the future directions.

2 Context and Motivations

2.1 The JavaScript Programming Language

Quoting [18], JavaScript is the programming language of the Web. The overwhelming majority of modern websites use the JavaScript programming language and all modern web browsers – either on desktops, game consoles, tablets or smart phones – include JavaScript interpreters making it the most ubiquitous programming language in history.

More concretely, JavaScript is a high-level, dynamic, untyped interpreted programming language which is well-suited to object oriented and functional programming styles. JavaScript derives its syntax from Java, its first-class functions from Scheme, and its prototype-based inheritance from Self. Initially, many professional programmers denigrated the language for various reasons, ranging from design errors to buggy implementation in the first versions of the language. The standardization of the language within the European Computer Manufacturer's Association (ECMA) and, more importantly, the advent of Asynchronous JavaScript and XML (AJAX) returned JavaScript to the spotlight and brought more professional programming attention. It resulted in the proliferation of comprehensive frameworks and libraries, improved JavaScript programming practices, together with an increased usage of JavaScript outside of web browsers within server-side JavaScript platforms.

Generally speaking, JavaScript has long since outgrown its scripting-language roots to become a robust and efficient general-purpose language. The latest version of the language defines new features for serious large-scale software developments, which also explains the interest of all major vendors such as Microsoft or Google. In parallel, the recent explosion of novel web services that goes along with the early advent of the Cloud Computing (CC) paradigm increase the widespread adoption of JavaScript at the core of the development of these services. To cite a few well-known examples, one can mention Google Office Apps (featuring GMail or Google Docs), Dropbox (a popular web-based storage service – see `https://www.dropbox.com/`) or Doodle (a web-based scheduling service – see `http://www.doodle.com/`). Google is so deeply dependent on this language that they released their home-made development framework for JavaScript under the banner of the Closure Tools project [1]. Of interest for the work presented in this article, we can cite the Closure Compiler which compiles JavaScript into compact, high-performance code. This compiler removes dead code, then rewrites and minimizes what's left so that it downloads and runs quickly on the client's browser. It also checks syntax, variable references, and types, and warns about common JavaScript pitfalls. These checks and optimization are meant to help writing applications that are less buggy and easier to maintain.

2.2 Evolutionary Algorithms (EAs)

EA is a class of solving techniques based on the Darwinian theory of evolution [15] which involves the search of a *population* X_t of solutions. Members of the population are feasible solutions and called *individuals*. Each iteration of an EA involves a competitive selection that weeds out poor solutions through the *evaluation* of a fitness value that indicates the quality of the individual as a solution to the problem. The evolutionary process involves at each generation a set of stochastic operators that are applied on the individuals, typically recombination (or cross-over) and mutation. Execution of simple EAs requires high computational resources in case of non-trivial problems, in particular the evaluation of the population is often the costliest operation in EAs. There exists many useful models of EAs yet a pseudo-code of a general execution scheme is provided in the Algorithm 2.2.

EAs are popular approaches to solve various hard optimization problems: on average, they generally converge to "*good*" solutions more quickly than the naive exhaustive

Algorithm 1. General scheme of an EA in pseudo-code.

```
t ← 0;
Generation(X_t); // generate the initial population
Evaluation(X_t); // evaluate population
while Stopping criteria not satisfied do
    X̂_t ← ParentsSelection(X_t); // select parents
    X'_t ← Modification(X̂_t); // cross-over + mutation
    Evaluation(X'_t); // evaluate offspring
    X_{t+1} ← Selection(X_t,X'_t); // select survivors of the next generation
    t ← t + 1;
end while
```

search algorithm. This article investigates the use of EAs for the protection of JavaScript programs by means of obfuscation, a notion reviewed in the next section. In this context, several criteria are optimized simultaneously to effectively explore and measure the trade-off that might be selected among these objectives. That's why our work comes into the framework of Multi-Objective Evolutionary Algorithms (MOEAs).

2.3 Code Obfuscation

Usually, when talking about security, the matter is about protecting a computer from intrusions or malicious software. Here, we are interested in the mechanisms that permit to protect software from piracy. More precisely, the objective is to deliberately obfuscate the source code of a program to conceal its purpose or its logic without altering its functionality, thus preventing the tampering or the reverse engineering of the program. We now provide the preliminary definitions required for the sequel of this paper. Most of them have been defined in the seminal work of Collberg [13]:

Definition 1 (Obfuscating Transformation)
Let $P \xrightarrow{\mathcal{T}} P'$ be a transformation of a source program P into a target P'. $P \xrightarrow{\mathcal{T}} P'$ is an obfuscation transformation *if P and P' have the same* observable behavior. *More precisely, if P fails to terminate or terminate with an error condition, then P' may or may not terminate. Otherwise P' must terminate and produce the same output as P.*

Observable behavior can be defined as being the behavior experienced by the user. This means everything the user can notice at first sight. Hence, if P' has side effects (new created files, network communications ...) that are not noticed by the user, it can still have the same observable behavior (provided it has the same user experienced effects as P).

Obfuscating transformations can affect different aspects of a program structure. They can be classified in three main classes:

1. *Data obfuscation*: this gathers all the transformations that obscure the data structures used in a program. This includes for instance the changes in variable

representation (from their encoding to their promotion[1]), the conversion from static data to procedural data, the split or the aggregation of variables etc.
2. *Layout obfuscation*. In this case, the transformations change the information included in the code formatting, typically by scrambling identifier names or the code indentation.
3. *Control obfuscation* which affect the aggregation, ordering or computations performed within the program control-flow. Applying control obfuscation technique often implies slowing down the program. Under the different approaches that fall under this category, we can mention the manipulation of predicates within the program to make them opaque, the insertion of dead code, the extension of loop conditions, the conversion of a reducible flow graph to a non-reducible one, the addition of redundant operands or interleaving functions, the inlining (or outlining) of function, the code parallelization or all the loop transformations (such as the loop unrolling).

In order to evaluate the obfuscation capacity induced by an obfuscating transformation, several metrics can be considered. McCabe proposes a graph theory oriented metric [23] in which the control flow of programs is seen as graphs. Here, a program complexity is measured by the number of linearly independent paths which is equal to $e - n + p$ in strongly connected graphs (e being the number of edges, n the number of vertices and p the number of connected components of the graph). Control flows of programs being assumed to have a strongly connected structure, we can see how adding more independent paths in a program can increase its complexity.

Chidamber and Kemerer listed several metrics for object oriented programs [12] like giving weight to classes, measuring coupling between classes (i.e. evaluating the interactions between classes) or the lack of cohesion in methods (i.e. measure the similarity between two methods counting the instance variables used in common). When not using object oriented program, some parallel lines can be drawn with data structures (*e.g.* Measuring global variable or data structures used by several functions, evaluation interactions between variables ...). The most well-known static metrics used to measuring software complexity are the following ones [14]:

μ_1 Program Length [19]. The more P has operators and operands, the more complex it gets.
μ_2 Cyclomatic Complexity [23]. The complexity of a function is measured by the number of predicates it contains.
μ_3 Nesting Complexity [20]. The more conditionals of a function are nested, the more complex that function is.
μ_4 Data Flow Complexity [24]. The complexity of a function increases with the number of variables references in inter-basic blocks.
μ_5 Fan-in/out Complexity [21]. A function is more complex if it has more formal parameters, its complexity also increases with number of global data structures it reads or writes.

[1] *Promoting* a variable means replacing a specialized storage structure by a more general one. For example, in a language such as Java, an integer typed variable can be replaced by an Integer class. The variable promotion could also be an increasing of its lifetime, like making a local variable global.

μ_e or μ_6 the efficiency of the code measured as the average execution time of the code on a reference machine, using one or more test cases representing normal execution of the program.

2.4 Obfuscation of JavaScript Programs

The obfuscation of a JavaScript program has been addressed by the Internet community as well as by hackers to embed malicious code in websites, for instance to redirect requests to another website so as to increase the number of visitors. In reaction, the research community had done many studies to detect malicious websites and thus obfuscated code through the analysis of JavaScript source code. For instance, the authors in [11] analyze the string variables contained in the JavaScript source code to classify the websites as malicious or not. The metrics used in this paper are string related metrics (this includes string length, frequency of particular function or entropy of the function or variable names). Following the same trend, the authors of [17] have patched the SpiderMonkey [6] JavaScript interpreter (which is used in the well known web browser `firefox`) to make some statistics about the code, like counting the number of newly generated strings or counting the number of `eval` calls during the execution of the program and thus can help to detect obfuscated code. As regards the obfuscation process in itself, there exists relatively few studies or tools in the literature. Indeed the current JavaScript obfuscation techniques mostly use data obfuscation on string variables and the `eval` function provided by the JavaScript language allowing the dynamic execution of strings. These techniques are used for instance by the on-line JavaScript obfuscator [3] or in packer [5] Another tool worth to mention is UgligyJS, a JavaScript obfuscator, compressor (minifier) or beautifier. Depending of the user's request, it performs many small optimizations and obfuscations to alter the initial JavaScript source code. The possible transformations are listed on the uglifyjs website [7]. ObfuscateJS has been as well included in the tools tested against JShadObf even if the last version of the software dates from 2006 [4]. The non-free JavaScript obfuscator, Jasob [2] has been used for the tests with the trial version. The other ones we wish to mention in this section are minifiers, an operation that can be seen as a partial obfuscation as it complexifies the JavaScript code. In this framework, we can cite the minifier of Yahoo, called YUI Compressor [8], which works on a few simple example but fail to parse complex codes such as the one of the `JQuery` library. A more powerful alternative is the minifier of Google called `closurecompiler` [1].

To sum up, obfuscation of JavaScript programs is still at a early stage and there is place for huge improvements. That's where comes the main contribution (and interest) of this article with the proposal of JSHADOBF, an obfuscation framework based on evolutionary heuristics designed to optimize *for a given input JavaScript program*, the sequence of transformations that should be applied to the source code to improve its obfuscation capacity.

3 JSHADOBF: An EA-Based JavaScript Obfuscator

This part is describing how is operating the JSHADOBF program, an overview of the full process is shown in figure 1. The implementation of the solution had to answer

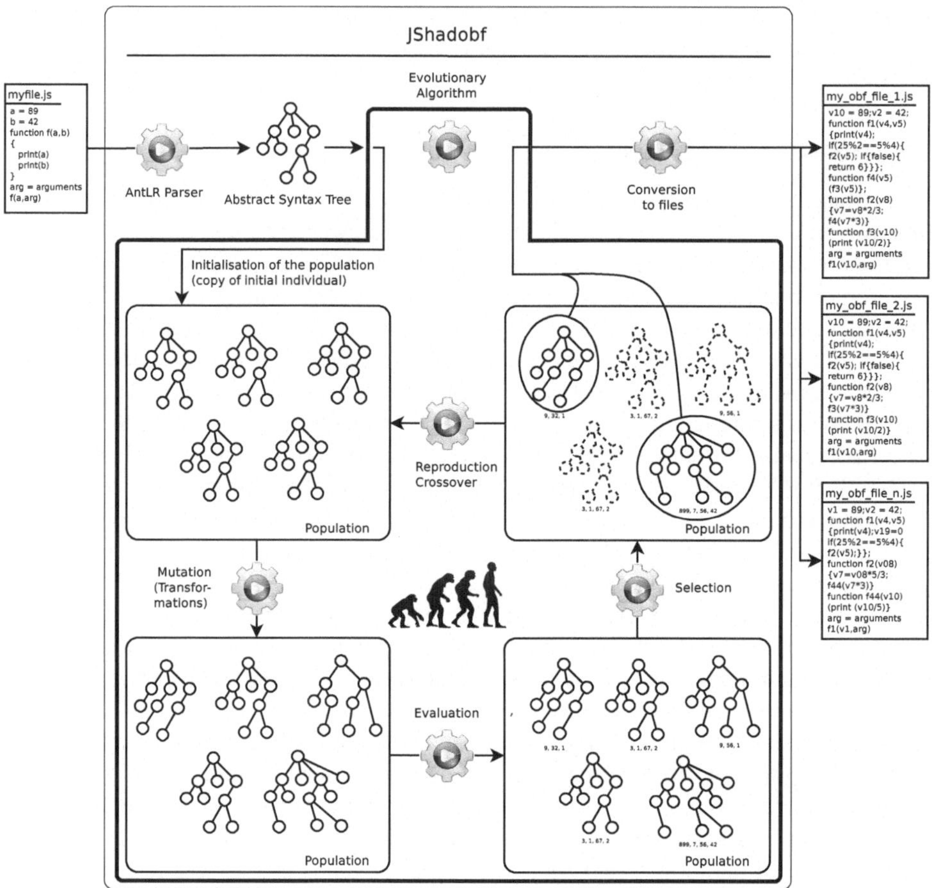

Fig. 1. Overview of JSHADOBF, describing the full process of the generation of new representations of the code

the four issues exposed in the following subsections. §3.1: How to parse a JavaScript program? §3.2: What transformations can be applied ? §3.3: How do you measure their efficiency? And §3.4: How to use EA to increase the obfuscation level of an *individual*?

3.1 AntLR Parsing

The JavaScript code is parsed using the grammar AntLR [25] developed with the help of the ECMAScript Standardization document [22]. Thanks to this grammar, the AntLR Parser is able to parse a file containing complex JavaScript source code and some JavaScript 1.8 "dialect" syntax. This grammar has been validated on the well known `JQuery` framework [9]. AntLR generates the Abstract Syntax Tree (AST) representation of a JavaScript source code. The Abstract Syntax Tree (AST) is a standard type of representation of a source code and almost all compilers (source to source or source to binary) are using to apply modification, optimization or to generate other representations of the code *e.g* binary. It is a tree-based representation of the source code containing all the information about the source code, and the structure tree embeds the structure of the source code *i.e.*, without the parenthesis, brackets. Source code of programs translated into an AST representation are easier to work with when dealing with any kind of modifications. Indeed this representation allow the programming of a generic `tree_walker` used to compute the metrics but as well to perform the different transformations. This `tree_walker` is given in parameter the function to used depending on the desired action, either the computation of a metric or some modifications on the AST. The following subsections §3.2 and §3.3 describe computation applied using this standard way of walking into the AST.

3.2 Considered Transformations

The different transformations developed within the framework of JSHADOBF are applied directly on the AST, and are not modifying the output of the program. They are simple in order to be easier to check, but applied many times on different parts of the program, they make the program harder to read. Here is the list of the transformations already developed:

- Renaming. This transformation is modifying and changing the name of some identifier randomly (except the identifiers which are used globally, or the one specified not to be).
- Outlining. The outlining transformation takes a set of statements and outline them. This create a new function either in the same scope or in an higher scope depending on the side effects of the selected set.
- Dummy If insertion: adds dummy if statements with randomly generated predicate.
- Dummy variable insertion: adds unused variables in the code.
- Dummy expression insertion: generation of random expressions and insertion at random position in the code.
- Changing place of variable declaration: when applicable, moving the variable declaration.
- Re-formatting string constants: replacement of the string constants, by concatenation of sub strings contained in variables declared in the same scope of the program.

These transformations have been tested on a test-suite of JavaScript programs, to ensure that the first requirement of the definition of a obfuscation holds *i.e.* keeping the functionality of the program intact. Because transformations applied on the source code can interfere between themselves, JSHADOBF uses very simple transformations tested on multiple JavaScript programs as well as many different combinations to ensure their validity. This aggregation of modifications used with the power of EA increases a lot the level of obfuscation of the program. However in order to determine the level of obfuscation of a source code, some metrics are needed. The next subsection will present the selected ones.

3.3 Metrics Used to Measure JSHADOBF Individual Quality

The metrics used to evaluate a source code complexity are the metrics presented in the §2.3. They will be used in the fitness functions to compute the fitness values. As we decided to explore the search space to minimize all these values, the fitness function are defined as follows: $\forall x \in [1..5], fitness_x(I) = 1/\mu_x$. Only the time of execution μ_e is directly the fitness value: $fitness_e(I) = \mu_e$.

The AST representation has been helpful also to compute the static metrics. In order to compute the time of execution, test-cases which are representatives to normal executions of the program are needed, preferably covering every portion of code within the program, in order to verify that transformations do not lead to a too important time of execution. The next section explains how the transformations are used in the EA at the heart of JSHADOBF.

3.4 Evolutionary Algorithms (EAs) Used within JSHADOBF

As the different metrics used are nearly independent from each others, they have to be taken into account in the EA, thus JSHADOBF relied on Multi-Objective Evolutionary Algorithm (MOEA) to search for solutions of the obfuscating process. We now review the classical steps EA as presented in the §2.2 in the context of JSHADOBF. The figure 1 illustrated all these phases.

Reproduction and Crossover. The reproduction selected is a simple recopy of *individuals*, we didn't implement any crossover, due to the nature of *individuals*. As stated in [26] there is no reason to say that crossover should always be used. Indeed one could think that a quite straight forward crossover could be the exchange of functions between *individuals*, however transformations such as outlining, and renaming make it more difficult, this is nonetheless a subject to be studied in future work.

Mutation. *Individual* mutation corresponds to the application of a randomly selected transformation, on a randomly selected portion of the AST assuming it makes sense for the considered transformation. This transformation is applied at most n times, with n selected by the user at the beginning of the process, allowing the limitation of the number of transformations at each step.

Evaluation. This stage is performed by computing the fitness functions defined previously. First, the five static metrics are computed by browsing through the AST representation, then a sub-process is launched to run the *individual* with standard input, leading preferably to a deterministic output, and the time taken by the sub-process to complete its task is the sixth metric. To counter the non-regularity of the execution time of process, this dynamic metric is computed n times, and the average is taken as the result of the computation. This dynamic evaluation of the *individuals* guarantees as well that the population stays valid according to the definition of obfuscation.

Selection. We use here NSGA-II [16], which is one of the reference selection algorithm for MOEAs. It is selecting the *individuals* by taking into account the non-domination criteria and the distance from one to the others to guarantee a good diversity as well as the leading *individuals* of the population. The selection uses the values of the fitness function computed during the evaluation part of the EA.

The cycle of the EA then continues until a certain number of generations has been reached, or until the different fitness values obtained are small enough for the user of JSHADOBF.

4 Experiments and Validations

We have validated our approach over two concrete examples: one pedagogical (a classical matrix multiplication program `matmul.js` which is outputting the result of the multiplication of two matrix) and one more serious on the most popular and widely used JavaScript library, named *JQuery* [9]. For the Matrix multiplication program the MOEA used a population of a size 1000 *individuals*, performing over 50 generations. The size of the population for the JQuery framework is 100 *individuals* which is smaller due to the size of the initial program which is approximately 8000 lines of code (160ko without comments), and the number of generations as well 50. JSHADOBF can as well be run with as target not the number of generation but rather some values for the objective functions. This however could lead to infinite computation if the objective are not reachable *e.g.* time of execution too small.

4.1 Experiments on a Matrix Multiplication Program

The graphs in the figures 2 are showing the relation between different metrics every tenth generation after the first generation for the Matrix multiplication program.

The pareto fronts are easily distinguishable on the different figures, they have different shapes as they are projections of the results of a MOEA algorithm with six objectives. On the different graphs may appear some alignment of the *individuals* (like

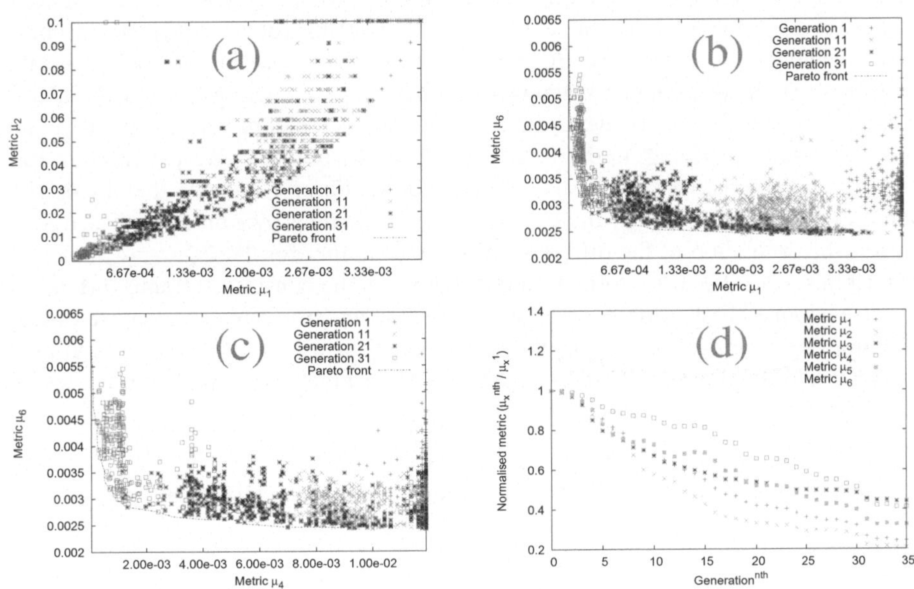

Fig. 2. Experimental results obtained for the obfuscation of a Matrix Multiplication program by JSHADOBF. (a), (b), (c): Example of 2D pareto fronts. (d): Evolution of the mean values of the different metrics.

when comparing μ_2 and μ_6, or when evaluating μ_1 and μ_2), this is explained by way the fitness function is computed, indeed it is often the inverse of an integer value.

The figure 2(d) represents the means values $mean_x(n^{th})$ of the fitness function $fitness_x$ of a generation n^{th} of size m which is computed as follows:

$$mean_x(n^{th}) = \frac{\sum_{i=1}^{m} fitness_x(I_i^{n^{th}})}{m}$$

These mean values are then normalised with the mean values of the first generation to be able to represent them on the same graphic:

$$f_x(n^{th}) = \frac{mean_x(n^{th})}{fitness_x(I^{1^{st}})}$$

The function f_x is computed with in argument the generation's number n^{th} for all the six metrics μ_x selected. We can then see the evolution of mean of the population regarding the selected metrics. On one of the individuals of the last generation, which has been chosen a priori, the metrics presented in the table 1 has been computed to show the evolution from the initial program and to compare with other obfuscator / minifier.

4.2 Experiments on `JQuery`

For the second experiment, we decided to apply JSHADOBF on a more serious application. For this reason, we selected one of the most popular and widely used JavaScript library *i.e.* `JQuery` [9], in the hope that it can illustrate the robustness and the usability of the technique presented here. `JQuery` is a fast and concise JavaScript Library that simplifies HTML document traversing, event handling, animating, and AJAX interactions for rapid web development. `JQuery` in its development version, is distributed with a test-suite verifying, in the version used, 3884 assertions. We use this test suite as a way to demonstrate the correct behaviour or the library, knowing that the original non-obfuscated version of `jquery.js` fails on 7 assertions over the 3884. The figure 3 depicts the evaluation of the different obfuscator/minifier for the `JQuery` framework against this test suite. It is worth to notice that when the considered framework is able to parse completely the library and thus to generate an obfuscated version, we observe the same behavior *i.e.* 7 assertions failed. Obviously, it would have been very unlikely to decrease this value as all framework derive the original code. At least it proves that the obfuscated/minified versions do have the expected action.

4.3 Comparison of JSHADOBF with Other Obfuscators/Minifiers

We compared the results obtain with the JSHADOBF program with other existing Obfuscator/Minifier. The comparison uses the metrics already shown in the §2.3. The results shown in table 1 reveal that JSHADOBF program performs better than the others on the selected metric. This is quite obvious because it uses EA to increase these values, whereas the others do not target these specific metrics. Indeed the transformations used by UglifyJS are not inserting dead code, but rather modifying a bit the different

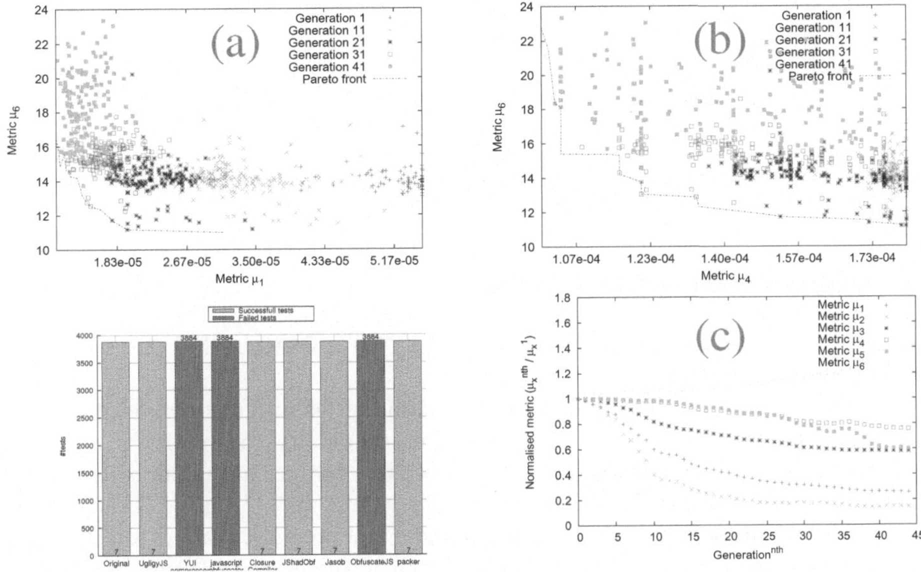

Fig. 3. Experimental results obtained for the obfuscation of the `jquery.js` program by JSHADOBF. (a), (b): Example of 2D pareto fronts, JQuery Unit test suite results, and (c) evolution of the mean values of the different metrics.

Table 1. Summary of the obtained results. Green cells indicate the best results so far.

`matmul.js`	μ_1	μ_2	μ_3	μ_4	μ_5	μ_e/μ_e(**ref**)
Original sources	254	10	4	84	51	1
UgligyJS [7]	252	8	4	84	51	1.0024
YUI compressor [8]	254	10	4	84	51	1.0086
`javascriptobfuscator` [3]	318	10	4	97	35	1.6055
Closure Compiler [1]	243	8	4	81	51	0.992706
Jasob [2]	254	10	4	84	51	1.0052
ObfuscateJS [4]	254	10	4	84	51	1.0058
Packer [5]	127	4	3	40	91	1.7918
JSHADOBF	6343	355	11	955	952	6.30254

`jquery.js`	μ_1	μ_2	μ_3	μ_4	μ_5	μ_e/μ_e(**ref**)
Original sources	18169	673	9	5519	16511	1
UgligyJS [7]	17990	359	9	5318	18673	1.009
Jasob [2]	18005	669	10	5463	16405	1.0074
Packer [5]	127	4	3	40	91	1.008
Closure Compiler [1]	17677	374	8	5486	28051	1.000
JSHADOBF	88843	7030	15	7410	20735	1.013

expressions and even removing unreachable code. Closure Compiler is as well reducing the source code and not only the length but the number of operand, indeed this is shown by the values in the two tables. The μ_1 which takes into account the number of operand *i.e.* the length of the variable name does not matter, is inferior than the initial value.

Table 2. Correlation of the metrics for the 20 first generations of the `JQuery` program

	μ_1	μ_2	μ_3	μ_4	μ_5	μ_e
μ_1	1.0000000	0.9585020	0.8961660	0.5712278	0.3797580	-0.5521950
μ_2		1.0000000	0.8407987	0.4467864	0.2861682	-0.4422623
μ_3			1.0000000	0.5999287	0.3358829	-0.5806230
μ_4				1.0000000	0.7937583	-0.5900691
μ_5					1.0000000	-0.4642683
μ_e						1.0000000

4.4 Summary of the Obtained Results

The table 1 summarised the results obtained with JSHADOBF and the other obfuscator available in the literature.

The table 2 shows the coefficients of correlation of the different metrics computed for the 200 *individuals* of the 40 first generations on the `JQuery` program, the green cells reflect highly correlated values. This shows that for the selected transformations the $\mu 1$, μ_2 and μ_3 are correlated and the μ_4 and μ_5 are as well correlated. This however is dependent to the selected transformations and might not occurs on the selection of a different set of modifications. Some *individuals* are available on JSHADOBF. website[2].

5 Conclusion

We have presented in this article JSHADOBF, a source to source JavaScript obfuscator based on Multi-Objective Evolutionary Algorithms (MOEAs). Our proposed framework optimizes simultaneously six metrics – five evaluating the obfuscation capacity of the population being evolved and one quantifying the performance of each individual solution by measuring the execution time on a reference computing machine. Experimental results on two concrete JavaScript applications have been provided. We first tested JSHADOBF on a simple pedagogical example, *i.e.* a matrix multiplication function where we outperformed the few existing tools. We then decided to validate our approach on one of the most popular and widely used JavaScript library *i.e.* JQuery. When the existing tools were not even able to parse successfully the library, JSHADOBF managed to parse it completely and to generate the different obfuscated versions to effectively explore and measure the trade-off that might be selected among the six objectives analyzed.

Of course, this work opens many perspectives. We are currently investigating the implementation of additional transformations (such as the modification of strings, the loop unrolling, the inlining of functions...) but also other metrics. In particular, we are investigating ways to adapt the data structure complexity to the case of the JavaScript programming language, and also ways to take into account the string length and the number of calls to the `eval` function which most of the time decrease the readability of a program, like in [17] because the complexity added by packer [5] cannot be measure by the selected metrics. Also, to accelerate the convergence of the evolutionary process and permit a distributed execution, we are adapting the island model to JSHADOBF and the first results are promising.

[2] `http://jshadobf.gforge.uni.lu/`

Acknowledgments. The experiments presented in this paper were carried out using the HPC facility of the University of Luxembourg. This work is supported by the Fonds National de la Recherche (FNR), Luxembourg *PHD-09-142*.

References

1. Closure compiler, `https://developers.google.com/closure/compiler/`
2. Jasob, `http://www.jasob.com/`
3. Javascriptobfuscator, `http://www.javascriptobfuscator.com/`
4. Obfuscatejs, `http://tools.2vi.nl/`
5. Packer, `http://dean.edwards.name/packer/`
6. Spidermonkey, `https://developer.mozilla.org/en-US/docs/SpiderMonkey`
7. Ugligyjs, `https://github.com/mishoo/UglifyJS`
8. Yui compressor, `http://developer.yahoo.com/yui/compressor/`
9. Jquery (2012), `http://www.jquery.org/`
10. Barak, B., Goldreich, O., Impagliazzo, R., Rudich, S., Sahai, A., Vadhan, S., Yang, K.: On the (Im)possibility of obfuscating programs. In: Kilian, J. (ed.) CRYPTO 2001. LNCS, vol. 2139, pp. 1–18. Springer, Heidelberg (2001)
11. Byung-Ik Kim, H.-C.J., Im, C.-T.: Suspicious malicious web site detection with strength analysis of a javascript obfuscation. International Journal of Advanced Science and Technology
12. Chidamber, S.R., Kemerer, C.F.: A metrics suite for object oriented design (1994)
13. Collberg, C., Nagra, J.: Surreptitious Software: Obfuscation, Watermarking, and Tamperproofing for Software Protection. Addison-Wesley Professional (2009)
14. Collberg, C., Thomborson, C., Low, D.: A taxonomy of obfuscating transformations. Rapport technique l'Université d'Auckland, -1 (1997)
15. Darwin, C.: The Origin of Species. John Murray (1859)
16. Deb, K., Agrawal, S., Pratap, A., Meyarivan, T.: A fast elitist non-dominated sorting genetic algorithm for multi-objective optimization: NSGA-II. In: Deb, K., Rudolph, G., Lutton, E., Merelo, J.J., Schoenauer, M., Schwefel, H.-P., Yao, X. (eds.) PPSN 2000. LNCS, vol. 1917, pp. 849–858. Springer, Heidelberg (2000)
17. Feinstein, B., Peck, D.: Caffeine monkey: Automated collection, detection and analysis of malicious javascript. In: DEFCON 15 (2007)
18. Flanagan, D.: JavaScript: The Definitive Guide Activate Your Web Pages, 6th edn. O'Reilly Media, Inc. (2011)
19. Halstead, M.H.: Elements of software science (1977)
20. Harrison, W.A., Magel, K.I.: A complexity measure based on nesting level. SIGPLAN Notices 16(3), 63–74 (1981)
21. Henry, S., Kafura, D.: Software structure metrics based on information flow. IEEE Transactions on Software Engineering SE-7(5) (1981)
22. E. C. M. A. International. ECMA-262: ECMAScript Language Specification. ECMA (European Association for Standardizing Information and Communication Systems), 3rd edn., Geneva, Switzerland (December 1999)
23. McCabe, T.J.: A complexity measure. IEEE Transactions on Software Engineering SE-2(4) (1976)
24. Oviedo, E.I.: Control flow, data flow, and program complexity. In: Proceedings of IEEE COMPSAC, pp. 146–152 (1980)
25. Parr, T.J., Parr, T.J., Quong, R.W.: Antlr: A predicated-ll(k) parser generator (1995)
26. Reeves, C.R., Rowe, J.E.: Genetic algorithms: principles and perspectives. A guide to GA theory. Kluwer Academic Publishers (2003)

Forward Secure Certificateless Proxy Signature Scheme

Jiguo Li*, Yanqiong Li, and Yichen Zhang

College of Computer and Information Engineering, Hohai University,
Nanjing 210098, China
ljg1688@163.com

Abstract. In order to deal with key exposure problem, we introduce forward secure technique into certificateless proxy signature scheme, and propose the formal definition and security model of forward secure certificateless proxy signature. Furthermore, we present a construction of forward secure certificateless proxy signature scheme with bilinear maps. Based on the difficulty of computational Diffie-Hellman problem, we prove the scheme is secure against chosen message attack in the random oracle model.

Keywords: forward secure, certificateless proxy signature, computational Diffie-Hellman problem, random oracle model.

1 Introduction

In 1996, Mambo, Usuda and Okamoto [1] firstly proposed a proxy signature scheme, in which the proxy signer can sign the message on behalf of the original signer. Proxy signature has a lot of practical applications, such as mobile communications, distributed system and electronic auction, etc. In order to satisfy different situations, researchers proposed many extensions of proxy signature, including designed verifier proxy signature [2], ID-based proxy signature [3], one-time proxy signature [4] and so on. However, we found that most of the proxy signatures are proposed in the identity based cryptography (IBC) setting or the traditional public key cryptography (PKC) setting. We know that IBC has key escrow problem while PKC has certificate management problem.

In order to solve the above problems, Al-Riyami and Paterson [5] firstly presented the certificateless public key cryptography (CL-PKC). Compared with PKC, CL-PKC does not require any certificates to ensure the authenticity of public keys. Moreover, CL-PKC overcomes the key escrow problem of IBC. Due to its advantage, many researchers have been interested in CL-PKC and some certificateless proxy signatures [6-8] have been proposed.

---

* This work is supported by the National Natural Science Foundation of China (60842002, 61272542, 61103183, 61103184), the Fundamental Research Funds for the Central Universities (2009B21114, 2010B07114), China Postdoctoral Science Foundation Funded Project under Grant No. 20100471373, the "Six Talent Peaks Program" of Jiangsu Province of China (2009182) and Program for New Century Excellent Talents in Hohai University.

J. Lopez, X. Huang, and R. Sandhu (Eds.): NSS 2013, LNCS 7873, pp. 350–364, 2013.

Key exposure is an important threat to the security of signature scheme. In 2009, Schuldt et al. [9] presented a proxy signature against proxy key exposure, which effectively solved the problem. It is obviously that there also exists key exposure problem in certificateless proxy signature. If the secret key of proxy signer is exposed, a malicious user can forge proxy signature instead of proxy signer, which will damage the benefit of original signer. Furthermore, all signatures that have ever been generated by proxy signer become invalid. How to minimize the damage caused by key exposure has been an open problem.

Forward secure technique can efficiently deal with key exposure problem. In 1997, Anderson [10] firstly introduced the concept of forward security in digital signature. In the forward secure signature scheme, the public key keeps unchanged in all time periods, while the private key updates in every time period. By this means, the past signature is still valid even if the private key in a time period is exposed. In 1999, Bellare and Miner [11] proposed a concrete construction of forward secure signature scheme. In their construction, they use the numbers of a binary tree to denote the total life time periods of the scheme. In every time period, the scheme derives a new private key from the private key of the last time period and uses it to sign messages. The public key remains unchanged in all time periods. In 2001, Itkis and Reyzin [12] put foward another forward secure signature scheme. The scheme can be verified effectively, but costs much time on private key generation and evocation algorithm. In 2004, Kang et al. [13] presented two forward secure signature schemes based on Diffie-Hellman group. The scheme is superior to Bellare and Miner's scheme in the time of key generation and evocation, and the time is fixed within the total time periods. In 2009, Nakanishi et al. [14] proposed a forward secure group signature scheme based on the group signature with paring, in which the complexity of the key evocation and signature verification is $O(\log T)$. At present, many scholars and experts have proposed effective forward secure signature schemes [15-17].

In 2010, Chen et al. [18] firstly proposed a forward secure cerficateless proxy signature scheme, but they didn't give the formal definition and security model of the scheme. Moreover, they didn't prove the security of the scheme in the random oracle model. In this paper, we firstly introduce the formal definition and security model of the scheme, and propose another forward secure certificateless proxy signature with bilinear maps. The security of our scheme is reduced to computational Diffie-Hellman problem. The scheme is not only avoiding certificate management problem, but also solving key escrow problem. At the same time, the scheme has forward secure property, which can solve the key exposure problem in certificateless proxy signature.

2 Preliminaries

Bilinear Pairing

Let G_1 denote an additive group of prime order q and G_2 be a multiplicative group of the same order. Let P denote a generator in G_1. Let $e: G_1 \times G_1 \rightarrow G_2$ be a bilinear mapping with the following properties:

— Bilinear: $e(aP,bQ)=e(P,Q)^{ab}$ for all $P,Q\in G_1$, $a,b\in \mathbb{Z}_q^*$.

— Non-degenerate: $e(P,Q)\neq 1$ for $P,Q\in G_1$.

— Computable: There is an efficient algorithm to compute $e(P,Q)$ for any $P,Q\in G_1$.

Definition 1. Computational Diffie-Hellman (CDH) Problem

Let G_1 denote an additive group of prime order q, and P denote a generator in G_1. Given (P,aP,bP), for some $a,b\in \mathbb{Z}_q^*$, compute abP.

The success probability of any probabilistic polynomial-time algorithm A solving CDH problem in G_1 is defined to be:

$$Succ_{A,G_1}^{CDH}=\Pr[A(P,aP,bP)=abP : a,b\in \mathbb{Z}_q^*].$$

The CDH assumption states that for every probabilistic polynomial-time algorithm A, $Succ_{A,G_1}^{CDH}$ is negligible.

3 The Concept and Security Model of forward Secure Certificateless Proxy Signature

3.1 The Concept of forward Secure Certificateless Proxy Signature

A forward secure certificateless signature scheme is defined by nine probabilistic polynomial-time algorithms: Setup, Partial-Private-Key-Extract, User-Key-Generate, Partial-Proxy-Key-Generate, Partial-Proxy-Key-Verify, Initial-Proxy-Key-Generate, Proxy-Key-Update, Proxy-Sign and Proxy-Verify.

- **Setup:** Takes a security parameter k and a total numbers of time periods N as input, it returns the master key s and system public parameters $params$. This algorithm is run by key generation center (KGC).
- **Partial-Private-Key-Extract:** Takes the master key s and a user's identifier ID as input, it outputs a partial private key D_{ID}. This algorithm is run by KGC.
- **User-Key-Generate:** Takes system public parameters $params$, a user's identifier ID as input, it outputs a secret value x_{ID} and a public key P_{ID}. This algorithm is run by the original signer A and the proxy signer B.
- **Partial-Proxy-Key-Generate:** Takes system public parameters $params$, a warrant m_w, an original signer's identity ID_A, partial private key D_A, secret value x_A and public key P_A as input, it outputs a partial proxy key σ_A. This algorithm is run by the original signer A.
- **Partial-Proxy-Key-Verify:** Takes system public parameters $params$, a warrant m_w, an original signer's identity ID_A and public key P_A, and a partial proxy

key σ_A as input, it returns true if the partial proxy key σ_A is correct or false otherwise. This algorithm is run by a proxy signer *B*.

— **Initial-Proxy-Key-Generate:** Takes system public parameters *params*, a partial proxy key σ_A, an original signer's identity ID_A and public key P_A, a proxy signer's identity ID_B, partial private key D_B, secret value x_B and public key P_B as input, it outputs a initial proxy key σ_B^0. This algorithm is run by a proxy signer *B*.

— **Proxy-Key-Update:** Takes system public parameters *params*, the current time period $t(t>0)$, a partial proxy key σ_A, an original signer's identity ID_A and public key P_A, a proxy signer's identity ID_B, partial private key D_B, secret value x_B and public key P_B, a proxy key σ_B^{t-1} of last time period as input, it outputs the proxy key σ_B^t of current time period, and deletes the proxy key σ_B^{t-1} of last time period completely. This algorithm is run by a proxy signer *B*.

— **Proxy-Sign:** Takes system public parameters *params*, the current time period t, a message m, a warrant m_w, a proxy signer's identity ID_B and public key P_B, a proxy key σ_B^t as input, it outputs a proxy signature ψ. This algorithm is run by a proxy signer *B*.

— **Proxy-Verify:** Takes system public parameters *params*, a message m, a warrant m_w, an identity ID_A and public key P_A of the original signer *A*, an identity ID_B and public key P_B of the proxy signer *B*, the current time period t and a proxy signature ψ as input, it returns true if the signature ψ is correct or false otherwise. This algorithm is run by a verifier.

3.2 The Security Model of forward Secure Cerificateless Proxy Signature

According to the security model of forward secure signature scheme proposed in [11] and the super adversary security model of cerificateless signature scheme defined in [19], we put forward the security model of forward secure certificateless proxy signature.

There are two types of adversary in forward secure certificateless proxy signature: A_I and A_{II}. A_I simulates malicious users (anyone except the KGC) who have the following capabilities. (1) A_I does not know the master key, but A_I can replace any user's public key. (2) A_I can get any proxy signer's message/proxy signature in any time period t ($0 \le t \le T$, T is the key exposure time period). A_{II} simulates a dishonest KGC who has the following capabilities. (1) A_{II} knows the master key, but A_I cannot replace the target user's public key. (2) A_{II} can get any proxy signer's message/proxy signature in any time period t ($0 \le t \le T$, T is the key exposure time period).

We define the security model of forward secure certificateless proxy signature scheme by using the game between a challenger C and an adversary $\Gamma \in \{A_{\mathrm{I}}, A_{\mathrm{II}}\}$ as follows.

Game 1

Setup: C runs the algorithm to generate master key s and system parameters $params$, C then sends $params$ to A_I while keeping master key secret.

Chosen Message Attack Phase: A_I can perform the following queries:

— **Public-Key-Query:** On receiving a user's identity ID_i, the challenger C performs User-Key-Generate algorithm to generate a public key P_i of ID_i, and returns P_i to A_I.

— **Partial-Private-Key-Query:** On receiving an identity ID_i, C runs Partial-Private-Key-Extract algorithms to generate the partial private key D_i, and returns D_i to A_I.

— **Public-Key-Replacement-Query:** On receiving an identity ID_i and a new public key $P_i^{'}$. C replaces the public key of ID_i with the new one.

— **Secret-Value-Query:** On receiving an identity ID_i, C performs User-Key-Generate algorithm to generate a secret value x_i of ID_i, and returns x_i to A_I.

— **Partial-Proxy-Key-Query:** On receiving a warrant m_w and an identity ID_A of an original signer A, C runs Partial-Proxy-Key algorithm to generate a partial proxy key σ_A, and return it to A_I.

— **Proxy-Key-Query:** On receiving a time period t, a warrant m_w, an identity ID_A of an original signer A and an identity ID_B of a proxy signer B, if $t = 0$, C runs Initial-Proxy-Key-Generate algorithms to generate initial proxy key σ_B^0, and returns it to A_I. Otherwise, C runs Proxy-Key-Update algorithms to generate a proxy key σ_B^t and returns it to A_I.

— **Proxy-Signature-Query:** On receiving a time period t, an identity ID_A of an original signer A, an identity ID_B of a proxy signer B, a message m and a warrant m_w, C returns a proxy signature ψ of the current time period to A_I.

At the end of every time period, A_I can continue to make chosen message attack or enter the *breakin* phase, while A_I must query according to the sequence of the time period strictly.

Breakin Phase: When A_I puts forward a *breakin* query, C simulates the key exposure situation, and will give all proxy signer's (including the target proxy signer) proxy key of time period T (T is key exposure period) to A_I. Here, A_I cannot achieve the partial private key and secret value of the proxy signer, but can replace the public key of the proxy signer.

Forgery Phase: A_I outputs $\{m^*, m_w^*, ID_A^*, P_A^*, ID_B^*, P_B^*, \mu^*, \psi^*\}$ of the time period μ^* $(0 \le \mu^* < T)$ as its forgery. We say A_I wins the game, if $\{m^*, m_w^*, ID_A^*, P_A^*, ID_B^*, P_B^*, \mu^*, \psi^*\}$ satisfies the following conditions. The advantage of A_I winning the game is defined as $Succ_{A_I}^{cma,cida,breakin}$.

(1) Verify $\{m^*, m_w^*, ID_A^*, P_A^*, ID_B^*, P_B^*, \mu^*, \psi^*\}$ = True.

(2) A_I has never made Partial-Private-Key-Query on ID_A^*.

(3) A_I has never made Partial-Proxy-Key-Query on $\{m_w^*, ID_A^*, P_A^*\}$.

(4) In the time period μ^*, A_I has not made Proxy-Key-Query on $\{m_w^*, ID_A^*, P_A^*, ID_B^*, P_B^*\}$.

(5) In the time period μ^*, A_I has not made Proxy-Signature-Query on $\{m^*, m_w^*, ID_A^*, P_A^*, ID_B^*, P_B^*\}$.

Definition 2. The forward secure certificateless proxy signature is existentially unforgeable against chosen message attack of adversary A_I, if the probability of A_I winning in the Game 1 is negligible in polynominal time. In other words, $Succ_{A_I}^{cma,cida,breakin} \le \varepsilon$, where ε is negligible.

Game 2

Setup: C runs the algorithm to generate master key s and system parameters *params*, C then sends *params* and master key to A_{II}.

Chosen Message Attack Phase: In this phase, A_{II} can ask Public-Key-Query, Public-Key-Replacement-Query, Secret-Value-Query, Partial-Proxy-Key-Query, Initial-Proxy-Key-Query, Updated-Proxy-Key-Query and Proxy-Signature-Query, and C will respond respectively. The operation is same as Game 1.

Breakin Phase: When A_{II} puts forward a *breakin* query, C simulates the key exposure situation, and will give all proxy signer's (including the target proxy signer) proxy key of time period T (T is key exposure period) to A_{II}.

Forgery Phase: A_{II} outputs $\{m^*, m_w^*, ID_A^*, P_A^*, ID_B^*, P_B^*, \mu^*, \psi^*\}$ of the time period μ^* $(0 \le \mu^* < T)$ as its forgery. We say A_{II} wins the game, if $\{m^*, m_w^*, ID_A^*, P_A^*, ID_B^*, P_B^*, \mu^*, \psi^*\}$ satisfies the following conditions. The advantage of A_{II} winning the game is defined as $Succ_{A_{II}}^{cma,cida,breakin}$.

(1) Verify $\{m^*, m_w^*, ID_A^*, P_A^*, ID_B^*, P_B^*, \mu^*, \psi^*\} = \text{True}$.

(2) A_{II} has never made Secret-Value-Query on ID_A^*, and has never made Public-Key- Replacement-Query on ID_A^* and ID_B^*.

(3) A_{II} has never made Partial-Proxy-Key-Query on $\{m_w^*, ID_A^*, P_A^*\}$.

(4) In the time period μ^*, A_{II} has not made Proxy-Key-Query on $\{m_w^*, ID_A^*, P_A^*, ID_B^*, P_B^*\}$.

(5) In the time period μ^*, A_{II} has not made Proxy-Signature-Query on $\{m^*, m_w^*, ID_A^*, P_A^*, ID_B^*, P_B^*\}$.

Definition 3. The forward secure certificateless proxy signature is existentially unforgeable against chosen message attack of adversary A_{II}, if the probability of A_{II} winning in the Game 2 is negligible in polynominal time. In other words, $Succ_{A_{II}}^{cma,cida,breakin} \le \varepsilon$, where ε is negligible.

4 The Construction of forward Secure Certificateless Proxy Signature

In this section, we present the construction of forward secure certificateless proxy signature scheme. We let k be a security parameter and N be system total time periods.

Setup: This algorithm runs as follows.

(1) Let G_1, G_2 be groups of the same order q where G_1 is an additive group and G_2 is a multiplicative group, and $e: G_1 \times G_1 \rightarrow G_2$ is a bilinear paring.

(2) Choose a random generator $P \in G_1$, and select $s \in \mathbb{Z}_q^*$ randomly. Let s be the master key and set $P_0 = sP$.

(3) Choose cryptographic hash functions $H_1: \{0,1\}^* \rightarrow G_1^*$, $H_2: \{0,1\}^* \times G_1^* \times \{0,1\}^* \times G_1^* \rightarrow \mathbb{Z}_q^*$, $H_3: \{0,1\}^* \times G_1^* \times \{0,1\}^* \times G_1^* \times \{0,1\}^* \times G_1^* \rightarrow \mathbb{Z}_q^*$, $H_4: \{0,1\}^* \times \{0,1\}^* \times G_1^* \times \{0,1\}^* \times G_1^* \rightarrow \mathbb{Z}_q^*$.

The system parameters are $params = (G_1, G_2, e, q, P, P_0, N, H_1, H_2, H_3, H_4)$.

Partial-Private-Key-Extract: Given a user's identity $ID_i \in \{0,1\}^*$, the algorithm computes $Q_i = H_1(ID_i)$ and outputs the user's partial private key $D_i = sQ_i$.

User-Key-Generate: Given system parameters $params$ and a user's identity ID_i, the algorithm selects $x_i \in \mathbb{Z}_q^*$ randomly as the user's secret value, and computes the user's public key $P_i = (X_i, Y_i) = (x_i P, x_i P_0)$.

Partial-Proxy-Key-Generate: Given system parameters $params$, a warrant m_w, an original signer A's identity ID_A, partial private key D_A, secret value x_A and public key P_A, the algorithm computes the proxy signer B's partial proxy key as follows.

(1) Randomly pick $r_A \in \mathbb{Z}_q^*$ and compute $R_A = r_A P$.
(2) Compute $h_A = H_2(m_w, ID_A, P_A, R_A)$ and $I_A = h_A D_A + (x_A + r_A)Q_A$.
(3) Output (m_w, σ_A) to B, and take $\sigma_A = (R_A, I_A)$ as the partial proxy key.

Partial-Proxy-Key-Verify: Given (m_w, σ_A), the algorithm computes $h_A = H_2(m_w, ID_A, P_A, R_A)$. If $e(I_A, P) = e(h_A P_0 + X_A + R_A, Q_A)$, accept σ_A. Otherwise, reject σ_A.

Proxy-Key-Generate: If (m_w, σ_A) is accepted, the algorithm generates the initial proxy key according to the following steps:

(1) Randomly pick $r_B^0 \in \mathbb{Z}_q^*$ and compute $R_B^0 = r_B^0 P$.
(2) Compute $h_B^0 = H_3(m_w, ID_A, P_A, ID_B, P_B, R_B^0)$ and $K_B^0 = I_A + h_B^0 x_B D_B + r_B^0 Q_B$.
(3) Output $\sigma_B^0 = (R_B^0, K_B^0)$ as the initial proxy key of time period 0.

Proxy-Key-Update: Given the current time period $t \in [1, N-1)$, the algorithm computes the σ_B^t of time period t from σ_B^{t-1} of time period $t-1$.

(1) Randomly pick $r_B^t \in \mathbb{Z}_q^*$ and compute $R_B^t = R_B^{t-1} + r_B^t P = \sum_{t=0}^{t} r_B^t P = u_B^t P$, while $u_B^t = \sum_{t=0}^{t} r_B^t$.
(2) Compute $h_B^t = H_3(m_w, ID_A, P_A, ID_B, P_B, R_B^t)$ and $z_B^t = \sum_{t=0}^{t} h_B^t = \sum_{t=0}^{t-1} h_B^t + h_B^t = z_B^{t-1} + h_B^t$.
(3) Compute $K_B^t = K_B^{t-1} + h_B^t x_B D_B + r_B^t Q_B = I_A + \sum_{t=0}^{t} h_B^t x_B D_B + \sum_{t=0}^{t} r_B^t Q_B = I_A + z_B^t x_B D_B + u_B^t Q_B$.
(4) Output $\sigma_B^t = (R_B^t, z_B^t, K_B^t)$ as the proxy key of the time period t, and delete r_B^t and σ_B^{t-1}.

Proxy-Sign: Given the current time period t and a message m, the algorithm performs the following steps to generate the proxy signature.

(1) Compute $h = H_4(m, m_w, ID_B, P_B, R_B^t)$.

(2) Compute $V = hK_B^t$.

(3) Output $\psi = (R_A, R_B^t, z_B^t, V)$ as the proxy signature of the time period t.

Proxy-Verify: Given the message/signature (m, m_w, ψ), the algorithm performs the following steps to verify the validity of proxy signature:

(1) Check whether the message m is consistent with m_w. If not, return false and abort. Otherwise, continue (2).

(2) Compute $h_A = H_2(m_w, ID_A, P_A, R_A)$, $h = H_4(m, m_w, ID_B, P_B, R_B^t)$. If $e(V,P) = e(h(h_A P_0 + X_A + R_A), Q_A)e(h(z_B^t Y_B + R_B^t), Q_B)$, return true. Otherwise, return false.

5 Security Analysis

5.1 Correctness

We can easily verify the proposed scheme is correct.

$$\begin{aligned}
e(V,P) &= e(hK_B^t, P) = e(h(I_A + \sum_{t=0}^{t} h_B^t x_B D_B + \sum_{t=0}^{t} r_B^t Q_B), P) \\
&= e(hh_A D_A + h(x_A + r_A)Q_A, P)e(h(\sum_{t=0}^{t} h_B^t x_B D_B + \sum_{t=0}^{t} r_B^t Q_B), P) \\
&= e(hh_A D_A, P)e(h(x_A + r_A)Q_A, P)e(h(z_B^t x_B D_B + u_B^t Q_B), P) \\
&= e(hh_A P_0, Q_A)e(h(X_A + R_A), Q_A)e(h(z_B^t Y_B + R_B^t), Q_B) \\
&= e(h(h_A P_0 + X_A + R_A), Q_A)e(h(z_B^t Y_B + R_B^t), Q_B)
\end{aligned}$$

5.2 Strong Unforgeability

According to the definition and security model of forward secure certificateless proxy signature provided in section 3, we prove our scheme is unforgeable as follows.

Theorem 1. Suppose there exists a polynomial bounded adversary A_I against our scheme with the success probability $Succ_{A_I}^{cma,cida,breakin}$ after asking at most q_{PK} Public-Key-Query, q_{PPK} Partial-Private-Key-Query, q_{ProK} Proxy-Key-Query. Then there exists an algorithm C that can solve the CDH problem with the success probability $Succ_C^{CDH} = \frac{1}{Nq_{PK}}(1 - \frac{1}{q_{PK}})^{q_{PPK}+q_{ProK}}\ Succ_{A_I}^{cma,cida,breakin}$ in polynomial time.

Proof: We construct an algorithm C to solve the CDH problem. Let $(P, P_1 = aP, P_2 = bP)$ be a random instance of the CDH problem in G_1, and C will play as a challenger to interact with A_I. We show how C compute abP with the ability of A_I.

Setup: C sets N as the total numbers of time periods, and $T(0 \le T \le N-1)$ as the key exposure time period. In time period T, adversary will make *breakin* query. C sets $P_0 = aP = P_1$ and the system parameters $params = (G_1, G_2, e, q, P, P_0, N, H_1, H_2, H_3, H_4)$, and returns $params$ to A_I.

C initializes the time period $t = 0$, and adversary A_I will output a value of d after every time period query. If $d = 0$, A_I will continue to make chosen message attack. If $d = breakin$, then A_I will enter *breakin* phase. At the end of chosen message attack of time period 0, A_I outputs $d = 0$. If $d \ne breakin$ and $T \ne N$, then A_I will enter the next time period to continue the chosen message attack.

Chosen Message Attack Phase: In this phase, C regards hash functions as the random oracles. A_I can ask Public-Key-Query, Partial-Private-Key-Query, Secret-Value-Query, Public-Key- Replacement-Query, Partial-Proxy-Key-Query, Proxy-Key-Query and Proxy-Signature-Query. Without loss of generality, we assume that A_I doesn't repeat any two identical query. C keeps seven lists L_1, L_2, L_3, L_4, H_2, H_3, H_4 to store the user's answers, where each list includes items of the form $(ID_i, x_i, P_i, \alpha_i, Q_i, D_i)$, $(m_{w_i}, ID_{A_i}, P_{A_i}, r_{A_i}, \beta_{A_i}, R_{A_i}, I_{A_i})$, $(m_{A_i}, ID_{A_i}, P_{A_i}, ID_{B_i}, P_{B_i}, t, r_{A_i}, R_{A_i}, \beta_{A_i}, r_{B_i}^t, \gamma_{B_i}^t, R_{B_i}^t, z_{B_i}^t, K_{B_i}^t)$, $(m_i, m_{w_i}, ID_{A_i}, P_{A_i}, ID_{B_i}, P_{B_i}, t, R_{A_i}, R_{B_i}^t, z_{B_i}^t, V)$, $(m_{w_i}, ID_{A_i}, P_{A_i}, R_{A_i}, \beta_{A_i})$, $(m_{w_i}, ID_{A_i}, P_{A_i}, ID_{B_i}, P_{B_i}, R_{B_i}^t, \gamma_{B_i}^t)$, $(m_i, m_{w_i}, ID_{B_i}, P_{B_i}, R_{B_i}^t, \kappa_{B_i}^t)$.

— **Public-Key-Query:** C randomly picks $f \in \{1, 2, \cdots, q_{PK}\}$. On receiving each of public key query, if $i \ne f$, C will randomly select $\alpha_i, x_i \in \mathbb{Z}_q^*$, and set $P_i = (x_i P, x_i P_0)$, $Q_i = \alpha_i P$, $D_i = \alpha_i P_0$. Otherwise, C sets $P_f = (x_f P, x_f P_0)$, $Q_f = \alpha_f P + P_2$, $D_f = \perp$. Finally, C adds $(ID_i, x_i, P_i, \alpha_i, Q_i, D_i)$ into the L_1 list, and returns P_i to A_I.

— **Partial-Private-Key-Query:** On receiving such a query on ID_i, if $i = f$, C aborts. Otherwise, C checks whether the ID_i has been created in L_1 list. If not, C randomly select $\alpha_i, x_i \in \mathbb{Z}_q^*$, and set $P_i = (x_i P, x_i P_0)$, $Q_i = \alpha_i P$, $D_i = \alpha_i P_0$. C adds $(ID_i, x_i, P_i, \alpha_i, Q_i, D_i)$ into the L_1 list, and returns D_i to A_I. Otherwise, C returns D_i to A_I directly.

— **Public-Key-Replacement-Query:** On receiving such a query on $(ID_i, P_i^{'})$, C checks whether the ID_i has been created in L_1 list. If not, C adds $(ID_i, \perp, P_i^{'}, *, *, *)$ into the L_1 list. Otherwise, C updates the item of ID_i as $(ID_i, \perp, P_i^{'}, \alpha_i, Q_i, D_i)$.

— **Secret-Value-Query:** On receiving such a query on ID_i, C checks whether the ID_i has been created in L_1 list. If not, C randomly select $\alpha_i, x_i \in \mathbb{Z}_q^*$, and set $P_i = (x_i P, x_i P_0)$, $Q_i = \alpha_i P$, $D_i = \alpha_i P_0$. C adds $(ID_i, x_i, P_i, \alpha_i, Q_i, D_i)$ into the L_1 list, and returns x_i to A_I. Otherwise, if $x_i = \perp$, C returns $\perp$ to A_I. Otherwise, C returns x_i to A_I directly.

— **H_2 Query:** On receiving such a query on $(m_{w_i}, ID_{A_i}, P_{A_i}, R_{A_i})$, C randomly selects $\beta_{A_i} \in \mathbb{Z}_q^*$ that hasn't appeared in the H_2 list. Then C adds $(m_{w_i}, ID_{A_i}, P_{A_i}, R_{A_i}, \beta_{A_i})$ into the H_2 list and returns β_{A_i} to A_I.

— **H_3 Query:** On receiving such a query on $(m_{w_i}, ID_{A_i}, P_{A_i}, ID_{B_i}, P_{B_i}, R_{B_i}^t)$, C randomly selects $\gamma_{B_i}^t \in \mathbb{Z}_q^*$ that hasn't appeared in the H_3 list. Then C adds $(m_{w_i}, ID_{A_i}, P_{A_i}, ID_{B_i}, P_{B_i}, R_{B_i}^t, \gamma_{B_i}^t)$ into the H_3 list and returns $\gamma_{B_i}^t$ to A_I.

— **H_4 Query:** On receiving such a query on $(m_i, m_{w_i}, ID_{B_i}, P_{B_i}, R_{B_i}^t)$, C randomly selects $\kappa_{B_i}^t \in \mathbb{Z}_q^*$ that hasn't appeared in the H_4 list. Then C adds $(m_i, m_{w_i}, ID_{B_i}, P_{B_i}, R_{B_i}^t, \kappa_{B_i}^t)$ into the H_4 list and returns $\kappa_{B_i}^t$ to A_I.

— **Partial-Proxy-Key-Query:** On receiving such a query on (ID_{A_i}, m_{w_i}), C firstly browses the L_1 list to get the current public key of the ID_{A_i}. Then C generates the partial proxy key according to the following steps.

(1) Randomly pick $r_{A_i}, \beta_{A_i} \in \mathbb{Z}_q^*$ that β_{A_i} hasn't appeared in the H_2 list.

(2) Set $H_2(m_{w_i}, ID_{A_i}, P_{A_i}, R_{A_i}) = \beta_{A_i}$ and compute $R_{A_i} = r_{A_i} P - (\beta_{A_i} P_0 + X_A)$.

(3) Compute $I_{A_i} = r_{A_i} Q_{A_i}$.

C adds $(m_{w_i}, ID_{A_i}, P_{A_i}, r_{A_i}, \beta_{A_i}, R_{A_i}, I_{A_i})$ into the L_2 list and returns $\sigma_{A_i} = (R_{A_i}, I_{A_i})$ to A_I.

— **Proxy-Key-Update:** This process is completed by C alone, which makes preparations for A_I's proxy key query and *breakin* query, and A_I can't make any query in the process. Given the current time period, C simulates the proxy key update process from the initial time period 0. The specific steps are as follows:

(1) Firstly check whether the item (ID_{A_i}, m_{w_i}) is in the L_2 list. If not, C performs Partial-Proxy-Key-Query to obtain the tuple $(r_{A_i}, \beta_{A_i}, R_{A_i}, I_{A_i})$. Otherwise, C returns the tuple $(r_{A_i}, \beta_{A_i}, R_{A_i}, I_{A_i})$ directly.

(2) Randomly pick $r_{B_i}^t, \gamma_{B_i}^t \in \mathbb{Z}_q^*$ that $\gamma_{B_i}^t$ hasn't appeared in the H_3 list.

(3) Set $H_3(m_{w_i}, ID_{A_i}, P_{A_i}, ID_{B_i}, P_{B_i}, R_{B_i}^t) = \gamma_{B_i}^t$ and compute $z_{B_i}^t = z_{B_i}^{t-1} + \gamma_{B_i}^t$.

(4) Compute $R_{B_i}^t = r_{B_i}^t P - z_{B_i}^t Y_B$ and $K_{B_i}^t = (r_{A_i} Q_{A_i} + r_{B_i}^t Q_{B_i})$.

C adds $(m_{w_i}, ID_{A_i}, P_{A_i}, ID_{B_i}, P_{B_i}, t, r_{A_i}, R_{A_i}, \beta_{A_i}, r_{B_i}^t, \gamma_{B_i}^t, R_{B_i}^t, z_{B_i}^t, K_{B_i}^t)$ into the L_3 list.

— **Proxy-Key-Query:** On receiving such a query on $(m_{w_i}, ID_{A_i}, ID_{B_i})$ in the time period $t\ (0 \le t < N)$, C firstly checks the L_1 list. If $x_{B_i} = \perp$, C returns $\perp$ to A_I. Otherwise, C checks L_3 list according to $(ID_{A_i}, ID_{B_i}, m_{w_i}, t)$. If $ID_{B_i} = ID_f$, C aborts. Otherwise, C returns $\sigma_{B_i}^t = (R_{B_i}^t, z_{B_i}^t, K_{B_i}^t)$ to A_I.

— **Proxy-Sign-Query:** On receiving such a query on $(m_i, m_{w_i}, ID_{A_i}, ID_{B_i})$ in the time period $t\ (0 \le t < N)$, C generates the proxy signature according to the following steps:

(1) Firstly check whether the item $(ID_{A_i}, ID_{B_i}, m_{w_i}, t)$ is in the L_3 list. If not, C performs Proxy-Key-Query to obtain the tuple $(r_{A_i}, R_{A_i}, \beta_{A_i}, r_{B_i}^t, \gamma_{B_i}^t, R_{B_i}^t, z_{B_i}^t, K_{B_i}^t)$. Otherwise, C returns the tuple $(r_{A_i}, R_{A_i}, \beta_{A_i}, r_{B_i}^t, \gamma_{B_i}^t, R_{B_i}^t, z_{B_i}^t, K_{B_i}^t)$ directly.

(2) Randomly pick $\kappa_{B_i}^t \in \mathbb{Z}_q^*$ that hasn't appeared in the H_4 list.

(3) Set $H_4(m_i, m_{w_i}, ID_{B_i}, P_{B_i}, R_{B_i}^t) = \kappa_{B_i}^t$ and compute $V = \kappa_{B_i}^t (r_{A_i} Q_{A_i} + r_{B_i}^t Q_{B_i})$.

C adds $(m_i, m_{w_i}, ID_{A_i}, P_{A_i}, ID_{B_i}, P_{B_i}, t, R_{A_i}, R_{B_i}^t, z_{B_i}^t, V)$ into the L_4 list and returns $\psi = (R_{A_i}, R_{B_i}^t, z_{B_i}^t, V)$ to A_I.

Breakin Phase: A_I outputs a decision value d, and C decides whether to enter the *breakin* phase. If $0 \le t < T$ and $d = 0$, A_I enters the next time period to continue the chosen message attack. If $t = T$ and $d = breakin$, C returns all proxy signer's (including the target proxy signer) proxy key of the current time period to A_I. Otherwise, C aborts.

Once A_I enters into the *breakin* phase, he can't continue the chosen message attack. After the *breakin* query, A_I enters into the forgery phase.

Forgery Phase: If C doesn't aborts in the simulation, then A_I outputs a validly forged proxy signature $\{m^*, m_w^*, ID_A^*, P_A^*, ID_B^*, P_B^*, \mu^*, \psi^*\}$ of the time period $\mu^*(0 \le \mu^* < T)$.

Analysis: If $ID_A^* \ne ID_f$, aborts. If $ID_A^* = ID_f$ and $\{m^*, m_w^*, ID_A^*, P_A^*, ID_B^*, P_B^*, \mu^*, \psi^* = (R_A^*, R_B^{\mu*}, z_B^{\mu*}, V^*)\}$ satisfies the requirements as defined in game 1, according to forking lemma[20], C selects different hash function $H_2^{'}$ and uses A_I's capability to get another valid tuple $\{m^*, m_w^*, ID_A^*, P_A^*, ID_B^*, P_B^*, \mu^*, \psi^{*'} = (R_A^*, R_B^{\mu*}, z_B^{\mu*}, V^{*'})\}$. Then C gets two tuples $e(V^*, P) = e(hh_A^* P_0 + h(X_A^* + R_A^*), Q_A^*)e(h(z_B^{\mu*} Y_B^* + R_B^{\mu*}), Q_B^*)$ and $e(V^{*'}, P) = e(hh_A^{*'} P_0 + h(X_A^* + R_A^*), Q_A^*)e(h(z_B^{\mu*} Y_B^* + R_B^{\mu*}), Q_B^*)$, thus $e(V^* - V^{*'}, P) = e(h(h_A^* - h_A^{*'})P_0, Q_A^*)$. Then $e(V^* - V^{*'}, P) = e(h(h_A^* - h_A^{*'}) \cdot aQ_A^*, P)$, and $V^* - V^{*'} = h(h_A^* - h_A^{*'})aQ_A^* = h(h_A^* - h_A^{*'})a(a_f P + bP)$. C checks L_1 list, H_2 list and H_4 list to get α_f, $h_A^* = \beta_A^*$, $h_A^{*'} = \beta_A^{*'}$ and $h = \kappa_B^{\mu*}$ respectively, and computes $abP = (V^* - V^{*'})(\beta_A^* - \beta_A^{*'})^{-1}\kappa_B^{\mu*-1} - \alpha_f P_1$.

Probability of Success: Event E_1 denotes that the algorithm C does not exit throughout the simulation. Event E_2 denotes that A_I outputs $t = T$ and $d = breakin$. Event E_3 denotes that A_I forges a valid proxy signature in the time period $\mu^*(0 \le \mu^* < T)$. Event E_4 denotes that A_I outputs a valid tuple $\{m^*, m_w^*, ID_A^*, P_A^*, ID_B^*, P_B^*, \mu^*, \psi^*\}$, and $ID_A^* = ID_f$ when event E_3 occurs. Then $Succ_C^{CDH} = \Pr[E_1 \Lambda E_2 \Lambda E_3 \Lambda E_4] = \Pr[E_1]\Pr[E_2 \mid E_1]\Pr[E_3 \mid E_1 \Lambda E_2]\Pr[E_4 \mid E_1 \Lambda E_2 \Lambda E_3]$. Among that $\Pr[E_1] = (1 - \frac{1}{q_{PK}})^{q_{PPK} + q_{ProK}}$, $\Pr[E_2 \mid E_1] = \frac{1}{N}$, $\Pr[E_3 \mid E_1 \Lambda E_2] = Succ_{A_I}^{cma,cida,breakin}$, $\Pr[E_4 \mid E_1 \Lambda E_2 \Lambda E_3] = \frac{1}{q_{PK}}$. Hence

$$Succ_C^{CDH} = \frac{1}{Nq_{PK}} \cdot (1 - \frac{1}{q_{PK}})^{q_{PPK} + q_{ProK}} Succ_{A_I}^{cma,cida,breakin}.$$

Due to the space limitation, we delete the proof of theorem 2. The reader refers to that of theorem 1 or our full version.

6 Conclusion

In this paper, we propose a forward secure certificateless proxy signature in the random oracle model. Our security model takes into account the super adversary in certificateless signature. We prove our scheme is existentially unforgeable against chosen message attack under CDH assumption. What is worth mentioning is that the proxy signature phase has no pairing operation and the proxy signature verification phase only requires three paring operations. Moreover, the scheme has effectively dealt with the key exposure problem and has no certificate management problem.

Acknowledgments. We would like to thank anonymous referees for their helpful comments and suggestions.

References

1. Mambo, M., Usuda, K., Okamoto, E.: Proxy Signature: Delegation of the Power to Sign Messages. IEICE Transactions on Fundamentals E79-A(9), 1338–1353 (1996)
2. Huang, X.Y., Mu, Y., Sulilo, W., Zhang, F.T.: Short Designed Verifier Proxy Signature from Pairings. In: Enokido, T., Yan, L., Xiao, B., Kim, D.Y., Dai, Y.-S., Yang, L.T. (eds.) EUC Workshops 2005. LNCS, vol. 3823, pp. 835–844. Springer, Heidelberg (2005)
3. Zhang, F.G., Kim, K.: Efficient ID-Based Blind Signature and Proxy Signature from Bilinear Pairings. In: Safavi-Naini, R., Seberry, J. (eds.) ACISP 2003. LNCS, vol. 2727, pp. 312–323. Springer, Heidelberg (2003)
4. Wang, H., Pieprzyk, J.: Efficient One-Time Proxy Signatures. In: Laih, C.-S. (ed.) ASIACRYPT 2003. LNCS, vol. 2894, pp. 507–522. Springer, Heidelberg (2003)
5. Al-Riyami, S.S., Paterson, K.G.: Certificateless Public Key Cryptography. In: Laih, C.-S. (ed.) ASIACRYPT 2003. LNCS, vol. 2894, pp. 452–473. Springer, Heidelberg (2003)
6. Yap, W., Heng, S., Goi, B.: Cryptanalysis of Some Proxy Signature Schemes without Certificates. In: Sauveron, D., Markantonakis, K., Bilas, A., Quisquater, J.-J. (eds.) WISTP 2007. LNCS, vol. 4462, pp. 115–126. Springer, Heidelberg (2007)
7. Chen, H., Zhang, F.T., Song, R.S.: Certificateless Proxy Signature with Provable Security. Journal of Software 20(3), 692–701 (2009)
8. Xiong, H., Li, F.G., Qin, Z.G.: A Provably Secure Proxy Signature Scheme in Certificateless Cryptography. International Journal of Informatica 21(2), 277–294 (2010)
9. Schuldt, J.C.N., Matsuura, K., Paterson, K.G.: Proxy Signatures Secure against Proxy Key Exposure. In: Cramer, R. (ed.) PKC 2008. LNCS, vol. 4939, pp. 141–161. Springer, Heidelberg (2008)
10. Anderson, R.: Two Remarks on Public Key Cryptology. Invited lecture. In: Proceedings of the 4th ACM Conference on Computer and Communications Security (1997)
11. Bellare, M., Miner, S.: A Forward-Secure Digital Signature Scheme. In: Wiener, M. (ed.) CRYPTO 1999. LNCS, vol. 1666, pp. 431–448. Springer, Heidelberg (1999)
12. Itkis, G., Reyzin, L.: Forward-Secure Signatures with Optimal Signing and Verifying. In: Kilian, J. (ed.) CRYPTO 2001. LNCS, vol. 2139, pp. 332–354. Springer, Heidelberg (2001)
13. Kang, B.G., Park, J.H., Hahn, S.G.: A New Forward Secure Signature Scheme (2004), `http://eprint.iacr.org/2004/183/`
14. Nakanishi, T., Hira, Y., Funabiki, N.: Forward-Secure Group Signatures from Pairings. In: Shacham, H., Waters, B. (eds.) Pairing 2009. LNCS, vol. 5671, pp. 171–186. Springer, Heidelberg (2009)
15. Malkin, T., Micciancio, D., Miner, S.: Efficient Generic Forward-Secure Signatures with an Unbounded Number of Time Periods. In: Knudsen, L.R. (ed.) EUROCRYPT 2002. LNCS, vol. 2332, pp. 400–417. Springer, Heidelberg (2002)

16. Alomair, B., Sampigethaya, K., Poovendran, R.: Efficient Generic Forward-Secure Signatures and Proxy Signatures. In: Mjølsnes, S.F., Mauw, S., Katsikas, S.K. (eds.) EuroPKI 2008. LNCS, vol. 5057, pp. 166–181. Springer, Heidelberg (2008)
17. Yu, J., Kong, F.Y., Cheng, X.G., Hao, R., Li, G.W.: Construction of Yet Another Forward Secure Signature Scheme Using Bilinear Maps. In: Baek, J., Bao, F., Chen, K., Lai, X. (eds.) ProvSec 2008. LNCS, vol. 5324, pp. 83–97. Springer, Heidelberg (2008)
18. Chen, H.B., Yang, X.Y., Liang, Z.Y., Wu, X.G.: Forward Secure Certificateless Proxy Signature Scheme. Computer Engineering 36(2), 156–157 (2010)
19. Huang, X., Mu, Y., Susilo, W., Wong, D.S., Wu, W.: Certificateless Signature Revisited. In: Pieprzyk, J., Ghodosi, H., Dawson, E. (eds.) ACISP 2007. LNCS, vol. 4586, pp. 308–322. Springer, Heidelberg (2007)
20. Pointcheval, D., Stern, J.: Security Arguments for Digital Signatures and Blind Signatures. Journal of Cryptology 13(3), 361–396 (2000)

Leakage-Resilient Zero-Knowledge Proofs of Knowledge for NP*

Hongda Li, Qihua Niu, and Bei Liang

State Key Lab of Information Security, Institute of Information Engineering
Chinese Academy of Sciences, Beijing 100093, China
{lihongda,niuqihua,liangbei}@iie.ac.cn

Abstract. Leakage-resilient zero-knowledge proofs for all NP was presented by Garg et al in 2011. How to construct leakage-resilient zero-knowledge proofs of knowledge for all NP languages is an interesting problem. This paper focuses on this problem and presents a constructions of leakage-resilient zero-knowledge proofs of knowledge for HC (Hamiltonian Cycle) problem.

Keywords: zero-knowledge proofs, leakage-resilient, proofs of knowledge, black-box simulation.

1 Introduction

Zero-knowledge proofs (ZKP), first introduced by Goldwasser et al.[9], are protocols that allow the prover to convince the verifier that an assertion is true without providing the verifier with any additional information about the assertion being proved. It is proved that any language in NP has a zero-knowledge proof system [10]. ZKP is required to protect the honest verifier from an all-powerful prover. Zero-knowledge arguments (ZKA) are a relaxation of the zero-knowledge proofs, in which the soundness property is required to hold only with respect to a computationally bounded prover.

Proofs of knowledge [9] are proofs that allow the prover to convince the verifier that it knows a secret witness w about a given common input x. If a ZKP or ZKA system for L is also a proof of knowledge system, it is known as a zero knowledge proof of knowledge (ZKPoK) or zero knowledge argument of knowledge (ZKAoK) for L. Now, ZKP (or ZKA) and ZKPoK (or ZKAoK) playe a crucial role in the design of cryptographic schemes and protocols.

In the conventional zero-knowledge, it is assumed that the verifier is given only black-box access to the honest prover's algorithm. That is, the prover's internal state, including the witness and the random coins, is perfectly hidden from the verifier. Unfortunately, this assumption is too strong to be met in many settings

* This work was partially supported the National Natural Science Foundation of China (Grant No. 60970139), Strategic Priority Program of Chinese Academy of Sciences (Grant No. XDA06010702), and IIEs Cryptography Research Project.

J. Lopez, X. Huang, and R. Sandhu (Eds.): NSS 2013, LNCS 7873, pp. 365–380, 2013.

where a malicious verifier has the ability to use different type of side-channel attacks to obtain leakage about prover's internal state.

Very recently, Garg et al. [7] first investigated zero knowledge proof in such a leaking setting (known as leakage-resilient zero-knowledge proof, LR-ZKP), where the malicious verifier is able to learn an arbitrary amount of leakage on the internal state of the honest prover by making a series of leakage queries $f_1, f_2, \cdots$ throughout the execution of the protocol. Their definition of LR-ZK requires that no such malicious verifier can learn anything beyond the validity of the assertion and the leakage.

An interesting problem left by this work is whether it is possible to obtain leakage-resilient ZKPoK. In fact, [7] discussed how to modify their protocol such that the modified protocol is a proof of knowledge. The presented method needs a public-coin zero knowledge proof of knowledge. Concretely, the modified protocol requires V only to reveal ch in stage 3 and then to prove that it is one that was committed in Stage 1 by a public-coin zero knowledge proof of knowledge. We will focus on this problem and give a new simpler construction under perfectly hiding commitment schemes.

1.1 Related Works

In the past few years there have been many works on developing cryptographic primitives resilient against such leakage attacks in various models, such as leakage-resilient encryption schemes, leakage-resilient signature schemes and leakage-resilient interactive protocols. Bitansky et. al. [1] considered leakage-resilient protocols for general functionality which are secure against semi-honest adversaries in the UC framework. Boyle et. al. [5] studied leakage-resilient multi-party coin tossing protocol. Damgard et. al. [6] considered leakage-resilient two-party secure protocols against semi-honest adversary. Two types of leakage attack are considered in their model: global leakage model (the adversary use a leakage function on the input and the entire randomness of an honest party) and local leakage model (the adversary chooses different leakage functions at different points of time during the protocol execution). Very recently, Boyle et. al. [4] constructed a general leakage-resilient multiparty computation (MPC) protocol with stronger security notion: an adversary obtaining leakage on the honest party's secret state is guaranteed to learn nothing beyond the input and output of corrupted parties.

2 Preliminaries

In this paper, we use some standard notations. If $A(\cdot)$ is a probabilistic algorithm, $A(x)$ is the result of running A on input x and $y = A(x)$ (or $y \leftarrow A(x)$) denotes that y is set to $A(x)$. For a finite set $\mathcal{S}$, we denote by $y \in_R S$ that y is uniformly selected from $\mathcal{S}$. We write $[n]$ for any $n \in \mathbb{N}$ to denote the set $\{1, \cdots, n\}$ and $poly(\cdot)$ to denote an unspecified polynomial.

We use the following standard definitions and tools.

2.1 Leakage-Resilient Zero-Knowledge Proof

We recall the definitions of leakage-resilient zero-knowledge from [7].

Let P and V be a pair of randomized interactive Turing machines, $\langle P, V\rangle(x)$ be a random variable representing the local output of Turing machine V when interacting with machine P on common input x, when the random input to each machine is uniformly and independently chosen. Customarily, machine P is called the prover and machine V is called the verifier. We denote by $\langle P, V\rangle(x) = 1$ ($\langle P, V\rangle(x) = 0$) that machine V accepts (rejects) the proofs given by machine P.

Definition 1. *A pair of interactive Turing machines $\langle P, V\rangle$ is called an interactive proof system for a language L if machine V is polynomial-time and the following two conditions hold:*

- *Completeness: there exists a negligible function c such that for every $x \in L$,*
$$\mathbf{Pr}[\langle P, V\rangle(x) = 1] > 1 - c(|x|)$$
- *Soundness: there exists a negligible function s such that for every $x \notin L$ and every interactive machine B, it holds that*
$$\mathbf{Pr}[\langle B, V\rangle(x) = 1] < s(|x|)$$

$c(\cdot)$ is called the completeness error, and $s(\cdot)$ the soundness error.

In the execution of interactive proofs, P has the ability to select a random coin r_i at the beginning of round i and uses it in round i. Synchronously, P updates his current secret state. Denote by *state* (initialized to the private input w) the current secret state of P. P updates *state* by setting $state = state||r_i$ in round i. The cheating verifier V launches a leakage attack by means of any number of arbitrary leakage queries throughout the interaction. A leakage query on provers state in round i is a leakage function f_i, to which the prover responds with $f_i(state)$. We denote by ℓ the number of leaking bits, i.e. $\ell = \sum_i |f_i(state_i)|$.

Classic zero knowledge is formalized by requiring that for any polynomial-time verifier V^* there exists a polynomial-time algorithm $\mathcal{S}$ (a.k.a the simulator) such that the view of V^* can be simulated by $\mathcal{S}$. Under the leakage attack setting, leakage information $f_i(state)$ obtained by V^* cannot be simulated by any polynomial-time algorithm $\mathcal{S}$ only upon common input x. To formulate leakage-resilient zero-knowledge, $\mathcal{S}$ is allowed to access to an leakage oracle by a series of query. A query to the leakage oracle is an efficiently computable function $f'_j(\cdot)$, to which the oracle responds with $f'_j(w)$. We denote by ℓ' the number of bits that $\mathcal{S}$ received from the leakage oracle, i.e. $\ell' = \sum_j |f'_j(state_j)|$. It is required that $\ell' \leq \lambda \cdot \ell$, where λ is a leakage parameter. The leakage oracle only holds the witness w and is denoted by $L_w^{n,\lambda}(\cdot)$.

Leakage-resilient zero knowledge require that no malicious verifier, launching leakage attack, can learn anything beyond the validity of the assertion and the leakage. This is formulated by requiring that for any polynomial-time verifier V^* with any auxiliary input z there exists a polynomial-time algorithm $\mathcal{S}$ (a.k.a the simulator) such that the view of V^* is indistinguishable from the output of $\mathcal{S}^{L_w^{n,\lambda}(\cdot)}(x, z)$.

Definition 2 (Leakage-Resilient Zero Knowledge). *An interactive proof system (P, V) for a language L with a witness relation $\mathcal{R}$ is said to be λ-**leakage-resilient zero knowledge** if for every* PPT *machine V^* that makes any arbitrary polynomial number of leakage queries on P's state (in the manner as described above) with ℓ bits of total leakage L_P, there exists a* PPT *algorithm $\mathcal{S}$ that obtains at most $\lambda \cdot \ell$ bits of total leakage $L_{\mathcal{S}}$ from a leakage oracle $L_w^{k,\lambda}(\cdot)$ (as defined above) such that for every $(x, w) \in \mathcal{R}$, every $z \in \{0,1\}^*$, $\{View_{V^*}(x, z)\}_{x \in L, z \in \{0,1\}^*}$ and $\left\{\mathcal{S}^{L_w^{k,\lambda}(\cdot)}(x, z)\right\}_{x \in L, z \in \{0,1\}^*}$ are computationally indistinguishable.*

To formulate that no malicious verifier can learn anything beyond the validity of the assertion and the leakage, it is natural to require $\lambda \leq 1$. However, [7] had showed that it is impossible to realize the above definition for any $\lambda < 1$. On the other hand, black-box λ-leakage-resilient zero knowledge proofs exist only when $\lambda > 1$.

2.2 Proof of Knowledge

In a proof of knowledge for a relationship R, the prover, holding a secret input w such that $(x, w) \in R$, and the verifier interact on a common input x. The goal of the protocol is to convince the verifier that the prover indeed knows such w. This is in contrast to a regular interactive proof, where the verifier is just convinced of the validity of the statement.

The concept of "knowledge" for machines is formalized by saying that if a prover can convince the verifier, then there exists an efficient algorithm that can "extract" a witness from this prover (thus the prover knows a witness because it could run the extraction procedure on itself).

Definition 3. *An interactive protocol $\langle P, V\rangle$ is a system of proofs of knowledge for a (poly-balanced) relation R with knowledge error κ if the following conditions hold:*

- *(efficiency): $\langle P, V\rangle$ is polynomially bounded, and V is computable in probabilistic polynomial time.*
- *(non-triviality): There exists an interactive machine P such that for every $(x, w) \in R$ all possible interactions of V with P on common input x and auxiliary y are accepting.*
- *(validity with knowledge error κ): Denote by $p(x, y, r)$ the probability that the interactive machine V accepts, on input x, when interacting with the prover specified by $P^*_{x,y,r}$ (the prover's strategy when fixing common x, auxiliary input y and random tape r). There exists an expected polynomial-time oracle machine $\mathcal{K}$ and a polynomial q such that on input x and access to oracle $P_{x,y,r}$, $\mathcal{K}^{P_{x,y,r}}(x)$ outputs w, such that $(x, w) \in R$, with probability of at least $(p(x, y, r) - \kappa(|x|))/q(|x|)$*

2.3 Commitment Schemes

In this paper, we use two types of commitment schemes. One is Naor's statistically binding commitment scheme[16]. This scheme is constructed using a pseudorandom generator $g : \{0,1\}^n \rightarrow \{0,1\}^{3n}$. Recall that in this scheme, the receiver first selects $\tau \in_R \{0,1\}^{3n}$ and sends it to the sender. To commit to bit b, the sender selects $v \in_R \{0,1\}^n$, and then sends to the receiver $c = g(v)$ if $b = 0$, or $c = \tau \oplus g(v)$ otherwise. Obviously, when the first message $\tau \in \{g(s_0) \oplus g(s_1) : s_0, s_1 \in \{0,1\}^n\}$, the commitment to b, by sending $g(s_0)$ to the receiver, can be decommit to two different values: $b = 0$ by revealing s_0, or $b = 1$ by revealing s_1.

The other is a two-round statistically hiding commitment scheme $Comm_{sh}(\cdot;\cdot)$. In such a scheme, the first message denoted by m is from the receiver, and a corresponding commitment algorithm is denoted by $Comm_{sh}^m(\cdot;\cdot)$. In particular, this scheme can be constructed based on claw-free collections [8].

3 A Leakage-Resilient Zero-Knowledge Proof of Knowledge for HC

Suppose that the language HC consists of all directed graphs that contain a Hamiltonian cycle. Our goal in this section is to construct a LR-ZKPoK for HC.

We start by reviewing Blum's 3-round zero knowledge proof for HC.

Common input: $G = (V, E) \in HC$, $|V| = n$.

- Prover's first step(P1): The prover randomly selects a permutation π, and sends the commitments to the adjacency of $G_i = \pi(G)$ to the verifier.
- Verifier's first step(V1): The verifier uniformly selects a challenge $ch \in_R \{0,1\}$ and sends it to the prover.
- Prover's second step(P2): If $ch = 1$, the prover reveals the partial commitments corresponding to the edges of the Hamiltonian cycle $\pi(H)$. If $ch = 0$ then the prover reveals all the commitments and π.
- Verifier's second step(V2): The verifier V checks P's revealment.

The protocol of [7] adds a preamble to n parallel Blum's protocol. Roughly speaking, their construction proceeds in three stages. In Stage 1, V commits to its challenge ch and a random string r_V using a public-coin statistically hiding commitment scheme. In Stage 2, P selects a random string r_P and V reveals r_V. And then, P and V compute $r = r_P \oplus r_V$. Finally, in Stage 3, P and V run n (where n denotes the security parameter) parallel repetitions of the 3-round Blum protocol, described as follows. In the first round, P uses Naor's commitment scheme to commit to the adjacency of the permuted graphs, where the string generated in Stage 2 is used as the first massage. In the second round, V reveals the commitment to its challenge ch. Finally, P responds to this challenge and V verifies the response from P. To allow the simulator to extract the challenge ch committed by V and to force r to obey a special distribution of its choice with minimal use of the leakage oracle, the commitment schemes in Stage 1 need a preamble of iterating challenge-response many times as in [18]

In the protocol of [7], V commits to its challenges ch before P sends its commitment. This implies that the permutation that P use to compute its commitments may depend on the challenge selected by V. This results in knowledge extractor cannot work efficiently. Therefore, the protocol in [7] is no longer a proof of knowledge. The LR-zero-knowledge property requires that for any V^* there exists a simulator (with a leakage oracle) that can simulate the view of V^*, while proofs of knowledge require that there exists a knowledge extractor that accesses to the prover's strategy P^* to extract a witness from P^*. The approach of requiring the verifier to commit to its challenges ch in advance ensures that the simulator $\mathcal{S}$ can output a simulated view indistinguishable from the view of V^* by rewinding the algorithm of V^* to obtain the challenge ch in advance, but then seemingly destroys the proof of knowledge property.

To solve the above problem, our protocol requires P first sends its commitments before the verifier's challenge is generated. Zero-knowledge property requires that the simulator can simulate the view of V^* without the witness. Therefore, the simulator must learn the real challenge before generating the prover's commitments. To this end, we use a jointly coin-flipping to generate real challenge, as in [13,15]. It results in that the simulator has the ability to control over the real challenge by rewinding the coin-flipping process.

Our protocol consists of four stages. Let $t = 3n^4$ and $k = \omega(n)$. In Stage 1, V commits to a random string $r_V \in \{0,1\}^t$ and two sequences $\{r^b_{i,j}\}_{i=1,j=1}^{i=\frac{k}{\varepsilon},j=k}$, $b = 0, 1$, using a public-coin statistically hiding commitment scheme, where $r^0_{i,j} \oplus r^1_{i,j} = r_V$ for every i, j. After this, n iterations follows. In the ith iteration P sends a random k-bit string $\sigma_i = \sigma_{i,1} \cdots \sigma_{i,k}$, and V reveal the commitments to $r^{\sigma_{i,1}}_{i,1}, \cdots, r^{\sigma_{i,k}}_{i,k}$. Finally, the prover sends a random string $r_P \in \{0,1\}^t$ to the verifier, which responds with the decommitments to r_V and to $r^{1-\sigma_{i,1}}_{i,1}$ for every i.

In Stage 2, the prover commits n random permuted graphes by Naor's commitment scheme with $r = r_V \oplus r_P$ as the first message. In Stage 3, P and V jointly generate a random string $ch \in \{0,1\}^n$. First, V commits to a random string $q \in \{0,1\}^n$ and two sequences $\{q^b_{i,j}\}_{i=1,j=1}^{i=\frac{k}{\varepsilon},j=k}$, $b = 0, 1$, using a public-coin statistically hiding commitment scheme, where $q^0_{i,j} \oplus q^1_{i,j} = q$ for every i, j. Subsequently, n iterations follows. In the ith iteration P sends a random k-bit string $\delta_i = \delta_{i,1} \cdots \delta_{i,k}$, and V reveal the commitments to $q^{\delta_{i,1}}_{i,1}, \cdots, q^{\delta_{i,k}}_{i,k}$. Finally, the prover selects a random string $q' \in \{0,1\}^n$ and sends the commitment to q' to the verifier.

In Stage 4, P computes $ch = q \oplus q'$, and uses it as challenge to execute P2 (Prover's second step of Blum's protocol). Then, V executes V2 with $ch = q \oplus q'$. The details of our protocol Π is described in Figure 1.

Theorem 1. *Protocol Π is a LR-ZKPoK for HC, assuming $Comm_{sh}(\cdot;\cdot)$ is a two-round statistically hiding commitment scheme and g is a pseudorandom generator meeting with $|g(x)| = 3|x|$.*

Common input: $G = (V, E) \in HC$, $|V| = n$.
Auxiliary input to the prover: A Hamilton cycle H in G.

- Stage 1: Jointly coin-tossing:
  - P sends the first random message m to V.
  - V selects $r_V \in \{0,1\}^t$ and $r^0_{i,j}, r^1_{i,j} \in \{0,1\}^t$, $i \in [\frac{k}{\varepsilon}], j \in [k]$, such that $r_V = r^0_{i,j} \oplus r^1_{i,j}$. Then, V sends $R_V = Comm^m_{sh}(r_V)$ and $R^e_{i,j} = Comm^m_{sh}(r^e_{i,j})$ for $i \in [\frac{k}{\varepsilon}], j \in [k]$ and $e = 0, 1$.
  - For $i = 1, \cdots, \frac{k}{\varepsilon}$:
    * P selects $\sigma_i = \sigma_{i,1} \cdots \sigma_{i,k} \in_R \{0,1\}^k$ and sends σ to V.
    * V decommits to $r^{\sigma_{i,j}}_{i,j}$, $j \in [k]$.
  - P selects $r_P \in_R \{0,1\}^t$, sets $s = r_P \oplus r_V$, and sends r_P to V.
  - V decommits to r_V and $r^{1-\sigma_{i,j}}_{i,j}$, $i \in [\frac{k}{\varepsilon}], j \in [k]$, and sets $r = r_P \oplus r_V$.
  - P aborts if the decommitments fails.
- Stage 2: The prover's commitment.
  - Let $r = r_1 \cdots r_n$, where $r_i = r_{i,1} \cdots r_{i,n^2}$ satisfying $|r_{i,v}| = 3n$ for $i \in [n]$ and $v \in [n^2]$. For every $i \in [n]$, P selects a random permutation π_i and commits to the adjacency of $G_i = \pi_i(G)$ using Naor's scheme with r_i as the first message for $i \in [n]$.
- Stage 3: Jointly coin-tossing
  - V selects $q \in_R \{0,1\}^n$ and $q^0_{i,j}, q^1_{i,j} \in \{0,1\}^n$, $i \in [\frac{k}{\varepsilon}], j \in [k]$, such that $q = q^0_{i,j} \oplus q^1_{i,j}$. Then, V sends $Q = Comm^m_{sh}(q)$ and $Q^e_{i,j} = Comm^m_{sh}(q^e_{i,j})$ for $i \in [\frac{k}{\varepsilon}], j \in [k]$ and $e = 0, 1$.
  - For $i = 1, \cdots, \frac{k}{\varepsilon}$:
    * P selects $\delta_i = \delta_{i,1} \cdots \delta_{i,k} \in_R \{0,1\}^k$ and sends δ to V.
    * V decommits to $q^{\delta_{i,j}}_{i,j}$, $j \in [k]$.
  - P selects $q' \in_R \{0,1\}^n$, and sends it to V.
  - V decommits to q and $q^{1-\delta_{i,j}}_{i,j}$, $i \in [\frac{k}{\varepsilon}], j \in [k]$, and computes $ch = q \oplus q'$.
  - P aborts if the decommitment fails.
- Stage 4: The prover open its commitments corresponding to $ch = ch_1 \cdots ch_n$.
  - P reveals the partial commitments to the adjacency of G_i corresponding to the edges of the Hamiltonian cycle $\pi_i(H)$ if $ch_i = 1$ or all the commitments to the adjacency of G_i and π_i if $ch_i = 0$.
  - For every $i \in [n]$, V checks wether P correctly reveals a simple Hamiltonian cycle when $ch_i = 1$, or a graph G_i and a permutation π_i such that $G_i = \pi_i(G)$ when $ch_i = 0$.

Fig. 1. LR-ZKPoK

Proof. **Completeness:** Completeness is obvious.

Soundness: It follows directly from the statistically hiding property of $Comm_{sh}(\cdot;\cdot)$ and the statistically binding property of Naor's commitment.

Let the message that P sends in Stage 2 be $\widetilde{C} = (C_1, \cdots, C_n)$. Say that $\widetilde{C}$ matches with $ch = ch_1 \cdots ch_n$ if P can answer every ch_i correctly. Let

$$Bad = \{r : \exists s_0, s_1 \in \{0,1\}^k, \ such\ that\ r = g(s_0) \oplus g(s_1)\}$$
$$Match = \{(\widetilde{C}, ch) : \widetilde{C} = (C_1, \cdots, C_n)\ match\ with\ ch = ch_1 \cdots ch_n\}$$

For any r generated in Stage 1, define an event $Event_r = \{r \in Bad\}$. For every $(\widetilde{C}, ch)$, where $\widetilde{C}$ is generated in Stage 2 and ch is defined by q and q' in Stage 3, define an event $Match_{(\widetilde{C},ch)} = \{(\widetilde{C}, ch) \in Match\}$.
Obviously,

$$\begin{aligned} Pr[\langle P^*, V\rangle(G) = 1] &= Pr[Match_{(\widetilde{C},ch)}] \\ &= Pr[Event_r \wedge Match_{(\widetilde{C},ch)}] + Pr[\overline{Event_r} \wedge Match_{(\widetilde{C},ch)}] \\ &\leq Pr[Event_r] + Pr[\overline{Event_r} \wedge Match_{(\widetilde{C},ch)}] \end{aligned}$$

It has been proved in [7] that $Pr[Event_r]$ is negligible. Next, we show that $Pr[\overline{Event_r} \wedge Match_{(\widetilde{C},ch)}]$ is negligible.

If $G \notin HC$ and $Event_r$ does not occur, it follows from the statistically binding property of Naor's commitment scheme that for any fixed $\widetilde{C} = (C_1, \cdots, C_n)$ there exists only one ch, denoted by $\widetilde{ch}$, such that $(\widetilde{C}, \widetilde{ch}) \in Match$ takes place. Hence, it holds that,

$$\begin{aligned} Pr[\overline{Event_r} \wedge Match_{(\widetilde{C},ch)}] &= Pr\begin{bmatrix} q \oplus q' = \widetilde{ch} : q \leftarrow_R \{0,1\}^n \\ Q = Comm_{sh}^m(q) \\ q' \leftarrow P^*(\widetilde{C}, Q, \cdots) \end{bmatrix} \\ &= Pr\begin{bmatrix} q' = q \oplus \widetilde{ch} : q \leftarrow_R \{0,1\}^n \\ Q = Comm_{sh}^m(q) \\ q' \leftarrow P^*(\widetilde{C}, Q, \cdots) \end{bmatrix} \end{aligned}$$

So, that $\overline{Event_r} \wedge Match_{(\widetilde{C},ch)}$ takes place implies that P^* can guess q from the commitment to q. From the statistically hiding property of $Comm_{sh}$, we have that $Pr[\overline{Event_r} \wedge Match_{(\widetilde{C},ch)}]$ is negligible.

Leakage-Oblivious Simulator: Leakage-oblivious simulator[7] is permitted to directly receive leakage query $f(state)$ from V^* as a real prover, where *state* consists of the witness and all random value used so far. Without holding any witness, however, the simulator cannot respond leakage query f directly. It is just well that the simulator can access a leakage oracle $L_w^{n,\lambda}$ that holds the witness. To respond the leakage query, the simulator first generates a new leakage query function f' (takeing the witness as input) and sends it to leakage oracle $L_w^{n,\lambda}$. Instead of returning leakage information $f'(w)$ to the simulator, leakage oracle $L_w^{n,\lambda}$ leaks $f'(w)$ directly to verifier V^*, and does not leak any information to the simulator. What the simulator does is to construct a new function f' such that $f'(w)$ is indistinguishable from $f(state)$ with which the prover responds directly to f.

Note that leakage query f takes the form of $f(w;R)$, where w is the prover's witness, $R = R(w)$ is a function that, on inputting the prover's witness w, outputs the prover's random coins. To creates a new query f' after receiving a query $f(w, R(w))$ from the verifier, the simulator first define $R(w)$ to be an appropriate random coins and lets f' be residual $f(w, R(w))$ with $R(w)$ hardwired in such that $f'(w) = f(w; R(w))$.

Leakage resilient zero knowledge: Let $t = 3n^4$ and $\varepsilon > 0$ such that $\frac{n}{\varepsilon}$ is an integer. On inputting common n-vertex graph G, the leakage-oblivious simulator $\mathcal{S}^{V^*}$ showing its zero-knowledge property operates as follows:

Simulating Stage 1:

▲ **V^*'s Commitment**:

1. $S \rightleftharpoons V^*$: $\mathcal{S}$ acts just like a real prover and obtains the commitments to $r_V, r_{i,j}^e \in_R \{0,1\}^t$ from V^* for $i \in [\frac{k}{\varepsilon}], j \in [k]$ and $e = 0, 1$.
2. $S \leftrightarrow V^*$: V^* could make multiple leakage queries in the above step. $\mathcal{S}$ uses $L_w^{n,\lambda}(\cdot)$ to answer all these leakage queries (in the manner as described in the main text). $\mathcal{S}$ aborts when V^* aborts.

▲ **Challenge-Response**: For $0 \leq a \leq k-1$, proceed as follows:

3. For $1 \leq b \leq \frac{1}{\varepsilon}$, do the following. Let $i = \frac{a}{\varepsilon} + b$.
   - 3.1 $S \to V^*$: $\mathcal{S}$ chooses k-bit random strings $\sigma_i = \sigma_{i,1} \cdots \sigma_{i,k}$, and sends σ_i to V^*.
   - 3.2 $S \leftrightarrow V^*$: $\mathcal{S}$ uses $L_w^{n,\lambda}(\cdot)$ to answer the leakage queries (in the manner as described in the main text). Let the output length of the leakage query be ℓ_i bits.
   - 3.3 $S \leftarrow V^*$: V^* reveals the commitments to $r_{i,j}^{\sigma_{i,j}}$ for $j = 1, \cdots, k$. If the decommitments is not correct, $\mathcal{S}$ aborts.
4. Find i_a ($\frac{a}{\varepsilon} + 1 \leq i_a \leq \frac{a+1}{\varepsilon}$), such that $\ell_{i_a} = min_{\frac{a}{\varepsilon}+1 \leq i \leq \frac{a+1}{\varepsilon}} \ell_i$.
   - 4.1 $S \to V^*$: $\mathcal{S}$ rewinds V^* to 3.1 of i_a iteration. Then $\mathcal{S}$ Chooses n-bit random strings $\sigma'_{i_a} = \sigma'_{i_a,1} \cdots \sigma'_{i_a,k}$, and sends σ'_{i_a} to V^*.
   - 4.2 $S \leftrightarrow V^*$: Let the output length of the leakage query be ℓ'_{i_a} bits. If $\ell'_{i_a} \leq \ell_{i_a}$, then $\mathcal{S}$ uses $L_w^{n,\lambda}(\cdot)$ to answer the leakage queries. Otherwise $\mathcal{S}$ aborts.
   - 4.3 $S \leftarrow V^*$: V^* reveals the commitments to $r_{i_a,j}^{\sigma'_{i_a,j}}$, $j = 1, \cdots, k$. If the decommitments in 4.3 is correct and $\sigma_{i_0} \neq \sigma'_{i_a}$, $\mathcal{S}$ extracts r_V and proceeds next step. Otherwise, $\mathcal{S}$ executes the next iteration or aborts when $a = k-1$.

▲ **Generating** r:

5. Assume $r_V = r'_1 \cdots r'_n$, where $r'_i = r'_{i,1} \cdots r'_{i,n^2}$ and $|r'_{i,j}| = 3n$. For $i \in [n]$, $j \in [n^2]$, $\mathcal{S}$ selects $z^0_{i,j}, z^1_{i,j} \in \{0,1\}^n$ and computes $r''_{i,j} = r'_{i,j} \oplus g(z^0_{i,j}) \oplus g(z^1_{i,j})$.
   5.1 $S \rightarrow V^*$: $\mathcal{S}$ sends $r_P = r''_1 \cdots r''_n$ to V^*, where $r''_i = r''_{i,1} \cdots r''_{i,n^2}$, and sets $r = r_P \oplus r_V$.
   5.2 $S \leftrightarrow V^*$: $\mathcal{S}$ uses $L^{n,\lambda}_w(\cdot)$ to answer the leakage queries.
   5.3 $S \leftarrow V^*$: V^* reveals the commitments to $r_V, r^{1-\sigma_{i,j}}_{i,j}$, $i \in [\frac{k}{\varepsilon}]$, $j \in [k]$. If the decommitments is not correct, $\mathcal{S}$ abort.

Response to Query Leakage in Simulating for Stage 1: In this stage, the response to the query leakage is very easy since P only reveals its random coin. In fact, $R(w)$ at any point is just the concatenation of all public cion. Assume that R' is the concatenation of all public cion sent by the simulator.

Then, the simulator sets $R(w) \triangleq R'$ and $f'(w) \triangleq f(w, R(w))$. The simulator then queries the leakage oracle with $f'(\cdot)$ and V^* obtains $f'(w)$. Since R that is used by an honest prover is identical to R', it is easy to see that $f'(w) = f(w; R(w))$.

Lemma 1. *That $\mathcal{S}$ reaches the end of Stage 1 but fails to extract r_V is negligible.*

Proof. Let E be the event that $\mathcal{S}$ reaches the end of Stage 1 but fails to extract r_V. Let E_i be the event that V^* does not abort in the ith challenge response slot, E'_i be the event that $\mathcal{S}$ rewinds V^* in the ith challenge response slot, and V does not abort. E''_i be the event that $\ell'_i > \ell_i$, where ℓ_i is the output length of the leakage query in the ith challenge response slot, ℓ'_i is the output length of the leakage query in the rewound i^{th} challenge response slot. Then, we obtain the following

$$E = (\bigwedge_{i=1}^{k\varepsilon^{-1}} E_i) \bigwedge_{a=0}^{k-1} (\overline{E'_{i_a}} \vee (E'_{i_a} \wedge E''_{i_a})) \subseteq \bigwedge_{a=0}^{k-1} (E_0 \wedge (\overline{E'_{i_a}} \vee (E'_{i_a} \wedge E''_{i_a})))$$

where $E_0 = \bigwedge_{i=1}^{k\varepsilon^{-1}} E_i$. Since the rewinds are independent, it holds that

$$\begin{aligned} Pr[E] &\leq \prod_{a=0}^{k-1} Pr[E_0 \wedge (\overline{E'_{i_a}} \vee (E'_{i_a} \wedge E''_{i_a})] \\ &\leq \prod_{a=0}^{k-1} Pr[E_{i_a} \wedge (\overline{E'_{i_a}} \vee (E'_{i_a} \wedge E''_{i_a})] \\ &\leq \prod_{a=0}^{k-1} (Pr[E_{i_a} \wedge \overline{E'_{i_a}}] + Pr[E_{i_a} \wedge E'_{i_a} \wedge E''_{i_a}]) \\ &\leq \prod_{a=0}^{k-1} (Pr[E_{i_a} \wedge \overline{E'_{i_a}}] + \tfrac{1}{2} Pr[E_{i_a} \wedge E'_{i_a}]) \\ &= \prod_{a=0}^{k-1} (Pr[E_{i_a}] - \tfrac{1}{2} Pr[E_{i_a} \wedge E'_{i_a}]) \\ &= \prod_{a=0}^{k-1} (Pr[E_{i_a}] - \tfrac{1}{2} Pr[E_{i_a}]^2) \end{aligned}$$

Note that $Pr[E_{i_a}] - \frac{1}{2} Pr[E_{i_a}]^2 \leq \frac{1}{2}$. It follows that $Pr[E] \leq \frac{1}{2^k}$ is negligible.

Simulating Stage 2:

1. $\mathcal{S} \to V^*$: For every $i \in [n]$, $\mathcal{S}$ chooses a random permutation π_i and sets $G_i = \pi_i(G)$. Then, $\mathcal{S}$ sends to V^* the commitments to the adjacency of G_i using Naor's commitment scheme with r_i as the first message, $i \in [n]$. Accurately, $\mathcal{S}$ sends $C_i = \{g(z^0_{i,j})\}_{j=1}^{j=n^2}$, $i \in [n]$ to V^*.
2. $\mathcal{S} \leftrightarrow V^*$: $\mathcal{S}$ uses $L^{n,\lambda}_w(\cdot)$ to answer the leakage queries.

Response to Query Leakage in Simulating for Stage 2: It is not a simple thing to deal with query leakage in this stage although $\mathcal{S}$ acts seemly as the same as an honest prover.

Let $\omega = H$ be a Hamiltonian cycle in G and R be the concatenation of all random cion used by the simulator before Stage 2. $\mathcal{S}$ simply constructs a a new leakage query f', after receiving leakage query $f(H, R(H))$ from V^*, by letting $f'(H) = f(H, R||\pi_1||\widetilde{r}_1||\cdots||\pi_n||\widetilde{r}_n)$ (here, π_i is used by $\mathcal{S}$ in Stage 2, $\widetilde{r}_i$ is related to r_i which is used in Naor's commitment), $\mathcal{S}$ does not have ability to make the response (to the challenge ch in Stage 4) consistent with $f'(H)$. To solve this problem, $\mathcal{S}$ must define a random function, denoted as $Select(H, \{z^0_{i,j}, z^1_{i,j}\})$, to determine the random coins used by $\mathcal{S}$. $Select(H, \{z^0_{i,j}, z^1_{i,j}\}_{i,j})$ proceeds as follows:

- Randomly select a challenge $ch = ch_1 \cdots ch_n \in \{0,1\}^n$.
- For every $i \in [n]$
  - If $ch_i = 0$, define $\rho(0, H)$ and $\varphi(0, H, \{z^0_{i,j}, z^1_{i,j}\})$ as follows:
    (1) $\rho(0, H)$ returns the permutation π_i selected by $\mathcal{S}$ in Stage 2. Let $\{g_{i,j}\}_{j \in [n^2]}$ be the adjacency matrix of $G_i = \pi_i(G)$.
    (2) $\varphi(0, H, \{z^0_{i,j}, z^1_{i,j}\})$ returns $y_{i,1}||\cdots||y_{i,n^2}$, where $y_{i,j} = z^b_{i,j}$ if $g_{i,j} = b$ for each $j \in [n^2]$.

    Then, set $\widetilde{r}_i = \rho(0, H)||\varphi(0, H, \{z^0_{i,j}, z^1_{i,j}\})$.
  - If $ch_i = 1$, select a random cycle H_i, and define two functions $\rho(1, H, H_i)$ and $\varphi(1, H, H_i, \{z^0_{i,j}, z^1_{i,j}\})$ as follows:
    (1) $\rho(1, H, H_i)$ first selects a permutation π' such that $H_i = \pi'_i(\pi_i(H))$. Thus, $\rho(1, H, H_i)$ returns $\pi'_i \circ \pi_i$. Let $\{g'_{i,j}\}_{j \in [n^2]}$ be the adjacency matrix of $G_i = \pi'_i(\pi(G))$.
    (2) $\varphi(1, H, H_i, \{z^0_{i,j}, z^1_{i,j}\})$ returns $y_{i,1}||\cdots||y_{i,n^2}$, where $y_{i,j} = z^b_{i,j}$ if $g'_{i,j} = b$ for each $j \in [n^2]$.

    Then, set $\widetilde{r}_i = \rho(1, H, H_i)||\varphi(1, H, H_i, \{z^0_{i,j}, z^1_{i,j}\})$.
- Output $R' = \widetilde{r}_1||\cdots||\widetilde{r}_n$.

Then, $\mathcal{S}$ defines a new leakage query $f'(H) = f(H, R||Select(H, \{z^0_{i,j}, z^1_{i,j}\}))$, where R is the concatenation of all random cion used by the simulator before Stage 2. $\mathcal{S}$ then queries $L^n_w(\cdot)$ with $f'(\cdot)$ and V^* obtain $f'(H)$. It is easy to see that $f'(H)$ is the same as one leaked from P.

Simulating Stage 3:

▲ **V^*'s Commitment**:

1. $S \rightleftharpoons V^*$: $\mathcal{S}$ acts just like a real prover and obtains the commitments to $q, q^e_{i,j}, i \in_R \{0,1\}^n$ from V^* for $i \in [\frac{k}{\varepsilon}], j \in [k]$ and $e = 0, 1$.
2. $S \leftrightarrow V^*$: V^* could make multiple leakage queries in the above step. $\mathcal{S}$ uses $L^{n,\lambda}_w(\cdot)$ to answer all these leakage queries (in the manner as described in the main text). $\mathcal{S}$ aborts whenever V^* aborts.

▲ **Challenge-Response**: For $0 \leq a \leq k-1$, proceed as follows:

3. For $1 \leq b \leq \frac{1}{\varepsilon}$, do the following. Let $i = \frac{a}{\varepsilon} + b$.
   - 3.1 $S \to V^*$: $\mathcal{S}$ chooses n-bit random strings $\delta_i = \delta_{i,1} \cdots \delta_{i,k}$, and sends δ_i to V^*.
   - 3.2 $S \leftrightarrow V^*$: $\mathcal{S}$ uses $L^{n,\lambda}_w(\cdot)$ to answer the leakage queries (in the manner as described in the main text). Let the output length of the leakage query be ℓ_i bits.
   - 3.3 $S \leftarrow V^*$: V^* reveals the commitments to $q^{\sigma_{i,j}}_{i,j}$ for $j = 1, \cdots, k$.
4. Find i_a such that $\ell_{i_a} = min_{\frac{a}{\varepsilon}+1 \leq j \leq \frac{a+1}{\varepsilon}} \ell_j$, proceeds as follows:
   - 4.1 $S \to V^*$: $\mathcal{S}$ rewinds V^* to 3.1 of i_a iteration. Then $\mathcal{S}$ Chooses n-bit random strings $\delta'_{i_a} = \delta'_{i_a,1} \cdots \delta'_{i_a,k}$, and sends δ'_{i_a} to V^*.
   - 4.2 $S \leftrightarrow V^*$: Let the output length of the leakage query be ℓ'_{i_a} bits. If $\ell'_{i_a} \leq \ell_{i_a}$, then $\mathcal{S}$ uses $L^{n,\lambda}_w(\cdot)$ to answer the leakage queries . Otherwise $\mathcal{S}$ aborts.
   - 4.3 $S \leftarrow V^*$: V^* reveals the commitments to $q^{\delta'_{i_a,j}}_{i_a,j}$, $j = 1, \cdots, k$. If the decommitments in 4.3 is correct and $\delta_{i_a} \neq \delta'_{i_a}$, $\mathcal{S}$ extracts q and proceeds next step. Otherwise, $\mathcal{S}$ executes the next iteration or abort when $a = k-1$.

▲ **Generating challenge** ch:

5. $\mathcal{S}$ computes $q' = ch \oplus q$, where ch is selected when responding to query leakage in simulating for Stage 2, $q = q_1 \cdots q_n$ is extracted in 4.3.
   - 5.1 $S \to V^*$: $\mathcal{S}$ sends q' to V^*.
   - 5.2 $S \leftrightarrow V^*$: $\mathcal{S}$ uses $L^{n,\lambda}_w(\cdot)$ to answer the leakage queries.
   - 5.3 $S \leftarrow V^*$: V sets $ch = q \oplus q'$, and reveals the commitments to q and $q^{1-\delta_{i,j}}_{i,j}$, $i \in [\frac{k}{\varepsilon}]$, $j \in [k]$.

Response to Query Leakage in Simulating for Stage 3: Assume that R' is the concatenation of all public cion sent by the simulator in Stage 3. The simulator set $R(w) \triangleq R||R'$ and $f'(w) \triangleq f(w, R(w))$, where R denotes the concatenation of all random cion used by the simulator before Stage 3. The simulator then queries the leakage oracle with $f'(\cdot)$ and V^* obtain $f'(w)$. Since R used by an honest prover is identical to R', it is easy to see that $f'(w) = f(w; R(w))$.

Lemma 2. *That $\mathcal{S}$ reaches the end of Stage 3 but fails to extract q is negligible.*

Proof. Similar to the proof of Lemma 1.

Simulating Stage 4:

1. $S \to V^*$: $\mathcal{S}$ reveals π_i and the commitments to the adjacency of $G_i = \pi_i(G)$ when $ch_i = 0$, or the commitments of C_i corresponding to the edges to H_i when $ch_i = 1$, for every $i \in [n]$.

Simulator's Output Distribution: Note that one difference between $\mathcal{S}$ and the honest prover is that $\mathcal{S}$ does not have ability to reveal the commitments (of C_i) corresponding to $h_{i,j} = 0$ when $ch_i = 1$. Very fortunately, the protocol does not require P to reveal these commitments. The other difference between $\mathcal{S}$ and the honest prover is that all the first messages, used by $\mathcal{S}$ in Naor's commitment in Stage 2, take the form of $g(z_{i,j}^0) \oplus g(z_{i,j}^1)$. Hence, assuming g is a pseudorandom generator, it is follows from the hiding property of Naor's scheme that the Simulator's output distribution is indistinguishable from the view of the verifier.

Define two hybrid simulators $\widehat{\mathcal{S}}_0$ and $\widehat{\mathcal{S}}_1$: $\widehat{\mathcal{S}}_0$ is the same as $\mathcal{S}$ except that it obtains a valid Hamiltonian cycle H_0 as auxiliary input and then directly reply to the leakage queries. $\widehat{\mathcal{S}}_1$ is the same as $\mathcal{S}_0$ except that it responds to the leakage queries as the honest prover. More precisely, instead of selecting a random cycle H_i, $\widehat{\mathcal{S}}_1$ sets $H_i = \pi_i(H)$ when replying to the query in Stage 2.

Lemma 3. *Assume that $g : \{0,1\}^n \to \{0,1\}^{3n}$ is a pseudorandom generator. Then, $\left\{\widehat{\mathcal{S}}_0^{L_w^{k,\lambda}(\cdot)}(G)\right\}_{G \in HC}$ and $\left\{\mathcal{S}^{L_w^{k,\lambda}(\cdot)}(G)\right\}_{G \in HC}$ are computationally indistinguishable.*

Proof. Note that the only difference between $\widehat{\mathcal{S}}_0$ and $\mathcal{S}$ is that, for any simple Hamiltonian cycle H_i, $\widehat{\mathcal{S}}_0$ can find π_i' such that $H_i = \pi_i'(H_0)$ and then can reveal C_i to be the commitments to $\pi_i'(G)$ whereas $\mathcal{S}$ cannot. Fortunately, $\widehat{\mathcal{S}}_0$ only reveals what $\mathcal{S}$ does. It follows from the hiding property of $Comm_{sh}(\cdot)$ that $\left\{\widehat{\mathcal{S}}_0^{L_w^{k,\lambda}(\cdot)}(G)\right\}_{G \in HC}$ and $\left\{\mathcal{S}^{L_w^{k,\lambda}(\cdot)}(G)\right\}_{G \in HC}$ are computationally indistinguishable.

Lemma 4. *Assume that $Comm_{sh}(\cdot)$ is a two round statistically hiding commitment scheme. Then, $\left\{\widehat{\mathcal{S}}_1^{L_w^{k,\lambda}(\cdot)}(G)\right\}_{G \in HC}$ and $\{View_{V^*}(G)\}_{G \in HC}$ are computationally indistinguishable.*

Proof. The only difference between $View_{V^*}(G)$ and $\widehat{\mathcal{S}}_1$ is that, owing to obtain r_V in advance, $\widehat{\mathcal{S}}_1$ can select a special r_P such that $r = r_P \oplus r_V$ obeys a predetermined distribution whereas P selects randomly r_P such that $r = r_P \oplus r_V$ obeys a uniform distribution. Suppose $r = r_1 \cdots r_n$ and $r_i = r_{i,1} \cdots r_{i,n^2}$. It is clear that $r_{i,j}$ is uniformly distributed on $\{0,1\}^{3n}$ in the real running. However, $\mathcal{S}$ selects a special r_P such that $r_{i,j} = g(z_{i,j}^0) \oplus g(z_{i,j}^1)$ is uniformly distributed on $\{g(z^0) \oplus g(z^1) : z^0, z^1 \in_R \{0,1\}^n\}$. If there exists a PPT algorithm $\mathcal{D}$ such that it can distinguish $\left\{\widehat{\mathcal{S}}_1^{L_w^{k,\lambda}(\cdot)}(G)\right\}_{G \in HC}$ from $\{View_{V^*}(G)\}_{G \in HC}$, then there exists a PPT algorithm $\widehat{\mathcal{D}}$ to distinguish the uniform distribution on $\{g(z^0) \oplus g(z^1) : z^0, z^1 \in_R \{0,1\}^n\}$ from the uniform distribution on $\{0,1\}^{3n}$. It is contradiction with the assumption that g is pseudorandom generator.

In addition, the difference between $\widehat{\mathcal{S}}_0^{L_w^{k,\lambda}(\cdot)}$ and $\widehat{\mathcal{S}}_1^{L_w^{k,\lambda}(\cdot)}$ is that $\widehat{\mathcal{S}}_0^{L_w^{k,\lambda}(\cdot)}$ interprets C_i (the commitment to $\pi_i(G)$) as the commitment to $\pi_i'\pi_i(G)$, where π_i' is determined by H and a random cycle H_i. it is easy to see that $\left\{\widehat{\mathcal{S}}_0^{L_w^{k,\lambda}(\cdot)}(G)\right\}_{G\in HC}$ and $\left\{\widehat{\mathcal{S}}_1^{L_w^{k,\lambda}(\cdot)}(G)\right\}_{G\in HC}$ are indistinguishable.

Over all, it follows that $\left\{\mathcal{S}^{L_w^{k,\lambda}(\cdot)}(G)\right\}_{G\in HC}$ and $\{View_{V^*}(G)\}_{G\in HC}$ are computationally indistinguishable.

Simulator's Getting Leakage: The following lemma is proved in [7].

Lemma 5. *he simulator $\mathcal{S}$ at most requires $(1+\varepsilon)\ell$ bits of leakage, assuming that V^* receives ℓ bits of leakage.*

Proof of Knowledge: To show that the protocol is a proof of knowledge, we need to construct an knowledge extractor $\mathcal{K}$, which has access to the prover-strategy oracle P^*.

On input G, $\mathcal{K}$ first interacts with P^* to execute the protocol acting as a honest verifier. If the proof is rejected, $\mathcal{K}$ aborts. Otherwise, $\mathcal{K}$ rewinds P^* to the beginning of Stage 3 to rerun the residual protocol with a fresh q. $\mathcal{K}$ repeats this until another acceptable proof occurs. Thus, $\mathcal{K}$ obtains two accepting proofs corresponding to two different challenge strings respectively. Finally, $\mathcal{K}$ extracts a Hamiltonian cycle from these proofs. The details is in Figure 2.

Step 1 $\mathcal{K}$, playing the role of the honest verifier, interacts with P^* to complete Stage 1 and Stage 2. Then, $\mathcal{K}$ obtains the commitment C_i to the adjacency of G_i ($i \in [n]$) from P^*.

Step 2 $\mathcal{K}$ honestly executes Stage 3. After selecting $q \in_R \{0,1\}^n$), $\mathcal{K}$ obtains q' and computes $ch = q \oplus q'$.

Step 3 After receiving the response to ch sent by P^* in Stage 4, $\mathcal{K}$ verifies the response. If the verification fails, $\mathcal{K}$ aborts. Otherwise, $\mathcal{K}$ proceeds next step.

Step 4 $\mathcal{K}$ rewinds P^* to the point of the beginning of Step 3. After selecting $\widehat{q} \in_R \{0,1\}^n$, $\mathcal{K}$ obtains $\widehat{q}'$ and computes $\widehat{ch} = \widehat{q} \oplus \widehat{q}'$.

Step 5 $\mathcal{K}$ receives the response to $\widehat{ch}$ from P^*. $\mathcal{K}$ verifies the response. If the verification fails, $\mathcal{K}$ return to the point of the beginning of Step 4.

Step 6 If $ch = \widehat{ch}$, $\mathcal{K}$ fails and aborts. Otherwise, let i be such that $ch_i \neq \widehat{ch}_i$, $\mathcal{K}$ obtains two accepting responses corresponding to two different queries ch_i and $\widehat{ch}_i$ respectively. That is, $\mathcal{K}$ obtains a random permutation π_i and a cycle H_i of $\pi_i(G)$. Thus, $\mathcal{K}$ can extract a Hamiltonian cycle $\pi_i^{-1}(H_i)$.

Fig. 2. Knowledge extractor

It is clear that $\mathcal{K}$ outputs a Hamiltonian cycle when it does not abort. In addition, $\mathcal{K}$ runs in expected polynomial time. In fact, let p be the probability that P^* convinces the verifier, p' be the probability that $\mathcal{K}$ terminates the repetition successfully in Step 4 and Step 5. It is easy to see that $p' \geq p$. Note that $\mathcal{K}$ clearly runs in strict polynomial time when $p = 0$. So we assume that $p > 0$ in what follows. Therefore, the expected running time of $\mathcal{K}$ is given by $(1-p) \cdot poly(n) + p \cdot \frac{1}{p'} \cdot poly(n) = poly(n)$.

Next, we show that the probability for $\mathcal{K}$ to output a Hamiltonian cycle is at least $p - 2^{-n}$ when $p > 2^{-n}$.

Let $Accept_{ch}$ denote the event that $\mathcal{K}$ obtains $ch = ch_1 \cdots ch_n$ and P^*'s acceptable response to ch, $Terminate$ denote the event that $\mathcal{K}$ terminates the repetition. Obviously, $p = \sum_{ch} Pr[Accept_{ch}]$. Assuming $p = \frac{m}{2^n} > 2^{-n}$, we have the following

$$\begin{aligned} Pr[(G,H) \in R_{HC} : H \leftarrow \mathcal{K}(G)] &= \textstyle\sum_{ch} Pr[Accept_{ch} \wedge Terminate \wedge (ch \neq \widehat{ch})] \\ &= \textstyle\sum_{ch} Pr[Accept_{ch}] \cdot Pr[Terminate \wedge (ch \neq \widehat{ch}) | Accept_{ch}] \end{aligned}$$

where $\widehat{ch}$ is determined when $Terminate$ occurs. Since
$Pr[Terminate \wedge (ch \neq \widehat{ch}) | Accept_{ch}] = (\frac{m-1}{2^n} + \cdots + (1 - \frac{m}{2^n})^k \cdot \frac{m-1}{2^n} + \cdots) = \frac{m-1}{m}$

we obtain the following $Pr[(G,H) \in R_{HC} : H \leftarrow \mathcal{K}(G)] = p\frac{m-1}{m} \geq p - 2^{-n}$. That is, $\mathcal{K}$ succeeds in computing a Hamiltonian cycle in G with probability of at least $p - 2^{-n}$ when $p > 2^{-n}$.

4 Conclusions and Open Problems

We constructed a leakage-resilient zero-knowledge proof of knowledge for HC (Hamiltonian Cycle) problem under perfectly hiding commitment schemes. Recently, Pandey [17] present a construction of constant round LR-ZK, so it is also interesting to construct a constant round LR-ZKoK.

References

1. Bitansky, N., Canetti, R., Halevi, S.: Leakage tolerant interactive protocols. Cryptology ePrint Archive, Report 2011/204 (2011)
2. Bellare, M., Goldreich, O.: On defining proofs of knowledge. In: Brickell, E.F. (ed.) CRYPTO 1992. LNCS, vol. 740, pp. 390–420. Springer, Heidelberg (1993)
3. Bellare, M., Goldreich, O.: On probabilistic versus deterministic provers in the definition of proofs of knowledge. Electronic Colloquium on Computational Complexity Report TR06-136
4. Boyle, E., Goldwasser, S., Jain, A., Kalai, Y.T.: Multiparty computation secure against continual memory leakage. In: Proceedings of the 44th Symposium on Theory of Computing, STOC 2012, pp. 1235–1254 (2012)
5. Boyle, E., Goldwasser, S., Kalai, Y.T.: Leakage-resilient coin tossing. In: Peleg, D. (ed.) DISC 2011. LNCS, vol. 6950, pp. 181–196. Springer, Heidelberg (2011)
6. Damgard, I., Hazay, C., Patra, A.: Leakage resilient two-party computation. Cryptology ePrint Archive, Report 2011/256 (2011)
7. Garg, S., Jain, A., Sahai, A.: Leakage-resilient zero knowledge. In: Rogaway, P. (ed.) CRYPTO 2011. LNCS, vol. 6841, pp. 297–315. Springer, Heidelberg (2011)

8. Goldreich, O., Kahan, A.: How to construct constant-round zero-knowledge proof system for NP. Journal of Cryptology 9(3), 167–189 (1996)
9. Goldwasser, S., Micali, S., Rackoff, C.: The knowledge complexity of interactive proof systems. SIAM Journal on Computing 18(16), 186–208 (1989)
10. Goldreich, O., Micali, S., Wigderson, A.: Proofs that yield nothing but their validity or all languages in NP have zero-knowledge proof systems. J. of the ACM 38(3), 691–729 (1991)
11. Goldreich, O.: Foundations of Cryptography - Basic Tools. Cambridge University Press (2001)
12. Halevi, S., Micali, S.: More on proofs of knowledge, `http://eprint.iacr.org/1998/015`
13. Li, H., Feng, D., Li, B., Xu, H.: Round-optimal zero-knowledge proofs of knowledge for NP. Science China: Information Science 55(11), 2417–2662 (2012)
14. Toshiya, I., Kouichi, S.: On the Complexity of Constant Round ZKIP of Possession of Knowledge. IEICE Trans. Fundamentals E76-A(1), 31–39 (1993)
15. Lindell, Y.: Constant-Round Zero-Knowledge Proofs of Knowledge, `http://eprint.iacr.org/2010/656`
16. Naor, M.: Bit commitment using pseudo-randomness (Extended abstract). In: Brassard, G. (ed.) CRYPTO 1989. LNCS, vol. 435, pp. 128–136. Springer, Heidelberg (1990)
17. Pandey, O.: Achieving constant round leakage-resilient zero knowledge, `eprint.iacr.org/2012/362.pdf`
18. Prabhakaran, M., Rosen, A., Sahai, A.: Concurrent zero knowledge with logarithmic round-complexity. In: FOCS (2002)

On the Security of an Efficient Attribute-Based Signature*

Yan Zhang, Dengguo Feng, Zhengfeng Zhang, and Liwu Zhang

Institute of Software, Chinese Academy of Sciences, Beijing, China
{janian,feng,zfzhang,zlw}@is.iscas.ac.cn

Abstract. In CT-RSA 2011, Maji et.al proposed an attribute-based signature (ABS) scheme, which is the most efficient ABS scheme that supports general predicates until now. They claimed that their ABS scheme is unforgeable under generic group model. Unfortunately, we found a forgery attack on this ABS scheme. In this paper, we firstly give a forgery example, then analyze the reason cause this attack and gives the conditions this attack worked. We found this attack is fatal to Maji et.al's ABS scheme.

Keywords: Attribute-based, signature, cryptoanalysis.

1 Introduction

Background. As a novel cryptographic primitive, attribute-based signature (ABS) enables a party to sign a message with expressive access policies. In a typical ABS system, users obtain private keys containing their attribute information from an authority, with which they can later sign messages for any predicate satisfied by their attributes. This signature could be verified to be satisfied with the predicate without leaking signer's identity. Since ABS provides good expression ability and privacy protection, it is very useful in a wide range of applications including private access control, anonymous credential, distributed access control, etc.

Since Maji et.al proposed the conception of ABS proposed in 2008[1], many ABS schemes have been proposed[2–9]. According to the predicates they supported, we can divide the existing ABS schemes into two types: ABS schemes supporting only simple predicates(usually threshold gates)[6–9] and expressive ABS supporting more generic predicates[2–5]. In practical applications, the latter type is much more useful, but the construction is difficult and the signature size is much longer.

In 2011, Maji et.al proposed three expressive ABS schemes in paper[2], in the third instantiation(denoted as MPR-ABS for short), similar construction with mesh signatures[10] and novel randomization method were used, instead of using

* Supported by the National Natural Science Foundation of China under Grant Nos. 60803129, 91118006; The National High-Tech Research and Development Plan of China under Grant Nos. 2011AA01A203, 2012AA01A403; The National Basic Research Program of China under Grant No. 2013CB338003.

J. Lopez, X. Huang, and R. Sandhu (Eds.): NSS 2013, LNCS 7873, pp. 381–392, 2013.

heavy-weight Non-Interactive Witness-Indistinguishable proofs[11], and achieves the shortest signature size among ABS schemes supporting general predicates.

Compared with other expressive ABS schemes, we can learn that the signature size of MPR-ABS scheme is over 80% shorter than the other four schemes (detailed comparison can be found in Table 1). Due to the high efficiency, this scheme was considered as the most practical ABS scheme and was cited by many other papers[3–5] as an important reference.

Unfortunately, we found that the MPR-ABS cannot resist the forgery attack. In this paper, we will propose our forgery attack on the MPR-ABS scheme and give the reason that cause this forgery.

Outline. The remainder of this paper is organized as follows: In section 2, we firstly introduce the cryptographic primitives and notations used in this paper, then we propose some Lemmas. In section 3, we review the formal definition and security requirements of attribute-based signature, as well as the concrete construction of MPR-ABS scheme. In section 4, we give the security analysis of the MPR-ABS scheme and propose a forgery attack on it. In section 5, we give the conclusion of this paper.

2 Preliminaries

2.1 Bilinear Groups

Let $\mathbb{G}, \mathbb{H}$ and $\mathbb{G}_T$ be groups of prime order q, then bilinear pairing is a map $e : \mathbb{G} \times \mathbb{H} \to \mathbb{G}_T$ satisfy the following properties:

`Bilinearity`. For all $g \in \mathbb{G}, h \in \mathbb{H}, a, b \in \mathbb{Z}_p$, $e(g^a, h^b) = e(g, h)^{ab}$;
`Non-degeneracy`. For all generators $g \in \mathbb{G}, h \in \mathbb{H}$, $e(g, h)$ generates $\mathbb{G}_T$;
`Efficiency`. There exists an efficient algorithm to compute $e(g, h)$ for any $g \in \mathbb{G}, h \in \mathbb{H}$.

2.2 Monotone Span Programs

Let $\Upsilon : \{0,1\}^n \to \{0,1\}$ be a monotone boolean function. A monotone span program for Υ over a field $\mathbb{F}$ is an $l \times t$ matrix $\mathbb{M}$ with entries in $\mathbb{F}$, along with a labeling function $a : [l] \to [n]$ that associates each row of $\mathbb{M}$ with an input variable of Υ, that, for every $(x_1, \ldots, x_n) \in \{0,1\}^n$, satisfies the following:

$$\Upsilon(x_1, \ldots, x_n) = 1 \Longleftrightarrow \exists \boldsymbol{v} \in \mathbb{F}^{1 \times l} : \boldsymbol{v}\mathbb{M} = [1, 0, 0, \ldots, 0]$$

and $(\forall i : x_{a(i)}) = 0 \Rightarrow v_i = 0$.

2.3 Notations

Let $\mathbb{M}$ be a matrix, then $rk(\mathbb{M})$ denotes the rank of $\mathbb{M}$, moreover, if $\mathbb{M}$ is a square matrix, $|\mathbb{M}|$ denotes the value of the determinant of $\mathbb{M}$. E indicates an identity matrix and O indicates a zero matrix over field $\mathbb{F}$.

If Υ is a predicate, then an attribute a is "Key Attribute" of Υ if it satisfy the following property:

Definition 1. *(Key Attribute) For a predicate Υ, we say attribute a is a key attribute of Υ if for all attributes set A satisfied with $\Upsilon(A) = 1$, we have $a \in A$.*

2.4 Lemmas

Lemma 1. *For any finite number of non-zero n-dimension vectors $(\boldsymbol{v}_1, \boldsymbol{v}_2, \ldots, \boldsymbol{v}_k)$, we can find $n-1$ extra n-dimension vectors $(\boldsymbol{y}_1, \boldsymbol{y}_2, \ldots, \boldsymbol{y}_{n-1})$ that for any $i \in [1, k]$, the vector group $(\boldsymbol{y}_1, \boldsymbol{y}_2, \ldots, \boldsymbol{y}_{n-1}, \boldsymbol{v}_i)$ is linearly independent.*

Proof. Denote $\boldsymbol{v}_i = (v_{i1}, \ldots, v_{in}), \boldsymbol{y}_i = (y_{i1}, \ldots, y_{in})$, then we can find $(\boldsymbol{y}_1, \boldsymbol{y}_2, \ldots, \boldsymbol{y}_{n-1})$ fulfil the requirements by executing the following procedure:

1. Set $x_1 = 1$, then for each $v_{i2} \neq 0$, compute $-\frac{x_1 v_{i1}}{v_{i2}}$, and select x_2 different from these values.
2. For each $v_{i3} \neq 0$, we can compute $-\frac{x_1 v_{i1} + x_2 v_{i2}}{v_{i3}}$, and select x_3 different from these values.
3. Repeat step 1 and 2 we can finally generate a group of values $x_1, \ldots, x_n$. Since $(\boldsymbol{v}_1, \boldsymbol{v}_2, \ldots, \boldsymbol{v}_k)$ are all non-zero vectors, it is easy to see that

$$\Sigma_{j=1}^{n} x_j v_{ij} \neq 0$$

4. Now set $\boldsymbol{y}_1 = (-x_2, 1, 0, \ldots, 0), \boldsymbol{y}_2 = (-x_3, 0, 1, \ldots, 0), \ldots, \boldsymbol{y}_{n-1} = (-x_n, 0, \ldots, 0, 1)$, then the value of determinant

$$|V_i| = |\boldsymbol{v}_i, \boldsymbol{y}_1, \boldsymbol{y}_2, \ldots, \boldsymbol{y}_{n-1}| = \Sigma_{j=1}^{n} x_j v_{ij} \neq 0$$

which means the corresponding vector group is linearly independent.

Lemma 2. *For any predicate Υ with corresponding attribute set Ω and MSP matrix $\mathbb{M}$, if $\forall a \in \Omega$, a is not a key attribute of Υ. Then the rank of $\mathbb{M}_{l \times t}$ is less than l.*

Proof. It is obvious that $rk(\mathbb{M}_{l\times t}) \leq l$, if $rk(\mathbb{M}_{l\times t}) = l$, then the corresponding equation $\boldsymbol{v}\mathbb{M} = (1, 0, \ldots, 0)$ has unique solution. For any non-zero value in the solution, the corresponding attribute a will be a key attribute of Υ, which leads to a contradiction.

Lemma 3. *Assume $u_1, \ldots, u_n \in \mathbb{Z}_p$ are n distinct numbers, denote $P_i(a, b) = \prod_{j=1,\ldots,n, j\neq i}(a + u_j b)$, then for any homogeneous polynomial $Y(a, b)$ with order $n-1$, we can find $k_1, \ldots, k_n \in \mathbb{Z}_p$ that $Y(a, b) = k_1 P_1(a, b) + \ldots + k_n P_n(a, b)$.*

Proof. If the coefficients of $P_i(a, b)$ are linearly independent, then it is easy to find $k_1, \ldots, k_n \in \mathbb{Z}_p$ for any $Y(a, b)$. Otherwise, we can find $k_1, \ldots, k_n \in \mathbb{Z}_p$ that

$$k_1 P_1(a, b) + \ldots + k_n P_n(a, b) = 0$$

with at least one $k_i \neq 0$, when we set $a = -u_i, b = 1$, we have

$$k_i \cdot \prod_{j=1,\ldots,n, j\neq i} (u_j - u_i) = 0$$

since $u_1, \ldots, u_n$ are distinct numbers, this means $k_i = 0$, which leads to a contradiction.

3 Attribute-Based Signatures: Definition and Security

3.1 Syntax of Attribute-Based Signatures

In this section, we will review the syntax of Attribute-Based Signatures proposed in [2]. Let $\mathbb{A}$ be the universe of possible attributes. A claim-predicate over $\mathbb{A}$ is a monotone boolean function, whose inputs are associated with attributes of $\mathbb{A}$. We say that an attributes set $\mathcal{A} \subseteq \mathbb{A}$ satisfies Υ if $\Upsilon(\mathcal{A}) = 1$, then an Attribute-based Signature scheme is defined as follow:

An Attribute-based Signature(ABS) scheme consists of the following five algorithms:

`TSetup`. (Run by a signature trustee): Generates public parameters params.
`ASetup`. (Run by an attribute authority): Generates a key pair APK, ASK from the params.
`AttrGen`. On input $(ASK, \mathcal{A} \subseteq \mathbb{A})$,outputs a signing key $SK_{\mathcal{A}}$.
`Sign`. On input $(PK = (\mathsf{params}, APK, SK_{\mathcal{A}}, m, \Upsilon)$,where $\Upsilon(\mathcal{A}) = 1$,outputs a signature σ.
`Ver`. On input $(PK = (\mathsf{params}, APK, m, \Upsilon, \sigma)$,outputs accept or reject.

3.2 Security of Attribute-Based Signatures

According to [2], an ABS scheme should be satisfied with the following unforgeability:

An ABS scheme is unforgeable if the success probability of any polynomial-time adversary in the following game is negligible:

1.Run $\mathsf{params} \leftarrow \mathsf{TSetup}$ and $ASK, APK \leftarrow \mathsf{ASetup}$. Give $PK = (\mathsf{params}, APK)$ to the adversary.
2.The adversary is given to access to two oracles: $\mathsf{AttrGen}(ASK, \cdot)$ and $\mathsf{Sign}(ASK, \cdot)$.
3.At the end the adversary outputs $(m^*, \Upsilon^*, \sigma^*)$

We say the adversary succeeds if (m^*, Υ^*) was never queried to the Sign and $\mathsf{Ver}(PK, m^*, \Upsilon^*, \sigma^*) = \mathsf{accept}$ and $\Upsilon^*(A) = 0$ for any A queried to the $\mathsf{AttrGen}$ oracle.

Furthermore, we have the weak unforgeability under selective predicate model where the challenge predicate is submitted before TSetup.

3.3 MPR-ABS Scheme

Then we will review the MPR-ABS scheme, according to [2], the detailed scheme was proposed as follow:

`TSetup`. Choose suitable cyclic groups $\mathbb{G}$ and $\mathbb{H}$ of prime order p and a bilinear pairing $\mathbb{G} \times \mathbb{H} \rightarrow \mathbb{G}_T$. Then choose a collision-resistant hash function $H : \{0,1\}^* \rightarrow \mathbb{Z}_p^*$. Choose random generators $g \leftarrow \mathbb{G}, h_0, \ldots, h_{t_{max}} \leftarrow \mathbb{H}$, where t_{max} is the maximum width of monotone span program the supported by the scheme. Finally, the public parameter is $\mathsf{params} = (\mathbb{G}, \mathbb{H}, H, g, h_0, \ldots, h_{t_{max}})$

ASetup. Choose random $a_0, a, b, c \leftarrow \mathbb{Z}_p^*$ and set:

$$C = g^c, A_0 = h_0^{a_0}, A_j = h_j^a, B_j = h_j^b (\forall j \in [t_{max}])$$

The master key is $ASK = (a_0, a, b)$. The public key

$$APK = (A_0, \dots, A_{t_{max}}, B_1, \dots, B_{t_{max}}, C)$$

AttrGen. On input ASK and attribute set $\mathcal{A} \subseteq \mathbb{A}$, randomly choose $K_{base} \leftarrow \mathbb{G}$. Set:

$$K_0 = K_{base}^{1/a_0}, K_u = K_{base}^{1/(a+bu)} (\forall u \in \mathcal{A})$$

The signing key is then $SK_{\mathcal{A}} = (K_{base}, K_0, \{K_u | u \in \mathcal{A}\})$

Sign. On input $(PK, SK_{\mathcal{A}}, m, \Upsilon)$ such that $\Upsilon(\mathcal{A}) = 1$, first convert Υ to its corresponding monotone span program $\mathbb{M} \in (\mathbb{Z}_p)^{l \times t}$, with row labeling $u : [l] \rightarrow \mathbb{A}$. Also compute the vector $\boldsymbol{v}$ that corresponds to the satisfying assignment $\mathcal{A}$. Compute $\mu = H(m||\Upsilon)$. Then pick random $r_0 \leftarrow \mathbb{Z}_p^*$ and $r_1, \dots, r_l \leftarrow \mathbb{Z}_p$ and compute:

$$Y = K_{base}^{r_0}, S_i = (K_{u(i)}^{v_i})^{r_0} \cdot (Cg^{\mu})^{r_i} (\forall i \in [l]),$$

$$W = K_0^{r_0}, P_j = \prod_{i=1}^{n} (A_j B_j^{u_i})^{M_{ij} r_i} (\forall j \in [t])$$

Since the signer may not have $K_{u(i)}$ for every attribute $u(i)$, but when this is the case, $v_i = 0$, and so the value is not needed. After all, the signature is $\sigma = (Y, W, S_1, \dots, S_l, P_1, \dots, P_t)$.

Ver. On input $PK, \sigma = (Y, W, S_1, \dots, S_l, P_1, \dots, P_t), m, \Upsilon)$, first convert Υ to its corresponding monotone span program $\mathbb{M} \in (\mathbb{Z}_p)^{l \times t}$, with row labeling $u : [l] \rightarrow \mathbb{A}$. Compute $\mu = H(m||\Upsilon)$. if $Y = 1$, then output reject. Otherwise check the following constraints:

$$e(W, A_0) = e(Y, h_0)$$

$$\prod_{i=1}^{l} e(S_i, (A_j B_j^{u_i})^{M_{ij}}) = \begin{cases} e(Y, h_1) e(Cg^{\mu}, P_1), j = 1 \\ e(Cg^{\mu}, P_j), j > 1 \end{cases}$$

for $j \in [t]$. Return accept if all the above checks succeed, and reject otherwise.

4 Forgery Attack on MPR-ABS Scheme

4.1 A Simple Example of OR Predicate

In this section, we will propose a forgery example on an OR predicate $\Upsilon = (u_1 \vee u_2 \dots \vee u_n)$. The corresponding matrix $\mathbb{M}$ is a $n \times 1$ matrix $\mathbb{M} = (M_1, \dots, M_n)^T$ $(M_i \neq 0)$. Then the adversary $\mathcal{A}$ executes as follows:

1. $\mathcal{A}$ first obtain a secret key for an irrelevant attribute u ($u \notin \{u_1, \ldots, u_n\}$) from the AttrGen oracle. The MPR-ABS secret key of $\mathcal{A}$ will be $\{K_b, K_0 = K_b^{1/a_0}, K_u = K_b^{1/(a+bu)}\}$, where a_0, a, b is the master secret key.
2. Now $\mathcal{A}$ can compute $\alpha_1 = \frac{u-u_2}{M_1(u_1-u_2)}, \alpha_2 = \frac{u_1-u}{M_2(u_1-u_2)}$ and set $\alpha_i = 0 (i > 2)$, we have the following equations:
$$\sum_{i=1}^{n} M_i \alpha_i = \frac{M_1(u-u_2)}{M_1(u_1-u_2)} + \frac{M_2(u_1-u)}{M_2(u_1-u_2)} = 1$$
and
$$\sum_{i=1}^{n} M_i u_i \alpha_i = \frac{M_1 u_1(u-u_2)}{M_1(u_1-u_2)} + \frac{M_2 u_2(u_1-u)}{M_2(u_1-u_2)} = u$$
3. $\mathcal{A}$ randomly selects $r_0 \in \mathbb{Z}_p^*, r_1, \ldots, r_n \in \mathbb{Z}_p$ and computes $Y = K_b^{r_0}, W = K_0^{r_0}, P_1 = \prod_{i=1}^{n}(A_1 B_1^{u_i})^{M_i r_i}$ and $S_i = K_u^{\alpha_i r_0} \cdot (Cg^{\mu})^{r_i} (i = [1, \ldots, n])$

then the tuple $(Y, W, P_1, S_i (i = [1, \ldots, n]))$ will be satisfied with the verification equations of MPR-ABS scheme, the correctness can be verified by the following equations:

$$e(W, A_0) = e(K_0^{r_0}, h_0^{a_0}) = e(K_b^{r_0/a_0}, h_0^{a_0}) = e(K_b^{r_0}, h_0) = e(Y, h_0)$$

and

$$\begin{aligned}
&\prod_{i=1}^{n} e(S_i, (A_1 B_1^{u_i})^{M_i}) \\
&= \prod_{i=1}^{n} e(K_u^{\alpha_i r_0} \cdot (Cg^{\mu})^{r_i}, (A_1 B_1^{u_i})^{M_i}) \\
&= \prod_{i=1}^{n} e((Cg^{\mu})^{r_i}, (A_1 B_1^{u_i})^{M_i}) \prod_{i=1}^{n} e(K_u^{\alpha_i r_0}, (A_1 B_1^{u_i})^{M_i}) \\
&= \prod_{i=1}^{n} e((Cg^{\mu}), (A_1 B_1^{u_i})^{r_i M_i}) \prod_{i=1}^{n} e((K_b^{1/(a+bu)})^{\alpha_i r_0}, (h_1^{(a+bu_i)})^{M_i}) \\
&= e((Cg^{\mu}), \prod_{i=1}^{n} (A_1 B_1^{u_i})^{r_i M_i}) \prod_{i=1}^{n} e((K_b^{1/(a+bu)})^{\alpha_i r_0}, (h_1^{(a+bu_i)})^{M_i}) \\
&= e((Cg^{\mu}), P_1) \prod_{i=1}^{n} e((K_b^{1/(a+bu)})^{r_0}, h_1))^{\alpha_i (a+bu_i) M_i} \\
&= e((Cg^{\mu}), P_1) e((K_b^{1/(a+bu)})^{r_0}, h_1))^{\sum_{i=1}^{n} \alpha_i (a+bu_i) M_i} \\
&= e((Cg^{\mu}), P_1) e((K_b^{1/(a+bu)})^{r_0}, h_1))^{(a \cdot \sum_{i=1}^{n} \alpha_i M_i + b \cdot \sum_{i=1}^{n} \alpha_i u_i M_i)} \\
&= e((Cg^{\mu}), P_1) e((K_b^{1/(a+bu)})^{r_0}, h_1))^{(a+bu)}
\end{aligned}$$

$$= e((Cg^{\mu}), P_1)e(K_b^{r_0}, h_1)$$
$$= e((Cg^{\mu}), P_1)e(Y, h_1)$$

Finally, we get a forgery signature $\sigma = (Y, W, P_1, S_i(i = [1, \ldots, n]))$ of the MPR-ABS scheme.

4.2 Forgery Attack on General Predicates

In this section, we will propose the forgery attack on general predicates, to forge a predicate with matrix size $l \times n$, we demand that the $\mathcal{A}$ has secret keys $sk_{\mathcal{A}} = \{K_b, K_0, K_u(u \in \Omega_{\mathcal{A}})\}$ with at least l attributes. These attributes could be arbitrary values, which may be disjoint with the attributes set defined by the predicate at all, so it is easy to get them from the AttrGen oracle.

1. The usage of values $r_0, r_1, \ldots, r_n \in \mathbb{Z}_p$ is to randomize the signature, so the adversary $\mathcal{A}$ can randomly choose these values. Then $\mathcal{A}$ compute $Y = K_b^{r_0}, W = K_0^{r_0}, P_j = \prod_{i=1}^{n}(A_j B_j^{u_i})^{M_{ij} r_i}$ and the first verification equation $e(W, A_0) = e(Y, h_0)$ will be automatically satisfied.
2. For the second equation, if we set $T_i = [\frac{S_i}{(Cg^{\mu})^{r_i}}]^{1/r_0}$, then T_i should be satisfied with the following equation:

$$\prod_{i=1}^{n} e(T_i, (A_j B_j^{u_i})^{M_{ij}}) = \begin{cases} e(K_b, h_1), j = 1 \\ 1_{\mathbb{G}_T}, j > 1 \end{cases}$$

3. Let t_i be the discrete logarithm of T_i to the base of K_b, then t_i satisfied with the following equation:

$$\sum_{i=1}^{n} t_i M_{ij}(a + bu(i)) = \begin{cases} 1, j = 1 \\ 0, j > 1 \end{cases}$$

4. Since $\mathcal{A}$ has the secret key of more than l attributes, he select l attributes $\tilde{u}_1, \ldots, \tilde{u}_l$ from $\Omega_{\mathcal{A}}$ to form a set Ω^*.
5. If we denote $\Omega^*(a, b) = \prod_{i=1}^{l}(a + b\tilde{u}_i)$, then by Lemma 3, it is easy for $\mathcal{A}$ to compute $F = K_b^{F(a,b)/\Omega^*(a,b)}$ using $K_{\tilde{u}_i} = K_b^{1/(a+b\tilde{u}_i)}$ for any homogeneous polynomial

$$F(a, b) = f_1 a^{l-1} + f_2 a^{l-2} b + \ldots + f_l b^{l-1}$$

with order $l - 1$.
6. $\mathcal{A}$ set $t_i = f_i(a, b)/\Omega^*(a, b)$, where

$$f_i(a, b) = f_{i1} a^{l-1} + f_{i2} a^{l-2} b + \ldots + f_{il} b^{l-1}$$

is homogeneous polynomials with undetermined coefficients. Then we have:

$$\sum_{i=1}^{n} f_i(a, b) M_{ij}(a + bu(i)) = \begin{cases} \Omega^*(a, b), j = 1 \\ 0, j > 1 \end{cases}$$

7. Although $\mathcal{A}$ did not know the value a, b, he could still try to solve these equations to make all coefficients equal. After he gets the solution of f_{ik}, he could compute the corresponding $T_i = K_b^{f_i(a,b)/\Omega^*(a,b)}$ and then compute $S_i = T_i^{r_0}(Cg^{\mu})^{r_i}$ and find a forgery signature $\sigma = (Y, W, P_i(i = [1, \ldots, l]), S_j(j = [1, \ldots, n]))$.

4.3 Applicable Situations of Our Attack

In section 4.2, we show a forgery attack on MPR-ABS scheme, in this section, we will give the precisely condition this method works. At first, we have Theorem 1:

Theorem 1. *For any predicate Υ with corresponding attribute set Ω and MSP matrix $\mathbb{M}$, if $\forall a \in \Omega$, a is not a key attribute of Υ, then any adversary $\mathcal{A}$ with attributes set Ω^* where $|\Omega^*| \geq |\Omega|$ could use our method mentioned in section 4.2 to forge a signature of MPR-ABS scheme on any message.*

Proof. According to section 4.2, if $\mathcal{A}$ could find $(f_{11}, f_{12}, \ldots, f_{1l}, f_{21}, \ldots, f_{2l}, \ldots, f_{ll}) \in \mathbb{Z}_p$ to make $f_i(a,b) = f_{i1}a^{l-1} + f_{i2}a^{l-2}b + \ldots + f_{il}b^{l-1}$ satisfy the following equations:

$$\sum_{i=1}^{n} f_i(a,b) M_{ij}(a + bu(i)) = \begin{cases} \Omega^*(a,b), j = 1 \\ 0, j > 1 \end{cases}$$

Then he can successfully generate a forgery of MPR-ABS scheme, we will show the existence of these values when there is no key attribute in the predicate.

At first, consider the $v_i(a,b) = f_i(a,b)(a + bu(i))/\Omega^*(a,b)$ as a whole, then $\boldsymbol{v} = (v_1(a,b), \ldots, v_l(a,b))$ satisfied with the equation $\boldsymbol{v} \cdot \mathbb{M} = (1, 0, \ldots, 0)$, we can simplify $\mathbb{M}$ to a equivalent full rank matrix $\mathbb{M}_{full}$ as follows:

1. If $\mathbb{M}$ is full-ranked, then $\mathbb{M}_{full} = \mathbb{M}$, otherwise, we can find a subset $(m_1, \ldots, m_k)$ consisting of the column vectors of $\mathbb{M}$ and $a_1, \ldots, a_k \in \mathbb{Z}_p$ where
$$a_1 m_1 + \ldots + a_k m_k = 0$$
2. Since there exists at least one vector $\boldsymbol{v}$ satisfied with this equation (otherwise, the corresponding predicate will be a full negation predicate), then the first column of $\mathbb{M}$ cannot appear in this subset. We can discard any one column in this subset, it is clear that for all vectors satisfied with the new equation, it will automatically be satisfied with the original one.
3. Repeat step 1 and 2 we will finally get a full rank matrix $\mathbb{M}_{full}$.

Then we use Gaussian elimination method to simplify the equations $\boldsymbol{v} \cdot \mathbb{M}_{full} = (1, 0, \ldots, 0)$, and $\mathbb{M}_{full}$ will be transformed to its row canonical form. Since $\mathbb{M}_{full}$ is full-ranked, there will be no zero column in it and we can exchange the rows of it to get a matrix with the form

$$\mathbb{M}' = (E|\hat{M})^T$$

Since exchanging the rows of $\mathbb{M}$ only means to change the order of attributes, it will not affect the existence of solution. If we denote the new equations as $\boldsymbol{v}\mathbb{M}' = \boldsymbol{y}'$, the solution $\boldsymbol{v}$ will still satisfy the same predicate Υ as $\mathbb{M}$.

After that, we can extend the equations as follows:

1. Since all attributes defined by the predicate Υ are not the key attributes, then the width of $\mathbb{M}'$ is less than l by Lemma 2. If we denote $\hat{M}$ as $(\hat{\boldsymbol{m}}_1, \ldots, \hat{\boldsymbol{m}}_t)$, then $\hat{\boldsymbol{m}}_i$ is a n-dimension vector where $n = l - t \geq 1$.
2. Moreover, we have $\hat{\boldsymbol{m}}_1, \ldots, \hat{\boldsymbol{m}}_t \neq \boldsymbol{0}$, otherwise, there will be a row of $\mathbb{M}'$ which is all 0 except one 1 in it, then the corresponding attribute has unique solution, if the solution is non-zero then it means there is a key attribute in Υ. Else, the attribute will be redundant and we can remove it from the predicate.
3. By Lemma 1, we can find $n-1$ extra vectors $\boldsymbol{p}_1, \ldots, \boldsymbol{p}_{n-1}$ that for each $\hat{\boldsymbol{m}}_i (i \in [1, \ldots, t])$, $(\boldsymbol{p}_1, \ldots, \boldsymbol{p}_{n-1}, \hat{\boldsymbol{m}}_i)$ is linearly independent.
4. Extend the equations as $\boldsymbol{v}\mathbb{M}'' = (\boldsymbol{y}', 0, \ldots, 0)$, where

$$\mathbb{M}''_{l \times (l-1)} = \begin{pmatrix} E & \hat{M} \\ O & \boldsymbol{p}_1 \\ & \cdots \\ O & \boldsymbol{p}_{n-1} \end{pmatrix}^T$$

It is easy to see all solutions of this extended equations will match the original constraints $\boldsymbol{v}\mathbb{M} = (1, 0, \ldots, 0)$, too.

Now we use the Gaussian elimination method again, since $\boldsymbol{p}_1, \ldots, \boldsymbol{p}_{n-1}$ was chosen to be linearly independent with $\hat{\boldsymbol{m}}_1, \ldots, \hat{\boldsymbol{m}}_t$, it is easy to see that $\mathbb{M}''$ is full-ranked and $rk(\mathbb{M}'') = t + n - 1 = l - 1$. The final result will be equations like $\boldsymbol{v}\mathbb{M}''' = \boldsymbol{y}'''$, where

$$\mathbb{M}''' = (E|\hat{M}''')^T$$

and $\hat{M}''' = (m_1''', \ldots, m_{l-1}''')^T$ is a $(l-1)$-dimension vector. Furthermore, since $\boldsymbol{p}_1, \ldots, \boldsymbol{p}_{n-1}$ was linearly independent with $\hat{\boldsymbol{m}}_1, \ldots, \hat{\boldsymbol{m}}_t$, we have $m_i''' \neq 0$ for all $i \in [1, \ldots, l-1]$.

Now we expand this simplified matrix by setting $v_i(a,b) = f_i(a,b)(a + bu(i)) / \Omega^*(a,b)$, then the equations will be $\boldsymbol{f}(\boldsymbol{a}, \boldsymbol{b})\mathbb{M}''' = \boldsymbol{z}'''(\boldsymbol{a}, \boldsymbol{b})$, where

$$\boldsymbol{f}(\boldsymbol{a}, \boldsymbol{b}) = (f_1(a,b)(a + u(1)b), \ldots, f_l(a,b)(a + u(l)b))$$

Since we did not know the value of secret key a, b, we can let the polynomials on both sides of equations exactly match, which means all terms of these polynomials equal. Then the question becomes to solve the following equations:

$$(f_{11}, f_{12}, \ldots, f_{1l}, f_{21}, \ldots, f_{2l}, \ldots, f_{ll})\bar{\mathbb{M}} = \boldsymbol{z}$$

where

$$\bar{\mathbb{M}} = \begin{pmatrix} E_1 & O & \ldots & O & N_1 \\ O & E_2 & \ldots & O & N_2 \\ \vdots & & \ddots & & \vdots \\ O & O & \ldots & E_{l-1} & N_{l-1} \end{pmatrix}^T$$

with

$$E_i = \begin{pmatrix} 1 & 0 & \dots & 0 \\ u(1) & 1 & \dots & 0 \\ \vdots & \ddots & & \vdots \\ 0 & \dots & u(1) & 1 \\ 0 & 0 & \dots & u(1) \end{pmatrix}, N_i = \begin{pmatrix} m_i''' & 0 & \dots & 0 \\ m_i'''u(l) & m_i''' & \dots & 0 \\ \vdots & \ddots & & \vdots \\ 0 & \dots & m_i'''u(l) & m_i''' \\ 0 & 0 & \dots & m_i'''u(l) \end{pmatrix}$$

Then we can use elementary transformation to simplify the coefficient matrix $\bar{\mathbb{M}}$ to

$$\bar{\mathbb{M}}' = \begin{pmatrix} E & O & \dots & O & N_1' \\ O & E & \dots & O & N_2' \\ \vdots & & \ddots & & \vdots \\ O & O & \dots & E & N_{l-1}' \\ v_1 & O & \dots & O & y_1 \\ O & v_2 & \dots & O & y_2 \\ \vdots & & \ddots & & \vdots \\ O & O & \dots & v_{l-1} & y_{l-1} \end{pmatrix}^T$$

where

$$N_i' = \begin{pmatrix} m_i''' & 0 & 0 & \dots & 0 & 0 \\ m_i'''\Delta_(i) & m_i''' & 0 & \dots & 0 & 0 \\ m_i'''\Delta_(i)(-u(i)) & m_i'''\Delta_(i) & m_i''' & \dots & 0 & 0 \\ \vdots & & \ddots & & \vdots & \\ m_i'''\Delta_(i)(-u(i))^{l-3} & m_i'''\Delta_(i)(-u(i))^{l-4} & m_i'''\Delta_(i)(-u(i))^{l-5} & \dots & m_i''' & 0 \\ m_i'''\Delta_(i)(-u(i))^{l-2} & m_i'''\Delta_(i)(-u(i))^{l-3} & m_i'''\Delta_(i)(-u(i))^{l-4} & \dots & m_i'''\Delta_(i) & m_i''' \end{pmatrix}, \Delta_(i) = u(l) - u(i)$$

and

$$v_i = (0, \dots, 0, u(i)), y_i = (0, \dots, 0, m_i'''u(l))$$

This matrix could be further simplified to

$$\bar{\mathbb{M}}'' = \begin{pmatrix} E & O & \dots & O & N_1' \\ O & E & \dots & O & N_2' \\ \vdots & & \ddots & & \vdots \\ O & O & \dots & E & N_{l-1}' \\ O & O & \dots & O & Z \end{pmatrix}^T$$

where

$$Z = \begin{pmatrix} m_1'''\Delta_(1)(-u(1))^{l-1} & m_1'''\Delta_(1)(-u(1))^{l-2} & \dots & m_1'''\Delta_(1) \\ m_2'''\Delta_(2)(-u(2))^{l-1} & m_2'''\Delta_(2)(-u(2))^{l-2} & \dots & m_2'''\Delta_(2) \\ \vdots & & \ddots & \vdots \\ m_{l-1}'''\Delta_(l-1)(-u(l-1))^{l-1} & m_{l-1}'''\Delta_(l-1)(-u(l-1))^{l-2} & \dots & m_{l-1}'''\Delta_(l-1) \end{pmatrix}$$

Since $u(i)$ are distinct attribute values, we have $\Delta_(i) = u(l) - u(i) \neq 0$ and $m_i''' \neq 0 (i \in [1, l-1])$. According to the properties of Vandermonde matrix, it is obvious that $rk(Z) = l - 1$ and $rk(\bar{\mathbb{M}}) = rk(\bar{\mathbb{M}}'') = (l-1) \times (l+1) = l^2 - 1$. As we have l^2 undetermined coefficients, we can know that the solution will always exist no matter which value the $\boldsymbol{z}$ is. Thus we have proved Theorem 1.

Moreover, if the adversary have some of the attributes in the predicate, we can extend the Theorem 1 to more general situations as follow:

Theorem 2. *For any predicate Υ with corresponding attribute set Ω and MSP matrix $\mathbb{M}$, and adversary $\mathcal{A}$ with attributes set Ω^*, if $|\Omega^*| \geq |\Omega|$ and $\forall a \in \Omega - \Omega^*$, a is not a key attribute of Υ, then $\mathcal{A}$ could use our method mentioned in section 4.2 to forge a signature of* MPR-ABS *scheme on any message.*

Proof. Since all private keys of these key attributes were held by the adversary, he can normally generate $S_i = (K_{u(i)}^{v_i})^{r_0} \cdot (Cg^{\mu})^{r_i}$. If we eliminate these v_is from the equations, we can use the similar method to forge the reminder part. The existence of forgery could be proved similarly as Theorem 1.

4.4 Discussions

Applicability in Practical Applications. From Theorem 2, we learn the applicability of our attack. As we know, for any predicate other than the AND gate, the attribute set containing all key attributes won't satisfy the predicate. Then the adversary could ask the AttrGen oracle to get all the key attributes and sufficient irrelevant attributes and generate a forgery signature, i.e. for all predicates other than the AND gate in MPR-ABS scheme, our forgery attack could successful works.

Moreover, our attack cannot be prevent by introducing extra verification procedure: according to the forgery procedure, the value $r_0, r_1, \ldots, r_l$ is randomly selected by the adversary, so the value of $Y, S_1, \ldots, S_l$ was uniformly distributed over group $\mathbb{G}$. Since $W, P_1 \ldots, P_t$ was uniquely determined by $Y, S_1, \ldots, S_l$ and the predicate Υ, the distribution of the forgery signature is exactly the same with a true signature.

Table 1. Comparison of Expressive ABS Schemes

(l, t denotes the length and width of the span program, λ is the security parameter)

	MPR11[2] Instantation3	MPR11[2] Instantation2	EHM11[3]	OT11[4]	OT12[5]
Signature Size	$l+t+2$	$36l + 2r + 9\lambda + 12$	$8l + t + 7$	$7l + 11$	$13l$
Security Model	generic group	standard	standard	standard	random oracle
Predicates	monotone	monotone	monotone	non-monotone	non-monotone
Sig. size example1 ($l = 10, t = 5, \lambda = 128$)	17	1534	92	81	130
Sig. size example2 ($l = 100, t = 50, \lambda = 128$)	152	4864	857	711	1300

Main Flaw of MPR-ABS. Then we discuss the main reason causes this attack, according to [2], the MPR-ABS was inspired by the mesh signatures proposed by Boyen[10]. In the original mesh signatures, the master secret key related to each atom-signature(i.e. the attribute private key) is different. However, Maji et. al simplified this construction to a single key pair (a, b) in the MPR-ABS. This flaw allows the adversary to generate a forgery signature by using the linear relation between the private keys, which leads to our attack.

5 Conclusion

In this paper, we proposed a forgery attack on the ABS scheme proposed by Maji et.al in paper [2]. This attack can be implemented under both selective and adaptive security model, and works on almost all predicates, which totally breaks the unforgeablity of Maji et.al's ABS scheme.

Acknowledgements. We thank Mr. Nan Zhang of New York University for his kindly help in advanced algebra and other fields of mathematics.

References

1. Maji, H., Prabhakaran, M., Rosulek, M.: Attribute-based signatures: Achieving attribute privacy and collusion-resistance. Technical Report, Cryptology ePrint Archive, Report 2008/328 (2008), http://eprint.iacr.org/2008/328
2. Maji, H.K., Prabhakaran, M., Rosulek, M.: Attribute-based signatures. In: Kiayias, A. (ed.) CT-RSA 2011. LNCS, vol. 6558, pp. 376–392. Springer, Heidelberg (2011)
3. Escala, A., Herranz, J., Morillo, P.: Revocable attribute-based signatures with adaptive security in the standard model. In: Nitaj, A., Pointcheval, D. (eds.) AFRICACRYPT 2011. LNCS, vol. 6737, pp. 224–241. Springer, Heidelberg (2011)
4. Okamoto, T., Takashima, K.: Efficient attribute-based signatures for non-monotone predicates in the standard model. In: Catalano, D., Fazio, N., Gennaro, R., Nicolosi, A. (eds.) PKC 2011. LNCS, vol. 6571, pp. 35–52. Springer, Heidelberg (2011)
5. Okamoto, T., Takashima, K.: Decentralized attribute-based signatures. Technical Report, Cryptology ePrint Archive, Report 2011/701 (2011), http://eprint.iacr.org/2011/701
6. Li, J., Kim, K.: Attribute-Based Ring Signatures. Technical Report, Cryptology ePrint Archive, Report 2008/394 (2008), http://eprint.iacr.org/2008/394
7. Li, J., Au, M., Susio, W., Xie, D., Ren, R.: Attribute-based signature and its applications. In: ASIACCS 2010, pp. 60–69 (2010)
8. Shahandashti, S.F., Safavi-Naini, R.: Threshold attribute-based signatures and their application to anonymous credential systems. In: Preneel, B. (ed.) AFRICACRYPT 2009. LNCS, vol. 5580, pp. 198–216. Springer, Heidelberg (2009)
9. Herranz, J., Laguillaumie, F., Libert, B., Ràfols, C.: Short attribute-based signatures for threshold predicates. In: Dunkelman, O. (ed.) CT-RSA 2012. LNCS, vol. 7178, pp. 51–67. Springer, Heidelberg (2012)
10. Boyen, X.: Mesh signatures. In: Naor, M. (ed.) EUROCRYPT 2007. LNCS, vol. 4515, pp. 210–227. Springer, Heidelberg (2007)
11. Groth, J., Sahai, A.: Efficient Non-interactive Proof Systems for Bilinear Groups. In: Smart, N.P. (ed.) EUROCRYPT 2008. LNCS, vol. 4965, pp. 415–432. Springer, Heidelberg (2008)

Factoring RSA Modulus with Known Bits from Both p and q: A Lattice Method

Yao Lu[1,2], Rui Zhang[1], and Dongdai Lin[1]

[1] State Key Laboratory of Information Security (SKLOIS),
Institute of Information Engineering (IIE),
Chinese Academy of Sciences (CAS)
[2] University of Chinese Academy of Sciences (UCAS)
lywhhit@gmail.com, {r-zhang,ddlin}@iie.ac.cn

Abstract. This paper investigates the problem of factoring RSA modulus $N = pq$ with some known bits from both p and q. In Asiacrypt'08, Herrmann and May presented a heuristic algorithm to factorize N with the knowledge of a random subset of the bits (distributed over small contiguous blocks) of a factor. However, in a real attack, an adversary often obtain some bits which distributed in both primes. This paper studies this extended setting and introduces a lattice-based approach. Our strategy is an extension of Coppersmiths technique on more variables, thus it is a heuristic method, which we heuristically assumed that the polynomials resulting from the lattice basis reduction are algebraically independent. However, in our experiments, we have observed that the well-established assumption is not always true, and for these scenarios, we also propose a method to fix it.

Keywords: lattices, RSA, Coppersmith's method, factoring with known bits.

1 Introduction

Factoring large integer is an old and fascinate problem in number theory which is important for cryptographic applications, especially after the birth of the public-key cryptosystem RSA. However, until now, there is no known deterministic or randomized polynomial-time algorithm without the help of quantum computers to solve it, the best algorithm to date is Number Field Sieve (NFS), which has an expected runtime $\mathcal{O}(\exp(c(\ln N)^{1/3}(\ln \ln N)^{2/3}))$ where c is a constant.

In practice, an attacker might obtain partial information from both p and q via side-channel attacks, it is important to investigate that how these affect the hardness of factorization problem. In Eurocrypt'85, Rivest and Shamir [11] first introduced the factoring with known bits problem, they applied Integer Programme technique and factored N given two-thirds of the least significant bits (LSBs) of either p or q. In Eurocrypt'96, Coppersmith [3] improved the above result, and showed that N can be factored given half of the LSBs or most significant bits (MSBs) of a factor. He used the lattice reduction technique to output

J. Lopez, X. Huang, and R. Sandhu (Eds.): NSS 2013, LNCS 7873, pp. 393–404, 2013.

small solutions to a bivariate polynomial. Note that for the above results, the unknown bits are within one consecutive block. Then in Asiacrypt'08, Herrmann and May [6] presented a heuristic algorithm that extend to n blocks, they also used the lattice reduction technique but for a linear modular polynomial. However, the running time of this algorithm is polynomial only for $n = \mathcal{O}(\log \log N)$ blocks.

A scenario different from the above setting is based on the cold boot attack [4], where one may only recover information stored in the computer memory with certain probability less than 1. Heninger and Shacham [5] studied the problem and presented a new algorithm to factorize N given a certain fraction of the random bits of the primes. Since the known bits are randomly distributed, their algorithm cannot make use of the lattice reduction or integer programming techniques. The reconstruction method is a modified brute-force search exploiting the known bits to prune wrong branches of the search tree, thereby reduced the total search space towards possible factorization.

To summarize, in practice we prefer to use the lattice-based approach for its better performance, on the other hand, the lattice-based approach requires strigent constraints: the knowledge of contiguous blocks. We notice that the previous lattice-based methods only consider the scenario which the leaked bits lie in a single prime. While in a real attack, we may obtain known bits from both primes. This raises the question whether we have any efficient lattice-based approach to utilize such additional information?

Our Treatments. In this paper we present a new heuristic algorithm to factorize N with the knowledge of a random subset of the bits (distributed over small contiguous blocks) in both primes. Suppose that p has n_1 unknown blocks, q has n_2 unknown blocks, it leads to a multivariate polynomial equation $f(x_1, \cdots, x_{n_1}, y_1, \cdots, y_{n_2}) = N - (a_0 + a_1x_1 + \cdots + a_{n_1}x_{n_1})(b_0 + b_1y_1 + \cdots + b_{n_2}y_{n_2}) = 0$ ($a_k = 2^l$: the k-th unknown block of p starts in the l-th bit position, $b_i = 2^j$: the i-th unknown block of q starts in the j-th bit position). Then we can use Coppersmith's method to recover the small solution of f.

Our algorithm relies on a heuristic assumption that the polynomials output by the LLL algorithm are algebraically independent, which is also assumed in many works [1,8,10,6]. However, in our experiments, we met some unsuccessful instances, in particular, if the unknown blocks are significantly unbalanced in size, the polynomials output are not always algebraically independent, thus one may not find enough independent polynomials to recover all the unknown bits. Therefore, for completeness, we give a detailed report for the failure of the assumption, and also present a method to fix these "unsuccessful" situations.

The rest of the paper is organized as follows. In Section 2, we introduce some useful background on lattice basis reduction and list some previous results. In Section 3, we give the analysis of the factoring with four unknown blocks of primes p, q, and provide various data obtained through numerical experiments. In Section 4, we generalize the analysis to an arbitrary number n of unknown blocks. At last, in Section 5 we give a conclusion.

2 Preliminaries

2.1 Lattices

Consider a set of linearly independent vectors $u_1, \cdots, u_w \in \mathbb{Z}^n$, with $w \leqslant n$. The lattice L, spanned by $\{u_1, \cdots, u_w\}$, is the set of all integer linear combinations of the vectors $u_1, \cdots, u_w$. The number of vectors is the dimension of the lattice. The set $u_1, \cdots, u_w$ is called a basis of L. In lattices with arbitrary dimension, finding the shortest vector is a very hard problem, however, approximations of a shortest vector can be obtained in polynomial time by applying the well-known *LLL* basis reduction algorithm [9].

Lemma 1. (**LLL**) *Let L be a lattice of dimension w. With polynomial time, the LLL-algorithm outputs reduced basis vector v_i, $1 \leqslant i \leqslant w$ that satisfy*

$$\| v_1 \| \leqslant \| v_2 \| \leqslant \cdots \leqslant \| v_i \| \leqslant 2^{\frac{w(w-1)}{4(w+1-i)}} \det(L)^{\frac{1}{w+1-i}}$$

We state Howgrave's result [7] to find small solutions of integer equations.

Lemma 2. (**Howgrave – Graham**) *Let $g(x_1, \cdots, x_k) \in \mathbb{Z}[x_1, \cdots, x_k]$ be an integer polynomial that consists of at most w monomials. Suppose that*

1. *$g(y_1, \cdots, y_k) = 0 \bmod p^m$ for $| y_1 | \leqslant X_1, \cdots, | y_k | \leqslant X_k$ and*
2. *$\| g(x_1X_1, \cdots, x_kX_k) \| < \frac{p^m}{\sqrt{w}}$*

Then $g(y_1, \cdots, y_k) = 0$ holds over the integers.

Let $g(x_1, \cdots, x_k) = \sum_{i_1, \cdots, i_k} a_{i_1, \cdots, i_k} x_1^{i_1} \cdots x_k^{i_k}$. We define the norm of g by the Euclidean norm of its coefficient vector: $\| g \|^2 = \sum_{i_1, \cdots, i_k} a^2_{i_1, \cdots, i_k}$.

The approach we used in the rest of the paper relies on the following heuristic assumption for computing multivariate polynomials.

Assumption 1. *The lattice-based construction yields algebraically independent polynomials, the common roots of these polynomials can be efficiently computed using techniques like calculation of the resultants or finding a Gröbner basis.*

The first part of Assumption 1 assures that the constructed polynomials allow for extracting the common root, while the second part assures that we are able to compute these common roots efficiently.

2.2 Previous Results

Let l_N denote the bit size of N, we have the following lemma [12]:

Lemma 3. (**Sarkar**) *Let $N = pq$ where p, q are of the equal bit-size. If one knows t MSBs of p: p_m, then we can compute the approximation $q_m = \lceil N/p_m \rceil$ of q, the probability that q and q_m share the first $t - t' - 1$ MSBs is at least $P_{t'} = 1 - \frac{1}{2^{t'}}$ which $0 \leq t' \leq t$. If one knows t LSBs of p: p_l, then we can compute t LSBs of q: q_l.*

In [12], the authors presented another lattice based method to handle the following situation:

Lemma 4. **(Sarkar)** *Let $N = pq$ where p, q are of equal bit-size. Suppose τl_N LSBs of p, q are unknown but the subsequence ηl_N LSBs of p, q are known. Then, under Assumption 1, one can recover the τl_N unknown LSBs of p, q in polynomial time, if $\tau < \frac{\eta}{2}$.*

3 Factoring with Four Unknown Blocks

In this section, we present an algorithm to factorize N with four unknown blocks of p and q. This attack model is illustrated in Figure 1.

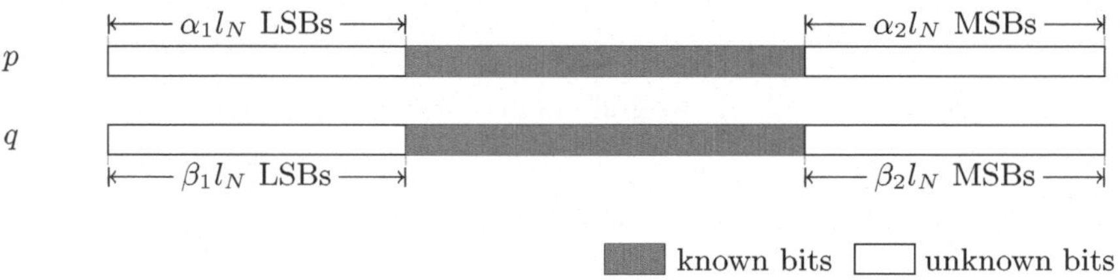

Fig. 1. Four unknown blocks of p, q

3.1 Our Algorithm

Let p_0, p_1, p_2 denote the known bits, the unknown $\alpha_1 l_N$ LSBs, the unknown $\alpha_2 l_N$ MSBs of p, let q_0, q_1, q_2 denote the known bits, the unknown $\beta_1 l_N$ LSBs, the unknown $\beta_2 l_N$ MSBs of q, respectively. Then we have

$$p = 2^{\alpha_1 l_N} p_0 + p_1 + 2^{(1/2-\alpha_2) l_N} p_2$$
$$q = 2^{\beta_1 l_N} q_0 + q_1 + 2^{(1/2-\beta_2) l_N} q_2$$

Hence we are interesting in finding the small root (p_1, p_2, q_1, q_2) of

$$f(x_1, x_2, y_1, y_2) = N - (2^{\alpha_1 l_N} p_0 + x_1 + 2^{(1/2-\alpha_2) l_N} x_2)(2^{\beta_1 l_N} q_0 + y_1 + 2^{(1/2-\beta_2) l_N} y_2)$$

Furthermore, we have the upper bounds

$$|p_i| \le X_i = N^{\alpha_i}, |q_i| \le Y_i = N^{\beta_i} \text{ for } i \in \{1, 2\}.$$

Following we use Coppersmith's method [3] to find the small integer root of polynomial f. Notice that the maximal coefficient of $f(x_1 X_1, x_2 X_2, y_1 Y_1, y_2 Y_2)$ is $N - p_1 q_1$, and the corresponding monomial is 1. Therefore, we define two sets: the set S is defined as the set of all monomials of f^{m-1} for a given positive integer m; the set M is defined as the set of all monomials that appear in

$x_1^{i_1}x_2^{i_2}y_1^{j_1}y_2^{j_2}f(x_1,x_2,y_1,y_2)$ with $x_1^{i_1}x_2^{i_2}y_1^{j_1}y_2^{j_2} \in S$. We introduce the shift polynomials

$$h_{i_1i_2j_1j_2}(x_1,x_2,y_1,y_2) = x_1^{i_1}x_2^{i_2}y_1^{j_1}y_2^{j_2}f(x_1,x_2,y_1,y_2)$$

for $x_1^{i_1}x_2^{i_2}y_1^{j_1}y_2^{j_2} \in S$.

We also use the notations $s = |S|$ for the total number of shift polynomials and $d = |M| - |S|$ for the difference of the number of monomials and the number of shift polynomials. Next we build a $(d+s) \times (d+s)$ matrix L.

The upper left $d \times d$ block is diagonal, where the rows represent the monomials $x_1^{i_1}x_2^{i_2}y_1^{j_1}y_2^{j_2} \in M \backslash S$. The diagonal entry of the row corresponding to $x_1^{i_1}x_2^{i_2}y_1^{j_1}y_2^{j_2}$ is $(X_1^{i_1}X_2^{i_2}Y_1^{j_1}Y_2^{j_2})^{-1}$. The lower left $s \times d$ block contains only zeros.

The last s columns of the matrix L represent the shift polynomials $h_{i_1i_2j_1j_2}$. The first d rows correspond to the monomials in $M \setminus S$, and the last s rows to the monomials of S. The entry in the column corresponding to $h_{i_1i_2j_1j_2}$ is the coefficient of the monomial in $h_{i_1i_2j_1j_2}$. If we sort the shift polynomials according to some ordering, the corresponding matrix defines a upper triangular lattice basis.

The determinant of the matrix L is

$$\begin{aligned}\det(L) &= \left(\prod_{x_1^{i_1}x_2^{i_2}y_1^{j_1}y_2^{j_2} \in M\backslash S} (X_1^{i_1}X_2^{i_2}Y_1^{j_1}Y_2^{j_2})^{-1}\right) \cdot (N - p_1q_1)^s \\ &= X_1^{s_1}X_2^{s_2}Y_1^{s_1^*}Y_2^{s_2^*} \cdot (N - p_1q_1)^s\end{aligned}$$

For the lattice attack to work, we require the enabling condition $\det(L) > 1$ (see [3] and [8] for detail). Then after some computations, we yield the bound:

$$(X_1X_2Y_1Y_2)^{\frac{5}{12}m^4+o(m^4)} < N^{\frac{1}{4}m^4+o(m^4)}$$

To obtain the asymptotic bound, we let m grow to infinity, and substitute the values of X_1, X_2, Y_1, Y_2. Finally we obtain

$$\alpha_1 + \alpha_2 + \beta_1 + \beta_2 < 0.6$$

Then under this condition and Assumption 1, we can compute another three polynomials that share the same root (p_1, p_2, q_1, q_2) over the integers, which finally find the desired root.

3.2 Experimental Results

Our algorithm is heuristic, therefore, we state some experimental results in Table 1 to illustrate the performance of the above algorithm. All the experiments have been performed in Magma [2] over Windows 7 on a laptop with Intel(R) Core(TM) i5-2430M CPU 2.40 GHz, 2 GB RAM. In all the cases, we suppose N is an 1000-bit RSA modulo with equal-size prime p, q.

Table 1. Experimental results for the attack in case of partial leakage of p, q

	m	p(MSBs/LSBs)	q(MSBs/LSBs)	expt(bit)	theory(bit)	dim(L)	time(sec)	result
1	2	107/107	107/107	428	428	27	3.463	success
2	2	84/130	130/84	428	428	27	4.321	success
3	2	84/130	84/130	428	428	27	3.682	x_2, y_2
4	2	90/150	90/150	480	428	27	3.479	x_2, y_2
5	3	119/119	119/119	476	473	64	1932.681	success
6	3	50/185	185/50	470	473	64	3071.519	success
7	3	50/185	50/185	470	473	64	657.638	x_2, y_2
8	3	50/250	50/250	600	473	64	2603.844	x_2, y_2

[1] The word "success" in the column "*result*" means that we can successfully recover the desired small root; whereas the symbol "x_2, y_2" means that we can only recover the values of x_2 and y_2.

For given lattice parameter m, we presented the number of bits that one should theoretically be able to recover from p and q (column *theory* of Table 1). For simplicity, we suppose that p and q have equal size of unknown bits in our experiments.

We observe that Assumption 1 does not always hold in our experiments. In our experiments, if the unknown blocks are equal in bit size ($X_1 \approx X_2 \approx Y_1 \approx Y_2$), we will recover the unknown bits of p, q just as theoretically predicted (see the second row and the sixth row of Table 1)). However in the unbalanced case, the situation is more complicated, the success of the experiment greatly depends on the location of the unknown blocks.

For instance, if the unknown blocks with smaller size are located at MSB side of p and LSB side of $q(X_1 \gg X_2, Y_1 \ll Y_2)$, we can also successfully recover the unknown bits (see the third row and the seventh row of Table 1)). Otherwise if they are both located at MSB side of p, q ($X_1 \gg X_2, Y_1 \gg Y_2$), we observe that only smaller variables x_2 and y_2 are eliminated (see the fourth row and the eighth row of Table 1)), in this case, we notice that the smaller vectors lie in a sublattice of small dimension, which may be the reason why Assumption 1 fails; on the other hand, the sublattice structure is helpful to recover the unknown blocks with smaller size, which require less exposed bits practically (see the fifth row and the ninth row of Table 1)).

3.3 Main Theorem

The method of Coppersmith is able to exploit the algebraic relation among the variables, but it completely ignores the coefficients of the polynomial. That is may be the main reason why Assumption 1 fails in many experiments of Section 3.2. However, based on the experimental results, we observe that though sometimes we may not get enough algebraic independent polynomials to recover all variables, we can still recover some smaller unknown variables with only limited number of polynomials we got. With this observation we can summarize a weaker assumption which is more close to the real fact.

Assumption 2. *The lattice-based construction of Section 3.1 at least yields two algebraically independent polynomials, and the smaller unknown variables of these polynomials can be efficiently computed using Gröbner basis technique.*

Based on Assumption 2, we can get our theorem.

Theorem 1. *Let $N = pq$ where p, q are of equal bit-size. Let $\alpha_1, \alpha_2, \beta_1, \beta_2$ be parameters satisfy $0 < \alpha_1, \alpha_2, \beta_1, \beta_2 < 1$. Suppose $\alpha_1 l_N$ LSBs of p, $\alpha_2 l_N$ MSBs of p, $\beta_1 l_N$ LSBs of q, $\beta_2 l_N$ MSBs of q are unknown, and the rest bits of p, q are known. Then one can factorize N in polynomial time if one of the following conditions is satisfied:*

1. $\alpha_1 + \alpha_2 < 0.207$ or $\beta_1 + \beta_2 < 0.207$ (Under Assumption 1).
2. $\alpha_1 + \alpha_2 + \beta_1 + \beta_2 < 0.6$ and $\alpha_i < 0.25$ or $\beta_i < 0.25$ for $i \in \{1, 2\}$ (Under Assumption 2).

Proof. We can get Condition 1 directly from Herrmann and May's result [6], we focus on Condition 2.

In our algorithm, under the condition $\alpha_1 + \alpha_2 + \beta_1 + \beta_2 < 0.6$ and Assumption 1, we are able to recover the root efficiently. However, sometimes we only get two algebraic independent polynomials (Assumption 2), in these cases two smaller variables are eliminated, we bring the two of known variables back to the polynomial f, and construct a new polynomial with two variable. Then we can apply Coppersmith's method [3] which acts on two variables to find the desired root. There are only two cases which this method fails:

- $\alpha_1 > 0.25$ and $\beta_1 > 0.25$. In this case the unknown blocks with smaller size are both located at MSB side of p, q, we can only recover the unknown variables x_2, y_2, however, we can not get x_1, y_1 using Coppersmith's method which requires the knowledge of half of the LSBs of p or q.
- $\alpha_2 > 0.25$ and $\beta_2 > 0.25$. In this case the unknown blocks with smaller size are both located at LSB side of p, q, we can only recover the unknown variables x_1, y_1, however, we can not get x_2, y_2 using Coppersmith's method which requires the knowledge of half of the MSB of p or q.

Combining with the above discussions, we can get Condition 2.

Remark 1. Our algorithm can be improved if the the unknown blocks are significantly unbalanced (see experiment performances in Table 1), one could employ additional extra shifts in the smaller variables, which intuitively means that the smaller variable gets stronger weight since it cases smaller costs. We do not give the optimization process because of the enormous modes of the location of the unknown blocks.

4 Extension to Arbitrary Number of Unknown Blocks

In this section, we consider the scenario the number of the unknown blocks of the factors p, q is arbitrary. Suppose there are n_1 blocks unleaked whose respective length is $\alpha_i l_N$ $(1 \leq i \leq n_1)$, similarly, the length of unleaked blocks for q is $\beta_i l_N$ $(1 \leq i \leq n_2)$ respectively. Figure 2 illustrates the description of this attack model.

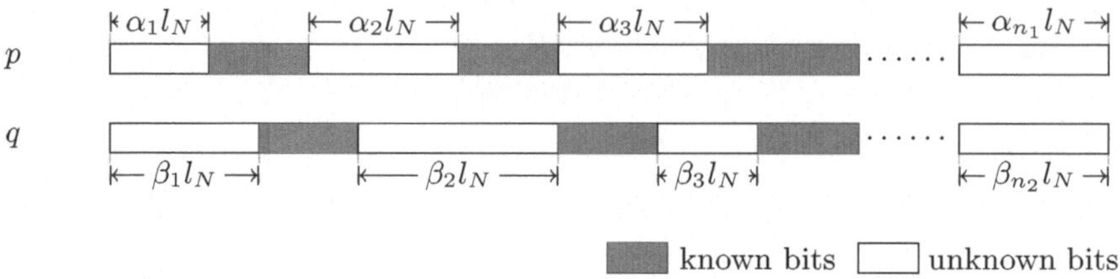

Fig. 2. Arbitrary number of unknown blocks of p and q

4.1 A General Algorithm

Since p is unknown for n_1 blocks, q is unknown for n_2 blocks, we can write $p = a_0 + a_1p_1 + \cdots + a_{n_1}p_{n_1}$, $q = b_0 + b_1q_1 + \cdots + b_{n_2}q_{n_2}$, where $p_i, q_j (1 \le i \le n_1, 1 \le j \le n_2)$ are unknowns, and $a_k = 2^l$ is the k-th unknown block of p starts in the l-th bit position, $b_i = 2^j$ is the i-th unknown block of q starts in the j-th bit position. This gives the following two equations:

$$p = a_0 + a_1x_1 + a_2x_2 + \cdots + a_{n_1}x_{n_1}$$
$$q = b_0 + b_1y_1 + b_2y_2 + \cdots + b_{n_2}y_{n_2}$$

with unknown variables $x_1, \cdots, x_{n_1}, y_1, \cdots, y_{n_2}$. We multiply the two equations, then get a multivariate polynomial:

$$f'(x_1, \cdots, x_{n_1}, y_1, \cdots, y_{n_2}) = N - \sum_{i=1}^{n_1}\sum_{j=1}^{n_2} a_ib_jx_iy_j - a_0\sum_{j=1}^{n_2} b_jy_j - b_0\sum_{i=1}^{n_1} a_ix_i - a_0b_0$$

In particular, suppose that the leaked bits include $\gamma_m l_N$ MSBs and $\gamma_l l_N$ LSBs of p, q, we redefine the polynomial as follows:

$$f(x_1, \cdots, x_{n_1}, y_1, \cdots, y_{n_2}) = f'(x_1, \cdots, x_{n_1}, y_1, \cdots, y_{n_2})/2^{\gamma_l l_N}$$

Furthermore, we have the upper bounds:

$$|p_i| \le X_i = N^{\alpha_i}, |q_j| \le Y_j = N^{\beta_j} \text{ for } i \in \{1, 2, \ldots, n_1\} \ j \in \{1, 2, \ldots, n_2\}.$$

Following we use Coppersmith's method [3] to find the small integer root of polynomial f. Notice that the maximal coefficient of $f(x_1X_1, x_2X_2, y_1Y_1, y_2Y_2)$ is $(N - p_1q_1)/2^{\gamma_1 l_N}$, and the corresponding monomial is 1. Therefore, we define two sets: the set S is defined as the set of all monomials of f^{m-1} for a given positive integer m; the set M is defined as the set of all monomials that appear in $x_1^{i_1}x_2^{i_2}y_1^{j_1}y_2^{j_2}f(x_1, x_2, y_1, y_2)$ with $x_1^{i_1}x_2^{i_2}y_1^{j_1}y_2^{j_2} \in S$. We introduce the shift polynomials

$$h_{i_1i_2j_1j_2}(x_1, x_2, y_1, y_2) = x_1^{i_1}x_2^{i_2}y_1^{j_1}y_2^{j_2}f(x_1, x_2, y_1, y_2)$$

for $x_1^{i_1}x_2^{i_2}y_1^{j_1}y_2^{j_2} \in S$.

At first we define two sets:

$$S = \bigcup\{x_1^{i_1}\cdots x_{n_1}^{i_{n_1}} y_1^{j_1}\cdots y_{n_2}^{j_{n_2}} : x_1^{i_1}\cdots x_{n_1}^{i_{n_1}} y_1^{j_1}\cdots y_{n_2}^{j_{n_2}} \text{ is a monomial of } f^{m-1}\},$$

$$M = \{\text{monomials of } x_1^{i_1}\cdots x_{n_1}^{i_{n_1}} y_1^{j_1}\cdots y_{n_2}^{j_{n_2}} f : x_1^{i_1}\cdots x_{n_1}^{i_{n_1}} y_1^{j_1}\cdots y_{n_2}^{j_{n_2}} \in S\}$$

Next we built a matrix L to find at least n_1+n_2-1 polynomials that share the root $(p_1,\cdots,p_{n_1},q_1,\cdots,q_{n_2})$ over the integers. Then the matrix has triangular form if the coefficient vectors are sorted according to the order. Then we have to satisfy the following condition to get these polynomials:

$$X_1^{s_1}\cdots X_{n_1}^{s_{n_1}} Y_1^{s_1^*}\cdots Y_{n_2}^{s_{n_2}^*} < W^s$$

for $s_k = \sum_{x_1^{i_1}\cdots x_{n_1}^{i_{n_1}} y_1^{j_1}\cdots y_{n_2}^{j_{n_2}} \in M\backslash S} i_k$, $s_t^* = \sum_{x_1^{i_1}\cdots x_{n_1}^{i_{n_1}} y_1^{j_1}\cdots y_{n_2}^{j_{n_2}} \in M\backslash S} j_t$ with $k \in \{1,\cdots,n_1\}, t \in \{1,\cdots,n_2\}$, $s = |S|$ and $W = ||f(x_1X_1,\cdots,x_{n_1}X_{n_1},y_1Y_1,\cdots,y_{n_2}Y_{n_2})||_\infty = N^{1-\gamma_m-\gamma_l}$.

The explicit computation of s, $s_1,s_2,\cdots,s_{n_1}$, $s_1^*,s_2^*,\cdots,s_{n_2}^*$ is given in Appendix A, while we only state the results here.

$$\begin{aligned}
\dim(L) = |M| &= \binom{m+n_1}{m}\binom{m+n_2}{m}\\
s &= \binom{m+n_1-1}{m-1}\binom{m+n_2-1}{m-1}\\
s_1 = \cdots = s_{n_1} &= \binom{m+n_2-1}{m}\binom{m+n_1-1}{m-2} + \binom{m+n_2}{m}\binom{m+n_1-1}{m-1}\\
s_1^* = \cdots = s_{n_2}^* &= \binom{m+n_1-1}{m}\binom{m+n_2-1}{m-2} + \binom{m+n_1}{m}\binom{m+n_2-1}{m-1}
\end{aligned}$$

Put the above values to the condition, we can get

$$\frac{\sum_{i=1}^{n_1}\alpha_i}{n_2+1} + \frac{\sum_{j=1}^{n_2}\beta_j}{n_1+1} < \frac{1-\gamma_m-\gamma_l}{n_1+n_2+1}$$

The runtime of our algorithm is dominated by the time to run LLL reduction algorithm on the lattice L, which takes polynomial time in the dimension of the lattice and in the bit-size of the entries. Thus the total time complexity of our algorithm is polynomial in log$N$ but exponential in n_1+n_2.

Let $n_1 = n_2 = 1$, after some calculations, we can get $\gamma_m + \gamma_l > 0.25$. It means that we can factorize N given $\gamma_m l_N$ MSBs and $\gamma_l l_N$ LSBs of a prime p if $\gamma_m + \gamma_l > 0.25$. If we assume $\gamma_l = 0$, then $\gamma_m > 0.25$, that is exactly Coppersmith's result on the problem of factoring with high bits known. Note that our result can be regard as an extension of Coppersmith's result.

This seems a perfect solution to the problem we posed at the beginning: Check whether or not the bit-size of unknown blocks satisfies the above conditions, if so, applies the above lattice method to recover the unknowns. However, in practice it not always works because of the failure of Assumption 1. Therefore, a natural problem is asked how we can repair this flaw.

4.2 A Combined Algorithm

In this section we present a combined algorithm to fix it. The main idea behind is as follows: Apply the lattice method to the original polynomial, though we may not recover all the unknown variables once, we still can get a part of them, then we reconstruct a new polynomial with the variables we recovered, and repeat the process until the lattice method fails. Now we give the detail.

Step 1. In this routine, we try to recover the MSBs and LSBs of p, q as much as possible. First check whether or not it satisfies the conditions of 4, if so, apply it. Secondly try to recover LSBs and MSBs of p, q using Lemma 3.

Step 2. Construct the polynomial with the known blocks of p, q, and apply the lattice method to this attack scenario.

Step 3. Check whether or not the algorithm of Step 2 recovers all the unknown variables of the polynomial, if so, terminate and return p, q; if not, test whether or not the algorithm recovers a part of variables, if that happens, go back Step 1 with the information of bits we have recovered, but if not, terminate and return fail.

This combined algorithm is a complement for the general algorithm of Section 4, it can not fully resolve the problem of the failure of Assumption 1, but it works in practice (see the discussions of Section 3).

5 Conclusion

In this paper we propose a lattice-based approach to factorize N with partial known bits of factors. Unlike previous works, we focus on the setting of the known bits from both primes. We give the detailed analysis for this extend setting, and provide the numerical experiments to support our theoretical bounds.

Acknowledgments. We would like to thank the anonymous reviewers for helpful comments. This work is supported by the National 973 Program of China under Grant No. 2011CB302400, IIEs Research Project on Cryptography under Grant No. Y3Z001C102, One Hundred Person Project of the Chinese Academy of Sciences under Grant No. NSFC61100225, the Strategic Priority Research Program of the Chinese Academy of Sciences under Grant No. XDA06010701.

References

1. Boneh, D., Durfee, G.: Cryptanalysis of RSA with private key d less than $n^{0.292}$. IEEE Transactions on Information Theory 46(4), 1339–1349 (2000) 394
2. Cannon, J., et al.: Magma computional algebraic sydstem (version: V2. 12-16) (2012), `http://magma.maths.usyd.edu.au/magma/` 397

3. Coppersmith, D.: Small solutions to polynomial equations, and low exponent RSA vulnerabilities. Journal of Cryptology 10(4), 233–260 (1997) 393, 396, 397, 399, 400
4. Halderman, J.A., Schoen, S.D., Heninger, N., Clarkson, W., Paul, W., Calandrino, J.A., Feldman, A.J., Appelbaum, J., Felten, E.W.: Lest we remember: cold-boot attacks on encryption keys. Communications of the ACM 52(5), 91–98 (2009) 394
5. Heninger, N., Shacham, H.: Reconstructing RSA private keys from random key bits. In: Halevi, S. (ed.) CRYPTO 2009. LNCS, vol. 5677, pp. 1–17. Springer, Heidelberg (2009) 394
6. Herrmann, M., May, A.: Solving linear equations modulo divisors: On factoring given any bits. In: Pieprzyk, J. (ed.) ASIACRYPT 2008. LNCS, vol. 5350, pp. 406–424. Springer, Heidelberg (2008) 394, 399
7. Howgrave-Graham, N.: Finding small roots of univariate modular equations revisited. In: Darnell, M. (ed.) Cryptography and Coding 1997. LNCS, vol. 1355, pp. 131–142. Springer, Heidelberg (1997) 395
8. Jochemsz, E., May, A.: A polynomial time attack on RSA with private CRT-exponents smaller than $n^{0.073}$. In: Menezes, A. (ed.) CRYPTO 2007. LNCS, vol. 4622, pp. 395–411. Springer, Heidelberg (2007) 394, 397
9. Lenstra, A.K., Lenstra, H.W., Lovász, L.: Factoring polynomials with rational coefficients. Mathematische Annalen 261(4), 515–534 (1982) 395
10. May, A.: New RSA vulnerabilities using lattice reduction methods. PhD thesis (2003) 394
11. Rivest, R.L., Shamir, A.: Efficient factoring based on partial information. In: Pichler, F. (ed.) EUROCRYPT 1985. LNCS, vol. 219, pp. 31–34. Springer, Heidelberg (1986) 393
12. Sarkar, S.: Partial key exposure: Generalized framework to attack RSA. In: Bernstein, D.J., Chatterjee, S. (eds.) INDOCRYPT 2011. LNCS, vol. 7107, pp. 76–92. Springer, Heidelberg (2011) 395, 396

A Counting $s, s_1, s_2, \cdots, s_{n_1}, s_1^*, s_2^*, \cdots, s_{n_2}^*$

Note that s is the number of solutions of $0 \leq i_1 + i_2 + \cdots + i_{n_1} \leq m-1$, $0 \leq j_1 + j_2 + \cdots + j_{n_2} \leq m-1$. Thus

$$\begin{aligned} s &= \left(\sum_{i_1=0}^{m-1}\sum_{i_2=0}^{m-1-i_1}\cdots\sum_{i_{n_1}=0}^{m-1-i_1-\cdots-i_{n_1-1}} 1\right)\left(\sum_{j_1=0}^{m-1}\sum_{j_2=0}^{m-1-j_1}\cdots\sum_{j_{n_2}=0}^{m-1-j_1-\cdots-j_{n_2-1}} 1\right) \\ &= \left(\sum_{t=0}^{m-1}\binom{t+n_1-1}{t}\right)\left(\sum_{t=0}^{m-1}\binom{t+n_2-1}{t}\right) \\ &= \binom{m+n_1-1}{m-1}\binom{m+n_2-1}{m-1} \end{aligned}$$

Next we consider s_1, we have

$$s = \sum_{i_1=0}^{m}\sum_{i_2=0}^{m-i_1}\cdots\sum_{i_{n_1}=0}^{m-i_1-\cdots-i_{n_1-1}}\sum_{j_1=0}^{m}\sum_{j_2=0}^{m-j_1}\cdots\sum_{j_{n_2}=0}^{m-j_1-\cdots-j_{n_2-1}} i_1$$

$$
\begin{aligned}
&-\sum_{i_1=0}^{m-1}\sum_{i_2=0}^{m-1-i_1}\cdots\sum_{i_{n_1}=0}^{m-1-i_1-\cdots-i_{n_1-1}}\sum_{j_1=0}^{m-1}\sum_{j_2=0}^{m-1-j_1}\cdots\sum_{j_{n_2}=0}^{m-1-j_1-\cdots-j_{n_2-1}} i_1 \\
&=\binom{m+n_2}{m}\sum_{i_1=0}^{m} i_1\binom{m-i_1+n_1-1}{m-i_1}-\binom{m+n_2-1}{m-1}\sum_{i_1=0}^{m-1} i_1\binom{m-i_1+n_1-2}{m-i_1-1} \\
&=\binom{m+n_2}{m}\sum_{T=0}^{m}(m-T)\binom{T+n_1-1}{T}-\binom{m+n_2-1}{m-1}\sum_{T=0}^{m-1}(m-1-T)\binom{T+n_1-1}{T} \\
&=\binom{m+n_2}{m}\binom{m+n_1}{m-1}-\binom{m+n_2-1}{m-1}\binom{m+n_1-1}{m-2} \\
&=\binom{m+n_2-1}{m}\binom{m+n_1-1}{m-2}+\binom{m+n_2}{m}\binom{m+n_1-1}{m-1}
\end{aligned}
$$

According to the structure of f, we have $s_1 = \cdots = s_{n_1}$.

Because of the symmetric characteristic of x and y in f, we have

$$
s_1^* = \cdots = s_{n_2}^* = \binom{m+n_1-1}{m}\binom{m+n_2-1}{m-2}+\binom{m+n_1}{m}\binom{m+n_2-1}{m-1}
$$

Performance Prediction Model for Block Ciphers on GPU Architectures

Naoki Nishikawa, Keisuke Iwai,
Hidema Tanaka, and Takakazu Kurokawa

Department of Computer Science and Engineering
National Defense Academy of Japan
1-10-20 Hashirimizu, Yokosuka-shi, Kanagawa-ken, 239-8686, Japan
{ed11001,iwai,hidema,kuro}@nda.ac.jp

Abstract. This paper presents a proposal of a performance prediction model of block ciphers on GPU architectures. The model comprises three phases: micro-benchmarks, analyzing code, and performance equations. Micro-benchmarks are developed in OpenCL considering scalability for GPU architectures of all kinds. Performance equations are developed, extracting some features of GPU architectures. Overall latencies of AES, Camellia, and SC2000, which covers all types of block ciphers, are inside the range of estimated latencies from the model. Moreover, assuming that out-of-order scheduling by Nvidia GPU works well, the model predicted overall encryption latencies respectively with 2.0 % and 8.8 % error for the best case on Nvidia Geforce GTX 580 and GTX 280. This model supports algebraic and bitslice implementation, although evaluation of the model is conducted in this paper only on table-based implementation.

Keywords: Performance prediction, GPU, OpenCL, AES, Camellia, SC2000, Micro-benchmark.

1 Introduction

High-speed encryption processing on Graphics Processing Units (GPUs) has been noticed for encryption of a large amount of data because it is benefited from software flexibility and hardware-based computing performance. Block cipher primitives in practical use are very numerous, as seen in recommended cipher lists of CRYPTREC[1] and NESSIE[2]. Several vendors (Nvidia, AMD, Intel, and ARM) provide individual GPU architectures. Consequently, the number of combinations of block ciphers and GPU architectures has doubled, forcing programmers to undertake implementation through trial-and-error. However, if a model exists that estimates prospective performance of the implementation on GPUs, programmers can predict the performance improvement rate a priori. In addition, such a model contributes to the design of next-generation of cryptographic algorithms appropriate for GPU architectures.

Therefore, in the paper, we propose a performance prediction model of block ciphers on GPU architectures. The most important aspect of the model is its

J. Lopez, X. Huang, and R. Sandhu (Eds.): NSS 2013, LNCS 7873, pp. 405–423, 2013.

design based not on vendor-dependent language or tools such as CUDA[3] or Nvidia Visual Profiler[4], but on micro-benchmarks in OpenCL[5], a common framework for parallel processing.

The remainder of this paper is organized as follows. Section 2 reviews related works about performance estimation to highlight important points of our model. In Section 3, we overview OpenCL-compliant GPU architectures and extract the fundamental features. In Section 4, from achievements of previous works about block cipher implementations on a GPU, we summarize the implementation methodology. In Section 5, on the basis on the above findings, we design a performance prediction model for block ciphers on a GPU. The points of the design are as follows: In a workflow of the model, we first obtain these latencies from micro-benchmarks and do their numbers from GPU code. Next we calculate encryption latency for one batch using their products and sum. Finally we obtain the range of estimated overall latencies using prediction equations designed by extracting some features of GPU architectures. Section 6 presents the evaluation of our model. Measured values of three block ciphers (AES[6], Camellia[7], and SC2000[8]) on Nvidia Geforce GTX 580 and GTX 280 are each generally within the range of estimated encryption latencies. In particular, assuming that out-of-order scheduling works well on Nvidia GPUs, the model predicted overall latencies of the three block ciphers with 2.0–15.7 % error on GTX 580 and with 8.0–22.0 % error on GTX 280. This paper ends in Section 7, with some concluding remarks and future works.

2 Related Works

2.1 Performance Estimation of Block Cipher Primitives

Matsui used an approach similar to ours to calculate the latency of AES and Camellia on two x86_64 processors[9]. He obtained overall encryption latencies from multiplying latencies of S-Box and instructions by their numbers respectively and then summing the products. The instruction latencies were each measured using code written in x86_64 assembly language. However, Matsui's technique presents a tough challenge for GPU programmers because native-assembly languages such as Nvidia SASS[10] are certainly published in some GPU architectures but the languages are never made uniform even in single vendor circumstances[11]. Therefore our model is designed based on simple micro-benchmarks.

2.2 Performance Prediction of GPU Applications

No research has been reported of performance prediction of block ciphers on GPUs or of performance modeling with OpenCL framework for other applications. However, some investigations of other GPGPU applications with CUDA language have been reported.

Kotohapalli et al. proposed simple and beneficial performance prediction model for the Nvidia GPU and evaluated it on Nvidia Geforce GTX 280 using three applications with different characteristics (matrix multiplication, list ranking, and histogram generation)[12]. In the model, latency for one thread was calculated first.

Then the overall latency was computed by multiplying the result by the number of all threads and dividing by the number of processor cores and pipeline stages. Moreover, to discuss a latency hiding effect by scheduling multiple warps, they defined the calculation method for one thread's latency in two ways: the MAX model (in which the latency of all computation instructions is hidden under that of memory access instructions) and the SUM model (in which it never does). The authors assume that the measured value is sandwiched between values estimated from the two models. Using their prediction model, they predicted histogram generation with 6,400 million element size at 18 % relative error, which includes many shared memory accesses. For calculation of one-thread latency, they used literature data published in the Nvidia programming guide[3] as instruction latencies. However, in accordance with the result of our micro-benchmarks, the latency fluctuates at various batch sizes; the literature data at what batches in the programming guide are unclear. Moreover, instruction latencies in some GPU architectures are not even published. Therefore, their technique is flawed for calculation of the latency of GPU applications.

Guo et al. proposed performance modeling for 32 cases of sparse matrix–vector multiplication (SpMV), which is the combination of eight sparse matrices and four SpMV formats (e.g. Compressed Sparse Row) with the use of micro-benchmark matrices partitioned from the target matrix[13]. Using the model, they predicted their execution times at less than 10 % error on an Nvidia Tesla C2050, but they neglect features of GPU architectures (e.g. scheduling between multiple warps).

Hong et al. proposed an analytical model for Nvidia GPU architectures abstracting scheduling between multiple warps, and geometric means of estimated CPI error for six different benchmarks (Sepia, Linear, SVM, Mat.(naive), Mat.(tiled), and Blackscholes) was 13.3 % on four Nvidia GPUs (8800GTX, FX5600, 8800GT, and GTX 280)[14]. However, they used Nvidia PTX, a vendor-dependent and virtual assembly language, of which the scope is limited to Nvidia GPUs. In addition, 27 parameters are used in the model, which is complicated for programmers. Moreover, the model does not consider cache memory built into memory hierarchy of GPU. However, our model absorbs such cache effects through the use of micro-benchmarks.

Zhang et al. developed a performance model for Nvidia Geforce 200-series GPUs based on micro-benchmarks, of which the error was 5–15 % for three algorithms (dense matrix multiply, tridiagonal solver, and sparse matrix vector multiply) on Nvidia Geforce GTX 285[15]. Unlike Hong's model, they used Decuda[16], a specialized disassembler for Nvidia GPUs, to obtain real code executed on actual GPUs. Moreover, to obtain input parameters for their model, they used an existing Nvidia GPU simulator Barra[17]. Unfortunately, these tools were all dependent on a particular vendor.

Baghsorkji et al. also proposed performance modeling on GPU architectures and evaluated it on Nvidia Geforce 8800[18]. This model has similar characteristics as ours: Scalability was considered so as not to be tightly coupled to any specific GPU architectures or high-level programming interface. Moreover, it captured performance effect of major GPU microarchitecture features and then showed the breakdown of overall encryption latency. Based on graphs presented in the paper, the errors between estimated and measured values were approximately 13–48 %, 3–25 %, 1–14 %, and 4–14 % for dense matrix multiplication, FFT, prefix sum scan, and sparse matrix-vector multiplication, respectively. However, their model used an approach based on Program Dependency Graph (PDG), which targets all GPGPU applications but is complicated for beginner programmers. In contrast, we offer a simple performance prediction model of block ciphers primitives, by focusing on a characteristic of implementation of the applications. Moreover, their model also does not support cache memory effect, unlike our model.

3 GPU Architecture and the Programming Model

Some leading processor vendors have announced their own GPUs supporting OpenCL technology. OpenCL-compliant GPU architectures are comprised of hierarchical structure of processor cores, of which the chip has N $\times$ Compute Units (CUs) and for which each CU includes several Processor Elements (PEs), registers, an instruction unit, and a local memory. High-capacity but low-speed global memory is outside of the chip and is connected to CUs via an interconnection network. Moreover, the programming model in OpenCL is large-scale thread-level parallel processing corresponding to the architecture. A GPU scheduler distributes thread blocks to CUs evenly and each thread of a thread block is executed on a PE. The thread block and thread are designated respectively as work-group and work-item in OpenCL.

These are the requirements for OpenCL-ready GPU architectures, but the design details depend strongly on the GPU vendor. Most successful GPU architectures of the present day come from Nvidia Corp., whose design is natural considering the OpenCL requirement with parallel processing for use of quite a few work-items. The fundamental points are the following. (i) Instruction issue for batch grouping of a specific number of work-items on a single instruction to lessen the area of instruction units and increase the percentage of processor cores in a GPU chip (ii) Deeply pipelined PEs to raise the efficiency to execute instructions of work-items in lock-step (iii) High-bandwidth memory system to receive memory requests concurrently from several PEs (iv) Out-of-order scheduling to hide the latency of arithmetic and logical instructions by a batch when PE pipelines stall attributable to memory access instructions by another batch. For that reason, we decided to incorporate the four points above into the design of our performance prediction model.

The point (iii) is realized, for example, as the mechanism by which local memory is split into several banks to receive memory requests from several PEs in parallel. However, if indexes of work-items belong to the same bank, then bank conflict occurs and the effective bandwidth decreases. In the case of Nvidia GPUs, because the indexes are exactly the same address, broadcast access occurs as conflict-free[19]. In addition, some GPU architectures such as Nvidia Fermi have cache memory inserted to the data path between PE and global memory[20].

Incidentally AMD Corp., another leading GPU vendor, has up to now promoted VLIW-based GPU architecture different from Nvidia's, but has now changed its development guidelines to a similar architecture to that of Nvidia's[21]. In fact, the above four points are also shared with AMD GPUs[22]. Therefore, our model is available for other GPUs such as AMD Radeon HD Graphics, although we evaluated the model only on Nvidia GPUs in this study.

4 Implementation of Block Ciphers on a GPU

4.1 Targeted Block Cipher Primitives

To test our model, we targeted three 128-bit block cipher primitives (AES[6], Camellia[7], and SC2000[8]), which cover all types of structure (see Table 1). Also, we deal only with 128-bit key size.

Electronic Code Book (ECB), CountTeR (CTR), or Xor-encrypt-xor Tweakable code book mode with ciphertext Stealing (XTS)[23] are known as parallelizable modes in block cipher. ECB use a single key applied to all plaintexts, and CTR uses a key stream generated from a secret key and combined to plaintexts. In the CTR mode, the generation of the key stream is conducted in the same manner as ECB. In the XTS mode, plaintexts are encrypted using two ECB modes. Therefore, we deal only ECB mode in this study.

4.2 Outline of the Implementation

For implementation of block ciphers on a GPU, we take advantage of achievements of previous works[24][25]. Almost all the modern block cipher primitives on a GPU are composed mainly of arithmetic and logical instructions and accesses to substitution tables and a key deployed in a memory with low latency. The implementation has some phases, as presented in Fig. 1.

Kernel Invocation Phase. The first phase is invoking a kernel. For encryption on a GPU, we only invoke single kernel because all plaintext blocks are encrypted in a kernel.

Load Data Phase. In spite of frequently accessed data, tables and key are located in global memory at the beginning of the encryption kernel. Therefore, before the encryption primitive phase starts, to lessen the access latency, we deploy them to local memory in CUs with parallel processing by work-items. However, synchronization between work-items is necessary before moving on to the next phase.

Encryption Primitive Phase. At the beginning of this phase, plaintexts are also located in global memory. Then work-items load a 128-bit plaintext to individual registers before encrypting the plaintext. During encryption, work-items process 128-bit plaintext blocks independently in parallel and therefore

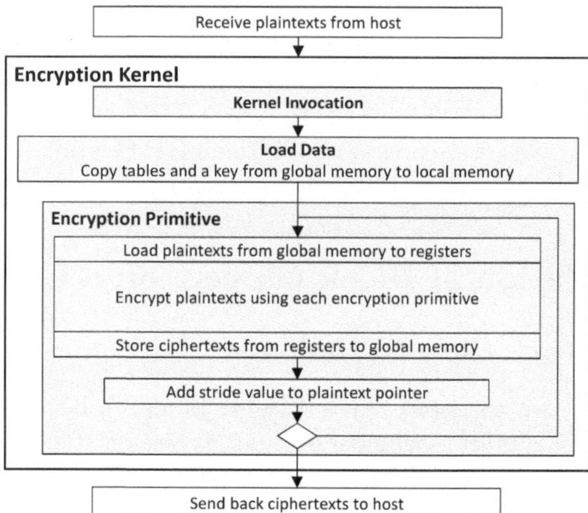

Fig. 1. Abstraction of implementation of block cipher on a GPU

keep hold on the plaintext data in registers. After encryption, each work-item stores a 128-bit ciphertext to global memory. Additionally work-items access tables in a random manner, although they access the same address of a key in a regular manner because the key is not changed during the process. This "regular" means a somewhat tricky pattern in which all work-items load a value from the same address because the encryption mode is ECB. When encrypting a large amount of data, after encryption of a plaintext, each work-item adds stride value to plaintext pointers and then continues to encrypt other one. Although extra registers for loop counter is necessary, once tables and key are deployed to local memory, the work-items can use the same tables and key directly.

5 Performance Modeling for Implementation of Block Ciphers on a GPU

5.1 Workflow

The workflow of our prediction model is presented in Fig. 2. In the model, four per-batch latencies are obtained from micro-benchmarks, whereas their numbers are collected from encryption primitive part of kernel program. The obtained parameters become inputs for a prediction equation (see (3)).

5.2 Performance Modeling

For expedience, we first discuss performance modeling. Letting L_{ker}, L_{ld}, and L_{enc} respectively denote latency of kernel invocation, load data, and encryption primitive phases as shown in Fig. 1, latency of overall encryption kernel on a GPU, L_{enc_total}, is represented simply as

$$L_{enc\_total} = L_{ker} + L_{ld} + L_{enc}. \tag{1}$$

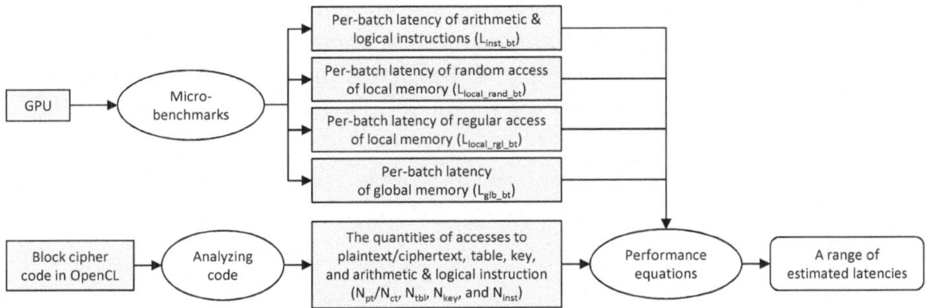

Fig. 2. Workflow of our prediction model

Latency of last subphase of encryption primitive phase (i.e., "Add stride value to plaintext pointer" in Fig. 1) is disregarded because it is lightweight compared to other main phases.

Next, we describe a calculation procedure of L_{enc}. In the model we refer to latency for one batch in one loop of encryption primitive phase as L_{enc_bt}, the number of batches and work-groups specified by a programmer respectively as N_{batch} and N_{wg}, and the number of CUs in a GPU and iterations of encryption primitive respectively as N_{cu} and N_{iter}. Then similar processing is executed for the number of work-groups assigned to a CU. Because identical processing is executed on all CUs in parallel, L_{enc} is represented as shown below.

$$L_{enc} = L_{enc\_bt} \times N_{iter} \times N_{batch} \times \frac{N_{wg}}{N_{cu}} \tag{2}$$

Therein, $\frac{N_{wg}}{N_{cu}}$ stands for the number of work-groups evenly distributed on CUs by a GPU scheduler. In Nvidia GPUs, the number of work-items in a batch are 32 and N_{batch} obtained dividing the number of work-items per work-group by 32. Point (i) described in Section 3 is incorporated in (2).

Finally, we describe the calculation procedure of L_{enc_bt}. In our model, latency for one batch of access to plaintext/ciphertext, table access, key access, and arithmetic and logical instructions are respectively designated as L_{glb_bt}, $L_{local\_rand\_bt}$, $L_{local\_rgl\_bt}$, and L_{inst_bt} and their numbers in each encryption primitive as N_{pt}/N_{ct}, N_{tbl}, N_{key}, and N_{inst}. As presented in Section 4.2, L_{glb_bt}, $L_{local\_rand\_bt}$, and $L_{local\_rgl\_bt}$ are obtained respectively as latency for one batch of global memory, of local memory in random, and of local memory in regular. N_{pt}/N_{ct} are the numbers of loading/storing plaintext/ciphertext from/to global memory, as presented in Section 4.2. Consequently, L_{enc_bt} is represented simply as products of a latency and a number for respective component and their sum. Out-of-order scheduling of point (iv) in Section 3 is incorporated not into (2) but into (3). Out-of-order scheduling has a strong impact on overall latency. We draw on Kothapalli's work[12] described in Section 2 for our model. Our model is based on latency per batch, although his model does on one thread latency because per-batch latencies of the input components fluctuate greatly depending on the number of working batches (see Section 6.2). According to Kothapalli's work, L_{enc_bt} is calculated in the following two submodels: scheduling-aware submodel (SA submodel), in which latency of all arithmetic and logical instructions are assumed to be hidden completely under that of memory access instructions; and scheduling-ignored submodel (SI submodel), in which they are never hidden. Consequently L_{enc_bt} is represented as

$$L_{enc\_bt} = \begin{cases} L_{glb\_bt}\times(N_{pt}+N_{ct})+L_{local\_rand\_bt}\times N_{tbl}+L_{local\_rgl\_bt}\times N_{key} & \text{(SA submodel)} \\ L_{glb\_bt}\times(N_{pt}+N_{ct})+L_{local\_rand\_bt}\times N_{tbl}+L_{local\_rgl\_bt}\times N_{key}+L_{inst\_bt}\times N_{inst} & \text{(SI submodel).} \end{cases} \tag{3}$$

Therefore, overall encryption latency is expected to be between two L_{enc_total}, as estimated from both submodels.

5.3 Analyzing Code

The quantities of input components for (3) (i.e., N_{pt}, N_{ct}, N_{tbl}, N_{key}, and N_{inst}) are derived from GPU code of each block cipher primitive. For getting N_{inst}, a methodology of counting up the quantities of operators is used. Additionally, in a 128-bit block cipher, the number of loading/storing plaintext/ciphertext from/to global memory is 4/4 because a unit of loading or storing by a work-item is 32-bit. A summary of these parameters is presented in Table 1.

In AES, the structure is an SPN network. The algorithm of 128-bit key defines 10-round processes. In AES, each round process is a transformation including 16 lookup tables (T-Boxes) and an XOR instruction with a 32-bit key.

In Camellia, the structure is a Feistel network. The algorithm of the 128-bit key defines 18-round processes. Each round includes an F-function which includes 8 table substitutions, 2 XOR instructions with two 32-bit keys, and several logical operations. Furthermore, FL and FL^{-1}-functions consisting of logical operations are inserted.

In SC2000, the structure is a hybrid of SPN and Feistel. The algorithm of 128-bit key defines seven-round processes. In each round, a plaintext is encrypted through five functions in sequence (I, B, I, R, and R). I-function is XORs with four 32-bit keys and B-function consists of logical operations. The R-function includes several table substitutions and logical operations. The inputs of these tables are separation of 32-bit and can be selected from multiple options such as (6-bit, 10-bit, 10-bit, 6-bit) or (11-bit, 10-bit, 11-bit) depending on the computer memory capacity. In the former, two tables with 6-bit input and two tables with 10-bit are used for substitution. In the latter, two tables with 11-bit input and one table with 10-bit input are done.

5.4 Micro-benchmark

As shown in Fig. 4, we developed micro-benchmarks to obtain latencies of input components of (3). Unfortunately in OpenCL, no built-in function to measure thread execution cycles inside of a kernel such as `clock()` in the CUDA platform is available. Therefore we first run an empty kernel eliminating a sequence

```
// The "l_Te0", "l_Te1", "l_Te2", and "l_Te3" are T-Boxes in local memory.
// The "l_key" is the round key on local memory. The "in" is plaintext.
// Start AES encryption
*(u32*)s0=GETU32(in+   tid*16)^l_key[0];   *(u32*)s1=GETU32(in+ 4+tid*16)^l_key[1];
*(u32*)s2=GETU32(in+ 8+tid*16)^l_key[2];   *(u32*)s3=GETU32(in+12+tid*16)^l_key[3];
// Round 1
t[0]=l_Te0[s0[0]]^l_Te0[s1[0]]^l_Te0[s2[0]]^l_Te3[s3[0]]^l_key[4];
t[1]=l_Te0[s1[1]]^l_Te0[s2[1]]^l_Te1[s3[1]]^l_Te0[s0[1]]^l_key[5];
t[2]=l_Te0[s2[2]]^l_Te0[s3[2]]^l_Te2[s0[2]]^l_Te1[s1[2]]^l_key[6];
t[3]=l_Te0[s3[3]]^l_Te0[s0[3]]^l_Te3[s1[3]]^l_Te2[s2[3]]^l_key[7];
```

Fig. 3. Code of implementation of AES on GPU (snippet)

Table 1. Summary of parameters of block cipher primitive. In SC2000 left side separated by a comma for (11-bit, 10-bit, 11-bit) option and right side for (6-bit, 10-bit, 10-bit, 6-bit).

	Structure	# tables (N_{tbl})	# keys (N_{key})	# arith. and logical instructions (N_{inst})	# loading plaintexts (N_{pt})	# storing ciphertexts (N_{ct})
AES	SPN	160	44	436	4	4
Camellia	Feistel	144	48	642	4	4
SC2000	Hybrid	72, 96	56, 56	506, 590	4	4

of instructions as well as the original micro-benchmark kernel, measuring both the elapsed times using `clGetEventProfilingInfo` API, thereby obtaining the difference between the two values as instruction latency. Micro-benchmarks comprised of the sequence of instructions are executed twice, throwing away the initial iteration to avoid a cold instruction cache miss. Then we obtained elapsed cycles by dividing the elapsed time by the reciprocal of the GPU core clock frequency.

First, we discuss a micro-benchmark of arithmetic and logical instructions. A micro-benchmark for L_{inst_bt} is designed to run a kernel of a sequence of their dependent arithmetic and logical instructions in an unrolled loop. Instruction latency is adopted as the average value. The number of work-groups is configured to one because the measurement is wrapped up in a single CU.

Next we discuss micro-benchmarks of latency of memory access. Micro-benchmarks of L_{glb_bt}, $L_{local\_rand\_bt}$, and $L_{local\_rgl\_bt}$ are all set to run a sequence of dependent reads from array in global or local memories. The access patterns of work-items to the array are controlled by a given initial value to work-items as well as arrays with precomputed data. Like L_{inst_bt}, memory access latencies are adopted as the average value. For $L_{local\_rand\_bt}$, note that the choice of random values in an array is critical for accuracy in the measurement. More specifically, if generated by imperfect random number function such as `rand()` in standard C library, then random values might be duplicated; the index of multiple work-items might be matched during several iterations. Then the obtained latency is no longer for purely random access. Therefore, for random values, we take advantage of S-Box out of AES, which is designed from 0–255 values over $GF(2^8)$ and which are random but never duplicated. However, considering the case of a number of work-item that exceeds the number of the S-Box array, a remainder divided work-item ID by 256 is set to the initial value of the work-item, as shown in line 15 of Fig. 4. For $L_{local\_rgl\_bt}$, we only replace `j=lid%256` to `j=0` in the line to realize the regular access pattern described in Section 4.2. For $L_{local\_rand\_bt}$ and $L_{local\_rgl\_bt}$, the number of work-groups is set as one for the same reason as L_{inst_bt}.

As described briefly in Section 4.2 and Section 5.3, the access pattern of global memory for loading/storing 128-bit plaintext/ciphertext by work-items is 32-bit (1-word) access four consecutive times with 128-bit stride. L_{glb_bt} is the latency for one batch. Therefore, to measure L_{glb_bt}, specific initial variables are prepared for work-items and value sorted in ascending order. They are set to the array as the 23rd line of Fig. 4. Moreover unlike $L_{local\_rand\_bt}$ and $L_{local\_rgl\_bt}$, the number of work-groups in the micro-benchmark is configured as the number of CUs in a GPU because global memory is connected to all CUs and because L_{glb_bt} should be measured in case memory requests from all CUs arise concurrently.

```
1  // Kernel for instructions (XOR)
2  __kernel void inst_latency(__global uint out, uint p1, uint p2, int its){
3    uint lid=get_local_id(0);
4    unsigned int a=p1, b=p2;
5    for(int i=0; i<its; i++) repeat256(a^=b; b^=a;)
6    out[lid]=a+b;
7  }
8  // Kernel for local memory latency (Random)
9  // "aes_sbox" is an array with S-Box of AES.
10 __kernel void local_latency(__global uint aes_s_box, __global uint out, int its){
11   uint lid=get_local_id(0);
12   __local l_data[256]; // l_data are an array in local memory.
13   if(lid==0){for(i=0; i<256; i++) l_array[i]=aes_s_box[i];}
14   barrier(CLK_LOCAL_MEM_FENCE);
15   uint j=lid%256;  // If j=0, the access pattern becomes regular.
16   for(int i=0; i<its; i++) repeat256(j=l_array[j];)
17   out[lid]=j;
18 }
19 // Kernel for global memory latency
20 // "data" is an array with precomputed data in global memory.
21 __kernel void global_latency(__global uint data, __global uint out, int its){
22   uint gid=get_global_id(0);
23   uint j=4*gid, k=4*gid+1, l=4*gid+2, m=4*gid+3; // Specialized in 128-bit encryption
24   for(int i=0; i<its; i++) repeat256(j=data[j]; k=data[k]; l=data[l]; m=data[m];)
25   out[gid]=j+k+l+m;
26 }
```

Fig. 4. Micro-benchmark for respective instructions. In micro-benchmark for memory access, the access patterns by multiple work-items are controlled by the initial value of work-items and array data for the access.

6 Evaluation

6.1 Evaluation Environment

For the evaluation of our model, we used Nvidia Geforce GTX 580 with Fermi architecture of recent generation and Nvidia Geforce GTX 280 with GT200 architecture of one generation earlier. The quantities of CUs of GTX 580 and GTX 280 are, respectively, 16 and 30; the quantities of PEs in a CU are, respectively, 32 and 8. Local memory capacities in a CU on GTX 580 and GTX 280 are, respectively, 64 KB and 16 KB. The maximum available number of work-item batches per work-group differs depending on their architectures as most 32 and 16 batches on GTX 580 and GTX 280, respectively. The quantities of split banks of local memory in a CU are, respectively, 32 and 16 on GTX 580 and GTX 280; local memory bandwidth on GTX 580 is wider than that on GTX 280. In addition, global memory bandwidths are, respectively, 193 GB/s and 142 GB/s on GTX 580 and GTX 280. The two GPUs are equipped alternatively with a machine for evaluation which has an Intel Core i7-2600K 2.66 GHz CPU and CentOS 6.0 operation system. Kernel programs are built by OpenCL driver bundled with Nvidia CUDA toolkit ver. 4.2 on both GPUs.

6.2 Acquisition of Component Latency of GPUs

Arithmetic and Logical Instructions (L_{inst_bt}). First, as an example, this report describes measurement results of latency and throughput of XOR at various batch sizes, as presented in Fig. 5. They are the data justifying our micro-benchmark, although parameters used for our model are latency per batch. Throughput increases linearly when the PE pipeline is not full, but once the pipeline is full, throughput saturates at about 31.1 ops/cycle for GTX 580 and about 7.5 ops/cycle for GTX 280, of which the values roughly coincide with the number of PEs in a CU. This fact indicates that XOR instructions of batches of work-items are processed ideally in parallel through PE pipelines. Incidentally in GTX 580, the latencies at the number of 2N-1 and 2N (N: natural number) are almost identical values, as derived from scheduling by Fermi architecture that instructions are issued to two batches in parallel[20]. Next, we display measurement results of XOR latency per batch in Fig. 6, which is divided latency at various batch sizes by their quantities of batches. When the PE pipeline is full, the XOR latencies per batch each become flat.

With the same micro-benchmark as that described above, results of micro-benchmarks for several arithmetic and logical instructions often used in block cipher primitives are presented in Table 2. However, MUL and MAD instructions are used for comparison to other instructions. Throughput is measured as the maximum available number of batches in a CU and latency for use of a single batch. In contrast, latency per batch is the value of latency at maximum number of batches divided by the batch number. In accordance with the result, we know that arithmetic and logical instructions in block cipher primitives are processed efficiently in PE pipeline for each GPU. In many instructions, our results match the values measured using the CUDA-based micro-benchmark previously reported in [26] and [27]. In this paper, for simplicity, 1.0 cycle/batch and 4.3 cycle/batch are adopted as L_{inst_bt} of GTX 580 and GTX 280, respectively.

Memory Access Instructions ($L_{local\_rand\_bt}$, $L_{local\_rgl\_bt}$, and L_{glb_bt}). First, latency and latency per batch of random and regular access to local memory at various batch sizes are presented, respectively, in Fig. 7 and Fig. 8. The latencies per batch on GTX 580 and GTX 280 become flat roughly at 18 batches

Table 2. List of throughputs, latencies, latencies per batch of arithmetic and logical instructions on GPUs. Digits in parentheses are the numbers of batches when latency per batch becomes flat.

GPU		Geforce GTX 580			Geforce GTX 280		
		Throughput (ops/cycle)	Latency (cycles)	**Latency per batch (cycles/batch)**	Throughput (ops/cycle)	Latency (cycle)	**Latency per batch (cycles/batch)**
Arithmetic	ADD, SUB	31.1	18.3	**1.0 (18)**	7.5	24.9	**4.3 (8)**
	MUL	15.9	18.3	**2.0 (9)**	1.7	111.1	**18.5 (9)**
	MAD	15.9	20.3	**2.0 (10)**	1.4	138.7	**22.6 (10)**
Logical	XOR, AND, OR	31.1	18.3	**1.0 (18)**	7.5	27.9	**4.3 (8)**
	SHL, SHR	15.6	37.0	**2.0 (18)**	3.9	53.3	**8.2 (9)**

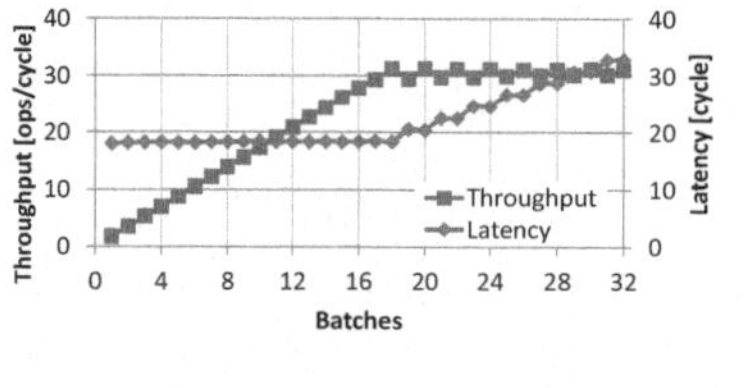

(a) Geforce GTX 580

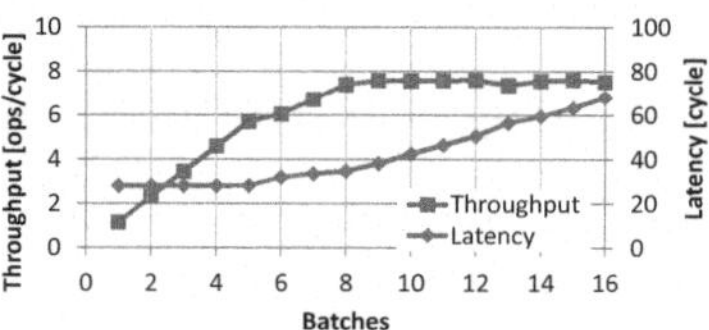

(b) Geforce GTX 280

Fig. 5. Throughput and latency of XOR instructions

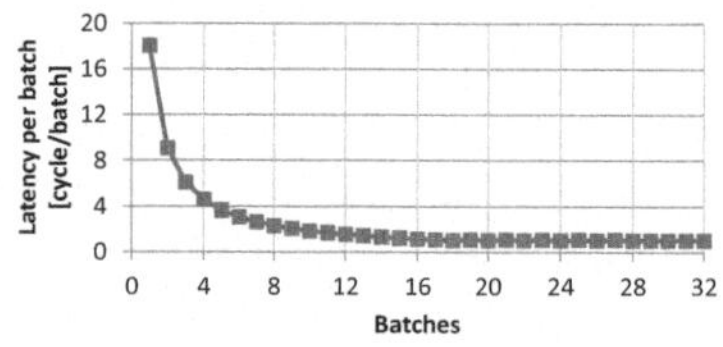

(a) Geforce GTX 580

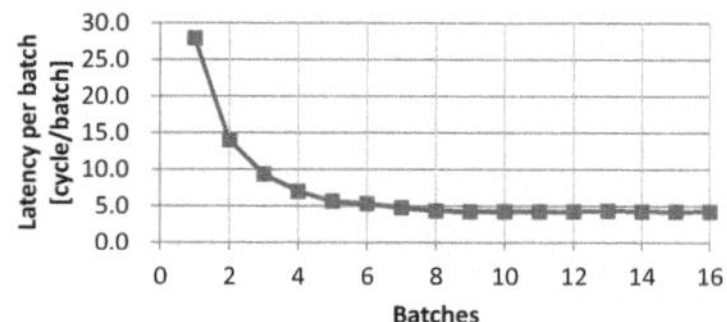

(b) Geforce GTX 280

Fig. 6. Latency per batch of XOR instructions

and 8 batches respectively, which indicates that local memory bandwidth reaches the maximum values at the number of batches above, irrespective of the access patterns. Their numbers are almost identical to the number of batches that execute arithmetic and logical instructions used in block ciphers at maximum efficiency. With regard to block cipher encryption primitives, the CUs in an Nvidia GPU are apparently designed to endanger maximum power at a specific number of batches (GTX 580: 18 batches, GTX 280: 8 batches). Moreover the latencies with both the access patterns in GTX 580 increase in a staircase pattern, which is derived from a two-batch instruction issue in parallel in common with the measurement of L_{inst_bt}. More interestingly, random access latency on GTX 580 at $2N - 1$ batches is worse than that at $2N$. This reason is not describable from Nvidia's documents or from findings of previous works in Section 2. However, we conjecture that the Fermi architecture is designed to optimize for scheduling at $2N$ batches and extra procedures are inserted in the case of random access to local memory at $2N - 1$ batches. Next, latency and latency per batch of global memory access at various batch sizes are presented in Fig. 9. The latency per batch on GTX 580 and GTX 280 become flat respectively once they become roughly at 8 batches and 2 batches, which are fewer batches than those of local memory access. The reason is that global memory is connected to all CUs via interconnection network. Therefore, memory requests from CUs concentrate and reached the maximum bandwidth with fewer batches, unlike local memory. Consequently, the latencies per batch for $L_{local\_rand\_bt}$, $L_{local\_rgl\_bt}$, and L_{gbl_bt} are each measured as the maximum available number of bathces in a CU, like L_{inst}.

A list of per-batch latencies of input components for (3) is presented in Table 3. The difference between local memory latency on GTX 580 and GTX 280 results from effective bandwidth caused by the number of banks. Moreover, the effective bandwidth for each GPU differs depending on access patterns, as described in Section 3. Additionally, latency per batch of global memory access in GTX 580 is considerably small compared to that in GTX 280, which results from cache memory with 128-bit line width inserted between PEs and global memory[20]. Micro-benchmarks for global memory make the best use of this cache line size. In this way, our prediction model based on micro-benchmarks offers programmers a single and easy-to-use methodology with or without cache memory.

Kernel Invocation (L_{ker}) and Load Data (L_{ld}). Finally, let us present a measurement result of latency of both Kernel Invocation and Load Data phases

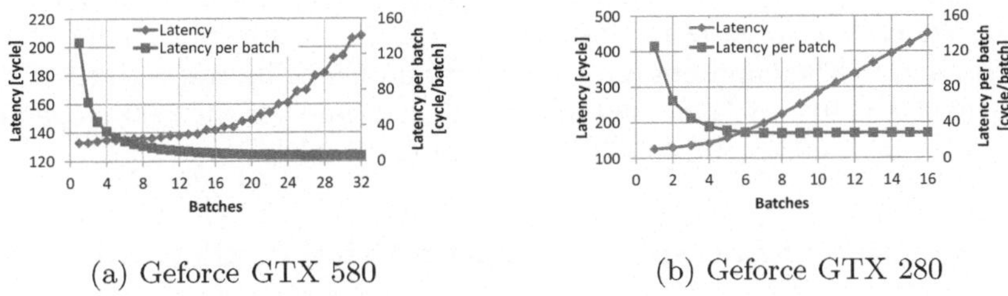

(a) Geforce GTX 580 (b) Geforce GTX 280

Fig. 7. Random access latency to local memory

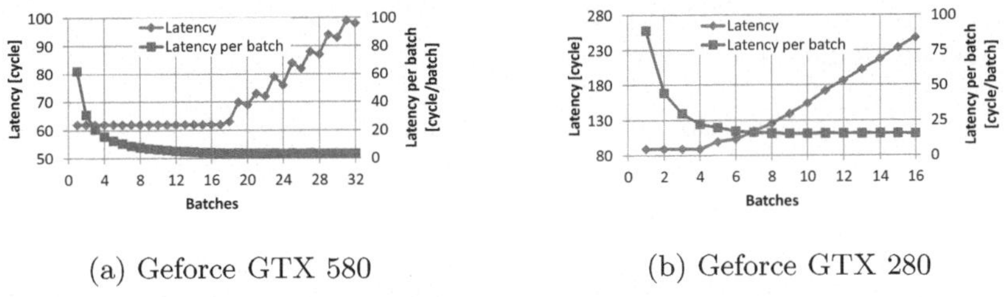

(a) Geforce GTX 580 (b) Geforce GTX 280

Fig. 8. Regular access latency to local memory

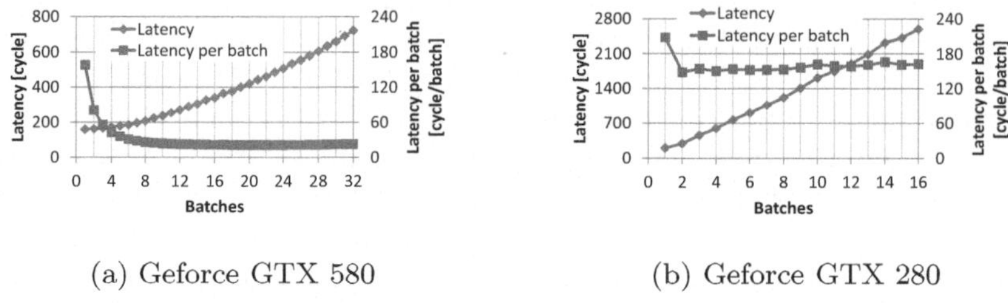

(a) Geforce GTX 580 (b) Geforce GTX 280

Fig. 9. Access latency to global memory

Table 3. List of per-batch latencies of input components on GPUs

	Geforce GTX 580 (cycles/batch)	Geforce GTX 280 (cycles/batch)
$L_{local\_rand\_bt}$	6.5	28.0
$L_{local\_rgl\_bt}$	3.1	15.5
L_{glb_bt}	22.6	162.4
L_{inst_bt}	1.0	4.3

in Fig. 1. For encryption of a large amount of data, L_{ker} and L_{ld} become much lower than L_{enc}.

We ran an empty kernel for L_{ker} and obtained 0.002×10^7 and 0.0007×10^7 cycles respectively on a GTX 580 and GTX 280 irrespective of the number of batches. We each ran kernels comprised of only the deployment part of AES, Camellia, and SC2000 and obtained for AES and Camellia respectively 0.003×10^7 and 0.002×10^7 on GTX 580 and GTX 280, and for SC2000 respectively 0.004×10^7 and 0.003×10^7 on GTX 580 and GTX 280.

6.3 Estimation of Encryption Latencies Using Prediction Equations

As an example of a procedure of estimating the range of overall encryption latency, we present the calculation process of AES encryption for 256 MB data size on GTX 580. Using (3) L_{enc_bt} is calculated in two ways based on SI and SA submodels. The number of input components and their latencies required in (3) are, respectively, in Table 1 and Table 3. Consequently, L_{enc_bt} of AES on GTX 580 is calculated as follows:

$$L_{enc\_bt} = \begin{cases} 22.6\times(4+4)+6.5\times160+3.1\times44=1357.2(\text{cycles}) & \text{(SA submodel)} \\ 22.6\times(4+4)+6.5\times160+3.1\times44+1.0\times436=1793.2(\text{cycles}) & \text{(SI submodel)} \end{cases} \quad (4)$$

Next we present a procedure of L_{enc} using (4) assuming that a programmer specified 64 work-groups and 1024 work-items per work-group for the encryption kernel. In Nvidia GPUs, a batch has 32 work-items and then $N_{batch} = 1024/32 = 32$ and $N_{wg} = 64$. Moreover, the number of CUs is 16 and then $N_{cu} = 16$. Next we discuss N_{iter}. Each work-item encrypts 128-bit data (16 Bytes). Therefore, $16 \times N_{wg} \times (32 \times N_{batch})$ Bytes of plaintext are encrypted for one iteration shown in Fig. 1. Therefore, N_{iter} required for 256 MBytes encryption is calculated as $N_{iter} = \frac{256\times1024\times1024}{16\times N_{wg}\times(32\times N_{batch})} = 256$. Consequently, using (2) L_{enc} based on the SA submodel is calculated as shown below.

$$L_{enc} = 1357.2 \times 256 \times 32 \times \frac{64}{16} = 44472729.6 \simeq 4.447 \times 10^7 \text{ (cycles)} \quad (5)$$

L_{enc} based on SI submodel is similarly calculated as 5.876×10^7 cycles. Finally, L_{ker} and L_{ld} on GTX 580 are, respectively, 0.002×10^7 and 0.003×10^7. Using (1) L_{enc_total} based on SA submodel is calculated as shown below.

$$L_{enc\_total} = (0.002 + 0.003 + 4.447) \times 10^7 = 4.452 \times 10^7 \text{ (cycles)} \quad (6)$$

Therein, L_{enc_total} based on SI submodel is similarly calculated as 5.881×10^7. Thereby, the range of overall estimated latency of AES encryption on GTX 580 is obtained.

Fig. 10 and Fig. 11 present a comparison of measured latency and a range of estimated encryption latencies of three block ciphers on GTX 580 and GTX 280 using respective specific quantities of work-groups and work-items per work-group to extract best performance for each GPU (GTX 580: 64 work-groups and 1024 work-items per work-group, GTX 280: 90 work-groups and 512 work-items per work-group). As for SC2000, (11-bit, 10-bit, 11-bit) and (6-bit, 10-bit, 10-bit, 6-bit) options are adopted, respectively, for implementation on GTX 580 and GTX 280 because of local memory capacity on each GPU. A range subtracting latency on the SI submodel from that on SA submodel represents the range of estimated latencies. Differences between the estimated value on the SI submodel and the measured one represent the number of cycles of arithmetic and logical instructions hidden under latency of memory access instructions.

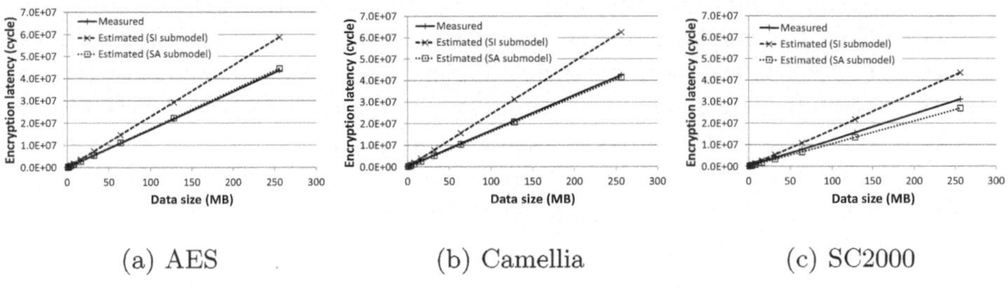

(a) AES (b) Camellia (c) SC2000

Fig. 10. Comparison of measured and the range of estimated encryption latency on Geforce GTX 580

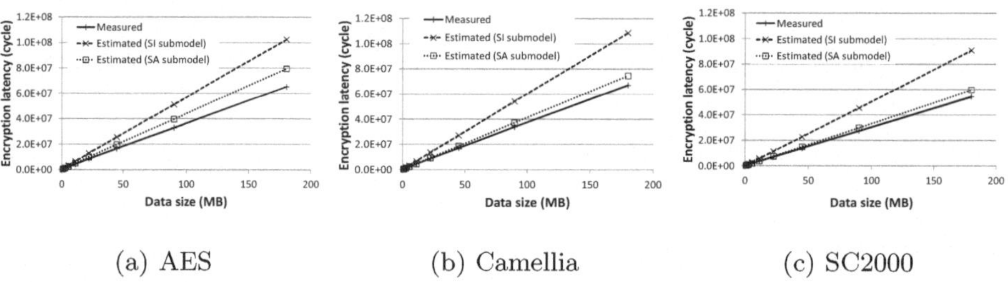

(a) AES (b) Camellia (c) SC2000

Fig. 11. Comparison of measured and the range of estimated encryption latency on Geforce GTX 280

6.4 Discussions

As shown in Fig. 10 and Fig. 11, comparisons between the measured latencies and the range of estimated encryption latencies on GTX 580 and GTX 280 each show different tendencies. In the former GPU, the measured values of three block ciphers are each within the range of estimated latencies. In the latter GPU, the measured values are each slightly below the estimated value based on the SA submodel. This reason results from very different instruction sets of the two GPUs (GTX 580: Fermi instruction set, GTX 280: GT200 instruction set), as published in an Nvidia document[11]. Moreover, assuming that out-of-order scheduling works well on Nvidia GPUs and the estimated values follow the SA submodel, the model predicted overall encryption latencies of three block ciphers with 8.8–22.0 % error on GTX 280 and particularly did those with 2.0–15.7 % error on GTX 580. Therefore, our prediction model can predict latency of block cipher encryption kernel on recent Nvidia GPUs with absolute accuracy.

As shown in Fig. 10 and Fig. 11, in accordance with comparison of AES and Camellia, irrespective of GPUs, the Camellia latency estimated from the SI submodel is worse than that of AES, which results from the numbers of arithmetic and logical instructions: 642 is for Camellia and 436 is for AES. That difference is reflected in the estimated value based on the SI submodel. Surprisingly, measured latencies of Camellia become nearly the same or less than that of AES because, in Camellia, the arithmetic and logical instructions are almost hidden under the access to tables, key, and plaintext/ciphertext. In fact, Camellia has 144 tables compared to 160 in AES, whereas the numbers of other components with memory access such as key are almost identical. Therefore, Camellia has less margins for latency hiding than AES, but actually 144 table access and the other instructions with memory access in Camellia are sufficient to hide 642 arithmetic and logical instructions which surpasses 432 arithmetic and logical instructions of AES. The SC2000 has 72 tables for the implementation on GTX 580 and 96 tables on GTX 280; each is fewer than those of Camellia. As a result, the latency of arithmetic and logical instructions does not be hidden as much as Camellia. For that reason, we know that the Camellia cipher algorithm benefits considerably from the out-of-order scheduling of Nvidia GPU architectures.

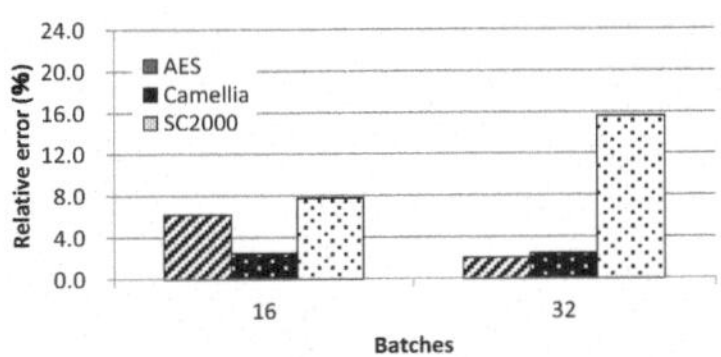

(a) Nvidia Geforce GTX 580

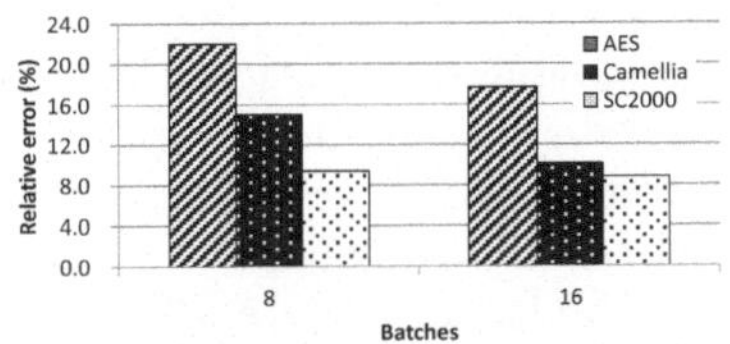

(b) Nvidia Geforce GTX 280

Fig. 12. Relative error between measured overall encryption latency and estimated one based on SA submodel

In the model, the quantities of input components are assessed directly from GPU code as that shown in Fig. 3. The OpenCL compiler optimizes the code, but the impact is absolutely limited only on the numbers of arithmetic and logical instructions because fluctuation of the number of table or key accesses implies generation of the wrong ciphertext. For a similar reason, skill of writing code by programmers also affects only them. However, latency of a arithmetic and logical instruction is less than that of a memory access instruction, as presented in Table 3. Furthermore, using several batches, out-of-order scheduling allows the latencies of arithmetic and logical instructions to be hidden. Therefore, the decrease of the arithmetic and logical instructions caused by the compiler optimization has lesser impact on overall latency. For that reason, this methodology of counting up the quantities of input components of each GPU code is excellent considering the simplicity of modeling.

Our model also supports algebraic and bitslicing implementation[28] for block ciphers because their estimated latencies are calculated based on the SI submodel. For example, bitslicing DES implementation methodology on a GPU was previously reported[29]. However, using a bitslicing implementation on a GPU, programmers have to accept the fact that it does not benefit from out-of-order scheduling effect of GPU architecture, because the implementation methodology includes no memory access to key and tables and then arithmetic and logical instructions are never hidden.

7 Conclusion and Future Works

We developed a performance prediction model of block ciphers on GPU architectures based on vendor-independent OpenCL micro-benchmarks. From the evaluation results, we confirm that the overall encryption latencies are inside of the range of estimated values calculated from our prediction model. Moreover, assuming that out-of-order scheduling works well on Nvidia GPUs, the model predicts overall encryption latencies respectively with 2.0 % and 8.8 % errors for the best case on GTX 580 and GTX 280.

Our future work will evaluate our model on other GPUs such as AMD Radeon HD Graphics and Intel HD Graphics.

References

1. Cryptography Research and Evaluation Committees, http://www.cryptrec.go.jp/english/index.html
2. New European Schemes for Signatures, Integrity and Encryption, https://www.cosic.esat.kuleuven.be/nessie/
3. NVIDIA Corp.: NVIDIA CUDA Programming Guide 4.2 (2012)
4. NVIDIA Corp.: Profiler User's Guide (2012)
5. Khronos Group: Open Compute Language, http://www.khronos.org/
6. National Institute of Standards and Technology (NIST): FIPS-197 Advanced Encryption Standard, AES (2001)
7. Aoki, K., Ichikawa, T., Kanda, M., Matsui, M., Moriai, S., Nakajima, J., Tokita, T.: *Camellia*: A 128-bit block cipher suitable for multiple platforms - design and analysis. In: Stinson, D.R., Tavares, S. (eds.) SAC 2000. LNCS, vol. 2012, pp. 39–56. Springer, Heidelberg (2001)
8. Shimoyama, T., Yanami, H., Yokoyama, K., Takenaka, M., Itoh, K., Yajima, J., Torii, N., Tanaka, H.: The Block Cipher SC2000. In: Matsui, M. (ed.) FSE 2001. LNCS, vol. 2355, pp. 312–327. Springer, Heidelberg (2002)
9. Matsui, M.: How far can we go on the x64 processors? In: Robshaw, M. (ed.) FSE 2006. LNCS, vol. 4047, pp. 341–358. Springer, Heidelberg (2006)
10. NVIDIA Corp.: NVIDIA Nsight Visual Studio Edition 2.2 User Guide (2011)
11. NVIDIA Corp.: cuobjdump Application Note version 03 (2011)
12. Kothapalli, K., Mukherjee, R., Rehman, M.S., Patidar, S., Narayanan, P.J., Srinathan, K.: A performance prediction model for the cuda gpgpu platform. In: Yang, Y., Parashar, M., Muralidhar, R., Prasanna, V.K. (eds.) HiPC, pp. 463–472. IEEE (2009)
13. Guo, P., Wang, L.: Accurate cuda performance modeling for sparse matrix-vector multiplication. In: HPCS, pp. 496–502 (2012)
14. Hong, S., Kim, H.: An analytical model for a gpu architecture with memory-level and thread-level parallelism awareness. In: Proceedings of the 36th Annual International Symposium on Computer Architecture, ISCA 2009, pp. 152–163. ACM, New York (2009)
15. Zhang, Y., Owens, J.D.: A quantitative performance analysis model for gpu architectures. In: HPCA, pp. 382–393 (2011)
16. van der Laan, W.J.: Decuda and Cudasm, the cubin utilities package (2009), https://github.com/laanwj/decuda
17. Collange, S., Daumas, M., Defour, D., Parello, D.: Barra: A parallel functional simulator for gpgpu. In: MASCOTS, pp. 351–360. IEEE (2010)
18. Baghsorkhi, S.S., Delahaye, M., Patel, S.J., Gropp, W.D., Hwu, W.-M.W.: An adaptive performance modeling tool for gpu architectures. In: PPOPP, pp. 105–114 (2010)
19. NVIDIA Corp.: OpenCL Programming Guide for the CUDA Architecture (2012)
20. NVIDIA Corp.: Whitepaper for NVIDIA's Fermi Architecture (2009)
21. AMD Corp.: Reference Guide of Southern Islands Series Instruction Set Architecture (2012)
22. AMD Corp.: AMD Accelerated Parallel Processing OpenCL Programming Guide rev. 2.4 (2012)
23. The IEEE Security in Storage Working Group: XTS block cipher-based mode (XEX-based tweaked-codebook mode with ciphertext stealing), http://siswg.net/

24. Osvik, D.A., Bos, J.W., Stefan, D., Canright, D.: Fast software AES encryption. In: Hong, S., Iwata, T. (eds.) FSE 2010. LNCS, vol. 6147, pp. 75–93. Springer, Heidelberg (2010)
25. Biagio, A.D., Barenghi, A., Agosta, G., Pelosi, G.: Design of a parallel AES for graphics hardware using the CUDA framework. In: International Parallel and Distributed Processing Symposium, pp. 1–8 (2009)
26. Resios, A., Holdermans: GPU performance prediction using parametrized models. Master Thesis of Utrecht University (2009)
27. Wong, H., Papadopoulou, M.M., Sadooghi-Alvandi, M., Moshovos, A.: Demystifying gpu microarchitecture through microbenchmarking. In: 2010 IEEE International Symposium on Performance Analysis of Systems Software, ISPASS, pp. 235–246 (2010)
28. Biham, E.: A fast new DES implementation in software. In: Biham, E. (ed.) FSE 1997. LNCS, vol. 1267, pp. 260–272. Springer, Heidelberg (1997)
29. Agosta, G., Barenghi, A., De Santis, F., Pelosi, G.: Record setting software implementation of des using cuda. In: Proceedings of the 2010 Seventh International Conference on Information Technology: New Generations, ITNG 2010, pp. 748–755 (2010)

Threshold-Oriented Optimistic Fair Exchange

Yang Wang[1], Man Ho Au[1], Joseph K. Liu[2], Tsz Hon Yuen[3], and Willy Susilo[1,⋆]

[1] Centre for Computer and Information Security Research, School of Computer Science and Software Engineering, University of Wollongong, Australia
[2] Cryptography and Security Department, Institute for Infocomm Research, Singapore
[3] Department of Computer Science, University of Hong Kong, Hong Kong
`yw990@uowmail.edu.au`, `{aau,wsusilo}@uow.edu.au`, `ksliu@i2r.a-star.edu.sg`, `thyuen@cs.hku.hk`

Abstract. Fair exchange protocol aims to allow two parties to exchange digital items in a fair manner. It is well-known that fairness can only be achieved with the help of a trusted third party, usually referred to as arbitrator. A fair exchange protocol is optimistic if the arbitrator is not involved in the normal execution of the fair exchange process. That is, its presence is necessary only when one of the exchanging parties is dishonest. Traditionally, the items being exchanged are digital signatures. In this paper, we consider the items to be threshold signatures. Specifically, the signatures are created by a subset of legitimate signers instead of a single signer. We define a security model for this new notion, and provide an concrete instantiation. Our instantiation can be proven secure in the random oracle model. Our definition covers the case when the item being exchanged is a secret key of an identity-based encryption where the master secret key is split amongst a set of authorities.

1 Introduction

Optimistic fair exchange (OFE), first introduced by Asokan, Schunter and Waidner [1], is a kind of protocols aiming to guarantee fairness for two parties exchanging digital items. In OFE, a trusted third party named "arbitrator" is needed but only involved when there is a dispute between the participants. Traditionally the digital items of interest are digital signatures and the optimistic fair exchange of digital signatures constitutes an important part of any business transaction. Typically such a protocol comprises three message flows. First Alice the signer initiates the exchange by sending a partial signature to the receiver, say Bob. The partial signature serves as a commitment assuring Bob of Alice's full signature at the end of the protocol. After verifying the validity of Alice's partial signature, Bob sends its full signature to Alice in the second message flow. Later, Alice should send her full signature back to Bob and complete the exchange. In the case there is a network failure or Alice attempts to cheat by

⋆ This work is supported by ARC Future Fellowship FT0991397.

J. Lopez, X. Huang, and R. Sandhu (Eds.): NSS 2013, LNCS 7873, pp. 424–438, 2013.

refusing to send her own full signature, Bob can ask the arbitrator to make a resolution with Alice's partial signature and his own full signature. In this case the arbitrator will convert Alice's partial signature into a full one and send it back to Bob. Note that at the end of this exchange, either both Alice and Bob gain the other's full signature, or neither does. Thus the exchange is fair.

1.1 Related Work

As a useful tool in applications such as contract signing, electronic commerce and even peer-to-peer file sharing, OFE has been extensively researched since its introduction. There are several approaches in the construction of OFE, including schemes based on verifiably encrypted signatures [2,6,5,16,21,19], and sequentially two-party multisignatures [8]. It was further showed that OFE can be constructed from OR signature [7], and conventional signatures and ring signatures [12]. Some desirable properties such as setup-free [22], stand-alone [22], abuse-free [9], signer ambiguity [11], resolution ambiguity [17] and accountability [13] are proposed in literatures as well.

In [3] and [15], OFE employing multiple arbitrators are discussed to reduce the trust placed on the single arbitrator. Unfortunately, the existing techniques are either expensive or rely on synchronized clocks, which is undesirable as achieving synchronization in a peer-to-peer setting in which the arbitrators do not even know each other is hard.

Most of the previous works on OFE are done in the individual setting, in which the two involving parties are individual users and they represent themselves. An interesting scenario in OFE is that either party consists of a group of users. In such a scenario, every single user in the group can represent its party to execute transactions with another party. In [18], the authors employ a ring signature such that all the group of users' public keys are involved in the ring to ensure that each signer can sign on behalf of the party. Later, optimistic fair exchange of group signatures is considered in [10].

To the best of our knowledge, there is no previous work on OFE discussing about the scenario that only a least number of users together can represent a party. That is, for a party involving a group of n users, only at least t users of them together can sign on behalf of the party and make exchanges with other parties. We introduce the notion of *threshold-oriented optimistic fair exchange* (TOFE), which in essence is optimistic fair exchange of threshold signatures. This can be viewed as a natural way to reduce the trust placed on every single user of the group.

Besides, TOFE has other practical applications. For example, consider the case in which two parties intend to exchange a secret key of an identity-based encryption (IBE) [4]. In an identity-based setting, the key generation centre (KGC) is a high value target to adversaries as compromising the master key will break the whole system. Thus the master key is typically split amongst a set of authorities so that only when a threshold of authorities together can create a secret key for an identity [14]. Remember that the secret key of an identity can be viewed as a digital signature on the user's identity from the KGC [4]. Thus, fair exchange of secret key of an identity-based encryption also falls within the model of OFE. In case when the master key is split amongst a set of authorities and two KGCs, perhaps each for a certain geographic location, would like to exchange a secret key of a specific identity, TOFE would be useful.

The table below summarizes the categories of exchanged digital items that have been discussed in the literatures.

Table 1. digital items that are exchanged in OFE

Schemes	Digial Items Exchanged
traditional OFE	individual signatures
Qu et al. [18]	ring signatures
Huang et al. [10]	group signatures
Our Scheme	threshold signatures / secret keys of an IBE

1.2 Contribution

In this paper, we study optimistic fair exchange in a threshold-oriented setting. Specifically, we present a formal definition for TOFE. We propose a concrete construction and demonstrate that our construction is secure in the random oracle model.

Organization. The rest of the paper is organized as follows. In Section 2, we review notations and technical preliminaries. In Section 3, the syntax of TOFE and its security definitions are presented. We present our construction and prove the security of our construction under well-known assumptions in Section 4. Finally, we conclude our paper in Section 5.

2 Preliminary

If n is a positive integer, we use $[n]$ to denote the set $\{1, \ldots, n\}$. If p is a prime, we use $\mathbb{Z}_p$ to denote the set $\{0, \ldots, p-1\}$ and $\mathbb{Z}_p^*$ to denote the set $\{a | a \in \mathbb{Z}_p \wedge \gcd(a, p) = 1\}$.

2.1 Bilinear Pairing

Let $\mathbb{G}$, $\mathbb{G}_T$ be two cyclic groups such that $|\mathbb{G}| = |\mathbb{G}_T| = p$. We say that $\hat{e}$ is a bilinear map if $\hat{e} : \mathbb{G} \times \mathbb{G} \to \mathbb{G}_T$ possesses the following properties.

- the group operation in $\mathbb{G}$ and the map $\hat{e}$ are both efficiently computable.
- For all elements of $g, h \in \mathbb{G}$, $a, b \in \mathbb{Z}_p$, it holds that

$$\hat{e}(g^a, h^b) = \hat{e}(g, h)^{ab}$$

- There exists $g, h \in \mathbb{G}$ such that $\hat{e}(g, h)$ is not the identity element of $\mathbb{G}_T$.

2.2 Number-Theoretic Assumptions

We review the following well-known computational assumptions.

Definition 1 (DL Assumption). *Let $\mathbb{G} = \langle g \rangle$ be a cyclic group of prime order p. The discrete logarithm assumption states that given a tuple $(g, Z) \in (\mathbb{G}, \mathbb{G})$, it is computationally infeasible to compute the value $z \in \mathbb{Z}_p$ such that $Z = g^z$.*

Definition 2 (CDH Assumption). *Let $\mathbb{G} = \langle g \rangle$ be a cyclic group of prime order p. The computational Diffie-Hellman assumption states that given a tuple $(g, g^a, g^b) \in (\mathbb{G}, \mathbb{G}, \mathbb{G})$, it is computationally infeasible to compute the value g^{ab}.*

2.3 Secret Sharing

We review the principle of the well-known Shamir secret sharing scheme [20] here. Roughly speaking, a secret sharing scheme allows a user to divide a secret into n pieces, called shares, so that any t share holders together can recover the secret. The major idea is that it takes t points to define a polynomial, say, $f(x)$ of degree $t-1$. One could generate f in such a way that $f(0)$ is the secret to be shared. Each share is then a point $(i, f(i))$. Now with t points, one could recover the polynomial and thus the value $f(0)$. On the other hand, with only $t-1$ points, nothing about $f(0)$ would be revealed since there are exponentially many curves that pass through those $t-1$ points.

Preparation Let x be the secret to be shared. Randomly pick a polynomial f of degree $t-1$ such that $f(0) = x$. Each share is defined as $(i, f(i))$ for $i = 1$ to n.

Reconstruction One could make use of Lagrange interpolation to recover the value $f(0)$ when t points are given.

- Let $\mathcal{I}$ be a set such that $|\mathcal{I}| = t$ and that for all $i \in \mathcal{I}$, $f(i)$ is known.
- The Lagrange polynomial interpolation technique states that

$$f(x) := \sum_{i \in \mathcal{I}} f(i)\lambda_i(x),$$

  where $\lambda_i(x)$, called the Lagrange basis polynomials, is defined as

$$\lambda_i(x) := \prod_{j \in \mathcal{I} \setminus \{i\}} \frac{x-j}{i-j}.$$

  Since we are interested in $f(0)$ in the secret sharing scheme, we use λ_i to denote the value of $\lambda_i(0)$ and refer to it as the Lagrange coefficient.
- Thus, to recover the secret, one first computes the Lagrange coefficient λ_i as

$$\lambda_i := \prod_{j \in \mathcal{I} \setminus \{i\}} \frac{-j}{i-j}.$$

- Then, $f(0)$ can be recovered as

$$f(0) := \sum_{i \in \mathcal{I}} f(i)\lambda_i.$$

3 Definition of TOFE

3.1 Syntax

We adapt the definitions and security models of OFE from various literatures for our TOFE. For efficiency consideration, our definition of TOFE consists of non-interactive algorithms only. The following is the syntax of a construction of TOFE, which consists of seven algorithms. In addition, we adopt the common reference string model.

- *Common Reference String Generation* On input a security parameter 1^k, this algorithm outputs a common reference string param_{CRS} which includes the security parameter 1^k. We assume param_{CRS} is an implicit input to all algorithms described below.
- $(\mathsf{pk}_A, \mathsf{sk}_A) \leftarrow \mathsf{AGen}()$ This algorithm outputs the arbitrator key pairs $(\mathsf{pk}_A, \mathsf{sk}_A)$.
- $(\mathsf{pk}_U, \{\mathsf{sk}_{U,i}\}_{i=1}^n) \leftarrow \mathsf{UGen}(n,t)$ This algorithm takes as input the required number of signers n, the threshold t and output the public key of the user pk_U, together with n secret signing keys for the signers $\mathsf{sk}_{U,i}$.
- $\mathsf{PSign} = (\mathsf{PSign}_{(s)}, \mathsf{PSign}_{(v)}, \mathsf{PSign}_{(g)})$ This is a suite of three algorithms which allows a subset of signers to create a partial signature.
  - $\hat{\sigma}_i \leftarrow \mathsf{PSign}_{(s)}(\mathsf{pk}_A, M, \mathsf{sk}_{U,i})$ On input the public key of the arbitrator pk_A, a message M and a secret signing key of signer i, this algorithm outputs a partial signature share for signer i.
  - $\mathtt{valid/invalid} \leftarrow \mathsf{PSign}_{(v)}(\mathsf{pk}_A, \mathsf{pk}_U, M, \hat{\sigma}_i, i)$ On input the public key of the arbitrator pk_A and that of the user pk_U, a message M, a partial signature share $\hat{\sigma}_i$ from signer i, this algorithm checks the validity of the partial signature share created by signer i.
  - $\hat{\sigma} \leftarrow \mathsf{PSign}_{(g)}(\mathsf{pk}_A, \mathsf{pk}_U, M, \{\hat{\sigma}_i\}_{i\in\mathcal{I}}, \mathcal{I})$ On input the public key of the arbitrator pk_A and that of the user pk_U, a message M, t partial signature shares $\{\hat{\sigma}_i\}$ for $i \in \mathcal{I}$ such that $\mathcal{I} \subset [n]$ and $|\mathcal{I}| = t$, this algorithm outputs a partial signature.
- $\mathtt{valid/invalid} \leftarrow \mathsf{PVer}(\mathsf{pk}_A, \mathsf{pk}_U, M, \hat{\sigma})$ This algorithm checks the validity of a partial signature $\hat{\sigma}$ on message M based on the public key of the arbitrator pk_A, the public key of the user pk_U.
- $\mathsf{Sign} = (\mathsf{Sign}_{(s)}, \mathsf{Sign}_{(v)}, \mathsf{Sign}_{(g)})$ Similar to the partial signature generation process, the signing algorithm is also a set of three algorithms which allows a subset of signers to create a signature.
  - $\sigma_i \leftarrow \mathsf{Sign}_{(s)}(\mathsf{pk}_A, M, \mathsf{sk}_{U,i})$ On input public key of the arbitrator pk_A, message M and secret signer key of signer i, this algorithm outputs a signature share for signer i.
  - $\mathtt{valid/invalid} \leftarrow \mathsf{Sign}_{(v)}(\mathsf{pk}_A, \mathsf{pk}_U, M, \sigma_i, i)$ This algorithm checks the validity of the signature share σ_i created by signer i based on the public key of the arbitrator pk_A, the public key of the user pk_U and message M.

- $\sigma \leftarrow \mathsf{Sign}_{(g)}(\mathsf{pk}_A, \mathsf{pk}_U, M, \{\sigma_i\}_{i\in\mathcal{I}}, \mathcal{I})$ On input the public key of the arbitrator pk_A and that of the user pk_U, a message M, t signature shares $\{\sigma_i\}$ for $i \in \mathcal{I}$ such that $\mathcal{I} \subset [n]$ and $|\mathcal{I}| = t$, this algorithm outputs a signature.

– *valid*/*invalid* $\leftarrow \mathsf{Ver}(\mathsf{pk}_A, \mathsf{pk}_U, M, \sigma)$ This algorithm checks the validity of a signature σ on message M based on the public key of the arbitrator pk_A and that of the user pk_U.

– $\sigma \leftarrow \mathsf{Res}(\mathsf{pk}_A, \mathsf{pk}_U, M, \hat{\sigma}, \mathsf{sk}_A)$ Given a valid partial signature $\hat{\sigma}$, a message M, public key of the user pk_U, key pair of the arbitrator $(\mathsf{pk}_A, \mathsf{sk}_A)$, this algorithm allows the arbitrator to output a signature on message M. Note that $\perp$ is returned if `invalid` $\leftarrow \mathsf{PVer}(\mathsf{pk}_A, \mathsf{pk}_U, M, \hat{\sigma})$.

Correctness. A construction of TOFE is correct if the following conditions hold:

1. Any partial signature created by any t honest signers using PSign will be valid under PVer.
2. Any signature created by any t honest signers using Sign will be valid under Ver.
3. Any signature created by the arbitrator using Res based on a valid partial signature will be valid under Ver.

Furthermore, it is required that any signature created by the arbitrator using Res based on a valid partial signature will be indistinguishable from the signature created by any t honest signers using Sign.

3.2 A Typical Usage of the TOFE Algorithms

Note that in OFE with three message flows between the initiator Alice and the receiver Bob, the item to be sent by Bob is not restricted to any format. It could be a digital item such as electronic money. For simplicity we assume the item to be sent by Bob is a digital signature. Nonetheless, it could be a ring signature, a group signature or a threshold signature. Below we show how Alice and Bob can conduct an exchange based on our definition of TOFE. Note that the party Alice in TOFE consists of a group of n signers, and an exchange is possible only when at least t-out-of-n signers agree to participate.

Our definition of TOFE does not require the set of t signers to communicate with each other. Below is a typical usage of our definition of TOFE algorithms.

1. *Partial Signature Shares Collection* Bob approaches each signer independently and the signers agree on the items to be exchanged. The signer, say signer i, invokes $\mathsf{PSign}_{(s)}$ and sends the share of the partial signature $\hat{\sigma}_i$ to Bob. Bob uses $\mathsf{PSign}_{(v)}$ to verify the share.
2. *Partial Signature Generation* Upon collecting t partial signature shares, Bob invokes $\mathsf{PSign}_{(g)}$ to generate a partial signature $\hat{\sigma}$. He invokes PVer to ensure its validity.
3. *Obligation Fulfillment* If the partial signature Bob obtained is valid, he fulfills his obligations. In this example, Bob sends his digital signature to all the signers involved.

4. *Signature Shares Collection* Each signer validates that Bob has fulfilled his obligations. In this example, each signer checks that the digital signature sent by Bob is valid. If yes, each signer, say signer i, invokes $\mathsf{Sign}_{(s)}$ and sends the share of the signature σ_i to Bob, who checks its validity with $\mathsf{Sign}_{(v)}$.
5. *Signature Generation* Upon collecting t signature shares, Bob invokes $\mathsf{Sign}_{(g)}$ to generate a signature σ. He invokes Ver to ensure its validity. If yes, the exchange process is completed.
6. *Resolution* Suppose some signers refuse to send their signature shares, or that the signature created in signature generation is invalid, Bob can approach the arbitrator for assistance. Specifically, he approaches the arbitrator and proves that he has fulfilled his obligation. After that, Bob submits the valid partial signature $\hat{\sigma}$ to the arbitrator. The arbitrator sends back the signature σ by invoking Res and this completes the exchange.
7. *Remarks* In this example, Bob can send his digital signature to the arbitrator as a proof of obligation fulfillment. Even if Bob is lying, the arbitrator can still give this digital signature to the signers should they also complain and thus the exchange could be completed regardless of what happens afterwards.

3.3 Security Model

Traditionally, any construction of optimistic fair exchange should be secure in three aspects, namely, security against signers, security against verifiers and security against the arbitrator respectively. As suggested by the respective names, they intend to cover the scenarios when the named party is dishonest. We modify the traditional model in the threshold setting. Specifically, the verifier can collude with $t-1$ malicious signers in our consideration of security against verifiers.

Security against Signers. This property guarantees that even when all the signers collude together, they cannot create a partial signature that passes the partial signature verification algorithm PVer yet it cannot be resolved into a full signature by the arbitrator. This property intends to protect honest verifiers. Specifically, we use the following three-phase game between a challenger $\mathcal{C}$ and an adversary $\mathcal{A}$ to define this property.

Initialization $\mathcal{A}$ specifies the number of signers n and the threshold t. $\mathcal{C}$ creates the common reference string param_{CRS} and invokes

$$(\mathsf{pk}_A, \mathsf{sk}_A) \leftarrow \mathsf{AGen}(),$$

$$(\mathsf{pk}_U, \{\mathsf{sk}_{U,i}\}_{i=1}^{n}) \leftarrow \mathsf{UGen}(n, t).$$

$\mathcal{C}$ gives $(\mathsf{param}_{CRS}, \mathsf{pk}_A, \mathsf{pk}_U, \{\mathsf{sk}_{U,i}\}_{i=1}^{n})$ to $\mathcal{A}$.

Query $\mathcal{A}$ can adaptively issue the following query to $\mathcal{C}$.

– Res Query. $\mathcal{A}$ gives $(\hat{\sigma}, M)$ to $\mathcal{C}$, who invokes

$$\sigma \leftarrow \mathsf{Res}(\mathsf{pk}_A, \mathsf{pk}_U, M, \hat{\sigma}, \mathsf{sk}_A)$$

and returns σ to $\mathcal{A}$.

End-Game $\mathcal{A}$ submits $(M^*, \hat{\sigma}^*)$ and wins the game if

$$\texttt{valid} \leftarrow \mathsf{PVer}(\mathsf{pk}_A, \mathsf{pk}_U, M^*, \hat{\sigma}^*)$$

$$\texttt{invalid} \leftarrow \mathsf{Ver}(\mathsf{pk}_A, \mathsf{pk}_U, M^*, \mathsf{Res}(\mathsf{pk}_A, \mathsf{pk}_U, M, \hat{\sigma}^*, \mathsf{sk}_A))$$

Security against Verifiers. This property guarantees that even when the verifier colludes with $t-1$ signers, they cannot create a valid full signature. This property intends to protect honest signers. Our model is static in the sense that the subset of signers to be controlled by the attacker is fixed during the initialization phase. Specifically, we use the following three-phase game between a challenger $\mathcal{C}$ and an adversary $\mathcal{A}$ to define this property.

Initialization $\mathcal{A}$ specifies the number of signers n and the threshold t, together with an index set $\mathcal{I}' \subset [n]$ such that $|\mathcal{I}'| = t-1$. $\mathcal{C}$ creates the common reference string param_{CRS} and invokes

$$(\mathsf{pk}_A, \mathsf{sk}_A) \leftarrow \mathsf{AGen}(),$$

$$(\mathsf{pk}_U, \{\mathsf{sk}_{U,i}\}_{i=1}^n) \leftarrow \mathsf{UGen}(n, t).$$

$\mathcal{C}$ gives $(\mathsf{param}_{CRS}, \mathsf{pk}_A, \mathsf{pk}_U, \{\mathsf{sk}_{U,i}\}_{i \in \mathcal{I}'})$ to $\mathcal{A}$.

Query $\mathcal{A}$ can adaptively issue the following query to $\mathcal{C}$.

- $\mathsf{PSign}_{(s)}$ Query. $\mathcal{A}$ gives (M, i) to $\mathcal{C}$, who invokes $\hat{\sigma}_i \leftarrow \mathsf{PSign}_{(s)}(\mathsf{pk}_A, M, \mathsf{sk}_{U,i})$ and returns $\hat{\sigma}_i$ to $\mathcal{A}$.
- $\mathsf{Sign}_{(s)}$ Query. $\mathcal{A}$ gives (M, i) to $\mathcal{C}$, who invokes $\sigma_i \leftarrow \mathsf{Sign}_{(s)}(\mathsf{pk}_A, M, \mathsf{sk}_{U,i})$ and returns σ_i to $\mathcal{A}$.
- Res Query. $\mathcal{A}$ gives $(\hat{\sigma}, M)$ to $\mathcal{C}$, who invokes $\sigma \leftarrow \mathsf{Res}(\mathsf{pk}_A, \mathsf{pk}_U, M, \hat{\sigma}, \mathsf{sk}_A)$ and returns σ to $\mathcal{A}$.

End-Game $\mathcal{A}$ submits $(M^*, \hat{\sigma}^*)$ and wins the game if

$$\texttt{valid} \leftarrow \mathsf{Ver}(\mathsf{pk}_A, \mathsf{pk}_U, M^*, \hat{\sigma}^*)$$

and that $(M^*, \cdot)$ did not appear in any $\mathsf{Sign}_{(s)}$ query. Furthermore, if there exists a $\mathsf{PSign}_{(s)}$ query with input $(M^*, \cdot)$, $(\cdot, M^*)$ should not appear as input in any Res query.

Security against the Arbitrator. This property guarantees that the arbitrator cannot create a signature on behalf of the user unless it is given a valid partial signature. In TOFE, we allow the arbitrator to collude with $t-1$ signers. As in the case of security against verifiers, our model is static in the sense that the subset of signers to be controlled by the attacker is fixed during the initialization phase. Specifically, we use the following three-phase game between a challenger $\mathcal{C}$ and an adversary $\mathcal{A}$ to define this property.

Initialization $\mathcal{A}$ specifies the number of signers n and the threshold t, together with an index set $\mathcal{I}' \subset [n]$ such that $|\mathcal{I}'| = t-1$. $\mathcal{C}$ creates the common reference string param_{CRS} and invokes

$$(\mathsf{pk}_A, \mathsf{sk}_A) \leftarrow \mathsf{AGen}(),$$

$$(\mathsf{pk}_U, \{\mathsf{sk}_{U,i}\}_{i=1}^n) \leftarrow \mathsf{UGen}(n,t).$$

$\mathcal{C}$ gives $(\mathsf{param}_{CRS}, \mathsf{pk}_A, \mathsf{pk}_U, \{\mathsf{sk}_{U,i}\}_{i\in\mathcal{I}'}, \mathsf{sk}_A)$ to $\mathcal{A}$.

Query $\mathcal{A}$ can adaptively issue the following query to $\mathcal{C}$.

- $\mathsf{PSign}_{(s)}$ Query. $\mathcal{A}$ gives (M, i) to $\mathcal{C}$, who invokes $\hat{\sigma}_i \leftarrow \mathsf{PSign}_{(s)}(\mathsf{pk}_A, M, \mathsf{sk}_{U,i})$ and returns $\hat{\sigma}_i$ to $\mathcal{A}$.
- $\mathsf{Sign}_{(s)}$ Query. $\mathcal{A}$ gives (M, i) to $\mathcal{C}$, who invokes $\sigma_i \leftarrow \mathsf{Sign}_{(s)}(\mathsf{pk}_A, M, \mathsf{sk}_{U,i})$ and returns σ_i to $\mathcal{A}$.

End-Game $\mathcal{A}$ submits $(M^*, \hat{\sigma}^*)$ and wins the game if

$$\mathtt{valid} \leftarrow \mathsf{Ver}(\mathsf{pk}_A, \mathsf{pk}_U, M^*, \hat{\sigma}^*)$$

and that $(M^*, \cdot)$ did not appear in any $\mathsf{Sign}_{(s)}$ query nor $\mathsf{PSign}_{(s)}$ query.

4 Construction

Our TOFE is motivated by the ordinary OFE by [5]. Indeed, when $t = n = 1$, our construction degenerates to their scheme.

Common Reference String Our construction works in the common reference string model. For a security parameter 1^k, let $\mathbb{G}$, $\mathbb{G}_T$ be cyclic groups of prime order p with g as a generator of $\mathbb{G}$, where p is a k-bit prime. Further, let $\hat{e} : \mathbb{G} \times \mathbb{G} \rightarrow \mathbb{G}_T$ be a bilinear map. The common reference string is defined to be

$$\mathsf{param}_{CRS} := (1^k, \mathbb{G}, \mathbb{G}_T, p, g, \hat{e}).$$

AGen On input param_{CRS}, the arbitrator picks at random $y \in_R \mathbb{Z}_p$ and computes $Y = g^y$. The public key and secret key of the arbitrator is defined as

$$(\mathsf{pk}_A, \mathsf{sk}_A) := (Y, y).$$

UGen On input param_{CRS}, the required number of signers n and the threshold t, the user picks at random a polynomial of degree $t-1$ in $\mathbb{Z}_p$, say f. Assume the signers are indexed by i, for $i = 1$ to n, with $n \geq t \geq 1$. The user further picks at random a hash function $H : \{0,1\}^* \rightarrow \mathbb{G}$. Note that H is to be modelled as a random oracle.

For $i = 1$ to n, the secret signing key of signer i is defined as $f(i)$.

The user computes the public key as

$$\mathsf{pk}_U := (H, X, X_1, \ldots, X_n) := (H, g^{f(0)}, g^{f(1)}, \ldots, g^{f(n)}).$$

The value $f(0)$, which is the actual master secret, should be deleted. This ensures only a set of t signers together could create a threshold signature.

PSign. The partial signature generation process consists of three sub-algorithms.

- *Generation of a Partial Signature Share* On input param_{CRS}, pk_A, a message M and the signing key of signer i $f(i)$, signer i randomly picks $r_i \in_R \mathbb{Z}_p$ and outputs the partial signature share as
$$\hat{\sigma}_i := (\alpha_i, \beta_i) := \big(H(M)^{f(i)} Y^{r_i}, g^{r_i}\big).$$
- *Verification of a Partial Signature Share* The partial signature share $\hat{\sigma}_i$ can be verified by evaluating the following relation:
$$\hat{e}(\alpha_i, g) \stackrel{?}{=} \hat{e}(H(M), X_i)\hat{e}(Y, \beta_i).$$
- *Generation of a Partial Signature* When t partial signature shares, say, $\hat{\sigma}_i$ for $i \in \mathcal{I} \subset [n]$ such that $|\mathcal{I}| = t$ on the same message, say M, have been collected, anyone can output the partial signature on message M as:
$$\hat{\sigma} := (\alpha, \beta) := (\prod_{i \in \mathcal{I}} \alpha_i^{\lambda_i}, \prod_{i \in \mathcal{I}} \beta_i^{\lambda_i}).$$
where λ_i is defined as
$$\lambda_i := \prod_{j \in \mathcal{I} \setminus \{i\}} \frac{-j}{i-j}.$$
As discussed, $f(0) = \sum_{i \in \mathcal{I}} f(i)\lambda_i$.

PVer. On input param_{CRS}, pk_A, pk_U, a message M and a partial signature $\hat{\sigma}$, the algorithm outputs `valid` if and only if the following equality holds:
$$\hat{e}(\alpha, g) = \hat{e}\big(H(M), X\big)\hat{e}(Y, \beta).$$

Sign. The full signature generation process consists of three sub-algorithms as well.

- *Generation of a Signature Share* On input param_{CRS}, pk_A, a message M and the signing key of signer i $f(i)$, signer i outputs the signature share as
$$\sigma_i := H(M)^{f(i)}.$$
- *Verification of a Signature Share* The signature share σ_i can be verified by evaluating the following relation:
$$\hat{e}(\sigma_i, g) \stackrel{?}{=} \hat{e}(H(M), X_i).$$
- *Generation of a Signature* When t signature shares, say, σ_i for $i \in \mathcal{I} \subset [n]$ such that $|\mathcal{I}| = t$ on the same message, say M, have been collected, anyone can output the signature on message M as:
$$\sigma := \prod_{i \in \mathcal{I}} \sigma_i^{\lambda_i}$$
where λ_i is defined as
$$\lambda_i := \prod_{j \in \mathcal{I} \setminus \{i\}} \frac{-j}{i-j}.$$

Ver. On input param_{CRS}, pk_A, pk_U, a message M and a signature σ, the algorithm outputs `valid` if and only if the following equality holds:

$$\hat{e}(\sigma, g) = \hat{e}(H(M), X).$$

Res. On input param_{CRS}, pk_A, pk_U, a message M, a partial signature $\hat{\sigma}$ and the secret key of the arbitrator y, the full signature can be computed as follows.

- Check that $\hat{\sigma}$ is a valid partial signature by evaluating the relation

$$\hat{e}(\alpha, g) \stackrel{?}{=} \hat{e}(H(M), X)\hat{e}(Y, \beta).$$

- Output σ as

$$\sigma := \alpha/\beta^y.$$

Regarding the security of our construction of TOFE, we have the following theorem.

Theorem 1. *Our construction of TOFE is secure against signers, verifiers and the arbitrator under the CDH assumption in the random oracle model.*

Proof. Security against signers. Given a valid partial signature $\hat{\sigma}^* := (\alpha^*, \beta^*)$ on message M^*, such that

$$\hat{e}(\alpha^*, g) = \hat{e}(H(M^*), X)\hat{e}(Y, \beta^*),$$

the resolved signature σ is defined as $\alpha^*/(\beta^*)^y$ where $Y = g^y$.

Note that

$$\hat{e}(\sigma, g) = \frac{\hat{e}(\alpha^*, g)}{\hat{e}((\beta^*)^y, g)} = \frac{\hat{e}(H(M^*), X)\hat{e}(Y, \beta^*)}{\hat{e}((\beta^*), g^y)} = \hat{e}(H(M^*), X),$$

any valid partial signature will always be resolved to a valid full signature.

Security against verifiers. Suppose the final output of $\mathcal{A}$ is (M^*, σ^*). If $\mathcal{A}$ has not made a $\mathsf{PSign}_{(s)}$ query with input $(M^*, \cdot)$, the analysis of this type of attack is covered in the security against the arbitrator to be discussed later. Thus without loss of generality, we safely assume that $\mathcal{A}$ has made a $\mathsf{PSign}_{(s)}$ query with input $(M^*, \cdot)$. In this setting, we show how to construct a simulator $\mathcal{S}$ that is given $A = g^a$, $B = g^b$ and tries to solve the CDH problem by outputting g^{ab}.

Initialization $\mathcal{A}$ specifies the number of signers n and the threshold t, together with an index set $\mathcal{I}' \subset [n]$ such that $|\mathcal{I}'| = t - 1$. $\mathcal{S}$ sets the common reference string param_{CRS}, $\mathsf{pk}_A = B^y$ for some randomly picked $y \in_R \mathbb{Z}_p$. For each $i \in \mathcal{I}'$, $\mathcal{S}$ picks $s_i \in_R \mathbb{Z}_p$ and computes $X_i = g^{s_i}$. $\mathcal{S}$ sets $X = g^a$. Consider a degree $t-1$ polynomial $f(x)$ such that $f(0) = a$ and $f(i) = s_i$ for $i \in \mathcal{I}'$. Note that the set of points $(0, a) \cup \{(i, s_i)\}_{i \in \mathcal{I}'}$ uniquely determines this polynomial yet the coefficients are unknown to $\mathcal{S}$. However, $\mathcal{S}$ can still compute $X_i = g^{f(i)}$ for $i \in [n] \setminus \mathcal{J}$ where $\mathcal{J} := 0 \cup \mathcal{I}'$ using the Lagrange polynomial interpolation technique discussed in Section 2. Specifically, for $i \in [n] \setminus \mathcal{J}$,

$$g^{f(i)} = g^{\sum_{j \in \mathcal{J}} f(j)\lambda_j(i)} = \prod_{j \in \mathcal{J}} \left(g^{f(j)}\right)^{\lambda_j(i)}.$$

Note that both $\lambda_j(i)$ and $g^{f(j)}$ for all $j \in \mathcal{J}$ are computable by $\mathcal{S}$ and thus $\mathcal{S}$ can compute $X_i = g^{f(i)}$ for all $i = 1$ to n. $\mathcal{S}$ also specifies the random oracle H. pk_U is set to be $(H, X, X_1, \ldots, X_n)$. $\mathcal{S}$ gives $(\mathsf{param}_{CRS}, \mathsf{pk}_A, \mathsf{pk}_U, \{s_i\}_{i \in \mathcal{I}'})$ to $\mathcal{A}$.

Query $\mathcal{A}$ can adaptively issue the following query to $\mathcal{S}$.

- Random Oracle H Query. Suppose $\mathcal{A}$ makes q queries of this type. $\mathcal{S}$ picks an index $z \in [q]$ at random. For the h-th query, $\mathcal{A}$ submits a value M_h and is expecting the value of $H(M_h)$. If $h \neq z$, $\mathcal{S}$ replies with g^{d_h} for a random $d_h \in_R \mathbb{Z}_p$. For the z-th query, $\mathcal{S}$ replies with g^b.
- $\mathsf{PSign}_{(s)}$ Query. $\mathcal{A}$ gives (M, i) to $\mathcal{S}$. Then, $\mathcal{S}$ locates the random oracle H query for M. If there exists h such that $M = M_h$ and that $h \neq z$, $\mathcal{S}$ picks $r \in_R \mathbb{Z}_p$ at random and responses with $(\alpha, \beta) = (Y^r X_i^{d_h}, g^r)$. If M has not been queried, $\mathcal{S}$ makes such a random oracle query on input M. If $M = M_z$, $\mathcal{S}$ responses as follows.
  - Note that each X_i for $i \in [n] \setminus \mathcal{I}'$ is of the form $g^{u_i a + v_i}$ for some constant $u_i \neq 0$, v_i known by $\mathcal{S}$.
  - $\mathcal{S}$ computes r such that $u_i = -yr$.
  - $\mathcal{S}$ randomly picks $t_i \in_R \mathbb{Z}_p$, computes $\beta_i = (g^a)^r g^{t_i}$ and $\alpha_i = (g^b)^{v_i + y t_i}$ and returns (α_i, β_i) to $\mathcal{A}$.
- $\mathsf{Sign}_{(s)}$ Query. $\mathcal{A}$ gives (M, i) to $\mathcal{S}$. If $M = M_z$, $\mathcal{S}$ aborts. Otherwise, $\mathcal{S}$ can locate h such that $H(M) = g^{d_h}$. Next, $\mathcal{S}$ computes $\sigma_i = X_i^{d_h}$ and returns σ_i to $\mathcal{A}$.
- Res Query. $\mathcal{A}$ gives $(\hat{\sigma}, M)$ to $\mathcal{S}$. $\mathcal{S}$ first checks the validity of $\hat{\sigma}$ and proceeds if it is valid. Otherwise it returns $\perp$. Then, $\mathcal{S}$ locates the random oracle H query for M. If $M = M_z$, $\mathcal{S}$ aborts. Otherwise, there exists h such that $H(M) = g^{d_h}$. Next, $\mathcal{S}$ computes $\sigma = X^{d_h}$ and returns σ to $\mathcal{A}$.

End-Game $\mathcal{A}$ submits $(M^*, \hat{\sigma}^*)$. If $M^* \neq M_z$, $\mathcal{S}$ aborts. In the random oracle model, M must have been submitted as an input in the random oracle H-query. Thus, with probability $1/q$, $\mathcal{S}$ does not abort. $\mathcal{S}$ outputs σ as the solution to the CDH problem. Note that in order to win,

$$\hat{e}(\sigma, g) = \hat{e}\big(H(M^*), X\big).$$

It implies that $\sigma = g^{ab}$.

Security against the arbitrator. We show any adversary $\mathcal{A}$ that breaks the security against the arbitrator can be converted into a simulator $\mathcal{S}$ that solves the CDH problem. $\mathcal{S}$ is given $A = g^a$, $B = g^b$ and its goal is to output g^{ab}.

Initialization $\mathcal{A}$ specifies the number of signers n and the threshold t, together with an index set $\mathcal{I}' \subset [n]$ such that $|\mathcal{I}'| = t - 1$. $\mathcal{S}$ sets the common reference string param_{CRS}, $\mathsf{pk}_A = g^y$ for some randomly picked $y \in_R \mathbb{Z}_p$.

For each $i \in \mathcal{I}'$, $\mathcal{S}$ picks $s_i \in_R \mathbb{Z}_p$ and computes $X_i = g^{s_i}$. $\mathcal{S}$ sets $X = g^a$. Consider a degree $t-1$ polynomial $f(x)$ such that $f(0) = a$ and $f(i) = s_i$ for $i \in \mathcal{I}'$. Note that the set of points $(0, a) \cup \{(i, s_i)\}_{i \in \mathcal{I}'}$ uniquely determines this polynomial yet the coefficients are unknown to $\mathcal{S}$. However, $\mathcal{S}$ can still compute $X_i = g^{f(i)}$ for $i \in [n] \setminus \mathcal{J}$ where $\mathcal{J} := 0 \cup \mathcal{I}'$ as

$$g^{f(i)} = g^{\sum_{j \in \mathcal{J}} f(j)\lambda_j(i)} = \prod_{j \in \mathcal{J}} \left(g^{f(j)}\right)^{\lambda_j(i)}.$$

$\mathcal{S}$ also specifies the random oracle H. pk_U is set to be $(H, X, X_1, \ldots, X_n)$. $\mathcal{S}$ gives $(\mathsf{param}_{CRS}, \mathsf{pk}_A, \mathsf{pk}_U, \{s_i\}_{i \in \mathcal{I}'}, y)$ to $\mathcal{A}$.

Query $\mathcal{A}$ can adaptively issue the following query to $\mathcal{S}$.

- Random Oracle H Query. Suppose $\mathcal{A}$ makes q queries of this type. $\mathcal{S}$ picks an index $z \in [q]$ at random. For the h-th query, $\mathcal{A}$ submits a value M_h and is expecting the value of $H(M_h)$. If $h \neq z$, $\mathcal{S}$ replies with g^{d_h} for a random $d_h \in_R \mathbb{Z}_p$. For the z-th query, $\mathcal{S}$ replies with g^b.
- $\mathsf{PSign}_{(s)}$ Query. $\mathcal{A}$ gives (M, i) to $\mathcal{S}$. Then, $\mathcal{S}$ locates the random oracle H query for M. If there exists h such that $M = M_h$ and that $h \neq z$, $\mathcal{S}$ picks $r \in_R \mathbb{Z}_p$ at random and responses with $(\alpha, \beta) = (Y^r X_i^{d_h}, g^r)$. If M has not been queried, $\mathcal{S}$ makes such a random oracle query on input M. If $M = M_z$, $\mathcal{S}$ aborts.
- $\mathsf{Sign}_{(s)}$ Query. $\mathcal{A}$ gives (M, i) to $\mathcal{S}$. If $M = M_z$, $\mathcal{S}$ aborts. Otherwise, $\mathcal{S}$ can locate h such that $H(M) = g^{d_h}$. Next, $\mathcal{S}$ computes $\sigma_i = X_i^{d_h}$ and returns σ_i to $\mathcal{A}$.

End-Game $\mathcal{A}$ submits $(M^*, \hat{\sigma}^*)$. If $M^* \neq M_z$, $\mathcal{S}$ aborts. In the random oracle model, M must have been submitted as an input in the random oracle H-query. Thus, with probability $1/q$, $\mathcal{S}$ does not abort. $\mathcal{S}$ outputs σ as the solution to the CDH problem. Note that in order to win,

$$\hat{e}(\sigma, g) = \hat{e}\big(H(M^*), X\big).$$

It implies that $\sigma = g^{ab}$.

This completes the proof of the theorem. □

5 Conclusion

We present the first threshold-oriented fair exchange protocol which allows a subset of signers to exchange a digital item with a counter party. Indeed, in our specific construction, the item being exchanged is a threshold signature. We define formal security model for TOFE, present an efficient construction and show that it is secure in the random oracle model under well-known assumptions. We leave construction of TOFE in the standard model as an open problem.

References

1. Asokan, N., Schunter, M., Waidner, M.: Optimistic protocols for fair exchange. In: ACM Conference on Computer and Communications Security, pp. 7–17 (1997)
2. Asokan, N., Shoup, V., Waidner, M.: Optimistic fair exchange of digital signatures. In: Nyberg, K. (ed.) EUROCRYPT 1998. LNCS, vol. 1403, pp. 591–606. Springer, Heidelberg (1998)
3. Avoine, G., Vaudenay, S.: Optimistic fair exchange based on publicly verifiable secret sharing. In: Wang, H., Pieprzyk, J., Varadharajan, V. (eds.) ACISP 2004. LNCS, vol. 3108, pp. 74–85. Springer, Heidelberg (2004)
4. Boneh, D., Franklin, M.K.: Identity-based encryption from the weil pairing. In: Kilian, J. (ed.) CRYPTO 2001. LNCS, vol. 2139, pp. 213–229. Springer, Heidelberg (2001)
5. Boneh, D., Gentry, C., Lynn, B., Shacham, H.: Aggregate and verifiably encrypted signatures from bilinear maps. In: Biham, E. (ed.) EUROCRYPT 2003. LNCS, vol. 2656, pp. 416–432. Springer, Heidelberg (2003)
6. Camenisch, J., Damgård, I.: Verifiable encryption, group encryption, and their applications to separable group signatures and signature sharing schemes. In: Okamoto, T. (ed.) ASIACRYPT 2000. LNCS, vol. 1976, pp. 331–345. Springer, Heidelberg (2000)
7. Dodis, Y., Lee, P.J., Yum, D.H.: Optimistic fair exchange in a multi-user setting. In: Okamoto, T., Wang, X. (eds.) PKC 2007. LNCS, vol. 4450, pp. 118–133. Springer, Heidelberg (2007)
8. Dodis, Y., Reyzin, L.: Breaking and repairing optimistic fair exchange from podc 2003. In: DRM 2003, pp. 47–54 (2003)
9. Garay, J.A., Jakobsson, M., MacKenzie, P.D.: Abuse-free optimistic contract signing. In: Wiener, M. (ed.) CRYPTO 1999. LNCS, vol. 1666, pp. 449–466. Springer, Heidelberg (1999)
10. Huang, Q., Wong, D.S., Susilo, W.: Group-oriented fair exchange of signatures. Inf. Sci. 181(16), 3267–3283 (2011)
11. Huang, Q., Yang, G., Wong, D.S., Susilo, W.: Ambiguous optimistic fair exchange. In: Pieprzyk, J. (ed.) ASIACRYPT 2008. LNCS, vol. 5350, pp. 74–89. Springer, Heidelberg (2008)
12. Huang, Q., Yang, G., Wong, D.S., Susilo, W.: Efficient optimistic fair exchange secure in the multi-user setting and chosen-key model without random oracles. In: Malkin, T. (ed.) CT-RSA 2008. LNCS, vol. 4964, pp. 106–120. Springer, Heidelberg (2008)
13. Huang, X., Mu, Y., Susilo, W., Wu, W., Zhou, J., Deng, R.H.: Preserving transparency and accountability in optimistic fair exchange of digital signatures. IEEE Transactions on Information Forensics and Security 6(2), 498–512 (2011)
14. Kate, A., Goldberg, I.: Distributed private-key generators for identity-based cryptography. In: Garay, J.A., De Prisco, R. (eds.) SCN 2010. LNCS, vol. 6280, pp. 436–453. Springer, Heidelberg (2010)
15. Küpçü, A., Lysyanskaya, A.: Optimistic fair exchange with multiple arbiters. In: Gritzalis, D., Preneel, B., Theoharidou, M. (eds.) ESORICS 2010. LNCS, vol. 6345, pp. 488–507. Springer, Heidelberg (2010)
16. Lu, S., Ostrovsky, R., Sahai, A., Shacham, H., Waters, B.: Sequential aggregate signatures and multisignatures without random oracles. In: Vaudenay, S. (ed.) EUROCRYPT 2006. LNCS, vol. 4004, pp. 465–485. Springer, Heidelberg (2006)

17. Markowitch, O., Kremer, S.: An optimistic non-repudiation protocol with transparent trusted third party. In: Davida, G.I., Frankel, Y. (eds.) ISC 2001. LNCS, vol. 2200, pp. 363–378. Springer, Heidelberg (2001)
18. Qu, L., Wang, G., Mu, Y.: Optimistic fair exchange of ring signatures. In: Rajarajan, M., Piper, F., Wang, H., Kesidis, G. (eds.) SecureComm 2011. LNICST, vol. 96, pp. 227–242. Springer, Heidelberg (2012)
19. Rückert, M., Schröder, D.: Security of verifiably encrypted signatures and a construction without random oracles. In: Shacham, H., Waters, B. (eds.) Pairing 2009. LNCS, vol. 5671, pp. 17–34. Springer, Heidelberg (2009)
20. Shamir, A.: How to share a secret. Commun. ACM 22(11), 612–613 (1979)
21. Zhang, J., Mao, J.: A novel verifiably encrypted signature scheme without random oracle. In: Dawson, E., Wong, D.S. (eds.) ISPEC 2007. LNCS, vol. 4464, pp. 65–78. Springer, Heidelberg (2007)
22. Zhu, H., Bao, F.: Stand-alone and setup-free verifiably committed signatures. In: Pointcheval, D. (ed.) CT-RSA 2006. LNCS, vol. 3860, pp. 159–173. Springer, Heidelberg (2006)

Secure Storage and Fuzzy Query over Encrypted Databases

Zheli Liu[1], Haoyu Ma[1], Jin Li[2], Chunfu Jia[1,*], Jingwei Li[1], and Ke Yuan[1]

[1] College of Information Technical Science, Nankai University
{liuzheli,hyma,cfjia,lijw,keyuan}@nankai.edu.cn
[2] School of Computer Science, Guangzhou University
lijin@gzhu.edu.cn

Abstract. Outsourcing database has attracted much attention recently due to the emergence of Cloud Computing. However, there are still two problems to solve, 1) how to encipher and protect the sensitive information before outsourcing while keeping the database structure, and 2) how to enable better utilization of the database like fuzzy queries over the encrypted information. In this paper we propose a new solution based on format-preserving encryption, which protects the privacy of the sensitive data and keeps the data structure as well in the encrypted database. We also show how to perform fuzzy queries over such enciphered data. Specially, our scheme supports fuzzy queries by simply exploiting the internal storing and query mechanism of the databases, thus the influence on both the inner relation of databases and the construction of applications are minimized. Evaluation indicates that our scheme is able to efficiently perform fuzzy query on encrypted database.

1 Introduction

In recent years, the blossoming of internet and the rise of cloud computing makes outsourced (or remote) database a popular choice for applications. Meanwhile, since in practice oursourced databases are considered as running on some untrusted servers, privacy of data in such databases has becoming a major concern for network users. An extreme case of the problem is remotely stored sensitive information, for the consequence of leaking such data can be severe. Accordingly, protecting sensitive information in outsourced databases has become a burning problem needed to be solved.

To encipher on databases where massive data are processed frequently, symmetry ciphers (or block ciphers) becomes the most obvious choice. The problem is, traditional block ciphers have the following problems: (1) If the length of the plaintext is not a multiple of that of the cipher's block, the ciphertext will be longer than the plaintext, called *ciphertext expansion.* (2) All plaintexts, regardless of their types and formats, are simply treated as binary strings. It means that the types and formats of ciphertexts are uncontrollable.

* Corresponding author.

J. Lopez, X. Huang, and R. Sandhu (Eds.): NSS 2013, LNCS 7873, pp. 439–450, 2013.

As a result, applying such block ciphers requires changing either the innards of databases or the basic structure of applications (which come at tremendous cost). Otherwise, the enciphered data could not be stored properly. Enciphering will also disrupt characteristics of the original data. In this way, it will be unable to perform many common database operations such as SQL query, data sorting, statistical analysis and data collection. This makes database encryption a disaster for system designing, since anything involves the mentioned database operations cannot work. Conversely, for ensuring availability, such problem becomes a main restriction in providing systematic protection for sensitive information.

Related works. The notion of *format-preserving encryption* (FPE) [4] was proposed to design block ciphers whose output could fit the requirement of different applications like databases. Black and Rogaway (2002) formalized the FPE problem, and proposed three basic methods for implementing such cipher [7]. Several FPE schemes [5, 18, 21, 22, 28] with provable-security have been presented in the last decade, such as *FFSEM*, *Thorp Shuffle*, *FFX mode* and *Swap-or-not* et al. The idea of FPE is to encipher target data without disrupting their format, which makes it a promising solution for protecting sensitive information on databases.

Table 1. A brief summary on the existing cryptographic methods of supporting queries over enciphered data in database

method	requires index	supports exact query	supports fuzzy query
Hacigumus et. al. [16]	Yes	Yes	No
Amanatidis et. al. [2]	No	Yes	No
Bao et. al. [3]	Yes	Yes	No
Evdokimov et. al. [13]	No	Yes	No
Ge et. al. [14]	Yes	Yes	No
Wang et. al. [32]	No	Yes	Partial
Yang et. al. [34]	Yes	Yes	No
Raluca et. al. [26]	Yes	Yes	Partial

On the other hand, several cryptographic tools were also developed in order to provide solutions for operating on encrypted databases, such as *order-preserving encryption* for sorting enciphered data [1, 8], and *homomorphic encryption* for performing any function computations [12, 15]. Specifically, researchers have developed schemes for searching keywords over encrypted data [9, 11, 27] and processing queries on encrypted databases [2, 3, 13, 14, 16, 26, 32, 34]. Although these works have provided some methods to solve the outsourcing database problem, as shown in Table 1, they are impractical: (1) the methods from [2],[13] and [32] works without changing innards of databases. However, [2] and [13] provide only equality comparisons, while [32] is only able to acquire a coarse result from fuzzy querying over enciphered data, precise matching still needs to be done over deciphered data ; (2) the symmetry searchable encryption methods (as [9, 11, 20, 27, 29–31]) require severs for data storage to be capable of performing test operations for querying, therefore they are impractical for databases where such operations are not supported; (3) other methods need to change the innards of databases, due to the need of maintaining indexes on the data at the server, meanwhile fuzzy queries are still not supported.

Considering sensitive information (e.g. name, ID, account, password, e-mail and address) exists in the form of character data, and are usually required to be queryable, how to perform SQL queries (especially fuzzy queries due to the practical utility) on enciphered character data is certainly a critical problem in designing protection mechanism for such information. Though many existing work were proposed as mentioned, they are still insufficient to support such complex queries in a practical and efficient way.

Our contributions. In this paper, we propose a secure system model for outsourced database by introducing the cryptographic notions of FPE and universal hashing. We also show how to support fuzzy query over the enciphered data. Unlike existing work, the proposed model is database-independent since: (1) we exploit FPE to ensure the encipherment do not change the format of data; (2) we maintain the assistant messages for searching enciphered data by adding extra fields to the database instead of making more fundamental modifications; (3) it supports fuzzy queries on the basis of database inner query mechanism.

We propose a scheme for the proposed model. The scheme supports fuzzy queries on the enciphered data by transforming their SQL statements from searching for patterns of the data. It generates keywords for each character and forms keyword strings of the same length as the corresponding data, thus it performs fuzzy query at a cost of $O(n)$ times of AES and negligible redundancies in the query results. Generally the scheme is practically secure, while there exists a potentially of leaking semantical structure of the enciphered data.

2 System Model

2.1 Our Model

Our system model provides secure modules for the application, which handles security-involved processes, respectively are enciphering, deciphering and what we called *query interpretation*. The purpose is to implement secure storage and basic queries (in specific, exact queries and fuzzy queries) over sensitive information, without deciphering data in advance, or changing either the inner relations of present databases or the construction of application systems. For each encrypted data field in databases, an extra keyword field is added to maintain the corresponding keyword strings.

Two secure modules are in our model consist. One is enciphering/deciphering module, which handles data storage to the databases (connected with enciphering), and responding for queries from the applications (connected with deciphering). On enciphering, the module takes string data from the applications, then generates its keyword string so that all substrings of the data can be represented using the keywords. After that, the module enciphers the data, and respectively stores the ciphertext into the target field of the database, and the keyword string

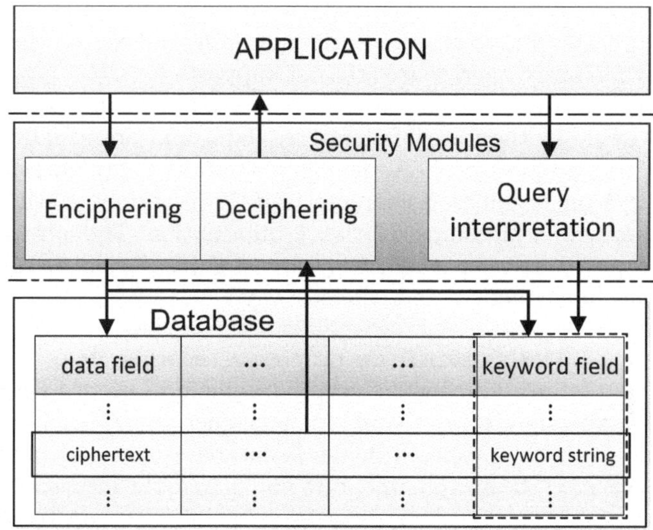

Fig. 1. System model of secure storage and fuzzy query over encrypted database

into the corresponding keyword field. The deciphering part is simpler, when the module receives encrypted records from the database as the result of queries, it directly deciphers data in the records and send them to the application. The other is query interpretation module, which explains the queries into that on the encrypted data. Using the same method as the former module, it transforms terms in the original query into combinations of keywords, and generates a new query where such combinations are used as terms, which searches for matches on the keyword field instead of directly for the data.

Implementation requirements. The main purpose of the proposed model is to support fuzzy query on encrypted databases, considering the practice, certain requirements need to be emphasized: 1) For exploiting the query mechanism of the database itself in performing secure fuzzy query, the keyword strings generated for the enciphered data must be stored in *nvarchar* fields. 2) To minimize the storage burden caused to databases, the keyword strings should not be too long (expected to be less than 512 characters).

Advantages. Overall, the proposed model has the following advantages over existing work: (1) it stands independently, neither the encipher/decipher nor the query interpretation process needs any specific constructional support from the target databases. Thus it's considered to be database-independent. (2) since adding new field to a database do not affect its original construction, the proposed model can be applied in reforming existing databases without making any fundamental modification, thus significantly reduce the reform cost. This makes it highly practical.

2.2 Security Notions

Firstly, the challenge scenario of the problem should be declared. In this paper, the enciphered data and the keyword strings are supposed to be stored in the same unprotected database (or say, untrusted server), where the adversary is assumed to be fully authorized to access any data. Therefore, no auxiliary protection from any part of the system other than our model, is expected.

As mentioned above, unprotected data never appears in the communication between the security modules and the database. In another word, even if an adversary breaks into the database and observes communications between the database and the middleware, it learns nothing but enciphered information. Therefore, an adversary can only perform ciphertext-only attack. This means that traditional attack modes on symmetry ciphers, such as known plaintext attack (KPA), chosen plaintext attack (CPA) and chosen ciphertext attack (CCA), have no practical meaning against this model.

However, as a famous work on cryptographic schemes for querying enciphered data, Song et. al. once termed a few useful security notions for the scenario [27], respectively are: (1) *Query isolation*, meaning that the untrusted server cannot learn anything more about the plaintext than the search result; (2) *Controlled searching*, meaning that the untrusted server cannot search for an arbitrary word without the user's authorization; (3) *Hidden queries*, meaning that the user may ask the untrusted server to search for a secret word without revealing the word to the server.

The above notions are used in describing the security of our scheme.

3 Technical Preliminaries

3.1 Format-Preserving Encryption

We will first give a review to the classical definition of FPE [4], which is described as follows:

Definition 1 (FPE). *A format-preserving encryption scheme is a function*

$$F : \mathcal{K} \times \mathcal{N} \times \mathcal{T} \times \mathcal{X} \to \mathcal{X} \times \{\perp\}, \tag{1}$$

where $\perp \neq \mathcal{X}$, and nonempty sets $\mathcal{K}$, $\mathcal{N}$, $\mathcal{T}$, $\mathcal{X}$ are respectively called the key space, format space, tweak space *and* domain.

3.2 Universal Hash Function

Universal hash functions (or UTF), which was first introduced by Carter and Wegman [10, 33], can be described as:

Definition 2 (UTF-1). *Define M, K and b the bit length of the message, the key and the output, denote $\mathcal{R} = \{0,1\}^K$, $\mathcal{X} = \{0,1\}^M$ and $\mathcal{Y} = \{0,1\}^b$, a universal hash function, denote as $h(k,m)$, is then described a function*

$$F_{uh} : \mathcal{R} \times \mathcal{X} \to \mathcal{Y} \tag{2}$$

for any $k \in \mathcal{R}$ and $m \in \mathcal{X}$.

Normally, the requirement of a UHF is that for any pair of distinct messages $m, m_0 \in \mathcal{X}$, the collision probability $h(k,m) = h(k,m_0)$ is small when key k is randomly chosen from $\mathcal{R}$, described as:

Definition 3 (UTF-2). *An ϵ_d-balanced and ϵ_c-almost universal hash function, $F_{uh} : \mathcal{R} \times \mathcal{X} \rightarrow \mathcal{Y}$, satisfies*

$$\begin{cases} \forall\, m \in \mathcal{X}/\{0\}, y \in \mathcal{Y} : Pr_{\{k \in \mathcal{R}\}}[h(k,m) = y] \leqslant \epsilon_d \\ \forall\, m, m^{'} \in \mathcal{X}(m \neq m^{'}) : Pr_{\{k \in \mathcal{R}\}}[h(k,m) = h(k,m^{'})] \leqslant \epsilon_c \end{cases} \tag{3}$$

3.3 Notations

Throughout the rest of the paper, let $Chars$ be the set of all possible characters, and $Chars^*$ be character strings over $Chars$ of any length. Given any two character strings $A, B \in Chars^*$, denote $A \parallel B$ as their concatenation, therefore $\forall\, X \in Chars^* \Leftrightarrow X = x_1 \parallel x_2 \parallel \cdots \parallel x_i \parallel \cdots \parallel x_*, x_i \in Chars$. Since fuzzy query is involved in our model, denote "%" as the wildcard used in the queries, which is also treated as a character.

Moreover, given secret keys $k_1 \in \mathcal{KS}_1, k_2 \in \mathcal{KS}_2, k_3 \in \mathcal{KS}_3$, where $\mathcal{KS}_1$,$\mathcal{KS}_2$, $\mathcal{KS}_3$ are *key spaces*, we define the following functions:

- $E_{k_1}(\cdot)$ and $E^{'}_{k_1}(\cdot)$ denote FPE schemes for character strings, which take in a character string and return an enciphered string of the same length and size.
- $H_{k_2}(\cdot)$ denotes a short-output UHF, which takes in a for fixed-length (say n bits) binary string and returns a 2-byte digest. In correspondence to function H, we let DIG be the set of all possible digests.
- $P_{k_3}(\{\cdot\})$ denotes a key-based pseudo-random permutation (or PRP) on an arbitrary set.
- $Exp(\cdot)$ denotes a string expansion function, for expanding any l-bit binary string μ ($l \leqslant n$) into an n-bit binary string by:

$$Exp(\mu) \leftarrow \mu \parallel \overbrace{11 \cdots 1}^{n-l \text{ bits}} . \tag{4}$$

- $Ksg(\cdot)$ denotes a keyword generater, which takes a digest generated by H, and transforms it into a unicode character (a keyword). Each distinct 2-byte digest is represented with a unique character by $Ksg(\cdot)$.

Finally, for concision, we now denote $DATA$ as the data field in the database for storing enciphered character strings, and $KeyW$ as the keyword field, where keyword strings of data in $DATA$ are kept.

4 Practical Scheme for Our Model

In this section, we give a detailed scheme for the proposed model.

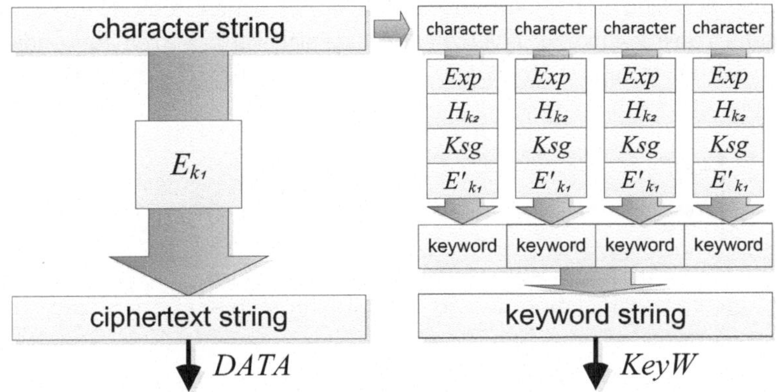

Fig. 2. Demonstration of storage procedure (given a character string of 4 characters)

4.1 Our Scheme

Since the system model consists of two modules, our scheme is described by a storage procedure and a querying procedure.

Storage procedure. As demonstrated in Figure 2, for a character string $D = d_1 \parallel d_2 \parallel \cdots \parallel d_n$, the storage procedure includes a keyword generation process (denote as $\mathcal{KG}_{\mathcal{A}}$) and an enciphering process (denote as $EncA$), respectively described as:

Definition 4 **($\mathcal{KG}_{\mathcal{A}}$).** *Given secret keys k_1 and k_2, the keywords generater $\mathcal{KG}_{\mathcal{A}}$ sets D's keywords by*

$$\mathcal{KG}_{\mathcal{A}}(D, k_1, k_2) = \{ka_1, ka_2, ..., ka_n\}, \tag{5}$$

where

$$\forall\, 1 \leqslant i \leqslant n, ka_i \leftarrow E^{'}_{k_1}(Ksg(H_{k_2}(Exp(d_i)))). \tag{6}$$

Definition 5 **($EncA$).** *Given FPE schemes $E_{k_1}(\cdot)$ and $E^{'}_{k_1}(\cdot)$ and master key $k_m = k_1 \parallel k_2$, for plaintext D, enciphering process of scheme A is described as:*

$$(D^{'}, KW_D) \leftarrow EncA_{k_m}(D), \tag{7}$$

where

$$\begin{cases} D^{'} \leftarrow E_{k_1}(D) \\ KW_D = ka_1 \parallel \cdots \parallel ka_n, ka_* \in \mathcal{KG}_{\mathcal{A}}(D, k_1, k_2) \end{cases}. \tag{8}$$

After the above processes, the scheme inserts/updates a record in the database, where the value of $DATA$ is D's ciphertext $D^{'}$, and the value of $KeyW$ is the keyword string KW_D.

Fuzzy query procedure. It is supposed that applications know the fact that enciphered data are stored in $DATA$, but can still only search for unencrypted patterns with statements described in section 3.3. Let the data aimed by the searched pattern be $SeD = sd_1 \parallel \cdots \parallel sd_t, sd_* \in Chars$. Assume pattern is:

$$\begin{cases} keyw_1 = sd_1 \parallel \cdots \parallel sd_{i_1} \\ keyw_2 = sd_{i_2} \parallel \cdots \parallel sd_{i_3} \\ keyw_3 = sd_{i_4} \parallel \cdots \parallel sd_n \end{cases}, 1 \leqslant i_1 < i_2 < i_3 < i_4 \leqslant n, \tag{9}$$

the query interpretation module will extract the terms, and generate their corresponding keyword strings by:

$$\begin{cases} keyw_1^{'} \leftarrow \mathbf{ka}_1 \parallel \cdots \parallel \mathbf{ka}_{i_1} \\ keyw_2^{'} \leftarrow \mathbf{ka}_{i_2} \parallel \cdots \parallel \mathbf{ka}_{i_3} \\ keyw_3^{'} \leftarrow \mathbf{ka}_{i_4} \parallel \cdots \parallel \mathbf{ka}_n \end{cases} \tag{10}$$

where $\mathbf{ka}_* \in \mathcal{KG}_{\mathcal{A}}(SeD)$.

After that, the module interprets the original query sentence into

select $*$ from $Table$ where $KeyW$ like '$keyw_1^{'}\%keyw_2^{'}\%keyw_3^{'}$'

which is able to find $D^{'}$ (as mentioned above, the ciphertext of D) from $DATA$, while both $DATA$ and $KeyW$ remains enciphered during the procedure. The result is handed to the deciphering module of the model, which recovers D and send it to the applications.

4.2 Security Analysis

In consideration of provable security, we suggest using existing FPE and UHF schemes in our model. Options for FPE schemes include FFX [5] and *generalized Numeric Feistel*[19], since the security bound of such structures has already been proved to be strong [24, 25]. Different FPE schemes are required respectively for enciphering data and keywords. Besides the reason that schemes like FFX cannot work on single characters, such deployment also increases security of the scheme. For the UHF function, several short-output schemes, like *MMH*[17], *NH*[6] and *digest()*[23], are available, whose main properties are given in Table 2.

Cryptographically, the ciphertext and keyword string of a data are generated in two independent procedures. Although the same key k_1 is shared, the FPE schemes in the two procedures are completely different. Additionally, due to the UHF invoked in generating keywords, given the ciphertext and the keyword

Table 2. A summary on the main properties of digest(), MMH and NH

Scheme	Key length	ϵ_c	ϵ_d	Output length
MMH	M	6×2^{-b}	2^{2-b}	b
NH	M	2^{-b}	2^{-b}	$2b$
digest()	$M + b$	2^{1-b}	2^{-b}	b

string, the adversary cannot learn anything about the plaintext, or the relation between the keywords and the ciphertext. I.e., the security of enciphered data can be reduced to that of the FPE schemes $E_{k_1}(\cdot), E^{'}_{k_1}(\cdot)$, and that of the UHF $H_{k_2}(\cdot)$.

Specifically, our scheme

- provides **query isolation** for searches, since the untrusted server can only get access to the ciphertexts and the keyword strings of data;
- provides **controlled searching**, untrusted server is free to search for any keyword or ciphertext, but it is unable to locate a record with a query that search for an unprotected data.
- provides **hidden queries**, since the scheme queries in the implied way (using keywords), unprotected data never appears in such queries.

Remark. In this scheme, the same keyword will be encrypted to the same character (required by its correctness). Therefore, the keyword strings could leak semantic information of the corresponding data. In this case, the adversary can perform frequency attack. However, the frequency attack relies on experience of adversary and the statistical validity of character frequency. Considering the following two practical aspects

- The different sensitive information(For example, postal code in different countries, mailing address in different countries, et al.) may lead to different statistical distribution.
- It is difficult to perform frequency attack when the number of character set is large, because the character frequency statistics becomes hard. For example, the character number of GBK is 21886, which is more bigger than ASCII.

Therefore, considering the tradeoff between efficiency and security, we believe that the scheme provides enough security for the practical characteristic of supporting fuzzy query efficiently.

4.3 Performance Evaluation

First of all, it is easy to see that compared with the storage procedure, query procedure of our scheme works much faster, therefore we will mainly analyze the efficiency of the scheme's storage procedure. Based on the construction, it can be considered that the time cost lies mainly on that of the functions $E_{k_1}(\cdot), E^{'}_{k_1}(\cdot), H_{k_2}(\cdot)$ and $P_{k_3}(\{\cdot\})$. Consider the following implementation:

- Use the FFX mode as $E_{k_1}(\cdot)$, and the unbalanced numeric Feistel as $E^{'}_{k_1}(\cdot)$, where in each Feistel round constructed from CBC-MAC, AES is invoked for 2 times (for security, 6 or more rounds is suggested for both scheme);
- Use any of MMH, NH or digest() as $H_{k_2}(\cdot)$;
- implement $P_{k_3}(\{\cdot\})$ with AES-based Prefix (given in [7]), where for each member of the input set, AES is invoked once.

Since the short-output UHFs available for $H_{k_2}(\cdot)$ are all multiplicative universal hashing in nature, where only addition, multiplication and modular addition for short integers (those can be represented using *short* or *int*) are involved, the time cost of $H_{k_2}(\cdot)$ is negligible compared to the other functions where block cipher is involved in each round.

Suppose both $E_{k_1}(\cdot)$ and $E'_{k_1}(\cdot)$ have 6 rounds, for enciphering a character string of length n needs $n+1$ times of FPE processing, our scheme invokes AES with $12(n+1)$ times. Therefore, given the length n of a character string, our scheme is able to encipher it in a searchable way with $O(n)$ times of AES operations.

5 Conclusion

To protect sensitive information in outsourced databases, we proposed a new model for secure storage on databases, as well as fuzzy query over enciphered data. FPE and UHF were applied in the model for enciphering and keyword generation, while the inner mechanisms of storage and query provided by the database itself are also fully exploited. The model provides an original solution towards data enciphering that supports both format-preserving structure and keyword search. Moreover, we proposed one practical scheme. Analysis indicated that our scheme is secure under the proposed model. Performance evaluation showed that our scheme is efficient and practical.

Acknowledgements. This work is supported by the National Natural Science Foundation of China (Nos. 60973141 and 61272423), National Key Basic Research Program of China (No. 2013CB834204), Fundamental Research Funds for the Central Universities, Specialized Research Fund for the Doctoral Program of Higher Education of China (Nos. 20100031110030 and 20120031120036), and Funds of Key Lab of Fujian Province University Network Security and Cryptology (No. 2011004).

References

1. Agrawal, R., Kiernan, J., Srikant, R., Xu, Y.: Order preserving encryption for numeric data. In: Proceedings of the 2004 ACM SIGMOD International Conference on Management of Data, pp. 563–574. ACM (2004)
2. Amanatidis, G., Boldyreva, A., O'Neill, A.: Provably-secure schemes for basic query support in outsourced databases. In: Barker, S., Ahn, G.-J. (eds.) Data and Applications Security 2007. LNCS, vol. 4602, pp. 14–30. Springer, Heidelberg (2007)
3. Bao, F., Deng, R.H., Ding, X., Yang, Y.: Private query on encrypted data in multi-user settings. In: Chen, L., Mu, Y., Susilo, W. (eds.) ISPEC 2008. LNCS, vol. 4991, pp. 71–85. Springer, Heidelberg (2008)
4. Bellare, M., Ristenpart, T., Rogaway, P., Stegers, T.: Format-preserving encryption. In: Jacobson Jr., M.J., Rijmen, V., Safavi-Naini, R. (eds.) SAC 2009. LNCS, vol. 5867, pp. 295–312. Springer, Heidelberg (2009)

5. Bellare, M., Rogaway, P., Spies, T.: The ffx mode of operation for format-preserving encryption, NIST submission (February 2010)
6. Black, J., Halevi, S., Krawczyk, H., Krovetz, T., Rogaway, P.: UMAC: Fast and secure message authentication. In: Wiener, M. (ed.) CRYPTO 1999. LNCS, vol. 1666, pp. 216–233. Springer, Heidelberg (1999)
7. Black, J., Rogaway, P.: Ciphers with arbitrary finite domains. In: Preneel, B. (ed.) CT-RSA 2002. LNCS, vol. 2271, pp. 114–130. Springer, Heidelberg (2002)
8. Boldyreva, A., Chenette, N., Lee, Y., O'Neill, A.: Order-preserving symmetric encryption. In: Joux, A. (ed.) EUROCRYPT 2009. LNCS, vol. 5479, pp. 224–241. Springer, Heidelberg (2009)
9. Boneh, D., Waters, B.: Conjunctive, subset, and range queries on encrypted data. In: Vadhan, S.P. (ed.) TCC 2007. LNCS, vol. 4392, pp. 535–554. Springer, Heidelberg (2007)
10. Carter, J., Wegman, M.N.: Universal classes of hash functions. Journal of Computer and System Sciences 18(2), 143–154 (1979)
11. Curtmola, R., Garay, J., Kamara, S., Ostrovsky, R.: Searchable symmetric encryption: Improved definitions and efficient constructions. Journal of Computer Security 19(5), 895–934 (2011)
12. van Dijk, M., Gentry, C., Halevi, S., Vaikuntanathan, V.: Fully homomorphic encryption over the integers. In: Gilbert, H. (ed.) EUROCRYPT 2010. LNCS, vol. 6110, pp. 24–43. Springer, Heidelberg (2010)
13. Evdokimov, S., Günther, O.: Encryption techniques for secure database outsourcing. In: Biskup, J., López, J. (eds.) ESORICS 2007. LNCS, vol. 4734, pp. 327–342. Springer, Heidelberg (2007)
14. Ge, T., Zdonik, S.: Fast, secure encryption for indexing in a column-oriented dbms. In: IEEE 23rd International Conference on Data Engineering, pp. 327–342. IEEE (2007)
15. Gentry, C.: Fully homomorphic encryption using ideal lattices. In: Proceedings of the 41st Annual ACM Symposium on Theory of Computing, pp. 169–178. ACM (2009)
16. Hakan, H., Bala, L., Chen, L., Sharad, M.: Executing sql over encrypted data in the database-service-provider model. In: Proceedings of the 2002 ACM SIGMOD International Conference on Management of Data, pp. 216–227. ACM (2002)
17. Halevi, S., Krawczyk, H.: MMH: Software message authentication in the gbit/Second rates. In: Biham, E. (ed.) FSE 1997. LNCS, vol. 1267, pp. 172–189. Springer, Heidelberg (1997)
18. Hoang, V.T., Morris, B., Rogaway, P.: An enciphering scheme based on a card shuffle. In: Safavi-Naini, R., Canetti, R. (eds.) CRYPTO 2012. LNCS, vol. 7417, pp. 1–13. Springer, Heidelberg (2012)
19. Hoang, V.T., Rogaway, P.: On generalized feistel networks. In: Rabin, T. (ed.) CRYPTO 2010. LNCS, vol. 6223, pp. 613–630. Springer, Heidelberg (2010)
20. Li, J., Wang, Q., Wang, C., Cao, N., Ren, K., Lou, W.: Fuzzy keyword search over encrypted data in cloud computing. In: 2010 IEEE INFOCOM, pp. 1–5. IEEE (2010)
21. Li, M., Liu, Z., Li, J., Jia, C.: Format-preserving encryption for character data. Journal of Networks 7(8), 1239–1244 (2012)
22. Morris, B., Rogaway, P., Stegers, T.: How to encipher messages on a small domain: Deterministic encryption and the thorp shuffle. In: Halevi, S. (ed.) CRYPTO 2009. LNCS, vol. 5677, pp. 286–302. Springer, Heidelberg (2009)

23. Nguyen, L.H., Roscoe, A.W.: Short-output universal hash functions and their use in fast and secure data authentication. In: Canteaut, A. (ed.) FSE 2012. LNCS, vol. 7549, pp. 326–345. Springer, Heidelberg (2012)
24. Patarin, J.: Luby-rackoff: 7 rounds are enough for $2^{n(1-\varepsilon)}$ security. In: Boneh, D. (ed.) CRYPTO 2003. LNCS, vol. 2729, pp. 513–529. Springer, Heidelberg (2003)
25. Patarin, J.: Security of random feistel schemes with 5 or more rounds. In: Franklin, M. (ed.) CRYPTO 2004. LNCS, vol. 3152, pp. 106–122. Springer, Heidelberg (2004)
26. Popa, R.A., Redfield, C.M.S., Zeldovich, N., Balakrishnan, H.: Cryptdb: protecting confidentiality with encrypted query processing. In: Proceedings of the Twenty-Third ACM Symposium on Operating Systems Principles, pp. 85–100. ACM (2011)
27. Song, D.X., Wagner, D., Perrig, A.: Practical techniques for searches on encrypted data. In: Proceedings of the 21st IEEE Symposium on Security and Privacy, pp. 44–55. IEEE (2000)
28. Spies, T.: Feistel finite set encryption, NIST submission (February 2008)
29. Wang, C., Cao, N., Li, J., Ren, K., Lou, W.: Secure ranked keyword search over encrypted cloud data. In: IEEE 30th International Conference on Distributed Computing Systems, pp. 253–262. IEEE (2010)
30. Wang, C., Ren, K., Yu, S., Urs, K.: Achieving usable and privacy-assured similarity search over outsourced cloud data. In: 2012 IEEE INFOCOM, pp. 451–459. IEEE (2012)
31. Wang, C., Wang, Q., Ren, K.: Towards secure and effective utilization over encrypted cloud data. In: The 31st International Conference on Distributed Computing Systems Workshops, pp. 282–286. IEEE (2011)
32. Wang, Z.F., Dai, J., Wang, W., Shi, B.L.: Fast query over encrypted character data in database. In: Zhang, J., He, J.-H., Fu, Y. (eds.) CIS 2004. LNCS, vol. 3314, pp. 1027–1033. Springer, Heidelberg (2004)
33. Wegman, M.N., Carter, J.: New hash functions and their use in authentication and set equality. Journal of Computer and System Sciences 22(3), 265–279 (1981)
34. Yang, Z., Zhong, S., Wright, R.N.: Privacy-preserving queries on encrypted data. In: Gollmann, D., Meier, J., Sabelfeld, A. (eds.) ESORICS 2006. LNCS, vol. 4189, pp. 479–495. Springer, Heidelberg (2006)

A Highly Efficient RFID Distance Bounding Protocol without Real-Time PRF Evaluation

Yunhui Zhuang[1], Anjia Yang[1], Duncan S. Wong[1], Guomin Yang[2], and Qi Xie[3]

[1] City University of Hong Kong, Hong Kong
{yhzhuang2-c,ayang3-c}@my.cityu.edu.hk, duncan@cityu.edu.hk
[2] University of Wollongong, Australia
gyang@uow.edu.au
[3] Hangzhou Normal University, China

Abstract. There is a common situation among current distance bounding protocols in the literature: they set the fast bit exchange phase after a slow phase in which the nonces for both the reader and a tag are exchanged. The output computed in the slow phase is acting as the responses in the subsequent fast phase. Due to the calculation constrained RFID environment of being lightweight and efficient, it is the important objective of building the protocol which can have fewer number of message flows and less number of cryptographic operations in real time performed by the tag. In this paper, we propose a new highly efficient mutually-authenticated RFID distance bounding protocol that enables pre-computation which is carried out off-line by the tag. There is no evaluation on any PRF during the real time protocol running which makes the tag significantly more efficient at a low-cost. The protocol requires only O(1) complexity for achieving tag privacy. In addition, we give a detailed security analysis to prove that our protocol is secure against all common attacks in distance bounding.

Keywords: RFID, Distance Bounding, Privacy, Mutual Authentication.

1 Introduction

Radio Frequency IDentification (RFID) technology mainly consists of tags and readers that can be used to identify and encode a variety of information. It has been widely applied in many applications in the modern world. For example, the building access control, library book borrowing services, and E-channel for immigration, etc. In general, there are two types of RFID tags, namely active and passive tags. Active tags contain an internal power source while the low-cost passive tags don't. Nowadays, many RFID-enabled authentication protocols are based on symmetric-key encryption system in order to keep them low-cost.

In 1987, Desmedt et al. [4] introduced the Mafia fraud that could defeat any authentication protocol. An adversary can successfully pass the protocol by

J. Lopez, X. Huang, and R. Sandhu (Eds.): NSS 2013, LNCS 7873, pp. 451–464, 2013.

relaying the messages between the legitimate reader and a remote legitimate tag. One way to prevent such attack is using distance-bounding protocol. It was first designed by Brands and Chaum in 1993 [1]. The concept of distance bounding is based on the combination of distance checking and authentication, under the measurement of the *Round Trip Time* (RTT) of messages exchanged by the reader and a tag. Based on RTT, the reader can evaluate the distance between itself and a tag in order to compare the value with an upper bound which can be estimated according to the assumption that nothing propagates faster than light. Brands and Chaum's protocol is too expensive in practice because there is a signature at the end in order to realize mutual authentication. In 2005, Hancke and Kuhn [2] designed another protocol without the final signature that contains only one slow phase and one fast bit exchange phase. Their protocol has been treated as a key-reference in the state-of-art publications regarding to RFID distance-bounding.

Since then quite a few distance bounding protocols have been published [3,7,8,9,10,11,14,15,16,17]. There are five common attacks in RFID distance bounding scenario: Impersonation fraud [1], Distance fraud [1], Mafia fraud [4], Terrorist fraud [4], and Distance hijacking attack [6]. In this paper, we only consider distance hijacking attack in the single-protocol environment defined in [6]. In 2011, Avoine et al. [5] used secret-sharing scheme to defeat terrorist frauds. They made the conclusion that at least a (3, 3) threshold secret-sharing scheme should be applied to resist terrorist fraud, while most existing works only used (2, 2) schemes that is susceptible to the terrorist fraud attack.

We introduce in this paper a prominent feature called "Pre-Computation" in RFID distance bounding protocols. This idea let us break away from traditional approach that the slow phase should always be ahead of the fast phase. Actually, the computation in the very beginning can be carried out off-line. In fact, the pre-computation in RFID is not new [13], but it has never been deployed in distance bounding. The existing protocols proposed recently require the tag to perform one/more time-consuming PRFs or signatures in real time. It is susceptible to the high power and high cost. The pre-computation is done by an ultra low power micro-controller which is powered by a large capacitor. It has been implemented and proved in [12]. And most important of all, the cost for planting a large capacitor in an RFID tag is negligible.

We find most distance bounding protocols use the idea of the fast bit exchange by transmitting only one-bit challenges for each round. In fact, the communication channels used in nowadays have a much bigger bandwidth to transmit more than one bit. As pointed out in [16], the two-bit challenges sent in the fast phase can be encapsulated to a much bigger packet over the communication channels. In addition, [18] pointed out a practical terrorist attack to the protocol proposed by Yang et al.[15] due to only one-bit challenges sent in each round. Having these observations in mind, our proposed protocol is designed by adopting two-bit challenges in the fast phase in order to prevent such attacks and make better use of the communication channels.

Our Contributions
In this paper, we combine all the features described above in an RFID authentication system and propose a highly efficient RFID distance bounding protocol with tag privacy.

The protocol features pre-computation on the tag, mutual authentication, resistance to all common attacks, and significantly more efficient at a low cost. It eliminates all online PRF evaluation and leaves only two if-else decisions to make in runtime for the tag. One more advantage of this elimination can minimize the processing time for response and make the propagation time of the bits dominate the round trip time (RTT), and at the same time, make the response processing time as invariant as possible. Consequently, we can get a more accurate estimation on the distance between the reader and a tag. To the best of our knowledge, our protocol is the first distance bounding protocol that realizes the tag online PRF-free by introducing the concept of pre-computation.

We also provide privacy-preserving in our protocol by an anonymous way, which requires only O(1) complexity for achieving privacy. We show our protocol is much more efficient in terms of tag's cost when compared with existing ones.

To show our contributions more precisely, we make a detailed comparison between our proposed protocol and others in Table 2, Section 4.

Paper Organization
The rest of the paper is organized as follows. In Section 2, we show our protocol with detailed description. In section 3, we give the security analysis with respect to the five attacks and how reader authentication is realized. In section 4, there will be a comparison between our protocol and previous proposed protocols. In the last section, we conclude the paper.

2 Our Proposed Protocol

In this section, we first give some preliminaries including the system description, the adversary model, and the definition of Pseudo-Random Function that we used as the underlying cryptographic primitive. Then we describe our proposed protocol in detail. At last, we have a discussion of several important issues in our protocol.

2.1 Preliminaries

System Description. The RFID system consists of multiple tags T_1,T_2,$\cdots$,T_n and a reader R, associated with a database. Each tag T_i stores a secret key x_i which is shared with the reader R, its identity ID, pseudonym ID', as well as the counter N_T which is initialized to zero. The reader maintains tag's identity ID, counter N'_T as well. In addition, the reader also maintains TID and TID' for achieving tag privacy. The reader and a tag communicate via the wireless channel. The upper bound for the transmission speed cannot exceed the speed of light.

Adversary's Capabilities. It is important to define a generic model for adversary's capabilities in a realistic and fair condition. In our model, an adversary $\mathcal{A}$ can be "active" which means she can eavesdrop, intercept, modify messages. $\mathcal{A}$ can control the transmission time between the reader and a tag. But $\mathcal{A}$ cannot perform unlimited computations. In addition, we assume that an honest tag will not give its security parameters to any third party.

Pseudo-random Function. Our protocol uses an *Pseudo-Random Function* (PRF) as the underlying cryptographic primitive. A family of efficiently computable functions $\boldsymbol{f} = \{F_K : \mathcal{D} \rightarrow \mathcal{R} | K \in \mathcal{K}\}$ is called a pseudo-random function family, if for any polynomial time algorithm $\mathcal{C}$,

$$\mathbf{Adv}^{prf}_{\boldsymbol{f},\mathcal{C}}(k) = \mathbf{Pr}[\mathcal{C}^{F_K(\cdot)}(1^k) = 1] - \mathbf{Pr}[\mathcal{C}^{\mathsf{RF}(\cdot)}(1^k) = 1].$$

is a negligible function of the security parameter k, where K is randomly selected from the key space $\mathcal{K}$, F_K is an instance of function family $\boldsymbol{f}$, and $\mathsf{RF} : \mathcal{D} \rightarrow \mathcal{R}$ is a truly random function.

2.2 Protocol Description

Our protocol has two stages, namely the pre-computation stage and real-time stage as shown in Figure 1.

Pre-computation Stage. We introduce two flag bits to facilitate the steps during the pre-computation stage: $Flag^{pre}$ and $Flag^{sync}$, where the former indicates whether the pre-computation has been done successfully; while the latter is to determine whether the reader authentication was successful in last execution. The $Flag^{pre}$ should be set to 1 before performing the pre-computation by the tag. In the meantime, $Flag^{sync}$ has to be 1 before updating pseudonym ID'.

We use a counter N_T (initialized to zero) as one of the three inputs to compute the Pseudo-Random Function (PRF) f and N_T should be updated each time at the very beginning whenever the tag is powered up. It is also worth mentioning that N_T cannot be a random number. Otherwise, it may suffer from the replay attack due to the absence of reader's nonce.

Because the contents of the input for computing of f and ID' are independent from the reader. Therefore, they can be computed before the protocol starts. This stage can cope with the limited resources of RFID tags, who will compute $v = f(x, ID, N_T)^{3n}$. Then split v into three shares: v^1, v^2, and v^3, respectively. Each of them carries n bits. After that the tag needs to check the value of $Flag^{sync}$ such that it will update ID' in pre-computation only when $Flag^{sync}=1$, which means the reader authentication was successful in the last execution. The update is computed as $ID' = f(x, ID')$. In the meanwhile, the tag is going to flip $Flag^{pre}$ to 0 indicating that the pre-computation has been finished. The tag now has the updated value of v^1, v^2, v^3, and k for running the real-time stage.

The pre-computation is carried out off-line as follows: by using an ultra low power micro-controller and a large capacitor, each time during the protocol running, the tag will receive enough RF (Radio Frequency) energy and rectifies it

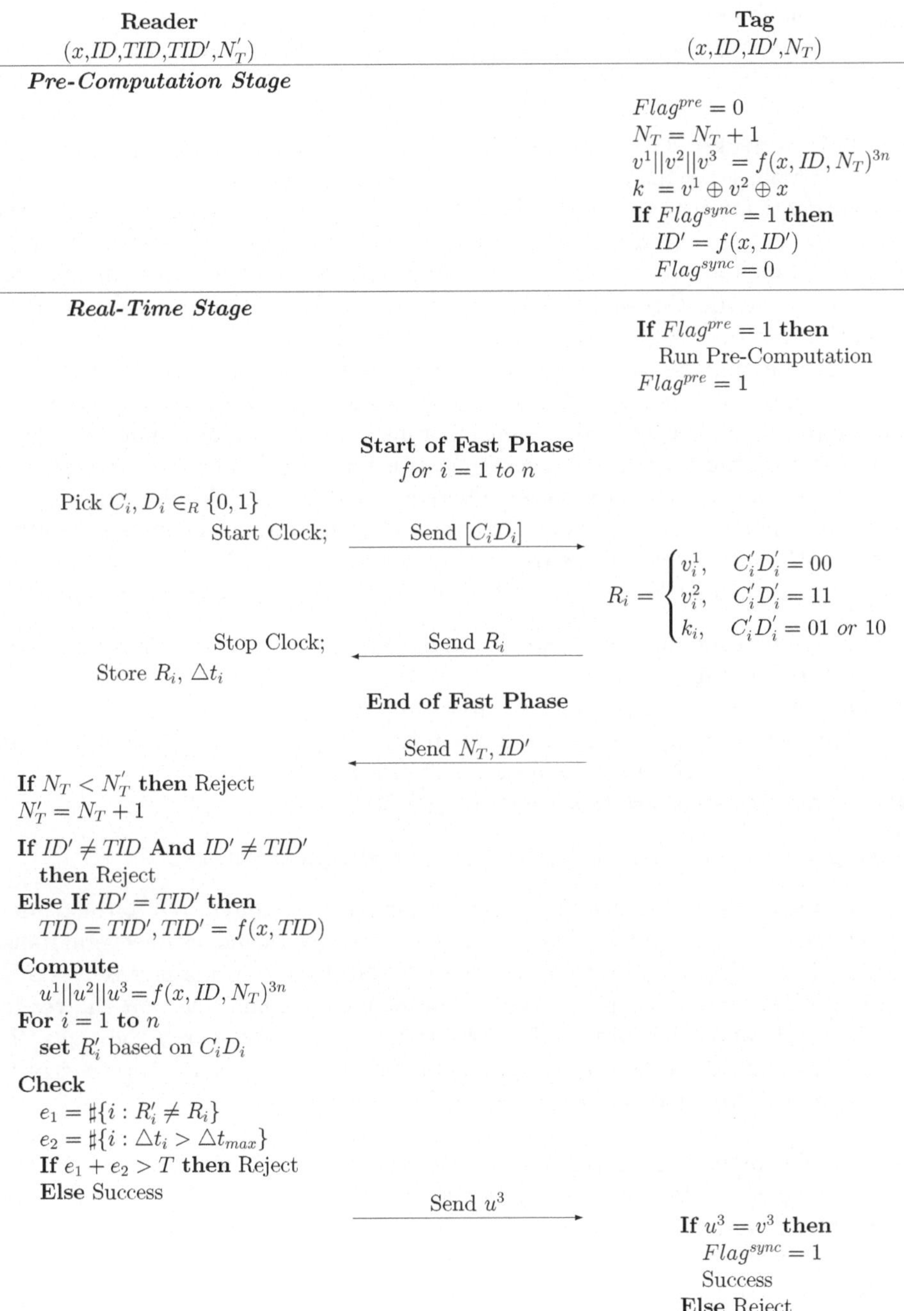

Reader
(x, ID, TID, TID', N'_T)
Tag
(x, ID, ID', N_T)
Pre-Computation Stage
$Flag^{pre} = 0$
$N_T = N_T + 1$
$v^1||v^2||v^3 = f(x, ID, N_T)^{3n}$
$k = v^1 \oplus v^2 \oplus x$
If $Flag^{sync} = 1$ then
$ID' = f(x, ID')$
$Flag^{sync} = 0$
Real-Time Stage
If $Flag^{pre} = 1$ then
Run Pre-Computation
$Flag^{pre} = 1$
Start of Fast Phase
for $i = 1$ to n
Pick $C_i, D_i \in_R \{0, 1\}$
Start Clock;
Send $[C_i D_i]$
$R_i = \begin{cases} v_i^1, & C_i' D_i' = 00 \\ v_i^2, & C_i' D_i' = 11 \\ k_i, & C_i' D_i' = 01 \text{ or } 10 \end{cases}$
Stop Clock;
Send R_i
Store R_i, $\triangle t_i$
End of Fast Phase
Send N_T, ID'
If $N_T < N'_T$ then Reject
$N'_T = N_T + 1$
If $ID' \neq TID$ And $ID' \neq TID'$
then Reject
Else If $ID' = TID'$ then
$TID = TID', TID' = f(x, TID)$
Compute
$u^1||u^2||u^3 = f(x, ID, N_T)^{3n}$
For $i = 1$ to n
set R'_i based on $C_i D_i$
Check
$e_1 = \sharp\{i : R'_i \neq R_i\}$
$e_2 = \sharp\{i : \triangle t_i > \triangle t_{max}\}$
If $e_1 + e_2 > T$ then Reject
Else Success
Send u^3
If $u^3 = v^3$ then
$Flag^{sync} = 1$
Success
Else Reject

Fig. 1. The Protocol without Real-Time PRF Evaluation

into DC (Direct Current) voltage stored in the large capacitor. After protocol finished, the tag will use this stored DC voltage to power the system in order to compute two PRFs and then stored in the non-volatile memory for next round protocol execution.

Real-Time Stage. The real-time stage consists of one fast bit exchange phase (a.k.a. fast phase), which has total n rounds, and one slow phase in which mutual authentication is provided. The communication channel used during the fast phase may suffer from noises. Hence the reader should setup a checking mechanism by a given error threshold (Fault Tolerance). The reader must abort the protocol if the threshold has been exceeded. This stage requires no PRF evaluation but only if-else decisions to make for the tag.

Before starting the fast phase, the tag needs to check the status of the flag bit once more. If $Flag^{pre} = 1$, the tag is aware that the pre-computation is not completed due to several reasons (details in Section 2.3). Under whatever circumstances, the tag needs to ensure the pre-computation has been completely done before running the fast phase. Therefore, the tag should perform the pre-computation in real time for once if $Flag^{pre} = 1$. In contrast, if the tag identifies that $Flag^{pre} = 0$, which means the pre-computation stage has been successfully finished, then it flips $Flag^{pre}$ to 1. The protocol now moves to the fast phase:

(1) The reader randomly picks two-bit challenge $C_i D_i$, starts the clock and sends $C_i D_i$ to the tag.
(2) The tag sends corresponding R_i according to both $C_i' D_i'$.
(3) Upon receiving R_i, the reader immediately stops the clock, stores the time delay $\triangle t_i$, and R_i. There will be no checking at this time.
(4) Above three steps are repeated for n rounds.

When proceed to the last slow phase, no time delays are measured:

(1) The tag sends the counter N_T together with its pseudonym ID' to the reader.
(2) The reader then produces the checking procedures by means of several if-else decision makings. Note that the reader's database also maintains N_T', TID and TID', where N_T' is the tag's counter which maintained on the reader side; TID and TID' are used as the index to quickly search the tag's ID, they are initialized as $TID = f(x, ID)$ and $TID' = f(x, f(x, ID))$, respectively. There are three parts during the checking mechanism.

   (2.1) **Counter Checking.** When received all the information from the tag, the reader will first check whether the received counter N_T is equal to or greater than its stored value N_T'. If N_T is small than N_T', the reader is going to reject the tag and abort the protocol in the sense that a replay attack has been launched because an honest tag will never use an old counter value when initiating a new protocol execution. If it is satisfied, then the reader's counter N_T' will be updated as $N_T' = N_T + 1$. Otherwise the reader will reject the tag and leave the counter unchanged.

(2.2) **Index Searching on Tag's ID.** After checking the counter, the reader moves to the 2nd part by comparing ID' with either TID or TID'. If none of them is equal to ID', there may be an attack launched by the adversary (i.e. de-synchronization attack). Therefore, the reader will reject the tag and abort the protocol immediately. In contrast, if ID' is indeed equal to TID', the reader is going to update its local stored TID and TID' to synchronize with the tag in the sense that there may be one step ahead by the tag. Similarly, if ID' is equal to TID, which means the reader has already catch up with the tag and no update is needed.

(2.3) **Fault Tolerance.** The reader is going to compute $u = f(x, ID, N_T)^{3n}$ and split it into three shares, u^1, u^2, and u^3, respectively. Each of them carries n bits. Based on challenge $C_i D_i$ picked in the fast phase, the reader should set R_i' in order to facilitate the fault tolerance. Now the reader will perform two concurrent checking on the validity of two different values:
 – it counts the number of errors e_1 of positions for the responses $R_i' \neq R_i$;
 – it counts the number of errors e_2 of the transmission delay $\triangle t_i > \triangle t_{max}$;
If $e_1 + e_2 > T$, where T is the fault tolerance threshold, the reader will reject the tag and abort the protocol. Otherwise, the reader can accept the tag.

(3) After above three checking parts, the reader is able to tell whether the protocol succeeds or not and sends u^3 to the tag for mutual authentication.
(4) Finally, the tag is going to check the validity of the u^3 computed by the reader and flip the flag bit $Flag^{sync}$ to 1 if reader authentication is successful. But on the tag side, the counter N_T is always updated at the very beginning no matter what decision the tag made.

2.3 Discussions

The Counter. Intuitively, the counter N_T' stored on the reader side should be synchronized with the counter N_T that stored on the tag. However, if some attacks are launched (i.e. de-synchronization attack), the tag's counter N_T is always greater than reader's N_T'. But it has no effect on the protocol execution in the sense that the checking mechanism only ensures N_T should be equal to or greater than N_T' to prevent replay attack.

The Flag Bit. The RFID chip can loose power at any time. If that happens, it might be possible to force a tag to reuse pre-computed values more than once. If there is no flag bit presented in the tag, the adversary is able to extract the secret key. Nevertheless, we use in our protocol two flag bits $Flag^{pre}$ and $Flag^{sync}$ to ensure the integrity of the RFID environment and the pre-computation has been completely done before the real-time protocol execution. The purpose for $Flag^{pre}$ is to guarantee the counter N_T is updated each time before computing f. If the $Flag^{pre} = 1$ before starting the fast phase, the tag is aware that either insufficient power stored in the large capacitor so that the tag cannot perform the pre-computation or some sort of attacks have been launched, such as the reset attack. Even this kind of attack has been identified, the tag only needs to perform the pre-computation in real time once. This makes our protocol much more robust. On the other hand, $Flag^{sync}$ can prevent the de-synchronization attack in the sense that the tag should only update ID' after reader authentication is successful. Otherwise, if the adversary modifies/blocks u^3 twice, then the tag can no longer be identified by the reader anymore.

3 Security Analysis

We will make a detailed security analysis against all common attacks in the distance bounding protocols.

Impersonation Fraud Resistance. In the impersonation attack, the adversary $\mathcal{A}$ does not know the tag's secret key x and must correctly answer the challenge C_iD_i during the fast phase. Thus, the success probability of the impersonation attack for one round is given by:

$$P_{imp} = \mathbf{Pr}[\mathcal{A}\ guesses\ R_i\ correctly] = \frac{1}{2}$$

The overall success probability is $\left(\frac{1}{2}\right)^n$ since there are n rounds in the fast phase.

Distance Fraud Resistance. The adversary $\mathcal{A}$ is the tag itself in a distance fraud. There are three choices for $\mathcal{A}$ to launch the distance fraud attack. In addition, $\mathcal{A}$ has to carry out the early-reply strategy (to send each reply before receiving the challenges) for all choices during the fast phase in order to make the RTT within the threshold $\triangle t_{max}$.

(1) **Randomly Reply.** $\mathcal{A}$ can choose the most naive way to get a probability of $\frac{1}{2}$ for each round by randomly picking the responses regardless of reader's challenges. Therefore, the success probability for one round is given by:

$$P_{dis-1} = \mathbf{Pr}[\mathcal{A}\ randomly\ replies\ R_i] = \frac{1}{2}$$

Up to n rounds in the fast phase, the overall success probability is $\left(\frac{1}{2}\right)^n$.

(2) **Challenge Guessing.** $\mathcal{A}$ may perform PRF computation during the pre-computation stage to get v^1, v^2, v^3, and k, respectively. With this choice, $\mathcal{A}$ needs to guess the reader's challenges correctly and send the response R_i in advance. Hence the success probability for one round is given by:

$$\begin{aligned}
P_{dis-2} &= \mathbf{Pr}[\mathcal{A}\ guesses\ C_iD_i\ correctly] \\
&= \mathbf{Pr}[C_i'D_i' = 00 \mid C_iD_i = 00] \times \mathbf{Pr}[C_iD_i = 00] \\
&\quad + \mathbf{Pr}[C_i'D_i' = 11 \mid C_iD_i = 11] \times \mathbf{Pr}[C_iD_i = 11] \\
&\quad + \mathbf{Pr}[C_i'D_i' = 01\ or\ 10 \mid C_iD_i = 01] \times \mathbf{Pr}[C_iD_i = 01] \\
&\quad + \mathbf{Pr}[C_i'D_i' = 01\ or\ 10 \mid C_iD_i = 10] \times \mathbf{Pr}[C_iD_i = 10] \\
&= \left(\frac{1}{4}\cdot\frac{1}{4}+\frac{1}{4}\cdot\frac{1}{4}+\frac{1}{2}\cdot\frac{1}{4}+\frac{1}{2}\cdot\frac{1}{4}\right) = \frac{3}{8}
\end{aligned}$$

Up to n rounds in the fast phase, the overall success probability is $\left(\frac{3}{8}\right)^n$.

(3) **"Majority Vote" Attack.** Although the presence of PRF guarantees the pure random output each time, it could happen that v_i^1, v_i^2 and k_i will have the same value. By Dirichlet's Box principle[1], at least two of them are the same.

Table 1. "Majority Vote" Attack

v_i^1	0	0	0	0	1	1	1	1
v_i^2	0	0	1	1	0	0	1	1
k_i	0	1	0	1	0	1	0	1
Success Probability	1	$\frac{1}{2}$	$\frac{3}{4}$	$\frac{3}{4}$	$\frac{3}{4}$	$\frac{3}{4}$	$\frac{1}{2}$	1

Table 1 shows all possible success probabilities for three registers with respect to the "Majority Vote" attack. The 1st column provides three registers v_i^1, v_i^2, and k_i, together with the success probability for each i. There are eight different combinations for three registers in the table (From 2nd to 9th columns). With this attack, the adversary $\mathcal{A}$ can simply select the value which has a majority, that is, two or three equal registers (Majority wins) and reply this particular value to the reader. Since k_i is determined by either 01 or 10 for C_iD_i, it has the higher probability if the majority wins. Thus, the probability that $\mathcal{A}$ can succeed in this case is given by:

$$\begin{aligned} P_{dis-3} &= \mathbf{Pr}[Majority\ Wins] \\ &= \left(\frac{1}{8} \cdot \left(1 + \frac{1}{2} + \frac{3}{4} + \frac{3}{4} + \frac{3}{4} + \frac{3}{4} + \frac{1}{2} + 1\right)\right) = \frac{3}{4} \end{aligned}$$

Up to n rounds in fast phase, the overall success probability is $\left(\frac{3}{4}\right)^n$.

Remark 1. $\mathcal{A}$ may choose the "Majority Vote" attack since it provides the highest success probability among three different choices in distance fraud attack.

Mafia Fraud Resistance. The tag does not collude with the adversary $\mathcal{A}$ in the Mafia fraud. $\mathcal{A}$ may launch the attack by using one of the following strategies.

(1) **Post-ask strategy.** By acting as a malicious tag, $\mathcal{A}$ first executes the fast phase with the reader in order to learn the correct challenges C_iD_i. After knowing all challenges $\mathcal{A}$ pretends to be a fake reader and runs the fast phase with the legitimate tag so that $\mathcal{A}$ can obtain valid response R_i. At last, $\mathcal{A}$ relays the final slow phase. With this strategy, $\mathcal{A}$ has to answer to the reader with arbitrary answers. This strategy has the same probability as in the impersonation fraud. Thus, the success probability in the post-ask strategy is given by:

$$P_{maf-1} = \mathbf{Pr}[\mathcal{A}\ guesses\ R_i\ correctly] = \frac{1}{2}$$

For n rounds in fast phase, the overall success probability is $\left(\frac{1}{2}\right)^n$.

[1] Dirichlet's Box principle: Given n boxes and m ($m > n$) objects, if m objects are placed into n boxes, at least one box must contain more than one (m/n) object.

(2) **Pre-ask strategy.** $\mathcal{A}$ needs to pretend to be a fake reader and execute the fast phase with the tag before the reader to do so. Afterwards, $\mathcal{A}$ runs the fast phase by acting as the malicious tag with the reader and relays the final slow phase. With this strategy, $\mathcal{A}$ needs to transmit the anticipated challenge bits $C_i'D_i'$ to the tag before the reader sends out its real challenge C_iD_i. However, there are two special cases with this strategy.

(i) $\mathcal{A}$ chooses C_iD_i solely from [00,11,01,10]. Thus, the success probability in this case is given by:

$$\begin{aligned} P_{maf-2} &= \mathbf{Pr}[\mathcal{A}\ guesses\ C_iD_i\ correctly] \\ &\quad + \mathbf{Pr}[\mathcal{A}\ guesses\ C_iD_i\ incorrectly \wedge \mathcal{A}\ randomly\ replies\ R_i\ correctly] \\ &= \mathbf{Pr}[\mathcal{A}\ guesses\ C_iD_i\ correctly] + \frac{1}{2}[1 - \mathbf{Pr}[\mathcal{A}\ guesses\ C_iD_i\ correctly]] \\ &= \frac{1}{2}[1 + \mathbf{Pr}[\mathcal{A}\ guesses\ C_iD_i\ correctly]] \\ &= \left(\frac{1}{2}\left(1 + \frac{3}{8}\right)\right) = \frac{11}{16} \end{aligned}$$

The overall success probability is $\left(\frac{11}{16}\right)^n$ for n rounds in fast phase. This approach provides a higher success probability when compared with the post-ask strategy. But $\mathcal{A}$ may choose another special case.

(ii) $\mathcal{A}$ only sends $C_i'D_i'$=01 (or 10) to the tag in the first fast phase execution in order to obtain the whole share of k. Then $\mathcal{A}$ runs the second fast phase with the reader. Therefore, $\mathcal{A}$ can succeed in this case will be:

$$\begin{aligned} P_{maf-3} &= \mathbf{Pr}[\mathcal{A}\ replies\ R_i\ correctly \mid C_iD_i = 01\ or\ 10] \times \mathbf{Pr}[C_iD_i = 01\ or\ 10] \\ &\quad + \mathbf{Pr}[\mathcal{A}\ guesses\ R_i\ correctly \mid C_iD_i = 00\ or\ 11] \times \mathbf{Pr}[C_iD_i = 00\ or\ 11] \\ &= \left(1 \cdot \frac{2}{4} + \frac{1}{2} \cdot \frac{2}{4}\right) = \frac{3}{4} \end{aligned}$$

For n rounds in fast phase, the overall success probability is $\left(\frac{3}{4}\right)^n$.

Remark 2. For any strategy, the success probability is upper bounded by $\left(\frac{3}{4}\right)^n$. It is obvious that the pre-ask strategy has the higher success probability.

Terrorist Fraud Resistance. In a terrorist fraud attack, the malicious tag colludes with the adversary who will run the fast phase and relay the last slow phase on behalf of the malicious tag. The tag could give some sensitive information to the adversary so that she could defeat the protocol for one session. To be more specific, the malicious tag cannot give all registers v^1, v^2, and k to $\mathcal{A}$, since $\mathcal{A}$ will be able to recover the secret key x by $x = v^1 \oplus v^2 \oplus k$. But N_T and ID' can be passed to $\mathcal{A}$ directly. Hence there are three scenarios to be considered.

(1) $\mathcal{A}$ has k and v^1 (same probability for k and v^2) at hand. When receiving the challenge C_iD_i, $\mathcal{A}$ knows the exact response from v_i^1 or k_i. But $\mathcal{A}$ needs to guess the value of v_i^2 when $C_iD_i = 11$. Thus, for $\mathcal{A}$ has $(k,\ v^1)$, the success probability in this situation is given by:

$$\begin{aligned} P_{terr-1} &= \mathbf{Pr}[\mathcal{A}\ guesses\ R_i\ correctly \mid C_iD_i = 11] \times \mathbf{Pr}[C_iD_i = 11] \\ &+ \mathbf{Pr}[\mathcal{A}\ replies\ R_i\ correctly \mid C_iD_i \neq 11] \times \mathbf{Pr}[C_iD_i \neq 11] \\ &= \left(\frac{1}{2}\cdot\frac{1}{4} + 1\cdot\frac{3}{4}\right) = \frac{7}{8} \end{aligned}$$

For n rounds in fast phase, the overall success probability is $\left(\frac{7}{8}\right)^n$

(2) $\mathcal{A}$ has both v^1 and v^2. $\mathcal{A}$ can reply with good answer when $C_i = D_i$. But $\mathcal{A}$ needs to randomly guess when $C_i \neq D_i$ since she has no knowledge of k. Then the success probability in this situation is given by:

$$\begin{aligned} P_{terr-2} &= \mathbf{Pr}[\mathcal{A}\ guesses\ R_i\ correctly \mid C_iD_i = 01\ or\ 10] \times \mathbf{Pr}[C_iD_i = 01\ or\ 10] \\ &+ \mathbf{Pr}[\mathcal{A}\ replies\ R_i\ correctly \mid C_iD_i = 00\ or\ 11] \times \mathbf{Pr}[C_iD_i = 00\ or\ 11] \\ &= \left(\frac{1}{2}\cdot\frac{2}{4} + 1\cdot\frac{2}{4}\right) = \frac{3}{4} \end{aligned}$$

For n rounds in fast phase, the overall success probability is $\left(\frac{3}{4}\right)^n$

(3) It's the opposite of case (2) when $\mathcal{A}$ only obtains k. Therefore, the success probability in this situation is given by:

$$\begin{aligned} P_{terr-3} &= \mathbf{Pr}[\mathcal{A}\ replies\ R_i\ correctly \mid C_iD_i = 01\ or\ 10] \times \mathbf{Pr}[C_iD_i = 01\ or\ 10] \\ &+ \mathbf{Pr}[\mathcal{A}\ guesses\ R_i\ correctly \mid C_iD_i = 00\ or\ 11] \times \mathbf{Pr}[C_iD_i = 00\ or\ 11] \\ &= \left(1\cdot\frac{2}{4} + \frac{1}{2}\cdot\frac{2}{4}\right) = \frac{3}{4} \end{aligned}$$

For n rounds in fast phase, the overall success probability is $\left(\frac{3}{4}\right)^n$

Distance Hijacking Attack Resistance. We only consider the distance hijacking attack in the single-protocol environment. Under this situation, the adversary $\mathcal{A}$ outside the legal authentication region exploits an inside legitimate tag to execute the fast phase so that $\mathcal{A}$ can cheat on its real distance to the reader. To launch such attack, $\mathcal{A}$ first does nothing during the fast phase as she is far away from the reader. When the fast phase ends, $\mathcal{A}$ will impersonate a fake reader to communicate with the exploited tag in order to get the counter N_T, and tag's pseudonym ID'. Upon receiving these information, $\mathcal{A}$ is going to act as a fraudulent tag to send N_T (untouched) and her own pseudonym $ID'_{\mathcal{A}}$ to the legitimate reader. Finally, the reader will make decision on acceptance of the fraudulent tag. It is obvious that $\mathcal{A}$ cannot win because she does not have the secret key x of the exploited tag. Besides, the $ID'_{\mathcal{A}}$ is different so that the output of the PRF is absolutely different. Therefore, the success probability of $\mathcal{A}$ is $(\frac{1}{2})^n$.

Reader Authentication. Up to now, many distance bounding protocols do not feature reader authentication. They focus on unilateral authentication where the tag tries to convince the reader of a statement related identity and the physical distance between them. They make the assumption that the reader should be honest, but we would like to argue that this may not be the case when considering the Mafia fraud attack, the adversary launches the attack by exchanging the roles of the reader and a tag. Therefore, it is crucial to support mutual authentication in distance bounding protocol as well. In fact, our protocol is the one providing reader authentication by introducing v^3. The presence of v^3 as one of the three registers let the tag be able to make a decision on reader's authenticity.

4 Comparison

In Table 2, we make a comparison between our proposed protocol and others with respect to several properties: the success probabilities of the Mafia fraud and terrorist fraud; mutual authentication (MA); tag privacy; number of message flows in slow phase; real-time tag computation, as well as the pre-computation.

Table 2. Comparison of distance bounding protocols

	Mafia	Terrorist	MA	Privacy	# of Msg Flows	Real-time Tag Comp	Pre-Comp
BC [1]	$(\frac{1}{2})^n$	No	No	No	2	1 commit, 1 signature	No
SP [14]	$(\frac{1}{2})^n$	No	No	No	2	1 commit, 1 MAC, ECC	No
HK [2]	$(\frac{3}{4})^n$	No	No	No	2	1 PRF	No
MP [7]	$(\frac{1}{2})^n$	No	Partial	No	3	2 Hash	No
KA [11]	$(\frac{1}{2})^n$	No	Partial	No	2	1 PRF	No
Swiss-Knife [3]	$(\frac{1}{2})^n$	$(\frac{3}{4})^n$	Yes	Yes	4	3 PRF	Partial
YZW [15]	$(\frac{3}{4})^n$	No	Yes	Yes	2	2 PRF	No
Our Protocol	$(\frac{3}{4})^n$	$(\frac{3}{4})^n/(\frac{7}{8})^{n\dagger}$	Yes	Yes	2	0 PRF	Yes

† The success probability for the terrorist fraud depends on how many registers the adversary obtains. There are three situations discussed in Section 3.

As we can see from the table, most protocols achieve the success probability of $\left(\frac{1}{2}\right)^n$ for the Mafia fraud resistance except HK's [2] and YZW's [15] since the absence of the signature in the last slow phase. It might be high risk but more efficient. MP [7] and KA [11] used mixed challenges in the fast phase that could converge toward the expected probability of $\left(\frac{1}{2}\right)^n$. Our proposed protocol, which does not have a signature, has two strategies that yield three different success probabilities by using two-bit challenges in the fast phase.

Speaking of the terrorist fraud attack, only the Swiss-Knife [3] and ours which are secure against it. However, [15] is not secure against terrorist fraud when considering the attack in [18]. Regarding to the distance hijacking attack [6], it seems that most protocols are secure in the single protocol environment with an ideal probability except Brands and Chaum's [1].

Next we consider mutual authentication (MA) of the distance bounding protocols. Most protocols assume that the reader should be honest, but this may not be the case when considering the Mafia fraud attack. Among all previous protocols in Table 2, only the Swiss-Knife [3] and YZW [15] are mutually authenticated that is achieved in our proposed protocol as well. For MP [7] and KA [11], their protocols are based on (binary) mixed challenges that enable partially mutual authentication during the fast phase.

When referring to the privacy of the tag, the Swiss-Knife [3], YZW [15] and ours support tag privacy protection. Our protocol realizes the privacy by using an index on tag's *ID* in an anonymous way. Note that our protocol requires only O(1) complexity for achieving privacy in the sense that the reader's cost is O(1) PRF, rather than O(n) PRF (For example, in Swiss-Knife [3]) in order to protect tag's privacy. Our protocol prevents the de-synchronization attack with the presence of both *TID* and TID'. When launching a de-synchronization attack, the adversary either prevents the tag updating ID' or prevents the reader updating *TID* and TID'. It is obvious that no matter what the adversary does, the value of ID' sent by the tag will always be the same as either *TID* or TID' so that the tag is synchronized with the reader, and vice versa.

The number of message flows in the slow phase is essential to the protocol execution time and power consumption. As for most protocols including ours have only one single slow phase when compared with the Swiss-Knife which needs four message flows in two slow phases. It is susceptible to much power consumption for a low-cost tag.

Finally, we make a special comparison in terms of the real-time tag computation and pre-computation. As all previous proposed protocols do not explicitly have the pre-computation stage, their protocols must have at least one time-consuming PRF, hash or signature evaluation in the real-time stage. But for the Swiss-Knife [3], they state that, one of three PRFs can be pre-computed before starting the protocol in the sense that the contents of the input for this PRF are irrelevant to the reader. It means that they still need two computations of PRFs in real time for achieving mutual authentication. Our proposed protocol, however, let the tag finish two PRF computations in the pre-computation stage by using a large capacitor which makes the real-time stage extremely faster than any of previous protocols.

5 Conclusion

In this paper, we proposed a highly efficient pre-computed RFID distance bounding protocol with tag privacy. It makes use of a large capacitor to store the DC voltage which can power the tag in order to compute the PRF off-line. Our protocol is mutually authenticated and secure against all common attacks in distance bounding. To the best of our knowledge, our proposed protocol is the first one that provides online PRF-free for the tag meaning that there is no evaluation on any PRF during the real-time protocol running which significantly makes the tag more efficient and low-cost. We also take tag's privacy into account through the method of index to search tag's *ID* which requires only O(1) complexity for achieving privacy. We give the detailed security analysis for our protocol and make a comprehensive comparison against others.

References

1. Brands, S., Chaum, D.: Distance Bounding Protocols. In: Helleseth, T. (ed.) EUROCRYPT 1993. LNCS, vol. 765, pp. 344–359. Springer, Heidelberg (1994)
2. Hancke, G., Kuhn, M.: An RFID Distance Bounding Protocol. In: SecureComm 2005, pp. 67–73. IEEE Computer Society (2005)
3. Kim, C.H., Avoine, G., Koeune, F., Standaert, F.-X., Pereira, O.: The Swiss-Knife RFID Distance Bounding Protocol. In: Lee, P.J., Cheon, J.H. (eds.) ICISC 2008. LNCS, vol. 5461, pp. 98–115. Springer, Heidelberg (2009)
4. Desmedt, Y.: Major security problems with the 'unforgeable' (Feige)- Fiat- Shamir proofs of identify and how to overcome them. In: SecuriCom 1988, pp. 15–17 (1988)
5. Avoine, G., Lauradoux, C., Marin, B.: How Secret-sharing can Defeat Terrorist Fraud. In: ACM Wisec 2011, pp. 145–156. ACM SIGSAC (2011)
6. Cremers, C., Rasmussen, K.B., Čapkun, S.: Distance Hijacking Attacks on Distance Bounding Protocols. In: IEEE S&P 2012, pp. 113–127 (2012)
7. Munilla, J., Peinado, A.: Distance Bounding Protocols for RFID Enhanced by Using Void-challenges and Analysis in Noisy Channels. Wireless Communications & Mobile Computing 8(9), 1227–1232 (2008)
8. Kardaş, S., Kiraz, M.S., Bingöl, M.A., Demirci, H.: A Novel RFID Distance Bounding Protocol Based on Physically Unclonable Functions. In: Juels, A., Paar, C. (eds.) RFIDSec 2011. LNCS, vol. 7055, pp. 78–93. Springer, Heidelberg (2012)
9. Avoine, G., Tchamkerten, A.: An Efficient Distance Bounding RFID Authentication Protocol: Balancing False-Acceptance Rate and Memory Requirement. In: Samarati, P., Yung, M., Martinelli, F., Ardagna, C.A. (eds.) ISC 2009. LNCS, vol. 5735, pp. 250–261. Springer, Heidelberg (2009)
10. Tu, Y.J., Piramuthu, S.: RFID Distance Bounding Protocols. In: EURASIP Workshop in RFID Technology, Vienna, Austria (2007)
11. Kim, C.H., Avoine, G.: RFID Distance Bounding Protocol with Mixed Challenges to Prevent Relay Attacks. In: Garay, J.A., Miyaji, A., Otsuka, A. (eds.) CANS 2009. LNCS, vol. 5888, pp. 119–133. Springer, Heidelberg (2009)
12. Chae, H.J., Yeager, D.J., Smith, J.R., Fu, K.: Maximalist Cryptography and Computation on the WISP UHF RFID Tag. In: RFIDSec (2007)
13. Hofferek, G., Wolkerstorfer, J.: Coupon Recalculation for the GPS Authentication Scheme. In: Grimaud, G., Standaert, F.-X. (eds.) CARDIS 2008. LNCS, vol. 5189, pp. 162–175. Springer, Heidelberg (2008)
14. Singelée, D., Preneel, B.: Distance Bounding in Noisy Environments. In: Stajano, F., Meadows, C., Capkun, S., Moore, T. (eds.) ESAS 2007. LNCS, vol. 4572, pp. 101–115. Springer, Heidelberg (2007)
15. Yang, A., Zhuang, Y., Wong, D.S.: An Efficient Single-Slow-Phase Mutually Authenticated RFID Ddistance Bounding Protocol with Tag Privacy. In: Chim, T.W., Yuen, T.H. (eds.) ICICS 2012. LNCS, vol. 7618, pp. 285–292. Springer, Heidelberg (2012)
16. Nikov, V., Vauclair, M.: Yet Another Secure Distacne-Bounding Protocol. IACR ePrint Archive, http://eprint.iacr.org/2008/319 and SECRYPT 2008
17. Rasmussen, K.B., Čapkun, S.: Location Privacy of Distance Bounding Protocols. In: ACM CCS 2008, pp. 149–160. ACM SIGSAC (2008)
18. Fischlin, M., Onete, C.: Provably Secure Distance-Bounding: an Analysis of Prominent Protocols. In: IACR ePrint Archive (2012), http://eprint.iacr.org/2012/128

Privacy Preserving Context Aware Publish Subscribe Systems

Mohamed Nabeel[1], Stefan Appel[2], Elisa Bertino[1], and Alejandro Buchmann[2]

[1] Purdue University, West Lafayette, IN, USA
{nabeel,bertino}@cs.purdue.edu
[2] TU Darmstadt, Darmstadt, Germany
{appel,buchmann}@dvs.tu-darmstadt.de

Abstract. Modern pub/sub systems perform message routing based on the message *content* and allow subscribers to receive messages related to their subscriptions and the current *context*. Both content and context encode sensitive information which should be protected from third-party brokers that make routing decisions. In this work, we address this issue by proposing an approach that assures the confidentiality of the messages being published and subscriptions being issued while allowing the brokers to make routing decisions without decrypting individual messages and subscriptions, and without learning the context. Further, subscribers with a frequently changing context, such as location, are able to issue and update subscriptions without revealing the subscriptions in plaintext to the broker and without the need to contact a trusted third party for each subscription change resulting from a change in the context. Our approach is based on a modified version of the Paillier additive homomorphic cryptosystem and a novel group key management scheme. The former construct is used to perform privacy preserving matching, and the latter construct is used to enforce fine-grained encryption-based access control on the messages being published. We optimize our approach in order to efficiently handle frequently changing contexts. We have implemented our approach in a prototype using an industry strength JMS broker middleware. The experimental results show that our approach is highly practical.

1 Introduction

The publish/subscribe (pub/sub) paradigm is a well known approach for disseminating information between multiple interested parties in a decoupled and asynchronous manner [7]. Message producers submit messages to a broker network which routes them to interested subscribers. Subscribers express their interest by issuing subscriptions. Content-based pub/sub systems allow subscribers to express their interest based on the message content. This content can be an arbitrary payload, e.g., a set of attribute-value (att/val) pairs, XML documents, or combinations of different types. The supported message content depends on the pub/sub middleware which performs message routing and matching. In many systems it is common to use att/val pairs to describe content and to express subscription filters as logical expressions on these attributes (e.g., MessageType == StockTickMessage $\wedge$ StockPrice > 38).

Context-sensitive message dissemination extends pub/sub content dissemination by taking into account the subscriber context [6]. Subscribers express interest in messages

J. Lopez, X. Huang, and R. Sandhu (Eds.): NSS 2013, LNCS 7873, pp. 465–478, 2013.

based on their current context, e.g., their current location. A major challenge for context-sensitive message dissemination is that the context of subscribers, and thus the subscriptions, change frequently over time, e.g., as the location changes. Context-dependent information dissemination is however a crucial requirement in many application scenarios. One example is a traffic information system (TIS) where information about the traffic situation is provided. Due to the characteristics of this scenario a pub/sub middleware supporting context-sensitive message dissemination is an appropriate infrastructure. Information about the current traffic situation is published and participants express their interest in information with subscriptions. As subscribers move and thus their contexts constantly change, subscriptions need to change accordingly, e.g., subscribers would typically be interested in traffic information along the route they are traveling.

A major shortcoming of existing context-based pub/sub approaches is that they do not assure privacy. In such systems, the broker receives subscriptions in plaintext and is thus aware of the context of subscribers. In case of the TIS example, this implies that brokers are aware of the exact position of subscribers. In order to assure privacy, we propose an approach to construct a privacy-preserving context-based pub/sub system. We extend and improve our preliminary work [15] in order to propose a new security model and construct our privacy preserving context-based pub/sub system.

In our previous model [15], each subscriber is required to submit a new subscription via a secure channel to a trusted third-party (TTP) that encrypts the subscription in a special way. This special encryption operation is called *blinding* and the encrypted value *blinded value*. Such blinded values are semantically secure (IND-CPA secure) where two blindings of the same value result in two different blinded values. The subscriber then registers with such blinded subscriptions at an untrusted broker. Such an approach allows the use of honest-but-curious brokers[1] to perform matching and routing on encrypted notifications using the blinded subscriptions. Although such an approach is privacy preserving, it is not suitable for context-based pub/sub systems. The reason is that as the context of subscribers changes frequently, subscriptions have to be updated often and involving a TTP to blind every subscription is not any longer feasible. Further, the previous model does not support fine-grained access control of notifications. Thus, a new security model and mechanisms are required whereby subscribers are allowed to create their own blinded subscriptions without compromising the security of the overall system and enforce fine-grained access control of notifications. In this work, we achieve our first objective by allowing authorized subscribers to create blinded subscriptions after obtaining some public security parameters at the time of registration. After the initial interactions, subscribers are not required to contact a TTP unless the public security parameters are updated. We achieve the second objective by introducing a fine-grained encryption-based access control mechanism. An advantage of such an approach compared to approaches based on shared secrets is that no secret information is given to subscribers to generate blinded subscriptions and therefore our approach avoids the problem of leakage of shared secrets by malicious subscribers.

Each notification in our approach is encrypted twice. The first encryption, referred to as blinding operation, is performed to blind each attribute value in the notification that is

[1] Brokers are obliged to follow the protocol, but they are curious to learn as much as possible during the execution of the protocol.

used by brokers to perform matching operations. The notification blinding is similar to the subscription blinding operation mentioned earlier except that the two operations use different blinding parameters so that certain parameters cancel off when a blinded notification and a subscription are homomorphically added by multiplying them. It should be noted that brokers cannot decrypt individual blinded values and they only learn a randomized difference between subscription and notification values when they perform matching operations. The second encryption, referred to as broadcast encryption, is performed to encrypt the payload of notifications based on fine-grained access control policies (ACPs). According to current initiatives on identity management [17], fine-grained ACPs are specified using the attributes of subscribers, referred to as *identity attributes*. Our broadcast encryption is based on a recently proposed group key management (GKM) scheme, referred to as attribute based GKM (AB-GKM) [20,14,16]. In the AB-GKM scheme, unlike conventional GKM schemes [2,9], subscribers are allowed to dynamically derive the data decryption keys based on the attribute credentials they possess and some public information provided by publishers.

We also provide support for multiple publishers that produce messages with overlapping attribute sets; a blinded subscription may match notifications from several publishers. Especially for context-based pub/sub, it is crucial to support multiple publishers located in the same context, e.g., the same geographical region. We thus introduce context managers as TTPs in our approach. Context managers provide publishers as well as subscribers with information required to publish encrypted/blinded notifications and to issue blinded subscriptions. Once publishers and subscribers obtain the required security parameters, the context manager is responsible for controlling the level of protection. It decides when to renew and redistribute security parameters to publishers and subscriber in order to reduce the risk of adversaries learning the content of notifications and subscriptions.

We implement our scheme based on the Java Message Service (JMS), the de-facto industry standard for messaging. We chose Apache ActiveMQ as JMS broker and extended it to support subscription evaluation on encrypted data. This allows us to perform a realistic evaluation of our approach since ActiveMQ is used in many real-world production pub/sub systems.

Our paper is structured as follows. Section 2 introduces the cryptographic constructs used in our approach. Section 3 introduces context-based pub/sub systems and presents an overview of our solution. Sections 4 and 5 present the technical details of the modified Paillier cryptosystem which is used to blind subscriptions and notifications, and our overall scheme. Section 6 shows experimental results for various algorithms and the overall system implemented in Apache ActiveMQ. Section 7 discusses related work and Section 8 concludes the paper.

2 Background

2.1 Paillier Homomorphic Cryptosystem

The *Paillier homomorphic cryptosystem* is a public key cryptosystem by Paillier [18] based on the "Composite Residuosity assumption (CRA)". The Paillier cryptosystem is homomorphic in that, by using a public key, the encryption of the sum $m_1 + m_2$ of two messages m_1 and m_2 can be computed from the encryption of m_1 and m_2. Our approach and protocols are inspired by how the Paillier cryptosystem works. Hence, we provide some internal details of the cryptosystem below so that readers can follow the rest of the paper.

Key Generation
Set $n = pq$, where p and q are two large prime numbers. Set $\lambda = \text{lcm}(p-1, q-1)$, i.e., the least common multiple of $p-1$ and $q-1$. Randomly select a base $g \in \mathbb{Z}/(n^2)^\times$ such that the order of g_p is a multiple of n. Such a g_p can be efficiently found by randomly choosing $g_p \in \mathbb{Z}/(n^2)^\times$, then verifying that $\gcd(L(g_p^\lambda \pmod{n^2}), n)) = 1$, where $L(u) = (u-1)/n$. for $u \in S_n = \{u < n^2 | u = 1 \pmod{n}\}$. In this case, set $\mu = \left(L(g_p^\lambda \pmod{n^2})\right)^{-1} \pmod{n}$. The public encryption key is a pair (n, g_p). The private decryption key is (λ, μ), or equivalently (p, q, μ).

Encryption $E(m, r)$
Given plaintext $m \in \{0, 1, \ldots, n-1\}$, select a random $r \in \{1, 2, \ldots, n-1\}$, and encrypt m as $E(m, r) = g_p^m \cdot r^n \pmod{n^2}$. When the value of r is not important to the context, we sometimes simply write a short-hand $E(m)$ instead of $E(m, r)$ for the Paillier ciphertext of m.

Decryption $D(c)$
Given ciphertext $c \in \mathbb{Z}/(n^2)^\times$, decrypt c as $D(c) = L(c^\lambda \pmod{n^2}) \cdot \mu \pmod{n}$.

In the construction of our pub/sub system, the Paillier homomorphic cryptosystem is used in a way that public and private keys are judiciously distributed among publishers, subscribers, and brokers such that the confidentiality and privacy are assured based on homomorphic encryption. A detailed description of the construction is presented in Section 4.

2.2 Attribute Based Group Key Management

Broadcast Group Key Management (BGKM) schemes [24,20] are a special type of GKM scheme whereby the rekey operation is performed with a single broadcast without requiring private communication channels. Unlike conventional GKM schemes, BGKM schemes do not give subscribers private keys. Instead subscribers are given a secret which is combined with public information to obtain the actual private keys. Such schemes have the advantage of requiring a private communication only once for the initial secret sharing. The subsequent rekeying operations are performed using one broadcast message. Further, in such schemes achieving forward and backward security requires only to change the public information and does not affect the secrets given to existing subscribers. However, BGKM schemes do not support group membership policies over a set of attributes. A recently proposed attribute based GKM (AB-GKM) scheme [13] provides all the benefits of BGKM schemes and also supports attribute based access control policies (ACPs).

Subscribers are required to show their identity attributes to the group controller to obtain secrets using the AB-GKM scheme. In order to hide the identity attributes from the group controller while allowing only valid subscribers to obtain secrets, we utilize oblivious commitment based envelope (OCBE) protocols [8]. We omit the details of the OCBE protocols due to the page limit.

The idea behind the AB-GKM scheme is as follows. A separate BGKM instance for each attribute condition, which is a predicate over an attribute, is constructed. The ACP, a Boolean expression over attribute conditions, is embedded in an access structure $\mathcal{T}$. $\mathcal{T}$ is a tree with the internal nodes representing threshold gates and the leaves representing BGKM instances for the attributes. $\mathcal{T}$ can represent any monotonic policy. The goal of the access tree is to allow deriving the group key for only the subscribers whose attributes satisfy the access structure $\mathcal{T}$.

The AB-GKM scheme consists of five algorithms: **Setup**, **SecGen**, **KeyGen**, **KeyDer** and **ReKey**. **Setup** initializes the system. **SecGen** generates a unique secret for each attribute condition. For a given ACP, **KeyGen** creates a symmetric key, public information and an access structure. **KeyDer** derives the symmetric key given one or more secrets and public information. **ReKey** regenerates the symmetric key and public information.

3 Overview

Our approach requires a modification of the matching algorithm inside the message broker to support the evaluation of blinded subscriptions against blinded notifications without decrypting them. Our system also supports fine-grained encryption based access control over notifications. Publishers encrypt notifications so that only authorized subscribers can derive the key and decrypt the notifications. In order to assure privacy, publishers and subscribers must perform an initialization to obtain secrets and public parameters that they later need for encryption and blinding operations. In this section, we give an overview of the modified Paillier cryptosystem and our context-based pub/sub model and present our system architecture. We describe the initialization phase as well as the regular runtime behavior. Finally, we present the trust model assumed in our approach.

3.1 Modified Paillier Cryptosystem

In our work, we adapt the Paillier cryptosystem so that brokers can perform matching operations without decrypting individual subscriptions and notifications. A high level overview of the modifications we perform to the Paillier cryptosystem and the rationale behind our modifications are provided below. We first shift the computation towards encryption so that decryption is computationally more efficient than the Paillier decryption. We also allow brokers to perform certain operations without knowing the private key. Such shifting of computation improves the performance of the overall pub/sub system since publishers and subscribers, which perform encryption, are typically distributed to many nodes while brokers have to handle notifications from many publishers and subscribers. Thus, by making decryption efficient, we eliminate a bottleneck in the system and improve the overall efficiency. We also blind the encrypted values and make μ, a parameter of the Paillier cryptosystem, public so that individual values cannot be decrypted, but a blinded subscription and a blinded notification can be multiplied together to obtain the difference. In order to make the correct matching decision by calculating the difference, we limit the domain size (l bits) of the subscription and notification values. We assume that l is much smaller compared to the plaintext space of the Paillier cryptosystem, n. For example, the subscription and notification for the attribute age, which may take values from 0 to 200, can be represented using a domain size of 8 bits. Since the domain size is much smaller than the plaintext space, brokers can make the matching decision by calculating the difference as follows: If the difference between a notification and a subscription value is in the first half of the plaintext space, the difference is positive and the notification value is greater than or equal to the subscription value. Otherwise, the difference is negative and the notification value is less than the subscription value.

The above modifications allow brokers to make matching decisions without learning the actual values. However the modified matching protocol still reveals the actual difference between the notification value and subscription values which leaks information about these values. In order to address this issue, we introduce controlled random values to the subscription and notification blinding operations so that the difference is randomized. The brokers can still make correct matching decisions by comparing which half the computed difference falls in the plaintext space, without however learning the actual difference.

3.2 System Architecture

We assume that logical expressions based on att/val pairs are used by subscribers to express their interest in notifications. We distinguish between two sets of attributes, namely context set and static set, and an additional payload which by itself can be a set of att/val pairs. The context set contains attributes representing the subscriber context, e.g., location. The static set represents general attributes describing the message, e.g., message type.

Our approach consists of four entities (see Figure 1a and Figure 1b): publisher, subscriber, broker, and context manager. In order to assure the privacy of subscriptions, subscribers must hide the content of their subscriptions from brokers. Further, since the attributes in the context set frequently change, subscribers must be able to update their subscriptions without contacting a TTP, referred to as the context manager. In our

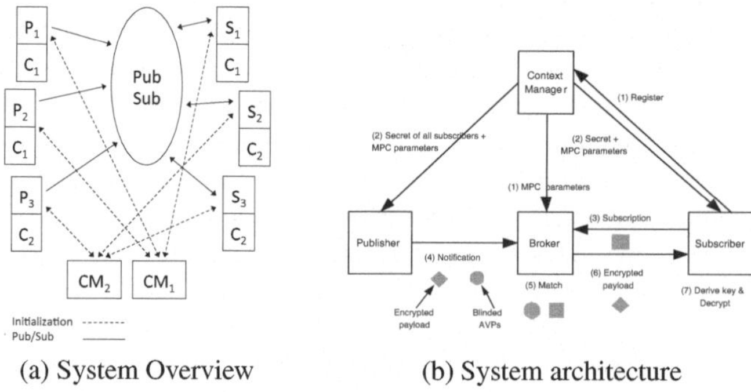

(a) System Overview (b) System architecture

Fig. 1. System details: Relations between publishers (P), subscribers (S), contexts (C), and context managers (CM)

approach, publishers and subscribers communicate with context managers only either during the initialization phase or when security parameters change in order to obtain secrets and public parameters.

A context manager is responsible for a certain context in the system. The context is described by a set of attributes, such as location with attributes *latitude* and *longitude*. To assure the privacy of the context, subscribers must be able to issue and update subscriptions with blinded context set attribute values and publishers must be able to publish notifications and blind context set attribute values.

When publishers join the system and want to publish messages for a certain context, they first contact the responsible context manager. After successful authentication the context manager provides some security parameters and a set of secrets corresponding to valid subscribers to the publishers which allow them to blind and encrypt notifications. The blinding operation is performed using the modified Paillier cryptosystem described in the next section and the encryption is performed using the symmetric key generated using the AB-GKM's key generation algorithm.

A similar bootstrapping process is necessary for subscribers. They contact the context manager and receive some other security parameters which allow them to issue blinded subscriptions for a certain context and secrets for identity attributes they have. Further, our scheme allows the subscribers to update their subscriptions within a context without contacting the context manager.

Brokers only receive blinded and encrypted notifications, and blinded subscriptions. Upon receiving a notification, they execute the matching operation on the blinded notification and the blinded subscriptions to make forwarding decisions. If a notification matches a subscription, the broker strips the blinded portion of the notification and sends only the encrypted notification to matching subscribers. It should be noted that brokers do not learn the individual notification and subscription values during matching operations.

Once subscribers receive encrypted notifications, using the secrets obtained from the context manager during the initialization phase, they can derive the decryption key using the AB-GKM's key derivation algorithm. The AB-GKM scheme makes sure that only valid subscribers can derive the key and hence decrypt notifications. Since subscribers are not given decryption keys during the registration and they must dynamically derive the keys, our approach can efficiently handle subscriber revocations and additions as well as access control policy changes without affecting the existing subscribers.

3.3 Trust Model

We consider threats and assumptions from the point of view of publishers and subscribers with respect to third-party brokers. We assume that brokers are honest but curious; they perform pub/sub operations correctly, but are curious to know the notifications and subscriptions. In other words, brokers are not trusted for the confidentiality of the notifications and subscriptions. The context manager is fully trusted. Publishers are trusted to keep the secrets obtained from the context manager confidential and to perform notification blinding and encryption as specified. Subscribers are not trusted in our system. They can decrypt encrypted notifications only if they have valid credentials. Brokers may collude with one another as well as with malicious subscribers.

4 Modified Paillier Cryptosystem

In this section we provide the details of our modified Paillier cryptosystem.

Making μ Public
Recall that in the original Paillier cryptosystem, the tuple (λ, μ) is the private key. However, μ does not need to be private since it is hard to decrypt an encrypted message by only knowing μ. In order to decrypt, one needs to know both λ and μ. It can be shown that if a probabilistic polynomial time (PPT) adversary can obtain λ from μ, it can solve the discrete logarithm problem (DLP). Since DLP is a known hard problem, it is hard to obtain λ from μ. Hence, we can make μ public while achieving the same security guarantees as the unmodified Paillier cryptosystem. We take advantage of this fact in order to shift the computation towards encryption and make decryption light weight.

Shifting the Computation
With the above modification, the new public and private keys are (n, g_p, μ) and λ respectively. First, we modify the Paillier cryptosystem so that anyone can decrypt using the new public key, but only those holding the private key can encrypt. This is similar to how digital signatures work. The following equations show the modifications to the encryption and decryption algorithms: **Encryption** $E'(m, r, \lambda) = E(m, r)^{\lambda} = g_p^{m\lambda} \cdot r^{n\lambda} \pmod{n^2} = c$. and **Decryption** $D(c) = L(c \pmod{n^2}) \cdot \mu \pmod{n}$.

It should be noted that one can perform all the homomorphic operations on the modified Paillier cryptosystem similar to the unmodified Paillier cryptosystem as the above modification only shift the computation from decryption to encryption.

Computing Differences (but not Individual Values)
With the shift of computation described above, anyone can find the difference by simply decrypting each value. However, such an approach does not assure the privacy of individual values. Therefore, we introduce an additional parameter to the encryption operation in order to allow one to compute the difference while at the same time not allowing the decryption of individual values.

Assume that there are two values x_1 and x_2. We perform the following modification to the encryption operation so that a decryptor can learn the difference $(x_1 - x_2)$ without learning either x_1 or x_2. We call the modified encryption as blinding operation. The modified encryption $E''(x_1, x_2)$ outputs x_1' and x_2' where $x_1' = g^t \cdot E'(x_1, r_1) \pmod{n^2}$ and $x_2' = g^{-t} \cdot E'(-x_2, r_2) \pmod{n^2}$.

Notice that even though the decryptor knows μ, it can decrypt neither x_1' nor x_2' as they are modular multiplied with g^t and g^{-t} respectively. Due to the additive homomorphic property, the following holds: $x_1' \cdot x_2' = E'(x_1 - x_2, r_3)$.

Since the multiplication of x_1' and x_2' cancels the blinding parameters, anyone can compute the difference as follows using the public key of the modified Paillier cryptosystem: $D(x_1' \cdot x_2') = x_1 - x_2$.

Allowing Comparison
Recall that in Section 3.1 we introduced the notion of domain size which is much smaller than the plaintext space of the Paillier cryptosystem. According to our assumptions, $0 \leq x_1, x_2 \leq 2^l$ where l is the domain size and $2^l << n$. Let the difference of

x_1 and x_2 be d. Due to the restriction on the domain size, d is either between 0 and 2^l or $n - 2^l$ and n. We use this fact to compare the numbers; if $d \leq 2^l$, then $x_1 \geq x_2$ and if $d > n - 2^l$, then $x_1 < x_2$.

During the above comparison process, the party performing the comparison learns the difference d which leaks certain information about the actual values. Hence, the comparison is not privacy preserving. We introduce a technique to randomize the difference so that it is difficult to learn the difference yet the party can learn the exact comparison result.

Notice that in the above calculation, we only utilize a small range of the plaintext space to make the comparison decision. We utilize the unused space in the plaintext space in the above calculation to randomize the difference while still allowing one to make the correct matching decision. The key idea is to expand the difference from $0 - 2^l$ to $0 - n/2$ and $(n - 2^l) - n$ to $n/2 - n$ by introducing controlled random values to the encryption operation. We introduce two random values r_p and r_q during the encryption operation shown below: $x_1'' = g^t \cdot E'(x_1, r_1)^{r_p} E'(r_q) \pmod{n^2}$ and $x_2'' = g^{-t} \cdot E'(-x_2, r_2)^{r_p} \pmod{n^2}$. The decryption results in the following output: $D(x_1'' \cdot x_2'') = r_p(x_1 - x_2) + r_q = d'$.

r_p and r_q are randomly selected so that $d' \leq n/2$ if $x_1 \geq x_2$ and $d' > n/2$ if $x_1 < x_2$. Each time a party performs the comparison it gets a different d' due to the random values and thus the difference preserves the privacy of the individual values under comparison.

5 Privacy-Preserving Brokering Scheme

In this section, we describe in detail our approach to construct a privacy preserving context-aware publish subscribe system using the modified Paillier cryptosystem presented in Section 4 and the AB-GKM scheme.

As introduced in Section 3, there are four entities in our system: context manager, publisher, subscriber, and broker. The context manager acts as a TTP and generates the parameters for the modified Paillier cryptosystem and manages secrets obtained by the SecGen algorithm of the AB-GKM scheme to subscribers based on the identity attributes they possess. The context manager maintains a set of contexts $\mathcal{C}$ and a set of secrets issued to subscribers. Each context $C_i \in \mathcal{C}$ is a tuple of the following form: $C_i = \langle \lambda_i, \mu_i, t_i, r_i \rangle$, where λ_i and μ_i are Paillier parameters for E' and D' algorithms. t_i and r_i are random values.

Brokers match notifications with subscriptions within the same context only. μ_i values are public. λ_i and t_i values are private to the context manager.

Subscriber Registration

Each subscriber registers with the context manager. Let the context of a random subscriber be C_i. During the registration, the subscriber receives the following values from the context manager: $E'(-r_i)$, $E'(-1)$, and $g^{-t_i} \cdot E'(-r_i)$.

These parameters are used by the subscriber to blind subscriptions. Since μ_i is public, the subscriber may decrypt $E'(-r_i)$ using D' and obtain r_i. However, the subscriber can recover neither g^{-t_i} nor t_i from $g^{-t_i} \cdot E'(-r_i)$.

Using the SecGen algorithm of the AB-GKM scheme, each subscriber i also obtains secrets s_{ij} for each identity attribute j they possess from the context manager. These secrets are later used to derive the decryption key using the key derivation (KeyDer) algorithm of the AB-GKM scheme and decrypt notifications.

It should be noted that the identity attributes are not revealed to the context manager in plaintext as the SecGen algorithm internally utilizes the OCBE protocols. Thus the privacy of the identity attributes are preserved from the context manager.

Publisher Registration

Each publisher also registers with the context manager. Let the context of a random publisher be C_i. During the registration, the publisher receives the following values from the context manager: $E'(r_i)$, $E'(1)$, and $g^{t_i} \cdot E'(r_i)$.

Similar to subscriber registration, these parameters are used by the publisher to blind notifications. Since μ_i is public, the publisher may decrypt $E'(r_i)$ using D' and obtain r_i. Notice that the context manager may provide $E'(1)$ and r_i, and allow the publisher to compute $E'(r_i)$ homomorphically instead of providing the value directly. Also, notice that the publisher can recover neither g^{t_i} nor t_i from $g^{t_i} \cdot E'(r_i)$.

In addition to the above modified Paillier cryptosystem parameters, each publisher also obtains the set of secrets issued to subscribers using the SecGen algorithm. These secrets are used to selectively encrypt notifications based on the identity attributes that subscribers possess. The publisher first uses the key generation (KeyGen) algorithm of the AB-GKM scheme to generate the encryption key based on these secrets and then encrypts the notifications using the generated key. Notice that these secrets do not reveal the actual identity attributes of subscribers to publishers. Thus the identity attributes of subscribers are preserved from publishers as well.

Notifications

Assume that a publisher wants to publish a notification for the attributes a_1 and a_2 with values v_1 and v_2 respectively. The publisher first blinds v_1 and v_2 to create v_1' and v_2' respectively using the modified Paillier cryptosystem presented in Section 4. We show the blinding operation for a general value v as follows: $v' = g^{t_i} \cdot E'(r_i) \cdot E'(r_i(v - 1)) \cdot E'(r_v) = g^{t_i} \cdot E'(r_i v + r_v)$, where r_v is a controlled random value selected by the publisher. $E'(r_i(v - 1))$ is homomorphically computed using $E'(r_i)$. Notice that this value can be computed efficiently using fast multiplication.

Based on the ACP and the secrets issued to subscribers, the publisher generates the encryption key k using the KeyGen algorithm of the AB-GKM scheme. It then encrypts the payload of the notification $(a_1 = v_1, a_2 = v_2)$ using the key k. We denote the encrypted payload as $E_k(payload)$. The publisher sends the blinded and encrypted notification $((a_1 = v_1', a_2 = v_2'), E_k(payload))$ to brokers. Notice that brokers cannot decrypt any of the blinded values as well as the encrypted payload.

An advantage of having two sets of encrypted values for each notification is that our approach allows to perform privacy preserving matching and enforce fine-grained ACPs independently.

Subscriptions

Assume that a subscriber wants to subscribe for the attribute a_1 with the value x. The subscriber blinds x and creates x' as follows: $x' = g^{-t_i} \cdot E'(-r_i) \cdot E'(r_i(1-x)) = g^{-t_i} \cdot E'(-r_i x)$. $E'(r_i(1-x))$ is homomorphically computed using $E'(-r_i)$.

The tuple (a, x', α), where $\alpha = \{<, >\}$, is sent to brokers. Similar to the blinded notifications, notice that brokers cannot decrypt x'.

The tuple (a, x', α) represents a single attribute condition and we call such a subscription an *atomic subscription*. A subscription, in general, can be a Boolean expression over a set of atomic subscriptions and is called a *composite subscription*. Notice that the atomic subscription intentionally leaves the equality comparison operator. The motivation behind such a scheme is to further hide subscriptions and notifications from brokers. In our scheme, equality subscriptions are performed using range queries so that brokers cannot distinguish between equality subscriptions and range queries. In order to submit an equality subscription for attribute a with the value x, the subscriber submits the query $(a, x_1, >) \wedge (a, x_2, <)$, where x_1 and x_2 are the blinded values of $x - 1$ and $x + 1$. Since the blinded values are semantically secure, the conjunctive query does not reveal any information about the range and therefore brokers cannot distinguish an equality subscription from a general range subscription.

Broker Matching

For each context C_i, brokers receive μ_i. Assume that for the context C_i, a broker has received the blinded notification and subscription values v'_1 and x' respectively for the attribute a_1. As mentioned above, we emphasize that the broker can decrypt neither v'_1 nor x'. As described in Section 4, the broker computes the randomized difference d' as follows: $d' = D'(v' \cdot x') = r_i(v - x) + r_v$

It decides $v_1 > x$ if $d' \leq n/2$ and $d' \neq 0$, $v_1 < x$ otherwise. The above matching algorithm is described for an atomic subscription. Usually notifications contain more than one attribute and the broker has to match such notifications with either atomic or composite subscriptions. The matching for a composite subscription is performed by evaluating each atomic subscription in the subscription and evaluating the Boolean expression. After successful matching, the broker forwards only the encrypted payload $E_k(payload)$ to matching subscribers. Subscribers having valid credentials can derive the key k using the KeyDer algorithm of the AB-GKM scheme and access the payload of the notification.

6 Implementation and Evaluation

We extended Apache ActiveMQ, a production strength and widely used messaging middleware, with our proposed mechanisms for privacy preserving pub/sub. We used a distributed setup with one 8 core and one 16 core Intel Xeon machine as message generating clients connected to an 8 core Intel Xeon 3.5 GHz machine running Linux 2.6 that acts as our extended ActiveMQ broker. An extended discussion of the evaluation is presented in our technical report [11].

Figures 2a, 2b, and 2c show CPU utilization and latency for the CONSTANT scenario where a constant number of entities are used.

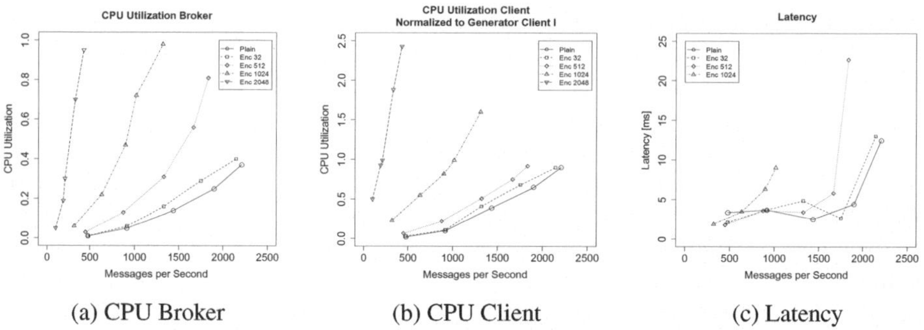

(a) CPU Broker (b) CPU Client (c) Latency

Fig. 2. Results CONSTANT Scenario: CPU Utilization and Latency for Different Message Rates and Blinding Strength

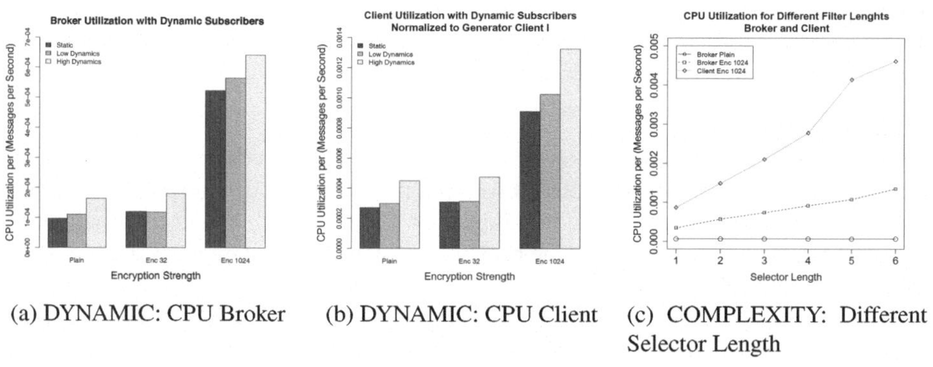

(a) DYNAMIC: CPU Broker (b) DYNAMIC: CPU Client (c) COMPLEXITY: Different Selector Length

Fig. 3. Results DYNAMIC and COMPLEXITY Scenarios: Frequent Re-Subscriptions and Different Filter Lengths

Figures 3a and 3b show the CPU utilization for the DYNAMIC scenario where subscribers leave and join the system at a certain rate to simulate context changes and user churn. The results show that the additional overhead of joining subscribers is not the factor that dominates CPU utilization at the broker. Further, the increase occurs independent of blinding which shows that the overhead of joining is inherent to the broker. On the client side CPU utilization is increased by about one third in the High Dynamics configuration compared to the Static configuration.

The results for the COMPLEXITY scenario, where subscribers use different message selector lengths, are shown in Figure 3c. For unencrypted subscriptions an increase in CPU utilization is not observable. For blinded subscriptions the CPU utilization of the broker increases slightly with increasing complexity. The utilization on the client side increases faster since for each message all attributes have to be blinded, but the broker does not necessarily evaluate the whole message selector.

7 Related Work

In this section, we compare our approach with existing work on secure content based pub/sub systems, and search over encrypted data.

Secure Content Based pub/sub Systems: Most of prior work on data confidentiality in the context of content based pub/sub systems is based on the assumption that brokers are trusted with respect to the privacy of the subscriptions [1,22,12]. However, when such an assumption does not hold, both publication confidentiality and subscription privacy are at risk. Further, such approaches limit brokers' ability to make routing decisions based on the content of the messages and thus their applicability is very limited. Approaches have also been proposed to assure confidentiality/privacy in the presence of untrusted third-party brokers. These approaches however suffer from several limitations [19,23,10,5]: inaccurate content delivery, because of the limited ability of brokers to make routing decisions based on content; weak security protocols; lack of privacy guarantees. For example, some of these approaches are prone to false positives, that is, sending irrelevant content to subscribers.

Search over Encrypted Data: Search on encrypted data is a privacy-preserving technique used in the *outsourced storage model* where a user's data are stored on a third-party server and encrypted using the user's public key. The user can use a query in the form of an encrypted token to retrieve relevant data from the server, whereas the server does not learn any more information about the query other than whether the returned data matches the search criteria. There have been efforts to support simple equality queries [21,3] and more recently complex ones involving conjunctions and disjunctions of range queries [4]. These approaches cannot be applied directly to the pub/sub model.

8 Conclusions

We proposed an approach to construct a privacy preserving context-based pub/sub system. Our approach assures the confidentiality of notifications and subscriptions from third-party brokers while allowing the brokers to perform matching operations. Further, publishers are able to enforce fine grained ACPs over encrypted notifications. Our solution is based on a modified Paillier cryptosystem and a recent group key management scheme. Unlike the existing approaches, in our approach, publishers and subscribers are able to generate notifications and subscriptions without contacting a TTP. We implemented our approach in ActiveMQ and the experimental results show that our approach is practical and efficient. As part of future work, we plan to investigate performance improvement techniques and specifically the trade-off between subscriber privacy and the message routing efficiency.

References

1. Bertino, E., Carminati, B., Ferrari, E., Thuraisingham, B., Gupta, A.: Selective and authentic third-party distribution of XML documents. IEEE TKDE 16(10), 1263–1278 (2004)
2. Bertino, E., Ferrari, E.: Secure and selective dissemination of XML documents. ACM TISS 5(3), 290–331 (2002)

3. Boneh, D., Di Crescenzo, G., Ostrovsky, R., Persiano, G.: Public key encryption with keyword search. In: Cachin, C., Camenisch, J. (eds.) EUROCRYPT 2004. LNCS, vol. 3027, pp. 506–522. Springer, Heidelberg (2004)
4. Boneh, D., Waters, B.: Conjunctive, subset, and range queries on encrypted data. In: Vadhan, S.P. (ed.) TCC 2007. LNCS, vol. 4392, pp. 535–554. Springer, Heidelberg (2007)
5. Choi, S., Ghinita, G., Bertino, E.: A privacy-enhancing content-based publish/Subscribe system using scalar product preserving transformations. In: Bringas, P.G., Hameurlain, A., Quirchmayr, G. (eds.) DEXA 2010, Part I. LNCS, vol. 6261, pp. 368–384. Springer, Heidelberg (2010)
6. Cugola, G., Margara, A., Migliavacca, M.: Context-aware publish-subscribe: Model, implementation, and evaluation. In: ISCC (2009)
7. Eugster, P., Felber, P.A., Guerraoui, R., Kermarrec, A.: The many faces of publish/subscribe. ACM Computing Surveys 35(2), 114–131 (2003)
8. Li, J., Li, N.: OACerts: Oblivious attribute certificates. IEEE TDSC 3(4), 340–352 (2006)
9. Miklau, G., Suciu, D.: Controlling access to published data using cryptography. In: VLDB (2003)
10. Minami, K., Lee, A.J., Winslett, M., Borisov, N.: Secure aggregation in a publish-subscribe system. In: WPES (2008)
11. Nabeel, M., Appel, S., Bertino, E., Buchmann, A.: Privacy preserving context aware publish subscribe systems. Technical Report 2013-1, Purdue University, CERIAS (2013)
12. Nabeel, M., Bertino, E.: Secure delta-publishing of XML content. In: ICDE (2008)
13. Nabeel, M., Bertino, E.: Towards attribute based group key management. In: CCS (2011)
14. Nabeel, M., Bertino, E., Kantarcioglu, M., Thuraisingham, B.M.: Towards privacy preserving access control in the cloud. In: CollaborateCom (2011)
15. Nabeel, M., Shang, N., Bertino, E.: Efficient privacy preserving content based publish subscribe systems. In: SACMAT (2012)
16. Nabeel, M., Shang, N., Bertino, E.: Privacy preserving policy based content sharing in public clouds. In: IEEE TKDE (2012)
17. OpenID, `http://openid.net/` (last accessed: July 18, 2012)
18. Paillier, P.: Public-key cryptosystems based on composite degree residuosity classes. In: Stern, J. (ed.) EUROCRYPT 1999. LNCS, vol. 1592, pp. 223–238. Springer, Heidelberg (1999)
19. Raiciu, C., Rosenblum, D.S.: Enabling confidentiality in content-based publish/subscribe infrastructures. In: Securecomm (2006)
20. Shang, N., Nabeel, M., Paci, F., Bertino, E.: A privacy-preserving approach to policy-based content dissemination. In: ICDE (2010)
21. Song, D.X., Wagner, D., Perrig, A.: Practical techniques for searches on encrypted data. In: SP (2000)
22. Srivatsa, M., Liu, L.: Securing publish-subscribe overlay services with eventguard. In: CCS (2005)
23. Srivatsa, M., Liu, L.: Secure event dissemination in publish-subscribe networks. In: ICDCS (2007)
24. Zou, X., Dai, Y., Bertino, E.: A practical and flexible key management mechanism for trusted collaborative computing. In: INFOCOM (2008)

A New Unpredictability-Based RFID Privacy Model

Anjia Yang[1], Yunhui Zhuang[1], Duncan S. Wong[1], and Guomin Yang[2]

[1] City University of Hong Kong, Hong Kong
{ayang3-c,yhzhuang2-c}@my.cityu.edu.hk,
duncan@cityu.edu.hk
[2] University of Wollongong, Australia
gyang@uow.edu.au

Abstract. Ind-privacy and unp-privacy, later refined to unp*-privacy, are two different classes of privacy models for RFID authentication protocols. These models have captured the major anonymity and untraceability related attacks regarding RFID authentication protocols with privacy, and existing work indicates that unp*-privacy seems to be a stronger notion when compared with ind-privacy. In this paper, we continue studying the RFID privacy models, and there are two folds regarding our results. First of all, we describe a new traceability attack and show that schemes proven secure in unp*-privacy may not be secure against this new and practical type of traceability attacks. We then propose a new unpredictability-based privacy model to capture this new type of attacks. Secondly, we show that this new model, where we called it the unp$^\tau$-privacy, is stronger than both unp*-privacy and ind-privacy.

Keywords: RFID, privacy models, mutual authentication protocol.

1 Introduction

RFID (Radio Frequency Identification) technology has been widely applied in many applications such as payments, supply chain management, tracking goods, and electronic passports. Generally speaking, an RFID system comprises a reader, a set of tags and a database. RFID tags authenticate themselves to an RFID reader through an authentication protocol and the reader may also need to authenticate itself to the tags if mutual authentication is required. However, there may exist privacy issues if the authentication protocol is not designed with a proper privacy protection mechanism. We mainly focus on the RFID tags' privacy since once the tags' privacy is disclosed, their owners or bearers will also suffer from privacy problems. To keep the tags' privacy means that the adversary cannot identify, trace or link tag appearances.

There are mainly two ways to deal with the RFID tags' privacy issues. The first one is to construct RFID protocols which can preserve the tags' privacy and the second one is to formalize privacy models for RFID systems. As to the former way, lots of protocols have been proposed in recent years [2,5,8–10,18,19],

J. Lopez, X. Huang, and R. Sandhu (Eds.): NSS 2013, LNCS 7873, pp. 479–492, 2013.

while many of them are claimed to have privacy flaws according to [11]. For the latter way, many privacy models have been proposed [1,3,4,6,7,11–17]. Among them, there are two major notions: one based on the indistinguishability of two tags [7], denoted as ind-privacy, and the other one based on the unpredictability of RFID protocol's outputs [4], denoted as unp-privacy. Ind-privacy is reasonably good; however, it is difficult to apply ind-privacy model to prove whether a given protocol is ind-private. To address this problem, Ha *et al.* [4] proposed the unp-privacy model and it has been rectified to eunp-privacy by Ma *et al.* [12]. In [11], Li *et al.* pointed out the limitation of eunp-privacy and proposed a new privacy model called unp*-privacy.

In this paper, we focus on the privacy models for RFID authentication protocols and point out some limitations of unp*-privacy. Then we propose a new privacy model and explore the relations between our proposed model and the previous models.

1.1 Our Contributions

(1) We revisit the unpredictability-based RFID privacy model denoted as unp*-privacy [11], and we point out the limitations of the unp*-privacy model by giving a protocol as a counterexample that is secure under unp*-privacy model while vulnerable to a practical attack given in Section 4.1. In this new attack, the adversary can observe the protocol results, i.e., the reaction of the reader and the tag, in an RFID authentication protocol. Through this attack the adversary can trace RFID tags.
(2) We propose a new unpredictability-based privacy model, denoted as unp$^\tau$-privacy (τ is short for traceability), and prove that our new model can handle the new attack and thus is more appropriate.
(3) We investigate the relationship among ind-privacy, unp*-privacy and unp$^\tau$-privacy and obtain the result that unp$^\tau$-privacy is stronger than both ind-privacy and unp*-privacy.

Fig. 1 illustrates the relations among the previous privacy models and the unp$^\tau$-privacy model that we elaborate in this paper. Note that the ind*-privacy model is a "bridge" which is proven to be equivalent to ind-privacy model and is used to explore the relation between ind-privacy and unp$^\tau$-privacy.

2 RFID Security Architecture

2.1 RFID System Model

We consider an RFID system which consists of n tags belonging to a set $\mathcal{T}$, and a reader R that is connected with a database. The reader and the tags are probabilistic polynomial time (PPT) interactive Turing machines. Each tag $\mathcal{T}_i$ stores an internal secret key k_i which is shared with the reader R, and some optional state information st_i. The reader R has a database to store k_i, st_i, ID_i which is the identifier of $\mathcal{T}_i$, and some other information for each tag $\mathcal{T}_i$.

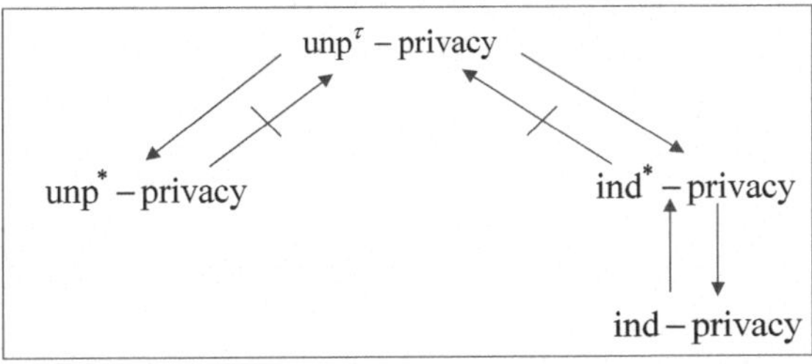

Fig. 1. Relations among privacy models

To start an authentication session, the reader R first sends a fresh challenge message c to a tag $\mathcal{T}_i$. Then $\mathcal{T}_i$ responds with a message r computed based on its secret key k_i, c, st_i, and random coins cn_i. We write r as $r = F_T(k_i, cn_i, st_i, c)$, where F_T denotes the function used by the tag. Upon receiving r, the reader verifies the response and will output either 'accept' or 'reject' as its reaction. If there is a third round (i.e. for mutual authentication), R will respond to $\mathcal{T}_i$ with a final message f which is computed according to the tag's response r, k_i, c, the reader's own state information st_R and random coins cn_R. We write it as $f = F_R(k_i, cn_R, st_R, c, r)$, where F_R is the function used by the reader. Similarly, when the tag receives f, it will verify whether f is valid or not and will output either 'accept' or 'reject' as its reaction, and terminate the session. Typically, in this paper, we focus on three-round RFID authentication protocols.

Definition 1. *An RFID system RS is composed of a tuple (R,$\mathcal{T}$,SetupReader, SetupTag, ReaderStart, TagCompute, ReaderCompute,π), where*

SetupReader. It is a function used to initialize the system with some system parameters and make the reader R ready to work.

SetupTag. It is a function used to generate the secret keys and set the initial state information for the tags. It also associates each tag with an unique *ID*.

ReaderStart. It is a function for R to generate a session identifier of a fresh session, denoted as *sid*, and a fresh challenge message c_{sid} of this session.

TagCompute($\mathcal{T}_i, sid, c_{sid}$). It is a function for $\mathcal{T}_i$ to compute its response message r_{sid}, with *sid* and c_{sid} as inputs.

ReaderCompute(sid, c_{sid}, r_{sid}). It is a function for R to compute the final message f_{sid}, with sid, c_{sid} and r_{sid} as inputs.

Protocol $\pi(R, \mathcal{T}_i)$. It is a polynomial time interactive protocol between R and $\mathcal{T}_i$. When executing the protocol, it will invoke the functions of ReaderStart,TagCompute, ReaderCompute.

We say a protocol $\pi(R, \mathcal{T}_i, sid)$ is successful if R and $\mathcal{T}_i$ accept each other.

For the completeness and soundness of RFID systems, we adopt the definitions by Li *et al.* [11]. Informally, completeness means that valid tags should always be accepted by a legitimate reader and soundness means that only valid tags/reader should be accepted. In the following sections, when we mention an RFID system, we mean it is complete and sound.

Remark 1. We assume any tag $\mathcal{T}_i$ can be involved in only one protocol session at a time and it will overwrite the old k_i and st_i when updating them.

2.2 Adversary Model

We consider a PPT adversary $\mathcal{A}$ who has the ability to eavesdrop, intercept, modify and remove messages transmitted between the reader and the tag. $\mathcal{A}$ also can generate its own messages. We assume that $\mathcal{A}$ can obtain the reaction of the reader and tag, i.e. $\mathcal{A}$ will know if the reader or any tag makes a decision ('accept' or 'reject'). In a word, we allow the adversary to adaptively query the following oracles.

InitReader. It invokes the reader R to start a new protocol session. R generates and returns a fresh session identifier sid and challenge message c_{sid}.

SendTag$(\mathcal{T}_i, sid, c_{sid})$. It invokes the tag $\mathcal{T}_i$ to start a new protocol session with the inputs sid and c_{sid}, and return a message r_{sid}.

SendReader(sid, c_{sid}, r_{sid}). It invokes R to compute and return the final message f_{sid} with the inputs sid, c_{sid} and r_{sid}.

Result(sid, f_{sid}). $\mathcal{A}$ queries the reaction of the tag in the session sid with the message f_{sid}.

SetTag$(\mathcal{T}_i)$. $\mathcal{A}$ obtains the secret key and internal state information of $\mathcal{T}_i$.

For convenience, we use O_1, O_2, O_3, O_4, O_5 to denote **InitReader, SendTag, SendReader, Result, SetTag** oracles respectively. We define some parameters for the adversary as follows. κ is the security parameter and n is the number of tags in $\mathcal{T}$, and q, s, u, v, and w are the number of O_1, O_2, O_3, O_4 and O_5 queries respectively allowed for the adversary in one game.

2.3 Mathematical Notations

Definition 2. *A function f is negligible if for every polynomial $p(\cdot)$ there exists an integer N such that for all integers $n > N$ it holds that $f(n) < \frac{1}{p(n)}$.*

Let $F : \mathcal{K} \times \mathcal{D} \rightarrow \mathcal{R}$ be a family of functions, where $\mathcal{K}$ is the set of indices of F, $\mathcal{D}$ is the domain of F and $\mathcal{R}$ is the range of F. Let $|\mathcal{K}| = m$, $|\mathcal{D}| = n$, $|\mathcal{R}| = p$. Let $RF : \mathcal{D} \rightarrow \mathcal{R}$ be the family of all functions with domain $\mathcal{D}$ and range $\mathcal{R}$. A polynomial time test (PTT) for F is an experiment, where a probabilistic polynomial time algorithm T with inputs m, n, p and access to an oracle O_f, guesses whether the function f is chosen from whether $F(\cdot)$ or $RF(\cdot)$. $b \in_R \{0,1\}$ means that b is chosen uniformly at random from $\{0,1\}$. We illustrate the PTT experiment in Fig. 2.

Definition 3. *An algorithm T passes the PTT experiment for the function family F if the advantage that it guesses the correct value of bit b is non-negligible, where the advantage of T is defined as $Adv_T(m,n,p) = \left|\Pr[b' = b] - \frac{1}{2}\right|$, k and f chosen uniformly at random from $\mathcal{K}$ and $RF(\cdot)$, respectively.*

Definition 4. *A function family $F : \mathcal{K} \times \mathcal{D} \rightarrow \mathcal{R}$ is a pseudorandom function family (PRF) if there is no probabilistic polynomial time algorithm which can pass the PTT experiment for F with non-negligible advantage.*

Experiment $\mathbf{Exp}_T^{PTT}(F, m, n, p)$

1. Select $b \in_R \{0, 1\}$;
2. If $b = 1$, select a random $k \in \mathcal{K}$ and set $f = F_k$; otherwise, select a random $f' \in RF(.)$ and set $f = f'$;
3. $b' \leftarrow T^{O_f}$;
4. The experiment outputs 1 if $b' = b$, 0 otherwise.

Fig. 2. Polynomial time test for F

3 Ind-Privacy and Unp*-Privacy

3.1 Ind-Privacy

Fig. 3 describes the ind-privacy experiment, denoted by $\mathbf{Exp}_{\mathcal{A}}^{ind}[\kappa, n, q, s, u, w]$. At first, the experiment sets up the RFID system by initializing a reader R and a set of tags $\mathcal{T} = (\mathcal{T}_1, \mathcal{T}_2, \cdots, \mathcal{T}_n)$ according to the system security parameter κ. It associates each tag $\mathcal{T}_i$ with a secret key k_i and an internal state information st_i, and also stores these keys and state information in the database connected with R. Then in the learning stage, the adversary can issue O_1, O_2, O_3, O_5 oracle queries at most q, s, u and w overall calls, respectively. The adversary also selects two uncorrupted tags $(\mathcal{T}_i, \mathcal{T}_j)$, which it has not sent SetTag (O_5) queries to, and outputs the state information st which will be used in the guess stage. Next, the experiment randomly selects a bit b and sets the challenge tag $\mathcal{T}_c = \mathcal{T}_i$ if $b = 0$, and $\mathcal{T}_c = \mathcal{T}_j$ otherwise. Finally, in the guessing stage, the adversary $\mathcal{A}$ is required to guess the random bit b by outputting a bit b'. During the guessing stage, $\mathcal{A}$ can issue O_1, O_2, O_3, O_5 oracle queries on $\mathcal{T}_c \cup (\mathcal{T} - \{\mathcal{T}_i, \mathcal{T}_j\})$ at most q, s, u and w overall calls respectively, with the restriction that it cannot query SetTag($\mathcal{T}_c$). We use $\mathbf{Exp}_{\mathcal{A}}^{ind}$ to represent the ind-privacy experiment.

Let

$$\mathbf{Adv}_{\mathcal{A}}^{ind}[\kappa, n, q, s, u, w] = \left| \Pr[\mathbf{Exp}_{\mathcal{A}}^{ind} = 1] - \frac{1}{2} \right|.$$

Experiment $\mathbf{Exp}_{\mathcal{A}}^{ind}[\kappa, n, q, s, u, w]$

1. Initialize the RFID system with a reader R and a set of tags $\mathcal{T}$ with $|\mathcal{T}| = n$;
2. $\{\mathcal{T}_i, \mathcal{T}_j, st\} \leftarrow \mathcal{A}^{O_1, O_2, O_3, O_5}(R, \mathcal{T})$; //learning stage
3. Set $\mathcal{T}' = \mathcal{T} - \{\mathcal{T}_i, \mathcal{T}_j\}$;
4. $b \in_R \{0, 1\}$;
5. If b=0, let $\mathcal{T}_c = \mathcal{T}_i$, else $\mathcal{T}_c = \mathcal{T}_j$;
6. $b' \leftarrow \mathcal{A}^{O_1, O_2, O_3, O_5}(R, \mathcal{T}', st, \mathcal{T}_c)$; //guess stage
7. The experiment outputs 1 if $b' = b$, 0 otherwise.

Fig. 3. Ind-privacy experiment

Definition 5. *An RFID system RS is said to be ind-private if for any PPT adversary $\mathcal{A}$, $\boldsymbol{Adv}_{\mathcal{A}}^{ind}[\kappa, n, q, s, u, w]$ is negligible.*

Discussion. In Juels and Weis' ind-privacy experiment [7], we cannot conclude directly whether the adversary has the ability to observe the reaction of the reader, that is, either accepts or rejects a tag. Nevertheless, in their following Section 3.1 where the OSK/AO protocols are analyzed, they described a kind of attack in which the adversary can observe the reaction of the reader. We believe they presume the adversary has this ability. In addition, Juels and Weis considered two-round RFID authentication protocols. However, Li *et al.* [11] proved Juels and Weis' ind-privacy model also works for three-round protocols. In this paper, we consider ind-privacy for three-round RFID authentication protocols, which support mutual authentication.

3.2 Unp*-Privacy

Fig. 4 illustrates unp*-privacy experiment, denoted by $\mathbf{Exp}_{\mathcal{A}}^{unp^*}[\kappa, n, q, s, u, v, w]$. In the learning stage, the adversary $\mathcal{A}$ selects an uncorrupted challenge tag $\mathcal{T}_c$ which it has not sent SetTag queries to. Next, the challenger picks a random bit b. When receiving an oracle query, the challenger will decide what to respond to $\mathcal{A}$ according to the value of b. $\mathcal{A}$ is required to guess the value of b. We use $\mathbf{Exp}_{\mathcal{A}}^{unp^*}$ to represent unp*-privacy experiment. Let

$$\mathbf{Adv}_{\mathcal{A}}^{unp^*}[\kappa, n, q, s, u, w] = \left|\Pr[\mathbf{Exp}_{\mathcal{A}}^{unp^*} = 1] - \frac{1}{2}\right|.$$

Definition 6. *An RFID system RS is said to be unp*-private if for any PPT adversary $\mathcal{A}$, $\boldsymbol{Adv}_{\mathcal{A}}^{unp^*}[\kappa, n, q, s, u, w]$ is negligible.*

Experiment $\mathbf{Exp}_{\mathcal{A}}^{unp*}[\kappa, n, q, s, u, w]$

1. Initialize the RFID system with a reader R and a set of tags $\mathcal{T}$ with $|\mathcal{T}| = n$;
2. $\{T_c, st\} \leftarrow \mathcal{A}^{O_1,O_2,O_3,O_5}(R, \mathcal{T})$; //learning stage
3. $b \in_R \{0,1\}$
4. $b' \leftarrow \mathcal{A}^{O_1,O_2,O_3}(R, T_c, st)$ //guess stage
   - 4.1 When $\mathcal{A}$ queries O_1, O_2, O_3 oracles, if b=1, run the algorithm **ReaderStart, TagCompute, ReaderCompute** respectively, and return the results (c, r, f);
   - 4.2 else b=0 pick c, r, f randomly from their respective domains and return them to $\mathcal{A}$.
5. The experiment outputs 1 if $b' = b$, 0 otherwise.

Fig. 4. Unp*-privacy experiment

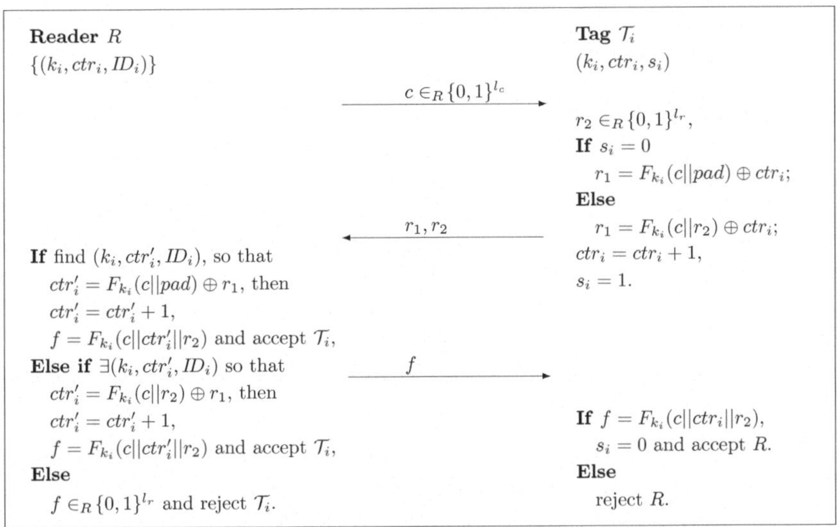

Fig. 5. A Counterexample

4 Limitation of Unp*-Privacy

Note that in unp*-privacy experiment, the adversary $\mathcal{A}$ can not observe the reaction of R and $\mathcal{T}_i$. However, in practice, for most RFID tag applications, this ability is easily obtainable. For example, a staff card either opens a door when authenticated successfully or fails to open a door when failed to be authenticated to the reader equipped in the door; a payment card is either accepted or rejected by a sale device. In the following section, we will show a counterexample which is secure under unp*-privacy model, while vulnerable to a kind of attack that is easy to launch in our daily life. This example implies a limitation of unp*-privacy when it is applied to RFID authentication protocols.

4.1 A Counterexample

Let $F : \{0,1\}^{l_k} \times \{0,1\}^{l_d} \rightarrow \{0,1\}^{l_r}$ be a PRF family. Let $ctr \in \{0,1\}^{l_r}$ be a counter, and $pad \in \{0,1\}^{l_{pad}}$ be a padding such that $l_r + l_{pad} = l_d$. When the system calls SetupTag($\mathcal{T}_i$), it will initialize $ctr_i = 1$ and set $s_i = 0$. After the initialization phase, the system will go on as the following steps.

(1) The reader R generates a random challenge message c to the tag $\mathcal{T}_i$.
(2) $\mathcal{T}_i$ randomly selects r_2 and computes r_1 according to the value of s_i: $r_1 = F_{k_i}(c||pad) \oplus ctr_i$ if $s_i = 0$, else $r_1 = F_{k_i}(c||r_2) \oplus ctr_i$.
(3) $\mathcal{T}_i$ sends the response r_1, r_2 to R, updates $ctr_i = ctr_i + 1$, and sets $s_i = 1$.
(4) R searches from the database for the tuple $(k_i,\, ctr_i',\, ID_i)$ such that $ctr_i' = F_{k_i}(c||pad) \oplus r_1$ or $ctr_i' = F_{k_i}(c||r_2) \oplus r_1$. If such a tuple exists, then update $ctr_i' = ctr_i' + 1$, compute $f = F_{k_i}(c||ctr_i'||r_2)$, send it to $\mathcal{T}_i$ and accept $\mathcal{T}_i$; else response with $f \in_R \{0,1\}^{l_r}$ and reject $\mathcal{T}_i$.

(5) Upon receiving f, $\mathcal{T}_i$ checks if $f = F_{k_i}(c||ctr_i||r_2)$. If yes, $\mathcal{T}_i$ accepts R and sets $s_i = 0$, else $\mathcal{T}_i$ rejects R.

A Traceability Attack. Now we launch a traceability attack against this protocol. We consider an adversary $\mathcal{A}$ who has the ability to know whether R accepts $\mathcal{T}_i$ or not and vice versa. $\mathcal{A}$ can find out the value of a tag's state s_i easily, for if $s_i = 0$, then $r_1 = F_{k_i}(c||pad) \oplus ctr_i$ which means the value of r_1 is not related with r_2. Therefore, $\mathcal{A}$ can change the value of r_2 that is sent by $\mathcal{T}_i$ and observe whether R will accept $\mathcal{T}_i$. If R accepts $\mathcal{T}_i$, then it means $s_i = 0$; otherwise, it means $s_i = 1$. Note that under normal circumstances the value of s_i is 0. Thus, an active attacker can flag a tag by setting its state $s_i = 1$ and then trace the tag. However, we can prove this counterexample is secure under unp*-privacy model.

Theorem 1. *The counterexample is unp*-private, given that the function family* $F : \{0,1\}^{l_k} \times \{0,1\}^{l_d} \rightarrow \{0,1\}^{l_r}$ *is a PRF family.*

Proof. Assume the counterexample in Fig. 5 is not unp*-private. That is, there exists an adversary $\mathcal{A}$ who can win the unp*-privacy game with advantage at least ϵ, and the running time at most t. We construct an algorithm $\mathcal{B}$ that uses $\mathcal{A}$ as a subroutine and can pass the PTT experiment for PRF family F. Algorithm $\mathcal{B}$ can simulate unp*-privacy experiment for $\mathcal{A}$ as follows.

Simulate the learning stage. At the beginning, $\mathcal{B}$ selects a random index $i \in [1, n]$ and sets $ctr_i = 1, s_i = 0$. The key of $\mathcal{T}_i$ is set as k_i implicitly, which is unknown to $\mathcal{B}$. For any tag $\mathcal{T}_j \in \{\mathcal{T} - \mathcal{T}_i\}$, $\mathcal{B}$ sets $ctr_j = 1, s_j = 0$ and sets the secret key of $\mathcal{T}_j$ as k_j which is selected randomly from the secret key space. When $\mathcal{A}$ queries O_1, O_2, O_3, O_5, $\mathcal{B}$ invokes O_f and the keys k_1, k_2, $\cdots$, k_{i-1}, k_{i+1}, $\cdots$, k_n to respond. Note that when $\mathcal{A}$ queries O_5 on tag $\mathcal{T}_i$, $\mathcal{B}$ aborts and randomly outputs a bit.

Simulate the challenge stage. $\mathcal{A}$ submits an uncorrupted challenge tag $\mathcal{T}_c$. Note that if $\mathcal{T}_c \neq \mathcal{T}_i$, $\mathcal{B}$ aborts and randomly outputs a bit.

Simulate the guess stage. Every time when $\mathcal{A}$ queries about O_1, O_2, O_3, $\mathcal{B}$ will answer $\mathcal{A}$ using O_f and the keys k_1, k_2, $\cdots$, k_{i-1}, k_{i+1}, $\cdots$, k_n as follows.

① When $\mathcal{A}$ queries O_1, $\mathcal{B}$ selects a random session sid and a random challenge message c and returns sid, c to $\mathcal{A}$.

② When $\mathcal{A}$ queries O_2, $\mathcal{B}$ selects a random string $r_2 \in_R \{0,1\}^{l_r}$. If $s_i = 0$, $\mathcal{B}$ queries O_f on $x = c||pad$, gets the response y and sets $r_1 = y \oplus ctr_i$; else queries O_f on $x = c||r_2$, gets the response y and sets $r_1 = y \oplus ctr_i$. Then update $ctr_i = ctr_i + 1$ and $s_i = 1$, and return r_1, r_2 to $\mathcal{A}$.

③ When $\mathcal{A}$ queries O_3, $\mathcal{B}$ queries O_f on $c||ctr_i||r_2$, gets the response f and sends f to $\mathcal{A}$.

Output. When $\mathcal{A}$ outputs a bit b', $\mathcal{B}$ also takes b' as its output.

We can see that when $O_f = F_{k_i}$, then the simulation is identical to the experiment with $b = 1$; otherwise, if $O_f = RF$, then the simulation is identical to the experiment with $b = 0$. Thus, if $\mathcal{B}$ does not abort during the simulation,

Experiment $\mathbf{Exp}_{\mathcal{A}}^{unp^{\tau}}[\kappa, n, q, s, u, v, w]$

1. Initialize the RFID system with a reader R and a set of tags $\mathcal{T}$ with $|\mathcal{T}| = n$;
2. $\{\mathcal{T}_c, st\} \leftarrow \mathcal{A}^{O_1,O_2,O_3,O_4,O_5}(R, \mathcal{T})$; //learning stage
3. $b \in_R \{0, 1\}$
4. $b' \leftarrow \mathcal{A}^{O_1,O_2,O_3,O_4}(R, \mathcal{T}_c, st)$ //guess stage
   4.1 When $\mathcal{A}$ queries O_1, O_2, O_3, O_4 oracles, if b=1, run the algorithm **ReaderStart, TagCompute, ReaderCompute, Result** respectively, and return the results; the challenger also returns the reaction of the reader R to $\mathcal{A}$, either *accept* or *reject*, when O_3 is queried.
   4.2 else b=0
      4.2.1 When $\mathcal{A}$ queries O_1, O_2 oracles, pick random elements sid, c and r from their respective domains, and return them to $\mathcal{A}$;
      4.2.2 When $\mathcal{A}$ queries O_3, the challenger compares whether r is equal to the output of $O_2(\mathcal{T}_c, sid, c)$. If yes, the challenger returns a random element f from its domain, and returns the reader's reaction as *accept*; else it returns a random element f from its domain and returns the reader's reaction as *reject*;
      4.2.3 When $\mathcal{A}$ queries O_4, the challenger checks whether f is equal to the output of $O_3(sid, c, r)$ and the reaction of the reader for this session sid is *accept*. If yes, the challenger returns the tag's reaction as *accept*; else it returns the tag's reaction as *reject*;
5. The experiment outputs 1 if $b' = b$, 0 otherwise.

Fig. 6. Unp$^{\tau}$-privacy experiment

$\mathcal{B}$'s simulation is perfect. The probability that $\mathcal{B}$ does not abort during the simulation is $\frac{1}{n}$. Thus, if the adversary $\mathcal{A}$ can pass unp*-privacy experiment with the advantage at least ϵ, then the advantage that $\mathcal{B}$ passes the PTT experiment is at least $\frac{\epsilon}{n}$. In addition, the running time of $\mathcal{B}$ is approximate to that of $\mathcal{A}$. This completes the proof. □

5 Our Proposed Privacy Model: Unp$^{\tau}$-Privacy

Fig. 6 illustrates the unp$^{\tau}$-privacy experiment, denoted by $\mathbf{Exp}_{\mathcal{A}}^{unp^{\tau}}[\kappa, n, q, s, u, v, w]$. In this experiment the adversary $\mathcal{A}$ can query O_4. Note that when $b = 1$ and O_3 is queried, the challenger will return f as well as the reaction of the reader, and when $b = 0$ and O_3 is queried, the challenger needs to send the reader's reaction to $\mathcal{A}$, since it's in accordance with the situation when $b = 1$ so that $\mathcal{A}$ can not distinguish $b=0$ or $b=1$ only according to the reaction of the reader R.

We use $\mathbf{Exp}_{\mathcal{A}}^{unp^{\tau}}$ to represent the unp$^{\tau}$-privacy experiment. Let

$$\mathbf{Adv}_{\mathcal{A}}^{unp^{\tau}}[\kappa, n, q, s, u, v, w] = \left|\Pr[\mathbf{Exp}_{\mathcal{A}}^{unp^{\tau}} = 1] - \frac{1}{2}\right|.$$

Definition 7. *An RFID system RS is said to be unp$^{\tau}$-private if for any PPT adversary $\mathcal{A}$, $\mathbf{Adv}_{\mathcal{A}}^{unp^{\tau}}[\kappa, n, q, s, u, v, w]$ is negligible.*

Note that the counterexample in Fig. 5 does not satisfy our privacy model. In unp$^{\tau}$-privacy experiment, when the adversary modifies the second message r_2

randomly, if $b = 1$, the reader R will accept the tag $\mathcal{T}_c$ with overwhelming probability, since the value of r_1 is not related with r_2 under normal circumstances; otherwise, if $b = 0$, the reader R will reject the tag $\mathcal{T}_c$. That is, the adversary can distinguish the two cases with overwhelming probability. Hence the counterexample is not unp$^\tau$-private.

5.1 Relation between Unp$^\tau$-Privacy and Ind-Privacy

In order to explore the relation between unp$^\tau$-privacy and ind-privacy, we first introduce a restricted ind-privacy model, denoted as ind*-privacy, as a "bridge", which is equivalent to ind-privacy.

Ind*-Privacy Fig. 7 illustrates the ind*-privacy experiment, denoted by $\mathbf{Exp}_{\mathcal{A}}^{ind^*}[\kappa, n, q, s, u, v, w]$, which is identical to the ind-privacy experiment given in Fig. 3 except that the adversary $\mathcal{A}$ in ind*-privacy experiment is not allowed to query oracles on other tags except for $\mathcal{T}_c$ in the guess stage. Since we have showed that the adversary in the ind-privacy model has the ability to know the result of the reader's reaction, we explicitly allow $\mathcal{A}$ to query O_4 in ind*-privacy experiment. We use $\mathbf{Exp}_{\mathcal{A}}^{ind^*}$ to simply represent ind*-privacy experiment. Let

$$\mathbf{Adv}_{\mathcal{A}}^{ind^*}[\kappa, n, q, s, u, v, w] = \left|\Pr[\mathbf{Exp}_{\mathcal{A}}^{ind^*} = 1] - \frac{1}{2}\right|.$$

Experiment $\mathbf{Exp}_{\mathcal{A}}^{ind^*}[\kappa, n, q, s, u, v, w]$

1. Initialize the RFID system with a reader R and a set of tags $\mathcal{T}$ with $|\mathcal{T}| = n$;
2. $\{\mathcal{T}_i, \mathcal{T}_j, st\} \leftarrow \mathcal{A}^{O_1,O_2,O_3,O_4,O_5}(R, \mathcal{T})$; //learning stage
3. Set $\mathcal{T}' = \mathcal{T} - \{\mathcal{T}_i, \mathcal{T}_j\}$;
4. $b \in_R \{0, 1\}$;
5. If b=0, let $\mathcal{T}_c = \mathcal{T}_i$, else $\mathcal{T}_c = \mathcal{T}_j$;
6. $b' \leftarrow \mathcal{A}^{O_1,O_2,O_3,O_4}(R, \mathcal{T}_c, st)$; //guess stage
7. The experiment outputs 1 if $b' = b$, 0 otherwise.

Fig. 7. Ind*-privacy experiment

Definition 8. *An RFID system RS is said to be ind*-private if for any PPT adversary $\mathcal{A}$, $\boldsymbol{Adv}_{\mathcal{A}}^{ind^*}[\kappa, n, q, s, u, v, w]$ is negligible.*

Ind*-Privacy $\Longleftrightarrow$ Ind-Privacy On the one hand, the adversary in ind-privacy experiment can query oracles on any tag from $\mathcal{T}' \cap \mathcal{T}_c$ in the guess stage, while the adversary in ind*-privacy experiment can only query oracles on $\mathcal{T}_c$ in the guess stage. There is no any other difference between ind-privacy and ind*-privacy. That is, there are more restrictions on the adversary in ind*-privacy experiment, and thus ind-privacy implies ind*-privacy. On the other hand, the adversary in ind*-privacy experiment can launch O_5 queries on all tags in $\mathcal{T}'$

before the guess stage in order to obtain the secret keys and internal state information of all the tags in $\mathcal{T}'$ and then store them in a list **TagKey-List**. Then in the guess stage when the adversary queries those oracles on any tag in $\mathcal{T}'$, the adversary itself can obtain the corresponding answers using the list **TagKey-List**. That is, the adversary's power in ind*-privacy experiment is not weakened compared with that in ind-privacy experiment.

Theorem 2. *Ind*-privacy is equivalent to ind-privacy for an RFID system RS.*

Proof. First, it is obvious that ind-privacy $\Longrightarrow$ ind*-privacy as what we have analyzed above. In the following, we will prove ind-privacy $\Longleftarrow$ ind*-privacy.

Assume that RS is not ind-private. That is, there exists an adversary $\mathcal{A}$ which can win the ind-privacy game with advantage at least ϵ, and the running time at most t. We construct an algorithm $\mathcal{B}$ that uses $\mathcal{A}$ as a subroutine and can pass ind*-privacy experiment. Algorithm $\mathcal{B}$ can simulate ind-privacy experiment for $\mathcal{A}$ as follows.

Simulate the learning stage. When $\mathcal{A}$ queries O_1, O_2, O_3, O_5 oracles, algorithm $\mathcal{B}$ queries these oracles in ind*-privacy experiment and sends the results it receives to $\mathcal{A}$. Actually, we have shown that in ind-privacy experiment, the adversary $\mathcal{A}$ also has the ability to observe the protocol results, which means it can query O_4 (can be seen in ind*-privacy experiment).

Simulate the challenge stage. When $\mathcal{A}$ outputs two uncorrupted tags $\mathcal{T}_i, \mathcal{T}_j$, algorithm $\mathcal{B}$ will also submit $\mathcal{T}_i$ and $\mathcal{T}_j$ to the challenger in ind*-privacy experiment, and get the response with a challenge tag $\mathcal{T}_c \in \{\mathcal{T}_i, \mathcal{T}_j\}$. Then $\mathcal{B}$ sends O_5 oracles on all the tags in $\mathcal{T}' = \mathcal{T} - \{\mathcal{T}_i, \mathcal{T}_j\}$ and stores the results in **TagKey-List**. Then $\mathcal{B}$ forwards $\mathcal{T}_c$ to $\mathcal{A}$.

Simulate the guess stage. When $\mathcal{A}$ queries O_1, O_2, O_3, O_5 oracles on $\mathcal{T}' \cup \mathcal{T}_c$, $\mathcal{B}$ also uses the oracles O_1, O_2, O_3, together with the list **TagKey-List** to answer $\mathcal{A}$.

Output. When $\mathcal{A}$ outputs a bit b', $\mathcal{B}$ also takes b' as its own output.

We can see the simulation of $\mathcal{B}$ is perfect. Thus if $\mathcal{A}$ can pass ind-privacy experiment with the advantage at least ϵ, then the advantage that $\mathcal{B}$ passes ind*-privacy experiment is at least ϵ, too. In addition, the running time of $\mathcal{B}$ is approximate to that of $\mathcal{A}$. This completes the proof. □

Unp$^\tau$-Privacy $\Longrightarrow$Ind*-Privacy

Theorem 3. *Given an RFID system RS, if RS is unp$^\tau$-private, then it is ind*-private.*

Proof. Assume that RS is not ind*-private. That is, there exists an adversary $\mathcal{A}$ which can win ind*-privacy game with advantage at least ϵ, and the running time at most t. We construct an algorithm $\mathcal{B}$ that uses $\mathcal{A}$ as a subroutine and can pass unp$^\tau$-privacy experiment. Algorithm $\mathcal{B}$ can simulate ind*-privacy experiment for $\mathcal{A}$ as follows.

Simulate the learning stage. When $\mathcal{A}$ queries O_1, O_2, O_3, O_4, O_5 oracles, algorithm $\mathcal{B}$ queries these oracles in unp$^\tau$-privacy experiment and sends the results it receives to $\mathcal{A}$.

Simulate the challenge stage. When $\mathcal{A}$ outputs two uncorrupted tags $\mathcal{T}_i, \mathcal{T}_j$ which it has not queried O_5 oracle on, algorithm $\mathcal{B}$ will pick a random bit b and set the challenge tag $\mathcal{T}_c = \mathcal{T}_i$ if $b = 0$ and $\mathcal{T}_c = \mathcal{T}_j$ otherwise. Then $\mathcal{B}$ sends $\mathcal{T}_c$ to $\mathcal{A}$ as its challenge tag and $\mathcal{B}$ also submits $\mathcal{T}_c$ as its own challenge tag to the challenger in unp$^{\tau}$-privacy experiment.

Simulate the guess stage. When $\mathcal{A}$ queries O_1, O_2, O_3, O_4 oracles on $\mathcal{T}_c$, $\mathcal{B}$ also queries these oracles on $\mathcal{T}_c$ in unp$^{\tau}$-privacy experiment and sends the results it receives to $\mathcal{A}$

Output. When $\mathcal{A}$ outputs a bit b', if $b' = b$, $\mathcal{B}$ outputs 1, otherwise it outputs 0.

We can see the simulation of $\mathcal{B}$ is perfect. Let b_0 be the random bit selected in unp$^{\tau}$-privacy experiment. If $b_0 = 0$, then the challenge tag $\mathcal{T}_c$ is in fact a virtual tag in $\mathcal{A}$'s view since $\mathcal{A}$ will always obtain the random responses when it queries O_1, O_2, O_3 in the guess stage. Hence, in this case, the probability of $b' = b$ is equal to $\frac{1}{2}$. Otherwise, if $b_0 = 1$, the probability of $b' = b$ is $\frac{1}{2} + \epsilon$. That means the advantage of $\mathcal{B}$ in unp$^{\tau}$-privacy experiment is equal to $|\frac{1}{2} - (\frac{1}{2} + \epsilon)| = \epsilon$, which is the same as that of $\mathcal{A}$ in ind*-privacy experiment. Thus if $\mathcal{A}$ can pass ind*-privacy experiment with the advantage at least ϵ, then the advantage that $\mathcal{B}$ passes unp$^{\tau}$-privacy experiment is at least ϵ, too. In addition, the running time of $\mathcal{B}$ is approximate to that of $\mathcal{A}$. This completes the proof. □

Unp$^{\tau}$-Privacy $\Longrightarrow$Ind-Privacy From Theorem 2 and Theorem 3, we can obtain the following Theorem 4:

Theorem 4. *Given an RFID system RS, if RS is unp$^{\tau}$-private, then it is ind-private.*

Unp$^{\tau}$-Privacy$\not\Longleftarrow$ Ind-Privacy

Theorem 5. *Given an RFID system RS, if RS is ind-private, then it does not imply RS is unp$^{\tau}$-private.*

Proof. (Sketch) We can use the same RFID system as in Li *et al.*'s paper [11]: $RS = \{R, \mathcal{T}, SetupReader, SetupTag, \pi\}$ such that the protocol transcripts will have the format $(c, r||r, f)$. Then we can show that RS is ind-private since for any PPT adversary, $r_1||r_1$ and $r_2||r_2$ are just two independent random strings. However, in unp$^{\tau}$-privacy experiment, the adversary can easily distinguish if the output $r_1||r_2$ comes from a real protocol transcript or it is chosen randomly by the challenger. If $r_1||r_2$ is chosen by the challenger randomly, then we know $r_1 \neq r_2$ with overwhelming probability; otherwise, if it is from the real protocol transcript, then $r_1 = r_2$ definitely. That is to say, RS is not unp$^{\tau}$-private. This completes the proof. □

5.2 Relation between Unp$^{\tau}$-Privacy and Unp*-Privacy

According to the counterexample in Fig. 5, we have known that unp*-privacy does not imply unp$^{\tau}$-privacy. Since the adversary are more powerful in unp$^{\tau}$-privacy experiment than in unp*-privacy experiment, intuitively we can understand that unp$^{\tau}$-privacy implies unp*-privacy.

Theorem 6. *Given an RFID system RS, if RS is unp$^\tau$-private, then it is unp*-private.*

Proof. Assume that RS is not unp*-private. That is, there exists an adversary $\mathcal{A}$ which can win the unp*-privacy game with advantage at least ϵ, and the running time at most t. We construct an algorithm $\mathcal{B}$ that uses $\mathcal{A}$ as a subroutine and can pass the unp$^\tau$-private experiment. Algorithm $\mathcal{B}$ can simulate the unp*-private experiment for $\mathcal{A}$ as follows.

Simulate the learning stage. When $\mathcal{A}$ queries O_1, O_2, O_3, O_5 oracles, algorithm $\mathcal{B}$ queries these oracles in unp$^\tau$-privacy experiment and sends the results it receives to $\mathcal{A}$.

Simulate the challenge stage. When $\mathcal{A}$ outputs one uncorrupted tag $\mathcal{T}_c$ as its challenge tag, algorithm $\mathcal{B}$ also makes $\mathcal{T}_c$ as its own challenge tag in unp$^\tau$-privacy experiment.

Simulate the guess stage. When $\mathcal{A}$ queries O_1, O_2, O_3 oracles on $\mathcal{T}_c$, $\mathcal{B}$ also queries these oracles on $\mathcal{T}_c$ in unp$^\tau$-privacy experiment and sends the results it receives to $\mathcal{A}$.

Output. When $\mathcal{A}$ outputs a bit b', $\mathcal{B}$ also takes b' as its output.

We can see the simulation of $\mathcal{B}$ is perfect. Thus if $\mathcal{A}$ can pass unp*-privacy experiment with the advantage at least ϵ, then the advantage that $\mathcal{B}$ passes unp$^\tau$-privacy experiment is at least ϵ, too. In addition, the running time of $\mathcal{B}$ is approximate to that of $\mathcal{A}$. This completes the proof. □

Up to now, we have explored all these relations among ind-privacy, unp*-privacy and our newly proposed unp$^\tau$-privacy. As shown in Fig. 1, we can obtain the following claim:

Claim. Unp$^\tau$-privacy is stronger than both unp*-privacy and ind-privacy.

6 Conclusion

In this paper, we revisited the unp*-privacy model which is based on the unp-privacy and pointed out its limitations by giving a counterexample and demonstrating a new traceability attack on it. Then we proposed a new unpredictability-based privacy model, denoted as unp$^\tau$-privacy. We investigated the relationship among ind-privacy, unp*-privacy and unp$^\tau$-privacy and formally proved that our unp$^\tau$-privacy is stronger than both ind-privacy and unp*-privacy.

References

1. Avoine, G.: Adversarial model for radion frequency identification. Cryptology ePrint Archive, Report 2005/049 (2005), `http://eprint.iacr.org/`
2. Burmester, M., Le, T.V., de Medeiros, B., Tsudik, G.: Universally composable RFID identification and authentication protocols. ACM TISSEC 2009 12(4) (2009)
3. Deng, R.H., Li, Y., Yung, M., Zhao, Y.: A new framework for RFID privacy. In: Gritzalis, D., Preneel, B., Theoharidou, M. (eds.) ESORICS 2010. LNCS, vol. 6345, pp. 1–18. Springer, Heidelberg (2010)

4. Ha, J., Moon, S., Zhou, J., Ha, J.: A new formal proof model for RFID location privacy. In: Jajodia, S., Lopez, J. (eds.) ESORICS 2008. LNCS, vol. 5283, pp. 267–281. Springer, Heidelberg (2008)
5. Henrici, D., Müller, P.: Hash-based enhancement of location privacy for radio-frequency identification devices using varying identifiers. In: IEEE PerCom Workshops 2004, pp. 149–153 (2004)
6. Hermans, J., Pashalidis, A., Vercauteren, F., Preneel, B.: A new RFID privacy model. In: Atluri, V., Diaz, C. (eds.) ESORICS 2011. LNCS, vol. 6879, pp. 568–587. Springer, Heidelberg (2011)
7. Juels, A., Weis, S.A.: Defining strong privacy for RFID. In: IEEE PerCom Workshops 2007, pp. 342–347 (2007); Also appears in ACM TISSEC 2009 13(1), 7 (2009)
8. Kim, C.H., Avoine, G., Koeune, F., Standaert, F.-X., Pereira, O.: The Swiss-Knife RFID distance bounding protocol. In: Lee, P.J., Cheon, J.H. (eds.) ICISC 2008. LNCS, vol. 5461, pp. 98–115. Springer, Heidelberg (2009)
9. Le, T.V., Burmester, M., de Medeiros, B.: Universally composable and forward-secure RFID authentication and authenticated key exchange. In: ASIACCS 2007, pp. 242–252 (2007)
10. Lee, S.M., Hwang, Y.J., Lee, D.-H., Lim, J.-I.: Efficient authentication for low-cost RFID systems. In: Gervasi, O., Gavrilova, M.L., Kumar, V., Laganá, A., Lee, H.P., Mun, Y., Taniar, D., Tan, C.J.K. (eds.) ICCSA 2005. LNCS, vol. 3480, pp. 619–627. Springer, Heidelberg (2005)
11. Li, Y., Deng, R.H., Lai, J., Ma, C.: On two RFID privacy notions and their relations. ACM TISSEC 2011 14(4) (2011)
12. Ma, C., Li, Y., Deng, R.H., Li, T.: Relation between two notions, minimal condition, and efficient construction. In: ACM CCS 2009, pp. 54–65 (2009)
13. Moriyama, D., Matsuo, S., Ohkubo, M.: Relations among notions of privacy for RFID authentication protocols. In: Foresti, S., Yung, M., Martinelli, F. (eds.) ESORICS 2012. LNCS, vol. 7459, pp. 661–678. Springer, Heidelberg (2012)
14. Ng, C.Y., Susilo, W., Mu, Y., Safavi-Naini, R.: RFID privacy models revisited. In: Jajodia, S., Lopez, J. (eds.) ESORICS 2008. LNCS, vol. 5283, pp. 251–266. Springer, Heidelberg (2008)
15. Ouafi, K., Phan, R.C.-W.: Traceable privacy of recent provably-secure RFID protocols. In: Bellovin, S.M., Gennaro, R., Keromytis, A.D., Yung, M. (eds.) ACNS 2008. LNCS, vol. 5037, pp. 479–489. Springer, Heidelberg (2008)
16. Paise, R.-I., Vaudenay, S.: Mutual authentication in RFID: Security and privacy. In: ASIACCS 2008, pp. 292–299 (2008)
17. Vaudenay, S.: On privacy models for RFID. In: Kurosawa, K. (ed.) ASIACRYPT 2007. LNCS, vol. 4833, pp. 68–87. Springer, Heidelberg (2007)
18. Weis, S.A., Sarma, S.E., Rivest, R.L., Engels, D.W.: Security and privacy aspects of low-cost radio frequency identification systems. In: Hutter, D., Müller, G., Stephan, W., Ullmann, M. (eds.) Security in Pervasive Computing 2003. LNCS, vol. 2802, pp. 201–212. Springer, Heidelberg (2004)
19. Yang, A., Zhuang, Y., Wong, D.S.: An efficient single-slow-phase mutually authenticated RFID distance bounding protocol with tag privacy. In: Chim, T.W., Yuen, T.H. (eds.) ICICS 2012. LNCS, vol. 7618, pp. 285–292. Springer, Heidelberg (2012)

Privacy-Preserving Multi-party Reconciliation Using Fully Homomorphic Encryption

Florian Weingarten[1], Georg Neugebauer[1], Ulrike Meyer[1], and Susanne Wetzel[2]

[1] LuFG IT-Security, UMIC Research Centre
RWTH Aachen University, D-52074 Aachen, Germany
{weingarten,neugebauer,meyer}@umic.rwth-aachen.de
[2] Department of Computer Science, Stevens Institute of Technology
NJ 07030, USA
swetzel@stevens.edu

Abstract. Fully homomorphic cryptosystems allow the evaluation of arbitrary Boolean circuits on encrypted inputs and therefore have very important applications in the area of secure multi-party computation. Since every computable function can be expressed as a Boolean circuit, it is theoretically clear how to achieve function evaluation on encrypted inputs. However, the transformation to Boolean circuits is not trivial in practice. In this work, we design such a transformation for certain functions, i.e., we propose algorithms and protocols which make use of fully homomorphic encryption in order to achieve privacy-preserving multi-party reconciliation on ordered sets. Assuming a sufficiently efficient encryption scheme, our solution performs much better than existing approaches in terms of communication overhead and number of homomorphic operations.

Keywords: privacy, secure group computation, cryptographic protocols, multi-party reconciliation protocols, fully homomorphic encryption.

1 Introduction

The problem of secure multi-party computation was first introduced by Yao [1]. It is about jointly computing a function on private inputs of multiple parties without involving another trusted party and without revealing the private inputs of any party. Privacy-preserving reconciliation protocols on ordered sets are protocols that solve a particular subproblem of secure multi-party computation. Here, each party holds a private input set in which the elements are ordered according to the party's preferences. The goal of a reconciliation protocol on these ordered sets is then to find all common elements in the parties' input sets that maximize the joint preferences of the parties. A reconciliation protocol is privacy-preserving, if it does not reveal anything about the private inputs of a party to any other party except from what can be deduced from the desired output of the protocol.

Two-party protocols that solve the reconciliation problem for totally ordered input sets of equal size have first been proposed in [2,3]. The performance of these two-party protocols was studied in [4]. They make use of a privacy-preserving set intersection protocol such as [5]. In [6,7] the first protocols were proposed which

J. Lopez, X. Huang, and R. Sandhu (Eds.): NSS 2013, LNCS 7873, pp. 493–506, 2013.

address the multi-party case. These protocols are based on privacy-preserving operations on multisets, i.e., sets in which elements may occur more than once. In particular, the protocols use set intersection, set union, and set reduction operations. Privacy-preserving protocols for these three operations were first introduced in [8]. Recently, further protocols for multi-party set intersection [9,10,11,12] and set union [13,14] have been proposed. An overview on a variety of applications of privacy-preserving reconciliation protocols, including scheduling applications, electronic voting, and online auctions, is provided in [15].

As a main contribution of this paper, we utilize fully homomorphic encryption [16,17] to design two new protocols for multi-party reconciliation on ordered sets and analyze their security properties and efficiency. Our two variants can guarantee more privacy regarding the output of the protocol compared to [6,7]. Our evaluation shows that the new protocols outperform the previously developed protocols in terms of communication and number of homomorphic operations.

The rest of this paper is structured as follows: In Sect. 2, we briefly review basic concepts used in our paper. In Sect. 3, we describe our two new reconciliation protocols. Sect. 4 presents the comparison of our new protocols with the previously developed protocols. In Sect. 5, we draw conclusions of our results.

2 Preliminaries

In this section, we will lay down some preliminaries. In particular, we will define the setting of reconciliation problems as well as outline the multi-party solution by Neugebauer et al. [6] since their core idea is the ground work for our solution in the next section. We introduce some necessary notation and tools from the area of Fully Homomorphic Encryption (FHE).

We consider n parties $\mathcal{A}_1, ..., \mathcal{A}_n$ with private input sets $P_{\mathcal{A}_1}, ..., P_{\mathcal{A}_n} \subseteq P$, each having exactly k (pairwise distinct) elements chosen from a common input domain P. Each party has certain "preferences" associated with its input set which orders a party's elements. The preference of a rule in this ordering is called its *rank* and is identified by a bijective function $\text{rank}_{\mathcal{A}_i} : P_{\mathcal{A}_i} \rightarrow \{1, ..., k\}$.

The goal of a reconciliation protocol is to find the "best" common input elements in a fair way, i. e., taking the preferences of all parties equally into account. The two notions of fairness introduced by Meyer et al. [3], called *preference order composition schemes*, are defined by the following two functions.

Definition 1. *For a common input* $x \in P_{\mathcal{A}_1} \cap ... \cap P_{\mathcal{A}_n}$, *define the functions* $f_{SR}, f_{MR} : \bigcap_{i=1}^{n} P_{\mathcal{A}_i} \rightarrow \mathbb{N}$ *by*

$$f_{SR}(x) := \text{rank}_{\mathcal{A}_1}(x) + ... + \text{rank}_{\mathcal{A}_n}(x) \text{ and}$$
$$f_{MR}(x) := \min(\text{rank}_{\mathcal{A}_1}(x), ..., \text{rank}_{\mathcal{A}_n}(x))$$

called sum of ranks (SR) *and* minimum of ranks (MR).

With f_{SR}, maximizing the combined rank means finding one or more rules which are ranked as high as possible by all parties, i.e., the ranks of all parties count. With f_{MR}, we want to find a rule which is not ranked very low by any party, i.e., only the smallest ranking of that rule counts. Depending on the concrete application, one of those two definitions of "fairness" might be preferred.

2.1 Reconciliation on Ordered Sets

We now give a formal definition of a reconciliation protocol.

Definition 2 (Reconciliation on Ordered Sets). *A* reconciliation protocol on ordered sets *for a preference composition scheme f is a multi-party protocol between n parties $\mathcal{A}_1, ..., \mathcal{A}_n$, each with an ordered input set $(P_{\mathcal{A}_i}, \text{rank}_{A_i})$ as described above. As output of the protocol, each party learns the maximal rank* $\max_{x \in I} f(x)$ *(if one exists) as well as the set of all rank-maximizing elements* $\arg\max_{x \in I} f(x) = \{x \in I \mid \forall y \in I \ : \ f(y) \leq f(x)\}$ *where* $I := P_{\mathcal{A}_1} \cap ... \cap P_{\mathcal{A}_n}$*.*

In the following, we will refer to the multi-party reconciliation problem on ordered sets as MPROS and the variants for minimum of ranks and sum of ranks as MPROS^{MR} and MPROS^{SR}, respectively.

2.2 Adversary Model

In this paper, we consider the honest-but-curious adversary model, which is also referred to as the *semi-honest model* [18]. In this model, all parties are assumed to act according to the prescribed actions in the protocols. They may, however, try to infer as much information as possible from all results obtained during the execution.

Definition 3 (Security of Reconciliation Protocols). *A reconciliation protocol on ordered sets (as defined in Definition 2) is said to be* privacy-preserving (in the semi-honest model) *if none of the participating parties gains any additional information about the other party's private inputs except from what can be deduced from the protocol output, i.e., the maximal rank and the set of rank-maximizing elements.*

2.3 Prior Privacy-Preserving MPROS Protocols

Neugebauer et al. [6,7] proposed an approach which is based on the work of Kissner and Song [8] about privacy-preserving multiset operations. The essential idea of the operations proposed by Kissner et al. is to encode the elements of multisets as the roots of an encrypted polynomial and compute the result of the set operations using an additively homomorphic cryptosystem, which allows to perform certain operations on encrypted polynomials.

The basic idea of Neugebauer et al. is to encode the ordered inputs as multisets where the rank of each element is encoded by the element's multiplicity in the set. The preference order composition schemes f_{SR} and f_{MR} can then be modeled using operations on these multisets. Privacy is preserved by the use of a semantically secure [19] additively homomorphic cryptosystem.

Let $P_{\mathcal{A}_1}, ..., P_{\mathcal{A}_n} \subseteq P$ be the inputs of the parties and $P \subseteq M$ be the set of possible inputs, encoded as elements of the plaintext space M of some semantically secure and additively homomorphic cryptosystem. Assume the rank of each input element $p \in P_{\mathcal{A}_i}$ is encoded by its multiplicity in the set $S_{\mathcal{A}_i}$, i.e., p appears $\text{rank}_{\mathcal{A}_i}(p)$ times in $S_{\mathcal{A}_i}$. Every such set $S_{\mathcal{A}_i}$ with k distinct elements can now be identified by a polynomial f_i of degree $\sum_{j=1}^{k} j = \frac{1}{2}k(k+1)$ such that the distinct roots of f_i correspond to the distinct set elements and the multiplicity of the root corresponds to the multiplicity of the element in $S_{\mathcal{A}_i}$. When using such multiset representations, the multiset intersection operation precisely coincides with the definition of f_{MR}. The MPROS^{MR} protocol computes $\text{Rd}_t(S_{\mathcal{A}_1} \cap ... \cap S_{\mathcal{A}_n})$ for $t = k-1, k-2, ..., 0$ until the resulting set is non-empty for the first time, where $\text{Rd}_t(A)$ for some multiset A denotes the set which results from *reducing* the multiplicity of each element in A by (up to) t. All elements in this non-empty set then maximize the minimum of ranks. The emptiness check is done by a threshold decryption of the result set and a computation of the roots of the decrypted polynomial. Threshold decryption is possible in a threshold version of an additively homomorphic cryptosystem. The private key is shared among the n parties with each party $\mathcal{A}_i$ holding a private share s_i. Using s_i, a party can now compute a *partial decryption* of a ciphertext. To successfully decrypt a given ciphertext, a certain number of key shares are required to compute the plaintext by combining the partial decryptions of the ciphertext.

The construction of [8,6] for the sum of ranks preference order composition scheme f_{SR} works as follows. At first glance, multiset union seems to coincide with f_{SR} because the multiplicity of an element in the union is defined as the sum of the multiplicities of the element in the single sets. However, we have to rule out all elements which are not in the intersection because there may be elements in the union that are not shared by all parties. Neugebauer et al. describe a protocol for MPROS^{SR} which computes $\text{Rd}_t((S_{\mathcal{A}_1} \cup ... \cup S_{\mathcal{A}_n}) \cap (S'_{\mathcal{A}_1} \cap ... \cap S'_{\mathcal{A}_n}))$ where $S'_{\mathcal{A}_i}$ contains the same elements as $S_{\mathcal{A}_i}$ but every element has multiplicity $n \cdot k$. Like before, the protocol continues for $t = kn-1, kn-2, ..., n-1$ until the resulting set is non-empty for the first time. All elements in this non-empty set then maximize the sum of ranks assigned by each party. The auxiliary sets $S'_{\mathcal{A}_i}$ ensure that only inputs that are common to all parties are contained in the resulting set.

2.4 Fully Homomorphic Encryption

In the following, we make use of an asymmetric *fully homomorphic encryption scheme* which operates on the binary plaintext space $M = \mathbb{F}_2 = \{0,1\}$ and generates ciphertexts from some set C via a probabilistic polynomial-time encryption algorithm E_{pk}. There is a (deterministic) polynomial-time decryption algorithm D_{sk} such that $\mathsf{D}(\mathsf{E}(m)) = m$ for all $m \in M$. Furthermore, we have algorithms $\boxplus_{\text{pk}}$ and $\boxtimes_{\text{pk}}$ which perform homomorphic operations, i.e., $\mathsf{D}(\mathsf{E}(m_1) \boxplus \mathsf{E}(m_2)) = m_1 + m_2$ and $\mathsf{D}(\mathsf{E}(m_1) \boxtimes \mathsf{E}(m_2)) = m_1 \cdot m_2$, where $+$ and $\cdot$ denote addition and multiplication in $\mathbb{F}_2$, i.e., binary XOR and AND. We also use the notations $\mathsf{E}, \mathsf{D}, \boxplus$ and $\boxtimes$ on tuples to denote component-wise application.

We use the notation $T_{\mathsf{B}}^{\mathsf{A}}(\ell)$ to denote the number of times algorithm A calls algorithm B on inputs of bit-length ℓ, for example $T_{\boxplus}^{\mathsf{A}}(\ell)$, $T_{\boxtimes}^{\mathsf{A}}(\ell)$, $T_{\mathsf{E}}^{\mathsf{A}}(\ell)$, or $T_{\mathsf{D}}^{\mathsf{A}}(\ell)$

to denote the runtime of A in terms of number of homomorphic additions, homomorphic multiplications, encryptions, or decryptions. We will write $T^{\mathsf{A}}(\ell)$ to denote the total number of homomorphic operations (both additions and multiplications). For a probabilistic algorithm, we write $x \leftarrow \mathsf{A}(x)$ to denote that x is one possible output of algorithm A on input x.

Furthermore, we use a couple of common "tool" algorithms which operate on Boolean inputs and only use XOR and AND operations and can therefore be adapted to operate on encrypted data by using a fully homomorphic encryption scheme. We omit the description of those algorithms due to lack of space, but their implementation is straightforward and mimics the common circuit implementations of those gadgets, see e.g. [20]. In particular, for inputs $c, d \in C^{\ell}$ with plaintext bit-length ℓ, we use the following algorithms:

- Negation: $\mathsf{Not}(c)$ for $\ell = 1$ flips a bit, i.e., $\mathsf{D}(\mathsf{Not}(c)) = \mathsf{D}(c) + 1$. $O(1)$
- Equality: $\mathsf{Equal}(c, d)$ returns an encryption of 1 if $\mathsf{D}(c) = \mathsf{D}(d)$ and an encryption of 0 otherwise. This can be generalized to $m \geq 2$ inputs. $O(m\ell)$
- Greater than: $\mathsf{GT}(c, d)$ returns an encryption of 1 if $\mathsf{D}(c) > \mathsf{D}(d)$ and an encryption of 0 otherwise. Here, $>$ denotes the order on M^{ℓ}, interpreted as binary representations of natural numbers. $O(\ell)$
- If-Then-Else: $\mathsf{IFE}(b, c, d)$ for $b \in C$ returns an encryption of $\mathsf{D}(c)$ if $\mathsf{D}(b) = 1$ and an encryption of $\mathsf{D}(d)$ otherwise. $O(\ell)$
- Maximum and Minimum: $\mathsf{Max}(c, d)$ and $\mathsf{Min}(c, d)$ which return encryptions of $\max(\mathsf{D}(c), \mathsf{D}(d))$ and $\min(\mathsf{D}(c), \mathsf{D}(d))$. This can be generalized to $m \geq 2$ inputs. $O(m\ell)$
- Addition: $\mathsf{Add}(c, d)$ returns an encryption of $\mathsf{D}(c) + \mathsf{D}(d)$, where $+$ denotes addition of binary numbers with carry. The output ciphertext tuple has length $\lceil \log_2(m) \rceil + \ell$. $O(m(\log(m) + \ell))$

The asymptotic complexities are given in terms of homomorphic operations, i.e., homomorphic additions and multiplications. More details on the tool algorithms are given in [21].

3 Our Contribution

3.1 FHE-Based Algorithm

We assume that $P_{\mathcal{A}_i} \subseteq \{0,1\}^{\ell} \setminus \{0^{\ell}\}$, so all parties agree on an ℓ-bit binary encoding of the possible inputs such that 0^{ℓ} is not a valid input encoding. Let χ_i denote an "extended" rank function $\mathrm{rank}_{\mathcal{A}_i}$ which assigns the rank 0 to all elements which are not included in the input of party $\mathcal{A}_i$ at all:

$$\chi_i : \{0,1\}^{\ell} \rightarrow \{0, ..., k\},\ x \mapsto \begin{cases} \mathrm{rank}_{\mathcal{A}_i}(x) & x \in P_{\mathcal{A}_i} \\ 0 & x \notin P_{\mathcal{A}_i} \end{cases}$$

If $k := |P_{\mathcal{A}_1}| = ... = |P_{\mathcal{A}_n}| \leq |P| < 2^{\ell}$ is the number of inputs, we can assume that every χ_i maps to $\{0,1\}^K$ instead of $\{0, ..., k\}$ where $K = \lceil \log_2(k+1) \rceil$. In practice, the rank function χ_i of a party $\mathcal{A}_i$ could for example be described by an ordered list of $|P|$ bit-strings each of length K, i.e., a complete truth table of all K output components. Let $X_1, ..., X_n$ be "encryptions" of the extended rank functions such that we have $X_i : \{0,1\}^\ell \rightarrow C^K$ with $\mathsf{D}(X_i(x)) = \chi_i(x)$ for all $x \in \{0,1\}^\ell$. For an input element $x \in \{0,1\}^\ell$, the value $X_i(x) \in C^K$ is an encryption of the rank of x in the input of $\mathcal{A}_i$.

Example. Let $P = \{a, b, c, d, e, f\}$ be the possible inputs and $P_{\mathcal{A}_1} = \{a, b, e\}$ the input of $\mathcal{A}_1$ with ranking $a <_{\mathcal{A}_1} e <_{\mathcal{A}_1} b$. We need at least $\ell = 3$ bits for encoding the possible inputs, for example $a = 001$, $b = 010$, $c = 011$, $d = 100$, $e = 101$, and $f = 110$. Assume that the parties agreed to use $k = 3$ input elements in their inputs, we therefore need $K = \lceil \log_2(3 + 1) \rceil = 2$ bits to encode each possible rank (including 0). The extended rank function of $\mathcal{A}_1$ and an encryption of it now look as follows:

Input $x \in P \subseteq \{0,1\}^\ell$	$\chi_1(x) \in \{0,1\}^K$	$X_1(x) \in C^K$
000 (invalid)	–	–
001 (a)	01 (1)	$\mathsf{E}(01)$
010 (b)	11 (3)	$\mathsf{E}(11)$
011 (c)	00 (-)	$\mathsf{E}(00)$
100 (d)	00 (-)	$\mathsf{E}(00)$
101 (e)	10 (2)	$\mathsf{E}(10)$
110 (f)	00 (-)	$\mathsf{E}(00)$

The ordered list of $|P| = 6$ ciphertext K-tuples of the third column of this table is what $\mathcal{A}_1$ sends to the other participants.

First, we look at the case of f_{MR} because this can be modeled as a multiset intersection as in [6] and as described in Sect. 2.3. We will use the tool algorithms from Sect. 2.4.

RECONCILIATION ALGORITHM FOR f_{MR}

Input: Encrypted $X_1, ..., X_n$ as described before and one $P_{\mathcal{A}_i}$ in plaintext.

1. Set $S := \emptyset$ and $R := \emptyset$.
2. $\forall x \in P_{\mathcal{A}_i}$, compute $y \leftarrow \mathsf{Min}(X_1(x), ..., X_n(x))$ and add (x, y) to S.
3. Set $max_y \leftarrow \mathsf{E}(0) \in C^K$.
4. For each $(x, y) \in S$, compute $max_y \leftarrow \mathsf{Max}(y, max_y)$.
5. For each $(x, y) \in S$, compute $x' \leftarrow \mathsf{E}(x) \boxtimes \mathsf{Equal}(y, max_y)$ and add it to the set R.
6. Return (max_y, R).

Output: Encrypted maximal rank max_y and a set R of encrypted elements which either have maximal rank max_y or decrypt to 0^ℓ. If there exists no maximal rank (because the inputs are disjoint), max_y will decrypt to 0 and all elements in R will decrypt to 0^ℓ.

In Step 2, party $\mathcal{A}_i$ computes the value of f_{MR} for all elements. Since $P_{\mathcal{A}_1} \cap ... \cap P_{\mathcal{A}_n} \subseteq P_{\mathcal{A}_i}$, the set $P_{\mathcal{A}_i}$ is an upper bound for the intersection and party $\mathcal{A}_i$ never needs to process more than $k = |P_{\mathcal{A}_i}|$ elements. For each element, the minimum of ranks is computed and the result together with its encrypted rank is added to the set S. In Step 4, we iterate over all the elements from Step 2 and compute the maximum by comparing with the "largest" element known at this point. In Step 5, we iterate again over all elements (of length ℓ) and multiply them with the result of Equal, thus effectively canceling out all elements which have rank other than max_y. Elements which are not shared by all parties are also implicitly canceled because they all have rank 0.

Computational Complexity. In Step 2, we loop $|P_{\mathcal{A}_i}| = k$ times and call Min each time on n inputs of length K. In Step 4, we call Max on inputs of length K and in Step 5, we call Equal on inputs of length K. The result is multiplied with ℓ bits. This gives a total of

$$\underbrace{\overbrace{|P_{\mathcal{A}_i}|}^{=k} \cdot T^{n\mathsf{Min}}(K)}_{\text{Step 2}} + \underbrace{\overbrace{|S|}^{=k} \cdot T^{\mathsf{Max}}(K)}_{\text{Step 4}} + \underbrace{\overbrace{|S|}^{=k} \cdot \ell \cdot T^{\mathsf{Equal}}(K)}_{\text{Step 5}}$$

$$\in k \cdot (O(nK) + O(K) + O(\ell K)) \subseteq O(nk \log(k)\ell)$$

homomorphic operations. As already mentioned in the example above, we use $K \cdot |P|$ ciphertexts to encode every X_i. We want to point out that Step 5 can easily be modified to only return *one* maximal element instead of all of them, which would reduce the complexity to $O(nk\ell)$. Also, we could emit the output of the rank max_y, which would increase privacy. We chose this variant in order to be compatible to Definition 2 and to be comparable to Neugebauer et al. [6].

We now have a look at the sum of ranks composition scheme f_{SR}. The basic idea is to compute a multiset union but omit all the elements which are not in the intersection. This is achieved by adding the ranks using the Add algorithm in combination with negated Equal calls to filter out elements which are not shared by all parties. The basic idea is the same as before, only Step 2 differs. Here we compute the value of f_{SR} instead of f_{MR}. We use Add to compute the sum of ranks. Next, we check if any of the terms used in this sum was zero. If so, the result will be multiplied by zero thus eliminating this entry from the set of possible maximal elements. The algorithm is shown in detail on the next page.

Computational Complexity. In Step 2, we use Add to compute the sum of n ciphertexts, each having length K. The result has length $K + \lceil \log_2(n) \rceil$. Next, we compute Equal on inputs of length K and negate the result. This is done n times and the product of those n bits is then multiplied with every bit of y. In Step 4, we compute Max on inputs of length $K + \lceil \log_2(n) \rceil$. Summing up, we have

$$\underbrace{k \cdot (T^{n\mathsf{Add}}(K) + n \cdot (T^{\mathsf{Equal}}(K) + T^{\mathsf{Not}}(1)))}_{\text{Step 2}}$$
$$+ \underbrace{k \cdot T^{\mathsf{Max}}(K + \lceil \log_2(n) \rceil)}_{\text{Step 4}} + \underbrace{k \cdot \ell \cdot T^{\mathsf{Equal}}(K + \lceil \log_2(n) \rceil)}_{\text{Step 5}}$$
$$\in k \cdot (O(n(\log(n) + K)) + nO(K) + \ell \cdot O(K + \log(n)))$$
$$\subseteq O(n \log(n) k \log(k) \ell)$$

homomorphic operations.

Like before, we can reduce the complexity to $O(n \log(n) k \ell)$ by only computing one maximal element instead of all. Also, we do not have to return max_y.

RECONCILIATION ALGORITHM FOR f_{SR}

Input: Encrypted $X_1, ..., X_n$ as described before and one $P_{\mathcal{A}_i}$ in plaintext.

1. Set $S := \emptyset$ and $R := \emptyset$.
2. For every $x \in P_{\mathcal{A}_i}$, compute

$$y \leftarrow \mathsf{Add}(X_1(x), ..., X_n(x)) \in C^{K + \lceil \log_2(n) \rceil}$$
$$y' \leftarrow y \boxtimes \bigboxtimes_{i=1}^{n} \mathsf{Not}(\mathsf{Equal}(X_i(x), \mathsf{E}(0)))$$

   and add (x, y') to the set S.
3. Set $max_y \leftarrow \mathsf{E}(0) \in C^{K + \lceil \log_2(n) \rceil}$.
4. For each $(x, y) \in S$, compute $max_y \leftarrow \mathsf{Max}(y, max_y)$.
5. For each $(x, y) \in S$, compute $x' \leftarrow \mathsf{E}(x) \boxtimes \mathsf{Equal}(y, max_y)$ and add it to the set R.
6. Return (max_y, R).

Output: Encrypted maximal rank max_y and a set R of encrypted elements which either have maximal rank max_y or decrypt to 0^ℓ. If there exists no maximal rank (because the inputs are disjoint), max_y will decrypt to 0 and all elements in R will decrypt to 0^ℓ.

3.2 Reducing the Encoding Size

Our algorithm has runtime (almost) linear in the number of parties n but uses $\lceil \log_2(k+1) \rceil \cdot |P|$ ciphertexts to encode a k-element input where P is the input domain with $|P| < 2^\ell$. In certain situations, very large input domains P might be necessary and such a large number of ciphertexts may not be acceptable due to the communication overhead or bandwidth limitations.

The factor $|P|$ originates from the idea of using complete truth tables for representing the rank functions $\chi_i : \{0,1\}^\ell \to \{0,1\}^K$. We now give a smaller representation to allow our algorithm to use smaller encodings and therefore fewer ciphertexts. The price for this is a slightly higher computational complexity in terms of homomorphic operations. Let

$$X_i := \{(\underbrace{\text{rank}_{\mathcal{A}_i}(x)}_{\in\{1,\dots,k\}}, \underbrace{\mathsf{E}(x)}_{\in C^\ell}) \mid x \in P_{\mathcal{A}_i}\},$$

so for each rule, we save an encryption of the rule itself together with its (unencrypted) rank.

We will be able to reuse both variants of our algorithm (f_{SR} and f_{MR}), the only thing we change is the way $X_i(x)$, the encrypted rank of the element x in the input of party $\mathcal{A}_i$, is computed. Before, this was just a lookup from a table we have received from party $\mathcal{A}_i$, therefore, this can be done in constant time and without using any homomorphic operations. We can get that same value by computing

$$X_i(x) \leftarrow \boxplus_{(r,c)\in X_i} \left(\underbrace{\mathsf{E}(r)}_{\in C^K} \boxtimes \underbrace{\mathsf{Equal}(c, \mathsf{E}(x))}_{\in C^1} \right).$$

This basically just compares x to all inputs in X_i. If one of the inputs in X_i encrypts x, the rank of x is returned. This is correct since exactly one of the terms in this sum will encrypt a non-zero value.

Computational Complexity. Computing $X_i(x)$ this way takes $|X_i| = k$ calls to Equal on inputs of length ℓ. The result will be multiplied by $\mathsf{E}(r)$ which has length $K := \lceil \log_2(k+1) \rceil$. We then use $k-1$ calls to $\boxplus$ (in each component) for adding the results. In total, we get:

$$T_\boxplus(\ell) = k \cdot T_\boxplus^{\mathsf{Equal}}(\ell) + (k-1) \cdot K \in O(k\ell)$$
$$T_\boxtimes(\ell) = k \cdot (T_\boxtimes^{\mathsf{Equal}}(\ell) + K) \in O(k\ell)$$
$$T_{\mathsf{E}}(\ell) = k \cdot (K + \ell) \in O(k\ell)$$

Having a look at Step 2 again, we see that we need to compute $X_i(x)$ for every $x \in P_{\mathcal{A}_i}$ and every $1 \le i \le n$. In total, we use nk computations of the above kind, resulting in $O(nk^2\ell)$ additional homomorphic operations for Algorithm II which will lead to a complexity of $O(nk^2\ell)$ for f_{MR} and $O(n\log(n)k^2\ell)$ for f_{SR}.

Summarizing, we can change the number of ciphertexts we need for encoding an input from $|P| \cdot \lceil \log_2(k+1) \rceil$ to $\log_2(|P|) \cdot k$ by increasing the asymptotic number of homomorphic operations by a factor of k. Which method is preferable will depend on the application parameters. For large values of k but small values of ℓ, we might still be better off with the original "truth table approach".

3.3 Putting It All Together: FHE Reconciliation Protocols

Recall that our algorithms take encrypted encodings of the parties' sets as inputs and return an encryption of an element which is maximal with respect to some preference order composition scheme. Up until now, we did not clarify how to use those algorithms in a secure and privacy-preserving way in order to solve the reconciliation problem. Especially, how are ciphertexts exchanged and who holds the secret decryption key?

We assume a fully homomorphic encryption scheme $(\mathsf{G}, \mathsf{E}, \mathsf{D}, \boxplus, \boxtimes)$ with plaintext space $M = \mathbb{F}_2$ which is semantically secure. One way to implement a protocol is to assume that we have a *threshold fully homomorphic encryption scheme* such that the key generation algorithm G and the decryption algorithm D have to be jointly performed by all parties together and that no single party or collaboration of less than n parties can decrypt any ciphertext on its own but everyone can compute E, $\boxplus$ and $\boxtimes$. Recently, the authors of [22] published such a threshold version of Gentry's fully homomorphic encryption scheme.

MULTI-PARTY RECONCILIATION PROTOCOL USING THRESHOLD FHE

1. All parties agree on the preference order composition scheme they want to use, on the number of inputs k in each party's set, and on an ℓ-bit binary encoding of the possible input elements such that 0^ℓ is not a valid encoding.
2. All parties $\mathcal{A}_1, ..., \mathcal{A}_n$ jointly generate a key pair $(sk, pk) \leftarrow \mathsf{G}(\lambda)$ such that everybody knows pk and only a share of sk.
3. Every party A_i generates an encrypted encoding X_i of its input and sends it to the other $n-1$ parties.
4. Every party runs the selected algorithm.
5. All parties participate in a threshold decryption of all outputs.

If a semantically secure homomorphic encryption scheme is used and no party can decrypt any ciphertexts on its own, no information about the private inputs will leak except what can be deduced from the maximal elements and their rank.

As an alternative, we present a protocol which is based on a non-threshold fully homomorphic cryptosystem. However, we need the help of an additional instance which is not one of the parties participating in the actual protocol. This additional instance is used for key generation and certain decryptions and is therefore called the *keyholder* $\mathcal{K}$. We require that all parties trust $\mathcal{K}$ not to collude with any of the other parties. If $\mathcal{K}$ plays by our rules, nobody will learn any private inputs, not even $\mathcal{K}$ itself. However, $\mathcal{K}$ is not to be seen as a trusted third party in the traditional sense. We do not have to trust $\mathcal{K}$ with the entire computation or with our secret inputs. The protocol is shown on the next page.

Like before, Step 3 will be performed by every party on its own and requires no interaction at all. Abusing $\mathcal{K}$ as a decryption oracle is not possible because $\mathcal{K}$ will wait until it receives ciphertexts from all parties and only send the decrypted results back if they are all equal. Even if $\mathcal{K}$ is compromised, not all private inputs will necessarily leak. However, if $\mathcal{K}$ colludes with some other party, this might be the case. Assuming the semi-honest model, this will not happen.

MULTI-PARTY RECONCILIATION PROTOCOL USING KEYHOLDER $\mathcal{K}$

1. Keyholder $\mathcal{K}$ generates a key pair $(sk, pk) \leftarrow G(\lambda)$ and publishes the public key pk.
2. As before, each party generates an encrypted encoding of its k input elements, and sends it to the $n-1$ other parties.
3. Each party runs the selected algorithm and sends the result to $\mathcal{K}$.
4. $\mathcal{K}$ uses the secret key sk to decrypt the n results he received from the parties. If all results encrypt the same value, this (decrypted) value will be sent back to all parties.

A possible drawback of the above protocol might be that $\mathcal{K}$ learns the result of the algorithm. If this is a problem, the parties can use a blinding technique first. The results R of the algorithms have length $k\ell$. The parties agree on an $k\ell$-bit one-time pad $x \in \{0,1\}^{k\ell}$ to blind the results by computing $c' \leftarrow \mathsf{E}(x) \boxplus c$. If all parties use the same x, all c' will encrypt the same value as required in order for $\mathcal{K}$ to send back the results in Step 4. Without knowing the value of x used by the parties, the keyholder will not learn anything at all. The parties can just exchange x over some arbitrary confidential channel. After the decrypted result $\mathsf{D}(c')$ is received, all parties can obtain $\mathsf{D}(c) \in \{0,1\}^{k\ell}$ by computing $\mathsf{D}(c') + x$.

4 Comparing Results

We now compare our results using fully homomorphic encryption (FHE) with the results by Neugebauer et al. [6]. Table 1 summarizes the complexity results of our algorithms. Algorithm II denotes Algorithm I with reduced encoding size as described in Sect. 3.2. Recall that n is the number of parties, k is the number of inputs in each party's set, ℓ is the bit-length of the input elements (i.e., the logarithm of the size of the input domain).

Deriving the complexity for our *reconciliation protocol with keyholder* from Sect. 3.3 is now straightforward. We are counting the *total* number of operations, i.e., the sum of the number of operations each single party has to perform. We do not count key generation and distribution from Step 1 and we assume the parties already agreed on a fully homomorphic encryption scheme, its security parameter λ and on the one-time pad used for blinding in Step 4.

Table 1. Number of homomorphic operations

Algorithm	f	Homomorphic operations	Ciphertexts
I	f_{MR}	$O(nk\log(k)\ell)$	$\lceil\log_2(k+1)\rceil \cdot \lvert P\rvert \in O(\log(k)2^{\ell})$
II	f_{MR}	$O(nk^2\ell)$	$k \cdot \log_2(\lvert P\rvert) \in O(k\ell)$
I	f_{SR}	$O(n\log(n)k\log(k)\ell)$	
II	f_{SR}	$O(n\log(n)k^2\ell)$	

Beginning with Step 2, each party has to encrypt its own input. Each input consists of k input elements and each input element has bit-length ℓ. As Table 1 shows, with Algorithm I each party has to encrypt at most $\lceil \log_2(k+1) \rceil \cdot |P|$ bits and send those bits to all other parties. With Algorithm II, each party encrypts $k \cdot \ell$ bits. In Step 3, every party runs the selected algorithm on the inputs it received from the other $n-1$ parties. This step requires no communication or further encryption operations.

Finally, in Step 4, each party blinds its result with the agreed one-time pad $x \in \{0,1\}^{k\ell}$. This requires a total of $k\ell$ encryptions and homomorphic additions for each party. Every party sends the blinded result $c \in C^{k\ell}$ to the keyholder $\mathcal{K}$ for decryption. This requires $nk\ell$ calls to D. After verifying that all results encrypt the same value, $\mathcal{K}$ sends the decrypted blinded result back to all n parties.

Table 2. Complexities of reconciliation protocols

Protocol	f	$\boxplus, \boxtimes, \boxdot$	E	D	#Messages
Neugebauer et al. [6]	f_{MR}	$O(k^6 + nk^4)$	$O(nk^2)$	$O(n^2k^3)$	$O(n^2k^3)$
FHE with Algo. I	f_{MR}	$O(n^2k\log(k)\ell)$	$O(n\log(k)2^\ell)$	$nk\ell$	$O(n^2\log(k)2^\ell)$
FHE with Algo. II	f_{MR}	$O(n^2k^2\ell)$	$O(nk\ell)$	$nk\ell$	$O(n^2k\ell)$
Neugebauer et al. [6]	f_{SR}	$O(n^4k^6)$	$O(nk^2)$	$O(n^4k^3)$	$O(n^4k^3)$
FHE with Algo. I	f_{SR}	$O(n^2\log(n)k\log(k)\ell)$	$O(n\log(k)2^\ell)$	$nk\ell$	$O(n^2\log(k)2^\ell)$
FHE with Algo. II	f_{SR}	$O(n^2\log(n)k^2\ell)$	$O(nk\ell)$	$nk\ell$	$O(n^2k\ell)$

Table 2 shows the number of operations which have to be performed in the different protocols as well as the number of messages which are exchanged. The analysis shows total numbers for all parties combined rather than for each single party. Recall that the new parameter ℓ in our results stands for the length of the input encodings (so 2^ℓ is the size of the input domain). In [6], the size of the input domain is tightly coupled to the security parameter of the cryptosystem whereas with our solution, ℓ is chosen by the user and the protocol will run faster if only small input domains are required (which we believe to be the case in most practical applications).

Note that interpretation of those numbers themselves is complicated without mentioning the specific cryptosystems which are used. The number of messages are counted as number of ciphertexts. This is not the same as the actual amount of data which has to be transmitted, which relies on the bit-length of the ciphertexts and will depend on the security parameter λ. Also, the number of calls to $\boxplus, \boxtimes$, or $\boxdot$ does not reflect the actual computational complexity because we cannot precisely state how expensive each of those calls is. We could try to be more precise by comparing an instantiation of our scheme using the Gentry scheme [23] with an instantiation of [6] using the Paillier scheme [24]. However, since Gentry's scheme is still under active research and little is known about it's practical efficiency, we do believe that such a comparison would not yield reliable insights.

However, we are confident in saying that given a fully homomorphic encryption scheme with comparable efficiency to current homomorphic encryption schemes, our protocols will outperform [6] by several orders of magnitude. Further details on our protocols and results can be found in [21].

5 Conclusion

In this paper, we developed a privacy-preserving multi-party reconciliation protocol which utilizes fully homomorphic encryption. We showed how to use ideas from circuit theory in order to compose algorithms which operate on encrypted data by utilizing small tool algorithms. Our protocol consists of an initial setup phase in which parties exchange encrypted data, followed by an offline computation phase, and a final phase for aggregating the result of the protocol.

We compare our approach to Neugebauer et al. [6] and we observe that our protocol has several advantages. As already mentioned, our computation is performed mainly offline and we only need a small and constant number of protocol rounds. Furthermore, fewer messages have to be exchanged and we require considerably fewer homomorphic operations, encryptions and decryptions. Although the exact computational complexity (for a fixed security level) cannot be made precise, we argued that our approach is likely to outperform Neugebauer et al. [6] in practice, assuming our protocol is instantiated with a sufficiently practicable fully homomorphic encryption scheme. In terms of privacy, our protocol allows for a stricter definition than Neugebauer et al. [6], namely, we can easily adopt our algorithms to output only one randomly chosen maximal element (instead of all of them) and the maximal rank does not have to be part of the output.

Acknowledgments. This work has been supported by the DFG project ME 3704/1-1 and NSF Award CCF 1018616.

References

1. Yao, A.C.: Protocols for secure computations. In: Proceedings of the 23rd SFCS, pp. 160–164. IEEE Computer Society, Washington, DC (1982)
2. Meyer, U., Wetzel, S., Ioannidis, S.: Distributed privacy-preserving policy reconciliation. In: ICC, pp. 1342–1349 (2007)
3. Meyer, U., Wetzel, S., Ioannidis, S.: New Advances on Privacy-Preserving Policy Reconciliation. In: IACR eprint 2010/64, `http://eprint.iacr.org/2010/064`
4. Mayer, D.A., Teubert, D., Wetzel, S., Meyer, U.: Implementation and Performance Evaluation of Privacy-Preserving Fair Reconciliation Protocols on Ordered Sets. In: First ACM CODASPY (2011)
5. Freedman, M.J., Nissim, K., Pinkas, B.: Efficient Private Matching and Set Intersection. In: Cachin, C., Camenisch, J.L. (eds.) EUROCRYPT 2004. LNCS, vol. 3027, pp. 1–19. Springer, Heidelberg (2004)
6. Neugebauer, G., Meyer, U., Wetzel, S.: Fair and Privacy-Preserving Multi-party Protocols for Reconciling Ordered Input Sets. In: Burmester, M., Tsudik, G., Magliveras, S., Ilić, I. (eds.) ISC 2010. LNCS, vol. 6531, pp. 136–151. Springer, Heidelberg (2011)

7. Neugebauer, G., Meyer, U., Wetzel, S.: Fair and Privacy-Preserving Multi-Party Protocols for Reconciling Ordered Input Sets, Extended Version (2011), http://eprint.iacr.org/2011/200
8. Kissner, L., Song, D.: Privacy-preserving set operations. In: Shoup, V. (ed.) CRYPTO 2005. LNCS, vol. 3621, pp. 241–257. Springer, Heidelberg (2005)
9. Cheon, J.H., Jarecki, S., Seo, J.H.: Multi-party privacy-preserving set intersection with quasi-linear complexity. Cryptology ePrint Archive, Report 2010/512 (2010)
10. Li, R., Wu, C.: An unconditionally secure protocol for multi-party set intersection. In: Katz, J., Yung, M. (eds.) ACNS 2007. LNCS, vol. 4521, pp. 226–236. Springer, Heidelberg (2007)
11. Sathya Narayanan, G., Aishwarya, T., Agrawal, A., Patra, A., Choudhary, A., Pandu Rangan, C.: Multi party distributed private matching, set disjointness and cardinality of set intersection with information theoretic security. In: Garay, J.A., Miyaji, A., Otsuka, A. (eds.) CANS 2009. LNCS, vol. 5888, pp. 21–40. Springer, Heidelberg (2009)
12. Patra, A., Choudhary, A., Rangan, C.P.: Selected areas in cryptography, pp. 71–91. Springer, Heidelberg (2009)
13. Frikken, K.: Privacy-Preserving Set Union. In: Katz, J., Yung, M. (eds.) ACNS 2007. LNCS, vol. 4521, pp. 237–252. Springer, Heidelberg (2007)
14. Hong, J., Kim, J.W., Kim, J., Park, K., Cheon, J.H.: Constant-round privacy preserving multiset union. IACR Cryptology ePrint Archive, 138 (2011)
15. Mayer, D., Neugebauer, G., Meyer, U., Wetzel, S.: Enabling fair and privacy-preserving applications using reconciliation protocols on ordered sets. In: 34th IEEE Sarnoff Symposium. IEEE, Princeton (2011)
16. Gentry, C.: Fully Homomorphic Encryption using Ideal Lattices. In: Proceedings of the 41st STOC, pp. 169–178. ACM, New York (2009)
17. van Dijk, M., Gentry, C., Halevi, S., Vaikuntanathan, V.: Fully Homomorphic Encryption over the Integers. In: Gilbert, H. (ed.) EUROCRYPT 2010. LNCS, vol. 6110, pp. 24–43. Springer, Heidelberg (2010)
18. Goldreich, O., Micali, S.M., Wigderson, A.: How to play ANY mental game. In: Proceedings of the Nineteenth Annual ACM Symposium on Theory of Computing, STOC 1987, pp. 218–229. ACM, New York (1987)
19. Goldwasser, S., Micali, S.: Probabilistic encryption & how to play mental poker keeping secret all partial information. In: Proceedings of the 14th STOC, pp. 365–377. ACM Press, New York (1982)
20. Wegener, I.: The complexity of Boolean functions. John Wiley & Sons, Inc., New York (1987)
21. Weingarten, F.: Evaluating the Use of Fully Homomorphic Encryption in Secure Multi-Party Computation. Diploma Thesis, Research Group IT-Security, RWTH Aachen University (2011)
22. Myers, S., Sergi, M., Shelat, A.: Threshold fully homomorphic encryption and secure computation, vol. 2011 (2011)
23. Gentry, C.: A fully homomorphic encryption scheme. PhD thesis, Stanford University, Stanford, CA, USA, AAI3382729 (2009)
24. Paillier, P.: Public-key cryptosystems based on composite degree residuosity classes. In: Stern, J. (ed.) EUROCRYPT 1999. LNCS, vol. 1592, pp. 223–238. Springer, Heidelberg (1999)

Privacy-Preserving Password-Based Authenticated Key Exchange in the Three-Party Setting*

Weijia Wang[1], Lei Hu[2], and Yong Li[3]

[1] School of Science,
Beijing Jiaotong University, Beijing 100044, P.R.China
wangwj@bjtu.edu.cn

[2] State Key Laboratory of Information Security
(Institute of Information Engineering, Chinese Academy of Sciences)
Beijing 100049, P.R. China
hu@is.ac.cn

[3] School of Electronic and Information Engineering,
Beijing Jiaotong University, Beijing 100044, P.R. China
liyong@bjtu.edu.cn

Abstract. Security and privacy are two important objectives in modern communication environments. However, compared with security, privacy issues have not been well addressed, especially in the password-only setting, of which unique secret is the password. In this paper, we treat privacy in the password-only setting as an independent notion, and propose the first provable privacy-preserving 3-party password-based authenticated key exchange (PP-3PAKE) scheme under an unified security and privacy model.

Keywords: password-based authenticated key exchange, secret handshake, oblivious transfer, privacy.

1 Introduction

Motivation. With the increasing concern about erosion of electronic privacy, the importance of privacy-preserving techniques has been treated as the same as that of communication security ones in the security community. However, communication security techniques have been studied extensively and a lot of effective and efficient security schemes are available. Contrastingly, privacy concerns have not been addressed to the same extent, even if in some common settings. For instance, the privacy-preserving technique in password-based secure communications has not been widely recognized.

Let us consider the following the scenario. Alice and Bob, two members of single club, want to date at an internet cafe by using light-weight wireless devices such

* The work is partially supported by the Fundamental Research Funds for the Central Universities under Grant Nos.2012JBM104 and 2012JBM004.

J. Lopez, X. Huang, and R. Sandhu (Eds.): NSS 2013, LNCS 7873, pp. 507–520, 2013.

as mobile phones. Each member of the club has registered and authenticated their identity information (i.e. names and qualifications) on the club server by a certain physical way and stored their respective passwords in it previously. To keep the conversations secure and anonymous, each of them expects to make sure that the counterpart is a legitimate club member before establishing a shared session key, to leak to the counterpart no identity information except his/her affiliation, and to prevent the server from observing that their conversation ever happened.

The environments above are potentially hostile, where Alice and Bob succeed in authenticating each other and building a session key only if both of them are members of a group. Neither one can obtain any information on the other's identity except knowing that they belong to the same group. It is assumed that the server is honest but curious, that is, it does not deviate the protocol but attempt to obtain some information on participators such as the actions of the parties on line.

However, for the above two scenarios, conventional 3-party password-based authenticated key exchange (3PAKE or 3-party PAKE) schemes, which allow two group members to authenticate each other and establish a shared session key by the help of an on-line server, have no capability of protecting *privacy* of members within the same group. On the other hand, since passwords are assumed to be the only voucher for authenticating in the two aforementioned cases, more exotic cryptographic tools like conventional secret handshake schemes, group signatures and identity escrow are unsuited due to the absence of the public key infrastructure (PKI). Hence, the above two situations motivate us to explore privacy-preserving techniques in password-based setting. In this paper, we focus on the privacy-preserving mutual authentication and the session key establishment in the 3PAKE setting.

Related Work. In the last few years, password-based authenticated key exchange (PAKE) protocols have been received much attention due to their good ubiquitousness. Since Bellovin and Merritt started the seminal work on *Encrypted Key Exchange* (EKE) [7], different aspects of password-based protocols have been considered [5,4,8,13,15,1,2,9,14,10], from two-party settings and simple security analysis at the beginning to the multi-party ones and thorough provable security proofs recently. According to the distribution of secrets, PAKE protocols can be classified into two categories. The first kind is the shared password-authentication (SPWA) scheme [10] which uses a password shared among communication parties to implement authentication and session key establishment. The other kind is the different password-authentication (DPWA) scheme [10] in which parties authenticate each other and build a common session key by the help of a trusted server, with which each of them share a distinct password. For the SPWA protocols, one need not consider the privacy issue due to the same secret held by each user. For the DPWA schemes, since the secrets each party holds are different, there are some fresh privacy[1]properties, which

[1] Informally, *privacy* focus on protecting sensitive identity information, while *security* consider preventing the leakage of passwords or session keys.

until now have not been considered desirably. Abdalla et al. [1] firstly considered the *key-privacy* for the server in the DPWA PAKE (for simplicity, we refer to it as PAKE directly) setting in a formal way. Yet this notion is essentially an aspect of the security of session key. In fact, the seminal work on the PAKE privacy was introduced by Viet et al. [19], who preliminarily considered the anonymous authentication from client to server in the 2-party PAKE case and proposed corresponding 2-party anonymous PAKE schemes. Recently Shin et al. [16] and Yang et al. [22] continued to discuss on the threshold anonymous scheme in the 2-party PAKE setting. These are all the works in the literature, to the best of our knowledge, involving the privacy in the password-based settings.

Comparatively, *privacy* are more considered in the settings which is based on public key systems such as PKI. Secret handshake (SH), as a full-fledged mechanism, are being investigated to achieve a manner, by which users can authenticate each other and reveal no information about its own membership (or credential) unless the peer's legitimacy was already ensured of, even if there exists an active adversary who may act as a handshake initiator or responder. Since Balfanz et al. [3] presented the first secret handshake scheme, a large number of schemes involving various aspects of the secret handshake has emerged. For instance, Castelluccia, et al. [11] developed a scheme under standard assumption, Jarecki et al. [12] provided a multi-party protocol, Tsudik and Xu [17] introduced a group secret handshake scheme supporting reusable certificates and Xu and Yung [21] proposed an interesting 2-party scheme which enjoys reusable credentials.

Our Contribution. Different from most of the previous work on 3-party password-based authenticated key exchange protocols, in the paper we consider the *privacy* as an independent notion in the password-only setting, introduce a novel concept: Privacy-Preserving 3-party PAKE (or Secret Handshake in the Three-party Setting) and provide a complete resolution as follows.

In the first, to build an unified framework for the privacy-preserving 3-party PAKE protocols, which can formally treats both the securities and the privacies, we extend the security model [4,1] for 3PAKE schemes by from the Secret Handshake introducing into the 3PAKE setting three main privacy notions: *resistance to detection*, *unlinkability* and *indistinguishability to eavesdroppers*, and redefining them with the indistinguishability ideology.

In the second, inspirited by the idea of Viet et al.'s [19] constructing the anonymous 2-party PAKE protocol, we propose the first privacy-preserving 3-party password-based authenticated key exchange (PP-3PAKE) scheme which also implements the secret handshake in the password-only setting by embedding an oblivious transfer (OT) scheme of Tzeng [18] in a 3-party PAKE protocol.

In the third, facing with the highly complicated structure of the PP-3PAKE protocol, we do not deal with its securities directly but apply a novel proof technology which, essentially a target driven way, depends on seeking a modularized general construction relative to the objective scheme. As a result, from simplicity to intricacy, step by step, we prove both the securities and the above three privacies of the PP-3PAKE scheme under the unified formal model.

2 Model and Definitions

In this section, we put forward a new formal model for *privacy-preserving* 3-party password-based authenticated key exchange protocols, which is based on the prototypical one provided by Abdalla [1].

2.1 Communication Model

Protocol Participants. There are two classes of the participants in PP-3PAKE protocols: client and server. For simplicity, we consider the case with only a single semi-trusted (namely, honest but curious) server S . By regarding S as a group manager, we define a group G_S and say that a client user is a member of G_S only if he stores his real identity information on S and shares a password with it. Since protocol executions are assumed to be in an anonymous setting, we fix two nonempty sets: $\mathcal{V}$, the set of the real identities of group members and $\mathcal{U}$, the set of the pseudonyms of group members. This means that a member of group G_S has two identities: the former $V \in \mathcal{V}$ is used for the registration in the server S and the latter $U \in \mathcal{U}$ is used for anonymous communications in the networks. Due to anonymous executions, only the pseudonyms occur in the view of the adversary. Therefore, $U \in \mathcal{U}$ is directly used to refer to as a group member (or a client user) in the following. For the convenience of the following privacy definitions, we assume that each real identity $V \in \mathcal{V}$ corresponds to at least two pseudonyms and define a transformation function $\mathcal{F} : \mathcal{U} \rightarrow \mathcal{V}$ to obtain its real identity from a pseudonym client.

Here we further divide the set $\mathcal{U}$ into two disjoint subsets: $\mathcal{C}$, the set of honest group members and $\mathcal{E}$, the set of malicious group members. That is, the set of all users $\mathcal{U}$ is the union $\mathcal{C} \bigcup \mathcal{E}$. The malicious set $\mathcal{E}$ corresponds to the set of inside attackers in the 3-party setting.

Long-Lived Keys. Each anonymous client user $U \in \mathcal{U}$ (who is essentially a member of group G_S) holds a corresponding identity $V = \mathcal{F}(U)$ and a password pw_V. The server S holds a vector $pw_S = \langle pw_S[V] \rangle_{V \in \mathcal{V}}$ with an entry for each real name user in which $pw_S[V]$ may be equal to pw_V in symmetric model or a transformation of pw_V as defined in [4].

Protocol Execution. In our model, a protocol is treated as a probabilistic algorithm which determines how instances of the protocol principals behave in responds to messages from the communication environment. Similarly, adversary $\mathcal{A}$ is probabilistic algorithm which has full control over the communication channels. During the execution of the protocol, the interaction between an adversary and the protocol participants occurs only via oracle queries, which model the adversary capabilities in a real attack. These queries are as follows, where U^i (S^j, respectively) denotes the i-th (j-th, respectively) instance of a anonymous group member U (the server S, respectively):

1. *SendClient*(U^i, m): This query sends a message m to the instance U^i. In fact, it models an active attack against a group member. The oracle com-

putes what the protocol says to, and sends back the response. A query $SendClient(Start, U)$ initializes a unused instance of the group member U, and next the adversary $\mathcal{A}$ can receive the initial flows sent out by the instance.
2. $SendServer(S^j, m)$: This query sends a message to a server instance S^j, which models an active attack against the server. It outputs the message which the server instance S^j would respond upon receipt of message m according to the protocol.
3. $Execute(U_1^{i_1}, S^j, U_2^{i_2})$: This query models passive attacks, where the adversary $\mathcal{A}$ gets access to a honest execution of the protocol among the client instances $U_1^{i_1}$ and $U_2^{i_2}$ and server instance S^j by only eavesdropping the transcript of that execution. The output of this query consists of the message that was exchanged during the honest execution of the protocol.

2.2 Security

Following [1], which in turn builds on [6,4], we make a small modification and present our definitions of the protocol security as below.

Notation. An instance U^i is said to be *opened* if the query $Reveal(U^i)$ (see definition below) has been made by the adversary. We say an instance U^i is *unopened* if it is not *opened*. An instance U^i is said to be *accepted* if it goes into an accept state after receiving the last expected protocol message.

Partnering. By using the notion of session identifications (*sid*) [4], we say two instances U_1^i and U_2^j are partners if the following conditions are met: (1) Both U_1^i and U_2^j accept; (2) Both U_1^i and U_2^j share the same *sid*; (3) The partner identification for U_1^i is U_2^j and vice-versa; and (4) No instance other than U_1^i and U_2^j accepts with a partner identification equal to U_1^i or U_2^j.

Freshness. If an instance U^i has been *accepted* and both the instance and its partner are *unopened* and neither of them belongs to the malicious set, we say the instance U^i is *fresh*.

Semantic Security. The security notion is defined in the context of executing a PP-3PAKE protocol P in the presence of an adversary $\mathcal{A}$. To model the misuse of session keys and capture the adversary's ability to distinguish a real session key from a random one, we define two queries *Reveal* and *Test* as follows:

- $Reveal(U^i)$: Only if the session key of the instance U^i is defined, the query is available and returns to the adversary the session key.
- $Test(U^i)$: If the instance U^i is not fresh, it returns $\perp$. Otherwise, it returns either the session key held by the instance U^i (if $b = 0$) or a random number of the same size (if $b = 1$), where b is the hidden bit selected at random prior to the first call.

During executing the protocol, the adversary $\mathcal{A}$ is allowed to send multiple queries to the *Execute*, *SendClient*, *SendServer*, and *Test* oracles and asks at most one *Test* query to each fresh instance of each honest group member, while it is no longer allowed to ask *Reveal* queries. Finally $\mathcal{A}$ outputs its guess b' for the bit b hidden in the *Test* oracle. An adversary $\mathcal{A}$ is said to be successful if $b' = b$. We denote this event by *Succ*. Provided that passwords are drawn from dictionary $\mathcal{D}$, we define the advantage of $\mathcal{A}$ in violating the semantic security of the protocol P and the advantage function of the protocol P, respectively, as follows:

$$Adv_{P,\mathcal{D}}^{ake}(\mathcal{A}) = 2 \cdot Pr[Succ] - 1,$$
$$Adv_{P,\mathcal{D}}^{ake}(t, R) = \max_{\mathcal{A}}\{Adv_{P,\mathcal{D}}^{ake}(\mathcal{A})\},$$

where the *maximum* is taken over all $\mathcal{A}$ with time-complexity at most t and using resources at most R (such as the number of oracle queries).

We say a PP-3PAKE protocol P is semantically secure if the advantage $Adv_{P,\mathcal{D}}^{ake}(t, R)$ is only negligibly larger than $\lambda n/|\mathcal{D}|$, where n is the number of active sessions and λ is a constant. Certainly, one can hope for the best scenario in which $\lambda = 1$ and an adversary has an advantage of $n/|\mathcal{D}|$ since it simply guesses a password in each of the active sessions.

Server Authentication Security. To measure the capability of a 3PAKE protocol to resist undetectable on-line dictionary attacks, in this paper we consider the authentication securities between clients and the server. Let $Succ_{P,\mathcal{D}}^{auth(C\to S)}(\mathcal{A})$ (or $Succ_{P,\mathcal{D}}^{auth(S\to C)}(\mathcal{A})$) denote the probability that an adversary $\mathcal{A}$ successfully impersonates a client (or the server) instance during executing the protocol P without being detected. Also let $Succ_{P,\mathcal{D}}^{auth(C\to S)}(t, R) = \max_{\mathcal{A}}\{Succ_{P,\mathcal{D}}^{auth(C\to S)}(\mathcal{A})\}$ (or $Succ_{P,\mathcal{D}}^{auth(S\to C)}(t, R) = \max_{\mathcal{A}}\{Succ_{P,\mathcal{D}}^{auth(S\to C)}(\mathcal{A})\}$) denote the maximum over all $\mathcal{A}$ running in time at most t and using resources at most R. A 3-party PAKE protocol P is said to be client-to-server (or server-to-client) authentication secure if $Succ_{P,\mathcal{D}}^{auth(C\to S)}(t, R)$ (or $Succ_{P,\mathcal{D}}^{auth(S\to C)}(t, R)$) is at most $O(k/|\mathcal{D}|)$.

2.3 Privacy

In the secret handshake schemes based on public key systems, one always considers three privacy notions: *resistance to detection*, *unlinkability* and *indistinguishability to eavesdroppers*. In the paper, we focus on the privacy-preserving 3PAKE protocol which can also be treated as a SH scheme in the password-only setting. Consequently, we formally redefine the above three privacy notions in the 3PAKE setting as follows.

Resistance to Detection. Intuitively, the notion captures the idea that an adversary, who does not belong to the group G_S (in other words, does not share a password with the server S), is not able to decide whether other participants are legal members of the group G_S. Formally, to define this notion, we introduce a new query *Detect* in the following.

1. *Detect*(U): The query initializes an instance of U and returns a TRUE message by taking either the real password held by the group member U (if $b = 0$) or a random number of the same size (if $b = 1$) as the instance password in response to the subsequent various queries, where b is a bit selected randomly at the beginning of the experiment.

During the execution of the protocol, the adversary $\mathcal{A}_{rd}$ is allowed to ask multiple queries to *Detect* as well as *Execute*, *SendClient* and *SendServer* oracles. Finally $\mathcal{A}_{rd}$ outputs its guess b' for the bit b hidden in the *Detect* oracle. An adversary $\mathcal{A}_{rd}$ is said to be successful if $b' = b$. We denote this event by $Succ_{rd}$. Provided that passwords are drawn from dictionary $\mathcal{D}$, we define the advantage of $\mathcal{A}_{rd}$ in violating *resistance to detection* and the corresponding advantage function of the protocol P, respectively, as follows:

$$Adv_{P,\mathcal{D}}^{detect}(\mathcal{A}_{rd}) = 2 \cdot Pr[Succ_{rd}] - 1,$$
$$Adv_{P,\mathcal{D}}^{detect}(t, R) = \max_{\mathcal{A}_{rd}}\{Adv_{P,\mathcal{D}}^{detect}(\mathcal{A}_{rd})\},$$

The protocol P is said to be *resistance to detection* if any polynomial bounded $\mathcal{A}_{rd}$ can not guess successfully with the probability which is non-negligibly higher than 1/2.

Unlinkability. As a secret handshake scheme, it is important to guarantee the privacy of the actions of each legal member with respect to the other legal members and the server. The goal of the privacy notion in the 3PAKE setting is to keep the pseudonyms used in the protocol communications and the corresponding real identities unlinkable. That is, even though the adversaries are insider attackers or the server, they are not able to determine which member a pseudonym belongs to. In defining this notion, we consider the worst case and imagine that an adversary $\mathcal{A}_{ul}$ who knows the passwords for all users accesses to the *Execute* and *SendClient* oracles but not to a *SendServer* oracle. The reason for not providing the adversary with a *SendServer* oracle is because this oracle can be easily simulated by the adversary using the passwords. To measure the adversary's ability to tell apart the real owner from a random one from the group, we introduce a new query *Link* as follows.

1. *Link*(U_s^i): The oracle returns either $\mathcal{F}(U_s)$ (if $b = 0$) or an legal identity randomly chosen from the group (if $b = 1$), where b is a random bit as in the previous definition.

Consider an execution of the protocol P by an adversary $\mathcal{A}_{ul}$ who is given the passwords of all users and is allowed to access to the *Execute*, *SendClient* and *Link* oracles. The output of the adversary is b'. Let $Succ_{ul}$ denote the event in which $b' = b$. The advantage of $\mathcal{A}_{ul}$ in violating *unlinkable* and the advantage function of the protocol P are defined, respectively, as follows:

$$Adv_{P,\mathcal{D}}^{link}(\mathcal{A}_{ul}) = 2 \cdot Pr[Succ_{ul}] - 1,$$
$$Adv_{P,\mathcal{D}}^{link}(t, R) = \max_{\mathcal{A}_{ul}}\{Adv_{P,\mathcal{D}}^{link}(\mathcal{A}_{ul})\},$$

We say that P is *unlinkable* if its corresponding advantage function is negligible.

Indistinguishability to Eavesdroppers. This notion shows that no adversary who only eavesdrops on execution of the protocol is able to distinguish between a successful execution and an unsuccessful one. To define the privacy notion, the adversary is allowed to only access to its *Execute* oracle and a new one which is described as follows.

1. $Ind(U_s^i, U_t^j)$: If client instances U_s^i and U_t^j are not parters in the same session, then return the invalid symbol $\perp$, otherwise return either a random message if $b = 1$ or the real execution transcripts between them where b is still a random bit as in the previous definition.

The adversary $\mathcal{A}_{ind}$ drives the execution of the protocol P by asking multiple queries to its *Execute* oracles. After asking the *Ind* query, the adversary outputs its guess b' for the bit b. Let $Succ_{ind}$ be the event in which the adversary guesses b correctly. We can then define the advantage of $\mathcal{A}_{ind}$ in violating *indistinguishability* of the protocol P and the corresponding advantage function of P as follows.

$$Adv_{P,\mathcal{D}}^{ind}(\mathcal{A}_{ind}) = 2 \cdot Pr[Succ_{ind}] - 1,$$
$$Adv_{P,\mathcal{D}}^{ind}(t, R) = \max_{\mathcal{A}_{ind}}\{Adv_{P,\mathcal{D}}^{ind}(\mathcal{A}_{ind})\},$$

The protocol P is said to be *indistinguishability to eavesdroppers* if its corresponding advantage function is negligible.

3 Security Primitives

Let $\mathbb{G}$ be a cyclic group of prime order q and let g be an arbitrary generator of $\mathbb{G}$.

Decisional Diffie-Hellman Assumption (DDH): Let us consider the following two distributions:

$$\mathcal{D}_{\mathbb{G}}^{ddh-real} = \{g^x, g^y, g^{xy} | x, y \in_R \mathbb{Z}_q\},$$
$$\mathcal{D}_{\mathbb{G}}^{ddh-rand} = \{g^x, g^y, g^z | x, y, z \in_R \mathbb{Z}_q\}.$$

Let Γ be a probabilistic polynomial time (PPT) algorithm for these two cases: On input a triple of $\mathbb{G}$, outputting 0 or 1. And let the advantage function $Adv_{\mathbb{G}}^{ddh}(t)$ be the maximum value, over all probabilistic polynomial algorithms Γ running in time at most t, of:

$$|Pr[\Gamma(\mathcal{D}_{\mathbb{G}}^{ddh-real}) = 1] - Pr[\Gamma(\mathcal{D}_{\mathbb{G}}^{ddh-rand}) = 1)]|.$$

We say that the DDH assumption holds in $\mathbb{G}$ if $Adv_{\mathbb{G}}^{ddh}(t)$ is a negligible function of t.

4 The Protocol

Inspired by the prior works of Abdalla et al. [2] and Viet et al. [19], we introduce a new protocol, privacy-preserving 3-party password-based authenticated key exchange protocol (PP-3PAKE), which enjoys both security and privacy. The basic idea of our PP-3PAKE scheme is embedding an oblivious transfer (OT) scheme of Tzeng [18] in a 3-party PAKE protocol.

4.1 Description of the Protocol

Let $\mathbb{G}$ are cyclic group of prime order q, and g be a generator of $\mathbb{G}$. Let l_1 be a security parameter, and $\mathcal{G}_1$,$\mathcal{G}_2$,H_0,H_1 be random hash functions from $\{0,1\}^*$ to $\{0,1\}^{l_1}$.

It is assumed that G_S are a group managed by a semi-trusted server S. Let $\mathcal{V} := \{V_1, V_2, ..., V_n\}$ be the set of the real identities of the group members registered on the server S, and $\mathcal{U} := \{U_1, U_2, ..., U_m\}$ be the set of the pseudonyms, with which each of group members participates in the execution of the protocol P. In the following, we directly denote by an anonymous group member U_i a group member with a pseudonym. All pw_i shared between anonymous group members U_i and the server S are assumed to be uniformly drawn from the dictionary $\mathcal{D}$.

The description of the PP-3PAKE protocol is as follows (also see Figure 1).

Phase 0.(Initialization)

1. In the beginning, two anonymous group members U_i and U_j who are going to perform the protocol, choose at random two nones n_i,n_j, respectively and then exchange them.

Phase 1.

1. U_i chooses at random $x_i, r_i \in Z_p$, computes $X_i = g^{x_i}$ and $M_i = g^{r_i} \cdot PW_{i,1}$, and then sends to S the message including X_i, M_i and the additional information $\Delta_i := U_i|n_i|U_j|n_j$.
2. Similarly, U_j selects randomly x_j and r_j, calculates X_j and M_j, and send X_j, M_j and $\Delta_j := U_j|n_j|U_i|n_i$ to S.

Phase 2.

1. The server S chooses a random numbers $s \in Z_p$ and two group random numbers $k_1^0, k_2^0, ..., k_n^0 \in Z_p$ and $k_1^1, k_2^1, ..., k_n^1 \in Z_p$, and in turn computes A_l^0, A_l^1, B_l^0 and B_l^1 for $1 \le l \le n$ as follows:

$$A_l^0 = H_0((M_i/PW_{l,1})^{k_l^0}|g^{x_j s}|\Delta_s^0), A_l^1 = H_0((M_j/PW_{l,1})^{k_l^1}|g^{x_i s}|\Delta_s^1)$$

$$B_l^0 = g^{x_j s} \oplus H_1((M_i/PW_{l,1})^{k_l^0}|\Delta_s^0), B_l^1 = g^{x_i s} \oplus H_1((M_j/PW_{l,1})^{k_l^1}|\Delta_s^1)$$

where an additional message $\Delta_s^0 = S|U_i|U_j|n_s|n_i|n_j|X_i$, $\Delta_s^1 = S|U_j|U_i|n_s|n_j|n_i|X_j$ and n_s is a nonce selected by S.

2. S sets $W_i = \{g^{k_1^0} \cdot PW_{1,2}, ..., g^{k_n^0} \cdot PW_{n,2}, A_1^0, ..., A_n^0, B_1^0, ..., B_n^0\}$ and $W_j = \{g^{k_1^1} \cdot PW_{1,2}, ..., g^{k_n^1} \cdot PW_{n,2}, A_1^1, ..., A_n^1, B_1^1, ..., B_n^1\}$, and transfers them to U_i and U_j, respectively.

Phase 3.

1. Upon receipt of W_i and Δ_s^0, U_i computes $N_i = B_i^0 \oplus H_1(g^{k_i^0 \cdot r_i} | \Delta_s^0)$ by using its password pw_i . Next, it checks $A_i^0 \stackrel{?}{=} H_0(g^{k_i^0 \cdot r_i} | N_i | \Delta_s^0)$. If true, it generates the session key $SK_i = (N_i)^{x_i}$ for later secure communications.
2. After getting W_j and Δ_s^1, U_j does same as U_i. It in turn computes N_j and checks A_j^1. Finally it also computes the session key $SK_j = (N_j)^{x_j}$.

Public information: $\mathbb{G}, g, q, \mathcal{G}_1, \mathcal{G}_2, H_0, H_1$
$pw_i \in \mathcal{D}$, $PW_{i,1} = \mathcal{G}_1(pw_i)$, $PW_{i,2} = \mathcal{G}_2(pw_i)$

User U_i | Server S | User U_j

User U_i:
$x_i, r_i \in_R Z_p$
$X_i = g^{x_i}$
$M_i = g^{r_i} \cdot PW_{i,1}$

$\xrightarrow{M_i, X_i, \Delta_i}$

User U_j:
$x_j, r_j \in_R Z_p$
$X_j = g^{x_j}$
$M_j = g^{r_j} \cdot PW_{j,1}$

$\xleftarrow{M_j, X_j, \Delta_j}$

Server S:
$s \in_R Z_p$
$k_1^0, k_2^0, ..., k_n^0 \in_R Z_p$
$k_1^1, k_2^1, ..., k_n^1 \in_R Z_p$
For $l = 1$ to n, compute:
$A_l^0 = H_0((M_i/PW_{l,1})^{k_l^0} | g^{x_j s} | \Delta_s^0)$
$A_l^1 = H_0((M_j/PW_{l,1})^{k_l^1} | g^{x_i s} | \Delta_s^1)$
$B_l^0 = g^{x_j s} \oplus H_1((M_i/PW_{l,1})^{k_l^0} | \Delta_s^0)$
$B_l^1 = g^{x_i s} \oplus H_1((M_j/PW_{l,1})^{k_l^1} | \Delta_s^1)$
Let:
$W_i = \{g^{k_1^0} \cdot PW_{1,2}, ..., g^{k_n^0} \cdot PW_{n,2}, A_1^0, ..., A_n^0, B_1^0, ..., B_n^0\}$
$W_j = \{g^{k_1^1} \cdot PW_{1,2}, ..., g^{k_n^1} \cdot PW_{n,2}, A_1^1, ..., A_n^1, B_1^1, ..., B_n^1\}$

$\xleftarrow{W_i, \Delta_s^0}$ $\qquad$ $\xrightarrow{W_j, \Delta_s^1}$

User U_i:
$N_i = B_i^0 \oplus H_1(g^{k_i^0 \cdot r_i} | \Delta_s^0)$
$A_i^0 \stackrel{?}{=} H_0(g^{k_i^0 \cdot r_i} | N_i | \Delta_s^0)$
If true, accept$\leftarrow$ true
$SK_i = (N_i)^{x_i}$

User U_j:
$N_j = B_j^1 \oplus H_1(g^{k_j^1 \cdot r_j} | \Delta_s^1)$
$A_j^1 \stackrel{?}{=} H_0(g^{k_j^1 \cdot r_j} | N_j | \Delta_s^1)$
If true, accept$\leftarrow$ true
$SK_j = (N_j)^{x_j}$

Fig. 1. The PP-3PAKE protocol

4.2 Security

In the following theorem, we show that the PP-3PAKE protocol enjoys both the semantic security and the authentication one from server to clients.

Theorem 1. *Let $\mathbb{G}$ be a cyclic group of prime order q and $\mathcal{D}$ be uniformly distributed dictionary of size $|\mathcal{D}|$. Let q_{exe} and q_{test} denote the numbers of queries to Execute and Test oracles, $q_{send}^{U_i}$ and $q_{send}^{U_j}$ denote the numbers of queries to the SendClient oracle to U_i and U_j , and q_{ake} be the number of client oracle instances motivated by querying SendClient(Start) oracles. Then,*

$$Adv^{ror-ake}_{PP-3PAKE,\mathcal{D}}(t, q_{exe}, q_{test}, q^{U_i}_{send}, q^{U_j}_{send}, q_{ake}) \leq$$
$$4 \cdot Adv^{ror-ake}_{mdhke,\mathcal{D}}(t, q_{exe}, q_{exe} + q^{U_i}_{send}, q^{U_i}_{send})$$
$$+ 4 \cdot Adv^{ror-ake}_{mdhke,\mathcal{D}}(t, q_{exe}, q_{exe} + q^{U_j}_{send}, q^{U_j}_{send})$$
$$+ 2 \cdot (\frac{{q_{ake}}^2 + {q_H}^2}{2q} + \frac{q_{ake}}{2^{l_1}})$$
$$+ 4 \cdot Adv^{ddh}_{\mathbb{G}}(t + 10(q_{exe} + q_{ake})\tau_{\mathbb{G}})$$

and

$$Succ^{auth(S \to C)}_{PP-3PAKE,\mathcal{D}}(t, q_{exe}, q_{test}, q^{U_i}_{send}, q^{U_j}_{send}, q_{ake}) \leq$$
$$2Adv^{ror-ake}_{mdhke,\mathcal{D}}(t, q_{exe}, q_{exe} + q^{U_i}_{send}, q^{U_i}_{send})$$
$$+ 2Adv^{ror-ake}_{mdhke,\mathcal{D}}(t, q_{exe}, q_{exe} + q^{U_j}_{send}, q^{U_j}_{send})$$
$$+ \frac{{q_{ake}}^2 + {q_H}^2}{2q} + \frac{q_{ake}}{2^{l_1}},$$

where q_H represents the total number of queries to the random oracles and $\tau_{\mathbb{G}}$ denotes the exponentiation computational time in $\mathbb{G}$.

Proof Idea. Consider the complicated structure of PP-3PAKE, we use the modular technique as in [20]: Firstly, we introduce a new general construction for 3PAKE protocol and prove its securities; Next, we instantiate the general construction to obtain a specific 3PAKE protocol, which is actually a simplified version of the PP-3PAKE protocol without the OT components and fully inherits the securities of the general construction. Finally, the only thing that remains to be done is to reduce the securities of S-3PAKE to the ones of PP-3PAKE. The proofs of the theorem above will be found in the full version of this paper.

4.3 Privacy

Resistance to Detection. As the following theorem states, the PP-3PAKE shown in Figure 1 enjoys the privacy protection of *resistance to detect* as long as it holds the semantic secure.

Theorem 2. *Let PP-3PAKE be the privacy-preserving 3-party password-based authenticated key exchange protocol depicted in Figure 1. Then,*

$$Adv^{detect}_{PP-3PAKE,\mathcal{D}}(t, q_{exe}, q_{test}, q^{U_i}_{send}, q^{U_j}_{send}, q_{ake}) \leq Adv^{ror-ake}_{PP-3PAKE,\mathcal{D}}(t, q_{exe}, q_{test}, q^{U_i}_{send}, q^{U_j}_{send}, q_{ake})$$

where q_{detect} are the upper bounds of detect queries and the other parameters are defined as in Theorem 1.

Proof Idea. The main idea of the proof for the semantic security of PP-3PAKE is to randomize the involving passwords. Therefore, obviously, this protocol privacy can be reduced to its semantic security.

Unlinkability As the following theorem states, the PP-3PAKE shown in Figure 1 enjoys the privacy protection of *unlinkability* even if the adversary against the privacy notion is the server.

Theorem 3. *Let PP-3PAKE be the privacy-preserving 3-party password-based authenticated key exchange protocol depicted in Figure 1. Then, it is unconditionally unlinkable.*

Proof Idea. For any $PW_{t,1}$ in the password set and random number r_i, there is r_i' that satisfies $g^{r_i} \cdot PW_{i,1} = g^{r_i'} \cdot PW_{t,1}$. Therefore, the adversary cannot get any information about which password the instance uses in the execution of the protocol even if it occupies all the user passwords and unlimited computing power.

Indistinguishability to Eavesdroppers. As the following theorem states, the PP-3PAKE shown in Figure 1 enjoys the privacy protection of *indistinguishability to eavesdroppers* as long as the DDH assumption holds in $\mathbb{G}$.

Theorem 4. *Let PP-3PAKE be the privacy-preserving 3-party password-based authenticated key exchange protocol depicted in Figure 1. Then,*

$$Adv^{ind}_{PP-3PAKE,\mathcal{D}}(t, q_{exe}, q_{ind}) \leq Adv^{ddh}_{\mathbb{G}}(t + 10q_{exe}\tau_{\mathbb{G}}).$$

where q_{id} are the upper bounds of Ind queries and the other parameters are defined as in Theorem 1.

Proof Idea. The proof of the privacy notion uses the techniques similar to the ones of the reduction proof for authenticator forgeries in [20]. The detail proofs will appear in the full version of this paper.

Actually, it is obvious that many 3PAKE protocols also hold *resistance to detection* and *indistinguishability to eavesdroppers.* PP-3PAKE enjoying *unlinkability* benefits from its OT components. Whether all normal 3PAKE with the semantic security keep the above first or third privacy notion is another interesting thing.

5 Conclusion and Discussion

The client computation and communication cost of our scheme are almost equivalent to those of generic 3PAKE protocols, but the corresponding complexity of the server side in our scheme is much greater than those in a generic one, especially in the case that the group size is large. It is a natural strategy to divide the user group into several sub-groups and let our protocol perform in a certain sub-group, which would effectively reduce the communication and computation complexity of the server. But this method will lead to the decrease of the privacy of our scheme. So, to seek a better tradeoff between the level of privacy and the size of sub-group will be our future work.

On the other hand, it is assume that the application of our scheme would be in a wireless setting where all communication is done via broadcast which offers receiver anonymity as a built-in feature. This means that the identity of a party is not directly derivable from the routing address that must appear in the clear in the protocol message, namely, there is no easy way to figure out the user who sent/received a certain message. Otherwise it is easy for an adversary to figure out who is interacting with whom or to observe that the peers continue talking with each other after finishing the protocol. This assumption is actually also implied in previous privacy-preserving authentication mechanisms.

References

1. Abdalla, M., Fouque, P.-A., Pointcheval, D.: Password-based authenticated key exchange in the three-party setting. In: Vaudenay, S. (ed.) PKC 2005. LNCS, vol. 3386, pp. 65–84. Springer, Heidelberg (2005)
2. Abdalla, M., Pointcheval, D.: Interactive diffie-hellman assumptions with applications to password-based authentication. In: S. Patrick, A., Yung, M. (eds.) FC 2005. LNCS, vol. 3570, pp. 341–356. Springer, Heidelberg (2005)
3. Balfanz, D., Durfee, G., Shankar, N., Smetters, D.K., Staddon, J., Wong, H.-C.: Secret handshakes from pairing-based key agreements. In: IEEE Symposium on Security and Privacy, pp. 180–196. IEEE Computer Society (2003)
4. Bellare, M., Pointcheval, D., Rogaway, P.: Authenticated key exchange secure against dictionary attacks. In: Preneel, B. (ed.) EUROCRYPT 2000. LNCS, vol. 1807, pp. 139–155. Springer, Heidelberg (2000)
5. Bellare, M., Rogaway, P.: Entity authentication and key distribution. In: Stinson, D.R. (ed.) CRYPTO 1993. LNCS, vol. 773, pp. 232–249. Springer, Heidelberg (1994)
6. Bellare, M., Rogaway, P.: Provably secure session key distribution: the three party case. In: ACM Symposium on Theory of Computing - STOC 1995, pp. 57–66. ACM (1995)
7. Bellovin, S.M., Merritt, M.: Encrypted key exchange: Password-based protocols secure against dictionary attacks. In: Proceedings of the 1992 IEEE Symposium on Security and Privacy, pp. 72–84. IEEE Computer Society Press (1992)
8. Bresson, E., Chevassut, O., Pointcheval, D.: New security results on encrypted key exchange. In: Bao, F., Deng, R., Zhou, J. (eds.) PKC 2004. LNCS, vol. 2947, pp. 145–158. Springer, Heidelberg (2004)
9. Bresson, E., Chevassut, O., Pointcheval, D.: Provably authenticated group diffie-hellman key exchange - the dynamic case. In: Boyd, C. (ed.) ASIACRYPT 2001. LNCS, vol. 2248, pp. 290–309. Springer, Heidelberg (2001)
10. Byun, J.W., Lee, D.H.: N-party encrypted diffie-hellman key exchange using different passwords. In: Ioannidis, J., Keromytis, A.D., Yung, M. (eds.) ACNS 2005. LNCS, vol. 3531, pp. 75–90. Springer, Heidelberg (2005)
11. Castelluccia, C., Jarecki, S., Tsudik, G.: Secret handshakes from CA-oblivious encryption. In: Lee, P.J. (ed.) ASIACRYPT 2004. LNCS, vol. 3329, pp. 293–307. Springer, Heidelberg (2004)
12. Jarecki, S., Kim, J., Tsudik, G.: Authentication for paranoids: Multi-party secret handshakes. In: Zhou, J., Yung, M., Bao, F. (eds.) ACNS 2006. LNCS, vol. 3989, pp. 325–339. Springer, Heidelberg (2006)
13. Katz, J., Ostrovsky, R., Yung, M.: Efficient password-authenticated key exchange using human-memorable passwords. In: Pfitzmann, B. (ed.) EUROCRYPT 2001. LNCS, vol. 2045, pp. 475–494. Springer, Heidelberg (2001)
14. Katz, J., Yung, M.: Scalable protocols for authenticated group key exchange. In: Boneh, D. (ed.) CRYPTO 2003. LNCS, vol. 2729, pp. 110–125. Springer, Heidelberg (2003)

15. MacKenzie, P.D.: The pak suite: Protocols for password-authenticated key exchange. Submission to IEEE P1363.2 (2002)
16. Shin, S., Kobara, K., Imai, H.: A secure threshold anonymous password-authenticated key exchange protocol. In: Miyaji, A., Kikuchi, H., Rannenberg, K. (eds.) IWSEC 2007. LNCS, vol. 4752, pp. 444–458. Springer, Heidelberg (2007)
17. Tsudik, G., Xu, S.: A flexible framework for secret handshakes. In: Danezis, G., Golle, P. (eds.) PET 2006. LNCS, vol. 4258, pp. 295–315. Springer, Heidelberg (2006)
18. Tzeng, W.-G.: Efficient 1-out-n oblivious transfer schemes. In: Naccache, D., Paillier, P. (eds.) PKC 2002. LNCS, vol. 2274, pp. 159–171. Springer, Heidelberg (2002)
19. Viet, D.Q., Yamamura, A., Tanaka, H.: Anonymous password-based authenticated key exchange. In: Maitra, S., Veni Madhavan, C.E., Venkatesan, R. (eds.) INDOCRYPT 2005. LNCS, vol. 3797, pp. 244–257. Springer, Heidelberg (2005)
20. Wang, W., Hu, L., Li, Y.: How to construct secure and efficient three-party password-based authenticated key exchange protocols. In: Lai, X., Yung, M., Lin, D. (eds.) Inscrypt 2010. LNCS, vol. 6584, pp. 218–235. Springer, Heidelberg (2011)
21. Xu, S., Yung, M.: k-anonymous secret handshakes with reusable credentials. In: Atluri, V., Pfitzmann, B., McDaniel, P.D. (eds.) ACM Conference on Computer and Communications Security, pp. 158–167. ACM (2004)
22. Yang, J., Zhang, Z.: A new anonymous password-based authenticated key exchange protocol. In: Chowdhury, D.R., Rijmen, V., Das, A. (eds.) INDOCRYPT 2008. LNCS, vol. 5365, pp. 200–212. Springer, Heidelberg (2008)

Light Weight Network Coding Based Key Distribution Scheme for MANETs

Jianwei Liu[1], Abdur Rashid Sangi[1], Ruiying Du[2], and Qianhong Wu[1,2,3]

[1] School of Electronics and Information Engineering, Beihang University, China
{liujianwei,sangi}@catbuaa.edu.cn
[2] School of Computer Science, Wuhan University, Wuhan, China
durayingΘgmail.com
[3] Department of Computer Engineering and Mathematics
Universitat Rovira i Virgili, Tarragona, Catalonia
qianhong.wu@urv.cat

Abstract. We present a lightweight network coding based key distribution scheme to secure communications in mobile ad hoc network. Our scheme only needs simple XOR network coding operations and message authentication codes to achieve data confidentiality and guarantee the integrity of the distributed keys, respectively. Security analysis shows the effectiveness of our scheme against eavesdropping and impersonation attacks as well as brute force attacks. The proposed scheme employs a cluster-based hierarchical network topology. Simulation analysis show that for key exchange between two nodes in the same cluster, the scheme achieves more than 95% key delivery ratio with an ignorable average delay of 2 m.s.; for key exchange between nodes in different clusters, 58% key delivery ratio is achieved with around 10 m.s. of average delay.

Keywords: network coding, key distribution scheme, message authentication code (MAC), wireless ad hoc network, network simulator-2.

1 Introduction

A mobile ad-hoc network (MANET) is a system composed of wireless mobile nodes. These nodes are equipped with computing, wireless communication and networking capabilities. MANET has been proposed as an effective networking system facilitating data exchange between mobile devices even without fixed infrastructures. MANETs have found applications in various scenarios such as battlefield or disaster rescue scenarios [21]. Since communication in wireless networks is via open channels, the risk of unsecured sensitive information being intercepted by unintended recipients is a realistic concern [10]. Consequently, efforts to secure communications in MANETs are essential.

Secure communications among ad-hoc nodes have attracts much attentions in academia. These efforts fall into two approaches referred to as group key agreement and key distribution systems. Group key agreement allows a group of users to negotiate a common secret key via open insecure networks. In this way,

J. Lopez, X. Huang, and R. Sandhu (Eds.): NSS 2013, LNCS 7873, pp. 521–534, 2013.

a confidential intragroup broadcast channel can be established without relying on a centralized key server to generate and distribute secret keys to the potential members. The earlier efforts [2] focuses on efficient establishment of the initial group key. Subsequent studies [24] enable efficient member joins but the cost for a member leave is comparatively high. A tree key structure has been further proposed to achieve better efficiency for member joins and leaves [17]. By using a ring-based key structure, a recent proposal in [5] can cope with member changes in a constant number of rounds. The state-of-the art in group key agreement due to Wu *et al.* [29] allows fast transmission to remote cooperative nodes in MANETs. This goal is achieved by exploiting their novel notion of asymmetric group key agreement [30,28]. The great advantage of asymmetric group key agreement lies in that it allows member changes with little extra communication or computation costs, while the initial communication and computation overhead is comparatively high.

In a key distribution system, a trusted and centralized key server presets and allocates the secret keys to potential users, such that only the privileged users can read the transmitted message. The dynamic network topology, multi-hop, decentralized and self-organizing properties pose security challenges [27] in MANETs. One of the most important problems is how to distribute and update secret keys to ensure secure communication among all participating nodes. The early key distribution protocol [11] does not support member addition/deletion after the system is deployed. The up-to-date schemes [9] strengthen the security concept in the key distribution scenario while keeping the same $O(\sqrt{N})$ complexity as [4], where N is the maximum number of users. These schemes allow secure group communications in MANETs while the computation and communication costs are expensive.

Network coding is a recently proposed technique which can be used to improve a network's, especially, a MANET's throughput, efficiency and scalability. The core idea of network coding [1] is to allow and encourage mixing of data at intermediate network nodes. A receiver sees these data packets and deduces from them the messages that were originally intended for the data sink. With network coding, instead of simply storing-and-relaying the packets of information the nodes received, the nodes of a network take several packets and combine them together for transmission. This can be used to attain the maximum possible information flow in a network.

In addition to the above gains to improve network information flow, a few works have noticed that network coding can improve a MANET's resilience to attacks and eavesdropping. Lima *et al.* discussed the attacks and countermeasures in wireless network coding [1]. Dong *et al.* identified some security threats and challenges in several network coding-based systems proposed for unicast in wireless network [6]. Gkantsidis and Roddriguez proposed a large scale contents distribution scheme [8] in network scenarios. Vilela et al. proposed a low-complexity cryptographic scheme [25] based on random linear network coding [16]. Yu *et al.* proposed the algorithms to resist Byzantine attacks [12] in a broadcast scenario. Recently, several secret key distribution protocols have been proposed for wireless networks based on network coding [19,20]. These proposals require considerable memory space on each participating nodes and rely on a mobile privileged node to bootstrap the participating network nodes. A recent network coding based key distribution [14] has less storage overhead but the computation cost has not been evaluated. The efficient network coding-based protocol [19] proposed for wireless sensor network assumes that there is a mobile node and other nodes are static. This assumption is not consistent with our MANET setting in which all nodes are mobile, and so-called neighbors of any node are not fixed any more.

In this paper, we investigate key distribution for secure communications in MANETs in which the nodes are clustered. We propose a network coding based scheme consisting of an intra-cluster key distribution protocol and an inter-cluster protocol. The scheme allows any pair of nodes to efficiently setup a shared key through a multi-hop route. In the initialization stage, a trusted third party (TTP) is employed to pre-install a secret key and all padded key materials of the other nodes to each ad hoc node. Each node only knows its own secret key. Besides, it also keeps an encrypted version of keys of all other nodes pre-installed by TTP in the initialization stage. After the initialization stage, end-to-end key distribution can be performed efficiently based on a network coding paradigm.

We realize our lightweight scheme by exploiting the inherent security property of network coding. The scheme only needs simple XOR network coding operations and well-established message authentication codes (MACs) to achieve data confidentiality and guarantee the integrity of the distributed keys, respectively. With the help random ounces, our scheme allows secure session key updates in an very efficient way. Security analysis shows the effectiveness of our scheme against eavesdropping and impersonation attacks. Under reasonable assumptions, our scheme can also withstand brute force attacks.

Analyses imply that our key distribution is lightweight and suitable for MANETs. By consuming rational memory space, our scheme avoid complicated online mechanism to distribute more secret key materials. Compared with the network coding based key distribution protocols in [19,20], our scheme requires less memory space on each participating nodes and does not expect a mobile (super) node to bootstrap the participating network nodes. We distinguish our scheme from the recent network coding based key distribution scheme [14] with tighter design and extensive experiments. The experimental results show that, for key exchange between nodes in the same cluster, our scheme achieves more than 95% key delivery ratio with an ignorable average delay of 2 m.s., and for key exchange between nodes in different clusters,58% key delivery ratio is achieved at only a cost of about 10 m.s. average delay.

2 The System Model

2.1 A Cluster-Based Hierarchical Network Topology

To host and enable a large number of nodes in a MANET, we employ a cluster-based hierarchical network topology in MANETs. In the clustering approach to topology control, a set of clusterheads is first selected; each node is associated with a clusterhead, and clusterheads are connected with each other directly or by means of gateways; the union of gateways and clusterheads constitute a connected backbone. As illustrated in Fig. 1 and Fig. 2, a subset of the network nodes is selected to serve as the network backbone. Once selected, the clusterheads and the gateways are exploited to reduce the complexity of maintaining topology information, and simplify essential network management functions such as routing, bandwidth allocation, channel access, power control or virtual-circuit support. For clustering to be effective, the links and nodes that are part of the backbone (i.e., clusterheads, gateways, and the links that connect them) must be close to minimum and must also be connected [3]. The characteristics of cluster-based topology of ad hoc network will be leveraged to distribute secret keys based on network coding paradigm in our security design.

Fig. 1. Clustering nodes in MANET

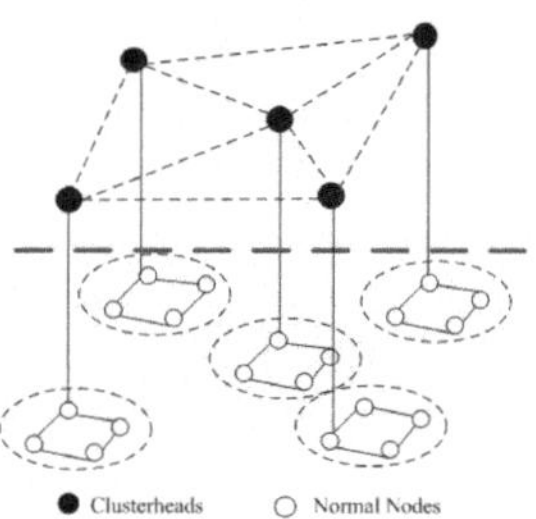

Fig. 2. A hierarchical network topology

2.2 Adversarial Threats and Design Goals

There are numerous security threats in MANETs. In this paper, we concentrate on typical adversarial threats to the secrecy of communications in MANETs. These typical security threats [27] are listed as follows.

- **Eavesdropping Attack.** The attacker can eavesdrop every traffic over the wireless medium in the MANET and can perform analysis upon receiving the traffic, given that the attacker knows all the cryptographic algorithms used in the MANET, but has limited computing resources and thus unable to break the underlying cryptographic primitives.
- **Impersonation Attack.** The attacker can intercept traffic on wireless link and try to impersonate as a legitimate user by replaying (and modifying) some traffics obtained during the previous sessions.
- **Brute-force Attack.** The attacker may try to exhaust the secret keys or inputs of the target nodes. The attack may also launch this attack against some cryptographic operations, e.g., to find a collision of hash operations.

The main goal our network coding-based scheme is to efficiently set up a secret key between two communication nodes, or set up a conference key among a group of nodes, so that non-compromised nodes can securely communicate in a hostile communication environment where there exist above adversarial threats. Another goal is that the proposed scheme should be efficient enough to be deployed in MANETs with resource-limited nodes.

With key pre-distribution and clustering-based network topology, several mitigating features can be exploited to achieve the above goals. First, before the nodes are deployed, some secret key materials can be preloaded. This can formalized in a scenario where, in the initialization stage, there exists an offline trusted third party (TTP) in the network. Second, as a managing node, each clusterhead knows all identifiers of nodes within its jurisdiction and can route the traffic to other clusterhead, and the latter will deliver the data to the designated node in the other cluster. Third, in many MANETs, each ad hoc node has minimum memory to store the encrypted keys of other nodes.

3 Proposed Network Coding Based Key Distribution Scheme for MANETs

In this section, a new key distribution scheme is proposed based on network coding paradigm. As the XOR operations are used in the scheme, so it requires only a few lightweight computations and provides a level of security of probabilistic key sharing scheme [7].

3.1 A High-Level View of Our Key Distribution Scheme

We adopt a cluster-based hierarchical network topology. The clusterheads are elected through a recommendation algorithm automatically [3], and every ad hoc node is associated with a clusterhead. Once any pair of node wants to setup a common secret key and communicate securely, they must first contact their own clusterheads. The clusterheads with the help of gateways can compute and deliver data between the two communication nodes. There are two cases here. In the first case, both nodes are associated with one same clusterhead. In the second case, both nodes are associated with two different clusterheads. Hence, the proposed scheme is made up of an intra-cluster key distribution protocol and an inter-cluster key distribution protocol.

Our key distribution protocols consists of *the initialization phase*, *the key distribution phase* and *the key updating phase*. The three phases are as follows.

- **Initialization Phase:** In this phase, an offline trusted third party (TTP) is employed to setup security parameter, such as generating secret key for each node, and choose cryptographic hash functions and algorithms. The TTP will initialize each ad hoc node and injects the security data into the node's memory. Once this phase is finished, all network nodes are ready for deployment.
- **Key Distribution Phase:** Two kinds of protocols will be executed based on whether two communication nodes belong to a same cluster or not. If the

two nodes belong to the same cluster, then key distribution fulfilled with the aid of the clusterhead. Whereas, if the two nodes belong to different clusters, the key distribution will be realized with the help of two different clusterheads playing the role of gateways.

- **Key Updating Phase:** When the network topology changes or new nodes enter the network, new session keys should be securely and efficiently established. When a node wants to update its current secret key, it needs to send an update request to its clusterhead. Then key updating procedure will be executed with the aid of clusterheads.

3.2 Proposed Intra-cluster Key Distribution Protocol

The data flow of our intra-cluster key distribution is illustrated in Fig. 3. The protocol is detailed as follows.

- **Initialization Phase:** An offline TTP generates a secret key $K_i \in P$, where P is the large key pool generated by TTP, and the corresponding identifiers $ID_i, i \in \{0, \cdots, N-1\}$ for each ad hoc node. TTP stores a list of an encrypted version of the other node's keys $K_j \oplus a_{ij}, i = 0, \cdots, i-1, i+1, \cdots, N-1$ (notice that $a_{ij} = a_{ji}$) into node i alone with all corresponding identifiers of the nodes. Then TTP chooses a secure hash function $h(x)$. After the initialization phase, each node only knows its own secret key and the encrypted version of other nodes. This minimizes the risk of secret key leakage when one node is compromised.
- **Key distribution phase:** This phase consist of the following procedures.
  1. Node A sends a challenge random r_A, a message authentication code $MAC_A = h(r_A \parallel K_A \oplus (K_B \oplus a_{AB}))$ and ID_A, ID_B to its clusterhead $H_l, l \in \{1, \cdots, N\}$, where N is the current maximum number of clusterheads in ad hoc network.
  2. When clusterhead H_l receive the message from node A, it first checks if node A and node B are associated with it. If the two nodes belong to the same cluster, then H_l recodes r_A, MAC_A, ID_A, ID_B and delivers ID_A, ID_B to node B.

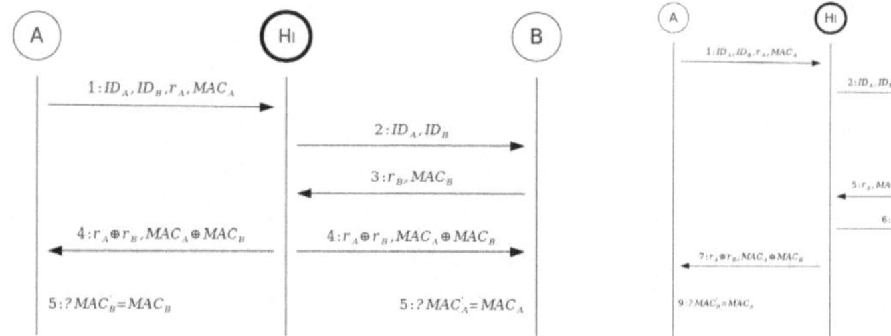

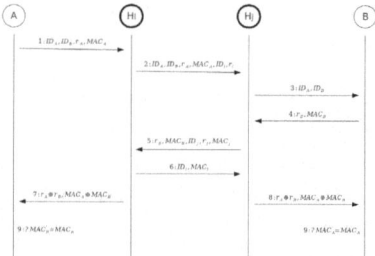

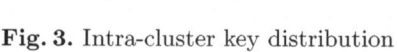

Fig. 3. Intra-cluster key distribution

Fig. 4. Inter-cluster key distribution

3. When node B receives ID_A, ID_B, node B knows that A wants to communicate with it. Then it sends a challenge random r_B and $MAC_B = h(r_B \parallel K_B \oplus (K_A \oplus a_{AB}))$ to H_l.
4. H_l first performs a simple table look-up and then uses network coding paradigm to broadcast the value of $\{r_A \oplus r_B \parallel MAC_A \oplus MAC_B\}$.
5. Upon receiving the message, node A computes $r_A \oplus \{r_A \oplus r_B\} = r'_B$ and $MAC_A \oplus \{MAC_A \oplus MAC_B\} = MAC_B$ and then computes $MAC'_B = h(r'_B \parallel K_A \oplus (K_B \oplus a_{AB}))$; Node B computes $r_B \oplus \{r_A \oplus r_B\} = r'_A$ and $MAC_B \oplus \{MAC_A \oplus MAC_B\} = MAC_A$ and then computes $MAC'_A = h(r'_A \parallel K_B \oplus (K_A \oplus a_{AB}))$.
6. Node A verifies to confirm if $MAC'_B = MAC_B$; Node B verifies to confirm if $MAC'_A = MAC_A$. If they are equal, then both node A and node B will compute a shared secret key $SK = h(K_A \oplus K_B \oplus a_{AB} \parallel r_A \parallel r_B)$.

- **Key Updating phase:** Note that the new session key between arbitrary two ad hoc nodes is $SK = h(K_A \oplus K_B \oplus a_{AB} \parallel r_A \parallel r_B)$. The two random numbers r_A, r_B guarantee that the session key is fresh for each execution. When one node want to update its session key with the other nodes, it can get the new session keys with the designated nodes by choosing two new random numbers r_A and r_B.

3.3 Proposed Inter-cluster Key Distribution Protocol

The data flow of the proposed inter-cluster key distribution protocol is illustrated in Fig. 4. The initial and key updating phases are similar to their counterparts of the intra-cluster protocol. What follows only specifies the key distribution phase.

1. Node A initiates the protocol by sending a challenge random r_A, a message authentication code $MAC_A = h(r_A \parallel K_A \oplus (K_B \oplus a_{AB}))$ and ID_A, ID_B to its cluserhead $H_l, l \in \{1, \cdots, N\}$.
2. Upon receiving the message from node A, H_l first checks if node A and node B are associated with it. If not, H_l records ID_A, ID_B, r_A, MAC_A and broadcasts a 6-tuple $ID_A, ID_B, r_A, MAC_A, r_l, ID_l$ to the other clusterheads, where r_l is the new random challenge generated by H_l.
3. Suppose clusterhead H_j receives the 6-tuple $ID_A, ID_B, r_A, MAC_A, r_l, ID_l$ broadcasted from H_l, H_j knows that node A want to communicate with a node B that is subscribed under its jurisdiction. Then H_j records the 6-tuple $ID_A, ID_B, r_A, MAC_A, r_l, ID_l$ and broadcasts ID_A, ID_B to node B.
4. Upon receiving ID_A, ID_B, node B knows A sends a random challenge r_B and $MAC_B = h(r_B \parallel K_B \oplus (k_A \oplus a_{AB}))$ to H_j.
5. Upon receiving r_B, MAC_B, H_j just performs a simple table look-up and generates a new random challenge r_j and sends a 5-tuple r_B, MAC_B, ID_j, r_j, MAC_j to H_l.
6. Upon receiving the 5-tuple, H_l performs a simple table look-up and computes $MAC'_j = h(r_l \parallel K_l \oplus (K_j \oplus a_{ji}))$. Then H_l check if $MAC_j = MAC'_j$. If the two values are equal, then H_l authenticates H_j. H_l performs a simple table look-up and computes $MAC_l = h(r_l \parallel K_l \oplus (K_j \oplus a_{ji}))$, then unicasts ID_l, MAC_l to H_j.

7. At almost the same time, H_l computes the value $\{r_A \oplus r_B \parallel MAC_a \oplus MAC_B\}$ and uses network coding paradigm to broadcasts the value to node A.
8. Upon receiving ID_l, MAC_l, H_j performs a simple table look-up and computes $MAC_l' = h(r_j \parallel K_j \oplus (K_l \oplus a_{ij}))$. Then H_j check if $MAC_l = MAC_l'$. If the two values are equal, then H_j authenticates H_l. H_j computes the value $\{r_A \oplus r_B \parallel MAC_A \oplus MAC_B\}$ and broadcasts the value to node B.
9. Upon receiving the message, node A computes $r_A \oplus \{r_A \oplus r_B\} = r_B'$ and $MAC_A \oplus \{MAC_A \oplus MAC_B\} = MAC_B$, and then computes $MAC_B' = h(r_B' \parallel K_A \oplus (K_B \oplus a_{AB}))$; Node B computes $r_B \oplus \{r_A \oplus r_B\} = r_A'$ and $MAC_B \oplus \{MAC_A \oplus MAC_B\} = MAC_A$, and then computes $MAC_A' = h(r_A' \parallel K_B \oplus (K_A \oplus a_{AB}))$.
10. Node A verifies to confirm if $MAC_B' = MAC_B$; Node B verifies to confirm if $MAC_A' = MAC_A$. If they are equal, then both node A and node B will compute a shared secret key $SK = h(K_A \oplus K_B \oplus a_{AB} \parallel r_A \parallel r_B)$.

4 Evaluation of the Proposal

4.1 Security Analysis

In the following, we discuss the main attack types that emerge in MANETs [27].

- **Eavesdropping attack:** We first consider an attacker who can listen to all the traffic over the wireless medium. If the TTP and the nodes are not compromised, the eavesdropper can not get any keys from the key pool but the users' identifiers, message authentication codes and random challenges. Note that these data except the identifiers will be changed during the next protocol execution. The attacker can not obtain any useful secret information by eavesdropping the traffic.
- **Impersonation attack:** We next consider an attacker who can intercept traffic on wireless link and impersonate as a legitimate user by replaying some intercepted private information. If the attacker could just intercept the data traffic and simply replay them during the current session, it can not obtain any benefit from the transaction. If the attacker wants to replay the intercepted data from the last protocol execution, then it will be easily detected by verifying the MAC values on both ad hoc nodes and clusterheads, because the attacker can not get the correct keys.
- **Brute-force attack:** Finally, an adversary could launch an attack against the XOR and hash operations used in the protocols. One may notice that the keys stored in the ad hoc nodes are XOR-ed by a random number R, which can be considered as an encryption operation using one-time padding cipher. It has been proved that the one-time padding cipher can achieve information-theoretic security. If the hash function used in the protocol is collision-resistant, the adversary can not find collisions of the $MACs$. Thus, the protocols proposed in paper are secure against brute-force attack.

4.2 Performance Analysis

We evaluate the performance of our scheme with extensive experiments. We implemented this scheme in network simulator-2 [18,22,23]. As mentioned above, this scheme requires a cluster based formation, i.e., cluster based routing protocol. We implemented the Cluster Based Routing Protocol [13] and modified this protocol to work with our key distribution scheme. OPENSSL [26] was incorporated into NS-2 to compute message authentication code. Table 1 shows simulation parameter and below is the simulation performance metrics:

Table 1. Simulation Parameters

Parameters	**Values**
Simulation Time	100, 300, 500, 700, 900, 1100, 1300 & 1500 Seconds
Space	1000x1000
Total Number of Nodes	50
Mobility	Moderate Mobility
Transmit Range	250m
Connections	5 & 10 Pairs
Traffic Type	Constant Key Packet
Node Speed	5 m//s
Key Distribution Packet Rate	1 packet//s
MAC Protocol	802.11
Mobility Model	Random Waypoint

- **Key Distribution Ratio (KDR):** Ratio of total number of key distribution packets sent to the number of successfully received key distribution packets, for exchanging keys between nodes in the same or different cluster.
- **Average Key Distribution Delay at Source (AKDDS):** The average delay that each key distribution packet faced till it finally received back at source nodes, for exchanging keys between nodes in the same or different cluster.
- **Average Key Distribution Delay at Destination (AKDDD):** It is the average delay that each key distribution packet faced till it finally received by the destination nodes, for exchanging keys between nodes in the same or different cluster.
- **Normalized Routing Overhead (NRO):** It is the number of routing discovery packets that were sent on an average for each key distribution packet. During key distribution between nodes in the same cluster, we do not require a route and only need clusterhead's help to finish the key distribution.
- **Average Number of Hops (ANH):** It is the average number of hops that each key distribution packet traversed to finally received by both ends, i.e., source and destination, only for exchanging keys between nodes in different clusters because hop count would remain the same, i.e., 4 hops, while keys are exchanged between nodes in the same cluster.

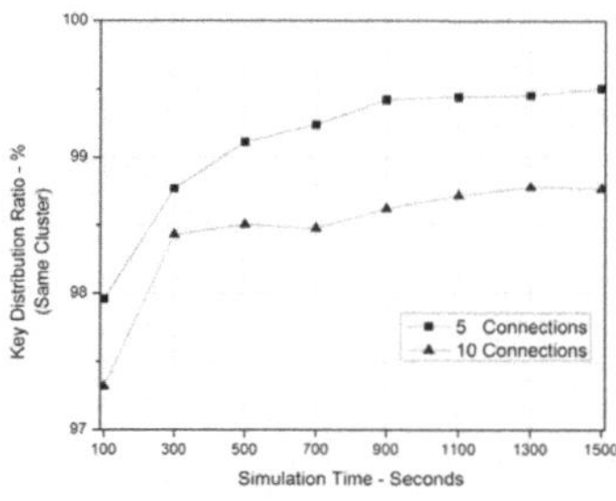

Fig. 5. Intra-Cluster KDR

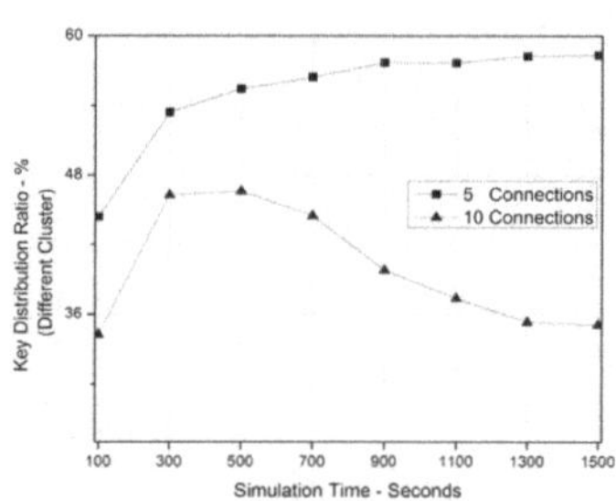

Fig. 6. Inter-Cluster KDR

Varied amount of key distribution packets were sent between 5 and 10 pair of nodes. The source node in each pair of nodes was configured to send one key exchange request per second.

Figure 5 shows the ratio of total keys that were successfully distributed to number of key distribution packets that were sent between nodes in the same cluster. Key distribution ratio was increased as the simulation time increased under both traffic scenarios. During low traffic i.e. 5 connections; the packet delivery ratio was higher than during high traffic i.e. 10 connections. Traffic congestion was noticed and key distribution packet dropped due to higher amount of traffic.

Each pair of node was configured to constantly sending one key exchange packet per second. Such configuration caused performance degradation as soon as the number of pairs was increased to ten.

Unlike key distribution in the same cluster, a route to destination is required to forward key distribution packet to another cluster. Results shown in figure 6 that key distribution ratio improved while low traffic but decreased under higher amount of traffic. We can avoid this performance degradation by reducing the sending rate of key distribution packets or disabling the constant key packet traffic. A trade off mechanism could help to replace constant key packet traffic.

Average delay that each key distribution packet faced to be successfully received back to source node in the same cluster is presented in figure 7. Key

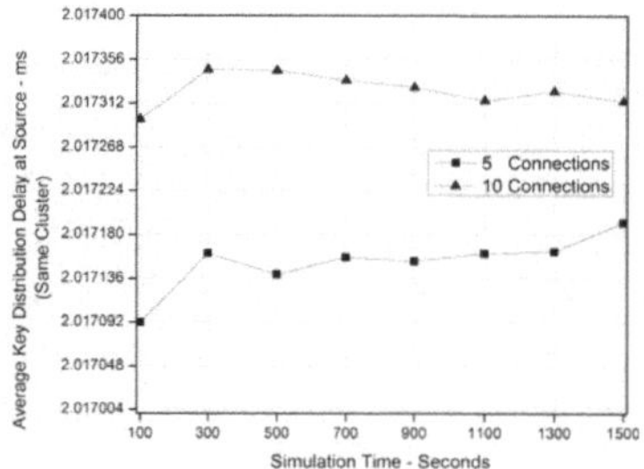

Fig. 7. Intra-Cluster AKDDS

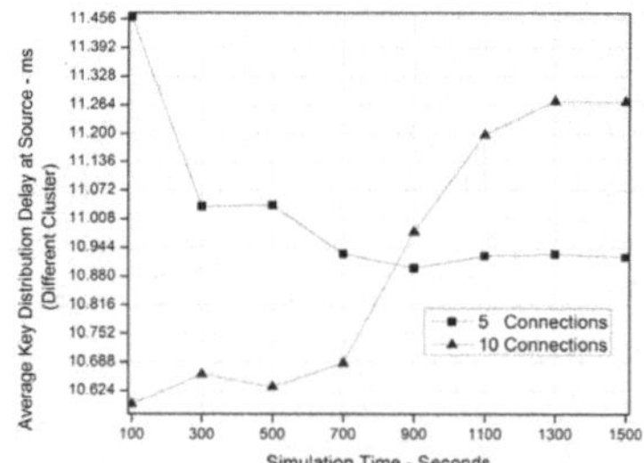

Fig. 8. Inter-Cluster AKDDS

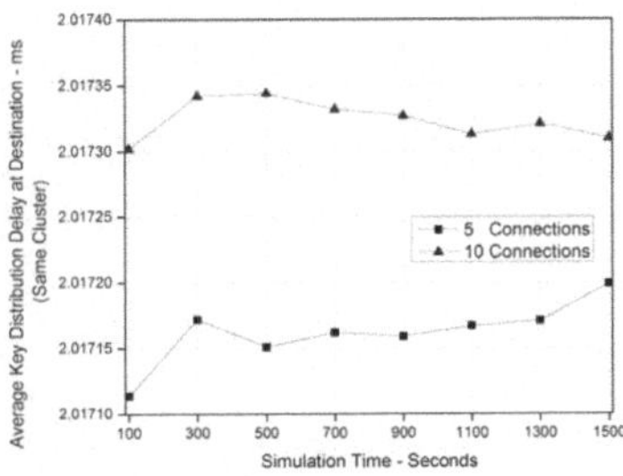

Fig. 9. Intra-Cluster AKDDD

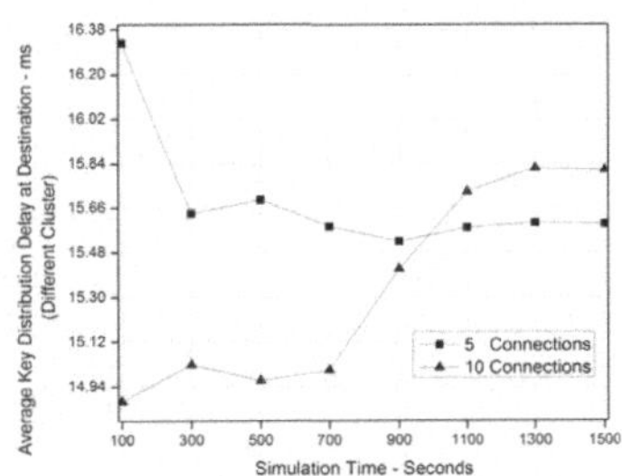

Fig. 10. Inter-Cluster AKDDD

distribution in the same cluster does not require any routing mechanism and these requests are handled by local information that is kept in cluster head.

Delay remained identical even the simulation time was increased from 100 to 1500 seconds. Key exchange packets during lower traffic i.e. 5 connections faced less delay as compared to higher traffic i.e. 10 connections.

Average delay that each key distribution packet faced to be successfully received back to source node in different cluster is presented in figure 8. Route acquisition is needed to reach destination node and thus each key packet need to face the delay caused by route discovery mechanism. A huge decline was noticed while low traffic but the delay increased and became higher after 900 seconds simulation and so on under high traffic scenario.

Higher amount of route discovery caused network congestion as well as the routing packet drop. Rate of unsuccessful route discoveries increased with increased duration of simulation.

Average delay that each key distribution packet faced to be successfully received at destination node in the same cluster is presented in figure 9. Average delay was slightly lower as compared to it was observed at source node (figure 7). Higher amount of traffic caused more delay during higher amount of traffic.

Fig. 10 illustrates the average delay that each key distribution packet faced to be successfully received at destination node in different cluster. An additional delay was observed due to route acquisition to reach destination that were in another cluster. At lower traffic load, the delay was higher in the beginning but it reduced tremendously when the simulation time approached 700 seconds and onward.

While higher traffic load, lower delay was faced by each packet till the simulation time was less than 700 seconds but it became huge as the simulation approached 900 seconds and onward.

Routing overhead was there only when both source and destination were in different clusters. Figure 11 shows this overhead in context of successful key distribution attempts. Lower traffic load generated comparatively less amount of routing overhead and this overhead declined as the simulation time was increased to 1500 seconds. On the contrary, higher amount of traffic load suffered enormous routing overhead in context of successful key distribution attempts.

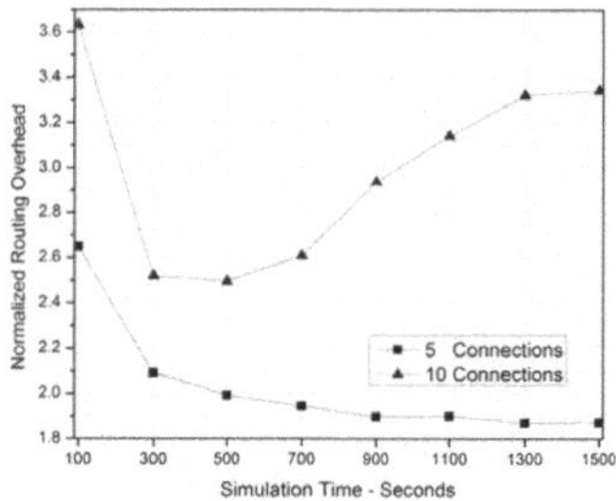

Fig. 11. Normalized Routing Overhead

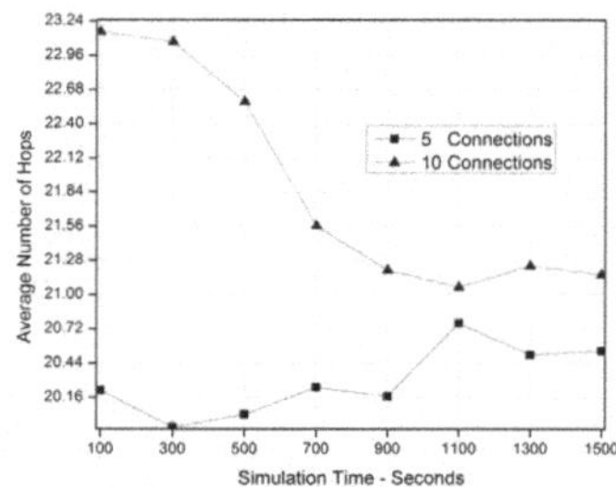

Fig. 12. Average Number of Hops

Higher rate of key distribution packets that were sent caused more routing overhead to discover destination nodes. A back off mechanism could improve this overhead. Limited amount of route discoveries should be generated and a new route discovery should be avoided until a previous route discovery is successful or timeout.

Number of hops that the key distribution packets traversed on an average is shown in figure 12. Results reveal that the key distribution packets traversed longer during higher traffic loads and number of hops was fewer on average during low traffic load.

5 Concluding Remarks

Wireless ad hoc network are vulnerable to various attacks, such as eavesdropping, impersonation and brute-force attacks. In this paper, we propose two lightweight key distribution protocols based on network coding paradigm. The security, memory requirements and computation overhead of the protocols are thoroughly analyzed. Analysis shows that the new protocols provide a lightweight solution for distributing keys while ensure communication confidentiality and authentication of nodes against typical attacks.

Acknowledgment. This paper is partly supported by the NSF of China through grants 60970116, 61173154, 61003214, 61272501, 61202465 and 61173192, by MOST of China through National Key Basic Research Program under 973 grant 2012CB315905, by the EU 7FP through project "DwB", the Spanish Government through projects CTV-09-634, PTA2009-2738-E, TSI-020302-2010-153, TIN2009-11689, TIN2011-27076-C03-01, CONSOLIDER INGENIO 2010 "ARES" CSD2007-0004 and TSI2007-65406-C03-01 and by the Catalonia Government through grant SGR2009-1135. For the authors with the UNESCO Chair in Data Privacy, this paper does not necessarily reflect the position of UNESCO nor does it commit that organization.

References

1. Ahlswede, R., Cai, N., Li, S.-Y.R., Yeung, R.W.: Network Information Flow. IEEE Transactions on Information Theory 46(4), 1204–1216 (2000)
2. Burmester, M., Desmedt, Y.: A Secure and Efficient Conference Key Distribution System (Extended Abstract). In: De Santis, A. (ed.) EUROCRYPT 1994. LNCS, vol. 950, pp. 275–286. Springer, Heidelberg (1995)
3. Li, B., Garcia-Luna-Aceves, J.J.: Tology Management in Ad Hoc Networks. In: Proc. of MOBIHOC 2003, pp. 129–140. ACM (2003)
4. Boneh, D., Gentry, C., Waters, B.: Collusion Resistant Broadcast Encryption with Short Ciphertexts and Private Keys. In: Shoup, V. (ed.) CRYPTO 2005. LNCS, vol. 3621, pp. 258–275. Springer, Heidelberg (2005)
5. Dutta, R., Barua, R.: Provably Secure Constant Round Contributory Group Key Agreement in Dynamic Setting. IEEE Transactions on Information Theory 54(5), 2007–2025 (2008)
6. Dong, J., Curtmola., S.R., Nita-Rotaru, C.: Toward Secure Network Coding in Wireless Networks: Threats and Challenges. In: Proc. of 4th Workshop on Secure Network Protocols (NPSEC 2008), pp. 33–38. IEEE (2008)
7. Du, W., Deng, J., Han, Y.S., Varshney, P.K., Katz, J., Khalili, A.: A Pairwise Key Predistribution Scheme for Wireless Sensor Networks. ACM Transactions on Information and System Security 8(2), 228–258 (2005)
8. Gkantsidis, C., Rodriguez, P.: Network Coding for Large Scale Content Distribution. In: Proc. of INFOCOM 2005, pp. 2235–2245. IEEE (2005)
9. Gentry, C., Waters, B.: Adaptive Security in Broadcast Encryption Systems (with Short Ciphertexts). In: Joux, A. (ed.) EUROCRYPT 2009. LNCS, vol. 5479, pp. 171–188. Springer, Heidelberg (2009)
10. Huang, Y.-M., Yeh, C.-H., Wang, T.-I., Chao, H.-C.: Constructing Secure Group Communication over Wireless Ad Hoc Networks Based on a Virtual Subnet Model. IEEE Wireless Communications 14(5), 71–75 (2007)
11. Ingemarsson, I., Tang, D.T., Wong, C.K.: A Conference on Key Distribution System. IEEE Transactions on Information Theory 28(5), 714–720 (1982)
12. Jaggi, S., Langberg, M., Katti, S., Ho, T., Katabi, D., Médard, M.: Resilient Network Coding in the Presence of Byzantine Adversaries. In: Proc. of INFOCOM 2007, pp. 616–624. IEEE (2007)
13. Jiang, M., Li, J., Tay, Y.C.: Cluster Based Routing Protocol (CBRP): Functional Specification. In: Mobile Ad-hoc Network (MANET) Working Group, IETF (1998)
14. Liu, J., Du, R., Chen, J., He, K.: A Key Distribution Scheme Using Network Coding for Mobile Ad Hoc Network. Security and Communication Networks 5(1), 59–67 (2012)
15. Lima, L., Vilela, J.P., Oliveira, P.F., Barros, J.: Network Coding Security: Attacks and Countermeasures. Cryptography and Security, CoRR abs/0809.1366 (2008), `http://arxiv.org/pdf/0809.1366v1.pdf`
16. Li, S., Yeung, R., Cai, N.: Linear Network Coding. IEEE Transactions on Information Theory 49(2), 371–381 (2003)
17. Mao, Y., Sun, Y., Wu, M., Liu, K.J.R.: JET: Dynamic Join-Exit-Tree Amortization and Scheduling for Contributory Key Management. IEEE/ACM Transactions on Networking 14(5), 1128–1140 (2006)
18. Network Simulator-2 (2011), `http://www.isi.edu/nsnam/ns`
19. Oliveira, P.F., Barros, J.: Mobile Secret Key Distribution with Network Coding. In: Proc. of the International Conference on Security and Cryptography (SECRYPT 2007), pp. 171–174 (2007)

20. Oliveira, F., Barros, J.: Network Coding Protocols for Secret Key Distribution. IEEE Transactions on Information Forensics and Security 3(3), 414–423 (2008)
21. Rong, B., Chen, H.-H., Qian, Y., Lu, K., Hu, R.Q., Guizani, S.: A Pyramidal Security Model for Large-Scale Group-Oriented Computing in Mobile Ad Hoc Networks: The Key Management Study. IEEE Transactions on Vehicular Technology 58(1), 398–408 (2009)
22. Sangi, A.R.: Route Information Poisoning in MANETs: Analysis and Defenses. In: Proc. of Fourth IITA Conference (2010)
23. Sangi, A.R., Liu, J., Liu, Z.: Performance Comparison of Single and Multi-Path routing Protocol in MANET with Selfish Behaviors. Proc. of World Academy of Science, Engineering and Technology (WASET) 65, 828–832 (2010)
24. Steiner, M., Tsudik, G., Waidner, M.: Key Agreement in Dynamic Peer Groups. IEEE Transactions on Parallel Distributed System 11(8), 769–780 (2000)
25. Vilela, J.P., Lima, L., Barros, J.: Lightweight Security for Network Coding. In: Proc. of ICC 2008, pp. 1750–1754. IEEE (2008)
26. Viega, J., Messier, M., Chandra, P.: Network Security with OpenSSL, 1st edn. O'Reilly, Cambridge (2002)
27. Wu, B., Chen, J., Wu, J., Cardei, M.: A Survey on Attacks and Countermeasures in Mobile Ad Hoc Networks. In: Xiao, Y., Shen, X., Du, D.-Z. (eds.) Wireless/Mobile Network Security, pp. 103–135. Springer (2006)
28. Wu, Q., Mu, Y., Susilo, W., Qin, B., Domingo-Ferrer, J.: Asymmetric Group Key Agreement. In: Joux, A. (ed.) EUROCRYPT 2009. LNCS, vol. 5479, pp. 153–170. Springer, Heidelberg (2009)
29. Wu, Q., Qin, B., Zhan, L., Domingo-Ferrer, J.: Fast Transmission to Remote Cooperative Groups: A New Key Management Paradigm. IEEE/ACM Transactions on Networking (2012) ISSN : 1063-6692, doi:10.1109/TNET.2012.2208201
30. Wu, Q., Qin, B., Zhang, L., Domingo-Ferrer, J., Farràs, O.: Bridging Broadcast Encryption and Group Key Agreement. In: Lee, D.H., Wang, X. (eds.) ASIACRYPT 2011. LNCS, vol. 7073, pp. 143–160. Springer, Heidelberg (2011)

Identity-Based Dynamic Authenticated Group Key Agreement Protocol for Space Information Network

Chao Wang[1,2], Kefei Mao[1], Jianwei Liu[1], and Jianhua Liu[1]

[1] School of Electronics and Information Engineering, Beihang University, Beijing 100191, China
wangchaopaper@126.com
[2] Department of PLA Air Force, China

Abstract. A novel identity-based authenticated group key agreement (ID-AGKA) protocol is proposed to implement secure group communication in space information network. Cluster-based hierarchical mechanism is applied to generate group session key through the intra-cluster phase, inter-cluster phase and key distribution phase. Not only is the cost of establishment and management in public key infrastructure reduced, but also the dynamic situations that satellite node joins or exits the group are supported in the proposed protocol. Authentication, forward and backward secrecy and semantic security are proved under difficult mathematical problem assumptions. Compared with the previous ID-AGKA protocols, the proposed protocol has lower computation complexity and communication cost, and achieves optimal overall performance for space information network.

Keywords: space information network, group key agreement, forward and backward secrecy, semantic security.

1 Introduction

Group key agreement (GKA) protocol, as an important technique of establishing the group session key, can be used to guarantee the confidentiality in the group communication. In the secure GKA protocols only when all of the group members cooperate together, can the group session key be established while any unauthorized sets of the group members cannot conspire to induce the group session key in advance. With the speedy growth of the wireless network, GKA protocols have become more and more important and many useful GKA schemes have been proposed in recent years. The classic GKA protocols proposed in Refs. [1-3] are only robust against the passive attack strategy. To overcome this drawback, the authenticated group key agreement (AGKA) protocols were proposed subsequently [4-10]. However, all above-mentioned GKA schemes can only work well under the certain wireless network circumstance where the numbers of the network nodes are invariant. Consequently, the dynamic AGKA protocols were put forward [11-14], in which the dynamic member joining or leaving scenarios

J. Lopez, X. Huang, and R. Sandhu (Eds.): NSS 2013, LNCS 7873, pp. 535–548, 2013.

are investigated adequately. Unfortunately, those dynamic AGKA protocols are only suitable for the traditional wireless network requirements.

Space information network (SIN), composed of varieties of satellites constellations, aircrafts and ground equipments, is a very complex interconnection network. Most of GKA protocols which are suitable for traditional wireless network cannot work well due to the high speed and the variable number of the satellite network nodes in SIN. In 2007, Wang and Zhao et al. [15] introduced a general framework for SIN, but failed to present a feasible AGKA scheme. Then, in 2012, Zhong and Ma et al. [16] further proposed an applicable AGKA scheme for SIN framework. Nevertheless, their AGKA scheme is based on a strong assumption that there is a secure and efficient signature scheme in advance, and the corresponding solutions are not given when a satellite node joins or leaves the SIN dynamically. Thereafter, the universally composable (UC) bidirectional AGKA protocol was designed for SIN without needing the strong signature assumptions [17], but it is unfeasible for n-party ($n \geq 3$). Moreover, the mechanism based on the public key certificates introduces higher calculation and storage cost, especially for SIN. Hence, the additional communication cost is also brought in along with the certificates' transmission, which significantly increases the difficulty of the key management. Afterwards, in 2011, the improved ID-AGKA scheme was proposed [18], in which the key management mechanism is relative simpler and the cost of public key infrastructure (PKI) in establishment and management is reduced. Although this scheme also has the dynamic authentication synchronously, it is vulnerable to the replay attack strategies. Additionally, the ID-AGKA schemes proposed in Refs. [19-27] also need improving in efficiency and performance, which are analyzed and compared in detail in later sections. In this study, utilizing the traditional cluster-based hierarchical mechanism we propose a novel ID-AGKA scheme which can work well when the satellite node joins or leaves the SIN. Furthermore, the security of the proposed scheme is analyzed and proved, and the performance in communication cost and computation complex is compared with many existing competitive schemes.

2 Preliminaries

2.1 Bilinear Pairing

Let G_1 be a cyclic additive group, G_2 be a cyclic multiplicative group of same prime order q. Let P be a generator of G_1, and $\hat{e}$ be a bilinear map such that $\hat{e}$: $G_1 \times G_2 \rightarrow G_2$ with the following properties [28, 29]:

- Bilinearity. For any $P, Q \in G_1$ and $a, b \in Z_q^*$, $\hat{e}(aP, bQ) = \hat{e}(P, Q)^{ab}$.
- Non-degeneracy. There exists $P \in G_1$, such that $\hat{e}(P, P) \neq 1$.
- Computability. For any$P, Q \in G_1$, it is efficient to compute $\hat{e}(P, Q)$.

2.2 Computational Problems

Two mathematically hard problems on which the proposed scheme is based are described, namely discrete logarithm problem (DLP) and computational Diffie-Hellmen problem (CDHP) [28, 29]:

- DLP. Given $P, Q \in G_1$, to find the integer a whenever such an integer $a \in Z_q^*$ exists, such that $Q = aP$.
- CDHP. Given aP and bP, to compute abP, where $P \in G_1$ and $a, b \in Z_q^*$.

2.3 Cluster-Based Hierarchical Model

The satellite network, composed of the geostationary earth orbit (GEO), medium earth orbit (MEO) and low earth orbit (LEO) satellites networks, can be generally regarded as the three-layer network architecture according to the SIN longitudinal hierarchical network model. Each satellite orbit network can be simply taken as a cluster such as GEO cluster, MEO cluster and LEO cluster, respectively. The most powerful satellite node acts as the cluster head in the same cluster, such as the satellite nodes ID_0^G, ID_0^M and ID_0^L, while other satellite nodes are the ordinary intra-cluster nodes, which are described in Fig.1. To describe the proposed scheme clearly the following notations are defined.

- $ID_i^G(ID_i^M, ID_i^L)$: each satellite node's ID in GEO (MEO, LEO) cluster, where $ID_0^G(ID_0^M, ID_0^L)$ is the cluster head and $ID_i^G(ID_i^M, ID_i^L)(i \neq 0)$ is the ordinary node in GEO(MEO, LEO) cluster.
- $C1(C2, C3)$: intra-cluster (inter-cluster, key distribution) phase.
- (u_i^G, v_i^G): the long-term public/private keys pair of the satellite node $ID_i^G(0 \leq i \leq n)$ generated by KGC.
- $K^G(K^M, K^L)$: the intra-cluster temporary key in GEO (MEO, LEO) cluster.
- K: the final group session key.

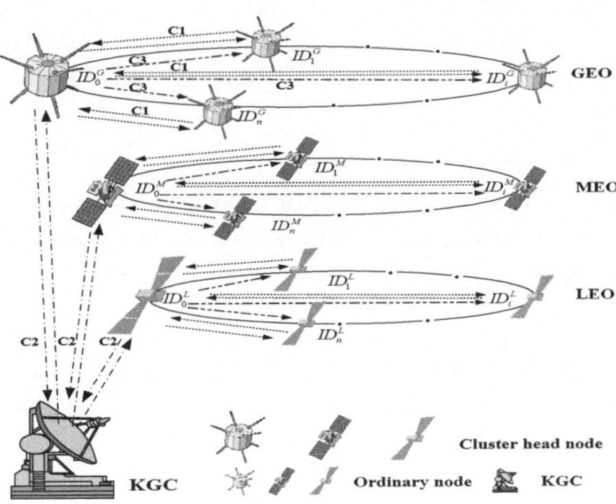

Fig. 1. The sketch of ID-AGKA protocol based on SIN longitudinal hierarchical network model

3 The Proposed Scheme

In this section, the proposed scheme for SIN is depicted in detail. Each satellite node generates a key contribution value and sends the contribution information to the key generation center (KGC) on the ground. When all the contribution values are received, KGC generates a group session key and distributes the key to all the satellite nodes in a secure manner. Moreover, the dynamic group key agreement is supported when the satellite node joins or exits the group. The proposed protocol consists of the following steps.

3.1 System Setup

Given a security parameter $k \in Z$, the credible KGC generates a set of system parameter denoted with $SP = \{G_1, G_2, \hat{e}, P, q, H\}$ by running a probably algorithm for polynomial time as follows.

- Run the parameter generator on input k to generate a prime q, a cyclic additive group G_1 and a cyclic multiplicative group G_2 of the same prime order q, a generator P of G_1 and an admissible pairing $\hat{e}$: $G_1 \times G_2 \rightarrow G_2$.

- Randomly select a system master key $s \in Z_q^*$, and compute $P_s = sP$ as the corresponding system public key.

- Choose cryptographic one-way hash functions with collision-resistance assumption H_1: $\{0,1\}^* \rightarrow G_1$ and H_2: $\{0,1\}^* \rightarrow Z_q^*$.

Finally, the KGC's master key s is kept secret and the system parameters P_s and $SP = \{G_1, G_2, \hat{e}, P, q, H\}$ are published. For each satellite node, KGC computes $u_i = H_2(ID_i)$ as the long-term public key and $v_i = su_i$ as the long-term private key, where ID_i is the identity of each satellite node. Then, KGC sends each public/private keys pair to the corresponding satellite node by a secure manner.

3.2 Key Agreement

The process of key agreement is carried out through intra-cluster (C1), inter-cluster (C2) and key distribution (C3) three phases, which are depicted in Fig.1 and presented as follows.

Phase 1: Intra-Cluster Phase. Within intra-cluster phase, the intra-cluster temporary key, such as K^G,K^M and K^L, are established for GEO, MEO and LEO cluster, respectively. Meanwhile, the two-way authentication between each ordinary satellite node and cluster head is implemented in the same cluster. Taking GEO cluster as an example, the following three steps are conducted.

- The ordinary node $ID_i^G (1 \leq i \leq n)$ chooses a random number $r_i \in Z_q^*$ and computes r_i^{-1}, $v_i^{G^{-1}}$ and $R_i = r_i P$, $S_i = v_i^G R_i$. Then $ID_i^G (1 \leq i \leq n)$ sends the message (ID_i^G, R_i, S_i) to the cluster head ID_0^G while keeping $(r_i^{-1}, v_i^{G^{-1}}, R_i, S_i)$ in the local memory.

- Once the message (ID_i^G, R_i, S_i) is received, ID_0^G verifies the identity of $ID_i^G(1 \leq i \leq n)$. That is, if $\hat{e}(S_i, P) \neq \hat{e}(u_i R_i, P_s)$, ID_i^G is illegal. Otherwise, ID_i^G is legal. Then ID_0^G chooses a random number $r_0 \in Z_q^*$ and computes $R_0 = r_0 P, T_i = r_0 v_0^G S_i (1 \leq i \leq n), W = H_1(ID_0^G, T_1, T_2, ..., T_n, t_0)$ and $S_0 = v_0^G W$. Where, t_0, used for a timestamp, is the system time of the cluster head ID_0^G. Then, ID_0^G can compute the intra-cluster temporary key $K^G = \hat{e}(r_0 v_0^G P, \sum_{i=1}^{n} T_i)$ and further obtains $h_0 = H_2(ID_0^G, K^G, t_0)$. Subsequently, ID_0^G broadcasts the message $(ID_0^G, S_0, T_1, T_2, ..., T_n, t_0, h_0)$ to ID_i^G.
- When the message $(ID_0^G, S_0, T_1, T_2, ..., T_n, t_0, h_0)$ is received, $ID_i^G(1 \leq i \leq n)$ verifies the cluster head ID_0^G by computing the equation that $W = H_1(ID_0^G, T_1, T_2, ..., T_n, t_0), \hat{e}(S_0, P) = \hat{e}(u_0 W, P_s)$. If the verification succeeds, ID_i^G calculates the intra-cluster temporary key $K^G = \hat{e}(T_i r_i^{-1} v_i^{G^{-1}}, \sum_{i=1}^{n} T_i)$ and $h_0' = H_2(ID_0^G, K^G, t_0)$. If the equation that $h_0' = h_0$ holds, the intra-cluster temporary key is established successfully. Otherwise, the intra-cluster phase should be restarted. Meanwhile, the timestamp information t_0 is both contained in h_0 and h_0', so the method can be used for avoiding the replay attacks. Finally, the intra-cluster temporary key K^G is established among all the satellite nodes in GEO cluster.
  Similarly, the intra-cluster temporary key K^M and K^L also can be established in MEO cluster and LEO cluster.

Phase 2: Inter-Cluster Phase. Each cluster head $ID_0^G(ID_0^M, ID_0^L)$ sends the corresponding $K^G(K^M, K^L)$ to KGC in this phase. Then these datas used for generating the final group session key are returned back to each cluster head after KGC's calculation as the following three steps. Meanwhile, the two-way authentication between each cluster head and KGC is accomplished in the similar way utilized in intra-cluster phase.

- $ID_0^G(ID_0^M, ID_0^L)$ computes $K_P^G = K^G P$ $(K_P^M = K^M P$, $K_P^L = K^L P)$ and sends $K_P^G(K_P^M$, $K_P^L)$ to KGC, respectively.
- Once the message from each cluster head is received, KGC implements the identity authentication. If the cluster head is legal, KGC chooses a rand number $K_r \in Z_q^*$ and computes $K_{rP} = K_r P$ and $K_{KGC} = H_1(K_P^G, K_P^M, K_P^L, K_r)$. Then, KGC can further obtain that $K_{KGC}^G = K_{KGC} \oplus K_r K_P^G$, $K_{KGC}^M = K_{KGC} \oplus K_r K_P^M$ and $K_{KGC}^L = K_{KGC} \oplus K_r K_P^L$, and send the message (K_{rP}, K_{KGC}^G), (K_{rP}, K_{KGC}^M) and (K_{rP}, K_{KGC}^L) to the corresponding cluster heads ID_0^G, ID_0^M and ID_0^L, respectively.
- After the message from KGC is arrived, each cluster head authenticates KGC's identity and computes K_{KGC}, respectively. That is, $K_{KGC} = K_{KGC}^G \oplus K_{rP} K^G, K_{KGC} = K_{KGC}^M \oplus K_{rP} K^M, K_{KGC} = K_{KGC}^L \oplus K_{rP} K^L$.

Phase 3: Key Distribution Phase. GEO (MEO, LEO) cluster performs the following steps independently and obtains the final group session key K successfully. Let's take GEO cluster as an example.

- For each $ID_i^G(1 \leq i \leq n)$, ID_0^G computers the corresponding $K_i^G = R_i K_{KGC}$, and broadcasts the message $(K_1^G, K_2^G, ..., K_n^G)$ to ID_i^G.

- After the message is received, each ID_i^G carries out the identity authentication. If the cluster head is legal, each ID_i^G computes the final group session key $K = K_i^G r_i^{-1}$ successfully. Similarly, each satellite node $ID_i^M(ID_i^L)$ in MEO cluster (LEO cluster) also can obtain the final group session key K.

3.3 Dynamic Member Joining/Leaving

The proposed scheme can work well when the satellite node joins or leavings the group, which is depicted detailedly in the following two scenarios.

Scenario 1: Satellite Node's Joining Scenario. Suppose that the new satellite node, denoted with ID_{n+1}^G, will join the GEO cluster, and its long-term public key and long-term private keys pair is (u_{n+1}^G, v_{n+1}^G) where $u_{n+1}^G = H_2(ID_{n+1}^G)$ and $v_{n+1}^G = su_{n+1}^G$.

(1) ID_{n+1}^G chooses a random number $r_{n+1} \in Z_q^*$, computes $R_{n+1} = r_{n+1}P$ and $S_{n+1} = v_{n+1}^G R_{n+1}$ and saves the set of $(r_{n+1}^{-1}, {v_{n+1}^G}^{-1}, R_{n+1}, S_{n+1})$ in the local memory. Then, ID_{n+1}^G broadcasts a request message $(ID_{n+1}^G, R_{n+1}, S_{n+1})$ to join the GEO cluster.

(2) After the request message is received, ID_0^G verifies ID_{n+1}^G's identity. If it succeeds, ID_0^G further computes that $T_{n+1} = r_0 v_0^G S_{n+1}, W' = H_1(ID_0^G, T_1, T_2, ..., T_n, T_{n+1}, t_0)$, $S_0' = v_0^G W'$. Therefore, the intra-cluster temporary key updates to $K^{G'} = \hat{e}(r_0 v_0^G P, \sum_{i=1}^{n+1} T_i) = \hat{e}(P,P)^{(r_0 v_0^G)^2 (r_1 v_1^G + ... + r_n v_n^G + r_{n+1} v_{n+1}^G)}$, and thus ID_0^G gets a new $h_0 = H_2(ID_0^G, K^{G'}, t_0)$. Then, ID_0^G broadcasts the message $(ID_0^G, S_0', T_1, T_2, ..., T_n, T_{n+1}, t_0, h_0)$ to ordinary satellite node $ID_i^G(1 \leq i \leq n+1)$.

(3) The original satellite node $ID_i^G(1 \leq i \leq n)$ can obtain the new intra-cluster temporary key by either of the following two ways.

  - According to the received broadcast message, $ID_i^G(1 \leq i \leq n)$ calculates $K^{G'} = \hat{e}(T_i r_i^{-1} {v_i^G}^{-1}, \sum_{i=1}^{n+1} T_i) = \hat{e}(P,P)^{(r_0 v_0^G)^2 (r_1 v_1^G + ... + r_n v_n^G + r_{n+1} v_{n+1}^G)}$.
  - ID_0^G encrypts $K^{G'}$ with the original intra-cluster temporary key K^G and multicasts the secret message to $ID_i^G(1 \leq i \leq n)$. Then, $ID_i^G(1 \leq i \leq n)$ can decrypt the secret message to obtain $K^{G'}$.

Specially, the new satellite node ID_{n+1}^G can obtain the new intra-cluster temporary key $K^{G'}$ as follows. According to the received broadcast message $(ID_0^G, S_0', T_1, T_2, ..., T_n, T_{n+1}, t_0, h_0)$, ID_{n+1}^G computes $W' = H_1(ID_0^G, T_1, T_2, ..., T_n, T_{n+1}, t_0)$ and verifies its legitimacy according to the equation that $\hat{e}(S_0', P) = \hat{e}(u_0^G W', P_s)$. If it is legal, ID_{n+1}^G can obtain $K^{G'}$, and further

compute $h_0^{'}$, that is,
$K^{G'} = \hat{e}(T_{n+1}r_{n+1}^{-1}v_{n+1}^{G}{}^{-1}, \sum_{i=1}^{n+1} T_i) = \hat{e}(P,P)^{(r_0 v_0^G)^2 (r_1 v_1^G + ... + r_n v_n^G + r_{n+1} v_{n+1}^G)}$,
$h_0^{'} = H_2(ID_0^G, K^{G'}, t_0)$. Therefore, the new intra-cluster temporary key is established if $h_0^{'} = h_0$ holds. Otherwise, the communication should be aborted.

(4) The new $K_{KGC}^{'}$ used for generating the new group session key can be obtained through inter-cluster phase mentioned in subsection 3.2. Finally, the new group session key is established among all the satellite nodes in GEO cluster through key distribution phase as introduced in subsection 3.2, that is, $K^{'} = K_i^{G'} r_i^{-1} (1 \le i \le n+1)$. Similarly, all the satellite nodes in MEO cluster (LEO cluster) also can compute the new group session key $K^{'}$.

Scenario 2: Satellite Node's Leaving Scenario. Two cases should be discussed when satellite node leaves the group, that is, the ordinary node's leaving and the cluster head's leaving.

- Ordinary node's leaving. The ordinary node ID_j^G sends a request for leaving the group to ID_0^G. When the message is received, ID_0^G reselects a random number $r_0^{'} \in Z_q^*$ with $r_0^{'} \neq r_0$, and computes that $T_i^{'} = r_0^{'} v_0^G S_{n+1} (1 \le i \le n, i \neq j)$, $W^{'} = H_1(ID_0^G, T_1^{'}, T_2^{'}, ..., T_{j-1}^{'}, T_{j+1}^{'}, ..., T_n^{'})$, $S_0^{'} = v_0^G W^{'}$. Therefore, ID_0^G can compute the new intra-cluster temporary key $K^{G'} = \hat{e}(r_0^{'} v_0^G P, \sum_{i=1, i\neq j}^{n+1} T_i^{'})$. Then, ID_0^G broadcasts the message $(ID_0^G, S_0^{'}, T_1^{'}, T_2^{'}, ..., T_{j-1}^{'}, T_{j+1}^{'}, ..., T_n^{'})$ to other nodes in the same cluster. After the message is received, each node verifies its legitimacy according to the equation that $\hat{e}(S_0^{'}, P) = \hat{e}(u_0^G W^{'}, P_s)$, where $W^{'} = H_1(ID_0^G, T_1^{'}, T_2^{'}, ..., T_{j-1}^{'}, T_{j+1}^{'}, ..., T_n^{'})$. If the verification succeeds, then the new intra-cluster temporary key $K^{G'}$ is

$$K^{G'} = \hat{e}(T_i^{'} r_i^{-1} v_i^{G-1}, \sum_{i=1, i\neq j}^{n} T_i^{'})$$
$$= \hat{e}(P,P)^{(r_0 v_0^G)^2 (r_1 v_1^G + r_2 v_2^G + ... + r_{j-1} v_{j-1}^G + r_{j+1} v_{j+1}^G + ... + r_n v_n^G)}$$

- Cluster head's leaving. After cluster head sends the request for leaving the group, other satellite nodes $ID_i^G (1 \le i \le n)$ reselect a powerful satellite node as the new cluster head denoted with $ID_0^{G'}$. Then, each satellite node reselects a random number $r_i^{'} \in Z_q^*$ and performs the intra-cluster phase mentioned in section 3.2 in order to update the intra-cluster temporary key to the new $K^{G'}$.

Finally, according to the new intra-cluster temporary key $K^{G'}$ obtained from case 1 or case 2, the new $K_{KGC}^{'}$ can be generated after the inter-cluster phase is performed as introduced in subsection 3.2. Then, after the key distribution phase, the new group session key is established, that is, $K^{'} = K_i^{G^{'}} r_i^{-1}$.

Similarly, the new group session key $K^{'}$ also can be established among all the satellite nodes in MEO cluster (LEO cluster).

4 Protocol Analysis

In 2000, Joux proposed a tripartite key agreement protocol based on parings over the elliptic curves [25]. However, it cannot resist the man-in-the-middle attack because of lacking of the authentication between the communicating parties. Barua et al. attempted to extend Joux's tripartite scheme to an ID-AGKA scheme [24], but their scheme requires $\lfloor \log_3^n \rfloor$ rounds which lowers the efficiency seriously. Subsequently, Choi et al. [19] and Du et al. [20] proposed two ID-AGKA protocols from bilinear and BD schemes [1]. Unfortunately, Zhang and Chen [26] demonstrated an impersonation attack on these two schemes and suggested adding a time parameter to prevent from replaying transcripts of the past session. Then, SHIM [27] showed that the protocol is still vulnerable to the participation attack. In 2006 and 2008, Lin et al. [21] and Tang et al. [22] put forward two GKA protocols with authentication respectively, but their protocols have shortcomings in number of rounds, pairing-computation and communication bandwidth. Although Li et al. [23] proposed an ID-AGKA protocol providing authentication with less rounds and pairing-computations, the larger required bandwidth brings out the bigger larger propagation delay which is a relatively important indicator in SIN.

In this section, we show that our ID-AGKA protocol is strong secure and has the powerful applicability and communication efficiency owing to considering the characteristic of SIN.

4.1 Correctness Analysis

Correctness Analysis of Intra-cluster Temporary Key. Within intra-cluster phase, the cluster head ID_0^G generates the intra-cluster temporary key K^G by virtue of the received message from the ordinary node ID_i^G, that is, $K^G = \hat{e}(r_0 v_0^G P, \sum_{i=1}^{n} T_i)$. Meanwhile, the ordinary node ID_i^G computes the intra-cluster temporary key K^G according to the broadcast message sent by the cluster head ID_0^G, that is, $K^G = \hat{e}(T_i r_i^{-1} v_i^{G^{-1}}, \sum_{i=1}^{n} T_i)$. The following equation can be established by the properties of the bilinear pairing, that is
$K^G = \hat{e}(T_i r_i^{-1} v_i^{G^{-1}}, \sum_{i=1}^{n} T_i) = \hat{e}(r_0 v_0^G P, \sum_{i=1}^{n} T_i) = \hat{e}(P,P)^{(r_0 v_0^G)^2 (r_1 v_1^G + \ldots + r_n v_n^G)}$.
Therefore, the correctness of the intra-cluster temporary key is guaranteed.

Correctness Analysis of Group Session Key. Within key distribution phase, each cluster head $ID_0^G(ID_0^M, ID_0^L)$ can compute the corresponding K_{KGC}, respectively, owing to the equation that $K_r K_P^G = K_r K_G P = K_{rP} K_G$. That is,

$K_{KGC} = K_{KGC}^G \oplus K_{rP}K^G$, $K_{KGC} = K_{KGC}^M \oplus K_{rP}K^M$, $K_{KGC} = K_{KGC}^L \oplus K_{rP}K^L$. Therefore, all the satellite nodes can compute the group session key K and its correctness is guaranteed by the following equation:
$K = K_i^G r_i^{-1} = R_i K_{KGC} r_i^{-1} = K_{KGC}P \quad (0 \leq i \leq n)$.
Similarly, for the situations that the satellite node joins or leaves the group, the same conclusion also can be deduced.

4.2 Security Analysis

In this section we show that our ID-AGKA protocol is strong secure and the security of the proposed protocol is proved under the DLP, CDHP and one-way hash functions with collision-resistance assumptions.

Two-Way Authentication. Cluster head and intra-cluster satellite nodes can authenticate each other.

Lemma 1. *Cluster head can authenticate intra-cluster satellite nodes.*

Proof. During intra-cluster phase, the cluster head can authenticate the intra-cluster satellite nodes by judging whether the equation that $\hat{e}(S_i, P) = \hat{e}(u_i R_i, P_s)$ holds or not. Assume that an adversary, namely Mallory, acting as an ordinary satellite node, wants to be authenticated successfully without being detected in the phase. Mallory would have to first derive r_i and v_i^G and further forge a reasonable R_i and S_i from the eavesdropping message (ID_i^G, R_i, S_i). Hence, it is equivalent to solving the discrete logarithm problem, which is computationally unfeasible. Therefore, without the knowledge of R_i and S_i, the adversary cannot pass the authentication.

Lemma 2. *Intra-cluster satellite nodes can authenticate cluster head.*

Proof. During intra-cluster phase, intra-cluster satellite node can authenticate the cluster head by computing the equation that $\hat{e}(S_0, P) = \hat{e}(u_0^G W, P_s)$. The adversary Mallory, as a forge cluster head, would have to first compute the correct v_0^G and further obtain S_0 to pass the authentication. However, it is very hard to compute the cluster head's private key v_0^G under the discrete logarithm problem assumption.
Therefore, the proposed schemes can provide the two-way authentication between the cluster head and intra-cluster satellite nodes.

Semantic Security. We prove that the proposed protocol is designed with semantic security as follows.

Theorem 1. *Under the DLP and CDHP assumptions, the proposed schemes can satisfy the semantic security of GKA.*

Proof. The semantic security of GKA requires that the key value and the random value in key space are indistinguishable to outside adversary even though the adversary can eavesdrop on all of the communicated messages throughout the protocol.

For intra-cluster phase, outside adversary can eavesdrop on the transmitted messages (ID_i^G, R_i, S_i) and $(ID_0^G, S_0, T_1, T_2, ..., T_n, t_0, h_0)$. As mentioned above, the intra-cluster temporary key K^G is that $K^G = \hat{e}(T_i r_i^{-1} v_i^{G^{-1}}, \sum_{i=1}^{n} T_i) = \hat{e}(r_0 v_0^G P, \sum_{i=1}^{n} T_i)$.

Obviously, K^G is decided by the random numbers r_0, r_i and the generated long-term private keys v_0^G and v_i^G. However, it is a fact that solving v_0^G and v_i^G is equivalent to solving the DLP and CDHP assumptions, which has been proved in Lemma 1 and Lemma 2. Consequently, K^G can keep the same randomness with r_0 and r_i that are never public and unable to be calculated to outside adversary. Therefore, outside adversary cannot distinguish K^G from r_0 and r_i randomly distributed in the intra-cluster temporary key space.

For inter-cluster phase, the transmitted messages obtained by outside adversary are (K_P^G, K_P^M, K_P^L) and $(K_{rP}, K_{KGC}^G, K_{KGC}^M, K_{KGC}^L)$. For the KGC side, the equation that $K_{KGC} = H_1(K_P^G, K_P^M, K_P^L, K_r)$ is established. The generated variable K_{KGC} is closely related with the intra-cluster temporary key K^G and the random number K_r. Additionally, the chose random number K_r is never public and the hash function is defined with collision-resistance assumption. Hence, the outside adversary cannot distinguish the variable K_{KGC} from the random value K_r distributed in the corresponding key space. For each cluster head side, the equations that $K_{KGC} = K_{KGC}^G \oplus K_{rP} K^G$, $K_{KGC} = K_{KGC}^M \oplus K_{rP} K^M$ and $K_{KGC} = K_{KGC}^L \oplus K_{rP} K^L$ are established. Since that the outside adversary cannot distinguish the intra-cluster temporary key K^G from the chose random number, which has been proved, and the random number K_r is never public, the variable K_{KGC} and the random number K_r in the corresponding key space are undistinguishable to outside adversary.

For key distribution phase, the messages intercepted by outside adversary are $(K_1^G, K_2^G, ..., K_n^G)$ and $R_i = r_i P$. The adversary would have to induce r_i to obtain group session key K owing to the equation that $K = K_i^G r_i^{-1}$. Therefore, it is also impossible to distinguish r_i from K, which is equivalent to solving the DLP assumption.

Forward and Backward Secrecy. In the following, we demonstrate that the proposed protocol provides forward and backward secrecy for dynamic member joining or leaving.

Theorem 2. *Under the hash function with collision-resistance assumption, the new member cannot compute the previous group key when he or she joins the group, and the leaving member also cannot compute the future group key when he or she leaves the group.*

Proof. Forward secrecy is that when a new member joins the group, he cannot compute the previous group keys and decrypt past-encrypted messages. Without loss of generality, suppose that a new satellite node ID_{n+1}^G joins the group. He might have intercepted the transmitted message $(ID_0^G, S_0, T_1, T_2, ..., T_n, t_0, h_0)$ before joining the group. Therefore, he can elicit the hash value which contains the useful information of the intra-cluster temporary key K^G. However, the hash function involved in the proposed scheme is one-way with collision-resistance, so it is too hard to compute K^G from the hash value. Furthermore, since the final group session key $K = K_i^G r_i^{-1}$ is based on the intra-cluster temporary key K^G, that is, $K^G = \hat{e}(T_i r_i^{-1} v_i^{G-1}, \sum_{i=1}^{n} T_i) = \hat{e}(P, P)^{(r_0 v_0^G)^2 (r_1 v_1^G + r_2 v_2^G + ... + r_n v_n^G)}$. Obviously, K^G consists of the contribution information of each intra-cluster node's long-term private key. For the new member ID_{n+1}^G, he would have to calculate the random numbers r_i and the long-term private key v_i^G to obtain the previous group key, which is unfeasible according to Theorem 1. Likewise, the new member ID_{n+1}^G is unable to induce K^G by means of the following equation $K^{G'} = \hat{e}(T_i r_i^{-1} v_i^{G-1}, \sum_{i=1}^{n+1} T_i) = \hat{e}(P, P)^{(r_0 v_0^G)^2 (r_1 v_1^G + r_2 v_2^G + ... + r_n v_n^G + r_{n+1} v_{n+1}^G)}$.

Therefore, the proposed protocol can provide the forward secrecy.

Backward secrecy is that when a group member leaves the group, he cannot compute future group keys and decrypt future encrypted messages. Assume that an old node ID_j^G leaves the group. Similar to the proof of dynamic member joining case, he also cannot calculate the future group session key K' after his leaving. Therefore, the proposed protocol can provide the backward secrecy.

4.3 Performance Analysis and Comparisons

In this section, we compare the performance and efficiency of the proposed protocol and existing competitive protocols. Here we assume that there are n satellite nodes including one powerful cluster head node and $n-1$ ordinary satellite nodes would like to establish a group session key only within the intra-cluster phase. Suppose that all the existing schemes compared with each other are carried out in the SIN scenario with the character of dynamic topology, high speed and large time-delay. The computation complexity, communication cost and other important performances are compared with six other competitive protocols, which is summarized in Table 1. For convenience, the following notations are used to analyze the performance.

- *Round*(R): The total number of rounds.
- *Bandwidth*(B): The total number of messages sent by each node.
- *Authentication*(A): Whether the protocol provides the authentication or not (Y/N).
- *Dynamic*(D): Whether the protocol satisfies dynamic member joining or leaving(Y/N).
- *Pairings*(P): The total number of pairing computations.
- *ScalMulti*(SM): The total number of scalar multiplications (i.e., computing kP, where $P \in G_1$).

Specially,the total amount of the computations does not include the computation complexity of the hash functions and the preliminary operations $(r_i^{-1}, v_i^{G^{-1}},$

Table 1. Comparisons between the previously protocols and our proposed protocol

Protocol	R	B	A	D	P	SM
Choi's[19]	2	$2n$	N	N	$2n$	n^2
Du's[20]	2	$3(n-1)$	Y	N	$4n$	$n(n+5)$
Lin's[21]	2	$2n$	Y	N	$2n$	n
Tang's[22]	2	$2n$	Y	N	$3n$	$2n(n-1)$
Li's[23]	1	$n(n-1)$	Y	N	n	n^2
Barua's[24]	$\lfloor \log_3^n \rfloor$	$< 5n(n-1)$	N	N	$\leq 5n \lfloor \log_3^n \rfloor + 3$	$\leq 9(n-1)$
Ours	2	n	Y	Y	$3(n-1)$	$3(n-1)$

R_i, S_i) by the satellite nodes, as the former complexity is relatively lower and the latter operations are offline.

From Table 1, we can observe that the proposed protocol not only has the lowest computation complexity and communication cost compared with Choi's protocol [19], Du's protocol [20] , Tang's protocol [22] and Barua's protocol [24], but also provides the two-way authentication and dynamic member joining or leaving situations. In addition, although the computation cost such as pairing computations and scalar multiplications of Lin's protocol [21] is slightly better, the communication cost is two times higher than the our proposed protocol. Considering that the big propagation delay (even up to a few milliseconds) is an intrinsic characteristic, the higher communication cost gives rise to the further larger propagation delay, a much more important indicator in SIN, which completely covers the computational advantage of Lin's protocol [21]. Moreover, Lin's protocol [21] is not suitable for dynamic member joining or leaving scenario. Li's protocol [23] can execute only one round communication to implement mutual authentication and has the lower computation cost in pairing computations, but the computation complexity and communication cost are increased quickly with n^2 (n usually is a very large number in SIN), which will decrease the communication efficiency seriously. Additionally, the preliminary operations $(r_i^{-1}, v_i^{G^{-1}}, R_i, S_i)$ of the satellite nodes saved in local memory are offline, which further reduces the scalar multiplications. Therefore, compared with the previous competitive protocols the proposed protocol is optimal in overall performance and has the most powerful applicability for the practical applications in space information network.

5 Conclusions

We have presented a new cluster-based ID-AGKA scheme according to the longitudinal hierarchical network model of the space information network. The proposed protocol not only reduces the cost of establishment and management in public-key infrastructure, but also satisfies the dynamic satellite nodes joining or leaving situation. Security analysis shows that the proposed protocol has two-way authentication, forward and backward secrecy and semantic security, and is also secure against common attack strategies. Compared with the previous ID-AGKA protocols, the proposed protocol has lower computation complexity and communication cost, and thus its overall performance is optimal in the space information network.

Acknowledgements. The authors would like to thank the anonymous reviewers for their helpful and valuable comments. This work is supported Supported by the Projects of National Natural Science Foundation of China under Grants (61272501), National Key Basic Research Program (NKBRP) (973 program) (2012CB315905) and Beijing Natural Science Foundation(4132056).

References

1. Burmester, M., Desmedt, Y.: A secure and efficient conference key distribution system. In: De Santis, A. (ed.) EUROCRYPT 1994. LNCS, vol. 950, pp. 275–286. Springer, Heidelberg (1995)
2. Kim, Y., Perrig, A., Tsudik, G.: Group key agreement efficient in communication. IEEE Transactions on Computers 53(7), 905–921 (2004)
3. Steiner, M., Tsudik, G., Waidner, M.: Key agreement in dynamic peer groups. IEEE Transactions on Parallel and Distributed Systems 11(8), 769–780 (2000)
4. Tsai, J.L.: A novel authenticated group key agreement protocol for mobile environment. Ann. Telecommun. 66(11), 663–669 (2011)
5. You, Z.Y., Xie, X.Y.: A novel group key agreement protocol for wireless mesh network. Computers and Electrical Engineering 37(2), 218–239 (2011)
6. Park, C., Hur, J., Hwang, S., Yoon, H.: Authenticated public key broadcast encryption scheme secure against insiders' attack. Mathematical and Computer Modelling 55(2), 113–122 (2012)
7. Xiong, H., Chen, Z., Qin, Z.G.: Efficient three-party authenticated key agreement protocol in certificateless cryptography. International Journal of Computer Mathematics 88(13), 2707–2716 (2011)
8. Hlbl, M., Welzer, T., Brumen, B.: An improved two-party identity-based authenticated key agreement protocol using pairings. Journal of Computer and System Sciences 78(1), 142–150 (2012)
9. Cheng, Q.F., Ma, C.G., Wei, F.S.: Analysis and improvement of a new authenticated group key agreement in a mobile environment. Ann. Telecommun. 66, 331–337 (2011)
10. Tan, Z.W.: Efficient identity-based authenticated multiple key exchange protocol. Computers and Electrical Engineering 37, 191–198 (2011)
11. Chuang, Y.H., Tseng, Y.M.: An efficient dynamic group key agreement protocol for imbalanced wireless networks. Int. J. Network Mgmt. 20(4), 167–180 (2010)
12. Zhao, X.W., Zhang, F.G., Tian, H.B.: Dynamic asymmetric group key agreement for ad hoc networks. Ad Hoc Networks 9(5), 928–939 (2011)
13. Sood, S.K., Sarje, A.K., Singh, K.: A secure dynamic identity based authentication protocol for multi-server architecture. Journal of Network and Computer Applications 34(2), 609–618 (2011)

14. Guo, H., Li, Z.J., Mu, Y., Zhang, F.: An efficient dynamic authenticated key exchange protocol with selectable identities. Computers and Mathematics with Applications 61(9), 2518–2527 (2011)
15. Wang, K., Zhao, Z.W., Yao, L.: An agile reconfigurable key distribution scheme in space information network. In: Proceedings of Second IEEE Conference on Industrial Electronics and Applications, Harbin, China, pp. 2742–2747 (2007)
16. Zhong, Y.T., Ma, J.F.: Efficient secure group key exchange protocol in space information networks. Journal of Jilin University (Engineering and Technology Edition) 42(1), 203–206 (2012)
17. Guo, Y.B., Wang, C., Wang, L.M.: Universally composable authentication and key exchange protocol for access control in spatial information networks. Acta Electronica Sinica 38(10), 2358–2364 (2010)
18. Cao, S., Zhang, C.R., Song, C.Y.: Identity-base dynamic authenticated group key agreement protocol for mobile networks. Journal of Air Force Engineering University (Natural Science Edition) 12(5), 67–71 (2011)
19. Choi, K.Y., Hwang, J.Y., Lee, D.-H.: Efficient ID-based group key agreement with bilinear maps. In: Bao, F., Deng, R., Zhou, J. (eds.) PKC 2004. LNCS, vol. 2947, pp. 130–144. Springer, Heidelberg (2004)
20. Du, X., Wang, Y., Ge, J., Wang, Y.: ID-based authenticated two Round multi-party key agreement. Cryptology ePrint Archive: Report 2003/247
21. Lin, C.H., Lin, H.H., Chang, J.H.: Multiparty key agreement for secure teleconferencing. In: IEEE International Conference on Systems, Man and Cybernetics, ICSMC 2006, pp. 3702–3707 (2006)
22. Tang, H., Zhu, L., Zhang, Z.: Efficient ID-based two round authenticated group key agreement protocol. In: WiCOM 2008: 4th International Conference on Wireless Communication, Networking and Mobile Computering, pp. 1–4. IEEE press, New York (2008)
23. Li, L.C., Tsai, Y.P., Liu, R.S.: A Novel ID-based authenticated group key agreement protocol using bilinear pairings. In: WOCN 2008: 5th IEEE and IFIP International Conference on Wireless and Optical Communications Networks (2008)
24. Barua, R., Dutta, R., Sarkar, P.: Extending joux's protocol to multi party key agreement. In: Johansson, T., Maitra, S. (eds.) INDOCRYPT 2003. LNCS, vol. 2904, pp. 205–217. Springer, Heidelberg (2003)
25. Joux, A.: A one round protocol for tripartite Diffie-Hellman. In: Bosma, W. (ed.) ANTS 2000. LNCS, vol. 1838, pp. 385–394. Springer, Heidelberg (2000)
26. Zhang, F.G., Chen, X.F.: Attack on two ID-based authenticated group key agreement schemes. Cryptology ePrint Archive: Report 2003/259 (2003)
27. Shim, K.A.: Further analysis of ID-based authenticated group key agreement protocl from bilinear maps. IEICE Trans. on Fundamentals of Electronics, Communications and Computer Sciences 90(1), 288–295 (2007)
28. Barreto, P.S.L.M., Kim, H.Y., Lynn, B., Scott, M.: Efficient algorithms for pairing-based cryptosystems. In: Yung, M. (ed.) CRYPTO 2002. LNCS, vol. 2442, pp. 354–368. Springer, Heidelberg (2002)
29. Boneh, D., Franklin, M.: Identity-based encryption from the Weil Pairing. In: Kilian, J. (ed.) CRYPTO 2001. LNCS, vol. 2139, pp. 213–229. Springer, Heidelberg (2001)

Authentication and Key Agreement Based on Hyper-sphere Using Smart Cards

Shaohua Tang and Lingling Xu

School of Computer Science & Engineering,
South China University of Technology, Guangzhou, China
shtang@IEEE.org, csshtang@scut.edu.cn

Abstract. A new geometry-based authentication and key agreement scheme, without invoking traditional strong symmetric and/or asymmetric encryption functions, is constructed by taking advantage of the geometric property that $(n+1)$ generic points in an n-dimensional space can determine a unique hyper-sphere under certain conditions. The security and performance of the scheme are analyzed. Experiments are also conducted to show that the scheme is efficient and is easy to implement.

Keywords: Authentication, Key Agreement, Hyper-Sphere, Geometric Approach, Smart Cards.

1 Introduction

Authentication and key agreement plays an important role in information security. Authentication ensures that the communicating entity is the one that it claims to be. Key agreement can let two communication parties negotiate a common session key.

Password authentication is one of the widely adopted authentication approaches. But usually the server side needs to keep some secret information related to users' passwords, which brings a lot of potential security vulnerabilities [7,10,11]. In order to solve these problems, smart card-based password authentication schemes [14,17] were proposed.

A smartcard-oriented remote login authentication approach based upon geometric properties was proposed by Wu [15]. Different from previous authentication methods, the principle of Wu's scheme [15] is based upon some geometric properties, which adopts the axiom that two points can uniquely determine a straight line. If a user and an authentication server can reconstruct the same straight line, then user authentication is successful. But Hwang [5] found that an illegitimate user can easily launch an attack via eavesdropping the login message in Wu's scheme. Chien-Jan-Tseng's scheme [3] was proposed to amend faults of Wu's scheme. Another more complex authentication system to enhance the security of remote login system based on geometric approach was proposed by Wang [13], which adopts the geometric properties of hyper-sphere in n-dimensional space, and its theoretical foundation is that $(n+1)$ points can uniquely determine a hyper-sphere in n-dimensional space under certain conditions. However,

J. Lopez, X. Huang, and R. Sandhu (Eds.): NSS 2013, LNCS 7873, pp. 549–562, 2013.

there are still some effective attacks [4] against Wang's scheme, for example, replay and off-line password guessing attacks. Besides, some other attacks [16], such as dictionary attacks, and user/central authority impersonation attacks, and user/central authority impersonation attacks, can also be launched against Wang's scheme.

Recently, some smartcard-based authenticated key agreement methods using chaotic maps [2] were proposed, and some using elliptic curve cryptography [6,12,8]. Some smartcard-based schemes are for some specific application areas, for example, wireless communications [1], VOIP SIP [18], and multi-server environments [9].

Our Contributions. An authentication system based on geometric properties of hyper-sphere is proposed in this paper, which can not only let the server efficiently authenticate the users using geometrical approach, but also let two communication parties agree on a common session key.

Organization. The remainder of this paper is organized as follows. Section 2 describes the preliminaries required in this paper. Our newly designed authentication and key agreement scheme based on geometric properties is described in Section 3. Section 4 discusses the security by analyzing some possible attacks. The experiment is presented in Section 5. Finally, Section 6 concludes the paper.

2 Preliminaries

2.1 Notation

Some notations that are used by this paper are given as follows.

p is a large prime number;

$GF(p)$ is a Galois field determined by p;

$f(x, y)$ is a cryptographic hash function taking x and y as input parameters.

2.2 Hyper-sphere

Hyper-sphere in Euclidean Space. A hyper-sphere is a generalization of the surface of an ordinary sphere to arbitrary dimension. In particular, a hyper-sphere in a 2-dimensional space is called circle. The formula for a hyper-sphere in n-dimensional Euclidean space can be expressed as:

$$(x_1 - c_1)^2 + (x_2 - c_2)^2 + \cdots + (x_n - c_n)^2 = r^2, \tag{1}$$

where $(c_1, c_2, \ldots, c_n)$ is the center of the hyper-sphere, r is the radius, and $(x_1, x_2, \ldots, x_n)$ is an arbitrary point on the hyper-sphere.

Hyper-sphere over Finite Fields. The concept of hyper-sphere and (1) can be extended to finite fields. For simplicity, the Galois field $GF(p)$ is adopted as the ground field in our scheme, where p is a large prime number. Then the equation for the hyper-sphere over $GF(p)$ can be expressed as:

$$(x_1 - c_1)^2 + (x_2 - c_2)^2 + \cdots + (x_n - c_n)^2 \equiv r^2 \pmod{p}, \tag{2}$$

where $x_i \in GF(p)$ and $c_i \in GF(p)$, for $i = 1, 2, \ldots, n$.

Notice that only r^2 is needed in our scheme, and r is never required throughout this paper. We remind that square-root may not always be a valid operation over $GF(p)$.

Determining a Hyper-sphere by Given Points. As we know, three different points in a 2-dimensional space that are not in the same straight line can determine a circle uniquely. The situation is similar in n-dimensional space. By taking $(n+1)$ points as input parameters, we can determine the center and r^2 of a hyper-sphere via Algorithm 1 shown in Fig. 1 if certain conditions are met.

As long as the center of the hyper-sphere and r^2 are fixed, then the formula for the hyper-sphere can be determined uniquely.

Finding Different Points on a Hyper-sphere. By given the center of a hyper-sphere and r^2, we can find n different points on the hyper-sphere [13]. We present the basic idea of [13] in the form of pseudo-code in Algorithm 2 shown in Fig. 2.

Verifying Whether a Given Point is on a Given Line. Our proposed authentication and key agreement scheme adopts not only the principles of hyper-spheres, but also properties of straight lines. It is a basic mathematical theorem to verify whether or not a given point is on a given line, and we formalize it in pseudo-code described in Algorithm 3 shown in Fig. 3.

3 The Proposed Scheme

3.1 Overview

Suppose that there are a lot of users and an authentication server ("AS" for short hereafter) in the system. The AS and a user should share a secret hyper-sphere firstly. If the user can prove to the AS that it can reconstruct the shared secret hyper-sphere, then the identity of the user is authenticated to be valid. In order to prevent eavesdropping attacks, however, the user will not directly present the parameters of the secret hyper-sphere, but to present the transformed parameters related to the secret hyper-sphere, instead. The basic idea is that after user U_i owning the center $\boldsymbol{C}$ of the hyper-sphere, U_i can determine another point $\boldsymbol{W}$ related to $\boldsymbol{C}$ and the current time stamp t. Then U_i can have a line L across points $\boldsymbol{C}$ and $\boldsymbol{W}$. After that, U_i randomly selects a point $\boldsymbol{G}$ on L, and the login message is related to $\boldsymbol{G}$. Obviously, point $\boldsymbol{G}$ is varied from each login session since the time stamp t is changed each time.

The authentication scheme can be divided into five stages: the initial stage, the user registration stage, the user login stage, the verification stage, and the session key computation stage. The initial stage is for the AS to select some initial parameters used during the whole authentication process. At the stage of user registration, the AS assigns a unique identifier for each user. The user takes

Algorithm 1: To determine a hyper-sphere by given $(n+1)$ points

Input: $(a_{i1}, a_{i2}, \dots, a_{in})$, which are the coordinates of $(n+1)$ points $\boldsymbol{A}_i$, where $i = 0, 1, \dots, n$;

Output: $(\boldsymbol{C}, R)$, where $\boldsymbol{C} = (c_1, c_2, \dots, c_n)$ is the center of a hyper-sphere, and $R = r^2$ is the square of the radius, respectively;

Procedure:

1 **begin**

2 Apply the coordinates of $\boldsymbol{A}_i$, $i = 0, 1, \dots, n$, to Eqn (1) and obtain:

$$\begin{cases} (a_{01}-c_1)^2 + (a_{02}-c_2)^2 + \cdots + (a_{0n}-c_n)^2 \equiv r^2 \pmod p \\ (a_{11}-c_1)^2 + (a_{12}-c_2)^2 + \cdots + (a_{1n}-c_n)^2 \equiv r^2 \pmod p \\ \cdots\cdots \\ (a_{n1}-c_1)^2 + (a_{n2}-c_2)^2 + \cdots + (a_{nn}-c_n)^2 \equiv r^2 \pmod p \end{cases}$$

3 Subtract the above j-th equation from the $(j+1)$-th equation, $j = 1, 2, \dots, n$, and obtain:

$$\begin{cases} 2(a_{11}-a_{01})c_1 + \cdots + 2(a_{1n}-a_{0n})c_n \equiv \sum_{j=1}^{n}(a_{1j}^2 - a_{0j}^2) \pmod p \\ \cdots\cdots \\ 2(a_{n1}-a_{n-1,1})c_1 + \cdots + 2(a_{nn}-a_{n-1,n})c_n \equiv \sum_{j=1}^{n}(a_{nj}^2 - a_{n-1,j}^2) \pmod p \end{cases}$$

which is a system of linear equations with n unknowns $c_1, c_2, \dots, c_n$.

4 Let $\boldsymbol{B}$ be the coefficient matrix and $\boldsymbol{D}$ be the vector of constants of the above system of linear equations respectively,

$$\boldsymbol{B} = \begin{bmatrix} 2(a_{11}-a_{01}) & \dots & 2(a_{1n}-a_{0n}) \\ \dots & \dots & \dots \\ 2(a_{n1}-a_{n-1,1}) & \dots & 2(a_{nn}-a_{n-1,n}) \end{bmatrix},$$

$$\boldsymbol{D}^T = (\sum_{j=1}^{n}(a_{1j}^2 - a_{0j}^2), \dots, \sum_{j=1}^{n}(a_{nj}^2 - a_{n-1,j}^2)),$$

where $\boldsymbol{D}^T$ stands for the transpose of vector $\boldsymbol{D}$. Now, the system of linear equations in the above step can be re-written as

$$\boldsymbol{B} \times \boldsymbol{C}^T = \boldsymbol{D};$$

5 Let $\triangle = |\boldsymbol{B}| \pmod p$; /* Calculate the determinant of matrix $\boldsymbol{B}$. */

6 **if** $(\triangle \neq 0)$ **then**

7 $\boldsymbol{C}^T = \boldsymbol{B}^{-1} \times \boldsymbol{D}$; /* Solve the unknowns $c_1, c_2, \dots, c_n$. */

8 **end**

9 **else**

10 **return** $(NULL, NULL)$;

11 **end**

12 Apply the values of $c_1, c_2, \dots, c_n$ to the first equation in Step 2, and obtain:

$$R \triangleq r^2 = (a_{01}-c_1)^2 + (a_{02}-c_2)^2 + \cdots + (a_{0n}-c_n)^2 \pmod p;$$

13 **return** $(\boldsymbol{C}, R)$;

14 **end**

Fig. 1. Algorithm To Determine a Hyper-sphere by Given $(n+1)$ Points

advantage of its smart card to generate an authentication message at the user login stage and delivers the authentication message to the AS via an open channel. At the verification stage, the AS verifies the received message to determine whether the user's identity is valid or not. After that, both the AS and the user can compute a shared session key at the session key computation stage.

Algorithm 2: To find n different points on a hyper-sphere

Input: $(\boldsymbol{C}, R)$, where $\boldsymbol{C} = (c_1, c_2, \ldots, c_n)$ is the center of a hyper-sphere and R is the square of the radius;

Output: $\boldsymbol{B}_1, \boldsymbol{B}_2, \ldots, \boldsymbol{B}_n$, which are different points on the hyper-sphere;

Procedure:

begin
    for $(i = 1; i \leq n; i++)$ **do**
        repeat
            for $(j = 1; j \leq n-2; j++)$ **do**
                Find integers e_{ij} and d_{ij} that satisfy $e_{ij} \equiv d_{ij}^2 \pmod p$;
                Let $x_{ij} = (d_{ij} + c_j) \pmod p$;
            end
            Find integers $e_{i,n-1}$, $d_{i,n-1}$, e_{in}, and d_{in} that satisfy

$$e_{i,n-1} \equiv d_{i,n-1}^2 \pmod p,$$

$$e_{i,n} \equiv d_{i,n}^2 \pmod p,$$

            and

$$e_{i,n-1} + e_{in} \equiv (R - \sum_{j=1}^{n-2} e_{ij}) \pmod p;$$

            Let $x_{i,n-1} = (d_{i,n-1} + c_{i,n-1}) \pmod p$,
              and $x_{in} = (d_{in} + c_{in}) \pmod p$;
            Let $\boldsymbol{B}_i = (x_{i1}, x_{i2}, \ldots, x_{in})$;
        until $\boldsymbol{B}_i \notin \{\boldsymbol{B}_1, \ldots, \boldsymbol{B}_{i-1}\}$;
    end
    return $\boldsymbol{B}_1, \boldsymbol{B}_2, \ldots, \boldsymbol{B}_n$;
end

Fig. 2. Algorithm To Find n Different Points on a Hyper-sphere

Algorithm 3: To verify whether a given point $\boldsymbol{G}$ is on a given line crossing given points $\boldsymbol{C}$ and $\boldsymbol{W}$

Input: $\boldsymbol{G} = (g_1, g_2, \ldots, g_n)$, $\boldsymbol{C} = (c_1, c_2, \ldots, c_n)$ and $\boldsymbol{W} = (w_1, w_2, \ldots, w_n)$, which are three points in n-dimensional space over $GF(p)$;

Output: $true/false$; if the point $\boldsymbol{G}$ is on the line across $\boldsymbol{C}$ and $\boldsymbol{W}$, $ture$; otherwise, $false$;

Procedure:

begin
    for $(i = 1; i \leq n; i++)$ **do**
        if $((c_i - w_i) \equiv 0 \pmod p)$ **then**
            return $false$;
        end
        else
            Let $\lambda_i = (g_i - w_i) \times (c_i - w_i)^{-1} \pmod p$;
        end
        if $(\lambda_i \neq \lambda_1)$ **then**
            return $false$;
        end
    end
    return $true$;
end

Fig. 3. Algorithm To Verify Whether a Given Point $\boldsymbol{G}$ Is on a Given Line

3.2 The Initial Stage

The AS chooses some initial parameters for the whole authentication system at this stage.

The AS selects a large prime p with the form $p = 8m+3$, where m is an integer. All computations hereafter are over the Galois field $GF(p)$. The AS chooses a positive integer n, a cryptographic hash function $f(x, y)$. The parameters p and n, and the hash function $f(\cdot, \cdot)$ are known to the public. Note that it will be more convenient to resolve the quadratic congruence to let p take the form of $p = 8m + 3$.

The AS randomly selects n linearly independent n-dimensional secret vectors $\boldsymbol{S}_1 = (s_{11}, s_{12}, \ldots, s_{1n})^T, \ldots, \boldsymbol{S}_n = (s_{n1}, s_{n2}, \ldots, s_{nn})^T$, where $s_{ij} \in GF(p)$. The vectors $\boldsymbol{S}_1, \boldsymbol{S}_2, \ldots, \boldsymbol{S}_n$ should be kept secret by the AS. Notice that the vectors can be regarded as points in n-dimensional space.

3.3 The User Registration Stage

The AS assigns a unique identifier for each user at this stage. A smart card containing some information dedicated to a user is also issued by the AS.

The protocol executed between a user and the AS is described as follows.

Step 1. User U_i selects a password PW_i, and calculates a point

$$\boldsymbol{A}_0 \triangleq (a_{01}, a_{02}, \ldots, a_{0n}) = (f(PW_i, 1) \pmod p, \ldots, f(PW_i, n) \pmod p).$$

The point $\boldsymbol{A}_0$ is sent to the AS in a secure way.

Step 2. The AS assigns U_i a unique identifier ID_i representing the identity of U_i, then calculates points $\boldsymbol{A}_1, \ldots, \boldsymbol{A}_n$ by invoking the secret vectors $\boldsymbol{S}_1, \ldots, \boldsymbol{S}_n$:

$$\boldsymbol{A}_1 \triangleq (a_{11}, a_{12}, \ldots, a_{1n}) = (f(ID_i, s_{11}) \pmod p, \ldots, f(ID_i, s_{1n}) \pmod p),$$

$$\cdots\cdots$$

$$\boldsymbol{A}_n \triangleq (a_{n1}, a_{n2}, \ldots, a_{nn}) = (f(ID_i, s_{n1}) \pmod p, \ldots, f(ID_i, s_{nn}) \pmod p).$$

The AS calls Algorithm 1 by using $\boldsymbol{A}_0, \boldsymbol{A}_1, \ldots, \boldsymbol{A}_n$ as input parameters, and obtains returned values $(\boldsymbol{C}, R)$.

If $(\boldsymbol{C} == NULL)$ or $(R == NULL)$

then

the AS repeats **Step 2** to select a new ID_i and re-compute points $\boldsymbol{A}_1, \boldsymbol{A}_2, \ldots, \boldsymbol{A}_n$ until Algorithm 1 returns non-$NULL$ values;

else

$(\boldsymbol{C}, R)$ identifies a hyper-sphere determined by points $\boldsymbol{A}_0, \boldsymbol{A}_1, \ldots, \boldsymbol{A}_n$, we denote it by UC_i and the formula of which can be expressed as:

$$UC_i : \quad (x_1 - c_1)^2 + (x_2 - c_2)^2 + \cdots + (x_n - c_n)^2 \equiv R \pmod p.$$

Step 3. The AS, by calling Algorithm 2, randomly chooses n points $\boldsymbol{B}_1, \boldsymbol{B}_2, \ldots, \boldsymbol{B}_n$ on the hyper-sphere UC_i except points $\boldsymbol{A}_1, \boldsymbol{A}_2, \ldots, \boldsymbol{A}_n$, i.e., $\{\boldsymbol{B}_1, \boldsymbol{B}_2, \ldots, \boldsymbol{B}_n\} \cap \{\boldsymbol{A}_1, \boldsymbol{A}_2, \ldots, \boldsymbol{A}_n\} = \varnothing$.

Step 4. The AS writes p, ID_i, and $f(\cdot, \cdot)$ to the firmware of a smart card, and writes $\boldsymbol{B}_1, \boldsymbol{B}_2, \ldots, \boldsymbol{B}_n$ to the secure storage area of the smart card. The access to $\boldsymbol{B}_1, \boldsymbol{B}_2, \ldots, \boldsymbol{B}_n$ is protected by U_i's password PW_i. After that, the AS delivers the smart card to user U_i via a safe way.

Remark. User U_i's password PW_i is always kept by U_i itself, and is never required to be known by the AS. Therefore, the AS is not necessary to store U_i's password.

3.4 The User Login Stage

A user generates a login message by using its smart card, and presents the login message to the AS at this stage. The protocol among a user, its smart card, and the AS are described as follows:

Step 1. User U_i inserts its smart card into a card reader attached to a login terminal. Then parameters $p, ID_i, \boldsymbol{B}_1, \boldsymbol{B}_2, \ldots, \boldsymbol{B}_n$ are loaded.

Step 2. User U_i inputs its password PW_i, and then the smart card computes

$$\boldsymbol{B}_0 = (f(PW_i, 1) \pmod p), \ldots, f(PW_i, n) \pmod p))$$

Step 3. The smart card, by calling Algorithm 1, reconstructs the secret hyper-sphere UC_i by taking points $\boldsymbol{B}_0, \boldsymbol{B}_1, \ldots, \boldsymbol{B}_n$ as input parameters, and obtains returned values $(\boldsymbol{C}, R)$, where $\boldsymbol{C} = (c_1, c_2, \ldots, c_n)$ is the center of UC_i.

Step 4. The smart card fetches the current time stamp t, and computes

$$w_1 = f(c_1, t) \pmod p,$$
$$w_2 = f(c_2, t) \pmod p,$$
$$\cdots\cdots$$
$$w_n = f(c_n, t) \pmod p.$$

Let point $\boldsymbol{W} = (w_1, w_2, \ldots, w_n)$.
If $(\boldsymbol{W} == \boldsymbol{C})$
then the smart card repeats **Step 4** to get a new time stamp t and calculate a new point $\boldsymbol{W}$, until $\boldsymbol{W} \neq \boldsymbol{C}$.

Step 5. The smart card randomly selects $\lambda \in GF(p) \setminus \{0, 1\}$, and computes

$$\begin{cases} g_1 \equiv w_1 + (c_1 - w_1) \times \lambda \pmod p \\ g_2 \equiv w_2 + (c_2 - w_2) \times \lambda \pmod p \\ \cdots\cdots \\ g_n \equiv w_n + (c_n - w_m) \times \lambda \pmod p \end{cases} \tag{3}$$

Let $\boldsymbol{G} = (g_1, g_2, \ldots, g_n)$, which is a point on a line L across points $\boldsymbol{W}$ and $\boldsymbol{C}$, with $\boldsymbol{G} \neq \boldsymbol{W}$ and $\boldsymbol{G} \neq \boldsymbol{C}$.

Step 6. User U_i sends the login message $M = \{t, ID_i, \boldsymbol{B}_1, \boldsymbol{G}\}$ to the AS.

Algorithm 4: To verify whether a user's login message M is valid or not

Input: $M = \{t, ID_i, \boldsymbol{B}_1, \boldsymbol{G}\}$, where t is the time stamp, ID_i is user U_i's identity, $\boldsymbol{B}_1$ and $\boldsymbol{G}$ are points in n-dimensional space;
Output: $true/false$; if the login message M is valid, $true$; otherwise, $false$;
Procedure:

```
begin
    if ( t is expired ) or ( t is invalid ) then
        return false;
    end
    for (j = 1; i ≤ n; i++) do
        Let A_j = (f(ID_i, s_j1) (mod p), ..., f(ID_i, s_jn) (mod p));
        /* s_j1, ..., s_jn are the AS's secret parameters; */
    end
    (C, R)=Algorithm_1(B_1, A_1, ..., A_n);
    /* Call Algorithm 1 by using B_1, A_1, ..., A_n as input parameters; */
    if (C == NULL) or (R == NULL) then
        return false;
    end
    else
        Let C ≜ (c_1, c_2, ..., c_n);   /*c_1, c_2, ..., c_n are components of C; */
        for (j = 1; j ≤ n; j++) do
            Let w_j = f(c_j, t) (mod p);
        end
        Let W = (w_1, w_2, ..., w_n);
        result = Algorithm_3(G, C, W);
        /* Call Algorithm 3 by using G, C, W as inputs to judge if G is on a
        line L across C and W; */
        if ( result == NULL ) then
            return false;
        end
        else
            return true;
        end
    end
end
```

Fig. 4. Algorithm To Verify Whether a User's Login Message M Is Valid or Not

3.5 The Verification Stage

At this stage, by calling Algorithm 4, the AS judges whether user U_i's login message is valid or not. The returned value $true$ or $false$ indicates "valid" or "invalid" about user U_i's identity.

3.6 The Session Key Computation Stage

Both user U_i and the AS can compute a shared common session key at this stage. Since user U_i generates a point $\boldsymbol{W}$ at its login stage, and the AS will re-construct the same point $\boldsymbol{W}$ at the verification stage if U_i's authentication message is valid. Thus, $\boldsymbol{W} = (w_1, w_2, \ldots, w_n)$ can be used to compute a common secret between U_i and the AS.

Let $k' = w_1||w_2||\ldots||w_n$, where "$||$" stands for concatenation operation, then k' is a common secret. We can fetch desired length of bits from k' by some pre-defined specifications to become a session key, for example, we define k to be the leading 128 odd bits of k':

$$k = leading\_128\_odd\_bits\_of(k');$$

As a result, k is a 128-bit session key shared between user U_i and the AS.

Notice that the computation of $\boldsymbol{W}$ invokes time stamp t, therefore, k is also a function of t, which means that k is varied from each session and will be statistically independent from its previous instance.

4 Security and Performance Analysis

4.1 Security Analysis

We analyze the security issues against some existing typical attacks.

1) Replay attack

   The login message M contains time stamp and the AS will check the validity of the time stamp. Therefore, replay attacks can be prevented by our scheme.

2) Forging login message

   If the attacker intercepts the authentication message M, what he can get is a point on the hyper-sphere. The attacker cannot reconstruct the hyper-sphere UC_i, and has no knowledge about the coordinates of the hyper-sphere's central point. If the attacker modifies the time stamp, he cannot construct a legal point $\boldsymbol{G}$ corresponding to the modified time stamp, and cannot construct a legal login message, either. Even though the attacker can intercept multiple authentication messages, he still cannot get enough information to reconstruct the hyper-sphere. Therefore, an attacker cannot forge a legal login message.

3) Off-line dictionary attack

   The dictionary attack has no effect to our approach. On the one hand, since $f(PW_i, j)$ is not exposed to the open network, the dictionary attack is hard to launch against our approach. On the other hand, even though the password PW_i was guessed and the login message M was intercepted, only $\boldsymbol{B}_0$, $\boldsymbol{B}_1$,and $\boldsymbol{G}$ were got by the attacker, but it is still lack of enough information to reconstruct the hyper-sphere.

4) Impersonating the AS

   Since the secret information of the AS might be exposed to the legal user in the approach described in [13], there is a security leak that a legal user might be able to forge the AS. A legal user can reconstruct other user's ID and secret shared with the AS, and then it can forge the AS to generate other legal user's login message. This problem is considered to be the biggest leak in [13]. But this problem doesn't exist in our approach. The legal user can know only $(n+1)$ points on the reconstructed secret hyper-sphere, but the AS will use other different n points plus the points $\boldsymbol{B}_0$ to calculate the secret hyper-sphere. Thus the user has no knowledge on the AS's n points, let alone n secret vectors to generate the points. Therefore, it is unable for a legal user to forge the AS.

5) Impersonating user

   Suppose that a legal user U_i might modify its user identifier ID_i in the login message and try to forge another user U_j. However, user U_i will not know the secret shared between the AS and U_j, then it is unable to generate a legal point $\boldsymbol{G}$ corresponding to U_j's information. Therefore, it is unable to forge another user to generate the legal login message.

6) Breaking cryptographic hash function

   The cryptographic hash function is usually considered to be secure. Even if the hash function was broken, the approach proposed in this paper is still secure. During all the procedures of computations, a user's $f(PW_i, j)$ or the AS's $f(ID_i, s_{ij})$ will never be exposed to the open channel. Therefore, it is unable for the attacker to get a user's PW_i or the AS's secret s_{ij} via breaking the hash function.

7) Brute force attacks

   The attackers might try to guess the center $\boldsymbol{C} = (c_1, \ldots, c_n)$ of the hyper-sphere shared between a user and the AS. Since each $c_j \in GF(p), j = 1, 2, \ldots, n$, then the complexity to guess $\boldsymbol{C}$ is $\mathcal{O}(2^{n \times |p|})$, where $|p|$ is the length of p in bits. For an ordinary application, we can choose a small positive integer for n, for example, let $n = 3$, and let $|p| = 128$ bits, then the attacking complexity is $\mathcal{O}(2^{384})$. A cryptosystem is usually considered to be practically secure if the complexity of the best attacking method against it is higher than $\mathcal{O}(2^{80})$.

4.2 Performance Analysis

We summarize the computation complexity, storage, and communication overhead required by each user and the AS respectively in this subsection.

Computation. Firstly, the computation complexity of Algorithms 1, 2, 3, and 4 are given in Table 1. Notice that all computations in Table 1, 2, and 3 are over $GF(p)$, and n denotes the dimension of the hyper-sphere.

The major computation of Algorithm 1 is to solve a system of linear equations (2), the complexity of which is less than $\mathcal{O}(n^3)$ by invoking a standard Gaussian elimination method. The major computation of Algorithm 4 needs to call Algorithm 1. Therefore, both Algorithm 1 and 4 require $\mathcal{O}(n^3)$ complexity of computation, but other algorithms require only $\mathcal{O}(n^2)$, or $\mathcal{O}(n)$, or 0 complexity.

Secondly, the computation complexity required by user U_i at each stage is summarized in Table 2. The user registration stage is executed only once during the lifetime of a password, but both the user login stage and the session key computation stage are implemented at each authentication session. From the

Table 1. Computation Complexity of Algorithms

	Multiplicative Inversion	Multiplication	Addition	Hash Function
Algorithm 1	$\mathcal{O}(n^3)$	$\mathcal{O}(n^3)$	$\mathcal{O}(n^3)$	0
Algorithm 2	0	$\mathcal{O}(n^2)$	$\mathcal{O}(n^2)$	0
Algorithm 3	$\mathcal{O}(n)$	$\mathcal{O}(n)$	$\mathcal{O}(n)$	0
Algorithm 4	$\mathcal{O}(n^3)$	$\mathcal{O}(n^3)$	$\mathcal{O}(n^3)$	$\mathcal{O}(n^2)$

performance analysis in Table 2, we observe that the most time consuming computation required by a user is only $\mathcal{O}(n^3)$ multiplicative inversions. For an usual application, as analyzed in the previous subsection, a small positive integer n, for example, $n = 3$ or $n = 5$ can lead to a practical security level. Therefore, it is fast for a smart card to execute a login procedure, and our scheme is suitable for smartcard-oriented applications.

Table 2. Computation Complexity of a User at each Stage

Stage	Multiplicative Inversion	Multiplication	Addition	Hash Function	Concatenation
User Registration	0	0	0	$\mathcal{O}(n)$	0
User Login	$\mathcal{O}(n^3)$	$\mathcal{O}(n^3)$	$\mathcal{O}(n^3)$	$\mathcal{O}(n^2)$	0
Session Key Computation	0	0	0	0	$\mathcal{O}(n)$

Thirdly, the computation complexity required by the AS at each stage is summarized in Table 3. Similarly, the most time consuming computation required by the AS is only $\mathcal{O}(n)$ multiplicative inversions, which means that our scheme is also efficient for the AS to verify a user's identity.

Table 3. Computation Complexity of the AS at each Stage

Stage	Multiplicative Inversion	Multiplication	Addition	Hash Function	Concatenation
User Registration	$\mathcal{O}(n^3)$	$\mathcal{O}(n^3)$	$\mathcal{O}(n^3)$	$\mathcal{O}(n^2)$	0
Verification	$\mathcal{O}(n^3)$	$\mathcal{O}(n^3)$	$\mathcal{O}(n^3)$	$\mathcal{O}(n^2)$	0
Session Key Computation	0	0	0	0	$\mathcal{O}(n)$

Storage. In the user side, the data needed to be kept by each user is stored in its smart card, which is $p, ID_i, f(\cdot,\cdot), \boldsymbol{B}_1, \boldsymbol{B}_2, \ldots, \boldsymbol{B}_n$. Then the storage requires $((n^2+1)|p| + |ID_i| + sizeof(f))$ bits, where $|p|$ stands for the length of p in bits, $|ID_i|$ for the length of ID_i, $sizeof(f)$ for the size of executable code of the hash function f in bits.

In the AS side, it is not necessary for the AS to store each user's password nor other private information. What the AS needs to store are n set of secret vectors

$\boldsymbol{S}_1 = (s_{11}, s_{12}, \ldots, s_{1n})$, ..., $\boldsymbol{S}_n = (s_{n1}, s_{n2}, \ldots, s_{nn})$ for the whole authentication system, and the length of which are $n^2|p|$ bits. For a practical instance, if we choose $n = 3$ and $|p| = 128$, then the AS needs to store $n^2|p| = 3^2 \times 128 = 1152$ bits, or 144 bytes of secret information for the whole system. Hence, the AS needs to store only small amount of data.

Communication Overhead. The login message sent from a user to the AS is $M = \{t, ID_i, \boldsymbol{B}_1, \boldsymbol{G}\}$, the length of which is $(|t| + |ID_i| + 2n|p|)$ bits, where $|t|$ stands for the length of time stamp in bits.

5 Experiment

We implement the authentication system in Java language. All the computations are over the Galois field $GF(p)$. The AS side program runs on a PC whose CPU is Pentium IV 2.5GHz processor, the memory is 512MB, and the operating system is Window XP. The user side program runs on Pocket PC to simulate the smart card. We use Asus A620BT Pocket PC, with InterPXA255 processor, and Window CE operating system. For different values of p and n, the time consumptions for the stages of authentication are shown in Table 4, 5 and 6 respectively, where p is the order of $GF(p)$, $|p|$ stands for the length of p in bits, and n is the dimension of the hyper-sphere. The time consumed by the AS side program is presented in Table 4 and 5, and the time taken by the user side program running on Pocket PC is shown in Table 6.

Table 4. Time Consumed by the AS side Program at the User Registration Stage (in second)

	$\|p\| = 64$	$\|p\| = 128$	$\|p\| = 256$	$\|p\| = 512$	$\|p\| = 768$	$\|p\| = 1024$
$n = 3$	0.019	0.025	0.041	0.069	0.172	0.434
$n = 5$	0.031	0.038	0.053	0.113	0.259	0.694
$n = 7$	0.031	0.040	0.063	0.178	0.328	0.690
$n = 10$	0.047	0.053	0.091	0.219	0.597	1.278
$n = 12$	0.066	0.062	0.097	0.278	0.622	1.534
$n = 15$	0.084	0.084	0.128	0.372	0.953	1.931

Table 5. Time consumed by the AS Side Program at the Verification Stage (in second)

	$\|p\| = 64$	$\|p\| = 128$	$\|p\| = 256$	$\|p\| = 512$	$\|p\| = 768$	$\|p\| = 1024$
$n = 3$	0.006	0.006	0.006	0.006	0.009	0.013
$n = 5$	0.006	0.009	0.009	0.017	0.019	0.028
$n = 7$	0.009	0.009	0.013	0.022	0.031	0.050
$n = 10$	0.012	0.016	0.022	0.041	0.066	0.097
$n = 12$	0.022	0.025	0.031	0.059	0.097	0.159
$n = 15$	0.028	0.031	0.050	0.094	0.153	0.241

Table 6. Time consumed by the User Side Program running on Pocket PC at the User Login Stage (in second)

	$\|p\| = 64$	$\|p\| = 128$	$\|p\| = 256$	$\|p\| = 512$	$\|p\| = 768$	$\|p\| = 1024$
$n = 3$	0.556	0.594	0.835	1.464	2.166	3.557
$n = 5$	0.809	1.013	1.669	3.028	4.76	8.111
$n = 7$	1.479	1.828	2.847	5.463	8.335	12.425
$n = 10$	2.459	3.242	5.208	9.923	15.966	23.496
$n = 12$	3.245	4.305	7.735	14.158	22.757	32.552
$n = 15$	5.251	6.811	10.897	20.503	34.025	48.643

6 Conclusion

An authentication and key agreement system based on the properties of n-dimensional hyper-sphere, without invoking traditional strong encryption functions, is proposed in this paper. It's essentially based on system of linear equations, which can only be solved by n set of linear equations that their coefficients are linearly independent. By analyzing some typical attacks, it's shown that our approach can resist these attacks. Compared with other geometry-based authentication approaches, our approach owns better security by overcoming their disadvantages. Theoretical analysis and experiment results confirm that the computation of our approach is relatively simple and requiring only small amount of overhead. The storage for both a user and the AS is reasonable. Therefore, it's suitable for smartcard-oriented application.

Acknowledgment. This paper is financially supported by the National Natural Science Foundation of China under Grant No. U1135004, 61170080 and 61202466, and Guangdong Province Universities and Colleges Pearl River Scholar Funded Scheme (2011), and Guangzhou Metropolitan Science and Technology Planning Project under grant No. 2011J4300028, and High-level Talents Project of Guangdong Institutions of Higher Education (2012), and Guangdong Provincial Natural Science Foundation of under grant No. 9351064101000003.

The authors are most grateful for the constructive advice on the revision of the manuscript from the anonymous reviewers. The authors thank Ms. Hua Zhang, who were the former students of the first author, for doing implementations to verify the applicability of our scheme.

References

1. Das, A.: A secure and effective user authentication and privacy preserving protocol with smart cards for wireless communications. Networking Science, 1–16 (2012), http://dx.doi.org/10.1007/s13119-012-0009-8
2. Guo, C., Chang, C.: Chaotic maps-based password-authenticated key agreement using smart cards. Communications in Nonlinear Science and Numerical Simulation 18(6), 1433–1440 (2013), http://www.sciencedirect.com/science/article/pii/S1007570412004698

3. Chien, H.-Y., Jan, J.-K., Tseng, Y.-M.: A modified remote login authentication scheme based on geometric approach. Journal of Systems and Software 55, 287–290 (2001)
4. Wang, S.H., Bao, F., Wang, J.: Comments on yet another log-in authentication using n-dimensional construction. IEEE Transaction on Consumer Electronics 50, 606–608 (2004)
5. Hwang, M.S.: Cryptanalysis of a remote login authentication scheme. Computer Communications 22, 742–744 (1999)
6. Juang, W., Chen, S., Liaw, H.: Robust and efficient password-authenticated key agreement using smart cards. IEEE Transactions on Industrial Electronics 55(6), 2551–2556 (2008)
7. Lennon, R., Matyas, S., Meyer, C.: Cryptographic authentication of time-invariant quantities. IEEE Transactions on Communications 29(6), 773–777 (1981)
8. Li, X., Qiu, W., Zheng, D., Chen, K., Li, J.: Anonymity enhancement on robust and efficient password-authenticated key agreement using smart cards. IEEE Transactions on Industrial Electronics 57(2), 793–800 (2010)
9. Li, X., Ma, J., Wang, W., Xiong, Y., Zhang, J.: A novel smart card and dynamic id based remote user authentication scheme for multi-server environments. Mathematical and Computer Modelling (2012), `http://www.sciencedirect.com/science/article/pii/S0895717712001720`
10. Luby, M., Rackoff, C.: A study of password security. Journal of Cryptology I, 151–158 (1989)
11. Menkus, B.: Understanding the use of passwords. Computers and Security 7, 132–136 (1988)
12. Sun, D., Huai, J., Sun, J., Li, J., Zhang, J., Feng, Z.: Improvements of Juang et al 's password-authenticated key agreement scheme using smart cards. IEEE Transactions on Industrial Electronics 56(6), 2284–2291 (2009)
13. Wang, S.J.: Yet another login authentication using n-dimensional construction based on circle property. IEEE Transaction on Consumer Electronics 49, 337–341 (2003)
14. Wang, S., Chang, F.: Smart card based secure password authentication scheme. Computers and Security 15, 231–237 (1996)
15. Wu, T.C.: Remote login authentication scheme based on a geometric approach. Computer Communications 18, 959–963 (1995)
16. Yang, F.Y., Jan, J.K.: Cryptanalysis of log-in authentication based on circle property. IEEE Transaction on Consumer Electronics 50, 625–628 (2004)
17. Yang, W., Shieh, S.: Password authentication schemes with smart cards. Computers and Security 18, 727–733 (1999)
18. Zhang, L., Tang, S., Cai, Z.: Efficient and flexible password authenticated key agreement for voice over internet protocol session initiation protocol using smart card. International Journal of Communication Systems (2013), `http://dx.doi.org/10.1002/dac.2499`

An Efficient Constant Round ID-Based Group Key Agreement Protocol for Ad Hoc Networks

Elisavet Konstantinou

Department of Information & Communication Systems Engineering,
University of the Aegean, Karlovassi, 83200, Samos, Greece
ekonstantinou@aegean.gr

Abstract. We present an authenticated ID-based Group Key Agreement (GKA) protocol which requires only one round for its execution. The protocol is contributory, energy-balanced and does not require an online TTP. All these properties and in particular the minimum round requirement, makes the protocol especially suited for ad hoc networks. In the paper, we will demonstrate the security properties of the new GKA protocol and present its communication/computation efficiency. Finally, we will compare the new protocol with all the one-round GKA protocols proposed so far in the literature and show that it outperforms all the ID-based protocols of this category.

Keywords: Group key agreement, Constant round, ID-based cryptography, Ad hoc networks.

1 Introduction

Group key agreement (GKA) protocols have been designed for the establishment of a secret, session group key between three or more participants who exchange for this purpose ephemeral messages over an open network. This secret key is used afterwards for the secure communication between the participants providing the basic security attributes, such as confidentiality, data and entity authentication, key confirmation etc. In such protocols, it is clear that the open network can be controlled by adversaries who aim to infiltrate the protocol. Therefore, a GKA protocol should be secure not only against passive attacks but also against active attacks.

The necessary authentication mechanisms are usually provided via asymmetric techniques, such as Public Key Infrastructures (PKI). However, the management of public key certificates requires a large amount of computation, storage and communication. For the elimination of these costs, ID-based cryptography was introduced by Shamir in 1984 [18]. In ID-based cryptography, each entity's public key is derived from its identity. This property eliminates the need for certificates and solves the public key management issues that arise in conventional public key cryptosystems.

In real world applications, the round efficiency of a GKA protocol is critical (the basic advantages are referred for example in [13,23]). The most important and obvious advantage is that all participants should not be necessarily online in the same time. This advantage is especially important in wireless ad hoc networks where the network topology changes frequently. Clearly, group key establishment is more suitable than

J. Lopez, X. Huang, and R. Sandhu (Eds.): NSS 2013, LNCS 7873, pp. 563–574, 2013.

pairwise key establishment for these networks as devices do not waste energy every time they wish to communicate with another device by establishing a new shared secret key. In group key agreement protocols, all the nodes of the group collaborate and finally form a shared secret key. Key distribution techniques require a central authority or an on-line trusted third party (TTP) to distribute the session keys which is not usually a realistic scenario in wireless ad hoc networks.

Our Contribution. We here present a new authenticated ID-based group key agreement protocol which requires only one round for its execution. The group key is the result of all participants' contributions and it is energy balanced since all participants play the same role in the protocol. Also there is no need for an online TTP or a particular network topology. These attributes make the proposed GKA protocol ideal for application in ad hoc networks.

The protocol is secure against passive and active attacks. The secrecy of the group key is based on the difficulty of Bilinear Diffie-Hellman (BDH) problem, while the security against active attackers is achieved with a batch verification technique. A batch verification algorithm for a digital signature scheme verifies a list of n (message, signature) pairs as a group [25]. It outputs 1 if all n signatures are valid and it outputs 0 if at least one signature is invalid. This property improves considerably the efficiency, since one verification for n signatures is significantly faster than n different verifications. Finally, we will compare the proposed protocol with all one round GKA protocols reported so far in the literature and we will see that it outperforms all the ID-based protocols.

The remainder of the paper is organized as follows. In Section 2 we elaborate on the proposed protocol. In Section 3 we discuss the security properties of the protocol and mention its communication and computation efficiency. In Section 4 we compare the proposed protocol with other one round GKA protocols and we give our conclusions in Section 5.

2 One Round Group Key Agreement Protocol

The proposed protocol is based on elliptic curve cryptography and bilinear maps. Recall that a bilinear map is a mapping $e : G_1 \times G_1 \rightarrow G_2$ which satisfies the following properties:

- Bilinearity: $e(aP, bQ) = e(P, Q)^{ab}$ for all $P, Q \in G_1$ and $a, b \in Z_q^*$.
- Non-degeracy: If P is a generator of G_1, then $e(P, P) \neq 1$ is a generator of G_2.
- Computability: There exists an efficient algorithm to compute $e(P, Q)$ for all $P, Q \in G_1$.

G_1 is an additive group, G_2 is a multiplicative group and both groups have prime order q. In order to use bilinear maps for cryptographic purposes we assume that the discrete logarithm problem (DLP) is hard in both G_1 and G_2. Examples of cryptographic bilinear maps are Weil pairing [2] and Tate pairing [1].

Before the execution of the group key agreement protocol, all nodes should agree upon the use of the same elliptic curve parameters, the same base point $P \in G_1$ and the same hash functions $H : \{0,1\}^* \rightarrow G_1$ and $H_1 : G_1 \rightarrow Z_q^*$. Every new member who wishes to join the group can acquire these parameters from its neighbors. We will suppose that the number of members in the group are n and we will denote them by M_i for $1 \leq i \leq n$. The protocol completes in the following stages:

Setup Stage: In order to provide authentication, we will need a Key Generation Centre (KGC). The public key of the KGC is equal to $P_{pub} = sP$ where s is a secret value and P is the base point. Every user M_i sends her public key $Q_i = H(ID_i)$ to the KGC which computes her secret key $S_i = sQ_i$.

First Stage: Every member M_i randomly generates a value $r_i \in Z_q^*$ and computes $R_i = r_i P$, $h_i = H_1(R_i)$ and $A_{i,j} = h_i S_i + r_i Q_j$ for $i \neq j$. Then, she broadcasts the values $(R_i, A_{i,1}, ..., A_{i,n})$. The only value that is not sent is $A_{i,i}$. We suppose that every user M_j can recognize her corresponding value $A_{i,j}$.

Second Stage: Every member M_j computes the value

$$K = \frac{e(\sum_{i=1}^{i=n} A_{i,j}, P_{pub})}{e(S_j, \sum_{i=1}^{i=n} R_i)} = e(\sum_{i=1}^{i=n} h_i S_i, P_{pub}) \tag{1}$$

which will be the secret group key. Indeed, for every value j we have that

$$K = \frac{e(\sum_{i=1}^{i=n} A_{i,j}, P_{pub})}{e(S_j, \sum_{i=1}^{i=n} R_i)} = \frac{e(\sum_{i=1}^{i=n}(h_i S_i + r_i Q_j), P_{pub})}{e(sQ_j, \sum_{i=1}^{i=n} r_i P)}$$

$$= \frac{e(\sum_{i=1}^{i=n} h_i S_i, P_{pub}) e(\sum_{i=1}^{i=n} r_i Q_j, sP)}{e(sQ_j, \sum_{i=1}^{i=n} r_i P)} = e(\sum_{i=1}^{i=n} h_i S_i, P_{pub}).$$

Verification Stage: In order to secure the protocol against active attacks, we will add to it a batch verification process. Therefore, every member M_j will accept K as the group key only if the following equation holds:

$$\frac{e(\sum_{i=1}^{i=n} A_{i,j}, P)}{e(Q_j, \sum_{i=1}^{i=n} R_i)} = e(\sum_{i=1}^{i=n} h_i Q_i, P_{pub}). \tag{2}$$

Notice that the batch verification process is correct since

$$\frac{e(\sum_{i=1}^{i=n} A_{i,j}, P)}{e(Q_j, \sum_{i=1}^{i=n} R_i)} = \frac{e(\sum_{i=1}^{i=n}(h_i S_i + r_i Q_j), P)}{e(Q_j, \sum_{i=1}^{i=n} r_i P)} =$$

$$\frac{e(\sum_{i=1}^{i=n} h_i s Q_i, P) e(\sum_{i=1}^{i=n} r_i Q_j, P)}{e(Q_j, \sum_{i=1}^{i=n} r_i P)} = e(\sum_{i=1}^{i=n} h_i Q_i, P_{pub}).$$

Another property of our protocol is that it gives the opportunity to every group member M_j to authenticate any other group member M_i by using the equation:

$$\frac{e(A_{i,j}, P)}{e(R_i, Q_j)} = e(h_i Q_i, P_{pub}). \tag{3}$$

If the above equation holds, then the group member M_i is authenticated by M_j. The value $A_{i,j}$ is actually the signature of user M_i over the message Q_j.

3 Efficiency and Security Considerations

In this section, we will examine the security properties of the new GKA protocol, discuss the handling of membership events and compute its computational/communicational efficiency.

3.1 Security Properties

In the following we summarize the basic security properties that a GKA protocol must satisfy. For a more detailed description, the interested reader is referred to [17].

- **Key privacy/ Key confidentiality/ Key secrecy:** It must be computationally infeasible for a passive adversary to compute the group key.
- **Known-key security:** An adversary who knows group keys of past sessions (e.g. former members of the group) must not be able to compute new group keys.
- **Key freshness:** Every session key must be fresh, e.g. new group keys should not have been used in the past.
- **Key independence:** Previously used group keys should not be discovered by joined new group members and former group members should not be able to compute subsequent group keys.
- **(Implicit) key authentication:** Only legitimate group members can learn the established group key. In our case, legitimate members are those that have a valid pair of long-term private and public keys.
- **Resistance against impersonation attacks:** The knowledge of past session keys can not lead to the impersonation of any of the group members.
- **Resistance against key replication attacks:** An adversary should not be able to enforce the same value of the group key in two different sessions.
- **Forward secrecy:** The disclosure of long-term keys does not compromise the secrecy of previous session keys.

The first property concerns the security of the protocol against passive attackers. Our protocol is secure against such attacks since the values S_j and $\sum_{i=1}^{i=n} A_{i,j}$ in Equation 1 are secret. The sum $\sum_{i=1}^{i=n} A_{i,j}$ is secret since the value $A_{i,i}$ is unknown. Also notice that from the equation $A_{i,j} = h_i S_i + r_i Q_j$, even though the attacker knows the values $A_{i,j}$, h_i and Q_j, he can not find either S_i or r_i because this would mean that he can solve the ECDLP (elliptic curve dicrete logarithm problem). Being more specific, we notice that the security of our protocol is based on the *Bilinear Diffie-Hellman*-BDH problem in $< G_1, G_2, e >$:

Definition 1. *(BDH Problem): Given* (P, aP, bP, cP) *for* $P \in G_1$ *and* $a, b, c \in Z_q^*$, *find the value* $r = e(P, P)^{abc}$.

BDH Assumption: We assume that the BDH problem is hard. This means that there is no polynomial time algorithm to solve BDH problem with non-negligible probability.

Let examine first the value $e(\sum_{i=1}^{i=n} A_{i,j}, P_{pub})$ from Equation 1. The sum is analyzed as

$$e(\sum_{i=1}^{i=n} A_{i,j}, P_{pub}) = e(A_{i,i}, P_{pub}) e(\sum_{i \neq j} A_{i,j}, P_{pub}).$$

The value $e(\sum_{i \neq j} A_{i,j}, P_{pub})$ can be computed by any adversary, so we must guarantee the security of $e(A_{i,i}, P_{pub})$. We have that

$$e(A_{i,i}, P_{pub}) = e(h_i S_i + r_i Q_i, P_{pub}) = e(h_i S_i, sP) e(r_i Q_i, sP) = e(h_i Q_i, sP)^s e(Q_i, sP)^{r_i}.$$

Since Q_i is a random element in G_1, we can write it as $Q_i = a_i P$, where P is the base point. This immediately means that finding the values $e(h_i Q_i, sP)^s$ and $e(Q_i, sP)^{r_i}$ requires the solution of the BDH problem. In addition, since we can not find the value $e(Q_i, sP)^{r_i} = e(S_i, r_i P)$, we can neither find the value $e(S_j, \sum_{i=1}^{i=n} R_i)$ from Equation 1. Similarly, the security of $e(h_i Q_i, sP)^s = e(h_i S_i, P_{pub})$ which is a component of the secret group key K, guarantees the security of the whole key.

The properties of key freshness and known-key security are satisfied since every session's group key is not related in any way with previous group keys. The new key is fresh since the hash values $h_i = H_1(R_i)$ are different in every session. In order to see if the property of key independence is satisfied, we must discuss the handling of membership events. We distinguish the following four basic membership events:

- A *Join Event* occurs when a single member wants to join the existing group. The group key is updated to include the new member and all participants are informed about the new key.
- A *Leave Event* occurs when a member wishes to leave the group, or is forced to leave it. The group key must be properly modified so that the departing participant can no longer use the old group key in order to encrypt/decrypt the group's communications.
- A *Group Merge Event* occurs when multiple potential members want to join an existing group. The keys of the two groups are merged so that all participates can communicate with each other using a common shared key.
- A *Group Partition Event* occurs when multiple members leave the group with or without forming their own subgroup. A new key must be established for each partitioned subgroup to guarantee secrecy.

We will discuss only the single leave/join event because group leave/join events can be treated similarly. Suppose first that member M_n wishes to leave the group. Then the new group key could be equal to $e(\sum_{j=1}^{j=n-1} h_j S_j, P_{pub}) = \frac{K}{e(h_n S_n, P_{pub})}$, where K is the previous session group key. The value $e(h_n S_n, P_{pub})$ can be computed by any legitimate participant M_j from equation:

$$e(h_n S_n, P_{pub}) = \frac{e(A_{n,j}, P_{pub})}{e(S_j, R_n)} = \frac{e(h_n S_n + r_n Q_j, P_{pub})}{e(sQ_j, r_n P)}.$$

Similarly, if member M_{n+1} wishes to join the group, then the new key could be easily transformed to $e(\sum_{j=1}^{j=n+1} h_j S_j, P_{pub})$ adding the contribution $h_{n+1} S_{n+1}$ of the new member. This means that the new member M_{n+1} would have to broadcast the values $(R_{n+1}, A_{n+1,1}, ..., A_{n+1,n})$ to all previous members.

However, the following property of our protocol, implies that for any membership event, the protocol should be re-executed from the first step. In particular, notice that every legitimate (e.g. has a valid long-term key pair and has also participated in the particular session) group member M_j can compute all values $e(h_iS_i, P_{pub})$ for $i \neq j$ using the following equation:

$$e(h_iS_i, P_{pub}) = \frac{e(A_{i,j}, P_{pub})}{e(S_j, R_i)}. \tag{4}$$

Based on this property, we see that if we follow the previously mentioned approach for leave/join members, previously used group keys will be discovered by joined new group members and former group members would be able to compute subsequent group keys. Thus, the property of key independence is satisfied only if a join or leave event is handled by re-executing the key agreement protocol.

The (implicit) key authentication property should hold in every GKA protocol in order to ensure legitimate users that only them can compute the key. This property is satisfied in the proposed protocol due to the batch verification process. For example, suppose that an attacker E takes part in the protocol by sending her values $(R_E, A_{E,1}, ..., A_{E,n})$ to the legitimate users by using a pair of keys (S_E, Q_E). Then, Equation 2 will not hold since the pair (S_E, Q_E) is not connected with the relation $S_E = sQ_E$. Moreover, using Equation 3, the attacker can be found easily. More details on active attacks and the security of the batch verification process follow in the next Section.

The resistance against impersonation attacks is guaranteed because the knowledge of keys $K = e(\sum_{i=1}^{i=n} h_iS_i, P_{pub})$ can not lead to the long-term secret keys S_i or to the secret master key s due to the intractability of the BDH problem (as explained in previous paragraphs). Notice also that two different sessions keys K and K' are not related in any way since the values h_i change in every session. The new protocol is also resistant to key replication attacks and this is due to its contributory nature. Since the key is composed by the contributions of all participants, no attacker can enforce the same value of the group key in two different sessions.

The protocol provides forward secrecy compromising *at most* one user. If two or more participants are compromised, then the property of forward secrecy is not satisfied in our protocol. The reason is the protocol's property mentioned in Equation 4. For example, suppose that an adversary has acquired two different long-term secret keys S_k and S_m of users M_k and M_s correspondingly. If she has gathered all public information exchanged between the group members during the past sessions, then she can find all values $e(h_iS_i, P_{pub})$ using Equation 4 and consequently all group keys $K = e(\sum_{i=1}^{i=n} h_iS_i, P_{pub})$. However, notice that according to [11], constructing a one round group key exchange protocol that provides forward security is still an open problem. The authors of [11] have proposed as a solution a key evolving approach that allows the users to keep their long-term public keys but update their private keys. This key evolving approach does not increase the number of rounds and thus the round efficiency can remain optimal. Possibly, the lack of forward secrecy can be handled in other ways. One simple idea will be to compute the group key as $K = e(\sum_{i=1}^{i=n} h_iS_i, P_{pub}) \cdot K^*$ where K^* is the group key of the previous session. Another solution will be the encryption of *only* one value R_i, e.g. R_0 with the previous session key. Then, every adversary will not be able to compute the value $e(h_0S_0, P_{pub})$ and the group key as well. This solution will add only a symmetric encryption operation in one group member and one symmetric decryption to the rest of the group members.

3.2 Security against Active Attacks

In order to guarantee security against active attacks, we have adopted in our protocol a batch verification technique. The idea behind batch verification techniques is that they use multiple signatures generated by a single user. The main advantage of this technique is that only one verification is needed for the authentication of the whole group, while in conventional signature schemes n verifications will be needed. As mentioned also in the previous Section, the proposed protocol is secure against active attacks since everyone who participates in it must have a valid secret key S_i. In any other case Equation 2 will not hold and this will indicate that at least one group member has an invalid key S_i. In particular, using Equation 3 this user can be easily found.

However, our batch verification scheme can be also proved secure in the random oracle model against adaptively chosen message attacks. The proof can be easily deduced from [28], since the batch verification algorithm we use in our protocol is a modified version of the scheme presented in this paper. In what follows, in order to show the similarity of the two schemes, we summarize the scheme in [28] using as group G_1 in the bilinear map, an elliptic curve group with base point P:

- **Batch Signature:** To sign t messages $m_1, ..., m_t$ a signer with identity ID_i and private key S_i performs the following steps:
  1. Choose a random $r_i \in Z_q^*$ and compute $R_i = r_i P$.
  2. For $1 \leq j \leq t$ compute $f_j = H(m_j)$.
  3. For $1 \leq j \leq t$ compute $z_{i,j} = S_i + r_i f_j$.
  4. Output the batch signature $\sigma_i = (R_i, z_{i,1}, ... z_{i,t})$.
- **Batch Verification:** Each user M_j verifies that
  $e(\sum_{i=1}^{i=n} z_{i,j}, P) = e(f_j, \sum_{i=1}^{i=n} R_i) e(\sum_{i=1}^{i=n} Q_i, P_{pub})$.

Notice that the values $z_{i,j}$ are very close to the values $A_{i,j}$ in Equation 2, with the difference that in our case the message m_j is equal to ID_j (since $Q_j = H(ID_j)$) and the secret key S_i is replaced with $h_i S_i$. The key $h_i S_i$ is secret and can be considered the participant's session secret key. The batch verification step is also almost identical to Equation 2. It is clear that since the protocol in [28] is provable secure in the random oracle model, the same is true for our scheme.

Finally, another active attack could be achieved by malicious nodes simply by impersonating an entity M_i and repeating the broadcast of the values $(R_i, A_{i,1}, ..., A_{i,n})$ to the group. As suggested by Zhang et al. in [26], this problem can be easily solved by adding a time parameter.

3.3 Efficiency of the Protocol

The complexity of a GKA protocol is estimated by the total number of calculations and the total number of exchanged messages required for the generation of the final key. The addition of the computation and communication cost of a protocol gives us its total energy cost which should be small enough, especially in the case that we wish to apply the protocol in wireless ad hoc networks. The computation cost is highly dependent on heavy calculations like the public key calculations and much less on other calculations like hash functions, symmetric encryption-decryption algorithms and symmetric signing-verifying schemes. We will therefore, take into consideration only the number of public key calculations like modular exponentiations, scalar multiplications and pairing computations.

Concerning first the communication cost, we see that every user should broadcast a single message with size equal to n elliptic curve points. To guarantee the minimum required security, the elliptic curve parameters should have size at least 160 bits. The protocol also requires from each participant a number of elliptic curve scalar multiplication and pairing computations. In particular, each user M_i has to compute in the first stage one scalar multiplication for the computation of R_i, one for h_iS_i and $n-1$ for the values r_iQ_j. In total, $n+1$ scalar multiplications in the first stage. The second stage requires from every user to compute only 2 pairing computations. Finally, the batch verification process needs 3 pairing computations and n scalar multiplications for each participant. Therefore, the final computation cost for each group member is 5 pairing operations and $2n+1$ scalar multiplications.

We would like to note here, that an important advantage of our protocol is that it nicely distributes energy consumption among the participants as each node has the same role in terms of required computations and communication exchanges (energy-wise, the two most demanding events). Balancing the energy dissipation among the nodes in an ad hoc network is very important since early energy depletion of certain nodes can be avoided and this increases the lifetime of the system by preventing early network disconnection [20]. Finally, the new protocol does not require an online TTP or central authorities and the storage memory needed in every node is not large.

4 Related Work and Comparison

The first constant-round GKA protocol proposed in the literature was presented in [5] by Burmester and Desmedt. This is a very efficient, unauthenticated scheme which requires only two rounds. Two ID-based variants of Burmester-Desmedt (BD) scheme were presented in [6,9]. However, both schemes were shown to fail to achieve authentication by Zhang and Chen [26,27]. In order to resist the attacks a new scheme was proposed in [10] which has the disadvantage of using a synchronized counter. More recently, Desmedt and Lange (DL) [8] presented two variants of the BD protocol [5] based on pairings. Their variants make use of some specific structure of the nodes and their authenticated versions come from the application of the same authors' efficient compiler [7].

The first attempt for the construction of a single round GKA protocol was made by Tzeng and Tzeng in 2000 [22]. However, the two proposed protocols in the paper require a session identifier to be known by all participants and clearly if this is not agreed in a setup phase then the protocols are completed in two rounds. Moreover, the protocols include some proofs of knowledge that each user acquires the same inputs. As it was mentioned in [4], these proofs are useful only in the case that the broadcast channel provides integrity of all messages and for this reason we won't consider these proofs in the computation cost of the protocols. Boyd and Nieto [4] also proved that the second protocol in [22] does not provide authentication and they proposed the use of a new GKA protocol proven secure in the random oracle model. However, their protocol (as [22]) fails to provide forward secrecy and is not energy-balanced since a "group leader" is required who performs n public key encryptions.

The first one round ID-based protocol proposed in the literature was [14]. The protocol requires $O(n^2)$ scalar multiplications and $O(n^2)$ pairings. Another ID-based one round group key agreement protocol was proposed in [19]. However, the authors of [29] showed that this protocol is flawed and that is not actually an ID-based scheme since one's public key is no longer the identity. In [29] a single round authenticated GKA protocol was proposed which according to the authors was the first provably secure ID-based protocol in the literature that requires only one round.

Another ID-based GKA protocol was presented in [16]. The authors consider their protocol ID-based but it is not. Like the protocol in [19], the public keys of the users are not their identities. Even though the authors claim that their protocol requires one round only, an extra round is necessary. This extra round involves a pair-wise key agreement phase between all group members. Moreover, the authors mention that their protocol requires only n pairings in total, but this is not true since for the computation of the group key, pairwise-keys are needed requiring for their construction $3n^2$ pairings. What's more, every user has to perform n polynomial interpolations for the computation of n polynomials with degree $n-1$.

In [12], a new one-round authenticated GKA protocol is presented, which is based on a modification of the ID-PKI proposed in [19]. This modification provides security against impersonation attacks. Although both protocols are based on the same modified ID-PKI and on the same attributes of bilinear pairings, the protocol in [12] requires much more computations to be executed, since it involves verification procedures. The protocol is provably secure against insider attacks, such as impersonation attacks. Another ID-based GKA protocol, which is executed in network level, is introduced in [24]. The novelty of this protocol lies in the fact that different members, from different domains can agree upon a common secret key. The IP addresses, as well as the MAC addresses of the protocol participants, serve as their public keys.

In Table 1 we summarize the communication and computation cost of all one-round group key agreement protocols presented in the literature so far. We have named the protocols after the initials of the authors' last names and the year of publication. For the computation cost we only take into consideration the number of modular exponentiations, scalar multiplications and the pairings performed by all group members in each protocol. However, there are several other actions taking place during the execution of a protocol, such as hash functions, symmetric encryption and signature algorithms, which are much less energy consuming tasks compared to heavy public key calculations and we consider their cost negligible. In the case that the GKA protocol assumes the execution of a public key encryption scheme, but the authors do not mention the exact scheme (e.g. in [4]), we assume in our analysis that RSA is used. When a public key signature scheme is referred in the GKA protocol but the authors give no information about it, we assume that the DSA is used.

The communication cost refers to the number of messages transmitted and received by all entities of the group. For example, in our protocol each participant sends a broadcast message which has size equal to n elliptic curve points. Thus the total number

Table 1. Communication and Computation Cost of All One-Round Protocols

Protocol	Sent Msg	Received Msg	Scalar Mult.	Pairings	Expon.
TT00 [22] (flawed)	$2n^2 + 3n$	$2n^3+n^2-3n$	-	-	$5n^2 + 2n$
SCL05 [19] (flawed)	$n(n-1)$	$n(n-1)$	n^2	n	-
BN03 [4]	$2n-1$	$2n(n-1)$	-	-	$4n-3$
KKHY04 [14]	$3n$	$3n(n-1)$	n^2+4n	$4n^2-3n$	-
ZSM06 [29]	$n(n+1)$	n^3-n	-	$n(n-1)$	-
HH07 [12]	$3n(n-1)$	$3n(n-1)$	$3n^2$	$3n$	-
XHX09 [24]	$2n(n-1)$	$2n(n-1)$	$3n^2-2n$	n^2+n	-
Our protocol	n^2	n^2	$2n^2+n$	$5n$	-

of sent messages in the network is n^2. With a similar way, we can calculate the total number of received messages in the network.

According to Table 1, the most efficient protocol is BN03, both in communication and computation cost. Our protocol follows together with SCL05. Taking into consideration that a pairing operation is approximately equal to three scalar multiplications, our new GKA protocol is the most efficient computationally after BN03 and SCL05. However, SCL05 protocol is not ID-based and more importantly is flawed. On the other hand, neither BN03 is ID-based and is not energy balanced since the initiator takes almost all the computational burden. Moreover, if an entity achieves to impersonate the initiator, the session keys are revealed.

A very recent one round protocol is presented in [21]. The authors do not report exactly the efficiency of their protocol which requires from all participants some matrix multiplications. Comparing this protocol with ours, we notice that the pairing operations are the same, but our protocol requires less scalar multiplications and less memory storage. Thus, concerning all the one round ID-based GKA protocols, our protocol is the most efficient in the literature so far (to the best of our knowledge).

Finally, we would like to note that Boneh and Silverberg proposed the use of multilinear forms for the construction of one round group key agreement protocols [3] and some ID-based variants of this idea were presented in [15]. However, these solutions are far from practical implementations and finding a multilinear form for large n is a very difficult task. Moreover, in Eurocrypt 2009 an *asymmetric* one round group key agreement scheme was proposed based on pairings [23]. After its execution, all users in the group share the same encryption key but they have different decryption keys. The performance of this protocol is more efficient than ours, since every user computes n scalar multiplications and only one pairing. However, the advantage of our protocol is that once the secret group key has been established, it can be used in symmetric encryption and decryption, while the scheme in [23] requires public key operations which means 3 exponentiations for encryption and 2 pairings for decryption per user.

5 Conclusions

We have presented an authenticated ID-based GKA protocol which requires only one broadcast for each participant in order to establish a common, secret group key. In addition to its round efficiency, the protocol does not need for its execution an online TTP, it is energy balanced and it does not require any specific network topology. All these reasons make it ideal for employment in wireless ad hoc networks.

Acknowledgments. I would like to thank Prof. Kenny Paterson (Royal Holloway, University of London) for his guidance during my visit to Royal Holloway few years back, where the idea for this work emerged.

References

1. Barreto, P.S.L.M., Kim, H.Y., Lynn, B., Scott, M.: Efficient algorithms for pairing-based cryptosystems. In: Yung, M. (ed.) CRYPTO 2002. LNCS, vol. 2442, pp. 354–368. Springer, Heidelberg (2002)
2. Boneh, D., Franklin, M.: Identity-based Encryption from the Weil Pairing. In: Kilian, J. (ed.) CRYPTO 2001. LNCS, vol. 2139, pp. 213–229. Springer, Heidelberg (2001)
3. Boneh, D., Silverberg, A.: Applications of Multilinear Forms to Cryptography. In: Contemporary Mathematics, pp. 71–90, AMS (2003)
4. Boyd, C., Nieto, J.M.G.: Round-Optimal Contributory Conference Key Agreement. In: Desmedt, Y. (ed.) PKC 2003. LNCS, vol. 2567, pp. 161–174. Springer, Heidelberg (2002)
5. Burmester, M., Desmedt, Y.: A Secure and Efficient Conference Key Distribution System (Extended Abstract). In: De Santis, A. (ed.) EUROCRYPT 1994. LNCS, vol. 950, pp. 275–286. Springer, Heidelberg (1995)
6. Choi, K.Y., Hwang, J.Y., Lee, D.-H.: Efficient ID-based Group Key Agreement with Bilinear Maps. In: Bao, F., Deng, R., Zhou, J. (eds.) PKC 2004. LNCS, vol. 2947, pp. 130–144. Springer, Heidelberg (2004)
7. Desmedt, Y., Lange, T., Burmester, M.: Scalable Authenticated Tree Based Group Key Exchange for Ad-Hoc Groups. In: Dietrich, S., Dhamija, R. (eds.) FC 2007 and USEC 2007. LNCS, vol. 4886, pp. 104–118. Springer, Heidelberg (2007)
8. Desmedt, Y., Lange, T.: Revisiting Pairing Based Group Key Exchange. In: Tsudik, G. (ed.) FC 2008. LNCS, vol. 5143, pp. 53–68. Springer, Heidelberg (2008)
9. Du, X., Wang, Y., Ge, J., Wang, Y.: ID-based Authenticated Two Round Multi-Party Key Agreement. Cryptology ePrint Archive, Report 2003/247 (2003)
10. Du, X., Wang, Y., Ge, J., Wang, Y.: ID-based Authenticated Two Round Multi-Party Key Agreement. Cryptology ePrint Archive, Report 2003/260 (2003)
11. Gorantla, M.C., Boyd, C., Nieto, J.M.G.: One round group key exchange with forward security in the standard model. IACR Cryptology ePrint Archive, Report 2010/83 (2010)
12. He, Y.Z., Han, Z.: An efficient authenticated group key agreement protocol. In: 41st Annual IEEE International Carnahan Conference on Security Technology, pp. 250–254 (2007)
13. Joux, A.: A one round protocol for tripartite Diffie-Hellman. In: Bosma, W. (ed.) ANTS 2000. LNCS, vol. 1838, pp. 385–394. Springer, Heidelberg (2000)
14. Kim, J.-S., Kim, H.-C., Ha, K.-J., Yoo, K.-Y.: One Round Identity-Based Authenticated Conference Key Agreement Protocol. In: Freire, M.M., Chemouil, P., Lorenz, P., Gravey, A. (eds.) ECUMN 2004. LNCS, vol. 3262, pp. 407–416. Springer, Heidelberg (2004)

15. Lee, H.M., Ha, K.J., Ku, K.-M.: ID-based Multi-party Authenticated Key Agreement Protocols from Multilinear Forms. In: Zhou, J., López, J., Deng, R.H., Bao, F. (eds.) ISC 2005. LNCS, vol. 3650, pp. 104–117. Springer, Heidelberg (2005)
16. Li, L.C., Tsai, Y.P., Liu, R.S.: A Novel ID-based Authenticated Group Key Agreement Protocol Using Bilinear Pairings. In: International Conference on Wireless and Optical Communication Networks - WOCN 2008. IEEE Press (2008)
17. Manulis, M.: Survey on Security Requirements and Models for Group Key Exchange. Technical Report TR-HGI-2006-002, Ruhr-Universität Bochum (2008)
18. Shamir, A.: Identity-based cryptosystems and signature schemes. In: Blakely, G.R., Chaum, D. (eds.) CRYPTO 1984. LNCS, vol. 196, pp. 47–53. Springer, Heidelberg (1985)
19. Shi, Y., Chen, G., Li, J.: ID-based One Round Authenticated Group Key Agreement Protocol with Bilinear Pairings. In: International Conference on Information Technology: Coding and Computing - ITCC 2005, pp. 757–761 (2005)
20. Singh, M., Prasanna, V.: Energy-optimal and energy-balanced sorting in a single-hop wireless sensor network. In: 1st IEEE International Conference on Pervasive Computing and Comminications (PERCOM 2003), pp. 50–59 (2003)
21. Teng, J.K., Wu, C.K., Tang, C.M.: An ID-based authenticated dynamic group key agreement with optimal round. Science China Information Sciences 55(11), 2542–2554 (2012)
22. Tzeng, W.-G., Tzeng, Z.-J.: Round-Efficient Conference Key Agreement Protocols with Provable Security. In: Okamoto, T. (ed.) ASIACRYPT 2000. LNCS, vol. 1976, pp. 614–627. Springer, Heidelberg (2000)
23. Wu, Q., Mu, Y., Susilo, W., Qin, B., Domingo-Ferrer, J.: Asymmetric Group Key Agreement. In: Joux, A. (ed.) EUROCRYPT 2009. LNCS, vol. 5479, pp. 153–170. Springer, Heidelberg (2009)
24. Xia, M., He, M., Xie, L.: A New ID-based Group Key Agreement Protocol for the Network. Journal of Computational Information Systems 5(6), 1855–1860 (2009)
25. Zaverucha, G.M., Stinson, D.R.: Group Testing and Batch Verification. IACR Cryptology ePrint Archive, Report 2009/240 (2009)
26. Zhang, F., Chen, X.: Attack on two ID-based authenticated group key agreement schemes. IACR Cryptology ePrint Archive, Report 2003/259 (2003)
27. Zhang, F., Chen, X.: Attack on an ID-based authenticated group key agreement scheme from PKC 2004. Information Processing Letters 91, 191–193 (2004)
28. Zhang, L., Wu, Q., Qin, B., Domingo-Ferrer, J.: Identity-Based Authenticated Asymmetric Group Key Agreement Protocol. In: Thai, M.T., Sahni, S. (eds.) COCOON 2010. LNCS, vol. 6196, pp. 510–519. Springer, Heidelberg (2010)
29. Zhou, L., Susilo, W., Mu, Y.: Efficient ID-based Authenticated Group Key Agreement from Bilinear Pairings. In: Cao, J., Stojmenovic, I., Jia, X., Das, S.K. (eds.) MSN 2006. LNCS, vol. 4325, pp. 521–532. Springer, Heidelberg (2006)

Human Identification with Electroencephalogram (EEG) for the Future Network Security

Xu Huang[1], Salahiddin Altahat[1], Dat Tran[1,*], and Li Shutao[2]

[1] Faculty of Education Science Technology & Mathematics,
University of Canberra, Canberra, Australia
{Xu.Huang,Salahiddin.Altahat,Dat.Tran}@Canberra.edu.au
[2] College of Electrical & information Engineering, Hunan University, Changsha, China
shutao_li@yahoo.com.cn

Abstract. Human identification becomes huge demand in particular for the security related areas, in particular for the network security. EEG signals are confidential and hard to imitate, since EEG signals are a reflection of individual-dependent inner mental tasks. Generally speaking, it has several advantages, such as (i) it is confidential as it corresponds to a mental task, (ii) it is very difficult to mimic and (iii) it is almost impossible to steal as the brain activity is sensitive to the stress and the mood of the person, an aggressor cannot force the person to reproduce his/her mental pass-phrase. In this paper we first proposed a novel algorithm to create a spatial pattern of EEG signals obtained from the open public database. In our EEG signal processing, we have analyzed 64-electrode EEG samples for two databases, one is for 45 people and calculate the equivalent root mean square (rms) values for each electrode signal over 1 second period, by which created a 64-value input for each subject. With this neural network (NN) model, our analysis clearly showed that our designed classifier is able to identify all the 45 people correctly (successful rate of 100%) with a mean square error of 2.0334×10^{-7} and the same algorithm applying to the 2nd database with 116 out of 122 people can be fully identified (successful rate of 95.1%) with a mean square error value of 0.00186. We deeply believe that a low complexity, high resolution, effective and efficient is very attractive for the real life applications especially for network security in the foreseeable future.

Keywords: biometric nature, security system, neural network, EEG, signal processing.

1 Introduction

Recently, it is noted that non-invasive brain-computer interface (BCI) becomes very attractive area as it uses a variety of brain signals as input, for example, electroencephalography (EEG), magnetoencephalography (MEG), functional magnetic resonance imaging (fMRI), and near infrared spectroscopy (NIRS). MEG, fMRI, and NIRS are expensive or bulky, and fMRI and NIRS present long time

[*] Corresponding author.

J. Lopez, X. Huang, and R. Sandhu (Eds.): NSS 2013, LNCS 7873, pp. 575–581, 2013.

constants in that they do not measure neural activity cannot be deployed as ambulatory BCI systems.

EEG signals are the signatures of neural activities. They are captured by multiple-electrode EEG machines either from inside the brain, over the cortex under the skull, or certain locations over the scalp, and can be recorded in different formats.

Up to the present, EEG signals have been successfully applied to the research and development of brain-computer interfaces whose main goal is to enhance the communication and control abilities of motor-disabled people [1-5]. Comparing with other biometric features, EEG has several advantages as follows: (a) it is confidential (as it corresponds to a mental task), (b) it is very difficult to mimic (as similar mental tasks are person dependent), (c) it is almost impossible to steal (as the brain activity is sensitive to the stress and the mood of the person, an aggressor cannot force the person to reproduce his/her mental pass-phrase).

In this paper we are building a concept of brain print and assuming that EEG signal alone is able to create a unique pattern for each subject. In other words we are not going to combine any other human feature with EEG signal to identify people. We are considering working on large number of peoples with two public databases and using simple feature extraction and simple classification methods to provide strong evidence that our novel algorithm with EEG signal processing can provide unique patterns to identify people with other human features.

2 Related Works

With a data set of four subjects and 255 EEG trials (subjects were at first with eyes closed) Poulos *et al.* adopted two classification algorithms and obtained the accuracies of around 80% and 95% respectively [1-2]. Paranjape et al. analysed a data set of 40 subjects and 349 EEG trials (subjects were resting with eyes open and closed) and got a classification accuracy of about 80% [3].

Palaniappan and Mandic carried out a personal identification experiment with 102 subjects based on visual evoked potentials and the accuracies were around 95-98% [4]. Marcel and Mill´an got a highest accuracy rate for personal verification of 93.4% [5].

The above early work has played an important role in studying the feasibility of EEG signals for usage in biometrics. However, when learning a classifier, they all adopted only one kind of brain activity.

Recent research on multitask learning indicates that the performance of a main task can be improved by learning related tasks together [6, 7, 14].

An ***authentication*** (or *verification*) system involves confirming or denying the identity claimed by a person (one-to-one matching).

In contrast, an ***identification*** system attempts to establish the identity of a given person out of a closed pool of *N* people (one-to-*N* matching).

Shedeed in [6] used voting scheme for different features extraction methods which are Discrete Fourier Transform and Wavelet Packet Decomposition both with different measures, and used neural network back propagation classifier and it was claimed that it reached an accuracy of 100%, but the number of classes was only three subjects only. Yazdani *et al.* in [7] works on a partial set of the same dataset we worked for visual evoked potentials. They used different features extraction methods which are autoregressive model (AR) model parameters and the peak of power spectrum density (PSD). They also claimed that it reached 100% accuracy over 20 subjects when AR model equal to or greater than 14. They used LDA to reduce features and the K-nearest neighbour (KNN) classifier. However, the proposed method is more complex and the number of subjects is less than what we are considering in this work. Riera *et al.* in [8] select the best five features set among multifeatures preliminary work. They believe that the best five features are AR model, Fourier Transform, Mutual Information, Coherence and Cross Correlation. These features were selected on different channel configuration. The number of the sample was 51 peoples and 36 intruders. They used Fisher's Discriminant Analysis classifier with four different discriminant functions. They reached a performance between 87.5% to 98.1%. Their proposed method is depending on high computation, and the number of subjects considered in this work approximately doubled. Poulus have many contributions in this field all with small number of subjects. The latest one was Poulus *et al.* [9] where they reach a classification rate around 99.5%. Palaniappan [10] used a total of 61 channels to record Visual Evoked potential (VEP) EEG signals from 20 subjects. He used the spectral power for the gamma band (30 – 50) Hz as a feature. The reached average accuracy was 99.06 with a 10 fold cross validation. Also Palaniappan *et al.* in their work in [11] to update the used methods in [3] and test the used methods against larger sample, the result drops to less than 95% when reaching 40 peoples.

3 Proposed Algorithm

In order to make human identification system more effective and efficient, we particularly focus on the simplest algorithm for decreasing the calculations and shorten latency.

In this work we are trying to test the EEG uniqueness over a large number of subjects, and also try to use simpler method for feature extraction to make EEG identification more applicable.

So in this work we shall:

1. use EEG identification method on a large number of subjects to emphasize EEG uniqueness among peoples. This will enhance the opportunity to use EEG identification on large scale, or even to use it as a universal human identity.

2. use relatively low complexity and low computation cost methods in pre-processing and feature extraction, to enhance considering EEG as an online solution for human identification. In this work we tackled the above concerns by using large public database that contains EEG data for (i) 45 people and (ii) 122 people. Also all the processing are only considering rms spatial pattern only to create feature vector which is used for the first time in EEG.

There are many debates about EEG bandwidth and it is noted that significant signals are distributed within lower than 100 Hz, for example Howard *et al.* [2] where they suggest upper limit to gamma in EEG bandwidth to 60Hz. A typical set of EEG signal during a few seconds for an adult brain activity are as shown in Figure 1 [12]. Therefore, in the pre-processing step, all the EEG signals were filtered to get frequencies between 0 and 60 Hz. All frequency components above 60 Hz were disregarded. There shows an example of the effect of the filtration on of the EEG signals. For the extraction of the human feature, the whole processing will only take EEG low pass signals and mapping them into the rms value for each special position or each electrode and the rms value represents active potential of the signal where power of the signal $p(x)$ is directly proportional to the rms value.

We have designed the EEG sample from each electrode is divided into one second time period length signals including 256 values, and the rms values for all the 256 values are calculated with equation (1) then sending them to feature vector. For this case we obtained feature vectors of length 64 rms values that taken from the related electrodes as shown by Figure 1.

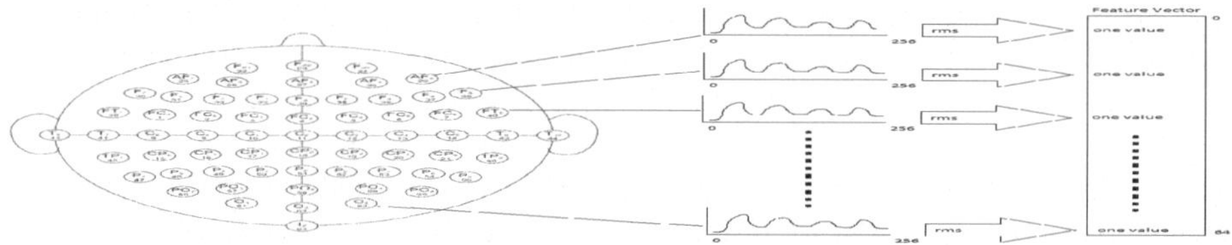

Fig. 1. 64 vectors transformed from corresponding 64 electrodes

A neural network (NN) classifier is designed to classify the obtained data. The NN classifier is feed forward error back propagation network. Training starts from a random weight set. The NN is designed with 64 nodes in the input layer, which is the same number of electrodes. The number of outputs depends on the number of subjects which is 45 for the first experiment and 122 for the second experiment. The network has 45 neurons hidden layer in the first experiment, and 70 neurons hidden layer in the second experiment. In the second experiment which was operated on 122 subjects. We used the MATLAB built in *nntraintool* tool to run the tests. The rms feature vector input was pre-processed by this tool by normalizing the data between [1, −1].

As mentioned in above that the dataset was taken from the public data repository for machine learning [1]. This dataset was collected through a study was performed at the *Neurodynamics Laboratory* of the State University of the New York Health Centre at Brooklyn. This study EEG correlates of genetic predisposition to alcoholism. The dataset contains multiple measurements from 64 electrodes placed on subject's scalps which were sampled at 256 Hz (3.9 ms epoch) for 1 second.

4 Experiments, Results and Discussion

The original data contains 77 alcoholic subjects and 45 control subjects. In the first experiment we consider half the samples available for all 45 control subjects.

The samples were selected randomly. The input layer size is 64 inputs which is the number of rms value for each electrode. The NN back propagation with one hidden layer with a number of neurons equal to the number of outputs (45), and the output layer which represent the number of subjects (45 control peoples). The NN engine by default normalizes the data between 1 and -1 for the input and output. The training stopped when the classifier reached below the minimum gradient which is set to 10^{-6}. Obviously, the results were so promising, and the classifier was able to identify all the 45 peoples correctly, with a mean square error value of 1.98842×10^{-7}. The similar design was used to the second dataset. The target is trying to check if this algorithm has generalization for dealing with other EEG signal. The second database is about 122 people in comparison the first database the size is almost three times as the previous one, which is obvious a good challenge to the designed algorithm. Also this will verify if the rms spatial pattern can be considered as a brain signature or brain print. In the second experiment the input size remain the same which 64 rms inputs for the EEG electrodes. The hidden layer size was increased to be 70 neurons arbitrarily. And the output size is 122 which is the number of peoples. As in the first experiment the NN engine by default normalizes the data between 1 and -1, and the continuous tan sigmoid activation function was used.

Although we consider bigger number of peoples, the results was also promising. The classifier was able to identify 113 peoples correctly out of 122, with a mean square error value of 0.00271. The other nine subjects were clarified the case that the classifier was not able to identify: four of nine were highly confused with other subject in the sample, and five were not identified totally. Figure 2 shows the mean square error and Figure 3 shows the gradient during the training.

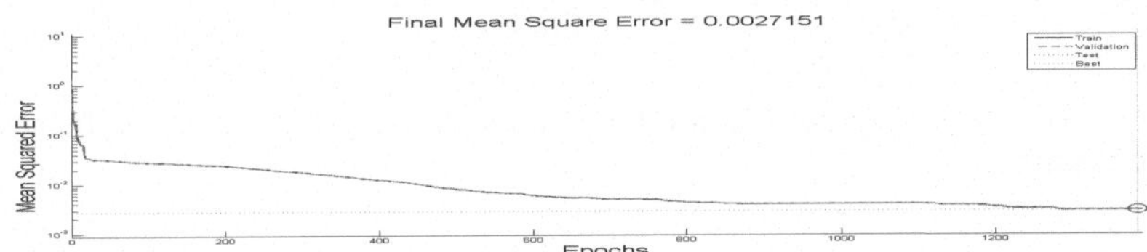

Fig. 2. Mean square errors for the second database, 122 people (subjects) during the training

To enhance the efficiency of the classifier in the second experiment, we add a weighted connection between the input layer and the output layer. The efficiency increases after this enhancement, and the classifier was able to identify 116 peoples correctly out of 122, in other words 95.1% successful rate.

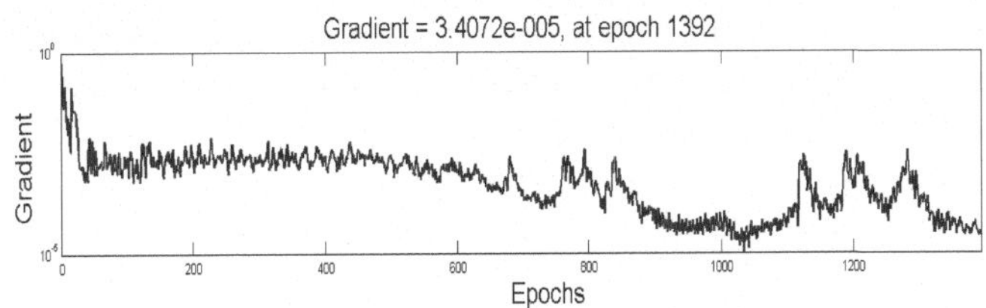

Fig. 3. Gradient for the second database for 122 people (subjects) during the training

The mean square error value was 0.00186. The other six subject that the classifier were not able to identify, four of them were highly confused with other subject in the sample, these four are different than the four in the first part of this experiment. The other two were not identified totally. This last experiment shows that by enhancing the classifier the result might enhance and a better classification rate might be achieved through using the rms spatial pattern as a feature vector. Figure 4 shows the mean square error and Figure 5 shows the gradient during the training of this experiment.

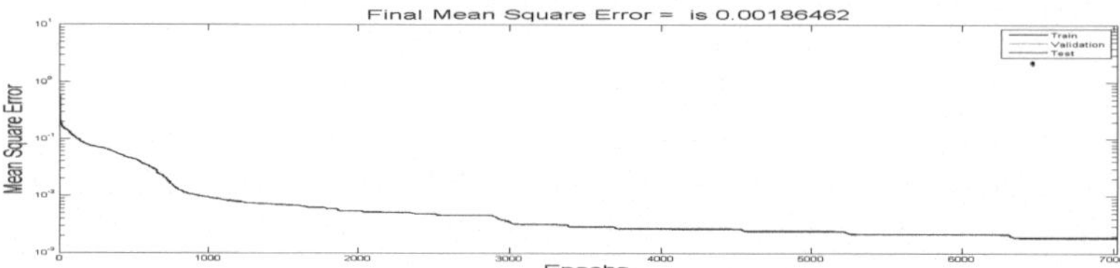

Fig. 4. mean square error for the second database for 122 people (subjects) during the training with enhanced classifier

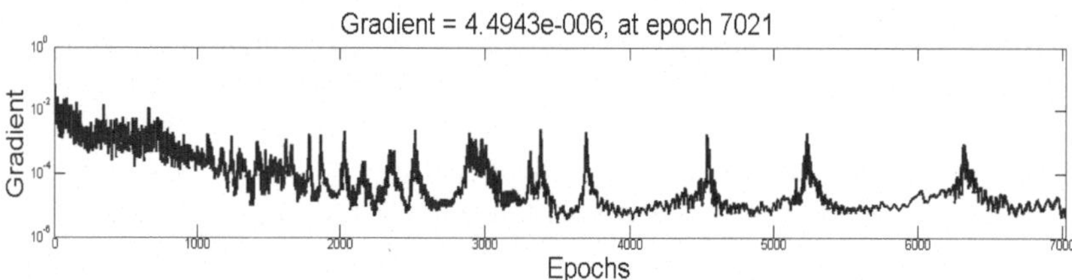

Fig. 5. Gradient for the second database for 122 people (subjects) during the training with enhanced classifier

5 Conclusion

In this paper we have been focusing on one of non-invasive brain computer interface (BCI) signal, a typical variety of brain signals, electroencephalography (EEG) as input to analysis its characteristics. Those characteristics are used to identify the people as other biometrics to recognize and distinguish people based on their physical or behavioral features. As using EEG signals to identify people has some advantages such as it is confidential, it is very difficult to mimic and it is almost impossible to steal, etc. EEG signal processing has drawn great attentions as this paper does. A novel algorithm is presented in this paper. Our designed classifier is able to identify all the 45 people correctly with a mean square error of 2.0334×10^{-7} for the first public open database and the same algorithm applying to the 2nd database with 116 out of 122 people can be fully identified (successful rate of 95.1%) with a mean square error value of 0.00186.

We deeply believe that a low complexity, high resolution, effective and efficient is very attractive for the real life applications become true in the foreseeable future.

Acknowledgment. This project is supported by the Commonwealth of Australia under the Australia-China Science and Research Fund (ACSRF02541).

References

[1] Akyildiz, I.F., Su, W., Sankarasubramaniam, Y., Cayirci, E.: Wireless sensor networks: a survey. Computer Networks 38(4), 393–422 (2002)

[2] Poulos, M., Rangoussi, M., Chrissikopoulos, V., Evangelou, A.: Parametric person identification from the EEG using computational geometry. In: Proceedings of the IEEE International Conference on Electronics, Circuits, and Systems, vol. 2, pp. 1005–1008 (1999)

[3] Paranjape, R., Mahovsky, J., Benedicenti, L., Koles, Z.: The electroencephalogram as a biometrics. In: Proceedings of the Canadian Conference on Electrical and Computer Engineering, vol. 2, pp. 1363–1366 (2001)

[4] Palaniappan, R., Mandic, D.: Biometrics from brain electrical activity: A machine learning approach. IEEE Transactions on Pattern Analysis and Machine Intelligence 29(4), 738–742 (2007)

[5] Marcel, S., del R. Millán, J.: Person authentication using brainwaves (EEG) and maximum a posteriori model adaptation. IEEE Transactions on Pattern Analysis and Machine Intelligence 29(4), 743–748 (2007)

[6] Marcel, S., del R. Millán, J.: Person authentication using brainwaves (EEG) and Maximum a posteriori model adaptation. IEEE Transactions on Pattern Analysis and Machine Intelligence Special Issue on Biometrics (2007)

[7] Shedeed, H.A.: A new method for person identification in a biometric security system based on brain eeg signal processing. In: 2011 World Congress Information and Communication Technologies (WICT), pp. 1205–1210 (December 2011)

[8] Yazdani, A., Roodaki, A., Rezatofighi, S.H., Misaghian, K., Setarehdan, S.K.: Fisher linear discriminant based person identification using visual evoked potential. In: 9th International Conference on Signal Processing, ICSP 2008, pp. 1677–1680 (October 2008)

[9] Riera, A., Soria-Frisch, A., Caparrini, M., Grau, C., Ruffini, G.: Unobtrusive biometric system based on electroenphalogram analysis. EURASIP, J. Adv. Signal Process. (2008)

[10] Poulos, M., Rangoussi, M., Alexandris, N., Evangelou, A.: Person identification from the EEG using nonlinear signal classification. Methods Inf. Med. 41(1), 64–75 (2002)

[11] Palaniappan, R.: Method of identifying individuals using vep signals and neural network. IEE Proceedings-Scince, Measurement and Technology 151(1), 16–20 (2004)

[12] Palaniappan, R., Mandic, D.P.: Eeg based biometric framework for automatic identity verification. J. VLSI Signal Process. 49(2), 243–250 (2007)

[13] Sanei, S., Chambers, J.A.: EEG Signal Processing. Centre of Digital Signal Processing, Cardiff & University, UK. John Wiley & Sons, Ltd. (2007)

[14] Huang, X., Altahat, S., Tran, D., Sharma, D.: Human Identification with Electroencephalogram (EEG) Signal Processing. In: Proceeding of 2012 International Symposium on Communications and Information Technologies (ISCIT), Holiday Inn, Gold Coast, Australia, October 2-5, p. 1026. IEEE catalog No.: CFP12830-USB (2012) ISBN: 978-1-4673-1155-7

Building Better Unsupervised Anomaly Detector with S-Transform

Sirikarn Pukkawanna, Hiroaki Hazeyama,
Youki Kadobayashi, and Suguru Yamaguchi

Nara Institute of Science and Technology
8916-5 Takayama, Ikoma, Nara 630-0192, Japan
{sirikarn-p,hiroa-ha,youki-k,suguru}@is.naist.jp

Abstract. Unsupervised anomaly detection is most widely applicable due to capabilities of detecting known and novel anomalies without prior knowledge. In this paper, we propose an unsupervised anomaly detection method based on time-frequency analysis. We firstly use S-Transform to reveal the frequency characteristics of a network signal. Secondly, heuristics are used for anomaly detection. We evaluate performance of our method on MAWI and DARPA datasets. Furthermore, we compare the results with an unsupervised Wavelet Transform-based anomaly detection method. The results indicate that our method achieves better detection performance compared with the Wavelet Transform-based method.

Keywords: Unsupervised anomaly detection, time-frequency analysis, signal processing, multi-resolution analysis, S-Transform.

1 Introduction

Several unsupervised anomaly detection techniques have been proposed due to limitations of signature-based or learning-based methods, which rely on labeled training data and can not detect unseen anomalies. Unsupervised anomaly detection detects anomalies without labeled data but by assuming that most traffic is normal and the remaining traffic is anomalous [2]. Clustering-based techniques [5, 6] group similar instances and use a distance measurement algorithm to detect outliers. The performance of these techniques depends on the clustering and distance measurement algorithms. [7, 8] use Principle Component Analysis (PCA) to decompose traffic feature distribution into normal and anomalous components. Gaining good results from PCA-based techniques requires proper parameter tuning [11]. [3, 4] apply time-frequency analysis by using Discrete Wavelet Transform (DWT) to reveal anomalies hidden in a network signal. A benefit of the DWT-based techniques is Multi-Resolution Analysis (MRA) which is able to detect various behaviors of anomalies. However, choosing a proper mother wavelet and decomposition level are considerable tasks.

In this paper, we developed an unsupervised anomaly detector based on time-frequency analysis called STAD, which consists of 3 stages: 1) Conversion of

J. Lopez, X. Huang, and R. Sandhu (Eds.): NSS 2013, LNCS 7873, pp. 582–589, 2013.

traffic to signal; 2) S-Transform; and 3) Detection of intense and hidden anomalies. Firstly, a packet stream is converted into network signals. Next, the STAD extracts frequency information of the signals by using S-Transform [1] which is less complex than DWT while preserving benefits of MRA. Finally, anomalies are detected by analysis of the previous outputs using heuristics. We evaluated our STAD with MAWI [12] and DARPA [13] datasets and compared the results with a DWT-based Anomaly detection method [3]. The evaluation results shown that the STAD could detect more anomalies than the DWT-based method in both datasets, especially hidden anomalies.

The rest of this paper is organized as follows. Section 2 describes our proposed anomaly detector. Section 3 describes the evaluation results and discussion. Conclusion and future work are described in Section 4.

2 S-Transform-Based Anomaly Detector (STAD)

In this section, we describe our developed S-Transform-based Anomaly Detector called STAD, which consists of 3 major stages described below.

Conversion of Traffic to Signal. In this stage, STAD converts a packet stream to 6 *network signals* which are typical used for traffic analysis, namely packet rate, bit rate, srcIP rate, dstIP rate, flow rate, and average flow size rate. The average flow size rate is computed by dividing the number of packets by the number of flows seen in 1-second timeslot. Next, the 6 *network signals* are individually normalized by using its mean value.

S-Transform. In this stage, the frequency characteristics of each *network signal* is revealed by using the original S-Transform (ST) [1]. The ST analyzes the *network signal* and stores results in a *ST matrix* of size $m \times n$, where m is the signal's timeslots, n is analyzed frequencies from 0 to $\lfloor m/2 \rfloor$ (Nyquist), and each element is an amplitude. For example, if the duration of the packet stream is 1 minute, thus the *ST matrix* has dimension of 60×30.

Detection of Intense and Hidden Anomalies. The aim of this stage is to detect anomalous timeslots by analysis the *ST matrices.* The pseudocode of this stage is shown in Algorithm 1. Firstly, STAD focuses on detecting intense anomalies by relying on Time Maximum Amplitude (*TMA*), Time Amplitude (*TA*), and Time Variance Amplitude (*TVA*). The *TMA*, *TA*, and *TVA* are vectors of the maximum value, the sum of all values, and the variance of all values in each *ST matrix* column, respectively. In order to detect suspicious timeslots, a threshold α is applied to the *TMA*, *TA*, and *TVA*. A timeslot's value that exceeds the α will be labeled as suspicious. Secondly, STAD detects hidden anomalies by using Frequency Amplitude (*FA*) computed by adding all values of each row of the *ST matrix.* Next, the FA is divided into equally 3 parts, and then each slope angle of each pair of maximum points among the 3 parts is computed. If the angle exceeds a threshold β, the *ST matrix* row vector at number which is equal to the

```
Data: 6 ST matrices Result: anomalous timeslots carrying intense and hidden anomalies
set all elements of lableCount to be 0
foreach STmatrix do
    for STmatrix column t ← 1 to m do          /* initial to detect intense anomalies */
        TMA[t] = max(STmatrix, t);  TA[t] = sum(STmatrix, t);
        TVA[t] = variance(ST matrix, t);
    end
    labelSuspiciousTime(TMA); labelSuspiciousTime(TA); labelSuspiciousTime(TVA);
    for STmatrix row f ← 1 to n do              /* initial to detect hidden anomalies */
        FA[f] = sum(STmatrix, f);
    end
    split FA into equally FA_L, FA_M, and FA_H ;
    degreeLM = slope(max(FA_L), max(FA_M));  degreeMH = slope(max(FA_M), max(FA_H));
    if (degreeLM≥ β) and (max(FA_L>FA_M)) then
        labelSuspiciousTime(STmatrix at row vector max(FA_L));
    end
    if (degreeLM≥ β) and (max(FA_L<FA_M)) then
        labelSuspiciousTime(STmatrix at row vector max(FA_M));
    end
    if (degreeMH≥ β) and (max(FA_M>FA_H)) then
        labelSuspiciousTime(STmatrix at row vector max(FA_M));
    end
    if (degreeMH≥ β) and (max(FA_M<FA_H)) then
        labelSuspiciousTime(STmatrix at row vector max(FA_H));
    end
end
for i ← 1 to m do                                  /* determine anomalous timeslots */
    if (labelCount[i]≥2 then  timeslot t is a anomalous timeslot;
end
funtion labelSuspiciousTime(vector) (  /* function for labelling suspicious timeslots */)
for t ← 1 to m do
    if (vector[t]≥ α) then labelCount[t]++
end
```

Algorithm 1: Intense and hidden anomaly detection algorithm

higher maximum value will be selected for suspicious timeslot detection. Finally, the timeslots which have been labeled as suspicious at least twice are anomalous timeslots. There are 2 parameters in this stage: α for detecting intense anomalies and β for detecting hidden anomalies. In this work, the α is empirically set to 1.8×mean of analyzing vector, and the β is 30.

3 Results and Discussion

We verified the performance of our STAD by testing on MAWI and DARPA'99 datasets and compared the results with an unsupervised Wavelet Transform-based anomaly detection method [3] called WTAD. In this section, we describe the parameter setting in the WTAD including evaluation results and discussion.

Based on the algorithm in [3], the parameters in the WTAD are set as follows. The mother wavelet is *Daubechies-4*, and the *V-part* is constructed by combining Wavelet coefficients of decomposition level 1 and 3. The anomaly detection threshold is set to 1.8×mean of the *V-part*.

3.1 Real Network Traffic

4 backbone traffic traces from MAWI dataset [12] are used to evaluate performance among the STAD and the WTAD, namely traffic data collected on August

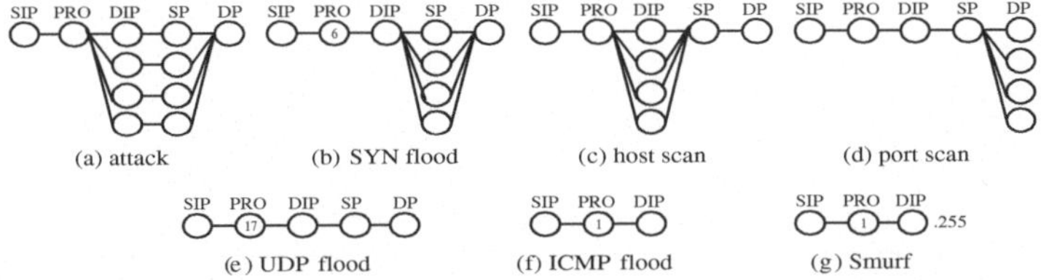

Fig. 1. Graph models presenting communication behavior of malicious activities

Table 1. Total alerts and alerts overlapped with graph-based classifiers on MAWI

Date	STAD		WTAD	
	#alert	#alert overlapped DARPA	#alert	#alert overlapped graph-based
1/Aug/04	119	116	200	195
6/Feb/09	449	443	90	87
6/Apr/09	431	174	180	65
2/Jan/10	425	160	100	41

1, 2004, February 6 and April 6 of 2009, and January 2, 2010. Unfortunately, the MAWI dataset lacks anomaly labels, thus manual analysis and 2 graph-based traffic classifiers [9,10] with 7 graph models (Fig. 1) are used for validation. The graph model needs a certain detection threshold, we thus empirically set the threshold for Fig. 1(a-d) is 20% of average number of flows per host per second. For Fig. 1(e-g) is 20% of average number of packets per host per second.

Table 1 shows the total number of anomalous timeslots detected by the STAD and the WTAD, and the number of overlapping results between the STAD/WTAD with graph-based classifiers. Mostly, the STAD generates much more alerts than the WTAD except on August 1, 2004 which shows similar results. [14] reports that the August 1 trace contains Sasser worm traffic and the graph-based classifiers classify 772 timeslots (from 900 timeslots) as malicious. On the other hand, the STAD and the WTAD similarly report small numbers of alerts, this is due to both detectors considering the large Sasser traffic as normal behavior. This is a weakness of unsupervised anomaly detection. For the results on February 6, 2009, our STAD gives more alerts than the WTAD. Manual analysis found that from the beginning of the trace until about 14:08, a host intermittently opened many connections to VNC port of many hosts. Fig. 2 shows that the STAD can detect those malicious activities similar to the graph-based classifiers, while the WTAD misses them. The spikes shown in Fig. 2 caused by a Dasher worm. Both the STAD and the WTAD can precisely detect that significant changes occurred. Fig. 2 also shows that the graph-based classifiers reports almost all timeslots as anomalous. This is because there are 2 anomalies (Fig. 1(a) and (e)) happened continuously throughout the trace and the graph-based classifiers determine anomalies based on pre-defined models without analysis of behavioral change like unsupervised anomaly detection. Fig. 3 shows the results on April 6, 2009, which consists of several anomalies such as

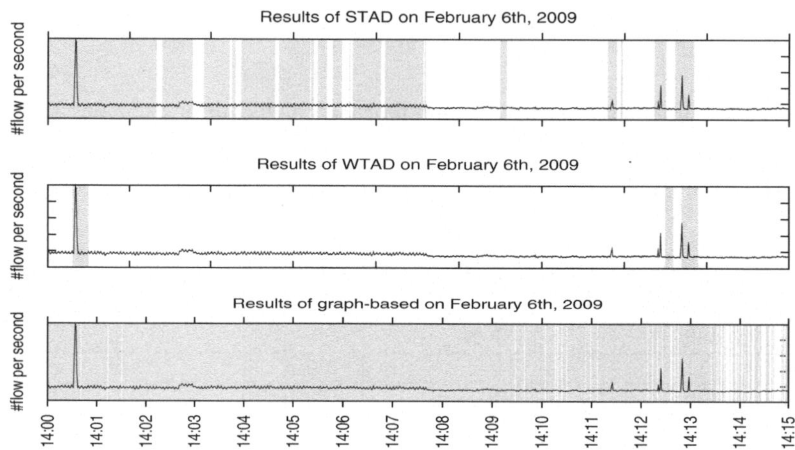

Fig. 2. Detection results of STAD, WTAD, and graph-based traffic classifiers on February 6, 2009 MAWI dataset

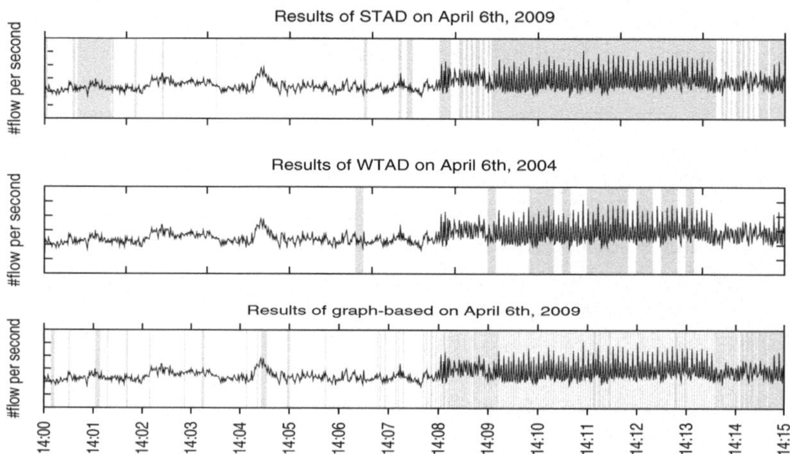

Fig. 3. Detection results of STAD, WTAD, and graph-based traffic classifiers on April 6, 2009, MAWI dataset

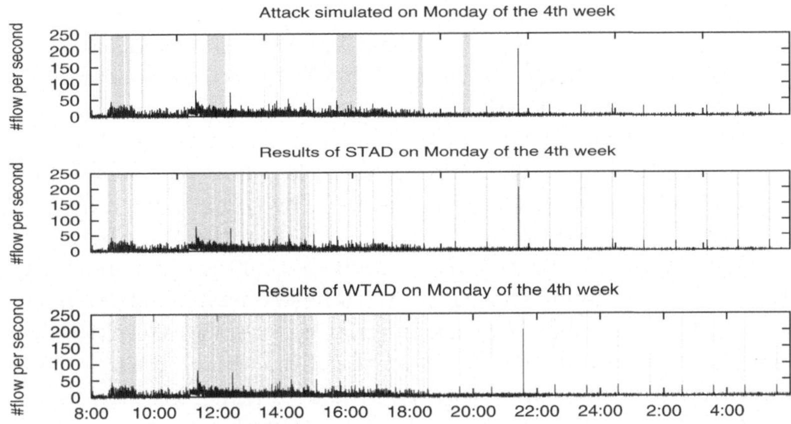

Fig. 4. Actual simulated attack times, detection results of STAD, and WTAD on DARPA'99 attack-present Monday of the 4th week

Table 2. Total alerts and alerts overlapped with DARPA report on DARPA'99

Date	STAD		WTAD	
	#alert	#alert overlapped DARPA	#alert	#alert overlapped DARPA
Monday	13,490	2,525	18,950	4,382
Wednesday	14,610	2,518	18,500	2,221
Thursday	14,350	3,580	20,110	1,721
Friday	12,860	1,600	15,460	1,338

heavy ICMP floods at around 14:01 and a long-lived anomaly displaying behavior like Fig. 1(a) from about 14:08. The results show that the WTAD missed some anomalous instances. By contrast, the STAD misses only some instances at the beginning and the end of the long-lived anomaly. Fig. 3 also shows that the graph-based classifiers do not report that all timeslots from 14:08 are anomalous. It is because that the connection numbers associated with the long-lived anomaly are lower than the threshold in some timeslots. This is a graph-based's drawback that if a host communication is matched against a graph model but the monitoring value (i.e., number of ports) does not exceed the threshold, those hosts will be ignored. The results on January 2, 2012 are similar to the results on April 6, 2009. The better detection performance of the STAD comes from the ability to detect hidden brute force SSH attacks occurred on January 2, 2012.

3.2 Simulated Attack-Present Network Traffic

In order to measure the effectiveness of our STAD, we also test the STAD on the 4th week data of DARPA'99 dataset [13] consisting simulated attacks.

Table 2 shows the total number of anomalous timeslots detected by the STAD and the WTAD, and the number of overlapping results between the

STAD/WTAD with DARPA report. The results show that the STAD mostly can detect more attack timeslots than the WTAD. By looking at the results, we found that the STAD can detect simulated DoS and probe attacks occurred in the traffic traces more precisely than the WTAD. Table 2 also shows that both detectors report significantly more timeslots as anomalous. The reasonable causes are shown in Fig. 4. The first subfigure is a flow rate signal of Monday traffic highlighted simulated attack timeslots. The second and third subfigures are anomalous timeslots reported by the STAD and the WTAD, respectively. Both of them labeled timeslots during 11:00 to 15:00 as anomalous. By using manual inspection, we found that there was a flash crowd anomaly which causes a lot number of connections between internal hosts with external web servers. The second and third subfigures also show that from about 16:00, both detectors labeled few timeslots which do not carry simulated attacks as anomalous at every constant interval. Manual analysis confirms that there was a communication between 2 hosts at constant interval in the traffic trace. One of the hosts use DNS port to create a large number of connections compared with the typical behavior which occurred during 22 hours. Furthermore, both the STAD and the WTAD report a heavy ICMP packet stream originated from external network at around 21:30 (a significant spike) as an anomaly. Traffic data from Monday, Thursday, and Friday also contain flash crowd events and anomalous DNS traffic caused both detectors to report many alerts as shown in Table 2. From These results, we can conclude that the STAD and the WTAD can both detect flash crowd events and some traffic that has deviant behavior, and the STAD is better at detecting more attacks simulated (especially DoS and probe attacks) on DARPA'99 dataset than the WTAD.

4 Conclusion and Future Work

This paper proposed an unsupervised S-Transform-based Anomaly Detector called STAD which is able to detect anomalies by using 2 threshold parameters. We verified the effectiveness of the STAD by testing it on real and simulated traffic from MAWI and DARPA datasets, and by comparing the results with an unsupervised Wavelet Transform-based Anomaly Detector (WTAD). The results indicated that our STAD outperforms the WTAD in terms of detection ability on both datasets. In the future work, we plan to evaluate our STAD in term of false positive. We also plan to investigate the ST-based method's performance by comparing to different anomaly detection techniques and traffic datasets.

References

1. Stockwell, R.G., Mansinha, L., Lowe, R.P.: Localization of the Complex Spectrum: The S-Transform. IEEE Trans. on Sig. Proc. 44(4), 998–1001 (1996)
2. Chandola, V., Banerjee, A., Kumar, V.: Anomaly detection: A Survey. In: ACM Computing Surveys (2009)
3. Barford, P., Kline, J., Plonka, D., Ron, A.: A Signal Analysis of Network Traffic Anomalies. In: IMW (2002)

4. Salagean, M., Firoiu, I.: Anomaly Detection of Network Traffic Based on Analytical Discrete Wavelet Transform. In: COMM (2010)
5. Münz, G., Li, S., Carle, G.: Traffic Anomaly Detection using K-means Clustering. In: GI/ITG-Workshop MMBnet (2007)
6. Portnoy, L., Eskin, E., Stolfo, S.: Intrusion Detection with Unlabeled Data using Clustering. In: CSS Workshop DMSA (2001)
7. Lakhina, A., Crovella, M., Diot, C.: Mining Anomalies using Traffic Feature Distributions. In: SIGCOMM (2005)
8. Callegari, C., Gazzarrini, L., Giordano, S., Pagano, M., Pepe, T.: A Novel PCA-based Network Anomaly Detection. In: ICC (2011)
9. Karagiannis, T., Papagiannaki, K., Faloutsos, M.: BLINC: Multilevel Traffic Classification in the Dark. In: SIGCOMM (2005)
10. Pukkawanna, S., Pongpaibool, P., Visoottiviseth, V.: LD^2: A System for Lightweight Detection of Denial-Of-Service Attacks. In: MILCOM (2008)
11. Ringberg, H., Soule, A., Rexford, J., Diot, C.: Sensitivity of PCA for traffic anomaly detection. In: SIGMETRICS (2007)
12. MAWI Working Group Traffic Archive, `http://mawi.wide.ad.jp/mawi/`
13. Lippmann, R., Haines, J., Fried, D., Korba, J., Das, K.: The 1999 DARPA Off-Line Intrusion Detection. Computer Networks 34(4), 579–595 (2000)
14. MAWILab, `http://www.fukuda-lab.org/mawilab/`

Fault-Tolerant Topology Control Based on Artificial Immune Theory in WMNs

Jing Chen[1], Ruiying Du[1], Li Zhao[1], Chiheng Wang[1], Minghui Zheng[2], and Yang Xiang[3]

[1] School of Computer Wuhan University, 430072
Hubei, China
[2] Department of Computer Science, Hubei University for Nationalities, 445000
Enshi, China
[3] School of Information Technology, Deakin University
Burwood, VIC 3125, Australia

Abstract. With more and more wireless city are constructed completely, the wireless mesh network is widely applied. However, the more applications are serviced in Wireless Mesh Network(WMN), the bigger influence when there is a failure in wireless mesh network. In order to enhance the reliability of WMN, we proposed a Fault-Tolerant topology control algorithm based on Artificial Immune(FTAI). FTAI controls network topology to ensure that the client nodes can maintain *k*-connectivity to the mesh router nodes, as a result, the network can tolerate *k*-1 nodes failure. For optimizing the process, FTAI designs a secondary immunization clonal selection algorithm to accelerate the computing speed. Through the analysis of experimental results, the WMN achieved optimum performance of many aspects in the premise of network fault-tolerant.

Keywords: Index Terms - Artificial Immune Theory, Topology Control, Wireless Mesh Network, Fault Tolerant.

1 Introduction

Wireless Mesh Network (WMN) is a promising network technology. It's able to provide economic and effective network coverage in a great distance scale[1]. The generation of WMNs comes from the development of mobile self-organizing network technology. In order to apply ad hoc wireless multi-hop technology in civilian domains, keep the connection with the Internet, and realize the ubiquitous communication, WMNs emerge as the times require[2]. Now there're numerous researches focused on WMNs, where the main purpose is to cover the shortage of some existing networks including wireless personal area networks (WPANs), wireless local area networks (WLANs) and wireless metropolitan area networks (WMANs) in some aspects[3]. With wide practicability, WMNs are well-suited for home, enterprise, public and any other networks[4].

As WMNs carry an increasing number of applications and services, once something is wrong, the impacts will be large, which indicates the fault-tolerance capacity of a network is really important[5]. Now the study of fault-tolerance is gradually

J. Lopez, X. Huang, and R. Sandhu (Eds.): NSS 2013, LNCS 7873, pp. 590–598, 2013.

becoming a hot spot due to WMN's unlimited potential application value[6]. Thus, topology control is generally needed to keep all the WMN nodes in certain connection even if some nodes break down.

In recent years, in those fields where Modern informatics and biology permeate each other alternately, Artificial Immune System (AIS) inspired by biological immune theory is receiving significant attention of more and more specialists and scholars[7]. The research areas cover optimization technique, data mining, pattern recognition, network security, virus detection, fault diagnosis and control engineering[8]. In this paper we will take the advantage of artificial immune computing optimization, and apply Artificial Immune Theory to topology control in WMNs. In order to realize fault-tolerance and optimize the performance of the whole network, we make a reasonable power distribution to the Mesh client nodes, which will result in a self-organized network being established, and k-connectivity to router nodes being achieved.

The remainder of this paper is organized as follows. In Section 2, relative work at home and abroad on topology control for wireless network is introduced. In Section 3, we present a fault-tolerant topology control model and algorithm based on artificial immune in WMNs. In Section 4, some simulation experiments are done to measure the proposed scheme by the analysis of network performance in all aspects. The paper is concluded in Section 5.

2 Relative Work

S.A.Borbash et al proposed Distributed algorithm based on the Relative Neighbourhood Graph (Dist_RNG)[9]. It defines the vertex set as the input and the topology structure of the neighbourhood graph as the output. To get the final outcome, we just need some local information about adjacent nodes. If a node can't reach its nearest neighbour node, its power should be increased. But the main drawback is that the lengths of some sides might have achieved the maximum communication range, which will lead to power consumed quickly. In this way, energy will exhaust too early to remain the topology structure of the whole network.

Xingjia Lu et al proposed Topology Control based on Artificial Immune Algorithm (TCAIA)[10] to solve Minimum Energy Network Connectivity (MENC) issue. In this algorithm, topology control on network nodes is implemented by using Clonal Selection Algorithm (CSA). No matter which node breaks down, the network can keep connected.

K-connected cluster topology control(KCCTC)[11] is composed of generating clusters which includes the selection of clustering nodes, gateway nodes and distributed gateway nodes, adjusting clusters which includes dealing with isolated clusters and adding redundancy to ordinary nodes, and finally scheduling sleeping nodes which includes four states, namely monitoring, cluster-head node sleeping, ordinary node sleeping, and being active.

3 Fault-Tolerant Topology Control Model and Algorithm Based on Artificial Immune

3.1 Network Model Design

Network topology is a weighted graph with direction $G = (V, E, c)$ in the two-dimensional plane, where V is the set of vertices $\{n_1, n_2..., n_N, n_{N+1}, ..., n_{N+M}\}$ and E is the set of edges. When $1 \le i \le N$, n_i refers to Mesh client node, while when $N+1 \le i \le N+M$, n_i refers to Mesh Router node. We define the edge set $E = \{(n_i, n_j) \mid dist(n_i, n_j) \le R_{max}\}$, where $dist()$ denotes the Euclidean distance function. The cost function $c(u,v)$ represents the power requirement of establishing a directional link between Node u and Node v, and it can also be expressed by $c(u, v) = (dist(u, v))^{\alpha}$. We define $\Gamma(n_i)$ as a collection of nodes that can be accessible by Node n_i according to the maximal transmission range $Rmax$, namely $\Gamma(n_i) = \{n_j \in V \mid (n_i, n_j) \in E\}$.

We care about whether Mesh client nodes can reach mesh router nodes instead of how many mesh router nodes can be accessible, so we can merge all the mesh router nodes into only one entity. Provided with a WMN structure model graph $G(V, E, c)$, accordingly we can build a simplified diagram of $G^r(V^r, E^r, c^r)$. Concrete steps are as follows, first replacing all the Mesh router nodes with a single node labeled n^*, which results in $V^r = \{n_1, n_2..., n_N, n^*\}$; The edges between any two mesh client nodes still stay the same, but the edges between mesh client nodes and mesh router nodes have changed into the edges between Mesh client nodes and Node n^*. Figure 1 is the simplified diagram G^r which is converted from Graph G (four mesh client nodes and two Mesh router nodes).

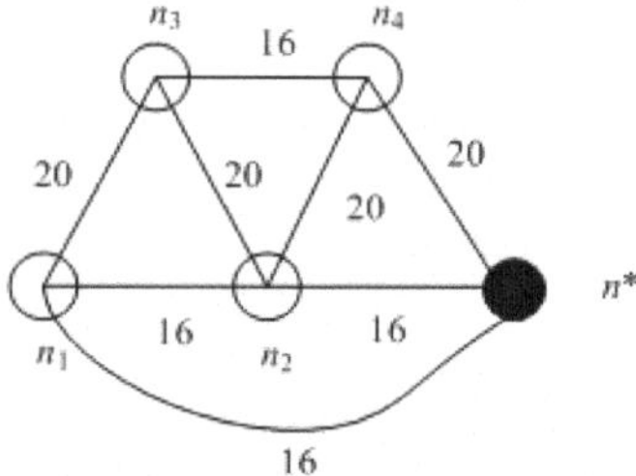

Fig. 1. The simplified structure diagram

3.2 Artificial Immune Model Design

Artificial immune system is an organization of various information processing technology and High-tech technology which develop relying on the principles and mechanism of biological immune system, as well as all kinds of intelligent system in engineering and scientific applications. It is designed for dealing with information and solving problems. In this paper we build an artificial immune model on the basis of WMN structural characteristics, to realize fault-tolerant topology control.

According to biological immune theory, the immune cells that should be selected, cloned, mutated, and then generate antibodies. To simplify the immune model and algorithm, immune cells and antibodies roll into a unique model, in other words, the same element in artificial immune model. The model we present is composed of antigens, antibodies and some operations such as antibody initialization, selection, cloning, mutation, and memory cells generating, etc. Select some antibodies that have a high affinity with antigens, clone, mutate, and then product new antibody population. After several cycles, we will get some solutions satisfying fault-tolerant topology control. In artificial immune model, these are some definitions.

Antigen: The problem is a simplified directional diagram G^r (V^r, E^r, c^r) where E^r is the set of edges within the maximum transmission range.

Antibody: all the answers to the immune model problem, namely to allocate power for each node in G^r. It can be expressed as $Ab = (p_1, p_2 \ldots p_n)$. According to the power allocated to each node, we can get the final network topology. Antibody (solution vector) $Ab_i = (p_{i,1}, p_{i,2} \ldots p_{i,n})$, stands for the i_{th} solution vector in the solution space; $p_{i,j}$, $j \in 1, 2 \ldots n$ stands for the power allocated to the j_{th} node in the i_{th} solution vector. And it is required that $p_j^{min} \le p_j \le p_j^{max}$, where p_j^{min} stands for the transmission power for the j_{th} node n_j to reach its nearest node, p_j^{max} stands for the transmission power for the j_{th} node n_j to reach its farthest node.

Population: the collection of solution vectors $pop_t = \{Ab_1, Ab_2 \ldots Ab_\mu\}$ in the immune model, or the antibody set in the immune clonal algorithm. pop_t suggests the t_{th} generation of population, and μ indicates every generation involves u solution vector.

The Degree of Affinity: the affinity between antibody and antigen in the immune model. Antibodies with high affinity should be selected, either to be cloned and mutated, or to be retained as members of the next generation. Accordingly, it stands for the number of mesh client nodes that have k disjoint paths to Node $n*$, and we set the proportion in all the nodes as a criterion of computing affinity degree; in a solution vector, we should refer to $p = \sum_{i=1}^{n} p_i$ to judge whether the total power of all Mesh client nodes is the smallest. Then the affinity degree function is:

$$f(*) = \theta \cdot \frac{\lambda}{n} + (1-\theta) \cdot \frac{p_{max}}{p + p_{max}} \tag{1}$$

Where * indicates antibody, $0<\theta<1$, λ indicates the number of nodes that keep k-connected, n is the number of all nodes, p indicates the total power of all the nodes, and p_{max} denotes the sum of maximum power.

Clonal Selection: in immune model, select those antibodies with high affinity. And half the population are retained, namely $m = \lfloor \mu/2+1 \rfloor$.

$$pop_t := f(pop_t) = \{f(Ab_1),\ f(Ab_2)\ldots f(Ab_\mu)\} \tag{2}$$

Clonal Propagation: in immunity model, antibodies with high affinity realize self-replication at a certain rate. The representation is :

$$\varphi(Ab) = \lfloor 10 \cdot [f(*)]^2 \rfloor \cdot Ab \tag{3}$$

Where φ is the clonal propagation function, m is the number of antibodies reproduced. Defining cluster as temporary population, it can be expressed:

$$cluster := \varphi(pop_t) = \{\varphi(Ab_1),\ \varphi(Ab_2)\ldots\} \tag{4}$$

Mutation Operation: in immune model, antibodies mutate after clonal propagation at a certain probability θ which is related to the affinity degree and produce new antibodies. Antibody $Ab = (p_1, p_2 \ldots p_i \ldots p_n)$ mutates into $Ab' = (p_1, p_2 \ldots pi' \ldots p_n)$, which can be described as $Ab' = \eta(Ab)$, where η is the mutation function. At every turn, mutation just occurs to a single node which is randomly decided. On the one hand, mutation is good to population variety and evolution, on the other hand, it may contribute to degeneration. Since the variation range can't exceed R_{max} in conventional clonal selection algorithms, we make some improvements. After altered, the minimal power need to keep the node k-connected, and the maximum one can be the minimum that can maintain connectivity with the farthest node. In this way can power varies in a small range, which promotes a faster convergence in power allocation. Thus, we can get better antibodies more quickly. The mutation function is :

$$cluster' := \eta(cluster) = \{\eta(Ab_1)\ ,\ \eta(Ab_2)\ldots\} \tag{5}$$

Immune Selection: After antibodies clone, propagate and mutate, we can select those qualified antibodies by immune selection function ψ. *cluster*' is the temporary population. A formal definition of this function is as follows:

$$pop_t := \psi(cluster') = \{\psi(Ab_1),\ \ \psi(Ab_2)\ldots\} \tag{6}$$

3.3 Fault-Tolerant Topology Control Algorithm Design Based on Artificial Immune

This paper plans to improve immune clonal selection algorithm, and takes advantage of the fact that memory cells respond quickly to antigen in the secondary immunization. Thus, the algorithm can not only assign power to the initial WMN nodes and maintain the connectivity, but also recover the connectivity and keep fault-tolerant as it was before, when network topology structure changes as a result of some nodes wrong or token.

Immune clonal selection algorithm is mainly used for the first antigen intrusion. But it ignores the response the immune system makes during the re-invasion of the same antigen or similar antigen.

Supposing something is wrong with Node n_i, the paths that go through Node n_i won't exist any more. Fig.2 shows the change of some network links.

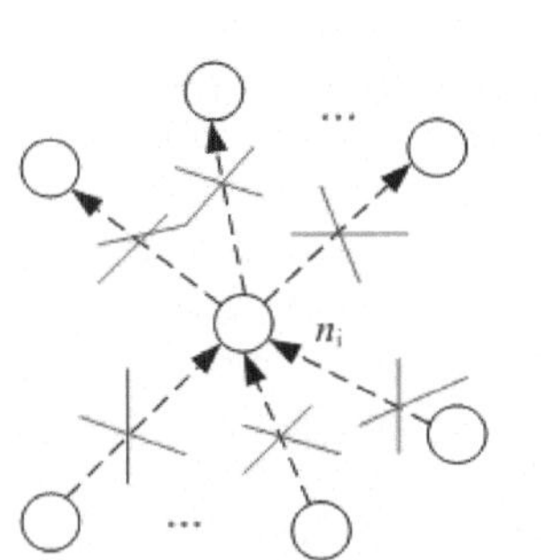

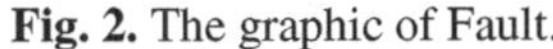

Fig. 2. The graphic of Fault.

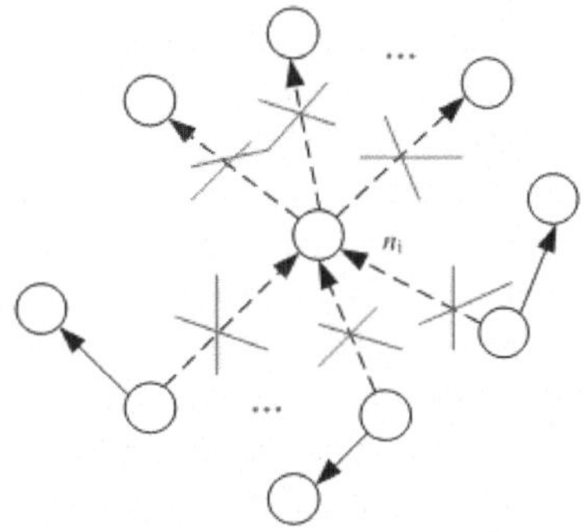

Fig. 3. The graphic of fault recovery

Algorithm 1. The pseudo-code improved immune clonal selection algorithm

Input:
directed graph of network structure, Ag

Output:
power allocated for all the nodes in the graph, Ab

$flag$: = 0, $count$: = 0;
IF (antigen's secondary invasion) **THEN** $flag$: = 1;
//whether antigen invades for the second time
END IF
IF ($flag$ = 0) **THEN** $pop_0 = \{Ab_1, Ab_2 \ldots Ab_\mu\}$;
//antibody initialization (allocate power randomly)
ELSE IF ($flag$=1) **THEN** $pop_0 = \{\text{memory cells} \ldots Ab_\mu\}$
END IF
WHILE (no existence of optimal antibody) **DO**
$pop_{count} := f(pop_{count}) = \{f(Ab_1), f(Ab_2) \ldots f(Ab_\mu)\}$;
//Clonal selection (to select the optimum power allocation)
$cluster := \varphi(pop_{count}) = \{\varphi(Ab_1), \varphi(Ab_2) \ldots \varphi(Ab_m)\}$;
//Clonal propagation (power allocation of cloned nodes)
$cluster' := \eta(cluster) = \{\eta(Ab_1), \eta(Ab_2) \ldots\}$;
//Mutation operation (power allocation of mutated nodes)
$pop_{count} := \{ pop_{count}, \psi(cluster') = \{\psi(Ab_1), \psi(Ab_2) \ldots\}\}$;
//Immune selection (select satisfactory power allocation)
IF $pop_{count} < \mu$ **THEN** $pop_{count} := \{ pop_{count} \ldots Ab_\mu\}$;
//complement random antibodies (power)
END IF
$count := count + 1$;
END WHILE

In the situation above, we just need to re-allocate larger power to the nodes mentioned above, which will help them rebuild a connection with other nearby nodes and return to the state of being k-connected, as well as keep the character of allowing errors on k-1 nodes. Of course, it only goes for the nodes that have lost k-connectivity, other than each one impacted. If the node still keeps k-connectivity, there is no need in altering its power. In Fig.3, a fault recovery after increasing power is depicted.

In this paper the algorithm is designed to redistribute power to all vertexes in the graph Gr, not only make them to maintain K connectivity to n*, but also make the total node power relatively small. Then it is required for the output of power distribution vector solution. This paper proposes an improved immune clone selection algorithm, and the core idea is that in the secondary immunization, due to memory cells with high affinity, a rapid reaction to another invasion of the antigens can be made, and in a short period of time better antibodies can be achieved by immune procedure, so that each Mesh client node's connectivity to Mesh router nodes can be quickly recovered. The pseudo-code of improved immune clonal selection algorithm is as follows:

4 The Experimental Results and Analysis

In order to evaluate the performance of FTAI in network topology control, this paper uses C++ programming to simulate the power distribution of the Mesh client nodes, and then make a comparative analysis of the experimental results.

4.1 Parameter Setting

If the communication range between Mesh router nodes is large enough, reliable connection can be ensured between them, however, the maximum transmission range of Mesh client nodes will be subject to certain restrictions. In this paper we assume that each node remains stationary, not moved once deployed. Particular parameter settings in the simulation process are as shown in table 1.

Table 1. Algorithm parameters

Parameter	value
Power dissipation coefficient α	2
K-connectivity degree	2
Mesh client node number N	20～40
Mesh router node number M	4
The maximum transmission range R_{max}	25m
Antibody population size μ	100～200
Selected clonal population size	0.33μ, 0.5μ, 0.66μ
Mutation probability θ	0.1

4.2 Performance Analysis

This chapter aims at simulating FTAI, and comparing it with the TCAIA[12] in all aspects of performance. Mainly due to the following several aspects the algorithms are verified:

1. When the Mesh client node number changes, the change of total power;
2. When the Mesh client node number changes, the change of the maximum power;

3. When the population size changes, the change of cloning, mutation, selection cycle numbers.

In order to observe how the total power changes when the Mesh client node number changes, we set up five circumstances in which the number is set 20, 25, 30, 35, 40 respectively, the population size 150, the retaining population size during clonal selection 0.5 μ. After repeated simulation and the average value is as shown as in Figure 4:

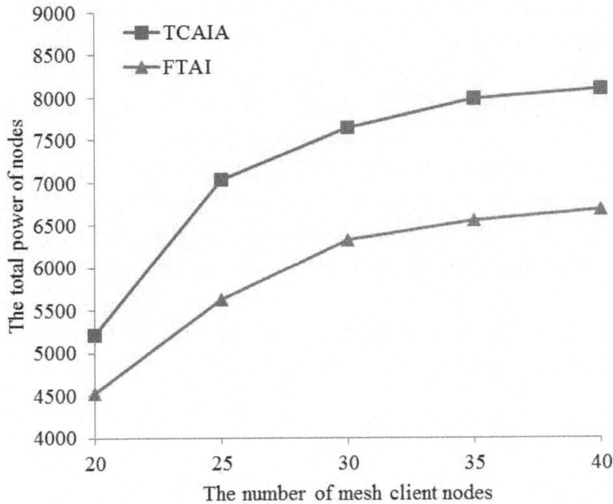

Fig. 4. The total power with different number of mesh client nodes

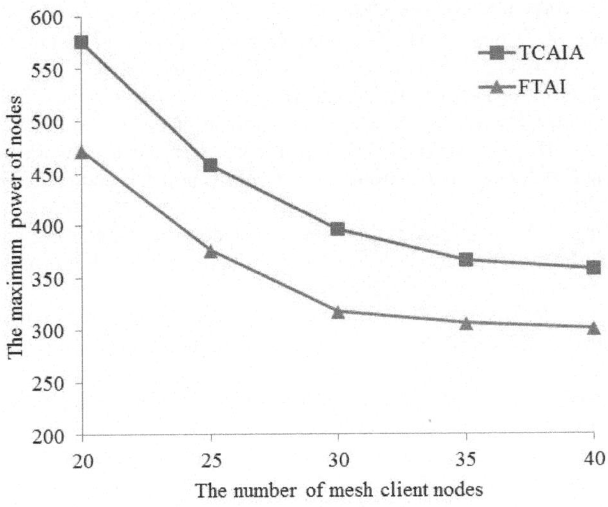

Fig. 5. The maximum power with different number of mesh client nodes

And when the Mesh client node number changes, how about the change of the maximum power? The circumstances we set up before also apply here. As well, the average value is as shown as in Figure 5.

5 Conclusion

WMN has a wide range of applications in households, enterprises and public places, once it goes wrong, communication will be seriously affected. Thus, fault-tolerant issue should be taken into consideration in network topology control. This paper takes advantage of artificial immune algorithm on solving the optimization problem, use an improved immune clonal selection algorithm to accomplish an optimal power allocation for each network nodes, and realize network topology control through changing the power level of WMN client nodes. In this way, better capabilities can be achieved. Mesh client nodes can maintain a certain connectivity to mesh router nodes, which achieves the purpose of being fault-tolerant. In the future work, we will focus on further improving the artificial immune model and algorithm, to make them more efficient and practical.

Acknowledgement. This work was partially supported by the National Natural Science Foundation of China under Grant No. 61272451, 61173175, 61272405.

References

1. Moraes, R., Ribeiro, C., Duhamel, C.: Optimal Solutions for Fault-tolerant Topology Control in Wireless Ad hoc Networks. IEEE Transactions on Wireless Communications 8(12), 1106–1109 (2012)
2. Chen, J., Du, R., Zhang, H.: Intrusion Detection Model Based on Incomplete Information Game in Wireless Mesh Networks. China Communication 9(10), 23–32 (2012)
3. Zhang, T., Yang, K., Chen, H.-H.: Topology Control for Service-Oriented Wireless Mesh Networks. IEEE Wireless Communications, 64–71 (August 2009)
4. Wen, J.: Wireless mesh network structural design on modern campus. 2009 International Forum on Computer Science-Technology and Applications 2, 127–129 (2009)
5. Wang, N., Wang, H.: A security architecture for wireless mesh network. In: International Conference on Challenges in Environmental Science and Computer Engineering, vol. 2, pp. 263–266 (2010)
6. Peng, M., Wang, Y.: Joint optimisation for power control, scheduling and routing algorithms in the infrastructure wireless mesh network. International Journal of Ad Hoc and Ubiquitous Computing 3, 122–131 (2008)
7. Gong, T., Cai, Z.: Robustness Reducing Model of Distributed Artificial Immune System. In: Third International Con-ference on Natural Computation (ICNC 2007), vol. 38, pp. 956–961 (2007)
8. Zheng, J., Chen, Y., Zhang, W.: A Survey of Artificial immune application. Artif. Intell. Rev. 34, 19–34 (2010)
9. Wang, L.: A Fault Tolerant Topology Control Algorithm for Large-scale Sensor Networks. In: Eighth International Conference on Parallel and Distributed Computing, Applications and Technologies, pp. 407–412 (2007)
10. Li, N., Hou, J.C., Sha, L.: Design and Analysis of an MST-Based Topology Control Algorithm. In: Proc. of IEEE INFOCOM, pp. 1702–1712 (2003)
11. Meng, Z.: Fault Tolerant Topology Control for Clustered Wireless Sensor Networks. IEEE

Virtually Reconfigurable Secure Wireless Networks Using Broadcast Tokens

Kannan Karthik

Department of Electronics and Electrical Engineering,
Indian Institute of Technology Guwahati,
Guwahati, Assam, 781039, India
{k.karthik}@iitg.ernet.in

Abstract. Secure multicast in a wireless network is possible only if subsets of nodes share different sets of encryption keys. In this paper we propose a key protection and release mechanism based on broadcast tokens, where each node is equipped with protected shares of several encryption keys (node-share) which can be unlocked only when the broadcast tokens arrive. If the node-shares are different for different nodes, each broadcast token could unlock a different set of keys in each node. This makes the network reconfigurable as the information shared between various nodes will change with the accumulation of each new token. A non-perfect secret sharing scheme has been used construct the node-shares and tokens based on a carefully designed codebook which must satisfy certain rules to ensure that the un-encrypted broadcast tokens and the node-shares do not leak the encryption keys. Construction for a three node re-configurable network is discussed under collusion-free conditions.

Keywords: Reconfigurable, Wireless networks, Broadcast, Key protection, Tokens, MIX-SPLIT, Non-perfect secret sharing.

1 Introduction

In any wireless sensor network, there arises a need to create secure virtual multicast connections either between subsets of nodes and/or dedicated unicast links between each of the nodes and the centre C. These secure connections are required to preserve confidentiality of the messages exchanged between the nodes. Any secure connection, requires the sharing of an encryption key, which can be pre-distributed by the centre at the time of forming the network and registering new nodes. Alternatively the centre may facilitate the generation of keys in a distributed fashion between several clusters of nodes. Key distribution mechanisms can be broadly classified into the following types:

Static direct key pre-distribution: In this framework the centre selects several subsets of keys from a large pool and embeds them in each of the nodes. Assignment of keys to the nodes can be done through random selection [1] [2] or

J. Lopez, X. Huang, and R. Sandhu (Eds.): NSS 2013, LNCS 7873, pp. 599–606, 2013.

deterministically based on combinatorial designs [3]. The main problem with static key pre-distribution is that the associations between nodes are static.

Dynamic and distributed key pre-distribution: By shifting the computation and key establishment between the nodes, the associations can be made dynamic. Key exhanges between pairs (or even clusters) of nodes are possible through public/private-key matrix constructions and protocols [4] [5]. Shared key computation is also possible through polynomial based key-sharing approaches [6][7]. Although these approaches are distributed and can be made network adaptive, the computational complexity associated with the generation of shares of the keys or public/private key fragments is expected to be large and may also require several exchanges of messages between the nodes.

Broadcast encryption and key management: The main idea here is to communicate a secret to a privileged group of nodes over a broadcast channel, without using any asymmetric key protocols. In Fiat et al. [8], k-resilient schemes were proposed, such that, k (or smaller) subset of nodes cannot reconstruct the *common group key* of a non-intersecting subset of nodes. The exchange is not possible unless each node is provided with private information such as a set of key encryption keys (KEKs) from a hierarchy of KEKs [9] [10]. There are two problems with this framework: (i) Group associations must be confined to a hierarchical structure to ensure efficient communication of the encrypted group keys, (ii) Multiple group keys can be delivered only at an increased communication cost.

Proposed model for key protection and release based on broadcast tokens: Each wireless node in this model is equipped with a protected share (node-share) of an encryption key set. However this stand alone node-share is of no use to the node, since the keys remain locked. When the centre releases a specific broadcast token, the combination *(token + node-share)* helps release some of the encryption keys. If the shares stored in different nodes are different, different sets of keys will be released in each node when the broadcast token is fused. Thus, the creation of a virtual multicast/unicast connection would depend on which set of keys are *exclusively* shared amongst the nodes. Several such inter-connections will be created upon fusion with the broadcast token in a *distributed fashion.* The evolution of this centre driven re-configurable network will depend on the design of the node-shares and the broadcast tokens. There are thus two reasons for introducing this form of key-protection: (i) To confine and control the virtual re-configurability of the network with the help of centre driven broadcast tokens, (ii) To restrict the damage incurred due to key information leakage when selective nodes are compromised.

In Section. 2 we discuss the framework for the proposed model. A construction methodology using a non-perfect secret sharing scheme called MIX-SPLIT is presented in Section. 3. Finally the codebook design for a 3-node system along with some analysis is presented in Section. 4.

2 Proposed Model Setting for Distributed Key Release

Consider a centre C and set of n wireless nodes $Node-1, Node-2, ...$, each of which, is in the listening range of C. Any message transmitted by any one of the nodes $Node-i$ (or the centre), can be tapped by all other nodes. Simultaneous broadcasts initiated by multiple nodes, is possible through orthogonal frequency division multiplexing. The mode of communication is always broadcast. The concern however in a broadcast channel, is the possibility that there could be several eavesdropping nodes who are not a part of the original space and could be tuning into the messages broadcasted. The centre generates a block of keys $\mathbb{K} = \{\bar{K}_1, \bar{K}_2, ..., \bar{K}_v\}$ and produces a set of shares $SH_1, SH_2, ..., SH_n$ corresponding to each node. Each share SH_i meant for $Node-i$ is self-contained i.e. has necessary information regarding all v keys, however this information is designed to be extracted only on a need to know basis. This information extraction can be triggered by the release of some carefully designed broadcast messages by the centre, which we may call as, broadcast tokens $\bar{T}$. Each broadcast token when fused with the share stored in a certain node $Node-i$, could help release a subset of keys which we represent by the set $\mathbb{SEC}_i \subseteq \mathbb{K}$. This set $\mathbb{SEC}_i$ is defined as the secret in the possession of $Node-i$ (some subset of $\mathbb{K}$), which is unlocked when a particular broadcast token $\bar{T}$ is fused with SH_i. All broadcast tokens sent by the centre are transmitted in the un-encrypted form.

Since different sets of keys $\mathbb{SEC}_i$ are released at different nodes, the fusion of the broadcast token may lead to the creation of several shared secrets (keys) amongst different clusters of nodes, which can be used for secure multicast. When the broadcast token is changed, the key configuration in each node also changes. Since the key configuration influences the virtual connectivity of the nodes, this will also influence the topology of the network.

3 Joint Construction of the Shares and Broadcast Tokens

The shares and broadcast tokens are created using non-perfect secret sharing scheme called MIX-SPLIT [11], [12] as follows:

Partitioning and Forming the Homogenous Block

Let $\bar{K}_1, \bar{K}_2, .., \bar{K}_v$ be v L_p-bit key strings. These strings are first concatenated and then shuffled to form a homogeneous block $\bar{X} = [x_1, x_2, .., x_L]$ of length $L = L_p \times v$ bits. Let $P = \{1, 2, 3, ..., L\}$ be the set of all possible bit-positions within the block $\bar{X}$. When the key-strings disperse, they occupy a certain group of positions within the homogeneous block, which, we define as a hidden *Partition*. There will be exactly v disjoint and equal length partitions $P_1, P_2, ..., P_v$ of length L_p such that $P = P_1 \cup P_2 \cup ..P_v$. From $\bar{X}$ another sequence $\bar{Y}$ is derived as $\bar{Y} = BIT\_CMP[\bar{X}]$, where, $BIT\_CMP[\,]$ is the complement of a binary string.

Mixing and Splitting $(\bar{X}, \bar{Y})$ into Node-Shares and Broadcast Tokens

A *macro-mixing* of the fragments of $(\bar{X}, \bar{Y})$ is done to produce m preliminary shares of the key block $\mathbb{S} = \{\bar{S}_1, \bar{S}_2, ..., \bar{S}_m\}$, a subset of which form the node-shares $SH_i, i = 1, 2, ..., n$ with $SH_i \subseteq \mathbb{S}$ and the others form broadcast tokens $\bar{T}_i, i = 1, 2, 3, ..., t$. Each of the preliminary shares can be written as,

$$\bar{S}_i = (\bar{S}_{i1}||\bar{S}_{i2}||...||\bar{S}_{iv}) \tag{1}$$

where, the sub-sequence $\bar{S}_{ij}$ is chosen according to a pre-designed codebook. The share inheritance is represented by the relation,

$$\begin{aligned} \bar{S}_{ij} &= \bar{X}(P_j) \text{ if } c_{i,j} = 1 \\ \bar{S}_{ij} &= \bar{Y}(P_j) \text{ if } c_{i,j} = 0 \end{aligned} \tag{2}$$

The binary value $c_{i,j} \in \{0, 1\}$ is a part of the codebook,

$$\mathbf{C} = \begin{pmatrix} c_{1,1} & c_{1,2} & \cdots & c_{1,v} \\ \cdots & \cdots & \cdots & \cdots \\ c_{m,1} & c_{m,2} & \cdots & c_{m,v} \end{pmatrix} = \begin{pmatrix} \mathbf{N} \\ \hline \mathbf{T} \end{pmatrix} \tag{3}$$

with m representing the number of shares and v the number of partitions (or number of keys). Thus each preliminary share $\bar{S}_i$ can be labeled as a v-bit codeword. The design of the node-shares and the tokens heavily relies on the structure of the codebook, which is partitioned into two parts, where, the $t \times v$ matrix $\mathbf{T}$ represents the t broadcast tokens and the $(m - t) \times v$ matrix $\mathbf{N}$ is used to form the node-shares $SH_i, i = 1, 2, .., n$.

Design Rules for Retrieval of Fragments of $\bar{X}$

All the v keys are contained in each of the shares defined by the codebook $\mathbf{C}$. An extraction of a subset of these keys, contained in the partitions of $\bar{X}$ is possible, by stacking selective shares one above the other [12]. Rules for conditional visibility and invisibility of the partitions (and subsequently the unlocking of the keys) are discussed in detail in [12] and have been re-stated here for completeness. If $\mathbf{A}$ is an $r \times v$ codebook containing a stack of r preliminary shares designed using the previous two steps, the following rules apply:
Rule 1: Complementary and repetitive columns lead to inseparable partitions
Rule 2: Rowsampling of a complementary pattern is complementary
Rule 3: Single share is always mixed (no partitions visible)
Rule 4: Atleast one partition becomes visible if a column is distinct

4 Codebook Design for a 3-Node System

Consider the design of the codebook for a reconfigurable 3-node system. Let the node share matrix be given by,

$$\mathbf{N} = \begin{pmatrix} 1\,0\,1\,0\,0\,1 \\ 1\,0\,0\,1\,1\,0 \\ 0\,1\,1\,0\,1\,0 \end{pmatrix} \tag{4}$$

Observe that every column in this codebook has a bit-complementary counterpart. Hence this node share matrix satisfies *Rule-1*. This implies that none of the partitions will be visible, even if all these preliminary shares are stacked one above the other. Using this node matrix **N** we generate the respective node shares SH_1, SH_2 and SH_3 as follows:

$$SH_1 = \begin{pmatrix} 1\,0\,1\,0\,0\,1 \\ 1\,0\,0\,1\,1\,0 \end{pmatrix} ; SH_2 = \begin{pmatrix} 1\,0\,1\,0\,0\,1 \\ 0\,1\,1\,0\,1\,0 \end{pmatrix} ; SH_3 = \begin{pmatrix} 1\,0\,0\,1\,1\,0 \\ 0\,1\,1\,0\,1\,0 \end{pmatrix} \tag{5}$$

Since the broadcast tokens $\bar{T}_i, i = 1, 2, ..., t$ must not leak any of the keys to the eavesdropper, the token matrix **T** must satisfy *Rule-1*. Since complementary columns were chosen for the node matrix **N**, we shall choose repetitive columns for the token matrix as this will help unlock some of the partitions and release some of the keys. Each token is encoded in the following format:

$$\bar{T} = [z_1\ z_2\ z_3\ z_2\ z_3\ z_1] \tag{6}$$

Observe here that bit-1 repeats as bit-6, bit-2 as bit-4 and bit-3 as bit-5 and $z_1, z_2, z_3 \in \{0, 1\}$. Since z_1, z_2, z_3 can be independently chosen the total number of unique tokens which satisfy *Rule-1* are $2^3 = 8$. However, since bit-complementary tokens do not alter the stack relation, they are redundant and will not add to the topological change in the network. Thus bit-complementary versions of the tokens need not be used. The number of useful tokens which will contribute to the topological change are $t = 2^2 = 4$. The token matrix is,

$$\mathbf{T} = \begin{pmatrix} \bar{T}_1 \\ \bar{T}_2 \\ \bar{T}_3 \\ \bar{T}_4 \end{pmatrix} = \begin{pmatrix} 1\,1\,0\,1\,0\,1 \\ 1\,0\,1\,0\,1\,1 \\ 1\,1\,1\,1\,1\,1 \\ 1\,0\,0\,0\,0\,1 \end{pmatrix} \tag{7}$$

We will assume a collusion free environment where the nodes do not combine their shares with other nodes. Under these circumstances the only information that is available to all the nodes are the transmitted broadcast tokens $\bar{T}_i$. When the token $\bar{T}_1$ is received, each $Node - i$ stacks this on top of the share set already present inside i.e. $SH_i, i = 1, 2, 3$. The results are shown in Fig. 1. Upon the fusion of SH_1 and $\bar{T}_1$, there are four distinct stack equations:

$$\begin{bmatrix} b \\ b \\ b \end{bmatrix} \quad \begin{bmatrix} b \\ \bar{b} \\ \bar{b} \end{bmatrix} \quad \begin{bmatrix} \bar{b} \\ b \\ \bar{b} \end{bmatrix} \quad \begin{bmatrix} b \\ b \\ \bar{b} \end{bmatrix} \tag{8}$$

The third stack equation is shared by columns 3 and 4 while the fourth stack equation is shared by columns 5 and 6, as a result of which the partitions P_3, P_4, P_5, P_6 remain in the mixed form as $P_3 \cup P_4$ and $P_5 \cup P_6$ respectively. Hence the keys $\bar{K}_3, \bar{K}_4, \bar{K}_5, \bar{K}_6$ cannot be unlocked even after stacking $\bar{T}_1$. However, the first and second stack equations are distinct, revealing the partitions P_1 and P_2 and subsequently the keys $\bar{K}_1$ and $\bar{K}_2$. Thus, $Node - 1$ acquires access to keys $[\bar{K}_1, \bar{K}_2]$ after receiving the broadcast token $\bar{T}_1$ (Fig. 1(a)). Continuing the analysis in a similar fashion one can show that nodes 2 and 3 acquire access to key $\bar{K}_2$ only (Fig. 1(b,c)). Since the shares stored at different nodes are different, the same broadcast token may release different sets of keys in different nodes. With every successive broadcast token there will be an addition to the stack and hence more keys will be released at the nodes. The keys available at the nodes at each stage (time slot) are shown in Table. 1.

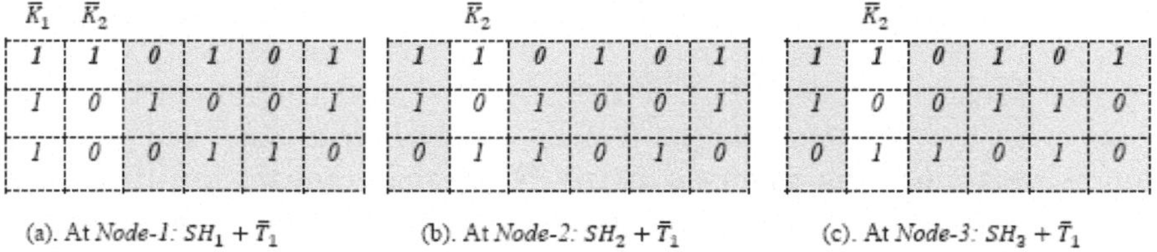

Fig. 1. Keys released when the broadcast token $\bar{T}_1$ is received and stacked on top of SH_1, SH_2 and SH_3 respectively at the three nodes

Table 1. Keys released at the nodes when broadcast tokens $\bar{T}_1, \bar{T}_2, \bar{T}_3, \bar{T}_4$ are received

Time-slot	Tokens	$\mathbb{SEC}_1$	$\mathbb{SEC}_2$	$\mathbb{SEC}_3$
Slot-1	$\bar{T}_1$	$\{\bar{K}_1, \bar{K}_2\}$	$\{\bar{K}_2\}$	$\{\bar{K}_2\}$
Slot-2	$\{\bar{T}_1, \bar{T}_2\}$	$\{\bar{K}_1, \bar{K}_2, \bar{K}_5\}$	$\{\bar{K}_2, \bar{K}_5\}$	$\{\bar{K}_2, \bar{K}_5, \bar{K}_6\}$
Slot-3	$\{\bar{T}_1, \bar{T}_2, \bar{T}_3\}$	$\{\bar{K}_1, \bar{K}_2, \bar{K}_5\}$	$\{\bar{K}_2, \bar{K}_5, \bar{K}_3, \bar{K}_4\}$	$\{\bar{K}_2, \bar{K}_5, \bar{K}_6\}$
Slot-4	$\{\bar{T}_1, \bar{T}_2, \bar{T}_3, \bar{T}_4\}$	$\{\bar{K}_1, \bar{K}_2, \bar{K}_5, \bar{K}_3, \bar{K}_6\}$	$\{\bar{K}_2, \bar{K}_5, \bar{K}_3, \bar{K}_4\}$	$\{\bar{K}_2, \bar{K}_5, \bar{K}_6, \bar{K}_1, \bar{K}_4\}$

4.1 Re-configurability

The impact of the broadcast tokens on the reconfigurability of the virtual network is seen in Fig. 2. With the arrival of each broadcast token a new set of keys could be available at each node, which could be utilized for selective unicast/multicast or broadcast (in case some of the keys are shared with all other nodes). When token $\bar{T}_1$ is broadcast, $Node-1$ extracts keys $[\bar{K}_1, \bar{K}_2$ while nodes 2 and 3 extract key $\bar{K}_2$. Since the key $\bar{K}_2$ is common to all three nodes, it can be used for secure broadcast (shown by the circle around the centre in Fig. 2(a)). On the other hand since key $\bar{K}_1$ is available only with $Node-1$, it can establish a secure virtual unicast link with the centre.

This cumulative process as a result of the reception of all four tokens is shown in Fig. 2(a-d) and is constructed based on the overlapping keys sets determined from Table. 1. Observe that for the first three token transmissions, the number of virtual connections increases linearly (Figs. 2(a,b,c)) and after the reception of $\bar{T}_3$, each node can now have a unique virtual link with the centre (Fig. 2(c)). However, upon the reception of token $\bar{T}_4$ these virtual unicast links are broken and are transformed into node-pair interconnections as seen in Fig. 2(d). This is the byproduct of an increase in the number of shared keys in each of the nodes. In a larger network, this change in the distribution of shared keys, initiated by token accumulation, results in the creation of larger multicast groups.

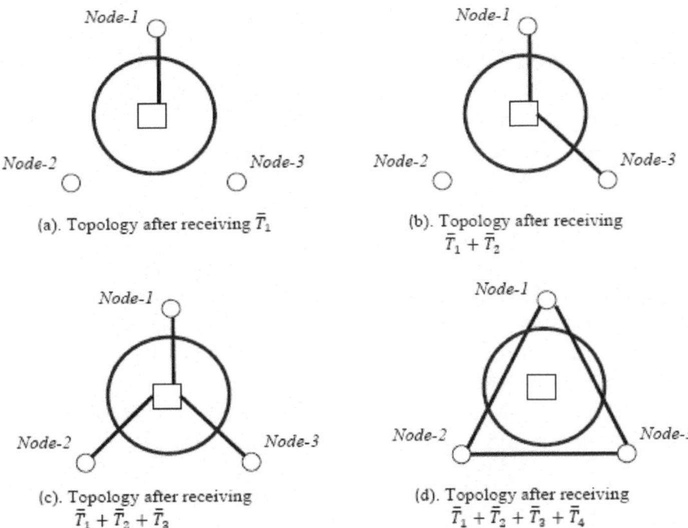

Fig. 2. Change in the virtual state of the network after receiving tokens $\bar{T}_1$ to $\bar{T}_4$

5 Conclusions

The paper proposes an architecture for dynamic virtual reconfiguration of a wireless network with the enforcement of key-protection at each node and by allowing the topological changes to be triggered by carefully designed broadcast tokens sent by the centre. With each broadcast token the changes in the virtual topology are enforced in a distributed fashion. The principal idea behind this architecture has been illustrated through the analysis of a 3-node network which uses a non-perfect secret sharing scheme called MIX-SPLIT to synthesize the node-shares and the broadcast tokens.

References

1. Eschenauer, L., Gligor, V.D.: A key-management scheme for distributed sensor networks. In: Proc. ACM Conf. on Computer and Communications Security (2002)
2. Chan, H., Perrig, A., Song, D.: Random key predistribution schemes for sensor networks. In: Proc. Symposium on Security and Privacy, pp. 197–213 (May 2003)
3. Camtepe, S.A., Yener, B.: Combinatorial design of key distribution mechanisms for wireless sensor networks. IEEE/ACM Transactions on Networking 15(2), 346–358 (2007)
4. Blom, R.: An optimal class of symmetric key generation systems. In: Beth, T., Cot, N., Ingemarsson, I. (eds.) EUROCRYPT 1984. LNCS, vol. 209, pp. 335–338. Springer, Heidelberg (1985)
5. Du, W., Han, J.D.Y.S., Varshney, P.K., Katz, J., Khalili, A.: A pairwise key predistribution scheme for wireless sensor networks. ACM Transactions on Information System Security 8(2) (May 2005)

6. Blundo, C., De Santis, A., Herzberg, A., Kutten, S., Vaccaro, U., Yung, M.: Perfectly-secure key distribution for dynamic conferences. In: Brickell, E.F. (ed.) CRYPTO 1992. LNCS, vol. 740, pp. 471–486. Springer, Heidelberg (1993)
7. Liu, D., Ning, P., Li, R.: Establishing pairwise keys in distributed sensor networks. ACM Transactions on Information System Security 8(1), 41–77 (2005)
8. Fiat, A., Naor, M.: Broadcast encryption. In: Stinson, D.R. (ed.) CRYPTO 1993. LNCS, vol. 773, pp. 480–491. Springer, Heidelberg (1994)
9. Wallner, D., Harder, E., Agee, R.: Key Management for Multicast: Issues and Architectures. Internet Draft (September 1998)
10. Wong, C.K., Mohamed, M., Lam, S.S.: Secure group communications using key graphs. IEEE/ACM Transactions on Networking 8(1) (February 2000)
11. Karthik, K., Hatzinakos, D.: Multimedia Encoding for Access Control with Traitor Tracing: Balancing Secrecy, Privacy and Traceability. VDM Verlag Dr. Muller (2008) ISBN: 978-3-8364-3638-0
12. Karthik, K.: A ramp code for fine-grained access control. In: Intl. Conf. on Computer Science and Information Technology, CCSIT (2013)

On the Use of Key Assignment Schemes in Authentication Protocols

James Alderman* and Jason Crampton

Information Security Group, Royal Holloway, University of London

Abstract. In this paper, we explore the use of Key Assignment Schemes in entity authentication protocols where authentication requires the claiment to demonstrate knowledge of a derivable key. By controlling the distribution of such keys, restrictions may be efficiently placed upon the circumstances under which an entity may be authenticated and the services to which they may gain access. We explore how standardized protocols may be extended to authenticate entities as members of a group associated to a particular security label, whilst protecting the long-term secrets in the system. We also see that such constructions may allow for authentication whilst preserving anonymity.

Keywords: Key assignment scheme, entity authentication, membership authentication, authentication policy.

1 Introduction

Key Assignment Schemes (KASs) have been studied since the work of Akl and Taylor [1] and permit an entity to derive many cryptographic keys by combining a small number of keys in its possession with some publicly available information. Traditionally, such schemes are used to support cryptographically-enforced access control, particularly for information flow policies; in this setting, derived keys are used to *decrypt* protected resources. However, we believe that KASs can also play a role in entity authentication protocols by using the derived keys as *encryption* keys instead. In this paper, we investigate methods by which KASs may be integrated into existing, standardized authentication protocols in order to authenticate an entity as a member of a specified group. Associating groups with specific services can allow for more control to be exerted over the conditions under which an entity may be authenticated, such as allowing authentication only during certain time periods or if assigned a specific security clearance. We shall also see that a KAS can help protect the long-term secret key, and allow a form of authentication to occur whilst preserving the anonymity of entities.

This paper focuses on two-party symmetric-key authentication protocols where we replace the usual long-term, shared key with one derived from a KAS construction. Authentication is achieved by constructing a fresh message using this

* The first author acknowledges support from BAE Systems Advanced Technology Centre under a CASE Award.

J. Lopez, X. Huang, and R. Sandhu (Eds.): NSS 2013, LNCS 7873, pp. 607–613, 2013.

shared secret. Keys in a KAS are associated with particular security labels which could represent security classifications, time periods or geo-spatial locations for example. Thus, by making appropriate choices of labels and KAS constructions, we can require the claimant to demonstrate knowledge of keys which satisfy an authentication policy for the system.

The full version of this paper [2] provides a more detailed discussion of the ideas presented in this short paper, as well as giving novel constructions that enable one-round authentication protocols without synchronised clocks and allow for individual authentication using a trusted third party.

2 Background

Notation: The statement $A \to B : \{m\}_\kappa$ is to be interpreted as: entity A sends the message m encrypted under the key κ to entity B. We write $\kappa_{A,B}$ to denote a symmetric key shared by entities A and B, while η_A denotes a nonce (number used only once) created by entity A.

Graph-based Access Control Policies: A *partially ordered set* (*poset*) is a set L equipped with a binary relation $\leqslant$ such that for all $x, y, z \in L$: $x \leqslant x$ (reflexivity); if $x \leqslant y$ and $y \leqslant x$ then $x = y$ (anti-symmetry); and if $x \leqslant y$ and $y \leqslant z$, then $x \leqslant z$ (transitivity). We may write $x < y$ if $x \leqslant y$ and $x \neq y$, and write $y \geqslant x$ if $x \leqslant y$. We say that x *covers* y, written $y \lessdot x$, if $y < x$ and no z exists in L such that $y < z < x$. The *Hasse Diagram* of a poset $(L, \leqslant)$ is the directed acyclic graph $(L, \lessdot)$ with vertices labelled by elements of L and an edge connecting vertex v to w if and only if $w \lessdot v$.

Let U be a set of entities, O be a set of resources to which access should be restricted, and $(L, \leqslant)$ be a poset of security labels. Also, let $\lambda : U \cup O \to L$ be a labelling function assigning security labels. The tuple $(L, \leqslant, U, O, \lambda)$ then denotes an *information flow policy* which can be represented by the Hasse Diagram of $(L, \leqslant)$. The policy requires that information flow from objects to entities preserves the partial ordering relation; for instance an entity $u \in U$ may read an object $o \in O$ if and only if $\lambda(u) \geqslant \lambda(o)$ [1].

Key Assignment Schemes: A Key Assignment Scheme (KAS) provides a generic, cryptographic enforcement mechanism for graph-based access control policies in which a unique cryptographic key, $\kappa(x)$, is associated to each node $x \in L$. Akl and Taylor [1] introduced the idea of a KAS to manage the problem of key distribution by allowing a trusted center to distribute a single cryptographic key, $\kappa(x)$, to each entity with security label x, who may then combine this knowledge with some publicly available information in order to derive $\kappa(y)$ for all $y < x$.

Henceforth, we write κ_x to represent the cryptographic key $\kappa(x)$. A well-known KAS construction, an *iterative key encrypting* (IKE) KAS [7], publishes $\{\kappa_y\}_{\kappa_x}$ for each directed edge (x, y) in the Hasse diagram. Then for any $x > y$, there

[1] Note that this statement is the *simple security property* of the Bell-LaPadula security model [4].

is a directed path from x to y and the key associated with each node on that path can be iteratively derived by an entity that knows κ_x. A survey of generic schemes is given in [7].

A fundamental security property of a KAS is that it should be secure against *key recovery* [3]: that is, the derivation of κ_y from a set of keys $\kappa_{x_1}, \ldots, \kappa_{x_n}$ should be possible if and only if there exists i such that $\kappa_{x_i} > y$. Thus, a set of users cannot recover a key for which no one of them isn't already authorized. An IKE KAS is known to be secure against *key recovery* provided the encryption function is chosen appropriately [3].

3 Using KASs for Authentication

KASs have previously been used to enforce graph-based access control policies, where a protected object is encrypted with the key associated with the object's security label and authorized entities may derive the key for decryption. However, we could also use derived keys for encrypting messages. Given that many authentication protocols use symmetric encryption to respond to challenges, we now explore how we can use KASs to build novel authentication protocols.

Traditional Entity Authentication. Consider, for example, Protocol 1 [10, Mechanism 2] – a unilateral, challenge-response authentication protocol – in which the verifier B sends a nonce η_B to the claimant A[2]. By encrypting a response that includes the nonce, the claimant demonstrates knowledge of the shared secret key $\kappa_{A,B}$ and the verifier knows that the message cannot be a replay. *Mutual authentication* is achieved by requiring both parties to encrypt a nonce (Protocol 2 [10, Mechanism 4]). Protocols in which the claimant encrypts a timestamp [10, Mechanism 1, Mechanism 3] requires fewer messages, however require the claimant and verifier to have (loosely) synchronized clocks and for there to be some "window of acceptability" for timestamps. Finally, a protocol may provide *authenticated key exchange* by including a session key in the verifier's response. Note that the protocols presented here use an authenticated encryption scheme to protect certain messages but could be modified to use a MAC, or other suitable cryptographic primitives if desired.

Authentication using KASs. We now consider how these protocols can be modified to use keys derived from a KAS. We assume the existence of a KAS associated with a *graph-based authentication policy* $(L, \leqslant, U, S, \lambda)$ which we define in an analogous manner to graph-based access control policies: U is a set of entities, S is a set of services (the claimants' intended interactions) and L is a set of distinct security labels that forms a poset under the relation $\leqslant$; $\lambda : U \cup S \to L$ is a function that assigns a security label to each entity and service. We write U_x to denote $\{u \in U : \lambda(u) = x\}$.

[2] Protocols 1 and 2 are taken from the ISO standard [10]. Some textual fields have been omitted from protocol descriptions in the interests of clarity and brevity.

Protocol 1

A → B: Hi
B → A: η_B
A → B: $\{\eta_B, B\}_{\kappa_{A,B}}$

Protocol 2

A → B: η_A
B → A: $\{\eta_A, \eta_B, A\}_{\kappa_{A,B}}$
A → B: $\{\eta_B, \eta_A\}_{\kappa_{A,B}}$

Fig. 1. Entity authentication protocols

Protocol 3

A → B: v
B → A: η_B
A → B: $\{\eta_B, B\}_{\kappa_v}$

Protocol 4

A → B: Hi
B → A: v, η_B
A → B: $\{\eta_B, B\}_{\kappa_v}$

Protocol 5

A → B: v, η_A
B → A: $\{\eta_A, \eta_B, A\}_{\kappa_v}, w$
A → B: $\{\eta_A, \eta_B\}_{\kappa_w}$

Fig. 2. Challenge-response authentication protocols using a KAS

In the following protocols, we replace the symmetric key $\kappa_{A,B}$ used in the protocols in Figure 1 with a key derived from a KAS. We assume that a trusted center initiates the setup of the system: defining a poset of security labels and a graph-based authentication policy, and instantiating the KAS construction. When an entity, u, joins the system, it is assigned a security label $\lambda(u)$ and given the associated cryptographic key $\kappa_{\lambda(u)}$. Henceforth, the entity may combine knowledge of this key with the public information from the KAS to derive all keys κ_x such that $x \leqslant \lambda(u)$ – that is, all keys that u is permitted to learn in accordance with the authentication policy. Thus, entities are assigned to groups, each associated with a particular security label and therefore permitted to interact with a specific service.

Protocol 3 illustrates one method for incorporating a KAS into a unilateral, challenge-response authentication protocol (this can easily be modified to accomodate time-variant parameters). The overall structure of the protocol is very similar to the traditional case in Protocol 1, however the claimant now presents the verifier with a security label, v, for which she wishes to be authenticated – for example, representing credentials that A claims to have, or a description of the desired service. Instead of using a symmetric key shared by the claimant and the verifier, the claimant now derives and uses the key κ_v. Given that the claimant is provided with the cryptographic key $\kappa_{\lambda(A)}$ by the trusted center, it is possible to prove knowledge of κ_v if and only if they can derive κ_v from $\kappa_{\lambda(A)}$.

Note that correctly encrypting the challenge demonstrates knowledge of κ_v, which means any entity with security label $w \geqslant v$ could compute this response. This authentication protocol is weaker in some sense than conventional authentication protocols in that it only proves that the claimant belongs to a group U_w, for some $w \geqslant v$. However, this form of authentication will suffice for many applications, in particular those for which no subsequent auditing or attribution of actions to individuals is required. Note also that conventional authentication may be thought of as a degenerate case of KAS-based authentication, in which the graph is an unordered set of labels, one label per entity.

The verifier must ensure that the chosen label satisfies the authentication policy for the requested service and that he himself has security clearance at least that of the chosen label: $\lambda(B) \geqslant v$. If not, a negotiation protocol could be run to determine the greatest common descendent of v and $\lambda(B)$ which is then acceptable to both parties. In some situations, it may be preferable to have the verifier choose the security label before issuing the challenge, as shown in Protocol 4. For example, in an environment where the required security label for all protocol runs is equal it may be more efficient for a verification server to issue the challenge than to check that labels chosen by claimants are sufficient. On the other hand, the first method may be more suitable in environments where peer-to-peer interactions are common, or the choice of services is greater. Mutual authentication can be achieved in a similar fashion, as shown in Protocol 5.

Protecting keys. In traditional entity authentication protocols, the claimant demonstrates knowledge of a long-term shared secret key. In the KAS authentication protocols above, however, the long-term secret key is the key issued to the entity upon joining the system, and the protocols use derived keys instead. Thus, if we restrict the challenge security labels to relate only to derived keys, the long-term secret is never used for encryption and is protected from known-plaintext attacks. In addition, it may be advantageous to ensure that all entities are issued with keys associated with non-root nodes of G so that if a entity is compromised, it may only reveal the subset of keys derived from those in its possession, while preserving the security of other keys in the KAS. We also note that the protocols above could encrypt the nonce from the verifier using the KAS derived key and require the claimaint to decrypt and use the nonce in order to prove knowledge of the key, thus protecting the derived key from known-plaintext attacks also.

Authenticated key exchange. Protocol 5 may be extended in the obvious way to distribute a session key, security label or a key relating to a specific group (or interval) from which many session keys may be derived. Compromising one session key should not reveal information about any other session keys [5]. Thus, if session keys are chosen to be from a KAS construction, they should be leaf nodes or the derived children of the given node must be distinct from session keys used elsewhere in the system. Also it is important to note that, if the session key is protected by the key κ_v, *any* member of a group associated with a label $w \geqslant v$ could learn the key. However, by definition, all members of the group associated with label v are authorized for services at that level and so session keys may be required only to protect the service from non-members.

Alternatively, by protecting the nonces as in Protocol 5, the participants have shared secrets that can be used to derive additional session keys using a pseudo-random function, in much the same way as the pre-master secret is used in the SSL/TLS protocol.

4 Related Work

Anonymous and membership authentication protocols [6, 8, 11, 13], wherein entities are authenticated as members of a group but the verifier does not learn the individual identities, largely use public-key cryptography to demonstrate knowledge of a shared secret. Whilst anonymity was not the prime focus of our work, we note that the protocols in this paper provide for some degree of anonymity; users within U_x are indistinguishable to the verifier (and so anonymous relative to the size of U_x). Previous work [12, 13] used the Akl-Taylor KAS [1] as a building block for anonymous authentication schemes but required additional public-key mechanisms, presumably because the security of the Akl-Taylor scheme is based on the RSA problem. Our work is the first, to our knowledge, to use purely symmetric constructions.

Some membership authentication schemes use *group signatures* [6, 8] or *ring signatures* [11] to prove knowledge of a secret known only to a group of entities in a public-key analogue of our (symmetric-key) protocols. In relation to group signatures, our proposal shares the requirement of a trusted authority for initialization of the system. However, that authority can reveal the identity of the signer, unlike our scheme(s) and ring signatures. Moreover, ring signatures do not require a trusted authority, but the ease with which ring signatures can be created and the inability to trace the source of a signature makes them unsuitable for authentication in many scenarios [9]. In short, we obtain the control provided by group signatures with the anonymity guaranteed by ring signatures.

5 Summary

In this paper, we have presented a novel use of Key Assignment Schemes to construct entity authentication protocols. Such protocols can be used to protect long-term secrets and to efficiently verify that a claimant satisfies an authentication policy. Example applications of such protocols include [2]: enforcing user clearance (for example, when accessing a secured database); authentication within a large, or rapidly changing, population where it is infeasible to maintain a list of active entities, but it is possible to issue keys valid for given time periods; ticket-based authentication or subscription services, where an entity is provided with a KAS key for a time interval representing a ticket lifetime – future interactions with services require that the entity authenticate using a derived key for the current time period[3]; authentication wherein entities prove authorization but wish to retain anonymity.

In future work, we hope to explore novel applications of our protocols, such as mitigating denial of service attacks on authentication servers by employing KASs in a proof of work scheme. In such a deployment, it is envisaged that a KAS be devised in which it is 'moderately hard' to derive keys and thus knowledge

[3] Similarly, a geo-spatial KAS construction where a mobile entity is provided with a KAS key representing locations (for example, attempting to authenticate using a smart card to a secure lock within an office building)

of a key proves that significant work has been done and that the server should dedicate resources to the authentication process. The difficulty of deriving keys may be adjusted according to demand by releasing additional public information.

We also intend to consider security definitions for KAS-based authentication and in particular whether security properties that hold separately for KASs and authentication protocols are preserved by our protocols.

References

1. Akl, S.G., Taylor, P.D.: Akl and Peter D. Taylor. Cryptographic solution to a problem of access control in a hierarchy. ACM Trans. Comput. Syst. 1(3), 239–248 (1983)
2. Alderman, J., Crampton, J.: On the use of key assignment schemes in authentication protocols. CoRR, abs/1303.4262 (2013), http://arxiv.org/abs/1303.4262
3. Atallah, M.J., Blanton, M., Fazio, N., Frikken, K.B.: Dynamic and efficient key management for access hierarchies. ACM Trans. Inf. Syst. Secur. 12(3) (2009)
4. Bell, D.E., LaPadula, L.J.: Secure computer systems: Mathematical foundations. Technical Report MTR-2547, MITRE Corporation (1973)
5. Bellare, M., Rogaway, P.: Entity authentication and key distribution. In: Stinson, D.R. (ed.) CRYPTO 1993. LNCS, vol. 773, pp. 232–249. Springer, Heidelberg (1994)
6. Boneh, D., Franklin, M.K.: Anonymous authentication with subset queries (extended abstract). In: Motiwalla, J., Tsudik, G. (eds.) ACM Conference on Computer and Communications Security, pp. 113–119. ACM (1999)
7. Crampton, J., Martin, K.M., Wild, P.R.: On key assignment for hierarchical access control. In: CSFW, pp. 98–111. IEEE Computer Society (2006)
8. Fujii, A., Ohtake, G., Hanaoka, G., Ogawa, K.: Anonymous authentication scheme for subscription services. In: Apolloni, B., Howlett, R.J., Jain, L. (eds.) KES 2007/WIRN 2007, Part III. LNCS (LNAI), vol. 4694, pp. 975–983. Springer, Heidelberg (2007)
9. Fujisaki, E., Suzuki, K.: Traceable ring signature. In: Okamoto, T., Wang, X. (eds.) PKC 2007. LNCS, vol. 4450, pp. 181–200. Springer, Heidelberg (2007)
10. International Organization for Standardization (ISO): ISO/IEC 9798-2:2008: Information technology - Security techniques - Entity authentication - Part 2: Mechanisms using symmetric encipherment algorithms (2008)
11. Naor, M.: Deniable ring authentication. In: Yung, M. (ed.) CRYPTO 2002. LNCS, vol. 2442, pp. 481–498. Springer, Heidelberg (2002)
12. Ohta, K., Okamoto, T., Koyama, K.: Membership authentication for hierarchical multigroups using the extended fiat-shamir scheme. In: Damgård, I. (ed.) EUROCRYPT 1990. LNCS, vol. 473, pp. 446–457. Springer, Heidelberg (1991)
13. Tzeng, W.-G.: A secure system for data access based on anonymous authentication and time-dependent hierarchical keys. In: Lin, F.-C., Lee, D.-T., Lin, B.-S.P., Shieh, S., Jajodia, S. (eds.) ASIACCS, pp. 223–230. ACM (2006)

On the Interactions between Privacy-Preserving, Incentive, and Inference Mechanisms in Participatory Sensing Systems

Idalides J. Vergara-Laurens[1], Diego Mendez-Chaves[2], and Miguel A. Labrador[1]

[1] University of South Florida, Tampa, FL, 33620
ijvergara@mail.usf.edu, mlabrador@usf.edu
[2] Pontificia Universidad Javeriana, Bogota, Colombia
diego-mendez@javeriana.edu.co

Abstract. In Participatory Sensing (PS) systems people agree to utilize their cellular phone resources to sense and transmit the data of interest. Although PS systems have the potential to collect enormous amounts of data to discover and solve new collective problems, they have not been very successful in practice, mainly because of lack of incentives for participation and privacy concerns. Therefore, several incentive and privacy-preserving mechanisms have been proposed. However, these mechanisms have been traditionally studied in isolation overseeing the interaction between them. In this paper we include a model and implement several of these mechanisms to study the interactions and effects that they may have on one another and, more importantly, on the quality of the information that the system provides to the final user. Our experiments show that privacy-preserving mechanisms and incentive mechanisms may in fact affect each other's performance and, more importantly, the quality of the information to the final user.

Keywords: Participatory sensing, privacy-preserving, incentive mechanisms, inference mechanisms, P-sense.

1 Introduction

Participatory Sensing (PS) is a new data collection paradigm based on the availability of millions of cellular users equipped with smart applications, a large diversity of sensors, and Internet connectivity at all times. The availability of such a large number of mobile nodes opens the possibility to collect very large amounts of data and from places not possible or economically feasible before. For example, P-Sense [8] is an application that requires users to sense the level of pollution as they travel to build accurate pollution maps that can be used by the community and governmental organizations for many different purposes. However, users might no be willing to participate in this system if they also have to spend their data plans and batteries without any direct benefit in return. Therefore, for some PS systems, incentive mechanisms need to be included to guarantee a minimum level of participation for the system to be able to actually work. Similarly, most users will not be willing to participate if as a result of their data reporting, their privacy is not guaranteed. Therefore, privacy-preserving mechanisms need to be in place for these PS systems. Finally, inference and data analysis mechanisms are

J. Lopez, X. Huang, and R. Sandhu (Eds.): NSS 2013, LNCS 7873, pp. 614–620, 2013.

also usually included as part of a PS system to make estimations of the variables of interest in places where no data have been collected from, to make predictions, or to make any other type of analysis that will bring additional information to the final users.

However, one important problem is that these mechanisms have been devised and studied in an isolated or independent manner, as if they were the only mechanisms working in the system. Therefore, this paper presents a model to study the interactions between privacy-preserving, incentive, and inference mechanisms that have not studied before. In particular, this paper answers to the following questions:

- What effect do privacy-preserving mechanisms have in the quality of the information that the system provides to the final user?
- What effect do incentive mechanisms have in the quality of the information that the system provides to the final user?
- What effect do privacy-preserving and incentive mechanisms working together have in the quality of the information that the system provides to the final user?

The rest of the paper is organized as follows. Section 2 includes a brief description of the privacy-preserving, incentive, and inference mechanisms available in the literature and the ones used in this paper. Section 3 describes the model and performance metrics utilized in this work to study the effects produced by these mechanisms. Section 4 presents the performance evaluation of available privacy-preserving and incentive mechanisms. Finally, Section 5 presents the most important conclusions and provides directions for additional research.

2 Related Work

This section provides a brief literature review on privacy-preserving, incentive, and inference mechanisms, as they related to the work in this paper.

Privacy-Preserving Mechanisms: The main idea of **anonimization** is to *generalize* the users' data to a group of users in such a way that the user cannot be distinguishable from the group [2]. On the other hand, **obfuscation** techniques assume that the identity of the participant is or could be known [10]. Differently from anonymization techniques, the key idea is to modify the real location of the participants without considering the location of other participants. Finally, **encryption-based** techniques rely on cryptographic methods to guarantee the privacy of the participants with no modification of the actual data [4].

Incentive Mechanisms: Most of these mechanisms are based on *reverse auction* techniques. For instance, in the *Reverse auction based dynamic price scheme (RADP-VPC-RC)* presented in [6], each user makes a bid offering her sensed data and the system buys the k cheapest ones. Further, RADP-VPC-RC tackles the problem of cost explosion and avoids users from dropping out of the system. The work presented in [5] extends this approach with the *Greedy Incentive Algorithm (GIA)*, which uses not only the price but also the locations of the users. The key idea is to buy the k cheapest samples that maximize the covered area avoiding to buy samples that are closely located.

Inference Mechanisms: They aim to estimate the variables of interest in those places where data are not available. In this area, Kriging is one of the most widely used techniques in geostatistics (a branch of statistics that focuses on spatio-temporal datasets) [7]. All the different variations of the kriging estimator are modified versions of the best linear regression estimator [3, 9].

3 System Model and Performance Metrics

The system model consists of four components: *Sensed Data, Privacy Mechanism, Incentive Mechanism* and *Inference Engine* (Figure 1). The sense data component corresponds to the data reported by the participants of the PS application and is used as the input to the other components of the system. The privacy mechanism, receives sensed data and produces modified data according to the selected privacy mechanism. The incentive mechanism, selects a subset of the input data according to the incentive mechanism implemented in the system. The last component, the inference engine, is used to produce estimations of the selected variables in the areas of interest.

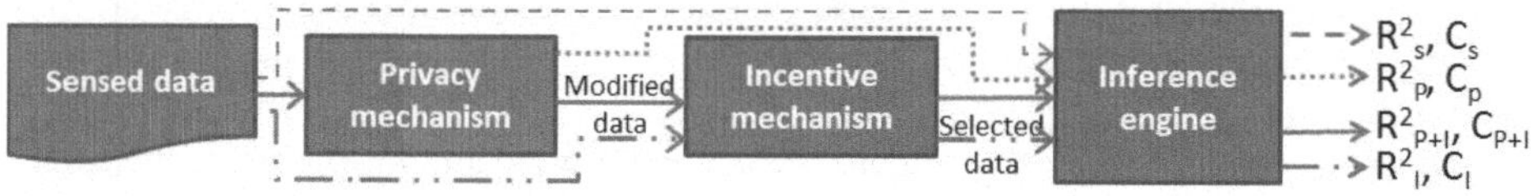

Fig. 1. System model and performance metrics

In addition, the proposed model includes several *data paths*. The first data path applies to those systems that implement neither privacy-preserving nor incentive mechanisms. The second data path considers a system that implements a privacy-preserving mechanism but it does not consider an incentive mechanism. The third path considers a system that does not implement a privacy-preserving mechanism but it does include an incentive mechanism. The fourth path considers a system that implements all components. Finally, the performance metrics for the model are: 1-**The quality of the estimation** R^2 measures how different the real data and the estimations are. 2-**The average displacement** as a result of changing the original location of the participant by privacy-preserving mechanisms. 3-**The coverage** of the area of interest C after the incentive mechanism is applied.

4 Performance Evaluation

In order to collect real environmental, we utilized the P-Sense system for measuring CO (ppm), CO_2 (ppm), combustible gases (ppm), air quality (4 discrete levels), temperature (F), and relative humidity (%) on the air [8]. Moreover, during three months data were collected 3 times a day for one hour, 3 to 4 days a week at the campus of the University of South Florida, in Tampa, Florida. The campus area is approximately 3.9 km^2, which is represented using a grid of 105x105 units in this project, i.e. each unit is equivalent to 20 meters. On the other hand, the implemented privacy-preserving mechanisms are: 1-**Tessellation** [2] (anonimization technique) varying the

k parameter from 3 to 9; 2-**Points of Interests** [10] (obfuscation technique) using a grid from 4x4 up to 11x11 cells; and 3-**Random Perturbation** [1] (obfuscation technique) using uniform distribution {[1,5],[5,15] and [10,20]}, normal distribution $\{[\mu = 5, 10, 10, 15, 15, 15, 20, 20, 20, \sigma = 1, 1, 3, 1, 3, 5, 1, 3, 5\}$, and exponential distribution, $\{\lambda = 5, 10, 15, 20\}$. Finally, the incentive mechanism utilized in the experiments is the GIA mechanism proposed in [5], as this is the only one in the literature that studies coverage considering the location of the users. The parameters used in the evaluation are the ones included in the GIA paper [5]: coverage radius=5, true valuation=uniform [0,10], and budget=[20,260].

4.1 Experiments and Results for Each Data Path

First Data Path: Neither Privacy nor Incentive Mechanisms. Table 1 presents the obtained R_S^2 and C_S when we apply the inference mechanism to the original data, i.e., without privacy nor incentive mechanism. Note the good quality of the estimations (R_S^2 is very close to 1), i.e., the estimated values are very close to the real values collected by the P-Sense system, and the coverage (33%) achieved by the system.

Table 1. The quality of the estimations (R_S^2) and coverage (C_S) for the first data path

Variable	Temperature	Relative humidity	Air Quality	CO_2	CO	Combustion gases	Coverage
R_S^2	0.92	0.89	0.91	0.92	0.88	0.96	33.14%

Second Data Path: Privacy but Not Incentive Mechanism. Figure 2 shows the quality of the estimations (R_P^2) produced by several privacy-preserving mechanisms for three of the environmental variables measured by the P-Sense system according to the average displacement. As it can be seen from the figure, all variables present a similar behavior regardless of the privacy-preserving mechanism: different privacy mechanisms with similar average displacement produce similar quality of estimation. This is an important conclusion because it means that none of the privacy-preserving schemes studied here is actually a good scheme in systems that do not tolerate low quality estimations. Moreover, Table 2 presents the relationship between the quality of the estimation (R_P^2), coverage (C_P), and average displacement for the temperature variable using the implemented privacy-preserving mechanisms. For example, *Points of Interest 6x6* and *Random Perturbation (all cases)* have similar average displacement and different coverage but very similar R_P^2. In conclusion, the impact of the average displacement over the quality is significantly greater than the impact of the coverage on the quality of estimation.

Third Data Path: Incentive but not Privacy Mechanism. Figure 3 shows the quality of the estimation (R_I^2) when the GIA mechanism is applied with different radii as a function of the budget. As the figure shows, the quality of estimation and number of selected participants decrease when the coverage radius increases. However, a very low radius implies the possibility of selecting participants that are very close to each other, which spend the budget but provide similar (redundant) information [5]. In conclusion,

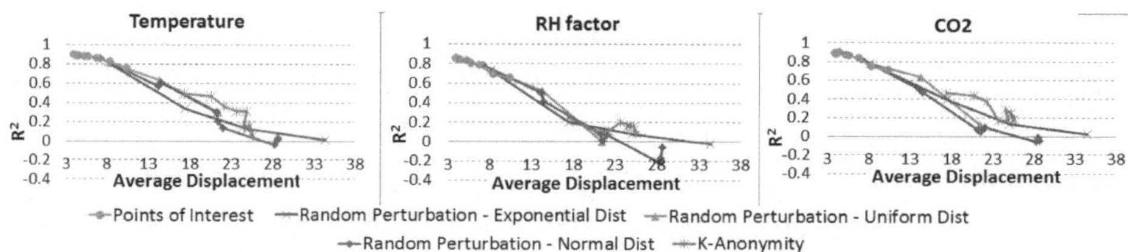

Fig. 2. R_P^2 as a function of the average displacement for several privacy-preserving mechanisms applied to each environmental variable

Table 2. Relationship between quality of estimation (R_P^2), coverage (C_P) and average displacement for the temperature

	Tessellation			Points of Interest				Random Perturbation		
–	$k=3$	$k=5$	$k=7$	$4x4$	$6x6$	$8x8$	$10x10$	Uniform [1; 10]	Normal ($\mu=5, \sigma=1$)	Exponential ($1/\lambda=5$)
R_P^2	0.47	0.31	0.16	0.76	0.86	0.88	0.89	0.82	0.86	0.82
C_P (%)	12.57	8.166	5.67	11.11	20.73	28.21	30.76	33.65	33.67	33.83
Avg Disp	20.66	23.66	24.45	10.45	6.8	5.25	4.21	8.42	7.18	8.12

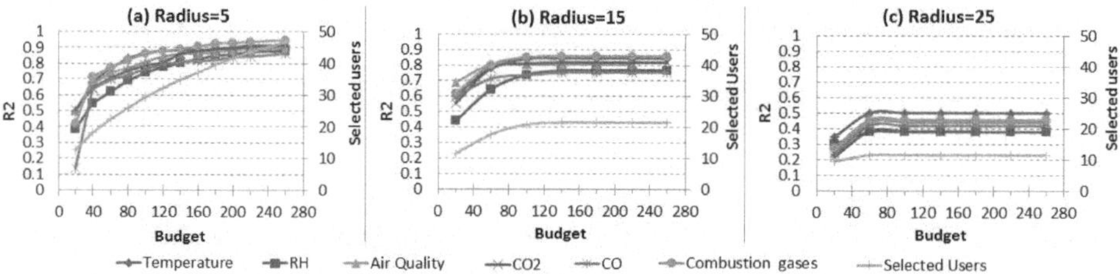

Fig. 3. R_I^2 as a function of the budget available to the GIA algorithm using different radii

selecting the appropriate radius should be function of the needed quality of estimation as well as the variability of the data being measured.

Figure 4-a shows the coverage (C_I) achieved by the GIA incentive mechanism. Note that, as expected, the coverage increases with the budget since a higher budget means more selected participants. However, although the effect of budget increments on the coverage is constant (figure 4-a), the effect of budget increments on quality of estimation is not significant after some value (figure 3-a). Therefore, the optimal budget depends mostly on the desired quality of estimation instead of the coverage.

Fourth Path: Privacy and Incentive Mechanisms. Figure 4 shows the coverage (C_{P+I}) achieved by the system as a function of the budget when the GIA mechanism is used along with the different privacy-preserving mechanism (three graphs on the right). Basically, the coverage increases with the budget. However, it can be seen how some privacy-preserving mechanisms limit the area of coverage of the GIA algorithm, providing a flat coverage value regardless of the budget available (Tessellation and Points of Interest). This is due to the number of selected points since a larger k as well as a smaller number of points of interest means fewer reporting points.

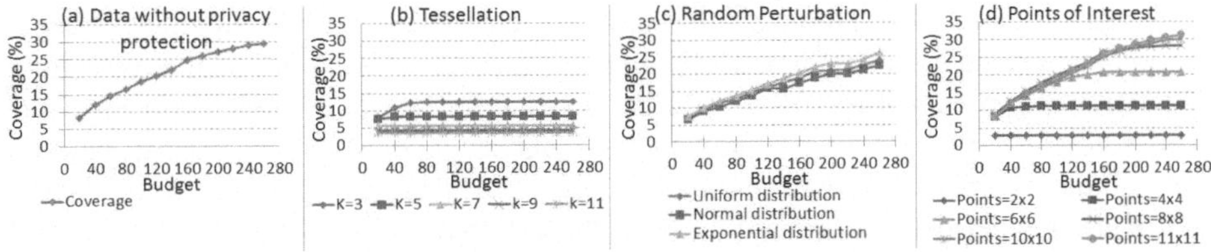

Fig. 4. Coverage achieved by the GIA mechanism as a function of the budget without privacy protection (C_I) (left) and when privacy-preserving mechanisms are present (C_{P+I})

Additionally, Figure 5 shows the quality of estimation (R^2_{P+I}) achieved by the system for different budgets and privacy-preserving mechanisms. In the case of Tessellation, the budget has no major effect on the quality of estimation because the incentive mechanism buys the anonymized locations and, when it buys one of the k users, the others are discarded. In the case of Points of Interest, the situation is similar: the budget affects the coverage but it does not affect the quality of estimation much because the number of point of interest defines the number of reporting locations. In conclusion, when privacy and incentive mechanisms work together, the most affecting factor is the average displacement produced by the privacy mechanisms.

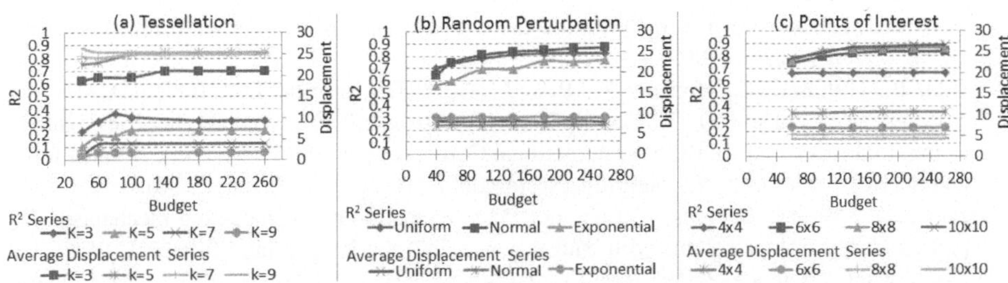

Fig. 5. Quality of estimation achieved by each privacy-preserving mechanism as a function of the budget used in the GIA mechanism (R^2_{P+I}) for temperature

5 Conclusions and Research Directions

This paper presents a model to study the interactions between privacy-preserving, incentive, and inference mechanisms in participatory sensing systems. A performance evaluation is carried out to evaluate the impact of these mechanisms on the quality of estimation (R^2), as provided by the inference system to the final user, as well as the area of coverage (C) achieved by the incentive mechanism. In the case where no incentive mechanism is included in the system, the impact of privacy-preserving mechanisms on the quality of the information to the final user depends on the average displacement that the privacy mechanism introduces to the real locations of the participants. Therefore, a system needing a high quality of information should avoid the use of privacy mechanisms that introduce large displacements, such as Tessellation, and rather utilize a privacy-preserving mechanism with low displacements, such as Points of Interest with a high number of points or Random Perturbation. In the case where the incentive mechanism is used, the information provided to the final user depends on the available budget, with the quality increasing with the budget. However, there is a point in which the effect of the budget decreases the quality of the estimation. Finally, when privacy and incentive mechanisms work together, the budget available to the incentive mechanism and the average displacements introduced by the privacy mechanism are the factors that affect the quality of the information to the user the most: for systems needing a high quality of estimation, a high budget should be used as well as a privacy mechanism with a low average displacement.

References

1. Agrawal, R., Srikant, R.: Privacy-preserving data mining. In: Proceedings of the 2000 ACM International Conference on Management of Data - SIGMOD, Dallas, Texas, USA, vol. 29, pp. 439–450 (May 2000)
2. Cornelius, C., Kapadia, A., Kotz, D., Peebles, D., Shin, M., Triandopoulos, N.: Anonysense: Privacy-aware people-centric sensing. In: Proceedings of the 6th International Conference on Mobile Systems, Applications, and Services - MobiSys, Breckenridge, Colorado, USA, pp. 211–224 (June 2008)
3. Goovaerts, P.: Geostatistics for Natural Resources Evaluation, volume 4th printing. Oxford University Press, USA (1997)
4. Hoh, B., Gruteser, M., Herring, R., Ban, J., Work, D., Herrera, J.C., Bayen, A.M., Annavaram, M., Jacobson, Q.: Virtual trip lines for distributed privacy-preserving traffic monitoring. In: Proceedings of the 6th International Conference on Mobile Systems, Applications, and Services - MobiSys, Breckenridge, Colorado, USA, pp. 15–28 (June 2008)
5. Jaimes, L., Vergara-Laurens, I., Labrador, M.: A location-based incentive mechanism for participatory sensing systems with budget constraints. In: Proceeding of the 2012 IEEE International Conference on Pervasive Computing and Communications - PERCOM, Lugano, Switzerland (March 2012)
6. Juong-Sik, L., Baik, H.: Sell your experiences: a market mechanism based incentive for participatory sensing. In: IEEE International Conference on Pervasive Computing and Communications - PerCom, Mannheim, Germany, pp. 60–68 (April 2010)
7. Mendez, D., Labrador, M., Ramachandran, K.: Data interpolation for participatory sensing systems. Submitted to the Pervasive and Mobile Computing Journal (Summer 2012)
8. Mendez, D., Perez, A., Labrador, M., Marron, J.: P-sense: A participatory sensing system for air pollution monitoring and control. In: Proceedings of IEEE International Conference on Pervasive Computing and Communications, pp. 344–347 (2011)
9. Moore, R.: Geostatistics in hydrology: Kriging interpolation. Technical report, Mathematics Department, Macquarie University, Sydney (1999)
10. Vergara-Laurens, I., Labrador, M.: Preserving privacy while reducing power consumption and information loss in lbs and participatory sensing applications. In: Proceedings of the 2011 IEEE Global Communication Conference Workshops - GLOBECOM Workshops, Houston, Texas, USA (December 2011)

Security Authentication of AODV Protocols in MANETs

Ahmad Alomari

Faculty of Mathematics and Computer Science, University of Bucharest,
Bucharest, Romania
alomari.jordan@gmail.com

Abstract. Mobile ad hoc networks are a collection of two or more devices equipped with wireless communication and networking capability and they move in dynamic and topology way. The nodes should deploy an intermediate node to be the router to route the packet from the source node to destination node. The wireless links in this network are prone to errors and can go down frequently due to mobility of nodes, interference and lack of infrastructure. Therefore, routing in MANET is a critical task due to highly dynamic environment. In recent years several routing protocols have been proposed for mobile ad hoc networks to increase the secure path between the nodes. We focus on our scheme on the authentication between the nodes and we choose Ad Hoc On-Demand Distance Vector (AODV) protocol to apply this scheme, which it depends on hash function, secret value and random number generation. This scheme is used to produce secure and authentic environment between the nodes In Mobile Ad Hoc Network.

Keywords: Black hole, hash function, Random hash function, AODV, MetaID.

1 Introduction

A mobile ad hoc network (MANET) is a self-organized wireless network where mobile nodes can communicate with each other without the assistance of a centralized authority. Each node is able to communicate with other nodes within its transmission range and relays on other nodes to communicate with nodes outside its transmission range [1]. The absence of centralized administration and the infrastructure less nature make MANETs good for military and fast deployment communications. For these reasons securing MANETs is hard to achieve. Current security technology brings a certain level of trust in obtaining communication. The trust relationships established between networks nodes could be used for the provision of higher level security solutions, such as key management. In [2], and [3], threshold cryptography has been proposed to provide a reliable, distributive key management for MANET by exploiting some nodes as a trust anchor for the rest of the network.

Some aspects of ad hoc networks have interesting security problems, routing is one such aspect. Several routing protocols for ad hoc networks have been developed to produce a secure environment between the nodes in ad hoc networks. We can apply this in our scheme and we choose the Ad Hoc on-demand Distance Vector (AODV)

J. Lopez, X. Huang, and R. Sandhu (Eds.): NSS 2013, LNCS 7873, pp. 621–627, 2013.

because it is the most popular routing protocol and it is used widely [4]. We focus in this paper on the authentication between the nodes, to make sure that the networks are accessible with authorization. Mobile ad hoc networks, for short MANET, have become a very important research area over the last past years. The structure of a MANET consists from mobile nodes which can act as a sender, and a forwarder which is used for messages. Our accent will be putted on the unique feature of these protocols, feature which is represented by the ability to trace routes in spite of dynamic topology. The attacks which can exist on ad-hoc network can be passive attacks and active attacks.

The paper has been organized in sections. Section 1 is the introduction; section 2 we make a security analysis of the most attacks of routing protocols and the main challenges in mobile ad hoc networks (MANETs); section 3 contains a review of AODV; section 4 speaks about our scheme: the main idea of this scheme is to use the hash function, secret value and time stamp to increase the authentication between the nodes when they start communicating in the ad hoc network.

2 Security Analysis

The structure of ad-hoc networks make them very vulnerable to many types of attacks such as passive eavesdropping, active interfering, impersonate, black hole, data tampering and one of the most important attack on which is very difficult to create a security solution, denial of service.

The idea of making AODV secure, represent a real challenge, because first of all we need to understand security attributes and mechanisms. Security is viewed as a structure composed from mixture of processes, procedures and systems. All this components ensure confidentiality, authentication, availability, integrity, access control and non-repudiation [5]. The triad CIA *(confidentiality, integrity, and authentication)* which can be applied in our solution means:

- *Confidentiality* is obtained by preventing the unauthorized nodes to access data.
- *Authentication* is used to ensure the identity of source as well as neighbor nodes to prevent a node from having an unauthorized access to resources and confidential information as well as to stop it from having interfering operations of the rest of the nodes.
- *Integrity* is very important, because it helps to prevent malicious nodes from altering data and resending it (sometimes called as replay attacks or wormhole attack).

In the following, we will go through different types of attacks and illustrating how they act. We mention that, some of the attacks they have been presented in real life, and we were able to see the experiments and how the components react at those attacks.

1. Impersonation – the attacker is able to spoof as an innocent node and join the network. In this situation, several such nodes join the network; they obtain control of the network and conduct malicious behavior. In this situation, they propagate fake routing information and they also gain access to confidential information's.

The network is very vulnerable to such attacks if it does not using a proper authentication mechanism.

2. Wormhole attack – the attacker connect two parts (which can be found at a specified distance) of the network and after this he tunnels the messages received in one part of the network to the other. In this case a low latency is used to pass the messages. Regarding the protection against the wormhole attack, our point of view is to have a "Packet Leash" mechanism in which all nodes in the MANET can obtain authenticated symmetric key of every other node [7]. The receiver can authenticate the information such as time and location from the received packet [8].

3. Black hole attack – the striker lures the traffic of the network in such a way that it compromises the node and forms a black hole, putting the opponent at the centre [8]. In this attack, malicious nodes trick all their neighboring nodes to attract all routing packets to them.

4. Sybil attack – a node tries to have multiple identities. In this situation the malicious node gains more information about the network [8]. There is a notable decrease of fault tolerant schemes like distributed storage, multi-path routing etc.

3 On-Demand or Reactive Routing Protocols

On-Demand protocols, routes are created as and when required. When a transmission occurs from source to destination, it initiates route discovery process within the network. Once a route is discovered and established, it is maintained by route maintenance procedure until either destination becomes inaccessible along every path from source or route is no longer desired. Some of examples on demand routing protocols are: DSR [9], AODV [4].

- Dynamic Source Routing (DSR)

Dynamic Source Routing (DSR) is an on-demand routing protocol, which is based on the theory of source-based routing rather than table-based. This protocol is source-initiated rather than hop-by-hop. Mobile nodes are required to maintain route caches that contain the source routes of which the mobile is aware. This is particularly designed for use in multi hop wireless ad hoc networks of mobile nodes. Basically, DSR protocol, like in other On-Demand routing, does not need any existing network infrastructure or administration and this allows the network to be completely self-organizing and self-configuring. The protocol consists of two major phases: route discovery and route maintenance. Every node maintains a cache to store recently discovered paths. When a node wants to send a packet to some destination, it first checks its route cache to determine whether it already has a path to the destination.

- Ad hoc on-demand distance vector (AODV)

AODV is an improvement of Destination-Sequenced Distance-Vector (DSDV) routing protocol which is collectively based on DSDV and DSR. The AODV have two main phases; first phase is route discovery: when a source node S wants to send a data packet to a destination node D, the source node initiates route discovery by broadcasting a route request (RREQ) to its neighbours. Second phase is route maintenance: a discovery routing between a source node and destination node is maintained as long as needed by the source node. Whenever there is a broken link between two nodes the route maintenance phase is carried out. The node that discovers the broken link initiates Route Error (RERR) message to the source node by the predecessor intermediate nodes. This process is repeated until the source node is reached.

4 Using Random Number with Secret Value and Timestamp to Protect the Privacy

This scheme proposes the use of random numbers with timestamp in the nodes to protect the privacy of the nodes. Random numbers are protected with secret values, and the use of hash functions to prevent forgery and copying. Also we use the time frame to provide a solution to prevent the replay attacks, and the protection of variable values makes it possible to solve synchronization problems.

The proposed scheme consists of four stages and provides security through random numbers and timestamp. Also providing anonymity can protect the privacy of nodes. We use also the secret value (SV), which is the exchange of messages in a secure way between any source and destination node in a network. This exchange can be made in two ways, first way: Secret Value (SV) Distribution with Confidentiality and Authentication: We can use the public key to exchange the secret value to provide protection against both active and passive attacks. Second way: Diffie-Hellman Key Exchange: The Diffie-Hellman algorithm efficiency depends on the hardness of computing discrete logarithms.

The proposed scheme gives an improvement for the authentication between the nodes on the insecure channel in the network. We can explain this stage as can be seen in figure 1.

Step1: When a node in Ad Hoc Network wants to communicate with other node in the same network or in another one as shown in figure 1, which explains the authentication process between the source (S) and the destination (D) node before they start send and receive the important data. The source node generates a random number r and timestamp Ts and conducts XoR calculating using secret value SV, which the component shares to produce $r \oplus SV$ and $Ts \oplus SV$, the two values are combined to form a hash value h (r \\ Ts). The source node sends the $r \oplus SV$ and $Ts \oplus SV$ which it is introduces to the destination node.

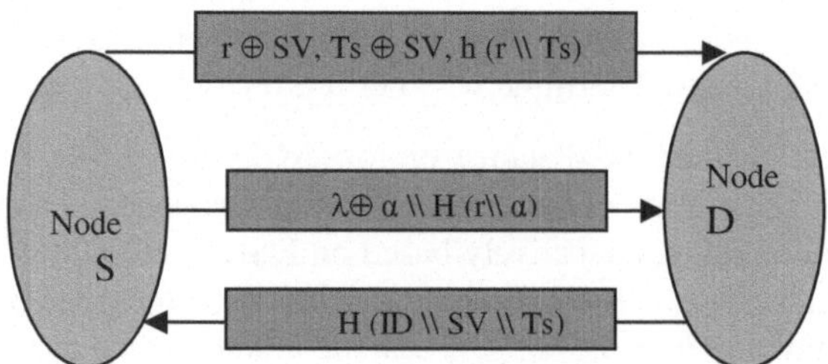

Fig. 1. Random number with secret value and timestamp authentication

Step2: This step is to authenticate the value transferred from the source. The destination conducts XoR calculating by inputting SV into r ⊕ SV and Ts ⊕ SV to acquire r and Ts. To authenticate r and Ts the destination hashes the two values to produce H (r\\Ts)' and compares it with H (r\\Ts) the hashed value transferred from the source node, when the two values are identical, r and Ts are authenticated. When the destination authenticate from the source values, it start to producesλ, where λ is the deference between r and Ts, and conducts a XoR calculation metaID, where metaID = α, to produce λ ⊕ α. The hash value H (r\\ α) is produces and combined with λ ⊕ α to form λ ⊕ α \\ H (r\\ α), which is to be sent to the source node for authentication.

Step 3: When the source receives λ ⊕ α \\ H (r\\ α) value from the destination it computes λ again by subtraction r from Ts (λ = r – Ts). Afterward the metaID value is acquired by conducting XoR calculation on the λ ⊕ α. To authenticate the acquired metaID (α), the transferred r is combined to form hash value H (r \\ α)'. If the transferred value H (r \\ α) is identical with produced H (r \\ α)', the metaID (α) is authenticated along with destination with the metaID. Also the source node computes metaID = H (ID)'to insure the ID belong to the destination. To acknowledge the authentication of the destination, the source combines the SV and the variable Ts to form a hash value of H (ID \\ SV \\ Ts) and send it to the destination node.

Step4: When the destination received the last value from the source node, it starts the verification process by authenticating the hash value H (ID \\ SV \\ Ts) that was transferred from the source node. The destination combines SV and Ts to produce hash value H (ID \\ SV \\ Ts). The source and destination mutually authenticate each other. Also after the hash value is authenticated, the destination ID that is included as a component of the hash value is authenticated.

Hash chain is used to verify the integrity of the hop count field of RREQ and RREP messages by allowing each node that receives the message to verify that the hop count has not been modified by malicious nodes. Hash chain consists of applying repeatedly a one-way hash function for a number of seeds.

Here we still use Destination Sequence Number (DSN) as in AODV to ensure that all routes are loop free and routing information is proper and valid. During the process of forwarding, the RREQ packets, the intermediate nodes record the address of the neighbor from whom the first copy of broadcast message is received in their routing tables. This helps to establish a reverse path [8][9].

AODV uses the hop count parameter to determine the shortest path between two nodes. A malicious node can set false hop counts and wrong values of the sequence number. This leads to redirection of network traffic or to a DoS attack.

When a path is not available for the destination, a route request packet is flooded along the network. The RREQ contains the following fields: sources address, request ID, source sequence number, destination address, destination sequence number, hop- count. The request ID is increased every time the source node sends new RREQ, so the pair (ID request, source address) defines a unique RREQ. On receiving RREQ message each node checks the request ID and the source address. If the node has already received a RREQ with the same pair of parameters the new RREQ packet will be ignored. Otherwise the RREQ will be forwarded (broadcast) or replied (unicast) with a RREP message:

- If the node doesn't have a route to the destination or it has one that is not updated, the RREQ will be re-broadcasted with increased hop-count;
- If the node has a path with a sequence number greater than or equal to that of RREQ, RREP message will be generated and sent back to the source. The number of RREQ messages that a node can send per second is limited.

AODV has an optimization using an expanding ring (ESR) technique for the flooding RREQ messages. Every RREQ has a time to live (TTL) value that specifies the number of times it should return this broadcasted message.

4.1 Comparison between Our Proposed Scheme and the Secure AODV (SAODV)

In MANET, the internal attacks are typically more severe, since malicious node already belongs to the network. To prevent internal attacks, we need to authenticate the unique identity of each node. Our proposed scheme provides an efficient way to verify the message authentication and message integrity. The receiver node can authenticate the sender of message as well as intermediate nodes using the shared secret key.

We compared our proposed scheme with secure AODV (SAODV) protocol in the presence of black hole attack [8]. A black hole attack is a kind of denial of service attack in which a malicious node assigns small hop count and high sequence number to the route reply message (RREP) and absorbs all packets by simply dropping it without forwarding them to the destination node. SAODV [10] is implemented as an extension to original AODV protocol. Although SAODV has proposed two alternatives to send RREP message, we used first alternative for implementation: only destination node can send RREP message. We also used hash function to secure hop count and RSA algorithm for digital signature and also the secret values and time stamp to increase the authentication process between the nodes.

In SAODV protocol, source node and intermediate node both verify signature before updating their routing table. A malicious node can impersonate a destination node but cannot generate signature of destination node. Similarly in proposed method, malicious node does not know the secret value shared between destination node and others node. The source node or intermediate node discards RREP packets coming from malicious node and hence does not establish route through malicious node.

Time delay of data packet means the difference between the time when the first data packet is received by the destination node and the time when the source node broadcasts a RREQ message. Time delay depends on both mobility and position of nodes. In case of the SAODV protocol and the proposed method, the time delay is more due to delay in establishing particular route as only destination node can send route reply message. Moreover the SAODV protocol has larger time delay compared to our scheme because SAODV uses asymmetric key cryptography so it requires significant processing time to compute or verify signatures and hashes at each node.

In proposed method, routing use extra bytes to store hashes and intermediate node addresses. Similarly in SAODV protocol, routing contain extra bytes to store digital signatures and hashes for providing security therefore both methods are the same from this point of view.

As shown our proposed protocol provides more security and authentication between nodes, improving also the security of the network.

5 Conclusion

In this paper, we describe the most and important attacks on the routing protocols and how the network can resist to these attacks in secure way, also we proposed a scheme used to increase the security between the nodes by enhancing and improving the authentication and confidentiality between the nodes. The proposed idea uses hash functions, time stamp and secret value, which it is shared between two nodes in a secure manner. Our solution expands the security scope and provides more authentication service between the nodes in MANET.

References

1. Conti, M.: Body, Personal and Local Ad Hoc Wireless Networks. In: The Handbook of Ad Hoc Wireless Networks, ch. 1. CRC Press LLC (2003)
2. Zhou, L., Hass, Z.J.: Securing Ad Hoc Networks. IEEE Networks
3. Zhang, Y., Lee, W.: Security in Mobile Ad-Hoc Networks. In: Ad Hoc Networks Technologies and Protocols, ch. 9. Springer (2005)
4. Perkins, C.E., Royer, E.M.: Ad hoc On-Demand Distance Vector Routing
5. Omala, C.R., Shetty, S., Padmashree, S., Elevarasi, E.: Wireless Ad hoc Mobile Networks. In: National Conference on Computing Communication and Technology, pp. 168–174 (2010)
6. Das, S.R., Perkins, C.E., Royer, E.M.: Performance Comparison of Two On-demand Routing Protocols for Ad Hoc Networks
7. Varaprasad, G., Venkataram, P.: The analysis of secure routing in mobile Ad Hoc network. In: International Conference on Computational Intelligence and Multimedia Applications, December 13-15, vol. 4, pp. 393–397 (2007)
8. Yi, Y., Naldurg, P., Kravets, R.: A security-aware routing protocol for wireless Ad Hoc networks, http://www-sal.cs.uiuc.edu/~rhk/pubs/SCI2002.pdf
9. Castelluccia, C., Mutaf, P.: Hash-Based Dynamic Source Routing. In: Mitrou, N.M., Kontovasilis, K., Rouskas, G.N., Iliadis, I., Merakos, L. (eds.) NETWORKING 2004. LNCS, vol. 3042, pp. 1012–1023. Springer, Heidelberg (2004)
10. Zapata, M.G.: Secure ad hoc on-demand distance vector (saodv) routing, internet-draft draftguerrero-manet-saodv-00.txt (October 2002)

Architecture for Trapping Toll Fraud Attacks Using a VoIP Honeynet Approach

Markus Gruber, Christian Schanes, Florian Fankhauser,
Martin Moutran, and Thomas Grechenig

Research Group for Industrial Software, Vienna University of Technology,
1040 Vienna, Austria
{markus.gruber,christian.schanes,florian.fankhauser,martin.moutran,
thomas.grechenig}@inso.tuwien.ac.at
http://security.inso.tuwien.ac.at/

Abstract. Voice over IP systems are more and more replacing Public Switched Telephone Network infrastructures. The number of voice telephony installations and the number of Session Initiation Protocol users is constantly increasing. Attacks against Voice over IP systems are becoming more imaginative and many attacks can cause financial damage, e.g., attackers gain money or create costs for the victim. Therefore, the dependency on available and secure Voice over IP systems to conduct secure business is given. We provide an environment to uncover real-world toll fraud attacks by collecting data using a Voice over IP honeynet solution.

1 Introduction

Today, Voice over IP (VoIP) systems are widely used in organizations, companies and also private households. Such systems represent a possible and valuable target for attackers. Although many attacks on VoIP systems are already known (see, e.g., Butcher et al. [3], Endler and Collier [5] and Blake [2]), there is not enough reliable information on the probability and nature of fraudulent calls on VoIP systems in the Internet. To establish countermeasures against attacks of VoIP systems the aim and methodology of attacks has to be known. Such information is not available for toll fraud attacks in current research work. To gain more understanding of existing real-world VoIP security attacks, in particular toll fraud, a VoIP honeynet with an Public Switched Telephone Network (PSTN) gateway was established. With this approach it is possible to collect data of attacks against the VoIP server as well as data of the abuse of our VoIP server for calls to the PSTN. The introduced approach allows to capture toll fraud attacks over a long period of time. Additionally, third party sources will be used for a detailed analysis. The implemented analyzing engine as part of the honeynet assists manual mining of the captured data.

The remainder of this paper is structured as follows. An overview of related work is given in Section 2. Section 3 introduces an architecture of a VoIP honeynet to gain information on toll fraud attacks via a PSTN uplink interface. In

J. Lopez, X. Huang, and R. Sandhu (Eds.): NSS 2013, LNCS 7873, pp. 628–634, 2013.

Section 4 an approach for detecting and analyzing toll fraud attacks was presented. The paper finishes with a conclusion and an outlook for possible further work in Section 5.

2 Related Work

Many attacks on VoIP systems are well described, e.g., malformed messages by Al-Allouni et al. [1], fraudulent calls by Nassar et al. [10] or registration hijacking by the authors of VOIPSA [15]. However, there is only a small amount of literature on the status of toll fraud attacks. An example of a lightweight VoIP security method to prevent toll fraud attacks via analyzing communication records with the focus on privacy was described in [8] by Hofbauer et al. The communication records contain personal information of the call participants, e.g., phone number or user names, with the focus on privacy. In [9] Hoffstadt et al. published an excerpt of toll fraud attacks. However, this analysis is only a short overview of fraudulent calls and not a detailed representation of fraudulent calls.

Our VoIP honeynet is based on the architecture and the ideas of Spitzner as described in [13], which can be used to gather information about attacks to protect IT systems. Our honeynet is focused on the collection of VoIP attacks with concentration on toll fraud attacks. One possibility to design a VoIP honeypot to detect attacks is described in [14] by Valli and Al-Lawati. This approach uses an Intrusion Detection System (IDS) and simple emulated honeypots to detect attacks. Our solution uses high interaction honeypots, i.e., vulnerable VoIP systems with an uplink interface to PSTN, which provides a realistic behavior to the attacker instead of emulated services. In [11] Ruiz-Agundez et al. present a fraud detection approach for next generation networks but not for Session Initiation Protocol (SIP) systems. A description of the scanning behavior of botnets is covered in [4] by Dainotti et al. Numerous websites feature information on VoIP attacks, e.g., SANS [12] shows the number of connections to port 5060 (which is the default port for SIP services), and Gauci's website on Sipviscious [6] gives details about sporadically recognized attacks. However, reliable data for custom analyses or automatic generated reports are not available.

3 Honeynet Architecture for Fraudulent Call Detection

Fraudulent calls are cost intensive for the operators of the VoIP system. This requires an architecture which supports capturing of the attacks with cost control for the honeynet operators.

3.1 Definition of Fraudulent Call Attacks

The term "toll fraud" is used if a person or a group of people uses paid services using another person's account without permission, described by Hoffstadt et al.

in [9]. In terms of SIP messages, the attacker first sends a REGISTER message containing the correct credentials to the SIP server. After the 200 OK response message from the server, the attacker can initiate calls by using INVITE messages.

Using a fraudulent VoIP call, an attacker calls a victim with fraudulent intentions. The aim of the attack varies, e.g., cause costs for the victim, advertising using voice calls without costs for the attacker, or the attackers use the hacked infrastructure to hide their own identity to call the potential victim.

The fraudulent call attack is a two-stage process. After the identification of a VoIP system an attacker starts the first phase and tries to gain access to the system, e.g., by brute force or social engineering attacks. In the second phase the attacker connects to the compromised system and attempts to make calls to endpoints in the PSTN.

3.2 Components and Processes of the VoIP/PSTN Honeynet Architecture

The main components of the proposed honeynet architecture are the honeywall, the VoIP honeypots, the VoIP Attack Analyzing Engine (VAAE) and the PSTN gateway, as shown in Figure 1. The architecture from our previous work [7] was extended with an uplink interface to a PSTN gateway and a voice pattern extraction functionality to be able to perform calls to PSTN endpoints and to analyze those calls.

Figure 1 also shows the processing steps for collecting toll fraud attacks with our proposed honeynet approach. First, the attacker tries to get access to a VoIP account on the honeypot for later abuse. As next step the caller (does not need to be the attacker) tries to call a phone number in the PSTN. The

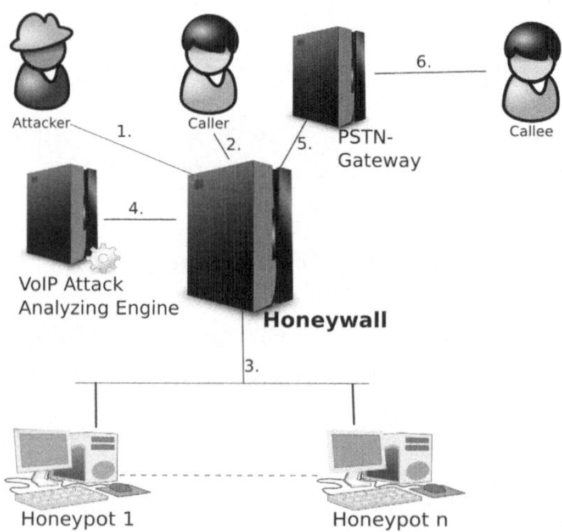

Fig. 1. Architecture of the VoIP honeynet with a PSTN uplink

honeywall captures all the VoIP packets, including the packets from the attacker, with *Data Capture* functionality, sends an alert and forwards the packets to the honeypot (step 3). The honeypot itself has a route to a PSTN gateway via the honeywall to support calls outside our infrastructure. The honeywall also controls the PSTN gateway to mitigate further risks, e.g., unintended calls, with the *Data Control* functionality. The honeywall allows configurations of predefined blacklists to block such calls, e.g., calls to law enforcement or a hospital. As fourth the honeywall sends the call to the VAAE to receive voice patterns of media data and forwards the call to the gateway afterwards. This architecture should help us to confirm the assumption that toll fraud attacks still exist and it is a business case for the attackers.

For the attackers the VoIP system of the honeypot seems to be a real VoIP gateway to perform calls to PSTN endpoints. For the analyses of the calls, the attackers and the attackers' behavior, our designed and implemented VAAE is used. The VAAE is able to perform various analyses of signaling data and media data of toll fraud attacks. The honeynet is extended with a feature to analyze media data via voice pattern extraction to be able to classify the calls, based on the assumed content. The VAAE can use all of the captured data from the VoIP honeynet. These are the timestamp of the data collection, the properties of the Internet Protocol (IP) stack, e.g., source and destination IP address, the properties of the SIP, e.g., SIP User Agent or SIP To Address and the properties of the Realtime Transport Protocol (RTP), e.g., media type, as well as the extracted voice patterns. The VAAE is connected via an own management network with the honeywall to avoid management data in the raw data. The VAAE can define various reports in templates to be able to reuse it and to be able to customize and automate the analyses.

As VoIP honeypot we use an Asterisk SIP server with four accounts with weak passwords to increase the probability of toll fraud attacks. Asterisk is a widely used VoIP system and very popular for attackers. If a caller tries to call a callee outside the local VoIP domain of the honeypot the call will be forwarded to our VoIP provider via the uplink interface, who will route the call to the specific PSTN endpoint.

3.3 Uplink Interface Setup – Connection to PSTN Endpoints

The uplink interface enables our VoIP system to call numbers in PSTN. The uplink interface can be, e.g., an Integrated Services Digital Network (ISDN) modem, a data modem or a third party provider. We decided to use a third party provider with a support for prepaid solutions to have better cost control. To activate the uplink interface and to allow calls to PSTN endpoints, credit must be bought first. The integrated VoIP provider sends a notification if a customized limit is reached to be able to top up the credit in time.

4 Capturing and Mining Honeynet Data – Approach for Detecting and Analyzing Toll Fraud Attacks

We implemented the approach and operated the honeynet to capture toll fraud attacks. Finally, one part of the approach is an analyzing engine which assists manual analysis.

4.1 Capturing Real-World VoIP/PSTN Attacks

While running our honeynet solution we found valuable insights into toll fraud attacks. The VoIP honeynet with PSTN gateway has been in operation since August 2011. The honeynet collected 98,447,971 incoming IP packets, including 30,025,621 VoIP packets up to and including December 2012.

In our honeynet we have different periods with an activated uplink interface, because we activated the uplink only for research purposes. We have an uplink period in October 2011, March, April and December 2012. Figure 2 shows the number of captured SIP packets in the honeynet from 2011-08-01 until 2012-12-31. The peak in March 2012 can be explained with the high number of SIP call attempts after the uplink interface has been activated. In comparison to the other uplink periods, in March 2012 the number of calls is much higher but the length of the calls is shorter as e.g., in December 2012. Between 2012-09-04 and 2012-12-06, maintenance was performed on our infrastructure which explains the low point in the chart during that time.

All captured calls in the evaluation period try to call an external number in a PSTN, in most cases an international number or a premium number. No calls and no tries to another VoIP user in the local domain were detected. The

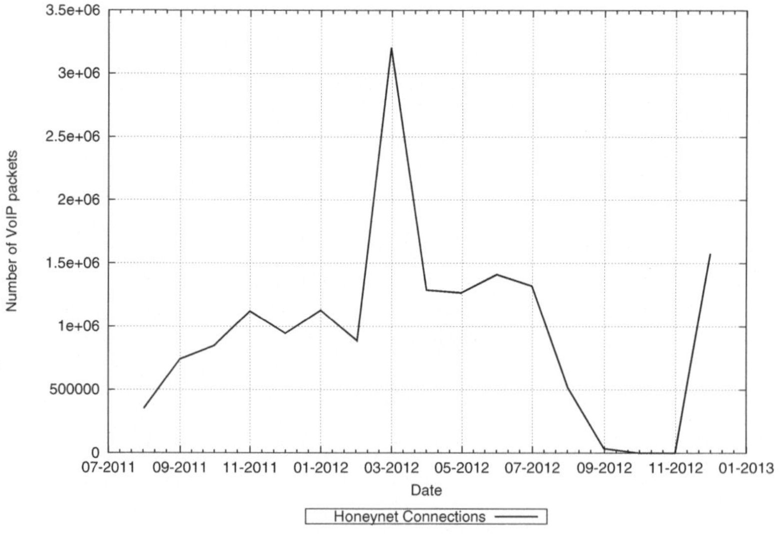

Fig. 2. Number of captured SIP packets in the honeynet

number of calls increases after the first successful call to PSTN. We guess the attackers are probing VoIP systems with PSTN gateways. If they find a system with a PSTN gateway they will perform further attacks, as we see in the peak in March 2012 in Figure 2. Thus, our assumption is supported that the attacker behaviour changes after a successful call to PSTN was performed.

4.2 Concept of a VoIP Attack Analyzing Engine for Toll Fraud Attacks

With the VAAE all data from the honeywall and the honeypot can be semi-automated analyzed to gain information about the attacks and the attackers. In addition to the collected data from the honeynet, the VAAE uses third party sources, e.g., the whois directory service, phone books, price tables of various VoIP services or User Agent (UA) databases, to gain even more information about the attacks and the attackers. Especially for fraudulent calls and the detection of the attacker intention, the VAAE uses a voice pattern analysis feature to identify similar noises, to identify unidirectional communication and to identify human conversations based on keywords for many languages.

With the use of templates the VAAE can be customized to perform various analyses, e.g., about the country of the callee's phone number, to show details of the signaling data or the possibility to classify the voice patterns of the content of the calls. These features help to identify the intention of the attackers, e.g., regular calls, Spam over IP Telephony (SPIT) messages or unidirectional communications.

5 Conclusion and Further Work

The number of VoIP users will likely increase in the future and, therefore, VoIP systems will get even more interesting for attackers. Our work presents a solution to capture toll fraud attacks for further analyzing with a VoIP honeynet approach. Our solution can be easily extended to gain information on attacks on other VoIP systems or to show attacks on the same system. This helps to learn more about VoIP toll fraud attacks.

The operation of the honeynet showed that toll fraud is one important aspect of VoIP system security. The costs of a misused system can be very expensive for the owner. Ongoing research on toll fraud attacks and, more generally, on the security status of VoIP systems is needed to better protect existing solutions. The introduced VoIP honeynet solution supports detailed analysis by collecting data on toll fraud attacks and by semi-automating analysis steps.

Further work include the analyzing of the collected data of toll fraud attacks with the presented VoIP honeynet approach and the derivation of countermeasures of the attacks based on the analyzed data.

References

1. Al-Allouni, H., Rohiem, A.E., Hashem, M., El-moghazy, A., Ahmed, A.E.-A.: Voip denial of service attacks classification and implementation. In: National Radio Science Conference (NRSC), pp. 1–12 (2009)
2. Blake, E.A.: Network security: Voip security on data network–a guide. In: InfoSecCD 2007: Proceedings of the 4th Annual Conference on Information Security Curriculum Development, pp. 1–7. ACM, New York (2007)
3. Butcher, D., Li, X., Guo, J.: Security challenge and defense in voip infrastructures. IEEE Transactions on Systems, Man, and Cybernetics, Part C: Applications and Reviews 37(6), 1152–1162 (2007)
4. Dainotti, A., King, A., Claffy, K., Papale, F., Pescapè, A.: Analysis of a "/0" stealth scan from a botnet. In: Proceedings of the 2012 ACM Conference on Internet Measurement Conference, IMC 2012, pp. 1–14. ACM, New York (2012)
5. Endler, D., Collier, M.: Hacking Exposed VoIP: Voice Over IP Security Secrets & Solutions. McGraw-Hill, Inc., New York (2007)
6. Gauci, S.: Distributed sip scanning during halloween weekend, `http://blog.sipvicious.org/2010/11/distributed-sip-scanning-during.html` (last accessed: January 12, 2013)
7. Gruber, M., Fankhauser, F., Taber, S., Schanes, C., Grechenig, T.: Trapping and analyzing malicious voip traffic using a honeynet approach. In: The 6th International Conference on Internet Technology and Secured Transactions (ICITST), pp. 442–447 (December 2011)
8. Hofbauer, S., Beckers, K., Quirchmayr, G., Sorge, C.: A lightweight privacy preserving approach for analyzing communication records to prevent voip attacks using toll fraud as an example. In: 2012 IEEE 11th International Conference on Trust, Security and Privacy in Computing and Communications (TrustCom), pp. 992–997 (June 2012)
9. Hoffstadt, D., Marold, A., Rathgeb, E.: Analysis of sip-based threats using a voip honeynet system. In: 2012 IEEE 11th International Conference on Trust, Security and Privacy in Computing and Communications (TrustCom), pp. 541–548 (June 2012)
10. Nassar, M., State, R., Festor, O.: Voip malware: Attack tool & attack scenarios. In: IEEE International Conference on Communications, ICC 2009, pp. 1–6 (June 2009)
11. Ruiz-Agundez, I., Penya, Y.K., Bringas, P.G.: Fraud detection for voice over IP services on next-generation networks. In: Samarati, P., Tunstall, M., Posegga, J., Markantonakis, K., Sauveron, D. (eds.) WISTP 2010. LNCS, vol. 6033, pp. 199–212. Springer, Heidelberg (2010)
12. SANS Internet Storm Center. Port details — sans internet storm center, `http://isc.sans.edu/port.html?port=5060` (last accessed: January 12, 2013)
13. Spitzner, L.: The honeynet project: trapping the hackers. IEEE Security & Privacy Magazine 1(2), 15–23 (2003)
14. Valli, C., Al-Lawati, M.: Developing robust voip router honeypots using device fingerprints. In: 1st International Cyber Resilience Conference (August 2010)
15. VoIP Security Alliance. Voipsa, voip security and privacy threat taxonomy, `http://www.voipsa.org/Activities/VOIPSA_Threat_Taxonomy_0.1.pdf` (last accessed: January 12, 2013)

Towards a Privacy-Preserving Solution for OSNs

Qiang Tang

APSIA Group, SnT, University of Luxembourg
6, rue Richard Coudenhove-Kalergi, L-1359 Luxembourg
qiang.tang@uni.lu

Abstract. In this short paper, we describe a solution to protect users' privacy in online social networks (OSNs). The solution achieves the following functionalities: (1) it enables users to store their private data securely; (2) it enables users, from the same or different OSNs, to compute their similarity through a secure protocol; (3) it enables similar users to establish a session key for secure communication. Different from existing solutions in the literature, which often rely on a global public key infrastructure or/and traditional key distribution techniques, the proposed solution leverages on the trust between friends and the entropy of users' private attributes.

1 Introduction

Online social networks (OSNs) provide the service that connects classmates, friends, and other people who share similar interests and activities across political, economic, and geographic borders. As surveyed in [1], a large number of OSNs exist, among which Facebook, MySpace, Google +, and Twitter are the most popular ones.

Due to their nature, OSNs can easily collect a huge amount of user data. Among all kinds of OSN data, a particularly important one is profile attributes. In most OSNs, profile attributes consist of a lot of information, ranging from name, address, education background to political views, hobbies, and daily activities. All attributes are available in plaintext to the OSN service providers and, depending on the configurations, some of them are available to third parties. It is not surprising that a subset of the profile attributes can already identify a user, even after anonymization [4,6]. Therefore, it is an interesting task to design a solution for users to: (1) protect their private profile attributes; (2) establish friendship with strangers based on their profile similarities (this is the main reason why users want to publish their profiles). This implies that the solution should partially resolve the privacy-functionality tension [8], by simultaneously providing privacy protection for profile attributes and allowing users to conveniently compute their profile similarities.

In reality, it is reasonable to assume that most users are involved in multiple OSNs. Now, suppose that both Alice and Bob are enrolled in Facebook and Myspace, and they have the same location attribute in Facebook and the same music taste attribute in Myspace. Due to the different focuses of the OSNs, Alice and Bob may not disclose their location information in Myspace, at the same time they may not disclose their music taste information in Facebook. It will not be a surprise that Alice and Bob are not friends in Facebook and Myspace, because they do not share much in common in either

J. Lopez, X. Huang, and R. Sandhu (Eds.): NSS 2013, LNCS 7873, pp. 635–641, 2013.

of the OSNs. If they realize their common attributes in both OSNs, Alice and Bob may like to consider each other as a friend and attend some music event together in the city. This indicates that it is desirable to have a solution which works across multiple OSNs.

1.1 Our Contribution

The contribution of this paper is threefold. Firstly, we describe some new cryptographic building blocks and briefly analyze their security properties, including a unilateral set intersection cardinality protocol and a unilateral comparison protocol. Secondly, we propose a solution for protecting users' private profile attributes in OSNs. In the solution, a transitive and uni-directional proxy re-encryption scheme [5] allows users to encrypt their private profile attributes with their own public keys. Based on the unilateral set intersection cardinality protocol, we design an Online-Offline profile matching protocol, which allows two users to compute their profile similarity and one of them can stay offline. Based on the unilateral comparison protocol and a fuzzy extractor scheme [3], we design an Online-Online profile matching protocol, which allows two online users to compute their profile similarity. Thirdly, we observe that users' communications are under surveillance by the OSN service providers. So, we propose a secure channel establishment protocol which allows two users to exchange a session key if they share a certain number of common private profile attributes.

1.2 Organization

The rest of this paper is organized as follows. In Section 2, we describe the new building blocks which will be used later on. In Section 3, we briefly describe the proposed solution. In Section 4, we provide the details of the profile matching protocols and a secure channel establishment protocol, employed in the proposed solution. In Section 5, we conclude the paper.

2 New Cryptographic Building Blocks

The proposed solution employs transitive and uni-directional proxy re-encryption cryptosystem , namely $(\mathsf{KeyGen}, \mathsf{Enc}, \mathsf{Dec}, \mathsf{Pextract}, \mathsf{Preenc})$ [5], and the following two new protocols.

2.1 Unilateral Set Intersection Cardinality Protocol

Let ℓ be the security parameter, $n > 1$ be an integer and $\mathbb{F} = \mathbb{Z}_q$ where q is a prime number (i.e. $\mathbb{F}$ is a finite field). We assume that the bit-length of q is a polynomial of the security parameter ℓ and $n < q$. Consider the following client-server setting: the server possesses a polynomial $\mathcal{R}(x) \in \mathbb{F}[x]$; the client possesses a polynomial $\mathcal{Q}(x) \in \mathbb{F}[x]$ and c_i $(1 \le i \le n) \in \mathbb{F}$. Suppose that $\mathcal{R}(x)$ and $\mathcal{Q}(x)$ are of degree n, and the roots of $\mathcal{F}(x) = \mathcal{R}(x) + \mathcal{Q}(x)$ are denoted as $d_i(1 \le i \le n) \in \mathbb{F}$. Based on Paillier scheme [7], the following protocol allows the client to learn the cardinality of the set intersection between c_i $(1 \le i \le n)$ and d_i $(1 \le i \le n)$, while the server learns nothing.

1. The server generates a paillier key pair (PK_s, SK_s), where the public key is $PK_s = (N_s, g_s)$. The client generates a paillier key pair (PK_c, SK_c), where the public key is $PK_c = (N_c, g_c)$. then, they exchange and validate their public keys. Here, we assume that $q^5 < N_s$ and $q < N_c$, so that the polynomial coefficients and roots can be directly encrypted by both public keys.
2. The server encrypts its polynomial $\mathcal{R}(x)$ and sends the ciphertext $[\mathcal{R}(x)]_{PK_s}$ to the client. Note that $[\mathcal{R}(x)]_{PK_s}$ is a vector, consisting of the ciphertexts of $\mathcal{R}(x)$'s coefficients under PK_s.
3. For every attribute c_i $(1 \leq i \leq n)$, the client does the following: (1) compute $[\mathcal{R}(c_i)]_{PK_s}$ based on $[\mathcal{R}(x)]_{PK_s}$ and c_i; (2) compute $Q(c_i)$ and its ciphertext $[Q(c_i)]_{PK_s}$; (3) compute $[\mathcal{F}(c_i)]_{PK_s}$ based on $[\mathcal{R}(c_i)]_{PK_s}$ and $[Q(c_i)]_{PK_s}$; (4) select $y_i \in_R \mathbb{Z}_{q^4}$ and compute the randomized value $[\mathcal{F}(c_i) + y_i]_{PK_s}$; (5) compute $y'_i = y_i \mod q$ and $[N_c - y'_i]_{PK_c}$. After all the computations, the client sends $\mathcal{F}(c_i) + y_i]_{PK_s}$, $[N_c - y'_i]_{PK_c}$ $(1 \leq i \leq n)$ to the server.
4. After receiving the values from the client, for every i $(1 \leq i \leq n)$, the server does the following: (1) decrypt $[\mathcal{F}(c_i) + y_i]_{PK_s}$ to obtain $\mathcal{F}(c_i) + y_i$; (2) compute $T_i = \mathcal{F}(c_i) + y_i \mod q$ which is equal to $\mathcal{F}(c_i) + y'_i \mod q$; (3) select $y''_i \in_R N_c$ and compute $R_i = ([T_i]_{PK_c} \cdot [N_c - y'_i]_{PK_c})^{y''_i} \mod N_c^2$. After all the computations, the server sends a randomly permuted version of $\{R_i\ (1 \leq i \leq n)\}$ to the client.
5. The client decrypts R_i $(1 \leq i \leq n)$, and count the number of 0s as the intersection size.

2.2 Unilateral Comparison Protocol

Let $\mathbb{G}$ be a group of prime order p, and $\mathsf{H}_2 : \{0,1\}^* \rightarrow \mathbb{G}$ and $\mathsf{H}_3 : \{0,1\}^* \rightarrow \{0,1\}^\ell$ be two hash functions. If a client wants to test whether his value S is equal to the value S' of the server, then the client initiates the protocol shown in Fig. 1.

Client (S)		**Server** (S')
$x \in_R \mathbb{Z}_p$		$y \in_R \mathbb{Z}_p$
	$\xrightarrow{\mathsf{H}_2(S)^x}$	
	$\xleftarrow{\mathsf{H}_3(\mathsf{H}_2(S')^y),\ \mathsf{H}_2(S)^{xy}}$	
$\mathsf{H}_3(\mathsf{H}_2(S')^y) \stackrel{?}{=} \mathsf{H}_3(\mathsf{H}_2(S)^{xyx^{-1}})$		

Fig. 1. Unilateral Comparison Protocol

3 The Proposed Solution for OSNs

We generally assume that there is a semi-trust relationship among friends in OSNs. By "semi-trust", we mean that if Alice semi-trusts Bob then she can assume that Bob will not collude with a third-party or reveal her private information. Moreover, we assume that the semi-trust relationship is unilateral, which means that "Alice semi-trusts Bob" does not immediately imply "Bob semi-trusts Alice". Furthermore, we assume that the semi-trust relationship is transitive: if Alice semi-trusts Bob, Bob semi-trusts Charlie, then Alice will semi-trust Charlie.

There is a PPCP server, which is semi-trusted to every user in the system. Therefore, users do not need to fully trust the PPCP server to store their plaintext attributes. Compared with any current OSN, where users need to fully trust the service providers, this is an improvement. Every user can communicate with the PPCP server through a secure channel. Moreover, the PPCP server is trusted to publish the following parameters, used by all users.

- Security parameter: ℓ.
- ElGamal parameter: a multiplicative group $\mathbb{G}$ of degree p, a generator g, and three cryptographic hash functions $\mathsf{H}_0 : \mathbb{G} \rightarrow \mathbb{Z}_p$, $\mathsf{H}_1 : \{0,1\}^* \rightarrow \{0,1\}^L$, $\mathsf{H}_2 : \{0,1\}^* \rightarrow \mathbb{G}$, and $\mathsf{H}_3 : \{0,1\}^* \rightarrow \{0,1\}^\ell$ where L is a polynomial of the security parameter.
- Profile encapsulation parameter: a finite field $\mathbb{F} = \mathbb{Z}_q$ where q is a prime number. We assume that the attributes fall into $\mathbb{F}$.

Let all the users be denoted as U_i $(1 \leq i \leq N)$, where N is an integer, and U_i's attributes be denoted as $\mathcal{A}_i = \{h_{i,j}\ (1 \leq j \leq n)\}$. The proposed solution is composed of three services, including the secure profile storage service, the secure profile matching service, and the secure communication service. They are described in detail below.

3.1 Secure Profile Storage Service

U_i registers at the PPCP server and obtains an identifier ID_i. Moreover, U_i generates an ElGamal public/private key pair (PK_i, SK_i), where $(SK_i = x_i, PK_i = g^{x_i})$, following the specification in [5] based on the ElGamal parameter. U_i sends the public parameters (ID_i, PK_i) to its friends.

1. U_i chooses a subset of his friends that he semi-trusts, denoted as U_{i_x} $(1 \leq x \leq N_i)$.
2. U_i performs the following operations.
   (a) Generate re-encryption keys $RK_{i \rightarrow i_x}$ for every $(1 \leq x \leq N_i)$, which is identified by (ID_i, ID_{i_x}).
   (b) Based on his attributes $h_{i,j}$ $(1 \leq j \leq n)$, generate $\mathcal{F}_i(x), \mathcal{Q}_i(x), \mathcal{R}_i(x) \in \mathbb{F}[x]$ of degree n as follows: $\mathcal{F}_i(x) = \prod_{j=1}^{n}(x - h_{i,j})$, $\mathcal{F}_i(x) = \mathcal{Q}_i(x) + \mathcal{R}_i(x)$, where the coefficients of $\mathcal{R}_i(x)$ are randomly chosen from $\mathbb{F}$.
   (c) Based on the ElGamal encryption algorithm Enc specified in [5], encrypt $\mathcal{Q}_i(x)$ using PK_i to obtain $[\mathcal{Q}_i(x)]_{PK_i} = (g^{r_i}, g^{r_i \cdot x_i} \cdot t_i, \mathsf{H}_1(t_i) \oplus \underline{\mathcal{Q}_i(x)})$, where $r_i \in_R \mathbb{Z}_p$, $t_i \in_R \mathbb{G}$, $\underline{\mathcal{Q}_i(x)}$ represents the coefficients of $\mathcal{Q}_i(x)$.
3. U_i stores $(PK_i,\ RK_{i \rightarrow i_x}\ (1 \leq x \leq N_i),\ \mathcal{R}_i(x),\ [\mathcal{Q}_i(x)]_{PK_i})$ at the PPCP server, and associates the data to his identifier ID_i. He keeps SK_i private locally.

With users' data, the PPCP server can construct a social graph $\mathcal{G}$ of the semi-trust relationships among users. In this graph, there is a directed edge from U_i to U_j if U_i semi-trusts U_j (i.e. U_i has generated a re-encryption key $RK_{i \rightarrow j}$).

3.2 Secure Profile Matching Service (i.e. Friendship Establishment)

Suppose that U_j has obtained some public information about U_i and consider him as a potential friend. For example, U_i may have publish his identifier ID_i and some hobby information at Facebook, and U_j surfed to U_i's page and obtained the information. Then, U_j can send ID_i to the PPCP server and request to match with U_i. When the PPCP server receives a request, it first checks whether U_i is online. If so, it check U_i's policy, which can have two possibilities.

1. If U_i prefers to run the Online-Online protocol described in Section 4.2 when he is online, then U_j and U_i run the protocol.
2. If U_i prefers not to be involved in the matching, the PPCP server tries to find the shortest semi-trust link from U_i to U_j. If the length of the link is within a threshold agreed by U_i, then the PPCP server represents U_i to run the Online-Offline protocol described in Section 4.1 with U_j. Otherwise, U_j's request is rejected.

If U_i is offline, the PPCP server checks U_i's policy to see whether he wants his profile to be matched when he is offline. If so, the PPCP server does the same as in the aforementioned possibility 2. Otherwise, U_j's request is rejected.

3.3 Secure Communication Service

Suppose that there is a semi-trust link from U_j to U_i, and these two users want to protect their communications. Then, then they can run the secure channel establishment protocol described in Section 4.3. Note that the existence of semi-trust link implies that U_j and U_i share a certain number of common profile attributes, therefore, the protocol will generate a common session key for them.

4 The Employed Protocols

In this section, we describe two profile matching protocols and a secure channel establishment protocol, that are refereed to in the previous section.

4.1 Online-Offline Matching Protocol

Suppose that a user U_j wants to match his profile with U_i and there is a semi-trust link from U_i to U_j, namely there is a chain of proxy re-encryption keys $(RK_{i\to i_1}, RK_{i_1\to i_2}, \cdots, RK_{i_t\to j})$ from U_i to U_j. In this case, the following protocol is carried out between U_j and the PPCP server.

1. In the first stage, the polynomial $Q_i(x)$ is transferred to U_j. In more detail, the PPCP server performs a series of re-encryptions to transform $[Q_i(x)]_{PK_i}$ into $[Q_i(x)]_{PK_j}$ using the chain of re-encryption keys. From $[Q_i(x)]_{PK_j}$, U_j can recover $Q_i(x)$ using his own private key SK_j. At the end of this stage, U_j has $Q_i(x)$ and his own attributes $\mathcal{A}_j = \{h_{j,t}\ (1 \le t \le n)\}$, and the PPCP server possess $\mathcal{R}_i(x)$.
2. In the second stage, U_j and the PPCP server run the unilateral set intersection cardinality protocol, specified in Section 2.1, where U_j and the PPCP server play the roles of the client and the server respectively. At the end of the protocol execution, U_j learns her profile simplicity with U_i.

4.2 Online-Online Matching Protocol

The proposed protocol makes use of a $(\mathcal{U}, \ell_1, \ell_2, t, \epsilon)$-fuzzy extractor [3], where $\mathcal{U}$ is the domain of profile attribute set. When U_j is the initiator, the proposed protocol proceeds in two stages.

1. In the first stage, U_j and U_i engage in a protocol, shown in Fig. 2, where H_1 is defined in Section 3.

$\mathbf{U_j}$		$\mathbf{U_i}$
$(\mathcal{A}_j = \{h_{j,t}\ (1 \le t \le n)\})$		$(\mathcal{A}_i = \{h_{i,t}\ (1 \le t \le n)\})$
$(r_j, h_j) = \mathsf{Gen}((h_{j,1}, \cdots, h_{j,n}))$		
	$\xrightarrow{h_j}$	
		$(r_i, h_i) = \mathsf{Gen}((h_{i,1}, \cdots, h_{i,n}))$
	$\xleftarrow{h_i}$	
$r'_i = \mathsf{Rep}(\mathcal{A}_j, h_i)$		$r'_j = \mathsf{Rep}(\mathcal{A}_i, h_j)$
$ck_j = \mathsf{H}_1(ID_i \| ID_j \| h_i \| r'_i \| h_j \| r_j)$		$ck_i = \mathsf{H}_1(ID_i \| ID_j \| h_i \| r_i \| h_j \| r'_j)$

Fig. 2. Online Matching Protocol (Stage 1)

2. In the second stage, U_j initiates the unilateral comparison protocol, specified in Section 2.2, to test whether $ck_j = ck_i$.

4.3 Secure Channel Establishment Protocol

As in Section 4.2, the proposed protocol combines a $(\mathcal{U}, \ell_1, \ell_2, t, \epsilon)$-fuzzy extractor scheme [3] and a secure password-based authenticated key exchange (PAKE) scheme. Note that a lot of PAKE schemes exist in the literature, Boyd and Mathuria [2] provided a survey for those proposed before 2004. In more detail, when U_j initiates the protocol with U_i, then they perform as follows.

1. In the first stage, they run the protocol shown in Fig. 2 to establish some ephemeral secrets. U_j generates $ck_j = \mathsf{H}_1(ID_i \| ID_j \| h_i \| r'_i \| h_j \| r_j)$ and U_i generates $ck_i = \mathsf{H}_1(ID_i \| ID_j \| h_i \| r_i \| h_j \| r'_j)$. Note that if the distance between $\mathcal{A}_i$ and $\mathcal{A}_j$ is smaller than t, then $ck_j = ck_i$.
2. In the second stage, they run a secure PAKE scheme to establish a session key. The key materials of ck_j and ck_i are used as the passwords.

5 Conclusion

In this short paper, we have briefly outlined a privacy-preserving solution for OSNs. The solution provides three services, including the secure profile storage service, the secure profile matching service, and the secure communication service. More details about the proposed solution and the associated protocols can be found in the full version of this paper, which is available at: http://tonyrhul.wordpress.com.

Acknowledgement. This work has been sponsored by the NLnet foundation in the Netherlands, when the author worked at University of Twente. The author thanks Arjan Jackmans from University of Twente for his helpful discussions.

References

1. Beye, M., Jeckmans, A., Erkin, Z., Hartel, P., Lagendijk, R., Tang, Q.: Literature overview - privacy in online social networks. Technical report, Centre for Telematics and Information Technology, University of Twente (2010)
2. Boyd, C., Mathuria, A.: Protocols for Authentication and Key Establishment. Springer (2004)
3. Dodis, Y., Reyzin, L., Smith, A.: Fuzzy extractors: How to generate strong keys from biometrics and other noisy data. In: Cachin, C., Camenisch, J.L. (eds.) EUROCRYPT 2004. LNCS, vol. 3027, pp. 523–540. Springer, Heidelberg (2004)
4. Hay, M., Miklau, G., Jensen, D., Towsley, D., Weis, P.: Resisting structural re-identification in anonymized social networks. Proc. VLDB Endow. 1(1), 102–114 (2008)
5. Jeckmans, A., Tang, Q., Hartel, P.: Privacy-preserving profile matching using the social graph. In: The Third International Conference on Computational Aspects of Social Networks, pp. 42–47 (2011)
6. Narayanan, A., Shmatikov, V.: De-anonymizing social networks. In: Proceedings of the 2009 30th IEEE Symposium on Security and Privacy, pp. 173–187 (2009)
7. Paillier, P.: Public-key cryptosystems based on composite degree residuosity classes. In: Stern, J. (ed.) EUROCRYPT 1999. LNCS, vol. 1592, pp. 223–238. Springer, Heidelberg (1999)
8. Palen, L., Dourish, P.: Unpacking "privacy" for a networked world. In: CHI 2003: Proceedings of the SIGCHI Conference on Human Factors in Computing Systems, pp. 129–136 (2003)

Measuring and Comparing the Protection Quality in Different Operating Systems

Zhihui Han, Liang Cheng, Yang Zhang, and Dengguo Feng

Institute of Software, CAS, China
{hanzhihui,chengliang}@is.iscas.ac.cn

Abstract. Host compromise is a serious computer security problem. It is necessary to understand the protection quality provided by various access control subsystems, which includes the likelihood of potential multi-step attacks and the damage effect. In this paper, we propose an approach to quantify the protection quality of access control subsystems. We compute a host attack graph to describe the protection quality of an access control subsystem from the point of threats it faces. By assessing attack actions with the help of CVSS, we make a quantitative risk evaluation for the system based on the attack graph.

Keywords: Operating System, Access Control, Quantitative Evaluation, Attack Graph, Protection Quality.

1 Introduction

Most Commercial-Off-The-Shelf (COTS) operating systems provide both Discretionary Access Control (DAC) and Mandatory Access Control (MAC) to protect our systems, such as Mandatory Integrity Control (MIC) for Windows Vista and 7, Security Enhanced Linux (SELinux) and AppArmor for Linux.

Given the existence of these access control subsystems, it is a natural desire to understand and compare the protection quality provided by them. In this paper, we present a tool called Access Control Quantitative Evaluation (ACQE) tool to quantify the protection quality. Our tool focuses on the privilege-escalation attack and can automatically discover all the privilege-escalation attack paths. An attack path consists of one or several actions performed by an attacker. Based on the Common Vulnerability Score System (CVSS) [6], we compute the probability and security impact of every action, and then the probability and security impact of every attack path. With the help of analytic hierarchy process(AHP) [1] and fault tree analysis(FTA) [2], we quantify the protection quality, which includes the probability of system compromised, and the impact on system confidentiality, integrity, and availability.

Our contributions are as follows:

1. We propose an approach to quantitatively analyze the security of a protection system. By introducing the evaluation of actions, we use FTA and AHP to quantitatively evaluate the security of a protection system.

J. Lopez, X. Huang, and R. Sandhu (Eds.): NSS 2013, LNCS 7873, pp. 642–648, 2013.

2. We implement a tool called ACQE based on our approach, which can help administrators to understand and harden their system security.
3. We use our tool ACQE to study the security of Windows 7, Ubuntu 10.04 with SELinux and AppArmor respectively.

The rest of this paper is organized as follows: Section 2 describes the overview of our approach. Section 3 discusses the experiments and results of comparing Windows 7 with Linux and some discussions. Section 4 discusses related work. Section 5 concludes the paper.

2 Design of Our Approach

To measure and compare the protection quality of access control subsystem, we first collect some security-related system information, and encode these information as logic predicates. Then, an attack graph [11] is generated. Next, we specify the *attack surface* of a protection system as the set of all the paths extracted from the attack graph. The *attack surface* intuitively reflects the security risk of a protection system. Finally, by assessing attack actions, we quantitatively evaluate the attack surface and output the result, where the result is the quantitative evaluation of protection quality. Fig.1 shows the overview of our approach.

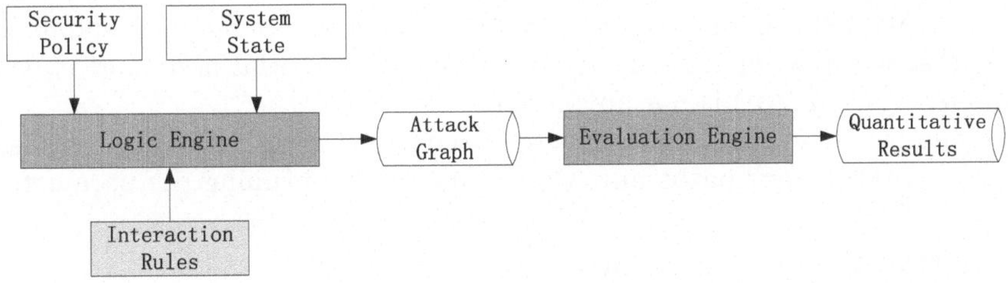

Fig. 1. Overview of our Approach

2.1 Logical Specifications of System Facts and Vulnerability

We first collect some security related system facts including system state and security policies. System facts related to our analysis include users, file system, network state and system process snapshot. We then encode the collected data to Prolog predicates, such as `File(file, attrList)`, which shows a file and its security attributes.

The specifications of vulnerability are the major component of interaction rules and the kernel part of logic engine.Since privilege escalation is the precondition for most of attacks, we focus on privilege escalation vulnerabilities and encode some escalation vulnerabilities to Prolog Horn clauses, one of which is listed below.

```
ControlProcess(p):- CriticalFile(p, file), ControlFileData(file).
```

This is the Wait-Execute vulnerability. The vulnerability enables an attacker to modify the critical file of the running process and hope the process will be run in the future by the same user, if the user is a privileged user, the new-running process can give the attacker some elevated privileges.

2.2 Attack Graph

An attack graph is used to demonstrate all possible attacks scenarios. With the input of security policies, system states and interaction rules, the logic engine can check which privileges an attacker can obtain from the initial abilities. By recording the inference trace, we can easily get the adjacent matrix of a host attack graph. There are two kinds of graph nodes in an attack graph: *ability nodes* and *action nodes.* An ability node represents an attacker's abilities and an action node indicates an action that an attacker may perform. Nodes representing initial abilities are called *initial nodes.* Nodes representing goals are called *goal nodes.* We specify the *attack surface* of an access control subsystem as the set of all the paths from initial nodes to goal nodes.

An attacker's goal is to get control of a process with administrator or system account in Windows or root user in Linux. An attack path is a sequence of abilities and actions, which shows the process that an attacker performs some actions to gain new abilities. We use a depth-first-search (DFS) to enumerate all the attack paths from initial nodes to goal nodes in the attack graph. In the DFS, we make following restrict to avoid unnecessary actions: if an enumerated path contains nodes: $v_1, ..., v_i, ..., v_n$, where v_1 is the initial node and v_n is the goal node, $v_i (1 < i < n)$ is not any goal node.

The number of attack paths extracted from attack graph could be very large, so we categorize attack paths into attack patterns by pruning the parameters.

2.3 Action Evaluation Approach

As basic events of attacks, attack actions should be assessed first, which is the foundation of Evaluation Engine in Fig. 1. Since the attack actions contained in attack paths correspond to vulnerability exploitations, we borrow CVSS [6] to assess these actions quantitatively.

We use exploitability metrics of CVSS to assess the level of exploitability needed for an attacker to exploit the vulnerabilities, which include three metrics: access vector AV, access complexity AC, authentication AU. We also use impact metrics of CVSS to assess the damage impact induced by exploiting the vulnerability on three classical security properties: confidentiality impact *ConfI*, integrity impact *IntegI*, availability impact *AvailI.* The possible values and quantitative number for every metric we adopt are the same with those defined in CVSS.

We convert the base score given by CVSS to probability by adopting normalization method, and derive following equations to evaluate an attack action:

$$Pr = AV * AC * AU \tag{1}$$

$$Impact = 1 - (1 - ConfI) * (1 - IntegI) * (1 - AvailI) \tag{2}$$

Where, *Pr* represents the likelihood of a successful attack action, and *Impact* represents the direct impact on the system if an attack action succeeds. And we use the quintuple (*ConfI*, *IntegI*, *AvailI*, *Impact*, *Pr*) to presents the evaluation result.

2.4 System Evaluation Approach

In this section, we will introduce a group of equations to evaluate the threat and cost to compromise the whole system. We use the quintuples (*Path_ConfI*, *Path_IntegI*, *Path_AvailI*, *Path_Impact*, *Path_Pr*) and (*System_ConfI*, *System_IntegI*, *System_AvailI*, *System_Impact*, *System_Pr*) to evaluate attack paths and the whole system respectively. We first use FTA [2] to compute the probability to represent the likelihood of system compromised, then adopt AHP [1] to evaluate the damage impact to reflect the average damage to the system caused by all the attack paths.

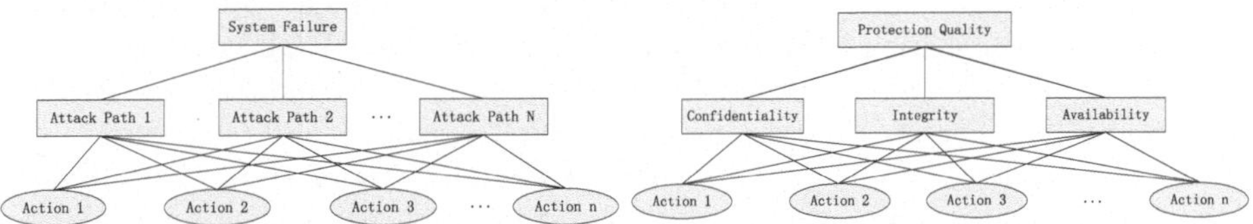

Fig. 2. The Fault Tree of Our Problem

Fig. 3. The Hierarchy of Our Problem

A Fault Tree Analysis (FTA) is a systematic top-down method of analyzing system performance. In the OS to analyze, the top event is the system failure, the basic events are the attack actions and the middle events are the attack paths. An attack path succeeds if all of the actions contained in the path succeed. The access control subsystem fails if any attack path succeeds. We assume that an attack path consists of n actions (AC) and there are N attack paths (AP) in total. The fault tree of our problem is represented by Fig.2, and the symbolic representations are listed as follows:

$$AP = AC_1 \wedge AC_2 \wedge \cdots \wedge AC_n \tag{3}$$

$$SF = AP_1 \vee AP_2 \vee \cdots \vee AP_N \tag{4}$$

We first compute a quintuple (*ConfI*, *IntegI*, *AvailI*, *Impact*, *Pr*) for every action. Then with the assumption that attack paths have independent probabilities, we compute the probability of attack paths and finally the probability of system failure with equations listed below:

$$Path\_Pr = \prod_{1 \le i \le n} Pr_i \tag{5}$$

$$System\_Pr = 1 - \prod_{i=1}^{N} (1 - Path\_Pr_i) \tag{6}$$

The analytic hierarchy process (AHP) is a structured technique for analyzing complex decisions. The hierarchy of our problem is shown in Fig.3. We first evaluate confidentiality, integrity and availability respectively, and then comprehend them to get the whole evaluation quintuple (*System_ConfI*, *System_IntegI*, *System_AvailI*, *System_Impact*, *System_Pr*) to describes the system protection quality with the following equations, where variable X indicates *ConfI*, *IntegI*, *AvailI* and *Impact* respectively.

$$Path\_X = \sum_{1 \leq i \leq n} Pr_i * X_i \tag{7}$$

$$System\_X = \frac{1}{N} \sum_{1 \leq i \leq N} Path\_X_i \tag{8}$$

3 Experiments and Results

We implement a tool called ACQE to evaluate our approach both on Windows 7 and Ubuntu 10.04 with SELinux and AppArmor. The ACQE consists of four components: *Fact Scanner*, *Attack Graph Generator*, *Path analyzer* and *Evaluation Engine*. The Fact Scanner scans the system to analyze, and retrieves system information, which is implemented using C++, consisting of about 3400 lines of code. Attack Graph Generator takes system state, security policies and vulnerability specifications as input, and generated the host attack graph. By initiating attacker's initial abilities, we use Prolog implementation XSB [12] to make an inference and generate the host attack graph. Path Analyzer is implemented to extract all the attack paths from initial nodes to goal nodes from the host attack graph. Through checking how an attack action to be performed and which new abilities gained after the action succeeds, we assess every action manually, and then evaluate the attack patterns.

During the experiments, some common software products are installed for evaluation, such as openssh-server, apache-server, mysql-server, bind, filezilla, firefox, and adobe reader. All the applications are running when the system security configuration information is being collected.

There are 11 attack patterns generated in our experiment. The number of instances of attack patterns and the quintuples for each access control subsystem are shown in table 1.

Table 1. The Result of Experiment

	P1	P2	P3	P4	P5	P6	P7	P8	P9	P10	P11
SELinux	4	116	0	352	0	7692	510356	6856	0	0	0
AppArmor	4	25	0	484	0	858	71523	19234	0	0	62436
Windows	6	30	15	41400	135	54	2064	27	74520	37260	0

SELinx quintuple is (0.117514, 0.224315, 0.117514, 0.320426, 1.00)
AppArmor quintuple is (0.140228, 0.219470, 0.140228, 0.343991, 1.00)
Windows quintuple is (0.167775, 0.222714, 0.167775, 0.381691, 1.00)

Comparing the two systems with their quintuples, we can see that an attacker makes less damage impact on confidentiality for the system with SELinux, and SELinux provides better protection for confidentiality. However, AppArmor gets a high score in protecting integrity because the additional pattern has a less *IntegI*, which conforms to the existing works [5] achieved by different approaches. Overall, SELinux provides higher and better security protection.

Similar comparison can be made between SELinux and Windows 7, AppArmor and Windows 7. Under our experiment settings, i.e., the default access control policies and the applications installed, we can see that SELinux provides the best confidentiality and availability protection, and AppArmor offers the best integrity protection. Unfortunately, Windows's performance in the overall security protection is the worst.

In our experiment, the success of some attacks depends on the success of identifying and exploiting software vulnerabilities. The actions defined to exploit the vulnerabilities are `CompromiseRead` and `CompromiseNetwork`. We could call these two actions malicious actions, and the attack patterns can be divided into to two groups: patterns in one group contain malicious actions and another not. Intuitively, malicious actions makes more damage impact on the security of system, which conforms to our compute results. Our computed results for every attack patterns illustrate that the attack patterns containing malicious actions make more security damage. Our experiment shows that it is very important to patch softwares regularly to eliminate known bugs.

4 Related Work

Windows access control has been studied in many research [10,4,7]. Govindavajhala and Appel construct a logical model to study Windows XP [7]. Host MulVAL [13] is a vulnerability analysis framework. NETRA [10] is a tool for systematically analyzing and detecting explicit information-flow vulnerabilities in access control configurations. WACCA [4] is an automatically tool to systematically analyze the Windows configurations. WACCA generates host attack graph and extracts attack patterns from the host attack graph to describe the protection quality.

The Access control of Unix-like systems can be dated back to the Kuang security analyzer for Unix [3]. Susan Hinrichs et al. [8] propose an attack-based model to analyze the transitive domain transitions of SELinux. SEAL [9] is logic-programming language and tool to model and analyze dynamic access control systems. VulSAN [5] is a tool to analyze and compare the quality of protection offered by different MAC systems.

Our approach differs from existed work is: (1) Our approach automatically constructs an attack graph and make a quantitative security evaluation by introducing probability to evaluate attack actions; (2) Our approach can be applied both to Windows and Linux; (3) Our approach analysis the comprehensive protection quality offered by MAC and DAC.

5 Conclusion and Future Work

In this paper, we propose a method to measure how secure a system is. Given the attacker's initial abilities and the vulnerability specifications, we can compute the host attack graph to automatically discover attack paths. By applying CVSS to our approach, we can first quantitatively assess attack actions related to our analysis and then evaluate the attack paths. Then we adopt AHP and FTA to compute a quintuple to quantize the protection quality. We have implemented a prototype of our approach called ACQE and applied it to analyze the protection quality of Windows 7 and Linux.

Acknowledgement. This work was supported in part by NSFC grant No.60970028, NSFC grant No.61100227 and National 863 Program of China under Grant 2011AA01A203.

References

1. Analytic hierarchy process., http://thequalityportal.com/q_ahp.htm
2. Fault tree analysis(fta), http://www.fault-tree-analysis-software.com/fault-tree-analysis-basics.html
3. Baldwin, R.W.: Rule based analysis of computer security. Phd, MIT (1987)
4. Chen, H., Li, N., Gates, C.S., Mao, Z.: Towards analyzing complex operating system access control configurations. In: Proceedings of the 15th ACM Symposium on Access Control Models and Technologies, pp. 13–22 (June 2010)
5. Chen, H., Li, N., Mao, Z.: Analyzing and comparing the protection quality of security enhanced operating systems. In: Proceedings of the 16th Network and Distributed System Security Symposium, NDSS 2009 (February 2009)
6. Gallon, L., Bascou, J.: Cvss attack graphs. In: 2011 Seventh International Conference on Signal-Image Technology and Internet-Based Systems (SITIS), pp. 24–31. IEEE (2011)
7. Govindavajhala, S., Appel, A.W.: Windows access control demystified. Technical report, Technical Report TR-744-06, Department of Computer Science, Princeton University (January 2006)
8. Hinrichs, S.: Attack-based domain transition analysis. In: Proceedings of the 2nd Annual Security Enhanced Linux Symposium (2006)
9. Naldurg, P., Seal, R.K.R.: A logic programming framework for specifying and verifying access control models. In: Proceedings of the 16th ACM Symposium on Access Control Models and Technologies, pp. 83–92 (June 2011)
10. Naldurg, P., Schwoon, S., Rajamani, S.K., Lambert, J.: Netra: seeing through access control. In: Proceedings of the 4th ACM Workshop on Formal Methods in Security Engineering, pp. 55–66 (2006)
11. Sheyner, O.: Scenario graphs and attack graphs. Phd. University of Wisconsin (2004)
12. T.X.R. Group: The xsb programming system, http://xsb.sourceforge.net/
13. Govindavajhala, S., Appel, A.W.: Automatic Configuration Vulnerability Analysis. Technical Report TR-773-07, Department of Computer Science, Princeton University (February 2007)

Collusion-Resistant Domain-Specific Pseudonymous Signatures*

Julien Bringer[1], Hervé Chabanne[1,2], and Alain Patey[1,2]

[1] Morpho
surname.name@morpho.com
[2] Télécom ParisTech
surname.name@telecom-paristech.fr
Identity and Security Alliance (The Morpho and Télécom ParisTech Research Center)

Abstract. At ISC 2012, Bender *et al.* introduced the notion of domain-specific pseudonymous signatures for ID documents. With this primitive, a user can sign with domain-specific pseudonyms, that cannot be linked across domains but that are linkable in a given domain. However, their security model assumes non-collusion of malicious users, which is a strong assumption. We therefore propose improvements to their construction. Our main contribution is a new pseudonymous signature scheme based on group signatures that is collusion-resistant.

1 Introduction

Several security mechanisms [1] are sequentially used when a *machine readable travel document* (MRTD) connects, via a reader, to a service provider. Using *Password Authenticated Connection Establishment* (PACE), the MRTD and the reader establish a secure channel, once the MRTD user has entered his password; Using *Extended Acces Control* (EAC), the MRTD and the service provider authenticate to each other and establish another secure channel; Optionally, using *Restricted Identification* (RI), the MRTD derives a pseudonym for the service such that the service provider can link the sessions when this particular user accessed the service, but such that it is impossible for two providers to link interactions of one user in their respective domains.

The original Restricted Identification of [1] is close to a Diffie-Hellman key exchange, with static keys, as can be seen in Figure 1a. The authenticity of the pseudonym sent by the card is not guaranteed. Furthermore, the domain-specific pseudonym of a user has limited applications, which motivates the work of Bender *et al.* [3], who suggest to use this pseudonym for digital signatures.

To augment security guarantees and provide the possibility of using the domain-specific pseudonyms as signature keys, Bender *et al.* [3] introduced the notion of

* This work has been partially funded by the European FP7 FIDELITY project (SEC-2011-284862). The opinions expressed in this document only represent the authors' view. They reflect neither the view of the European Commission nor the view of their employer.

J. Lopez, X. Huang, and R. Sandhu (Eds.): NSS 2013, LNCS 7873, pp. 649–655, 2013.

Inputs: • User U: Secret key x • Service Provider SP: Domain Identifier R **Protocol:** 1. SP sends R to U. 2. U computes $nym = Hash(R^x)$, the domain-specific pseudonym of U for SP. 3. U sends nym to SP. 4. SP optionally checks if nym belongs to a black list and/or a white list.	**Inputs:** • User U: Pseudonymous signature key x • Service Provider SP: Domain Identifier R **Protocol:** 1. SP sends R and a message m to U. 2. U derives a pseudonym nym from x and R. 3. U signs the message m using x and nym 4. U sends the signature σ and nym to SP. 5. SP checks σ, using public parameters and nym.
(a)The Original RI Protocol	(b)The RI Protocol with Pseudonymous Signatures

Fig. 1. The Restricted Identification Protocol

domain-specific pseudonymous signatures. This can be seen as a relaxation of the notion of group signatures [7,2]. Group signatures enable users to anonymously sign on behalf of a group. Anonymity guarantees are very strong: two signatures of the same user can only be linked by the group manager, who also issues keys. However, pseudonyms produced by the RI protocol for a given user and a given service should enable linkability, since pseudonyms serve as identifiers for the users.

Domain-specific pseudonymous signatures, as defined in [3], satisfy 3 properties: *unforgeability*, *cross-domain anonymity* and *seclusiveness*. The second property states that pseudonymous signatures cannot be linked across domains while seclusiveness is a relaxation of the notion of *traceability* [2] for group signatures.

Bender *et al.* [3] suggest a modification to the original Restricted Identification protocol [1] using pseudonymous signatures, as summed up in Figure 1b. In addition to his domain identifier, the service provider sends a message to be signed. This message is signed by the user using a pseudonymous signature. This pseudonymous signature at the same time guarantees that the user owns a valid unrevoked signature key and that the pseudonym is legitimate, *i.e.* that the same user key has been used to sign and to derive the pseudonym.

The pseudonymous signature scheme of Bender *et al.* [3] fulfills the security requirements exposed above (unforgeability, cross-domain anonymity and seclusiveness). However, the security model relies on a very strong assumption: they assume that no two malicious users can retrieve their keys and collude. Indeed, the relation between signature keys and issuing key being linear, with two signature keys, one is able to retrieve the issuing key and thus to issue as many new valid keys as they want. To justify their assumption, the authors invoke the fact that these keys are supposed to be stored on smartcards on ID documents, and that smartcards are supposed to be tamper-proof. It is however likely that, on a national scale, two users will be able to retrieve keys stored on their smartcards.

This is the motivation for our work. We propose a new construction of pseudonymous signatures, where we allow the users to access their keys and where collusion of malicious users does not break the security guarantees. To do so, we use (collusion-resistant) group signatures and combine them with Schnorr proofs of knowledge to guarantee validity of pseudonyms.

An extended version of this paper is available in [5].

2 Pseudonymous Signatures

2.1 Setting

Three entities are involved: the Issuing Authority (IA), users M_i, and service providers SP_j with specific domains D_j. The issuing authority issues secret keys to the users and domain parameters to the service providers. The users can generate, from their secret keys and the domain parameters, one pseudonym per domain. Using domain-specific pseudonymous signatures, users can sign messages linked to their pseudonyms. The pseudonym being attached to the signatures, the signatures of one user in one domain are obviously linkable. The construction guarantees that signatures of the same user for different domains are not linkable by (even colluding) service providers. However, the issuing authority can retrieve these links. There are six algorithms in the scheme:

PSKeyGen(k)**.** The Issuing Authority generates a master secret key msk and a master public key gpk.
The IA and the SP_j's generate domain-specific public keys dpk_j.

PSJoin(msk, gpk)**.** The Issuing Authority and the user M_i interact to generate a secret key sk_i for user M_i.

PSSign(gpk,sk_i,dpk_j,m)**.** The user M_i outputs his pseudonym nym_{ij} for domain D_j and a signature σ on m for domain D_j

PSVerify(gpk,nym_{ij},dpk_j,m,σ,RL_j)**.** The Service Provider for domain D_j checks the signature σ on message m and the link between σ and nym_{ij}. SP_j also performs a revocation check, using RL_j, the list of revoked pseudonyms for domain D_j

PSDomainRevoke(RL_j,nym_{ij})**.** SP_j runs this algorithm to prevent a member M_i from making valid signatures in D_j. It outputs an updated revocation list RL_j, where nym_{ij} has been added.

PSRevoke(gpk,x_i)**.** IA runs this algorithm to prevent a member M_i from making valid signatures in all domains. He sends an information x_i about the key of M_i that the SP_j's use to revoke M_i from their domains. Every service provider SP_j outputs an updated RL_j.

2.2 Security

The security properties of pseudonymous signatures are close to the properties of group signatures. We require a pseudonymous signature scheme to satisfy *Correctness*, *Cross-Domain Anonymity*, *Unforgeability* and *Seclusiveness*. We here sumarize these properties, formal definitions appear in [5].

Correctness. The scheme is *correct* if every signature-pseudonym couple created by an unrevoked member is verified as valid.

Cross-Domain Anonymity. Cross-Domain Anonymity guarantees that signatures are anonymous and that linkability is possible within a given domain only, even with colluding service providers.

Seclusiveness. The scheme achieves *Seclusiveness* if an adversary $\mathcal{A}$ is unable to forge a valid signature that cannot be opened properly.

Unforgeability. The aim of the *Unforgeability* property is to prevent anyone, including the Group Manager, from making signatures on behalf of a given user. Notice that, contrary to the security definitions of [3], we do not require the group manager to delete information about the users' keys after the *PSJoin* algorithm.

2.3 Overview of the Scheme of Bender *et al.*

We sum up the components of the pseudonymous signature scheme of [3] and the reasons why it does not resist to collusions.

Let $G = \langle g \rangle$ be a cyclic group of prime order q. The secret key of the IA is made of two randomly chosen integers $x, z \in_R \mathbb{Z}_q$. The public parameters of the system are g, g^x and g^z.

The key of a user M_i is a couple (x_{1i}, x_{2i}), chosen by the IA, such that $x_{1i} = x - z \cdot x_{2i}$.

The domain parameters for every domain D_j are chosen by the IA, by picking a random $r_j \in_R \mathbb{Z}_q^*$ and setting $dpk_j = g^{r_j}$. SP_j learns dpk_j, but not r_j.

The pseudonym of a user M_i for domain D_j is $dpk_j^{x_{1i}}$.

To sign, user M_i uses two intertwined proofs of knowledge, a Schnorr proof of knowledge [10] that he knows the discrete logarithm of the pseudonym and an Okamoto proof [9] that he owns a valid (x_1, x_2) key pair. The proofs are non-interactive and rely on the random oracle. The message to be signed is included in the entries of the hash function used to generate the challenge.

Limitations. First, it is noticeable, that when one finds two (x_1, x_2) couples, one easily retrieves the secret keys x and z of the IA and can thus generate as many valid key couples as one wants. The authors of [3] justify that, since these keys are supposed to be stored on smartcards, assumed to be tamper-proof, security will be guaranteed. We estimate that this assumption is optimistic, especially for the sensitive application of ID documents.

Second, the IA generates all the keys and, thus, is able to sign on behalf of the users. It is specified in [3] that these keys are supposed to be deleted by the IA, once delivered to the users, which is impossible to verify. This might raise some security issues, we also solve this problem in our proposal thanks to the *Exculpability* property of group signatures.

3 Our Proposal for a Collusion-Resistant Pseudonymous Signature Scheme

3.1 The Proposal

One of the main properties of group signatures is that they prevent from linking signatures. However, pseudonymous signatures are supposed to enable linkability of signatures if they are accompanied by the same pseudonym, but unlinkability otherwise. By combining the construction of [3] with the CL-BP group signature [8,6][1], we build pseudonymous signatures that are resistant to collusions. This construction requires more computation from the user to sign messages. It requires elliptic curve cryptography but the smartcard does not need to be able to compute pairings.

The *PSKeyGen* algorithm, described in Algorithm 1 is mostly an execution of the *GSKeyGen algorithm* of the CL-BP scheme by the Issuing Authority. IA also has to pick randomly chosen domain parameters $dpk_j = g_1^{r_j}$ that he sends to the service providers. It is essential, in order to preserve unlinkability, that the service providers do not learn r_j. The *PSJoin* algorithm, described in Algorithm 2[2] consists in an execution of the *GSJoin* algorithm. The *PSSign* algorithm, described in Algorithm 3 consists in a CL-BP signature, a domain-specific pseudonym derivation, and a proof of knowledge that the same key has been used in both operations. The *PSVerify* algorithm, described in Algorithm 4 is a verification of the proof of knowledge, followed by a revocation check, where the verifier checks if the pseudonym is on the revocation list or not. Notice that the verifier only performs a list membership test and not a linear number of arithmetic operations, as in the Revocation Check of the *GSVerify* algorithm. The revocation algorithms, *PSDomainRevoke*, described in Algorithm 5, and *PSRevoke*, described in Algorithm 6, consist in adding the pseudonym of the revoked user in the revocation list RL_j of the domain RL_j.

Algorithm 1. *PSKeyGen(k)*

1: Run the *GSKeyGen* algorithm of the CL-BP scheme, as Group Manager.
2: Thus obtain $gpk = (G_1, G_2, G_\mathcal{T}, e, p, g_1, g_2, \tilde{g}_1, \hat{g}_1, w, H, T_1, T_2, T_3, T_4)$ and $msk = \gamma$.
   $G_1 = \langle g_1 \rangle, G_2 = \langle g_2 \rangle, G_\mathcal{T}$ are bilinear groups of prime order p and $e : G_1 \times G_2 \to G_\mathcal{T}$ is a pairing. g_1 and $\tilde{g}_1$ are elements of G_1. γ is an element of $\mathbb{Z}_p^*$ and $w = g_2^\gamma$. $T_1 = e(g_1, g_2)$, $T_2 = e(\tilde{g}_1, g_2)$, $T_3 = e(\hat{g}_1, g_2)$, $T_4 = e(\hat{g}_1, w)$.
3: For every service provider SP_j, pick a random $r_j \in_R \mathbb{Z}_p$ and issue the domain parameters $dpk_j = g_1^{r_j}$ to SP_j.

---

[1] A full description of the CL-BP group signatures is available in the extended version of this paper [5].

[2] Optionally, during the execution of this algorithm, M_i also gets $e(A_i, g_2)$ to avoid pairing computations by the smartcard

Algorithm 2. *PSJoin(msk, gpk)*

IA runs a CL-BP *GSJoin* algorithm with the user M_i.
M_i gets a key $gsk_i = (x_i, A_i, f_i)$, such that $e(A_i, wg_2^{x_i}) = e(g_1\tilde{g}_1^{f_i}, g_2)$.
IA gets x_i and A_i.

Algorithm 3. *PSSign(gpk,sk$_i$,dpk$_j$,m)*

Choose $B \in_R G_1$ and compute $J = B^{f_i}$, $K = B^{x_i}$.
Choose $a \in_R \mathbb{Z}_p$, compute $b = ax_i$ and $T = A_i\hat{g}_1^a$.
Choose $r_f, r_x, r_a, r_b \in_R \mathbb{Z}_p$.
Compute $R_1 = B^{r_f}$, $R_2 = B^{r_x}$, $R_4 = K^{r_a}B^{-r_b}$, $R_3 = e(T, g_2)^{-r_x}T_2^{r_f}T_3^{r_b}T_4^{r_a}$ and $R_5 = dpk_j^{r_x}$.
Compute $c{=}H(gpk||B||J||K||T||R_1||R_2||R_3||R_4||R_5||m)$.
Compute $s_f = r_f + cf_i$, $s_x = r_x + cx_i$, $s_a = r_a + ca$ and $s_b = r_b + cb$.
Output: $\sigma = (B, J, K, T, c, s_f, s_x, s_a, s_b)$ and $nym_{ij} = dpk_j^{x_i}$

Algorithm 4. *PSVerify(gpk,nym$_{ij}$,dpk$_j$,m,σ,RL$_j$)*

Signature Check:
Check that $B, J, K, T \in G_1$ and s_f, s_x, s_a, $s_b \in \mathbb{Z}_p$.
Compute $R'_2 = B^{s_x}K^{-c}$, $R'_3 = e(T, g_2)^{-s_x}T_2^{s_f}T_3^{s_b}T_4^{s_a}T_1^c e(T, w)^{-c}$, $R'_4 = K^{s_a}B^{-s_b}$, $R'_1 = B^{s_f}J^{-c}$ and $R'_5 = dpk_j^{s_x}nym^{-c}$.
Check that $c{=}H(gpk||B||J||K||T||R'_1||R'_2||R'_3||R'_4||R'_5||m)$.
Revocation Check:
Check that $nym_{ij} \notin RL_j$.
Output **valid** if all checks succeed. Otherwise output **invalid**.

Algorithm 5. *PSDomainRevoke(RL$_j$,nym$_{ij}$)*

Add nym_{ij} to RL_j
Output RL_j

Algorithm 6. *PSRevoke(gpk,x$_i$)*

IA sends $rt_i = x_i$ to all SP'_js
Every SP_j adds $nym_{ij} = dpk_j^{rt_i}$ to RL_j and outputs RL_j.

3.2 Security

Our pseudonymous signature scheme achieves the security properties described in Section 2.2, under the same security conditions as the CL-BP scheme. Security is guaranteed is in the random oracle model.

Theorem 1 (Correctness). *The pseudonymous signature scheme described in Section 3.1 achieves Correctness.*

Theorem 2 (Cross-Domain Anonymity). *Under the Decisional Diffie-Hellman assumption, the pseudonymous signature scheme described in Section 3.1 achieves Cross-Domain Anonymity.*

Theorem 3 (Seclusiveness). *Under the q-Strong Diffie-Hellman assumption [4], the pseudonymous signature scheme described in Section 3.1 achieves Seclusiveness.*

Theorem 4 (Unforgeability). *Under the Discrete Logarithm assumption, the pseudonymous signature scheme described in Section 3.1 achieves Unforgeability.*

Implementation. In [6], parameters for the CL-BP scheme are suggested and a computation time analysis is performed. The computation required by our *PSSign* algorithm is the cost of the *GSSign* algorithm of the CL-BP scheme and an exponentiations necessary to compute R_5 and nym_{ij}. As noticed in [6], all the computation of *GSSign* but the hash function can be computed offline, before the knowledge of the message to be signed. This offline work consists in 6 multi-exponentiations in G_1 and 1 multi-exponentiation in $G_{\mathcal{T}}$. The remaining online work for our pseudonymous signature is then 1 hash function computation and 2 exponentiations in G_1. With the parameters of [6], this online computation requires less than 100 ms on a personal computer. The corresponding computation for *PSVerify* is 5 multi-exponentiations in G_1, 1 multi-exponentiation in $G_{\mathcal{T}}$ and 1 pairing. Contrary to the one of *GSVerify*, the cost of the *Revocation Check* of *PSVerify* is negligible. With the parameters of [6], the computation of *PSVerify* requires around 500 ms on a personal computer.

References

1. Advanced security mechanisms for machine readable travel documents. part 2 extended access control version 2 (EACv2), password authenticated connection establishment (PACE), and restricted identification (RI). Tech. Rep. TR-03110-2, BSI, version 2.10 (March 2012)
2. Bellare, M., Shi, H., Zhang, C.: Foundations of group signatures: The case of dynamic groups. IACR Cryptology ePrint Archive 2004, 77 (2004)
3. Bender, J., Dagdelen, Ö., Fischlin, M., Kügler, D.: Domain-specific pseudonymous signatures for the german identity card. In: Gollmann, D., Freiling, F.C. (eds.) ISC 2012. LNCS, vol. 7483, pp. 104–119. Springer, Heidelberg (2012)
4. Boneh, D., Boyen, X.: Short signatures without random oracles. In: Cachin, C., Camenisch, J.L. (eds.) EUROCRYPT 2004. LNCS, vol. 3027, pp. 56–73. Springer, Heidelberg (2004)
5. Bringer, J., Chabanne, H., Patey, A.: Collusion-resistant domain-specific pseudonymous signatures. IACR Cryptology ePrint Archive, `http://eprint.iacr.org/2013/182`
6. Bringer, J., Patey, A.: VLR group signatures - how to achieve both backward unlinkability and efficient revocation checks. In: SECRYPT, pp. 215–220 (2012)
7. Chaum, D., van Heyst, E.: Group signatures. In: Davies, D.W. (ed.) EUROCRYPT 1991. LNCS, vol. 547, pp. 257–265. Springer, Heidelberg (1991)
8. Chen, L., Li, J.: VLR group signatures with indisputable exculpability and efficient revocation. In: Elmagarmid, A.K., Agrawal, D. (eds.) SocialCom/PASSAT, pp. 727–734. IEEE Computer Society (2010)
9. Okamoto, T.: Provably secure and practical identification schemes and corresponding signature schemes. In: Brickell, E.F. (ed.) CRYPTO 1992. LNCS, vol. 740, pp. 31–53. Springer, Heidelberg (1993)
10. Schnorr, C.P.: Efficient signature generation by smart cards. J. Cryptology 4(3), 161–174 (1991)

On the Applicability of Time-Driven Cache Attacks on Mobile Devices[⋆,⋆⋆]

Raphael Spreitzer and Thomas Plos

Institute for Applied Information Processing and Communications (IAIK),
Graz University of Technology, Inffeldgasse 16a, 8010 Graz, Austria
{raphael.spreitzer,thomas.plos}@iaik.tugraz.at

Abstract. Cache attacks are known to be sophisticated attacks against cryptographic implementations on desktop computers. Recently, investigations of such attacks on specific testbeds with processors that are employed in mobile devices have been done. In this work we investigate the applicability of Bernstein's [2] timing attack and the cache-collision attack by Bogdanov *et al.* [4] in real environments on three state-of-the-art mobile devices: an *Acer Iconia A510*, a *Google Nexus S*, and a *Samsung Galaxy SIII*. We show that T-table based implementations of the Advanced Encryption Standard (AES) leak enough timing information on these devices in order to recover parts of the used secret key using Bernstein's timing attack. We also show that systems with a cache-line size larger than 32 bytes exacerbate the cache-collision attack of Bogdanov *et al.* [4].

Keywords: AES, ARM Cortex-A series processors, time-driven cache attacks, cache-collision attacks.

1 Introduction

Cache attacks are a specific form of implementation attacks that focus on the exploitation of variations within the execution time of a cryptographic algorithm due to different access times within the memory hierarchy. For instance, the central-processing unit (CPU) is able to access data within the CPU cache an order of magnitude faster than data within the main memory. Cache attacks can be separated into three categories: (1) *time-driven attacks*, (2) *access-driven attacks*, and (3) *trace-driven attacks*. Time-driven attacks [2] exploit the overall encryption time and, thus, require many measurement samples. In contrast, access-driven attacks [6, 12] and trace-driven attacks [3] focus on more fine-grained information leakage and require far less measurement samples than time-driven attacks. However, access-driven attacks and trace-driven attacks require sophisticated knowledge about the hardware and the software under attack.

Today's mobile devices also employ CPU caches and investigations of implementation attacks—and cache attacks in particular—are necessary in order to ensure the

⋆ An extended version of this paper can be found at [11].

⋆⋆ This work has been supported by the Austrian Science Fund (FWF) under grant number TRP 251-N23 (Realizing a Secure Internet of Things - ReSIT). Furthermore, it has been supported by the Austrian Research Promotion Agency (FFG) and the Styrian Business Promotion Agency (SFG) under grant number 836628 (SeCoS).

J. Lopez, X. Huang, and R. Sandhu (Eds.): NSS 2013, LNCS 7873, pp. 656–662, 2013.

user's privacy and security on these devices. Especially due to the wide-spread usage of mobile devices, *e.g.*, smartphones and tablet computers, and their manifold application scenarios, security and privacy issues on these devices are of utmost importance. Additional applications and widgets allow for further enhancements of capabilities on these devices and potentially contain security-relevant algorithms. Since these algorithms might be vulnerable to implementation attacks, the investigation of such attacks shall raise the awareness of implementation attacks among developers, leading to more secure systems in general. However, until recently these attacks mainly focused on desktop machines [2, 6, 8, 12]. Only minor efforts have been made towards the investigation of these attacks on mobile devices [10], where mainly testbeds simulating specific mobile-device configurations [4, 5, 13] have been used.

In 2010, Bogdanov *et al.* [4] proposed a cache-collision attack by exploiting collisions between consecutive encryptions of pairs of chosen plaintexts. The attack environment was an ARM9 board running the AES implementation of OpenSSL [9] which was queried via an Ethernet interface. Gallais and Kizhvatov [5] investigated trace-driven cache attacks on an ARM7 microcontroller. In 2012, Weiß *et al.* [13] investigated the applicability of Bernstein's [2] time-driven cache attack on a Beagleboard employing an ARM Cortex-A8 processor, running the *Fiasco.OC microkernel* and the *L4Re runtime environment* on top. Nevertheless, they claim that further research regarding the impact of real noise is necessary.

In this work, we focus on the investigation of time-driven cache attacks in more realistic environments by analyzing the applicability of the attack by Bernstein [2] and the attack by Bogdanov *et al.* [4] on three Android-based mobile devices. We aim at analyzing whether T-table based implementations of the Advanced Encryption Standard (AES) on state-of-the-art Android-based mobile devices, *i.e.*, featuring a full-blown operating system, leak enough timing information to deduce the used secret key.

The presented paper is organized as follows. Section 2 outlines the required preliminaries and illustrates the basic concepts of the two investigated cache attacks. We state the main findings regarding the analysis of these two attacks on mobile devices in Section 3. Finally, we conclude this work in Section 4.

2 Background Knowledge

In this section we introduce the necessary preliminaries and outline the basic concepts of the conducted attacks.

Advanced Encryption Standard. The Advanced Encryption Standard (AES) [7] is a block cipher operating on a 128-bit state denoted as a series of bytes $\mathbf{S} = \{\mathbf{s}_0, \ldots, \mathbf{s}_{15}\}$. The AES consists of four round transformations: *SubBytes*, *ShiftRows*, *MixColumns*, and *AddRoundKey*. Since *SubBytes* and *MixColumns* perform complex mathematical operations, software implementations usually operate on look-up tables $\mathbf{T}$ which hold precomputed values for these two round transformations. The fact that these look-up tables—each consisting of 256 4-byte values—are partially cached during the encryption and the fact that the look-up indices are key dependent, *i.e.*, $\mathbf{s}_i = \mathbf{p}_i \oplus \mathbf{k}_i$ within the first round, leads to AES implementations which are susceptible to cache attacks.

Table 1. Detailed device specifications for the three mobile devices under attack

	Acer Iconia A510	Google Nexus S	Samsung Galaxy SIII
Processor	Cortex-A9	Cortex-A8	Cortex-A9
Processor implementation	Nvidia Tegra 3 Quad 1.4 GHz	Exynos 3 Single 1 GHz	Exynos 4 Quad 1.4 GHz
L1 cache size	32 KB	32 KB	32 KB
L1 cache associativity	4 way	4 way	4 way
L1 cache-line size	32 byte	64 byte	32 byte
L1 cache sets	256	128	256
Operating system	Android 4.0.4	Android 2.3.4	Android 4.0.4

ARM Architecture. The ARM Cortex-A series processors [1] are employed in many modern mobile devices, *e.g.*, smartphones and tablet computers. Processors of this series typically employ a 4-way set-associative data cache with a cache-line size of either 32 or 64 bytes and a total size of 32 KB. The crucial difference between most desktop CPU caches and ARM CPU caches is the mechanism to evict a cache line from a cache set. While desktop CPU caches usually employ a deterministic replacement policy, ARM processors usually evict a cache line randomly. Since time-driven cache attacks rely on statistical analysis of measurement samples, the random replacement policy might have a negative impact on the number of required measurement samples.

Time-Driven Cache Attacks. The basic idea of these attacks is to exploit the overall execution time of cryptographic primitives employing precomputed look-up tables.

Timing Attack. In 2005, Bernstein [2] suggested a time-driven cache attack against the AES T-table implementation of OpenSSL [9]. The attack is based on the assumption that the overall encryption time correlates with the timing leakage of specific look-up operations. By correlating measurement samples of encryptions under a known key $\mathbf{K}$ with measurement samples under an unknown key $\tilde{\mathbf{K}}$ one tries to deduce the used secret key. For further details about this attack we refer to [2, 8].

Collision Attack. Cache-collision attacks exploit collisions between look-up indices of intermediate state bytes. Given information about such collisions an attacker tries to infer relations between key bytes. Bogdanov *et al.* [4] suggested to choose pairs of plaintexts $(\mathbf{P}_1, \mathbf{P}_2)$ such that five S-Box or T-table look-ups within the encryption of $\mathbf{P}_2$ collide with S-Box or T-table look-ups of $\mathbf{P}_1$. This is what they call a *wide collision*. The encryption time of the plaintext $\mathbf{P}_2$ is used as an indicator to determine whether such a *wide collision* occurred.

3 Analysis and Practical Results

We launch the above outlined attacks on state-of-the-art Android-based mobile devices: (1) an *Acer Iconia A510 tablet computer*, (2) a *Google Nexus S*, and (3) a *Samsung Galaxy SIII*. Table 1 provides a detailed specification of these devices. The attack runs in unprivileged mode, though we need root access once after powering up the device to grant unprivileged applications access to the cycle-count register. As already suggested

Table 2. Sample output of Bernstein's time-driven cache attack on a *Samsung Galaxy SIII*

# of key candidates	Key byte	Possible values									
3	0	**b5**	b4	b8							
125	1	00	a2	be	c2	b8	1d	f6	...	**93**	...
165	2	87	03	51	17	1b	1f	c7	...	**11**	...
⋮	⋮	⋮									
2	13	**4a**	4b								
40	14	6a	7a	7b	74	61	7c	64	**6b**	78	...
2	15	9c	**9d**								

by Neve [8] we perform the attacks within a single application, *i.e.*, the attack application performs the AES encryption (standard C implementation of OpenSSL [9]) and computes the relevant information. In this section we briefly state the main findings of the conducted attacks on the three mobile devices.

3.1 Timing Attack

The timing attack by Bernstein [2] requires measurement samples under a known key $\mathbf{K}$ and an unknown key $\tilde{\mathbf{K}}$. Gathering 2^{30} measurement samples under the known key $\mathbf{K}$ and the unknown key $\tilde{\mathbf{K}}$ takes about 6 hours on the *Google Nexus S* and about 4 hours on the *Acer Iconia A510* and the *Samsung Galaxy SIII*. Table 2 illustrates an excerpt of a sample output on the *Samsung Galaxy SIII* after correlating the measurement results. The columns state the number of remaining key candidates, the index of the corresponding key byte and all possible key bytes with the correct key marked in bold. A series of dots illustrates omitted key bytes. The possible key candidates are sorted according to the computed correlation and, thus, the position also indicates the probability of the corresponding key candidate being the correct key byte. One clearly observes that timing information is leaking, though the number of remaining key bits is still too large for an exhaustive key search. In order to retrieve more key bits one might apply the second-round attack as suggested by Neve [8]. From Table 2 we also observe that for some key bytes the number of possible key candidates has been reduced significantly, *e.g.*, to only 2 key candidates. However, some key bytes have not been reduced significantly.

Table 3 lists two runs with the lowest number of remaining key bits for each of the three mobile devices. The number of generated measurement samples seems to be a crucial part. For the same number of measurement samples we observed runs where the key space was not reduced significantly and runs where the key space was reduced too much, *i.e.*, the correct key byte was not present among the possible key candidates anymore in which case the attack would fail. Thus, more measurement samples do not necessarily yield better results in terms of remaining key bits.

Timing variations within the encryption time only occur if cache evictions happen frequently. Bernstein [2] generated the required cache evictions by sending data of different length to the server and the server in turn performed memory accesses on the transmitted data. We also launched this attack in a more realistic scenario where we mounted the attack while watching videos or while watching an image slideshow on the mobile devices. Nevertheless, running external applications on purpose did not leak

Table 3. Results of Bernstein's time-driven attack on the three mobile devices

Device	Samples in		Remaining key space
	study phase	attack phase	
Acer Iconia A510	2^{30}	2^{27}	73 bits
	2^{30}	2^{29}	78 bits
Google Nexus S	2^{30}	2^{29}	65 bits
	2^{29}	2^{28}	69 bits
Samsung Galaxy SIII	2^{30}	2^{29}	58 bits
	2^{30}	2^{30}	61 bits

more information and, hence, did not reduce the key space further. We conclude that these external applications either affected the wrong cache sets or lead to uncontrollable noise that corrupted the timing measurements. Furthermore, on multi-core devices, *e.g.*, the *Acer Iconia A510* and the *Samsung Galaxy SIII*, the two applications might be executed on different cores. Thus, a fairly realistic approach would be to wrap the attack in a fine-grained application and to control the memory accesses and potentially also the number of active cores within this application.

3.2 Collision Attack

Bogdanov *et al.* [4] aim at recovering 4-byte key chunks at once. After recovering all four potential 4-byte key chunks these are enumerated exhaustively in order to recover the whole key. Recovering 4-byte key chunks at once requires at least four real *wide collisions* between chosen pairs of plaintexts ($\mathbf{P}_1, \mathbf{P}_2$). However, given the overall encryption time of multiple plaintexts the critical part of this attack is to distinguish encryptions that lead to *wide collisions* from encryptions that do not lead to *wide collisions.* This in turn means that a high expectation rate of *false positives*[1] must be overcome by taking more plaintexts—that possibly lead to *wide collisions*—into consideration.

Figure 1 illustrates two histograms of encryption times of five plaintexts that lead to *wide collisions* in light gray and five plaintexts that do not lead to wide collisions in dark gray. The presented histograms are based on measurement samples gathered on the ARM Cortex-A8 processor. Due to reasons of noise each of the five chosen plaintexts is encrypted multiple times. In case of the 3-round AES implementation we clearly observe easily separable encryption times for plaintexts which lead to *wide collisions* and plaintexts which do not lead to *wide collisions.* Thus, by taking $n = 4$ plaintexts with the lowest encryption times we might indeed detect 4 real *wide collisions* with a high probability. In contrast, in case of the 7-round AES implementation we observe that the encryption times of these two categories of plaintexts cannot be distinguished anymore. Obviously, the number of false positives increases drastically and, hence, we need to consider a higher number n of plaintexts that possibly lead to *wide collisions.* The n plaintexts are used to find possible candidates of 4-byte subkeys by iterating over all possible 4-byte keys (2^{32}). Bogdanov *et al.* [4] state the number of expected

[1] False positives are diagonal pairs which are supposed to lead to *wide collisions* due to their encryption time, but in fact do not lead to wide collisions.

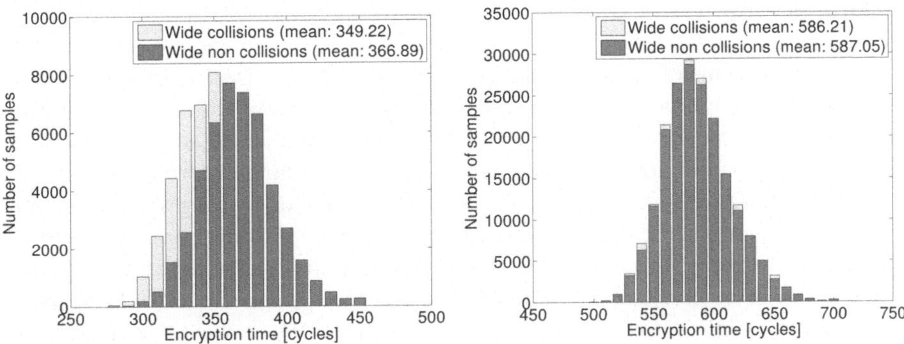

Fig. 1. Histogram of encryption times for a 3-round AES (left) and a 7-round AES (right)

4-byte subkey candidates per attacked 4-byte subkey as $(\binom{n}{4} \cdot 256)$ and since these subkeys must be enumerated exhaustively for all four 4-byte subkeys this yields an overall complexity of $(\binom{n}{4} \cdot 256)^4$ AES encryptions to recover the whole key.

We blame the larger cache-line size of 64 bytes on the ARM Cortex-A8 for the challenging detection of wide collisions. In contrast, Bogdanov *et al.* [4] launched the attack on an ARM9 board with a cache-line size of 32 bytes. Since each T-table is composed of 256 4-byte elements, a 32-byte cache line holds $\delta = 8$ T-table elements, whereas a 64-byte cache line holds $\delta = 16$ T-table elements. In case of a cache miss the Cortex-A8 loads 16 consecutive T-table elements into the cache, whereas the ARM9 board loads only 8 elements into the cache at once. If we take probability theory into consideration the problem becomes clear. Since the last round of the AES T-table implementation usually employs a different T-table, there are $4 \cdot 9$ look-up operations into the same T-table within the rounds 1–9. The probability for δ consecutive T-table elements—mapping to the same cache line—still not being cached after one encryption is $(1 - \frac{\delta}{256})^{4 \cdot 9}$. In case of $\delta = 16$ this yields a probability of 0.098 that a specific block of T-table elements is still not being cached after one encryption. In case of $\delta = 8$ this yields a probability of 0.319. Hence, the probability for a specific T-table element already being cached after the first encryption is $1 - 0.098 = 0.902$ and $1 - 0.319 = 0.681$. This in turn means that the probability for additional cache collisions, besides the required *wide collisions*, is far greater on systems with a cache-line size of 64 bytes. The overall encryption time of $\mathbf{P}_2$ decreases and makes *wide collisions* nearly indistinguishable from non wide collisions. We conclude that the larger cache-line size on the ARM Cortex-A8 exacerbates the detection of *wide collisions* and, thus, the applicability of this attack in general.

Even on the Cortex-A9 the detection of at least four *wide collisions* among a small number of chosen plaintexts, *e.g.*, $n \leq 6$, is a challenging task and a larger number of n drastically increases the remaining brute-force complexity. Our observations showed that we are able to detect enough *wide collisions* among $n = 7$ chosen plaintexts, but in this case the complexity of the exhaustive key search is impractical.

4 Conclusion

Recent investigations of cache attacks on mobile devices focused on specific testbeds and stressed the importance of analyzing these attacks in more realistic environments. Thus, we investigated the applicability of two time-driven cache attacks on state-of-the-art Android-based mobile devices. We observed that timing information also leaks on these devices and can be used to reduce the key space of cryptographic algorithms significantly. Though time-driven cache attacks usually require an enormous number of measurement samples we consider the attack of Bernstein [2] a threat for cryptographic implementations on mobile devices. In addition, we analyzed the attack of Bogdanov *et al.* [4] according to its applicability on mobile devices. We showed that a cache-line size of 64 bytes exacerbates this attack and even on systems with a cache-line size of 32 bytes the detection of *wide collisions* seems to be a challenging task. Our observations revealed that, in practice, encryptions where *wide collisions* occur and encryptions where no wide collisions occur are hardly distinguishable. Even though a high number of false positives might be overcome by taking more diagonal pairs into consideration, this drastically increases the complexity of the following key-search phase.

References

[1] ARM Ltd. Cortex-A Series (2012),
`http://www.arm.com/products/processors/cortex-a/index.php`

[2] Bernstein, D.J.: Cache-timing attacks on AES (2005),
`http://cr.yp.to/antiforgery/cachetiming-20050414.pdf`

[3] Bertoni, G., Zaccaria, V., Breveglieri, L., Monchiero, M., Palermo, G.: AES Power Attack Based on Induced Cache Miss and Countermeasure. In: ITCC (1), pp. 586–591 (2005)

[4] Bogdanov, A., Eisenbarth, T., Paar, C., Wienecke, M.: Differential Cache-Collision Timing Attacks on AES with Applications to Embedded CPUs. In: Pieprzyk, J. (ed.) CT-RSA 2010. LNCS, vol. 5985, pp. 235–251. Springer, Heidelberg (2010)

[5] Gallais, J.-F., Kizhvatov, I.: Error-Tolerance in Trace-Driven Cache Collision Attacks. In: COSADE, Darmstadt, pp. 222–232 (2011)

[6] Gullasch, D., Bangerter, E., Krenn, S.: Cache Games - Bringing Access-Based Cache Attacks on AES to Practice. In: IEEE SP, pp. 490–505 (2011)

[7] National Institute of Standards and Technology (NIST). FIPS-197: Advanced Encryption Standard (November 2001)

[8] Neve, M.: Cache-based Vulnerabilities and SPAM Analysis. PhD thesis, UCL (2006)

[9] OpenSSL Software Foundation. OpenSSL Project (2012),
`http://www.openssl.org/`

[10] Spreitzer, R., Plos, T.: Cache-Access Pattern Attack on Disaligned AES T-Tables. In: COSADE 2013. LNCS. Springer (in press, 2013)

[11] Spreitzer, R., Plos, T.: On the Applicability of Time-Driven Cache Attacks on Mobile Devices (Extended Version). Cryptology ePrint Archive, Report 2013/172 (2013),
`http://eprint.iacr.org/`

[12] Tromer, E., Osvik, D.A., Shamir, A.: Efficient Cache Attacks on AES, and Countermeasures. Journal of Cryptology 23(1), 37–71 (2010)

[13] Weiß, M., Heinz, B., Stumpf, F.: A Cache Timing Attack on AES in Virtualization Environments. In: Keromytis, A.D. (ed.) FC 2012. LNCS, vol. 7397, pp. 314–328. Springer, Heidelberg (2012)

Ancestor Excludable Hierarchical ID-Based Encryption Revisited

Fan Zhang[1], Hua Guo[1,2,⋆], and Zhoujun Li[1,⋆]

[1] State Key Laboratory of Software Development Environment,
Beihang University, Beijing 100083, PRC
[2] State Key Laboratory of Information Security,
Institute of Information Engineering, Chinese Academy of Sciences,
Beijing 100093, PRC
eastlilly@163.com, {hguo,lizj}@buaa.edu.cn

Abstract. A hierarchical ID-based encryption (HIBE) allows a root Private Key Generator (PKG) to delegate private key generation and identity authentication to lower-level PKGs. However, any ancestor in the path can generate a private key for any descendant node and thus decrypt the ciphertext. In an ancestor-excludable HIBE (AE-HIBE) scheme, ancestors with a level less than the designated one can be excluded from a set of privileged ancestors who have the right to decrypt a ciphertext to a target node. We find that the functional definition and the concrete scheme proposed by Miyaji are flawed. To fix the problem, we introduce a new functional definition of AE-HIBE and present a new AE-HIBE scheme. The new scheme is proved to be ID-CPA secure in the random oracle and can be converted to ID-CCA security by applying a conversional method.

Keywords: Identity-based Cryptography, Ancestor Excludable Hierarchical Identity-based Encryption, Provable Security.

1 Introduction

The advantage of identity-based encryption (IBE) [1, 2] lies in public key handling. In an identity-based encryption, a user's identity can serve as a public key without the need of a traditional public key infrastructure, and the corresponding private key is created by binding the identity string with a master secret of a trusted authority called Private Key Generator (PKG). However a single PKG is undesirable for a large network because the PKG could become a bottleneck in communication.

To overcome this problem, hierarchical identity-based encryption (HIBE) [3, 4] was introduced in 2002. After thet, many efficient HIBE schemes are proposed in the recent years [5–8]. HIBE allows a root PKG to distribute the workload by delegating private key generation and identity authentication to lower-level PKGs. An important feature of HIBE is that any ancestor in the path from the

⋆ Corresponding author.

J. Lopez, X. Huang, and R. Sandhu (Eds.): NSS 2013, LNCS 7873, pp. 663–670, 2013.

root PKG to a target node can decrypt the ciphertext to the target node even if the ancestor does not have the same private key as that of the target node, since an ancestor can generate a private key for any descendant node. This is reasonable for some strict hierarchical structures, in which the upper-level members may fully control the lower-level member and even disclose ciphertexts sent to the lower-level member in the case of necessarily. However, this feature is undesirable in some hierarchical structures, for example, in a consortium of corporations that engage in governmental projects or joint ventures [9]. In such a consortium, one company would be a leader and other companies would work in a part of the business as its sections, branches, or subsidiaries. Thus, such a consortium forms a hierarchical structure, but at the same time, each of the consortium companies is rather independent, and all upper-level members do not necessarily have to control the lower-level members.

Miyaji introduced the concept of ancestor-excludable HIBE (AE-HIBE) [9], where an AE-HIBE scheme should satisfy the ancestor excludable feature, i.e., ancestors with a level less than the designated one can be excluded from a set of privileged ancestors who have the right to decrypt a ciphertext to a target node. She also gave the functional definition together with the security definitions. Moreover, a concrete example of AE-HIBE is presented and proved to be selective-ID-CPA secure in the standard model. Unfortunately, we found that the functional definition and the concrete scheme are flawed.

In this paper, we analyze Miyaji's functional definition of AE-HIBE and the concrete AE-HIBE scheme. We then introduce a new functional definition of AE-HIBE and present a new AE-HIBE scheme. The new scheme is ID-CPA secure in the random oracle and can be converted to having ID-CCA security by applying a conversional method.

2 Preliminary

This section introduces the background knowledge, i.e., the "admissible bilinear map" [2], the Bilinear Diffie-Hellman problem, and the security model.

Definition 1. *(Bilinear Map) Let* $\mathbb{G}$ *be an additive group of prime order* q *and* $\mathbb{G}_T$ *a multiplicative group of the same order. Let* P *denote a generator of* $\mathbb{G}$*. An admissible pairing is a bilinear map* $\hat{e} : \mathbb{G} \times \mathbb{G} \to \mathbb{G}_T$ *which has the following properties: (1) Bilinear: given* Q*,* $R \in \mathbb{G}$ *and* $a, b \in \mathbb{Z}_q^*$*, we have* $\hat{e}(aQ, bR) = \hat{e}(Q, R)^{ab}$*, (2) Non-degenerate:* $\hat{e}(P, P) \neq 1_{\mathbb{G}_T}$*, (3) Computable:* $\hat{e}$ *is efficiently computable.*

Definition 2. *(Bilinear Diffie-Hellman Assumption) For* $a, b, c \in_R \mathbb{Z}_q^*$*,* aP*,* bP *and* cP *are computed. Given* (aP, bP, cP)*, compute* $\hat{e}(P, P)^{abc}$ *is hard.*

A HIBE scheme is semantically secure against adaptive chosen ciphertext and adaptive chosen target attack (IND-HID-CCA) if no polynomially bounded adversary $\mathcal{A}$ has a non-negligible advantage against the challenger in the following game [4].

- Setup: The challenger takes a security parameter K and runs the Root Setup algorithm. It gives the adversary the resulting system parameters $params$. It keeps the root key to itself.
- Phase 1: The adversary issues queries $q_1, \cdots, q_m$ where q_i is one of:
  1. Public-key query (ID-tuple$_i$): The challenger runs a hash algorithm on ID-tuple$_i$ to obtain the public key H(ID-tuple$_i$).
  2. Extraction query (ID-tuple$_i$): The challenger runs the Extraction algorithm to generate the private key d_i, and sends it to the adversary.
  3. Decryption query (ID-tuple$_i$, C_i): The challenger runs the Extraction algorithm to generate the private key d_i, runs the Decryption algorithm to decrypt C_i using d_i, and sends the resulting plaintext to the adversary.

  These queries may be asked adaptively. Note also that the queried ID-tuple$_i$ may correspond to a position at any level in the hierarchy.
- Challenge: Once the adversary decides that Phase 1 is over, it outputs two equal length plaintexts $M_0, M_1 \in \mathcal{M}$ and an ID-tuple on which it wishes to be challenged. The only constraints are that neither this ID-tuple nor its ancestors appear in any private key extraction query in Phase 1. Again, this ID-tuple may correspond to a position at any level in the hierarchy. The challenger picks a random bit $b \in \{0, 1\}$ and sets C = Encryption($params$, ID-tuple,M_b). It sends C as a challenge to the adversary.
- Phase 2: The adversary issues more queries $q_{m+1}, \cdots, q_n$ where q_i is one of:
  1. Public-key query (ID-tuple$_i$): Challenger responds as in Phase 1.
  2. Extraction query (ID-tuple$_i$ $\neq$ ID-tuple or ancestor): Challenger responds as in Phase 1.
  3. Decryption query ((ID-tuple$_i$, C_i) $\neq$ (ID-tuple or ancestor, C)): Challenger responds as in Phase 1.
- Guess: The adversary outputs a guess $b' \in \{0, 1\}$.

The adversary wins the game if $b = b'$. We define its advantage in attacking the scheme to be $|\Pr[b = b'] - \frac{1}{2}|$.

3 Analysis of Miyaji's AE-HIBE Scheme

In this section, we analyze Miyaji's functional definition and the concrete scheme. Due to limited space, the details are omitted here. More details on the functional definition and the concrete scheme can be find in [9]. For readability, we firstly analyze the concrete scheme and then explain the reason from the functional definition.

The problem about the concrete encryption scheme is the algorithms of KDer$_p$. Now we compute the private key of the first three levels step by step.

- Level 0: $\mathrm{SK}_\varepsilon = \{\mathrm{SK}_{\varepsilon,1}, \cdots, \mathrm{SK}_{\varepsilon,t}\}$;
- Level 1: Let $v = v_1$. Select $\alpha_v \in \mathbb{Z}_q$. Compute
  $A_{v,1} = \mathrm{SK}_{\varepsilon,1} + \alpha_v i_d(v_1)Q_1 + \alpha_v P_1 = \alpha R_1 + \alpha_v i_d(v_1)Q_1 + \alpha_v P_1$,
  $B_v = \alpha_v P, C_{v,2} = \alpha_v Q_2, \cdots, C_{v,t} = \alpha_v Q_t$.
  The secret key is $\mathrm{SK}_v = \{\mathrm{sk}_{v,1}\}$, where $\mathrm{sk}_{v,1} = \{A_{v,1}, B_v, C_{v,2}, \cdots, C_{v,t}\}$

- Level 2: Firstly we use KDer to compute the private key as following:
  (1) Let $v = v_1v_2$ $(l = 2)$;
  (2) Select $\alpha_v \in \mathbb{Z}_q$, and compute $A_{v,1} = \alpha R_1 + \alpha_v(id(v_1)Q_1 + id(v_1v_2)Q_2 + P_1)$, $A_{v,2} = \alpha R_2 + \alpha_v(id(v_1v_2)Q_2 + P_1)$.
  The private key is $\{\mathrm{sk}_{v_1v_2,1}, \mathrm{sk}_{v_1v_2,2}\}$, where $\mathrm{sk}_{v_1v_2,1} = \{A_{v_1v_2,1}, B_{v_1v_2}, C_{v_1v_2,3}, \cdots, C_{v_1v_2,t}\}$, $\mathrm{sk}_{v_1v_2,2} = \{A_{v_1v_2,2}\}$.
  Now we use $\mathrm{KDer_p}$ to compute the private key as following:
  1. $v = v_1$;
  2. Purse $\mathrm{SK}_v = \{\mathrm{SK}_{v,1}\}$;
  3. Select a random secret value $r_{v_1v_2} \in \mathbb{Z}_q$, compute $A_{v_1v_2,1} = \alpha R_1 + (\alpha_{v_1} + r_{v_1v_2})(i_d(v_1)Q_1 + i_d(v_1v_2)Q_2) + (\alpha_{v_1} + r_{v_1v_2})P_1$, $B_{v_1v_2} = (\alpha_{v_1} + r_{v_1v_2})P$, $C_{v_1v_2,3} = (\alpha_{v_1} + r_{v_1v_2})Q_3$, $\cdots$, $C_{v_1v_2,t} = (\alpha_{v_1} + r_{v_1v_2})Q_t$.

The private key is $\{\mathrm{sk}_{v_1v_2,1}\}$, where $\mathrm{sk}_{v_1v_2,1} = \{A_{v_1v_2,1}, B_{v_1v_2}, C_{v_1v_2,3}, \cdots, C_{v_1v_2,t}\}$. Note that $A_{v_1v_2,2} = A_{v_1,2} + i_d(v_1v_2)C_{v_1,2} + r_{v_1v_2}(i_d(v_1v_2)Q_2 + P_1)$ is unknown since $A_{v_1,2}$ does not exit.

According to the definition of KDer_p, the node v_1 can derive only $\{\mathrm{sk}_{v_1v_2,1}\}$ but not $\{\mathrm{sk}_{v_1v_2,2}\}$. Only the root center can compute both $\{\mathrm{sk}_{v_1v_2,1}\}$ and $\{\mathrm{sk}_{v_1v_2,2}\}$. Here is the problem: without $\{\mathrm{sk}_{v_1v_2,2}\}$, the node of the second level v_1v_2 can not generate the second part of the private key for his child node $v_1v_2v_3$. For the same reason, a node in level l ($l \geq h$, where h is the designated level) can only generate the first part of his child node's private keys. However, decrypting a ciphertext needs $\mathrm{sk}_{v,h}$, which leads the decryption unsuccessful. To obtain the valid decryption key $\mathrm{sk}_{v,h}$, the only way is that a node in level l $(l \geq h)$ asks the root PKG to generate his private key, and then uses this private key to derive other private keys for his descendent. However, this is not realistic since it is against the original motivation of the HIBE, i.e., Hierarchical ID-based encryption allows a root PKG to distribute the workload by delegating private key generation and identity authentication to lower-level PKGs.

4 A New Ancestor-Excludable HIBE Scheme

In this section, we introduce a new functional definition of AE-HIBE and present a new scheme. The new functional definition is defined as follows.

Definition 3. *AE-HIBE consists of a 5-tuple of PPT algorithms, where*

- *Root Setup: The root PKG takes a security parameter k and the level t of m-ary tree, and returns params (system parameters) and a root secret. The system parameters will be publicly available, while only the root PKG will know the root secret.*
- *Lower-Level Setup: Lower-level users obtain the system parameters of the root PKG. Moreover, Lower-level users generate local secrets and the corresponding local public parameters.*
- *Extraction: A PKG with ID-tuple $(ID_1, \cdots, ID_t)$ may compute a private key for any of its children by using the system parameters and its private key (and any other secret information).*

– *Encryption: A sender inputs params, $M \in \mathcal{M}$, the ID-tuple of the intended message recipient, and level h of a designated ancestor, outputs a ciphertext C together with the ID-tuple of the recipient and the level h.*
– *Decryption: A user inputs params, $C \in \mathcal{C}$, level h of a designated ancestor, and its private key d, and returns the message $M \in \mathcal{M}$.*

Now we are ready to propose the new AE-HIBE scheme.

– **Root Setup**: (1) Runs $\mathcal{IG}$ on input K to generate groups $\mathbb{G}_1$, $\mathbb{G}_2$ of prime order q and an admissible pairing $\hat{e} : \mathbb{G}_1 \times \mathbb{G}_1 \to \mathbb{G}_2$; (2) chooses an arbitrary generator $P_0 \in \mathbb{G}_1$; (3) picks a random $s_0 \in \mathbb{Z}/q\mathbb{Z}$ and sets $Q_0 = s_0 P_0$; (4) chooses hash functions $H_1 : \{0,1\}^* \to \mathbb{G}_1$ and $H_2 : \{0,1\}^* \to \mathbb{G}_1$.
The message space is $\mathcal{M} = \{0,1\}^n$. The ciphertext space is $\mathcal{C} = \mathbb{G}_1^t \times \{0,1\}^n$ where t is the level of the recipient. The system parameters are $params = (\mathbb{G}_1, \mathbb{G}_2, \hat{e}, P_0, Q_0, H_1, H_2)$. The root PKG's secret is $s_0 \in \mathbb{Z}/q\mathbb{Z}$.
– **Lower-Level Setup**. Entity $\mathrm{E}_t \in \mathrm{Level}_t$ picks a random $s_t \in \mathbb{Z}/q\mathbb{Z}$, which it keeps secret. E_t computes $s_t P_0$ and releases $s_t P_0$ as the public parameters.
– **Extraction**. Let E_t be an entity in Level_t with ID-tuple $(\mathrm{ID}_1, \cdots, \mathrm{ID}_t)$, where $(\mathrm{ID}_1, \cdots, \mathrm{ID}_i)$ for $1 \leq i \leq t$ is the ID-tuple of E_t's ancestor at Level_i. Set S_0 to be the identity element of $\mathbb{G}_1$. Then E_t's parent computes $P_t = H_1(ID_1, \cdots, ID_t) \in \mathbb{G}_1$, and sets E_t's secret point S_t to be $S_{t-1} + s_{t-1}P_t = \sum_{i=1}^{t} s_{i-1}P_i$;
– **Encryption**. To encrypt $M \in \mathcal{M}$ with the ID-tuple $(\mathrm{ID}_1, \cdots, \mathrm{ID}_t)$, the encrypter firstly chooses k as the designated level, then does the following:
  • Computes $P_i = H_1(ID_1, \cdots, ID_i) \in \mathbb{G}_1$ for $1 \leq i \leq t$.
  • Chooses a random $r \in \mathbb{Z}/q\mathbb{Z}$.
  • Sets the ciphertext to be: $C = [(rP_0, rP_1, \cdots, rP_{k-1}, rP_{k+1}, \cdots, rP_t, M \oplus H_2(g^r)), \mathrm{E}_t, k]$ where $g = \hat{e}(s_{k-1}P_0, P_k) \in \mathbb{G}_2$.
– **Decryption**. Let $C_1 = [U_0, U_1, \cdots, U_{k-1}, U_{k+1}, \cdots, U_t, V] \in \mathcal{C}$ be the ciphertext encrypted using the ID-tuple $(\mathrm{ID}_1, \cdots, \mathrm{ID}_t)$. To decrypt C, E_t computes:

$$V \oplus H_2\left(\frac{\hat{e}(U_0, S_t)}{\prod_{i=1}^{k-1} \hat{e}(s_{i-1}P_0, U_i) \cdot \prod_{i=k+1}^{t} \hat{e}(s_{i+1}P_0, U_i)}\right) = M.$$

This concludes the description of our AD-HIBE scheme.

5 Security Analysis

The security of Basic-AE-HIBE is based on the difficulty of the BDH problem, as stated in the following theorems (which are analogous to Theorem 2 in [4]):

Theorem 1. *Suppose there is an HIB-OWE adversary $\mathcal{A}$ that makes at most $q_{H_2} > 0$ hash queries to the hash function H_2 and at most $q_E > 0$ private key extraction queries and has advantage ε_t of successfully targeting a Basic AE-HIBE node in $Level_t$. If the hash functions H_1, H_2 are random oracles, then there is an algorithm $\mathcal{B}$ that solves the BDH in groups generated by $\mathcal{IG}$ with advantage at least $(\varepsilon_t(\frac{t}{e(q_E+t)})^t - \frac{1}{2^n})q_{H_2}^{-1}$ and running time $\mathcal{O}(time(\mathcal{A}))$.*

Proof: Similarly to the proof of the IBE scheme in [2] and the HIBE scheme in [4], we first define a related public-key encryption scheme called BasicPub, and then use two lemmas to show that the security of Basic AE-HIBE is based on the difficulty of the BDH problem. One lemma proves that breaking Basic AE-HIBE is as hard as breaking BasicPub, and the other one proves that breaking BasicPub is as hard as solving an instance of the BDH problem.

We begin our proof with defining BasicPub. BasicPub is a public-key encryption scheme specified by three algorithms.

- Key Generation: (1) Run $\mathcal{IG}$ on input K to generate two groups $\mathbb{G}_1$, $\mathbb{G}_2$ and a bilinear map $\hat{e}$. Choose an arbitrary generator $P_0 \in \mathbb{G}_1$. (2) Pick a random $s_0 \in \mathbb{Z}/q\mathbb{Z}$ and set $Q_0 = s_0 P_0$. (3) Pick random values $s_i \in \mathbb{Z}/q\mathbb{Z}$ and random points $P_i \in \mathbb{G}_1$ $(1 \leq i \leq t)$, and set $Q_i = s_i P_0$ and $S_i = s_{i-1} P_i$ $(1 \leq i \leq t)$. (4) Choose a cryptographic hash function $H_2 : \mathbb{G}_2 \to \{0,1\}^n$. The ciphertext space is $\mathcal{C} = \mathbb{G}_1 \times \{0,1\}^n \times \mathbb{N}$. The public key is $(\mathbb{G}_1, \mathbb{G}_2, \hat{e}, P_0, Q_0, Q_1, \cdots, Q_t, H_2)$. The private key is S_i $(1 \leq i \leq t)$.
- Encryption: To encrypt $M \in \mathcal{M}$, choose a random $r \in \mathbb{Z}/q\mathbb{Z}$ and $k \in \{1, \cdots, t\}$, set the ciphertext to be $C = ([rP_0, M \oplus H_2(g^r)], P_k, k)$, where $g = \hat{e}(Q_{k-1}, P_k) \in \mathbb{G}_2$.
- Decryption: Let $C_1 = [U, V] \in \mathcal{C}$ be the part of the ciphertext. To decrypt C, compute $V \oplus H_2(\hat{e}(U, S_k)) = M$.

Lemma 1. *Suppose that $\mathcal{A}$ is an HIB-OWE adversary that makes at most $q_E > 0$ private key extraction queries and has advantage ε_t of successfully targeting a Basic AE-HIBE node in Level$_t$, and suppose that the hash function H_1 is a random oracle. Then there is an OWE adversary $\mathcal{B}$ that has advantage at least $\varepsilon_t(t/e(q_E + t))^t$ against BasicPub and running time $\mathcal{O}(time(\mathcal{A}))$.*

The proof of Lemma 1 is similar to the proof of Lemma 2 in [4]. The only difference lies in the Challenge stage. In this stage, algorithm $\mathcal{B}$ sets $T_h = b_h P_h$ and $T_k = b_k P_0 (1 \leq k \leq t, k \neq h)$ where h is the designated level. Let $C = [U, V]$ be the challenge ciphertext given to algorithm $\mathcal{B}$. Algorithm $\mathcal{B}$ sets the Basic AE-HIDE ciphertext C' to be $[b_h^{-1}U, b_h^{-1}b_1 U, \cdots, b_h^{-1}b_{h-1}U, b_h^{-1}b_{h+1}U, \cdots, b_h^{-1}b_t U, V]$. Algorithm $\mathcal{B}$ responds to $\mathcal{A}$ with the challenge C'.

Observe that a valid private key for ID-tuple$_i$ has the form $S'_t = s'_{h-1}T_h + \sum_{k=1,k\neq h-1}^{t-1} s'_k T_{k+1}$, It is easy to check that

$$\frac{\hat{e}(b_h^{-1}U, S'_t)}{\prod_{k=1}^{h-1} \hat{e}(b_h^{-1}b_k U, s'_{k-1}P_0) \cdot \prod_{k=h+1}^{t} \hat{e}(b_h^{-1}b_k U, s'_{k-1}P_0)} = \hat{e}(U, s'_{h-1}P_h).$$

With the additional information $\{s'_k P_0 : 1 \leq k \leq t\}$ for some $(s'_1, \cdots, s'_{t-1}) \in (\mathbb{Z}/q\mathbb{Z})^{t-1}$ where s'_h is unknown to the simulator, we can find that the correct decryption of C' is M.

Similar to the proof of Lemma 2 in [4], the probability that $\mathcal{B}$ does not abort is at least $(t_i/e(q_E + t))^t$.

Lemma 2. *Suppose that $\mathcal{A}$ is an OWE adversary with advantage ε against BasicPub that makes a total of q_{H2} queries to the hash function H_2, and suppose that H_2 is a random oracle. Then there is an algorithm $\mathcal{B}$ that solves the BDH problem for $\mathcal{IG}$ with advantage at least $\varepsilon - \frac{1}{2^n}/q_{H_2}$ and running time $\mathcal{O}(time(\mathcal{A}))$.*

Proof: The proof is exactly the same as the proof for Boneh's IBE scheme in [2]. Combining Lemma 1 and 2, Theorem 1 for BasicHIDE can be proved.

6 Conclusion

Miyaji introduced the concept of ancestor-excludable hierarchical ID-based encryption (AE-HIBE) to prevent the ancestors with a level less than the designated one from decrypting a ciphertext to a target descendant node. Unfortunately, we found the functional definition and the concrete scheme she proposed are flawed. In this paper, we introduced a new functional definition of AE-HIBE, then presented a new AE-HIBE scheme, and proved that the new scheme is ID-CPA secure in the random oracle. The security can be converted to ID-CCA security by applying a general conversion method.

Acknowledgments. This work was supported by the National Natural Science Foundation of China (Grant Nos. 90718017, 61170189, 61202239), the Research Fund for the Doctoral Program of Higher Education (Grant No. 20111102130003, 20121102120017), and the Fund of the State Key Laboratory of Software Development Environment (Grant No. KLSDE-2011ZX-03, SKLSDE-2012ZX-11).

References

1. Shamir, A.: Identity-based cryptosystems and signature schemes. In: Blakely, G.R., Chaum, D. (eds.) CRYPTO 1984. LNCS, vol. 196, pp. 47–53. Springer, Heidelberg (1985)
2. Boneh, D., Franklin, M.: Identity based encryption from the Weil pairing. In: Kilian, J. (ed.) CRYPTO 2001. LNCS, vol. 2139, pp. 213–229. Springer, Heidelberg (2001)
3. Horwitz, J., Lynn, B.: Toward Hierarchical Identity-Based Encryption. In: Knudsen, L.R. (ed.) EUROCRYPT 2002. LNCS, vol. 2332, pp. 466–481. Springer, Heidelberg (2002)
4. Gentry, C., Silverberg, A.: Hierarchical ID-Based Cryptography. In: Zheng, Y. (ed.) ASIACRYPT 2002. LNCS, vol. 2501, pp. 548–566. Springer, Heidelberg (2002)
5. Agrawal, S., Boneh, D., Boyen, X.: Efficient lattice (H)IBE in the standard model. In: Gilbert, H. (ed.) EUROCRYPT 2010. LNCS, vol. 6110, pp. 553–572. Springer, Heidelberg (2010)
6. Gentry, C., Halevi, S.: Hierarchical Identity Based Encryption with Polynomially Many Levels. In: Reingold, O. (ed.) TCC 2009. LNCS, vol. 5444, pp. 437–456. Springer, Heidelberg (2009)
7. Lewko, A., Waters, B.: Unbounded HIBE and Attribute-Based Encryption. In: Paterson, K.G. (ed.) EUROCRYPT 2011. LNCS, vol. 6632, pp. 547–567. Springer, Heidelberg (2011)

8. Boneh, D., Boyen, X., Goh, E.-J.: Hierarchical Identity Based Encryption with Constant Size Ciphertext. In: Cramer, R. (ed.) EUROCRYPT 2005. LNCS, vol. 3494, pp. 440–456. Springer, Heidelberg (2005)
9. Miyaji, A.: Ancestor Excludable Hierarchical ID-based Encryption and Its Application to Broadcast Encryption. IPSJ Digital Courier 3, 610–624 (2007)
10. Boyen, X.: General Ad Hoc encryption from exponent inversion IBE. In: Naor, M. (ed.) EUROCRYPT 2007. LNCS, vol. 4515, pp. 394–411. Springer, Heidelberg (2007)

Think Twice before You Share: Analyzing Privacy Leakage under Privacy Control in Online Social Networks

Yan Li, Yingjiu Li, Qiang Yan, and Robert H. Deng

School of Information Systems, Singapore Management University
{yan.li.2009,yjli,qiang.yan.2008,robertdeng}@smu.edu.sg

Abstract. Online Social Networks (OSNs) have become one of the major platforms for social interactions. Privacy control is deployed in popular OSNs to protect user's data. However, user's sensitive information could still be leaked even when privacy rules are properly configured. We investigate the effectiveness of privacy control against privacy leakage from the perspective of information flow. Our analysis reveals that the existing privacy control mechanisms do not protect the flow of personal information effectively. By examining typical OSNs including Facebook, Google+, and Twitter, we discover a series of privacy exploits which are caused by the conflicts between privacy control and OSN functionalities. Our analysis reveals that the effectiveness of privacy control may not be guaranteed as most OSN users expect.

Keywords: Online Social Network, Privacy Control, Attacks, Information Flow.

1 Introduction

Online Social Network services (OSNs) have become an essential element in modern life where massive amount of personal data is published. Prior research [9,3,1] shows that it is possible to infer undisclosed personal data from *publicly* shared information. But the availability and quality of the public data causing privacy leakage are decreasing due to the following two factors: 1) privacy control mechanisms have become the standard feature of OSNs and keep evolving [4,2]. 2) the percentage of users who choose *not* to publicly share information is also increasing [3]. In this tendency, it seems that privacy leakage may be perfectly *prevented* as the increasingly comprehensive privacy control mechanism is available to the users. However, this may not be achievable according to our findings.

In this paper, we investigate privacy protection from a new perspective, referred to as *privacy leakage under privacy control* (PLPC). *PLPC* examines whether a user's private personal information is leaked *even if* the user properly configures privacy rules. The problem of PLPC in OSNs involves *distributor* and *receiver*. An *adversary* is a receiver who intends to learn private information published by a *victim* who is a distributor. An adversary's capabilities can be characterized according to two factors. The *first* factor is the distance between adversary and victim. Considering a social network as a directed graph, an n-hop adversary can be defined such that the length of the shortest connected

J. Lopez, X. Huang, and R. Sandhu (Eds.): NSS 2013, LNCS 7873, pp. 671–677, 2013.

path from victim to adversary is n hops. In our discussion, we consider 1-hop adversary (i.e. *friend*), 2-hop adversary (i.e. *friend of friend*), and k-hop adversary where $k > 2$ (i.e. *stranger*). The *second* factor is prior knowledge about a victim required by corresponding attacks.

We examine the underlying reasons that make privacy control vulnerable using information flow based analysis. We start with categorizing the personal information of an OSN user into three *attribute sets* according to *who the user is*, *whom the user knows*, and *what the user does*, respectively. We model the information flow between these attribute sets and examine the functionalities which control the flow. We inspect typical real-world OSNs including Facebook, Google+, and Twitter, where privacy exploits and corresponding attacks are identified.

Our analysis reveals that most of the privacy exploits are inherent due to the underlying conflicts between privacy control and essential OSN functionalities. Therefore, the effectiveness of privacy control may not be guaranteed even if it is technically achievable.

We summarize the contributions of this paper as follows:

- We investigate the interaction between privacy control and information flow in OSNs. We identify privacy exploits for current privacy control mechanisms in typical OSNs. Based on these privacy exploits, we introduce a series of attacks for adversaries with different capabilities to obtain private personal information.
- We analyze the discovered exploits caused by the conflicts between privacy control and the functionalities. These conflicts reveal that the effectiveness of privacy control may not be guaranteed as most OSN users expect.

2 Attribute Sets, Functionalities, and Information Flows in OSNs

In a typical OSN, Alice owns a *profile page* for publishing her personal information. The personal information can be categorized into three *attribute sets*: a) personal particular set (PP set), b) social relationship set (SR set), and c) social activity set (SA set), according to *who the user is*, *whom the user interact with*, and *what the user does*, respectively. We show corresponding personal information and attribute sets on Facebook, Google+, and Twitter in Table 1.

Table 1. Types of personal information on Facebook, Google+, and Twitter

Acronym	Attribute set	Facebook	Google+	Twitter
PP	Personal Particulars	Current city, hometown, sex, birthday, employer, university, religion, political views, music, emails, city, about me	Introduction, occupation, employment, education, places lived, phone, gender	Name, location, bio, website
SR	Social Relationship (incoming list, outgoing list)	Friends, friends	Have you in circles, your circles	Following, follower
SA	Social Activities	Status message, photo, link, video, comments, like	Post, photo, comments, link, video, plus 1's	Tweets

Alice's PP set describes persistent facts about Alice, such as gender and race. Alice's SR set stores her social relationships as connections. A *connection* represents information flow from a *distributor* to her *1-hop receiver*. Alice's SR set consists of an *incoming list* and an *outgoing list*. For each user u_i in Alice's incoming list, there is a connection from u_i to Alice. For each user u_o in Alice's outgoing list, there is a connection from Alice to u_o. Alice can receive information from the users in her incoming list, and distribute her information to the users in her outgoing list. The social relationships in certain OSNs such as Facebook are mutual. Such mutual relationship can be considered as a pair of connections linking two users with opposite directions. The incoming list and outgoing list in SR set and their corresponding names on FaceBook, Google+, and Twitter are shown in Table 1. Lastly, Alice's SA set describes her social activities, such as status messages and photos.

Most OSNs provide two basic functionalities including REC and TAG. REC functionality recommends to Alice a list of users that Alice may include in her SR set. The list of recommended users is composed based on the social relationships of the users in Alice's SR set. TAG functionality allows Alice to mention another user's name in her social activities, which provides a link to the user's profile page.

The attribute sets (illustrated as circles in Figure 1) of multiple users are connected within an OSN, where personal information may explicitly flow from a profile page to another profile page via REC and TAG, as represented by solid arrows and rectangles in Figure 1. It is also possible to access a user's personal information in PP set and SR set via implicit information flows marked by dashed arrows. The details about these information flows are described below.

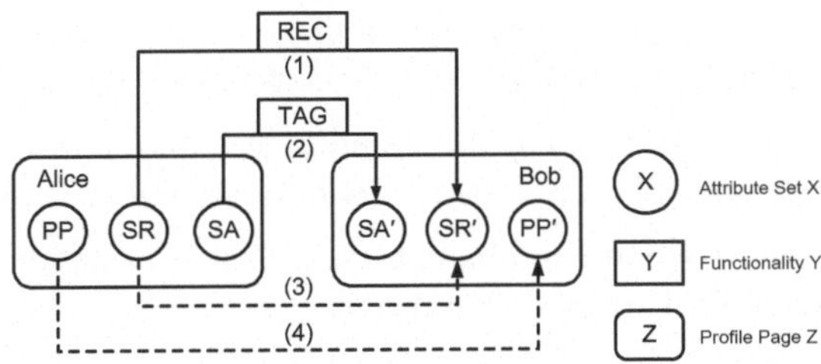

Fig. 1. Information flows between attribute sets

The first explicit flow is caused by REC, as shown in arrow (1) in Figure 1. REC recommends to Bob a list of users based on the social relationships of the users in Bob's SR set. Thus the undisclosed users in Alice's SR may be recommended to Bob via REC, if Bob is connected with Alice.

The second explicit flow is caused by TAG is shown in arrow (2) in Figure 1. An OSN user may mention other users' names in a social activity in his/her SA set via TAG, which creates explicit links connecting SA sets within different profile pages.

The third flow is an implicit flow caused by the design of information storage for SR sets, as shown in arrow (3) in Figure 1. Given a connection from Alice to Bob, Bob is included in Alice's outgoing list while Alice is included in Bob's incoming list.

The fourth flow is an implicit flow related to PP set, which is shown as the arrow (4) in Figure 1. Due to the homophily effect [6], a user is willing to connect with the users with similar personal particulars. This tendency can be used to link PP sets of multiple users.

It is difficult to prevent privacy leakage from all these information flows. A user may be able to prevent privacy leakage caused by explicit information flows by carefully using corresponding functionalities, as these flows are materialized only when the functionalities are used. However, it is difficult to avoid privacy leakage due to implicit information flows, as they are caused by inherent correlations among the information shared in OSNs. In fact, all these four information flows illustrated in Figure 1 correspond to inherent exploits, which will be analyzed in Section 3.

3 Exploits and Attacks

In this section, we analyze the exploits and attacks to a victim's PP set, SR set, and SA set. All of our findings have been verified on Facebook, Google+, and Twitter.

3.1 PP Set

The undisclosed information in PP set can be inferred by the following exploit, namely *inferable personal particular.*

Inferable Personal Particular. Human beings are more likely to interact with others who have the same or similar personal particulars [6]. The phenomenon is called homophily. This causes an exploit named *inferable personal particulars*, which corresponds to the information flow shown as dashed arrow (4) in Figure 1.

Exploit 1: *If most of a victim's friends have similar personal particulars, it could be inferred that the victim may have the same or similar personal particulars.*

An adversary may use Exploit 1 to obtain undisclosed information in a victim's PP set. The following is a typical attack on Facebook.

Attack 1: Considering a scenario on Facebook shown in Figure 2, Bob, Carl, Derek, and some other users are Alice's friends, and Bob is a friend of Carl, Derek, and most of Alice's friends. Alice shares her employer information "*XXX Agency*" with Carl and

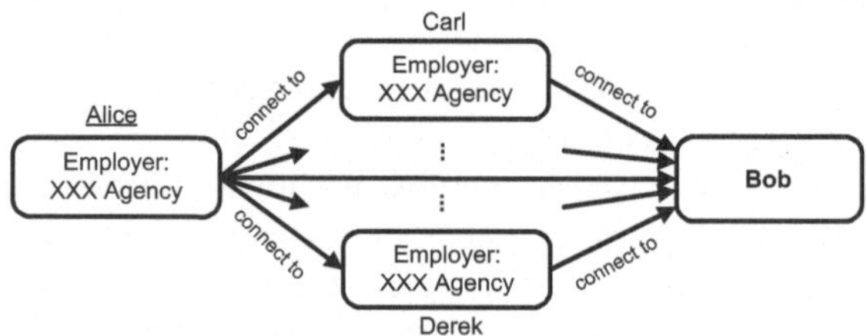

Fig. 2. Alice and most of her friends have common employer information

Derek. Most of Alice's friends may share their employer information with their friends due to different perceptions in privacy protection. Bob can collect the employer information of Alice's friends and infer that Alice's employer may be "*XXX Agency*".

The above attack works on Facebook, Google+, and Twitter. An adversary should have two types of knowledge. The first type of knowledge includes a large portion of users stored in the victim's SR set. The second type of knowledge includes the personal particulars of these users.

3.2 SR Set

The information in SR set can be leaked by two exploits, namely *inferable social relationship* and *unregulated relationship recommendation*.

Inferable Social Relationship. A user's SR set consists of incoming list and outgoing list. Given a connection from Alice to Carl, Carl is recorded in Alice's outgoing list while Alice is recorded in Carl's incoming list. This causes an exploit named *inferable social relationship*, which corresponds to the information flow shown as dashed arrow (3) in Figure 1.

Exploit 2: *Each social relationship in a victim's* SR *set indicates a connection between the victim and another user u. User u's* SR *set also stores a copy of this relationship for the same connection, which can be used to infer the relationship in the victim's* SR *set.*

An adversary may use Exploit 2 to obtain undisclosed social relationships in a victim's SR set, which is shown as the following exemplary attack on Facebook.

Attack 2: Considering a scenario on Facebook, where Bob is a stranger to Alice, and Carl is Alice's friend. Alice shares her SR set with a user group including Carl. Bob guesses Carl may be connected with Alice, but cannot confirm this by viewing Alice's SR set as it is protected against him. However, Carl shares his SR set publicly due to different concerns in privacy protection. Seeing Alice in Carl's SR set, Bob infers that Carl is Alice's friend.

Any adversary can use Exploit 2 as long as he has two types of knowledge: 1) a list of users in the victim's SR set; 2) social relationships in these users' SR sets. This attack could be a stepping stone for an adversary to infiltrate a victim's social network. Once the adversary discovers a victim's friends and becomes a friend of the victim's friends. After that, he is more likely to be accepted as the victim's friend [7].

Unregulated Relationship Recommendation. Most OSNs provide REC functionality to recommend a list of other users whom this user may know. The recommendation list is usually calculated based on the relationships in SR set but not regulated by the privacy rules chosen by the users in the recommendation list. This causes an exploit named *unregulated relationship recommendation*, which corresponds to the information flow shown as solid arrow (1) in Figure 1.

Exploit 3: *All social relationships in a victim's* SR *set could be automatically recommended by* REC *to all users in the victim's* SR *set, irrespective of whether or not the victim uses any privacy rules to protect her* SR *set.*

An adversary may use Exploit 3 to obtain undisclosed relationships in a victim's SR set, which is shown in the following attack on Facebook.

Attack 3: On Facebook, Bob is a friend of Alice, but not in a user group named `Close_Friends`. Alice shares her SR set with `Close_Friends` only. Although Bob is not allowed to view Alice's social relationships in her SR set, such information is automatically recommended by REC to Bob. If Bob is connected with Alice only, the recommendation list consists of the social relationships in Alice's SR set only.

Any adversary who is a *friend* of a victim can perform the attack on both Facebook and Google+. No prior knowledge is required for this attack.

3.3 SA Set

The undisclosed information in SA set protected by existing privacy control mechanisms can be inferred due to the following exploit, *inferable social activity*.

Inferable Social Activity. A user's name can be mentioned by the other in a social activity via TAG such that this social activity provides a link to the profile page of the mentioned user. Such links create correlations among all the users involved in the same activity. This causes an exploit named *inferable social activity*, which corresponds to the information flow shown as solid arrow (2) in Figure 1.

Exploit 4: *If a victim's friend uses* TAG *to mention the victim in a social activity published by the victim's friend, it implies that the victim may also attend the activity. Although this activity may involve the victim, the visibility of this activity is solely determined by the privacy rules specified by the victim's friend who publishes the activity, which is out of the control of the victim.*

An adversary may use Exploit 4 to obtain undisclosed social activities in a victim's SA set, which is shown in the following attack on Facebook.

Attack 4: Considering a scenario on Facebook, where Bob and Carl are Alice's friends, and Bob is Carl's friend. Alice publishes a social activity in her SA set regarding a party which Carl and she attended together and she allows Carl only to view this social activity. However, Carl publishes the same social activity in his SA set and mentions Alice via TAG. Due to different concerns in privacy protection, Carl allows all his friends to view this social activity. By viewing Carl's social activity, Bob can infer that Alice attended this party.

This attack may work on Facebook, Google+, and Twitter. Any adversary can perform this attack if he knows the social activities published by the victim's friends pointing to the victim via TAG.

To mitigate the threat, the privacy control should enforce privacy rules to an activity no matter who publishes it. To resolve privacy conflicts in collaborative data sharing, policy negotiation mechanisms have been proposed [5,8]. However, these policy negotiation mechanisms may significantly restrict the sharing nature of OSNs and frustrate users who intend to share that activity, as the consents of all involved users are required for each joint activity.

4 Conclusion

In this paper, we investigated privacy leakage under privacy control in online social networks. Our analysis showed that privacy leakage could still happen even when users correctly configure their privacy rules. We examined real-world OSNs including Facebook, Google+, and Twitter, and discovered the exploits which lead to privacy leakage. The detailed attacks were demonstrated by utilizing these exploits to learn undisclosed personal information that is supposed to be protected by the corresponding privacy rules. Our analysis further revealed that these exploits are associated with the underline conflicts between privacy control and functionalities, which are difficult to resolve.

Acknowledgment. This research is supported by the Singapore National Research Foundation under its International Research Centre @ Singapore Funding Initiative and administered by the IDM Programme Office.

References

1. Balduzzi, M., Platzer, C., Holz, T., Kirda, E., Balzarotti, D., Kruegel, C.: Abusing social networks for automated user profiling. In: Jha, S., Sommer, R., Kreibich, C. (eds.) RAID 2010. LNCS, vol. 6307, pp. 422–441. Springer, Heidelberg (2010)
2. Carminati, B., Ferrari, E., Heatherly, R., Kantarcioglu, M., Thuraisingham, B.: A semantic web based framework for social network access control. In: Proceedings of the 14th ACM Symposium on Access Control Models and Technologies, pp. 177–186 (2009)
3. Chaabane, A., Acs, G., Kaafar, M.A.: You are what you like! information leakage through users interests. In: Proceedings of the 19th Annual Network & Distributed System Security Symposium (2012)
4. Fong, P.W.L., Anwar, M., Zhao, Z.: A privacy preservation model for facebook-style social network systems. In: Backes, M., Ning, P. (eds.) ESORICS 2009. LNCS, vol. 5789, pp. 303–320. Springer, Heidelberg (2009)
5. Hu, H., Ahn, G.-J., Jorgensen, J.: Detecting and resolving privacy conflicts for collaborative data sharing in online social networks. In: Proceedings of the 27th Annual Computer Security Applications Conference, pp. 103–112 (2011)
6. McPherson, M., Smith-Lovin, L., Cook, J.M.: Birds of a feather: Homophily in social networks. Annual Review of Sociology 27, 415–444 (2001)
7. Watts, D.J.: Small worlds: the dynamics of networks between order and randomness. Princeton University Press (1999)
8. Yamada, A., Kim, T.-J., Perrig, A.: Exploiting privacy policy conflicts in online social networks. Technical report, Carnegie Mellon University (2012)
9. Zheleva, E., Getoor, L.: To join or not to join: the illusion of privacy in social networks with mixed public and private user profiles. In: Proceedings of the 18th International Conference on World Wide Web, pp. 531–540 (2009)

A Dynamic and Multi-layer Reputation Computation Model for Multi-hop Wireless Networks

Jia Hu[1], Hui Lin[2,*], and Li Xu[2]

[1] Department of Computer Science and Mathematics, Liverpool Hope University
[2] School of Mathematics and Computer Science, Fujian Normal University

Abstract. Multi-hop wireless networks have shown significant benefits in wireless communication, but they also face the internal multi-layer security threats. Since most security mechanisms require the cooperation of nodes, characterizing and learning the neighboring nodes' actions and the evolution of these actions over time is vital. This paper proposes a new dynamic and multi-layer reputation computation model named CRM that couples conventional layered reputation computation model with multi-layer design and multi-level security technology to identify malicious nodes and preserve security against internal multi-layer threats. Simulation results and performance analyses demonstrate that CRM can provide rapid and accurate malicious node identification and management, and implement the security preserving against the internal multi-layer and bad mouthing attacks more effectively.

Keywords: multi-hop networks, network security, reputation computation model.

1 Introduction

Security protection in MWNs [1, 2] is closely related to trust. In MWNs, trust can help characterize and learn the nodes' actions and the evolution of these actions over time, which facilitates secure cooperation and is vital to construct an efficient and robust solution for security-sensitive applications. As a key technique for managing trust, reputation computation models have been introduced as effective approaches to characterize and quantify a node's behavior. Luo et al. [6] proposed RFSTrust, a trust model based on fuzzy recommendation similarity to quantify and to evaluate the trustworthiness of nodes. Laniepce et al. [7] proposed a reputation cross-layer system which runs on the AP side and makes use of the TCP control mechanisms to evaluate node cooperation. Liu et al. [8] proposed a novel reputation computation model to recognize selfish nodes much earlier and decrease the convergence time for isolating selfish nodes. Although quite a few reputation computation models for MWNs have been proposed, all existing reputation computation models are based on the direct observation of layer-specifics to evaluate the node's reputation, thus ignoring many key factors of reputation in another layer. Meanwhile, they do not take the bad mouthing attack into account. However, multi-layer security mechanisms need to be implemented and enforced for MWNs to resist multi-layer and bad mouthing attacks.

J. Lopez, X. Huang, and R. Sandhu (Eds.): NSS 2013, LNCS 7873, pp. 678–684, 2013.

This paper designs a dynamic and multi-layer reputation computation model (CRM) for the MWNs. To the best of our knowledge, the proposed model is the first dynamic reputation computation model with consideration of the multi-layer design [3][4] and multi-level security [5] to identify and manage internal malicious nodes. To further enhance the reliability and validity of the dynamic reputation computation model, the proposed CRM model also adopts a unique combination of node role level relevancy and node security level relevancy to evaluate the reliability and credibility of the recommendation reputations that can further defense bad mouthing attack.

2 Multi-layer Dynamic Reputation Computation Model

This paper considers multi-hop 802.11s WMNs composed of mesh routers (or mesh nodes) and mesh clients [12]. For the multi-layer attacks, we consider the jamming attack in physical layer, selfish MAC attack in MAC layer, blackhole/grayhole attack in network layer. Moreover, the bad mouthing attack is considered.

This section proposes a novel dynamic multi-layer reputation computation model extended from our previous work [11-12]. CRM couples uncertainty based reputation computation models [8] [13-15] with multi-layer design [3-4] and multi-level security technology [5]. The multi-layer design combines network-layer node forwarding behavior observations with MAC-layer channel collision detections and physical-layer channel quality measures. Furthermore, CRM also adopts a unique combination of node role level relevancy and node security level relevancy to evaluate the reliability and the credibility of the recommendation reputations which will further defense bad mouthing attack. In CRM, we use a 4-tuple $\omega_{x:y} = (b_{x:y}, d_{x:y}, u_{x:y}, a_{x:y})$ to represent node *x*'s reputation toward *y* [11] and the final reputation of *x* toward *y* at time t_0, $\omega^{final}_{t_0,x:y}$, includes two components: the direct reputation $\omega^{dir}_{t_0,x:y}$ and the recommendation reputation $\omega^{rec}_{t_0,x:y}$.

2.1 Direct Reputation Computation

The direct reputation computation operates independently at every node and each node stores it in local reputation database. For neighbor nodes *x* and *y*, the direct reputation $\omega^{dir}_{t_0,x:y}$ can be denoted as (1).

$$\begin{cases} u^{cr-dir}_{t_0,x:y} = \alpha_1 * u^{Net-dir}_{t_0,x:y} + \alpha_2 * u^{MAC-dir}_{t_0,x:y} + \alpha_3 * u^{Phy-dir}_{t_0,x:y} \\ b^{cr-dir}_{t_0,x:y} = P_f * (1 - P^{Phy}_{loss}) * (1 - P^{MAC}_{col}) * (1 - u^{cr-dir}_{t_0,x:y}) \\ d^{cr-dir}_{t_0,x:y} = \left[1 - P_f * (1 - P^{Phy}_{loss}) * (1 - P^{MAC}_{col})\right] * (1 - u^{cr-dir}_{t_0,x:y}) \\ a^{cr-dir}_{t_0,x:y} = 0.5 \end{cases} \quad (1)$$

where $\alpha_1 + \alpha_2 + \alpha_3 = 1$. $u_{t_0,x:y}^{Net-dir}$, $u_{t_0,x:y}^{MAC-dir}$, $u_{t_0,x:y}^{Phy-dir}$ denote x's uncertainty on y at the network, MAC and physical layer respectively, and P_f is the node successful forwarding probability. They can be computed as (2).

$$\begin{cases} u_{t_0,x:y}^{Net-dir} = I_s / I_t \\ u_{t_0,x:y}^{Mac-dir} = P_{col}^{MAC} \\ u_{t_0,x:y}^{Phy-dir} = P_{loss}^{Phy} \\ P_f = N_s / N_t \end{cases} \tag{2}$$

where I_s is the number of successful interactions between nodes and I_t is the total number of interactions between nodes. N_s is the number of packets node has successfully forwarded and N_t is the total number of packets needs to be forwarded.

P_{col}^{MAC} is the packet collusion probability at MAC layer and can be computed as (3).

$$\begin{cases} r_{link-bussy} = 1 - \dfrac{f(P_{col}^{MAC}) * \lambda_{idle}}{f(P_{col}^{MAC}) * \lambda_{idle} + g(P_{col}^{MAC}) * \lambda_{suc} + h(P_{col}^{MAC}) * \lambda_{col}} \\ f(P_{col}^{MAC}) = (1 - P_{col}^{MAC})^{n/_{n-1}} \\ g(P_{col}^{MAC}) = n * (1 - P_{col}^{MAC})[1 - (1 - P_{col}^{MAC})^{1/_{n-1}}] \\ h(P_{col}^{MAC}) = 1 + (n-1)(1 - P_{col}^{MAC})^{n/_{n-1}} - n * (1 - P_{col}^{MAC}) \end{cases} \tag{3}$$

where $r_{link-bussy}$ is the link busyness ratio. λ_{idle}, λ_{suc} and λ_{col} denote the idle slot length, the durations of a successful transmission and a collision, respectively [16, 17].

P_{loss}^{Phy} is the packet loss probability caused by the bad channel quality. P_{loss}^{Phy} is estimated by modeling the underlying time varying channel as a GE model [3][16] and can be computed as (4).

$$\begin{cases} P_{loss}^{Phy} = P_{l-g} * \dfrac{q}{(p+q)} + P_{l-b} * \dfrac{p}{(p+q)} \\ p = \sum_{i=1}^{n-1} m_i \Big/ m_0 \\ q = \sum_{i=1}^{n-1} m_i \Big/ \sum_{i=1}^{n-1} m_i * i \end{cases} \tag{4}$$

where m_0 is the number of the delivered packets and m_i is the number of loss bursts having length i. P_{l-g} and P_{l-b} are the loss occur probability in good and bad states, respectively. How to estimate the parameters P_{l-g} and P_{l-b} can be referred to [16] [18].

2.2 Recommendation Reputation Computation

When there is not enough history interaction data for x to evaluate the direct reputation toward y or the direct reputation is not enough for x to make a decision on y, x will start a recommendation reputation query by broadcasting a Reputation Query message to the neighbors to ask for the reputation opinion on y. Whenever an x's neighbor receives the Query message, it will check its local reputation table whether there is a direct reputation on y with the uncertainty value of less than 1.0. If there is, the node sends a Reply message to x which contains its id, (sl, sc) (sl represents the security level of x's role and sc represents the security class of x's role), valid time period and its direct reputation on y, else it simply ignores the query.

Let R represent the set of recommenders ($|R| = n, n > 1$). After receiving the replies, x will execute the recommendation reputation evaluation phase as follows.

(1) If n=2 and the two recommendation reputations from y and k are conflict, x will evaluate the reliability of two recommenders as (5), and then select the recommendation opinion from the more trustworthy one.

$$\begin{cases} \xi_{x:y} = \beta_1 * \theta_1 + \beta_2 * \theta_2 \\ \theta_1 = 1 - \dfrac{|sc_{y/k} - sc_x|}{N_{sc}}, sc \in [1, N_{sc}] \\ \theta_2 = \begin{cases} \dfrac{sl_{y/k} - sl_x}{N_{sl}}, & sl_{y/k} \geq sl_x \\ 1 - \dfrac{|sl_{y/k} - sl_x|}{N_{sl}}, & sl_{y/k} < sl_x \end{cases}, sl \in [1, N_{sl}] \\ \beta_1 + \beta_2 = 1 \end{cases} \tag{5}$$

where θ_1 and θ_2 are the sl and sc relevancy between x and y/k. And, we say y is more trustworthy than k, if any of the conditions in (6) hold.

$$\begin{cases} \xi_{x:y} > \xi_{x:k} \\ \xi_{x:y} = \xi_{x:k} \wedge b_y > b_k \\ \xi_{x:y} = \xi_{x:k} \wedge b_y = b_k \wedge d_y < d_k \\ \xi_{x:y} = \xi_{x:k} \wedge b_y = b_k \wedge E(\omega_y) > E(\omega_k) \end{cases} \tag{6}$$

(2) If n>2, let $R'(|R'| = \tau)$ defined as (7) be the new set of the recommenders. Then, we allocate an appropriate weight f_i to each recommendation reputation and calculate the $\omega^{rec}_{t_0,x:y}$ by (8).

$$R' = \{ i | \xi_{x:i} \geq TH_{\xi} \} \tag{7}$$

$$\begin{cases} b_{t_0,x:y}^{\text{rec}} = \sum_{k=1,k\in R'}^{\tau} f_k \cdot b_{t_0,k:y}^{\text{dir}} \Big/ \tau \\ d_{t_0,x:y}^{\text{rec}} = \sum_{k=1,k\in R'}^{\tau} f_k \cdot d_{t_0,k:y}^{\text{dir}} \Big/ \tau \\ u_{t_0,x:y}^{\text{rec}} = \sum_{k=1,k\in R'}^{n} f_k \cdot u_{t_0,k:y}^{\text{dir}} \Big/ \tau \\ a_{t_0,x:y}^{\text{rec}} = \sum_{k=1,k\in R'}^{\tau} f_k \cdot a_{t_0,k:y}^{\text{dir}} \Big/ \tau \\ f_i = \xi_{x:i} * E(\omega_{t_0,x:i}) \Big/ \sum_{k\in R'} \xi_{x:k} * E(\omega_{t_0,x:k}) \end{cases} \tag{8}$$

After obtaining the direct reputation and the recommendation reputation, the dynamic final reputation can be calculated following the computations presented in [12].

3 Simulation Results and Analysis

The simulated network consists of 100 nodes located in a rectangular space of size 1000m x 1000m. Hybrid Wireless Mesh Protocol (HWMP) is used as the underlying routing protocol. Traffic source are constant bit-rate (CBR) and each source sends data packets of 1024 bytes. A practical scenario is considered where channel loss may be caused by attacks, or normal loss events such as medium access collisions or bad channel quality. We compare the proposed CRM against the models in [8] and [12], denoted by FSLR, and SLCRM, respectively. The performance is evaluated using the following metrics: the False Positive Rate (FPR) and the Packet Delivery Rate (PDR).

We build the experimental environment with bad link/channel quality and dishonest recommendations present. As shown in Fig. 1, we can see that the false positive rates of all the three models increase when the percentage of the malicious recommendation nodes increases and the fastest-growing and the slowest-growing model is the FSLR and the CRM, respectively. Because of the effective detection and defending mechanism against both bad mouthing and multi-layer attacks proposed in the CRM, its superiority is more obvious than FSLR and SLCRM.

We compare the PDR of the CRM to those of the SLCRM and FSLR. We consider the scenario with the honest recommendations and bad link/channel quality. As shown in Fig. 2, we can find that: (1) the average PDR of all the three models decreases when the percentage of the bad link/channel increases. (2) For FSLR, since it cannot detect the attacks launched in other layers in addition to the network layer, it cannot distinguish the reason of the packet loss, which will result in more normal nodes being classified as misbehaving nodes and then be isolated. Consequently, the average PDR of the FSLR falls at the highest pace. (3) The average PDR of the CRM drops slower than that of the SLCRM. The SLCRM can only detect the attacks launched in the network and MAC layer but ignoring the channel interrupt and packet loss caused by the attacks launched in the physical layer, which produces large impacts on the detection of malicious nodes and makes the average PDR of the SLCRM falls faster than that of the CRM .

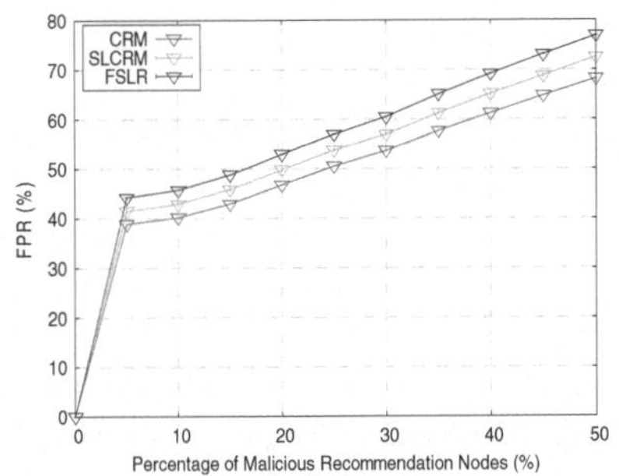

Fig. 1. Average FPR with multi-layer and bad mouthing attacks present

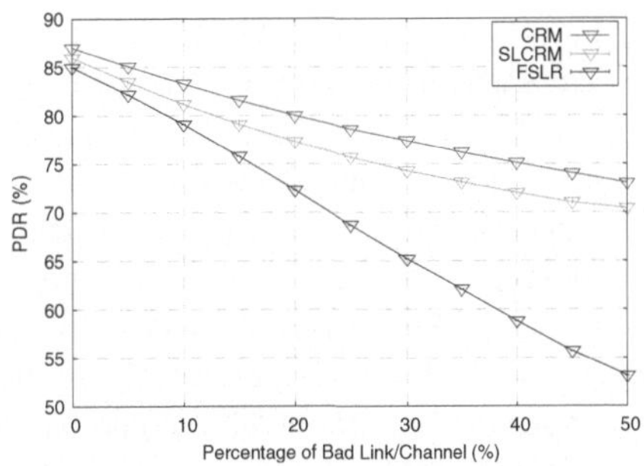

Fig. 2. Average PDR with multi-layer attacks present

4 Conclusions

This paper have investigated the problems of the internal multi-layer attack and bad mouthing attack in MWNs and have proposed a dynamic and multi-layer reputation computation model named CRM. Based on the innovative combination of the uncertainty based layered reputation computation model, multi-layer design, multi-level security technology and the proposed recommendation reputation reliability evaluation, CRM can effectively defend against the internal multi-layer security attacks and bad mouthing attack. Elaborate theoretical analyses have demonstrated that the CRM is secure and efficient. Furthermore, extensive simulation results have verified that the false positive rate and packet delivery ratio of the proposed CRM reputation computation model are better than those of the SLCRM and FSLR models.

Acknowledgement. This work is supported by the National Natural Science Foundation of China (61072080, 61202390, 61202452).

References

[1] Khan, S., Loo, K.K., Din, Z.U.: Cross Layer Design for Routing and Security in Multi-hop Wireless Networks. Journal of Information Assurance and Security 4, 170–173 (2009)

[2] Kamhoua, C.A., Pissinou, N., Makki, K.: Game Theoretic Modeling and Evolution of Trust in Autonomous Multi-Hop Networks. In: Proceeding of IEEE ICC 2011, Kyoto, Japan (2011)

[3] Salleh, N.M., Muhammad, M., Zakaria, M.S., Gannapathy, V.R., Suaidi, M.K., Ibrahim, I.M., AbdulAziz, M.Z.A., Johar, M.S., Ahmad, M.R.: Wireless Mesh Networks: Cross Layer Design Challenge. In: Proceeding of the ASIA-PACIFIC Conference on Applied Electromagnetics Proceedings, Melaka, Malaysia (2007)

[4] Akyildiz, I.F., Wang, X.: Cross-Layer Design in Wireless Mesh Networks. IEEE Transactions on Vehicular Technology 57(2), 1061–1076 (2008)

[5] Lu, W., Sundareshan, M.K.: A model for multilevel security in computer networks. IEEE Transactions on Software Engineering 16(6), 647–659 (1990)
[6] Luo, J., Liu, X., Fan, M.: A trust model based on fuzzy recommendation for mobile ad-hoc networks. Computer Network 53(14), 2396–2407 (2009)
[7] Laniepce, S., Lancieri, L., Achemlal, M., Bouabdallah, A.: A cross-Layer Reputation System for Routing Non-Cooperation Effects Mitigation Within Hybrid Ad-Hoc Networks. In: Proceeding of the IWCMC, Caen, France, pp. 296–300 (2010)
[8] Liu, Y., Li, K., Jin, Y., Zhang, Y., Qu, W.: A novel reputation computation model based on subjective logic for mobile ad hoc networks. Future Generation Computer Systems 27(5), 547–554 (2011)
[9] Long, X., Joshi, J.: BaRMS: A Bayesian Reputation Management Approach for P2P Systems. In: Proceeding of the IEEE IRI, Las Vegas, Nevada, USA, pp. 147–152 (2010)
[10] Khan, S., Loo, K.-K., Mast, N., Naeem, T.: SRPM: Secure routing protocol for IEEE 802.11 infrastructure based wireless mesh networks. Journal of Network and Systems Management 18(2), 190–209 (2010)
[11] Lin, H., Ma, J., Hu, J., Yang, K.: PA-SHWMP: a privacy-aware secure hybrid wireless mesh protocol for IEEE 802.11s wireless mesh networks. EURASIP Journal on Wireless Communications and Networking 2012, 69 (2012)
[12] Lin, H., Ma, J., Hu, J.: SLCRM: Subject Logic Based Cross layer Reputation Mechanism for Wireless Mesh Networks. China Communications 19(10), 40–49 (2012)
[13] Yu, H., Shen, Z., Miao, C., Leung, C., Niyato, D.: A Survey of Trust and Reputation Management Systems in Wireless Communications. Proceedings of the IEEE 98(10), 1755–1772 (2010)
[14] Li, F., Wu, J.: Uncertainty Modeling and Reduction in MANETs. IEEE Transactions on Mobile Computing 9(7), 1035–1048 (2010)
[15] Noack, A.: Trust agreement in wireless mesh networks. In: Ardagna, C.A., Zhou, J. (eds.) WISTP 2011. LNCS, vol. 6633, pp. 336–350. Springer, Heidelberg (2011)
[16] Shila, D.M., Cheng, Y., Anjali, T.: Mitigating Selective Forwarding Attacks with a Channel-Aware Approach in WMNs. IEEE Transactions on Wireless Communications 9(5), 1661–1675 (2010)
[17] Zhai, H., Chen, X., Fang, Y.: How well can the IEEE 802.11 wireless LAN support quality of service? IEEE Transactions on Wireless Communications 4(6), 3084–3094 (2005)
[18] Gandikota, V.R., Tamma, B.R., Siva Ram Murthy, C.: Adaptive FEC-Based Packet Loss Resilience Scheme for Supporting Voice Communication over Ad Hoc Wireless Networks. IEEE Transactions on Mobile Computing 7(10), 1184–1199 (2008)
[19] Chen, M.: OPNET Network Simulation. Tsinghua University Press, Beijing (2004)

Distributed and Anonymous Publish-Subscribe

Jörg Daubert, Mathias Fischer, Stefan Schiffner, and Max Mühlhäuser

Technische Universität Darmstadt, CASED,
Telecooperation Group, Hochschulstraße 10, 64283 Darmstadt
{joerg.daubert,mathias.fischer,stefan.schiffner}@cased.de,
max@informatik.tu-darmstadt.de

Abstract. Publish-subscribe is a scheme for distributing information based on interests. While security mechanisms have been added to publish-subscribe, privacy, in particular anonymous communication is hardly considered. We summarize security and privacy requirements for such systems, including an adversary model for privacy. We introduce a construction for publish-subscribe overlays that fulfills the requirements. Contrary to previous approaches, it does neither presume an online trusted third party, nor expensive cryptographic operations performed by brokers. Further, we informally discuss how our requirements are met.

Keywords: privacy, pub-sub, overlay.

1 Introduction

Publish-subscribe decouples producers (*publishers*) and consumers (*subscribers*) of information by introducing super nodes, the *brokers*. Subscribers announce their interests to the broker (subscription), while publishers send information (notification) to the broker. Brokers match and distribute notifications. Privacy is desirable, e.g., in private car sharing, dating services, or citizen journalism. In the latter, participants publish and consume news, and might be subject to repression, e.g., whistleblowers and politically prosecuted people. As a result, a publish-subscribe (pub-sub) system intended for a deployment in such a scenario has to fulfill several requirements to protect its users. We require a pub-sub system to comply with anonymity, confidentiality, scalability, integrity, authenticity, and availability: participants are anonymous w.r.t. an adversary if they are unidentifiable for the adversary within a set of participants, the anonymity set [9]. Information must be transmitted secretly between sender and receiver. The system must remain scalable in terms of number of supported nodes. Alteration of a message must be detectable by the receiver (integrity). Only authorized participants can send authentic notifications and can read notifications. The system must maintain availability in the presence of node failures and attacks.

We define privacy in pub-sub as the combination of participant anonymity and confidentiality. Both requirements are closely related, as the lack of one can lead to a violation of the other one [11]. Privacy adversaries can be structured w.r.t. their capabilities: a *passive* adversary only observes messages, while an

J. Lopez, X. Huang, and R. Sandhu (Eds.): NSS 2013, LNCS 7873, pp. 685–691, 2013.

active one can alter. An adversary with knowledge about pseudonyms or keys is an *insider*. Furthermore, it can have either *global* or *local* topology knowledge. Finally, the internal adversary can collude with other internal adversaries. We focus on an active insider with full topology information on the communication network, but it can only observe its own communication channels. It is strong as it can act adaptively, exploit the topology information, and force the system to react by sending valid messages.

A pub-sub system complies with subscriber anonymity, or publisher anonymity respectively, w.r.t. an adversary and an attribute, if the subscriber cannot be identified within the anonymity set. A pub-sub system complies with notification confidentiality, or subscription confidentiality respectively, w.r.t. an adversary, if the adversary does not learn the attribute, the notification, or the subscription content.

Several approaches for realizing privacy-preserving pub-sub schemes exist [1–3, 7, 8, 10, 12–15]. Most approaches focus on confidentiality [1–3, 7, 8, 10, 12, 14], but do not consider anonymity [16]. To ensure confidentiality, many contributions encrypt information [2, 3, 7, 8, 10, 12, 15], leverage a private matching scheme [1–3, 7, 8, 10, 12], and describe key management [12, 14, 15]. However, approaches [2, 8] assume an out-of-band key exchange. Moreover, approaches [2, 3, 8, 13] even require the knowledge of the cryptographic keys of participants. This violates anonymity as well as space decoupling, a functional pub-sub requirements that decouples publishers from subscribers. Approaches [10, 14] provide space decoupling, but depend on a central, online Trusted Third Party (TTP), which is a Single Point of Failure (SPoF) that violates availability and scalability. The key exchange protocols in [2, 3, 13] do not scale with the number of participants. Approaches [3, 12] only consider honest but curious brokers, but not malicious publishers and subscribers. Further, [15] is fully distributed, and therefore scalable as well as free of SPoFs, but does not sufficiently describe the membership management. Finally, multicast protocols, e.g., PIM-SM [4], can be used to establish distribution trees and scale well, but do not provide anonymity and confidentiality.

Summarizing the related work, none of the articles provides anonymity to both—publisher and subscriber—and scalability. Therefore, none of those systems achieves the listed requirements—most dominantly not anonymity, confidentiality and scalability at once.

In this paper, we bridge the gap between privacy by means of anonymity and confidentiality, as well as scalability for pub-sub systems. The main contribution of our article is a scalable, anonymous and confidential method for pub-sub overlay construction, which is described in the following Section. Moreover, we discuss our solution along these requirements and the attacker model in Section 3. Finally, Section 4 concludes the article.

2 Privacy-Preserving and Scalable pub-sub Overlay

We create pub-sub overlay topologies that enable efficient privacy-preserving notification distribution from publishers to subscribers. We assume a connected

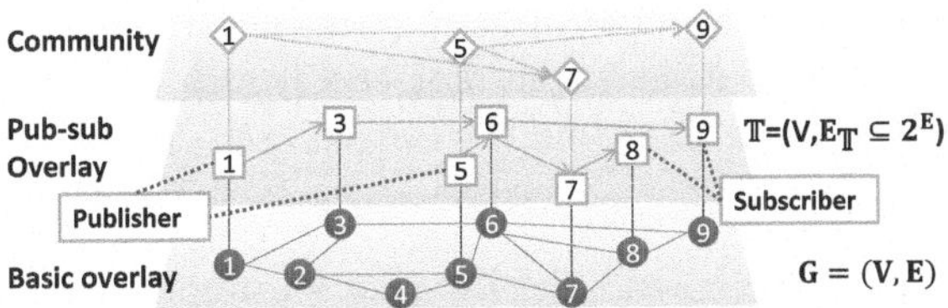

Fig. 1. Basic overlay (bottom), pub-sub overlay (middle), community (top)

basic overlay network G (lowest layer of Fig. 1), e.g., established via SCAMP [6]. This basic overlay provides each node with a neighborhood set, as well as confidential links between neighbors. On top, we construct a mesh network $\mathcal{M}_a$ per attribute a. Each mesh spans a subset of overlay members (middle layer of Fig. 1). The pub-sub overlay is a union of all meshes. The top layer in Fig. 1 depicts the desired notification flow. To establish mesh $\mathcal{M}_a$, we use advertisements and subscriptions prior to sending notifications. Though, we present the overlay construction with a single attribute, it is generalizable to multiple attributes.

We use the following notations: the set of publishers $\mathcal{P}$, subscribers $\mathcal{S}$, forwarders $\mathcal{F}$, and $\mathcal{S}_a \subseteq \mathcal{S}$ for the set of subscribers interested in an attribute $a \in \mathcal{A}$. Respectively, $\mathcal{P}_a \subseteq \mathcal{P}$ denotes the set of publishers publishing attribute a. The graph $G := (V, E)$ as basic overlay with participants $V := \mathcal{P} \cup \mathcal{S} \cup \mathcal{F}$ and edges E. Further, meshes $\mathcal{M}_a := (V_{\mathcal{M}} \subseteq V, E_{\mathcal{M}} \subseteq E)$ as subgraphs in overlay $\mathbb{T}$ for an attribute a and a subset of edges $E_{\mathcal{M}} \subseteq E$.

2.1 Overlay Construction

The overlay construction is split in an advertisement phase and a subscription phase. We use an offline TTP for the initial distribution of key material, which is used for confidentiality and authenticity. Confidentiality is achieved by using symmetric keys. Authenticity and message integrity are achieved using signatures and certificates issued by the TTP. Each participant initially connects to the TTP and presents its desired attributes. If the TTP grants access to the participant, the TTP releases the corresponding key material.

Cryptographic Primitives. The *TTP* owns a secret key sk_{TTP} and a public key pk_{TTP}. Furthermore, we use the following functions: $keyGen(\text{a}) \mapsto (sk_a, pk_a, K_a)$ generates a key triple: the signature key sk_a for attribute a, the signature verification key pk_a, and the symmetric key K_a. $enc(m, K) \mapsto \{m\}_K$ encrypts message m with key K to cipher text $\{m\}_K$. $sign(m, sk) \mapsto m_{sig}^{sk}$ signs a message m using a cryptographic hash function and the private key sk and creates the signature m_{sig}^{sk}. $cert(pk, t, sk_{TTP}) \mapsto cert_{pk}$ returns $cert_{pk} = (pk, t, sign(pk||t, sk_{TTP}))$, a certificate for public key pk and an associated token t. Here, $pk||t$ denotes the concatenation of pk and t. Function $verify(m, m_{sig}^{sk}, pk) \mapsto true$ or $false$ uses pk to verify that signature m_{sig}^{sk} is a valid signature of m that was created with the secret key sk.

The TTP prepares keys and certificates: for each attribute $a \in \mathcal{A}$, it executes $keyGen_A$ and stores the output triple. For certificates, the TTP obtains $t_a = enc(a, K_a)$, creates $cert_a$ by executing $cert(pk_a, t_a, sk_{TTP})$, and stores it together with the triple.

Advertisement Phase. We spread the information about attributes and where to obtain them in the basic overlay G. Further, we have to ensure that only legitimate subscribers for a are able to link a to the message due to notification confidentiality. For that, every new publisher need to contact the TTP to retrieve the keys for a: $(sk_a, pk_a, K_a, cert_a)$. Every new subscriber just obtains (K_a).

Each advertisement for attribute a contains a token t_a, so that subscribers can match their interest against it. Thus, only legitimate subscribers in possession of the respective K_a can link t_a to a. To spread the information about a, a publisher floods G by sending advertisements to its neighbors in G. As t_a is identical for all publishers in possession of the same a, every forwarder can suppress duplicates.

To prevent overlay partitioning, forwarders must be able to distinguish duplicates from the same publisher and two different publishers $p_1, p_2 \in \mathcal{P}_a$. However, publisher IDs contradict anonymity. Random time-to-live counters would allow adversaries to lie. This would enable them to capture more messages and to partition the overlay.

To overcome this problem, we use hash chains. They serve as transaction pseudonyms per advertisement. Hash chains allow the selection of the shortest path, while preventing adversaries from lying. Given a cryptographic hash function $H(h) = h'$ that takes h as input and outputs h', a hash chain is defined by all values h_i derived by repeatedly applying H to its output. The function $isChain$ tests if two hash values h_1 and h_2 belong to the same hash chain and have a maximum distance d_{max}:

$$isChain : (h_1, h_2) \mapsto \{true, false\} :$$
$$\forall_{i \in \{0..d_{max}\}} : \textit{if}\, H^{(i)}(h) \stackrel{?}{=} h' \vee H^{(i)}(h') \stackrel{?}{=} h \mapsto true, \text{ otherwise } false$$

The parameter d_{max} is equivalent to a time-to-live and has to be set according to the expected maximum diameter of G. The publisher generates a random h from the output domain of H and attaches it together with token t_a to an advertisement message (t_a, h). Forwarders keep routing tables, containing triples (t_a, h, v), where v is the neighbor from which the advertisement has been received from. If a forwarder f has not received token t_a before, f stores it in the routing table as (t_a, h, v) and forwards (t_a, h') with $h' := H(h)$ to all other neighbors. Otherwise, f already has a triple (t_a, h_2, v_2). Then it checks if the output of $isChain(h, h_2)$ returns $true$: hence, both advertisements belong to the same hash chain. Further, in case h is a predecessor of h_2 in the hash chain, a shorter path has been discovered and f replaces (t_a, h_2, v_2) by (t_a, h, v). If $isChain(h, h_2)$ returns $false$, h and h_2 belong to different hash chains. Thus, another publisher for the same t_a has been found, and f stores (t_a, h, v) in the routing table.

Tokens must be signed, so that an adversary cannot create arbitrary advertisements and flood G. For that, the publisher executes $sign(t_a, sk_a)$ and obtains ${t_a}_{sig}^{sk_a}$.

The advertisement is then extended to message $(t_a, t_a{}_{sig}^{sk_a}, cert_a, h)$. Every participant verifies advertisements by checking $cert_a$ and $t_a{}_{sig}^{sk_a}$. Hence, participants can detect non-authentic advertisements as well as duplicates.

Subscription Phase. Subscribers identify advertisements of interest, and establish distribution paths for notifications via subscription messages. The result is an overlay mesh $\mathcal{M}_a$.

For that, subscribers compare the token t_x from an advertisement triple (t_x, h', v) to their attributes of interests. A subscriber encrypts each own a with the corresponding key K_a and compares the result t_a with t_x. Once the t_x from the triple is confirmed to match t_a, the subscriber s joins the mesh $\mathcal{M}_a$ via a subscription.

Subscriptions are sent back the reverse path of the advertisements. A subscriber adds tuple (t_a, s) to the subscription table, where s is the subscribing node itself. Moreover, it sends a subscription message (t_a) towards the origin of the advertisement. Whenever a forwarder f receives a subscription (t_a) from neighbor v, f updates its subscription table with the tuple (t_a, v). If there is no subscription entry (t_a, v_x) for any neighbor v_x, f forwards the subscription. For that, f retrieves all records (t_a, h_m, v_m) matching t_a from the routing table and sends subscription (t_a) to each neighbor v_m.

In case there are multiple publishers for the same attribute, additional measures are required to ensure mesh $\mathcal{M}_a$ is connected. Let us assume two publishers p_1 and p_2, and p_2 joins after p_1. Then p_2 receives an advertisement from p_1 via a neighbor v. Now p_2 subscribes towards p_1 via v, and therefore establishes a directed connection between p_1 and p_2 in $\mathcal{M}_a$. In case a node leaves the system, the remaining nodes repair the mesh $\mathcal{M}_a$ with unsubscribe and unadvertise messages.

2.2 Content Distribution

After securely establishing the distribution overlays M_a per attribute a, notifications need to be transported. A notification for attribute a originated by a publisher p contains token t_a as routing identifier and some content m. The notification is flooded in the pre-established mesh $\mathcal{M}_a$. For that, p, and every subsequent forwarder, looks up all records matching t_a in its subscription and routing tables, and sends the notification to each v_x, except the one the notification was received from.

While t_a does not leak any plaintext information, m is accessible by every traversed node. Hence, m must be protected to ensure notification confidentiality. Both roles, $\mathcal{P}_a$ and $\mathcal{S}_a$, share a symmetric key K_a. Publisher p encrypts m using K_a and obtains $\{m\}_{K_a}$. Hence, a notification $(t_a, \{m\}_{K_a})$ does not leak any more information than an advertisement. Finally, the same signature scheme as for advertisements is applied to obtain an authentic notification $(t_a, \{m\}_{K_a}, sig)$, with $sig = sign(t_a || \{m\}_{K_a}, sk_a)$.

3 Discussion

A privacy-preserving pub-sub system has to comply with the requirements defined in Section 1 to be applicable to the citizen journalism scenario. We analyze our pub-sub overlay with respect to these requirements. We assume the TTP to be honest w.r.t. not disclosing information.

Anonymity. Our system provides publisher and subscriber anonymity. The adversary has full topology information on G. For subscriber anonymity, we assume a single adversarial publisher that publishes one attribute. Hence, the distribution mesh is a tree and the adversary is the root. As subscriptions are merged by branch nodes, at most one subscription per branch reaches the adversary. Thus, the adversary cannot distinguish subscribers from other nodes within each branch. Hence, the anonymity set size of a subscriber in a branch is the size of this branch. For publisher anonymity, we assume a single adversarial subscriber that subscribes only to one attribute. Further, the advertisement is received via the shortest path first. With G, the adversary can construct a tree from all shortest paths starting on its own node to all nodes. Hence, the anonymity set size of a publisher in a branch is the size of this branch.

Confidentiality. Nodes that are neither publisher nor subscriber cannot decipher messages. We use a symmetric crypto-system, which provides security to known plaintext attacks for end-to-end encryption. Still, due to decoupling in pub-sub [5], if a notification, or advertisement respectively, matches a subscription or not can be always learned [10] by observation.

Integrity and Authenticity. Our system provides message integrity and authenticity for advertisement and notifications by using digital signatures. However, subscriptions are not authentic. Moreover, an adversary in possession of a corresponding key may alter foreign advertisements and notifications.

Scalability A scalable system grows at most proportionally with the number of participants in terms of resources per participant. The required node memory for the basic overlay depends on the size of its neighborhood and remains constant [6]. Hence, the required memory for the overlay grows proportionally with the number of attributes.

Resilience. A robust system can compensate node failure or provide at least graceful degradation. The presented pub-sub construction method represents a Peer-to-Peer (P2P) network without online SPoFs and bottlenecks, as each peer can take over the role of the other ones.

4 Conclusion

We presented the citizen journalism scenario, stated security requirements for pub-sub systems in such a scenario, and categorized privacy adversaries. Further, we analyzed related approaches, and introduced our complementary construction to privacy-preserving pub-sub overlays. Finally, we discussed our construction w.r.t. the requirements. The construction protects participant anonymity, keeps information confidential, scales, and does not depend on central structures except the offline TTPs. Therefore, our work is applicable to citizen journalism. Future work will reduce the dependency on the offline TTPs and study the anonymity of different overlay types.

References

1. Barazzutti, R., Felber, P., et al.: Thrifty Privacy: Efficient Support for Privacy-Preserving Publish / Subscribe. In: DEBS, pp. 225–236. ACM (2012)
2. Chen, W., Jiangt, J., Skocik, N.: On the privacy protection in publish/subscribe systems. In: WCNIS, pp. 597–601. IEEE (2010)
3. Choi, S., Ghinita, G., Bertino, E.: A Privacy-Enhancing Content-Based Publish/Subscribe System Using Scalar Product Preserving Transformations. In: Bringas, P.G., Hameurlain, A., Quirchmayr, G. (eds.) DEXA 2010, Part I. LNCS, vol. 6261, pp. 368–384. Springer, Heidelberg (2010)
4. Fenner, B., et al.: Protocol Independent Multicast - Sparse Mode (PIM-SM): Protocol Specification (Revised). RFC 4601 (Proposed Standard) (2006)
5. Eugster, P.T., Felber, P., Guerraoui, R., Kermarrec, A.: The many faces of publish/subscribe. ACM Computing Surveys (CSUR) 35(2), 114–131 (2003)
6. Ganesh, A.J., Kermarrec, A., Massoulié, L.: Peer-to-Peer Membership Management for Gossip-Based Protocols. IEEE (TC) 52(2), 139–149 (2003)
7. Ion, M., Russello, G., Crispo, B.: Supporting Publication and Subscription Confidentiality in Pub/Sub Networks. In: Jajodia, S., Zhou, J. (eds.) SecureComm 2010. LNICS, vol. 50, pp. 272–289. Springer, Heidelberg (2010)
8. Nabeel, M., Shang, N., Elisa, B.: Efficient privacy preserving content based publish subscribe systems. In: SACMAT, pp. 133–144. ACM (2012)
9. Pfitzmann, A., Köhntopp, M.: Anonymity, Unobservability, and Pseudonymity - A Proposal for Terminology. In: Federrath, H. (ed.) Anonymity 2000. LNCS, vol. 2009, pp. 1–9. Springer, Heidelberg (2001)
10. Raiciu, C., Rosenblum, D.S.: Enabling Confidentiality in Content-Based Publish/Subscribe Infrastructures. In: SecureComm, pp. 1–11. IEEE (August 2006)
11. Schiffner, S., Clauß, S.: Using linkability information to attack mix-based anonymity services. In: Goldberg, I., Atallah, M.J. (eds.) PETS 2009. LNCS, vol. 5672, pp. 94–107. Springer, Heidelberg (2009)
12. Shikfa, A., Önen, M., Molva, R.: Privacy in context-based and epidemic forwarding. In: WoWMoM, pp. 1–7. IEEE (June 2009)
13. Shikfa, A., Önen, M., Molva, R.: Privacy-Preserving Content-Based Publish/Subscribe Networks. In: Gritzalis, D., Lopez, J. (eds.) SEC 2009. IFIP AICT, vol. 297, pp. 270–282. Springer, Heidelberg (2009)
14. Srivatsa, M., Liu, L.: Securing publish-subscribe overlay services with EventGuard. In: CCS, p. 289. ACM (2005)
15. Tariq, M.A., Koldehofe, B., Altaweel, A., Rothermel, K.: Providing basic security mechanisms in broker-less publish / subscribe systems. In: DEBS, pp. 38–49. ACM (July 2010)
16. Wang, C., Carzaniga, A., Evans, D., Wolf, A.L.: Security Issues and Requirements for Internet-Scale Publish-Subscribe Systems. In: HICSS, pp. 3940–3947. IEEE (2002)

Enhancing Passive Side-Channel Attack Resilience through Schedulability Analysis of Data-Dependency Graphs

Giovanni Agosta, Alessandro Barenghi, Gerardo Pelosi, and Michele Scandale

Department of Electronics, Information and Bioengineering – DEIB
Politecnico di Milano, 20133 Milano, Italy
surname@elet.polimi.it

Abstract. In this work, we provide an evaluation of the fitness of a cipher implementation for automated, low overhead, Side Channel Attack (SCA) countermeasure insertion through instruction re-scheduling. This evaluation is automated by means of an extension to the Clang/LLVM compiler framework and is thus amenable to be performed on a generic cipher implementation in C.

Keywords: Applied Cryptography, Embedded Systems Security.

1 Introduction

As electronic devices become increasingly interconnected and pervasive in consumer commodities, security, trustworthy computing, and privacy protection have emerged as worthy challenges for research and industrial activities. In particular, an effort towards designing of mathematically secure cryptographic primitives and engineering their effective implementations is currently in force.

Cryptographic designs are based on strong mathematical problems and traditionally it is assumed that the secret values (i.e., cryptographic keys or confidential configuration parameters) are manipulated in such a way not to expose any information except clearly designated inputs and outputs. By contrast, the secret parameters are securely held in a portion of the device memory without direct read access. However, even if the security margin warranted by the mathematical properties of the cipher is adequate, the security of the system can be undermined by information leakage via environmental parameters (i.e., by side-channel leakage). It is effectively proven that gaining physical access to an embedded device enables an attacker to recover sensitive information exploiting both implementation weaknesses of the cryptographic operations and specific features provided by the underlying hardware platform [7].

For instance, on-line measurements of the power supplied-to or EM radiations emitted-from an embedded device contain pieces of information about the operations being performed and the data being processed [4]. Attack techniques, commonly known as *passive side-channel attacks*, are able to retrieve the key from a secure device [3, 7, 9] exploiting this information. The key observation is

J. Lopez, X. Huang, and R. Sandhu (Eds.): NSS 2013, LNCS 7873, pp. 692–698, 2013.

that the operations combining the key material with the known input usually act bitwise: it is thus possible to regard them as independent one from the other and model their behavior separately. Thus, the attacker selects an operation combining a portion of the key, $k_{\mathtt{part}}$, with a the input and computes all the possible results of this operation for a large set of input values, In, and all the possible values taken by $k_{\mathtt{part}}$. Subsequently, the input values in In are fed to the actual circuit (the key of which is unknown), and the side-channel information (power consumption, EM emissions) is measured. Finally, the attacker obtains predictions for the value of the side-channel parameter during the computation for all the fixed value of $k_{\mathtt{part}}$, employing the previously computed results, comparing these predictions with the actual measurements through an appropriate statistical tool (e.g., Pearson's linear correlation coefficient). The prediction which turns out to be the best fit to the actual side-channel measurement is the one relying on the correct hypothesis on the value of the selected key portion $k_{\mathtt{part}}$. One crucial aspect of the aforementioned work-flow is the implicit assumption that the operations executed by each run of the algorithm are the same and computed in the same sequence. In such a way, the profiling obtained through measuring the device will yield a correlation with the a-priori predicted consumption as accurate as possible.

In this paper, we tackle the security of software implementations of cryptographic primitives, devoting our attention to their protection. It is common to employ software implementations either as a complement to hardware ones or as a safety fallback, in case the security of the hardware one is breached. In particular, we examine the possibility of exploiting the features of the data dependency graph of a cipher implementation to derive different, semantically equivalent, schedules for it. This in turn implies the possibility of employing different valid schedules for the cipher at runtime, effectively increasing the difficulty of modeling the execution flow of the cipher.

This paper proposes the first security evaluation of block cipher algorithms in terms of their schedulability properties formally analyzing their data dependency graph structures and individuating the maximal set of instructions amenable to rescheduling. This provides an effective improvement with respect to the state-of-the-art, which only contemplates some examples of ad-hoc rescheduling of the AES cipher, performed by hand by the developer [9], and the insertion of random length delays through dummy instructions [6]. Exploiting these reschedulability properties, we propose a new way to raise the resistance against side-channel attacks with a lower overhead than the current state-of-the-art techniques. To provide practical figures supporting our approach, we analyzed different implementations of the AES cipher, characterizing them in terms of reschedulability. The schedulability analysis is performed in an automated fashion by means of an extension to the Clang/LLVM compiler framework, following a live trend in current research which employs compilers to provide a sound security margin for secure cipher implementations [1,2,5]. To the end of evaluating the actual performance hit on a real world architecture, we report the distribution of the timings achieved by different (and thus possibly not performance-optimal) schedules of the AES cipher on an ARM architecture platform.

The work is organized as follows: in Section 2 we describe our compiler extension to the end of performing the analysis, and in Section 3 we provide the experimental evaluation for our case study (the AES cipher) through comparing different implementations and target architectures. Finally, Section 4 summarizes the contribution of the paper.

2 A Compiler Extension for SCA Resilience

The Clang/LLVM compiler framework [8] is a modular compiler toolchain developed as an open source project, providing a well-structured and extensible infrastructure to developers. Clang/LLVM is rapidly reaching an industry standard status, as it is widely employed and supported by significant players in innovation. We chose to integrate our schedulability analysis in this framework, so that the resulting code can be translated into actual executable code by a production grade compiler framework, yielding reliable results. The Clang/LLVM compiler is structured following the canonical structure of a compiler pipeline: the first stage is a front-end processor (Clang), which translates C/C++ code into a source-language-agnostic Intermediate Representation (IR). The IR is processed by the middle-end stage, which performs architecture-agnostic optimizations on it, (e.g., dead code elimination), obtaining a refined version of it. The last stage, known as the back-end, tackles the architecture dependent steps of the code emission up to the emission of the assembly code for the desired target architecture.

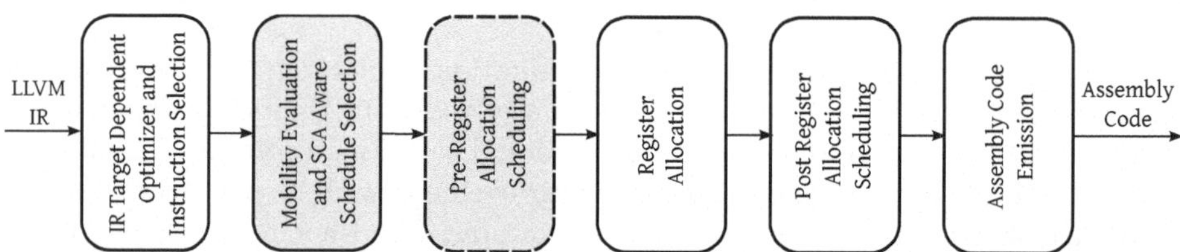

Fig. 1. LLVM Backend Pipeline

Figure 1 provides an overview of the LLVM backend stage, highlighting the pass we add to the pipeline thanks to the modular structure of LLVM. The first portion of the backend takes care of performing target dependent optimizations (e.g., strength reduction) and the instruction selection phase, which maps the IR instructions into actual machine instructions exposed by the ISA of the target architecture. We chose to perform our schedulability analysis and rescheduling pass right after the instruction selection pass, as it is the last point in the compiler backend where there are no physical resource-bound dependencies,

Algorithm 1. ComputeDepth

```
Input: G – basic block DAG; N – node
Output: G – nodes of the input DAG are updated w/ depth values
maxDepth ← 0
foreach pred ∈ Predecessors(G, N) do
    curDepth ← Depth(G, N) + Latency(G, N)
    if IsAntidependence(G, pred, N) then curDepth ← curDepth + 1
    if curDepth > maxDepth then maxDepth ← predDepth
SetDepth(G, N, maxDepth)
foreach succ ∈ Successors(G, N) do
    ready ← true
    foreach pred ∈ Predecessors(G, succ) do
        if not HasValidDepth(G, pred) then ready ← false
    if ready then ComputeDepth(G, succ)
```

(i.e., the input instruction flow has not yet been constrained by both register and functional unit association). The instructions composing the program flow at this stage have the maximum mobility as they are described employing an infinite number of registers, allowing us to explore fully the rescheduling possibilities (*Mobility Evaluation Pass*). Subsequently, our modified compiler pipeline should perform the *Pre-register Allocation Scheduling* pass. This pass can reduce the amount of randomness introduced by our rescheduling pass: we explore this performance-to-security tradeoff in our experimental evaluation. After running the two aforementioned new passes, the compiler computes the *register allocation* (RA) binding virtual registers to the actual target architecture registers, minimizing the register spill and fill actions. Since the RA does not necessarily enforce a single possible execution order for the instructions (as some of them can be run in a mutually interchangeable order even after RA), the pipeline pass following the RA performs a post-RA scheduling, effectively producing a linear sequence of instructions, trying to minimize pipeline stalls. The final pass of the compiler backend stage is the actual assembly code emission.

Instruction Mobility Evaluation

The compiler pass added to perform the schedulability analysis (see Figure 1) takes as input the CFG of the program routine to be analyzed and acts over each basic block. For each basic block our pass builds a directed acyclic graph (DAG) with data dependency information to compute the sets of independent instructions. Each incoming arc is labelled with the latency needed to produce an operand value for the destination node, and the outgoing arcs are labelled with the instruction latency of the node. Starting from a virtual root node of the DAG (to have a single entry point), for each node we compute its *depth* as the longest path from the entry point. Let I_d be the set of instructions at depth d: it follows that

$|I_d|$ gives us the *mobility* of each element in I_d and $\left(\prod_{j=1}^{\infty} |I_j|!\right)$ is the number of possible reschedules of the basic block instructions. Algorithm 1 reports the pseudo-code of the procedure employed to compute the depth of a given node w.r.t. the entry point. A valid schedule for the considered basic block is then computed through randomly selecting a possible permutation among each set I_d. In the subsequent compiler passes, the virtual registers will be mapped to physical ones and two or more instructions with the same depth in a basic block will be concurrently executed in case the underlying architecture is equipped with enough resources. The pre-register allocation pass (see Figure 1) re-arranges the code trying to limit the register pressure within the maximum number of registers available in the target architecture respecting the constraints on the functional units. The register allocation pass then will map virtual registers to physical ones, moving physical register values to memory when needed. The post-register allocation pass refines the execution performance of each basic block taking into account the pipeline structure of the target processor thus, swapping some instructions to reduce the number of stalls.

3 Experimental Results

As case study we employ two AES-128 implementations: the single S-Box NIST reference implementation and the 4 T-Tables OpenSSL one. We evaluated the reshuffled algorithms on two different ARM architectures. The first platform is a Pandaboard ES: a high end embedded development platform equipped with a Dual-core ARM 1.2 GHz Cortex-A9 MPCore and 1 GB of DDR2 RAM. The board runs Linaro Linux 12.11 compiled with the armv7l ABI. The second platform is the Pogoplug v2: a plug computer-type system equipped with a Marvell Feroceon 88FR131 based on an ARM 926 CPU clocked at 1.2 GHz and 256 MB of RAM. The board runs ArchLinux compiled with the `armv5tel` ABI.

The first step was to analyze the schedulability of both implementations of the AES: we considered the canonical loop based implementation and two variants where the first and second iterations of the loop were peeled (i.e., removed from the loop body and inserted as a straight-line code block in front of it). The structure of block ciphers makes them vulnerable mostly in the first two iterations (round) of the main loop. We refer to the aforementioned variants of the AES implementations as *no-lp*, *1-lp* and *2-lp*. The reschedulability analyses were performed before the RA pass took place (*preRA*) and after it did (*postRA*). In the *postRA* analysis, we considered instruction shuffling to be performed also before the *preRA* phase, and the *preRA* rescheduler acting to rearrange the instructions to mitigate performance penalties. Fig. 2 reports the results of the schedulability analysis. The *preRA* analysis shows that the instruction mobility of the S-Box version is higher than that of T-Table one. This is reasonable as the former operates independently on the 16 AES state bytes. The latter behaviour forces tighter data dependencies among the instructions, thus reducing the number of viable schedules. A key observation is the fact that, analyzing the mobility

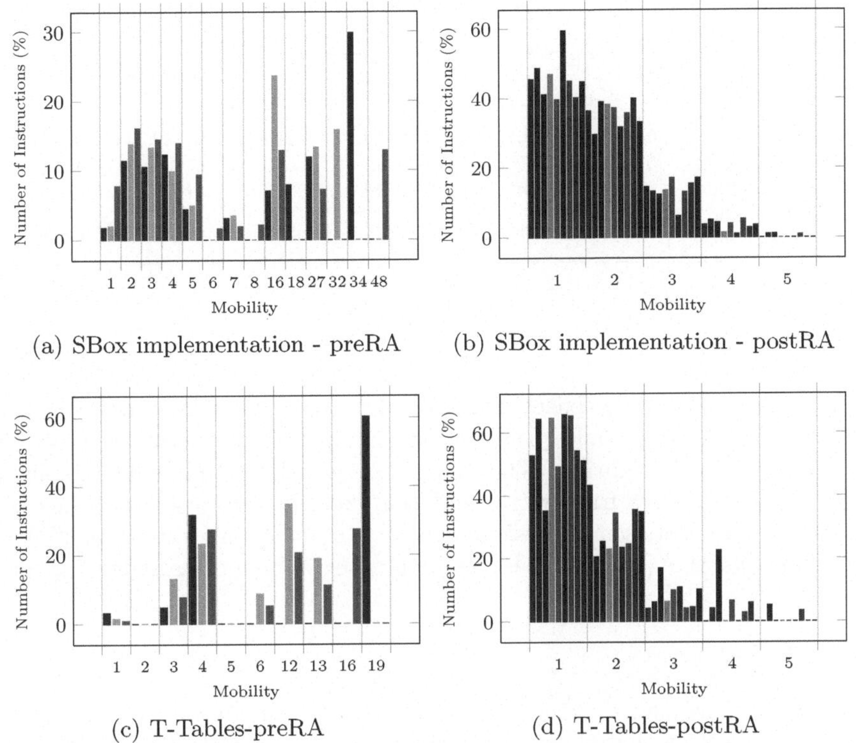

Fig. 2. Histograms of instruction mobility for the two AES implementations: pre RA colours are employed to point out their correspondent *postRA* analysis (blue=no peel, green=1 round peeled, red=2 rounds peeled). *postRA* analyses are performed without *preRA* shuffling (light), with *preRA* shuffling only (middle), and with *preRA* shuffling and the *preRA* scheduler from LLVM (dark).

of the instructions *postRA*, they do not exceed mobility 5. This decrease in the amount of viable schedules is to be ascribed to the constraints imposed by the use of a finite register set. We note that the *postRA* rescheduling may also be done at runtime at a low cost, as the actual hardware resource allocation has already been performed.

We also evaluate the performance overhead caused by rescheduling, by encrypting one million plaintexts for each variant to be tested, and computing the average execution times over 30 runs with different schedules. Table 1 reports the encryption throughput obtained on each platform. Except for the *no-lp* case, where the performance overhead is non negligible, protecting one or two rounds of the cipher through rescheduling still yields more than satisfactory throughput. Moreover, performing *preRA* and *postRA* shuffling yields a more efficient solution on our target platforms. We ascribe this, albeit minimal, speedup to the fact that the shuffled versions of the ciphers allow the values involved in the computation to be kept hot in the CPU caches, thus yielding a small speedup.

Table 1. Average throughput (MB/s) of the shuffled AES binaries

Transformation	ARM 926		Cortex-A9	
	S-Box	T-Table	S-Box	T-Table
Baseline	5.59/5.62/5.66	14.34/14.46/14.72	7.62/8.13/8.64	22.34/20.60/21.75
Post-RA Shuffle	5.54/5.59/5.65	14.26/14.47/14.65	7.65/8.11/8.61	20.62/20.45/21.20
Full Shuffle	3.74/5.21/5.20	12.59/13.49/14.04	5.88/7.61/7.71	22.21/18.68/24.72
Full Shuffle and Pre-RA resched	3.79/4.18/4.29	16.66/16.14/16.03	6.69/6.53/6.62	25.12/21.13/23.10

4 Conclusions

We presented a compiler-based framework to provide SCA countermeasures based on the *hiding-in-time* principle exploiting the instruction re-scheduling of an encryption primitive. The approach has been implemented in the Clang/LLVM compiler framework, and the experimental evaluation has highlighted how the proposed analysis allows to exploit the instruction mobility to realize effective SCA countermeasures with a negligible performance impact.

References

1. Agosta, G., Barenghi, A., Maggi, M., Pelosi, G.: Compiler-based Side Channel Vulnerability Analysis and Optimized Countermeasures Application. In: Alpert, C., Sciuto, D., Zorian, Y. (eds.) DAC, pp. 77–82. ACM (2013)
2. Agosta, G., Barenghi, A., Pelosi, G.: A Code Morphing Methodology to Automate Power Analysis Countermeasures. In: Groeneveld, P., Sciuto, D., Hassoun, S. (eds.) DAC, pp. 77–82. ACM (2012)
3. Barenghi, A., Pelosi, G., Teglia, Y.: Improving First Order Differential Power Attacks through Digital Signal Processing. In: Makarevich, O.B., Elçi, A., Orgun, M.A., Huss, S.A., Babenko, L.K., Chefranov, A.G., Varadharajan, V. (eds.) SIN, pp. 124–133. ACM (2010)
4. Barenghi, A., Pelosi, G., Terraneo, F.: Efficient and Cost Effective Design of Block Cipher Implementations on Embedded Devices. International Journal of Grid and Utility Computing (IJGUC) (2013); Xhafa, F. (ed.), Inderscience
5. Bayrak, A.G., Regazzoni, F., Brisk, P., Standaert, F.X., Ienne, P.: A First Step towards Automatic Application of Power Analysis Countermeasures. In: Stok, L., Dutt, N.D., Hassoun, S. (eds.) DAC, pp. 230–235. ACM (2011)
6. Coron, J.-S., Kizhvatov, I.: An Efficient Method for Random Delay Generation in Embedded Software. In: Clavier, C., Gaj, K. (eds.) CHES 2009. LNCS, vol. 5747, pp. 156–170. Springer, Heidelberg (2009)
7. Kocher, P.C., Jaffe, J., Jun, B., Rohatgi, P.: Introduction to Differential Power Analysis. Journal Cryptographic Engineering 1(1), 5–27 (2011)
8. Lattner, C., Adve, V.: LLVM: A Compilation Framework for Lifelong Program Analysis & Transformation. In: Proc. CGO 2004, Palo Alto, California (March 2004)
9. Mangard, S., Oswald, E., Popp, T.: Power Analysis Attacks - Revealing the Secrets of Smart Cards. Springer (2007)

Combining Dynamic Passive Analysis and Active Fingerprinting for Effective Bot Malware Detection in Virtualized Environments

Shun-Wen Hsiao[1,2], Yi-Ning Chen[1], Yeali S. Sun[1], and Meng Chang Chen[2]

[1] Department of Information Management, National Taiwan University, Taiwan
{r93011,r99725028,sunny}@im.ntu.edu.tw
[2] Institute of Information Science, Academia Sinica, Taiwan
{hsiaom,mcc}@iis.sinica.edu.tw

Abstract. We propose a detection mechanism that takes the advantage of virtualized environment and combines both passive and active detection approaches for detecting bot malware. Our proposed passive detection agent lies in the virtual machine monitor to profile the bot behavior and check against it with other hosts. The proposed active detection agent that performs active bot fingerprinting can send specific stimulus to a host and examine if there exists expected triggered behavior. In our experiments, our system can distinguish bots and the benign process with low false alarm. The active fingerprinting technique can detect a bot even when a bot does not do its malicious jobs.

Keywords: botnet, fingerprinting, virtual machine, intrusion detection.

1 Introduction

Generally, bot behavior can be divided into two categories: network activity and host activity. Correspondingly, there are two types of intrusion detection systems (IDS): network-based and host-based IDS. The former one targets on bot's network activities observed from the network; while the latter one focuses on the information collected directly from the host. They target on the following entities to detect malware: files, Windows registries, DLLs and networks.

One limitation of both detectors is their passivity. We can only detect bots after observing particular bot activities. Another issue is that bot may change it behavior if it detects a detector. In order to overcome the above issues, we propose a detection mechanism that takes the advantage of virtualized environment with combining both passive and active approaches.

The proposed *Passive Detection Agent* lies in the virtual machine monitor to examine and track the tainted data used by a suspicious host and check it against the bot behavior profile. It provides a transparency to the monitored host. Moreover, it can monitor multiple guest hosts simultaneously. The proposed *Active Detection Agent* that performs active bot fingerprinting can send specific stimulus (derived from the bot behavior profile) to a host and examine if it is a

J. Lopez, X. Huang, and R. Sandhu (Eds.): NSS 2013, LNCS 7873, pp. 699–706, 2013.

bot by observing whether certain expected behavior is triggered by the stimulus. Our experiment shows it can diminish the problem of passivity and is a good tool to evaluate a host without installing additional detection agents.

2 Related Work

Botnet Detection. BotHunter [2] constructs a botnet infection dialog model and uses it to detect the intrusion activities. BotSniffer [3] detects bots within the same botnet based on their spatial-temporal correlation and similarity. BotMiner [4] performs cross cluster correlation to identify the host that shares similar behavior patterns. Panorama [6] traces the information flow of predefined taint data in the host, and observes how and when a malware process leverages them. While BotTracer [5] detects malicious behavior by observing the process with the help of virtual machine technique, API hooking and network monitoring tool.

Virtual Machine Introspection. Garnkel [10] proposed a detection architecture using VM introspection (VMI). They provide six security policies and monitor them with a modified VMware Workstation. ReVirt [11] targets on moving security logging mechanism into a VM. Chen et al. [12] stated that secure logging and intrusion detection could benefit from the virtualized environment. A formal model [13] of VMI is even proposed for describing VMI techniques.

Fingerprinting. OS fingerprinting was developed by using the different configurations of each OS's TCP protocol implementation to detect the OS version of a remote host. Today, fingerprinting technology has been widely used in OS Fingerprinting, application fingerprinting and vulnerability fingerprinting. In this paper, we adopt the concept of fingerprinting and introduce a profiling system in the virtualized layer for bot fingerprinting.

3 Monitor and Detection Approach

3.1 Monitor the Guest OS in a Virtualized Environment

We implement the detection agents in the visualization layer to monitor the guest behavior through the VMM so that we can monitor it without modifying the guest OS or installing additional software, and reduce the risk of being detected by the malware. In addition, the detection agents can monitor all above guest OSes at the same time without affecting the guest OS performance. However, such virtual machine introspection (VMI) approach must consider the semantic gap between the OS-level semantics and low-level virtual machine observations.

3.2 Learning-Based Bot Behavior Profile

The initial bot process may create other processes to perform malicious activities. Our goal is to trace all these bot processes' behavior and generate a bot behavior profile. We adopt a learning approach to generate the profile from real world bot samples. In our observation, usually a bot needs to access or modify specific files or Windows registries to run the bot. Hence, we build the bot's behavior profile by using the file/registry access activities of the bot processes.

We define an *activity* as a system API call related to a file/registry access. The proposed PDA will generate a *bot process activity log* that contains the activities of the processes of a bot variant. Based on a set of collected activity logs of a bot family, we then generate a *bot behavior profile* that contains the common activities from each activity logs. Then, we collect the bot behavior profile of different bot families to build a *bot (malware) behavior database.*

3.3 Passive Bot Detection

Based on the database, we identify a set of files/registries subject to monitor and mark them *tainted*, and then the PDA checks unknown processes against the tainted objects in the runtime. If any process accesses the tainted objects, it is marked suspicious. Then immediately, the PDA starts to trace the activities of this process and generates the corresponding activity log.

The PDA then analyzes the collected activity log against the bot behavior profile database to determine the abnormality. We calculate the Jaccard similarity coefficient between a bot behavior profile and the activity log to measure the similarity of them. The Jaccard value for file, $\alpha_J(i,k)$, and for registry, $\beta_J(i,k)$ are computed for a possible bot k in guest host i based on the process activity log L_i and the bot behavior profile L_k.

$$\alpha(i,k) = \frac{\#\text{ of tainted file access activity in } L_i \cap L_k}{\#\text{ of tainted file access activity in } L_i \cup L_k} \tag{1}$$

$$\beta(i,k) = \frac{\#\text{ of tainted registry access activity in } L_i \cap L_k}{\#\text{ of tainted registry access activity in } L_i \cup L_k} \tag{2}$$

If both values are 1.0, it implies the guest i has exactly the same behavior with bot k. Proper thresholds α_k and β_k should be set for effective detection. Hence, if $\alpha(i,k) \geq \alpha_k$ and $\beta(i,k) \geq \beta_k$, we say the host i is infected by bot k.

3.4 Active Bot Fingerprinting

We observe a bot has certain hidden behavior only when it is properly triggered [7]. We derive such active fingerprinting from the bot behavior profile as follows.

1. We list the I/O-related activities invoked by the bot process in terms of API calls with the input parameters and output results.
2. Construct the bot dataflow digraph where a vertex is an API call and a directed edge from vertex u to vertex v indicates the relationship that an output value of u is passed to v as an input parameter.
3. From 2), generate a fingerprint that contains stimulus and response in pair. The stimulus is set to the API call u and the response is set to the API call v. If we change the value, theoretically it will be passed to v.

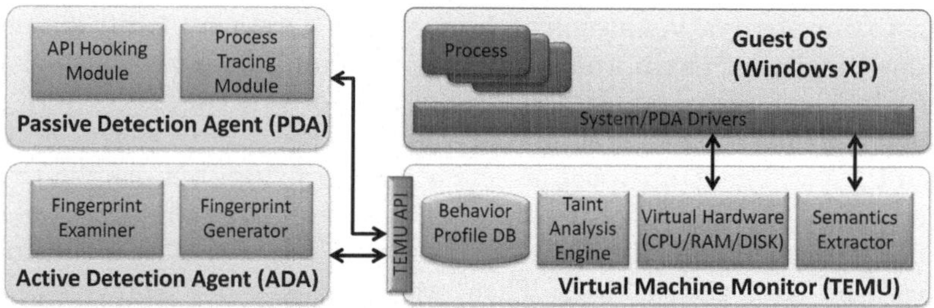

Fig. 1. The proposed system structure

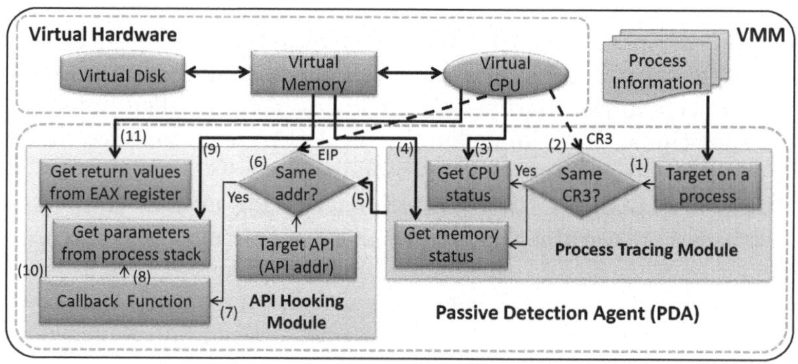

Fig. 2. The operation of the PDA

4. From 3), we perform the active bot fingerprinting through the stimulus (i.e., u), and then observe if v is triggered. In our experiments, a stimulus is most likely a file change, a registry change or network packet received.

4 System Design and Implementation

Our system (Fig. 1) consists of Passive Detection Agent (PDA) and Active Detection Agent (ADA) that are implemented as VMM plugins.

PDA Process Tracing Module. Before tracing a process, PDA acquires the process information of the guest OS sent by the PDA driver. It includes process name, `PID`, `CR3` value and the loaded modules. In Fig. 2, the module gets the current `CR3` value (step 1) of the current process. If the target process (specified by `CR3`, `PID` or process name) is executing (step 2), the current status of CPU (step 3) and memory (step 4) are retrieved for further inspection. Further, we call the API hooking module (step 5) to record the process behavior.

PDA API Hooking Module. API hooking [1] modifies the API address in the DLL file to a self-defined function for call interception. Our API hooking is stealthier by obtaining the call information through the virtual hardware.

Table 1. The number of API calls of collected bot families and the benign IE

	File			Registry			Others	
	Create	Copy	Delete	QueryValue	CreateKey	SetValue	LoadLibrary	Others
Korgo	8.6	1.0	0.0	131.3	12.0	10.7	24.0	5.9
Pinfi	16.5	1.2	0.1	189.6	19.5	20.2	25.9	6.5
Sality	12.3	0.8	2.3	466.3	18.1	388.0	23.0	13.6
Virut	7.0	1.0	0.0	119.1	16.7	14.4	23.8	5.2
IE	163.0	0.0	8.0	905.0	34.0	39.0	40.0	3.0

We monitor the `EIP` register to check if target API is called (step 6) and invoke the callback function (step 7). We obtain the inputs and outputs of the API from memory (step 8–9) and the `EAX` register (step 10–11). Three types of API are hooked: (1) File: CreateFile, ReadFile, WriteFile, CopyFile; (2) Registry: RegOpenKeyEx, RegQueryValueEx, RegSetValueEx, RegCreateKeyEx, RegDeleteKeyEx, RegDeleteValue; (3) Other: LoadLibrary, OpenProcess, CreateProcess, CreateProcessInternal, WinExec, ExitProcess.

Active Detection Agent (ADA). ADA contains a fingerprint generator and an examiner. Generator generates bot fingerprinting, and the examiner instructs the ADA driver to initiate the stimulus of a fingerprint and checks if the expected response is triggered. It can be performed periodically to check the bot infection situation, even when a bot is in its incubation period.

The PDA and ADA implementation (Fig. 1) is based on TEMU [8], a dynamic taint tracing platform built upon QEMU [9]. Xerces-c is used to generate and parse XML-based behavior profile. The host OS is Ubuntu 10.10, TEMU 1.0 is used with kqemu 1.3.0pre11, and the guest OS is Windows XP SP3. We also implement new features in TEMU including a multi-process tracing mechanism, parameters retrieval function for Windows API, and an event logging subsystem.

5 Experiment

The bot samples are provided the National Center for High-Performance Computing, Taiwan. We choose four families of botnet: `Virut`, `Sality`, `Korgo` and `Pinfi`. For each family, we have 10 variants that are the largest in the database. We also use Windows Internet Explorer (IE) as an example of benign process.

5.1 Learning-Based Bot Behavior Profiling

We infect vulnerable guest OS with bot samples and instruct the PDA to record the bot-related activities for 2 minutes. For generating the behavior profile for a bot family, we extract the common entries form the activity logs of the variants of this family. We expect that different bot families should have certain distinct behavior. Table 1 shows the number of file/registry accessed in our samples.

Table 2. The similarity coefficient of bot variants using file/registry related API

	Korgo	Pinif	Sality	Virut
Family Member (File)	(.1879, .0666)	(.0131, .0466)	(.1107, .0627)	(.2269, .0657)
Family Member (Registry)	(.2629, .0690)	(.2050, .0916)	(.3979, .1910)	(.2320, .0654)
with IE (File)	(.0323, .0132)	(.0394, .0154)	(.0251, .0138)	(.0365, .0119)
with IE (Registry)	(.0949, .0090)	(.0854, .0177)	(.0392, .0193)	(.0774, .0228)

LoadLibrary. `LoadLibrary` loads specified module into the address space of the calling process. There are total 22 common libraries for all bot families. `Pinfi` loads a library (`cja1.tmp`) from a temporary folder, which is abnormal.

Process-Related APIs. It is quite common to spawn new processes. However, IE only duplicates itself `IEXPLORER.EXE`. `Korgo` uses `WinExec` to execute `%system32%\zaegr.exe`. Alternatively, `Virut` uses `OpenProcess` to invoke `rundll32.exe`.

CopyFile and DeleteFile. All bots use `CopyFile` to make a copy of the bot binary to system or temporary folder. The filename looks like `zaegr.exe` or `vwjop.exe`. `Sality` deletes several temporary files that are created by itself, when IE only deletes HTTP cookies and HTML files in IE's temporary folder.

CreateFile. This API has a parameter `creationDisposition`, and it could be `CREATE_NEW`, `CREATE_ALWAYS` or `OPEN_EXISTING`. The bot samples use the first two values to create files in the system folder and use the last one to read/execute file, when IE uses `OPEN_EXISTING` for reading cookies, HTML and font files.

RegCreateKey and RegSetValue. Bot may modify registry to change the host behavior, such as adding services (all bots), change hostname/domain (`Korgo`), change firewall settings (`Sality`), or disable User Account (`Sality`).

Files and Registries. Table 2 shows the average Jaccard similarity coefficient and its standard deviation between every bot variants within its family, as well as the coefficient comparing with IE. As expected, the similarity within the bot family is higher than IE. From the viewpoint of registry, `Sality` variants have common behavior (.3979), but the variance (.1910) is large as well.

We observe (1) the number of file is small, which suggests detecting file is important but may have high false positive; (2) variants may use random filenames; (3) variants usually do not use random registry name; (4) bot variants in the same family have common activities which indicates using known bots may detect new variants; (5) IE is very different from others.

5.2 Passive Bot Detection

We randomly selection four of variants (out of ten) to generate the bot behavior profile, and use it to test the rest variants. Each test runs 20 times with different random selections. Take `Sality` for example; on the average, the behavior profile has 1.5 files and 447.65 registries; while `Virut`'s profile has 5 files and 129.55 registries. We then calculate the Jaccard value for each testing variants and IE.

Due to the page limit, we only use k = `Virut` as an example, the average $\alpha_J(V_i, k) = 0.2981$ and $\alpha_J(IE, k) = 0.0378$, so that the α difference is 0.2603. The average $\beta_J(V_i, k) = 0.3307$ and $\beta_J(IE, k) = 0.0925$, hence the β difference is 0.2382. The larger difference means we can more easily to distinguish a benign process and a bot process. For all bot families, the minimal difference for α_J is 0.0498 and for β_J is 0.1127. They are used as thresholds in our experiment.

5.3 Active Bot Detection

We generated an active fingerprinting for `Virut` for example. The stimulus is to set the value of registry `Domain` and `Hostname` in `HKEY_LOCAL_MACHINE\System\CurrentControlSet\Services\Tcpip\Parameters`. The former one is usually `NULL`, while the latter one is the host name. The response is a DNS query with a domain name combining the value of two registries. We test this fingerprinting on all the `Virut` variants and all variants access these two registries and send the DNS packet out, except one accesses them but does not send the DNS packet.

6 Conclusion

We propose a passive process activity analysis and active fingerprinting methods for bot detection in virtualized environments. Our system has the following benefits. (1) These methods are less intrusive than traditional host-based approach. (2) It can closely and more precisely monitor the behavior of bots. (3) The agents are in the hypervisor for monitoring the bots' API call without being detected by the bot. (4) The passive and active detection methods provide proactive and effective malware detection. The experiment results show that with bot behavior profiles, PDA can distinguish bot host and ADA can actively detect bot.

References

1. Willems, C., Holz, T., Freiling, F.: Toward Automated Dynamic Malware Analysis Using CWSandbox. In: IEEE Security & Privacy (2007)
2. Gu, G., Porras, P., Yegneswaran, V., Fong, M., Lee, W.: BotHunter: detecting malware infection through IDS-driven dialog correlation. In: USENIX Security (2007)
3. Gu, G., Zhang, J., Lee, W.: BotSniffer: Detecting Botnet Command and Control Channels in Network Traffic. In: NDSS (2008)
4. Gu, G., Perdisci, R., Zhang, J., Lee, W.: BotMiner: clustering analysis of network traffic for protocol- and structure-independent botnet detection. In: SECURITY (2008)
5. Liu, L., Chen, S., Yan, G., Zhang, Z.: BotTracer: Execution-Based Bot-Like Malware Detection. In: Wu, T.-C., Lei, C.-L., Rijmen, V., Lee, D.-T. (eds.) ISC 2008. LNCS, vol. 5222, pp. 97–113. Springer, Heidelberg (2008)

6. Yin, H., Song, D., Egele, M., Kruegel, C., Kirda, E.: Panorama: Capturing System-wide Information Flow for Malware Detection and Analysis. In: ACM CCS (2007)
7. Brumley, D., Hartwig, C., Liang, Z., Newsome, J., Song, D., Yin, H.: Automatically Identifying Trigger-Based Behavior in Malware. In: Botnet Analysis and Defense (2007)
8. Song, D., Brumley, D., Yin, H., Caballero, J., Jager, I., Kang, M.G., Liang, Z., Newsome, J., Poosankam, P., Saxena, P.: BitBlaze: A New Approach to Computer Security via Binary Analysis. In: Sekar, R., Pujari, A.K. (eds.) ICISS 2008. LNCS, vol. 5352, pp. 1–25. Springer, Heidelberg (2008)
9. QEMU, `http://wiki.qemu.org`
10. Garnkel, T., Rosenblum, M.: A Virtual Machine Introspection Based Architecture for Intrusion Detection. In: NDSS (2003)
11. Dunlap, G.W., King, S.T., Cinar, S., Basrai, M., Chen, P.M.: Revirt: Enabling intrusion analysis through virtual-machine logging and replay. In: OSDI (2002)
12. Chen, P.M., Noble, B.D.: When virtual is better than real. In: USENIX HotOS (May 2001)
13. Pfoh, J., Schneider, C., Eckert, C.: A Formal Model for Virtual Machine Introspection. In: ACM VMSec (2009)

Filtering Trolling Comments through Collective Classification

Jorge de-la-Peña-Sordo, Igor Santos, Iker Pastor-López, and Pablo G. Bringas

S[3]Lab, DeustoTech Computing, University of Deusto, Bilbao, Spain
{jorge.delapenya,isantos,iker.pastor,pablo.garcia.bringas}@deusto.es

Abstract. Nowadays, users are increasing their participation in the Internet and, particularly, in social news websites. In these webs, users can comment diverse stories or other users' comments. In this paper we propose a new method based for filtering trolling comments. To this end, we extract several features from the text of the comments, specifically, we use a combination of statistical, syntactic and opinion features. These features are used to train several machine learning techniques. Since the number of comments is very high and the process of labelling tedious, we use a collective learning approach to reduce the labelling efforts of classic supervised approaches. We validate our approach with data from 'Menéame', a popular Spanish social news site.

Keywords: information filtering, spam detection, web categorisation, content filtering, machine-learning.

1 Introduction

With the appearance of web 2.0 [1], the Internet Community became more sensitive about the primordial users' needs when surfing the net. Since then, the users' dynamic interaction and collaboration was drastically enhanced, and the development of the social networking sites, wikis or blogs, amongst others, started. Social news websites such as Digg[1] or 'Menéame'[2] are very popular among users. These sites work in a very simple and intuitive way: users submit their links to stories online, and other users of these systems rate them by voting. The most voted stories appear, finally, in the front-page [2].

In our previous work [3], we proposed an approach able to automatically categorise comments in these social news sites using supervised machine-learning algorithms. Nevertheless, supervised learning requires a high number of labelled data for each of the classes (i.e., trolling or normal comment). It is quite difficult to label this amount of data for a real-world problem such as the web mining. To generate this information, a time-consuming process of analysis is mandatory and, in the process, some comments may avoid filtering.

Collective classification [4] is a semi-supervised approach that employs the relational structure of labelled and unlabelled datasets combination to increase the

[1] http://digg.com/
[2] http://meneame.net/

J. Lopez, X. Huang, and R. Sandhu (Eds.): NSS 2013, LNCS 7873, pp. 707–713, 2013.

accuracy of the classification. With these relational models, the predicted label will be influenced by the labels of related samples. The techniques of collective and semi-supervised learning have been implemented satisfactorily in fields of computer science like text classification [4], malware detection [5] or spam filtering [6].

Considering this background, we present a novel text categorisation approach based on collective classification techniques to optimise classification performance when filtering controversial comments. This method employs a combination of statistical, syntactic and opinion features of the comments to represent them. Our main contributions are: (i) a new method to represent comments in social news websites, (ii) an adaptation of the collective learning approach to comment filtering, and (iii) an empirical validation which shows that our method can maintain high accuracy rates, minimising the effort of labelling.

The remainder of this paper is structured as follows. Section 2 describes the extracted features of the comments. Section 3 describes the experimental procedure and discussed the obtained results. Finally, Section 4 concludes and outlines the avenues of the future work.

2 Description of the Method

'Menéame' is a Spanish social news website, in which news and stories are promoted. It was developed in later 2005 by Ricardo Galli and Benjamín Villoslada and it is currently licensed as free software. We extracted several features from the comments that can be divided into 3 different categories: opinion, statistical and syntactic features.

- **Statistical Features**
  - **Comment body:** We used the information contained in the body of the comment. To represent the comments we have used the Vector Space Model (VSM) [7]. We used the *Term Frequency – Inverse Document Frequency* (TF–IDF) [8] weighting schema and the inverse term frequency idf_i. As the terming schema we have employed two different alternatives: using the word as the term to weigh and n-grams as terms to weigh. An n-gram is the overlapping subsequence of n words from a given comment.
  - **Number of references to the comment (in-degree):** It indicates the number of times the comment has been referenced in other comments of the same news story.
  - **Number of references from the comment (out-degree):** It measures the number of references of the comment to other comments of the same news story.
  - **Number of the comment:** It indicates the oldness of the comment.
  - **Similarity of the comment with the snippet of the news story:** We used the similarity of the VSM of the comment with the model of the snippet of the news story. In particular, we employ the cosine similarity [9].

  - **Number of coincidences** between words in the comment and tags of the news story.
  - **Number of URLs** in the comment body.
- **Syntactic Features** In this category we count the number of words in the different syntactic categories. To this end, we performed a Part-of-Speech tagging using FreeLing[3]. The following features were used, all of them expressed in numerical values extracted from the comment body: adjectives, numbers, dates, adverbs, conjunctions, pronouns, punctuation marks, interjections, determinants, abbreviations and verbs.
- **Opinion Features**
  - **Number of positive and negative words:** We employed an external opinion lexicon[4]. Since the lexicon contains English words and 'Menéame' is written in Spanish, we translated them to Spanish.
  - **Number of votes:** The number of positive votes of the comment.
  - ***Karma*:** The *karma* is computed by the website based on the users' votes.

3 Empirical Validation

We gathered comments from 'Menéame' from 5th of April, 2011 to 12th of April, 2011. This dataset of comments comprises one week of stories filled by 9,044 comment instances. We labelled each of the comments in one category into *Normal* and *Controversial*. *Normal* means that the comment is not hurtful or hurting, using ia restrained tone. *Controversial*, on the other hand, refers to a comment seeking to create polemic. Our data was finally formed by 6,857 normal comments and 2,187 controversial comments.

We performed two different procedures to generate the VSM of the comment body: (i) VSM with words and terms and (ii) n-grams with different values of n (n=1, n=2, n=3). Furthermore, we removed every word devoid of meaning in the text, called stop words, (e.g., 'a','the','is') [8]. In both cases, we employed an external stop-word list of Spanish words[5].

To evaluate our approach, we applied k-cross validation with $k = 10$. Next, for each training set, we extracted the most important features for each of the classification types using *Information Gain* (IG) [10], an algorithm that evaluates the relevance of an attribute by measuring the information gain with respect to the class and We removed every feature with an IG value of zero. Since the dataset is not balanced for the different classes, we also applied Synthetic Minority Over-sampling TEchnique (SMOTE) [11] to address unbalanced data.

We then accomplished the learning step using different learning algorithms depending on the specific model, for each fold. We employed the implementations of the collective classification provided by the *Semi-Supervised Learning and*

[3] Available in: `http://www.lsi.upc.edu/~nlp/freeling`

[4] Available in: `http://www.cs.uic.edu/~liub/FBS/opinion-lexicon-English.rar`

[5] The list of stop words can be downloaded at `http://paginaspersonales.deusto.es/isantos/resources/stopwords.txt`

Table 1. Results in terms of accuracy, TPR, FPR and AUC of the Controversy Level for Word VSM

Dataset	Accuracy (%)	TPR	FPR	AUC
KNN K = 10	67.14 ± 1.92	0.50 ± 0.04	0.27 ± 0.02	0.66 ± 0.02
Bayes K2	75.93 ± 0.65	0.04 ± 0.01	0.01 ± 0.01	0.64 ± 0.03
Bayes TAN	76.64 ± 0.36	0.05 ± 0.01	0.01 ± 0.01	0.64 ± 0.03
Naïve Bayes	74.13 ± 3.74	0.20 ± 0.11	0.09 ± 0.08	0.62 ± 0.03
SVM: PolyKernel	68.35 ± 2.06	0.59 ± 0.05	0.29 ± 0.03	0.65 ± 0.03
SVM: Norm. PolyKernel	69.53 ± 1.55	0.53 ± 0.03	0.25 ± 0.02	0.64 ± 0.02
SVM: PUK	69.54 ± 1.33	0.52 ± 0.04	0.25 ± 0.02	0.63 ± 0.02
SVM: RBFK	68.34 ± 3.33	0.44 ± 0.03	0.24 ± 0.05	0.60 ± 0.02
J48	71.72 ± 2.06	0.31 ± 0.04	0.15 ± 0.02	0.60 ± 0.04
Random Forest N = 100	77.08 ± 0.94	0.18 ± 0.04	0.04 ± 0.01	0.67 ± 0.03

Table 2. Results in terms of accuracy, TPR, FPR and AUC of the Controversy Level for N-gram VSM

Dataset	Accuracy (%)	TPR	FPR	AUC
KNN K = 10	57.32 ± 2.13	0.61 ± 0.05	0.44 ± 0.03	0.63 ± 0.03
Bayes K2	75.60 ± 0.74	0.06 ± 0.02	0.02 ± 0.01	0.65 ± 0.02
Bayes TAN	76.34 ± 0.43	0.06 ± 0.02	0.01 ± 0.00	0.65 ± 0.02
Naïve Bayes	53.81 ± 1.78	0.62 ± 0.02	0.49 ± 0.02	0.59 ± 0.02
SVM: PolyKernel	60.84 ± 1.38	0.74 ± 0.04	0.43 ± 0.01	0.65 ± 0.02
SVM: Norm. PolyKernel	70.72 ± 1.56	0.54 ± 0.05	0.24 ± 0.02	0.65 ± 0.02
SVM: PUK	70.83 ± 1.86	0.49 ± 0.05	0.22 ± 0.02	0.63 ± 0.03
SVM: RBFK	53.42 ± 2.98	0.74 ± 0.03	0.53 ± 0.04	0.60 ± 0.03
J48	71.04 ± 1.54	0.35 ± 0.04	0.17 ± 0.02	0.61 ± 0.02
Random Forest N = 100	76.88 ± 1.30	0.19 ± 0.04	0.05 ± 0.01	0.68 ± 0.03

Collective Classification[6] package for machine-learning tool WEKA [12]. In our experiment approaches, we used the following models: (i) *Collective IBK*, with $k = 10$; (ii) *CollectiveForest*, where the value of the trees to experiment is 100; (iii) *CollectiveWoods*, with 100 trees; and (iv) *RandomWoods*, with 100 trees. In our collective experiments, we examined various configurations of the collective algorithms with different sizes of the $\mathcal{X}$ set of known instances; the latter varied from 10% to 90% of the instances utilised for training (i.e., instances known during the test).

In order to evaluate the contribution of Collective Classification to categorisation comments, we compared the filtering capabilities of our method with some of the most used supervised machine-learning algorithms. Specifically, we used the following models: (i) *Bayesian networks (BN)*, with different structural learning algorithms: K2 and Tree Augmented Naïve (TAN) and a Naïve Bayes Classifier; (ii)Support Vector Machines (SVM), with a polynomial kernel, a normalised polynomial Kernel, a Pearson VII function-based universal kernel (PUK) and a radial basis function (RBF) based kernel; (iii) *K-nearest neighbour (KNN)*, with $k = 10$; and (iv) *Decision Trees (DT)*, trained with J48 (the *Weka* [12] implementation of the *C4.5* algorithm) and Random Forest [13], an ensemble

[6] Available at: `http://www.scms.waikato.ac.nz/~fracpete/projects/collective-classification`

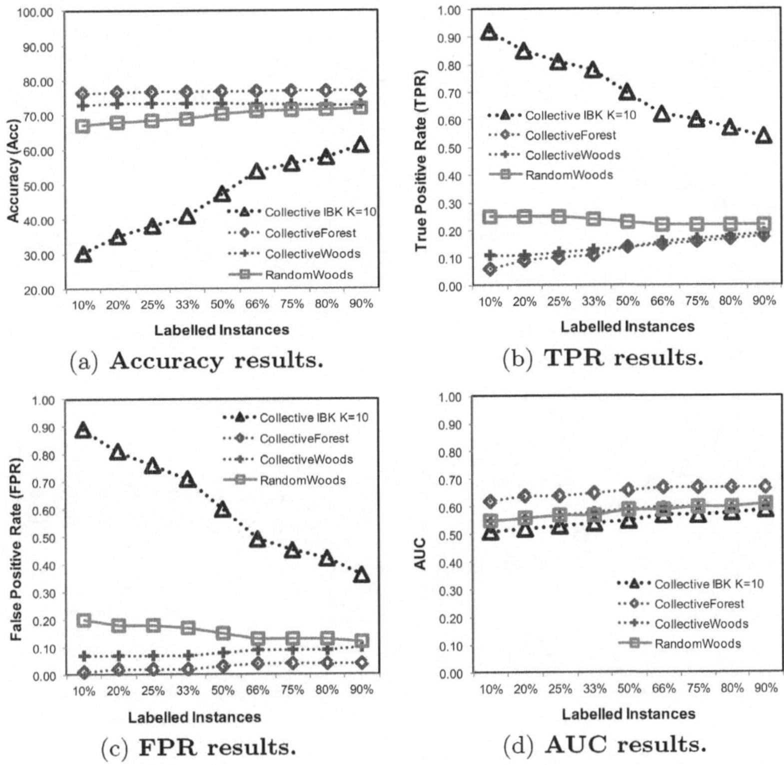

(a) **Accuracy results.**

(b) **TPR results.**

(c) **FPR results.**

(d) **AUC results.**

Fig. 1. Results performed with Word VSM features

of randomly constructed decision trees. In particular, we employed $N = 100$ for Random Forest.

Finally, in order to measure the effectiveness of the method, we measured the *True Positive Rate* (TPR) to test our procedure; i.e., the number of the controversial comments correctly detected divided by the total number of controversial comments. We also took in account the *False Positive Rate* (FPR); i.e., the number of normal comments misclassified as controversial divided by the total number of normal comments. In addition, we obtained the *Accuracy*; i.e., the total number of hits of the classifiers divided by the number of instances in the whole dataset. Finally, we recovered the *Area Under the ROC Curve* (AUC), that is computed by plotting the TPR against the FPR under different thresholds and computing the area formed under the generated curve.

Table 1 shows the results with words as tokens using classic supervised learning algorithms, and Table 2 shows the results with n-grams as tokens using classic supervised learning algorithms. Figure 1 shows the results with VSM generated with words, when collective learning algorithm are used, and Figure 2 shows the results with VSM generated with n-grams using collective learning approaches.

Regarding the supervised learning algorithms, Random Forest with N = 100 with words VSM, achieved significant results: 77.08% accuracy, 0.18 TPR, 0.04

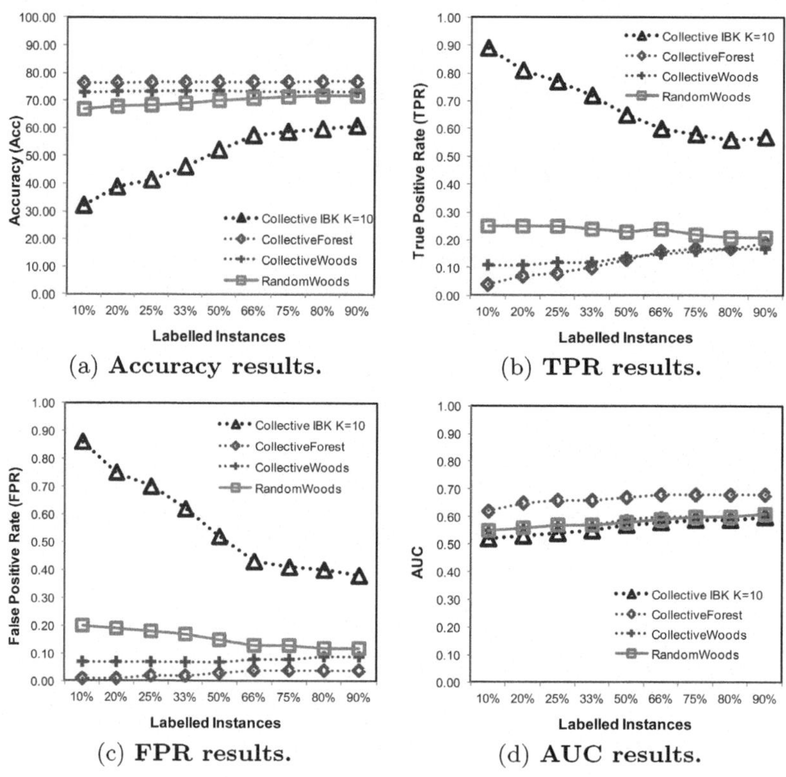

(a) **Accuracy results.**

(b) **TPR results.**

(c) **FPR results.**

(d) **AUC results.**

Fig. 2. Results performed with N-gram VSM

FPR and 0.67 AUC. For collective classification, CollectiveForest, using words as terms for the VSM, obtained a accuracy of 76.94% by only labelling the 75% of the dataset, a TPR of 0.16, a FPR of 0.04 and a AUC of 0.67. The results for collective classification are close to the supervised approaches, and the labelling effort has been reduced to 76.94% of the whole data.

4 Conclusions

The problem with supervised learning is that a previous work of comment labelling is required. This process in the field of web filtering can introduce a high performance overhead due to the number of new comments that appear everyday. In this paper, we proposed the first collective-learning-based trolling comment filtering method system that based upon statistical, syntactic and opinion features, is capable of determining when a comment is controversial. We empirically validated our method using a dataset from 'Menéame', showing that our technique, despite having much less labelling requirements, obtains nearly the same accuracy than the best supervised learning approaches.

The avenues of future work are oriented in three main ways. Firstly, we would like to apply additional algorithms to extend the study of filtering trolling comments in social news websites. Secondly, we will incorporate new and different features from the comment dataset to train the models. And finally, we will focus on executing an extended analysis of the effects of the labelled dataset dimension.

References

1. O'Reilly, T.: What is web 2.0: Design patterns and business models for the next generation of software. Communications & Strategies (1), 17 (2007)
2. Lerman, K.: User participation in social media: Digg study. In: Proceedings of the 2007 IEEE/WIC/ACM International Conferences on Web Intelligence and Intelligent Agent Technology-Workshops, pp. 255–258. IEEE Computer Society (2007)
3. Santos, I., de-la Peña-Sordo, J., Pastor-López, I., Galán-García, P., Bringas, P.: Automatic categorisation of comments in social news websites. Expert Systems with Applications (2012)
4. Neville, J., Jensen, D.: Collective classification with relational dependency networks. In: Proceedings of the Second International Workshop on Multi-Relational Data Mining, pp. 77–91 (2003)
5. Santos, I., Laorden, C., Bringas, P.: Collective classification for unknown malware detection. In: Proceedings of the 6th International Conference on Security and Cryptography (SECRYPT), pp. 251–256 (2011)
6. Laorden, C., Sanz, B., Santos, I., Galán-García, P., Bringas, P.G.: Collective classification for spam filtering. In: Herrero, Á., Corchado, E. (eds.) CISIS 2011. LNCS, vol. 6694, pp. 1–8. Springer, Heidelberg (2011)
7. Baeza-Yates, R.A., Ribeiro-Neto, B.: Modern Information Retrieval. Addison-Wesley Longman Publishing Co., Inc., Boston (1999)
8. Salton, G., McGill, M.: Introduction to modern information retrieval. McGraw-Hill, New York (1983)
9. Tata, S., Patel, J.M.: Estimating the Selectivity of tf-idf based Cosine Similarity Predicates. ACM SIGMOD Record 36(2), 75–80 (2007)
10. Kent, J.: Information gain and a general measure of correlation. Biometrika 70(1), 163–173 (1983)
11. Chawla, N., Bowyer, K., Hall, L., Kegelmeyer, W.: SMOTE: synthetic minority over-sampling technique. Journal of Artificial Intelligence Research 16(3), 321–357 (2002)
12. Garner, S.: Weka: The Waikato environment for knowledge analysis. In: Proceedings of the 1995 New Zealand Computer Science Research Students Conference, pp. 57–64 (1995)
13. Breiman, L.: Random forests. Machine Learning 45(1), 5–32 (2001)

Security Analysis of Touch Inputted Passwords

A Preliminary Study Based on the Resistance against Brute Force Attacks

Bruno Alves Pereira Botelho, Emilio Tissato Nakamura, and Nelson Uto

CPqD - Centro de Pesquisa e Desenvolvimento, Brazil
{bpereira,nakamura,uto}@cpqd.com.br

Abstract. In this paper, we present a security analysis of a few touch inputted authentication methods (Android´s PIN and pattern unlock, and iconographic password), based mainly on the resistance against brute force attacks. In order to support our study, we developed a set of specific tools for performing the tests against each method. Recommendations for improving the security of the aforementioned mechanisms are given based on the experimental results.

Keywords: authentication, brute force, iconographic, touch inputted password.

1 Introduction

This paper presents a set of recommendations based on a security analysis of Android authentication mechanisms, using a set of tools specifically developed for brute forcing touch inputted authentication methods, such as those used on mobile devices. Our solution targets two different mechanisms used in Android, the PIN (Fig. 1a) [1] and the pattern unlock (Fig. 1b) [1], and the iconographic authentication adopted by the mobile application shown in Fig. 1c.

The security analysis also takes into consideration, besides the image-based brute force attacks, other exploitation methods, such as dictionary attacks, shoulder surfing, password guessing, and attacks against the authentication system itself.

In turn, the set of recommendations considers the possible countermeasures against the aforementioned attacks ,and other important aspects in mobile devices, in special, the usability issues that must be balanced with the security aspects.

This paper is structured as follows: Section 2 discusses touch inputted passwords, while Section 3 presents the implementation aspects of image-based brute force tools. In Section 4 we show the experimental results of the tests, and Sections 5 and 6 present, respectivly, recommendations and final considerations.

2 Touch Inputted Passwords

The advent of touchscreen devices evolved the interaction between the user and the mobile devices. This evolution has had direct impact on security. One of the impacts

J. Lopez, X. Huang, and R. Sandhu (Eds.): NSS 2013, LNCS 7873, pp. 714–720, 2013.

has been to replace physical keyboards with virtual ones in order to enter PINs. Another one is the use of new security mechanisms that take advantage of a touch-screen, such as the pattern unlock and the iconographic authentication.

These authentication mechanisms are based on touch inputted passwords and can be used for protecting both the access to the device (unlocking) as well as the access to applications (in-app authentication) and data (service – multi-channel or not – authentication). The three touch inputted authentication mechanisms analyzed in this paper are briefly described in the following paragraphs.

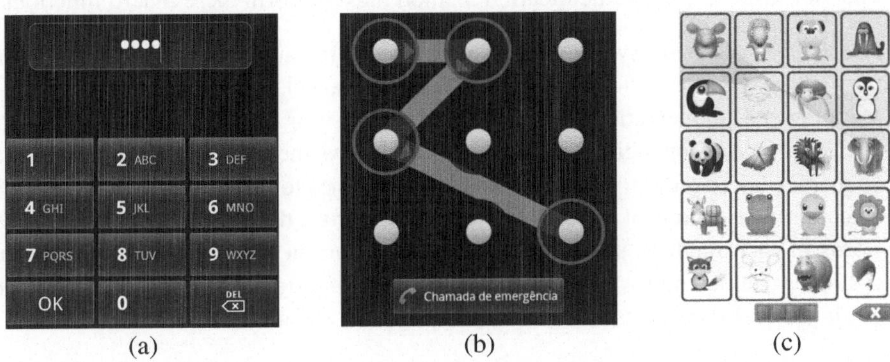

Fig. 1. Authentication methods. (a) PIN. (b) Pattern unlock. (c) Iconographic password.

PIN. Android's PIN mechanism consists in a screen containing a 4x3 grid of buttons. The disposition of the keys does not vary along the attempts, which makes an attack easier to perform. A delay of a 30 seconds is added after a user consecutively types a wrong PIN five times.

Pattern Unlock. This mechanism allows the user to define a path with 4 to 9 dots, in a 3x3 grid, and to use it to unlock the device. As a rule one cannot use a point more than once, since it is virtually removed after selection. Also, it is not possible to connect the extremities of a line with three circles, without selecting the middle one, unless the latter has been previously visited. As in the previous mechanism, there is a 30 seconds delay after five wrong and consecutive attempts.

Iconographic Passwords. This mechanism uses images and icons instead of the characters represented on virtual keyboards. This can be translated into combination of security with usability, with a greater facility to memorize passwords [4], more usability [5] and less correlation with passwords that can be guessed or be listed in dictionaries. In the analyzed system, the default configuration presents twenty icons in a 5x4 grid and the user should select, no matter the order, the four elements of a previously chosen set. Repetition of icons in the password is not allowed.

3 Image-Based Brute Force Tools

The image-based brute force tools simulate the user interaction on the mobile device to enter the touch inputted passwords. In every type of authentication (PIN, pattern unlock, and iconographic password) the tool simulates the user touch on the areas of the screen that represent the current element of the password. For this reason, an initial mapping of all images to be used is required: numeric keyboard for PIN, circles for pattern unlock, and icons for iconographic password.

The tools used in each authentication method must perform these macro functions:

1. Recognition of the password input screen: checks the authentication screen by distinguishing specific static items such as the OK, Cancel, and Clear buttons.
2. Mapping and segmentation of the screen distinguishing unique elements (numbers, circles, or icons, depending on each method): knows the coordinates of each button on the display in order to let the tool send the touches to the correct positions.
3. Selection and testing of a candidate password: from the set of all possible passwords in each method, selects and submits the current one to be tested. Different strategies can be employed to minimize the total duration of the brute force attack. For instance, PINs representing dates can be tested before the other ones.

In order to interact with the device, by sending touches and taking screenshots, we employ the MonkeyRunner tool [6] connected to the equipment's USB port. This communication requires the Android Debug Bridge daemon to be running on the device, which restricts the scenarios where the attack can be directly executed [7].

The paraghaphs below complement what was discussed in [7] regarding the implementation of the tools and the challenges we had to overcome.

PIN. Based on the disposition of the keys in the 4x3 grid, that does not vary along the attempts, the tool maps each element's position in the virtual keyboard, storing them on a static table, before performing the exhaustive PIN search. A thirty second delay must be added after five attempts, in order to cope with the countermeasure implemented by the device. We chose to sequentially select the PINs, starting from the minimum value, 0000, and ending with the maximum value, 9999.

Pattern Unlock. The mapping is accomplished via a static table with coordinates (x,y) from the center of each circle on the display, which are obtained from an initial screenshot. In order to simulate the drag gesture on the device's screen, one can use the method `MonkeyDevice.drag()`. However, since it only allows dragging along two points of the grid, we had to patch the method `drag()` from the `ChimpChat.AdbChimpDevice` class. Finally, instead of calculating all the possible patterns each time the tool is executed, we chose to generate them once and create a dictionary with the paths. This can be accomplished by a simple recursive algorithm that traverses the grid dots, which we illustrate by the following pseudocode:

```
function traverse(currentLen,desiredPathLen,path,
                  visitedNodes)
   if (currentLen == desiredPathLen)
      printPath(path, currentLen)else
      for each node n in neighborhood(lastNode(path))
         if (notVisited(n)) addNodeToPath(n, path)
            addToVisitedNodes(n, visitedNodes)
            if (isCenterNode(n) OR isMiddleNode(n))
               addNeighborsDueToRemovalOf(n)
               traverse(currentLen + 1, desiredPathLen,
                        path, visitedNodes)
               removeNeighborsDueToReinsertionOf(n)else
               traverse(currentLen + 1, desiredPathLen,
                        path, visitedNodes)
            removeFromVisitedNodes(n, visitedNodes)
```

Iconographic Password. The tool requires, initially, that one takes a screenshot, in order to obtain the set of icons used by the application. Those are processed, having their background colored with pink, and set as the baseline for icon classification. The objective of this step is to avoid mistakes in the matching process by removing all the pixels that do not belong to the icon, but result from the applications' wallpaper, due to the background transparency. For each authentication attempt, a screenshot needs to be taken, since the icon grid changes every time. The image is divided into twenty rectangles of same size and each one of them is compared to the icons in the baseline set. This step is performed by calculating a similarity score according to the pseudocode depicted in [7]. The candidate icon is considered to be the same as the one in the baseline set for which the smaller score is obtained, in the comparison process. This way, one can classify each icon in the grid and be able to test the current password. Due to the slowness of the `MonkeyImage.getPixel()` method, we had to get a raster representation of each icon, before invoking the `getPixel()` method.

4 Experimental Results

The tests were performed on a Samsung Galaxy SII running Android 2.3, connected to an Intel® Core™ i7@2934.00 MHz with 8 GBytes of RAM, running Linux Ubuntu 10.04. For each method, we randomly asked twenty people to choose a password of length 4 to be brute forced by the tools we developed for this experiment.

The tools were configured with the default values for each parameter, meaning we did not use any specific knowledge about the volunteers in order to try to accelerate the brute force attack. In other words, we started the PIN search with 0000, the pattern unlock by the top left circle, and the iconographic password by the icons corresponding to number 0123, no matter who chose the password.

Based on the amount of time for finding the correct value in each run, we calculated the following average times per attempt, already considering the delay added by the brute force countermeasure (30 seconds after 5 consecutive wrong attempts): PIN, 8 sec; pattern, 9 sec; iconographic password, 10 sec. These results indicate that the attack against iconographic password is more time consuming per attempt than the others mainly because of the time required for icon recognition.

Table 1 presents the minimum, maximum, and average times to crack the passwords defined by the volunteers. The PIN search takes the longer maximum and average times, which is related to the bigger number of possibilities [7]. On the other hand, PIN's minimum time is the second smaller, indicating that the password selection process depends on the user's memorization and information retrieval capabilities. For instance, users may choose the password based on the position of the keys or on dates, which tend to have a leading 0 or 1. Clearly, one can use such information to improve the search process, as previously stated.

Table 1. Minimum, maximum, and average times to break each type of password

Time to crack	PIN (hh:mm)	Pattern (hh:mm)	Iconographic (hh:mm)
Minimum	00:37	00:34	03:06
Maximum	21:18	03:51	12:19
Average	11:00	01:41	07:58

It is interesting to note that the average times resulting from the practical tests were lower than the mathematical estimates for all methods but the iconographic. Mathematically, the time for half the password space to be tested for the PIN, the pattern unlock, and the iconographic password is 11:06, 2:01, and 6:43, respectively. This fact, together with the bigger minimum time, makes iconographic passwords favorable in terms of security against brute force, if a larger password space could be used.

5 Recommendations

The most common strategy against brute force techniques consists in locking the device for a few seconds, after an arbitrary number of consecutive unsuccessful authentication attempts. However, a fixed delay facilitates the implementation of a tool, because one can stop the test for that specific amount of time. Hence, a better strategy to encumber an attack like this consists in locking the user a random amount of time after a random number of incorrect attempts.

Aditionally to the temporary locking countermeasure, one could demand the user to authenticate with a pre-configured secondary account in a remote server, once the number of consecutive and incorrect attempts reaches a predetermined threshold. This technique is implemented by newer versions of the Android operating system.

Another possibility is the use of biometrics, such as face recognition, which is already included in the latest versions of Android. Other options include voice authentication, which also does not require additional biometric sensors, as opposed to fingerprinting, for example. However, the adoption of biometric systems requires proper implementation of liveness detection techniques, in order to counter spoofing attacks.

For more critical accesses, multi-factor authentication, such as the use of biometric authentication together with PIN or iconographic password, is recommended. In some cases, even multimodal biometric authentication may be used with another factor. For instance, one can combine voice and face recognition with a password.

The iconographic authentication can also be improved by adopting parameters such as repeated icons and in which their order matters, as well as the expansion of the collection of icons. Nevertheless, with these new parameters, the usability of iconographic passwords must be reevaluated in order to balance security and usability, as this is directly linked with the facility to memorize and use the password.

If the same parameters are used for all the authentication methods covered in this paper, one obtains for each case the total number of passwords illustrated in Table 2.

Table 2. Passwords space of each authentication method with the same security parameters

Length	PIN	Pattern	Iconographic
4	10,000	6,561	160,000
5	100,000	59,049	3,200,000
6	1,000,000	531,441	64,000,000
7	10,000,000	4,782,969	1,280,000,000
8	100,000,000	43,046,721	25,600,000,000
9	1,000,000,000	387,420,489	512,000,000,000

Regarding other types of attacks against authentication, shoulder surfing, dictionary attacks, password guessing, and direct attacks against the authentication system itself should be considered. In shoulder surfing, where the attacker observes the user entering information, the attack on mobile devices is critical. Considering that the PIN and the pattern unlock are performed through a fixed keypad, the attacker can easily see and identify the position of circles/digits. In this case, the iconographic password system we analyzed is more secure than the other methods because the icons change position for each interaction. Here, the attacker must identify the icon itself and not its position on the display. In addition, for the pattern unlock, the user can leave marks while moving the fingers to swipe across the display to unlock the device.

Dictionary attacks in turn focus on alphanumeric passwords. Regarding PINs, the attack tools can be configured so that dates, which consists of days (from 01 to 31) and months (from 01 to 12), are tested before any other alternative. It is important to note that dictionary attack does not apply to iconographic authentication.

For password guessing attacks on PINs, all dates and phone numbers can be tested. For the other methods, this attack is less likely to happen due to the lack of connections between something concrete and the pattern unlock path or the iconographic password, although some icons can be linked to a given style or day-to-day routine.

Finally, direct attacks can be aimed at any type of authentication method and should be avoided by secure development, leaving no room for vulnerabilities that can be exploited by attackers. Furthermore, the infrastructure itself where the password database is stored must be secured. Note that, for short password, it is not effective to protect them by storing only their hashes, even with the use of salts, since an attacker can easily build a dictionary of all possible passwords. In this case, a probabilistic encryption method must be used together with a proper key management.

6 Final Considerations

We presented in this paper a security analysis of different authentication methods used by mobile devices. The experimental tests involved image-based brute force attacks performed by a set of tools we specially developed. In the present version we just intended to create a proof of concept, considering the basic countermeasures adopted by the target applications. Future implementations should consider ways to bypass additional protection mechanisms, such as the authentication with a secondary account or a random delay after a few number of authentication failure attempts.

These tools can also be used for testing the security of other methods, such as the face recognition authentication. Although the touchscreen is not used in this method, the tests can take advantage of some techniques developed for the image-based brute force tools. In this scope, a method to compose a database with several types of human faces, which can be used in an attack, is currently being studied.

Considering the size of the passwords space in each authentication method evaluated in this work, as well as the time to obtain access by using the developed tools, we can assert that iconographic passwords may be advantageous in terms of security, when compared to PIN and pattern unlock. However, usability tests must be performed in order to balance usability and security, as a secure method can still be discarded or avoided by the user if it is hard to use.

Acknowledgment. The authors thank the financial support given to the project "Biometric Multimodal and Iconographic Authentication for Mobile Devices, BIOMODAL", granted by FUNTTEL of the Brazilian Ministry of Communications, through Agreements Nr. 01.09.0627.00 with the FINEP / MCTI.

References

1. Hoog, A.: Android forensics: investigation, analysis and mobile security for Google Android. Syngress (2011)
2. Suo, X., Zhu, Y., Owen, G.: Graphical passwords: a survey. In: Proceedings of the 21st Annual Computer Security Applications Conference, ACSAC 2005, pp. 463–472 (2005)
3. Tambascia, C., Duarte, R., Menezes, E.: Usability evaluation of iconographic authentication for mobile devices using Eye tracking. In: MOBILITY 2011 (October 2011)
4. Ávila, I., Menezes, E., Braga, A.: Memorization Techniques in Iconic Passwords. In: IHCI 2012 (July 2012)
5. Tambascia, C., Braga, A., Menezes, E., Negrão, F.: User Experience Evaluation in the Creation and Use of Iconographic Passwords for Authentication in Mobile Devices. In: MOBILITY 2012 (October 2012)
6. Milano, D.: Android application testing guide. Packt Publishing (2011)
7. Botelho, B., Nakamura, E., Uto, N.: Implementation of tools for brute forcing touch inputted passwords. In: ICITST 2012 (December 2012)

A Pairing-Free Identity Based Authentication Framework for Cloud Computing

Dheerendra Mishra, Vinod Kumar, and Sourav Mukhopadhyay

Department of Mathematics
Indian Institute of Technology Kharagpur
Kharagpur 721302, India
{dheerendra,vinod,sourav}@maths.iitkgp.ernet.in

Abstract. Cloud Computing facilitates convenient on-demand access to networks, servers, storage, applications and services to the user with minimal management from user side. It is a client-server model in which user accesses a remote server to utilize resource or service cheaply and easily without owning. However, a user uses public network during access of cloud services while an adversary can get full control over the public network. Therefore, a user should adopt a mechanism in which user and server can authenticate each other and establish a secure session. Recently, Kang and Zhang proposed an Identity-Based mutual authentication in Cloud Storage Sharing using elliptic curve cryptography and claimed that their scheme can resist various attacks. However, we analyze the security aspects of the Kang and Zhang's scheme and identify some security flaws in their scheme. In this paper, we propose an enhanced identity based mutual authentication scheme for client-server cloud architecture. Further, we present security analysis of the scheme which shows that the proposed scheme supports flawless anonymous mutual authentication such that client-server can establish secure session.

Keywords: Cloud Computing, pairing-free identity based cryptosystem, anonymity, mutual authentication.

1 Introduction

Cloud Computing is an on-demand technology which employs computing resources to present convenient on-demand access to networks, servers, storage, services and application. A user can access or control over the Cloud infrastructure without knowledge, expertise and big investment [1]. However, there are many issues that need to be addressed to achieve flexible and secure infrastructure. Zhang et al. [7] presented a brief study of the research challenges which are occurring in Cloud. Takabi et al. [4] discussed the emerging security challenges in it. One of the challenge is to control the data breaching in cloud storage services. Since, user stores/access his/her data over the remote server, an adversary can get the opportunity to makes this mechanism vulnerable for attack as an adversary can achieve full control over the public network. Therefore, to

J. Lopez, X. Huang, and R. Sandhu (Eds.): NSS 2013, LNCS 7873, pp. 721–727, 2013.

achieve secure and authorized communication, a powerful mutual authentication and session key establishment protocol is necessary. Moreover, an adversary can link the communication and the login session of a user and can extract useful information. However, anonymous communication ensures that there is no way to link individual information to an identifiable natural person. Anonymity of user and server identity also enhances the security as an adversary is not able to relate previously gained information. Therefore, secure and anonymous mutual authentication mechanism is paramount requirement in cloud.

In recent years, many identity-based authentication protocols have been proposed for cloud [6,2,3]. In 2009, Yang and Chang [6] proposed an identity-based remote user authentication protocol for mobile users based on elliptic curve cryptography (ECC). Their scheme inherits the merits of both identity based cryptosystem and elliptic curve. Chen et al. [2] identified two security flaws, namely, insider attack and impersonation attack in Yang-Chang's scheme. To remove these security flaws, they presented an advanced password based authentication scheme. The authors claimed that their protocol is secured to provide mutual authentication and is appropriate for Cloud Computing environment. However, in 2012, Wang et al. [5] showed that Chen et al. protocol is not secure and is vulnerable to offline password guessing attack, and key compromise impersonation attack and also suffers from clock synchronization problem. Kang and Zhang [3] presented short key size identity based authentication scheme, which requires the computation of bilinear pairing on super singular elliptic curve group with large element size where the computation cost of the pairing is approximately three times higher than that of elliptic curve point multiplication. We also found that their scheme suffers some serious security flaws.

In this paper, we firstly review the Kang-Zhang's identity-based authentication protocol and show that their protocol is not secured to maintain authorized communication between remote user and the server. Further, we present a new pairing free identity based mutual authentication for cloud computing. In this scheme, cloud user and server mutually authenticate each other and establish a session key.

2 Review of Kang-Zhang's Scheme

In this section, we briefly review the Kang and Zhang [3] mutual authentication mechanism for Cloud Computing. We use the same notations as in [3]. For more details of Kang and Zhangs scheme one can refer to [3].

Let ID_A and ID_B are the identities of A and B respectively. (Q_A, SK_A) and (Q_B, SK_B) are the public-private key pair of A and B respectively where $Q = H(c||ID||ID_i)$ and $\mathsf{SK} = (s||s_i)Q = (s||s_i)H(c||ID||ID_i)$ for random $s, s_i, c \in Z_q^*$. Then, the mechanism of mutual authentication is summarized below:

- B computes $K_{BA} = e(SK_B, Q_A)$.
- B sends $< ID_B, Q_B, M, f(K_{BA}, M) >$ to A, where M is information of data requested above and $f(.)$ is a one-way hash function.
- Upon receiving the message, A evaluates $K_{AB} = e(SK_A, Q_B)$.
- A computes value $f(K_{AB}, M)$, then verifies that $f(K_{AB}, M) =? f(K_{BA}, M)$. If verification success, then Alice will believe Bob is valid user.

- Then, A sends the message tuple $< n, N', N, f(K_{AB}, N) >$, where n is the consentaneous identifier and N is a token which contains the information of data shared, token's period of validity, Bob's public key and identification string, etc., and N' is the token's signature.
- Upon receiving the the message tuple $< n, N', N, f(K_{AB}, N) >$, Bob exercises the similar authentication mechanism.

2.1 Cryptanalysis of Kang-Zhang's Scheme

In Kang and Zhang scheme, user and server mutually authenticate each other. However, the scheme does not maintain the key security attributes such as key freshness, known session key and forward secrecy as:

Key Freshness: In Kang and Zhang's scheme, common key $K_{AB} = e(SK_A, Q_B)$ does not include any session parameters such as random number or time-stamp. Once the key is established, user can use it for any number of session and any number of time, i.e., user and server do not create different session keys for different sessions. Therefore, scheme looses key freshness attribute.

Known Session Keys: Since, the entities use same key for different session rather than different key for different session. Therefore, scheme does not tolerate known session key attack.

Forward Secrecy: If the private key of Alice SK_A or Bob SK_B compromise, then an adversary can compute session key K_{AB} and K_{BA}, since $K_{AB} = K_{BA}$, Q_A and Q_B are public, and $K_{AB} = e(SK_A, Q_B)$ and $K_{BA} = e(SK_B, Q_A)$.

3 Proposed Scheme

In this section, we propose a mutual authentication protocol between Cloud user U and server S. In which, if authentication succeeds, user and server establish a session key. The protocol is composed of main three algorithms:

- Set Up.
- Extract.
- Mutual authentication and session key computation.

3.1 Set Up:

Private key generator (PKG) takes a security parameter k, return security parameter and master key. For given k, PKG takes the following steps:

- Choose an arbitrary generator $P \in G$
- Select a master key $\mathsf{m} \in Z_q^*$ and set public key $\mathsf{PK} = \mathsf{m}P$
- Choose collusion free one way hash functions $H_1 : \{0,1\}^* \times G \to Z_q^*$, $H_2 : \{0,1\}^* \times \{0,1\}^* \times \{0,1\}^k \times \{0,1\}^* \times \{0,1\}^* \to \{0,1\}^k$ & $H : \{0,1\}^* \times \{0,1\}^* \times G \times G \times \{0,1\}^* \times \{0,1\}^* \to \{0,1\}^k$.
- Publish system parameters $\langle E/F_q, G, k, P, \mathsf{PK}, H_1, H_2, H \rangle$ and keep master key m secret.

3.2 Extract

Server's Private Key Extraction: Server S submits its public identities ID_S to PKG. Then, PKG verifies the proof of the identity. If verification succeeds, then generates the partial private key as:

- Generate $x_S \in Z_q^*$.
- Compute $X_S = x_S P$ and $h_S = H_1(ID_S||X_S)$, and generate private key $Y_S = x_S + \mathsf{m}h_S \bmod q$. Then, PKG delivers (X_S, Y_S) to S through a secure channel.

On receiving private key, S verifies $Y_S P = X_S + H_1(ID_S||X_S)\mathsf{PK}$. If verification succeeds, S sets its public key $PK_S = Y_S P$. Then, It make its parameter $< ID_S, PK_S, P, H_1, H_2, H >$ public.

Users' Private Key Extraction: User U submits its identities ID_U to PKG. Then, PKG verifies the proof of identities. If verification succeeds, then PKG generates the partial private keys as:

- Generate $x_U \in Z_q^*$.
- Compute $X_U = x_U P$ and $h_U = H_1(ID_U||X_U)$.
- By using its master key m, PKG generates the U's private key $Y_U = x_U + \mathsf{m}h_U \bmod q$. Then, PKG delivers the key $< X_U, Y_U >$ to U through a secure channel.

On receiving private key, U verifies $Y_U P = X_U + H_1(ID_U||X_U)\mathsf{PK}$. If verification succeeds, U sets its public key $PK_U = Y_U P$ and keeps $< X_U, Y_U >$ secret.

3.3 Mutual Authentication and Session Key Computation

The Cloud user U knows servers public parameters, then U initiates and establishes a secure session with server S as follows:

- U sends "HELLO" message to S.
- S replies to U with a "HELLO" message.
- On receiving the S message, U performs the following steps:
  - Choose a random value $u \in Z_q^*$.
  - Compute uY_U, $T_U = uP, T_U' = uY_U P, uY_U PK_S = uY_U Y_S P$ and $W = H_1(t_1||uY_U Y_S P)$.
  - Send $\langle ID_U \oplus W, T_U, T_U', PK_U, t_1 \rangle$ to S where t_1 is the timestamp.
- On receiving the user message, S computes $t_2 - t_1 \leq \triangle t$, where t_2 is the message receiving time of server and $\triangle t$ is the valid time delay in message transmission. If time delay in message transmission is valid, then S performs the following steps:
  - Compute $Y_S T_U' = Y_S u Y_U P$ and $W^* = H_1(t_1||Y_S u Y_U P)$ then extract user's identity $ID_U = ID_U \oplus W \oplus W^*$ as $uY_U Y_S P = Y_S u Y_U P$, i.e., $W = W^*$.

- Verify ID_U's registration details and authenticity. If U is authorized and non-register user, S registers U. If U is unauthorized user then deny the request. Otherwise, it proceeds.
- Select a random value $s \in Z_q^*$ and compute $T_S = sP$ and $T_S' = sY_SP$.
- Compute $sY_SPK_U = sY_SY_UP, K_{SU} = sY_SY_UP + Y_SuY_UP$ and $sT_U = suP$.

  Then, finally compute the session key sk and message authentication code mac as:

$$sk = H(ID_U||ID_S||suP||K_{SU}||t_1||t_3)$$

$$\mathsf{mac} = H_2(ID_U||ID_S||sk||t_1||t_3)$$

- Send the message $\langle ID_S \oplus W^*, T_S, T_S', \mathsf{mac}, t_3\rangle$ to U at time t_3.

• On receiving the message, U computes $t_4 - t_3 \leq \Delta t$, where t_4 is the message receiving time of user's system. If time delay in message transaction is valid, then U achieves $ID_S = ID_S \oplus W^* \oplus W$. Then, U computes $uT_S = usP$ and $K_{US} = Y_UT'_S + uY_UY_SP$.
• Finally, U computes the session key sk^* and message authentication code mac^* as:

$$sk^* = H(ID_U||ID_S||usP||K_{US}||t_1||t_3)$$

$$\mathsf{mac}^* = H_2(ID_U||ID_S||sk||t_1||t_3).$$

  Then, U verifies the condition $\mathsf{mac}^* =? \mathsf{mac}$. If the condition holds, U ensures the validity of message. Then, U sends $\langle ID_U, \mathsf{mac}^*\rangle$ to S.
• On receiving the message, S verifies $\mathsf{mac} =? \mathsf{mac}^*$. If verification succeeds, a user and server agree upon the common session key sk. And, once the session establishes user can store/access his/her data securely over the public channel.

4 Security and Performance Analysis

4.1 Security Analysis

In this section, we will justify that proposed mutual authentication mechanism is secure against following attacks:

Anonymity: During communication, user send dynamic identity $ID_U \oplus H_1$ $(ID_U||\ uY_UY_SP)$ instead of real identity ID_U. The identity ID_U is XOR with the hashed value of the secret uY_UY_SP where to compute uY_UY_SP for given $< p, uY_YP, Y_SP >$ is equivalent to CDH problem on ECC.

Known-Key Secrecy: If a session key between user and server is compromised, which does not mean to compromise of other session keys because every session key evolves random values u and s, where u and s are selected arbitrary independently for each session by U and S respectively. In addition, every session key involves time stamps, which are different for each session.

Replay Attack: Replay Attack is most common attack in authentication process. However, the common countermeasures are time-stamp and random number mechanism. In our scheme, we adopt the time-stamp as a counter-measure. The messages, in phase $U \to S$ and $S \to U$ are with time-stamps, therefore, replay attack could not work in any phase.

Perfect forward Secrecy: If the long term private keys of two parties, U and S compromise, one can compute $Y_U Y_S P$. However, an adversary can not compute session key because to compute session key $sk = H(ID_U||ID_S||suP||K_{SU} ||t_1||t_3)$, one has to compute usP. And, to compute usP for given $< P, uP, sP >$ is equivalent to CDH problem in ECC.

PKG forward Secrecy: If the PKG's master key m compromise. Then adversary can not even compute the user or server private keys Y_U or Y_S respectively. As, private keys of user and server are $Y_U = x_U + \mathsf{m}h_U$ and $Y_S = x_S + \mathsf{m}h_S$ respectively, which includes random values $x_U, x_S \in Zq^*$. In addition, to compute session key sk, computation of usP is required. However, to compute usP for given $< P, uP, sP >$ is equivalent to CDH problem on ECC.

Man in the Middle Attack: User and server authenticate each other without knowing. An adversary or malicious PKG can try man in the middle attack by sending the forge message. However, to authenticate each other user and server exchange message authentication code (mac). To compute mac, knowledge of session keys sk is required, although, session key sk is assumed secret and can con not be achieved with publicly known values as discussed above.

Known Session-Specific Temporary Information Attack: If short term secret values u and s compromise, then adversary can compute usP. However, to achieve $K_{US} = uY_U Y_S P + sY_S Y_U P$ or $K_{SU} = sY_S Y_U P + uY_U Y_S P$, one has to compute $Y_S Y_U P$ or $Y_U Y_S P$ for given $\langle P, Y_U P, Y_S P\rangle$, which is equivalent to CDH problem on ECC.

Impersonation Attack: The adversary E can try to mount impersonation attack on the proposed protocol as follows:

- U initiates the session with S.
- U chooses a random number $u \in Z_q^*$ and computes uP, $uY_U P$ and $W = H_1(t_1||uY_U Y_S P)$. Then, U sends the message $\langle ID_U \oplus W, uP, uY_U P, t_1\rangle$ to S.
- E does not intercept the U's message.
- On receiving, S chooses a random number $s \in Z_q^*$ and computes $T_S = sP$, $sY_S P$ and mac. Then, S responds with the message $\langle ID_S \oplus W^*, sP, sY_S P, \mathsf{mac}, t_3\rangle$ to U.
- E intercepts the S's message and try to replace it, E chooses $e \in Z_q^*$ and computes eP and euP. However, E can not replace mac, as to compute mac, E has to compute sk as $\mathsf{mac} = H_2(ID_U||ID_S||sk||t_1||t_3)$, where to

compute sk, E has to compute $K_{EU} = uY_UY_SP + eY_SY_UP$. Although E can not compute neither eY_SY_UP nor uY_UY_SP with e, Y_UP, uP, Y_SP, P, as to compute uY_UY_SP for given $\langle uY_UP, Y_SP, P\rangle$ is equivalent to CDH problem on ECC and to compute eY_SY_UP value Y_SY_UP is needed where for given $< Y_UP, Y_SP, P >$ computation of Y_SY_UP is equivalent to CDH problem on ECC . Since, CDH problem is assumed to be a hard problem on ECC, therefore, impersonation attacks are not possible in proposed protocol.

5 Conclusion

In this paper, we have analyzed Kang and Zhang's scheme and showed some security flaws in their scheme. Furthermore, we have proposed a mutual authentication mechanism between cloud user and server, which is based on pairing-free identity based mechanism. In proposed protocol, user and server authenticate each other and establish a session key without disclosing their identities over the public channel. By using the session key, user and server can communicate securely over the public network. Moreover, this scheme does not require the computation of bilinear pairing which makes this scheme more efficient and usable for cloud infrastructure. Lastly, we have analyzed the security attributes of the scheme which prove that proposed scheme is secure to establish secure communication channel over the insecure channel.

References

1. Armbrust, et al.: A View of Cloud Computing. Communications of the ACM 53(4), 50–58 (2010)
2. Chen, T.H., Yeh, H., Shih, W.K.: An Advanced ECC Dynamic ID-Based Remote Mutual Authentication Scheme for Cloud Computing. In: 5th FTRA International Conference on Multimedia and Ubiquitous Engineering (MUE), pp. 155–159 (2011)
3. Kang, L., Zhang, X.: Identity-Based Authentication in Cloud Storage Sharing. In: International Conference on Multimedia Information Network and Security (MINES), pp. 851–855. IEEE Computer Society (2010)
4. Takabi, H., Joshi, J.B.D., Ahn, G.J.: Security and Privacy Challenges in Cloud Computing Environments. IEEE Security & Privacy 8(6), 24–31 (2010)
5. Wang, D., Mei, Y., Ma, C.-G., Cui, Z.-S.: Comments on an advanced dynamic ID-based authentication scheme for cloud computing. In: Wang, F.L., Lei, J., Gong, Z., Luo, X. (eds.) WISM 2012. LNCS, vol. 7529, pp. 246–253. Springer, Heidelberg (2012)
6. Yang, J.H., Chang, C.C.: An ID-Based Remote Mutual Authentication with Key Agreement Scheme for Mobile Devices on Elliptic Curve Cryptosystem. Computers & Security 28(3), 138–143 (2009)
7. Zhang, Q., Cheng, L., Boutaba, R.: Cloud Computing: State-of-the-art and Research Challenges. Journal of Internet Services and Applications 1(1), 7–18 (2010)

Formal Modeling and Automatic Security Analysis of Two-Factor and Two-Channel Authentication Protocols*

Alessandro Armando[1,2], Roberto Carbone[2], and Luca Zanetti[1,2]

[1] DIBRIS, Università degli Studi di Genova, Italy
{alessandro.armando,luca.zanetti}@unige.it
[2] Security & Trust Unit, FBK-irst, Trento, Italy
{armando,carbone}@fbk.eu

Abstract. As the number of security-critical, online applications grows, the protection of the digital identities of the users is becoming a growing concern. Strong authentication protocols provide additional security by requiring the user to provide at least two independent proofs of identity for the authentication to succeed. In this paper we provide a formal model and mechanical security analysis of two protocols for two-factor and two-channel authentication for web applications that relies on the user's mobile phone as a second authentication factor and the GSM/3G communication infrastructure as the second communication channel. By using a model checker we detected vulnerabilities in the protocols that allow an attacker to carry out a security-sensitive operation by using only one of the two authentication factors. We also present a fix that allows to patch the protocols.

1 Introduction

Strong authentication protocols supplement traditional authentication mechanisms based on user's credentials (namely, username and passwords) with other proofs of identity (e.g., a one-time password generated by a special purpose hardware token) possibly transmitted over an additional communication channel (e.g., GSM). When this is the case, the protocol is said to offer *two-factor* (and possibly also *two-channel*) *authentication*. *Secure Call Authorization* (hereafter *SCA*) is a commercial solution for two-factor and two-channel authentication developed by AliasLab S.p.A. that relies on the user's mobile phone as a second authentication factor and the GSM/3G communication infrastructure as the second authentication channel. Indeed a key feature of *SCA* is the tight integration with the GSM/3G TelCo operator that ensures the authenticity of the caller ID. Unlike traditional one-time password generators which are bound to a specific service provider, by using *SCA* the mobile phone can play the role of a universal token, meaning that it can be used to support the authentication to a variety of service providers. In order to secure access to a web application, *SCA* offers a number of functionalities through a sophisticated API [1], supporting a variety of authentication protocols which are exemplified in the available documentation through use case

* This work has partially been supported by the FP7-ICT Project SPaCIoS (no. 257876) and by the project SIAM in the context of the FP7 EU "Team 2009 - Incoming" COFUND action. We would like to thank Alessio Lepre and Gianluca Buelloni of AliasLab for their helpful comments on the paper.

J. Lopez, X. Huang, and R. Sandhu (Eds.): NSS 2013, LNCS 7873, pp. 728–734, 2013.

scenarios. In this paper we provide a formal model and mechanical security analysis of the protocols corresponding to the *SecureCall Authentication with Drop Call* and the *SecureCall Authentication with Personal PIN DTMF* use case scenarios, hereafter the SCA-basic and the SCA-PIN protocols, resp. The formal modeling activity allowed us to spell out precisely the details of the protocols, the necessary assumptions for their proper functioning, and the expected security goals. For the mechanical analysis we used the model checker SATMC [2], detecting vulnerabilities in both protocols. Both vulnerabilities can be exploited by an attacker in possession of the user's credentials and capable to induce her (through social engineering techniques) to place a call with her mobile phone to the authentication server. In both cases, the attacker succeeds in carrying out a security-sensitive operation by using only one of the two authentication factors, i.e. the user's credentials on the service provider, thereby witnessing the violation of the strong authentication property that the protocols aim to achieve. We also discuss a fix that allows to patch both of them, using the *SCA* API in a different way.

It must be noted that the protocols in *SCA* API references are not prescriptive. Developers are thus free (and also encouraged) to use the API as they deem appropriate, possibly defining custom authentication protocols meeting the application requirements and assessing their security. As a matter of fact our proposed fix can be readily implemented by using the functionalities available in the *SCA* API. Moreover, AliasLab upon request provides assistance to their customers to assess the security of their solutions. However developers tend to use the scenarios provided as examples in the documentation as a blueprint for their implementations. Indeed, by analyzing two strong authentication solutions based on *SCA* and deployed in two different real-world, security-critical applications, namely CloudPlus and LegalPro, we found that they implement the SCA-basic and SCA-PIN resp. and hence suffer from the aforementioned attacks as described in the sequel.[1]

2 Two-Factor and Two-Channel Authentication Protocols

The SCA-basic protocol enables web-based, two-factor authentication by asking the user to prove possession of a (registered) mobile phone in addition to the user's credentials by placing a call to a toll-free number. Four roles take part in the SCA-basic protocol: a mobile phone (`M`) and a web Browser (`B`) both controlled by the user, a Service Provider (`SP`), and an authentication server (`TAS`) controlled by the TelCo operator. The objective of the user, using

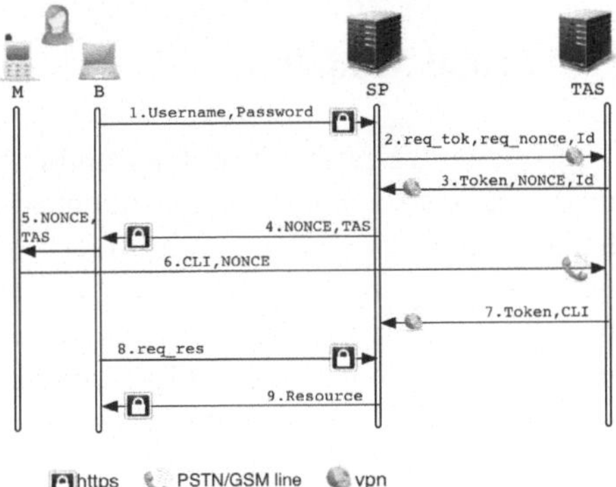

Fig. 1. The SCA-basic protocol

[1] Because of the sensitivity of the information contained in this paper the names of the real-world applications implementing the protocols and suffering from the attacks described in the paper (namely CloudPlus and LegalPro) are fictitious. We have promptly reported our findings to the developers of CloudPlus and LegalPro suggesting a better way to use the *SCA* API.

the web browser B, is to get access to a resource provided by SP. The SCA-basic protocol terminates when SP authenticates the user and grants access to the resource. Fig. 1 shows an excerpt of the messages exchanged during a typical execution of the SCA-basic protocol. In the first step the user using B provides her credentials (Username and Password) on the SP login web page. If the credentials are correct, in the second step, SP generates an identifier Id and sends it to TAS, making a request for a token (req_tok) and a nonce (req_nonce). In step 3, TAS replies with a four-digit NONCE and a new Token and stores their association locally in a database, say TAS_DB. SP uses Id to associate Token and NONCE to the corresponding browser session. In step 4, SP sends B the request to place a call to the toll-free number of TAS and to digit NONCE after the tone. The flow of this information from B to M is represented by step 5. In step 6, the user calls TAS using her mobile phone M and enters the number NONCE received from SP. The phone call has also the implicit effect of sending the Calling Line Identification (CLI) of M to TAS. TAS looks TAS_DB for the Token corresponding to NONCE and then forwards CLI and Token to SP (step 7). In step 8, B asks SP for Resource. Finally SP checks in SP_DB if CLI corresponds to Username and sends Resource to B (step 9).

Communications between the parties are subject to the following assumptions: (A1) communications between B and SP are carried over a unilateral SSL 3.0 or TLS 1.0 channel (henceforth SSL/TLS), established through the exchange of a valid certificate (from SP to B); (A2) communications between M and TAS are carried over a PSTN/GSM line, through the user's mobile phone. This ensures confidentiality and gives TAS the ability to authenticate the phone number of the phone placing the incoming call; (A3) communications between SP and TAS are carried over a secure channel, e.g. VPN.

The protocol is expected to meet the following security property: the user must be strongly authenticated on SP. The difference between the standard authentication property and the two-factor authentication one lies in the fact that the latter still must hold even if a malicious agent either *(i)* knows the credentials of the user or *(ii)* possesses the user's mobile phone.

3 Formal Modeling

We focus on the problem of determining whether the concurrent execution of a finite number of sessions of the protocol enjoys the expected security properties in spite of the interference of a malicious intruder. This problem can be recast into a model checking problem of the form $M \models (C \Rightarrow G)$, where M is a transition system modeling the initial state of the system and the behaviours of the principals, C is a conjunction of Linear Temporal Logic (LTL) formulae constraining the allowed behaviours of the intruder, and G is an LTL formula stating the expected security property.

We represent the states of M as sets of facts. In particular, the state of an honest agent a is represented by the state fact $\mathtt{state}_r(j, a, es)$. The informal meaning is that the agent a, playing role r, is ready to execute the protocol step j, and es is a list of expressions representing the internal state of a. Similarly, we use other facts to represent the reception and the sending of a message, the knowledge of the intruder, and to model sets (e.g. the database SP_DB). Here and in the sequel we use typewriter font to denote facts with the additional convention that variables are capitalized (e.g. TAS, NONCE),

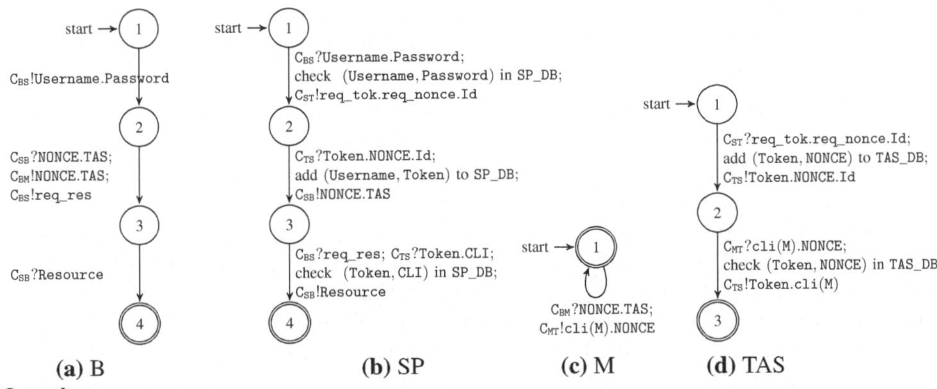

Legend:
- C_{BS}, C_{SB}, C_{BM}, C_{TS}, C_{ST}, C_{MT}: channels supporting the communication between B, SP; SP, B; B, M; TAS, SP; M, TAS resp.
- $c!m$: message m is sent over channel c.
- $c?x$: a message, say m, is read from channel c and variable x is set to m.
- add (x,y) to DB: pair (x,y) added to DB.
- check (x,y) in DB: if pair (x,y) is not in DB, the protocol stops.
- $m1.m2$: concatenation of messages $m1$ and $m2$.

Fig. 2. Process view of the SCA-basic protocol

while constants and function symbols begin with a lower-case letter (e.g. `tas`, `nonce`). The constant `i` denotes the intruder. While the initial state of the system defines the initial knowledge of the intruder and the initial state of all the honest principals involved in the protocol sessions considered, rewriting rules specify the evolution of the system. For the sake of simplicity, we present here the evolution of M using the process view of the protocol (which can be easily converted to rewriting rules). More details about the actual formalism can be found in [2]. The process view of the SCA-basic protocol is depicted in Fig. 2. Each state in the figure corresponds to the state fact of the agent playing that role. (See [3] for more details.) Notice that, we model the behaviour of the user defining two distinct processes (Fig. 2(a) and (c)), according to the specific device she uses (B and M). Moreover, in order to formalize the communication between these two processes, we consider a generic channel C_{BM}, modeling the user who reads the nonce on the web page and digits it on the phone. It is important to underline that a user u—in the expected execution of the protocol—plays both the roles B and M, but, as we show in Sect. 4, this is not true in general, and can lead to serious issues. For the sake of brevity, we omit the rules modeling the abilities of the Dolev-Yao [6] intruder.

The security-relevant properties of communication channels can be specified by adding suitable LTL formulae to C. We say that a channel c provides confidentiality if its output is exclusively accessible to a given receiver p. Thus, the condition $confidential(c, p)$ can be formalized by an LTL formula stating that globally (for all the states of the system) only p can receive messages sent on channel c. An authentic channel c provides authenticity if its input is exclusively accessible to a specified sender p, the condition $authentic(c, p)$ can be formalized by another LTL formula stating that globally only p can send messages on channel c. Similarly for the other channels, including the $unil\_conf\_auth(x, y, c_{xy}, c_{yx})$ channel relation that models a run of SSL/TLS in which agent y has a valid certificate but agent x has not. More details can be found in [2]. The assumptions on channels in Sect. 2 can be modeled including the following formulae in C: *(i)* $unil\_conf\_auth(b, sp, c_{bs}, c_{sb})$, *(ii)* $authentic(c_{mt}, m)$, $confidential(c_{mt}, tas)$, *(iii)* $authentic(c_{st}, sp)$, $confidential(c_{st}, tas)$, $authentic(c_{ts}, tas)$, $confidential(c_{ts}, sp)$, where b, sp, tas, and m are the agents playing the roles B, SP, TAS, and M resp., and c_{bs}, c_{sb}, c_{mt}, c_{st}, and c_{ts} are the corresponding channels among them. (Clearly, formulae *(i)*, *(ii)*, and *(iii)* capture assumptions (A1), (A2), and (A3) resp.) We assume confidential to m the channel c_{bm} between the agents playing the roles B and M, including the formula $confidential(c_{bm}, m)$ as well.

The use of LTL also allows for the specification of the security goals of the protocol. The language of LTL we consider here uses facts as atomic formulae, the usual propositional connectives (namely, $\vee$, $\wedge$, $\Rightarrow$), and the temporal operators **G** (globally) and **O** (once). To define the security goal we rely on the definition given in [9]: whenever sp (playing role SP) completes a run of the protocol apparently with user u (playing role B), then u has previously been running the protocol apparently with sp. This can be formally expressed by the following formula:

$$authentication(\mathtt{sp}, \mathtt{u}) := \mathbf{G}\,(\mathtt{state}_{\mathtt{SP}}(4, \mathtt{sp}, [\mathtt{u}, \ldots]) \Rightarrow \mathbf{O}\,\mathtt{state}_{\mathtt{B}}(2, \mathtt{u}, [\mathtt{sp}, \ldots])) \quad (1)$$

stating that, if sp reaches the last protocol step 4 (cf. Fig. 2(b)) believing to talk with u, then sometime in the past u, using the browser B, must have been in the state 2 (cf. Fig. 2(a)), in which she started the protocol speaking with sp. When this is the case, then we say that sp *authenticates* u. Of course, formula (1) must hold even if the attacker knows the credentials of the user or possesses the user's mobile phone. We focused on the first case: a compromised password should not enable an attacker to break in if a two-factor authentication is in place. Thus, we change the initial state of the intruder, assuming that he knows the credentials of the victim. Moreover, we make the assumption that the attacker knows a way to contact the victim user (e.g. email address).

4 Security Analysis

We have mechanically analyzed the formal model of the SCA-basic protocol using SATMC [2], a state-of-the-art model checker for security protocols. SATMC determined that the security property of Sect. 3 is violated and returned the attack depicted in Fig. 3. In the attack, the intruder i initiates a session of the protocol to access a resource provided by sp pretending to be the honest user u. (Indeed, we assume that i knows the credentials of u). At this point sp checks the credentials of u and sends nonce and tas phone number to i (step 4). Then i forwards nonce and tas phone number to u and induces her with social engineering techniques to call tas (e.g. in order to win a prize). The attack completes with the delivery of resource to i. The analysis reveals that u has no information about the SP she is currently placing the call for. The call is used by i to authenticate (or issue a request), on behalf of u, on

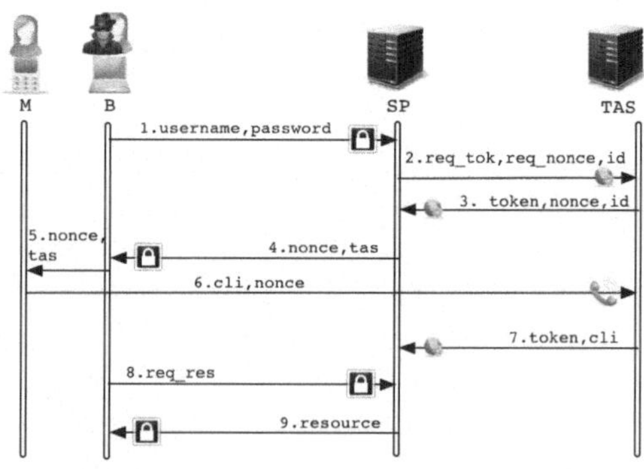

Fig. 3. Attack on the SCA-basic protocol

a service provider (sp) *different* from the one expected by u. The SCA-basic protocol could be improved by making the TAS issue a welcome message during the phone call, stating the purpose of the call (e.g. "Please enter the nonce to authenticate to sp."). An alternative solution is given by the SCA-PIN protocol. It extends the SCA-basic protocol by asking the user to additionally enter a PIN when placing the call to TAS. Then, in step 7, TAS forwards it to SP (together with CLI and Token). Since the PIN is assigned by SP to the user upon registration, the user knows which SP a given PIN corresponds to and therefore she can easily identify fake requests. When the user calls TAS (step 6), she enters the PIN. Notice that the welcome message—including the identity of SP—is not necessary anymore. To perform the attack, the attacker can provide the NONCE to the user, but he cannot provide the PIN. For the attack to work, he should also ask the user to enter the PIN associated with SP. By doing so, the user becomes aware of the SP the phone call is meant for, and this thwarts the attack. The positive aspect of this solution is that no customization of the welcome message is required for TAS. Yet, the usability is reduced and the user is asked to remember and provide the right PIN for each SP.

The two solutions proposed above allow to mitigate the issue. However, SATMC discovered another, subtler attack on the improved versions of the protocol whereby the call placed by the user to authorize an operation on a given SP is used by the attacker to authenticate (or issue a request) on the *same* SP on behalf of the user. The problem lies in the fact that she cannot ascertain (nor specify) for which operation she places the call with her mobile phone on the given SP. For instance, the attacker could send the following message: "Please, provide the pin to tas in order to unlock your access to sp", while his real purpose is to complete the protocol in order to authenticate himself. This shows that the user must be aware not only of the SP the PIN is meant for, but the operation she is performing as well. In Fig. 4 we propose a patched variant of the protocol. It is refined in such a way to provide the expected information to the user during the phone call, using the existing API. We indicate with Op the relevant information about the operation to be executed. This is not only provided to the user as a web page (steps 1 and 4), but it is also communicated during the phone call (step 7). According to the content of the vocal message, the user can choose either to provide the PIN or to abort the process. As expected, SATMC confirms that this variant does not suffer from the attacks reported above in the protocol sessions considered.

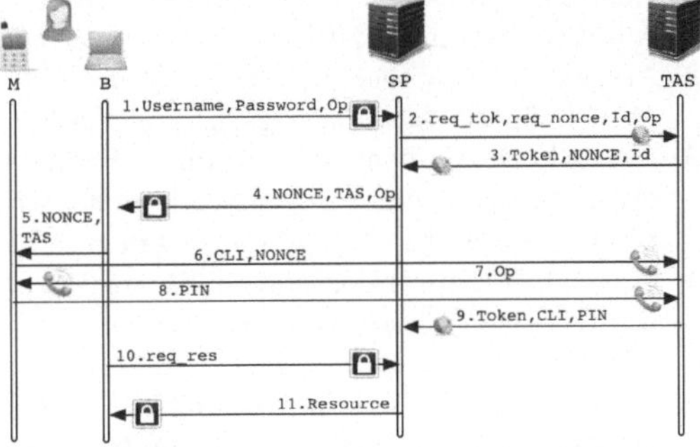

Fig. 4. The SCA-PIN protocol fixed

5 Related Work

The importance of two factor authentication is witnessed by the existence of various surveys. [4] performs an high-level analysis of a number of strong authentication protocols by providing concepts, implementation approaches, and challenges/additional concerns at the architectural level. Moreover it classifies strong authentication protocol in four categories: knowledge-based authentication, server-generated otp, client-generated otp and out-of-band authentication. The SCA-basic and SCA-PIN protocols are variants of out-of-band authentication that, as said by the author, should work to impede common phishing attacks. [5] gives an overview on strong authentication of mobile two-factor authentication. [11] proposes a study of the various ways the mobile phone can be used as an authentication token towards service providers on the Internet. RSA provides some guidelines, e.g. [10]. But all of them do not provide a formal analysis of strong authentication protocols. This is provided in [7], where some phishing attacks are found using the PROSA tool, a simulator implemented in Maude, based on rewriting logic. [7] uses an inference construction approach that attempts to use inference in modal logics to establish required beliefs at the protocol participants. Performing reachability analysis in PROSA [8], as the author remarks, is quite limited. Differently from him, we use an attack construction approach that uses model-checking techniques to search attacks.

6 Conclusions

We have presented the formal modeling and the mechanical analysis of two protocols for strong authentication. We reported vulnerabilities in both protocols and proposed a possible fix. Our finding confirms the difficulty of getting authentication protocols right and provides further evidence of the effectiveness of formal method techniques to support their security analysis.

References

1. AliasLab. SecureCall Authorization - Web Services Interface v3.0. Technical report, AliasLab (February 2010)
2. Armando, A., Carbone, R., Compagna, L.: LTL Model Checking for Security Protocols. In: JANCL, Special Issue on Logic and Information Security. Hermes Lavoisier (2009)
3. Armando, A., Carbone, R., Zanetti, L.: Formal modeling and automatic security analysis of two-factor and two-channel authentication protocols (2013), `http://www.ai-lab.it/armando/pub/nss13-extended.pdf`
4. Chou, D., Microsoft Corporation: Strong user authentication on the web, `http://msdn.microsoft.com/en-us/library/cc838351.aspx` (accessed September 20, 2012)
5. DeFigueiredo, D.: The Case for Mobile Two-Factor Authentication. S&P (2011)
6. Dolev, D., Yao, A.: On the Security of Public-Key Protocols. IEEE Transactions on Information Theory 2(29) (1983)
7. Hagalisletto, A.M.: Analyzing two-factor authentication devices. T.r., U. of Oslo (2007)
8. Hagalisletto, A.M.: Attacks are protocols too. In: ARES, pp. 1197–1206 (2007)
9. Lowe, G.: A hierarchy of authentication specifications. In: Proc. CSFW. IEEE (1997)
10. RSA. Enhancing one-time passwords for protection against real-time phishing attacks, `www.rsasecurity.com` (accessed September 20, 2012)
11. van Thanh, D., Jorstad, I., Jonvik, T., van Thuan, D.: Strong authentication with mobile phone as security token. In: MASS 2009, pp. 777–782 (October 2009)

Towards a More Secure Apache Hadoop HDFS Infrastructure

Anatomy of a Targeted Advanced Persistent Threat against HDFS and Analysis of Trusted Computing Based Countermeasures

Jason Cohen[1] and Subatra Acharya[2]

[1] Towson University/Hewlett Packard, Computer and Information Sciences, Towson, MD USA
[2] Towson University, Department of Computer and Information Sciences, Towson, MD USA
Jason.C.Cohen@hp.com, sacharya@towson.edu

Abstract. Apache Hadoop and the Hadoop Distributed File System (HDFS) have become important tools for organizations dealing with "Big Data" storage and analytics. Hadoop has the potential to offer powerful and cost effective solutions to Big Data analytics; however, sensitive data stored within an HDFS infrastructure has equal potential to be an attractive target for exfiltration, corruption, unauthorized access, and modification. As a follow-up to the authors' previous work in the area of improving security of HDFS via the use of Trusted Computing technology, this paper will describe the threat against Hadoop in a sensitive environment, describe how and why an Advanced Persistent Threat (APT) could target Hadoop, and how standards-based trusted computing could be an effective approach to a layered threat mitigation.

Keywords: Hadoop, HDFS, APT, Trusted Computing, Security.

1 Introduction and Motivation

Why talk about Advanced Persistent Threats (APT) in the context of Apache Hadoop? "Big Data" has become a hot topic in the enterprise space within recent years, perhaps even rivaling the popularity of "cloud" in the buzzword count within popular trade literature. But what does "Big Data" mean, and what are the implications to an organization's security posture when using popular platforms to store and process this data? "Big Data" is a singular term to describe an array of possible scenarios, meaning different things to different organizations. In the general case, it is being able to store and reason about large quantities of both structured and unstructured data. For instance, in the world of a search giant like Google, this means generating near instant responses to search queries from an enormous amount of raw data from an enormous quantity of web pages. What projects like Apache Hadoop have done is to bring this capability to the masses through non-proprietary, open-source software that can scale to fit practically any organization's needs in any business space. Advanced Persistent Threats (APTs) has become another popular buzzword emerging from the realm of information security into the vernacular, but what does this mean and how is it any

J. Lopez, X. Huang, and R. Sandhu (Eds.): NSS 2013, LNCS 7873, pp. 735–741, 2013.

different from any other threat? Typical defenses techniques are generally good enough to block the casual attack coming from script kiddies and known worms/viruses. Unfortunately, unknown vulnerabilities, insider threats, end user carelessness, and a persistent attacker represent difficult problems in network defense. APTs methodically attempt to exploit possible entry points in a patient manner with advanced techniques. The RSA SecurID breach of 2011 and Stuxnet (2010) are recent examples. Most literature associates APTs with Nation State or organized crime however, so called 'hacktivist' groups and other determined entities or individuals have the potential to become APTs.

For some organizations, the HDFS infrastructure becomes a catch-all for data that has an indeterminate purpose. Given the wide range of applications, it is not particularly hard to imagine that sensitive data could be contained within a HDFS infrastructure, making it a ripe place for an APT to target for long term exploitation. Depending on the business of the organization, this could have the potential to be a treasure trove of information that a potential adversary could become acutely interested in. A recent Forbes article estimates that the Big Data Industry is at about $5 billion in factory revenue, with projections to increase to $55 billion by 2017. The old adage of "follow the money" applies to cyber targeting. If the organization can gain financial benefit from the data stored within HDFS, someone else may be able to as well.

Trusted Computing, in the context of the Trusted Computing Group (TCG) standards, refers to a set of technology standards aimed at increasing the trustworthiness of computer systems through the use of hardware rooted trust. At the core of the TCG solution stack lays the Trusted Platform Module (TPM), an inexpensive cryptographic chip that is present in a number of commodity class PCs, servers, and other devices [1]. It is a cryptographic component which can enable a level of trust in the state of a system, as well as provide mechanisms to verify this state and enable higher-level functions such as key generation and secure storage. By applying this technology to an application specific problem, we can demonstrate some possible mitigations against APTs directed at an Apache Hadoop environment.

2 Anatomy of an APT against HDFS

The Security model of Hadoop makes assumptions assumptions made about the state of the networks that may not be realistic: "The security features in CDH4 meet the needs of most Hadoop customers because typically the cluster is accessible only to trusted personnel. In particular, Hadoop's current threat model assumes that users cannot: 1. Have root access to cluster machines. 2. Have root access to shared client machines. 3. Read or modify packets on the network of the cluster. " [2] In addition, there is no support for data at rest encryption. Until the most recent releases, encryption of data on the wire was not supported [2]. These limitations leave Hadoop vulnerable to a number of attack scenarios, even in a situation where the assumptions of the threat model are applied.

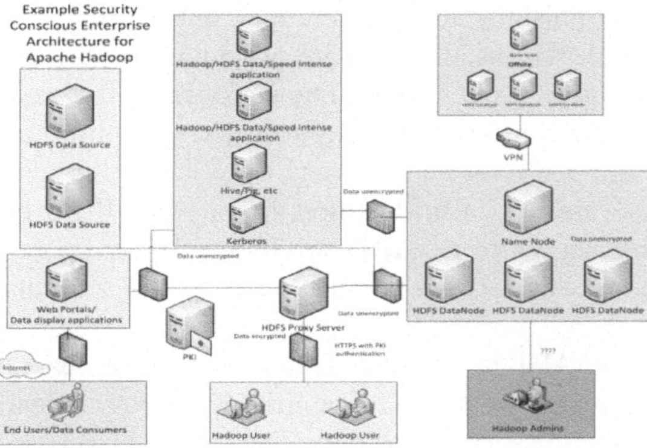

Fig. 1. An example of a Security Conscious Enterprise Architecture for Hadoop

The diagram above illustrates example Hadoop enterprise architecture in an organization that has taken reasonable security precautions to protect the sensitive elements of the infrastructure. The core idea in this design is to isolate the HDFS data sources in a layered approach. In this way, Hadoop users and applications utilizing Hadoop are connected to the data through firewalls and an HDFS proxy server. Along with other security best practices (OS patching, intrusion detection, malware scanners, etc) and proper configuration, this would be considered a reasonably secure implementation, and the data can be considered safe under most scenarios. This is the type of environment which Hadoop, even with security settings enabled, is designed to operate. Owen O'Malley, one of the chief contributors of the Hadoop security design and Hadoop in general stated "the motivation for adding security to Apache Hadoop actually had little to do with traditional notions of security in defending against hackers since all large Hadoop clusters are behind corporate firewalls that only allow employees access" [3] . However, an attacker specifically targeting this environment, given the right opportunities, could gain unauthorized access to HDFS.

APTs can be thought of as a seven step exploitation life cycle that includes reconnaissance, initial intrusion, establishment of a backdoor, credential acquisition, utility installation, privilege escalation/lateral movement/data exfiltration, and persistence maintenance [4]. An outside attacker looking to access HDFS data in our example needs to make initial inroads into the corporate network. First, he can look for a traditional entry point in front-facing services. The web portal application shown would be a first target, where he would use a traditional vulnerability scanner to find any open ports (management interfaces such as RDP/SSH) or exploitable services, or attempt to exploit known issues (or a zero- day exploit) that could be used to get a remote shell. If he is able to gain access to the web server with a remote shell, he can use this as a starting point into the network. From the portal, he could manipulate the application code to pull data from HDFS, or he will move on to compromise the HDFS proxy server. If there is no exploit available to do this, he will target user credentials, perhaps from an admin that accesses the web server. If he failed to gain access through the front facing services, he will move on to a social engineering attack. The attacker will target a particular individual (preferably someone with potential administrative access) with a spear-phishing attack where they will either disclose credentials or are directed to a website that installs malware providing a backdoor. He may be able to use a zero-day exploit to avoid detection by anti-virus software and network filters. In our diagram, we show Hadoop Administrators that have direct access to the protected HDFS infrastructure. An ideal scenario may be to infect this administrator's computer with malware, and use it as a bridge directly into the HDFS infrastructure via their administrative channel. Once in, APTs are known to set up easy-to-find back doors along with hidden, giving security administrators a false sense that they have solved a problem [4].

At this point, the APT has several options to gain access to the HDFS data. A straightforward approach would be to gain the Kerberos credentials for a service account or individual with access to the data. The issue with this approach is that, unless the attacker finds an account with super-user access to all files, he will be limited by the HDFS security to the set of files that they have access. Compromising the various Hadoop applications shown would have a similar effect. The attacker could monitor and exfiltration data which the applications have access to. If HDFS traffic is in the clear, the attacker could do this by simply monitoring the network traffic. Compromising the HDFS proxy would be a more ideal target, and could give the attacker a better access to the full contents of HDFS. Using open channels through the firewalls protecting the core HDFS services by either exploiting the network applications or via an administrative channel would allow the attacker to directly manipulate the HDFS environment. The symmetric encryption key used in token protection is distributed to each node and stored on the file system [5]. Accessing this key would allow further compromise by creating of delegation tokens to access restricted files. Likewise, with physical access to the DataNodes, the unencrypted blocks could be exfiltrated or modified. For long term persistence, without requiring continued physical presence, an attacker could craft a replacement HDFS software package that relayed data streams to another location as they are created or accessed. An attack like this would more fit the profile of an APT rather than a get the data and run effort.

3 Mitigations Based on Trusted Computing and Limitations

In our previously published work, we described various ways that Trusted Computing concepts could be used to enhance the confidentiality and integrity of data within a Hadoop HDFS infrastructure [6]. In the following, we will discuss how these integrations could help defend against the APT which we described. In addition, we describe our current efforts into integrating data block level encryption utilizing the TPM into the Hadoop source.

With the goal of establishing trustworthiness of the base operating system, we created a Hadoop environment where each node of the Hadoop Cluster creates a chain of trust using the TPM and Open Source components to take measurements of key components of the operating system and associated sensitive files. Specifically, each node will implement TrustedGrub to verify key files and extend platform control registers with platform integrity information. Each node implements file level integrity measurements protected by hardware trust, specifically, implementation of the Linux Integrity Subsystem (IMA) and Extended Validation Module (EVM), also augmenting the post-boot measurements of TrustedGrub. The idea of these boilerplate TCG approaches is to give insight into the integrity of the system at boot time. By using a boot loader which measures key operating system files and extends the platform control registers, a decision can be made whether to unlock critical files (such as configuration files, key files, etc.) that are needed for Hadoop. Also, measuring the Hadoop software can be one of these measurements, indicating whether this software was altered. In addition, IMA/EVM provides an access log and PCR value for all files that are part of the Trusted Computing Base (which is essentially all files opened by root) [7]. Under normal operational circumstances, this PCR value should be consistent, and checking this value would give insight into possible compromise. In the APT scenario where an attacker gained access to a Hadoop node directly, he could eventually be detected if the IMA PCR value is checked. Should the attacker modify OS files, Hadoop configuration files, or Hadoop software, this would be detected as well, either through IMA or during the next boot. After the node boots, a remote validation server will confirm the state of each node in the Hadoop cluster via a remote attestation protocol. Specifically, this will be an implementation of an Open Platform Trust Services Collector on each node and a central Verifier. Each node will attest to its status using a secure protocol. In our APT scenario, this protection measure will give insight into the state of the platform, and hence aid in detection of compromise. If the TCB IMA PCR is checked as part of this, then a runtime compromise can be detected, otherwise, the checked values are only valid when they are created at system boot. The trusted computing components can also aid in protecting the block and metadata of HDFS, although carte blanche block encryption in software will likely slow down performance beyond the 3% overhead that the Hadoop Security Design specifies [3]. Unfortunately, if we are relying on known PCR values and a TPM protected key to unlock a loop-back encrypted partition containing HDFS checksums or data block files, these files would be accessible to the attacker who compromised the system after the encrypted partition was opened.

Taking the use of trusted computing concepts into the software layer can offer some additional interesting options in limiting the attack surface. Although there are several ways in which the cryptographic engine could potentially be used, we will focus on an obvious use case of implementing block encryption on DataNodes, utilizing jTSS to provide a Java based interface to the TPM. Ultimately, this encryption concept would be user defined, such that a decision could be made on a case-by-case basis of security versus performance. For our initial implementation, we wanted to keep the integration as simple as possible, as there are a number of optimizations, error correction, and redundancy operation's going on within HDFS that we left out of the encryption picture. The diagram below shows a simplified HDFS dataflow, where a Client accesses the NameNode for metadata operations for the virtual file system (such as file location within the DataNodes) and the DataNodes handle storage and retrieval of the blocks from the actual file system on the node. The HDFS code is abstracted such that higher level operations involving blocks are abstracted from code that actually reads or writes the bytes from disk.

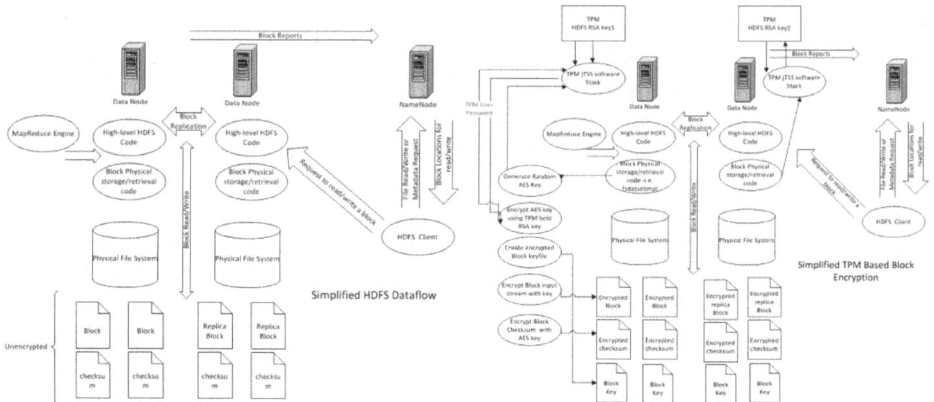

Fig. 2. Simplified HDFS Dataflow/Simplified TPM Based Block Encryption

To implement an encryption layer that would not require modification of the higher-level code logic, we implemented a solution where each data block would be individually encrypted and decrypted as the request comes in to store or read the block. In this scenario, each DataNode has an RSA key stored within the TPM which we are calling the HDFS key. This could be a migratable key that is shared between the nodes (a solution that would be more efficient for block replication), or, as in our initial solution, a different key in each node. This solution has the potential to limit a cascade compromise should the key be compromised. The core of this concept is the generation of a random AES key. The TPM's random number generator is used to enhance the randomness of this key over the Java based generator. This random AES key is then used to encrypt the block (typically configured to be 64-128MB in size) and the checksum file. The AES key is then encrypted using the TPM stored key and stored in a block key file associated with the block id. If the block is requested, the key is unwrapped and the file decrypted into the output stream. In this way, the block is only encrypted while on the disk. In our attack scenario, encrypting the blocks in this fashion present an attacker with physical access to the system the inability to directly access block files. In order to access the blocks, he would need to manipulate the HDFS software to extract the files for him. He would also be able to see the blocks as they are decrypted if he is able to monitor memory buffers. The other issue is protection of the TPM key. Although the RSA key itself is protected, an attacker with root access could simply ask the TPM to decode the block key file, giving access to the AES key. The TPM can be configured with a user password, otherwise it uses the "well known secret". If a user password is used, it needs to come from somewhere. We simply built this hash into the code for now, but ideally, the password would come via a remote server once the platform passes an attestation procedure. It would be delivered over an encrypted tunnel as a hash and only stored in memory. In this case, the attacker would have to find the password in memory, again adding to the skill and time needed to compromise the files.

4 Conclusions and Future Work

Future work will consist of further examination of the performance consequences of using Trusted Computing within a Hadoop architecture and further examination of software integration. Our current implementation is a proof of concept, and requires refinement, and integration into the client application, allowing for the goal of selectable encryption. Also, a purposeful attestation environment which would integrate into an overall portal to determine the state of the cluster would be desirable. Further, protection of the TPM authorization data needs to be explored in a more holistic fashion.

The prevalence of the Advanced Persistent Threat should give security organizations pause, and reason to evaluate solutions to make this style of attack more difficult to conduct. Along with providing sufficient boundaries, layers of security, and proactive monitoring and actions, implementing trusted computing concepts and utilizing these proven technologies can be an additional step to help protect sensitive resources.

References

1. Trusted Computing Group. TCG Specification Architecture Overview V. 1.4. Trusted Computing Group (August 2, 2007), http://www.trustedcomputinggroup.org/files/resource_files/AC652DE1-1D09-3519-ADA026A0C05CFAC2/TCG_1_4_Architecture_Overview.pdf (cited: June 15, 2012)
2. Cloudera. Cloudera CDH4 Security Guide, https://ccp.cloudera.com/download/attachments/21438266/CDH4_Security_Guide_4.1.pdf?version=3&modificationDate=1349900837000 (cited: November 23, 2012)
3. O'Malley, O.: Motivations for Hadoop Security (August 2011), http://hortonworks.com/blog/motivations-for-apache-hadoop-security/ (cited: December 04, 2012)
4. Mandiant corporporation. Mandiant M-Trends (2010), http://www.princeton.edu/~yctwo/files/readings/M-Trends.pdf (cited: November 1, 2012)
5. Becherer, A.: Hadoop Security Design: Just add Kerberos? Really? iSEC Partners, Inc., s.l. (2010)
6. Cohen, J.C., Subatra, A.: Incorporating hardware trust mechanisms in Apache Hadoop. IEEE, s.l. (2012), 978-1-4673-4942-0
7. Linx IMA Wiki. Sourceforge IMA Project (May 18, 2012), http://sourceforge.net/apps/mediawiki/linux-ima/index.php?title=Main_Page (cited: June 15, 2012)

A Formally Verified Initial Authentication and Key Agreement Protocol in Heterogeneous Environments Using Casper/FDR

Mahdi Aiash

School of Science and Technology, Middlesex University, London, UK
M.Aiash@mdx.ac.uk

Abstract. Future mobile networking will involve the convergence of different wireless networks such as 2G, 3G, WiMax and Long Term Evolution. The wide scale deployment of such heterogeneous networks will precipitate a radical change in the network infrastructure, where currently closed systems such as 3G will have to operate in an open environment. This brings to the fore certain security issues which must be addressed, the most important of which is the initial Authentication and Key Agreement to identify and authorize mobile nodes on these various networks. This paper proposes a new security protocol to authenticate the mobile terminal in heterogeneous networks.

Keywords: Authentication and Key Agreement Protocols, Casper/FDR, Heterogeneous Networks.

1 Introduction

Unlike current communication systems such as 2G and 3G [1] which introduce closed environments where the core network is controlled and owned by sole network operators and thus its security is mainly based on the assumption that, the core network is physically secure,the above discussion highlights the fact that we are moving towards an open, heterogeneous environment where the core network is not controlled by a single operator, so multiple operators will have to cooperate. This new open architecture, will bring about new security threats such as initially authenticating the mobile nodes in this open environment. This paper proposes a novel Authentication and Key Agreement (AKA) protocol that considers the open nature of heterogeneous networks.

The rest of this paper is organized as follows: Section 2 describes the open architecture of the future, heterogeneous networks as introduced in [2]. Section 3 presents the new proposed protocol. The paper concludes in Section 4.

2 Overview of Future Networks

In Next Generation Networks, multiple operators have to cooperate in order to provide continuous connectivity. However, since each network operator uses a

J. Lopez, X. Huang, and R. Sandhu (Eds.): NSS 2013, LNCS 7873, pp. 742–748, 2013.

different network architecture, interoperability might be a key challenge. One proposed solution for this problem is having a central management entity, called Core-End Point (CEP) to control the resource of the different networks and co-ordinate the multiple operators [3] [2] [4]. As shown in Fig 1, this future Internet

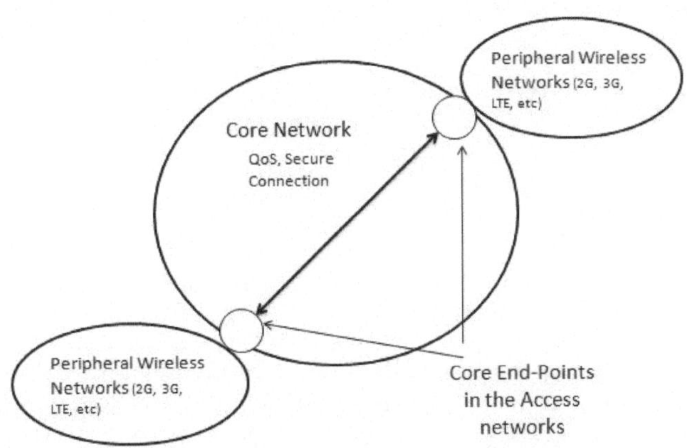

Fig. 1. The Future Internet Architecture

could be viewed as composed of several Core End-Points, interconnected over the super fast backbone of the Internet. Each CEP is responsible for managing multiple, wireless peripheral networks such as Wimax, WiFi or mobile technologies in a local context. A detailed view of the the Core End-Point's structure along with the attached networks is shown in Fig 2. The figure shows a hierarchical architecture, where the bottom level is represented by several Access Points (APs) and Access Routers (ARs), that communicate with the wireless interfaces in the mobile terminals. The middle level comprises a number of technology-specific domains, where each domain represents a certain network operator and technology such as 2G, 3G and Wi-Fi. For these domains to interoperate, the Core End-Point, which is residing at the top level acts as a central administrative domain to control the inter-domain functions and provide overall management. In order to deal with the QoS and security tasks in this architecture, a number of operational entities have been proposed as follows: The Central A3C server (CA3C), the Central QoS Broker (CQoSB), the Domain A3C Server (DA3C), the Domain QoS Broker (DQoSB), the Access Router (AR). These entities co-operate to provide security and QoS-related tasks as described in [2].

2.1 Verifying Security Protocols Using Formal Methods and Casper/FDR Tool

Previously, analysing security protocols used to go through two stages. Firstly, modelling the protocol using a theoretical notation or language such as Communication Sequential Processes (CSP) [6]. Secondly, verifying the protocol using

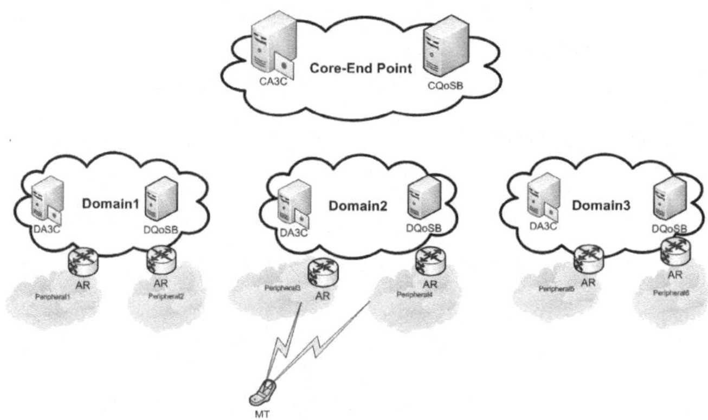

Fig. 2. The Network Structure

a model checker such as Failures-Divergence Refinement (FDR) [7]. However, describing a system or a protocol using CSP is a quite difficult and error-prone task; therefore, Gavin Lowe [5] has developed the CASPER/FDR tool to model security protocols, it accepts a simple and human-friendly input file that describes the system and compiles it into CSP code which is then checked using the FDR model checker. The proposed protocol in this paper has been verified using the Casper/FDR tool.

3 The Proposed Solution

In order to address the security threats in NGNs and to provide a better security in the core network, our proposed solution presumes the existence of secure connection between all the network entities (Auth, DA3C, CA3C) in the core network.

3.1 The Key Hierarchy

As shown in Fig 3, the security materials comprise a top level Unique Key uk(MT), which is pre-shared between the MT and the CA3C server. Similar to the (Ki) key in GSM [1] , the uk(MT) is stored into the MT's SIM card and is never used for encryption purposes rather, it is only used for deriving further security keys. The second level key is the Domain Specific Master Key (DSMS), as the name implies, this key is unique at the domain level and is derived using an irreversible function F1 as follows: DSMS=F1(uk(MT), seq1, Auth_Domain_Name), where seq1 is a fresh sequence number, the Auth_Domain _Name is the corresponding domain name. Since each domain might have more than one Authenticator, the MT could join the domain via any of its Auths, thus, a different Secret Key (SK) has to be used for each Authenticator. One Authentication Key (AK) is used for mutual authentication between the MT and the network. Similar to F1, two irreversible function F2 and F3 are used to derive AK and SK as follows: AK = F2 (seq1, DSMS), SK = F3(seq1, AuthID, DSMS). Where AuthID is the ID of the Auth and is broadcasted by the Auth in the form of AuthID@DomainName. Defining the Key Derivation Function (KDF) used by F1-F3 functions is beyond the scope of this paper.

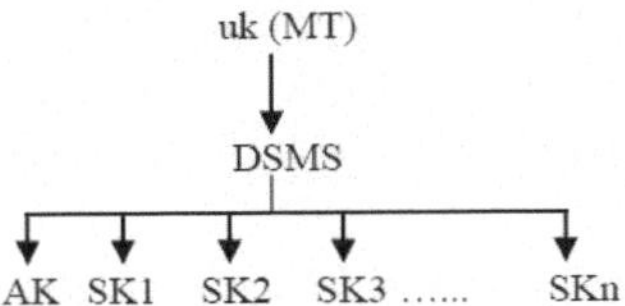

Fig. 3. The Key Hierarchy

Table 1. Notation

The Notation	Description
MT	The Mobile Terminal
Auth	Is the Access Router in the peripheral network
AuthID	The Authenticator unique ID has the format AuthID@domainname
CA3C	Core-endpoint entity, which has QoS and Security related responsibilities
se1(DA3C)	Pre-shared secret key between the CA3C and the DA3C
se2(Auth)	Pre-shared secret key between the DA3C and the Authenticator (Auth)
uk(MT)	Unique secret key shared between the CA3C and the MT
DSMS	Domain specific- Master Key DSMS= F1 (uk(MT), seq1, Auth-domain name)
AK	Authentication key AK= F2 (seq1, DSMS)
SK	Secret Key SK = F3 (Seq1, AuthID, DSMS), used to encrypt all the messages between the MT and the network
F1, F2, F3	Irreversible Key Derivation Functions
InitAuth flag	A flag set only in the initial authentication. In case of handover, this flag will not be set
HoAckm	Joining/Handover Acknowledgement message used by the DA3C server to inform the CA3C in the CEP about a successful authentication
seq1, seq2	Sequence numbers
{m}{K}	Encrypting the message (m) using the key (K)

3.2 The Security Protocol

To secure the core network, we propose the presence of a certain trust relationship between the network's entities and thus secure channels have already been established between the CA3C, the DA3Cs and between the DA3Cs, the Auths. Such secure channels could be guaranteed by using different mechanisms such as IP security (IPSec)or any other Virtual Private Network (VPN) protocols. Alternatively, this could be achieved using out-of-band approach such as agreeing on security materials among the multiple operators.

By considering the notation in Table 1, the AKA protocol is explained as follows:

After starting the mobile device, the MT picks the access routers' advertisements (Adv) which contain information about the access network such the AuthID and the domain name. The MT uses this information to generate a Domain-Specific Master Key (DSMS).

Phase 1
Msg 1: Auth → MT: Adv
Generate the DSMS= F1(uk(MT), seq1, AuthID)

The protocol starts when the MT sends a joining message Msg 2 to the Auth. The Auth responds by sending authentication request AuthReq as Msg 3.

Phase 2
Msg 2. MT → Auth: AccReq
Msg 3. Auth → MT: AuthReq

By using the DSMS, the MT derives the Authentication Key (AK) and composes Msg 4, this message consists of a fresh sequence number seq1 used as a challenge, Authentication ID (AuthID); the Mobile terminal identity (MT) , and a set Initauth flag (InitAuth=1). The Auth passes this message to the DA3C and from there to the CA3C as Msg 5 and Msg 6. Using the included mobile ID, the CA3C looks up the corresponding uk(MT) and uses it to generate a fresh Domain Specific Master key DSMS.

Phase 3
Generate the AK = F2(seq1, DSMS)
Msg 4. MT → Auth: MT, seq1, AuthID, Initauth
Msg 5. Auth → DA3C: {MT, seq1, AuthID, Initauth}{se2(Auth)}
Msg 6. DA3C → CA3C: {MT, seq1, AuthID, Initauth}{se1(DA3C)}
Generate the DSMS= F1(uk(MT), seq1, AuthID)

The DSMS key is included in Msg 7. Using the information in this message, the DA3C generates the Authentication Key (AK) and returns the previously sent sequence Seq1 and a new sequence number Seq2 all the way to the MT as Msg 8 and Msg 9. These messages are encrypted using the derived AK. Since the MT has the required information to derive all the keys (DSMS, SK, AK), the MT verifies the contents of Msg 9 and derives the Secret Key SK.

Phase 4
Msg 7. CA3C → DA3C: {DSMS, seq1, AuthID, MT, Initauth}{se1(DA3C)}
Generate the AK = F2(seq1, DSMS)
Msg 8. DA3C → Auth: {{seq1, seq2}{AK}}{se2(Auth)}
Msg 9. Auth → MT:{seq1,seq2}{AK}
Verify the message contents, then derive the SK:= F3(seq1, DSMS, AuthID)
The MT returns Seq2 all the way to the DA3C as Msg 10 and Msg 11. The DA3C verifies the contents of Msg 11 and derives the Secret Key SK.

Phase 5
Msg 10 . MT → Auth:{seq2}{AK}
Msg 11. Auth → DA3C :{{seq2}{AK}}{se2(Auth)}
Verify the message contents, then derive the SK:= F3(seq1, DSMS, AuthID)
Upon verifying the Msg 11, the DA3C authenticates the MT and acknowledges this to the CA3C, and then generates the Secret Key (SK) and passes it to the Auth in Msgs12, 13. Using the SK, the Auth sends an encrypted access response message to the MT as Msg 14.
Phase 6
Msg 12. DA3C → CA3C:{HoAckm}{se1(DA3C)}
Msg 13. DA3C → Auth:{SK}{se2(Auth)}
Msg 14. Auth → MT:{AccRes}{SK}

Formal Verification: A Casper input file describing the protocol was prepared. For conciseness, only the #Specification and the #Intruder Information headings are mentioned here. The security requirements of the system are defined under the # Specification heading. The lines starting with the keyword Secret define the secrecy properties of the protocol. The lines starting with Agreement and WeakAgreement define the protocol's authenticity properties.

 # Specification
```
Secret(MT,AK,[DA3C])
Secret(DA3C,AK,[MT])
Secret(MT,SK,[DA3C, Auth])
Agreement( MT, DA3C, [seq2])
Agreement(DA3C, MT, [AK])
WeakAgreement(MT, Auth)
WeakAgreement(Auth,MT)
WeakAgreement(Auth, DA3C)
WeakAgreement(DA3C, Auth)
```

The # Intruder Information heading specifies the Intruder identity, knowledge and capability. The first line identifies the Intruder as Mallory, the Intruder knowledge defines the Intruder's initial knowledge, i.e., we assume the Intruder knows the identity of the participants and can intercept and replay all the exchanged messages.

 # Intruder Information
```
Intruder = Mallory
IntruderKnowledge = {mt, da3c, Mallory, ca3c, Authid, auth,
uk(Mallory)}
```
After simulating the protocol, Casper/FDR found no attacks

4 Conclusion

This paper investigates the security issue in heterogeneous networks. In particular, it tries to address the issue of authenticating mobile nodes when initially joining the network. Therefore, a new AKA protocol has been proposed, the protocol is formally verified using formal methods approach based on the Casper/FDR tool.

References

1. Jochen, S.: Mobile Communications. Addison Wesley (2003)
2. Aiash, M., Mapp, G., Lasebae, A.: A QoS framework for Heterogeneous Networking. In: ICWN 2011 (2011)
3. International Telecommunication Union (ITU-T), Global Information Infrastructure, Internet Protocol Aspects and Next Generation Networks, Y.140.1 (2004)
4. Almeida, M., Corujo, D., Sargento, S., Jesus, V., Aguiar, R.: An End-to-End QoS Framework for 4G Mobile Heterogeneous Environments. In: OpenNet Workshop (2007)
5. Lowe, G., Broadfoot, P., Dilloway, C., Hui, M.: Casper, A compiler for the Analysis of security protocol, http://www.comlab.ox.ac.uk/gavin.lowe/Security/Casper/ (accessed January 1, 2013)
6. Ryan, P., Schneider, S., Goldsmith, M., Lowe, G., Roscoe, A.W.: The modelling and analysis of security protocols. Pearson Ltd. (2010)
7. Formal Systems (Europe) Ltd.: Failures-Divergence Refinement. FDR2 User Manual, http://www.fsel.com/documentation/fdr2/fdr2manual.pdf (accessed January 1, 2013)

A Comprehensive Access Control System for Scientific Applications

Muhammad I. Sarfraz, Peter Baker, Jia Xu, and Elisa Bertino

Purdue University, West Lafayette, Indiana 47906, USA
{msarfraz,pnbaker,xu222,bertino}@purdue.edu

Abstract. Web based scientific applications have provided a means to share scientific data across diverse groups and disciplines extending beyond the local computing environment. But the organization and sharing of large and heterogeneous data pose challenges due to their sensitive nature. In this paper we analyze the security requirements of scientific applications and present an authorization model that facilitates the organization and sharing of data without compromising the security of data.

Keywords: Access Control, Scientific Applications.

1 Introduction

Web based scientific applications provide an infrastructure that allows scientists and researchers to run scientific computations, data analysis and visualization through their web browsers. Moreover, such applications also provide a collaborative environment in which scientists and researchers can work together by sharing their tools and datasets. But the organization and sharing of large and heterogeneous data pose challenges due to their sensitive nature where data needs to be protected from unauthorized usage. An inadequate or unreliable authorization mechanism can significantly increase the risk of unauthorized use of scientific data. For this purpose, we present an access control system for scientific applications. We formulate a methodology that incorporates principles from security management and software engineering. From a security management perspective, the goal is to meet the requirements for access management in scientific applications. From a software engineering perspective, the goal is to incorporate the well-known principles of software engineering in the access control model design to yield a specification that allows authorizations to be developed and managed in a standardized manner.

The remainder of this paper is organized as follows: Section 2 describes the data model while Section 3 discusses the authorization requirements for scientific applications. In Section 4, we present the authorization model based on the requirements in Section 3. Section 5 discusses the key components of the access control system of Computational Research Infrastructure for Science (CRIS), a web-based scientific application. The related work is presented in Section 6 and Section 7 concludes the paper.

J. Lopez, X. Huang, and R. Sandhu (Eds.): NSS 2013, LNCS 7873, pp. 749–755, 2013.

2 Data Model

A model of authorization must be designed to be consistent with the objects being supported in a scientific application. This section describes the key concepts that characterize the various objects in the scientific domain and their impact on the design of an authorization model. ***Object Hierarchy:*** Data object hierarchies are a common approach to organize large amounts of data by exploiting relationships among the various data objects. An object hierarchy is represented as a tree structure. From access control perspective, the hierarchical organization of data objects should effectively reduce the total number of permission assignments, thus reducing the cost of permission administration. ***Datasets and Versions:*** Most of the large scientific datasets are assembled from samples collected over time and are versioned for the purpose of long-term preservation and re-use of primary research data. From access control perspective, authorizations must be specified on a versioned dataset and on individual versions of the dataset. ***Scientific Workflows:*** A key impediment for scientists is how to automate their manual repetitive scientific tasks. Workflows have emerged as an alternative to ad hoc approaches for constructing computational scientific experiments . From access control perspective, authorizations on workflows can be specified at two different granularities: (1) access is granted/denied on an individual workflow (2) access is denied/granted on an individual task within a workflow. We have adopted the latter as the default and support the first as user option. ***Computational Tools:*** Most of the research activities in Web based scientific applications have focused on the development of new computational tools to support scientific discovery. Since computational tools access large amounts of data, an important implication from access control perspective is to prevent unauthorized access to a dataset when invoked as part of the execution of the tool.

3 Authorization Requirements

This section highlights the security management issues that impact the design of an authorization model for scientific applications. In what follows, we assume a general notion of authorization by which an authorization is defined in terms of a subject, a permission, an object, an object owner and an object class.

Implicit Authorization. An inefficient way to implement an authorization mechanism is to explicitly store all authorizations for all system subjects desiring access and all system objects whose access has been requested. In contrast, the concept of implicit authorizations makes it unnecessary to store all authorizations explicitly.The idea behind implicit authorization is that a permission of certain type defined for a subject on a certain object implies other authorizations i.e. authorizations can be automatically propagated. Hence the authorization mechanism can compute authorizations from a minimal set of explicitly stored authorizations in order to prevent unauthorized access. Furthermore, in order to allow exceptions to an authorization, an authorization is distinguished as positive or negative authorization. A positive authorization is a granting authorization and a negative authorization is an explicit denial of an authorization.

Dataset Security. Scientific applications allow a user to develop a computational tool and then grant the run authorization on this tool to other users. An important question is whether the authorization to directly access a dataset d must be checked when d is invoked as part of the execution of the tool. There can be two approaches: In the case of first approach, all accesses made during the execution of the tool are further checked as necessary against the same user who invoked the tool. Thus a user must possess all authorizations on datasets accessed by the tool and therefore authorization controls embedded in the tool would be easily by-passed. While this can be fine in some situations, the second approach is exactly the opposite of what should be done as a means to protect data. In this case, a user having the authorization to execute a tool should not have any authorization to directly read or modify the dataset accessed by the tool. When the tool is executed, all datasets which are not granted to the tool, their permission will be checked against the user executing the tool. Note that only an owner may grant execution authorizations on a dataset.

Sandbox Search. Sandbox Search functionality allows a user to search whether certain data exists but this does not imply the right to see the actual data. The user must have permission to access data in order to retrieve the actual data. A question can be why forbid a user from searching when data cannot be accessed if the user does not have the permission on the data. This is due to two reasons: (1) users performing these queries will consume a lot of resources (2) in some cases one may not want to allow a browsing query to report the existence of their data as it may reveal information intended to be hidden.

Temporal Constraints. In many situations, permissions have a temporal dimension in that they are usually limited in time or may hold for specific periods of time. Therefore temporal constraints surrounding an access request must be evaluated to grant/deny access to objects. Each authorization has a time interval associated with it, representing the set of time instants for which the authorization is granted.

Conflict Resolution. Authorization rules must be specified correctly to ensure that authorized access is allowed while unauthorized access is denied. Identifying and resolving a conflict before it results in the denial of a legitimate access request is essential to improving the usability of any access control system.

4 Authorization Model Design

In this section, we present a general authorization model for scientific applications by formalizing the authorization requirements mentioned in Section 3. The authorization model is extension of the earlier work by Rabitti et al. [4].

Basic Definition An authorization is defined as (s, o, p, s', c) where: $s \in S$, the set of subjects; $o \in O$, the set of objects; $p \in P$, the set of permission; $s' \in$ owner$(o) \subseteq S$; $c \in C$, the set of class of objects. A function f is defined to determine if an authorization (s, o, p, s', c) is True or False;

$$f : S \times O \times P \times S \times C \rightarrow \text{(True,False)}$$

Definition 1. *A positive authorization is a tuple (s, o, p, s', c) with $s \in S$, $o \in O$, $p \in P$, $s' \in S$ and $c \in C$. A negative authorization is a tuple $(s, o, \neg p, s', c)$ with $s \in S$, $o \in O$, $p \in P$, $s' \in S$ and $c \in C$.*

Definition 2. *An authorization base (AB) is a set of explicit authorizations (s, o, p, s', c) with $s \in S$, $o \in O$, $p \in P$, $s' \in S$ and $c \in C$ where p positive or negative; that is,*

$$AB \subseteq S \times O \times P \times S \times C$$

The model in [4] is extended to include the owner of the object and class of the object as part of the authorization tuple. It is imperative for the purpose of *Dataset Security* mentioned in Section 3 to determine that the privilege being granted to a subject s on an object o is by the owner of o. The inclusion of object class is essentially to differentiate between the type of objects since all authorizations are being stored in one base, namely AB.

Implicit Authorization. An explicitly specified authorization may imply authorizations along any combination of two dimensions in authorization definitions, namely, the subject, and object. The function $\imath(s, o, p, s', c)$ computes True or False of an authorization (s, o, p, s', c) from the explicit authorization in AB if either the authorization (s, o, p, s', c) or $(s, o, \neg p, s', c)$ can be deduced from some $(s_1, o_1, p_1, s'_1, c_1)$.

Definition 3. *Function $\imath(s, o, p, s', c)$ is defined as*

$$\imath; S \times O \times P \times S \times C \rightarrow \textit{(True,False)}$$

If $(s, o, p, s', c) \in AB$, then $\imath(s, o, p, s', c) =$ True; else, if $(s_1, o_1, p_1, s'_1, c_1) \in AB$ such that $(s_1, o_1, p_1, s'_1, c_1) \rightarrow (s, o, p, s', c)$, then $\imath(s, o, p, s', c) =$ True; else, if $(s_1, o_1, \neg p_1, s'_1, c_1) \in AB$ such that $(s_1, o_1, \neg p_1, s'_1, c_1) \rightarrow (s, o, \neg p, s', c)$, then $\imath(s, o, p, s', c) =$ False.

We now formally define the three domains S, O and P and the rules used for deducing implicit authorizations from explicitly defined authorizations. ***Subjects*** are organized as a means of a group and authorizations are associated to groups thus reducing the number of explicit authorizations. The idea of groups is similar to user-role assignment in Role Based Access Control (RBAC). The groups form a hierarchy called a Group Hierarchy (GH) where a node on the hierarchy represents a group and a directed arc from group A to group B indicates that an authorization for group A subsume the authorizations for group B.

A user has permission p on object o if there exists a group s such that $f(s, o, p, s^{'}, c)$ = True and the user belongs to s. ***Permissions*** in our model take the value {read, write, create, delete, execute} and implication between two authorizations does *NOT* occur along the domain P. A permission in our model is stored as a cumulative permission represented by an integer bit mask where each bit represents a permission. Hence only one entry is needed to store an authorization for a particular object which reduces the need for implicit authorization along the domain P. ***Objects*** are organized in a Hierarchical Object Lattice (HOL) in the form of a rooted acyclic graph in which each node is a Project, Experiment, Job or Workflow. An arc from node A to node B in the HOL indicates that object A implies object B. Note that authorizations can only propagate in the O domain when objects are hierarchical and not in the case of tools. In the case of tools, each tool directly references the dataset(s) being utilized by the tool and each dataset directly references its versions. An authorization to a dataset must be explicitly defined and cannot imply authorization from a tool accessing the dataset.

Dataset Security. Whenever an authorization request for tool $t \in O$ is evaluated by function f to be true, the function *check* performs an additional check and returns *False* if the tool can be invoked by user but does not have authorization to execute this tool on the given dataset and *True* if the current user can execute the tool. Two other functions that we describe are: *grant* and *revoke* which respectively grant and revoke authorizations. They return True if authorization grant and revocation have been done correctly and return False otherwise. The function *grant* is organized as follows: First a check is done to verify that the user is the owner of the dataset since only owner can grant authorization. In this case, an error is returned since the owner already has all the authorizations and therefore the authorization is not needed. Otherwise, an authorization rule is added to the authorization base. The function *revoke* is organized in a similar way as the *grant* function by recalling that only an owner of the dataset may revoke authorizations on the dataset. The main difference is that a check is done to verify whether the authorization to be revoked exists in the authorization base.

Sandbox Search. A user is allowed to only execute a browsing query on the existence of data. If the function f return *False* then the user does not have the authorization to search and no search results are returned. If function f returns true, then the function *match* is called to check whether the object being searched exists.

Temporal Constraints. We consider a temporal constraint to be associated with each authorization and refer to an authorization together with a temporal constraint as a *temporal authorization.* Temporal authorization ([t_1,t_2],$(s, o, p, s^{'}, c)$) states that user s has permission p on object o between period t_1 and t_2. Note that an authorization without any temporal constraint can be represented as a temporal authorization whose validity spans from the time at which the authorization is granted to infinity.

Conflict Resolution. To prevent conflicts, we ensure that any operation on AB leaves AB in a state satisfying the resolution, consistency, and redundancy invariant. The resolution invariant adopts the negative takes precedence approach where if we have one reason to authorize an access, and another to deny it, then we deny it. The consistency invariant ensures false authorizations are not added to AB and the redundancy invariant ensures that an authorization is not in AB if it is implied by another authorization.

5 CRIS Access Control System

In this section, we discuss the key components and implementation of the CRIS access control system. We adopt the access control framework of Spring Security as it provides comprehensive authorization services and has been used quite widely in enterprise applications. This system illustrates the use of the authorization requirements in Section 3 and the authorization model in Section 4 for the design and enforcement of access control for scientific applications.

Authorization Base (AB). The AB reflects the authorization base mentioned in our model and consists of four tables provided by the default implementation of Spring Security as discussed below:

– *acl_sid* uniquely identifies any principal or authority in the system. A principal is a user and an authority is a group of users. Spring Security also provides support for group hierarchies and allows you to configure which groups should include others.
– *acl_class* uniquely identifies any domain object class in the system.
– *acl_object_identity* stores information for each unique domain object along with its parent, owner and whether authorization entries inherit from any parent.
– *acl_entry* stores the individual permissions assigned to each principal or authority and whether the permission is positive or negative.

Authorization Module (AM). The AM provides a CRIS user the ability to create and store authorizations in the authorization base for the various objects in the users workspace and consequently allow access to authorized objects. If the authorization specified by the user is not already stored in AB or implied by an existing authorization in AB, the authorization is inserted into AB. Note that after any operation on AB, the state of AB is checked to ensure AB satisfies the resolution, redundancy and consistency invariants mentioned in Section 3. To check whether a user has authorization on the requested object means to evaluate the function f which is defined in terms of function $\imath$. Then if $\imath$ returns True, user gets access to the desired object. In the case of tools, an additional check is done by invoking the *check* method in order to get access to the dataset(s) associated with the tool.

6 Related Work

Our work is related to many areas of access control, specifically access control specification in scientific applications. Andre et al. [3] propose a number of aspects or areas of security relevant to eScience projects and Ivan et al. [2] examine the steps that can be taken to ensure that security requirements are correctly identified and security measures are usable by the intended research community. The various authorization requirements addressed in our paper have also been discussed in different domains. Rabitti et al. [4] developed a comprehensive authorization model centered around implicit authorizations designed for next-generation database systems. Bertino [1] proposes a model to provide data hiding and security where authorizations specify privileges for users to execute methods on objects. In summary, we provide a comprehensive access control system for scientific applications. While some of the authorization requirements have been studied in detail, a comprehensive access control system in the domain of scientific applications has not been addressed in literature.

7 Conclusion

In this paper we present an access control system suited for Web based scientific applications. Given the scale and depth of modern-day scientific applications, it is imperative that the methodology to formulate an authorization model be based on standardized constructs. We formulated an authorization model based on authorization requirements and well known principles of software engineering to yield a specification that can be readily integrated into existing systems.

References

1. Bertino, E.: Data Hiding and Security in Object-Oriented Databases. In: 8th International Conference on Data Engineering, pp. 338–347. IEEE Computer Society (1992)
2. Flechais, I., Sasse, M.: Stakeholder Involvement, Motivation, Responsibility, Communication: How to Design Usable Security in eScience. International Journal of Human-Computer Studies 67(4), 281–296 (2009)
3. Martin, A., Davies, J., Harris, S.: Towards a Framework for Security in eScience. In: 6th IEEE International Conference on eScience, pp. 230–237. IEEE Computer Society (2010)
4. Rabitti, F., Bertino, E., Kim, W., Woelk, D.: A Model of Authorization for Next-Generation Database Systems. ACM Transactions on Database Systems 16(1), 88–131 (1991)

Partial Fingerprint Reconstruction with Improved Smooth Extension

Wei Zhou[1], Jiankun Hu[1], Ian Petersen[1], and Mohammed Bennamoun[2]

[1] School of Engineering and Information Technology,
The University of New South Wales,
Canberra, Australia ACT 2600
wei.zhou@student.adfa.edu.au,
{J.Hu,i.petersen}@adfa.edu.au

[2] School of Computer Science and Software Engineering,
The University of Western Australia,
Perth, Australia WA 6009
m.bennamoun@csse.uwa.edu.au

Abstract. Almost all existing attempts on partial fingerprints focus on one-to-one fingerprint matching using level 2 or level 3 features obtainable in the partial segment. Recently a model-based partial fingerprint reconstruction algorithm is introduced, which aims to extend the fingerprint ridge flows smoothly into the missing part from a different perspective. This novel idea has shown promising results for narrowing down the candidate lists before matching. On this basis we propose to improve the scheme of smooth extensions and take into account the boundary effect while retrieving the initial raw orientation field. The experiment results show that the orientation field reconstructed by our algorithm is more faithful to the ground truth.

Keywords: partial fingerprint, orientation field, smooth extension, image forensic, biometrics.

1 Introduction

Biometrics especially face and fingerprint have found many applications in modern security systems, ranging from access control [1][2], to the emerging biocryptography [3][4][5][6]. Fingerprint recognition has been the most practical and widely used biometric technique since 1980s. One of the most important areas in fingerprint biometrics is matching partial fingerprints to full (relatively larger or rolled) pre-enrolled fingerprints in the database. Although tremendous progress has been made in plain and rolled fingerprint matching, partial fingerprint matching continues to be a difficult problem. The major challenges are the absence of sufficient level 2 features (minutiae) and other structures such as core and delta due to the restricted usable parts in partial fingerprint images.

Previous attempts have been made to solve the partial fingerprint problem by application of various core-based alignment techniques and maximum feature

J. Lopez, X. Huang, and R. Sandhu (Eds.): NSS 2013, LNCS 7873, pp. 756–762, 2013.

extraction methods on the partial image before matching. Jea and Govindaraju [7] addressed the problem by using localized secondary features derived from minutiae points and obtaining one-to-one correspondence of these features. Chen and Jain [8] proposed an algorithm to extract two major level 3 features (dots and incipient) based on local phase symmetry to improve the efficiency of partial fingerprint matching.

Considering the huge size of fingerprint databases maintained by law enforcement agencies, these exhaustive one-to-one matching approaches are impractical. Therefore, the automatic generation of a narrowed down candidate list for a partial fingerprint is very important. Recently, Feng and Jain [9][10] proposed a multi-staged filtering system to reduce the search space while retrieving the potential candidates for large-scale latent fingerprint matching. However, the filtering scheme depends on the singular points which are found in the partial fingerprint segment. This approach fails if the partial fingerprint does not include the singular points.

Most recently, Y. Wang and J. Hu [11] applied their prior work, namely the FOMFE model [12] to address the partial fingerprint problem from another angle. Instead of extracting level 2 or level 3 features from the partial segment, [11] proposed an analytical approach for reconstructing the global Orientation Field (OF) by exploiting the global topological features. Specifically, they have developed algorithms to extend the partial ridge flows smoothly into the unknown segment while preserving the fidelity. This approach has shown very promising results in reducing the size of the candidate lists for matching, and what is more, the information of singular points is not a necessity.

Based on Y. Wang and J. Hu's work, we propose to improve the algorithm of smooth extensions by training the existing topological features using FOMFE model each time the extension is applied. Besides, we optimize the extraction approach of topological features on the boundary of the coarse orientation field, which is a decisive factor to the correctness of the initial FOMFE training result. We have tested our algorithm on certain partial fingerprints. The results show that the orientation field reconstructed by our method is more faithful to the one retrieved from corresponding full fingerprint.

2 Smooth Extension with FOMFE Training

2.1 Improved Algorithm

In the previous smooth extension model [11], the phase portrait in the known segment will not change with iteration, so the coefficient update will be heavily affected by the expanded area which can lead to large cumulated error. We improve the partial fingerprint reconstruction model by training the phase data using FOMFE model [12] every time the coefficient β is updated, as a result, the whole phase portrait is normalized (see Algorithm 1).

Algorithm 1: Smooth extension with FOMFE training

Initialize $k \leftarrow 0$;
$\Omega^{(0)} \leftarrow \Omega$, $\beta_l^{(0)} \leftarrow \widetilde{\Psi}_\Omega^T d_{\Omega,l} \quad (l = cos, sin)$;
while $S - \Omega^{(k)} \neq 0$ **do**
  Let $\Omega^{(k+1)} \leftarrow \Omega^{(k)} + \Delta$;
  Let $\Delta \leftarrow \Omega^{(k+1)} - \Omega^{(k)}$;
  Evaluate $\hat{d}_{\Delta,l} = \Psi_\Delta \beta_l^{(k)} \quad (l = cos, sin)$;
  `/* enforce the squared sum of cosine and sine components equals to one */`
  Normalize $\hat{d}_{\Delta,l}$;
  Update $\beta_l^{(k+1)} \leftarrow \beta_l^{(k)} + \widetilde{\Psi}_\Delta^T \hat{d}_{\Delta,l}$;
  Evaluate $\hat{d}_{\Omega^{(k+1)},l} = \Psi_{\Omega^{(k+1)}} \beta_l^{(k+1)} \quad (l = cos, sin)$;
  Let $\Omega^{(k)} \leftarrow \Omega^{(k+1)}$ and $k \leftarrow k + 1$;
end
Normalize $\hat{d}_{S,l} \quad (l = cos, sin)$;
Output $\hat{d}_{S,l} \quad (l = cos, sin)$;

2.2 Experiment Evaluation

We have done a series of comparison experiments to demonstrate the advantage of our algorithm.

Figure 1 is the orientation field estimated on a full fingerprint, wherein Subfigure (a) is the coarse OF evaluated by an improved gradient-based method [13]. The gray-scale image is first divided into blocks with equal size of 8×8 pixels, then the dominant orientation angle θ in each block is computed by a weighted averaging scheme from four neighboring blocks [13]. This scheme is more robust against noise compared with other gradient-based methods, except certain distortion on the boundary of the partial fingerprint. The FOMFE model takes the coarse OF as input and refines it, as shown in Subfigure (b), the OF trained by FOMFE is normalized over the whole fingerprint region.

Figure 2 shows the OF estimation on the corresponding partial fingerprint. The partial fingerprint is obtained by erasing certain parts of the full fingerprint. Subfigure (a) is the coarse OF and (b) is the refined OF trained by FOMFE.

Figure 3 provides a ground truth OF estimation as reference for the following experiments. The OF is trained by the FOMFE model on the full fingerprint, but plotted on the partial fingerprint image.

Figure 4 illustrates the final reconstruction results by Smooth Extension and our improve method. It is obvious that the OF reconstructed by the improved algorithm is more normalized and can better approximate the ground truth orientation field shown in Figure 3.

3 Discussion

Since the FOMFE model takes the coarse OF as input, the original OF estimation based on the gradient method will affect the subsequent reconstruction

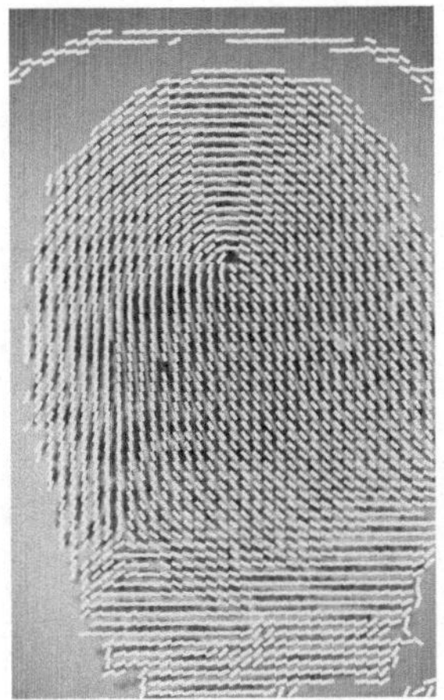

(a) Coarse OF estimated by the weighted averaging gradient-based method

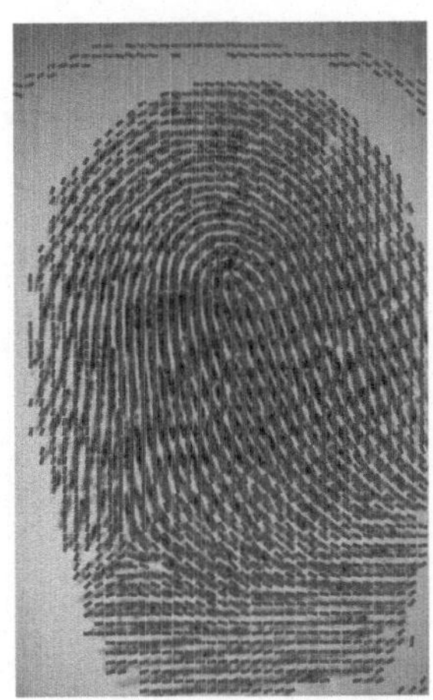

(b) OF trained by the FOMFE model

Fig. 1. Estimated Orientation Field on the full fingerprint

process, more specifically, the orientation angles on the boundary of the partial fingerprint will decide the extending trend of the fingerprint ridge flow. As stated before, the coarse OF on the boundary of the partial fingerprint is fuzzy to some extent, so the initial boundary OF trained by FOMFE is not accurate, and these errors will be amplified step by step during the reconstruction process. As shown in Figure 4(b), the overall estimated OF in the middle hole is flatter than that of the ground truth, and part of the estimated OF in the lowermost hole on the right side is not smoothly connected with the OF in the existing partial segment.

To overcome this problem, we propose to improve the coarse OF estimation on the boundary of the partial fingerprint. In practice, we locate the boundary blocks and replace their coarse angles with the one of their nearest neighbors. As shown in Figure 5(a), the initial coarse OF on the partial segment including the boundary is more smoother than that in Figure 2(a). Figure 5(b) is the final reconstruction result using the improved OF estimation method, which shows the reconstructed OF is nearly the same as that estimated on the full fingerprint. In principal, the proposed does not require registration. However, in practice it is hard to determine the symmetric peripheral area for the algorithm if rotation is not dealt with properly. It is well known that rotation can cause many other problems apart from this [14]. Also latent partial fingerprints are often of poor quality where OF retrieval could be difficult as well. Noise resistance methods such as [15] should be deployed before applying the proposed smooth extension method.

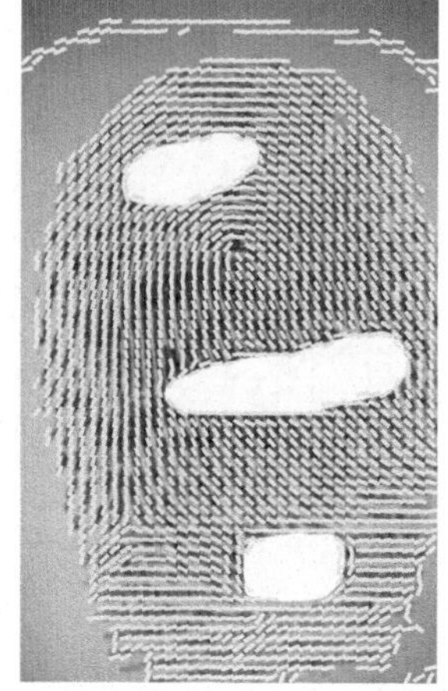

(a) Coarse OF estimated by the weighted averaging gradient-based method

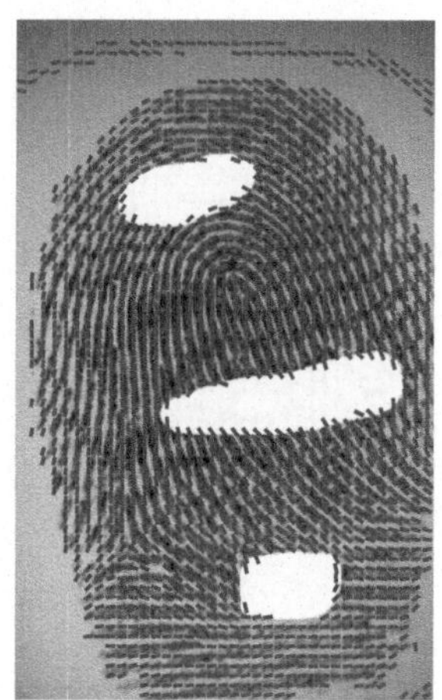

(b) OF trained by the FOMFE model

Fig. 2. Estimated Orientation Field on the partial fingerprint

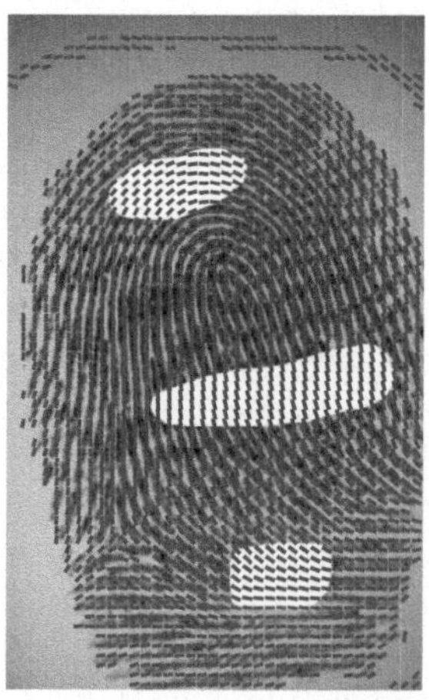

Fig. 3. Estimated OF by FOMFE on full fingerprint and shown on partial fingerprint

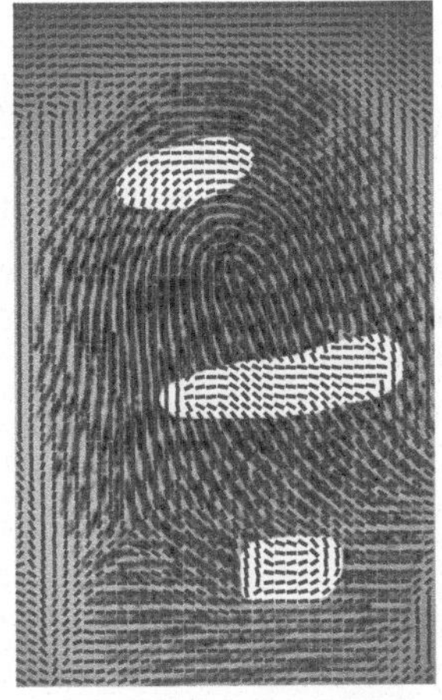

(a) Smooth Extension

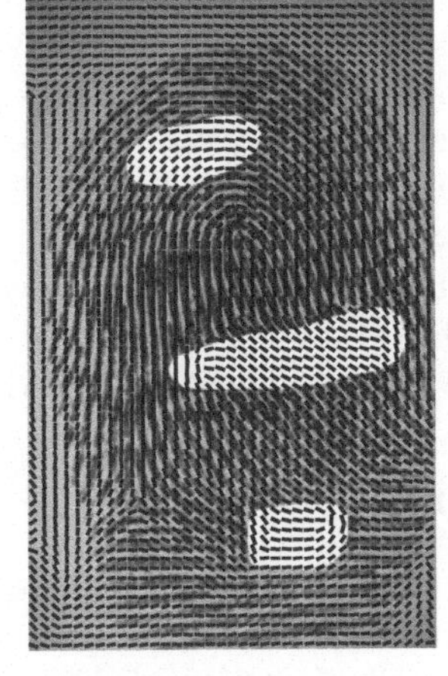

(b) Smooth Extension with FOMFE training

Fig. 4. Estimated OF after reconstruction on partial fingerprint

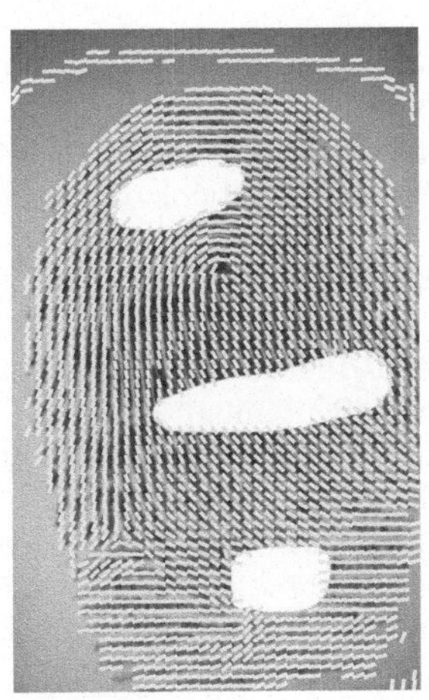

(a) Improved coarse OF estimation

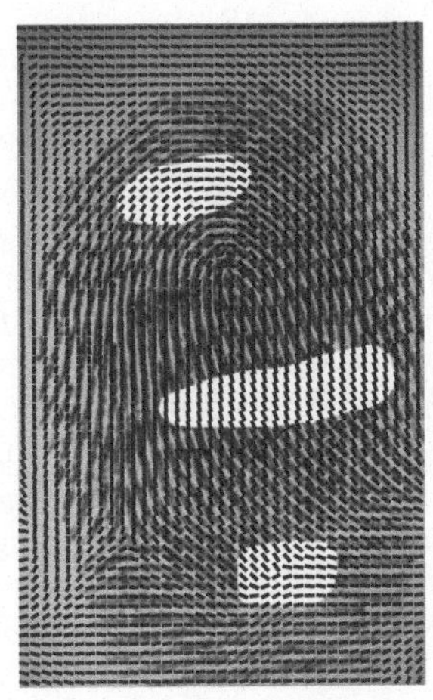

(b) Final reconstruction result

Fig. 5. Improved coarse OF and the subsequent reconstruction result

4 Conclusion

Previous works on partial fingerprints focus on extracting maximum features from the partial image and matching the partial image with the suitable sub-image from the full image. This one-to-one matching method is impractical when the size of the fingerprint database is huge. Another perspective is to reconstruct the partial fingerprint and utilize the reconstructed full image to narrow down the candidate list for matching. This opens up a novel direction for solving the partial fingerprint problem. We replayed this smooth extension based reconstruction method and improved it by considering the phase portrait in the expanded region and the known region as a whole. Besides, we tried to eliminate the errors of the coarse OF estimation on the boundary of the partial fingerprint. The experiment results show that the orientation field reconstructed by our algorithm is more close to the one estimated from the corresponding full fingerprint.

References

1. Xi, K., Hu, J., Han, F.: Mobile device access control: an improved correlation based face authentication scheme and its java me application. Concurr. Comput.: Pract. Exper. 24(10), 1066–1085 (2012)
2. Xi, K., Tang, Y., Hu, J.: Correlation keystroke verification scheme for user access control in cloud computing environment. Comput. J. 54(10), 1632–1644 (2011)
3. Ahmad, T., Hu, J., Wang, S.: Pair-polar coordinate-based cancelable fingerprint templates. Pattern Recogn. 44(10-11), 2555–2564 (2011)
4. Wang, S., Hu, J.: Alignment-free cancelable fingerprint template design: A densely infinite-to-one mapping (ditom) approach. Pattern Recogn. 45(12), 4129–4137 (2012)
5. Xi, K., Ahmad, T., Han, F., Hu, J.: A fingerprint based bio-cryptographic security protocol designed for client/server authentication in mobile computing environment. Journal of Security and Communication Networks 4(5), 487–499 (2011)
6. Xi, K., Hu, J.: Introduction to Bio-cryptography. In: Handbook of Information and Communication Security. Springer (2010)
7. Jea, T.Y., Govindaraju, V.: A minutia-based partial fingerprint recognition system. Pattern Recogn. 38(10), 1672–1684 (2005)
8. Chen, Y., Jain, A.K.: Dots and excipients extended features for partial fingerprint matching. In: Proc. Biometric Consortium Conf. (September 2007)
9. Feng, J., Jain, A.K.: Filtering large fingerprint database for latent matching. In: Proc. Int. Conf. on Pattern Recognition (ICPR 2008), pp. 1–4 (2008)
10. Jain, A.K., Feng, J.: Latent fingerprint matching. IEEE Transactions on Pattern Analysis and Machine Intelligence 33(1), 88–100 (2011)
11. Wang, Y., Hu, J.: Global ridge orientation modeling for partial fingerprint identification. IEEE Trans. Pattern Anal. Mach. Intell. 33(1), 72–87 (2011)
12. Wang, Y., Hu, J., Phillips, D.: A fingerprint orientation model based on 2d fourier expansion (fomfe) and its application to singular-point detection and fingerprint indexing. IEEE Trans. Pattern Anal. Mach. Intell. 29(4), 573–585 (2007)
13. Wang, Y., Hu, J., Schroder, H.: A gradient based weighted averaging method for estimation of fingerprint orientation fields. In: Proceedings of the Digital Image Computing: Techniques and Applications, DICTA 2005 (December 2005)
14. Zhang, P., Hu, J., Li, C., Bennamoun, M., Bhagavatula, V.: A pitfall in fingerprint bio-cryptographic key generation. Computers & Security 30(5), 311–319 (2011)
15. Wang, Y., Hu, J., Han, F.: Enhanced gradient-based algorithm for the estimation of fingerprint orientation field. Applied Mathematics and Computation 185(2), 823–833 (2007)

Modeling and Analysis for Thwarting Worm Propagation in Email Networks

Sheng Wen, Yang Xiang, and Wanlei Zhou

School of Information Technology,
Deakin University,
Melbourne, Australia VIC 3125
{wsheng,yang,wanlei}@deakin.edu.au

Abstract. Email worm has long been a critical but intractable threat to Internet users. In this paper, we propose an analytical model to present the propagation dynamics of email worms using difference equations. Based on this model, we further investigate the quarantine conditions for the number of infected users decreasing as soon as possible. In this field, previous works have found that a *static threshold* for worms fast dying out does not exist. In our work, we extend the modeling with *dynamical quarantine* processes to see if the previous viewpoint is still supported or not. By contrast, the results suggest that it is possible to have a sharp decline in the number of infected users within a short period of time. In the experiments, we implement both the empirical and theoretical methods to support our analysis. The work of this paper can provide practical values on protecting email networks.

Keywords: network security, email worms, quarantine.

1 Introduction

For over a decade, emails are chosen as primary carriers for transmission of worms. A typical email worm arrives on a computer as an attachment to an email message, which, when activated by the user, will infect this user and send further copies of itself to other recipients. The success of recent email worms, such as W32.Ismolk [1], indicates that email worms are still one of the major threats in current Internet.

In the real world, the entire email network has almost infinite users, and the topology exhibits scale-free and small world properties [2]. It has been proved that a constant threshold for email worms fast dying out does not exist in the entire email network [3,4,5]. Therefore, we try to find out dynamic quarantine conditions for email networks; in particular, we choose the recovery functions that change with time to measure the quarantine conditions. So the problems are: when an outbreak of email worms has been detected, will it be possible to thwart the propagation of the worms? If so, what quarantine conditions are to be satisfied to make the number of infected users decay as soon as possible?

In this paper, we show our recent work on managing security issues in email networks. Firstly, in order to understand the spreading of email worms, we model

J. Lopez, X. Huang, and R. Sandhu (Eds.): NSS 2013, LNCS 7873, pp. 763–769, 2013.

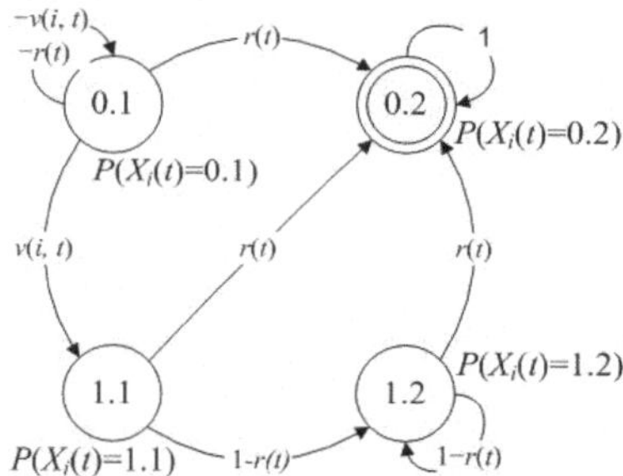

Fig. 1. State transition graph of a node. '0.1': healthy but susceptible; '1.1': a user is infectious and will send out malware email copies; '1.2': a user is infected but not yet infectious; '0.2': healthy and will never be infected again.

their propagation dynamics using difference equations. To the best of our knowledge, we are the first to propose an analytical model on the propagation of email worms. Validation based on simulation studies indicates our analytical model is accurate. Secondly, we investigate the quarantine conditions, under which the number of infected users will decrease as soon as possible (i.e. exponentially or linearly). The results of our investigation suggest that the condition for email worms fast dying out do exist in the email network and security staffs can eliminate infection incidents fast, but it is hard to eradicate all of them.

The rest of this paper is organized as follows: Section 2 presents the related work. Section 3 presents the analytical modeling method, followed by the validation of the modeling in Section 4. In Section 5, we discuss the dynamical quarantine strategies on the basis of the proposed model. Finally in Section 6 , we conclude this paper and discuss the future work.

2 Representation of Worm Propagation

To investigate the quarantine conditions for thwarting the propagation of email worms, we propose a model to present their spreading dynamics. Firstly, nodes and topology information are basic elements for the propagation of email worms. A node in the topology represents a user in email networks. Let the random variable $X_i(t)$ denote the status of an arbitrary node i at time t:

$$X_i(t) = \begin{cases} 0 \quad healthy \begin{cases} 0.1 & susceptible \\ 0.2 & immunized \end{cases} \\ 1 \quad infected \begin{cases} 1.1 & active \\ 1.2 & dormant \end{cases} \end{cases} \tag{1}$$

The "0.1" is not one tenth but a symbol of the susceptible state. The same applies to the symbols of "0.2", "1.1" and "1.2". As shown in Fig.1, node i transits to the infected state if it is at the susceptible state. The infection probability is presented by $v(i,t)$. Besides, no matter what state the node is at, it may transit to the immunized state. The recovery probability is presented by $r(t)$. Since the immunized state is an absorbing state, it can be predicted that the spread of worms will finally end. We have the probability of node i being infected or immunized at time t as in

$$P(X_i(t) = 1) = (1 - r(t)) \cdot P(X_i(t-1) = 1) + v(i,t) \cdot P(X_i(t-1) = 0.1) \tag{2}$$

$$P(X_i(t) = 0.2) = P(X_i(t-1) = 0.2) + r(t) \cdot [1 - P(X_i(t-1) = 0.2)] \tag{3}$$

Because email worms depend on email users checking the mailbox and opening malicious attachments to spread, we introduce a variable $open_i(t)$ to indicate the event of user i checking newly arrived emails at time t. In the real world, some users use outlook to receive emails almost instantly, some others may use email web services, like Gmail. Therefore, the email checking periods T_i for each user are different, and we have

$$P(open_i(t) = 1) = \begin{cases} 0, & otherwise \\ 1, & t \bmod T_i = 0 \end{cases} \tag{4}$$

Then, we derive the infection probability $v(i,t)$ as in

$$v(i,t) = s(i,t) \cdot P(open_i(t) = 1) \cdot [1 - r(t)] \tag{5}$$

wherein $s(i,t)$ is a conditional probability, which denotes the infection probability under the conditions of 1) user i opening the mailbox at time t and 2) user i having not been immunized at time t.

Secondly, we use an m by m square matrix T with element p_{ij} to indicate a network consisting of M nodes. If node i is susceptible, it can be compromised by any of its infected neighbors. The element p_{ij} in matrix T denotes the propagation probability from node i to node j. Thus, the probability that node i is infected at time t by any of its neighbors who send out worm emails at time $t-1$, $\Theta(t)$, is

$$\Theta(t) = 1 - \prod_{j=1}^{M} [1 - p_{ji} \cdot P(X_j(t-1) = 1.1)] \tag{6}$$

Since different users have different email checking periods, the worm emails will arrive at the mailboxes of their neighbors at different time. We assume the worm emails are neglected if users do not open the attachment in current checking period, therefore, a user can only be infected by worm emails which arrived at his or her mailbox within one email checking period. Then, we can iterate the computation of $s(i,t)$ as in

$$\begin{aligned} s(i,t) = 1 - [1 - s(i,t-1) \cdot (1 - P(open_i(t-1) = 1))] \\ \cdot \prod_{j=1}^{M} [1 - p_{ji} \cdot P(X_j(t-1) = 1.1)] \end{aligned} \tag{7}$$

$$P(X_j(t-1) = 1.1) = v(j,t-1) \cdot P(X_j(t-2) = 0.1) \tag{8}$$

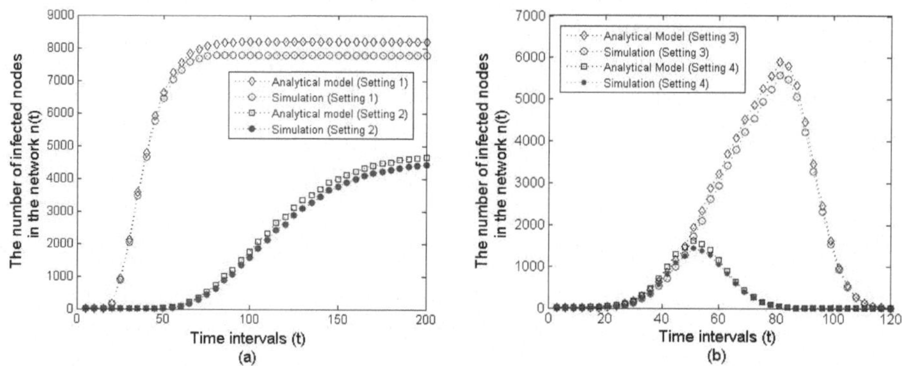

Fig. 2. Comparison of the simulation model and our analytical model. Setting 1: $T_i \sim N(20, 10)$, $p_{ij} \sim N(0.5, 0.2)$; Setting 2: $T_i \sim N(40, 20)$, $p_{ij} \sim N(0.25, 0.1)$; Setting 3: $d = 80$, $D = 40$; Setting 4: $d = 40$, $D = 80$.

Finally, the expected number of infected nodes at time t, $n(t)$, can be computed from $P(X_i(t) = 1)$, as in

$$n(t) = E\left(\sum_{j=1}^{M} X_i(t)\right) = \sum_{j=1}^{M} E\left(X_i(t)\right) = \sum_{j=1}^{M} P\left(X_i(t) = 1\right) \tag{9}$$

In equation (9), we can see that $n(t)$ is ascribed to the sum of the probabilities of each node being infected at time t.

3 Validation of Propagation Model

Before using the proposed analytical model, we validate its correctness by comparing it with simulation results. Firstly, we evaluate the correctness of our model without recovery ($r(t) = 0$). As shown in Fig.2(a), the simulation model and our analytical model are close to each other. Secondly, we validate the correctness of our proposed model with recovery effect. When a type of new email worm is born, email users have no knowledge about it. Irrespective of their vigilance, we assume 100 percent of the users are susceptible. Then, this type of worms can spread without any defense during a certain time period. We introduce a variable d to represent the length of this period. Besides, according to the statistics of Qualys Inc. [6], the number of vulnerabilities decreases by 50% of the remaining every 30 days in 2003 and 21 days in 2004. Therefore, we introduce another variable D to present the time interval for 50% decreasing. Then, we have the recovery probability $r(t)$ as: $r(t) = 0$, if $t < d$; $r(t) = 1 - 0.5^{\frac{(t-d)}{D}}$, if $t \geq d$. As shown in Fig.2(b), the results of the simulation model and our proposed analytical model are also close to each other. Thus, the following analysis based on our analytical model is convincible.

4 Analysis of Quarantine Strategy

Based on our analytical model, we introduce a variable $\Delta(t)$ to denote the reduction in the number of infected nodes in an email network, and we have

$$\begin{aligned}\Delta(t) &= n(t) - n(t-1) \\ &= \sum_{i=1}^{M} [(1 - r(t)) \cdot s(i,t) \cdot P(open_i(t) = 1) P(X_i(t-1) = 0.1)] \\ &\quad - r(t) \sum_{i=1}^{M} P(X_i(t-1) = 1)\end{aligned} \tag{10}$$

We also introduce a variable $\varsigma_i(t)$ to represent the infection probability when there is no defense applied, as in

$$\varsigma_i(t) = s(i,t) \cdot P(open_i(t) = 1) \tag{11}$$

Supposing $\Delta(t)$ is known, we then deduce the required recovery probability as

$$r(t) = \frac{\sum_{i=1}^{M} [\varsigma_i(t) \cdot P(X_i(t-1) = 0.1)] - \Delta(t)}{\sum_{i=1}^{M} [\varsigma_i(t) \cdot P(X_i(t-1) = 0.1)] + n(t-1)} \tag{12}$$

The value of $r(t)$ indicates the probability of email users (either infected or not) to be immunized to email worms. We therefore choose the required recovery probability $r(t)$ as the quarantine condition for email worms fast dying out in email networks.

In the following, we investigate the dynamical quarantine conditions for email worms fast dying out in two trends as follows:

Scenario 1: *the number of infected email users, $n(t)$, decays exponentially fast.*

Given a free spreading period d, if the number of infected users, $n(t)$, decays exponentially fast after this period, we have

$$n(t) = a^{-(t-d)} \cdot n(d) \qquad when \quad t > d \tag{13}$$

We then obtain the value of $\Delta(t)$ as

$$\Delta(t) = n(d) \cdot a^{d-t} \cdot (1 - a) \qquad when \quad t > d \tag{14}$$

We divide the whole spreading procedure of email worms into four phases: slow start, fast spread, slow finish and quarantine. Firstly, we assume email worms have already widely spread and security staffs begin to protect email users at the quarantine phase. As shown in Fig.3(a), the number of infected users declines sharply, and in Fig.3(b), the value of $r(t)$ stays steady (nearly a trapezoid zone) before the number of infected users has greatly decreased. Secondly, we further assume email users are protected at the fast spread phase. As shown in Fig.3(c), the value of $n(t)$ also declines sharply. However, the speed for email worms dying out exponentially fast leads to a long lag (logarithmic decline at the later stage). We can increase the base number a to reduce the negative effect of the long lag.

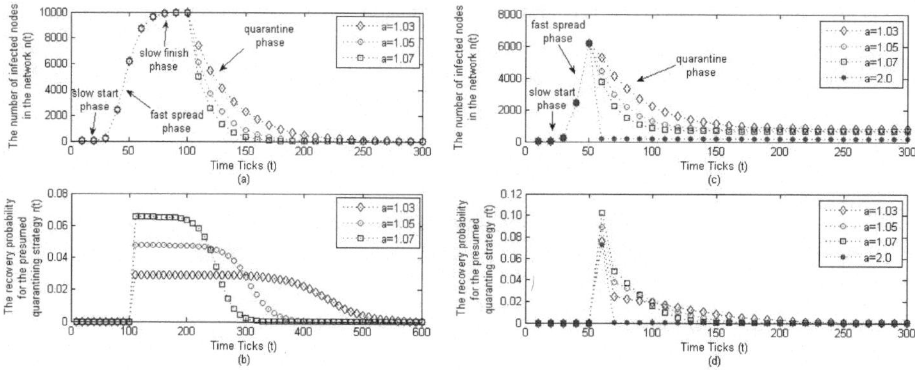

Fig. 3. The number of infected nodes $n(t)$ and the recovery probability for email worms dying out exponentially fast when $d = 100$ for (a) and (b), $d = 50$ for (c) and (d).

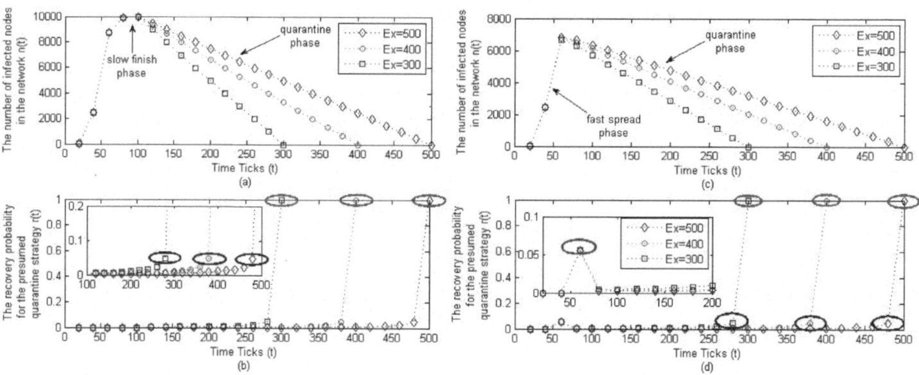

Fig. 4. The number of infected nodes $n(t)$ and the recovery probability for email worms dying out exponentially fast when $d = 100$ for (a) and (b), $d = 50$ for (c) and (d)

In Fig.3(d), we see that the value of $r(t)$ stays high for a shorter period (nearly a triangle zone) when $a = 2$.

Scenario 2: *the number of infected email users, $n(t)$, decays linearly fast.*

Given a free spreading period d, if the number of infected users, $n(t)$, decays linearly fast, we have

$$\Delta(t) = -\frac{n(t)}{Ex - t} \qquad t > d \tag{15}$$

In this case, we introduce a presumed time point Ex for email worms fast dying out. So we have $n(t) = 0$ if $t = Ex$. Then, we let the quarantine process start at the slow finish phase. Firstly, as shown in Fig.4(a), the number of infected email users declines linearly and reaches zero at Ex. In Fig.4(b), we can see that the value of $r(t)$ stays small for eliminating email worms on infected users. However, if security staffs want to eradicate all email worms from the email network, the value of $r(t)$ becomes close to one. In practical terms, this means security staffs have to quarantine all email users and make sure none of them would be infected any more. In Fig.4(b), we call the points with red circles as the ideal quarantine points and the points with blue circles as the practical quarantine points. Secondly, we let the quarantine process start at the fast spread phase. As shown in Fig.4(c), the number of infected user reaches zero at the Ex time point. Since there are many new infection incidents in the fast spread phase, we see in Fig.4(d) that email users should be more vigilant against email worms at the early quarantine stage. We highlight the peak value of $r(t)$ during this period with a green circle.

From the above analysis, we derive certain practical inspirations. Firstly, when an outbreak of email worms has been detected in an email network, it is possible to eliminate infected users as quickly as possible, for example, as shown in Fig.3(b), when the recovery probability keeps 6%, the number of infected users will decrease greatly in 50 time ticks. If we increase the recovery probability, less time will be needed. In the real world, if averagely 6 users out of 100 can be immunized in certain periods, it is possible to thwart the propagation of email worms. Secondly, as shown in Fig.3(c), it is difficult to eradicate all the worms in an email network, which is in accordance with the discussion in paper [7].

5 Conclusion

This paper presents an investigation on quarantine conditions of email worms in an email network. Our work can help model the propagation dynamics of email worms and analyze quarantine conditions for email worms dying out as quickly as possible in email networks. The discussion may also be applicable to other social networks that are exploitable by computer viruses and worms.

References

1. Marc, F., Trevor, M., et al.: Symantec internet security threat report 2010. Technical report, Symantec Corporation (2011)
2. Ebel, H., Mielsch, L.I., Bornholdt, S.: Scale-free topology of e-mail networks. Phys. Rev. E 66, 035103 (2002)
3. Wang, Y., Chakrabarti, D., Wang, C., Faloutsos, C.: Epidemic spreading in real networks: An eigenvalue viewpoint. In: Proceedings of SRDS, pp. 25–34 (2003)
4. Ganesh, A., Massoulie, L., Towsley, D.: The effect of network topology on the spread of epidemics. In: Proceedings of the 24th Annual Joint Conference of the IEEE Computer and Communications Societies, INFOCOM 2005, vol. 2, pp. 1455–1466. IEEE (March 2005)
5. Chakrabarti, D., Leskovec, J., Faloutsos, C., Madden, S., Guestrin, C., Faloutsos, M.: Information survival threshold in sensor and p2p networks. In: 26th IEEE International Conference on Computer Communications, INFOCOM 2007, pp. 1316–1324. IEEE (May 2007)
6. Eschelbeck, G.: The laws of vulnerabilities. Technical report, BlackHat Conference, Qualys Inc. (2004)
7. Newman, M.E.J., Forrest, S., Balthrop, J.: Email networks and the spread of computer viruses. Phys. Rev. E 66, 035101 (2002)

On Secure and Power-Efficient RFID-Based Wireless Body Area Network

Sana Ullah* and Waleed Alsalih

College of Computer and Information Sciences, King Saud University, Riyadh
sullah@ksu.edu.sa

Abstract. A Wireless Body Area Networks (WBAN) has emerged as a promising technology for pervasive healthcare systems. It allows the seamless integration of small and intelligent invasive or non-invasive sensor nodes in, on or around a human body for continuous health monitoring. This paper presents a secure RFID-based protocol for WBAN. This protocol introduces a separate wakeup process that is used for secure communication on the main channel. The performance of the proposed protocol is analyzed and compared with that of IEEE 802.15.6-based CSMA/CA and preamble-based TDMA protocols using extensive simulations. It is shown that the proposed protocol is power-efficient and is less vulnerable to different attacks compared to the other protocols. For a low traffic load and a single alkaline battery of capacity 2.6Ah, the proposed protocol could extend the WBAN lifetime to approximately five years.

Keywords: IEEE 802.15.6, WBAN, RFID, Security.

1 Introduction

Wireless Body Area Networks (WBANs) are becoming increasingly important for future health care systems. They have enough capabilities to collect biological information from the users in order to maintain their optimal health status. WBANs are able to detect and possibly predict the deteriorating conditions of patients and are also able to monitor chronic diseases including cardiovascular and asthma diseases [1]. This kind of unobtrusive health monitoring not only improves the quality of life but also provides computer-assisted rehabilitation to the patients. WBANs are generally comprised of in-body and on-body area networks. The in-body networks allow communication between invasive nodes and the coordinator using Medical Implant Communications Service (MICS) band, while the on-body networks use unlicensed Industrial, Scientific, and Medical (ISM) and Ultra-wideband (UWB) bands for communication between non-invasive nodes and the coordinator. Because both invasive and non-invasive sensor WBAN nodes are miniaturized and have limited power capacity, they require novel power-efficient solutions at network, Medium Access Control (MAC),

* Corresponding author.

J. Lopez, X. Huang, and R. Sandhu (Eds.): NSS 2013, LNCS 7873, pp. 770–776, 2013.

and physical layers. This paper proposes a secure Radio Frequency IDentification (RFID)-based protocol for low-power communication in WBAN. Extensive simulations are conducted to analyze performance of the proposed protocol with that of IEEE 802.15.6-based CSMA/CA [2] and preamble-based TDMA protocols [3] in terms of network lifetime, bandwidth utilization and security. The proposed protocol extends the WBAN network lifetime from months to years. It also supports a secure wakeup process that prevents adversaries from attacking the network.

The rest of the paper is organized as follows. Section 2 presents the related work on MAC protocols for WBAN. Section 3 presents the secure RFID-based protocol for WBAN and the simulation results. The final section concludes our work.

2 Related Work

Many researchers have directly adapted the contention-based or Carrier Sensor Multiple Access with Collision Avoidance (CSMA/CA) protocol defined in IEEE 802.15.4 [4] due to the fact that this standard supports low data rate applications with low-power consumption. The authors of [5] considered the contention-based IEEE 802.15.4 MAC for periodic and asymmetric WBAN traffic, however they have not considered the real-WBAN scenario where many nodes may generate aperiodic traffic. Similarly, Li et al. has proved that the performance of unslotted CSMA/CA IEEE 802.15.4 mode is better than that of the beacon mode in terms of throughput and latency [6]. Another study presented in [7] has discouraged the use of IEEE 802.15.4-based CSMA/CA because of unreliable Clear Channel Assessment (CCA) and heavy collision problems. The authors of [8] investigated the contention-based slotted ALOHA protocol for WBAN in terms of throughput and energy consumption. A random contention-based protocol is presented in [9], which enhances quality of service for multiple WBAN users by considering inter-WBAN interference. The schedule-based or Time Division Multiple Access (TDMA) protocols have also attracted the attention of many WBAN researchers. In [10], the authors proposed a novel TDMA protocol that solves overhearing and protocol overhead problems by exploiting the fixed WBAN topology. In order to prolong the WBAN network lifetime, the authors of [11] proposed a TDMA protocol that uses an out-of-band wakeup channel for low-power consumption. Another TDMA-based protocol is presented in [12] where the authors considered directional MAC with multi-beam antennas for enabling simultaneous communication in all directions. We proposed a dual-channel TDMA-based protocol in [13] and [14] where communication between nodes and the coordinator is based on traffic patterns. Another study presented in [15] proposed a battery-aware TDMA protocol that utilizes battery discharge dynamics, wireless channel models, and packet queuing characteristics.

Most of the above MAC protocols do not address the security and network lifetime issues in WBANs. For example, they consume significant power due to collision overhead and frequent synchronization, thus reducing the overall

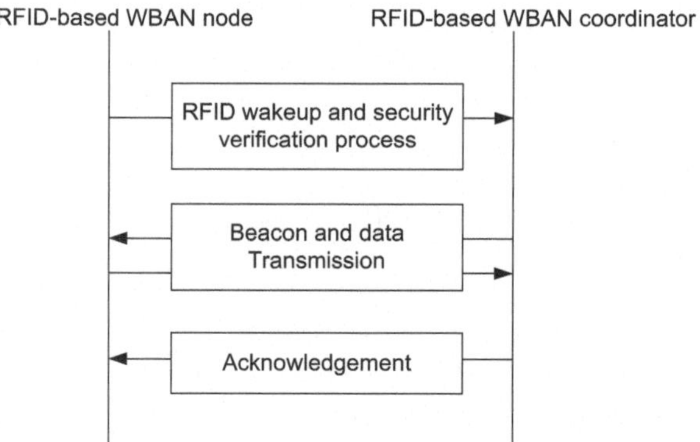

Fig. 1. Resource allocation process of the proposed protocol

network lifetime. The secure RFID-based protocol is able to solve these problems by providing a secure wakeup process that must be able to prevent adversaries from attacking the network and must also be able to extend the network lifetime from months to years.

3 RFID-Based Power Saving Mechanism

RFID systems have already played a significant role in a wide range of applications including manufacturing, object tracking, inventory control, smart environments, and healthcare systems. One of the main reasons of RFID success is its cheap and quick implementation without any additional cost. In a typical RFID systems, the RFID tags are attached to the objects for different applications. These tags store information that is further read by the RFID reader. The RFID tags are categorized into active, passive, and semi-passive tags. The active tags have enough power sources and have the ability to initiate communication. The passive tags can only receive data and can be powered up by the reader. The semi-passive tags have limited power source only for internal processing. Because these tags are inexpensive and power-efficient, they can be easily integrated into WBAN. They can be attached to WBAN nodes and can be used for wakeup purpose only (and not for storing information as done in traditional RFID systems). Our RFID-based protocol considers a secure RFID wakeup method that triggers the data channel for communication. The proposed protocol uses a separate control channel for wakeup and synchronization packets and a data channel for original data transmission.During the wakeup process, the nodes send an RFID security code (the security codes are randomly distributed by the coordinator) in the RFID wakeup packet, which is compared by the coordinator with the code already stored in its circuitry. When the two RFID security codes are same, the data channel is triggered for transmission. However, when the codes are different, the RFID wakeup circuitry aborts the wakeup process. The secure RFID wakeup process prevents adversaries from penetrating into network and from using different attacking methods including backoff manipulation, collision, and reply attacks [16]-[17]. One of the reasons is that the adversaries are unable to grab the beacon and the resource allocation information until they follow the secure wakeup process. Once the wakeup process is successfully done, the coordinator sends beacon on the data channel to the nodes for synchronization as given in Fig. 1. The beacon contains information about the superframe structure and data slot boundaries (the beacon and data frame formats are not included here to space limitation problems).

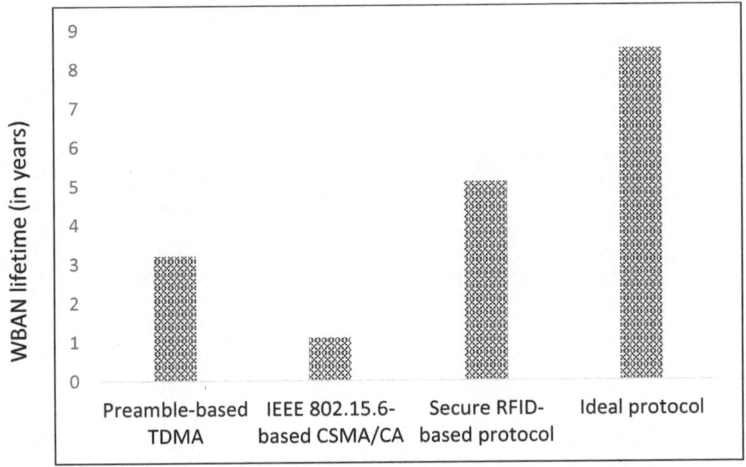

Fig. 2. WBAN network lifetime for an average packet generation period of 50 seconds

We conduct a preliminary study on analyzing the performance of the proposed protocol with that of IEEE 802.15.6-based CSMA/CA and preamble-based TDMA protocols in terms of network lifetime, bandwidth utilization and security. We develop a discrete event custom simulator in C++ that implements the basic operation of all the protocols including the secure RFID-based protocol. Because we are interested in MAC layer performance, the physical layer parameters are not considered in the simulations. We consider a single WBAN star topology where the communication flow is in upward direction towards the coordinator. The nodes are triggered to generate Poisson traffic. For the CSMA/CA, the minimum and maximum Contention Windows (CWs) are taken the same for all nodes. The CW is doubled for even number of failures and is unchanged for odd number of failures. The simulation parameters are listed in Table 1.

Fig. 2 shows the WBAN lifetime for a packet generation period of 50 seconds. The figure considers an alkaline battery of capacity 2.6Ah. The average lifetime of a node is around three months for IEEE 802.15.6-based CSMA/CA, one year for preamble-based TDMA, and five years for the secure RFID -based protocol. Since the proposed protocol adjusts the wakeup and sleep schedules of the nodes,

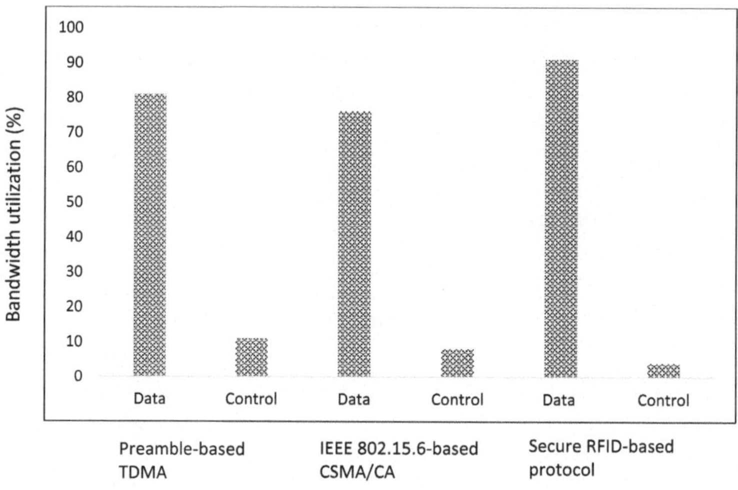

Fig. 3. Bandwidth utilization of the protocols

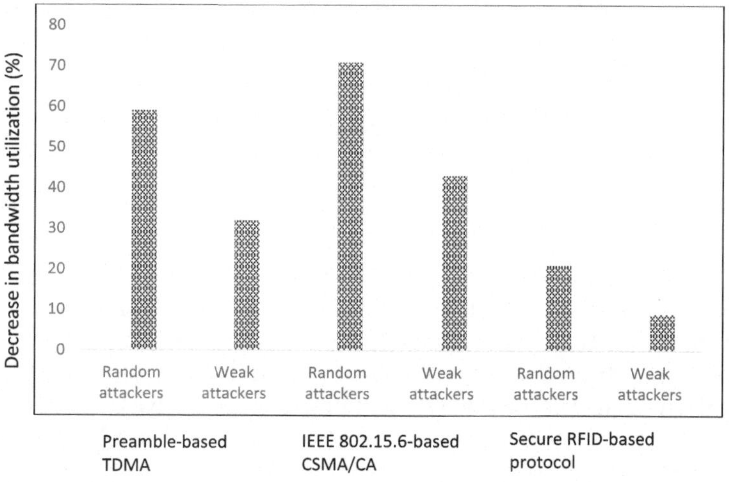

Fig. 4. Decrease in bandwidth utilization using random and weak attackers

the overall power consumption decreases as a function of larger wakeup or packet generation periods. This result is obvious as larger packet generation periods allow nodes to remain in sleep mood for enough duration. The results presented in Fig. 2 are valid for low traffic load with an error free channel. Fig. 3 shows the bandwidth efficiency for all protocols, where the data and control represent the

Table 1. Simulation parameters

CCA	63/Symbol rate	CW	16
pSIFS	$50\mu s$	Wakeup/Beacon packet	80 bits
CSMA slot length	$CCA + 20\mu s$	MAC header	56 bits
$MACFooter$	16 bits	Propagation delay	$1\mu s$
Idle power	$5\mu W$	Transmitting power	$27mW$
Receiving power	$1.8mW$	Switching time	$1.2ms$

time spent in transmitting data and control packets, respectively. The bandwidth utilization is almost the same for all protocols, however the overhead of control packets is different, for example, control packets transmitted by the preamble-based TDMA are overheard by all other nodes. In the proposed protocol, the overhead of control packets is almost negligible because it sends RFID wakeup signal whenever required, thus reducing overhearing and idle listening problems. In order to analyze different attacks on all the protocols, we consider two types of attackers: a random attacker, which has smart attacking capabilities and can use backoff manipulation, collision, and relay attacks, simultaneously, and a weak attacker, which has limited capabilities to attack the network. As illustrated in Fig. 4, random attackers decrease the bandwidth utilization of preamble-based TDMA, IEEE 802.15.6-based CSMA/CA, and secure RFID-based protocols by 60%, 70%, and 20%, respectively. The IEEE 802.15.6-based CSMA/CA is mostly affected by backoff manipulation and collisions attacks where the attackers tried to select a small CW in order to keep the channel busy all the time. The proposed protocol, however, is less vulnerable to attacks due to its strong and secured wakeup process.

4 Conclusion

This paper proposed a secure RFID-based protocol for WBAN. The proposed protocol used RFID for wakeup purpose only. The preliminary simulation study showed that the proposed protocol is power-efficient and is less vulnerable to different attacks compared to that of IEEE 802.15.6-based CSMA/CA and preamble-based TDMA protocols. In future, we will extend the secure RFID-based protocols for heterogeneous WBAN applications including heart activity monitoring.

Acknowledgment. This research is supported by the National Plan for Science and Technology at King Saud University, Project No: 11-INF1500.

References

1. Ullah, S., Higgins, H., et al.: A Comprehensive Survey of Wireless Body Area Networks - On PHY, MAC, and Network Layers Solutions. J. Medical Systems 36(3), 1065–1094 (2012)

2. IEEE 802.15.6, Wireless Medium Access Control (MAC) and Physical Layer (PHY) Specifications for Wireless Personal Area Networks (WPANs) used in or around a body (2012)
3. PB-TDMA website, `http://www.isi.edu/nsnam/ns/doc/node176.html` (Date visited: February 21, 2013)
4. IEEE Std.802.15.4: Wireless medium access control (MAC) and physical layer (PHY) specifications for low data rate wireless personal area networks (WPAN). IEEE, Piscataway (2006)
5. Timmons, N.F., Scanlon, W.G.: Analysis of the performance of IEEE 802.15.4 for medical sensor body area networking. In: The Proc. of IEEE SECON, Santa Clara, CA, USA, pp. 4–7 (2004)
6. Li, C., Li, H.B., Kohno, R.: Performance evaluation of IEEE 802.15.4 for wireless body area network. In: The Proc. of IEEE International Conference on ICC Workshops, Dresden, Germany, pp. 1–5 (2009)
7. Zhen, B., Li, H.B., Kohno, R.: IEEE body area networks and medical implant communications. In: The Proc. of the ICST 3rd International Conference on Body Area Networks, Tempe, Ariz, USA (2008)
8. Kynsijarvi, L., Goratti, L., Tesi, R., Iinatti, J., Hamalainen, M.: Design and performance of contention based MAC protocols in WBAN for medical ICT using IR-UWB. In: 21st International Conference on Personal, Indoor and Mobile Radio Communications Workshops (PIMRC Workshops), September 26-30, pp. 107–111 (2010)
9. Cheng, S., Huang, C.Y., Tu, C.C.: RACOON: A Multiuser QoS Design for Mobile Wireless Body Area Networks. Journal of Medical System 35, 1277–1287 (2011)
10. Marinkovi, Popovici, E.M., Spagnol, C., Faul, S., Marnane, W.P.: Energy-efficient low duty cycle MAC protocol for wireless body area networks. IEEE Transaction on Information Technology in Biomedicine 13(6), 915–925 (2009)
11. Al Ameen, M., Ullah, N., Sanaullah Chowdhury, M., Riazul Islam, S.M., Kwak, K.: A power efficient MAC protocol for wireless body area networks. EURASIP Journal on Wireless Communications and Networking (2012)
12. Hussain, M.A., Alam, M.N., Kwak, K.S.: Directional MAC Approach for Wireless Body Area Networks. Sensors 11(1), 771–784 (2011)
13. Ullah, S., Kwak, K.S.: An ultra low-power and traffic-adaptive medium access control protocol for wireless body area network. Journal Medical Systems 36(3), 1021–1030 (2012)
14. Kwak, K.S., Ullah, S.: A traffic-adaptive MAC protocol for WBAN. In: IEEE Globecom, pp. 1286–1289 (2010)
15. Su, H., Zhang, X.: Battery-dynamics driven TDMA MAC protocols for wireless body-area monitoring networks in healthcare applications. IEEE Journal of Selected Areas in Communication 27(4), 424–434 (2009)
16. Saleem, S., et al.: A Study of IEEE 802.15.4 Security Framework for Wireless Body Area Networks. Sensors 11(2), 1383–1395 (2011)
17. Radosavac, S., Cardenas, A.A., Baras, J.S., Moustakides, G.V.: Detecting IEEE 802.11 MAC layer misbehavior in ad hoc networks: Robust strategies against individual and colluding attackers. J. Comput. Secur. 15, 103–128 (2007)

Towards Authenticated Objects

Daniele Midi[1], Ashish Kundu[2], and Elisa Bertino[1]

[1] Department of Computer Science and CERIAS, Purdue University, West Lafayette, USA
{dmidi,bertino}@cs.purdue.edu
[2] IBM T J Watson Research Center, New York, USA
akundu@us.ibm.com

Abstract. In many application domains, objects are transferred, shared, and used across organizational and trust boundaries, which poses serious security concerns. Given the ubiquitous use of objects, it is important to assure at program run-time that the objects received and used have not been modified by any unauthorized program or entity, and are from the authorized programs. In this paper, we propose an authenticated model of objects that facilitates verification of authenticity of objects at program run-time and its possible Java-based implementations.

1 Introduction

With the advent of web services and mobile software, the security of distributed software and the data it manages has become a crucial requirement. Consider the following example of a communication between two remote applications: a smartphone application (app, for short) receives a serialized object from a server or another device; the object is then used for a computation by the smartphone app which then sends the result back to the server/device. This is a traditional remote method invocation model – via RPC and RMI, web services or based on web-based computing. Comprehensive security solutions require addressing several requirements: (1) How the receiver app verifies the authenticity of the object it receives. This means checking that the object has been sent by the authorized sender as claimed, and that the object has not been modified in an unauthorized manner. (2) How the receiver app validates the identity of the sender app. (3) How to guarantee that no sensitive data is disclosed to the receiver during the object transmission process. (4) How to guarantee that the object is not an attack vector that exploits vulnerabilities in the receiver system.

An object may be tampered with when it is on the network being transferred from the client to the service, or at the service-side before the object is processed and after the object is received. Similarly, an object may be tampered with at the client side after it was sent by the client process and before being transmitted on the network. Existing security solutions such as transport layer security protocols treat objects as bitstreams dis-regarding the semantics objects have, and thus cannot be used to verify authenticity of objects in a programming context – between remote processes or processes executing on one processor as part of one program. In order to prevent such attacks at the level of programming language objects, it is essential for the service to carry out authenticity verification of the received objects before processing them.

J. Lopez, X. Huang, and R. Sandhu (Eds.): NSS 2013, LNCS 7873, pp. 777–783, 2013.

In this paper, we focus on approaches addressing the security requirements (1) integrity – objects have not been modified in an unauthorized manner and (2) origin – objects are owned/authored by an authorized entity. Together, they are referred to as "authenticity of objects". Cryptographic protection of integrity and origin is referred to as "authenticity protection", and the process is called *object authentication* (different from user authentication that refers to schemes such as password-based verification) – known as *object signing*.

In this paper we propose an approach to sign and verify programming language objects for the Java language. We discuss several alternatives for integrating the signature and verification functions into Java programs. Using the proposed schemes and programming models, authentication of objects can be incorporated into programs during development, compilation or runtime.

2 Authenticated Objects in Java

The integration of the authentication scheme with the programming language is critical as the adopted integration approach affects the use of the authentication scheme and the efficiency of the code. In what follows we first describe a low level core application programming interface (API), followed by a description of four integration approaches.

2.1 Core API

Even if from the point of view of the programmer all approaches differ with respect to how the security is integrated in the code, they share the same core functions. In particular, the signature and verification functions, as well as the signature schemes themselves, provide the low-level layer of API on top of which all the approaches have been built. The current implementation includes two different signature schemes, based on the Merkle Hash Tree technique [5], and on the Redactable Set Signature technique [3] respectively.

Both signature schemes use the hashing and cryptographic functions provided by the standard Java 7 APIs. For the Merkle hash technique, we use the RSA signature algorithm. We chose to implement public-key schemes instead of private-key schemes primarily because public-key schemes simplify key distribution among programs and processes, and cover the use cases of private-key schemes also. For evaluation purposes, the public and private key pairs are dynamically generated using the built-in Java functions whenever the code execution starts. However, our core API provides an interface, called `IKeyProvider`, for which the developer can provide an implementation in order to support other approaches for provisioning the encryption keys to code, e.g. from a local file or a remote centralized repository. One such key provider can be implemented on top of Trusted Platform Module (TPM[1]). It may use a keypair derived from the RSA keys of TPM towards signing the objects. Key distribution is carried out by including the public key certificate along with the object that includes the signature – an instance of the class `ObjectAuthenticationSignature`.

[1] `http://www.trustedcomputinggroup.org/resources/tpm_main_specification`

In order to be processed by the Merkle Hash Tree-based signature function, the objects are transformed into a tree representation, using a conventional format that easily allows one to represent any object member, it being a primitive type, an array or another object. For the second scheme, the objects are treated as sets of members and thus do not include any edges as in trees.

2.2 Example programs

We will use the following two classes to demonstrate object authentication. Class `A` (in Listing 1.1) is annotated with signing and re-signing details. The annotation `@Sign` includes the principal whose keys are used for signing and verification and the method chosen for signing. The example shows that the annotation `@IncludeInSignature` is used to specify all the member fields that are to be included in the computation of the signature of the object. The annotation `@Resign` for method `setA()` requires the object to be re-signed every time the value of a is set through this method.

```
@Sign(identity="signer", method="Merkle")
public class A {
    public A (String a) { this.a = a; }
    @IncludeInSignature
    private String a;
    public String getA() { return a; }
    @Resign
    public void setA(String a) { this.a = a; }
}
```

Listing 1.1. Example class A with authentication behavior described via annotations

In Listing 1.2, the example class `B` demonstrates how the parameters passed to a method are verified for authenticity. The first implementation of `f()` uses programmer-driven verification of object `a` of class `A` passed as a parameter; it requires the signature of `a` too to be passed as a parameter to the method. In another definition of `f()`, the authenticity of `a` is verified automatically with no programmer input through the annotation `@VerifyAllParams`. If the signature of the parameter finds the object to be non-authentic, then it throws an exception `SignatureMismatchException`.

```
public class B {
    public void f(A obj, ObjectAuthenticationSignature signature) {
        try {
            if(!ObjectAuthentication.verify(obj, signature))
                throw new SignatureMismatchException();
        } catch (ObjectAuthenticationException | UnsupportedSignignMethodException e) {
            e.printStackTrace();
        }
    }
    @VerifyAllParams
    public void f(A obj) { }
}
```

Listing 1.2. Example class B demonstrating how parameters are verified via annotations

2.3 The Library Approach

The library approach (see Listing 1.3 for an example) exposes the internal core API through a simple interface. The programmer can therefore leverage the signature and

Annotation	Semantics
@Sign(identity, method="Merkle")	When used to annotate a class, it specifies that the instances of that class may/should be signed using the specified identity. The identity parameter is a string denoting an identifier for an identity, used by in the signing function to retrieve the correct public/private key pair. The method parameter specifies which signing method has to be used.
@IncludeInSignature	Used to annotate all the fields to be included in the signature.
@Resign	When used to annotate a method, it specifies that after the method execution the signing process should be carried out again to keep the signature up-to-date. It is useful for all the methods which modify object members included in the signature.
@AlwaysResign	When used to annotate a class, it specifies that the signing process should be carried out again to keep the signature up-to-date after the execution of any class method.
@VerifyAllParams	When used to annotate a method, it specifies that before the execution of that method, all the parameters should be verified as authenticated object proxies containing a valid signature. If the verification fails, an InvalidSignatureException exception is thrown.

Fig. 1. Annotations used in signing Java objects and their semantics

verification functions, as well as choose the preferred signature scheme to use. Under this approach, the object signing and verification processes only happen on demand, that is, when the appropriate method is invoked by the code.

```
try {
    KeyManager.setKeyProvider(new StaticKeyProvider());
    A a = new A("John");
    B b = new B();
    ObjectAuthenticationSignature signature =
        ObjectAuthentication.sign(a, "Merkle",
        KeyManager.getPrivateKey("signer"),
        KeyManager.getPublicKey("signer"));
    b.f(a, signature);
} catch (ObjectAuthenticationException | UnsupportedSignignMethodException e) {
    e.printStackTrace();
}
```

Listing 1.3. How library method is used to sign an object and verify its signature when passed as a parameter to a method.

2.4 Automatic Integration Approaches and Annotations

The Library approach has the drawback that the programmer must make sure to include all the proper method calls for signing and verifying objects. To reduce the programming costs, the other approaches support automatic signature and verification processes. They are based on the use of Java annotations that the developer can use to annotate classes, variables and methods to specify the expected behavior. These annotations are used by our integration approaches to take the appropriate actions to maintain the desired security level. The signature process is carried out as a post-condition for the object constructor and for all the methods that require an automatic object re-signing; the verification is executed as a pre-condition for the methods that require authenticated objects. Table in Figure 1 summarizes the main annotations that we have introduced.

2.4.1 The Proxy Approach

This approach leverages the notion of dynamic proxy (see Listing 1.4 for an example). When a developer wants to enhance a class with automatic authentication, instead of directly creating an instance of the class through the `new` keyword, they can request the generation of an authentication-enabled dynamic proxy. This proxy will have the exact same type of the original class, so that it can be used wherever the original object was used. However, it will automatically sign the object upon creation (if needed) and intercept calls to specific methods in order to update its signature and/or verify the authenticity of the parameters, according to the annotations specified by the developer. Even though the Java standard API already provides mechanisms to create dynamic proxies, some of their limitations made them unsuitable for our purposes. For this reason, we leveraged the open source library called CGlib, a high performance Code Generation Library, used to extend Java classes and implement interfaces at runtime.

```
KeyManager.setKeyProvider(new StaticKeyProvider());
A a = AuthProxy.create(A.class, new Object[]{ "John" });
B b = AuthProxy.create(B.class);
b.f(a);
```

Listing 1.4. How proxy method is used to sign an object `a` and verify the signature when `a` is passed as a parameter to `b.f()`

2.4.2 The Runtime Approach

This approach manipulates the Java classes at run-time (see Listing 1.5 for an example) to add the authentication capabilities. Unlike in the Proxy integration approach, the developer does not have to use particular methods to instantiate the object. At the very beginning of the program, just one instruction requires to authentication-enable all the classes needing to have that behavior (i.e. the classes previously decorated with the appropriate annotations). Our run-time support system manipulates the class definitions by injecting all the required features before the classes loaded by the standard Java class loader. From that moment on, the program can create instances of those classes by using the normal `new` operator. More in detail, this integration approach adds a protected member that will hold the current updated signature for the object and a protected method able to self-sign the object whenever needed, following the specifications provided by the annotations. The scheme automatically inspects the class hierarchy and takes care of the possible inheritances.

```
KeyManager.setKeyProvider(new StaticKeyProvider());
try {
    AuthRuntime.makeAuthenticated("edu.purdue.ObjectAuthentication.test.A");
    AuthRuntime.makeAuthenticated("edu.purdue.ObjectAuthentication.test.B");
} catch (RuntimeTransformationException e) { e.printStackTrace(); }
A a = new A("John");
B b = new B();
b.f(a);
```

Listing 1.5. How runtime method is used to sign an object `a` and verify the signature when `a` is passed as a parameter to `b.f()`

2.4.3 The Post-Compilation Approach

To avoid the startup runtime overhead incurred by the Proxy and Runtime approaches, we have developed a Post-compilation tool able to alter the compiled classes in order to make the object authentication features persistent (see Listing 1.6 for an example). We provide a self-contained runnable JAR file that can be simply run inside the folder containing the compiled .class Java files. It automatically discovers all the classes inside the current folder and its subfolders, analyzes the annotations and alters the compiled bytecode to inject the requested authentication-enabled behavior wherever needed. The changes made are saved on the original files, thus making them persistent. As the post-compilation tool depends on the core API, this JAR file contains all the references needed for the object authentication features. Through this post-compilation tool, the programmer can use the favorite development environment and tool chain and in the end, after the Java compilation, introduce the authentication mechanisms in the compiled classes. At that point, it is even possible to distribute those classes as a library for other projects, thus enabling a large variety of development scenarios, such as injecting the authentication mechanisms into the classes shared between the client and the server components in a Java RMI application.

```
KeyManager.setKeyProvider(new StaticKeyProvider());
A a = new A("John");
B b = new B();
b.f(a);
```

Listing 1.6. How postcompilation method is used to sign an object `a` and verify the signature when `a` is passed as a parameter to `b.f()`. All the authentication code is automatically injected

2.5 Comparison of the Integration Approaches

All four approaches have advantages and disadvantages, thus the developer has to choose the most appropriate one. The Library approach gives the programmer freedom about when in the code to require the signature and verification of objects, tailoring the frequency of these activities based on the specific code optimization requirements. However, the developer needs to make sure that the method calls for the object signature and verification are included in the code as well as always keep the signature up-to-date whenever the object's members are modified. On the other hand, the automatic approaches always guarantee that the signature is up-to-date and that no method that requires authenticated objects is executed with an invalidly signed object. Moreover, the developer does not need to worry about the implementation details of the object authentication layer. The last and maybe most significant advantage of the automatic approaches is the possibility of seamlessly adding the object authentication mechanisms to legacy applications. Of course, the automatic integration approaches do not allow the developer to fine-tune the object signature and verification activities and may thus result in lower execution performance.

We evaluated the performance overhead of our object authentication techniques by varying different parameters – such as the number of components to be signed and number of signings and verifications – and measuring the time taken for different operations in the program lifecycle – such as object instantiation, authentication-enabling and first signing and actual program body execution. Our results show that when the program body consists of very few instructions, the most costly operations are the authentication-enabling of objects and the initial signature. When the program body is more complex, though, the workload for this start-up becomes negligible with respect to the rest of the program. The Library approach proved faster in all the scenarios, as the developer can fine-tune the authentication operations, but the Post-compilation approach has comparable performance, as all the bytecode manipulation is already complete before the execution. The Proxy and Runtime approaches have similar performance. However, the Runtime approach is faster during the actual program execution (including the verification processes), while requiring a longer initialization phase in all the scenarios.

3 Related Work

Relevant approaches that are close to our work include proof-carrying code techniques [6], software attestation, and trusted system boot. Abadi et al. [1] have proposed techniques for verifying control flow integrity in software execution. Secure information flow control [2,7] has focused on analysis and control of flow of sensitive and tainted data. However, none of these approaches address the problem of integrity of data structures such as objects. Integration of security capabilities in programming languages has been investigated in contexts other than digital signatures. Authenticity of trees and graphs have been addressed by Kundu, Atallah and Bertino [4]. Sumii and Pierce et al [8] developed dynamic notions of sealed objects. Yip et al. [9] proposed notions of policy objects for program security.

4 Future Work

We plan to further investigate performance issues in authenticated object models. There are three dimensions to the performance problem that we need to address: development of more efficient cryptographic digital signature schemes and protocols suitable for programming language contexts, language runtime design keeping authentication in mind, and design of language constructs that can be used by programmers for better efficiency.

Acknowledgements. The work reported in this paper has been partially supported by NSF under grant CNS-1111512.

References

1. Abadi, M., Budiu, M., Erlingsson, U., Ligatti, J.: Control-flow integrity principles, implementations, and applications. TISSEC 13(1), 4 (2009)
2. Denning, D.E., Denning, P.J.: Certification of programs for secure information flow. Commun. ACM 20(7), 504–513 (1977)
3. Johnson, R., Molnar, D., Song, D., Wagner, D.: Homomorphic signature schemes. In: Preneel, B. (ed.) CT-RSA 2002. LNCS, vol. 2271, pp. 244–262. Springer, Heidelberg (2002)
4. Kundu, A., Atallah, M., Bertino, E.: Leakage-free redactable signatures. In: CODASPY 2012 (2012)
5. Merkle, R.C.: A certified digital signature. In: Brassard, G. (ed.) CRYPTO 1989. LNCS, vol. 435, pp. 218–238. Springer, Heidelberg (1990)
6. Necula, G.: Proof-carrying code. In: POPL, pp. 106–119. ACM (1997)
7. Smith, G., et al.: A new type system for secure information flow. In: CSFW. IEEE (2001)
8. Sumii, E., Pierce, B.: A bisimulation for dynamic sealing. ACM SIGPLAN Notices 39, 161–172 (2004)
9. Yip, A., Wang, X., Zeldovich, N., Kaashoek, M.: Improving application security with data flow assertions. In: SOSP 2009, pp. 291–304. ACM, New York (2009)

A Finger-Vein Based Cancellable Bio-cryptosystem

Wencheng Yang[1], Jiankun Hu[1,*], and Song Wang[2]

[1] School of Engineering and Information Technology, University of New South Wales at the Australia Defence Force Academy, Canberra ACT, 2600, Australia
[2] School of Engineering and Mathematical Sciences, La Trobe University, VIC 3086, Australia
Wencheng.Yang@student.adfa.edu.au, J.Hu@adfa.edu.au, Song.Wang@latrobe.edu.au

Abstract. Irrevocability is one major issue in existing bio-cryptosystems. In this paper, we proposed a cancellable bio-cryptosystem by taking the full advantage of cancellable and non-invertible properties of bio-hashing biometrics. Specifically, two transformed templates are generated by using the bio-hashing algorithm and applied into two different secure sketches, fuzzy commitment sketch and fuzzy vault sketch, respectively. These two secure sketches can be fused in two different ways: AND fusion and OR fusion, so as to emphasis either on the recognition accuracy or the security level of the system. Experimental results and security analysis show the validity of the proposed scheme.

Keywords: Cancellable biometrics, bio-cryptosystem, finger-vein, fuzzy commitment, fuzzy vault.

1 Introduction

Finger-vein pattern is unique to a specific individual, contact-less, difficult to forge, not affected by skin discolorations or race, and does not change with people's age [1]. Because of these good properties of finger-vein features, finger-vein recognition attracts more and more research attentions and becomes a hot research topic in recent years. In a standard biometric recognition system, templates are stored in the databases or smartcards at the enrollment stage and compared with queries at the authentication stage. However, the raw template in use will bring serious secure consequences. For example, finger-vein feature is permanently associated with a particular individual. Once it is compromised, it will be lost permanently. Moreover, one finger-vein template is usually used for different applications which can be compromised by the cross-match. If an individual's finger-vein template is compromised in one application, substantially all of the applications, in which the finger-vein template is used, are compromised. To reduce the security threats brought by the possible information leakage of finger-vein template, two possible techniques, named bio-cryptosystem and cancellable biometrics are proposed to achieve the template protection in this paper.

[*] Corresponding author.

J. Lopez, X. Huang, and R. Sandhu (Eds.): NSS 2013, LNCS 7873, pp. 784–790, 2013.

Bio-cryptosystem provides security by two ways, either by binding the cryptographic key using biometric features or generating the cryptographic key directly from biometric features [2]. These biometric features are not stored explicitly but in the encrypted domain protected by some secure techniques, e.g. fuzzy vault, fuzzy extractor [2-6]. However, one drawback of bio-cryptosystems is that the encrypted template is probable to be restored by the adversary if the encryption algorithm and the helper data are public. Once the template is restored, it will be lost forever, if it is not revocable. Cancellable biometrics, which is first introduced by Ratha et al [7], achieves authentication by using the transformed or distorted biometric data instead of the original biometric data. The templates can be cancelled and are unique in different applications [8]. Even if the adversary compromises the transformed templates, the original templates are still secure and cannot be recovered because the transformation is non-invertible [6, 8, 9].

Motivated by the above concerns, in this paper, we proposed a finger-vein based cancellable bio-cryptosystem which combines the changeable and non-invertible properties of cancellable biometrics into bio-cryptosystem to achieve irreversibility of the template, at the same time, enhance the security level of the system. The rest of the paper is organized as follows. The proposed finger-vein based cancellable bio-cryptosystem is presented in Section 2. In Section 3, experimental results and security analysis are demonstrated and discussed. The conclusion and future work are given in Section 4.

2 Proposed Method

In order to enhance the security level of the finger-vein template, we equip the finger-vein based bio-cryptosystem with the cancellable property by using bio-hashing technique [10]. To be more specific, firstly, the original template feature set T extracted by two mature techniques named Gabor filter and linear discriminate analysis (LDA) is bio-hashed into two non-invertible variants, T_1 and T_2 by using the bio-hashing algorithm in [10]. Secondly, these two template variants are secured by two different secure sketches, fuzzy commitment and fuzzy vault, respectively. Finally, to enhance the recognition accuracy or security level of the system comparing with single secure sketch based system, these two sketches can be fused in two different ways, AND fusion and OR fusion.

2.1 Generation of Finger-Vein Feature Set and Its Variants

Before feature extraction, the finger-vein impression should be processed like impression alignment and region of interest (ROI) chop. Since Gabor filter and linear discriminate analysis (LDA) have shown to be powerful in image-based face recognition in the spatial domain [11], we employ the scheme in [11] to extract the finger-vein feature set and a real-valued vector, which contains N real values, is generated. In order to make the extracted features to be revocable, we transform the finger-vein feature set (e.g. template, T) into two different variants (e.g. T_1 and T_2) by the bio-hashing algorithm [10], each of them in the form of a fixed-length binary string of r bits. These two binary strings are non-invertible, because through inversion of bio-hashing to recover original biometric data is impossible due to that factoring the inner products of biometric feature and the user specified random number is intractable [10].

2.2 Encoding Stage

In the encoding stage, the two variants, T_1 and T_2 of the original template T generated by bio-hashing are secured by two different secure sketches, fuzzy commitment and fuzzy vault, respectively.

1) Fuzzy commitment encoding: The template T_1 is encrypted by fuzzy commitment sketch and the BCH code is used for error correction in our application. Given a secret s_1, it is encoded by BCH code into a codeword C_{T1} in the length of r which is the same as the length of the binary template feature T_1. Then the template T_1 is bound with the codeword C_{T1} to generate the secure sketch ST_1, as $ST_1=T_1 \oplus C_{T1}$. Here, $\oplus$ denotes the XOR operation. Assuming that fuzzy commitment is information theoretically secure, the secure sketch ST_1 provides no information about the template T_1, the adversary can only carry out a brute force attack to compromise T_1 which is expected to be uniformly distributed [7]. The secure sketch ST_1 acts as helper data and is stored in the database.

2) Fuzzy vault encoding: The template T_2 is encrypted by fuzzy vault sketch. Since the elements secured by fuzzy vault are in the form of points, we divide the template T_2 into Q segments $\{T_{21}, T_{22}, \ldots, T_{2Q}\}$ and each segment is r_s bits. Correspondingly, Q random binary strings $\{S_1, S_2, \ldots, S_Q\}$ are generated and encoded by BCH code into Q codewords $\{CS_1, CS_2, \ldots, CS_Q\}$, each of them is also r_s bits. After that, each template segment from $\{T_{21}, T_{22}, \ldots, T_{2Q}\}$ is bound with the corresponding codeword from $\{CS_1, CS_2, \ldots, CS_Q\}$ sequentially to generate the transformed template segments $\{ST_{21}, ST_{22}, \ldots, ST_{2Q}\}$, as $ST_{2i} = T_{2i} \oplus CS_i$, where $i \in [1,Q]$. Given a secret s_2, we divided it into *num* fragments and encoded them into a (*num*-1) order polynomial $P(x)$ with *num* coefficients. Each elements of $\{S_1, S_2, \ldots, S_Q\}$ is evaluated on polynomial $P(x)$ to gain $\{P(S_1), P(S_2), \ldots, P(S_Q)\}$. The combination set $\{(S_1, P(S_1)), (S_2, P(S_2)), \ldots, (S_Q, P(S_Q))\}$ can be considered as the genuine point set GT_2. At the same time, a chaff point set CT_2 is generated to secure the genuine point set GT_2. The final vault sketch VT_2, obtained by the union of GT_2 and CT_2, is defined as $VT_2= GT_2 \cup CT_2$. Both VT_2 and $\{ST_{21}, ST_{22}, \ldots, ST_{2Q}\}$ act as helper data and are stored in the database.

2.3 Decoding Stage

Given a query feature set Q extracted from the query impression, its two variants, Q_1 and Q_2 are generated by the same procedure described in section 2.1. Then Q_1 and Q_2 are applied to the decode model of fuzzy commitment and vault sketches, respectively, to retrieve the secret s_1 and s_2.

1) Fuzzy commitment decoding: During the decoding procedure of commitment sketch, the variant query feature set $Q1$ and the secure sketch ST_1 are XORed and output a corrupted codeword, C'_{T_1} as $C'_{T_1} = Q_1 \oplus ST_1$. If the number of errors happening in C'_{T_1} (comparing to C_{T_1}) is within the error correcting capability of the BCH code, the secret s_1 can be correctly retrieved, vice verse.

2) Fuzzy vault decoding: During the decoding procedure of vault sketch, the inverse operation is applied to the transformed template segments $\{ST_{21}, ST_{22}, \ldots, ST_{2Q}\}$. To be specifically, the query feature set Q_2 are divided into Q segments,$\{Q_{21}, Q_{22}, \ldots, Q_{2Q}\}$ and an XOR operation is performed between the corresponding elements from $\{ST_{21}, ST_{22}, \ldots, ST_{2Q}\}$ and $\{Q_{21}, Q_{22}, \ldots, Q_{2Q}\}$, so as to get the reversed codewords, $\{CS'_1, CS'_2, \ldots, CS'_Q\}$. If the hamming distance between an element CS'_i from reversed codewords, $\{CS'_1, CS'_2, \ldots, CS'_Q\}$ and its corresponding element CS_i from the original codewords, $\{CS_1, CS_2, \ldots, CS_Q\}$ is smaller than the error correcting ability of the BCH code, the element CS'_i could be correctly decoded to obtain the string S_i. The decoded string set is expressed by $\{S_i\}_{i=1}^{DQ}$, where DQ is the number of the correctly decoded strings. If DQ is larger *num*, the vault sketch VT_2 can be successfully decoded and the polynomial $P(x)$ can be reconstructed. The secret s_2 can be retrieved by sequentially concatenating the *num* coefficients of polynomial $P(x)$.

2.4 Fusion of Commitment Sketch and Vault Sketch

In order to achieve better recognition accuracy or higher security level of the system, two secure sketches, commitment sketch and vault sketch could be fused in two different ways, AND fusion and OR fusion. If higher security level of the system is required, AND fusion can be executed. Specifically, the secret, s of the system is generated by concatenating secrets, s_1 and s_2, as $s = s_1 \| s_2$. If and only if both secure sketches are decoded, the secret, s could be retrieved. So the security level of the system will be the entropy of commitment sketch plus the entropy of vault sketch. However, under the AND fusion, the recognition accuracy of the system will be brought down, because the similarity between query feature set and template feature set have to satisfy both hamming distance threshold and set difference threshold. If high recognition accuracy of the system is required, the OR fusion can be adopted. To be specific, the secret, s of the system could be set to be the same as s_1 and s_2, as $s = s_1 = s_2$. Even if one secure sketch is decoded, the secret, s could still be retrieved. The recognition accuracy would be the better one of the single commitment sketch or vault sketch based system. However, the security level of the system would be the worse of them, because the adversary could compromise the secret, s by decoding any one sketch.

3 Experimental Results and Security Analysis

The performance of the proposed system is evaluated on the public available finger-vein database from the Homologous Multi-modal Traits Database [12] setup by the Group of Machine Learning and Applications, Shandong University (SDUMLA). The finger-vein database contains images from 106 individuals. Each individual was asked to provide images of his/her index finger, middle finger and ring finger of both hands and the collection for each of the 6 fingers are repeated for 6 times to obtain 36 finger-vein images. Therefore, there are 3,816 images composed in the database and each image is 320×240 pixels in size. We chose the 1st, 2nd impressions as the training samples, and the 3rd, 4th, 5th, 6th impressions from the first 100 fingers from the finger-vein database as testing samples. For genuine test, the 3rd is considered as the template and 4th, 5th and 6th impressions from the same finger are considered as query, so 300 (=100x3) genuine matching attempts are made. For imposter test, the 3rd is considered as the template and 3rd, 4th, 5th and 6th impressions from other fingers are considered as query, so 39600 (=100×99×4) imposter matching attempts will be made. The performance of the proposed system is evaluated by the false accept rate (FAR), genuine accept rate (GAR) and false reject rate (FRR).

In our application, the length of the variants generated from the original feature set by bio-hashing is r=288 bits. For the single fuzzy commitment scheme, we use the BCH(n, k, t) code for error correcting where we set n=r=255 bits, and k is the length of the secret s_1. We evaluate the recognition accuracy of the single commitment sketch based bio-cryptosystem on different length of k, where t is the error correction capability of BCH code. By sphere-packing bound [13], the security of single commitment sketch based system is equal to the entropy of T_1 by given ST_1 which can be expressed as

$$H_\infty(T_1 \mid ST_1) = log\left(2^r / \binom{r}{t}\right) \tag{1}$$

For the single vault sketch based scheme, we set the number of segment Q=17, so N_{GT2}, the number of the genuine point set GT_2 is also 17. Accordingly, we set N_{CT2}, the number of chaff point set CT_2 to be 400. We evaluate the performance of the single vault sketch based bio-cryptosystem based on different num which is the number of fragments from s_2. For the security of single vault sketch based system, the entropy of GT_2 by given VT_2 is expressed as

$$H_\infty(GT_2 \mid VT_2) = -\log\left(\frac{\binom{N_{GT_2}}{num}}{\binom{N_{GT_2}+N_{CT_2}}{num}}\right) \tag{2}$$

The recognition accuracy and security level of single commitment sketch and single vault based bio-cryptosystem are shown in table 1 and table 2, respectively. The recognition accuracy and security level of AND fusion or OR fusion based bio-cryptosystem are adjustable according to different parameters which we will not discuss in this paper.

Table 1. Performance of single fuzzy commitment sketch based bio-cryptosystem

k, length of secret s_1(bits)	FRR(%)	FAR(%)	Security (bits)
9	20.33	0	53
21	22.33	0	65
45	30.67	0	87
91	56.77	0	140
107	61.33	0	150

Table 2. Performance of single fuzzy vault sketch based bio-cryptosystem

num, number of fragments from secret s_2	FRR(%)	FAR(%)	Security (bits)
7	6.33	7.33	34
8	9.67	2.41	40
9	12.33	0.64	45
10	15.67	0.14	51
11	18.67	0.03	57
12	22.33	0.01	63
13	24.67	0	69

4 Conclusion and Future Work

The proposed finger-vein based cancellable bio-cryptosystem takes the full advantage of cancellable and non-invertible properties of bio-hashing technique to solve the problem of irrevocability in existing bio-cryptosystems. It uses two variants of the original biometric template and applies them into two different secure sketches, fuzzy commitment sketch and fuzzy vault sketch. Different fusion ways, AND fusion and OR fusion of these two secure sketches improve either the recognition accuracy or the security level of the cancellable bio-cryptosystem depending on the requirement of the real application. Because different similarity measures are used in fuzzy commitment and fuzzy vault, hamming distance for fuzzy commitment and set difference for fuzzy vault, it is difficult to calculate the best points that achieve the best recognition accuracy and security level of AND fusion based system and OR fusion based system. To find these points will be the future research topic. Multimodal bio-cryptosystems incorporating fingerprint [14, 15] and face [16] will also be an interesting research topic.

References

1. Mulyono, D., Jinn, H.S.: A study of finger vein biometric for personal identification. In: International Symposium on Biometrics and Security Technologies, ISBAST 2008, pp. 1–8. IEEE (2008)

2. Hu, J.: Mobile fingerprint template protection: progress and open issues. In: 3rd IEEE Conference on Industrial Electronics and Applications, ICIEA 2008, pp. 2133–2138. IEEE (2008)
3. Dodis, Y., Ostrovsky, R., Reyzin, L., Smith, A.: Fuzzy extractors: How to generate strong keys from biometrics and other noisy data. SIAM Journal on Computing 38, 97–139 (2008)
4. Ahmad, T., Hu, J., Wang, S.: Pair-polar coordinate-based cancelable fingerprint templates. Pattern Recogn. 44, 2555–2564 (2011)
5. Zhang, P., Hu, J., Li, C., Bennamoun, M., Bhagavatula, V.: A pitfall in fingerprint bio-cryptographic key generation. Computers & Security 30, 311–319 (2011)
6. Wang, S., Hu, J.: Alignment-free cancellable fingerprint template design: a densely infinite-to-one mapping (DITOM) approach. Pattern Recogn. (2012)
7. Ratha, N.K., Connell, J.H., Bolle, R.M.: Enhancing security and privacy in biometrics-based authentication systems. IBM Systems Journal 40, 614–634 (2001)
8. Xi, K., Ahmad, T., Han, F., Hu, J.: A fingerprint based bio-cryptographic security protocol designed for client/server authentication in mobile computing environment. Security and Communication Networks 4, 487–499 (2011)
9. Yang, W., Hu, J., Wang, S.: A Delaunay Triangle-Based Fuzzy Extractor for Fingerprint Authentication. In: 2012 IEEE 11th International Conference on Trust, Security and Privacy in Computing and Communications (TrustCom), pp. 66–70. IEEE (2012)
10. Jin, A.T.B., Ling, D.N.C., Goh, A.: Biohashing: two factor authentication featuring fingerprint data and tokenised random number. Pattern Recogn. 37, 2245–2255 (2004)
11. Vitomir, Š., Nikola, P.: The complete gabor-fisher classifier for robust face recognition. EURASIP Journal on Advances in Signal Processing (2010)
12. Yin, Y., Liu, L., Sun, X.: SDUMLA-HMT: a multimodal biometric database. Biometric Recognition, 260–268 (2011)
13. MacWilliams, F., Sloane, N.: The theory of error-correcting codes (2006)
14. Wang, Y., Hu, J., Phillips, D.: A fingerprint orientation model based on 2D Fourier expansion (FOMFE) and its application to singular-point detection and fingerprint indexing. IEEE Transactions on Pattern Analysis and Machine Intelligence 29, 573–585 (2007)
15. Wang, Y., Hu, J.: Global Ridge Orientation modelling for Partial Fingerprint Identification. IEEE Transactions on Pattern Analysis and Machine Intelligence 33, 16 (2011)
16. Xi, K., Hu, J., Han, F.: Mobile device access control: an improved correlation based face authentication scheme and its Java ME application. Concurrency and Computation: Practice and Experience 24, 1066–1085 (2012)

Author Index